brief

contents

office 2010

word 2010

excel 2010

chapter 1
Getting Started with Excel 2010 EX-2

chapter 2
Using Formulas and Functions EX-40

chapter 3
Formatting the Worksheet EX-76

access 2010

powerpoint 2010

preface

How well do you know Microsoft Office? Many students can follow specific step-by-step directions to re-create a document, spreadsheet, presentation, or database, but do they truly understand the skills it takes to create these on their own? Just as simply following a recipe does not make you a professional chef, re-creating a project step by step does not make you an Office expert.

The purpose of this book is to teach you the skills to master the Office applications in a straightforward and easy-to-follow manner. But *Microsoft® Office 2010: A Skills Approach* goes beyond the ***how*** and equips you with a deeper understanding of the ***what*** and the ***why.*** Too many times books have little value beyond the classroom. The *Skills Approach* series has been designed to be not only a complete textbook, but also a reference tool for you to use as you move beyond academics and into the workplace.

ABOUT TRIAD INTERACTIVE

Triad Interactive is a small business and a District of Columbia Qualified High Technology Company specializing in online education and training products.

Triad's flagship program is SimNet®—a simulated Microsoft Office learning and assessment application developed for the McGraw-Hill Companies. SimNet development began in 1999 with SimNet 2000, a CD-ROM-based program used to measure students' understanding of the Microsoft Office 2000 applications. In 2000, for Office XP, Triad expanded the SimNet platform to include a learning component with lessons written by Cheri Manning and Catherine Manning Swinson. Over the past 10 years, the SimNet series has continued to evolve from a simple CD-ROM program into a robust online learning and assessment system. More than 500,000 students worldwide have used SimNet to learn the skills necessary to master Microsoft Office.

Triad is also actively involved in cancer education and in research projects to assess the usefulness of technology for helping high-risk populations make decisions about managing their cancer risk and treatment.

about the **authors**

CHERI MANNING

Cheri Manning is the president and co-owner of Triad Interactive. She is the author of the Microsoft Excel and Microsoft Access content for the SimNet series of online assessment and learning programs. She has been authoring instructional content for these applications for over 10 years. Cheri is also the co-author of McGraw-Hill's *What's New in Microsoft Office 2003* and *What's New in Microsoft Office 2007*.

Cheri began her career as an Aerospace Education Specialist with the Education Division of the National Aeronautics and Space Administration (NASA), where she produced materials for K–12 instructors and students. Prior to founding Triad Interactive, Cheri was a project manager with Compact Publishing, where she managed the development of McGraw-Hill's Multimedia MBA CD-ROM series.

CATHERINE MANNING SWINSON

Catherine Manning Swinson is the vice president and co-owner of Triad Interactive. She is the author of the Microsoft Word, Microsoft PowerPoint, and Microsoft Outlook content for the SimNet series of online assessment and learning programs. She has been authoring instructional content for these applications for over 10 years. Catherine is also the co-author of *What's New in Microsoft Office 2003* and *What's New in Microsoft Office 2007*.

Catherine began her career at Compact Publishing, one of the pioneers in educational CD-ROM-based software. She was the lead designer at Compact and designed every edition of the *TIME Magazine Compact Almanac* from 1992 through 1996. In addition, she designed a number of other products with Compact, including the *TIME Man of the Year* program and the *TIME 20th Century Almanac.*

The authors would like to extend a special thank-you to the Triad staff especially to Torger Wuellner for keeping the show running while we were writing the text and to Katie Lawson and Jodi Sandvick for staying late and coming in on the weekends to help with graphics. Thanks to Marlena Pechan, Barrett Lyon, and Alan Palmer for their patience working with two authors new to the print world. Thanks to Liz Haefele and Scott Davidson for the opportunity to expand our digital collaboration into print. And a final thanks to Paul Altier for his extraordinary vision of what this series could be and for all of his encouragement and support throughout the process. We deeply appreciate all of the hard work by the contributors, technical editors, reviewers, and everyone at McGraw-Hill to develop this new series.

contributors

word projects

Randy Nordell
American River College

excel projects

Melissa Prinzing
Sierra College

access projects

Ralph De Arazoza
Miami Dade College

powerpoint projects

Debra Fells
Mesa Community College

from the perspective of

Bonnie Smith
Fresno City College

technical editors

Menka Brown
Piedmont Technical College

Patricia Casey
Trident Technical College

Elliot Cherner
Mesa Community College

Ranida Harris
Indiana University Southeast

Mary Carole Hollinsgworth
Georgia Perimeter College

Terri Holly
Indian River State College

Mary Locke
Greenville Technical College

Daniela Marghitu
Auburn University

Brenda Nielsen
Mesa Community College

Phil Nielson
Salt Lake Community College

Judy Settle
Central Georgia Technical College

Pam Silvers
Asheville-Buncombe Technical College

Candace Spangler
Columbus State Community College

Lynne Stuhr
Trident Technical College

reviewers

OUR THANKS GO TO ALL WHO PARTICIPATED IN THE DEVELOPMENT OF *MICROSOFT® OFFICE 2010: A SKILLS APPROACH.*

Rosalyn R. Amaro
Florida State College at Jacksonville

Wilma Andrews
Virginia Commonwealth University

Tom Ashby
Oklahoma City Community College

Robert Balicki
Cleary University

Alfred Basta
Kaplan University

Judy Bennett
Sam Houston State University

Jan Bentley
Utah Valley University

Judy Brierley
Seminole State College

Judy Brown
The University of Memphis

Katharine Brown
University of North Florida

Menka Brown
Piedmont Technical College

Sylvia Brown
Midland College

Peter Cardon
University of South Carolina

Patricia Casey
Trident Technical College

Gerianne Chapman
Johnson & Wales University

Sissy Copeland
Piedmont Technical College

Jami Cotler
Siena College

Don Danner
San Francisco State University

Raphael De Arazoza
Miami Dade College

Darren Denenberg
University of Nevada–Las Vegas

Kim Ellis
Virginia Western Community College

Jean Finley
Asheville Buncombe Technical Community College

Dave Fitzgerald
Jackson Community College

Deborah Franklin
Bryant & Stratton College

Amy Giddens
Central Alabama Community College

Barbara Gombetto
Bryant & Stratton College

Kemit Grafton
Oklahoma State University–Oklahoma City

Marilyn Griffin
Virginia Tech

Andrew Hardin
University of Nevada–Las Vegas

Michael Haugrud
Minnesota State University Moorhead

Terri Hayes
Broward College

Cheryl Heemstra
Anne Arundel Community College

Mary Carole Hollingsworth
Georgia Perimeter College

Lister W. Horn
Pensacola State College

Jennifer Ivey
Central Carolina Community College

Linda F. Johnsonius
Murray State University

Barbara Jones
Golden West College

Sally Kaskocsak
Sinclair Community College

Hazel Kates
Miami Dade College Kendall Campus

Judith Keenan
Salve Regina University

Hal Kingsley
Trocaire College

Linda Kliston
Broward College–North

Kitty Koepping
Shepherd University, Shepherdstown, WV

Charles Lake
Faulkner State

Jackie Lamoureux
Central New Mexico Community College

Nanette Lareau
University of Arkansas Community College at Morrilton

Patricia A. Lee
Florida State College at Jacksonville

Mary Locke
Greenville Technical College

Donna M. Lohn
Lakeland Community College

Nicki Maines
Mesa Community College

Daniela Marghitu
Auburn University

Juan Marquez
Mesa Community College

Phil Marshall
University of South Carolina

Prosenjit Mazumdar
George Mason University

Dr. Robert McCloud
Sacred Heart University

Daniel McKee
Mansfield University of PA

Patricia M. McMurray
Kaplan Career Institute ICM Campus

Dawn Medlin
Appalachian State University

Susan Mitchell
Davenport University

Kathleen M. Morris
University of Alabama

Carmen Morrison
North Central State College

Melissa Nemeth
Kelley School of Business Indianapolis

Brenda Nielsen
Mesa Community College

Philip H Nielson
Salt Lake Community College

Maria Osterhoudt
St. Petersburg College

Judy Pento
Seacoast Career School

Don Rhyne
San Joaquin Valley College

Steven Rosen
Keiser University

Kathy Ruggieri
Lansdale School of Business

Charles Salazar
Clackamas Community College

Diane Santurri
Johnson & Wales University

Steven A. Singer
Kapiolani Community College

Bonnie Smith
Fresno City College

Candice Spangler
Columbus State Community College

Diane Stark
Phoenix College

Allen Truell
Ball State University

Kari Walters
Louisianna State University

Eric Weinstein
Suffolk County Community College

Stu Westin
University of Rhode Island

Billie Jo Whary
McCann School of Business and Technology Sunbury Campus

Melinda White
Seminole State College

Judy Wynekoop
Florida Gulf Coast University

Laurie Zouharis
Suffolk University

Instructor Walkthrough

Microsoft Office 2010: A Skills Approach

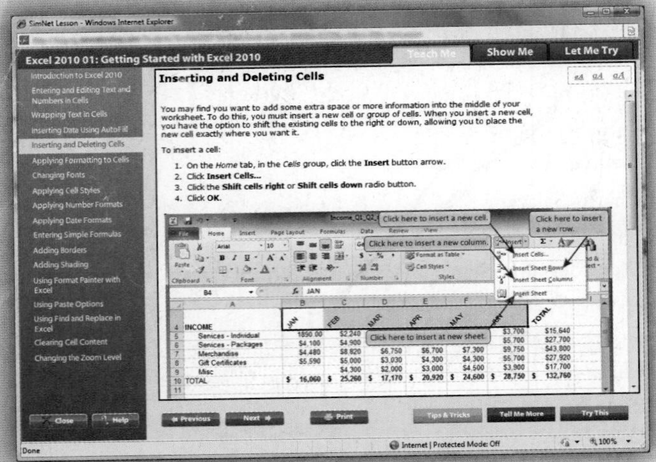

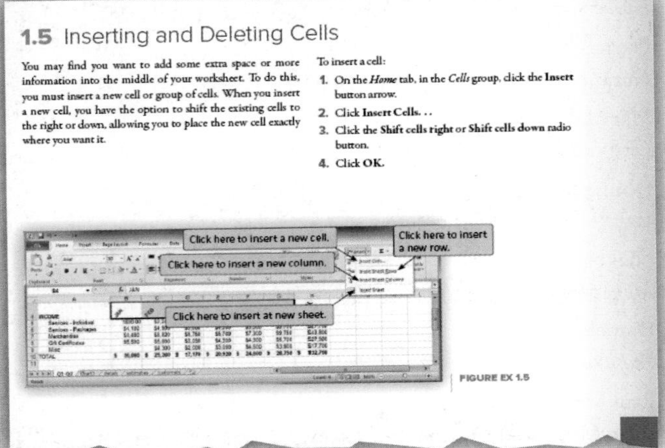

1.5 Inserting and Deleting Cells

You may find you want to add some extra space or more information into the middle of your worksheet. To do this, you must insert a new cell or group of cells. When you insert a new cell, you have the option to shift the existing cells to the right or down, allowing you to place the new cell exactly where you want it.

To insert a cell:

1. On the *Home* tab, in the *Cells* group, click the **Insert** button arrow.
2. Click **Insert Cells. . .**
3. Click the **Shift cells right** or **Shift cells down** radio button.
4. Click **OK.**

FIGURE EX 1.5

› **1-1 Content in SimNet for Office 2010**

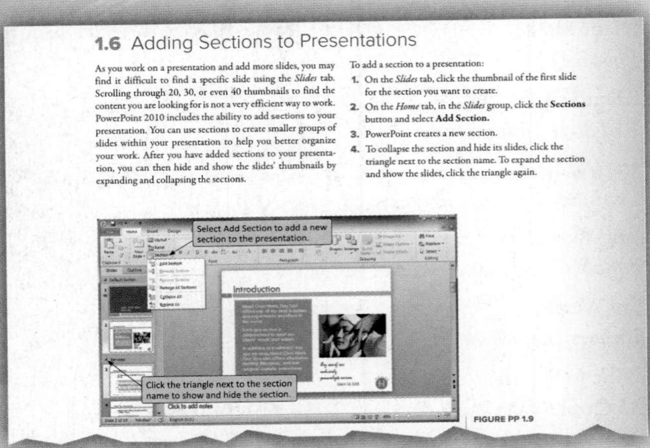

1.6 Adding Sections to Presentations

As you work on a presentation and add more slides, you may find it difficult to find a specific slide using the *Slides* tab. Scrolling through 20, 30, or even 40 thumbnails to find the content you are looking for is not a very efficient way to work. PowerPoint 2010 includes the ability to add sections to your presentation. You can use sections to create smaller groups of slides within your presentation to help you better organize your work. After you have added sections to your presentation, you can then hide and show the slides' thumbnails by expanding and collapsing the sections.

To add a section to a presentation:

1. On the *Slides* tab, click the thumbnail of the first slide for the section you want to create.
2. On the *Home* tab, in the *Slides* group, click the **Sections** button and select **Add Section.**
3. PowerPoint creates a new section.
4. To collapse the section and hide its slides, click the triangle next to the section name. To expand the section and show the slides, click the triangle again.

FIGURE PP 1.9

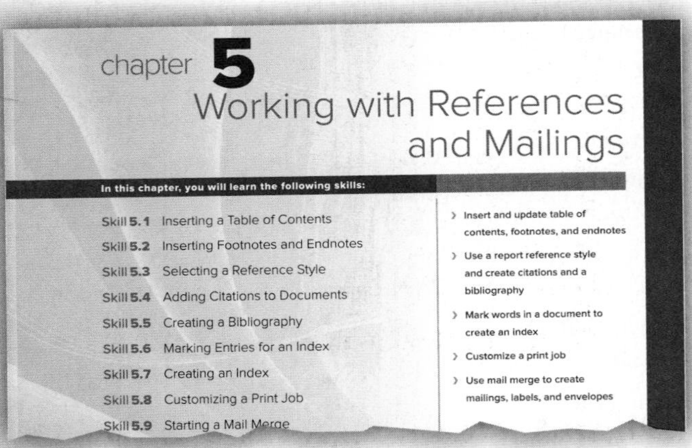

chapter **5**

Working with References and Mailings

In this chapter, you will learn the following skills:

- Skill **5.1** Inserting a Table of Contents
- Skill **5.2** Inserting Footnotes and Endnotes
- Skill **5.3** Selecting a Reference Style
- Skill **5.4** Adding Citations to Documents
- Skill **5.5** Creating a Bibliography
- Skill **5.6** Marking Entries for an Index
- Skill **5.7** Creating an Index
- Skill **5.8** Customizing a Print Job
- Skill **5.9** Starting a Mail Merge

- › Insert and update table of contents, footnotes, and endnotes
- › Use a report reference style and create citations and a bibliography
- › Mark words in a document to create an index
- › Customize a print job
- › Use mail merge to create mailings, labels, and envelopes

› **At-a-glance Office 2010 skills**

Quick, easy-to-scan pages, for efficient learning

› **Introduction—Learning Outcomes are clearly listed.**

Fix It

On Your Own

Skill Review

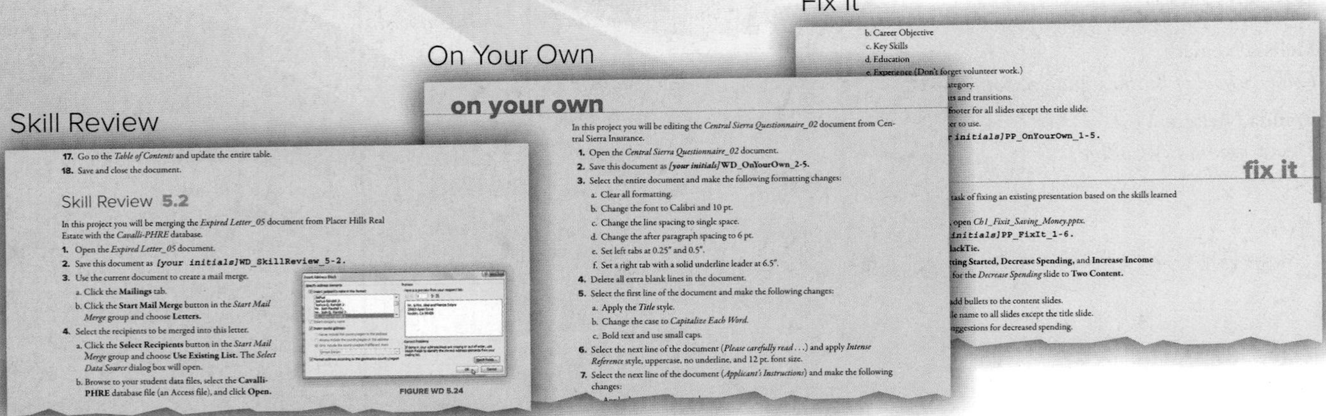

17. Go to the *Table of Contents* and update the entire table.
18. Save and close the document.

Skill Review 5.2

In this project you will be merging the *Expired Letter_05* document from Placer Hills Real Estate with the *Cavalli-PHRE* database.

1. Open the *Expired Letter_05* document.
2. Save this document as **[your initials]WD_SkillReview_5-2.**
3. Use the current document to create a mail merge.
   a. Click the **Mailings** tab.
   b. Click the **Start Mail Merge** button in the *Start Mail Merge* group and choose **Letters.**
4. Select the recipients to be merged into this letter.
   a. Click the **Select Recipients** button in the *Start Mail Merge* group and choose **Use Existing List.** The *Select Data Source* dialog box will open.
   b. Browse to your student data files, select the **Cavalli-PHRE** database file (an Access file), and click **Open.**

FIGURE WD 5.24

on your own

In this project you will be editing the *Central Sierra Questionnaire_02* document from Central Sierra Insurance.

1. Open the *Central Sierra Questionnaire_02* document.
2. Save this document as **[your initials]WD_OnYourOwn_2-5.**
3. Select the entire document and make the following formatting changes:
   a. Clear all formatting.
   b. Change the font to Calibri and 10 pt.
   c. Change the line spacing to single space.
   d. Change the after paragraph spacing to 6 pt.
   e. Set left tabs at 0.25" and 0.5".
   f. Set a right tab with a solid underline leader at 6.5".
4. Delete all extra blank lines in the document.
5. Select the first line of the document and make the following changes:
   a. Apply the *Title* style.
   b. Change the case to *Capitalize Each Word.*
   c. Bold text and use small caps.
6. Select the next line of the document (*Please carefully read. . .*) and apply *Intense Reference* style, uppercase, no underline, and 12 pt. font size.
7. Select the next line of the document (*Applicant's Instructions*) and make the following changes:

b. Career Objective
c. Key Skills
d. Education
e. Experience (Don't forget volunteer work.)
...egory.
...s and transitions.
...ooter for all slides except the title slide.
...er to use.
...**initials]PP_OnYourOwn_1-5.**

fix it

...task of fixing an existing presentation based on the skills learned

...open *Ch1_Fixit_Saving_Money.pptx.*
...**initials]PP_FixIt_1-6.**
...lackTie.
...ting Started, Decrease Spending,** and **Increase Income**
...for the *Decrease Spending* slide to **Two Content.**
...dd bullets to the content slides.
...le name to all slides except the title slide.
...ggestions for decreased spending.

› **Diverse end-of-chapter projects**

Projects that relate to a broad range of careers and perspectives, from nursing, education, business, and everyday personal uses.

Features:

From the Perspective of...

from the perspective of . . .

PARENT

My child uses word processing software to complete assignments and write simple reports. She even enjoys adding interesting clip art to make her work look good while having fun.

5.5 Creating a Bibliography

A bibliography is a compiled list of sources you referenced in your document. Typically, bibliographies appear at the end of a document and list all the sources you marked throughout the document. Microsoft Word 2010 comes with a number of prebuilt bibliography building blocks for you to use. When you select one of these building blocks, Word will search the document and compile all the sources from your document and format them according to the style you chose.

FIGURE WD 5.5

Tips and Tricks

tips & tricks

If you find yourself typing certain long phrases over and over again, you can use the AutoCorrect feature to replace short abbreviations with long strings of text that you don't want to type. For example, you could replace the text *hhspa* with *Head Over Heels Day Spa*. This will not only save you time when typing, but more importantly ensure accuracy in your documents.

Tell Me More

tell me **more**

Beginning with Office 2007, Microsoft changed the file format for Office files. Files created with Office 2007 and Office 2010 will not work with older versions of Office. If you want to share your files with people who are using Office 2003 or older, you should save the files in a different file format.

1. Click the **File** tab.
2. Click **Save As.**
3. The *Save As* dialog opens. Click the arrow at the end of the *Save as type:* box to expand the list of available file types.
4. To ensure compatibility with older versions of Office, select the file type that includes 97-2003 (for example,

Try This

try **this**

To apply the *cut, copy,* or *paste* command, you can also use the following shortcuts:

› **Cut** = Press Ctrl + X on the keyboard, or right-click and select **Cut.**

› **Copy** = Press Ctrl + C on the keyboard, or right-click and select **Copy.**

› **Paste** = Press Ctrl + V on the keyboard, or right-click and select **Paste.**

› **Instructor materials available on the online learning center, www.mhhe.com/office2010skills**

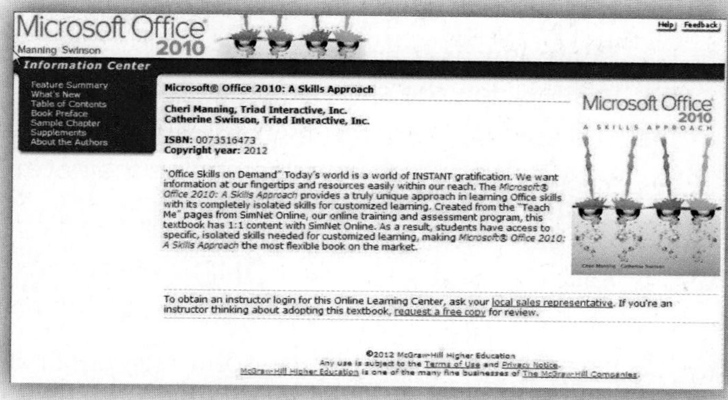

- Instructor Manual
- Instructor PowerPoints
- Test Bank

SimNet for Office **2010**

Online training and assessment

INCLUDES:

- Microsoft® Office Suite
- Microsoft® Outlook
- Windows XP
- Windows Vista
- Windows 7
- Internet Explorer 7
- Internet Explorer 8
- Computer Concepts

Since 1999, instructors have been using SimNet to measure student outcomes in a virtual Microsoft® Office environment. Now completely online, with nothing to install, students can practice and study their skills at home or in the school lab. Moreover, this resource is an ideal course solution, but even more valuable, as it can be used beyond the course for self-study! For more information, contact your McGraw-Hill sales representative or visit the SimNet Online Web site, **www.mhhe.com/simnet2010**

IT'S EASY!

SimNet is an EASY & INTUITIVE, true turnkey design. Instructors can quickly and efficiently assign content around the needs of your course, edit throughout the semester, and copy to multiple sections and instructors! SimNet is scannable so students can quickly scan the tasks in a lesson to identify the skills they know and the ones they don't…saving them time!

STUDENTS LEARN BEYOND THE BOOK!

SimNet offers a complete computer-based learning side that presents each skill or topic in several different modes:

- *Teach Me:* combines instructional text, graphics, and interactivity to present each skill.
- *Show Me:* uses animation with audio narration to show how the skill is implemented.
- *Let Me Try:* allows students to apply and practice what they have learned on their own to master the learning objective.

STUDENTS LEARN BEYOND THE COURSE!

SimNet allows students to perform their best in the course, and SimNet allows students to continue learning Office skills for future classes and beyond through its self-study material! Need to learn an advanced topic or a refresher on a certain skill? Use SimSearch to search or pull up specific content when you need it.

office 2010

chapter 1

Getting Started with Microsoft Office 2010 Common Features

In this chapter, you will learn the following skills:

- Learn about Microsoft Office 2010 and its applications: Word, Excel, PowerPoint, and Access
- Recognize Microsoft Office 2010 common features and navigation
- Perform basic editing tasks
- Demonstrate how to open, save, print, and close files
- Use Microsoft Help

skills

introduction

There are many shared features across the applications of Microsoft Office 2010. This chapter will prepare students to navigate the common features such as the user interface and the Ribbon. Readers will learn basic editing skills such as checking spelling and cut, copy, and paste. Other features that appear across applications such as managing files and folders, using Office Help, and previewing and printing are explained.

1.1 Introduction to Microsoft Office 2010

Microsoft® Office 2010 is a collection of business "productivity" applications (computer programs designed to make you more productive at work, school, and home). The most popular Office applications are

Microsoft Word—a word processing program. Word processing software allows you to create text-based documents, similar to how you would type a document on a typewriter. However, word processing software offers more powerful formatting and design tools, allowing you to create complex documents including reports, résumés, brochures, and newsletters.

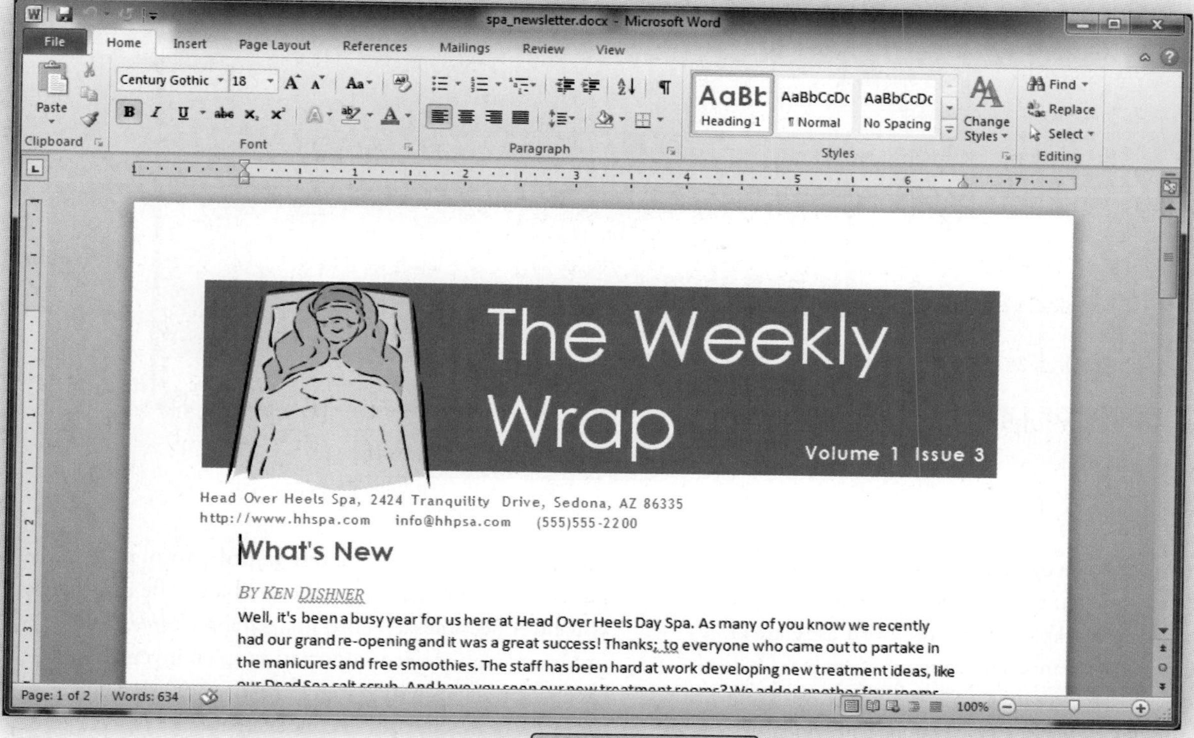

A Word Document

FIGURE OF 1.1

Microsoft Excel—a spreadsheet program. Originally, spreadsheet applications were viewed as electronic versions of an accountant's ledger. Today's spreadsheet applications can do much more than just calculate numbers—they include powerful charting and data analysis features. Spreadsheet programs can be used for everything from personal budgets to calculating loan payments.

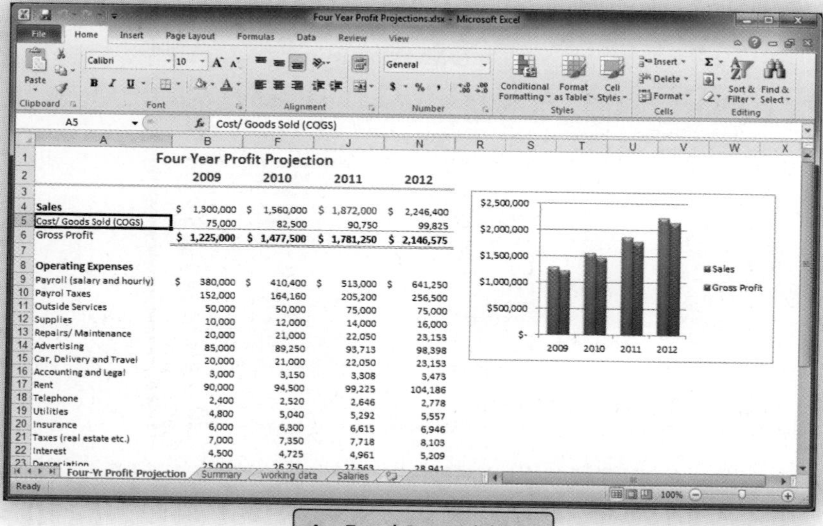

An Excel Spreadsheet

FIGURE OF 1.2

Microsoft PowerPoint—a presentation program. Such applications enable you to create robust, multimedia presentations. A presentation consists of a series of electronic slides. Each slide contains content, including text, images, charts, and other objects. You can add multimedia elements to slides, including animations, audio, and video.

FIGURE OF 1.3 A PowerPoint Presentation

Microsoft Access—a database program. Database applications allow you to organize and manipulate large amounts of data. Databases that allow you to relate tables and databases to one another are referred to as *relational* databases. As a database user, you usually see only one aspect of the database—a *form.* Database forms use a graphical interface to allow a user to enter record data. For example, when you fill out an order form online, you are probably interacting with a database. The information you enter becomes a record in a database *table.* Your order is matched with information in an inventory table (keeping track of which items are in stock) through a *query.* When your order is filled, a database *report* can be generated for use as an invoice or a bill of lading.

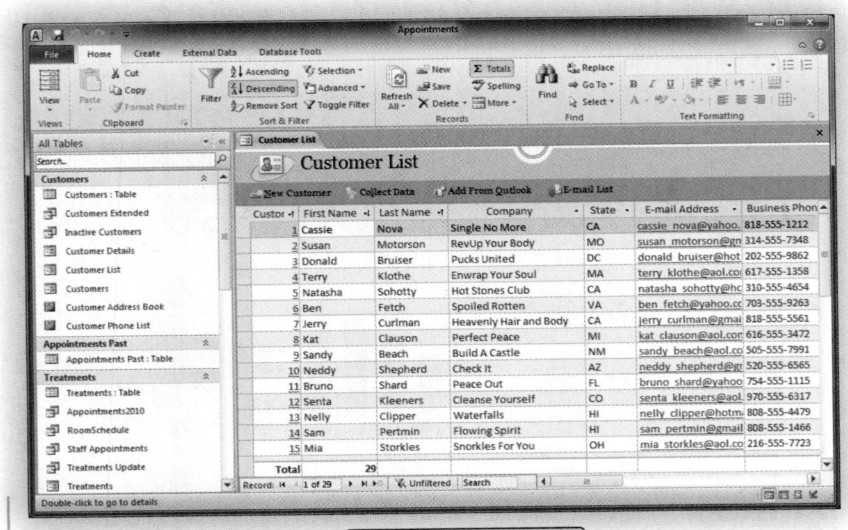

FIGURE OF 1.4 An Access Database

from the perspective of . . .

BUSY PARENT

I use a template to maintain a family calendar to keep track of everyone's activities. Word processing software is great for creating flyers for school projects, writing reports, and keeping a grocery list. Spreadsheets help me organize the family budget and do my accounting homework. I even use a database program to keep track of household items, just in case of an emergency.

To open one of the Office applications:

1. Click the Windows **Start** button (located in the lower left corner of your computer screen).
2. Click **All Programs.**
3. Click the **Microsoft Office** folder.
4. Click the application you want to open.

Word, Excel, and PowerPoint open a new blank file automatically; Access opens to Backstage view, where you are asked to give the database a file name first.

tips & tricks

You can download a free trial version of Microsoft Office from Microsoft's Web site (http://office.microsoft.com). The trial allows you to try the applications before buying them. When your trial period ends, if you haven't purchased the full software license yet, you will no longer be able to use the applications (although you will continue to be able to open and view any files you previously created with the trial version).

tell me **more**

There are three popular versions of Microsoft Office, each offering a different combination of programs.

Office Home and Student—includes *Word 2010, Excel 2010, PowerPoint 2010,* and *OneNote 2010* (a note-taking and organizational program). This version of Office is intended for home use only. Use by commercial or nonprofit businesses is prohibited.

Office Home and Business—includes the same applications as the Home and Student version, and adds *Outlook 2010* for e-mail, contacts, and calendar management.

Office Professional—includes the same applications as the Home and Business version, and adds *Access 2010* and *Publisher 2010* (a desktop publishing application).

try **this**

A shortcut for starting one of the Office applications is to type the application name in the *Instant Search* box at the bottom of the *Start* menu:

1. Click the **Start** button.
2. In the *Instant Search* box, type `Access`, `Excel`, `PowerPoint`, or `Word`, and then press ←Enter.
3. The application will open a new blank file.

1.2 Getting to Know the Office 2010 User Interface

THE RIBBON

If you have used a word processing or spreadsheet program in the past, you may be surprised when you open one of the Microsoft Office 2010 applications for the first time. Beginning with Office 2007, Microsoft redesigned the user experience—replacing the familiar menu bar/toolbar interface with a new Ribbon interface that makes it easier to find application functions and commands.

The **Ribbon** is located across the top of the application window and organizes common features and commands into tabs. Each **tab** organizes commands further into related **groups.** When a specific type of object is selected (such as a picture, table, or chart), a contextual tab will appear. **Contextual tabs** contain commands specific to the type of object selected and are only visible when the commands might be useful.

Each application includes a **Home tab** that contains the most commonly used commands for that application. For example, in Word, the *Home* tab includes the following groups: *Clipboard, Font, Paragraph, Styles,* and *Editing,* while the Excel *Home* tab includes groups more appropriate for a spreadsheet program: *Clipboard, Font, Alignment, Number, Styles, Cells,* and *Editing.*

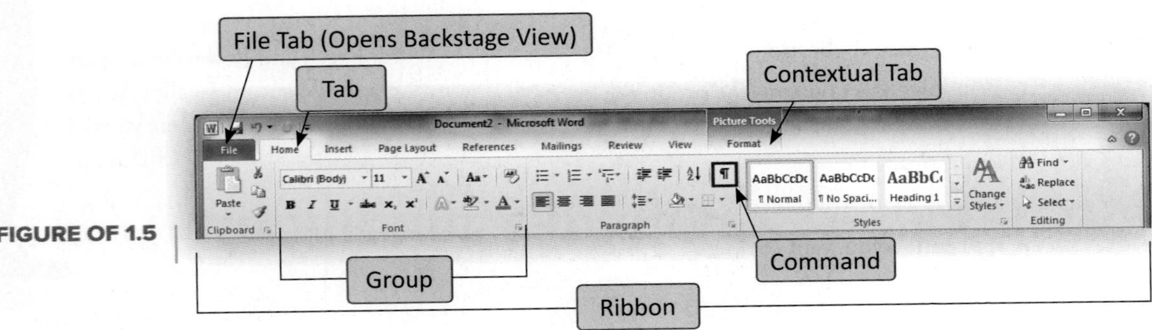

FIGURE OF 1.5

BACKSTAGE

Notice that each application also includes a **File tab** at the far left side of the Ribbon. Clicking the *File* tab opens the **Microsoft Office Backstage™ view,** where you can access the commands for managing and protecting your files including Save, Open, Close, New, and Print. Backstage replaces the Office Button menu from Office 2007 and the *File* menu from previous versions of Office.

tips & tricks

If you need more space for your document, you can minimize the Ribbon by clicking the **Minimize the Ribbon** button in the upper-right corner of the Ribbon (or press Ctrl + F1). When the Ribbon is minimized, the tab names appear along the top of the window (similar to a menu bar). When you click a tab name, the Ribbon appears. After you select a command or click away from the Ribbon, the Ribbon hides again. To redisplay the Ribbon permanently, click the **Expand the Ribbon** button in the upper-right corner of the window. Double-click the active tab to hide or display the Ribbon.

KEYBOARD SHORTCUTS

Many commands available through the Ribbon and Backstage are also accessible through keyboard shortcuts and shortcut menus.

Keyboard shortcuts are keys or combinations of keys that you press to execute a command. Some keyboard shortcuts refer to F keys or function keys. These are the keys that run across the top of the keyboard. Pressing these keys will execute specific commands. For example, pressing the F1 key will open Help in any of the Microsoft Office applications. Keyboard shortcuts typically use a combination of two keys, although some commands use a combination of three keys and others only one key. When a keyboard shortcut calls for a combination of key presses, such as Ctrl + V to paste an item from the Clipboard, you must first press the modifier key (Ctrl), holding it down while you press the V key on the keyboard.

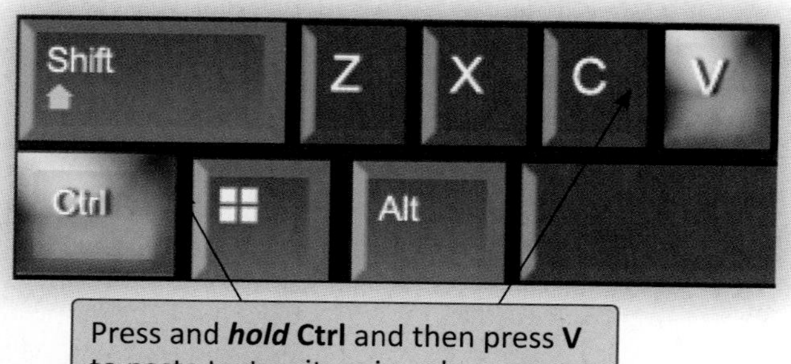
Shift
Z
X
C
V
Ctrl
Alt
Press and ***hold*** **Ctrl** and then press **V** to paste text or item in a document.

FIGURE OF 1.6

try **this**

Many of the keyboard shortcuts are universal across applications—all applications, not just Microsoft Office applications. Some examples of universal shortcut keys include

- Ctrl + C = Copy
- Ctrl + X = Cut
- Ctrl + V = Paste
- Ctrl + Z = Undo
- Ctrl + O = Open
- Ctrl + S = Save

SHORTCUT MENUS

Shortcut menus are menus of commands that display when you right-click an area of the application window. The area or object you right-click determines which menu appears. For example, if you right-click in a paragraph, you will see a shortcut menu of commands for working with text; however, if you right-click an image, you will see a shortcut menu of commands for working with images.

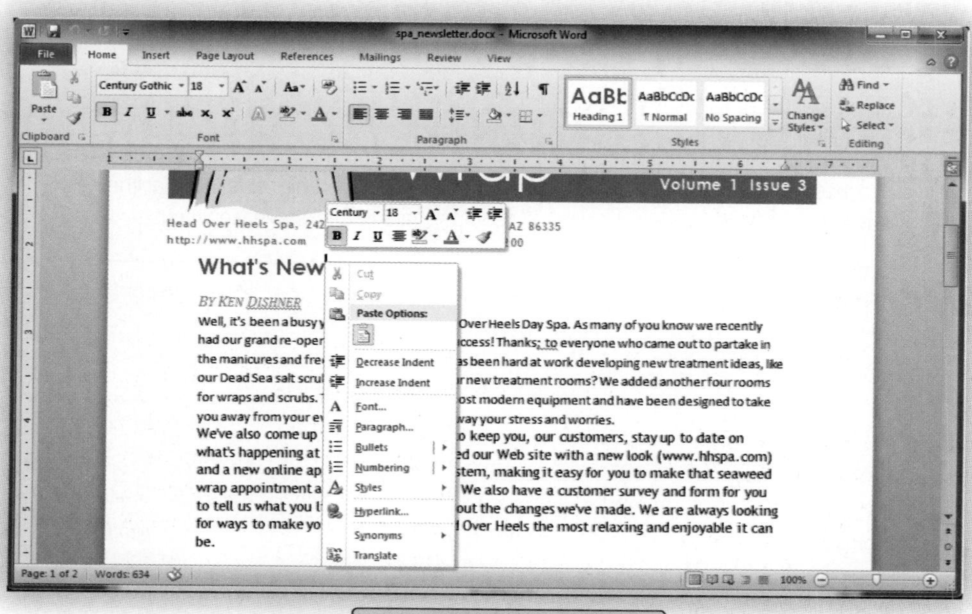
Right-Click Shortcut Menu

FIGURE OF 1.7

QUICK ACCESS TOOLBAR

The **Quick Access Toolbar** is located at the top of the application window above the *File* tab. The Quick Access Toolbar, as its name implies, gives you quick one-click access to common commands. You can add commands to and remove commands from the Quick Access Toolbar.

To modify the Quick Access Toolbar:

1. Click the **Customize Quick Access Toolbar** button located on the right side of the Quick Access Toolbar.
2. Options with check marks next to them are already displayed on the toolbar. Options with no check mark are not currently displayed.
3. Click an option to add it to or remove it from the Quick Access Toolbar.

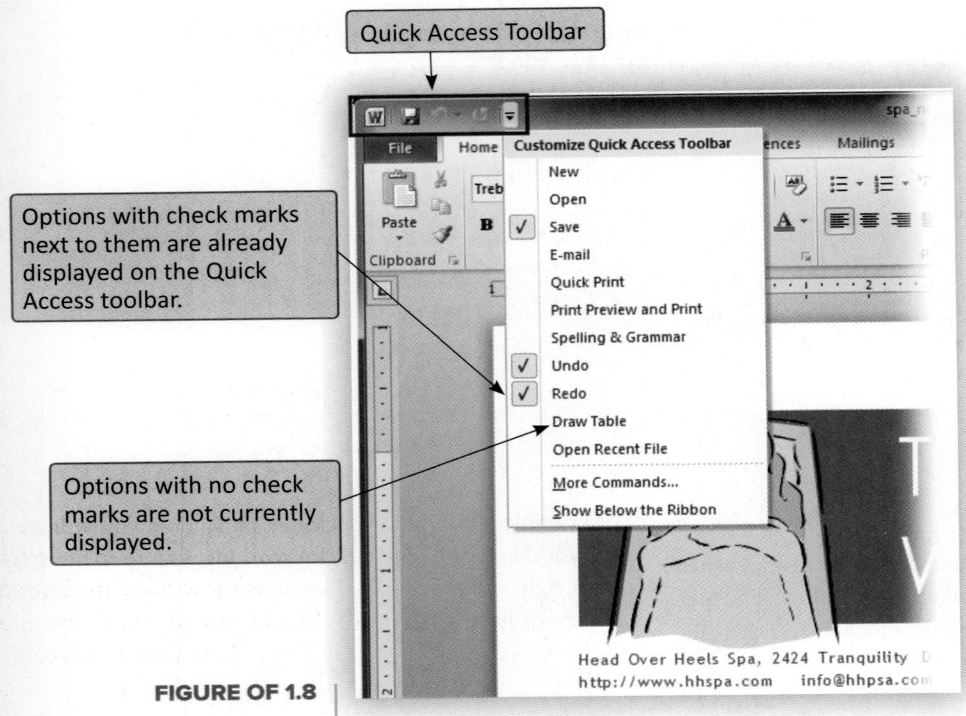

FIGURE OF 1.8

tips & tricks

If you want to be able to print with a single mouse click, add the *Quick Print* button to the Quick Access Toolbar. If you do not need to change any print settings, this is by far the easiest method to print a file because it doesn't require opening Backstage view first.

THE MINI TOOLBAR

The **Mini toolbar** gives you access to common tools for working with text. When you select text and then rest your mouse over the text, the Mini toolbar fades in. You can then click a button to change the selected text just as you would on the Ribbon.

To display the Mini toolbar, you can also right-click the text. The Mini toolbar appears above the shortcut menu.

try **this**

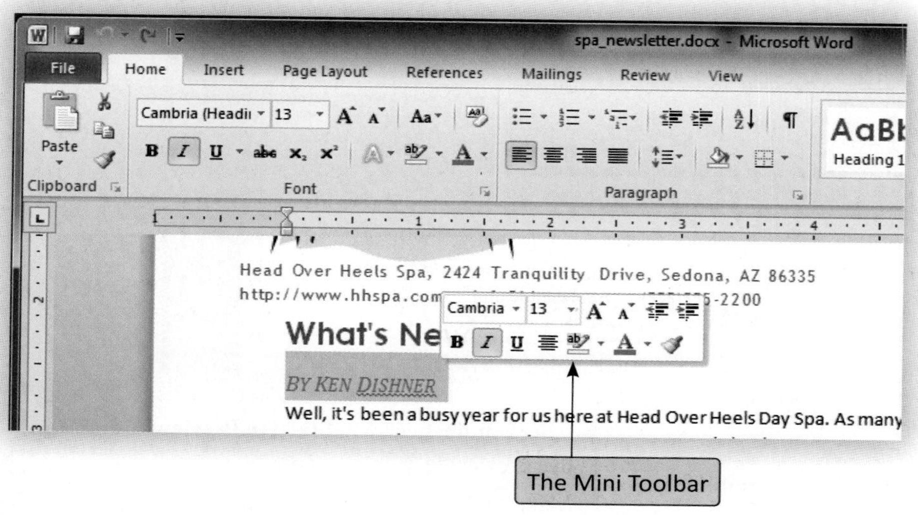

FIGURE OF 1.9

ENHANCED SCREENTIPS

A **ScreenTip** is a small information box that displays the name of the command when you rest your mouse over a button on the Ribbon. An **Enhanced ScreenTip** displays not only the name of the command, but also the keyboard shortcut (if there is one) and a short description of what the button does and when it is used. Certain Enhanced ScreenTips also include an image along with a description of the command.

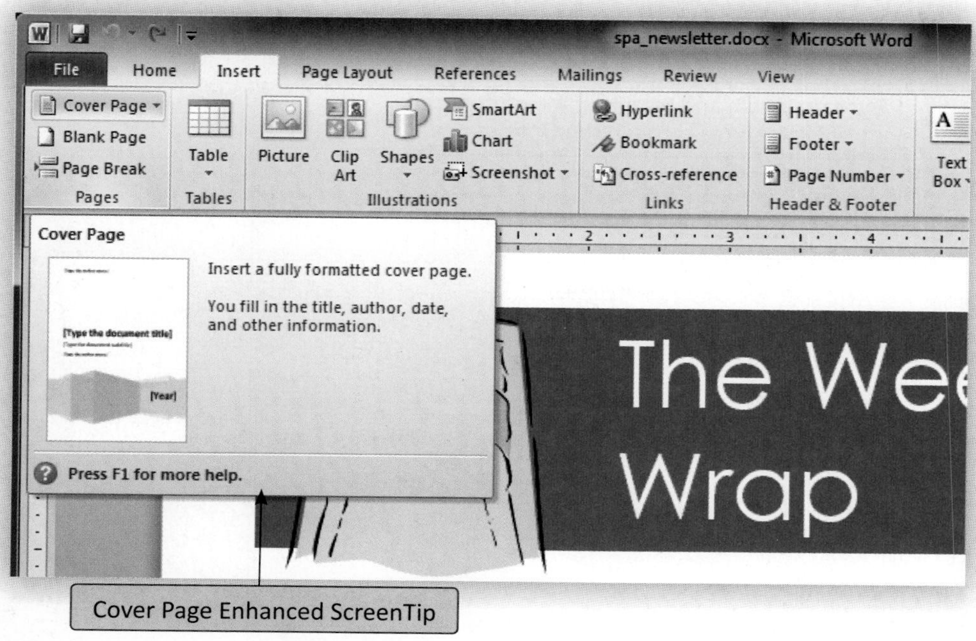

FIGURE OF 1.10

USING LIVE PREVIEW

The **Live Preview** feature in Microsoft Office 2010 allows you to see formatting changes in your file before actually committing to the change. When Live Preview is active, rolling over a command on the Ribbon will temporarily apply the formatting to the currently active text or object. To apply the formatting, click the formatting option.

Use Live Preview to preview the following:

- **Font Formatting**—including the font, font size, text highlight color, and font color
- **Paragraph Formatting**—including numbering, bullets, and shading
- **Quick Styles and Themes**
- **Table Formatting**—including table styles and shading
- **Picture Formatting**—including correction and color options, picture styles, borders, effects, positioning, brightness, and contrast
- **SmartArt**—including layouts, styles, and colors
- **Shape Styles**—including borders, shading, and effects

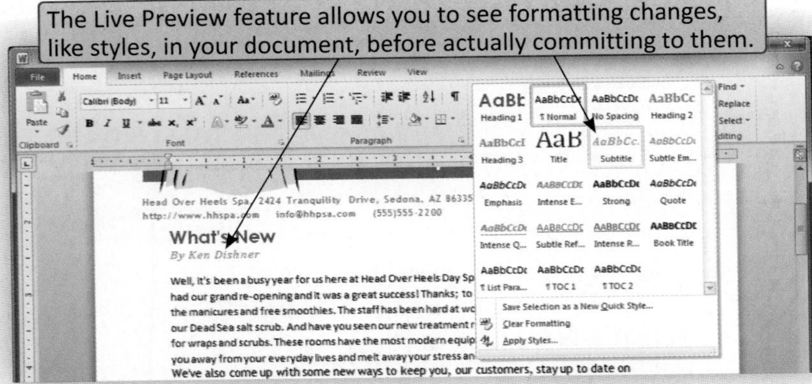

The Live Preview feature allows you to see formatting changes, like styles, in your document, before actually committing to them.

FIGURE OF 1.11

THE OPTIONS DIALOG

You can enable and disable some of the user interface features through the *Options* dialog.

1. Click the **File** tab to open Backstage view.
2. Click **Options.**
3. Make the changes you want, and then click **OK** to save your changes.
   - Check or uncheck **Show Mini toolbar on selection** to control whether or not the Mini toolbar appears when you hover over selected text. (This does not affect the appearance of the Mini toolbar when you right-click.)
   - Check or uncheck **Enable Live Preview** to turn the live preview feature on or off.
   - Make a selection from the *ScreenTip style:* list:
     - **Show feature descriptions in ScreenTips** displays Enhanced ScreenTips when they are available.
     - **Don't show feature descriptions in ScreenTips** hides Enhanced ScreenTips. The ScreenTip will still include the keyboard shortcut if there is one available.
     - **Don't show ScreenTips** hides ScreenTips altogether, so if you hold your mouse over a button on the Ribbon, nothing will appear.

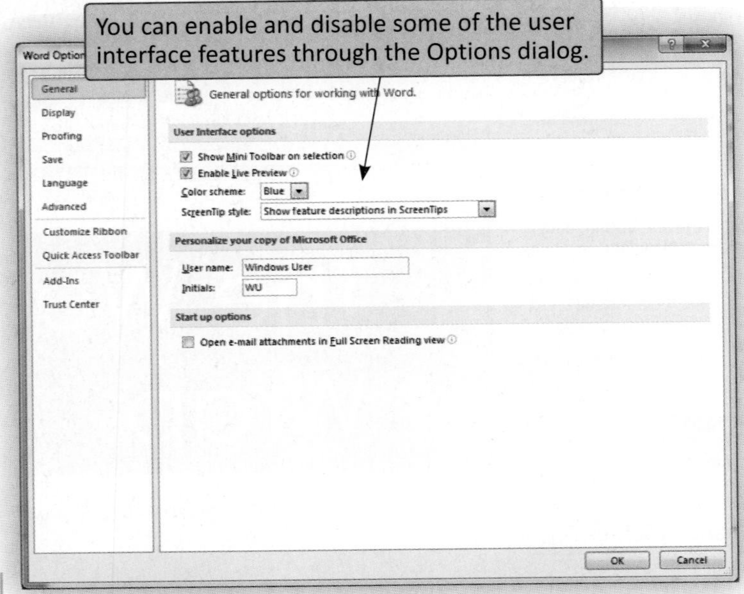

FIGURE OF 1.12

1.3 Opening Files

Opening a file retrieves it from storage and displays it on your computer screen. The steps for opening a file are the same for Word documents, Excel spreadsheets, PowerPoint presentations, and Access databases.

To open an existing file:

1. Click the **File** tab to open Backstage view.
2. Click **Open.**
3. The *Open* dialog box appears. If necessary, navigate to find the folder location where the file you want is stored.
4. Select the file name in the large list box.
5. Click the **Open** button in the dialog box.

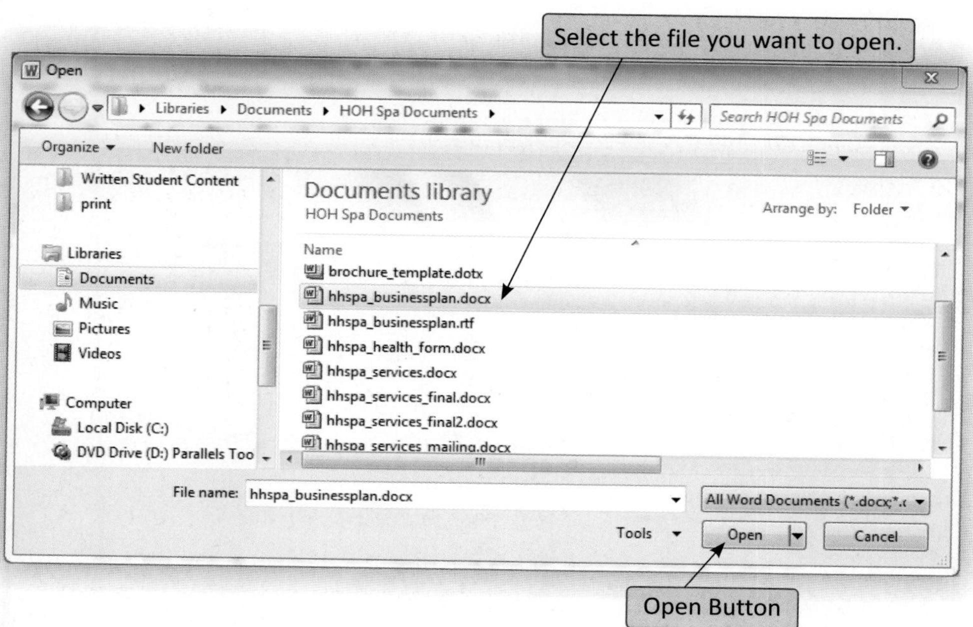

FIGURE OF 1.13

tips & tricks

The screen shot shown here is from Word 2010 running on the Microsoft Windows 7 operating system. Depending on the operating system you are using, the *Open* dialog box will appear somewhat different. However, the basic steps for opening a file are the same regardless of which operating system you are using.

tell me more

You can find files that you have recently worked on.

1. Click the **File** tab to open Backstage view.
2. Click **Recent.**
3. The **Recent Files** list shows the most recent files you have worked on. Click a file name to open it.

If you don't see the file you need in the *Recent Files* list, you can use the *Recent Places* list to browse to a specific folder. Click a folder in the *Recent Places* list to open the *Open* dialog showing files in that location.

try this

To open the *Open* dialog box, you can also press Ctrl + O on the keyboard.

To open the file from within the *Open* dialog box, you can also

- Press the ←Enter key once you have typed or selected a file name.
- Double-click the file name.

1.4 Creating New Files

When you open one of the Office applications from the *Start* menu, a new blank file appears on your screen ready for you to begin work. But what if you want to create another new file? Will you need to exit the program and then launch it again? The **New** command allows you to create new files without exiting and reopening the program.

To create a new blank file:

1. Click the **File** tab to open Backstage view.
2. Click **New.**
3. Under the *Home* section, the *Blank* option is selected by default. To create a new blank document, workbook, or presentation, simply click the **Create** button beneath the preview of the blank file. In Access, you will need to enter a file name for the new database before clicking **Create.**

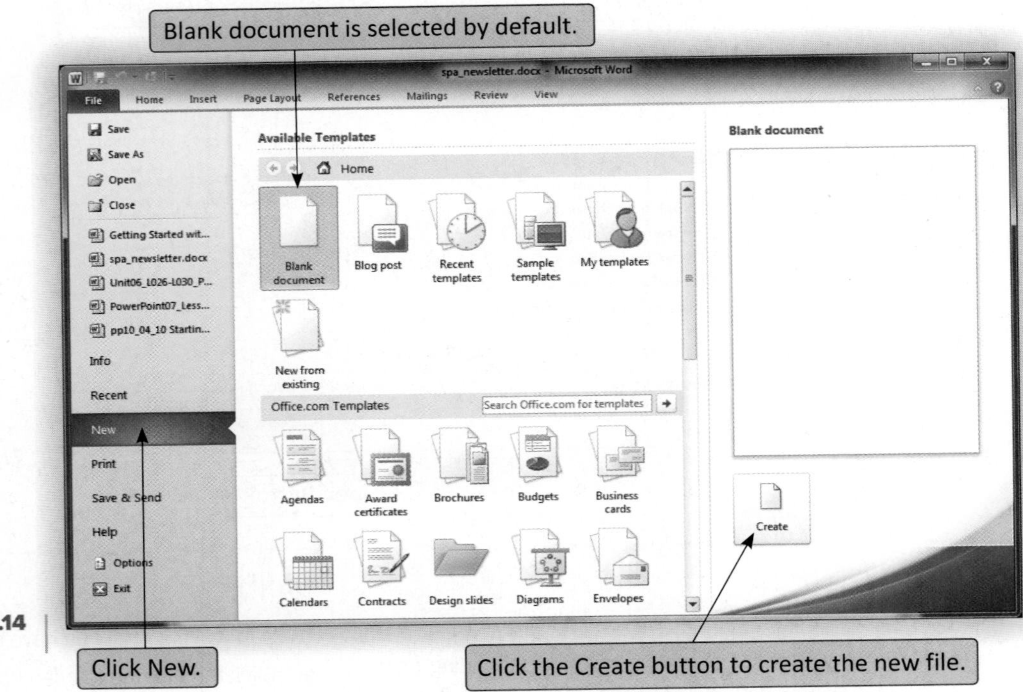
Blank document is selected by default.
Click New.
Click the Create button to create the new file.

FIGURE OF 1.14

A **template** is a file with predefined settings that you can use as a pattern to create a new file of your own. Using a template makes creating a fully formatted and designed new file easy, saving you time and effort. There are templates available for letters, memos, résumés, newsletters, budgets, expense reports, sales presentations, project management databases, and almost any other type of file you can imagine.

To create a new file from a template:

1. Click the **File** tab to open Backstage view.
2. Click **New.**
3. Notice that the entire right pane is labeled *Available Templates.* Even the *Blank* option is considered a template. The *Home* section gives you access to all the templates located on your computer. The *Office.com* section gives you access to hundreds of templates available from Office.com, but you must have an active Internet connection to download a template from this section.
4. To find a template from Office.com, click one of the categories in the *Office.com* section.
5. Click each template image to see a preview of the file and a brief description of the template.
6. When you find the template you want to use, click the **Download** button.
7. A new file opens, prepopulated with all of the template elements.

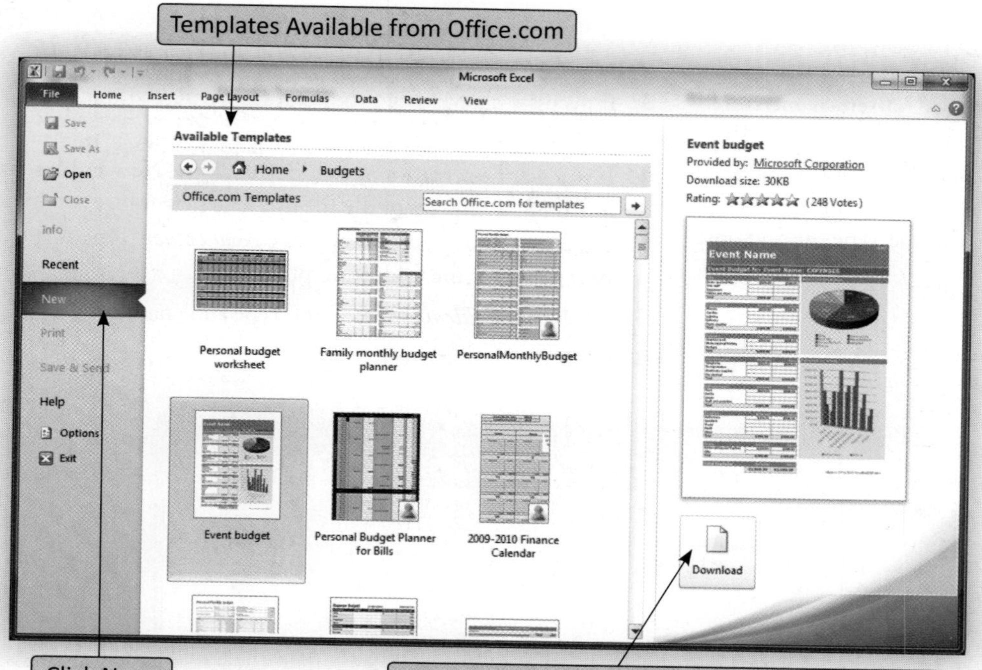

FIGURE OF 1.15

tell me **more**

Each of the Office applications includes a set of templates that are copied to your computer when you install the application. These templates are always available from the *Home* section of the *Available Templates* page, in the *Sample templates* category.

try **this**

To bypass the Backstage view and create a new blank file, press Ctrl + N on the keyboard.

1.5 Saving Files

As you work on a new file, it is displayed on-screen and stored in your computer's memory. However, it is not permanently stored until you save it as a file to a specific location. The first time you save a file, the *Save As* dialog box will open. Here you can enter a file name, select the file type, and choose where to save the file.

To save a file for the first time:

1. Click the **Save** button on the Quick Access Toolbar.
2. The *Save As* dialog box appears.
3. If necessary, navigate to the location where you want to save the file.
4. If you want to create a new folder, click the **New Folder** button near the top of the file list. The new folder is created with the temporary name *New Folder.* Type the new name for the folder and press **Enter.**
5. Click in the *File name:* box and type a file name.
6. Click the **Save** button.

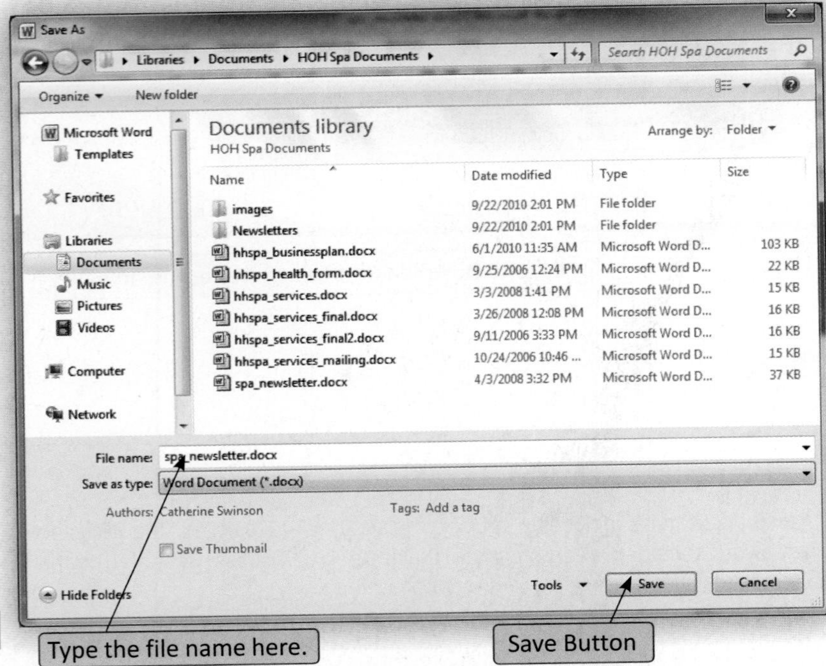

Type the file name here.
Save Button

FIGURE OF 1.16

The next time you save this file, it will be saved with the same file name and to the same location automatically. The *Save As* dialog will not open again.

As you are working with files, be sure to **save often!** Although Office 2010 includes a recovery function, it is not foolproof. If you lose power or your computer crashes, you may lose all the work done on the file since the last save.

tips & tricks

The screen shot shown here is from Word 2010 running on the Microsoft Windows 7 operating system. Depending on the operating system you are using, the *Save As* dialog box will appear somewhat different. However, the basic steps for saving a file are the same regardless of which operating system you are using.

try this

To save a file, you can also

› Press Ctrl + S on the keyboard.

› Click the **File** tab, and then select **Save.**

To open the *Save As* dialog box, you can also click the **File** tab, and then select **Save As.**

tell me more

Beginning with Office 2007, Microsoft changed the file format for Office files. Files created with Office 2007 and Office 2010 will not work with older versions of Office. If you want to share your files with people who are using Office 2003 or older, you should save the files in a different file format.

1. Click the **File** tab.
2. Click **Save As.**
3. The *Save As* dialog opens. Click the arrow at the end of the *Save as type:* box to expand the list of available file types.
4. To ensure compatibility with older versions of Office, select the file type that includes 97-2003 (for example, *Word 97-2003 Document* or *Excel 97-2003 Workbook*).

1.6 Checking Spelling

All of the Office applications include a built-in spelling checker. When you start the spelling checker, you will see that the *Spelling* dialog box varies slightly from application to application, but the basic spelling checker functionality is the same for all. In fact, the Office applications share the same dictionaries (the lists of words that the spelling checker checks against). With the spelling checker available in every application, there are no excuses for typos and misspelled words.

To check a file for spelling errors:

1. Click the **Review** tab on the Ribbon. In the *Proofing* group, click the **Spelling** button (**Spelling & Grammar** in Word). In Access, the *Spelling* button is on the *Home* tab, in the *Records* group.
2. The first spelling error appears in the *Spelling* dialog box.
3. Review the spelling suggestions and then select an action:
    - Click **Ignore Once** to make no changes to this instance of the word.
    - Click **Ignore All** to make no changes to all instances of the word.
    - Click **Add to Dictionary** to make no changes to this instance of the word and add it to the main dictionary, so future uses of this word will not show up as misspellings. When you add a word to the main dictionary, it is available for all of the Office applications.
    - Click the correct spelling in the *Suggestions:* list, and click **Change** to correct just this instance of the misspelling in your document.
    - Click the correct spelling in the *Suggestions:* list, and click **Change All** to correct all instances of the misspelling in your document.
4. After you select an action, the spelling checker automatically advances to the next suspected spelling error.
5. When the spelling checker finds no more errors, it displays a message telling you the check is complete. Click **OK** to close the dialog and return to your file.

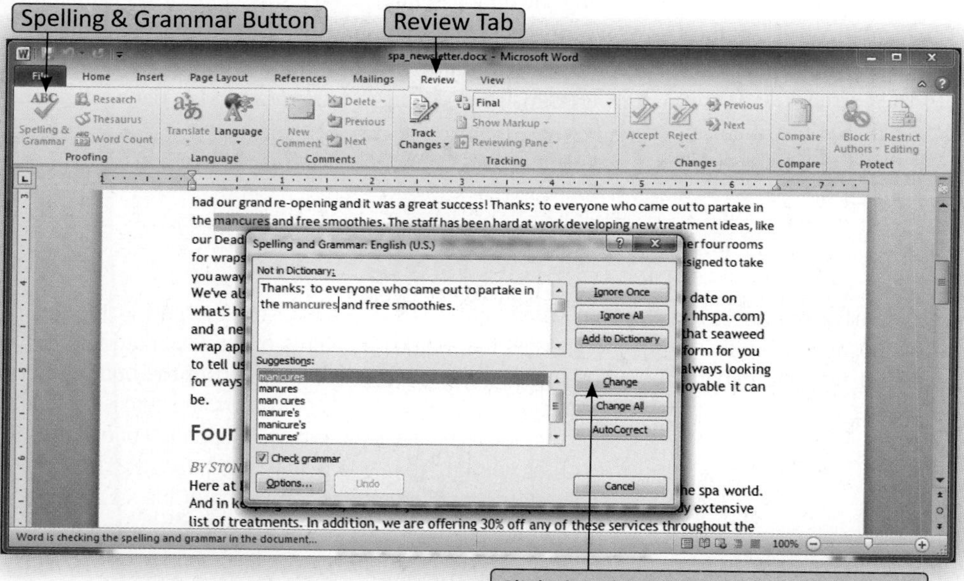
Spelling & Grammar Button
Review Tab
Click the Change button to replace the current word with the suggested word.

FIGURE OF 1.17

tips & tricks

Whether or not you use the Spelling tool, you should always proofread your files. Spelling checkers are not infallible, especially if you misuse a word, yet spell it correctly—for instance, writing "bored" instead of "board."

If you misspell a word often, the next time the spelling checker catches the misspelling, use this trick: Click the correct spelling in the *Suggestions:* list and then click the **AutoCorrect** button. Now, when you type the misspelled version of the word, it will be corrected automatically as you type.

tell me more

If you have repeated the same word in a sentence, Word will flag the second instance of the word as a possible error. In the *Spelling* dialog box, the *Change* button will switch to a *Delete* button. Click the **Delete** button to remove the duplicate word.

try this

To open the *Spelling* dialog box, you can also press the F7 key.

1.7 Using Cut, Copy, and Paste

The *cut, copy,* and *paste* commands are used to move text and other objects within a file and from one file to another. Text or an object that is **cut** is removed from the file and placed on the Office clipboard for later use. The **copy** command places a duplicate of the selected text or object on the Clipboard without changing the file. The **paste** command is used to insert text or an object from the Clipboard into a file.

To move text within a file:

1. Select the text to be cut or copied.
2. On the *Home* tab of the Ribbon, click the appropriate button:

   Cut

   or

   Copy

3. Place the cursor where you want to insert the text from the Clipboard.
4. Click the **Paste** button on the Ribbon.

These same steps apply whether you are cutting, copying, and pasting text, pictures, shapes, video files, or any type of object in an Office file.

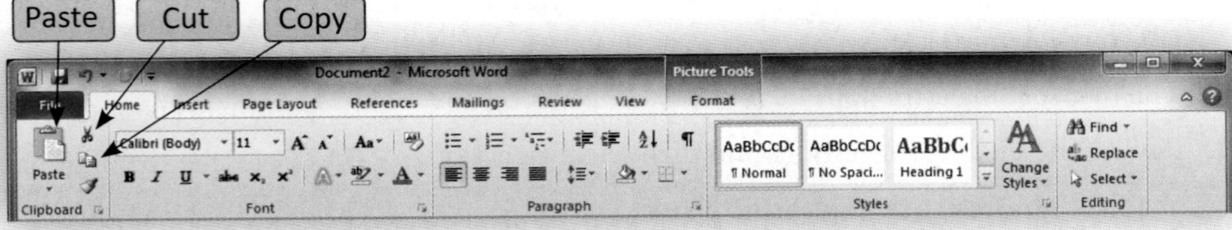

FIGURE OF 1.18

When you cut or copy items, they are placed on the **Office Clipboard.** The Office Clipboard can store up to 24 items. When you use the Paste command, the item most recently added to the Clipboard is pasted into the current file. If you want to cut or copy multiple items and then paste them in different places in your file, open the Office Clipboard by clicking the dialog launcher in the *Clipboard* group. Next to each item in the Clipboard is an icon that identifies the application from which the item originated (Word, Excel, PowerPoint, etc.). From the *Clipboard* task pane, click any item to paste it into the current file.

tips & tricks

The Office Clipboard is common across all Office applications—so you can cut text from a Word document and then paste that text into an Excel spreadsheet or copy a chart from Excel into a PowerPoint presentation.

tell me more

The *Paste* button has two parts—the top part of the button pastes the topmost contents of the Clipboard into the current file. If you click the bottom part of the button (the *Paste* button arrow), you can control how the item is pasted. Each type of object has different paste options. For example, if you are pasting text, you may have options to keep the source formatting, merge the formatting of the source and the current document, or paste only the text without any formatting. Move your mouse over the icon for each paste option to see a preview of how the paste would look, and then click the icon for the paste option you want.

try this

To apply the *cut, copy,* or *paste* command, you can also use the following shortcuts:

- **Cut** = Press Ctrl + X on the keyboard, or right-click and select **Cut.**
- **Copy** = Press Ctrl + C on the keyboard, or right-click and select **Copy.**
- **Paste** = Press Ctrl + V on the keyboard, or right-click and select **Paste.**

1.8 Using Undo and Redo

If you make a mistake when working, the **undo** command allows you to reverse the last action you performed. The **redo** command allows you to reverse the undo command and restore the file to its previous state. The Quick Access Toolbar gives you immediate access to both of these commands.

To undo the last action taken, click the **Undo** button on the Quick Access Toolbar.

To redo the last action taken, click the **Redo** button on the Quick Access Toolbar.

To undo multiple actions at the same time:

1. Click the arrow next to the *Undo* button to expand the list of your most recent actions.
2. Click an action in the list.
3. The action you click will be undone, along with all the actions completed after that. In other words, your file will revert to the state it was in before that action.

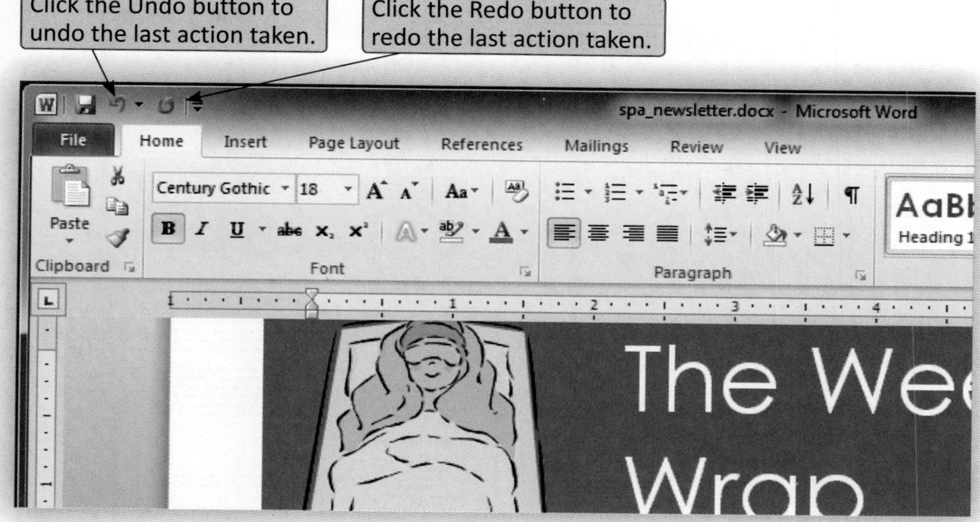

FIGURE OF 1.19

tips & tricks

Not every action can be undone. Often the application will warn you before you do something that you can't undo—but not always. For example, before you delete a database record, Access will warn you that the action cannot be undone. However, in Excel, if you delete a worksheet, Excel will ask you if you want to permanently delete the data in the sheet. The warning box does not explicitly tell you that this action cannot be undone.

try this

- To undo an action, you can also press Ctrl + Z on the keyboard.
- To redo an action, you can also press Ctrl + Y on the keyboard.

1.9 Previewing and Printing

In Office 2010, all of the print settings are combined in a single page along with a preview of how the printed file will look. As you change print settings, the preview updates. The page (referred to as the *Print* tab in Backstage view) is similar for Word, Excel, and PowerPoint, with each application offering different print settings. In Access, print preview is a special database view, not integrated into the *Print* tab.

To preview and print your file in Word, Excel, and PowerPoint:

1. Click the **File** tab.
2. Click **Print.**
3. At the right side of the page is a preview of how the printed file will look. Beneath the preview there is a page count. If there are multiple pages, use the *Next* and *Previous* arrows to preview all of the pages in the file. You can use the scrollbar to the right to scroll through the preview pages.
4. Click the **Print** button to send the file to your default printer.

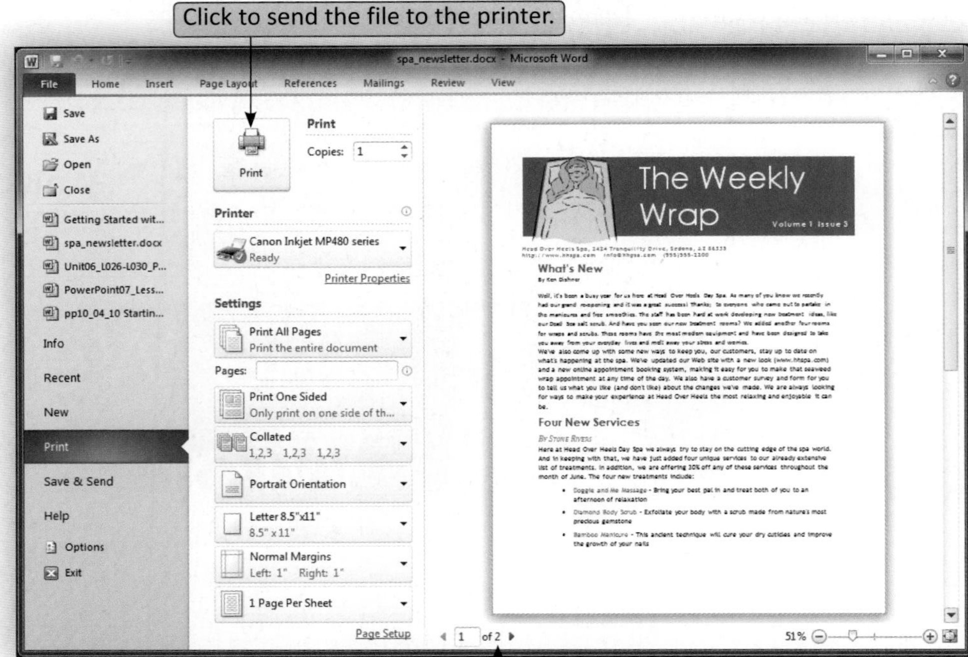

FIGURE OF 1.20

tips & tricks

Add the *Quick Print* command to the Quick Access Toolbar so you can print with a single mouse click. If you do not need to change the default print settings, you can click the *Quick Print* button instead of going through the *Print* tab in Backstage view.

try this

Press Ctrl + P to open the *Print* tab in Backstage view.

tell me more

To preview and print database objects in Access:

1. Click the **File** tab.
2. Click **Print.**
3. The *Print* tab offers three options:

Quick Print—sends the object to the printer without making any changes to the printer settings.

Print—opens the *Print* dialog, where you can control which pages to print, the number of copies to print, and other printer settings.

Print Preview—opens the object in Print Preview view. After viewing the preview, click the **File** tab again to return to Backstage view. Click **Print** again, and then choose one of the print options (*Quick Print* or *Print*).

1.10 Checking for Compatibility

Some features in Word 2010, Excel 2010, and PowerPoint 2010 are not available in previous versions of the applications. If a file uses one of the new features, opening it in a previous version of Office may have unintended consequences. For example, conditional formatting in an Excel 2010 workbook will be converted to static cell shading in Excel 2003. If you are sharing a file created in Office 2010 with someone who may be using an earlier version of Office, you should check the file for compatibility issues.

To check your file to see if it contains elements that are not compatible with earlier versions of Microsoft Office:

1. Click the **File** tab.
2. The *Info* tab in Backstage view opens automatically. Click the **Check for Issues** button, and then click **Check Compatibility.**
3. The *Compatibility Checker* dialog opens. This dialog is slightly different for each application, but the basic functionality is the same. The *Compatibility Checker* lists the items in your file that may be lost or downgraded if you save the document in an earlier Microsoft Office format. For each item, the dialog lists the number of times the issue occurs in the file (*Occurrences*).
4. Review the compatibility issues, and then click **OK** to close the *Compatibility Checker.*

Note: Running the Compatibility Checker does not change your document. It only lists the items that will lose functionality when the document is saved in an earlier Microsoft Office format. It is up to you whether or not you want to make any changes to the file.

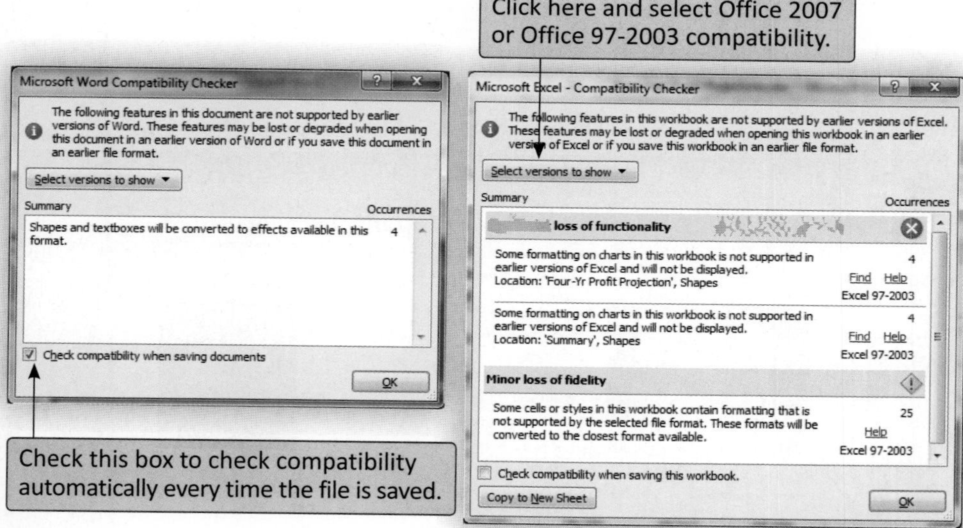

FIGURE OF 1.21

tips & tricks

If you often share files with people using an older version of Microsoft Office, you can set Compatibility Checker to run every time you save the file. Open the *Compatibility Checker* dialog, and then click the **Check compatibility when saving** check box to add a check mark. Click **OK.**

tell me more

In the Compatibility Checker, you can check for compatibility with Office 2007 or Office 97-2003. Click the **Select versions to show** button and click the option you want. There are few compatibility issues between Office 2010 and Office 2007, but there may be quite a few between Office 2010 and Office 97-2003.

1.11 Using the Status Bar

The status bar appears at the bottom of the application window and displays information about the current file. The information available on the status bar varies by application:

- In Word, the status bar may display the page number, number of words in the document, the current vertical position of the cursor in the document, and whether or not there are spelling and grammar errors.
- In Excel, the status bar displays whether the current cell is in *Ready* or *Edit* mode. When a group of cells is selected, the status bar may display the sum or average of the values, the number of cells selected, or the minimum or maximum value within the selected range.
- In PowerPoint, the status bar displays the slide number, the current theme, and whether or not there are spelling errors.
- In Access, the status bar displays the name of the current view and whether or not a filter has been applied to the current object.

To change the information shown on the status bar:

1. Right-click anywhere on the status bar.
2. In the *Customize Status Bar* menu, click an item to add it to or remove it from the status bar display.

Some status bar elements are common across applications:

- Word, Excel, and PowerPoint include a **zoom slider** at the right side of the status bar to allow you to control how the file appears on-screen. Drag the slider to the right to increase the zoom percentage and make text and images appear larger; drag the slider to the left to decrease the zoom percentage to make text and images look smaller.
- The status bar also displays buttons for changing the file view. Although Word, Excel, PowerPoint, and Access all offer different types of views, the buttons for changing the view appear in the same place for all the applications—near the right side of the status bar.

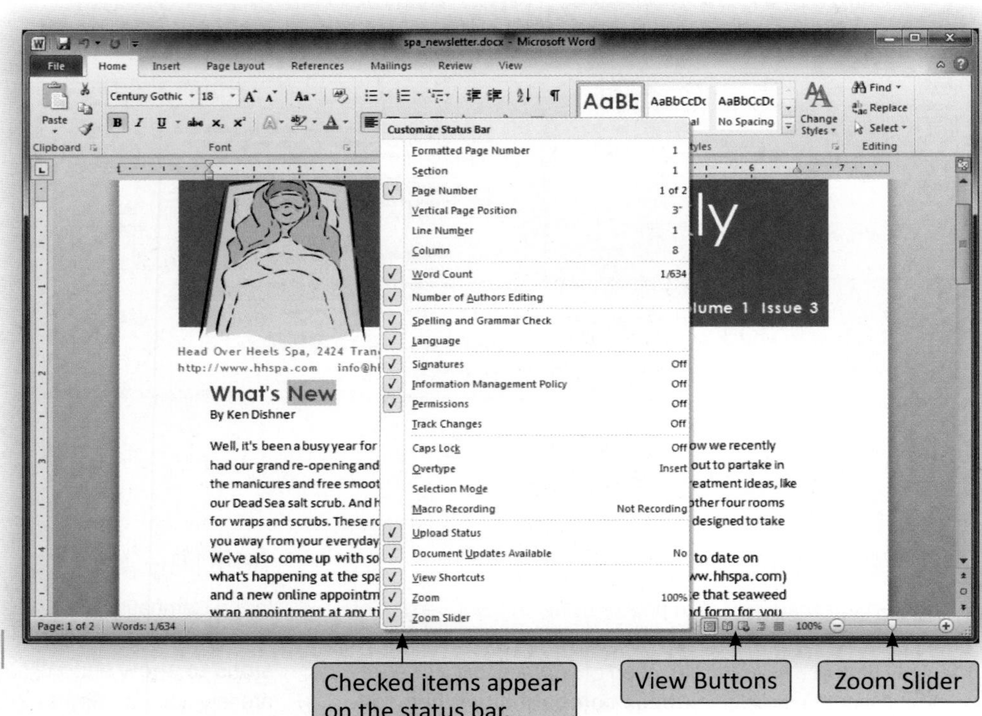

FIGURE OF 1.22

1.12 Using Help

If you don't know how to perform a task, you can look it up in the Office Help system. Each application comes with its own Help system with topics specifically tailored for working with that application.

To look up a topic using the Microsoft Office Help system:

1. Click the **Microsoft Office Help** button. It is located at the far right of the Ribbon.
2. In the *Type words to search for* box, type a word or phrase describing the topic you want help with.
3. Click the **Search** button.
4. A list of results appears.
5. Click a result to display the help topic.

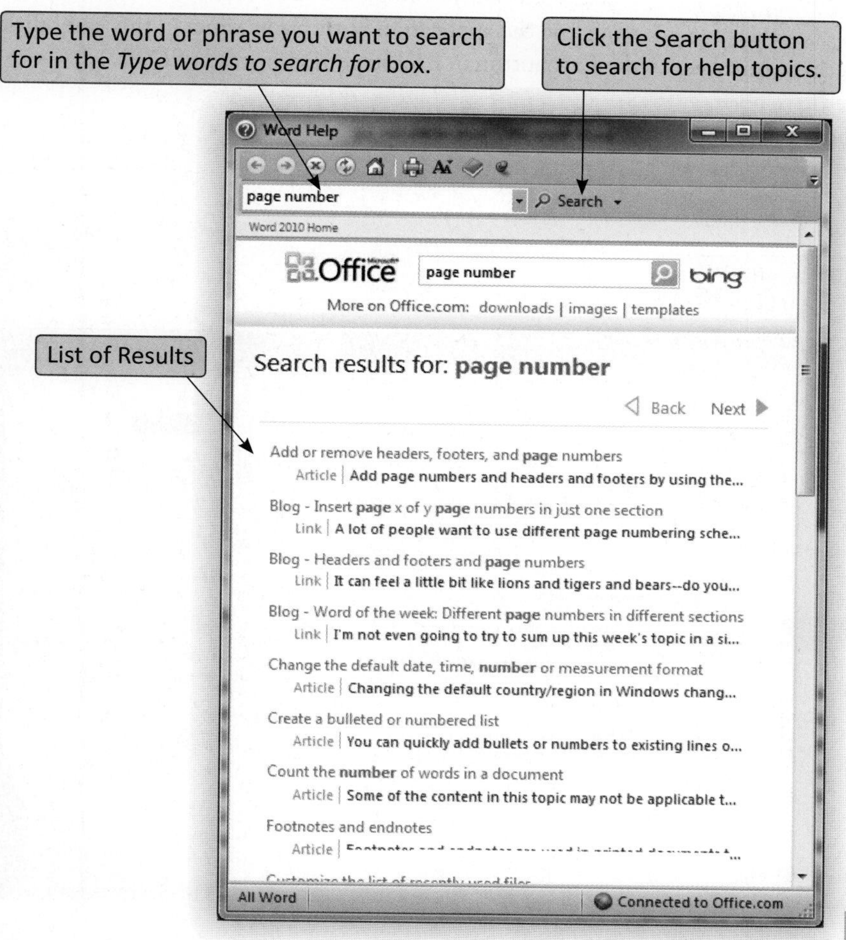

FIGURE OF 1.23

tips & tricks

At the bottom right of the Help window there is a button indicating if you are connected to Office.com or if you are working offline. If you are working offline (not connected to Office.com), Help is still available, but it is limited to the topics that are installed as part of the Office applications. If you are connected to Office.com, the Help system adds material from the Office.com Web site including templates and links to other Web sites.

tell me more

The Help toolbar is located at the top of the Help window. This toolbar includes buttons for navigating between screens, reloading the current screen, and returning to the Help Home page. Click the printer icon on the toolbar to print the current topic. Click the pushpin icon to keep the Help window always on top of the Microsoft Office application.

try this

To open the Help window, you can also press F1 on the keyboard.

1.13 Closing Files and Exiting the Application

Closing a document removes it from your computer screen and stores the last-saved version for future use. If you have not saved your latest changes, most applications will prevent you from losing work by asking if you want to save the changes you made before closing.

To close a file and save your latest changes:

1. Click the **File** tab to open Backstage view.
2. Click the **Close** button.
3. If you have made no changes since the last time you saved the file, it will close immediately. If changes have been made, the application displays a message box asking if you want to save the changes you made before closing.

Click **Save** to save the changes.

Click **Don't Save** to close the document without saving your latest changes.

Click **Cancel** to keep the document open.

When you close a file, the application stays open so you can open another file to edit or begin a new file. Often, when you are finished working on a file, you want to close the file and close the application at the same time. In this case, click the **Exit** button in Backstage view instead of *Close*.

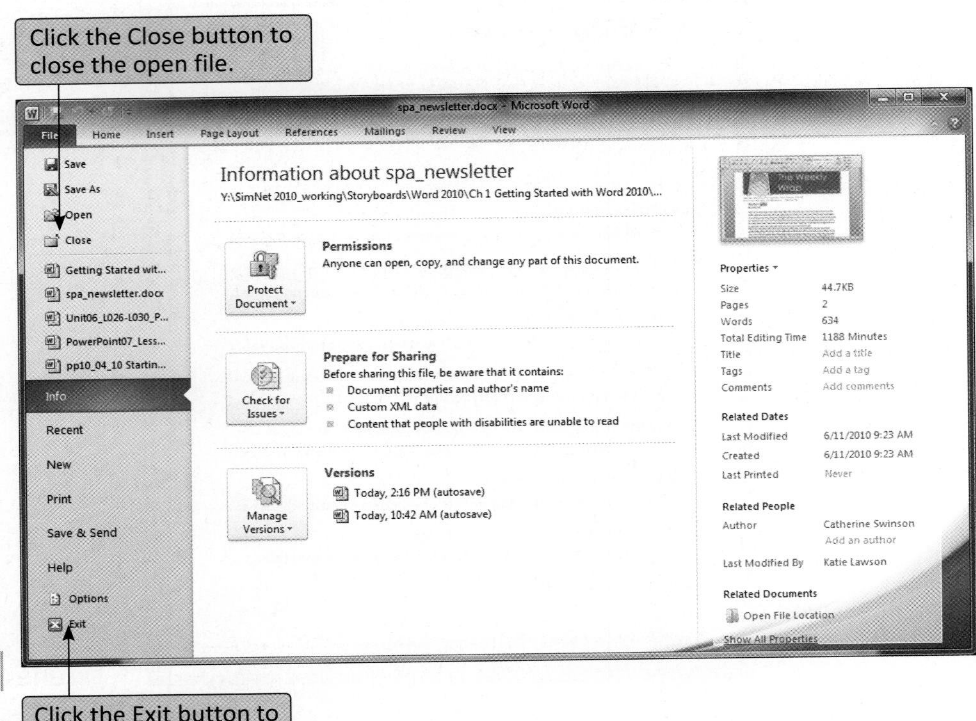

FIGURE OF 1.24

try this

To close a document, you can also press Ctrl + W on the keyboard.

Note: If you click the [X] in the upper-right corner of the application window or right-click the title bar of the application window and select **Close,** the application closes, not just the current file. This is similar to clicking the *Exit* button from Backstage view.

word 2010

chapter 1

Getting Started with Word 2010

In this chapter, you will learn the following skills:

- Enter, select, and delete text
- Use the AutoCorrect feature
- Use the spelling, grammar, and Thesaurus features
- Find and replace text in a document
- Change the way the document is viewed in the user interface

Skill 1.1 Introduction to Word 2010

Skill 1.2 Entering, Selecting, and Deleting Text

Skill 1.3 Using AutoCorrect

Skill 1.4 Checking Spelling and Grammar as You Type

Skill 1.5 Using the Thesaurus

Skill 1.6 Finding Text

Skill 1.7 Replacing Text

Skill 1.8 Using Views

Skill 1.9 Zooming a Document

skills

introduction

This introductory chapter will introduce students to some of the basic editing features of Microsoft Word 2010, and demonstrate changing how a document is displayed in the user interface. Students will learn how to save and edit documents, use the spell and grammar checker, use the Thesaurus, change the view and size of a document, use Find and Replace, and add AutoCorrect entries.

1.1 Introduction to Word 2010

Microsoft Office Word 2010 is a word processing program that enables you to create many types of documents including letters, résumés, reports, proposals, Web pages, blogs, and more. Word's advanced editing capabilities allow you to quickly and easily perform tasks such as checking your spelling and finding text in a long document. Robust formatting allows you to produce professional-looking documents with stylized fonts, layouts, and graphics. Building Blocks and Quick Styles allow you to insert complex desktop publishing elements to your document. Printing and file management can be managed directly from the Word window. In short, everything you need to create polished professional and personal documents is available in Microsoft Word.

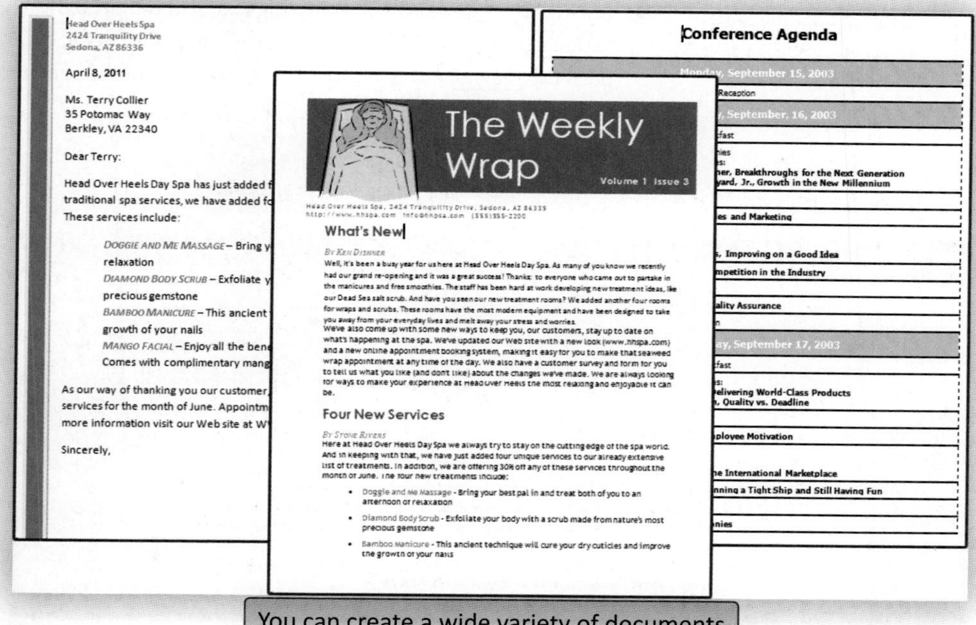

FIGURE WD 1.1

Here are some basic elements of a Word document:

Font—also called the typeface, refers to a set of characters of a certain design. You can choose from several pre-installed fonts available.

Paragraph—groups of sentences separated by a hard return. A hard return refers to pressing the ←Enter key to create a new paragraph. You can assign a paragraph its own style to help it stand out from the rest of the document.

Styles—complex formatting, including font, color, size, and spacing, that can be applied to text. Use consistent styles for headings, body text, notes, and captions throughout your document. Styles also can be applied to tables and graphics.

Tables—used to organize data into columns and rows.

Graphics—photographs, clip art, SmartArt, or line drawings that can be added to documents.

tips & tricks

Microsoft Office 2010 includes many other features that can help further enhance your documents. If you would like to learn more about these features, click the **Help** icon in the upper-right corner of the Word interface or visit Microsoft Office online through your Web browser.

tell me more

Some basic features of a word processing application include

Word wrap—places text on the next line when the right margin of the page has been reached.

Find and replace—searches for any word or phrase in the document. Also, allows all instances of a word to be replaced by another word.

Spelling and grammar—checks for errors in spelling and grammar and offers solutions to the problem.

1.2 Entering, Selecting, and Deleting Text

The basic function of a word processing application like Microsoft Word is to create written documents. Whether the documents are simple, such as a letter, or complex, such as a newsletter, one of the basic tasks you will perform in Word is entering text. **Word wrap** is a feature in Microsoft Word that automatically places text on the next line when the right margin of the document has been reached. There is no need to press ←Enter to begin a new line in the same paragraph. Only press ←Enter when you want to create a break and start a new paragraph.

To enter text in a document:

1. Place the cursor where you want the new text to appear.
2. Begin typing.
3. When the cursor reaches the end of the line, do not press ←Enter. Keep typing and allow word wrap to move the text to the next line.
4. If you make a mistake when entering text, you can press the ←Backspace key to remove text to the left of the cursor, or press the Delete key to remove text to the right of the cursor.

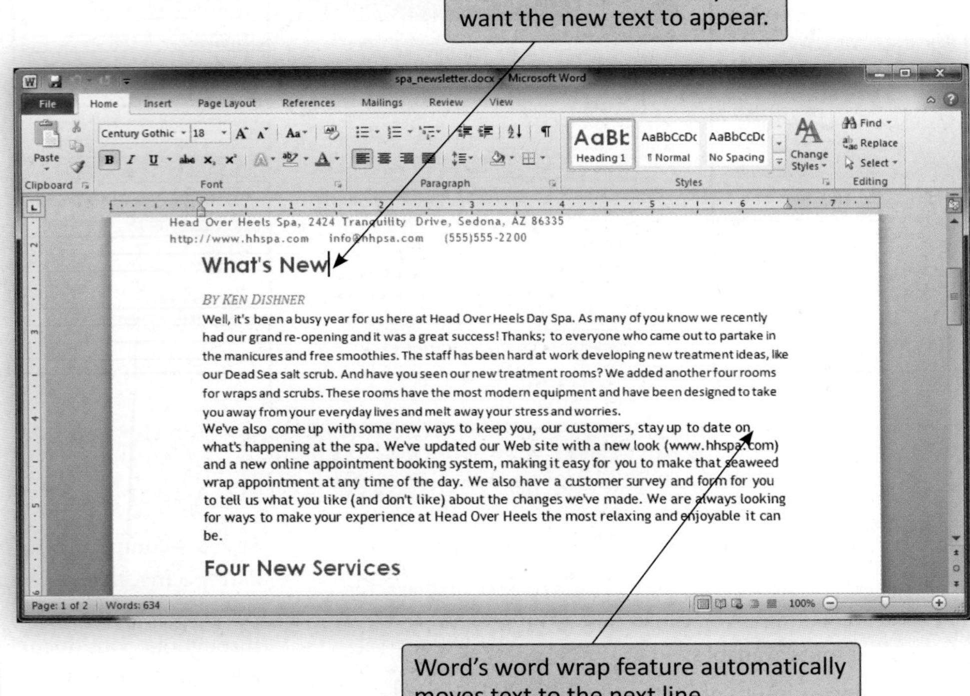
Place the cursor where you want the new text to appear.
Word's word wrap feature automatically moves text to the next line.

FIGURE WD 1.2

To select text in a document, click and drag the cursor across the text. A shaded background appears behind the selected text. Once the text is selected, you can apply commands, such as changing the font or applying the bold effect, to the text as a group.

tips & tricks

If you want to edit text you have typed, click in the text to place the cursor anywhere in the document. When you begin typing, the new text will be entered at the cursor point, pushing any existing text out to the right. You also can use the arrow keys to move the cursor around in the document and then begin typing.

tell me more

The cursor indicates the place on the page where text will appear when you begin typing. There are a number of cursors that display, but the default text cursor is a blinking vertical line.

try this

To select all the text in the document, you can press Ctrl + A on the keyboard.

1.3 Using AutoCorrect

While you are typing, Word's **AutoCorrect** feature analyzes each word as it is entered. Each word you type is compared to a list of common misspellings, symbols, and abbreviations. If a match is found, AutoCorrect automatically replaces the text in your document with the matching replacement entry. For example, if you type "teh," AutoCorrect will replace the text with "the."

You can create your own AutoCorrect entries, as well as modify preexisting ones. AutoCorrect also allows you to check for common capitalization errors. If you find yourself making spelling errors that are not recognized by AutoCorrect, you can add your own entries to the AutoCorrect replacement list.

To add a new entry to the AutoCorrect list:

1. Click the **File** tab.
2. Click the **Options** button.
3. In the *Word Options* dialog box, click the **Proofing** button.
4. Click the **AutoCorrect Options . . .** button.
5. Type your commonly made mistake in the *Replace:* box.
6. Type the correct spelling in the *With:* box.
7. Click **OK** in the *AutoCorrect* dialog box.
8. Click **OK** in the *Word Options* dialog box.

The next time you type the error, Word will automatically correct it for you.

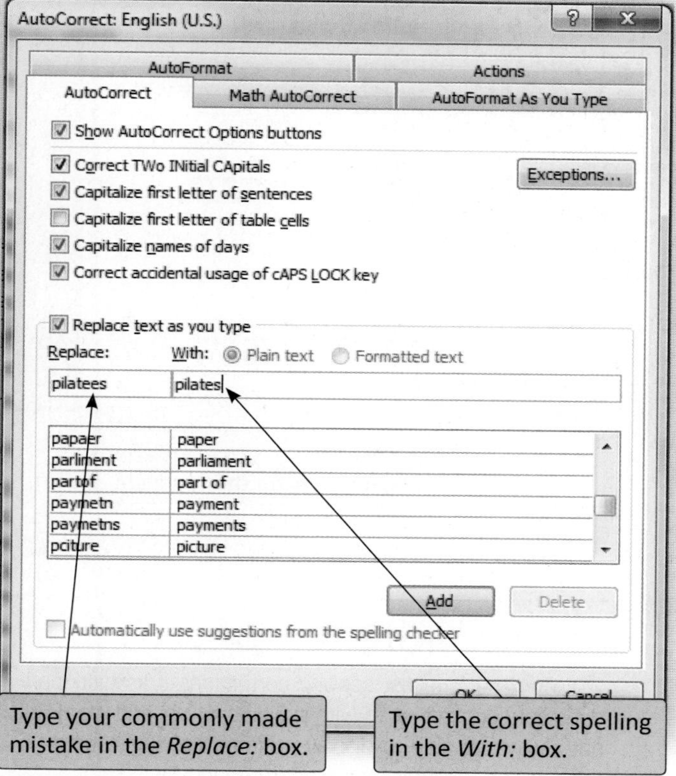

FIGURE WD 1.3

tips & tricks

If you find yourself typing certain long phrases over and over again, you can use the AutoCorrect feature to replace short abbreviations with long strings of text that you don't want to type. For example, you could replace the text *hhspa* with *Head Over Heels Day Spa.* This will not only save you time when typing, but more importantly ensure accuracy in your documents.

tell me **more**

AutoCorrect does more than just fix spelling errors. From the *AutoCorrect* dialog box you can set options to

- Correct accidental use of the Caps Lock key.
- Automatically capitalize the first letter in a sentence or the names of days.
- Automatically apply character formatting such as bold and italic, and format lists and tables.

Explore the *AutoCorrect* dialog box on your own to discover all the options available.

1.4 Checking Spelling and Grammar as You Type

Microsoft Word can automatically check your document for spelling and grammar errors while you type. Misspelled words, words that are not part of Word's dictionary, are indicated by a wavy red underline. Grammatical errors are similarly underlined in green, and are based on the grammatical rules that are part of Word's grammar checking feature. When you right-click either type of error, a shortcut menu appears with suggestions for correcting the error and other options.

To correct a misspelled word underlined in red:

1. Right-click the misspelled word.
2. Choose a suggested correction from the shortcut menu.

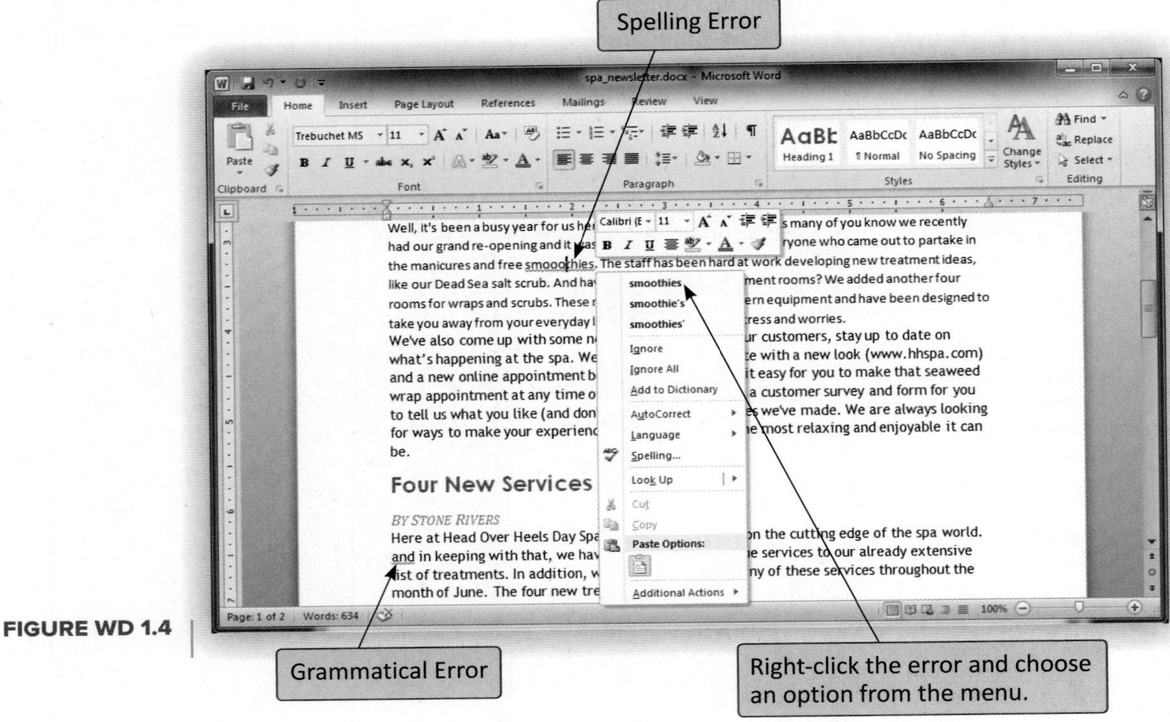
Spelling Error
Grammatical Error
Right-click the error and choose an option from the menu.

FIGURE WD 1.4

tips & tricks

Although checking spelling and grammar as you type is a useful tool when creating documents, there are times when you may find it distracting. You can choose to turn off checking spelling errors or grammar errors as you type. To turn the *Check Spelling as you type* and *Check Grammar as you type* features on and off:

1. Click the **File** tab.
2. Click the **Options** button.
3. In the *Word Options* dialog box, click the **Proofing** button.
4. In the *When correcting spelling and grammar in Word* section, deselect the *Check spelling as you type* option for spelling errors or the *Mark grammar errors as you type* option for grammatical errors.

tell me **more**

Word will not suggest spelling corrections if its dictionary does not contain a word with similar spelling, and Word will not always be able to display grammatical suggestions. In these cases, you must edit the error manually.

If the word is spelled correctly, you can choose the *Add to Dictionary* command on the shortcut menu. When you add a word to the dictionary, it will no longer be marked as a spelling error.

1.5 Using the Thesaurus

When writing documents, you may find that you are reusing a certain word over and over again, and that you would like to use a different word that has the same meaning. Microsoft Word's **Thesaurus** tool provides you with a list of synonyms (words with the same meaning) and antonyms (words with the opposite meaning).

To replace a word using the Thesaurus:

1. Place the cursor in the word you want to replace.
2. Click the **Review** tab.
3. In the *Proofing* group, click the **Thesaurus** button.
4. The selected word appears in the *Search for:* box of the *Research* task pane with a list of possible meanings below it. Each possible meaning has a list of synonyms (and, in some cases, antonyms).
5. Point to a synonym (or antonym) and click the arrow that appears to display a menu of options.
6. Click **Insert** on the menu to replace the original word with the one you selected.

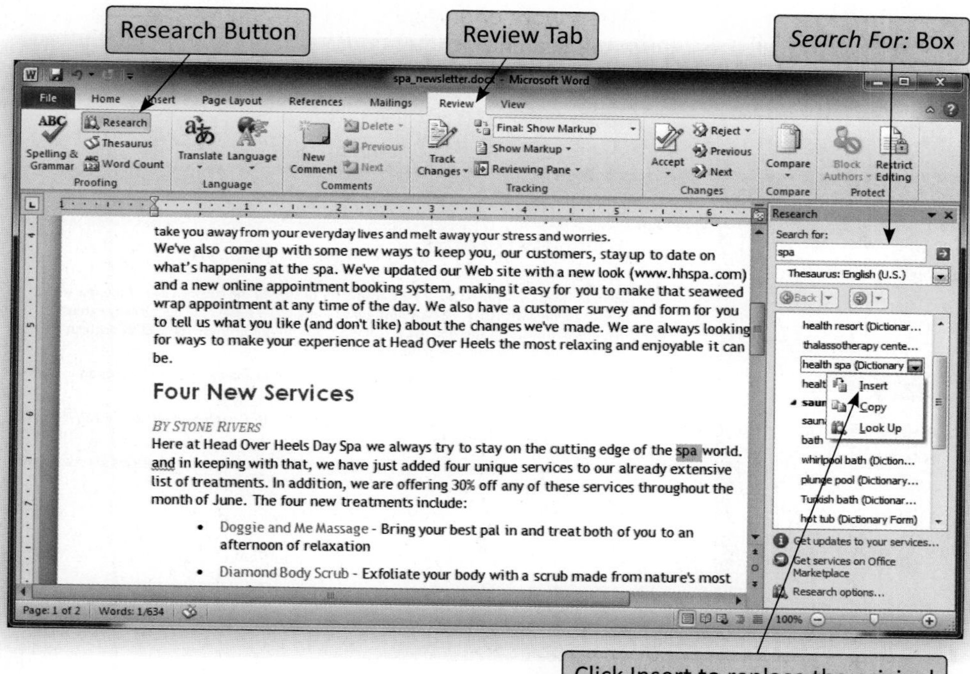

FIGURE WD 1.5

tips & tricks

If one of the synonyms is close to what you want, but not quite right, you can select **Look Up** from the menu to see a list of alternatives for the synonym. You also can click the synonym (without displaying the menu) to see the list of alternative synonyms.

tell me **more**

The *Research* task pane is a robust tool that contains more than just the English Thesaurus. The *Research* task pane also contains links to research Web sites, translation tools, and the Encarta Dictionary. Click the arrow next to *Thesaurus: English (US)* to select a different research tool.

try **this**

To look up a word using the Thesaurus, you also can

- Right-click the word, point to *Synonyms,* and select **Thesaurus . . .**
- With the cursor in the word you want to look up, press ⇧Shift + F7 on the keyboard.

1.6 Finding Text

In past versions of Microsoft Word, searching for text in a document was performed through the *Find and Replace* dialog box. In Word 2010, the default method for searching for text in a document is to use the *Navigation* task pane. When you search for a word or phrase using the *Navigation* task pane, Word will highlight all instances of the word or phrase in your document and display each instance as a separate result in the task pane.

To find a word or phrase in a document:

1. Start on the *Home* tab.
2. In the *Editing* group, click the **Find** button.
3. The *Navigation* task pane appears.
4. Type the word or phrase you want to find in the *Search Document* box at the top of the task pane.
5. As you type, Word automatically highlights all instances of the word or phrase in the document and displays any results in the task pane.
6. Click a result to navigate to that instance of the word or phrase in the document.

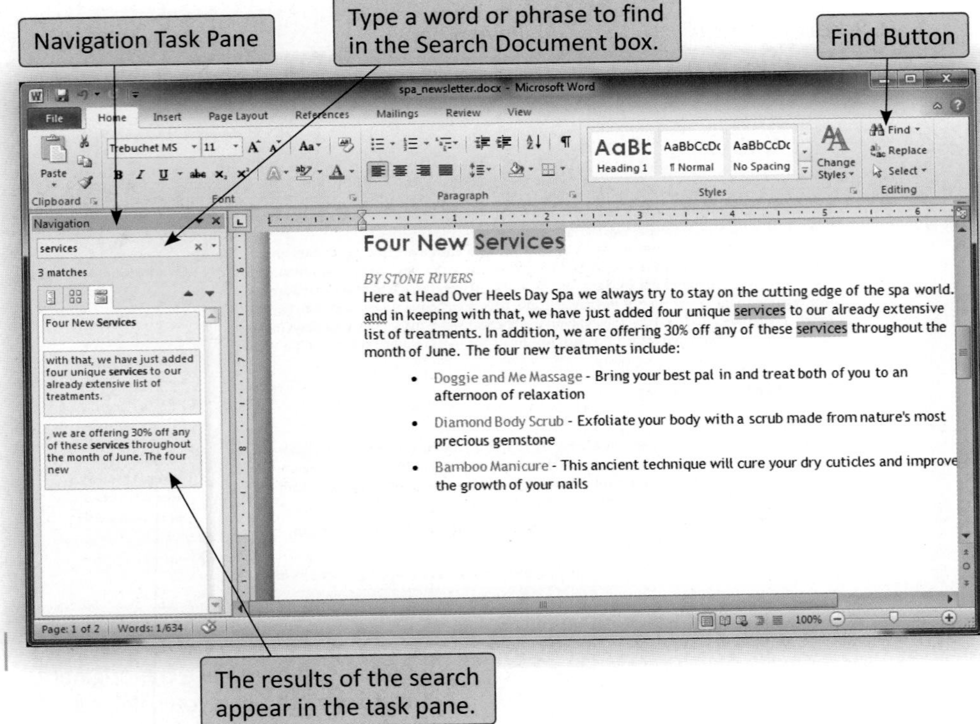

Navigation Task Pane
Type a word or phrase to find in the Search Document box.
Find Button
The results of the search appear in the task pane.

FIGURE WD 1.6

tips & tricks

If you are more comfortable using the *Find and Replace* dialog box, you can still use it to search for text in your document. To open the *Find and Replace* dialog box, start on the *Home* tab. In the *Editing* group, click the **Find** button arrow and select **Advanced Find . . .** The *Find and Replace* dialog box opens with the *Find* tab displayed. Use the dialog to search for text just as you would in previous versions of Word.

tell me more

- The magnifying glass in the *Search Document* box gives you access to more search options. You can choose to only search specific elements in your document, such as tables, graphics, or footnotes.
- Clicking the **X** next to a search word or phrase will clear the search, allowing you to perform a new search.

try this

To display the *Navigation* task pane with the *Search* tab displayed, you also can

- Click the **Find** button and select **Find** on the menu.
- Press Ctrl + F on the keyboard.

1.7 Replacing Text

The **Replace** command in Word allows you to locate specific instances of text in your document and replace them with different text. With the *Replace* command, you can replace words or phrases one instance at a time or all at once throughout the document.

To replace instances of a word in a document:

1. On the *Home* tab, in the *Editing* group, click the **Replace** button.
2. Type the word or phrase you want to change in the *Find what:* box.
3. Type the new text you want in the *Replace with:* box.
4. Click **Replace** to replace just that one instance of the text.
5. Click **Replace All** to replace all instances of the word or phrase.
6. Word displays a message telling you how many replacements it made. Click **OK** in the message that appears.
7. To close the *Find and Replace* dialog, click the **Cancel** button.

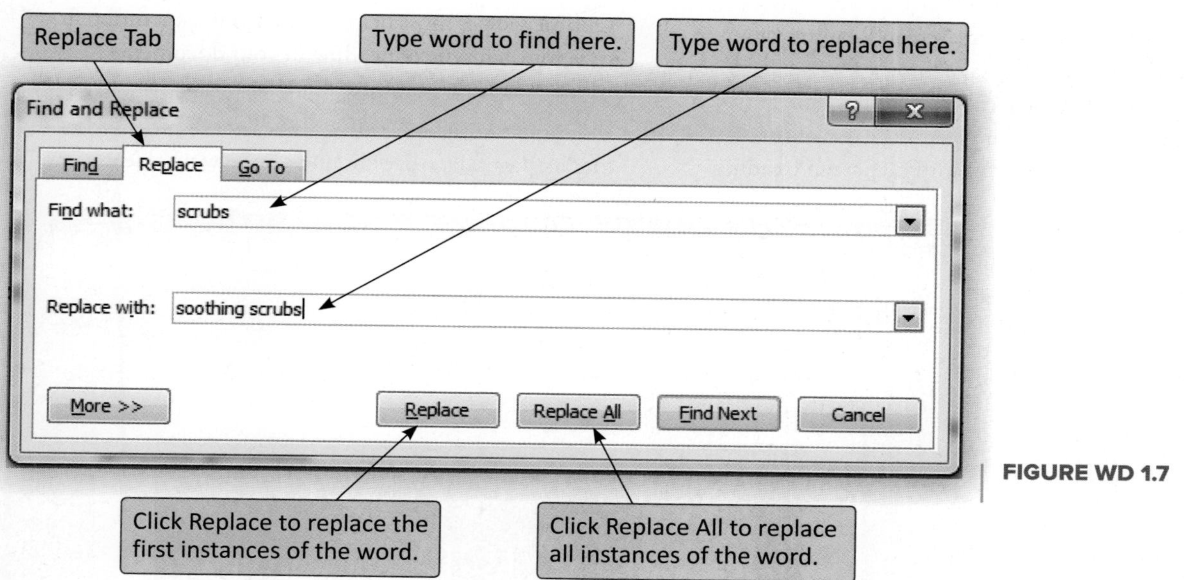

FIGURE WD 1.7

tips & tricks

In addition to text, the *Replace* command also can operate on formatting characters such as italicized text and paragraph marks. The *More >>* button in the *Find and Replace* dialog box displays additional options, including buttons that allow you to select formatting and other special characters in the document.

tell me **more**

The *Go To* tab in the *Find and Replace* dialog box allows you to quickly jump to any page, line, section, comment, or other object in your document.

try **this**

To open the *Find and Replace* dialog box with the *Replace* tab displayed, you also can press Ctrl + H on the keyboard.

1.8 Using Views

By default, Microsoft Word displays documents in Print Layout view, but you can display your documents in a number of other ways. Each view has its own purpose, and considering what you want to do with your document will help determine which view is most appropriate to use. To switch between different views, click the appropriate icon located in the lower-right corner of the status bar next to the zoom slider.

Word 2010 allows you to view your documents five different ways:

- **Print Layout view**—Use this view to see how document elements will appear on a printed page. This view will help you edit headers and footers, and adjust margins and layouts.
- **Full Screen Reading View**—Use this view when you want to review a document. Full Screen Reading view presents the document in an easy-to-read format. In this view, the Ribbon is no longer visible. To navigate between screens, use the navigation buttons at the top of the window. To change the options for Full Screen Reading view, click the **View Options** button. To return to the Print Layout view, click the **Close** button in the upper-right corner of the window.
- **Web Layout View**—Use this view when designing documents that will be viewed on-screen, such as a Web page. Web Layout view displays all backgrounds, drawing objects, and graphics as they will appear on-screen. Unlike Print Layout view, Web Layout view does not show page edges, margins, or headers and footers.
- **Outline View**—Use this view to check the structure of your document. In Outline view, you can collapse the document's structure to view just the top-level headings or expand the structure to see the document's framework. Outline view is most helpful when you use a different style for each type of heading in your document.
- **Draft View**—Use this simplified layout view when typing and formatting text. Draft view does not display headers and footers, page edges, backgrounds, or drawing objects.

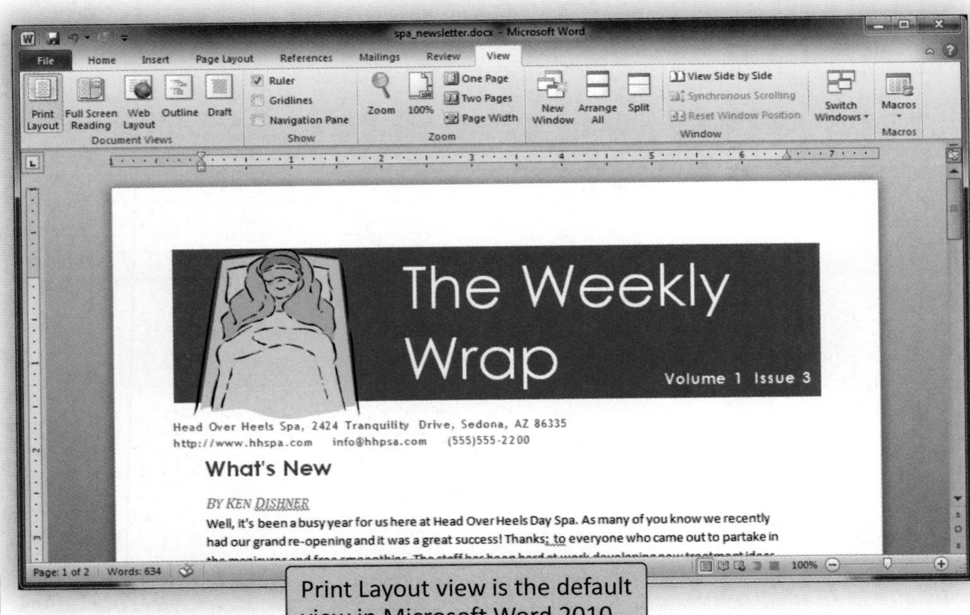

FIGURE WD 1.8

tips & tricks

Draft view is useful for checking the placement of page and section breaks in your document. You can easily remove a break in Draft view by selecting the break and pressing Delete on the keyboard.

tell me more

In Word 2003, the default view for documents was called *Normal* view and was the same as *Draft* view. In Word 2007 and Word 2010, Microsoft changed the default view for documents to *Print Layout* view.

try this

To switch views, you also can click the **View** tab on the Ribbon and select a view from the *Document Views* group.

1.9 Zooming a Document

When you first open a document, you may find that the text is too small to read, or that you cannot see the full layout of a page. Use the **zoom slider** in the lower-right corner of the window to zoom in and out of a document, changing the size of text and images on-screen. Zooming a document only affects how the document appears on-screen. It does not affect how the document will print.

To zoom in on a document, making the text and graphics appear larger:

- Click and drag the zoom slider to the right.
- Click the **Zoom In** button (the button with the plus sign on it) on the slider.

To zoom out of a document, making the text and graphics appear smaller:

- Click and drag the zoom slider to the left.
- Click the **Zoom Out** button (the button with the minus sign on it) on the slider.

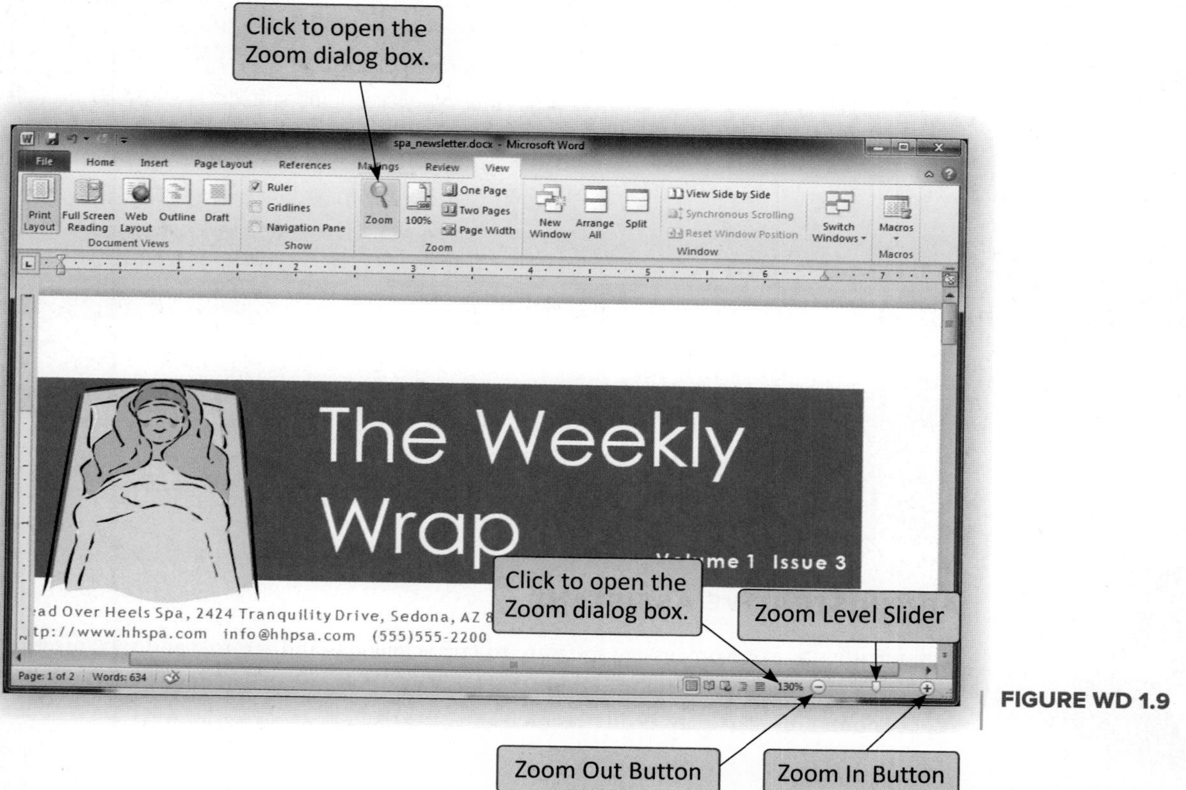

FIGURE WD 1.9

tips & tricks

As you move the slider, the zoom level displays the percentage the document has been zoomed in or out. When zooming a document, 100% is the default zoom level. If you change the zoom percentage and then save and close the document, the next time you open the document, it will display at the last viewed zoom percentage. If you work on a large monitor at a high resolution and need to display your document at a higher zoom percentage, it is a good idea to return the document back to 100% before sending it out to others.

tell me **more**

You can use the *Zoom* dialog box to apply a number of display presets:

Page width—changes the zoom so the width of the page including margins fills the screen.

Text width—changes the zoom so the width of the page not including margins fills the screen.

Whole page—changes the zoom so the entire page, both vertically and horizontally, displays on the screen. This is a helpful view when working with a page's layout.

Many pages—changes the zoom to display anywhere from one to six pages on the screen at once.

try **this**

You also can change the zoom level through the *Zoom* dialog box:

1. To open the *Zoom* dialog box:
   a. Click the zoom level number next to the zoom slider OR
   b. Click the **View** tab. In the *Zoom* group, click the **Zoom** button.
2. Click a zoom preset or type the zoom percentage in the *Percent:* box.
3. Click **OK.**

from the perspective of . . .

ADMINISTRATIVE ASSISTANT

I frequently use word processing software to create agendas and reports, and take meeting minutes. Using document, color, and font themes saves time and makes documents look like I spent hours creating them. I will never tell.

projects

Skill Review 1.1

In this project you will be editing the *Values Statement_01* document from Sierra Pacific Community College District.

1. Open Microsoft Word 2010.
2. Open the *Values Statement_01* document.
   a. Click the **File** tab. The Backstage view will open.
   b. Click the **Open** button. The *Open* dialog box will open.
   c. Browse to the location of your student data files for Chapter 1.
   d. Click the **Values Statement_01** document.
   e. Click the **Open** button (or double-click the document). The *Values Statement_01* document will open.
3. Save your document with a different file name.
   a. Click the **File** tab.
   b. Click the **Save As** button. The *Save As* dialog box will open.
   c. Navigate to the location where you will be saving your completed documents.
   d. In the *File name:* box, type: ***[your initials]*WD_SkillReview_1-1.**
   e. Click **Save.** Notice how the name of the document is now changed at the top of your Word window.
4. Change how the document is displayed on your computer.
   a. Click the **View** tab.
   b. In the *Zoom* group, click the **Page Width** button. The document will be displayed according to the width of your Word window.
5. Add an entry to the AutoCorrect feature of Word 2010.
   a. Click the **File** tab to open the Backstage view.
   b. Click the **Options** button. The *Word Options* dialog box will open.
   c. Click the **Proofing** button.
   d. Click the **AutoCorrect Options** button. The *AutoCorrect* dialog box will open.
   e. The *AutoCorrect* tab should be displayed. If not, click the **AutoCorrect** tab.
   f. In the *Replace:* box type: `SPCCD`
   g. In the *With:* box type: `Sierra Pacific Community College District`
   h. Click the **Add** button. Notice how this AutoCorrect entry has been added and it is displayed in alphabetical order in the list of AutoCorrect entries.
   i. Click **OK** to close the *AutoCorrect* dialog box.
   j. Click **OK** to close the *Options* dialog box.

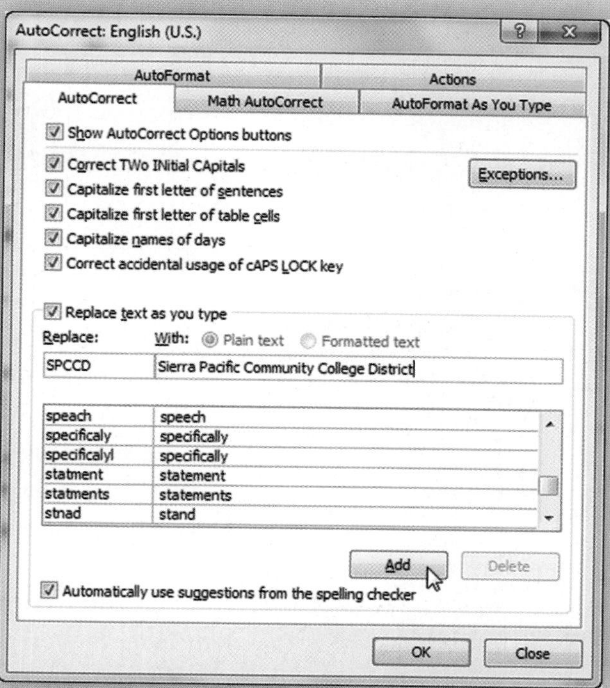

FIGURE WD 1.10

6. Add text to the document.
   a. Click in front of the *Student Learning Outcome* heading in the first column.
   b. Press **Enter.**
   c. Press the *up arrow* key on your keyboard to move your cursor to the blank line you just inserted. Or click on the blank line you just inserted.
   d. Type the following heading: `Leadership`
   e. Press **Enter.**
   f. Type the following text: `Responsible leadership and service among all SPCCD faculty, staff, and students are nurtured and encouraged so the college will be a leader for positive change, growth, and transformation in student-oriented educational practices.`

   Notice how *SPCCD* was changed to *Sierra Pacific Community College District.*
   g. Press **Enter.**
   h. In the *Communication* paragraph in the second column, click directly in front of the word *mission* and type: `SPCCD` (be sure to space after). Notice how *SPCCD* was changed to *Sierra Pacific Community College District.*
   i. Click before the word *Values* in the title of the document.
   j. Type: `SPCCD` and space after.

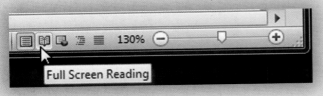

7. Change how your document is viewed in the window.
   a. At the bottom-right corner of your Word window, click the **Full Screen Reading** icon (second icon) to change the display view. This also can be done by clicking the **View** tab and clicking the **Full Screen Reading** button in the *Document Views* group.
   b. Click the **Close** button in the upper right to close this view and return to *Print Layout* view (the default view in Word).
   c. In the *Zoom Out* and *Zoom In* area at the bottom-right corner of your Word window, click the **Zoom Out** button until your document is displayed at 100%. This also can be done by clicking the **View** tab and clicking the **100%** button in the *Zoom* group.

FIGURE WD 1.11

FIGURE WD 1.12

FIGURE WD 1.13

8. Check spelling and grammar as you type. Notice how words that Word does not recognize are underlined in red and potential grammar errors are underlined in green.
   a. Right-click the heading *Access* at the top of the first column. A list of suggested changes is shown.
   b. Click **Access.** Word corrects the spelling of this word.
   c. Right-click the word *Of* in the heading *Benefits Of Education.*
   d. Click on **of** (lowercase).

9. Spell and grammar check the entire document with the *Spelling and Grammar* dialog box.
   a. Click the **Review** tab.
   b. In the *Proofing* group, click the **Spelling & Grammar** button. The *Spelling and Grammar* dialog box will open.
   c. The word *assesment* is indicated as *Not in Dictionary.*

d. Click **assessment** in the *Suggestions* area.

e. Click the **Change All** button. Both misspelled instances of this word are changed.

f. The next word not in the dictionary is *ageis.*

g. Click **age is.**

h. Click the **Change** button.

i. Continue to check the spelling and grammar on the remainder of the document. If Word prompts you to continue at the beginning of the document, click **Yes.**

j. Click **OK** when finished.

10. Save and close the document.

a. Click the **File** tab and click **Save.** You also can save your document by pressing **Ctrl+S** or clicking the **Save** icon on the *Quick Access* toolbar.

b. To close the document, click the **File** tab and click **Close.** You also can close a document by pressing **Ctrl+W.**

11. Close Microsoft Word.

a. Click the **File** tab and click **Exit.** You also can click the **X** button in the upper-right corner of the Word window.

b. If you have any unsaved documents, you will be prompted to save them.

Skill Review **1.2**

In this project you will be editing the *Employment Offer_01* document from Central Sierra Insurance.

1. Open Microsoft Word 2010.

2. Open the *Employment Offer_01* document.

a. Click the **File** tab. The Backstage view will open.

b. Click the **Open** button. The *Open* dialog box will open.

c. Browse to the location of your student data files for Chapter 1.

d. Click the **Employment Offer_01** document.

e. Click the **Open** button (or double-click the document). The *Employment Offer_01* document will open.

3. Save your document with a different file name.

a. Click the **File** tab.

b. Click the **Save As** button. The *Save As* dialog box will open.

c. Navigate to the location where you will be saving your completed documents.

d. In the *File name:* box, type: `[your initials]WD_SkillReview_1-2.`

e. Click **Save.** Notice how the name of the document is now changed at the top of your Word window.

4. Turn on the Show/Hide feature so you can view the paragraph marks and other formatting characters.

a. Click the **Home** tab.

b. In the **Paragraph** group, click the **Show/Hide** button. The formatting characters will be revealed in the document.

c. The *Show/Hide* button can be toggled on or off. *Ctrl+** also will toggle on/off this feature.

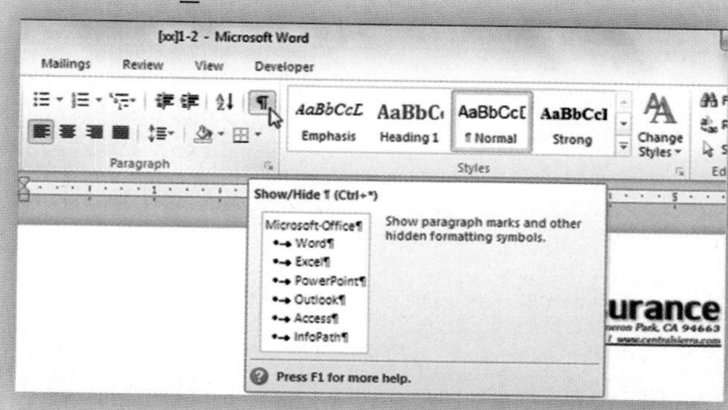

FIGURE WD 1.14

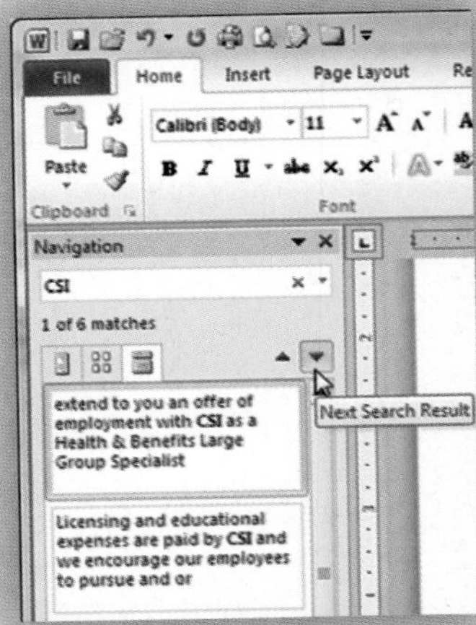

FIGURE WD 1.15

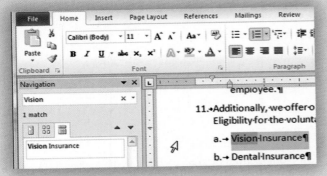

5. Find words in the document and display in the *Navigation* pane.

   a. On the *Home* tab, in the *Editing* group, click the **Find** button. The *Navigation* pane is displayed on the right side of the Word window. *Ctrl+F* also will open the *Find* feature in the *Navigation* pane.

   b. Click in the *Search Document* box and type: `CSI`

   c. Press **Enter.** Each occurrence of this word is displayed in the *Navigation* pane.

   d. Click the **Next Search Result** arrow to move to the next matching occurrence.

   e. Click the **X** button in the *Search Document* box to clear the current search.

   f. In the *Search Document* box type: `Vision`

   g. Press **Enter.** Only one occurrence is found.

   h. In the document select this entire line by clicking to the left of the lettered item outside of the left margin. The entire line will be selected.

   i. Press **Delete** to delete this line.

   j. Click the **X** in the upper-right corner of the *Navigation* pane to close it.

FIGURE WD 1.16

6. Use the *Find and Replace* feature to replace *CSI* with *Central Sierra Insurance.*

   a. Press **Ctrl+Home** to move to the top of the document.

   b. On the *Home* tab, in the *Editing* group, click the **Replace** button. The *Find and Replace* dialog box will open. *Ctrl+H* also will open the *Find and Replace* dialog box.

   c. In the *Find what:* box type: `CSI`

   d. In the *Replace with:* box type: `Central Sierra Insurance`

   e. Click the **More** button to view *Search Options.*

   f. Click the **Match case** check box.

   g. Click the **Find whole words only** check box.

   h. Click the **Replace** button. The first occurrence of this word is selected in the document.

   i. Click **Replace** to replace *CSI* with *Central Sierra Insurance.* The next occurrence will be selected.

   j. Click **Replace All** to replace all occurrences in the document.

   k. Click **OK** to finish the find and replace process.

   l. Click **Close** to close the *Find and Replace* dialog box.

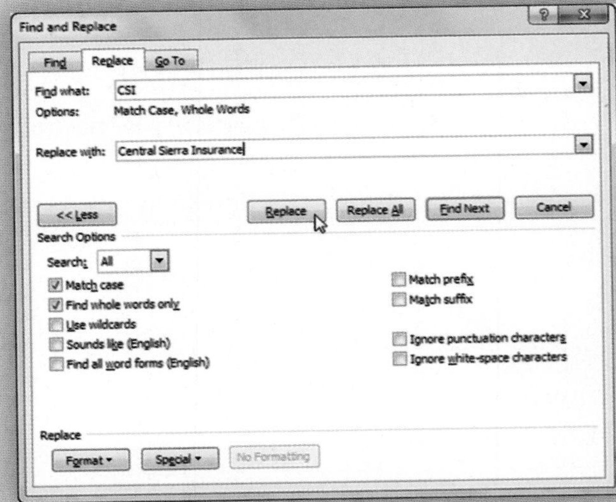

FIGURE WD 1.17

7. Use *Find and Replace* with wildcards to replace *percent* with *%.*

   a. Press **Ctrl+Home** to move to the top of the document.

   b. Click the **Replace** button.

   c. In the *Find what:* box type: `?percent` (The ? is a wildcard representing one character.)

   d. In the *Replace with:* box type: `%`

   e. Click the **Use wildcards** check box in the *Search Options* box.

   f. Click the **Replace All** button to replace all occurrences of *percent* with *%.*

g. Click **OK** to finish the find and replace process.

h. Click **Close** to close the *Find and Replace* dialog box.

8. Spell and grammar check the entire document.

a. Click the **Review** tab.

b. Click the **Spelling & Grammar** button in the *Proofing* group. The *Spelling and Grammar* dialog box will open.

c. Click the **Ignore All** button to skip the personal names not recognized by Word (for example *Skaar*).

d. Choose **days' vacation** when you come to this phrase.

e. Continue to check the spelling and grammar on the remainder of the document. If Word prompts you to continue at the beginning of the document, click **Yes.**

f. Click **OK** when finished.

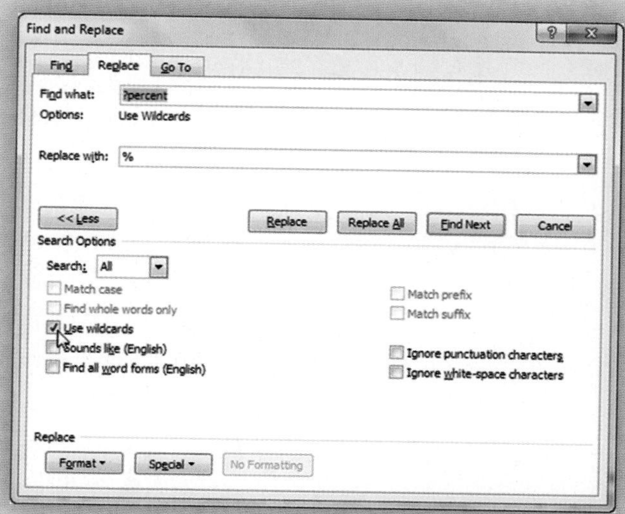

FIGURE WD 1.18

9. Find the words in the document, and use the *Thesaurus* to find an appropriate synonym.

a. On the *Home* tab, in the *Editing* group, click the **Find** button. The *Navigation* pane is displayed on the right side of the Word window.

b. Click in the *Search Document* box and type: `accrual`

c. Press **Enter.** One occurrence is found.

d. Click the **Review** tab.

e. In the *Proofing* group, click the **Thesaurus** button. The *Research* pane will open at the right side of the Word window.

f. Click the **arrow** to the right of the word *accumulation.*

g. Click **Insert.** The word *accumulation* replaces *accrual.*

h. Click the **X** to close the *Research* pane.

i. In the *Navigation* pane, clear the current search.

j. Click in the **Search Document** box and type: `construed`

k. Press **Enter.** One occurrence is found.

l. Right-click the word *construed* in the document.

m. Point to **Synonyms** and then click **understood.**

n. Close the *Navigation* pane.

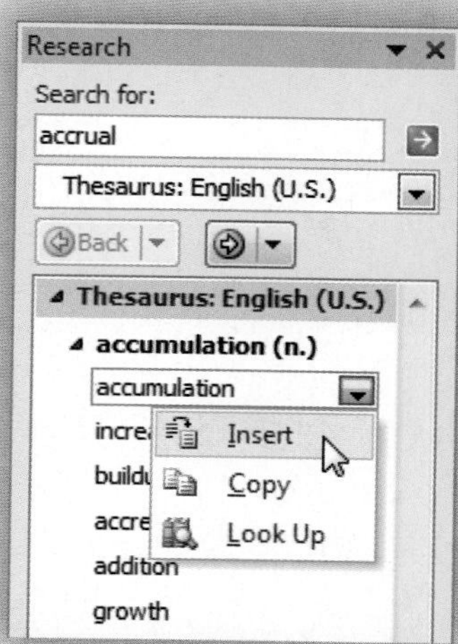

FIGURE WD 1.19

10. Save and close the document.

a. Click the **File** tab and click **Save.** You also can save your document by pressing **Ctrl+S** or clicking the **Save** icon on the *Quick Access* toolbar.

b. To close the document, click the **File** tab and click **Close.** You also can close a document by pressing **Ctrl+W.**

11. Close Microsoft Word.

a. Click the **File** tab and click **Exit.** You also can click the **X** button in the upper-right corner of the Word window.

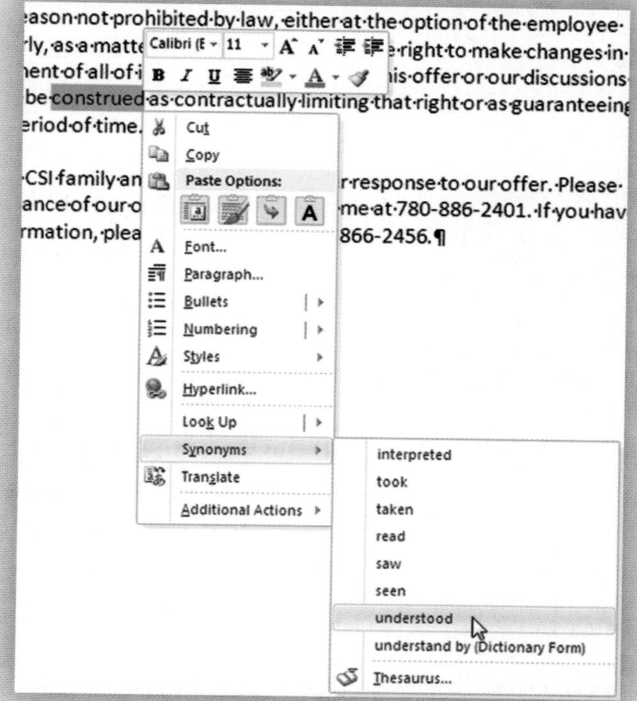

FIGURE WD 1.20

challenge yourself **1**

In this project you will be editing the *Notice of Privacy_01* document from Courtyard Medical Plaza.

1. Open Microsoft Word 2010.
2. Open the *Notice of Privacy_01* document.
3. Save this document as `[your initials]WD_Challenge_1-3`.
4. Turn on the *Show/Hide* feature so you can view the paragraph marks and other formatting characters.
5. Change the zoom level to view the document in *Page Width*.
6. Add an *AutoCorrect* entry to change *CMP* to *Courtyard Medical Plaza.* Close the *AutoCorrect* dialog box and the *Options* dialog box.
7. On the second line on the first page, select *Courtyard Medical Plaza* and delete this entire line including the paragraph mark at the end.
8. Click in front of *Notice of Privacy Practices* on the first line of the document, and type `CMP` and press **Enter.**
9. Click at the end of the sentence of the first numbered item on the first page.
10. Press **Enter.**
11. Type the following text: `tell you about your rights and our legal duties with respect to your protected heath information, and`
    a. If Word automatically capitalized *tell,* change it back to lowercase.
12. Press **Enter.**
13. Click at the end of the second bulleted item.
14. Replace the period with a semicolon, space once, and type `and`
15. Press **Enter** and type the following text: `Information about your relationship with CMP such as medical services received, claims history, and information from your benefits plan sponsor or employer about group health coverage you may have.`
    a. *CMP* will automatically be replaced with *Courtyard Medical Plaza.*
16. Use *Find and Replace* to replace *protected health information* with *PHI.*
    a. In the *Search Options* area, select **Match case.**
    b. Do not change this occurrence.
    c. Ignore any occurrences of this information in headings (bolded text). Click **Find Next** to skip an occurrence.
17. Use *Find and Replace* to replace *Privacy and Compliance Office* with *Office of Privacy & Compliance.*
18. Use the *Find* feature to find the word *utilization.*
19. Use the *Thesaurus* to change the word to *employment.*
20. Check the spelling and grammar on the entire document.
    a. Ignore the section heading text that is marked as a potential grammatical error (e.g., *Your*).
    b. Ignore all proper nouns.
    c. Ignore the lowercase letters at the beginning of the numbered list.

21. Delete the *AutoCorrect* entries you created in this exercise and *Skill Review 1.1* exercise.
   a. Open the *AutoCorrect* dialog box. The *AutoCorrect* tab should be displayed. If not, click the **AutoCorrect** tab.
   b. In the *Replace* box type: `CMP`
   c. Select this *AutoCorrect* entry.
   d. Click the **Delete** button.
   e. Repeat this process to delete the entry for *SPCCD.*
   f. Close the open dialog boxes.
22. Save and close this document.

challenge yourself **2**

In this project you will be editing the *Personal Training Program_01* document from American River Cycling Club.

1. Open the *Personal Training Program_01* document.
2. Save this document as ***[your initials]*WD_Challenge_1-4.**
3. Change the zoom level to view the document at 120%.
4. Turn on the *Show/Hide* feature so you can view the paragraph marks and other formatting characters.
5. In the *Training Intensity and Heart Rate* section, delete the second paragraph.
6. In the *Training Intensity and Heart Rate* section, add bulleted items.
   a. Press **Enter** after the second bulleted item and add the following bulleted items:
   `Recover back to 65%-75% (4-6 minutes)`
   `Pedal at 90% for 3-5 minutes`
   `Recover back to 65%-75% (4-6 minutes)`
   `Repeat this cycle 5-8 times depending on the duration of your training ride`
   `Warm down at 50-60% for the last 10 minutes`
7. Delete the *Tracking Training—Miles versus Hours* heading and the paragraph following the heading.
8. Replace all occurrences of *heartrate* (one word) with *heart rate* (two words).
9. Replace all occurrences of *personal training program* with *PTP.*
   a. Skip the occurrences in the title and section headings.
10. Replace all occurrences of the word *percent* with *%.*
    a. Be sure to use a single-character wildcard before percent so there will not be a space between the number and the percent symbol (e.g., 90%).
11. Use *Find* to locate the word *Incorporate.*
12. Use the *Thesaurus* to find an appropriate synonym to replace this word.
13. Use *Find* to locate the word *effectiveness.*
14. Use the *Thesaurus* to find an appropriate synonym to replace this word.
15. Find *40K* in the document and change it to `25 mile`
16. Find *BMI* in the document and change it to `body mass index (BMI)`
17. Check the spelling and grammar on the entire document.
    a. Ignore the word *criterium.*

18. View the document in *Draft* view.
19. Change the view to *Full Screen Reading* view.
20. Close the *Full Screen Reading* view, which will return you to *Print Layout* view.
21. Save and close the document.

on your own

In this project you will be editing the *Distance Education Plan_01* document from Sierra Pacific Community College District.

1. Open the *Distance Education Plan_01* document.
2. Save this document as **[your initials]WD_OnYourOwn_1-5.**
3. Change the zoom level to your preference.
4. Replace occurrences of *online learning* with *OL.*
   a. Make sure you look at the context of the sentence to make sure the replacement is appropriate.
   b. Do not make this replacement in headings.
5. Replace all *%* with *percent.*
   a. Make sure the replacement includes a space between the number and *percent* (e.g., 100 percent).
6. Replace *SPCCD* with *Sierra Pacific.*
   a. Make sure you look at the context of the sentence to make sure the replacement is appropriate.
   b. Do not make this replacement in headings.
7. In the *Planning Process* section, delete the last paragraph and the four bulleted items beneath it.
8. Locate *learning management system* in the body of the document and put the acronym in parentheses after these words. Use proper spacing.
9. Locate *Planning Coordination Council* in the body of the document and put the acronym in parentheses after these words. Use proper spacing.
10. Add an *AutoCorrect* entry to change *SPCCD* to *Sierra Pacific Community College District.*
11. In the *PURPOSE OF THIS PLAN* section, type the following as the first sentence in the paragraph: `The Online Learning Task Force was formed in February 2005 to develop an Online Learning Strategic Plan for the SPCCD.`
12. In the *Online Learning Offerings and Programs* section, type the following as the second paragraph: `SPCCD currently has no complete degree programs being offered entirely by distance methods, but there are several certificate programs which are available online. At least one course in each General Education area has been approved for online learning delivery, but not all of these courses are currently being offered. There are other graduation requirements that cannot currently be met through online learning methods.`
13. View the document in *Draft* view.
14. Delete an extra *Enters* (paragraph marks) in the document to ensure consistent spacing between paragraphs and sections.

15. Return to *Print Layout* view.
16. Use appropriate synonyms to replace the following words: *dramatic* and *strategically.*
17. The first fully online course offered at SPCCD was in *1997,* not *1998.* Find and make this change.
18. The current success rate for online courses is *72* percent. Find and make this change.
19. Delete the *AutoCorrect* entry you created in this exercise.
20. Check the spelling and grammar on the entire document and make appropriate changes.
21. Save and close the document.

fix it

In this project you will be editing the *Disclosure Letter_01* document from Placer Hills Real Estate.

1. Open the *Disclosure Letter_01* document.
2. Save this document as `[your initials]WD_FixIt_1-6`.
3. Change the zoom level to your preference.
4. Change the inside address of this block format business letter to:
   `David and Sharon Wing`
   `4685 Orange Grove`
   `Rocklin, CA 97725`
5. Make the necessary change to the salutation of the letter.
6. Find and replace all occurrences of *release* with *disclosure.*
7. The word *disclosure/disclose* is used too often in this document. Find the word *disclose* and use an appropriate synonym to replace it.
8. Find the word *transference* and use an appropriate synonym to replace it.
9. Change the date of the letter to the *current date.* Use proper date format.
10. Add the following sentence as the first sentence in the last body paragraph.
    `Please complete the enclosed disclosure statement by [`*`insert a date five days from today`*`] and return it to me.`
11. Whenever a letter refers to an attached or enclosed document, it is proper to include an *Enclosure* notation. Type the word `Enclosure` on the line directly below the reference initials.
12. On a block format business letter, all lines should begin at the left margin. Using the Word 2010 default line and paragraph spacing, there should be a blank line (two Enters) after the date line and after the complimentary close (Best regards). There should be one Enter after other parts of the letter. The inside address and the writer's name, title, and company are kept together using line breaks (Shift + Enter). Turn on Show/Hide and make any necessary changes to ensure the document has proper and consistent spacing between parts. This document will fit on one page.
13. Use *mixed punctuation* on this business letter. Mixed punctuation requires a *colon* after the salutation and a *comma* after the complimentary close.
14. Proofread the document carefully and make any necessary spelling and grammar changes.
15. There should be approximately the same amount of white space at the top and bottom of the document. Use *Enter(s)* before the date line to balance the letter on the page.
16. Save and close the document.

chapter **2**

Formatting Text and Paragraphs

In this chapter, you will learn the following skills:

- **Apply fonts and styles to text**
- **Incorporate different types of lists to organize information**
- **Use Quick Styles to enhance readability**
- **Change paragraph alignment and spacing to effectively use white space**
- **Set and use tabs and indents to improve document layout**

Skill 2.1 Applying Character Effects
Skill 2.2 Changing Fonts
Skill 2.3 Changing Font Sizes
Skill 2.4 Changing Text Case
Skill 2.5 Changing Font Colors
Skill 2.6 Applying Highlights
Skill 2.7 Using Format Painter
Skill 2.8 Clearing Formatting
Skill 2.9 Creating Bulleted Lists
Skill 2.10 Creating Numbered Lists
Skill 2.11 Creating Multilevel Lists
Skill 2.12 Using Quick Styles
Skill 2.13 Changing Paragraph Alignment
Skill 2.14 Changing Paragraph Spacing
Skill 2.15 Revealing Formatting Marks
Skill 2.16 Changing the Space between Paragraphs
Skill 2.17 Changing Indents
Skill 2.18 Using Tab Stops
Skill 2.19 Using Tab Leaders

skills

introduction

This chapter will cover character and paragraph formatting and alignment to enhance the presentation, professionalism, and readability of documents. Students will apply fonts and styles, incorporate lists, use Quick Styles, change paragraph alignment and spacing, and use tabs and indents.

2.1 Applying Character Effects

Character effects are special formatting you can apply to text that alters the text's appearance. You can call attention to text in your document by using the **bold,** *italic,* or underline effects. Remember that these effects are used to emphasize important text, and should be used sparingly—they lose their effect if overused.

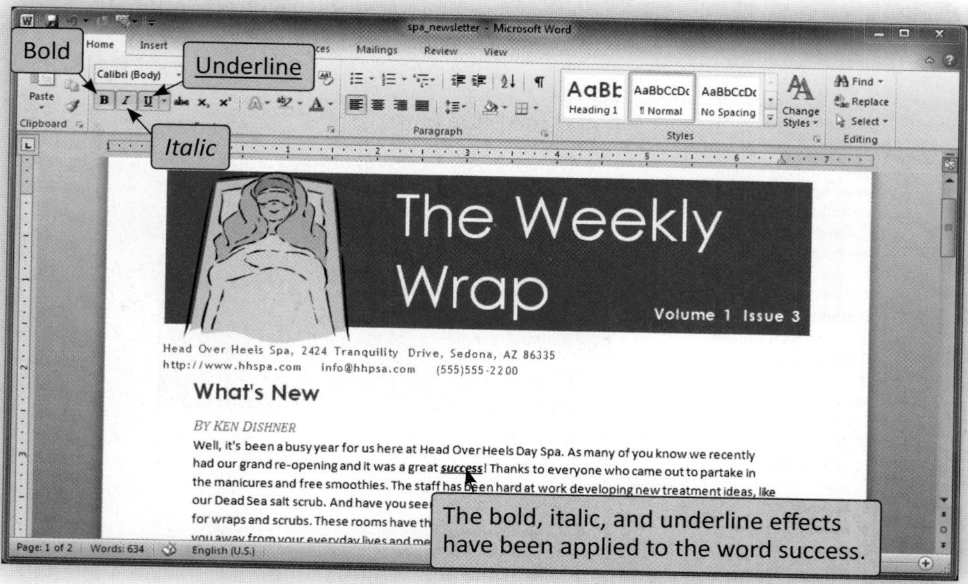

FIGURE WD 2.1

You can apply these effects using similar steps:

1. Select the text you want to emphasize.
2. On the *Home* tab, in the *Font* group click the button of the effect you want to apply:

B **Bold**—gives the text a heavier, thicker appearance.

I **Italic**—makes text slant to the right.

U **Underline**—draws a single line under the text.

Some of the other character effects available from the Ribbon include:

abc **Strikethrough**—draws a horizontal line through the text.

x_2 **Subscript**—draws a small character below the bottom of the text.

x^2 **Superscript**—draws a small character above the top of the text.

Aa **Change Case**—changes the capitalization on selected text.

tips & tricks

The *Font* dialog box contains other character formatting options not available from the Ribbon. These effects include **Shadow** and **Outline** among others. To open the *Font* dialog box, on the *Home* tab, in the *Font* group, click the dialog launcher. Select an option in the *Effects* section and click **OK** to apply the character effect to the text.

tell me more

When text is bolded, italicized, or underlined, the button appears highlighted on the Ribbon. To remove the effect, click the highlighted button, or press the appropriate keyboard shortcut.

try this

- The following keyboard shortcuts can be used to apply the bold, italic, and underline effects:
  - Bold = Ctrl + B
  - Italic = Ctrl + I
  - Underline = Ctrl + U
- To access the bold or italic commands, you can also right-click the selected text and click the **Bold** or **Italic** button on the Mini toolbar.
- To apply an underline style, click the **Underline** button arrow and select a style.

2.2 Changing Fonts

A **font**, or typeface, refers to a set of characters of a certain design. The font is the shape of a character or number as it appears on-screen or in a printed document.

To change the font:

1. Select the text to be changed.
2. On the *Home* tab, click the arrow next to the *Font* box.
3. As you roll over the list of fonts, the Live Preview feature in Word changes the look of the text in your document, giving you a preview of how the text will look with the new font applied.
4. Click a font name from the menu to apply it to the text.

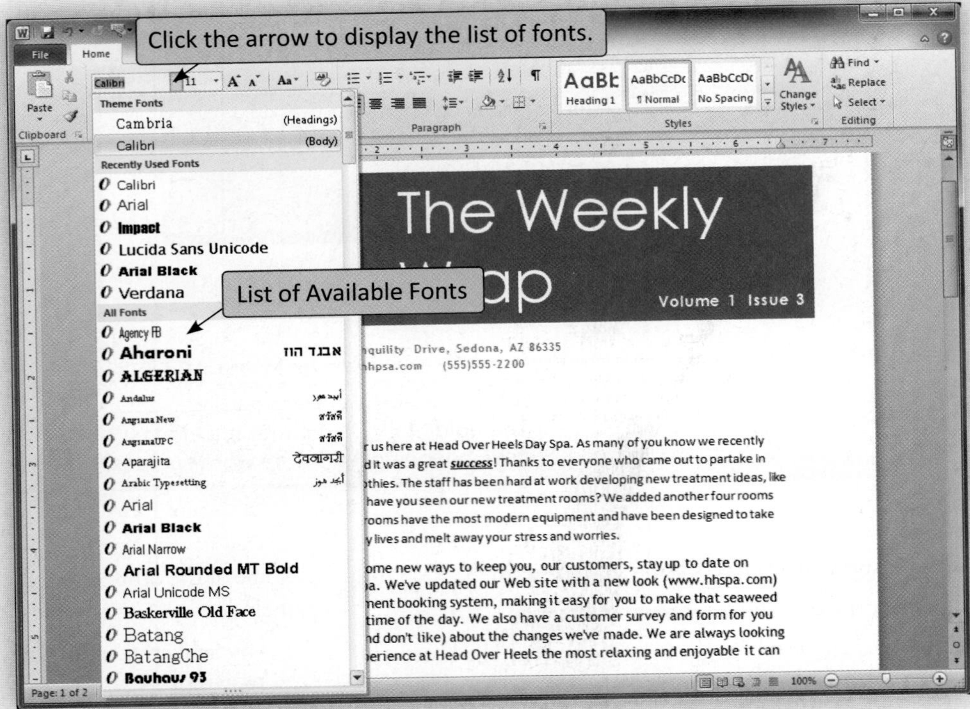

FIGURE WD 2.2

Word offers many fonts. **Serif fonts**, such as Cambria and Times New Roman, have an embellishment at the end of each stroke. **Sans serif fonts**, such as Calibri and Arial, do not have an embellishment at the end of each stroke.

Cambria is a serif font.

Calibri is a sans serif font.

FIGURE WD 2.3

tips & tricks

If you want to change the font of an individual word, you can place your cursor in the word you want to modify then select the new font.

try this

To change the font you can also right-click the text, click the arrow next to the *Font* box on the Mini toolbar, and select a font from the list.

tell me more

Using different fonts can enhance your document, giving it a polished look, but when writing a document it is best to limit the number of fonts you use. Using multiple fonts in one document can give it a cluttered and unprofessional appearance. It is good practice to use the same font for body text and the same font for headings in your document. Sans serif fonts are easier to read onscreen and should be used for the main body text for documents that will be delivered and read electronically, such as a blog. Serif fonts are easier to read on the printed page and should be used for documents that will be printed such as a report.

2.3 Changing Font Sizes

When creating a document it is important to not only choose the correct font, but also to use the appropriate font size. Fonts are measured in **points,** abbreviated "pt." On the printed page, 72 points equal one inch. Different text sizes are used for paragraphs and headers in a document. Paragraphs typically use 10 pt., 11 pt., and 12 pt. fonts. Headers often use 14 pt., 16 pt., and 18 pt. fonts.

To change the size of the text:

1. Select the text to be changed.
2. On the *Home* tab, in the *Font* group, click the arrow next to the *Font Size* box.
3. Scroll the list to find the new font size.
4. Click the size you want.

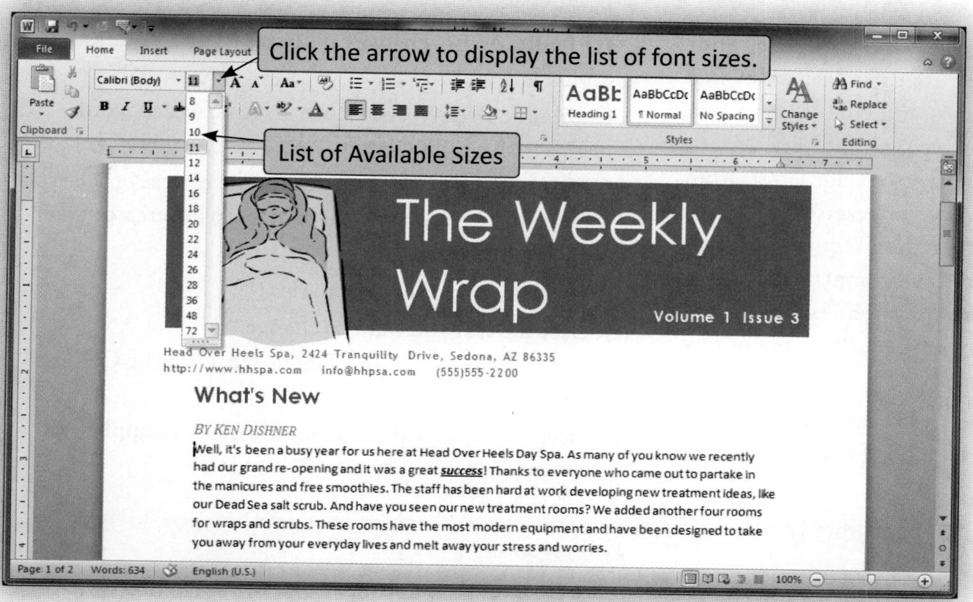

FIGURE WD 2.4

tips & tricks

Sometimes when you are formatting text, you may not be sure of the exact size you want your text to be. You can experiment with the look of text in your document by incrementally increasing and decreasing the size of the font. Use the *Grow Font* or *Shrink Font* button, available in the *Font* group, to change the font size by one increment.

tell me more

The *Font* dialog box gives you access to all the attributes for text fonts. In the *Font* dialog box, you can not only change the size of the font, but also the type, color, and effects applied to the font. To open the *Font* dialog box, click the dialog launcher in the *Font* group.

try this

To change the font you can also right-click the text, click the arrow next to the *Font Size box* on the Mini toolbar, and select a font size from the list.

from the perspective of . . .

COLLEGE GRADUATE

Word processing software is perfect to create my résumé. With fonts, themes, styles, and a spelling and grammar checker, my résumé is eye-catching and professional.

2.4 Changing Text Case

When you type on a keyboard you use the Shift key to capitalize individual letters and the Caps Lock key to type in all capital letters. Another way to change letters from lowercase to uppercase, and vice versa, is to use the *Change Case* command. When you use the **Change Case** command in Word, you are manipulating the characters that were typed, changing how the letters are displayed. There are five types of text case formats you can apply to text:

Sentence case—formats text as a sentence with the first word being capitalized and all remaining words beginning with a lowercase letter.

lowercase—changes all letters to lowercase.

UPPERCASE—changes all letters to uppercase, or capital letters.

Capitalize Each Word—formats text so each word begins with a capital letter.

tOGGLE cASE—formats text in the reverse of the typed format, converting uppercase letters to lowercase and lowercase letters to uppercase.

To apply text case formatting to text:

1. Select the text you want to change.
2. On the *Home* tab, in the *Font* group, click the **Change Case** button.
3. Select a text case option from the menu to apply it to the text.

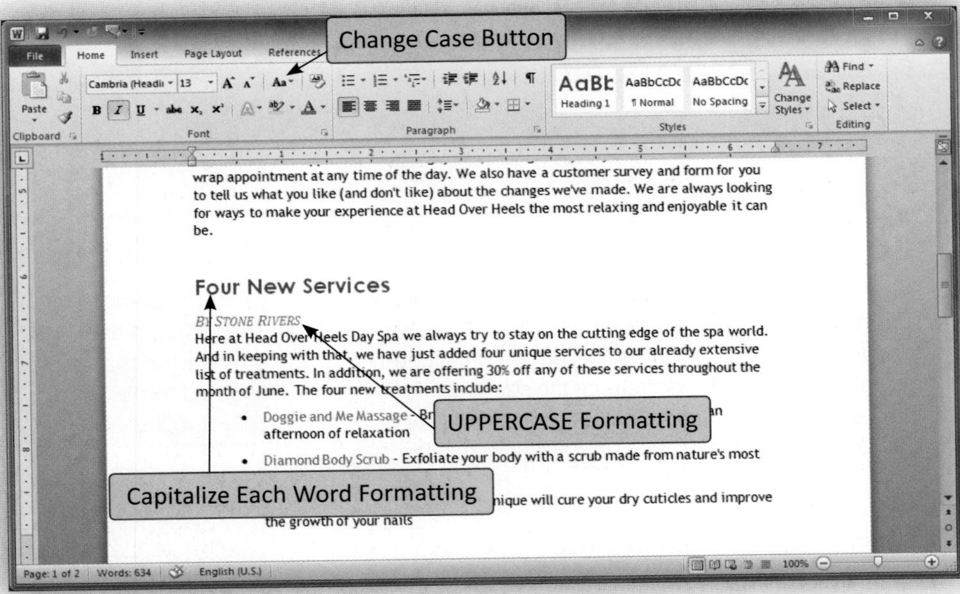

FIGURE WD 2.5

tips & tricks

Headers and titles often use the *Capitalize Each Word* format. One way to ensure that your headers and titles are consistent in text case is to use the *Change Case* command.

tell me **more**

From the *Font* dialog box, you can apply the *All caps* or *Small caps* character formatting to text. Although the *All caps* command has the same effect as the *UPPERCASE* case command, *All caps* applies character formatting, while *UPPERCASE* changes the underlying text that was typed.

2.5 Changing Font Colors

In the past, creating black and white documents was the standard for most business purposes. This was mostly because printing color documents was cost prohibitive. Today, color printing is more affordable and accessible. Business documents often include graphics, illustrations, and color text.

Adding color to text in your document adds emphasis to certain words and helps design elements, such as headers, stand out for your reader. It is important to be selective when adding color to your document. Using too many colors can often be distracting to the reader.

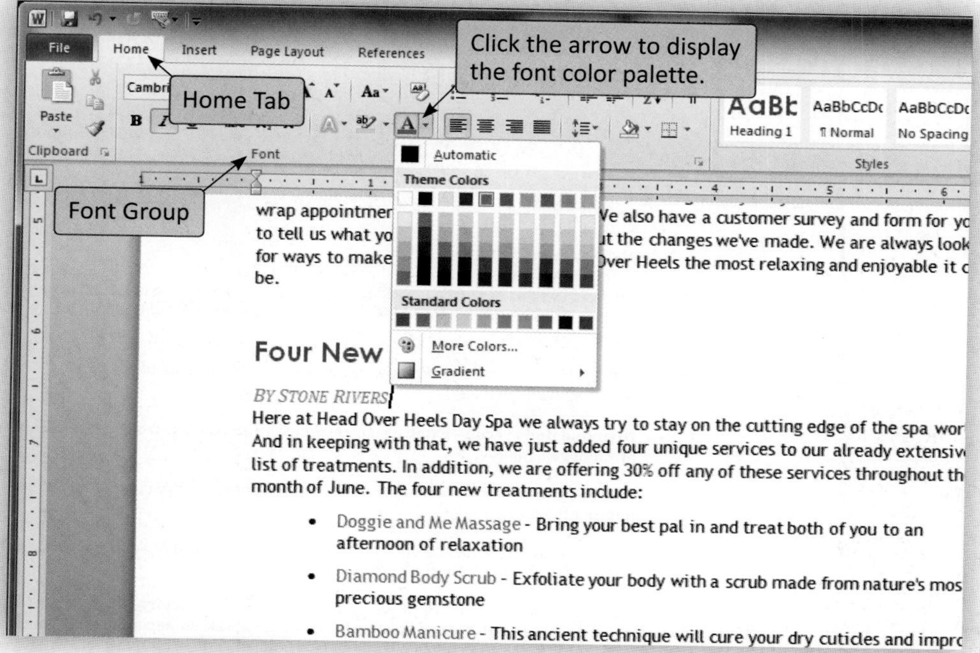

FIGURE WD 2.6

To change the color of the text:

1. Select the text to be changed.
2. On the *Home* tab, in the *Font* group, click the arrow next to the *Font Color* button.
3. Click the color you want from the color palette.

tips & tricks

When you change the color of text, the *Font Color* button changes to the color you selected. Click the **Font Color** button to quickly apply the same color to other text in the document.

tell me more

A color theme is a group of predefined colors that work well together in a document. You can apply a color theme to change the color of a number of elements at once. When you change the color theme, the color palette changes and displays only colors that are part of the color theme.

try this

You can change the font color from the Mini toolbar. To display the Mini toolbar, right-click in the text you want to change. Click the arrow next to the *Font Color* button and select the color you want.

2.6 Applying Highlights

Text in a Word document can be highlighted to emphasize or call attention to it. The effect is similar to that of a highlighting marker. When text is highlighted, the background color of the selected area is changed to make it stand out on the page.

Highlighting is very useful when you are sharing a document with coworkers or reviewers. It calls the other person's attention to elements that most need his or her attention. However, highlighting can sometimes be distracting as well. Be careful when using the highlighter in Word; only use it for small amounts of text.

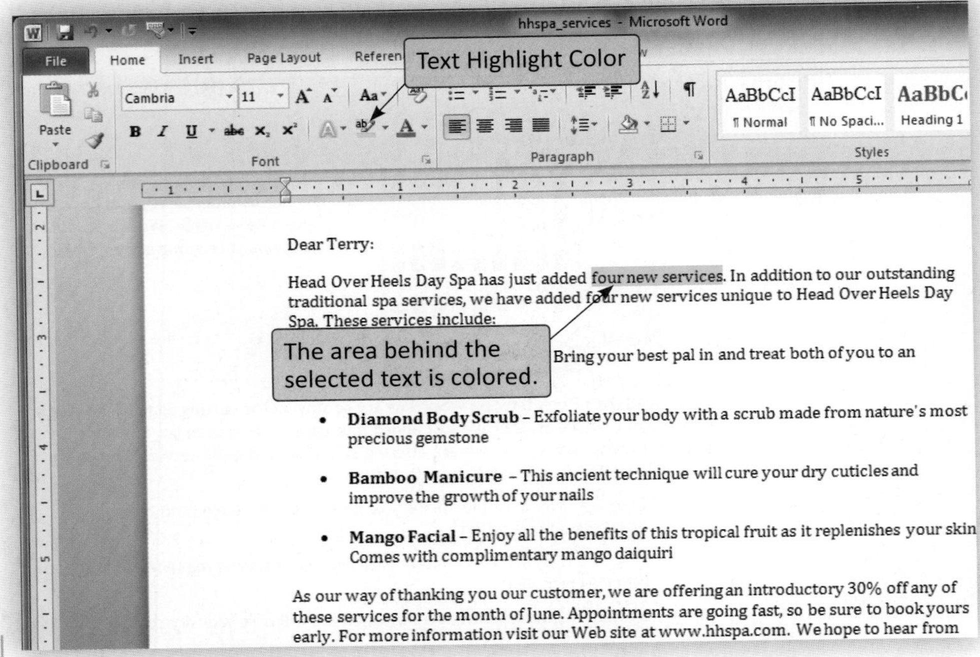

FIGURE WD 2.7

To highlight text in a document:

1. Select the text to be highlighted.
2. On the *Home* tab, in the *Font* group, click the arrow next to the *Text Highlight Color* button.
3. Click the color you want to use.

tips & tricks

Be careful when selecting colors to use for highlighting. If both the color of the text and the highlight color are dark, the text will be hard to read. If the highlight color is too light, it may not give the text enough emphasis.

tell me more

Rather than applying highlighting to text you have already selected, you can use the highlighter to apply highlighting to text throughout your document. Click the **Text Highlight Color** button without selecting any text first. Your cursor changes to a highlighter shape. Click and drag across text with the highlighter cursor to highlight text. To change your cursor back, click the **Text Highlight Color** button again.

try this

You can highlight text from the Mini toolbar. First, select the text you want to highlight; right-click the selected text to display the Mini toolbar. Click the arrow next to the *Text Highlight Color* button and select the color you want.

2.7 Using Format Painter

When you want to copy text from one part of your document to another, you use the copy and paste commands. What if you don't want to copy the text but instead copy all the formatting from text in one part of your document to text in another part of your document? The **Format Painter** tool allows you to copy formatting styles that have been applied to text. You can then "paste" the formatting, applying it to text anywhere in the document.

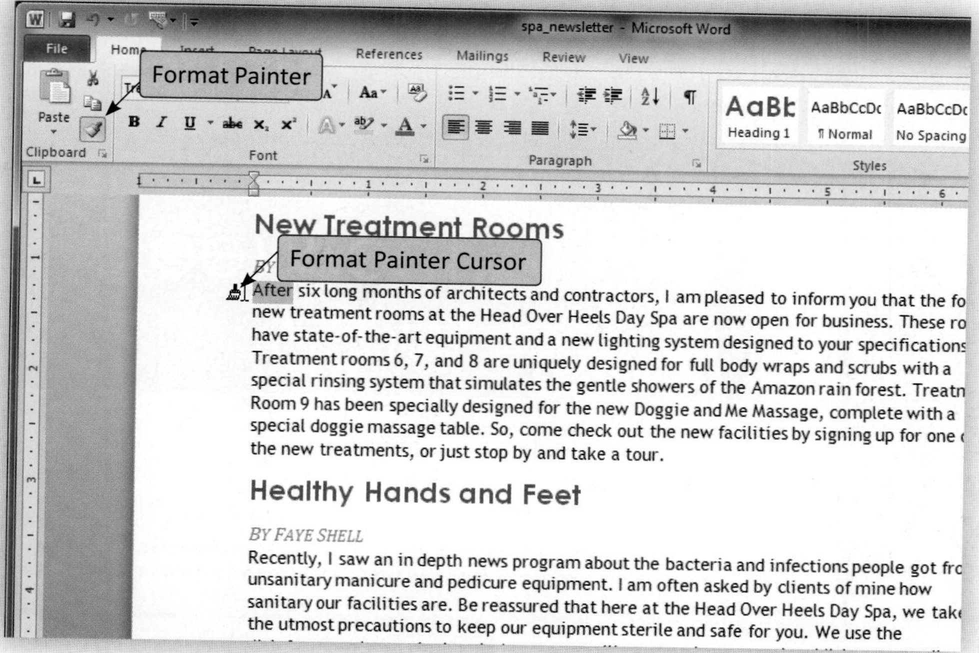

FIGURE WD 2.8

To use Format Painter:

1. Select the text that has the formatting you want to copy.
2. On the *Home* tab, in the *Clipboard* group, click the **Format Painter** button.
3. Select the text that you want to apply the formatting to.
4. The formats are automatically applied to the selected text.

tips & tricks

If the text you are copying the formatting from is formatted using a paragraph *style,* then you don't need to select the entire paragraph. Just place the cursor anywhere in the paragraph and click the **Format Painter** button. To apply the same paragraph style formatting to another paragraph, click anywhere in the paragraph to which you want to apply the formatting.

tell me more

If you want to apply the formats more than once, double-click the **Format Painter** button when you select it. It will stay on until you click the **Format Painter** button again or press Esc to deselect it.

try this

To activate *Format Painter,* you can right-click the text with formatting you want to copy and click the **Format Painter** button on the Mini toolbar.

2.8 Clearing Formatting

After you have applied a number of character formats and effects to text, you may find that you want to return your text to its original formatting. You could perform multiple undo commands on the text, or you could use the *Clear Formatting* command. The **Clear Formatting** command removes any formatting that has been applied to text, including character formatting, text effects, and styles, and leaves only plain text.

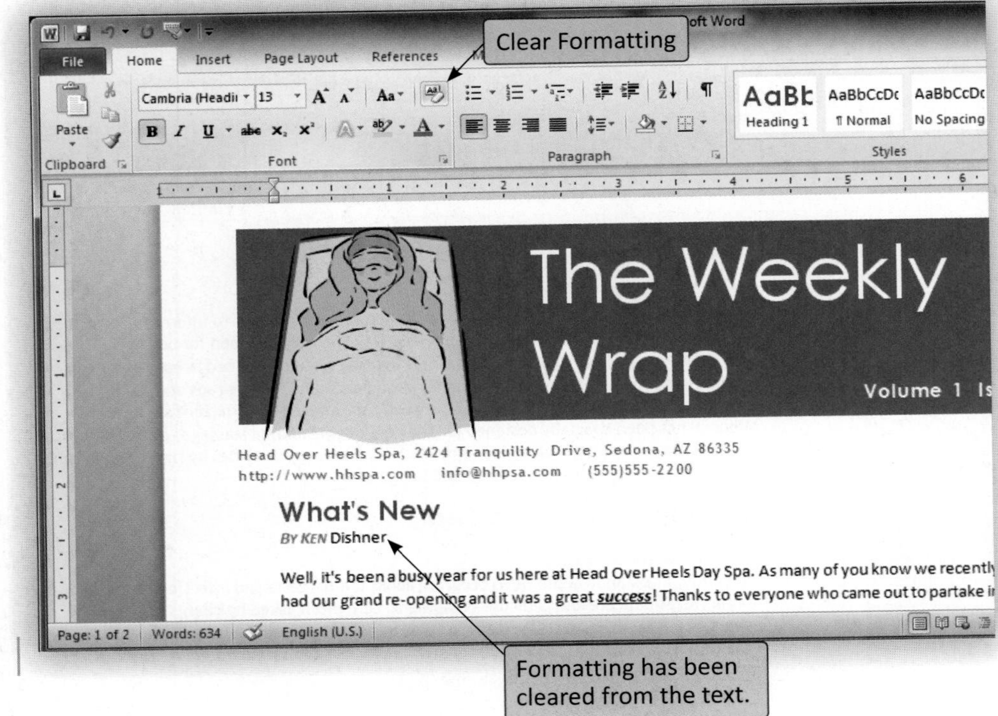

FIGURE WD 2.9

To remove formatting from text:

1. Select the text you want to remove the formatting from.
2. On the *Home* tab, in the *Font* group, click the **Clear Formatting** button.

tips & tricks

If you clear the formatting from text and then decide that you want to keep the formatting that was removed, you can use the undo command to apply the previous formatting to the text.

tell me more

The *Clear Formatting* command does not remove highlighting that has been applied to text. In order to remove highlighting from text, you must click the **Text Highlighting Color** button and select **No Color.**

try this

To clear the formatting from text, you can also:

1. On the *Home* tab, in the *Styles* group, click the **More** button.
2. Click **Clear Formatting.**

2.9 Creating Bulleted Lists

When typing a document you may want to include information that is best displayed in list format rather than paragraph format. If your list does not include items that need to be displayed in a specific order, use a bulleted list to help information stand out from surrounding text. A **bullet** is a symbol that is displayed before each item in a list. When a bullet appears before a list item, it indicates that the items in the list do not have a particular order to them.

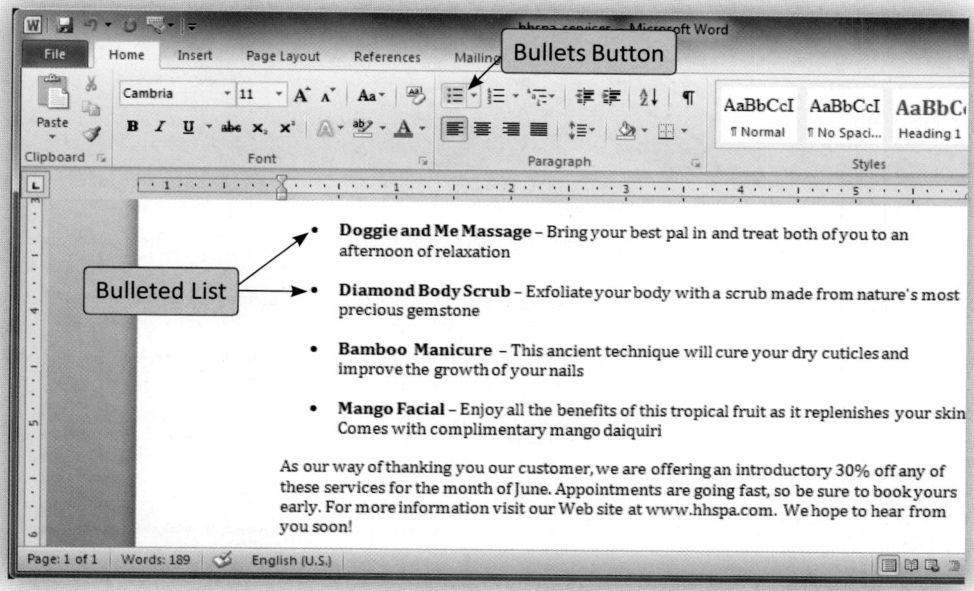

FIGURE WD 2.10

To create a bulleted list:

1. Select the text you want to change to a bulleted list. In order to appear as separate items within a bulleted list, each item must be followed by a hard return (press ←Enter).
2. On the *Home* tab, in the *Paragraph* group, click the **Bullets** button.
3. Click outside the list to deselect it.

tips & tricks

- Sometimes you will want to add more items to an existing list. Place your cursor at the end of a list item and press ←Enter to start a new line. A bullet will automatically appear before the list item.
- You can turn off the bullets formatting feature by pressing ←Enter twice.

tell me more

To change the bullet type, click the **Bullets** button arrow and select an option from the *Bullet Library.* You can create new bullets by selecting **Define New Bullet . . .**

try this

You can start a bulleted list by

- Typing an asterisk, a space, and your list item, then pressing the ←Enter key.
- Clicking the **Bullets** button, typing your list item, then pressing the ←Enter key.

You can convert text to a bulleted list by right-clicking the selected text, pointing to **Bullets,** and selecting an option.

2.10 Creating Numbered Lists

Some lists, such as directions to complete a task, need to have the items displayed in a specific order. **Numbered lists** display a number next to each list item and display the numbers in order. Numbered lists help you organize your content and display it in a clear, easy-to-understand manner.

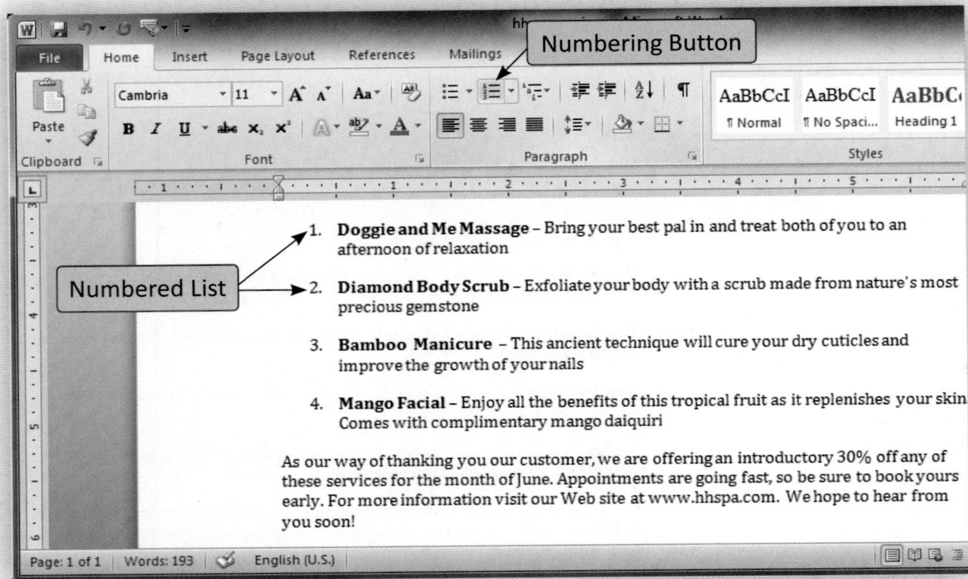

FIGURE WD 2.11

To create a numbered list:

1. Select the text you want to change to a numbered list. As with bulleted lists, in order to appear as separate items within a numbered list, each item must be followed by a hard return (press ←Enter).
2. On the *Home* tab, in the *Paragraph* group, click the **Numbering** button.
3. Click outside the list to deselect it.

tips & tricks

- Sometimes you will want to add more items to an existing list. To add another item to the list, place your cursor at the end of an item and press ←Enter to start a new line. The list will renumber itself to accommodate the new item.
- You can turn off the numbering feature by pressing ←Enter twice.

tell me more

To change the numbering list type, click the **Numbering** button arrow and select an option from the *Numbering Library*. You can create new numbered list styles by selecting **Define New Number Format . . .**

try this

You can start a numbered list by:

- Typing a 1, a space, and your list item, then pressing the ←Enter key.
- Clicking the **Numbering** button, typing your list item, then pressing the ←Enter key.
- You can convert text to a numbered list by right-clicking the selected text, pointing to **Numbering,** and selecting an option.

2.11 Creating Multilevel Lists

A **multilevel list** divides your content into several levels of organization.

1. For example, your top level organization might start with 1.
   a. The next level appears indented, and the numbering scheme restarts at the beginning.
2. When you return to the first outline level, the numbering scheme picks up with the next number.
   a. But the sublevels restart each time.

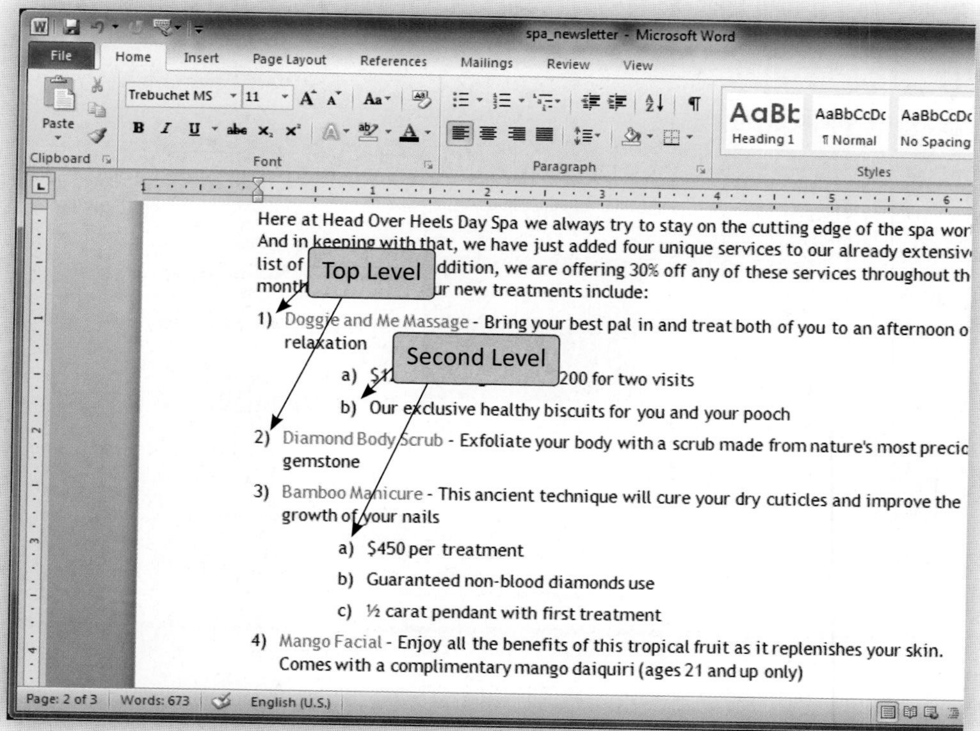

FIGURE WD 2.12

A multilevel numbered list can have up to nine levels of organization. The numbering for sublevels can be displayed in a variety of formats, available from the *Multilevel List* gallery.

To create a multilevel list:

1. Select the text you want to change into a list.
2. On the *Home* tab, in the *Paragraph* group, click the **Multilevel List** button.
3. The list has been created with each item at the same level.
4. To demote an item in the list, select the text, and click the **Increase Indent** button.
5. To promote an item in the list, select the text, and click the **Decrease Indent** button.

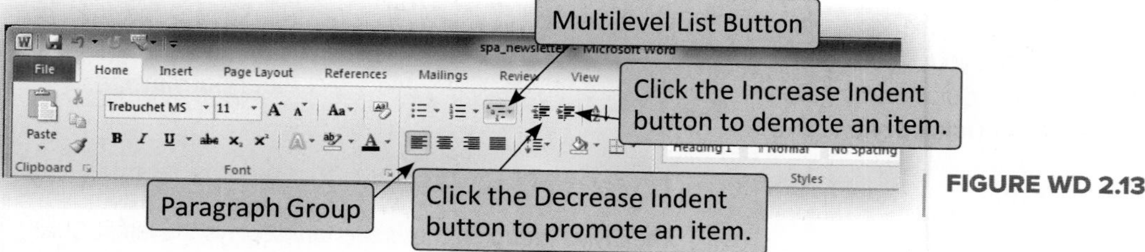

FIGURE WD 2.13

tips & tricks

Word comes with a number of predesigned multilevel list styles, but you also can choose to create your own multilevel list style. To create a custom multilevel list format, click the **Define New List Style . . .** item at the bottom of the *Multilevel List* gallery.

tell me more

Some multilevel lists show headings, which are based on predefined styles. Heading 1 text is placed at the topmost level of the list, followed by Heading 2 text, followed by Heading 3, etc.

2.12 Using Quick Styles

A **Quick Style** is a group of formatting, including character and paragraph formatting, that you can easily apply to text in your document. Quick Styles can be applied to body text, headers, quotes, or just about any type of text you may have in your document.

It is a good idea to use Quick Styles to format your documents. When you use Quick Styles to format text in your document, you can quickly change the look of that style across your document by changing the document's theme. Certain Quick Styles, such as headings, are also used by other features in Word, such as creating a table of contents and the Navigation task pane.

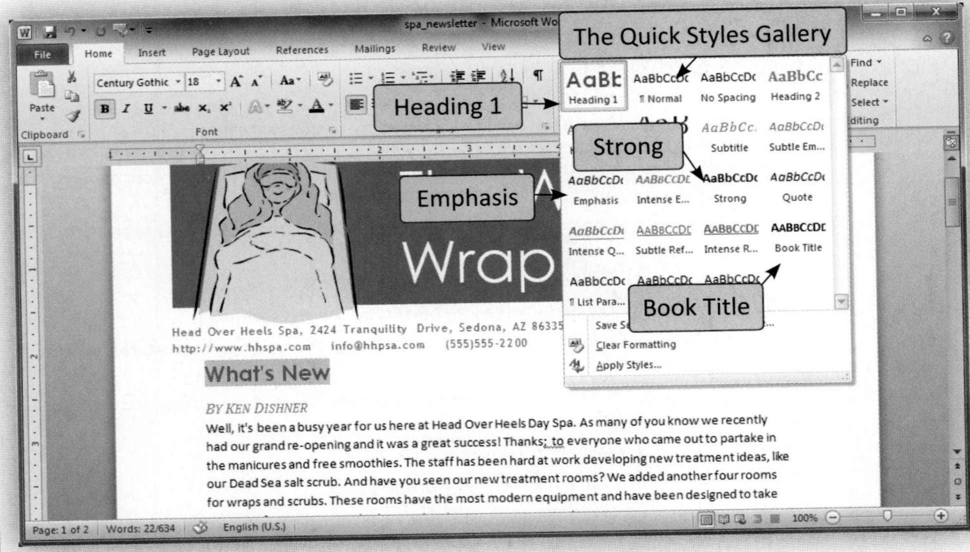

FIGURE WD 2.14

To apply a Quick Style to text:

1. Select the text you want to change.
2. On the *Home* tab, in the *Styles* group, click the **More** button.
3. Select a **Quick Style** from the *Quick Styles* gallery.

tips & tricks

If you modify a Quick Style, you can save the style with a new name and then use it throughout your document. To save a new text Quick Style, open the *Quick Styles* gallery and select **Save Selection as a New Quick Style . . .**

tell me more

When you select a new Quick Style, it replaces the style for the text. If you want to clear all the formatting for text, open the *Quick Styles* gallery and select **Clear Formatting.**

try this

The *Styles* group on the *Home* tab displays the latest Quick Styles you have used. If you want to apply a recently used Quick Style, you can click the option directly from the Ribbon without opening the *Quick Styles* gallery.

2.13 Changing Paragraph Alignment

Paragraph alignment refers to how text is aligned with regard to the left and right margins.

> **Left alignment** aligns the text on the left side, leaving the right side ragged.
>
> **Center alignment** centers each line of text relative to the margins.
>
> **Right alignment** aligns the text on the right side, leaving the left side ragged.
>
> **Justified alignment** evenly spaces the words, aligning the text on the right and left sides of the printed page.

It is important to understand common uses of different alignments. Paragraph text and headers are typically left aligned, but titles are often centered. Newspaper columns are often justified, and columns of numbers are typically right aligned.

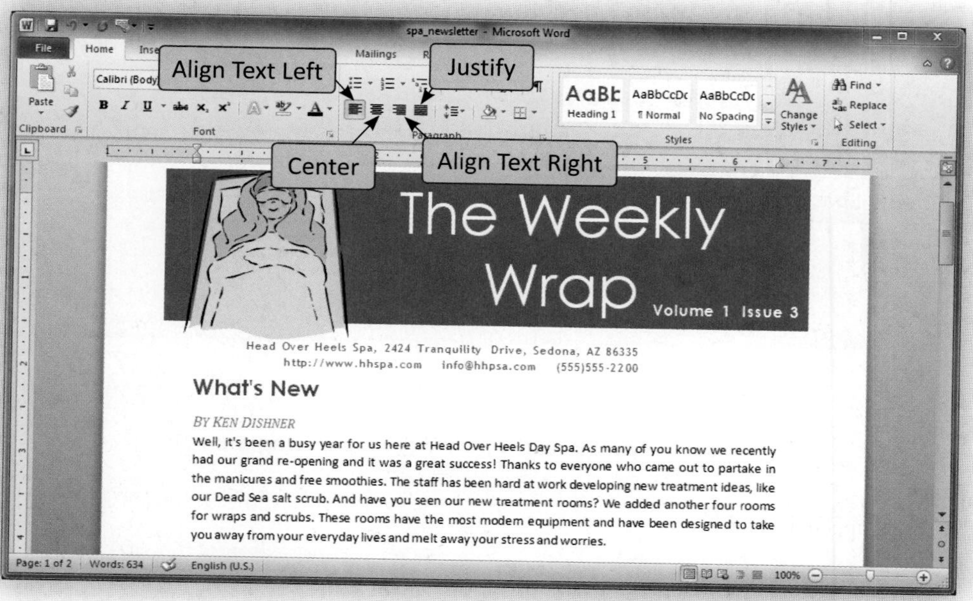

FIGURE 2.15

To change the alignment of text:

1. Click in the paragraph you want to change.
2. On the *Home* tab, in the *Paragraph* group, click an alignment button:

- **Align Text Left**
- **Center**
- **Align Text Right**
- **Justify**

tips & tricks

If you want to center text, you can right-click the text and select the **Center** button on the Mini toolbar. The Mini toolbar includes the *Center* button. However, it does not include any of the other alignment buttons. To apply other horizontal alignment, use the Ribbon or the keyboard shortcut.

try this

The following keyboard shortcuts can be used to apply horizontal alignment:

- **Align left** = Ctrl + L
- **Center** = Ctrl + E
- **Align Right** = Ctrl + R
- **Justify** = Ctrl + J

2.14 Changing Paragraph Spacing

Line spacing is the white space between lines of text. The default line spacing in Microsoft Word 2010 is 1.15 spacing. This gives each line the height of single spacing with a little extra space at the top and bottom. This line spacing is a good choice to use for the body of a document. Other commonly used spacing options include single spacing, double spacing, and 1.5 spacing.

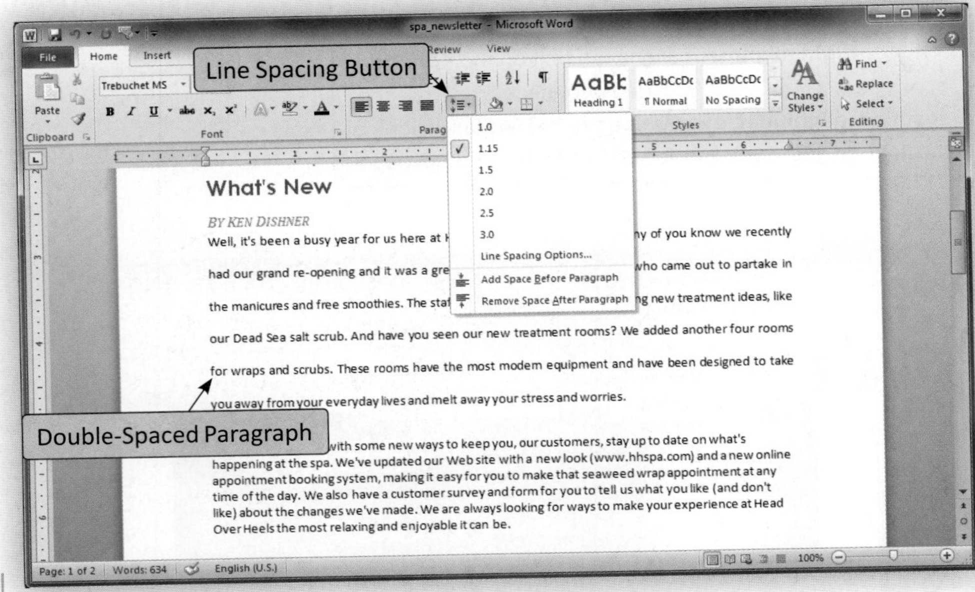

FIGURE WD 2.16

To change line spacing:

1. Select the text you want to change.
2. On the *Home* tab, in the *Paragraph* group, click the **Line Spacing** button.
3. Select the number of the spacing you want.

tips & tricks

You can add and remove space before and after your paragraphs by selecting the **Add Space Before Paragraph** and **Remove Space After Paragraph** options on the *Line Spacing* drop-down menu.

tell me more

Formatting marks control the appearance of your document and can be displayed by clicking the **Show/Hide** button ¶ on the *Home* tab.

A paragraph mark, ¶, is created every time the ←Enter key is pressed. Although these marks are hidden by default, revealing them can help you check your document for errors.

try this

- To apply single spacing, you can also press Ctrl + 1 on the keyboard.
- To apply double spacing, you can also press Ctrl + 2 on the keyboard.

2.15 Revealing Formatting Marks

When creating a document it is important to use consistent formatting, such as a single space after the period at the end of a sentence. As you create a document, Word adds formatting marks that are hidden from view. You can quickly check the formatting of your document by displaying these hidden formatting marks.

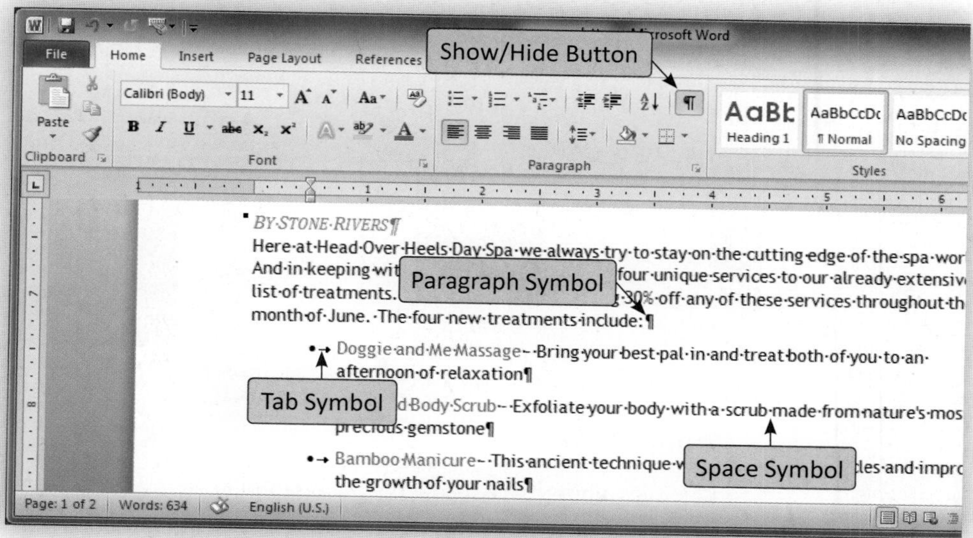

FIGURE WD 2.17

To display formatting marks in a document:

1. On the *Home* tab, in the *Paragraph* group, click the **Show/Hide** button.
2. The formatting marks are displayed in the document.
3. Click the **Show/Hide** button again to hide the formatting marks. Formatting marks include symbols that represent spaces, nonbreaking spaces, tabs, and paragraphs. The following table shows examples of formatting marks:

CHARACTER	FORMATTING MARK
Space	·
Nonbreaking Space	°
Tab	→
Paragraph	¶

tips & tricks

You can choose to always show specific formatting marks on-screen even when the *Show/Hide* button is inactive. To show specific formatting marks:

1. Click the **File** tab and select **Options.**
2. In the *Word Options* dialog box, click the **Display** category.
3. Select the formatting marks you want to display in the *Always show these formatting marks on the screen* section.
4. Click **OK.**

tell me more

- Formatting marks appear on-screen, but they do not appear in the printed document.
- A nonbreaking space is a space between two words that keeps the words together and prevents the words from being split across two lines.

try this

To show formatting marks, you can press Ctrl + Shift + 8.

2.16 Changing the Spacing between Paragraphs

When you set line spacing for a paragraph, Word creates new paragraphs based on that line height. This results in a very evenly spaced document, but also one where it can be difficult to differentiate between paragraphs, especially if your document is single spaced. To help differentiate between paragraphs in a document, you can change the spacing before and after paragraphs.

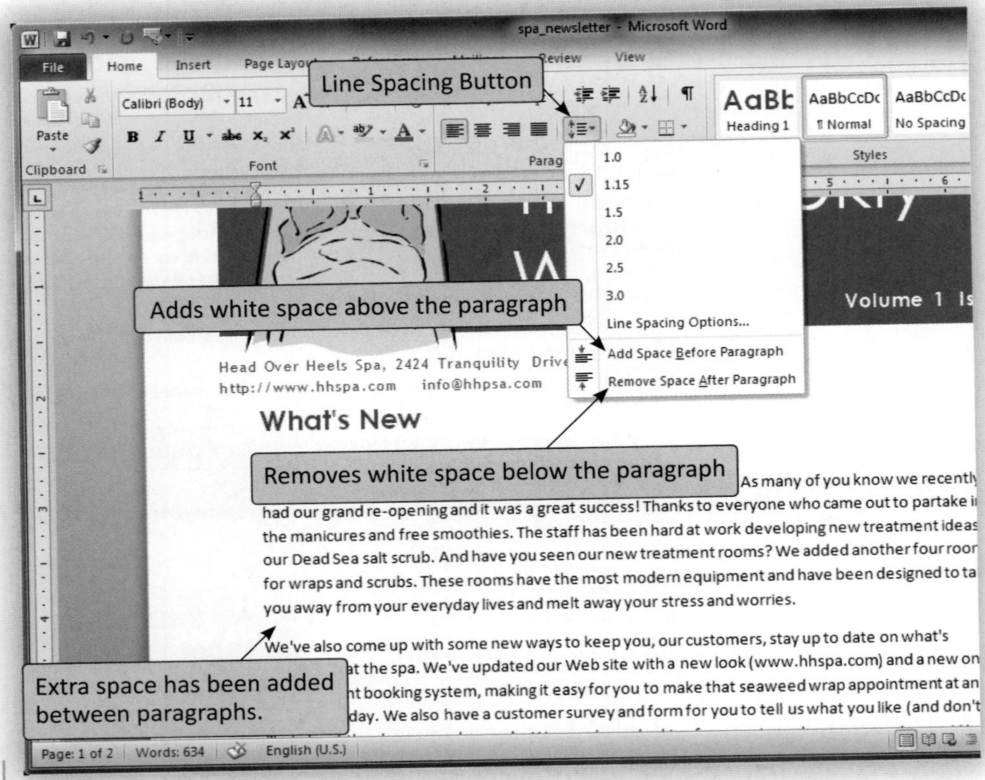

FIGURE WD 2.18

To increase and decrease the space before and after paragraphs:

1. Click in the paragraph you want to change.
2. On the *Home* tab, in the *Paragraph* group, click the **Line Spacing** button.
3. Choose one of the following options:

   Click **Add Space Before Paragraph** to add space above the first line of the paragraph.

   Click **Add Space After Paragraph** to add space below the last line of the paragraph.

   Click **Remove Space After Paragraph** to remove space from below the last line of the paragraph.

   Click **Remove Space Before Paragraph** to remove space from above the first line of the paragraph.

tips & tricks

You can control how much spacing appears before and after paragraphs.

1. Click the **Page Layout** tab.
2. In the *Paragraph* group, type a number in the *Before:* or *After:* box and press Enter to adjust the spacing between paragraphs. You can also click the arrows next to the boxes to adjust the spacing.

tell me more

Many of the Quick Styles available in the *Styles* group on the *Home* tab include spacing before and after paragraphs. Use Quick Styles to add text that includes text and paragraph formatting.

2.17 Changing Indents

When you create a document, the margins control how close the text comes to the edge of a page. But what if you don't want all your paragraphs to line up? Indenting paragraphs increases the left margin for a paragraph, helping it stand out from the rest of your document.

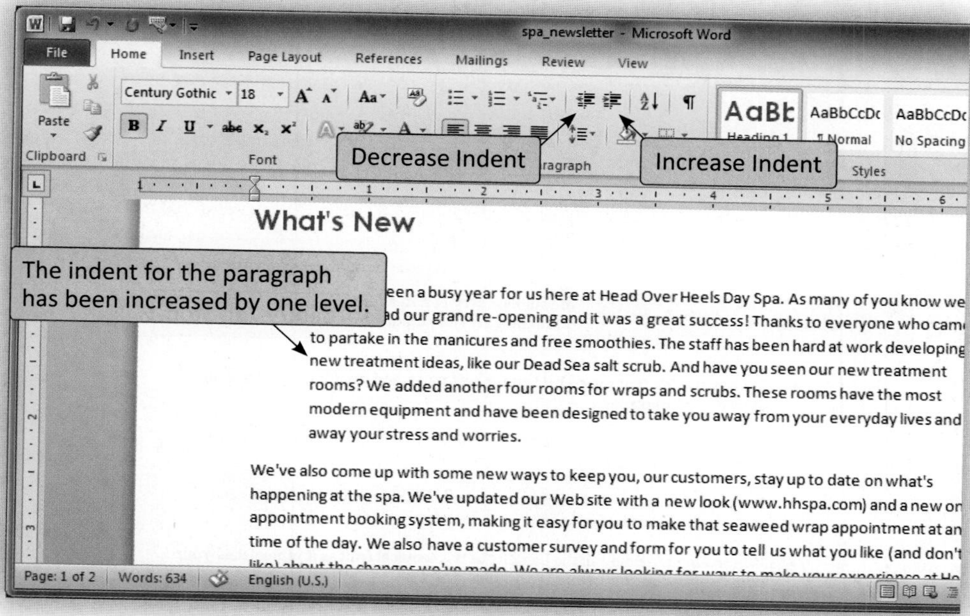

FIGURE WD 2.19

To change the indentation of a paragraph:

1. Place the cursor anywhere in the paragraph you want to change.
2. To increase the indent of the paragraph by one level, on the *Home* tab, in the *Paragraph* group, click the **Increase Indent** button.
3. To reduce the indent of the paragraph and bring it closer to the edge of the page by one level, click the **Decrease Indent** button.

tips & tricks

You can increase indents by one increment rather than by one level:

1. Click the **Page Layout** tab.
2. In the *Paragraph* group, click the arrows next to *Left:* and *Right:* to move paragraphs by one increment for each click.

try this

To change the indentation of a paragraph, you can right-click the paragraph and click the **Increase Indent** button or **Decrease Indent** button on the Mini toolbar.

tell me more

The *Indent* commands indent all lines in a paragraph the same amount. If you want only the first line of a paragraph to be indented and the remainder of the paragraph to be left-aligned, use a **First Line** indent. If you want the first line of a paragraph to be left-aligned and the remainder of the paragraph to be indented, use a hanging indent. In the *Format Paragraph* dialog box, you can precisely set options for first line indents and hanging indents. To open the *Format Paragraph* dialog box, click the **Dialog Launcher** in the *Paragraph* group on the *Home* tab or in the *Paragraph* group on the *Page Layout* tab.

2.18 Using Tab Stops

A **tab stop** is a location along the horizontal ruler that indicates how far to indent text when the Tab key is pressed.

There are five types of tab stops:

Left —Displays text to the right of the tab stop

Center —Displays text centered over the tab stop

Right —Displays the text to the left of the tab stop

Decimal —Aligns the text along the decimal point

Bar —Displays a vertical line through the text at the tab stop

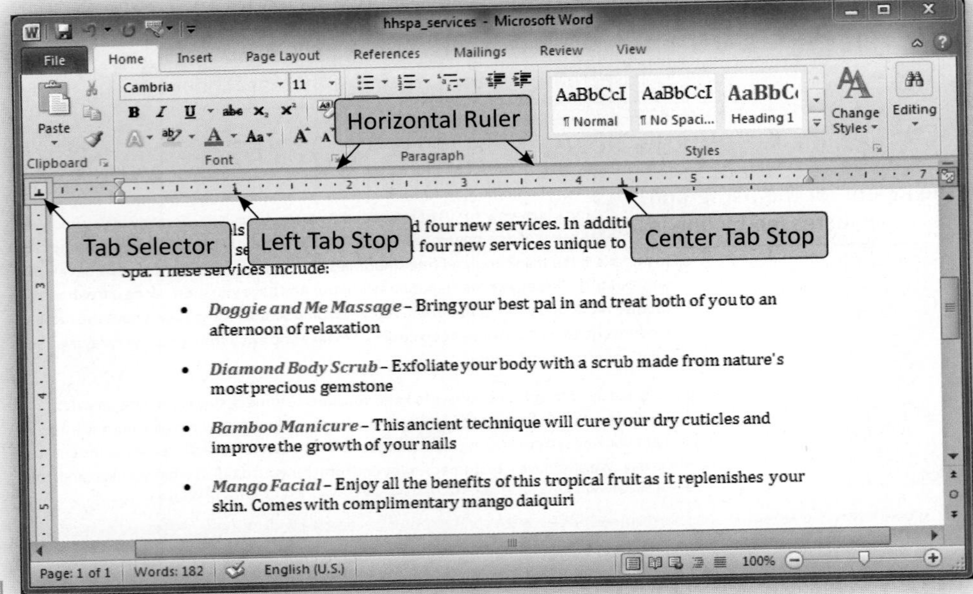

FIGURE WD 2.20

To set a tab stop:

1. Select the paragraph in which you want to set a tab stop.
2. Click the **tab selector** at the far left of the horizontal ruler until it changes to the type of tab you want.
3. Click the horizontal ruler where you want to set a tab stop.

tips & tricks

To clear a tab stop:

› Drag the tab marker down from the horizontal ruler to remove it.

To move a tab stop:

› Drag the tab marker to the right or left along the horizontal ruler to its new position.

If the ruler is not displayed, click the **View** tab and select the **Ruler** check box in the *Show* group.

tell me more

The tab selector also includes two options for adding indents to your document. The **First Line Indent** controls where the first line of a paragraph begins. The **Hanging Indent** controls where the remainder of the paragraph is indented.

try this

You can set tab stops in the *Tabs* dialog box:

1. Double-click the ruler to open the *Tabs* dialog box.
2. In the *Tab stop position:* box, type the number of where you want the tab stop to appear.
3. Click a radio button in the *Alignment* section.
4. Click **OK.**

2.19 Using Tab Leaders

Adding tab leaders can make data even easier to read. **Tab leaders** fill in the space between tabs with solid, dotted, or dashed lines. Using tab leaders helps associate columns of text by leading the reader's eye from left to right.

To add tab leaders:

1. Select the text to which you want to add the leader.
2. On the *Home* tab, in the *Paragraph* group, click the dialog launcher.
3. In the *Paragraph* dialog box, click the **Tabs . . .** button.
4. In the *Leader* section of the *Tabs* dialog box, select the leader option you want.
5. Click **OK.**

FIGURE WD 2.21

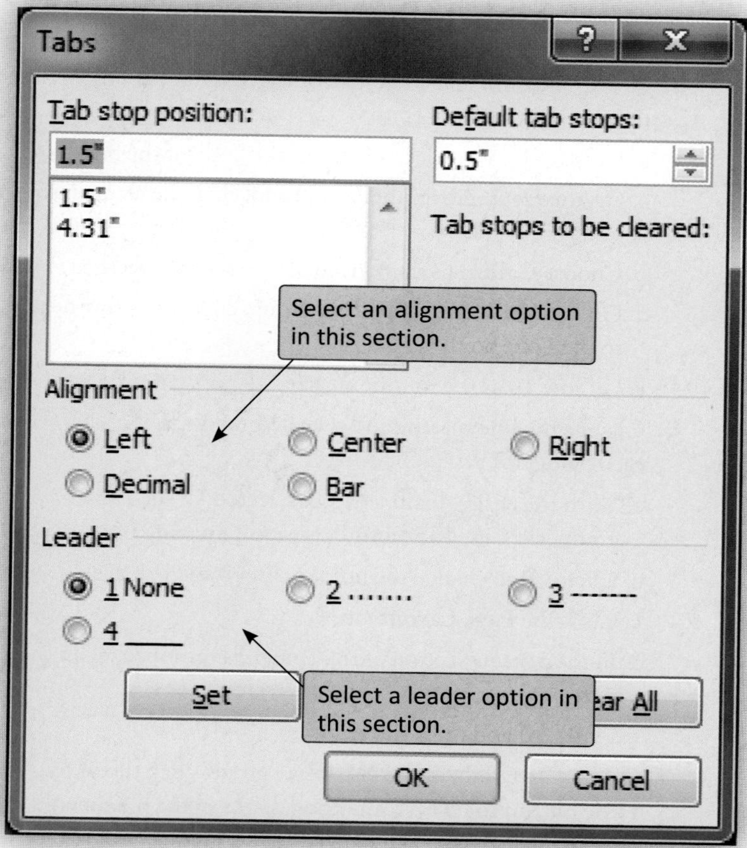

FIGURE WD 2.22

tips & tricks

When creating a table of contents for your document, use tab leaders to visually link section headings with page numbers.

try this

To open the *Tabs* dialog box, you can double-click a tab stop on the ruler.

projects

Skill Review 2.1

In this project you will be editing the *Brochure_02* document from Placer Hills Real Estate.

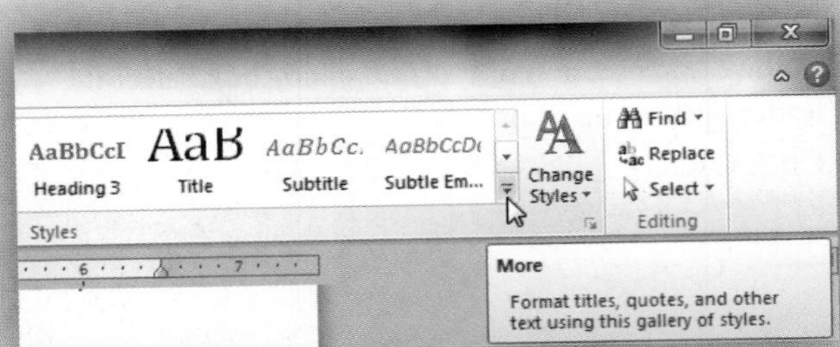

FIGURE WD 2.23

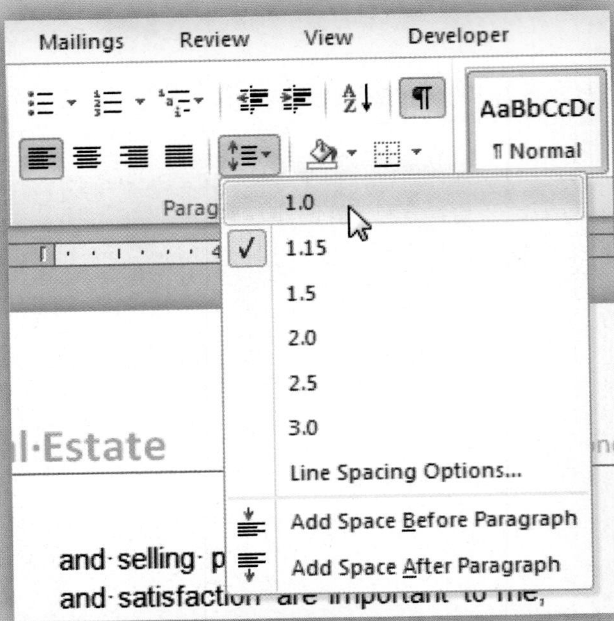

FIGURE WD 2.24

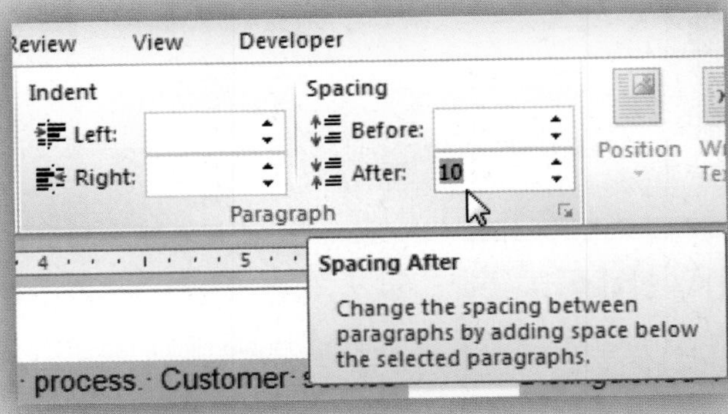

FIGURE WD 2.25

1. Open Microsoft Word 2010.
2. Open the *Brochure_02* document.
3. Save this document as
   ***[your initials]*WD_Projects_2-1.**
4. Clear the formatting on the first two lines of text in the first column.
   a. Select the first two lines of text in the first column.
   b. On the *Home* tab, in the *Styles* group, click the **More** button to expand the *Styles* gallery.
   c. Click the **Clear Formatting** selection below the *Styles* gallery. This will clear all current formatting and reset these lines to the default format from the Normal template.
5. Change the font and size on all of the text in the body of the document.
   a. Press **Ctrl+A** to select all text in the body of the brochure.
   b. On the *Home* tab, in the *Font* group, click the arrow next to the **Font** box.
   c. Choose **Calibri** as the font to use on the selected text.
   d. On the *Home* tab, in the *Font* group, click the arrow next to the **Font** box.
   e. Choose **10** as the font point size.
6. Change the line spacing and the paragraph spacing after each paragraph.
   a. With the entire document still selected, in the *Paragraph* group, click the **Line and Paragraph Spacing** button.
   b. Click **1.0** to change the line spacing to single space.
   c. Click the **Page Layout** tab.
   d. In the *Spacing* section of the *Paragraph* group, click in the **After** box.
   e. Type: `10` and press **Enter.**
7. On the *Home* tab, in the *Paragraph* group, click the **Show/Hide** button to reveal formatting marks in the document.
8. Delete all of the extra blank lines between paragraphs in the document.
9. Change after paragraph spacing to keep lines together.
   a. Select the lines of text containing the *Phone* and *Email* in the first column.
   b. Click on the **Page Layout** tab.
   c. In the *Paragraph* group, change the *After* spacing to **0 pt.**

10. Use *Quick Styles* to apply a heading format to a section heading in the document.
    a. Select the **Mission Statement** heading in the first column.
    b. Click the **Home** tab.
    c. In the *Styles* group, click the **Heading 1** style. The *Heading 1* style is applied to the selected section heading.
11. Change the spacing before paragraph on the selected heading.
    a. Make sure the *Mission Statement* heading is still selected.
    b. Click on the **Page Layout** tab.
    c. In the *Spacing* section of the *Paragraph* group, change *Before* to **0 pt.** You can either type **0 pt** or click on the down arrow to decrease the paragraph spacing to **0 pt.**
12. Use the *Format Painter* to change the format on all of the section headings to match the style and spacing of the first section heading.
    a. Select the **Mission Statement** heading in the first column.
    b. On the *Home* tab, in the *Clipboard* group, click the **Format Painter** button.
    c. Select the entire line of the next heading (*Real Estate Experience*). The formatting is applied to this heading and the *Format Painter* is turned off.
    d. With the *Real Estate Experience* heading selected, double-click the **Format Painter** button. Double-clicking the *Format Painter* button will allow you to use the *Format Painter* on more than one selection.
    e. Select each of the remaining headings one at a time. The format will be applied to each heading. Be careful not to click on or select any other text during this process or the style will be applied to that selection.
    f. Click the **Format Painter** button to turn it off after you have finished applying this style to all of the headings.
13. Add a numbered list to and decrease the indent on a section of the brochure.
    a. In the *Why I Am a Real Estate Agent* section, select all of the text.
    b. On the *Home* tab, in the *Paragraph* group, click the **Numbering** button. Numbering is applied to this section and it is indented.
    c. Click the **Decrease Indent** button once to change the left indent to 0″.
14. Add a bulleted list to and decrease the indent on a section of the brochure.
    a. In the *Professional Credentials* section, select all of the text.
    b. On the *Home* tab, in the *Paragraph* group, click the **Bullets** button. Bullets are applied to this section and it is indented.
    c. Click the **Decrease Indent** button once to change the left indent to 0″.
15. Change the paragraph spacing on selected text and use the *Format Painter.*
    a. Select all of the text in the *Education & Training* section. Do not include the heading.
    b. Click the **Page Layout** tab.
    c. In the *Paragraph* group, change the *After* spacing to *3 pt.*
    d. Select one line of the text in this section.
    e. Click the **Format Painter.**
    f. Select all of the text in the *The Placer Hills Belief System* section. Do not include the heading. The format will be applied to this section.
16. Apply a *Quick Style* to and change the paragraph spacing on selected text.
    a. In the *What Clients Are Saying* section, select the first quote and include the quotation marks.
    b. Click the **Home** tab.

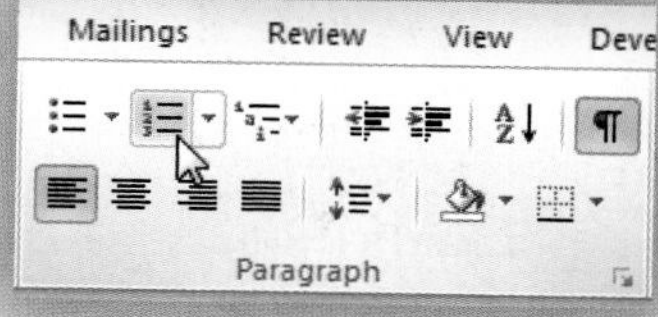

FIGURE WD 2.26

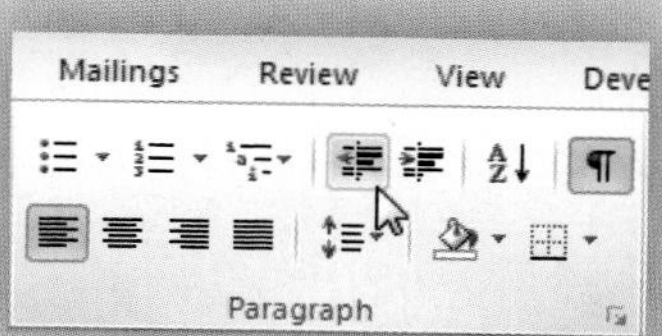

FIGURE WD 2.27

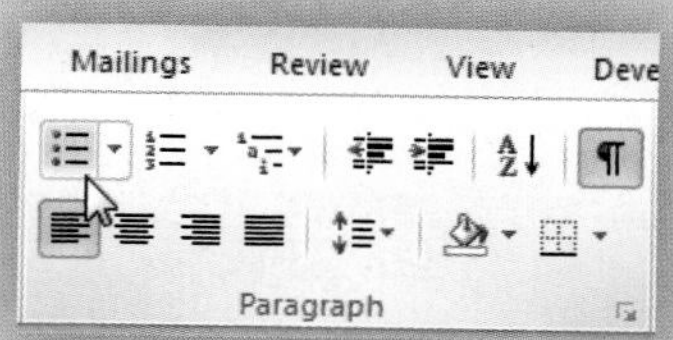

FIGURE WD 2.28

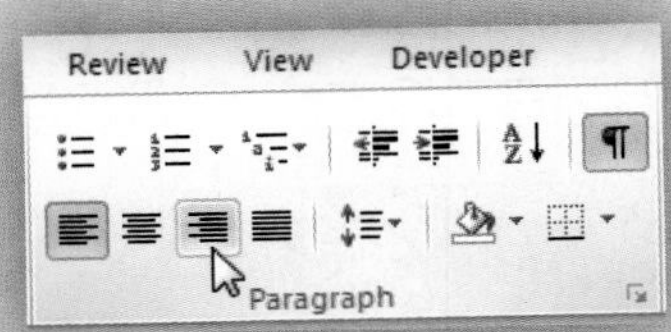

FIGURE WD 2.29

c. In the *Styles* group, apply the **Quote** style. You might have to click the **More** button to locate this style.

d. Click the **Page Layout** tab.

e. In the *Paragraph* group, change the *After* spacing to *3 pt.*

f. Use the *Format Painter* to apply this format to the second quote in this section.

g. Select **–Rod & Luisa Ellisor, Rocklin, CA.**

h. Click the **Home** tab.

i. In the *Paragraph* group, click the **Align Text Right** button or press **Ctrl+R.**

j. Select and right align **–Jon & Robin Anderson, Roseville, CA.**

17. Change font size, style, effects, and color on selected text.

a. Select **Emma Cavalli** and **Realtor Consultant** at the top of the first column.

b. On the *Home* tab, in the *Font* group, change the font to **Cambria.**

c. Click the **Bold** button in the *Font* group.

d. Change the *Font Size* to **14 pt.**

e. Click on the *Font Color* button, and change the color to **Dark Blue, Text 2.**

f. On the *Home* tab in the *Font* group, click the **Dialog Launcher.**

g. Click on **Small Caps** in the *Effects* area, and click **OK** to close the *Font* dialog box.

h. Select **Realtor Consultant.**

i. Click the **Italic** button in the *Font* group or press **Ctrl+I.**

j. Select the word **Commitment** in the *The Placer Hills Belief System* section.

k. Click on **Bold** in the *Font* group.

l. On the *Home* tab in the *Font* group, click the **Dialog Launcher.**

m. Click **Small Caps** in the *Effects* area, and click **OK** to close the *Font* dialog box.

n. Use the *Format Painter* to apply this format to all of the other introductory words in this section (Communication, Trust, Integrity, Customers, Teamwork, Success, Creativity, Win-Win).

18. Save and close the document.

Skill Review 2.2

In this project you will be editing the *Seller Escrow Checklist_02* document from Placer Hills Real Estate.

1. Open the *Seller Escrow Checklist_02* document.

2. Save this document as ***[your initials]*** **`WD_SkillReview_2-2`.**

3. Change font, font size, and line spacing on the entire document.

a. Press **Ctrl+A** to select the entire document.

b. On the *Home* tab, in the *Font* group, change the font to **Calibri** and the font size to **12 pt.**

c. In the *Paragraph* group, change the line spacing to **2.0.**

4. Click the **Show/Hide** button in the *Paragraph* group to reveal formatting marks in the document.

5. Delete all of the extra blank lines between paragraphs in the document.

6. Add tabs and leaders to selected lines using the *Tabs* dialog box.
   a. Select the **Seller** and **Escrow Company** lines.
   b. Click on the **Dialog Launcher** button in the bottom-right corner of the *Paragraph* group. The *Paragraph* dialog box will open.
   c. Click the **Tabs** button. The *Tabs* dialog box will open.
   d. Click **Clear All** to clear all existing tabs on these lines.
   e. Click in the *Tab stop position* box; type: `3`
   f. In the *Alignment* area click **Right.**
   g. In the *Leader* area click **4** (solid underline leader).
   h. Click the **Set** button to set this 3″ right tab with a solid underline leader.
   i. Set another tab with the following settings: 3.5″, Left alignment, no leader. Be sure to press **Set** to add the tab.
   j. Set another tab with the following settings: 6.5″, Right alignment, solid underline leader (4).
   k. Click **OK** to close the *Tabs* dialog box.

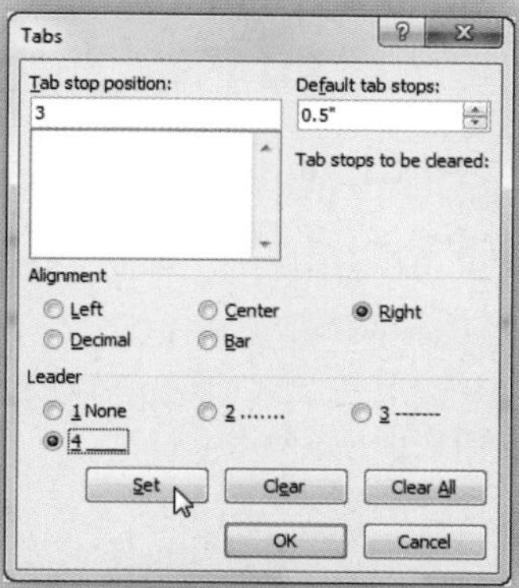

FIGURE WD 2.30

7. Add text and use tabs.
   a. Click after the word *Seller.*
   b. Press **Tab.** A solid underline will appear.
   c. Press **Tab** to move to 3.5″
   d. Type: `Property Address`
   e. Press **Tab.**
   f. Click after the words *Escrow Company.*
   g. Press **Tab.** A solid underline will appear.
   h. Press **Tab** to move to 3.5″
   i. Type: `Escrow #`
   j. Press **Tab.**

8. Add a center tab on the ruler and add text.
   a. Select the **Task to Be Completed** line.
   b. Click on the **Tab** selector to change the tab to a *Center Tab.* If the ruler is not visible below the ribbon, click on the **View Ruler** icon above the vertical scroll bar on the right side of the Word window. The ruler can also be turned on by clicking on the **View** tab and clicking on the **Ruler** check box in the *Show* group.
   c. Click on the Ruler at 5.5″ to set a center tab.
   d. Click after *Task to Be Completed.*
   e. Press **Tab.**
   f. Type: `Date Completed`**.** This text should be centered at 5.5″.

FIGURE WD 2.31

9. Set tabs on the remaining lines of the document.
   a. Select the remaining lines of text **Open Escrow with Escrow Company** through **Fax/Email Clear Pest Report.**
   b. Click the **Dialog Launcher** button in the bottom-right corner of the *Paragraph* group. The *Paragraph* dialog box will open.
   c. Click the **Tabs** button. The *Tabs* dialog box will open.
   d. Set a left tab at 4.5″.
   e. Set a right tab with a solid underline leader at 6.5″.

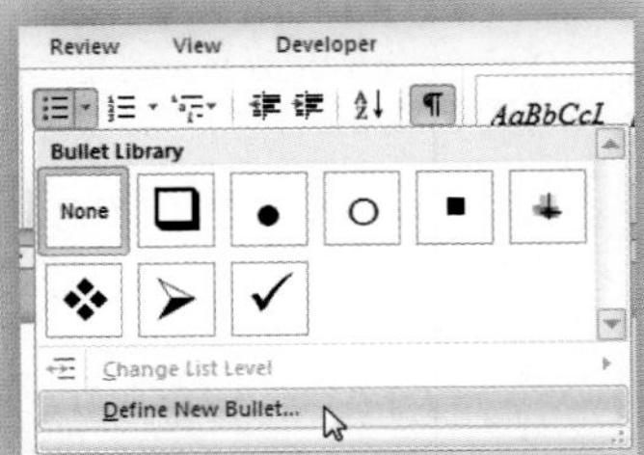

FIGURE WD 2.32

f. Click **OK** to close the *Tabs* dialog box.

g. Click after *Open Escrow with Escrow Company.*

h. Press **Tab** to move to 4.5″.

i. Press **Tab** to insert a solid underline leader to 6.5″.

j. Repeat this process after each of the remaining lines through *Fax/Email Clear Pest Report.*

10 Add bullets to selected lines of text.

a. Select the lines of text **Open Escrow with Escrow Company** through **Fax/Email Clear Pest Report.**

b. Click on the **arrow** to the right of the *Bullets* button in the *Paragraph* group to open the *Bullets* menu.

c. Select one of the bullets in the *Bullet Library* area. The selected lines will have this bullet applied.

d. In the *Paragraph* group, click on the **Decrease Indent** button once to move the bulleted list to the left margin.

11. Customize the bulleted list and add text.

a. Press **Ctrl+End** to move to the end of the document.

b. Press **Enter.**

c. Type: `Title` and press **Tab** twice.

d. Press **Enter.**

e. Type: `Lender` and press **Tab** twice.

f. Press **Enter.**

g. Type: `Buyer's Agent` and press **Tab** twice.

h. Click at the end of the *Fax/Email Clear Pest Report* line (after the underline tab).

i. Press **Backspace** twice to delete the two tabs.

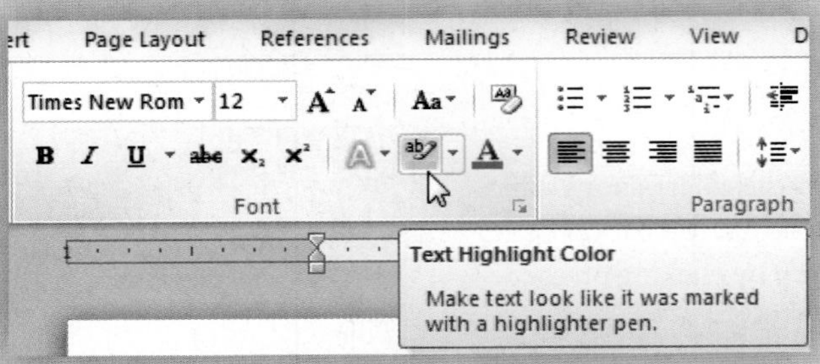

FIGURE WD 2.33

j. Click the **Bullets** button to turn off the bullet on this line.

k. Change the line spacing to **1.0** on this line.

l. Click the **Page Layout** tab.

m. Change the **After** spacing in *Paragraph* group to **6 pt.**

n. Select the word **Clear** on this line of text.

o. Click the **Home** tab.

p. Click the **Text Highlight Color** button in the *Font* group to highlight this text with yellow.

12. Change font case and style on selected text.

a. Select the entire line beginning with **Task to Be Completed.**

b. In the *Font* group, click on the **Change Case** button and select **UPPERCASE.**

c. Click the **Bold** button in the *Font* group.

d. In the *Font* group, click the **arrow** to the right of the *Font Color* button.

e. Select **Dark Blue.**

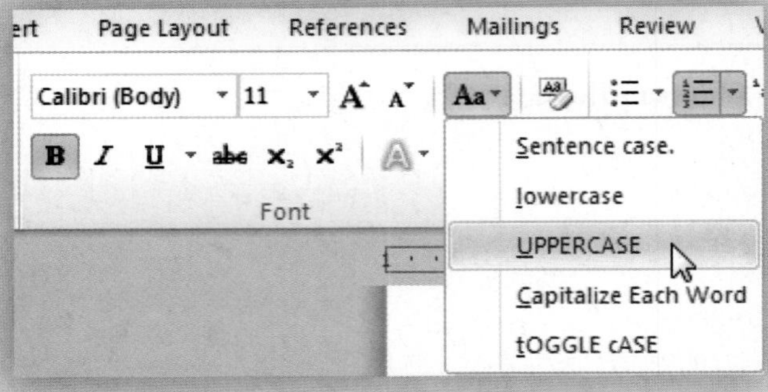

FIGURE WD 2.34

13. Apply a *Quick Style* to selected text.

a. Select the first line of the document (**Seller Escrow Checklist**).

b. In the *Styles* group, click the **Title** style.

c. Click the **Center** button in the *Paragraph* group, or press **Ctrl+E** to center the selected text.

14. Save and close the document.

challenge yourself 1

In this project you will be editing the *Staying Active_02* document from Courtyard Medical Plaza.

1. Open the *Staying Active_02* document.

2. Save this document as `[your initials]WD_Challenge_2-3.`

3. Change font, font size, line spacing, and paragraph spacing on entire document.

a. Change the font to Calibri and the size to 11 pt.

b. Change the line spacing to single (1.0).

c. Change the before paragraph spacing to 6 pt.

4. Delete all of the extra blank lines between paragraphs in the document.

5. Customize the title of the document.

a. Apply the **Intense Reference** *Quick Style* to the title of the document.

b. Change the font size to 18 pt.

c. Change the before paragraph spacing to 36 pt. and the after spacing to 12 pt.

d. Center the title.

6. Customize the first section heading in the document (*Try some of the following suggestions:*).

a. Apply the **Subtle Reference** *Quick Style.*

b. Change the font size to 14 pt.

c. Change the before paragraph spacing to 12 pt. and the after paragraph spacing to 6 pt.

7. Use the *Format Painter* to apply the formatting of the first section heading to the second section heading (*To keep exercise fun and interesting:*).

8. Change the case of both section headings to **Capitalize Each Word.**

9. Add a multilevel list to the four paragraphs after the first section heading.

a. Select all four paragraphs after the first section heading.

b. Apply numbered and lettered [1), a), i), etc.] multilevel list to selected text.

10. The first sentence in each paragraph will be a first-level numbered item. You will change the remaining sentences to be either a second- or third-level entry.

a. Click before the second sentence in the first paragraph of this multilevel list.

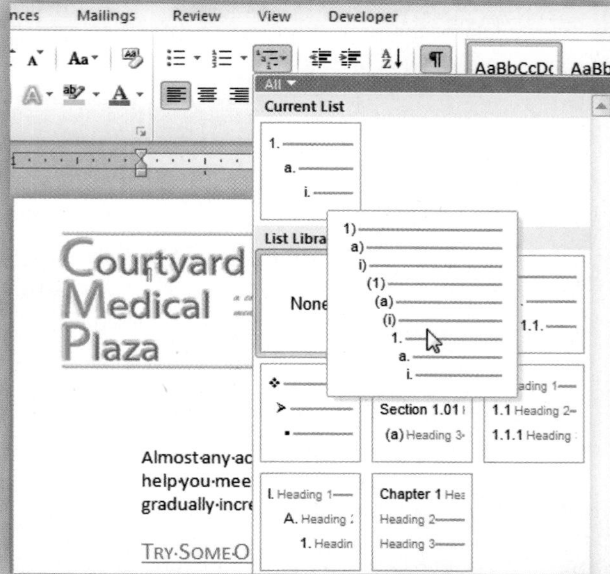

FIGURE WD 2.35

b. Press **Enter** and then press **Tab** (or **Increase Indent**). This sentence is now listed as *a).*

c. Click before the next sentence (*For example . . .*) and press **Enter.**

d. Press **Tab** (or **Increase Indent**) to change this sentence to *i)* (a third-level entry).

e. Click before the next sentence (*The more physical activity . . .*) and press **Enter.**

f. Press **Shift+Tab** (or **Decrease Indent**) to change this sentence to *b)* (a second-level entry).

11. In the second paragraph (*If you don't like counting calories . . .*), change the second and third sentences to second-level entries.

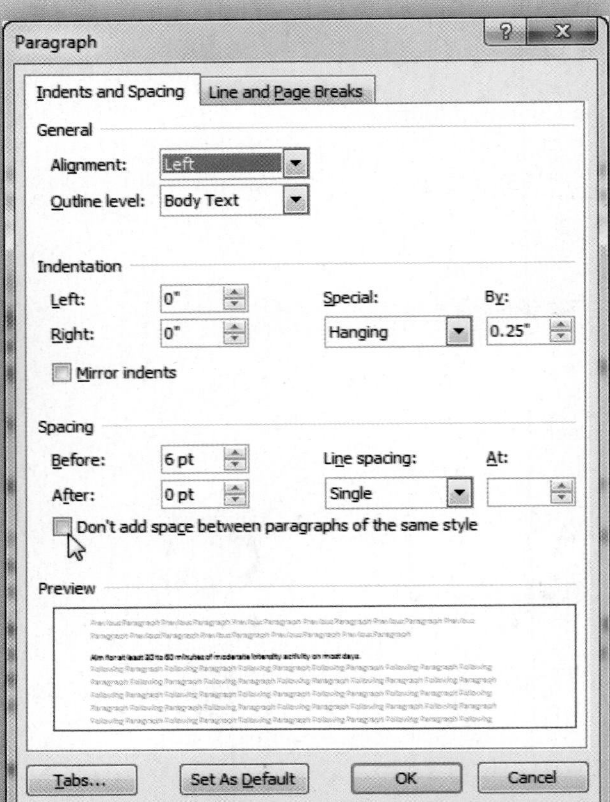

FIGURE WD 2.36

12. In the third paragraph (*Use both aerobic and strengthening . . .*), change the second and third sentences to second-level entries.

13. Press **Enter** after the fourth paragraph and add the following second- and third-level entries.

`Household chores` (second level)

`Cleaning windows` (third level)

`Vacuuming` (third level)

`Doing laundry` (third level)

`Yard work and gardening` (second level)

`Using stairs rather than an elevator` (second level)

`Getting up and moving regularly at work` (second level)

14. Customize the font style, effects, and paragraph spacing in the multilevel list.

a. Select the first line in the multilevel list.

b. Use bold and small caps on this line (Hint: Use the *Font* dialog box).

c. Open the *Paragraph* dialog box and deselect the *Don't add space between paragraphs of the same style* check box so the 6 pt. before paragraph spacing is applied to this selection.

d. Use the Format Painter to apply this formatting to the other first-level entries in this multilevel list.

15. Add a bulleted list to the four paragraphs after the second section heading (*To keep exercise fun and interesting:*).

a. Select all four paragraphs in this section and apply a bullet of your choice.

b. Decrease the indent of the bulleted list so the bullets are at the left margin.

c. Open the *Paragraph* dialog box and deselect the *Don't add space between paragraphs of the same style* check box so the 6 pt. before paragraph spacing is applied to this bulleted list.

16. Change the first sentence on each of the bulleted items to bold and small caps.

17. Save and close the document.

challenge yourself 2

In this project you will be editing the *Emergency Procedures_02* document from Sierra Pacific Community College District.

1. Open the *Emergency Procedures_02* document.

2. Save this document as ***[your initials]*** **WD_Challenge_2-4.**

3. Change the font on the entire document to Times New Roman and 12 pt.

4. Customize the title of the document.
   a. Apply the **Heading 1** *Quick Style* to the title of the document.
   b. Change the case to UPPERCASE.
   c. Change the before paragraph spacing to 18 pt.
5. Customize the section headings of the document.
   a. Apply the **Heading 2** *Quick Style* to the first section heading [*Emergency Telephones (blue phones)*] in the document.
   b. Underline this heading and change to small caps.
   c. Change the before paragraph spacing to 14 pt.
   d. Use the *Format Painter* to apply this formatting to the remaining headings in the document.
6. Customize the section headings of the document.
   a. Apply the **Heading 2** *Quick Style* to the first section heading [*Emergency Telephones (blue phones)*] in the document.
   b. Underline this heading and change to small caps.
   c. Use the *Format Painter* to apply this formatting to the remaining headings in the document.
7. Delete all of the extra blank lines in the document.
8. Change the bulleted list in the *Emergency Telephones* section to a numbered list.
   a. Change the left indent to 0.25″ (use the *Paragraph* group on the *Page Layout* ribbon).
9. Apply this numbered list formatting to the text in the following sections (do not include the section headings): *Assaults, Fights, or Emotional Disturbances; Power Failure; Fire; Earthquake; Bomb Threat.*
10. In the *Emergency Telephone Locations* section, change the left indent of the locations to 0.25″ (do not include the heading).
11. Bold each of the emergency telephone locations in this section (**Stadium Parking Lot, Barton Hall,** etc.).
12. In the *Emergency Phone Numbers* section, change the left indent of these lines to 0.25″ (do not include the heading).
13. Select the text in the *Emergency Phone Numbers* section and set a 6.5″ right tab with a dot leader (leader selection 2).
14. Press **Tab** before each of the phone numbers in this section to line up the numbers at the right margin. A dot leader will be inserted before each phone number.
15. Select the text in the *Accident or Medical Emergency* section and apply a bullet of your choice.
    a. Make sure the left indent is at 0.25″.
16. Use the *Format Painter* to apply this bulleted list format to the text in the following sections (do not include the section headings): *Tips to Professors and Staff, Response to Students.*
17. In the *Accident or Medical Emergency* section, bold, italicize, and underline **Life-threatening emergencies** and **Minor emergencies.**
18. Find all occurrences of *Phone 911* in the document. On each occurrence, change to red font color, bold, and all caps.
19. Save and close the document.

on your own

In this project you will be editing the *Central Sierra Questionnaire_02* document from Central Sierra Insurance.

1. Open the *Central Sierra Questionnaire_02* document.
2. Save this document as `[your initials]WD_OnYourOwn_2-5.`
3. Select the entire document and make the following formatting changes:
   a. Clear all formatting.
   b. Change the font to Calibri and 10 pt.
   c. Change the line spacing to single space.
   d. Change the after paragraph spacing to 6 pt.
   e. Set left tabs at 0.25″ and 0.5″.
   f. Set a right tab with a solid underline leader at 6.5″.
4. Delete all extra blank lines in the document.
5. Select the first line of the document and make the following changes:
   a. Apply the *Title* style.
   b. Change the case to *Capitalize Each Word.*
   c. Bold text and use small caps.
6. Select the next line of the document (*Please carefully read*. . .) and apply *Intense Reference* style, uppercase, no underline, and 12 pt. font size.
7. Select the next line of the document (*Applicant's Instructions*) and make the following changes:
   a. Apply the *Intense Quote* style.
   b. Change the left and right indents to 0″.
   c. Change the after paragraph spacing to 6 pt.
8. Apply the formatting from *Applicant's Instructions* heading to *Insurance Application Disclaimer* (on the second page).
9. Select all of the text after the *Insurance Application Disclaimer* heading to the end of the document and change the after paragraph spacing to 12 pt.
10. Click at the end of the *Name and Title of Insured* line and press **Tab** to insert a solid underline leader.
11. Add a tab after the *Signature of Insured* and *Date of Application* lines.
12. Add a multilevel list to all of the lines between the *Applicant's Instructions* and *Insurance Application Disclaimer* headings.
   a. Use the following multilevel style: 1), a), i)
   b. With the text still selected, open the *Paragraph* dialog box and deselect the *Don't add space between paragraphs the same style* check box.
   c. Use either *Tab* or *Increase Indent* to change each line that begins *If "yes,"*. . . to a second-level item.
   d. Click at the end of each paragraph in the multilevel list and press **Tab** to insert a solid underline leader after each question.
13. Click after the *Applicant's Instructions* heading and press **Enter.**
14. Add the following paragraph: `Answer ALL questions. If the answer to any is NONE, please write NONE. Questionnaire must be signed and dated by owner, partner, or officer.`

15. In the paragraph you just typed, use a text highlight color of your choice to highlight the words *ALL* and the second occurrence of *NONE*.
16. Select the entire document and change the paragraph alignment to *Justify*.
17. Save and close the document.

fix-it

In this project you will be editing the *Conference Registration Form_02* document from Central Sierra Insurance.

1. Open the *Conference Registration Form_02* document.
2. Save this document as `[your initials]WD_FixIt_2-6`.
3. Using the Microsoft Word 2010 features you have learned and practiced in this chapter, you will edit and customize this conference registration form to enhance readability and produce a more professional-looking document. *Note: You do not need to fill in the information requested in the registration form; you are just customizing this form.*
4. Use *Quick Styles* to attractively and professionally format the opening and closing lines of the document.
5. Delete unnecessary blank lines, tabs, indents, and spaces.
6. Change font, size, color, style, effects, and case as necessary.
7. Use line and paragraph spacing and alignment as necessary to consistently format this form.
8. Use an appropriate bullet for a check box.
9. Use indents as needed to align bulleted items.
10. Use tabs and solid underline leaders to provide fill-in areas on this form.
11. Change indents as necessary to attractively, professionally, consistently format this document.
12. Use the *Format Painter* as necessary to ensure consistent formatting.
13. Make all occurrences of *Agriculture Insurance Conference* bold and small caps.
14. On all occurrences of *Westfield Hotel & Spa* change the font color and make bold and italicize.
15. Highlight the due date of the conference registration form.
16. The document should be formatted to fit on one page.
17. Proofread and spell check the document carefully.
18. Save and close the document.

chapter 3

Formatting Documents

In this chapter, you will learn the following skills:

- Add consistency to document fonts and colors by using themes
- Use headers and footers to display page numbering and date/time
- Control document layout by adjusting margins and using page and section breaks
- Enhance document formatting and readability by using borders, watermarks, and hyperlinks
- Use building blocks, Quick Parts, and property controls to save time and provide consistency for commonly used information

skills

introduction

This chapter will cover additional features of document formatting to enhance the consistency of fonts and colors, to control margins and pagination, and to increase user efficiency by creating and storing commonly used information. Students will be using themes, borders, watermarks, headers and footers, building blocks and Quick Parts, margins, and page and section breaks to improve document readability.

3.1 Applying Document Themes

A **theme** is a group of formatting options that you apply to an entire document. Themes include font, color, and effect styles that are applied to specific elements of a document. Theme colors limit the colors available from the color palette for fonts, borders, and backgrounds. Theme fonts change the fonts used for built-in styles—such as Normal style and headings. Theme effects control the way graphic elements in your document appear. Applying a theme to your document is a quick way to take a simple piece of text and change it into a polished, professional-looking document.

To apply a theme to a document:

1. Click the **Page Layout** tab.
2. In the *Themes* group, click the **Themes** button.
3. Click an option in the *Built-In* section to apply it to your document.

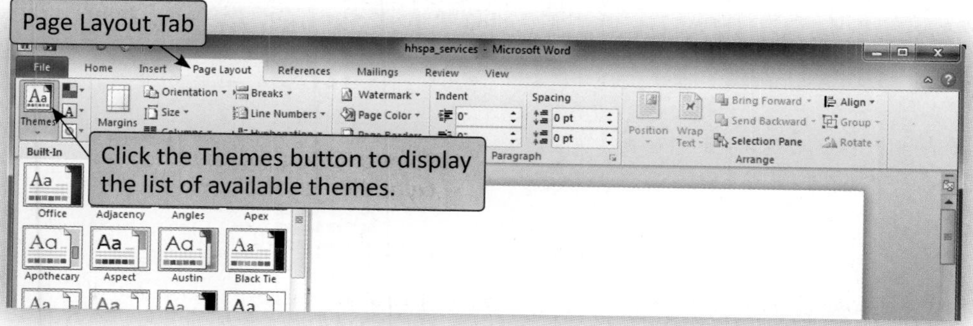

FIGURE WD 3.1

tips & tricks

To reset the theme to the original theme that came with the document's template, click the **Themes** arrow and select **Reset to Theme from Template.**

tell me **more**

You can modify any of the existing themes and save it out as your own custom theme. The file will be saved with the *.thmx* file extension. The theme will be saved in the *Document Themes* folder and will be available from Excel, PowerPoint, and Outlook as well as Word.

3.2 Using Color Themes and Font Themes

When creating a document, it can sometimes be difficult to choose colors that work well together. Documents can end up monochromatic or with too many colors that don't work well together. A **color theme** is a set of colors that are designed to work well together in a document. A color theme will change the color of text, tables, and drawing objects in a document. When you apply a theme to a document it includes a color theme, which has default theme colors for document elements. You can change the color theme without affecting the other components of the theme.

To apply a color theme to a document:

1. Verify you are on the *Home* tab.
2. In the *Styles* group, click the **Change Styles** button.
3. Point to **Colors** and select a color theme.

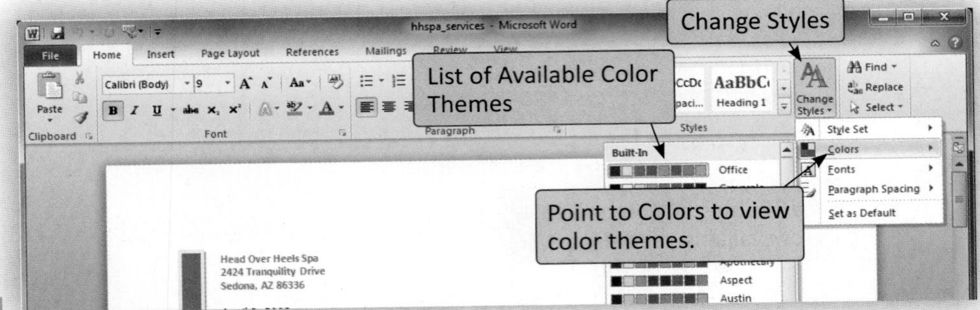

FIGURE WD 3.2

There are thousands of fonts for you to choose from to use in your documents. Some fonts are designed to work well as header text, such as Cambria, and others are designed to work well as body text, such as Calibri. When you apply a theme to a document, this includes a **font theme**, which includes default fonts for body text and header text. As with color themes, you can change the font theme without affecting the other components of the theme.

To apply a font theme to a document:

1. On the *Home* tab, in the *Styles* group, click the **Change Styles** button.
2. Point to **Fonts** and select a font theme.

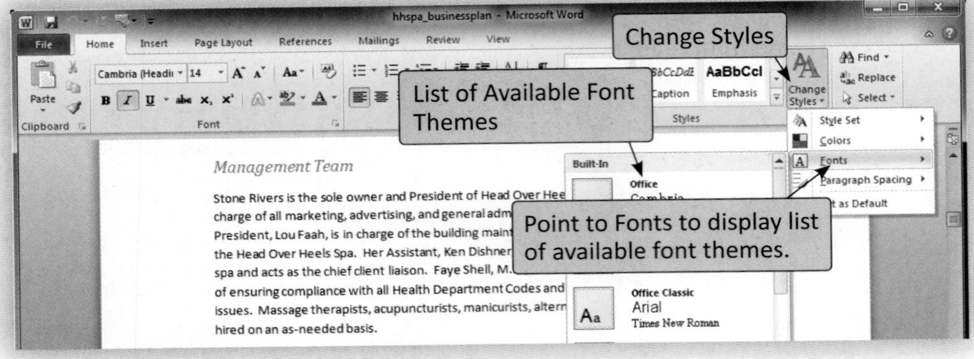

FIGURE WD 3.3

tell me **more**

- When you change the color theme for a document, the color options for document elements will change. The theme colors will appear in the *Font Color* menu, as well as in the *Table Styles* and *Shape Styles* galleries. Choose your colors from these preset theme colors to ensure your document has a consistent color design.
- The font theme menu displays a preview of the header font (on top) and the body font (on bottom). Notice that some themes include two different fonts, but others include the same font, only in different sizes. The default font theme for Word 2010 is the Office Cambria/Calibri font theme.

try **this**

- To apply a color theme, you can click the **Page Layout** tab, click the **Theme Colors** button, and select a color theme.
- To apply a font theme, you can click the **Page Layout** tab, click the **Theme Fonts** button, and select a font theme.

3.3 Adding Page Borders

Page borders are graphic elements that can give your document a more polished look. **Page borders** draw a decorative graphic element along the top, right, bottom, and left edges of the page. Borders can be simple lines or include 3-D effects and shadows. You can modify borders by changing the style and color. You can apply a border to the entire document or parts of a section.

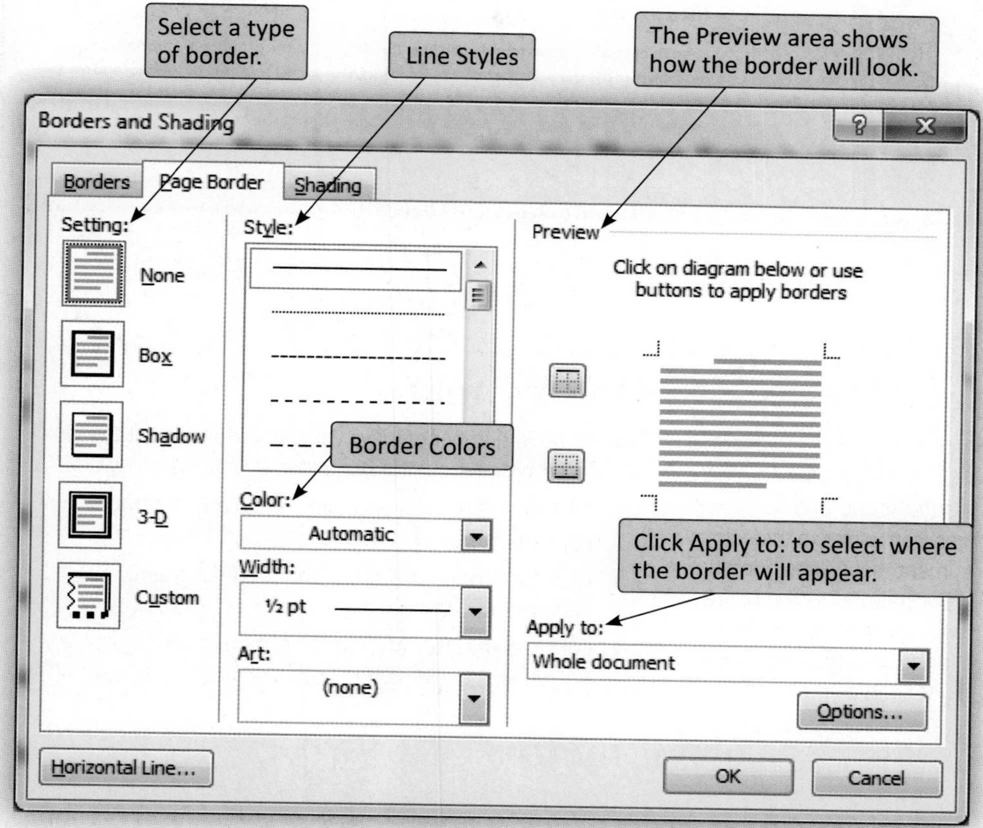

FIGURE WD 3.4

To add a border to a document:

1. Click the **Page Layout** tab.
2. In the *Page Background* group, click the **Page Borders** button.
3. The *Borders and Shading* dialog box opens with the *Page Border* tab displayed.
4. Click a setting for the border.
5. Select a style, color, and width for the page border.
6. The *Preview* area shows how the border will look.
7. Click the **Apply to:** arrow and select the part of the document to add the page border to.
8. Click **OK** to accept your changes and add the page border to the document.

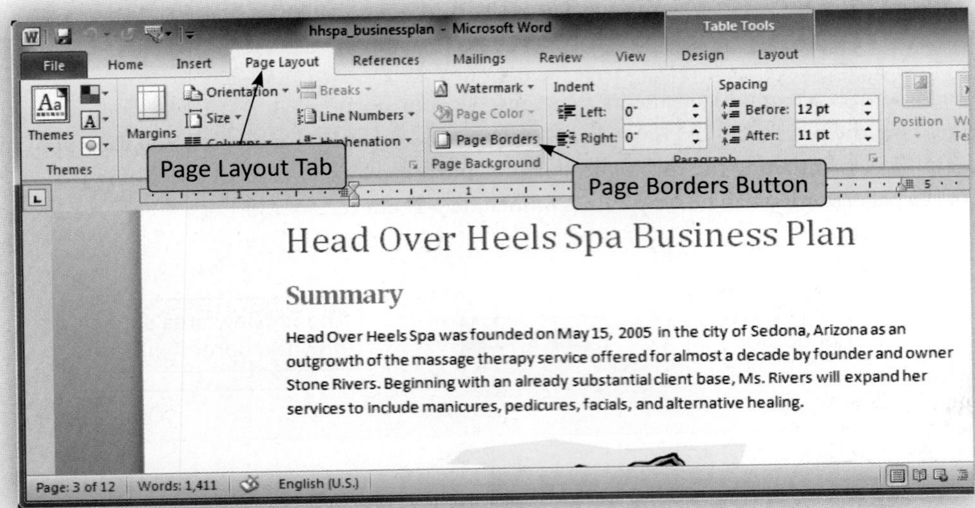

FIGURE WD 3.5

tips & tricks

If you want to add further visual interest to your document, you can change the page color. Click the **Page Color** button [Page Color] in the *Page Background* group and select a color. The page background changes from white to the color you chose. If you have a large document that will be printed, you may not want to add a color background to the entire document. Printing color takes longer than printing in black and white and is more expensive in the end. However, adding color to a cover page can add a refined element to your document.

tell me more

There are a number of ways you can further adjust the look of page borders from the *Borders and Shading* dialog box:

- Click on the *Preview* area diagram to add or remove parts of the border.
- Click the **Art:** drop-down menu to select graphic elements for the border.
- Click the **Horizontal Line . . .** button to add a graphic horizontal line element to your document.

try this

You can also open the *Borders and Shading* dialog box from the *Home* tab. In the *Paragraph* group, click the arrow next to the *Borders* button and select **Borders and Shading . . .**

3.4 Creating Watermarks

A **watermark** is a graphic or text that appears as part of the page background. Watermarks appear faded so that the text that appears on top of the watermark is legible when the document is viewed or printed.

There are three categories of watermarks:

- **Confidential**—Include the text "Confidential" or "Do Not Copy" in different layouts.
- **Disclaimers**—Include the text "Draft" or "Sample" in different layouts.
- **Urgent**—Include the text "ASAP" or "Urgent" in different layouts.

To add a watermark to a document:

1. Click the **Page Layout** tab.
2. Click the **Watermark** button and select an option from the gallery.

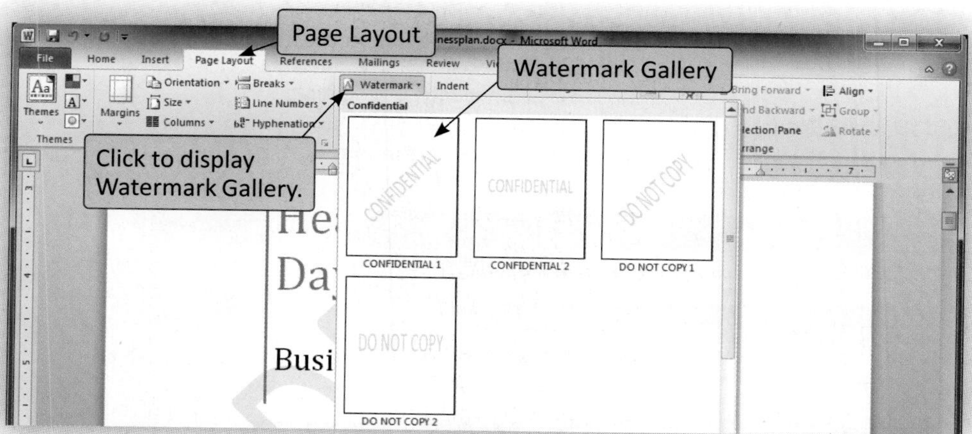

FIGURE WD 3.6

tips & tricks

You do not have to use one of the built-in watermarks from the *Watermark* gallery. You can create your own custom watermark, displaying whatever text or image you like. Click the **Custom Watermark . . .** command to open the *Printed Watermark* dialog box and choose different options for the text watermark. You can add pictures as watermarks from this dialog box. When you add a picture as a watermark, it appears faded so any text on top of it is still legible.

tell me more

To remove a watermark, click the **Watermark** button and select **Remove Watermark.**

try this

You can add watermarks through the *Building Blocks Organizer.*

3.5 Inserting Building Blocks

A **building block** is a piece of content that is reusable in any document. Building blocks can be text, such as AutoText, or they can include graphics, such as a cover page. You can insert building blocks from specific commands on the Ribbon or from the **Building Blocks Organizer**. The *Building Blocks Organizer* lists the building blocks in alphabetical order by which gallery they appear in and includes Bibliographies, Cover Pages, Equations, Footers, Headers, Page Numbers, Table of Contents, Tables, Text Boxes, and Watermarks.

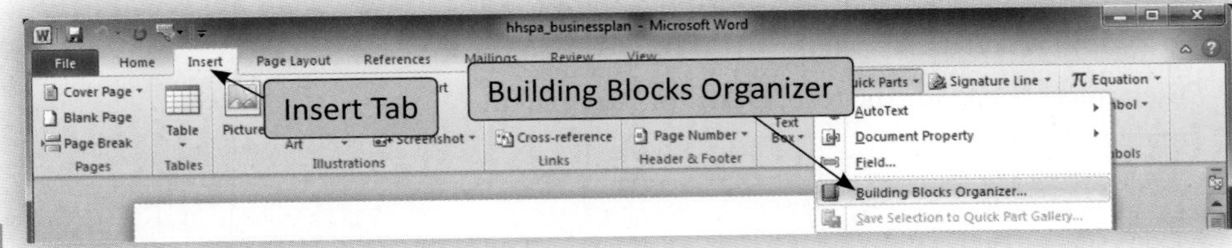

FIGURE WD 3.7

To insert a building block from the *Building Blocks Organizer:*

1. Click the **Insert** tab.
2. Click the **Quick Parts** button and select **Building Blocks Organizer . . .**
3. Select a building block in the list and click the **Insert** button.

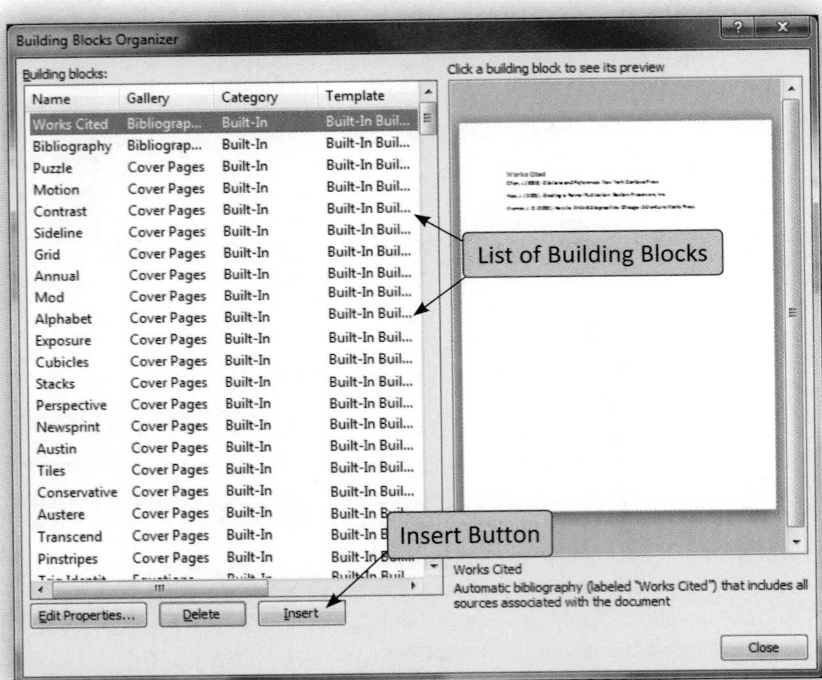

FIGURE WD 3.8

tips & tricks

If you find that the list of building blocks is too long, you can remove building blocks you don't use. To remove a building block from the *Building Blocks Organizer,* select a building block and click the **Delete** button. Be aware that the *Building Blocks Organizer* is used across all of Word 2010. If you delete a building block from the *Building Blocks Organizer,* it will no longer be available when you are working on other documents.

tell me more

You can sort the list of building blocks by clicking the *Name, Gallery, Category,* or *Template* button at the top of the *Building Blocks Organizer.* You can also modify the properties of a building block, changing properties such as the name or which gallery the building block appears in.

3.6 Adding Headers and Footers

A **header** is text that appears at the top of every page, just below the top margin; a **footer** is text that appears at the bottom of every page, just above the bottom margin. Typically, headers and footers display dates, page numbers, document titles, or authors' names. Word 2010 comes with a number of predesigned headers and footers that you can add to your document and then modify to suit your needs.

To add a header to a document:

1. Click the **Insert** tab.
2. In the *Header & Footer* group, click the **Header** button and select a header design from the gallery.
3. Word displays the *Header & Footer Tools* contextual tab and inserts a header with content controls for you to enter your own information. Click a content control and enter the information for your header.
4. To close the header and return to your document, click the **Close Header and Footer** button on the contextual tab.

To add a footer to a document:

1. Click the **Insert** tab.
2. In the *Header & Footer* group, click the **Footer** button and select a footer design from the gallery.
3. Word displays the *Header & Footer Tools* contextual tab and inserts a footer with content controls for you to enter your own information. Click a content control and enter the information for your footer.
4. To close the header and return to your document, click the **Close Header and Footer** button on the contextual tab.

If the first page of your document is a title page, you won't want the header text to display on the page. To display a different header on the first page of the document than the rest of the document, display the *Header & Footer Tools* contextual tab. In the *Options* group, click the **Different First Page** check box so it is selected.

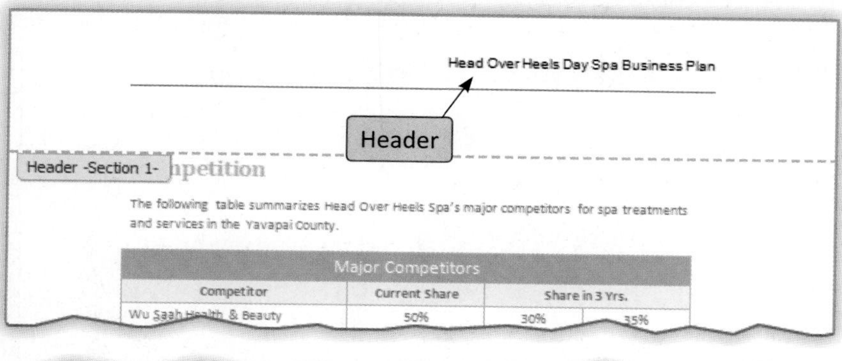

FIGURE WD 3.9

tips & tricks

Headers and footers appear faded out in Print Layout view. If you want to edit a header or footer, double-click it and make your changes. Click the **Close Header and Footer** button to return to the document.

tell me more

When you add a header or footer to your document, the *Design* tab under *Header & Footer Tools* displays. This tab is called a contextual tab because it only displays when a header or footer is the active element. Click the **Design** tab to modify the header or footer properties.

try this

You can add headers and footers through the *Building Blocks Organizer*.

3.7 Adding the Date and Time to the Header

In addition to information such as the company name and page numbers, headers and footers typically include the current date. You could manually type the date in the header or footer and then update the date every time you work on the document, or you could add an **automatic date stamp**. An automatic date stamp pulls the current date from the computer's system clock and displays the date in the document. The date is then automatically updated when the computer's date changes.

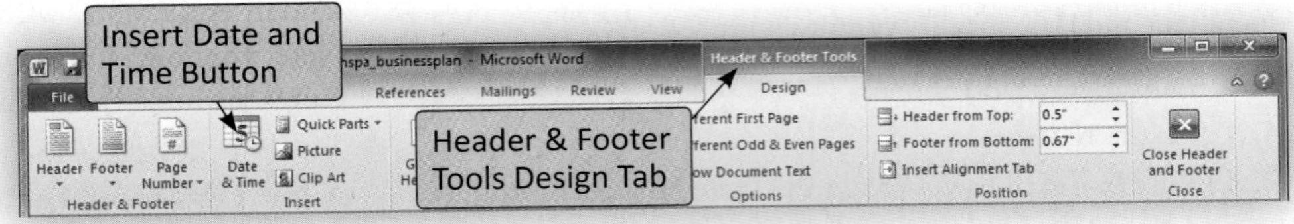

FIGURE WD 3.10

To add an automatic date stamp to the header of a document:

1. Double-click the header to switch to header view.
2. Under the *Header & Footer Tools,* in the *Insert* group, click the **Insert Date and Time** button.
3. In the *Date and Time* dialog box, click a date format in the *Available formats:* box.
4. Select the **Update automatically** check box.
5. Click **OK.**

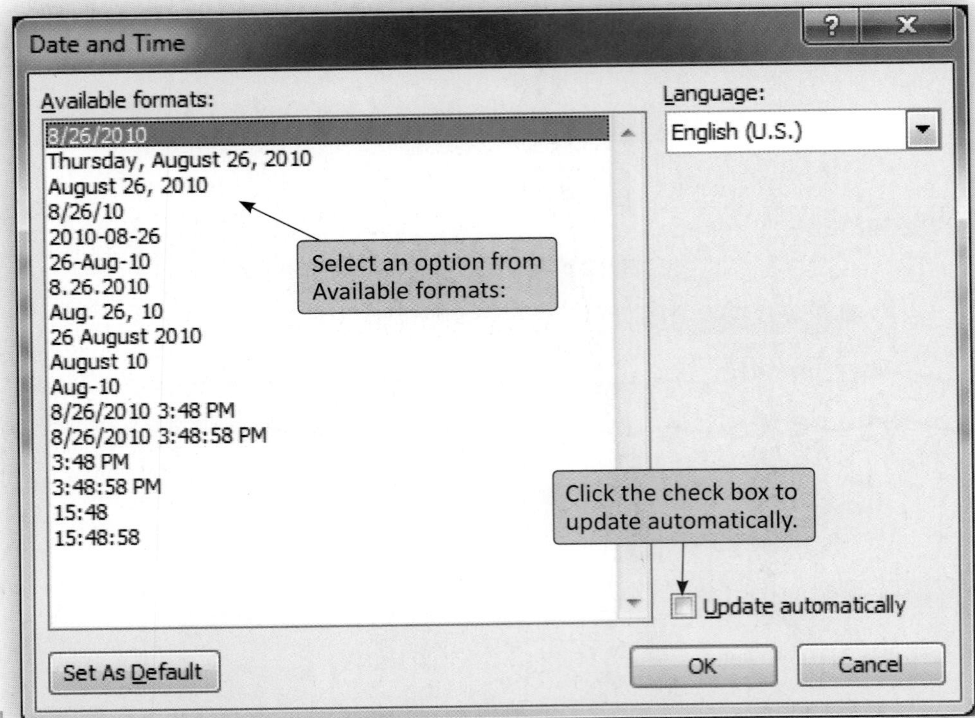

FIGURE WD 3.11

tips & tricks

To update the date in your document, click the date and then click the **Update** button. Word will automatically display the computer's current date. If you did not select the *Update automatically* check box when you inserted the date, the computer will not automatically update the date in your document.

try this

You can also use *Quick Parts* to add the date and time to the header or footer of your document:

1. Under the *Header & Footer Tools,* in the *Insert* group, click the **Quick Parts** button and select **Field . . .**
2. In the *Field* dialog box, click the **CreateDate** or the **Date** field.
3. Select a format for the date.
4. Click **OK.**

3.8 Inserting Page Numbers

Headers and footers often include page numbers, but they also include other information, such as author name, date, and document title. If all you want to do is add page numbers to a document, you don't need to use the header and footer feature. Instead, you can insert simple page numbers to a document through the *Page Number* gallery.

FIGURE WD 3.12

To add page numbers to the bottom of pages of a document:

1. Click the **Insert** tab.
2. In the *Header & Footer* group, click the **Page Number** button. Point to *Bottom of Page,* and select an option.
3. To remove a page number, click the arrow next to the *Page Number* button and select **Remove Page Numbers.**

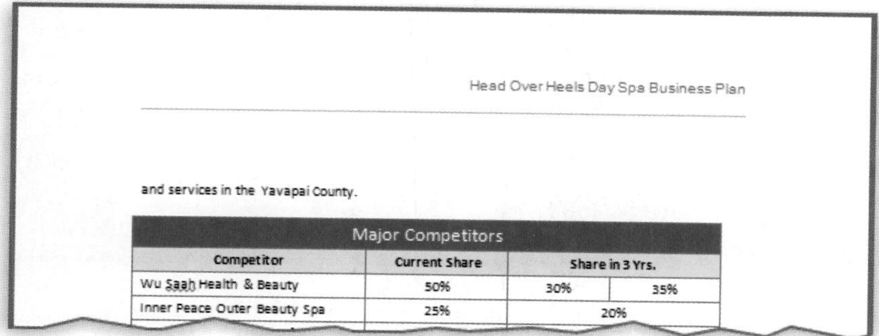

Head Over Heels Day Spa Business Plan

and services in the Yavapai County.

Major Competitors			
Competitor	Current Share	Share in 3 Yrs.	
Wu Saah Health & Beauty	50%	30%	35%
Inner Peace Outer Beauty Spa	25%	20%	

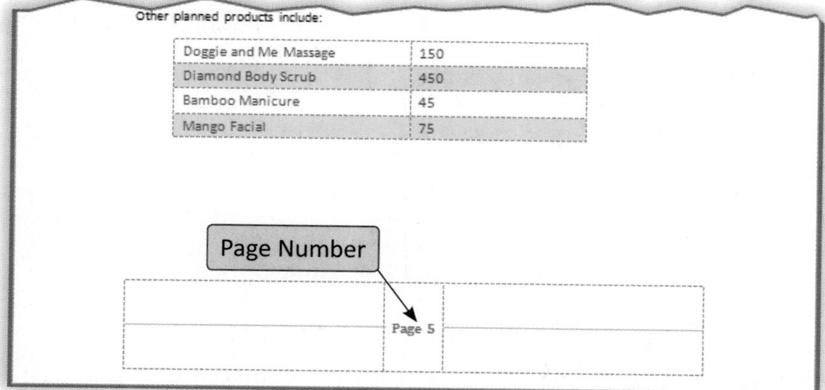

Other planned products include:

Doggie and Me Massage	150
Diamond Body Scrub	450
Bamboo Manicure	45
Mango Facial	75

FIGURE WD 3.13

tips & tricks

When adding page numbers to a document, you should always use Word's built-in building block. If you type page numbers into your document manually, they will not update when you add or remove pages.

tell me more

Traditionally, page numbers appear in the header or footer of the document. However, you can choose to display page numbers in the margin or at the current location of the cursor in the document.

try this

You can also add a page number through the *Building Blocks Organizer.*

3.9 Inserting Property Controls

A **property control** is an element you can add to your document to save time entering the same information over and over again. When you insert a property control and then replace the text with your own information, any time you add that control again it will include your custom text. Property controls can be used as shortcuts for entering long strings of text that are difficult to type. For example, instead of typing the company name Head Over Heels Day Spa, you can insert the *Company* property control. Word will add the text to the document and update the text automatically if any changes are made to the property control. By using property controls, you can be assured that all the information throughout the document is consistent.

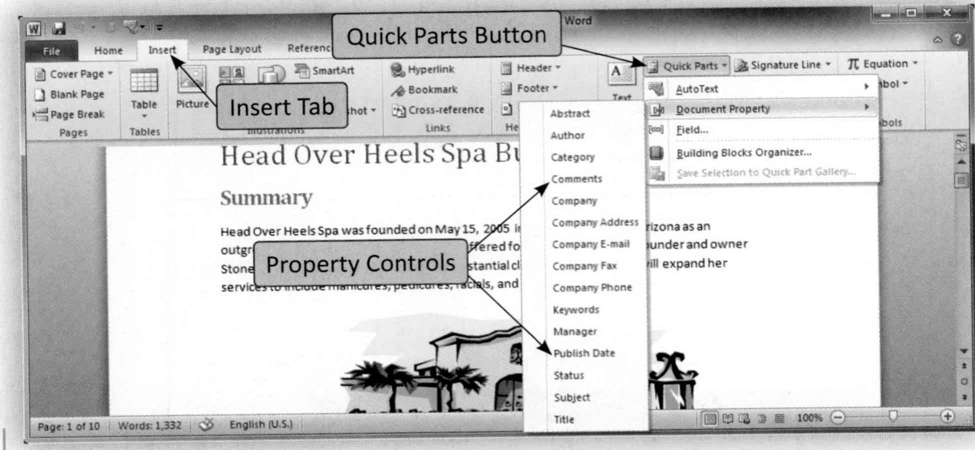

FIGURE WD 3.14

To add a property control to a document:

1. Click the **Insert** tab.
2. In the *Text* group, click the **Quick Parts** button, point to **Document Property,** and select a control.
3. Type your text in the control.
4. Select the same control from the *Document Property* menu to add the same text to the document.

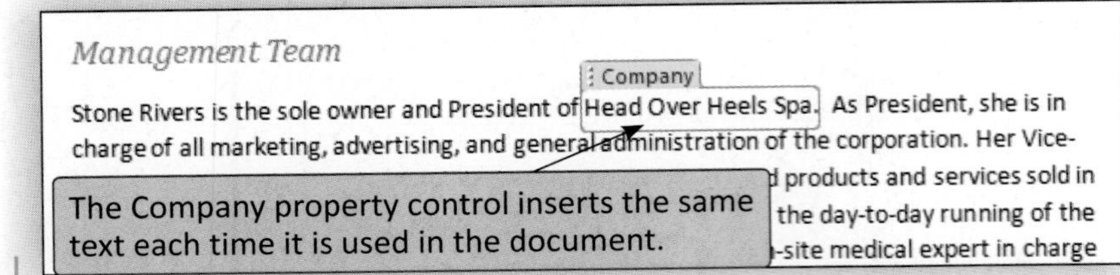

FIGURE WD 3.15

tips & tricks

If you need to update a property control, you only need to type the change once in the document. As you update any property control, all the other controls created from the same property control will update.

tell me more

Many of the built-in property controls, such as company name and author, pull their information from the document's properties. If you add a property control and modify the information, the document's related property will be updated as well.

3.10 Saving Quick Parts as Building Blocks

Quick Parts are snippets of text that you can save and then add to any document. They include the text and all the formatting that has been applied to it. Use Quick Parts when you want text to appear a certain way throughout your documents, such as a company's tag line.

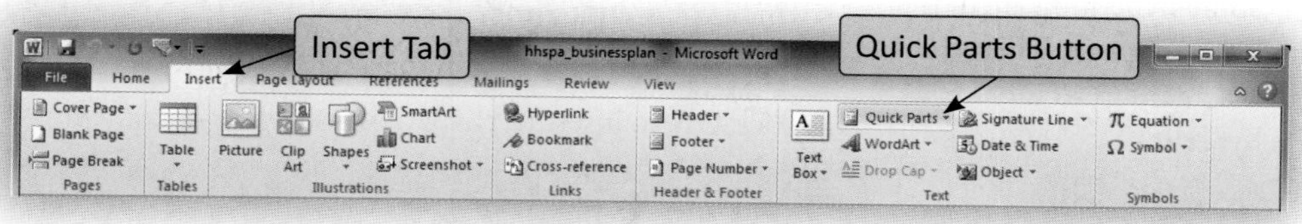

FIGURE WD 3.16

To add text to the *Quick Parts* gallery:

1. Select the text to add to the gallery.
2. Click the **Insert** tab.
3. In the *Text* group, click the **Quick Parts** button and select **Save Selection to Quick Part Gallery . . .**
4. The *Create New Building Block* dialog box opens.
5. Review the information for the Quick Part and make any changes.
6. Click **OK.**

To add a Quick Part to a document from the *Quick Part* gallery:

1. Click the **Insert** tab.
2. Click the **Quick Parts** button and select the Quick Part to add.

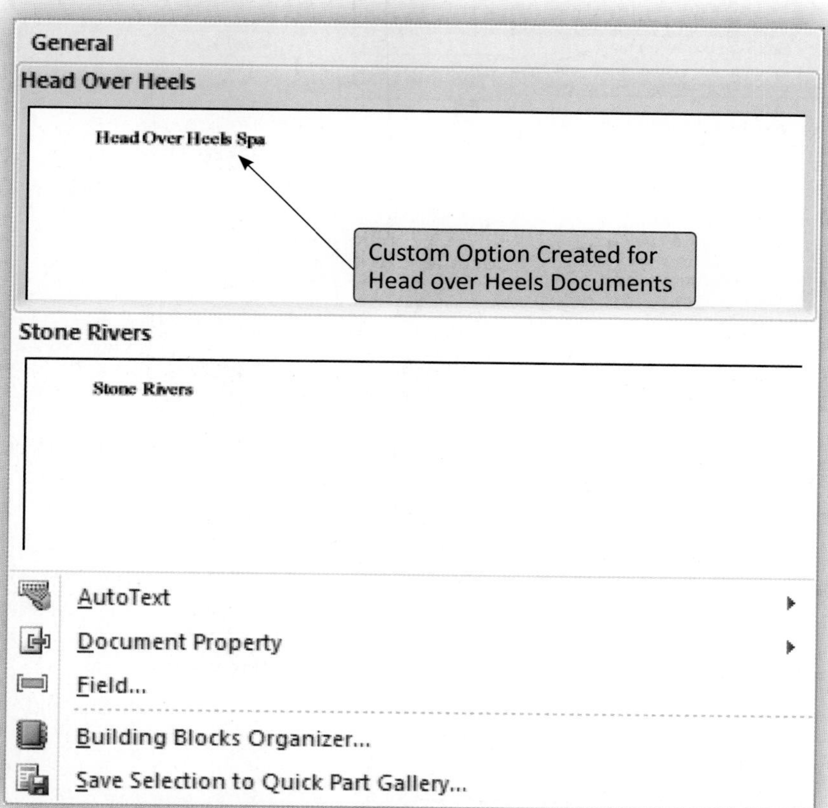

FIGURE WD 3.17

tips & tricks

When you save text to the *Quick Parts* gallery, you are actually creating a building block. The Quick Part you created appears in the *Building Blocks Organizer* under the category *Quick Parts.*

tell me more

To edit or delete a Quick Part, open the *Building Blocks Organizer,* select the Quick Part building block in the list, and click the **Edit Properties . . .** or **Delete** button.

3.11 Inserting Hyperlinks

A **hyperlink** is text or a graphic that, when clicked, opens another page or file. You can use hyperlinks to link to a section in the same document, to a new document, or to an existing document, such as a Web page. Some hyperlinks include ScreenTips. A **ScreenTip** is a bubble that appears when the mouse is placed over the link. Add a ScreenTip to include a more meaningful description of the hyperlink.

To insert a hyperlink:

1. Select the text or graphic you want to use as the link.
2. Click the **Insert** tab.
3. In the *Links* group, click the **Hyperlink** button to open the *Insert Hyperlink* dialog box.
4. Select an option under *Link to:* and select the file to which you want to link.
5. Type the text of the link in the *Text to display:* box.
6. Click **OK** to insert the hyperlink into your document.

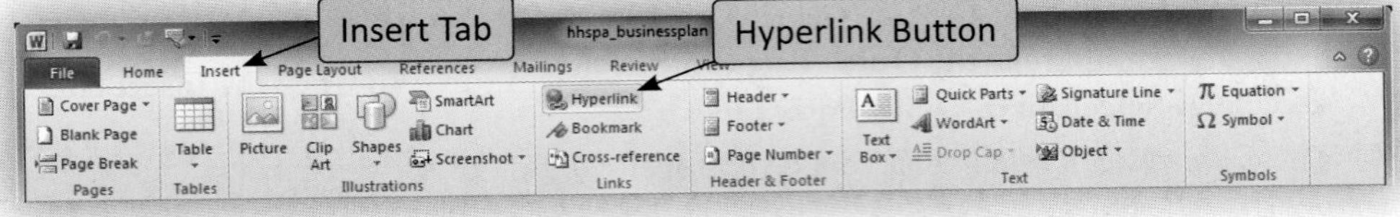

FIGURE WD 3.18

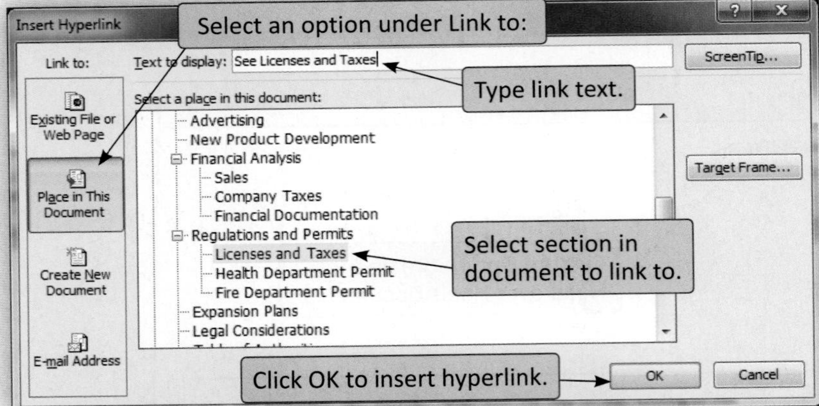

FIGURE WD 3.19

To edit a hyperlink, right-click the link and select **Edit Hyperlink . . .** from the menu. Make any changes in the *Edit Hyperlink* dialog box.

To remove a hyperlink, right-click the link and select **Remove Hyperlink** from the menu.

tell me **more**

You can add bookmarks to a long document to help you easily return to a specific place in the document. To add a bookmark:

1. Click the **Insert** tab.
2. In the *Links* group, click the **Bookmark** button. The *Bookmark* dialog box opens.
3. Type a name for the bookmark in the *Bookmark name:* box.
4. Click the **Add** button.

To return to a place in a document using bookmarks:

1. First open the *Bookmark* dialog box.
2. Click the name of the bookmark you want to navigate to.
3. Click the **Go To** button.

try **this**

To open the *Insert Hyperlink* dialog box, you can:

› Right-click the text or object you want as the link and select **Hyperlink . . .** from the shortcut menu.

› Press Ctrl + K on the keyboard.

from the perspective of . . .

POLICE OFFICER

I use word processing software to write my reports. I keep notes regarding complaints, disturbances, and accidents.

3.12 Adjusting Margins

Margins are the blank spaces at the top, bottom, left, and right of a page. Word's default margins are typically 1 inch for the top and bottom and 1 inch for the left and right. Word 2010 comes with a number of predefined margin layout options for you to choose from, including normal, narrow, wide, and mirrored.

To adjust the margins for a document:

1. Click the **Page Layout** tab.
2. In the *Page Setup* group, click the **Margins** button and select an option for the page layout.

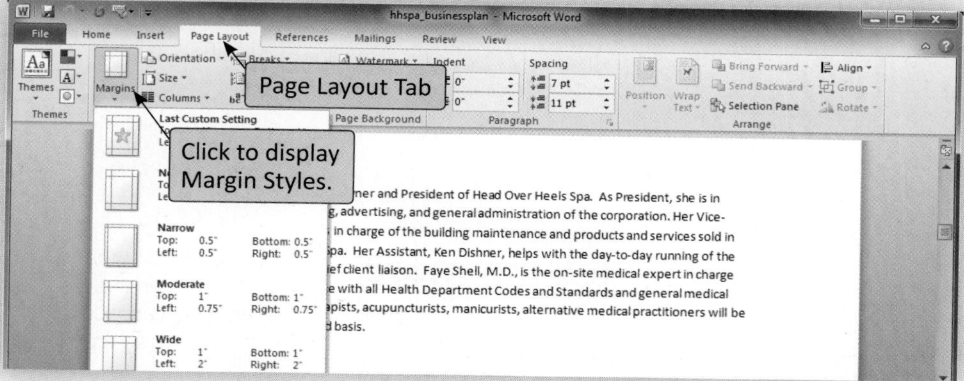

FIGURE WD 3.20

tips & tricks

While most documents you create will use the Normal or Moderate settings for margins, some documents will require either less or more space around the text. If you have a large exhibit or table, you may want to make the margins narrow so the content will still fit in portrait orientation. On the other hand, if you are writing a letter, you may want to increase your margins to accommodate preprinted stationery.

tell me **more**

The default settings for margins in Word 2003 used to be 1 inch for the top and bottom and 1.25 inches for the left and right. Starting in Word 2007, Microsoft changed this default setting to be 1 inch for all four margins.

try **this**

If you don't want to use one of Word's preset margins, you can set your own margin specifications in the *Page Setup* dialog box. To open the *Page Setup* dialog box, at the bottom of the *Margins* gallery, select **Custom Margins . . .**

3.13 Inserting Page Breaks and Section Breaks

When text or graphics have filled a page, Word inserts a soft page break and goes on to a new page. However, at times you may want to manually insert a **hard page break**—forcing the text to a new page no matter how much content is on the present page. Typically hard page breaks are used to keep certain information together—for instance, sections of a document.

To insert a hard page break:

1. Click the **Page Layout** tab.
2. In the *Page Setup* group, click the **Breaks** button, and select **Page.**

When you insert a page break, any remaining content in the document appears at the top of the next page. If you want an empty page to appear after the break, you can insert a blank page. When you insert a blank page, Word places a hard break, followed by a blank page, followed by the remaining content of the document.

To insert a blank page:

1. Click the **Insert** tab.
2. In the *Pages* group, click the **Blank Page** button.

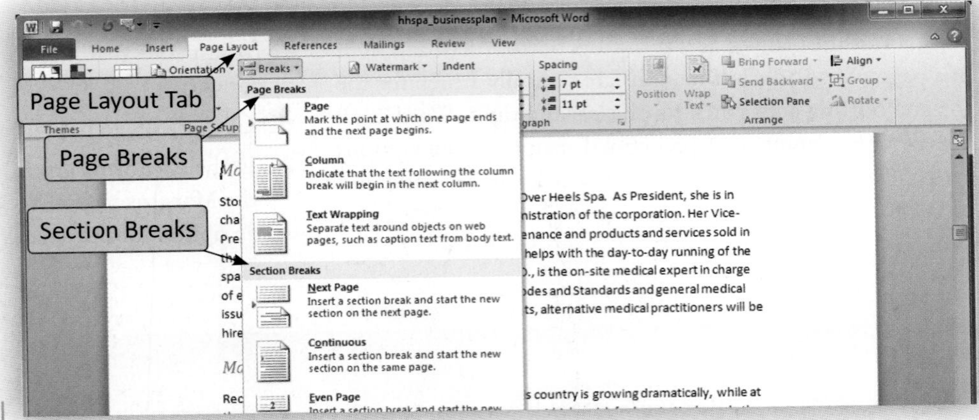

FIGURE WD 3.21

tips & tricks

If you want to remove a hard page break, switch to Draft view so you can see where the break is. Place your cursor below the break and press Delete on the keyboard.

tell me more

There are two basic types of breaks you can add to a document:

- **Page Break**—These breaks create visual breaks in your document but keep the content in the same section. Page breaks include Page, Column, and Text Wrapping.
- **Section Breaks**—These breaks create new sections in your document. Section breaks include Next Page, Continuous, Even Page, and Odd Page.

try this

To insert a hard page break, you can:

- On the *Insert* tab, in the *Pages* group, click the **Page Break** button Page Break.
- Press Ctrl + Enter on the keyboard.

3.14 Adding a Cover Page

When creating documents such as proposals or business plans, it is a good idea to include a cover page that contains the title of the document and the date. You can also add other information such as a subtitle, a short description of the document, and company information. Word 2010 comes with a number of prebuilt cover pages that you can quickly and easily add to your documents.

To add a cover page:

1. Click the **Insert** tab.
2. In the *Pages* group, click the **Cover Page** button and select an option.
3. Word inserts a cover page with content controls for you to enter your own information. Click a content control and enter the information for your document.

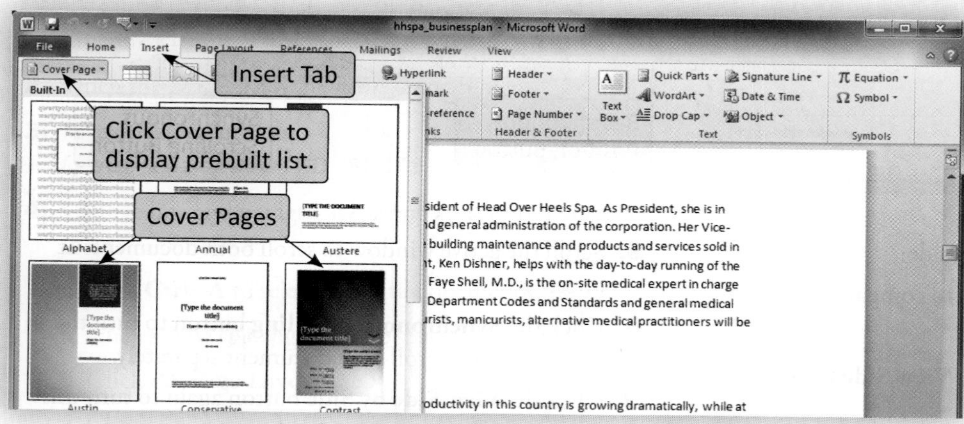

FIGURE WD 3.22

tips & tricks

Most content controls include instructions for adding text to the cover page. However, some content controls, such as the author, do not include text and are hidden from view. One way to see all the fields available in a cover page is to use the Select All command by pressing Ctrl + A on the keyboard.

tell me more

When you click a date content control, you will notice a calendar icon next to the text area. Click the icon to display the calendar to select a date to add to the cover page.

try this

You can also add cover pages through the *Building Blocks Organizer.*

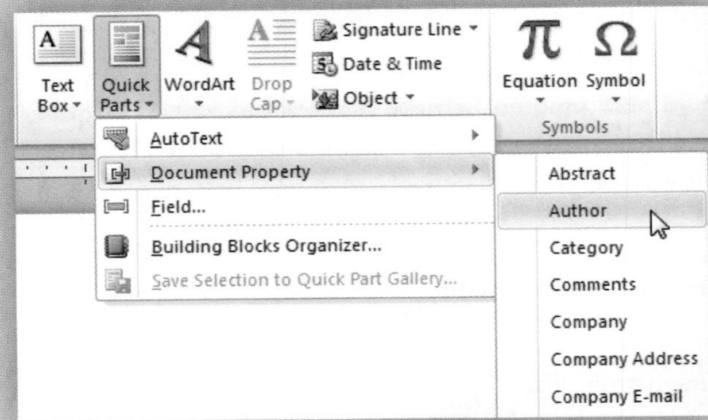

FIGURE WD 3.26

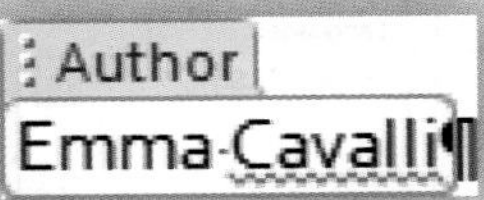

FIGURE WD 3.27

7. Customize *Property Controls.*

a. Click at the end of the document or press **Ctrl+End** to move the cursor to the end of the document.

b. Press **Enter** twice.

c. Click the **Insert** tab.

d. In the *Text* group, click the **Quick Parts** button.

e. Put your mouse pointer on *Document Property* and select **Author.** The *Author* property control will be inserted into your document.

f. If there is text in this property control, delete it and type `Emma Cavalli.`

g. Click after this property control to deselect it and press **Enter**. You also can use the *right arrow key* to deselect a property control.

h. Repeat the above steps to add the following property controls:

Company: `Placer Hills Real Estate`

Company Address: `7100 Madrone Road, Roseville, CA 95722`

Company E-mail: `ecavalli@phre.com`

Company Phone: `916-450-3333`

i. Select all five lines and text you just entered and delete them.

j. Delete any blank lines at the end of the document.

8. Insert text and *property controls* into the document to create the closing lines of the document.

a. Click at the end of the document or press **Ctrl+End** to move the cursor to the end of the document. Your cursor should be at the end of the last paragraph in the document.

b. Press **Enter** twice.

c. Type: `Best Regards` and press **Enter** four times.

d. Click on the **Quick Parts** button in the *Text* group on the *Insert* tab.

e. Put your mouse pointer on *Document Property* and select **Author**. The *Author* property control will be inserted into your document.

f. Click after *Emma Cavalli* and press **Enter.**

g. Type: `Realtor Consultant` and press **Enter.**

h. Insert the **Company** property control into your document.

9. Insert a paragraph of text and include property controls.

a. Click at the end of the last body paragraph in your document and press **Enter** twice.

b. Type the following paragraph inserting property controls where indicated: `As always, if you have any questions or concerns, please call me at` *[Company Phone]* `or e-mail me at` *[Company E-mail]*. `Best wishes and thank you for choosing` *[Company].*

*(Note: you might have to use the **right arrow** key to deselect the property control fields after inserting them.)*

10. Create a *Quick Part* and save as a *Building Block.*

a. Select the closing lines of the document (*Best Regards* through *Placer Hills Real Estate*).

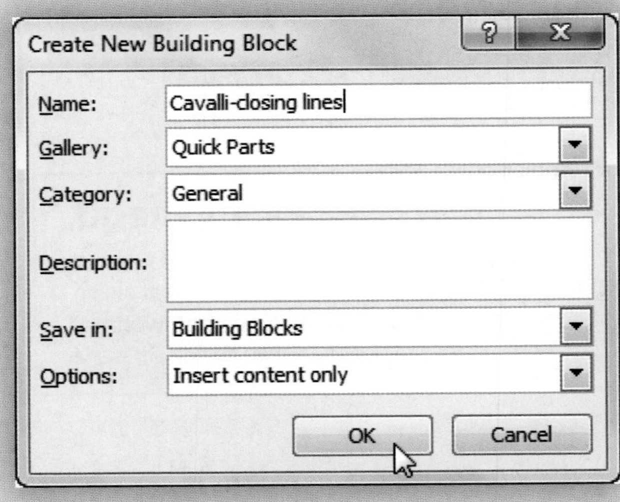

FIGURE WD 3.28

b. On the *Insert* tab, in the *Text* group, click the **Quick Parts** button.

c. Select **Save Selection to Quick Part Gallery.** The *Create New Building Block* dialog box will open.

d. In the *Name* box type: `Cavalli-closing lines`

e. Click **OK** to close the *Create New Building Block* dialog box. The selection will be saved and available to be used from Quick Parts.

f. Select the closing lines of the document (*Best Regards* through *Placer Hills Real Estate*) and press **Backspace** to delete these lines.

g. On the *Insert* tab, in the *Text* group, click the **Quick Parts** button.

h. Select **Cavalli-closing lines** to insert this *Quick Part* into the document.

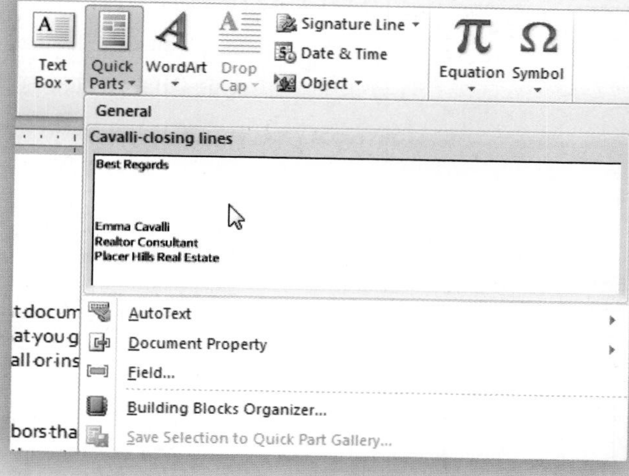

FIGURE WD 3.29

11. Use property controls and text to create information which will later be used as a footer.

a. Go to the end of the document and press **Enter** twice.

b. Set a right tab at 6″. You can use either the ruler or the *Tabs* dialog box.

c. Insert the **Author** property control, click at the end of this control, and press **Tab** to move to the right margin.

d. Insert the **Company** property control, click at the end of this control, and press **Enter** to move to the next line.

e. Insert the **Company Phone** property control, click at the end of this control, and press **Tab** to move to the right margin.

f. Insert the **Company Address** property control, click at the end of this control, and press **Enter** to move to the next line.

g. Insert the **Company E-mail** property control, click at the end of this control, and press **Tab** to move to the right margin.

h. Type: `www.phre.com`

i. Select and bold the first line of this text you just entered.

j. Select the second and third lines of text you just entered and change the font size to **10 pt**.

12. Add a border to text and save text as a *Quick Part*.

a. Select the first line of text entered in the step above (11).

b. Click the **Home** tab.

c. Click the **small arrow** to the right of the *Border* button in the *Paragraph* group.

d. Click **Top Border** to insert a border above the selected line of text.

e. Select all three lines of text.

f. On the *Insert* tab, in the *Text* group, click the **Quick Parts** button.

g. Select **Save Selection to Quick Part Gallery**. The *Create New Building Block* dialog box will open.

h. In the *Name* box type: `Cavalli-footer`

i. Click **OK** to close the *Create New Building Block* dialog box.

j. Select and delete these three lines of text.

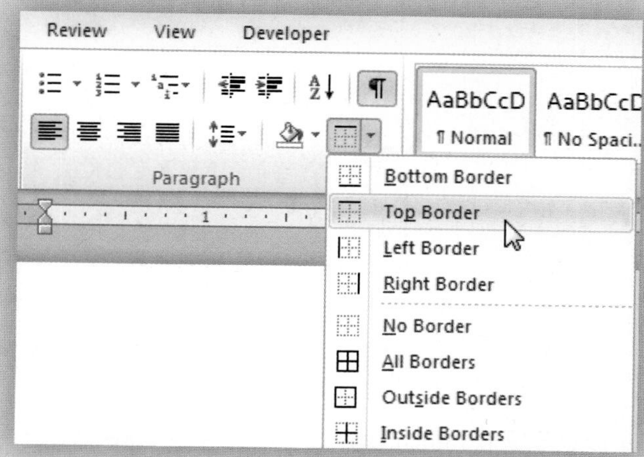

FIGURE WD 3.30

13. Insert a footer into the document.

a. Click the **Insert** tab.

b. Click the **Footer** button in the *Header & Footer* group.

c. Click **Edit Footer**. The footer will open at the bottom of the page.

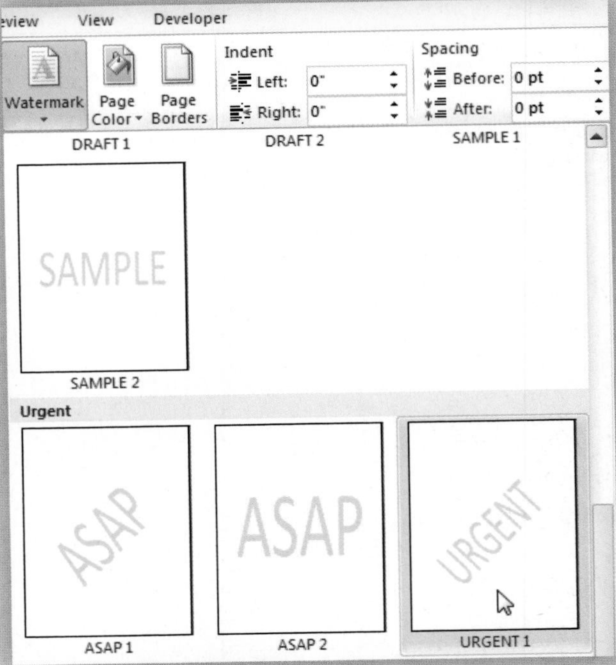

FIGURE WD 3.31

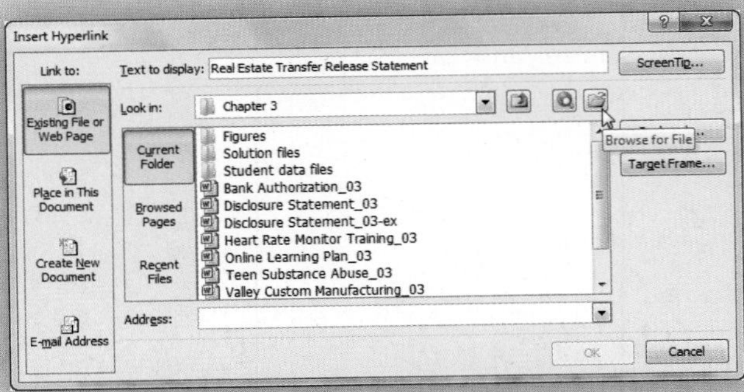

FIGURE WD 3.32

d. Click the **Insert** tab.

e. Click the **Quick Parts** button in the *Text* group.

f. Select **Cavalli-footer** to insert this *Quick Part* into the document.

g. Press **Backspace** to delete the blank line below the footer.

h. Click the **Design** tab and click the **Close Header and Footer** button in the *Close* group. Double-clicking in the body of the document will also close the *Header/Footer.*

14. Insert a watermark on the document.

a. Click the **Page Layout** tab.

b. Click the **Watermark** button in the *Page Background* group.

c. Click **Urgent 1** to insert this watermark into the document. You might have to scroll down to locate this watermark.

15. Insert hyperlinks into the document.

a. Find and select **Real Estate Transfer Release Statement** in the body of the letter.

b. Click the **Insert** button.

c. Click the **Hyperlink** button in the *Links* group. The *Insert Hyperlink* dialog box will open.

d. In the *Link to:* area click **Existing File or Web Page** if it is not already selected.

e. Click the **Browse for File** button. The *Link to File* dialog box will open.

f. In the menu to the right of the *File name:* box, click **Office Files** and select **All Files** to display all of the files in the selected folder.

g. Browse to the folder containing your student data files and select the **Form 521** .pdf file.

h. Click **OK** to close the *Link to File* dialog box.

i. Click **OK** to insert the hyperlink and close the *Insert Hyperlink* dialog box. The selected text now appears as a hyperlink.

16. Modify a property control.

a. Click the phone number (*Company Phone* property control) in the last body paragraph of the letter.

b. Change the phone number to **916-450-3334** and click outside of the property control. Notice that the phone number in the footer is also changed.

17. Use *View Side by Side* to view the edited document with the original document.
   a. Click the **File** tab to open the Backstage.
   b. Click the **Open** button. The *Open* dialog box will open.
   c. Browse to find the *Disclosure Statement_03* document from your student data files.
   d. Select the file and click the **Open** button. This document will open.
   e. Click the **View** tab.
   f. Click the **View Side by Side** button in the *Window* group. The two documents will be displayed side by side. Examine the two documents.
   g. Scroll down in one of the documents. Notice how they scroll down together.
   h. Click the **View Side by Side** button in the *Window* group to close this viewing option.
18. Close each document, saving the `[your initials]WD_SkillReview_3-1` file. Do not save the *Disclosure Statement_03* file.

Skill Review **3.2**

In this project you will be editing the *Heart Rate Monitor Training_03* document from American River Cycling Club.

1. Open the *Heart Rate Monitor Training_03* document.
2. Save this document as `[your initials]WD_SkillReview_3-2.`
3. Change the document margins, theme fonts, and theme colors.
   a. Click the **Page Layout** tab.
   b. Click the **Margins** button in the *Page Setup* group.
   c. Choose **Normal** (1″ top, bottom, left, and right margins).
   d. On the *page layout* tab, in the *Themes* group, click the **Colors** button.
   e. Choose **Grid** as the theme colors.
   f. On the *page layout* tab, in the *Themes* group, click the **Fonts** button.
   g. Choose **Austin** as the theme fonts.
   h. Select the entire document and change the font size to **10 pt**.
4. Apply *Quick Styles* to title and section headings.
   a. Select the title of the document.
   b. Apply the **Title** style to the title.
   c. Use the *Font* dialog box to make the title **22 pt.**, **small caps**, and **bold**.
   d. **Center** the title.
   e. Change the before paragraph spacing on the title to **24 pt**.
   f. Select the first bold heading (*Know Your Resting Heart Rate*).
   g. Apply the **Heading 1** style.
   h. Change the before paragraph spacing to **12 pt**.
   i. Use the *Format Painter* to apply this format to all of the other bolded headings. Remember to double-click the *Format Painter* button to apply to multiple selections and click the button again when finished applying formats.
   j. Select the first italicized heading (*Comparing Heart Rate Values with Others*).
   k. Apply the **Heading 2** style.
   l. Use the *Format Painter* to apply this format to all of the other italicized headings.

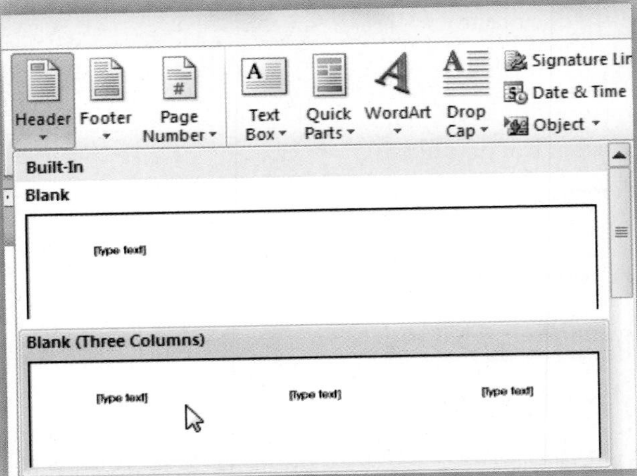

FIGURE WD 3.33

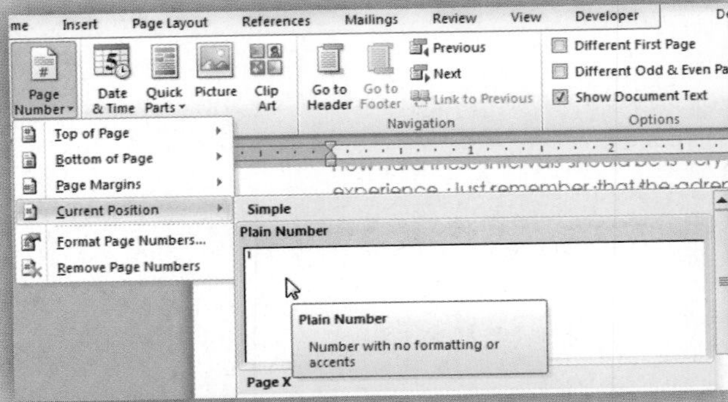

FIGURE WD 3.34

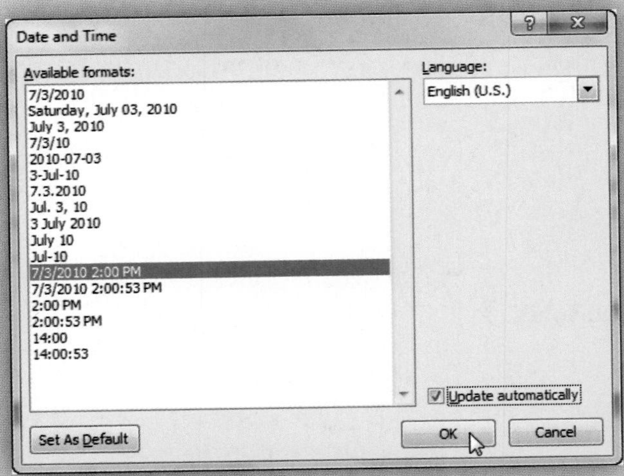

FIGURE WD 3.35

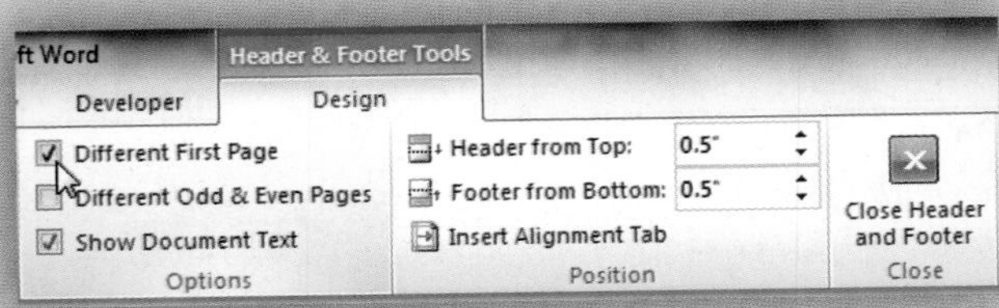

FIGURE WD 3.36

5. Insert a header in the document.

a. Click the **Insert** tab.

b. Click the **Header** button in the *Header & Footer* group.

c. Select **Blank (Three Columns)**. The header of the document will open with three *Type text* fields available.

d. Click in the first *Type text* field and type: `American River Cycling Club`

e. Click in the second *Type text* field and press **Delete** to remove this field.

f. Click in the last *Type text* field and type **your name**.

g. Select the entire line in the header.

h. Press **Ctrl+B** to make bold.

i. Click the **Home** tab.

j. Click the small arrow to the right of the *Border* button in the *Paragraph* group and select **Bottom Border**.

6. Insert a footer in the document.

a. With the header still open, scroll down to the bottom of the page to view the footer.

b. Click in the footer of the document and type `Page` and space once after the word.

c. Click the **Design** tab.

d. Click the **Page Number** button in the *Header & Footer* group.

e. Put your cursor on **Current Position** and then select **Plain Number**. The page number is inserted after the word *Page*.

f. Press **Tab** twice.

g. Type: `Last Modified` and space once after.

h. Click the **Date & Time** button in the *Insert* group. The *Date and Time* dialog box will open.

i. Select the format with the date and time (e.g., *7/3/2010 2:00 PM*).

j. Select the **Update automatically** check box.

k. Click **OK** to insert the date/time and close the *Date and Time* dialog box.

l. Select the entire footer.

m. Click the **Home** tab.

n. Change the font to **9 pt**. and add a **Top Border**.

o. Click the **Design** tab.

p. Click on the **Different First Page** check box. This will turn off the header/footer on the first page so the header/footer will only be displayed on second and continuing pages.

q. Click on the **Close Header and Footer** button in the *Close* group.

7. Add a page border and color to the document.

    a. Press **Ctrl+Home** to move to the top of the document.

    b. Click the **Page Layout** tab.

    c. Click the **Page Borders** button in the *Page Background* group. The *Borders and Shading* dialog box will open.

    d. In the *Setting:* area, click **Shadow**.

    e. In the *Style:* area, select the solid line.

    f. In the *Color:* area, the theme color should already be selected. If it is not, choose **Tan, Accent 1**.

    g. In the *Width:* area, choose **2¼ pt**.

    h. In the *Apply to:* area, choose **Whole document** if it is not already selected.

    i. Click **OK** to apply the page border and close the *Borders and Shading* dialog box.

    j. Click the **Page Color** button in the *Page Background* group.

    k. Select **Tan, Accent 2, Lighter 80%** for the page color.

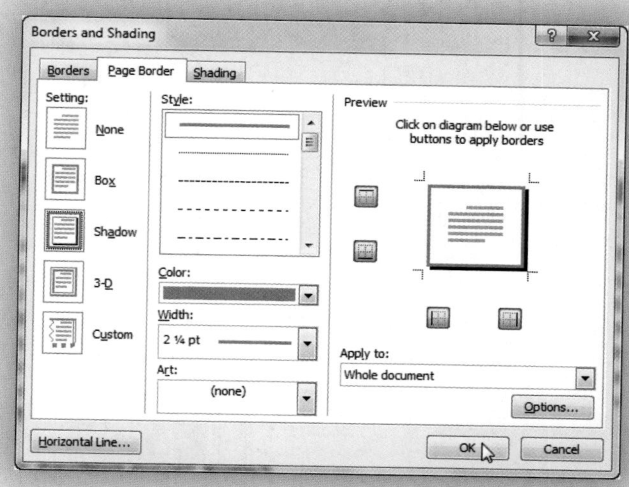

FIGURE WD 3.37

8. Insert page breaks.

    a. Click in front of the *Analyze Your Heart Rate Data* heading near the bottom of the first page.

    b. Click the **Page Layout** tab.

    c. Click the **Breaks** button in the *Page Setup* group.

    d. Select **Page** to insert a page break before the heading. The heading and text following are moved to the top of the second page.

    e. Click in front of the *Not Being Aware of Factors Affecting Heart Rate* heading near the bottom of the second page.

    f. Press **Ctrl+Enter** to insert a page break before this heading.

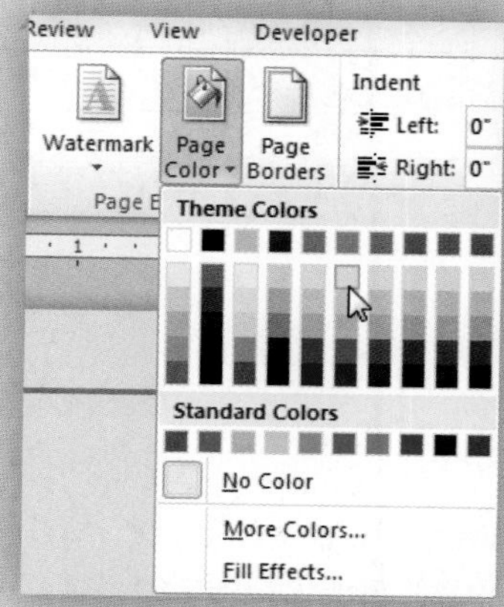

FIGURE WD 3.38

9. Add a cover page to the document.

    a. Press **Ctrl+Home** to move to the top of the document.

    b. Click the **Insert** tab.

    c. Click the **Cover Page** button in the *Pages* group.

    d. Select **Austin** as the cover page. The cover page is inserted before the first page of the document.

    e. Click in the **Abstract** area and type: `In this document are some tips to help you use your heart rate monitor to improve the effectiveness of your training rides.`

    f. Click in the **Title** area and type: `Tips For Better Heart Rate Monitor Training`

    g. Select the text in the *Title* area and change the font size to **24 pt.** and **bold** the text.

    h. Click in the **Subtitle** area and type: `American River Cycling Club`

    i. Select the text in the *Subtitle* area and change the font size to **14 pt.** and **bold** the text.

    j. Click in the **Author** area and type **your name**.

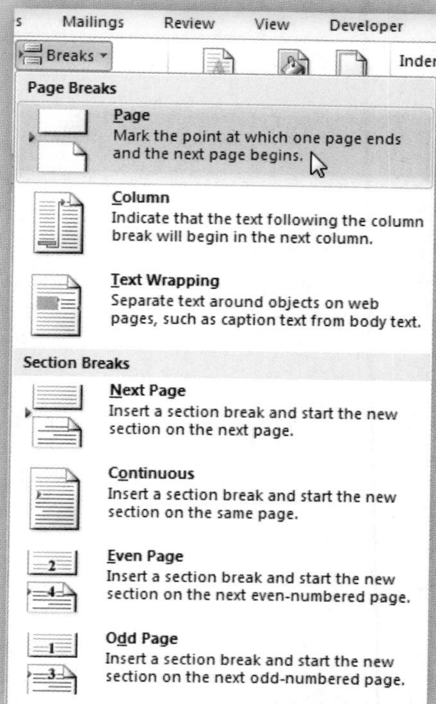

FIGURE WD 3.39

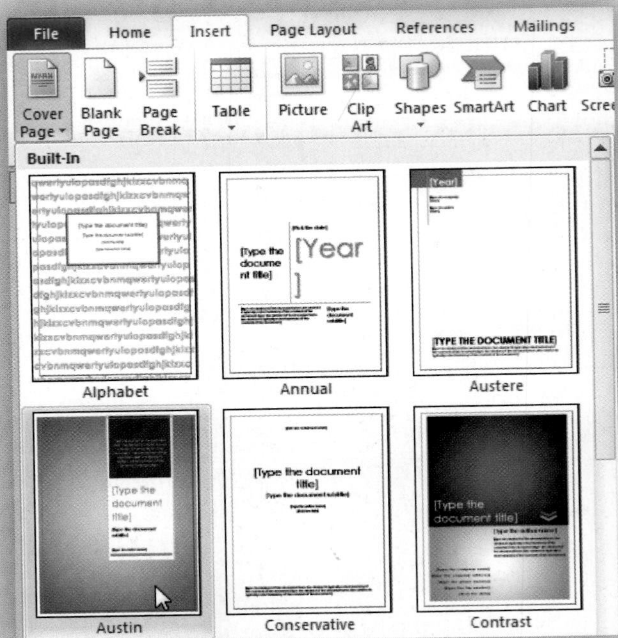

FIGURE WD 3.40

10. Insert a hyperlink into the document.
    a. Locate and select **American River Cycling Club** in the first body paragraph of the document.
    b. Click the **Insert** tab.
    c. Click the **Hyperlink** button in the *Links* group (or press **Ctrl+K**) to open the *Insert Hyperlink* dialog box.
    d. In the *Link to:* area click the **Existing File or Web Page** button.
    e. In the *Address:* area type: `http://www.americanrivercyclingclub.org`
    f. Click **OK** to insert the hyperlink and close the *Insert Hyperlink* dialog box. The selected text now appears as a hyperlink.
11. Save and close the document.

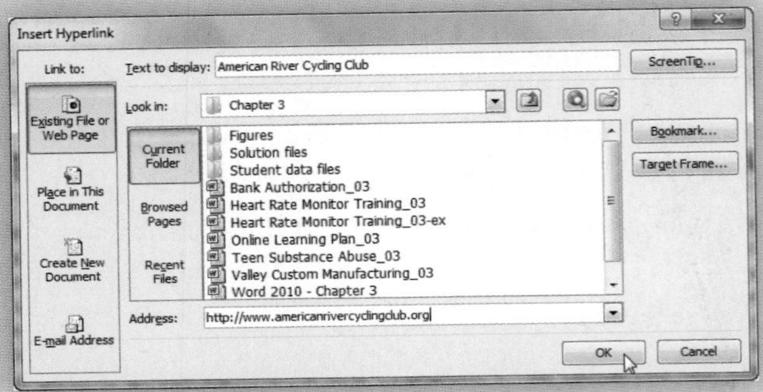

FIGURE WD 3.41

challenge yourself 1

In this project you will be editing the *Bank Authorization_03* document from Placer Hills Real Estate.

1. Open the *Bank Authorization_03* document.
2. Save this document as *`[your initials]`*`WD_Challenge_3-3`.
3. Change the margins to the **Office 2003 Default** setting.
4. Apply the **Thatch** theme to the document.
5. Select the entire document and make the following changes.
    a. Change the font size to **12 pt**.
    b. Change the after paragraph spacing to **18 pt**.
    c. Change the line spacing to single space.
6. Delete the extra blank lines in the document.

7. Click at the top of the document and insert the date in the proper business letter format (January 1, 2012). Make sure the date updates automatically.
8. Press **Enter** after the date.
9. Select **Authorization Letter to Lender**.
10. Apply the **Book Title** style and change the font size to **12 pt**.
11. Click at the end of the document and press **Enter**.
12. Add/modify the following property controls:

    Author: `Emma Cavalli`

    Company: `Placer Hills Real Estate`

    Company Address: `7100 Madrone Road, Roseville, CA 95722`

    Company E-mail: `ecavalli@phre.com`

    Company Phone: `916-450-3334`
13. Select and delete all of the property controls you just inserted and make sure there are no extra Enters after *Sincerely*.
14. Click after *Sincerely* and press **Enter** twice.
15. Insert the **Author, Company,** and **Company Phone** property controls. Use a line break (*Shift+Enter*) after each property control to place each on a separate line.
16. Open the footer (*Edit Footer*) of the document and insert the **Cavalli-footer** *Quick Part* created in *Skill Review 3.1*. Use **Backspace** to delete the extra line at the end of the footer and then close the footer.
17. Click at the end of the *Borrower Name(s)* line, press **Enter,** and type the following sentence inserting property controls where indicated: `Please consider this my/our authorization to you to provide any and all information regarding our above referenced loan to` *[Author]*, *[Company]* `as per my/our request.`
18. Press **Enter** at the end of the sentence you just entered.
19. Select the lines **Bank/Financial Institution** through **Borrower Name(s)**.

    a. Apply the **Small caps** font effect.

    b. Set a **5.5″** right tab with a solid underline leader.

    c. Press **Tab** at the end of each of these lines to insert the solid underline leader.
20. Select the first **Seller/Borrower Signature(s)** line.
21. Use the *Borders and Shading* dialog box to insert a **solid 1½ pt. top border** to the selection to create a line for a signature(s).
22. Insert a blank line above the date and insert the **Company** property control .
23. Apply the **Title** style to this line and make it **all caps**.
24. Select this line and save it to the *Quick Part* gallery. Save it as **PHRE**.
25. Insert the **Confidential 1** watermark into the document.
26. Open the original document (*Bank Authorization_03*) and compare it to the modified document.
27. Close both documents. When prompted, save the document you modified.

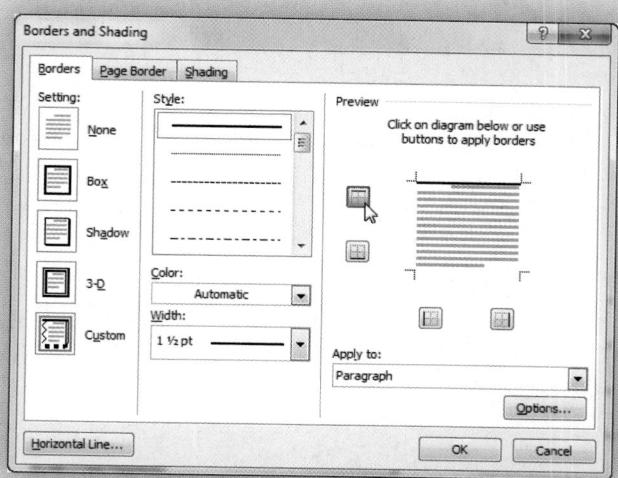

FIGURE WD 3.42

challenge yourself **2**

In this project you will be editing the *Teen Substance Abuse_03* document from Courtyard Medical Plaza.

1. Open the *Teen Substance Abuse_03* document.
2. Save this document as `[your initials]WD_Challenge_3-4`.
3. Change the margins to use the **Normal** setting.
4. Select the entire document and make the following changes.
   a. Change the font size to **12 pt**.
   b. Change the line spacing to single space.
   c. Change the after paragraph spacing to **10 pt**.
5. Change the theme font to **Waveform** and the theme color to **Opulent**.
6. Select the title of the document and apply the **Title** style, and use **bold** and **small caps**.
7. Select the first section heading (*What Is Teen Substance Abuse?*) and apply the **Intense Reference** style.
8. Change the font size of this heading to **13 pt**.
9. Use the *Format Painter* to apply this style to the remaining headings in the document.
10. In the *What Are The Signs of Substance Abuse?* section, select the second through fifth paragraphs in this section.
11. Apply a bullet of your choice. Using the *Paragraph* dialog box, deselect the **Don't add space between paragraphs of the same style** check box so the after paragraph spacing remains consistent.
12. Use the *Format Painter* to apply this bullet format to the last five paragraphs in the *Can Teen Substance Use and Abuse Be Prevented?* section.
13. Insert a header and footer into your document.
    a. Use the **Austere (Odd Page)** for the header.
    b. In the *Title* property control field, type `Courtyard Medical Plaza`
    c. In the *Date* property control field, select the **current date** and then center this field.
    d. Use the **Page Number** button to insert the **Bold Numbers 3** page number at the bottom right of the page. Use **Backspace** to remove the blank line after the page number in the footer.
    e. Set the header/footer to display only on second and continuing pages.
    f. Scroll through your document to ensure that the header and footer only appear on the second and continuing pages of the document.
14. Select the header and add it to the *Quick Part* gallery. Save this building block as **CMP-header**.
15. Select the footer and add it to the *Quick Part* gallery. Save this building block as **CMP-footer**.
16. Apply a page border and page color of your choice to the document. Make sure the colors match the theme of your document and the page color is light enough so that the text is readable.
17. Use page breaks where necessary to keep sections together.
18. Insert a cover page of your choice.
    a. Use **Courtyard Medical Plaza** as the *Title* property control. If you change this property control, it will also be changed in the header of the document.

b. Fill in other property controls as needed.

c. Change font size, alignment, and style as needed to make the cover page informative, attractive, and professional.

19. Go to the end of the document and press **Enter** twice.
20. Enter the following text: `For more information visit the Courtyard Medical Plaza Web site (www.cmp.com).`
21. Create a hyperlink to **Courtyard Medical Plaza,** use `www.cmp.com` as the URL.
22. Select this last line of text, center it, and apply a border of your choice to this paragraph.
23. Save and close the document.

on your own

In this project you will be editing the *Valley Custom Manufacturing_03* document from Central Sierra Insurance.

1. Open the *Valley Custom Manufacturing_03* document.
2. Save this document as ***[your initials]*****WD_OnYourOwn_3-5.**
3. Insert a **Page break** before the *Liability* heading.
4. Change the margins to use the **Normal** setting.
5. Click after the last of the first page and press **Enter** twice.
6. Type `Sincerely,` and press **Enter** four times.
7. Insert the **Author** property control and change the author to **Jennie Owings, Vice President.**
8. On the next line, insert the **Company** property control and change the company to **Central Sierra Insurance**.
9. Press **Enter** twice after the company name and type `Enclosure`.
10. Select the closing lines you just inserted and add it to the *Quick Part* gallery. Save this building block as **Owings-closing**.
11. Insert the current date at the top of the letter on the first page and press **Enter** four times after. Set the date so it does not update automatically.
12. Choose and apply a document theme of your choice. The letter should fit on the first page. If it does not, change the font size or theme as necessary. Make sure there is a consistent font and size throughout the document.
13. Select the first section heading (**Liability**:) and apply a Quick Style of your choice. Make this heading look professional by making changes to size, style, effects, and/or paragraph spacing.
14. Apply this style to the other section headings in the document (**Property** and **Autos & Trailers**).
15. Select the six building paragraphs in the *Property* section (**Manufacturing Building** through **Sales Building**) and apply numbering to these paragraphs. **Bold** each of the building names (e.g., **Manufacturing Building**).
16. Insert a header and footer and include the following information:

    a. On the first line of the header at the left, type: `Valley Custom Manufacturing`

b. On the next line insert the current date. Set the date so it does not update automatically.

c. On the next line insert the current page number.

d. Press **Enter** twice after the page number.

e. Insert a bottom border on the page number line.

f. In the footer, insert the **Author** property control field at the left and the **Company** property control field at the right. Adjust the right tab if necessary.

g. Insert a top border above the information in the footer.

h. Set the header and footer so they do not appear on the first page, but appear on the second and continuing pages.

17. Add the **Confidential 1** watermark to the document.
18. On the first page adjust the before paragraph spacing on the date line to balance the letter on the page.
19. Select **Central Sierra Insurance** in the first paragraph of the letter and insert a hyperlink. Use `www.centralsierra.com` as the URL.
20. If necessary, change the font and size of the text in the header and footer to match the font and size of the text in the body of the document.
21. Use page breaks where necessary to keep information together.
22. Save and close the document.

fix it

In this project you will be editing the *Online Learning Plan_03* document from Sierra Pacific Community College District. Use the Word features you have learned in this and previous chapters to enhance this report.

1. Open the *Online Learning Plan_03* document.
2. Save this document as ***[your initials]*WD_FixIt_3-6.**
3. Choose a color theme and font theme of your choice.
4. Change the margins to use the **Office 2003 Default** setting.
5. On the entire document, change the font size to **12 pt.**, the line spacing to **1.15**, and the after paragraph spacing to **10 pt**.
6. Delete any extra blank lines in the document.
7. On the bulleted list at the end of the document, edit the list so all of the bullets are at the same level and change the left indent so the bullets line up at the left margin.
8. Insert the **Company** property control at the top of the document. Change the company name to **Sierra Pacific Community College District**.
9. On the next line insert the **Title** property control. Change the title to **Online Learning Plan.** Press **Enter** after this property control field so it is on a line by itself.
10. Apply the **Title** style to the first line of the document. Decrease the size as necessary to make it fit on one line and center this line.
11. Apply the **Subtitle** style to the next line of the document (*Online Learning Plan*) and increase the size of this line, bold it, and make it small caps.
12. Apply the **Heading 1** style to each of the four main headings in the document.
13. Apply the **Heading 2** style to each of the subheadings in the *Where Are We Now with Online Learning* section.

14. Apply the **Heading 3** style to each of the course types in the *Definition of Online Learning Modes* section.

15. Apply a **1 pt.** bottom border to each of the *Heading 1* style headings. The color of the border should be consistent with the color theme of the document.

16. Modify the footer and header.

    a. Insert the current date after **Last Modified:**, and set the date to update automatically.

    b. Insert the **Title** property control field between the company name and *Last Modified.*

    c. Adjust the font size of the text in the footer so all of the information fits and there is space between each of the different items.

    d. Adjust the tabs so the center tab is in the middle of the typing line and the right tab is at the right margin.

    e. Remove the existing page number and insert a right-aligned page number in the header. Use a format that includes both the page number and the number of pages (e.g., 1 of 4).

    f. Set the header and footer so they do not appear on the first page.

17. Remove the page color from the document and add a page border of your choice.

18. Insert a cover page of your choice. Customize the control property fields as needed.

19. Include a watermark with the word **Draft.**

20. Use page breaks as necessary to control pagination.

21. Insert a hyperlink on **Sierra Pacific Community College District** in the first paragraph of the body of the report. Use `www.spccd.edu` as the URL.

22. Save and close the document.

Note to student: If you are using a public computer, you will want to delete the saved Quick Parts from this computer after you have completed these exercises. In the *Building Blocks Organizer,* select and delete the Quick Parts you have created in these exercises.

chapter **4**

Working with Tables and Graphics

In this chapter, you will learn the following skills:

- Create, enter text, and edit tables
- Merge cells, align data within cells, and sort data
- Apply borders and Quick Styles to tables
- Insert pictures, resize graphics, and organize graphics around text
- Insert clip art, WordArt, SmartArt, shapes; apply styles to graphics; and add captions to graphics.

skills

introduction

This introductory chapter will show students how to enhance the appearance and readability of a document by including tables and graphics within Word documents, editing these objects, and applying styles to these objects. Students will learn how to create and edit tables; use borders and Quick Styles on tables; insert and edit pictures, Clip Art, WordArt, SmartArt, and shapes; and apply styles and formatting to tables and graphics.

4.1 Creating a Table

A **table** helps you organize information for effective display. Tables are organized by rows, which display horizontally, and columns, which display vertically. The intersection of a row and column is referred to as a **cell**. Tables can be used to display everything from dates in a calendar to sales numbers to product inventory.

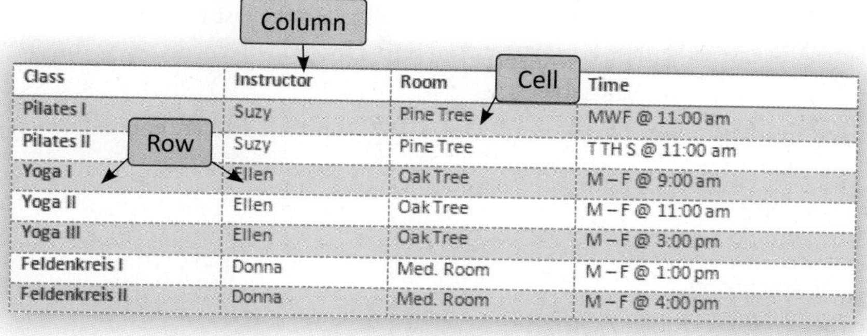

Class	Instructor	Room	Time
Pilates I	Suzy	Pine Tree	MWF @ 11:00 am
Pilates II	Suzy	Pine Tree	T TH S @ 11:00 am
Yoga I	Ellen	Oak Tree	M – F @ 9:00 am
Yoga II	Ellen	Oak Tree	M – F @ 11:00 am
Yoga III	Ellen	Oak Tree	M – F @ 3:00 pm
Feldenkreis I	Donna	Med. Room	M – F @ 1:00 pm
Feldenkreis II	Donna	Med. Room	M – F @ 4:00 pm

FIGURE WD 4.1

To create a simple table:

1. Click the **Insert** tab.
2. Click the **Table** button.
3. Select the number of cells you want by moving the cursor across and down the squares.
4. When the description at the top of the menu displays the number of rows and columns you want, click the mouse.
5. The table is inserted into your document.

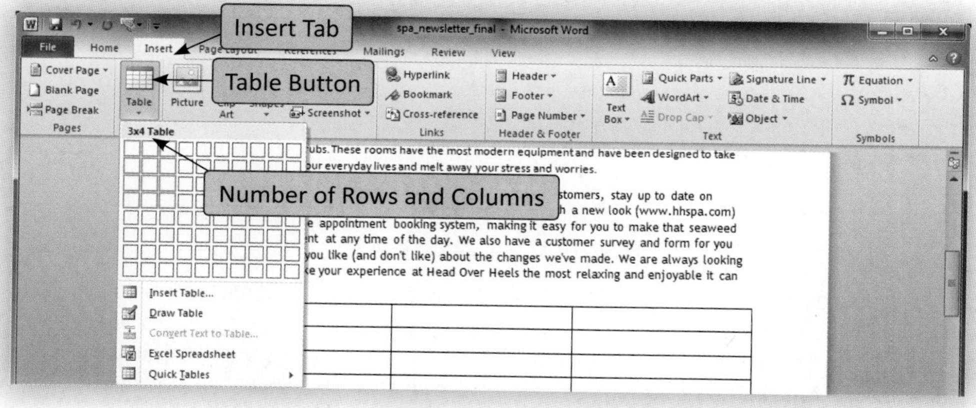

FIGURE WD 4.2

tips & tricks

Rather than inserting a table and then adding data, you can convert existing text into a table. After selecting the text to be converted, click the **Table** button and click **Insert Table . . .** The number of rows and columns will automatically be determined by the tabs and paragraphs in the selection.

tell me more

Word 2010 comes with a number of Quick Tables building blocks. These templates are preformatted for you and include sample data. To insert a Quick Table, click the **Tables** button, point to **Quick Tables,** and select a building block option from the gallery. After you insert a Quick Table, just replace the sample data with your own.

try this

To insert a table, you can:

1. Click the **Table** button and select **Insert Table . . .**
2. In the *Insert Table* dialog box, enter the number of rows and columns for your table.
3. Click **OK**.

4.2 Entering Data in a Table

Once you have inserted a blank table, you will need to enter data. When entering data in a table, it is a good idea to use the first row as a heading row by typing a short description of the content for the column in each cell. After you have labeled each column, continue entering the data into your table.

To enter data in a table:

1. Place the cursor in the cell where you want to enter the data.
2. Type the data just as you would in normal text.
3. Press Tab to move to the next cell and enter more data.
4. When you reach the last cell in the last row of a table, pressing Tab on the keyboard will create a new row in the table.
5. Continue pressing Tab until all data are entered.

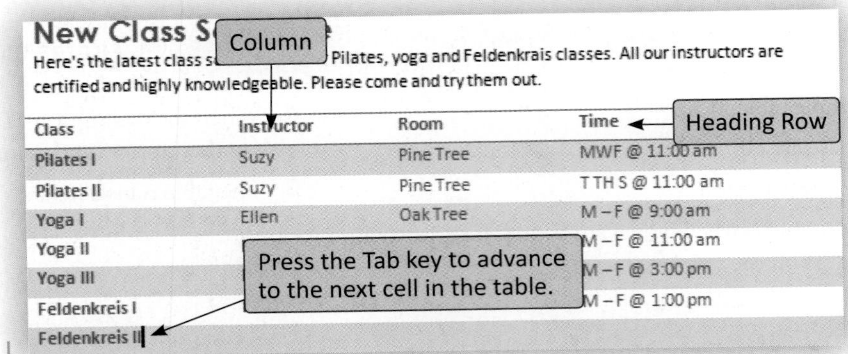

FIGURE WD 4.3

tips & tricks

Each cell is set up as one line, but if you type more data than will fit in one line, Word will automatically wrap and create another line within the cell, making the row taller. If this happens, all the cells in that row will be affected. You also can press ←Enter to force a new line within the cell.

tell me more

When working with tables, the conventional way to identify a cell is by column and row. Columns are typically referred to by letters, and rows by numbers. Thus, the first cell in the third row would be identified as "cell A3" and the third cell in the first row would be identified as "C1."

try this

To move to another cell, you can click in the cell or use the keyboard arrow keys to move across the rows and up and down the columns.

4.3 Inserting Rows, Columns, and Cells

Once you have created a table, you often find you need more rows or columns. With Word, you can easily insert additional rows and columns from the *Table Tools* contextual tabs.

When you place the cursor in a table, the *Table Tools* contextual tabs display. These tabs are called contextual tabs because they only display when a table is the active element. The *Design* tab contains tools to change the look of the table, such as shading and borders. The *Layout* tab contains tools to change how information is displayed in the table, such as row and column commands.

To insert an additional row and column:

1. Click the **Layout** tab under *Table Tools.*
2. To insert a new row, click the **Insert Above** button or the **Insert Below** button.
3. To insert a new column, click the **Insert Left** button or the **Insert Right** button.

To delete a row or column:

1. Click in the row or column you want to delete.
2. Click the **Layout** tab under *Table Tools.*
3. Click the **Delete** button and select an option.

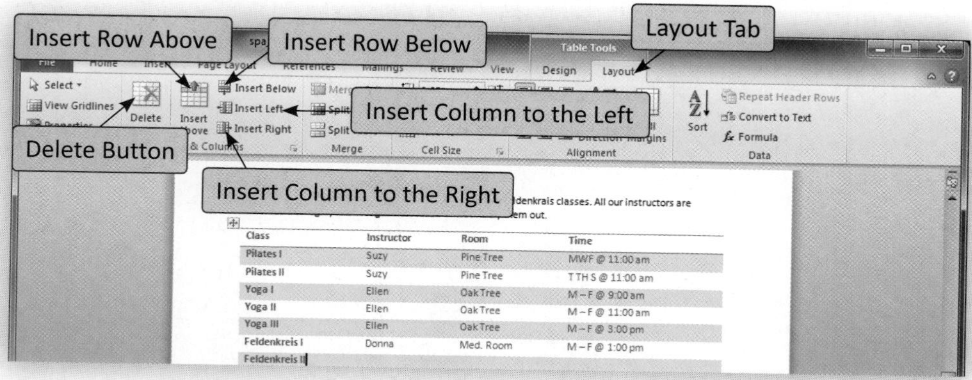

FIGURE WD 4.4

tips & tricks

A quick way to insert a new row at the end of a table is to place the cursor in the last cell in the last row and then press the Tab key. A new row is automatically added to the table, with your cursor in its first cell.

tell me more

Another way to add rows and columns to tables is to copy an existing row or column and then paste it into the table. To copy and paste a row, first select the row you want to copy and click the **Copy** button. Next, place your cursor in the first cell of the row below where you want the copied row to appear. Click the **Paste** button to insert the copied row. You can use the same method to copy and paste columns in tables as well.

try this

To insert rows and columns, you can right-click in a cell, point to **Insert,** and select **Insert Rows Above, Insert Rows Below, Insert Columns to the Left,** or **Insert Columns to the Right.**

4.4 Sizing Tables, Columns, and Rows

When you insert a table, it covers the full width of the page and the columns and rows are evenly spaced. Once you have entered your data, you will probably find that the table is larger than it needs to be and the columns and rows need adjusting. You can resize your table using Word's AutoFit commands.

To adjust the width and height of cells using the AutoFit command:

1. Click in the table you want to resize.
2. Click the **Layout** tab under *Table Tools*.
3. In the *Cell Size* group, click the **AutoFit** button.
4. Select **AutoFit Contents** to resize the cell to fit the text of the table.

To resize all the rows in a table so they have the same height, in the *Cell Size* group click the **Distribute Rows** button. Click the **Distribute Columns** to resize all the columns in a table so they have the same width.

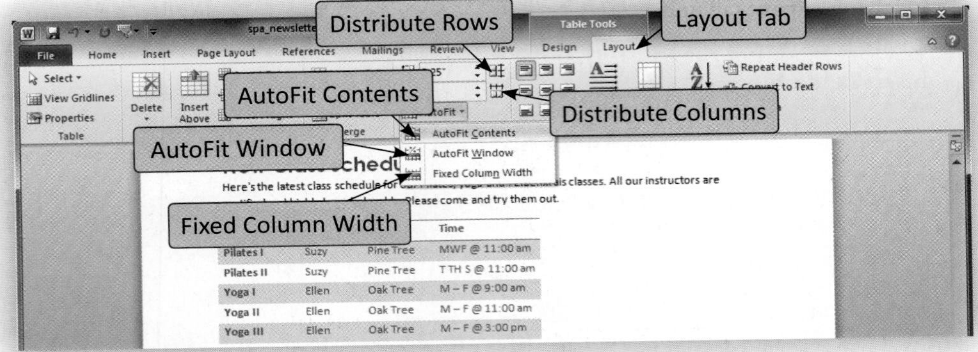

FIGURE WD 4.5

tips & tricks

Once you have resized a table, you will probably want to position it better on the page. You can do this by using the **move handle** tool that appears at the top-left corner of the table when the mouse pointer is placed over the table. Click the move handle and drag the table to where you want it.

tell me more

You can resize a table manually two different ways:

- Rest the mouse pointer anywhere over the table. When the **resize handle** appears at the bottom-right corner of the table, click and drag it until you achieve the desired size. This method can also be used to resize columns and rows.
- Click in the row or column you want to resize. In the *Cell Size* group, adjust the numbers for the **Table Row Height** and **Table Column Width** by clicking the up and down arrows in the control box.

try this

To use the AutoFit command to resize a table, you can right-click in the table, point to **AutoFit,** and select **AutoFit Contents.**

4.5 Merging and Splitting Cells

When you first create a table, it is a grid of rows and columns. But what if you want to display your content across columns or across rows? For instance, if the first row of your table includes the title for the table, then you will probably want to display the title in a single cell that spans all the columns of the table. In this case, you will want to ***merge*** the cells in the first row into one cell. On the other hand, if you have a cell that contains multiple values, you may want to ***split*** the cell so it can display each value in a separate row or column. Use the **merge cells** and **split cells** commands to customize the layout of tables. Merging cells entails combining multiple cells into one, whereas splitting a cell divides the cell into multiple cells.

To merge cells in a table:

1. Select the cells you want to merge into one.
2. Under *Table Tools,* click the **Layout** tab.
3. In the *Merge* group, click the **Merge Cells** button.

To split a cell in a table:

1. Select the cell you want to split.
2. In the *Merge* group, click the **Split Cells** button.
3. In the *Split Cells* dialog box, enter the number of columns and rows.
4. Click **OK** to split the cell.

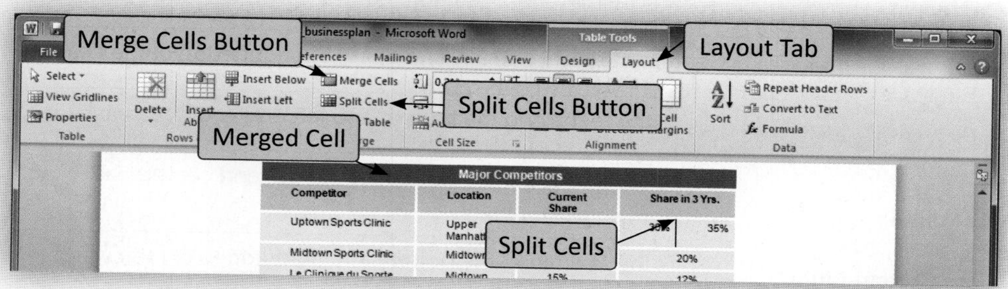

FIGURE WD 4.6

tips & tricks

In addition to splitting cells, you also split a table, creating two tables from one. To split a table into two tables:

1. Place the cursor in the row where you want to split the table.
2. In the *Merge* group, click the **Split Table** button.

tell me more

When you place the cursor in a table, the *Table Tools* tabs display. These tabs are called contextual tabs because they only display when a table is the active element.

try this

- To merge cells, you can right-click the selected cells and select **Merge Cells** from the menu.
- To split cells, you can right-click a cell and select **Split Cells . . .** from the menu.

4.6 Aligning Text in Tables

When entering data in tables, there will be times when you want to change the position of text within a particular cell. While most text in cells is left-aligned, titles and column headings are often center-aligned, and most columns of numbers are right-aligned. You can control both the vertical and horizontal alignment in cells.

To change the alignment of cells:

1. Click the cell you want to change.
2. Under *Table Tools,* click the **Layout** tab.
3. In the *Alignment* group, click one of the nine alignment options:

	Align Top Left	Aligns the text along the top and left edges of the cell.
	Align Top Center	Aligns the text along the top of the cell and centers the text horizontally in the cell.
	Align Top Right	Aligns the text along the top and right edges of the cell.
	Align Center Left	Centers the text vertically and along the left edge of the cell.
	Align Center	Centers the text vertically and horizontally in the cell.
	Align Center Right	Centers the text vertically and along the right edge of the cell.
	Align Bottom Left	Aligns the text along the bottom and left edges of the cell.
	Align Bottom Center	Aligns the text along the bottom of the cell and centers the text horizontally in the cell.
	Align Bottom Right	Aligns the text along the bottom and right edges of the cell.

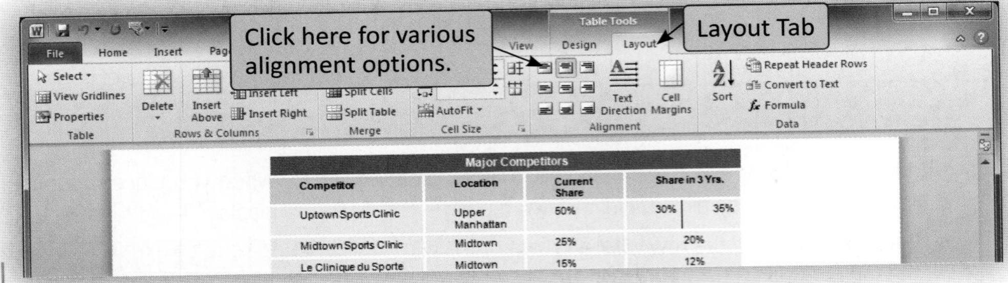

FIGURE WD 4.7

tips & tricks

To manually change the size of margins within cells, click the **Cell Margins** button in the *Alignment* group. The *Table Options* dialog box opens. Here you can adjust the left, right, top, and bottom margins of cells.

tell me more

You can change the direction of text in table cells by clicking the **Text Direction** button in the *Alignment* group on the *Layout* tab. The text rotates and is displayed vertically. Click the button again to flip the text the other direction. Click the button a third time to return the text to its original position.

try this

- To change the alignment of a cell, you can right-click in the cell, point to **Cell Alignment,** and select an alignment option.
- You can change the horizontal alignment of cells by clicking one of the alignment buttons in the *Paragraph* group on the *Home* tab.

4.7 Sorting Data in Tables

After you have entered data in a table, you may decide it needs to be displayed in a different order. **Sorting** rearranges the rows in your table by the text in a column or columns. Word allows you to sort data based on the first character of each entry. You can sort in alphabetical or numeric order, in either ascending (A–Z) or descending (Z–A) order.

To sort a column alphabetically:

1. Under *Table Tools,* click the **Layout** tab.
2. In the *Data* group, click the **Sort** button.
3. The *Sort* dialog box opens.
4. Click the **Sort by** arrow and select a field to sort by.
5. The *Ascending* radio button is selected by default.
6. Click **OK** to sort the text in the table.

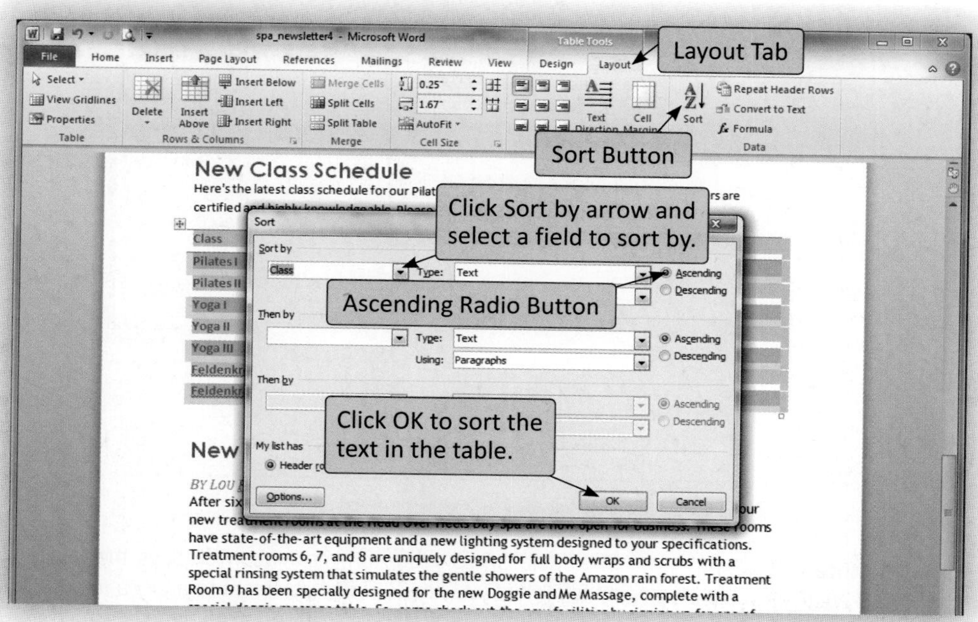

FIGURE WD 4.8

tips & tricks

You can sort by text, number, or date. You can refine the sort by choosing additional fields to sort by:

- If you want to sort the text in reverse order, from Z to A, click the **Descending** radio button.
- Word can sort upper- and lowercase letters differently. Click the **Options . . .** button in the *Sort* dialog box and then click the **Case sensitive** check box in the *Sort Options* dialog box.

try this

To open the *Sort* dialog box, from the *Home* tab, in the *Paragraph* group, click the **Sort** button.

4.8 Adding Table Quick Styles

Just as you can apply complex formatting to paragraphs using Quick Styles for text, you can apply complex formatting to tables using Quick Styles for tables. Using Quick Styles for tables, you can change the text color along with the borders and shading for a table, giving it a professional, sophisticated look without a lot of work.

To apply a Quick Style to a table:

1. Under *Table Tools,* click the **Design** tab.
2. In the *Table Styles* group, click the **More** button.
3. Select a Quick Style from the *Quick Styles* gallery.

By default, the Word *Table Styles* gallery displays styles that include header rows, banded rows, and first column layouts. If you want to change the options that display in the gallery, check or uncheck the options in the *Table Styles Options* group.

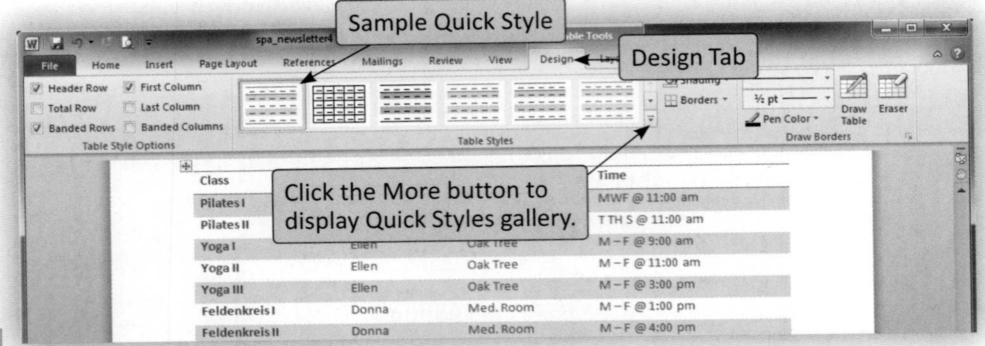

FIGURE WD 4.9

tips & tricks

To create your own table style, click the **More** button and select **New Table Style . . .** In the *Create New Style from Formatting* dialog box, you can create a new table style based on an existing table style, changing options such as grid lines and shading to suit your needs. When you save the style, it will appear in the *Table Styles* gallery.

try this

The *Table Styles* group on the Ribbon displays the latest Quick Styles you have used. If you want to apply a recently used Quick Style, you can click the option directly from the Ribbon without opening the *Quick Styles* gallery.

4.9 Adding Borders to a Table

When you first create a table, it uses the simple grid style. You can apply a Quick Style to your table to quickly add formatting, but what if you want to further adjust the look of a table after applying the Quick Style? You can choose different shading for your table and add and remove borders to change the look of the entire table or just parts of the table.

To change the borders for a table:

1. Select the table you want to change.
2. Under *Table Tools,* click the **Design** tab.
3. In the *Table Styles* group, click the arrow next to the **Borders** button.
4. On the menu that appears, all currently selected options appear active with a background color. Options that are not selected appear without a background color.
5. Click a border option to turn that border on or off in the table.

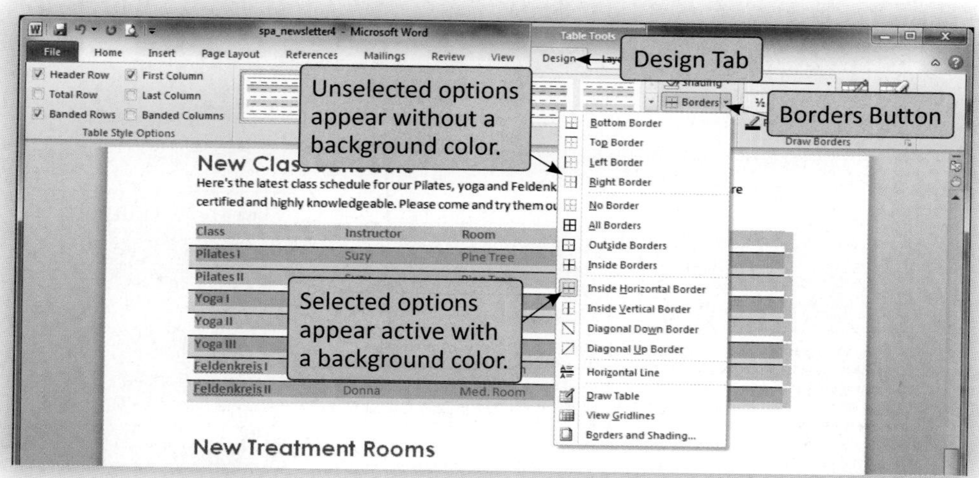

FIGURE WD 4.10

tips & tricks

If your table does not show borders, you can display gridlines to give you a visual guide. The gridlines appear as a dotted line on screen but do not print as part of the final document. To display gridlines, click the **Borders** button and select **View Gridlines.**

tell me **more**

In addition to changing the borders of a table, you can change the shading, or background color applied to the table. Adding shading to a table helps it stand out on a page. To apply shading to a table, click the **Shading** button [Shading] in the *Table Styles* group. A palette of colors displays. Select a color to change the background color for the table.

try **this**

You can change the borders of a table by clicking the *Home* tab. In the *Paragraph* group, click the arrow next to the *Borders* button and select an option.

You can change borders and shading through the *Borders and Shading* dialog box. To open the *Borders and Shading* dialog box:

- From the *Home* tab or from the *Design* tab, click the arrow next to the *Borders* button and select **Borders and Shading . . .**
- Right-click on the table and select **Borders and Shading . . .** from the menu.

4.10 Inserting Clip Art

Word's **clip art** feature allows you to easily insert clips into your document. These **clips** refer to media files from another source. They include images, photographs, scanned material, animations, sound, and video. By default, Word inserts these clips as embedded objects, meaning they become part of the new document (changing the source file will not change them in the new document). The Clip Art task pane allows you to search for different kinds of clips from many different sources.

To insert a clip art image into a document:

1. Click the **Insert** tab.
2. In the *Illustrations* group, click the **Clip Art** button.
3. When the *Clip Art* task pane opens, type a word describing the clip you want in the *Search for:* box.
4. Click the **Go** button.
5. Click the clip you want to insert it into the document

You can narrow your search by media type, only searching for illustrations or photographs or videos or audio clips. Click the **Results should be:** arrow and click the check box in front of a media type to include or exclude those types of files from your search. Click the **All media types** check box to select and deselect all types at once.

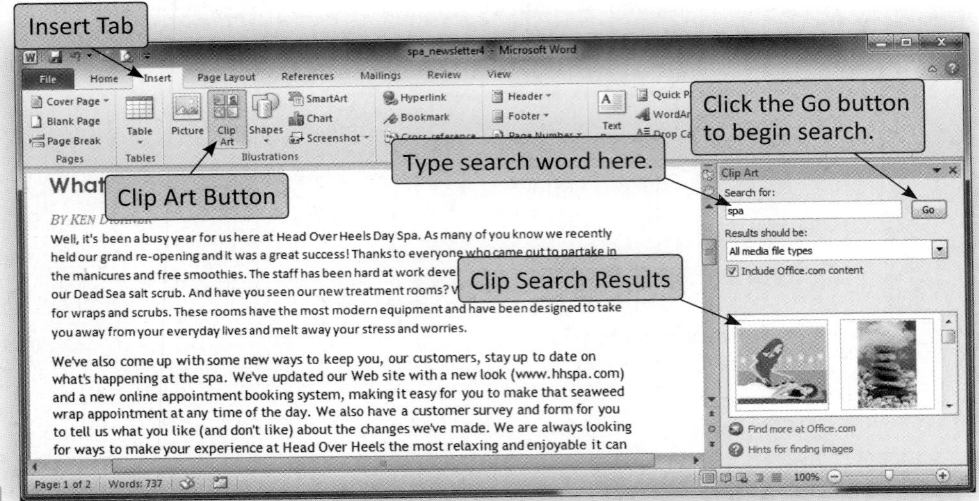

FIGURE WD 4.11

tips & tricks

Microsoft's Web site for office content, *Office.com,* contains more clips for you to use in your documents. If you are connected to the Internet, click the **Include Office.com content** check box to include content from the Web site in your search results.

try **this**

To insert an image from the *Clip Art* task pane, you can point to the image and click the arrow that appears. A menu of options displays. Click **Insert** on the menu to add the clip to your document.

4.11 Inserting a Picture

You can insert images that you created in another program into your document. By default, Word inserts images as embedded objects, meaning they become part of the new document. Changing the source file will not change or affect the newly inserted image.

To insert an image from a file:

1. Click the **Insert** tab.
2. In the *Illustrations* group, click the **Picture** button.
3. The *Insert Picture* dialog box opens.
4. Navigate to the file location, select the file, and click **Insert.**

To delete a picture, select the picture and press the **Delete** key on the keyboard.

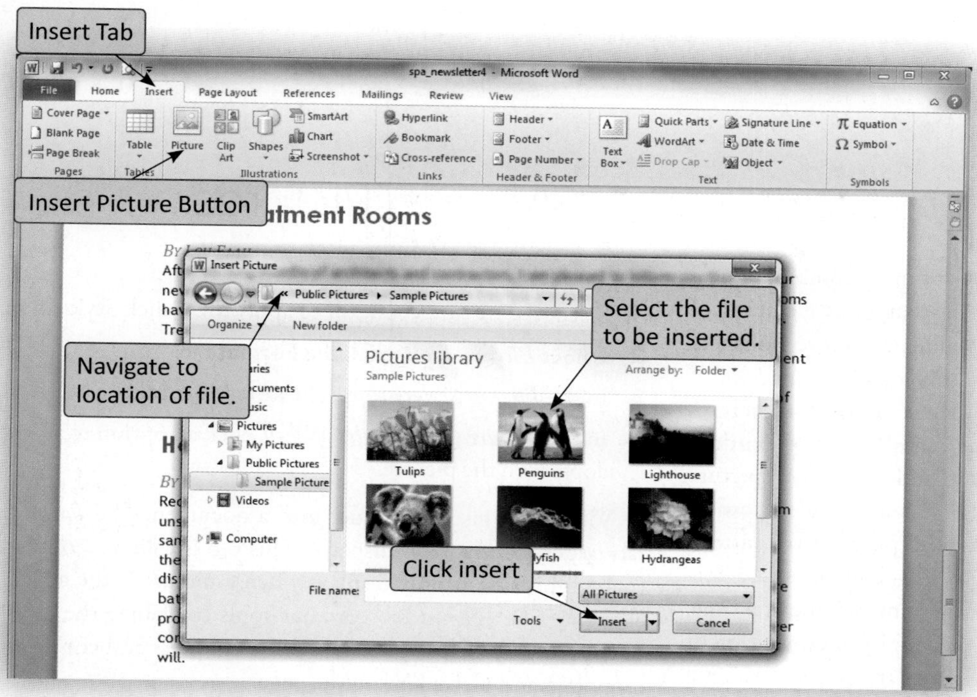

FIGURE WD 4.12

tell me **more**

When you insert a picture to a document, the *Format* tab under *Picture Tools* displays. This tab is called a contextual tab because it only displays when a picture is the active element. The *Format* tab contains tools to change the look of the picture, such as picture style, brightness and contrast, cropping, and placement on the page.

try **this**

To insert the file, you can click the **Insert** button arrow and select **Insert.**

from the perspective of . . .

MEDICAL PROFESSIONAL

Word processing software enables me to record a patient's history, medications, and symptoms. I can easily organize a patient's information using a table, creating an easy-to-read, professional document.

4.12 Applying Quick Styles to Pictures

Quick Styles are a combination of formatting that gives elements of your document a more polished, professional look without a lot of work. Quick Styles for pictures include a combination of borders, shadows, reflections, and picture shapes, such as rounded corners or skewed perspective. Instead of applying each of these formatting elements one at a time, you can apply a combination of elements at one time using a preset Quick Style.

To apply a Quick Style to a picture:

1. Select the picture you want to apply the Quick Style to.
2. Under *Picture Tools,* click the **Format** tab.
3. In the *Picture Styles* group, click the **More** button.
4. In the *Picture Quick Styles* gallery, click an option to apply it to the picture.

When you insert a picture into a document, the *Format* tab under *Picture Tools* displays. This tab is called a contextual tab because it only displays when a picture is the active element. The *Format* tab contains tools to change the look of the picture, such as picture styles, brightness and contrast, cropping, and placement on the page.

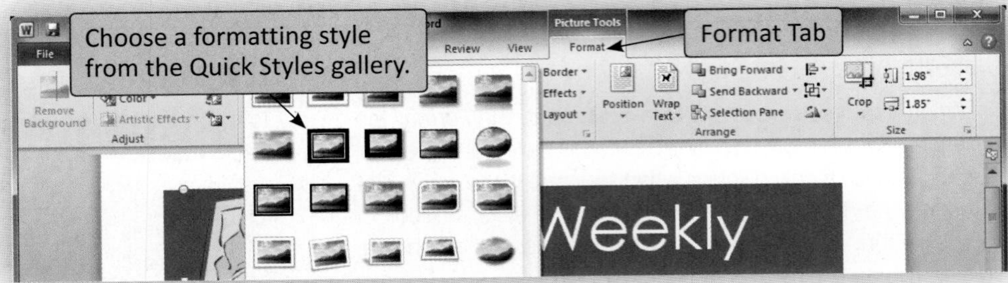

FIGURE WD 4.13

tips & tricks

Once you have applied a Quick Style to a picture, you can further modify the look of the picture using the **Picture Shape, Picture Border,** and **Picture Effects** options.

try this

The *Picture Styles* group displays the latest Quick Styles you have used. If you want to apply a recently used Quick Style, you can click the option directly from the Ribbon without opening the *Quick Styles* gallery.

4.13 Wrapping Text around Graphics

When you first add a graphic to your document, Word inserts the graphic at the insertion point and displays the graphic in line with the text. More often than not, you will want to place the graphic somewhere else on the page. Word comes with a number of preset image positions that include wrapping the text around the image.

To position the image on a page with text wrapping:

1. Under *Picture Tools,* click the **Format** tab.
2. In the *Arrange* group, click the **Position** button.
3. In the *With Text Wrapping* section, select an option.
4. The image is placed on the page according to the option you chose.

	In Line with Text
	Position in Top Left with Square Text Wrapping
	Position in Top Center with Square Text Wrapping
	Position in Top Right with Square Text Wrapping
	Position in Middle Left with Square Text Wrapping
	Position in Middle Center with Square Text Wrapping
	Position in Middle Right with Square Text Wrapping
	Position in Bottom Left with Square Text Wrapping
	Position in Bottom Center with Square Text Wrapping
	Position in Bottom Right with Square Text Wrapping

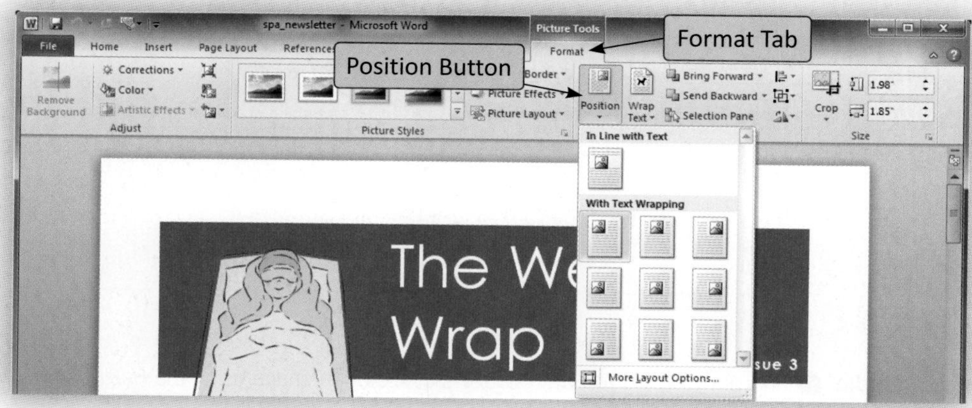

FIGURE WD 4.14

tips & tricks

If you have multiple images, you can layer the images and then arrange them using the **Bring to Front** button [Bring to Front] and **Send to Back** button [Send to Back] in the *Arrange* group.

tell me more

Word's **text wrapping** feature gives you the ability to lay out text and graphics in a number of ways. Other wrapping styles include **Square**, **Tight**, **Behind Text, In Front of Text, Top and Bottom**, and **Through**. Click the **Wrap Text** button in the *Arrange* group to apply one of these layout options.

try this

You can position images on the page from the *Page Layout* tab. In the *Arrange* group, click the **Position** button and select an option.

4.14 Resizing and Moving Graphics

When you first add an image to a document, you may find it does not appear the way you expected. The image may be too large for the page or it may be in the wrong place on the page. You can change the layout of a document by resizing and moving images.

To resize and move a graphic:

1. Select the graphic you want to change.
2. To resize a graphic, click a **resize handle** and drag toward the center of the image to make it smaller or away from the center of the image to make it larger.
3. To move a graphic, rest your mouse over the graphic. When the cursor changes to the **move cursor**, click and drag the image to the new location.

When an image is selected, you will see two types of resize handles:

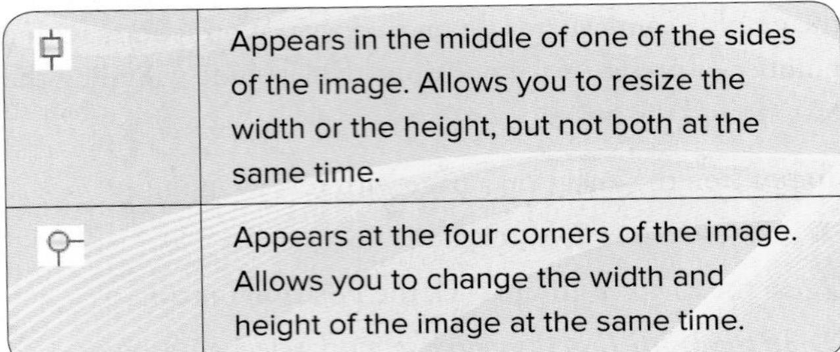

	Appears in the middle of one of the sides of the image. Allows you to resize the width or the height, but not both at the same time.
	Appears at the four corners of the image. Allows you to change the width and height of the image at the same time.

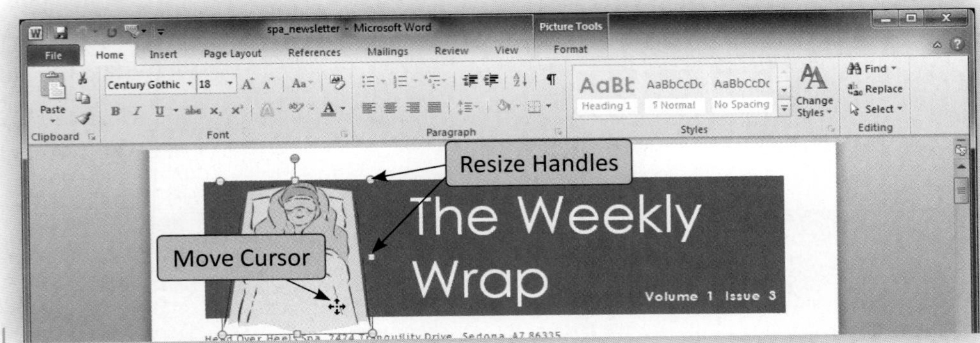

FIGURE WD 4.15

tell me **more**

To rotate a graphic, click the **rotate handle** and drag your mouse to the right to rotate the image clockwise or to the left to rotate the image counterclockwise.

try **this**

You can change the size of an image using the *Height:* and *Width:* boxes in the *Size* group on the *Format* tab under *Picture Tools.*

4.15 Adding WordArt to Documents

Sometimes you'll want to call attention to text you have added to your document. You could format the text by using character effects, or if you want the text to really stand out, use **WordArt**.

WordArt Quick Styles are predefined graphic styles you can apply to text. These styles include a combination of color, fills, outlines, and effects.

To add WordArt to a document:

1. Click the **Insert** tab on the Ribbon.
2. In the *Text* group, click the **WordArt** button and select a Quick Style from the gallery.
3. Replace the text "Your Text Here" with the text for your document.

After you have added WordArt to your document, you can modify it just as you would any other text. Use the *Font* box and *Font Size* box on the *Home* tab to change the font or font size of WordArt.

In previous versions of Microsoft Word, WordArt came with a predefined set of graphic styles that could be formatted, but on a very limited basis. In Word 2010, WordArt has been changed to allow a wide range of stylization. When you add WordArt to a document, the *Drawing Tools Format* contextual tab appears. In the *WordArt Styles* group you can apply Quick Styles to your WordArt, or modify it further by changing the text fill, text outline, and text effects.

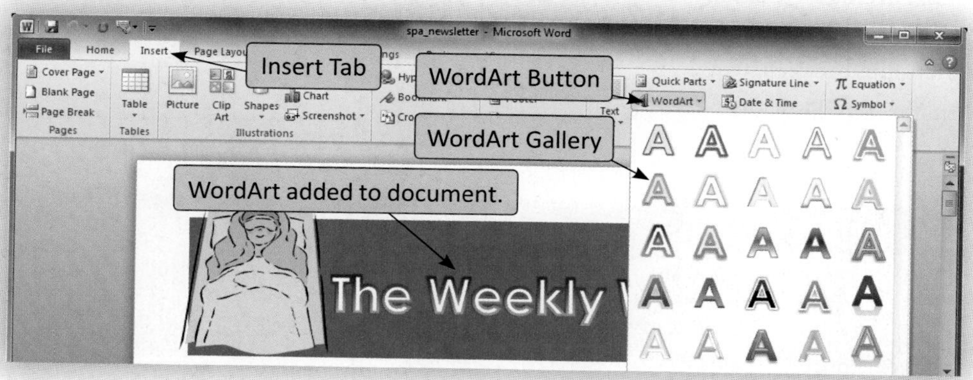

FIGURE WD 4.16

tips & tricks

Be sure to limit the use of WordArt to small amounts of text, such as a newsletter banner. Overuse of WordArt can be distracting to your readers.

tell me more

You can change the look of WordArt using the commands in the *Transform* gallery. You can choose to display the text along a path or to distort the letters creating a warped effect. To transform WordArt, under *Drawing Tools*, click the **Format** tab. In the *WordArt Styles* group, click the **Text Effects** button. Point to **Transform** and select an option from the gallery.

4.16 Inserting SmartArt

SmartArt is a way to take your ideas and make them visual. Where documents used to have plain bulleted and ordered lists, now they can have SmartArt, which are visual diagrams containing graphic elements with text boxes for you to enter your information in. Using SmartArt not only makes your document look better, but it helps convey the information in a more meaningful way.

There are eight categories of SmartArt for you to choose from:

List—Use to list items that do not need to be in a particular order.

Process—Use to list items that do need to be in a particular order.

Cycle—Use for a process that repeats over and over again.

Hierarchy—Use to show branching, in either a decision tree or an organization chart.

Relationship—Use to show relationships between items.

Matrix—Use to show how an item fits into the whole.

Pyramid—Use to illustrate how things relate to each other with the largest item being on the bottom and the smallest item being on the top.

Picture—Use to show a series of pictures along with text in the diagram.

To add SmartArt to a document:

1. Click the **Insert** tab.
2. Click the **SmartArt** button.
3. In the *Choose a SmartArt Graphic* dialog box, click a **SmartArt** option and click **OK.**
4. The Smart Art is added to your document.
5. Click in the first item of the *Text* pane and type your first item.
6. Enter the text for each item.
7. Click outside the SmartArt graphic to hide the *Text* pane.

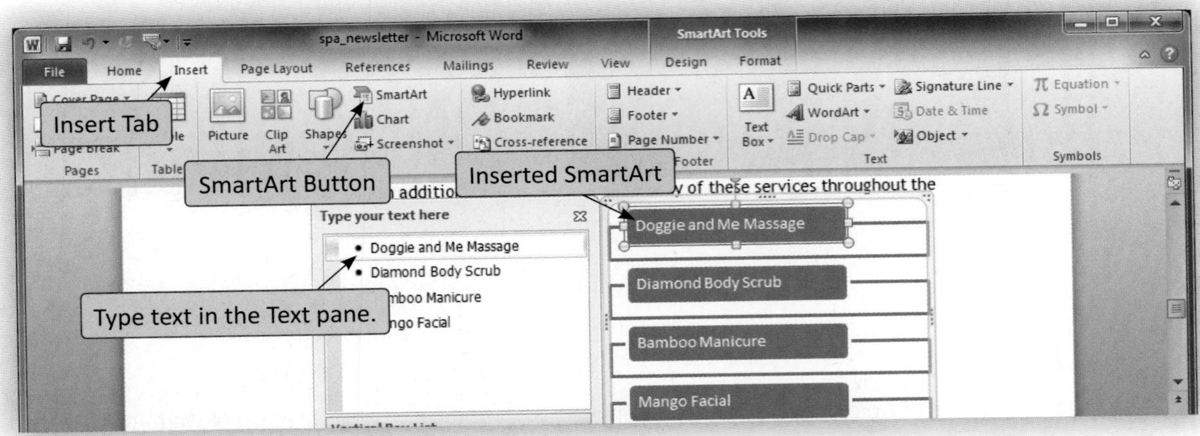

FIGURE WD 4.17

tips & tricks

When choosing a SmartArt diagram, it is important that the diagram type suits your content. In the *Choose a SmartArt Graphic* dialog box, click a SmartArt type to display a preview of the SmartArt to the right. The preview displays not only what the diagram will look like, but also includes a description of the best uses for the diagram type.

try this

To enter text in SmartArt, you can click in the text area of the SmartArt and type your text.

4.17 Inserting a Shape

A **shape** is a drawing object that you can quickly add to your document. Word comes with a number of shapes for you to choose from including lines, block arrows, callouts, and basic shapes such as smiley faces, rectangles, and circles.

To add a shape to a document:

1. Click the **Insert** tab.
2. In the *Illustrations* group, click the **Shapes** button and select an option from the *Shapes* gallery.
3. The cursor changes to a crosshair +.
4. Click anywhere on the document to add the shape.

Once you have added a shape to a document, there are a number of ways you can work with it:

- To resize a graphic: click a resize handle (or) and drag toward the center of the image to make it smaller or away from the center of the image to make it larger.
- To rotate a graphic: click the rotate handle and drag your mouse to the right to rotate the image clockwise or to the left to rotate the image counterclockwise.
- To move a graphic: point to the graphic and when the cursor changes to the move cursor click and drag the image to the new location.

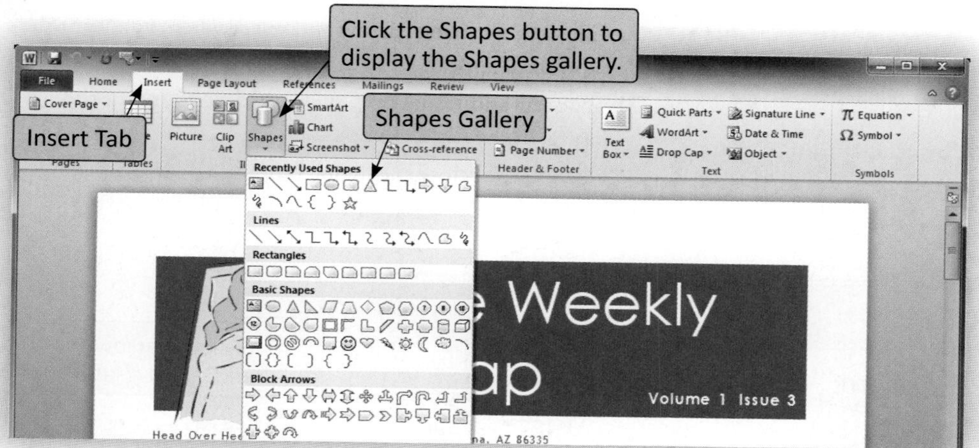

FIGURE WD 4.18

tips & tricks

Some shapes, such as callouts, are designed for displaying text. When you add a callout to a document, a text area automatically appears with the cursor ready for you to enter text. But what if you want to add text to another type of shape? You can add text to any shape you add to a document. To add text, right-click the shape and select **Add Text.** A text area displays in the shape. Type the text and click outside the shape.

tell me more

When you insert a shape into a document, the *Format* tab under *Drawing Tools* displays. This tab is called a contextual tab because it only displays when a drawing object is the active element. The *Format* tab contains tools to change the look of the shape, such as shape styles, effects, and placement on the page.

4.18 Adding a Caption

A **caption** is a brief description of an illustration, chart, equation, or table. Captions can appear above or below the image, and typically begin with a label followed by a number and the description of the image. Captions are helpful when referring to images within paragraphs of text (see Figure 1: An example of a caption).

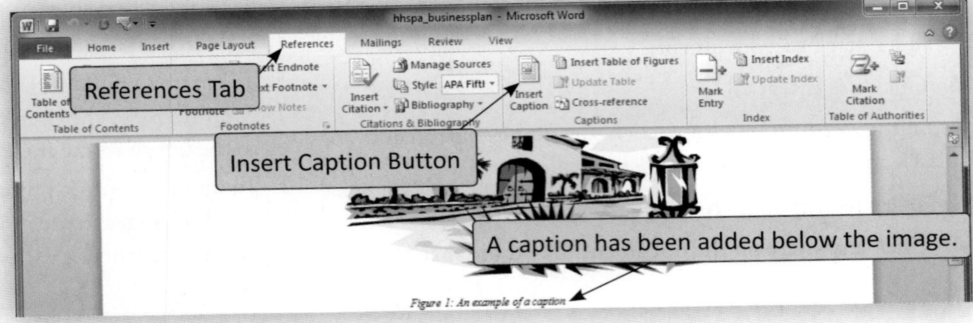

FIGURE WD 4.19

To add a caption to a figure:

1. Select the figure you want to add the caption to.
2. Click the **References** tab.
3. In the *Captions* group, click the **Insert Caption** button.
4. The *Caption* dialog box opens.
5. Click the **Label:** arrow and select a figure type.
6. Click the **Position:** arrow and select where you want the caption to appear.
7. Type any additional text, such as a description of the figure, in the *Caption:* box.
8. Click **OK** to close the dialog box and add the caption.

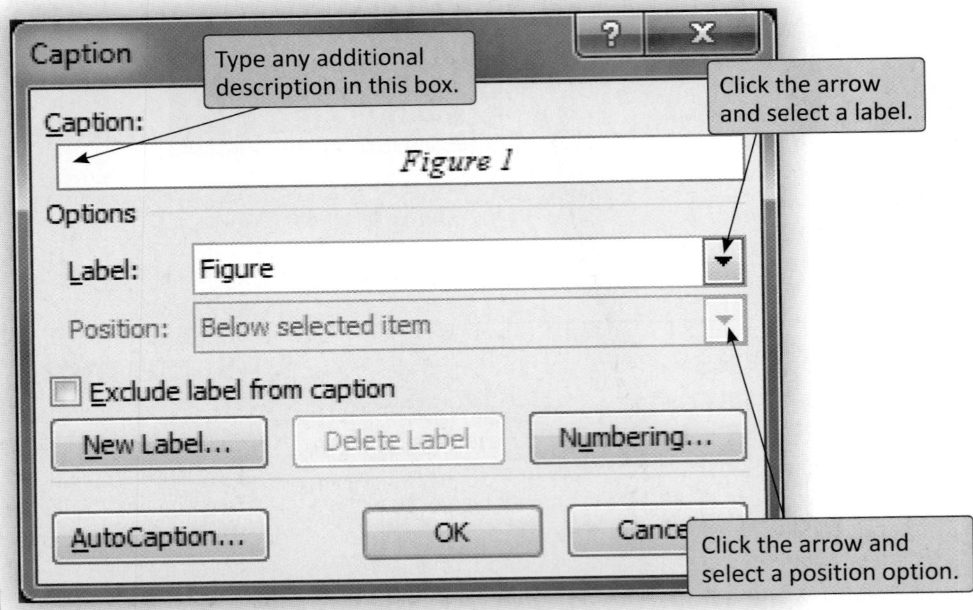

FIGURE WD 4.20

tips & tricks

Word automatically numbers the figures in your document based on the label type. For example, if you have several tables that use the "table" label, those captions will be numbered sequentially. If you have other figures labeled as "figures," those images will be numbered sequentially. If you go back and add a new caption or change the label of an existing caption, Word will renumber the existing captions for you.

tell me more

When you add certain types of images or objects to your document, such as a Microsoft Excel chart or an Adobe Acrobat document, you can have Word automatically add a caption to the figure. In the *Insert Caption* dialog box, click the **AutoCaption . . .** button. In the *AutoCaption* dialog box, select the type of object you want to automatically add captions to and click **OK**.

projects

Skill Review 4.1

In this project you will be editing the *Emergency Telephones_04* document from Sierra Pacific Community College District.

1. Open Microsoft Word 2010.
2. Open the *Emergency Telephones_04* document.
3. Save this document as `[your initials]WD_SkillReview_4-1`.
4. Insert and arrange a company logo picture in the document.
   a. Click the **Insert** tab.
   b. In the *Illustrations* group, click the **Picture** button. The *Insert Picture* dialog box will open.
   c. Browse to your student data file location, select the **SPCCD logo** file, and click **Insert**. The logo will be inserted into the document.
   d. On the *Picture Format* tab, in the *Arrange group,* click the **Wrap Text** button and choose **In Front of Text**.

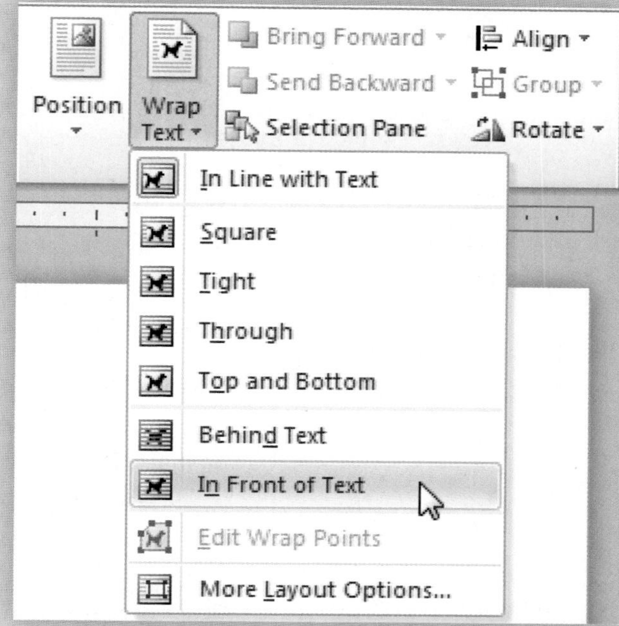

FIGURE WD 4.21

5. Position the company logo in the document.
   a. Click the logo picture and drag it to the upper-left corner of the document.
   b. With the logo still selected, in the *Arrange* group, click the **Position** button and select the top left with square wrapping option.
6. Add a table to the document and enter text into the table.
   a. Move to the end of the document and type `Emergency Phone Numbers` and apply the **Heading 2** style.
   b. Press **Enter** and click the **Insert** tab.
   c. In the *Tables* group, click the **Tables** button and select a **4 × 1** (four columns and one row) table.
   d. Type the information below into the table. Press **Tab** to move forward from cell to cell and press **Shift+Tab** to move back one cell. Press **Tab** at the end of a row to insert a new row. Don't worry about alignment or text wrapping at this point; just enter the data.

Emergency Response System	Fire, Medical, Sheriff	Available 24 hrs.	911
College Police	› South Library	› M-Su: 7 a.m.-7 p.m.	› (209) 658-7777
› Health Center	› Administration Building	› M-F: 7 a.m.-4 p.m.	› (209) 658-2239
› Information Center	› Counseling Building	› M-F: 8 a.m.-5 p.m.	› (209) 658-4466
› Evening Dean	› Asst. Dean, Math	› M-Th: 5 p.m.-8 p.m.	› (209) 658-7700
› Site Administrator	› VP of Administrative Services	› M-F: 8 a.m.-5 p.m.	› (209) 658-8501
› Weekend College Coordinator	› Area Deans	› S: 8 a.m.-5 p.m.	› (209) 658-6500

7. Delete a column from and insert a row into an existing table.

a. Click somewhere in the second column and click the **Layout** tab under *Table Tools.*

b. In the *Row & Columns* group, click the **Delete** button and select **Delete Columns.** The table should now be three columns and seven rows.

c. Click somewhere in the first row and click the **Insert Above** button in the *Rows & Columns* group.

d. Enter the following information in the first row.

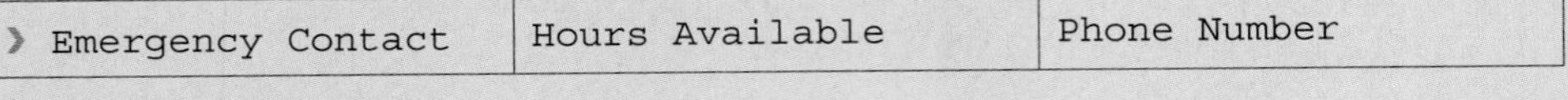

› Emergency Contact	Hours Available	Phone Number

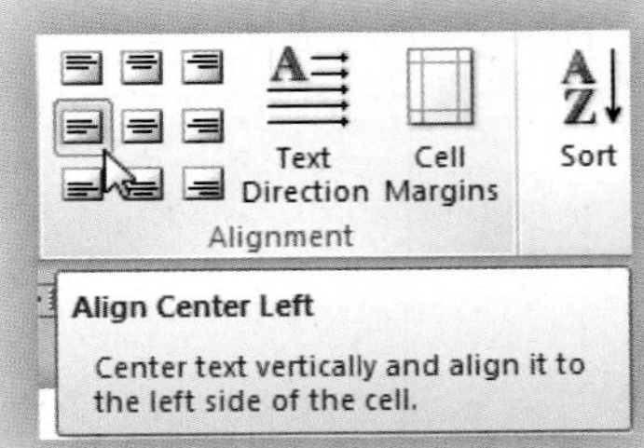

FIGURE WD 4.22

8. Change the size of the columns and rows, sort text within the table, and apply a table Quick Style.

a. On the *Layout* tab, in the *Table* group, click the **Select** button and choose **Select Table** to select the entire table.

b. In the *Cell Size* group, click the **AutoFit** button and choose **AutoFit Contents** to automatically adjust the column width to fit the contents of the table.

c. In the *Cell Size* group, change the *Height* to **0.2″**.

d. In *Alignment* group, click the **Align Center Left** button to vertically center and horizontally left-align the text in each cell.

e. Click the **Sort** button in the *Data* group. The *Sort* dialog box will open.

f. In the *My list has* area, click the **Header row** radio button. This will exempt the first row from being sorted with the rest of the text in the table.

g. In the *Sort by* area, select **Emergency Contact,** which is the first column of the table.

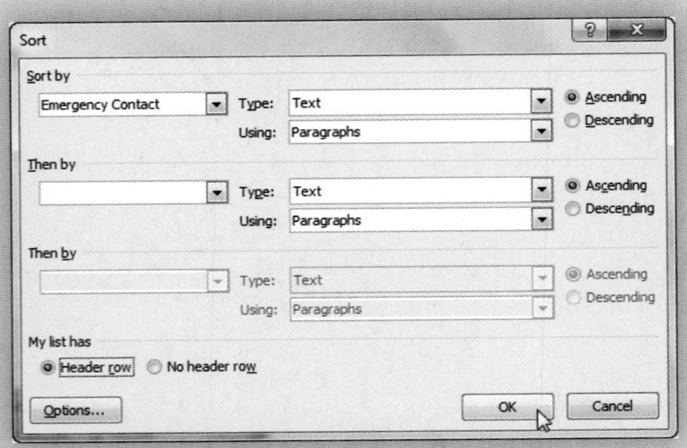

FIGURE WD 4.23

h. Choose **Text** as the *Type,* **Paragraphs** in the *Using* area, and **Ascending** as the sort order.

i. Click **OK** to apply the sort.

j. Click the **Design** tab under *Table Tools.*

k. In the *Table Styles* group, click the **Light Shading – Accent 1** style to apply this style to the table.

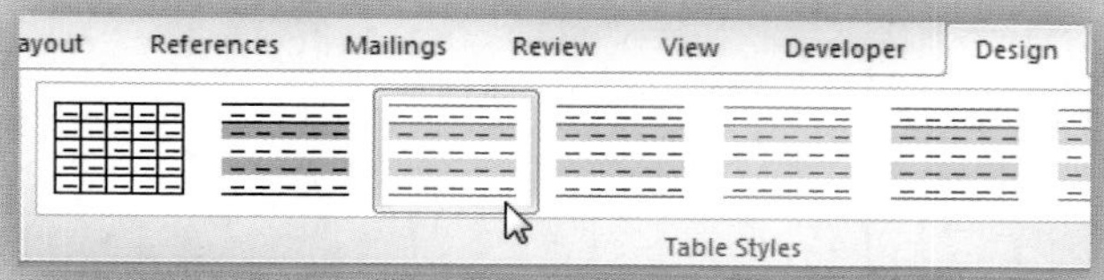

FIGURE WD 4.24

9. Convert existing text to a table.

a. Select the lines of text in the *Emergency Telephone Locations* section (do not include the section heading).

b. Press the **Decrease Indent** button to change the left indent to 0″.

c. On the *Insert* tab, in the *Tables* group, click the **Tables** button. Select **Convert Text to Table**. The *Convert Text to Table* dialog box will open. Word automatically detects the number of columns needed and uses tabs to separate text into cells. (Note: If the *Table size* area does not contain 3 columns and 10 rows, you have incorrectly selected the table.)

d. Click **OK** to convert the text to a table.

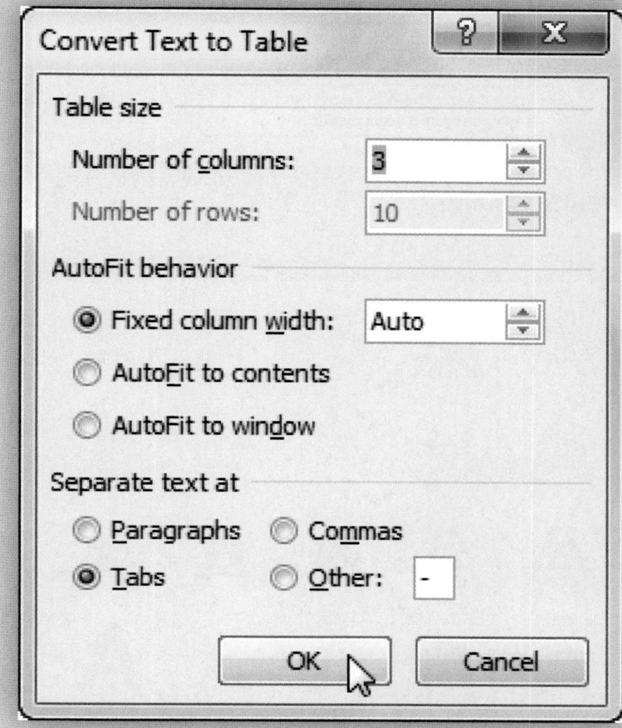

FIGURE WD 4.25

10. Insert a row, merge cells, and insert text in the table.

a. Click somewhere in the first row and click the **Insert Above** button in the *Rows & Columns* group.

b. Click in the first row of the table. On the *Layout* tab, in the *Table* group, click the **Select** button, and choose **Select Row.**

c. Click the **Merge Cells** button in the *Merge* group to merge the three columns in the first row into one column.

d. Enter the following information in the first row: `Blue Emergency Telephones`

11. Change the size of the columns and rows, sort text within the table, and apply a table Quick Style.

a. On the *Layout* tab, in the *Table* group, click the **Select** button and choose **Select Table** to select the entire table.

b. In the *Cell Size* group, click the **AutoFit** button and choose **AutoFit Contents**.

c. In the *Cell Size* group, change the *Height* to **0.2″**.

d. Select all of the rows of the table except for the first row.

e. In the *Alignment* group, click the **Align Center Left** button.

f. Click the **Sort** button in the *Data* group. The *Sort* dialog box will open.

g. In the *Sort by* area choose **Column 1,** and in the *Then by* area choose **Column 2.**

h. Click **OK** to apply the sort.

i. Select the entire table.

j. Click the **Design** tab under *Table Tools.*

k. In the *Table Styles* group, click the **Light Shading – Accent 1** style to apply this style to the table.

l. In the *Table Style Options* group, make sure that both the **Header Row** and **First Column** check boxes are checked.

m. Click in the first row of the table and horizontally center the text in this row.

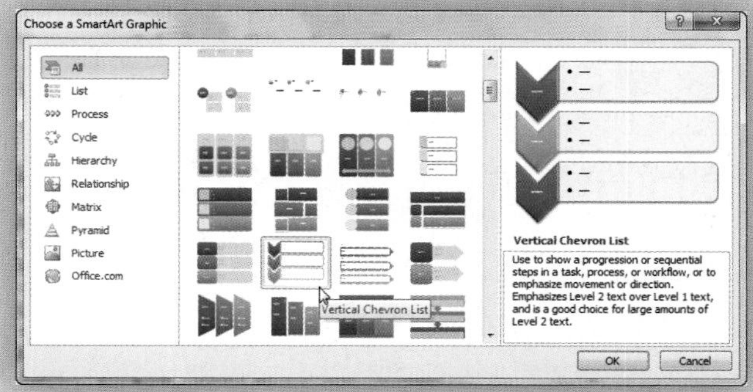

FIGURE WD 4.26

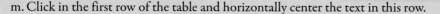

12. Add a SmartArt graphic to the document and resize it.

   a. Select the numbered list in the first section of the document and delete these lines of text.

   b. Click at the end of the first sentence in the first section and press **Enter** twice.

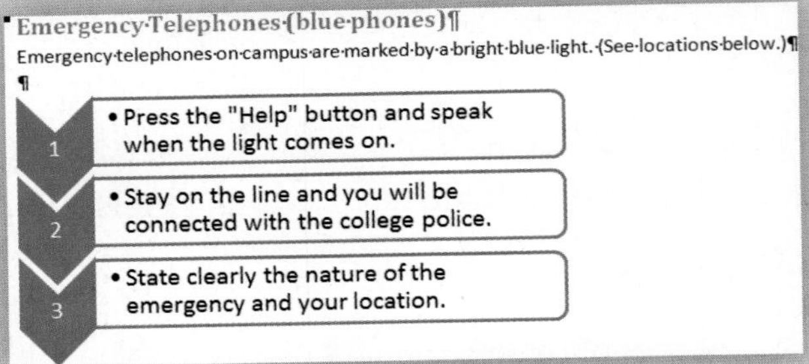

FIGURE WD 4.27

   c. On the *Insert* tab, in the *Illustrations* group, click the **SmartArt** button. The *Choose a SmartArt Graphic* dialog box will open.

   d. Scroll down the graphics options and select **Vertical Chevron List** and press **OK**.

   e. Type the text in the SmartArt graphic as shown in Figure WD 4.28. You will need to delete the extra bulleted *[Text]* field in each of the text areas by clicking it and pressing **Backspace**.

   f. After you have entered the numbers and text into the *SmartArt* graphic, click the outside edge of the graphic to select it.

   g. Click the **Format** tab under *SmartArt Tools*.

   h. In the *Size* group, change the *Height* to **2″** and the *Width* to **4″**.

13. Save and close the document.

FIGURE WD 4.28

Skill Review 4.2

In this project you will be editing the *Brochure_04* document from Placer Hills Real Estate.

1. Open the *Brochure_04* document.

2. Save this document as **[your initials]WD_SkillReview_4-2**.

3. Insert WordArt into the brochure and resize and reposition it.

   a. Select **Emma Cavalli** at the top of the first column.

   b. Click the **Insert** tab.

   c. In the *Text* group, click the **WordArt** button and select the **Fill – Blue, Accent1, Metal Bevel, Reflection** option (fifth item in the sixth row). The WordArt is inserted into the document.

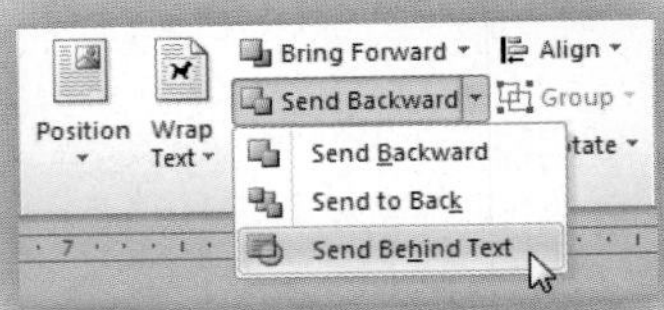

FIGURE WD 4.29

   d. On the *Format* tab, in the *Size* group, change the *Shape Height* to **0.9″** and the *Shape Width* to **4.5″**.

   e. In the *Arrange* group, click the small arrow to the right of the *Send Backward* button and choose **Send Behind Text**.

   f. Put your mouse pointer on the outside edge of the **WordArt** graphic and drag toward the upper-left corner of the document. Position the graphic so it is approximately 0.2″–0.3″ away from the top and left edge of the brochure.

FIGURE WD 4.30

4. Insert a clip art, arrange it in the brochure, and add a caption.

   a. Click at the end of the first column.

   b. On the *Insert* tab, in the *Illustrations* group, click the **Clip Art** button. The *Clip Art* pane will open at the right side of the Word window.

c. Type `House` in the *Search for:* box and click **Go.** *Clip Art* selections will appear below in the *Clip Art* pane.

d. On a clip art selection of your choice, click the small arrow to the right of the graphic and choose **Insert.** The clip art will be inserted into your brochure.

e. In the *Size* group, change the *Height* to **1″** and press **Enter.** The *Width* will automatically be adjusted to keep the graphic proportional.

f. Click on the **Wrap Text** button in the *Arrange* group and choose **Tight.**

g. Drag the graphic to the right of the last numbered item in the first column so the text wraps around the graphic. Make sure the text from the first column does not wrap to the second column.

h. With the clip art still selected, click on the **References** tab.

i. In the *Captions* group, click on the **Insert Caption** button. The *Caption* dialog box will open.

j. Click **OK** to add the caption.

k. Click in the caption below the graphic and delete the text.

l. In the caption area type: `Putting Your Needs First!`

m. Resize the caption by dragging the square sizing handle on the right edge to the right so all the text fits on one line.

n. Move the caption as necessary so it is centered below the clip art.

o. On the *Insert* tab, in the *Illustrations* group, click the **Clip Art** button to close the *Clip Art* pane.

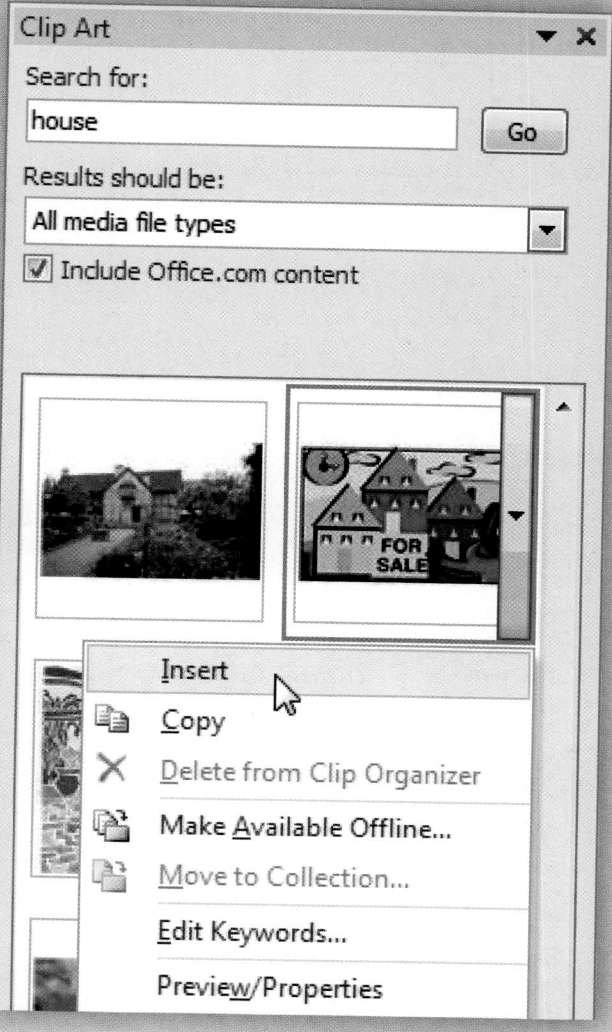

FIGURE WD 4.31

5. Add shapes to the brochure and adjust the fill color and arrangement.

a. Click at the end of the first quote in the second column (. . . *in just 3 days!*") and put in the line break (**Shift+Enter**). Do the same after the second quote.

b. Click the **Insert** tab.

c. In the *Illustrations* group, click the **Shapes** button and select the first option in the *Callouts* area (**Rectangular Callout**). A drawing cursor will appear (+).

d. Click and drag from the top left of the first quote to the bottom right and then release the mouse button. The callout will appear over the quote. You can resize the callout by dragging one of the sizing handles on the sides and corners.

e. On the *Format* tab, in the *Shape Styles* group, click on the **Shape Fill** button and choose a light blue shade.

f. In the *Arrange* group, click the small arrow to the right of the *Send Backward* button and choose **Send Behind Text.**

FIGURE WD 4.32

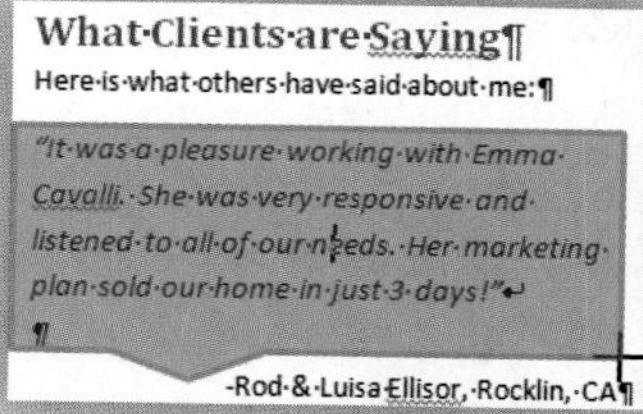

FIGURE WD 4.33

6. Use copy and paste to duplicate a callout. Copying a callout, rather than creating a new one, will allow for consistency in size and features.

a. Click on the callout you just created and press **Ctrl+C** to copy the callout.

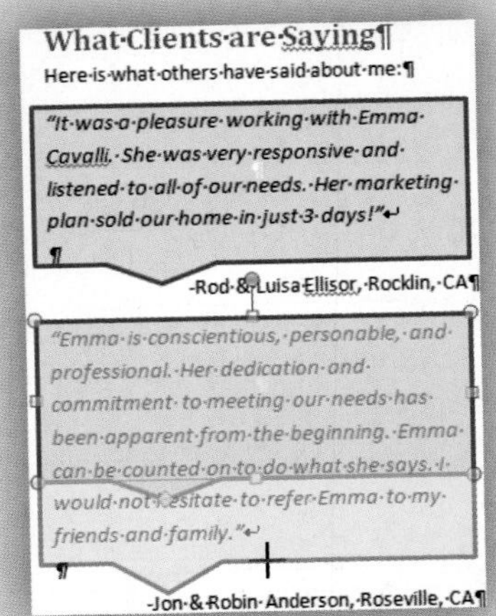

FIGURE WD 4.34

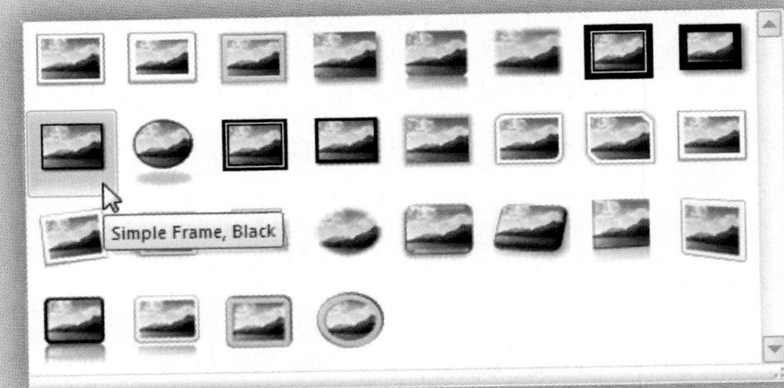

FIGURE WD 4.35

FIGURE WD 4.36

b. Press **Ctrl+V** to paste this item. The callout will be pasted slightly below and to the right of the original callout.

c. Use the left arrow key to drag the new callout so it aligns vertically with the first callout.

d. Use the down arrow key to move the new callout over the second quote.

e. Using the square resizing handle at the bottom of the callout, resize the callout to fit the second quote.

7. Convert text to a table and make formatting changes to the table.

a. Select all of the text in the *The Placer Hills Belief System* section (do not include the heading), and change the font size to **9 pt**. and the after paragraph spacing to **0 pt**.

b. On the *Insert* tab, in the *Tables* group, click the **Table** button and click **Convert Text to Table**. The *Convert Text to Table* dialog box will open.

c. Click **OK** to convert the text to a table.

d. On the *Design* tab in the *Styles* group, choose the **Colorful Grid – Accent 1** style.

e. In the *Table Style Options* group, deselect the **Header Row** check box.

f. On the *Layout* tab in the *Cell Size* group, click the **AutoFit** button and select **AutoFit Contents**.

g. In the *Cell Size* group, change the *Height* to **0.2″**.

h. In the *Alignment* group, click the **Align Center Left** button.

8. Insert a picture, apply a Quick Style, and reposition the picture.

a. Click at the end of the third column of the brochure.

b. On the *Insert* tab in the *Illustrations* group, click the **Picture** button. The *Insert Picture* dialog box will open.

c. Browse to your student data files, select the **PHRE logo** file, and click **Insert.**

d. In the *Arrange* group, click the **Wrap Text** button and choose **In Front of Text.**

e. In the *Picture Styles* group, click the **More** button and select the **Simple Frame, Black** Quick Style (first option in the second row).

f. With the logo still selected, in the *Arrange* group, click the **Position** button and select the bottom right with square wrapping option.

9. Save and close the document.

challenge yourself 1

In this project you will be editing the *Maximum Heart Rate_04* document from American River Cycling Club.

1. Open the *Maximum Heart Rate_04* document.

2. Save this document as `[your initials]WD_Challenge_4-3.`

3. Insert the **ARCC logo** picture into the document. This file is in your student data files.
4. Apply the **Center Shadow Rectangle** (fifth option in the second row; this location might vary depending on the size of your Word window) Quick Style to the logo.
5. Change the height and width of the logo to **120%** of its original size. Use the *Scale* option in the *Layout* dialog box.
6. Use **Square** text wrapping and reposition the logo so it appears in the top left corner of the page.
7. Select the predicted maximum heart rate formula after the first paragraph and insert the **Continuous Block Process** SmartArt (in the *Process* group). The formula will be deleted and the SmartArt inserted.
8. Type in the formula in the text boxes.
9. Change the height and width of the SmartArt graphic to **50%** of its original size.
10. Use the **Position** button to align the graphic at the top right with square text wrapping.

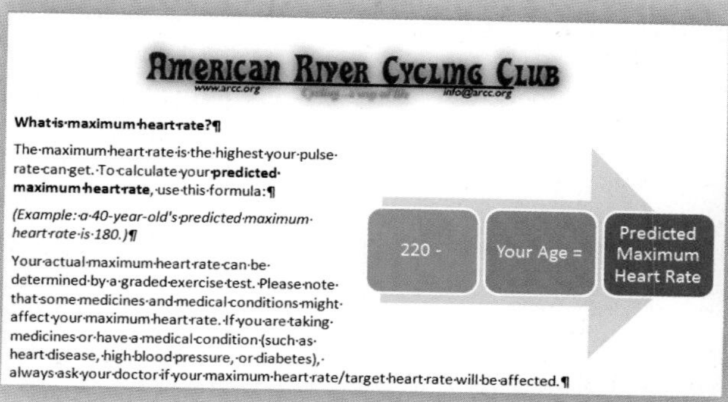

AMERICAN RIVER CYCLING CLUB
www.arcc.org info@arcc.org

What is maximum heart rate?¶

The maximum heart rate is the highest your pulse rate can get. To calculate your **predicted maximum heart rate**, use this formula:¶

(Example: a 40-year-old's predicted maximum heart rate is 180.)¶

Your actual maximum heart rate can be determined by a graded exercise test. Please note that some medicines and medical conditions might affect your maximum heart rate. If you are taking medicines or have a medical condition (such as heart disease, high blood pressure, or diabetes), always ask your doctor if your maximum heart rate/target heart rate will be affected.¶

FIGURE WD 4.37

11. Change the color of the graphic and apply a *SmartArt Style* of your choice.
12. Select all of the lines of tabbed text at the bottom of the document and convert it to a table.
13. Insert a row above the first row, merge all three columns in this row, and type in bold: `TARGET AND MAXIMUM HEART RATES`
14. Insert a row above the third row (age *25*) and type the following.

20	120-170	200

15. Insert a row after the last row of the table and type:

70	90-128	150

16. Use **AutoFit Window** to distribute the table between the margins.
17. Apply a table Quick Style of your choice. The **Header Row** option should be selected and the **First Column** option should be deselected.
18. Change the row height to **0.25″** and center all the text vertically and horizontally.
19. To the right of the first paragraph in the *Target Heart Rate* section, insert a clip art of a heart.
20. Change the size of the graphic to approximately **1″**, use **Tight** wrapping, and position the graphic to the right of the first paragraph in this section.
21. Apply a *Picture Style* of your choice to this graphic.
22. Insert a caption on the clip art graphic and type: `Know your target heart rate`
23. The document should fit on one page. Adjust the size and/or position of the graphics as necessary.
24. Save and close the document.

challenge yourself **2**

In this project you will be editing the *Buyer Escrow Checklist_04* document from Placer Hills Real Estate.

1. Open the *Buyer Escrow Checklist_04* document.
2. Save this document as `[your initials]WD_Challenge_4-4`.
3. Apply the **Title** style to the title of the document.
4. Select the five lines of text below the title and change the tab to a **5″** right tab with a solid underline leader.
5. To the right of these lines, insert a Clip Art of a check mark.
6. Resize the graphic so it is approximately **1.5″** and apply a *Picture Style* of your choice.
7. Apply **Tight** text wrapping and position the graphic to the right of these lines.
8. Insert the **PHRE logo** picture.
9. Apply the **Behind Text** text wrapping and position it in the upper-right corner of the document. Make sure the horizontal bottom border from the title is visible below the graphic.
10. Select the lines of text beginning with *Task* through *Verify Preliminary Report with Lender,* and convert this selected text to a table.
11. Insert a column to the right of the first column in the table and type `Initials` in the first row of this column.
12. Insert a column between the existing columns in the table and type `Date Completed` in the first row of this new column (second column).
13. Insert a row above the *Verify Preliminary Report with Buyer* and type `Disclosure Statement to Buyer` in the first column of this new row.
14. Change the row height of the entire table to **0.4″** and align all text vertically centered and left-aligned.
15. Select all of the text in the first column except the first row and apply an open square bullet. Decrease the indent of these bulleted items.
16. **AutoFit** the contents of the table.
17. Use the *Properties* dialog box to center the entire table horizontally (not the text, but the entire table.
18. Select the entire table and use the *Borders and Shading* dialog box to apply a **2¼ pt. Grid** border to the table.
19. On the first row of the table, apply a **2¼ pt**. bottom border and a light gray shading.
20. Insert a column to the right of the last column in the table and type `Notes` in the first row of this column.
21. Change the text alignment of this column so it is consistent with the rest of the table.
22. Change the width of this, the fourth column, to **1.5″**.
23. Change the text alignment in the first row so all text is centered vertically and horizontally.
24. This document should fit on one page.
25. Save and close the document.

on your own

In this project you will be creating a training calendar for the American River Cycling Club.

1. Open a new Word document.
2. Save this document as `[your initials]WD_OnYourOwn_4-5`.
3. Change the orientation to **Landscape** and change the margins to use the **Moderate** setting.
4. Insert a table with seven columns and six rows.
5. In the first row type the days of the week beginning with Sunday.
6. In the second through sixth rows type the number for each day of the month.
7. Change widths of all of the columns to **1.3"**.
8. Change the row height of the first row to **0.3"**.
9. Change the row height of rows 2–6 to **0.9"**.
10. Insert a row above the first row, merge all of the cells in this row, and type the current month and year.
11. Change the font size to **48 pt., bold, all caps,** and **centered.**
12. Select the second row and change the text to **14 pt., bold,** and **small caps,** and center the text vertically and horizontally.
13. Select the remaining rows and change the text to **10 pt**. and **bold**, and align the numbers in the upper right of each cell.
14. Horizontally center the entire table on the page (not the text, but the entire table).
15. Apply a Quick Style to the table. Make changes to the *Table Style Options* as necessary.
16. Insert shapes on the calendar and insert text into the shapes.
    a. Insert a shape of your choice on the first Monday of the month. Draw it large enough so it takes up most of the cell and leaves the date visible.
    b. Right-click on the shape and choose **Add Text** and type: `Morning Ride 6-8 a.m.`
    c. Change the font, size, line spacing, and paragraph spacing on the text as necessary. Use a line break (*Shift+Enter*) to wrap text if needed.
    d. Change the shape style, fill, outline, and/or effects to arrange the graphic and text attractively.
    e. Copy this shape and text and paste it on the other Mondays in the month and align to maintain consistency.
17. Use the steps above to create a shape and text on each Wednesday of the month. Use a different shape and add the following text: `River Ride 6-8 p.m.`
18. Use the steps above to create a shape and text on each Friday of the month. Use a different shape and add the following text: `Time Trial 5-6 p.m.`
19. Use the steps above to create a shape and text on each Saturday of the month. Use a different shape and add the following text: `Hilly Ride 8-11 a.m.`
20. Insert WordArt of your choice and type: `American River Cycling Club`. Customize using *WordArt Styles* and align at the top left above the table. (Note: you might have to click below the table to insert items in your document).
21. Insert a clip art of a bicycle and align at the upper right above the table. Resize and arrange as necessary to fit in the upper left. Customize using *Picture Styles.*

22. Insert a SmartArt of your choice (one with three boxes aligned horizontally) and type: `EAT`, `SLEEP`, and `RIDE!` (one word in each box). Center the SmartArt below the table. Resize and arrange as necessary to fit below the table. Customize using *Picture Styles.*
23. The entire document should fit on one page. Make any necessary adjustments to arrange the document attractively.
24. Save and close the document.

fix it

In this project you will be editing the *Vaccination Schedule_04* document from Courtyard Medical Plaza.

1. Open the *Vaccination Schedule_04* document.
2. Save this document as **`[your initials]WD_FixIt_4-6`.**
3. Using the Word features in the chapter, you will be editing and customizing this document to make a professional and readable one-page document.
4. Include in the table the vaccination information that is below the table.
5. A couple of the cells in the table have information about two vaccinations; edit the table so that each vaccination is in a separate row.
6. Delete any extra *Enters* in the table.
7. Sort the table by *Name of Vaccine.*
8. Insert a row at the top of the document and type `RECOMMENDED VACCINATION SCHEDULE` as the title of the table.
9. Apply a table Quick Style and adjust the *Table Style Options* as necessary.
10. Adjust column widths, row height, borders, shading, and text alignment as necessary.
11. Apply the Quick Style to the title of the document.
12. Insert the **CMP logo** picture into the document and position at the upper left of the document. Use text wrapping as needed and/or adjust the paragraph spacing on the title so the title does not wrap around the company logo.
13. Insert a vaccination clip art to the right of the first two paragraphs of the document. Adjust size and text wrapping as needed. Customize using *Picture Styles.*
14. Insert an appropriate caption on the clip art graphic.
15. Arrange the document so all of the information fits on one page making use of the entire page. Make changes to table row height and graphic(s) size, alignment, and text wrapping as needed to produce a professional-looking document.
16. Save and close the document.

chapter 5
Working with References and Mailings

In this chapter, you will learn the following skills:

- **Insert and update table of contents, footnotes, and endnotes**
- **Use a report reference style and create citations and a bibliography**
- **Mark words in a document to create an index**
- **Customize a print job**
- **Use mail merge to create mailings, labels, and envelopes**

skills

introduction

In this chapter, you will be introduced to long reports and the Word features that help users create properly formatted reports, which include table of contents, footnotes and endnotes, reference style, citations, bibliography, and index. You will also be shown how to use Word's mail merge feature to create mailings, envelopes, and labels.

5.1 Inserting a Table of Contents

If you have a long document with many sections and headings, it is a good idea to include a **table of contents** at the beginning of the document. A table of contents lists the topics and associated page numbers, so your reader can easily locate information. The table of contents is created from heading styles in the document. If you want your document's section titles to display in the table of contents, be sure to apply heading styles to that text.

To insert a table of contents:

1. Verify the insertion point is at the beginning of the document.
2. Click the **References** tab.
3. In the *Table of Contents* group, click the **Table of Contents** button and select an option from the gallery.
4. The table of contents is added to the beginning of the document.

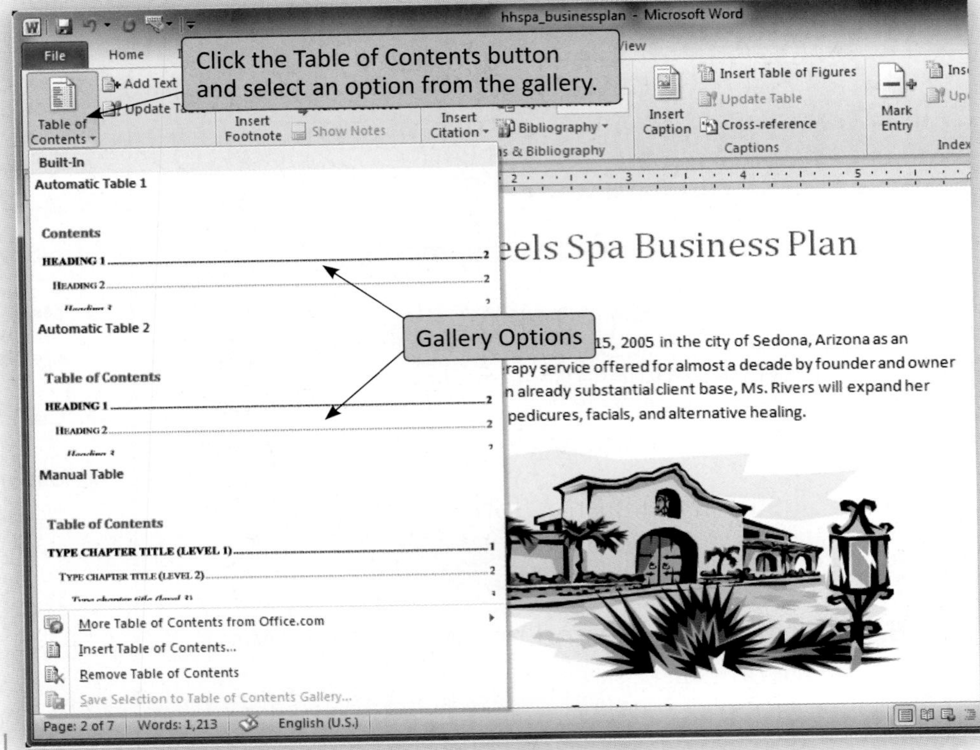

FIGURE WD 5.1

If you make changes to your document after you have inserted a table of contents, you should be sure to update the table of contents to keep the information accurate. To update the table of contents, click the **Update Table** button Update Table in the *Table of Contents* group. You can also update the table of contents by clicking on the table of contents and clicking the **Update Table. . .** button at the top of the control.

tips & tricks

To remove a table of contents, click the **Table of Contents** button and select **Remove Table of Contents** at the bottom of the gallery.

try this

If you want to add your own customized table of contents, click **Insert Table of Contents . . .** at the bottom of the gallery. The *Table of Contents* dialog box opens. Here you can choose different options for the table of contents including tab leaders, formats, and page number formatting.

tell me more

A table of contents is typically based on heading styles, but you can create a table of contents based on custom styles or from marked entries.

A table of contents is a building block that is added to the document. When you select the building block, extra controls appear at the top including the *Table of Contents* and the *Update Table . . .* buttons.

5.2 Inserting Footnotes and Endnotes

Footnotes and **endnotes** provide your reader with further information on a topic in a document. They are often used for source references. Footnotes and endnotes are comprised of two parts: a **reference mark** (a superscript character placed next to the text) and the associated text. Footnotes appear at the bottom of a page, whereas endnotes are placed at the end of the document.

To insert a footnote:

1. Place your cursor where you want the footnote to appear.
2. Click the **References** tab.
3. In the *Footnotes* group, click the **Insert Footnote** button.
4. The superscript number is added next to the text and the cursor is moved to the footnote area at the bottom of the page.
5. Type the text for your footnote. When you are finished, return to your document by clicking anywhere in the main document area.

To insert an endnote:

1. Place your cursor where you want the endnote to appear.
2. Click the **References** tab.
3. In the *Footnotes* group, click the **Insert Endnote** button.
4. The superscript number is added next to the text and the cursor is moved the endnote area at the end of the document.
5. Type the text for your endnote.

To convert footnotes to endnotes or vice versa, click the **dialog launcher** in the *Footnotes* group. In the *Footnote and Endnote* dialog box, click the **Convert. . .** button, choose an option, and click **OK.**

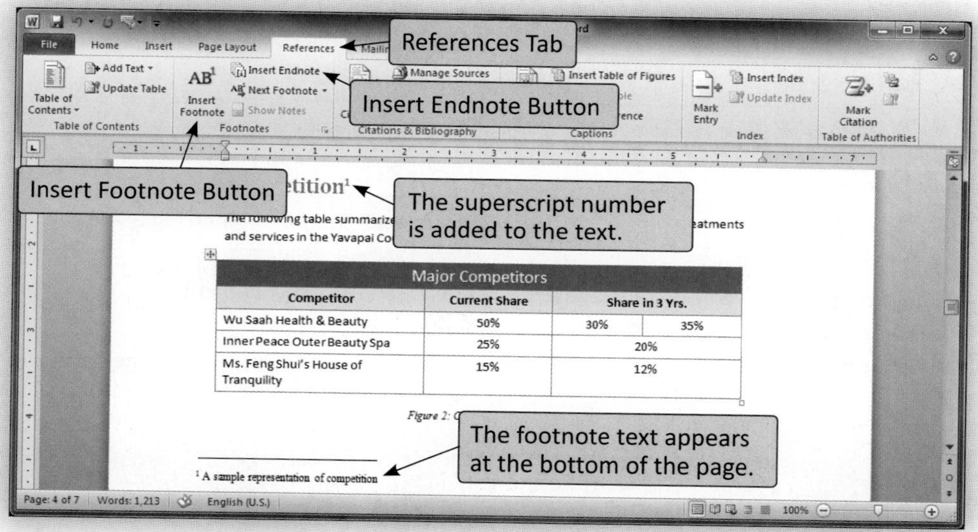

References Tab
Insert Endnote Button
Insert Footnote Button
The superscript number is added to the text.
The footnote text appears at the bottom of the page.

FIGURE WD 5.2

tips & tricks

- Click the **Next Footnote** button to navigate to the next footnote in the document. Click the arrow next to the **Next Footnote** button to display a menu allowing you to navigate to previous footnotes and between endnotes in the document.
- To delete a footnote, you must first select the reference mark in the document and press **Delete** on the keyboard. If you select and delete the text of the footnote, the reference mark will remain and the footnote will not be removed from the document.

tell me more

Once you have inserted and formatted your first footnote or endnote, Word automatically numbers all subsequent notes in your document for you. If you add a new footnote between two existing footnotes, Word will renumber all the footnotes in the document, keeping them in sequential order.

try this

To insert a footnote, you can also click the **dialog launcher** in the *Footnotes* group. In the *Footnote and Endnote* dialog box, verify that the **Footnote** radio button is selected and click **Insert.**

5.3 Selecting a Reference Style

A **reference style** is a set of rules used to display references in a bibliography. These rules include the order of information, when and how punctuation is used, and the use of character formatting, such as italics and bold. The two most common reference styles in use today are *APA* and *Chicago;* however, there are a number of other reference styles you can choose from. It is important that you use the correct reference style for the subject of your document. The following table lists the available styles in Word and when they are most commonly used:

STYLE ABBREVIATION	FULL NAME	PURPOSE
APA Fifth Edition	American Psychological Association	Education, psychology, and social sciences
Chicago Fifteenth Edition	*The Chicago Manual of Style*	Books, magazines, and newspapers
GB7714 2005	NA	Used in China
GOST – Name Sort	Russian State Standard	Used in Russia
GOST – Title Sort	Russian State Standard	Used in Russia
ISO 690 – First Element and Date	International Standards Organization	Patents and industry (both print and nonprint works)
ISO 690 – Numerical Reference	International Standards Organization	Patents and industry (both print and nonprint works)
MLA Sixth Edition	Modern Language Association	Arts and humanities
SIST02	NA	Used in Asia
Turabian Sixth Edition	Turabian	All subjects (designed for college students)

When creating a bibliography, it is important to use a consistent reference style for your citations. Word makes this easy by allowing you to set the reference style for the entire document at once.

To change the reference style for a document:

1. Click the **References** tab.
2. In the *Citations & Bibliography* group, click the arrow next to *Style:* and select a style from the list.

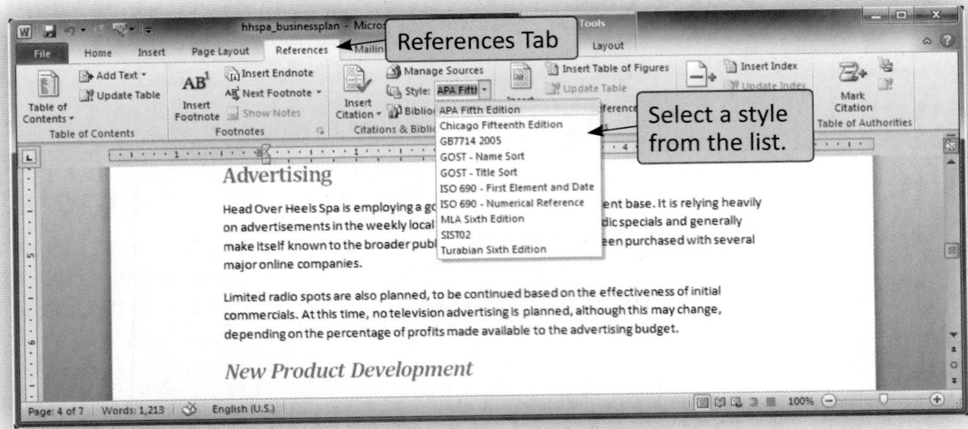

FIGURE WD 5.3

tips & tricks

When you change the reference style for a document, all citations are automatically updated to use the new style.

tell me more

To see a preview of the source style, click the **Manage Sources** button in the *Citations & Bibliography* group. The preview box at the bottom of the *Manage Sources* dialog box shows how the selected reference will appear as a citation and in the bibliography.

5.4 Adding Citations to Documents

When you use materials in a document from other sources, such as a book or a journal article, you need to give credit to the original source material. A **citation** is a reference to such source material. Citations include information such as the author, title, publisher, and the publish date.

To add a citation to a document, you must first create the source:

1. Place the cursor where you want to add the citation.
2. Click the **References** tab.
3. In the *Citations & Bibliography* group, click the **Insert Citation** button and select **Add New Source. . .**
4. In the *Create Source* dialog box, click the arrow next to *Type of Source* and select an option.
5. In the *Author* box, type the name of the author.
6. In the *Title* box, type the title of the book or article.
7. In the *Year* box, type the year the book or article was published.
8. Add other information about the source to the appropriate fields.
9. When you are finished, click **OK** to add the citation to the document.

After you have added a new source, it appears on the **Insert Citation** menu. To add the same source to another part of the document, click the **Insert Citation** button and select the source for the citation.

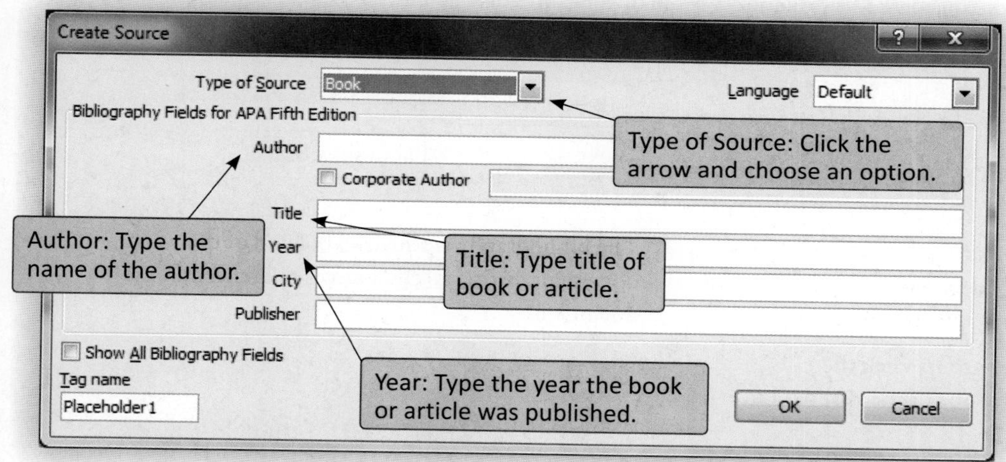

FIGURE WD 5.4

tips & tricks

When you add a citation, the citation appears inside parentheses at the place where you inserted it. A citation includes basic information from the source including the author, year, title, and pages. A bibliography lists all the citations in a document, and includes more of the source information than the citation.

tell me more

Citations appear in the document as a control. When you click the control, you will see an arrow on the right side. Click the arrow to display a menu for editing the source and the citation. In the *Edit Source* dialog box, you can change the information you added when you created the source. In the *Edit Citation* dialog box, you can change information specific to the citation, such as page numbers.

from the perspective of . . .

PARENT

My child uses word processing software to complete assignments and write simple reports. She even enjoys adding interesting clip art to make her work look good while having fun.

5.5 Creating a Bibliography

A **bibliography** is a compiled list of sources you referenced in your document. Typically, bibliographies appear at the end of a document and list all the sources you marked throughout the document. Microsoft Word 2010 comes with a number of prebuilt bibliography building blocks for you to use. When you select one of these building blocks, Word will search the document and compile all the sources from your document and format them according to the style you chose.

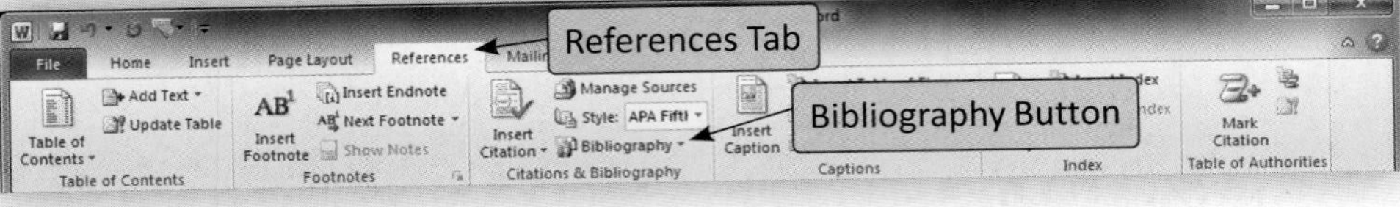

FIGURE WD 5.5

To add a bibliography to a document:

1. Place the cursor at the end of the document.
2. Click the **References** tab.
3. In the *Citations & Bibliography* group, click the **Bibliography** button and select one of the bibliography building blocks.
4. The bibliography is added to the end of the document, listing all the sources referenced in the document.

Bibliography

Rockland Falls Spa v. Ava Codas, IHAV-ENOC-LUE4 (United States Supreme Court May 21, 2009).

Chester, M. (2010). *Avoiding the Pedi-Scare: Health Code Do's and Don'ts.*

Chu, I. W. (2010). *Get Your Ohm On.* St. Louis: McGraw-Hill.

D.U. Tensionmeiser, M. (2009). The Case for Homeopathic Remedies.

Gemman, H. (2009). *How to Stand Out in the Booming Health Spa Industry.* Oklahoma City: McGraw-Hill.

Hammerhead, B. (2010). *Alternative Healing Methods Lead to Increased Wellness.* Detroit: McGraw-Hill.

Larson, K. D., Wild, J. J., & Chiappetta, B. (2007). *Fundamental Accounting Principles.* Irwin/McGraw-Hill.

Mallor, J. P., Barnes, A. J., Bowers, T., Phillips, M. J., & Langvardt, A. W. (2010). *Business Law and the Regulatory Environment: Concepts and Cases.* Irwin/McGraw-Hill.

Thompson, R., & Cats-Baril, W. (2008). *Future Trends in Spa Therapies and Meditation.* McGraw-Hill/Irwin.

FIGURE WD 5.6

tell me **more**

The bibliography building blocks include a formatted header for your bibliography. You can choose to have the section titled *Bibliography* or *Works Cited.*

try **this**

To add a simple bibliography, click the **Insert Bibliography** command at the bottom of the *Bibliography* gallery.

from the perspective of . . .

WEDDING CONSULTANT

Using mail merge, I can advertise my business with customized personal letters and send them to my customers. Word processing software makes creating wedding invitations easy too, and I can use mail merge to create the matching envelopes!

5.6 Marking Entries for an Index

When creating long documents, you may want to add an index to the document to help your readers quickly locate specific information. To create an index you must first mark the topics you want to include, and then create the index. When formatting marks are hidden, marked entries look no different from other text in the document. However, when the index is created, Word finds all the marked entries and adds them to the index.

To mark entries:

1. Select the word you want to add to the index.
2. Click the **References** tab.
3. In the *Index* group, click the **Mark Entry** button.
4. The word appears in the *Main entry:* box.
5. Click the **Mark** button to mark the entry.
6. Click the **Close** button to close the *Mark Index Entry* dialog box.

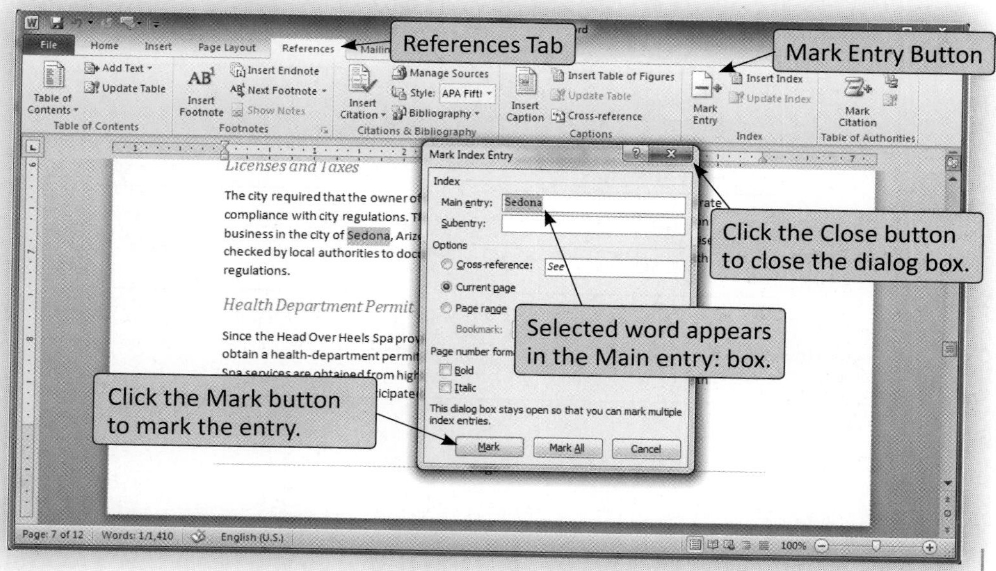

FIGURE WD 5.7

tips & tricks

After you mark an entry, Word adds the *XE (Index Entry)* formatting mark to the word and displays all formatting marks in the document, so you can double-check your page layout. However, formatting marks should be hidden before you create and insert the index to make it easier to view your final document.

tell me more

To add a reference to every instance of a word to the index, click the **Mark All** button in the *Mark Index Entry* dialog box.

try this

To open the *Mark Index Entry* dialog box, you can also click the **Insert Index** button in the *Index* group. In the *Index* dialog box, click the **Mark Entry . . .** button.

5.7 Creating an Index

An **index** is a list of topics and associated page numbers that typically appears at the end of a document. Adding an index to your document can help your readers find information quickly.

An index entry can reference a single word, a phrase, or a topic spanning several pages. You can also add cross-references to your index.

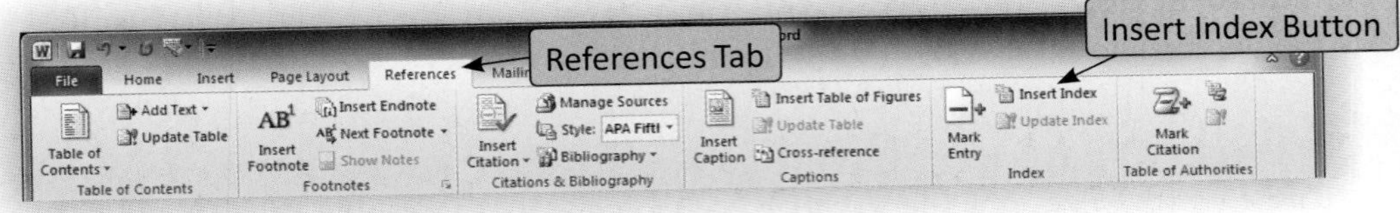

FIGURE WD 5.8

To add an index to a document:

1. Place the cursor at the end of the document.
2. Click the **References** button.
3. In the *Index* group, click the **Insert Index** button.
4. The *Index* dialog box opens.
5. Click the **Formats:** arrow and select a format.
6. Modify the other options until the preview looks the way you want.
7. Click **OK** to insert the index into your document.

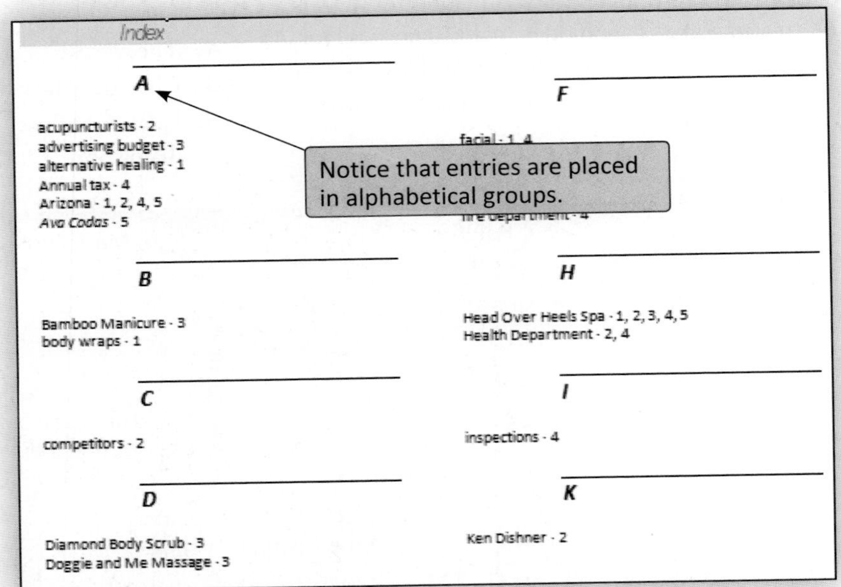

FIGURE WD 5.9

tips & tricks

To add new entries to an index, do not type directly in the index. Instead, mark the entries and then update the index. Any entries typed directly into the index will be deleted when the index is updated. To update an index, first select the index and then click the **Update Index** button in the *Index* group.

tell me **more**

A cross-reference is an index entry that refers to another entry in the index rather than to a page in the document. Cross-references are often used to direct readers from an uncommon entry to a more frequently used one.

5.8 Customizing a Print Job

The default *Print* command in Word prints one copy of the entire document. But what if you only want to print one section of your document or print five copies of your document at once? From the *Print* tab in Backstage view, you can customize how your document prints, including changing the number of copies and specifying which pages to print.

To modify print settings from Backstage view:

1. Click the **File** tab.
2. Click **Print.**
3. Verify that the correct printer name is displayed in the *Printer* section.
4. In the *Copies:* box, enter the number of copies you want to print.
5. In the *Pages:* box, type the range of pages you want to print.
6. Click **Print.**

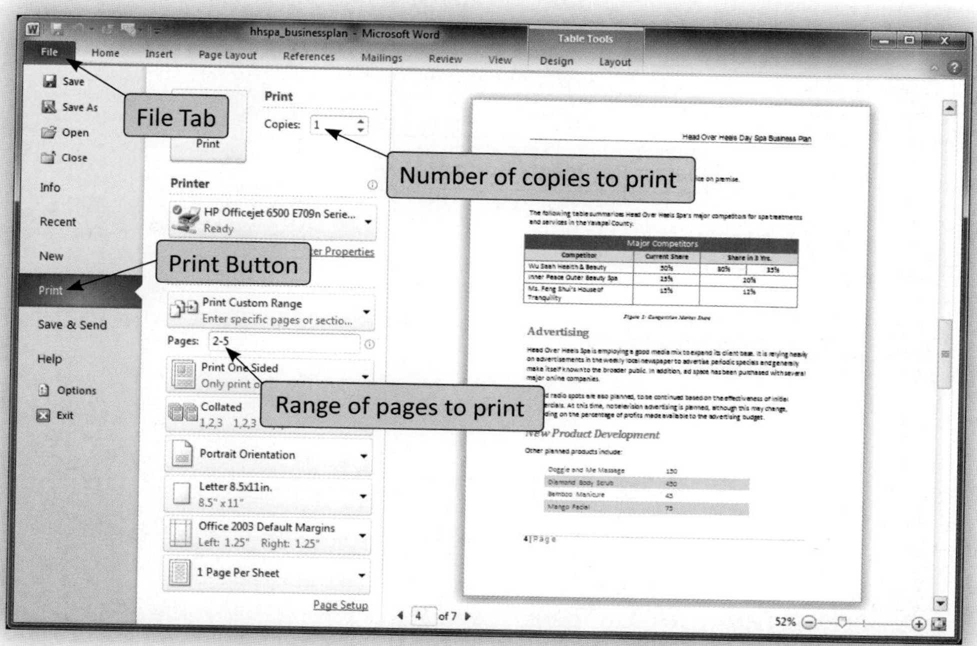

FIGURE WD 5.10

tips & tricks

Past versions of Microsoft Word included a *Print Preview* command that allowed you to see how your document would display on the printed page before printing the document. In Word 2010, *Print Preview* has been integrated into the *Print* tab in Backstage view. As you adjust the settings for printing your document, Word displays a live preview on the right side of the screen of how the document will look when printed.

tell me **more**

Use a hyphen to print a range of pages. Use a comma between page numbers to print individual pages. For example, if you type `1-5`, page 1 through page 5 will print. If you type `1,5`, page 1 and page 5 will print, but not pages 2, 3, and 4.

try **this**

To display the *Print* tab in Backstage view, you can also press Ctrl + P on the keyboard.

5.9 Starting a Mail Merge

Suppose you have a letter you want to send out to 20 recipients, but you want each person's name to appear on the letter, giving it a more personal touch. You could write the letter and save 20 versions—one for each recipient—but this is time-consuming and cumbersome. In Word, you can take a list of names and addresses and merge them with a standard document, creating a personalized document for each name on your list. This process is called a **mail merge**.

Before you can create a mail merge, you must first select a main document and select recipients. To set up the main document and select recipients:

1. Click the **Mailings** tab.
2. In the *Start Mail Merge* group, click the **Start Mail Merge** button and select **Letters.**
3. Click the **Select Recipients** button and select **Use Existing List . . .**
4. In the *Select Data Source* dialog box, select a data source and click **Open.**

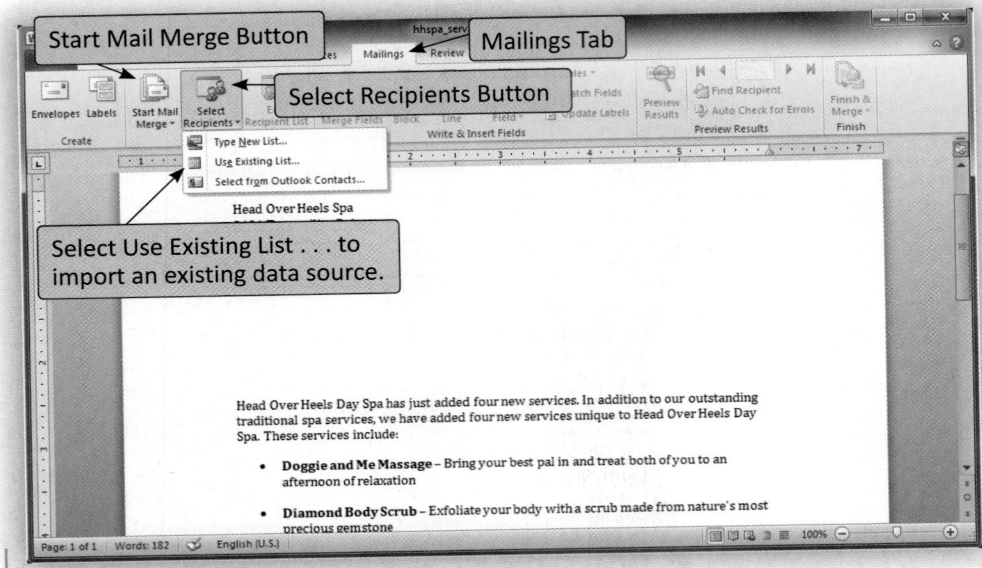

FIGURE WD 5.11

tips & tricks

Use mail merge to automatically create labels, envelopes, directories, and e-mails, as well as form letters.

tell me more

The recipients list for a mail merge can be entered in manually by selecting **Create New List. . .** from the *Select Recipients* menu or can be imported from the list of contacts from Microsoft Outlook. When you import the list of contacts from Outlook, you then have the option to remove any contacts you do not want to include in the merge.

try this

You can also create a mail merge using the *Mail Merge Wizard,* which will take you through creating the mail merge step by step. To display the *Mail Merge Wizard,* click the **Start Mail Merge** button and select **Step by Step Mail Merge Wizard . . .**

5.10 Inserting Fields and Writing the Mail Merge Document

The main document of a mail merge contains the text and merge fields, which appear on every version of the merged document. **Merge fields** are placeholders that insert specific data from the recipients list you created. You can choose to add address blocks, greeting lines, and specific fields such as first names, last names, and e-mail addresses.

The three basic types of merge fields are

Address Block—inserts a merge field with the name and address of the recipient.

Greeting Line—inserts a field with a greeting and the recipient's name.

Merge Fields—allows you to insert merge fields based on your data source, such as first names, last names, addresses, phone numbers, and e-mail addresses.

To add an address block merge field:

1. Click in the document where you want the merge field to appear.
2. On the *Mailings* tab, in the *Write & Insert Fields* group, click the **Address Block** button.
3. In the *Insert Address Block* dialog box, make any changes to the display and click **OK.**

To add a greeting line merge field:

1. Click in the document where you want the merge field to appear.
2. On the *Mailings* tab, in the *Write & Insert Fields* group, click the **Greeting Line** button.
3. In the *Insert Greeting Line* dialog box, make any changes to the display and click **OK.**

To add individual merge fields:

1. Click in the document where you want the merge field to appear.
2. Click the **Insert Merge Field** button and select an option to insert.

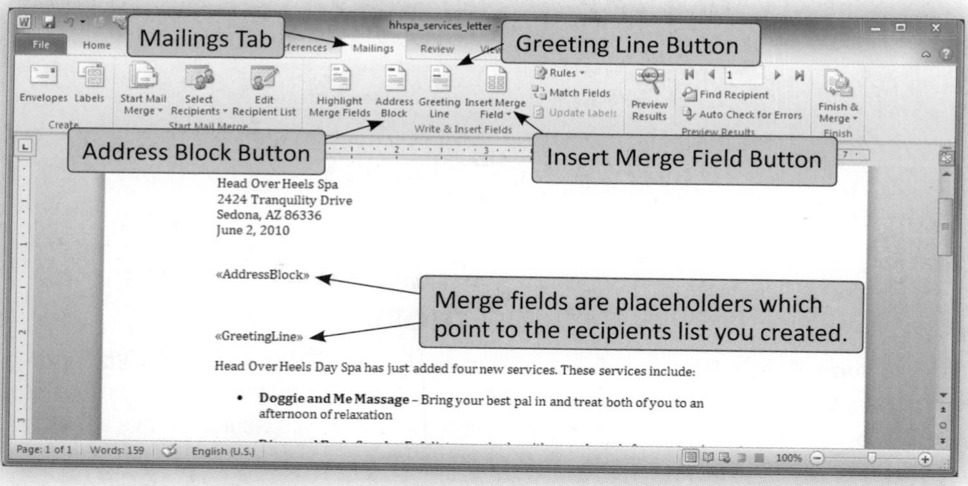

FIGURE WD 5.12

tips & tricks

Both the *Insert Address Block* and the *Insert Greeting Line* dialog boxes include a preview of how the merge fields will display in the document. Click the next and previous buttons to navigate through the list of recipients to see how each one will display before finalizing your choices.

5.11 Previewing and Finishing the Mail Merge

Before you complete the mail merge and print your documents, it is a good idea to review each document created in the merge.

To preview the mail merge:

1. In the *Preview Results* group, click the **Preview Results** button.
2. Click the **Next Record** and **Previous Record** buttons to navigate among different documents.

After you have previewed the mail merge, the last step is to finish the merge by printing the documents.

To print the documents in the mail merge:

1. In the *Finish* group, click the **Finish & Merge** button and select **Print Documents . . .**
2. In the *Merge to Printer* dialog box, click **OK.**

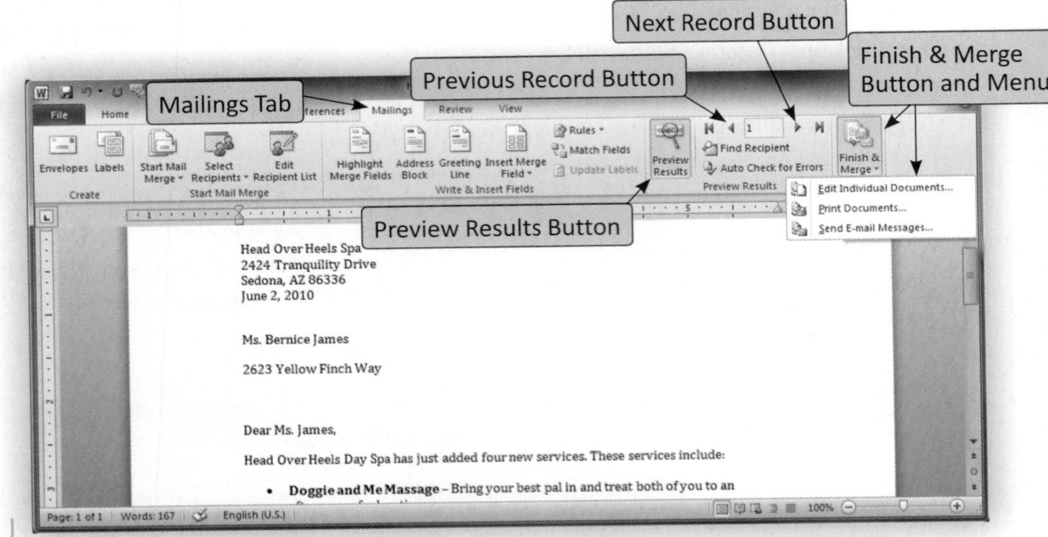

FIGURE WD 5.13

tips & tricks

Before you finish the merge, click the **Auto Check for Errors** button to review your documents for errors.

tell me more

If you want to modify letters individually, click **Edit individual letters . . .** Then, in the *Merge to New Document* dialog box, select the records you want to change and click **OK.** Word opens a new document based on the selected records. Make any changes you want, and then print or save the document just as you would any other file.

If you want to send the document via e-mail, click **Send E-mail Messages . . .** Enter the subject line and mail format. Select the recipients you want to send the document to and click **OK.**

5.12 Creating Envelopes and Labels

With Word you can create an envelope and print it without leaving the document you are working on. Word's preset formats take care of the measuring and layout for you.

To create and print an envelope:

1. Click the **Mailings** tab.
2. In the *Create* group, click the **Envelopes** button.
3. Type the address of the person you are sending the document to in the *Delivery address:* text box.
4. Type your address in the *Return address:* text box.
5. Click the **Options. . .** button.
6. Click the **Envelope size:** arrow and select an envelope size.
7. Click **OK** in the *Envelope Options* dialog box.
8. Click the **Print** button in the *Envelopes and Labels* dialog box.

Word also comes with a number of preset options for creating mailing labels. To create and print labels, in the *Create* group, click the **Labels** button. From the *Labels* tab, you can create a single label or an entire sheet of labels. You can also choose to send the labels directly to the printer or create a new document of labels to save and print whenever you need them.

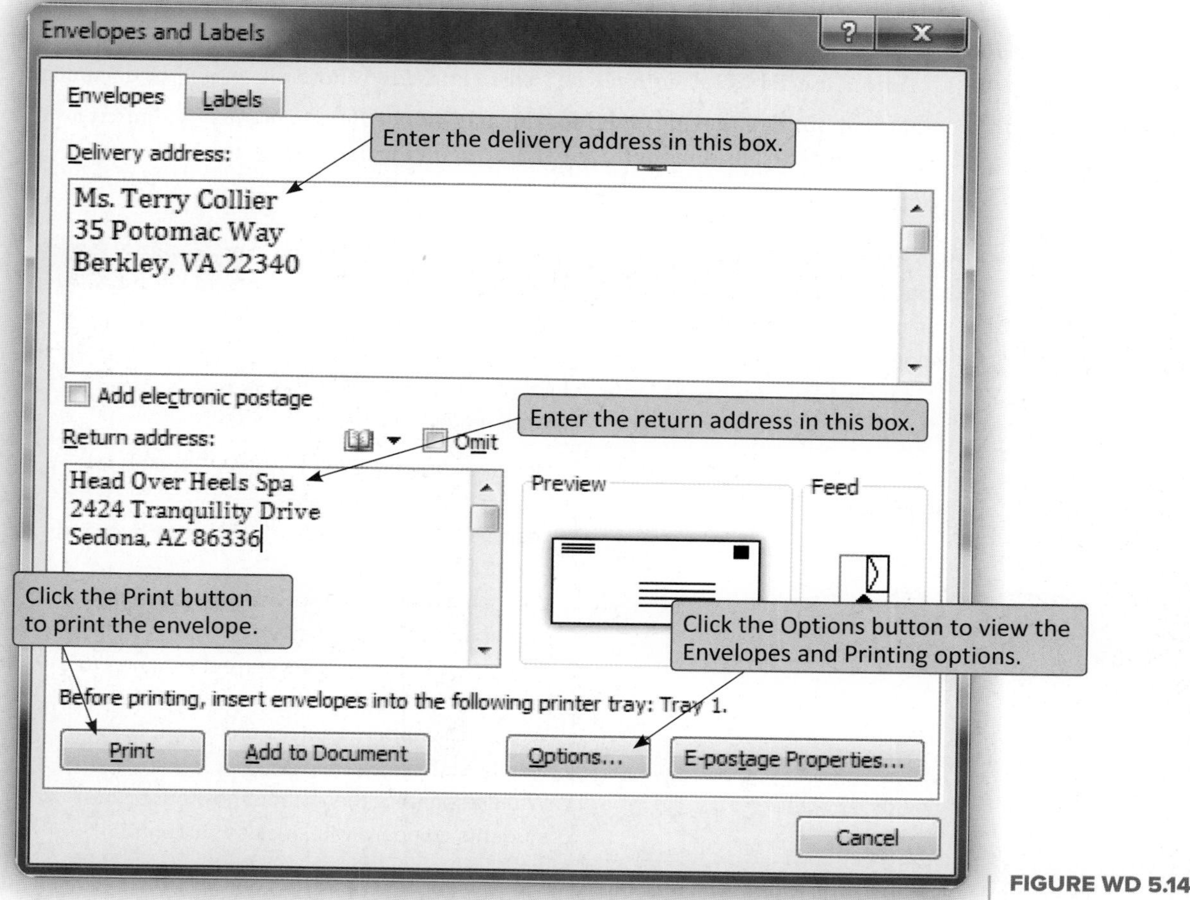

FIGURE WD 5.14

tips & tricks

You may not need to type an address. When you open the *Envelopes and Labels* dialog box, Word searches your document for an address. If it finds what looks like an address, it will copy it directly into the dialog box for you. Of course, you can always change this if it's not what you need.

try this

To open the *Envelopes and Labels* dialog box, you can also click the **Labels** button, and then click the **Envelopes** tab to create an envelope.

projects

Skill Review 5.1

In this project you will be editing the *Distance Education Plan_05* document from Sierra Pacific Community College District.

1. Open Microsoft Word 2010.
2. Open the *Distance Education Plan_05* document.
3. Save this document as `[your initials]WD_SkillReview_5-1.`
4. Apply the **Title** style to the title of the report.
5. Insert a *Table of Contents* at the beginning of the document.
   a. Move to the top of the document and click the **References** tab.
   b. Click the **Table of Contents** button in the *Table of Contents* group and select **Automatic Table 2.** The *Table of Contents* is inserted above the title of the document.
   c. Click in front of the title of the document (*Distance Education Plan*) and insert a **page break** to position the *Table of Contents* on the first page by itself.
6. Apply the **Heading 3** style to the following headings.

SECTION	APPLY HEADING 3 STYLE
Definition of Distance Education Modes	Online course Hybrid course Television or Tele-Web course Web-Enhanced course
Distance Education Offerings and Programs	How are Courses and Programs Selected for Distance Education Delivery? Leadership/Management of Distance Education at SPCCD What student support services are currently available to DE students? How are faculty members currently trained to teach online, hybrid or Web-enhanced courses? What tech support services are available for faculty, staff and students? What research is there about how our online students compare with in-class students?
Specific Goals for Distance Education at SPCCD	Goal #1 Goal #2 Goal #3 Goal #4 Goal #5
Top Priority Action Items for Distance Education	Leadership for DE at SPCCD Technical Infrastructure and Resources Student Services for DE Students Alignment of Instructional Resources Instructor Support and Training

Strategic Issue Areas	Recommendations on Course and Program Development Recommendations on Instructional Quality and Professional Development Recommendations on Student Success and Support Services Recommendations on Funding, Governance and Management

7. Update the *Table of Contents.*
   a. Click the *Table of Contents* on the first page of the report.
   b. Click the **Update Table** button at the top of the *Table of Contents,* or click the **Update Table** button in the *Table of Contents* group on the *References* tab. The *Update Table of Contents* dialog box will open.
   c. Select the **Update entire table** radio button and click **OK.** The *Table of Contents* entries and page numbers will be updated.

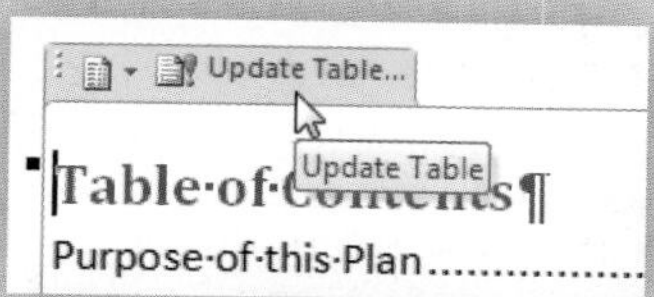

FIGURE WD 5.15

8. Insert footnotes into the report.
   a. Click after the *Web-Enhanced course* heading (on page 3).
   b. On the *References* tab, in the *Footnotes* group, click the **Insert Footnote** button. The number *1* footnote is inserted into the body of the report, and the footnote area opens at the bottom of the page.
   c. Type the following information in the footnote area: `Just for clarification, this is a non-DE course which uses DE tools.`
   d. Click at the end of the second paragraph in the *Distance Education Offerings and Programs* section (on page 4), insert a footnote, and type the following: `There are currently two fully online certificate programs going through the curriculum review process.`
   e. Click at the end of the *Top Priority Action Items for Distance Education* heading (on page 7), insert a footnote, and type the following: `These DE Action Items were presented to and approved by the Academic Senate during the fall semester.`

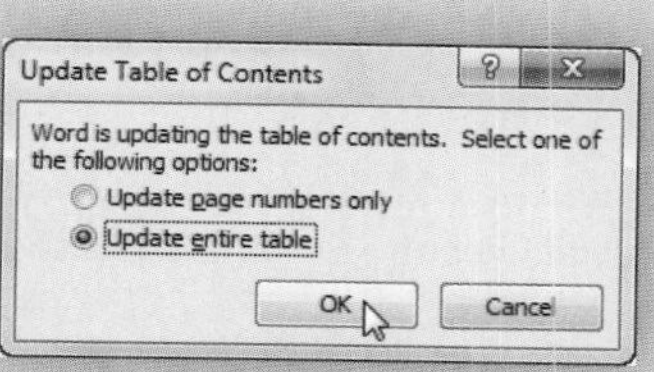

FIGURE WD 5.16

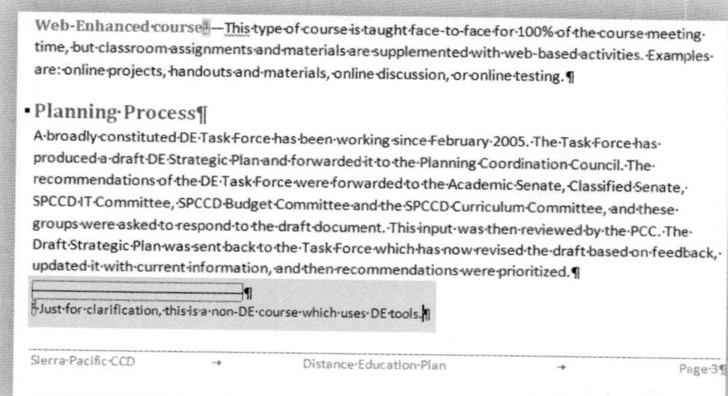
Web-Enhanced·course¹—This·type·of·course·is·taught·face-to-face·for·100%·of·the·course·meeting·time,·but·classroom·assignments·and·materials·are·supplemented·with·web-based·activities.·Examples·are:·online·projects,·handouts·and·materials,·online·discussion,·or·online·testing.¶

Planning·Process¶

A·broadly·constituted·DE·Task·Force·has·been·working·since·February·2005.·The·Task·Force·has·produced·a·draft·DE·Strategic·Plan·and·forwarded·it·to·the·Planning·Coordination·Council.·The·recommendations·of·the·DE·Task·Force·were·forwarded·to·the·Academic·Senate,·Classified·Senate,·SPCCD·IT·Committee,·SPCCD·Budget·Committee·and·the·SPCCD·Curriculum·Committee,·and·these·groups·were·asked·to·respond·to·the·draft·document.·This·input·was·then·reviewed·by·the·PCC.·The·Draft·Strategic·Plan·was·sent·back·to·the·Task·Force·which·has·now·revised·the·draft·based·on·feedback,·updated·it·with·current·information,·and·then·recommendations·were·prioritized.¶

¹Just·for·clarification,·this·is·a·non-DE·course·which·uses·DE·tools.¶

Sierra·Pacific·CCD → Distance·Education·Plan → Page·3¶

FIGURE WD 5.17

9. Select a *Reference Style* for the document, create a source, and insert a citation.
   a. On the *References* tab, in the *Citations & Bibliography* group, click the arrow next to *Style:* and choose **APA Fifth Edition.**
   b. Click at the end of the *Web-Enhanced course* paragraph (on page 3).
   c. In the *Citations & Bibliography* group, click the **Insert Citation** button and choose **Add New Source.** The *Create Source* dialog box will open.
   d. In the *Type of Source* area, choose **Web site.**
   e. Continue creating the source with the information shown in Figure WD 5.18.

Create Source

Type of Source: Web site

Bibliography Fields for APA Fifth Edition

Author	Chavez, R. M.
	Corporate Author
Name of Web Page	Understanding Online Modalities
Name of Web Site	Modern Education Trends
Year	2008
Month	October
Day	
Year Accessed	2011
Month Accessed	March
Day Accessed	9
URL	http://moderneducationtrends.org/online_modalities.htm

Show All Bibliography Fields

Tag name: Smi08 Example: http://www.adatum.com

OK Cancel

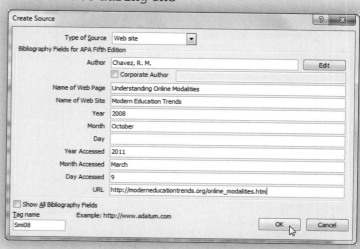

FIGURE WD 5.18

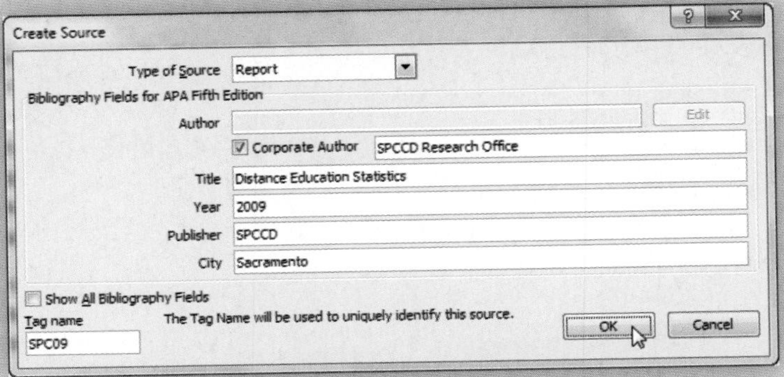

FIGURE WD 5.19

f. Click **OK** to add the source and insert the citation into the document. The parenthetical citation *(Chavez, 2008)* will be inserted into the report.

10. Create another source and edit the citation.

a. Click at the end of the first paragraph in the *What research is there about how our online students compare with in-class students* section (on page 5), click the **Insert Citation** button, click **Add New Source,** and type the source as shown in Figure WD 5.19.

b. Click **OK** to add the source and insert the citation into the document.

c. Click the citation you just inserted.

d. Click the small arrow on the right and choose **Edit Citation.** The *Edit Citation* dialog box will open. Since the author of this source is already mentioned in the paragraph, it does not need to be included in the citation.

e. In the *Suppress* area, click the **Author** check box to suppress this information in the citation.

f. Click **OK** to finish editing this citation. The citation will now contain the title of the report and the date *(Distance Education Statistics, 2009).*

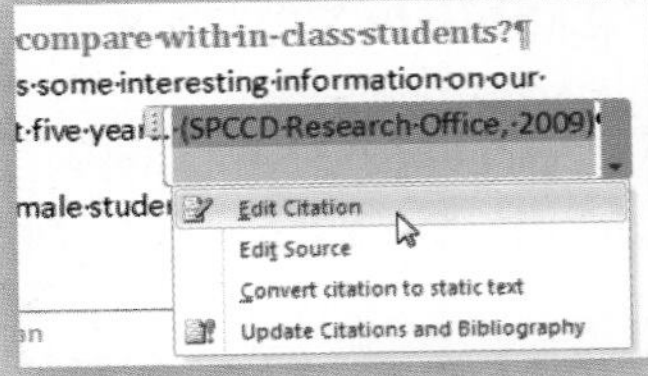

FIGURE WD 5.20

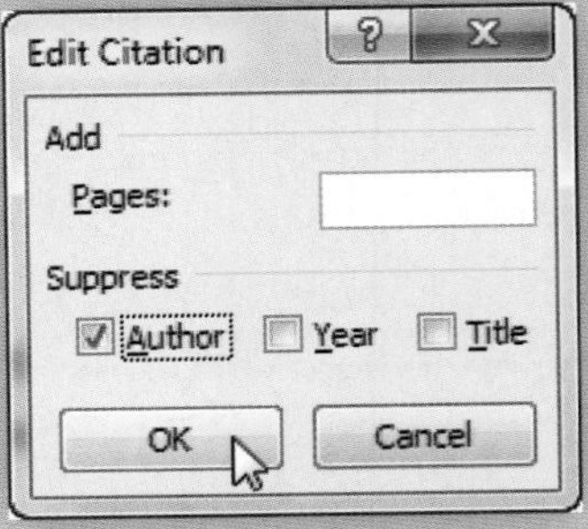

FIGURE WD 5.21

11. Insert a *Works Cited* page at the end of the report and update the *Table of Contents.*

a. Go to the end of the report and insert a page break.

b. On the *References* tab, in the *Citations & Bibliography* group, click the **Bibliography** button and choose **Works Cited.** A works cited page is added to your report with the sources you have added. The *Works Cited* heading is inserted as a *Heading 1* style so it will be included in the *Table of Contents.*

c. Center the *Works Cited* heading.

d. Go to the *Table of Contents* and update the entire table. Notice how the *Works Cited* page is included at the end of the *Table of Contents.*

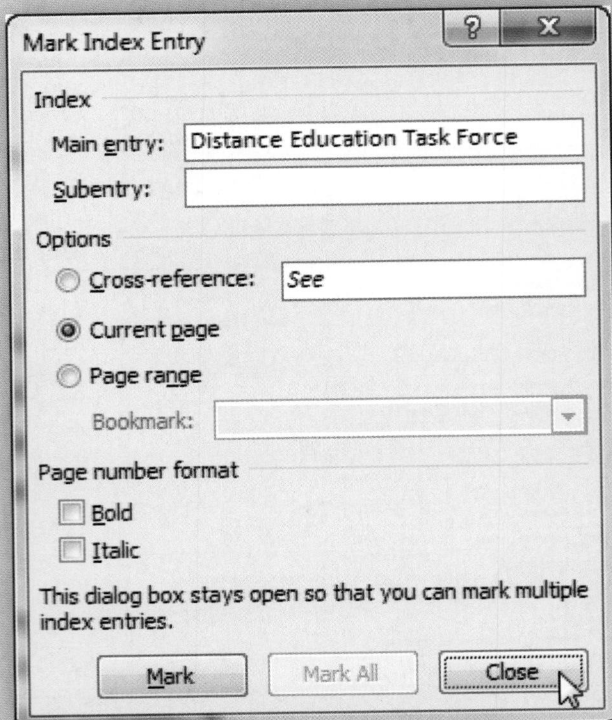

FIGURE WD 5.22

12. Mark entries in the report to be included in the *Index.*

a. Select **DE Task Force** in the *What student support services are currently available to DE students?* section (on page 3).

b. On the *References* tab, in the *Index* group, click the **Mark Entry** button. The *Mark Index Entry* dialog box will open and the selected text is included in the *Main Entry* area.

c. Confirm that the **Current page** option is selected and click on **Mark.**

d. Click **Close** to close the *Mark Index Entry* dialog box. This index entry is created. When the *Show/Hide* feature is turned on, the index code (*{ XE "Distance Education Task Force" }*) will be visible.

e. Use *Find* to find **online course.**

f. Select the first occurrence of **online course** that is not in the *Table of Contents* or in a heading.

g. Click the **Index** button, click **Mark All,** and click on **Close.** All occurrences of these words in the report should be marked for indexing.

h. Find and mark the following index entries. Do not select a heading or *Table of Contents* entry to mark as an index entry. On each of these choose **Mark All.** (Note: If there is more than one occurrence of an entry in a paragraph, Word will only mark the first occurrence of that entry.)

hybrid	web-enhanced	Planning Coordination Council
Academic Senate	Classified Senate	Curriculum Committee
ITC	Help Desk	Strategic Plan

13. Turn off the **Show/Hide** button to hide the index entry codes.
14. Create an *Index* for the report.
    a. Go to the end of the report (after the *Works Cited* page) and insert a page break.
    b. Type `Index` at the top of the new page, apply the **Heading 1** style to this line, and press **Enter.**
    c. On the *References* tab, in the *Index* group, click the **Insert Index** button. The *Index* dialog box will open.
    d. In the *Formats:* area, choose **Formal.**
    e. The *Type:* should be **Indented** and *Columns:* should be **2.**
    f. Click **OK** to insert the *Index.*
    g. Center the *Index* title.
15. Scroll through the report and insert page breaks as necessary to keep information together.
16. Update the *Index.*
    a. Click the *Index* at the end of the document.
    b. On the *References* tab, in the *Index* group, click the **Update Index** button.
17. Go to the *Table of Contents* and update the entire table.
18. Save and close the document.

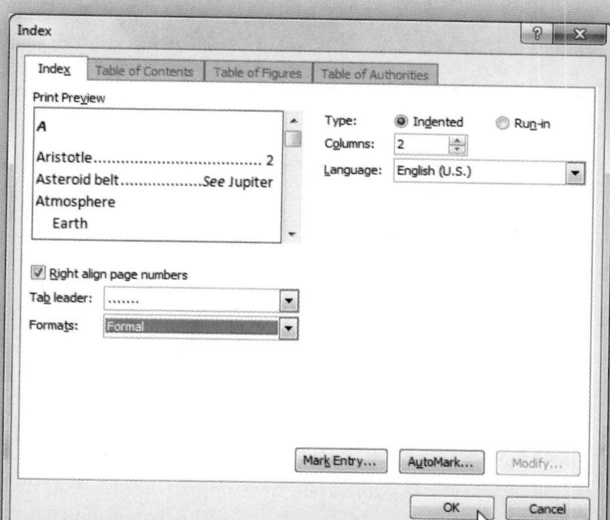

FIGURE WD 5.23

Skill Review 5.2

In this project you will be merging the *Expired Letter_05* document from Placer Hills Real Estate with the *Cavalli-PHRE* database.

1. Open the *Expired Letter_05* document.
2. Save this document as **`[your initials]WD_SkillReview_5-2.`**
3. Use the current document to create a mail merge.
    a. Click the **Mailings** tab.
    b. Click the **Start Mail Merge** button in the *Start Mail Merge* group and choose **Letters.**
4. Select the recipients to be merged into this letter.
    a. Click the **Select Recipients** button in the *Start Mail Merge* group and choose **Use Existing List.** The *Select Data Source* dialog box will open.
    b. Browse to your student data files, select the **Cavalli-PHRE** database file (an Access file), and click **Open.**

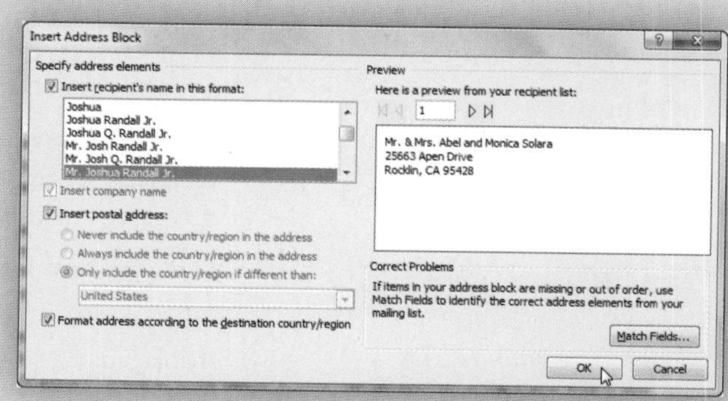

FIGURE WD 5.24

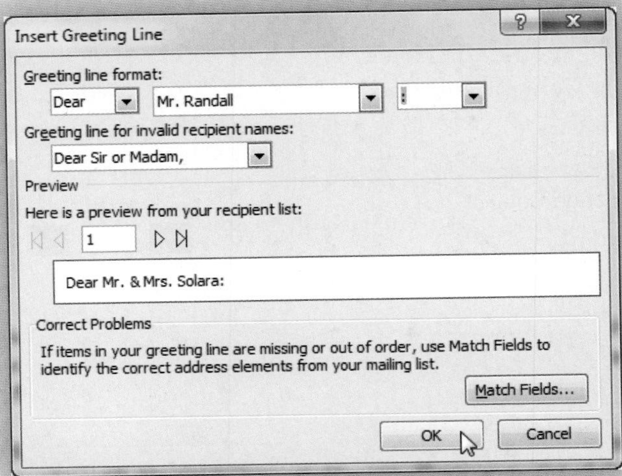

FIGURE WD 5.25

5. Insert the *Address Block* merge field into the business letter as the inside address.
   a. Click in front of the *[Inside Address]* placeholder text in the business letter.
   b. On the *Mailings* tab, in the *Write & Insert Fields* group, click the **Address Block** button. The *Insert Address Block* dialog box will open.
   c. In this dialog box, you can customize how the *Address Block* will be displayed. In the *Preview* area you can see how each record will be displayed in the letter.
   d. Click **OK** to accept the *Address Block* settings and insert the *Address Block* into the letter.
   e. The merge field code <<*AddressBlock*>> is inserted into the letter before the placeholder text *[Inside Address]*.
   f. Select and delete **[Inside Address]** after the *AddressBlock* merge code. Be sure not to delete any *Enters.*

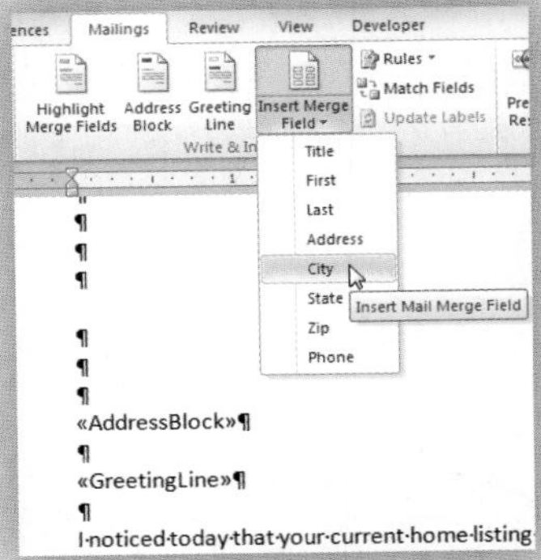

FIGURE WD 5.26

6. Insert the *Greeting Line* merge field into the business letter as the salutation.
   a. Click in front of the *[Salutation]* placeholder text in the business letter.
   b. On the *Mailings* tab, in the *Write & Insert Fields* group, click the **Greeting Line** button. The *Insert Greeting Line* dialog box will open.
   c. In the *Greeting line format:* area, confirm that the greeting line consists of *Dear,* a courtesy title (*Mr., Mrs.,* etc.), and the last name, and change the ending punctuation to a **colon.**
   d. Click **OK** to accept the *Greeting Line* settings and insert the *Greeting Line* into the letter.
   e. The merge field code <<*GreetingLine* >> is inserted into the letter before the placeholder text *[Salutation].*
   f. Select and delete **[Salutation]** after the *GreetingLine* merge code. Be sure not to delete any *Enters.*

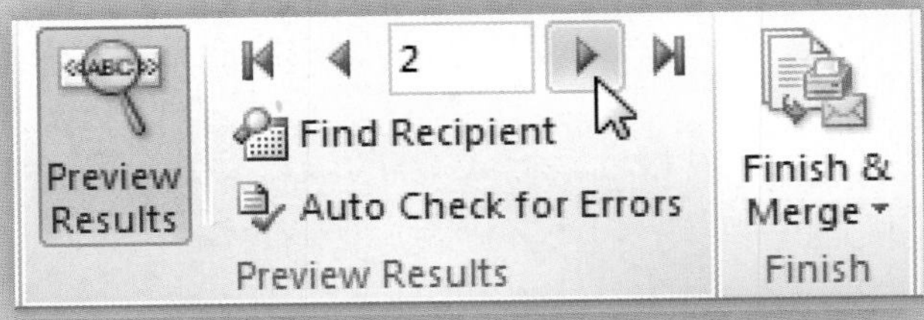

FIGURE WD 5.27

7. Insert a merge field code into the body of the letter.
   a. Select and delete the **[City]** placeholder text in the first sentence in the first paragraph of the letter.
   b. In the *Write & Insert Fields* group, click the **Insert Merge Field** button and select **City.**
   c. The <<*City*>> merge code will be inserted into the letter.
   d. Make sure there is a space before and after this merge field.
8. Save the *[your initials]WD_SkillReview_5-2* document.
9. Preview the results of your merge.
   a. Click the **Preview Results** button in the *Preview Results* group. Data from the recipient list are displayed in the <<*AddressBlock*>>, <<*GreetingLine*>>, and <<*City*>> fields in the document.
   b. Click the **Next Record** button to display the contents of the next record in the letter.
   c. Click the **Preview Results** button to return to the letter with the merge field codes displayed.

10. Finish and review the results of your mail merge.
    a. Click the **Finish & Merge** button in the *Finish* group and choose **Edit Individual Documents.** The *Merge to New Document* dialog box will open.
    b. Click the **All** radio button and click **OK** to complete the merge. The letter will be merged with the recipient list into a new document.
    c. Save this new document as `[your initials]WD_merge_5-2.`
    d. Scroll through the document to verify that there are six letters and that the merged information from the recipient list is correctly placed in the document.
11. Add an envelope to the first letter.
    a. On the *Mailings* tab, in the *Create* group, click the **Envelopes** button. The *Envelopes and Labels* dialog box will open. The inside address from the first letter is included in the *Delivery address:* area.
    b. In the *Return address:* area type:
       Emma Cavalli
       Placer Hills Real Estate
       7100 Madrone Road
       Roseville, CA 95722
    c. Click the **Add to Document** button.
    d. A dialog box will open asking if you want to save the return address as the default address; click **No.** The envelope will be inserted on a separate page before the first letter.
12. Create a custom print to print only the merged letters and not the envelope.
    a. Click the **File** tab to open the BackStage.
    b. Click the **Print** button to display the print options.
    c. In the *Pages:* area in the *Settings* section type: 2-7
    d. Click the **Print** button to print the six merged letters. The BackStage will close and you will be returned to the merged document.
13. Save and close both open documents.

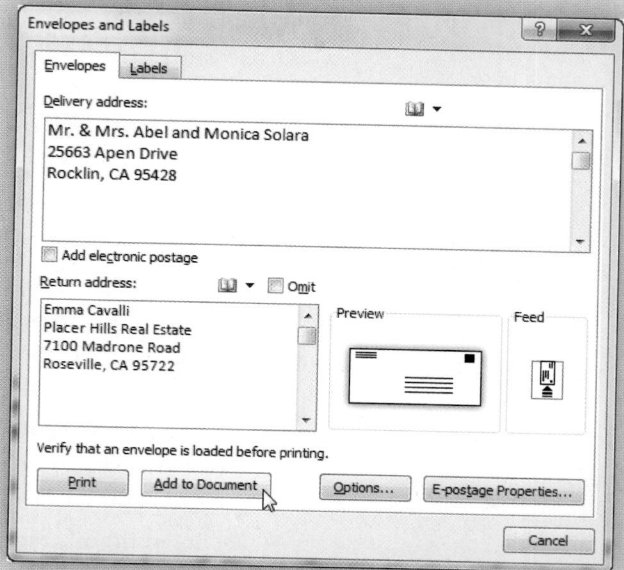

FIGURE WD 5.28

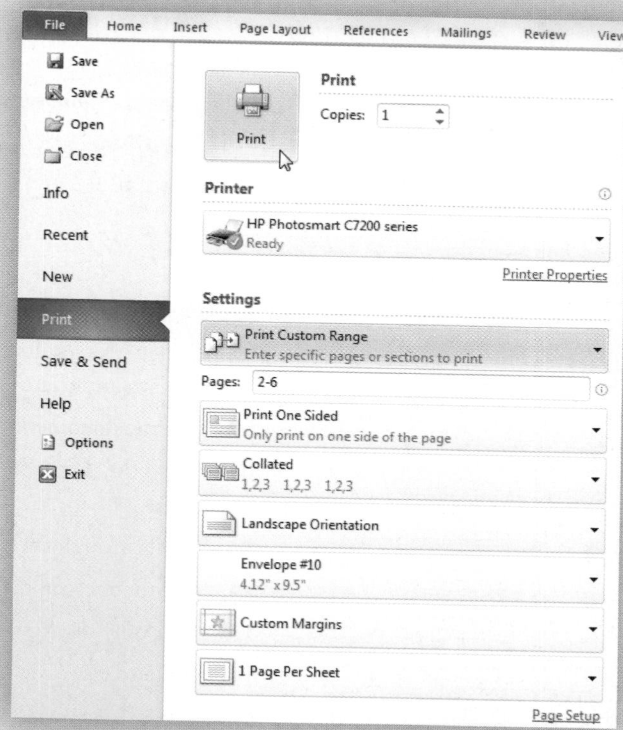

FIGURE WD 5.29

challenge yourself 1

In this project you will be merging the *Renewal Letter_05* document from Central Sierra Insurance with the *CSI_Souza_Renewals* database.

1. Open the *Renewal Letter_05* document.
2. Save this document as `[your initials]WD_Challenge_5-3.`

3. Click at the end of *Premium Basis* in the second column of the first row of the table and insert a footnote.
4. Type the following in the footnote: `Note: The actual premium will be determined by your actual sales following a final audit at policy year-end.`
5. Create a mail merge using this letter.
6. Use the **CSI_Souza_Renewals** database as your recipient list. This file is in your student data files.
7. Insert the **Address Block** merge field in the document where indicated by the bracketed placeholder text (e.g., *[Address Block]*). Make sure the company name is on the second line of the *Address Block.* Delete the bracketed placeholder text.
8. Insert the **Greeting Line** merge field in the document where indicated by the bracketed placeholder text. Edit the *Greeting Line* so there is no punctuation at the end of the line. Delete the bracketed placeholder text.
9. Insert the other merge fields as indicated by the bracketed placeholder text and delete the bracketed placeholder text. The merge fields you will be inserting are indicated by the bracketed placeholder text below:

   [Policy Number]

   [Company]

   [Insurance Company]

   [Policy Description]

   [Premium Basis]

   [Cost per $1000]

   [Total Premium]

   [First Name]
10. Preview the results of the mail merge. Make sure all the merge fields are in the correct location and there is proper spacing around them.
11. Save the document.
12. Finish the merge so you can edit the individual documents. There should be eight letters.
13. Scroll through the document to make sure the mail merge worked properly.
14. Save the merged document as **`[your initials]WD_merge_5-3.`**
15. Print only the first page of the merged document.
16. Save and close the open documents.

challenge yourself 2

In this project you will be editing the *Personal Training Program_05* document from American River Cycling Club.

1. Open the *Personal Training Program_05* document.
2. Save this document as **`[your initials]WD_Challenge_5-4.`**
3. Apply the **Austin** theme to the document.
4. Apply the **Heading 1** style to each of the bold section headings.
5. Apply the **Heading 2** style to each of the underlined section headings.

6. Use **MLA Sixth Edition** reference format.
7. At the end of the *Pace of Rides* section, add the following citation.

Type of Source	**Book**
Author	Burke, E. R.
Title	The Complete Book of Long-Distance Cycling
Year	2000
City	New York
Publisher	Rodale Books

8. At the end of the *Number of Rides per Week* section, add the following citation.

Type of Source	**Book**
Author	Chapple, T.
Title	Base Building for Cyclists
Year	2007
City	San Francisco
Publisher	VeloPress

9. At the end of the *Duration of Rides* section, add the following citation.

Type of Source	**Web site**
Corporate Author	USA Cycling
Name of Web Page	Training Guidelines
Year	2009
Month	April
Year Accessed	2011
Month Accessed	January
Day Accessed	12
URL	http://www.usacycling.com/training_guidelines

10. Insert a page break at the end of the document and insert a **Bibliography.**
11. Insert a blank page at the beginning of the document and insert a **Table of Contents** on this blank page. All headings marked as *Heading 1* and *Heading 2* should be displayed in the *Table of Contents.*
12. Find the first occurrence of each of the acronyms below and insert a footnote for each using the information below.

INSERT FOOTNOTE AFTER	TYPE TEXT IN FOOTNOTE
PTP	Personal training program
RPM	Revolutions per minute
VO2	The highest rate of oxygen consumption attainable during maximal or exhaustive exercise
BMI	Body mass index

13. Find and mark for index all occurrences of each of the words below. Use *Mark All* and don't mark an occurrence in the *Table of Contents* or in a heading.

PTP	Max VO2
heart rate	rest day
recovery	training log
BMI	muscles

14. On a separate page at the end of the document, type `Index` and apply the **Heading 1** style.
15. Insert a one-column *Index* of your choice.
16. Insert a footer of your choice into the document. Make sure the footer has a page number and that you set the footer to not appear on the first page (hint: different first page).
17. At the beginning of the document, insert a **Cover Page** of your choice. Add text as needed in the document property fields.
18. Turn off **Show/Hide** and scroll through your document inserting page breaks where necessary.
19. Update the *Table of Contents* and the *Index.*
20. Save and close the document.

on your own

In this project you will be creating mailing labels and return address mailing labels for Central Sierra Insurance.

1. Open a new Word document.
2. Save this document as ***[your initials]*WD_OnYourOwn_labels_5-5.**
3. Start a new mail merge job to create labels for all of the employees from Central Sierra Insurance. Use *Avery US Letter 5160* labels.
4. Use the *Central Sierra Insurance* database as the recipient list.
5. Insert an **Address Block** on the labels and do not include the company name.
6. Click on the **Update Labels** button so the *Address Block* is placed in each label.
7. Preview the labels to make sure they fit correctly on each label. You might have to adjust the before or after paragraph spacing.
8. Save the document.
9. Finish the merge to a new document and save as ***[your initials]*WD_OnYourOwn_merge_5-5.**
10. Open a new Word document.
11. Create **Labels** (don't start a new mail merge) to create return mailing labels for Central Sierra Insurance.
12. Type the address for Central Sierra Insurance:

    Central Sierra Insurance
    5502 Ridley Way
    Cameron Park, CA 94663
13. Use *Avery US Letter 5160* labels and use a full page of the same label.

14. Insert these return labels into a new document and save the document as `[your initials]WD_OnYourOwn_return_5-5.`
15. Close the open documents.

In this project you will be editing the *Society Training Guide_05* document from Courtyard Medical Plaza.

1. Open the *Society Training Guide_05* document.
2. Save this document as `[your initials]WD_FixIt_5-6.`
3. Apply a theme to this document to complement the colors of the Courtyard Medical Plaza logo.
4. Apply **Heading 1** and **Heading 2** styles to the main and subheadings in the document.
5. Apply the **Heading 3** style to each of the *Skiing Procedures* in the *Four-Track (4T) and Three-Track (3T)* and *Bi-Ski and Mono-Ski* sections.
6. Insert a **Table of Contents** before the first page. Make sure all three levels of headings are displayed.
7. Use text wrapping to appropriately position the picture next to the *Introduction to Equipment* subsection in the *Bi-Ski and Mono-Ski* section.
8. In each of the *Disabilities* sections, mark each disability as an entry for the *Index.*
9. Insert an **Index** of your choice after the last page of the document. Include a heading on the Index page and apply a style so it will appear in the *Table of Contents.*
10. Insert a footnote after each of the *Skiing Procedures* headings, and inform the reader that these procedures will vary based on the experience of both the participant and ski instructor.
11. Remove any extra lines in the document.
12. Insert a footer of your choice into the document. Include a page number and the title of the document.
13. Add a **Cover Page** to the document.
14. Turn off **Show/Hide** and insert any page breaks where necessary.
15. Update the *Table of Contents* and *Index.*
16. Print only the *Table of Contents* pages.
17. Save and close the document.

excel 2010

chapter 1

Getting Started with Excel 2010

In this chapter, you will learn the following skills:

- Enter text and numbers
- Format worksheets
- Enter simple formulas
- Apply borders and shading
- Edit worksheets

Skill 1.1 Introduction to Excel 2010
Skill 1.2 Entering and Editing Text and Numbers in Cells
Skill 1.3 Wrapping Text in Cells
Skill 1.4 Inserting Data Using AutoFill
Skill 1.5 Inserting and Deleting Cells
Skill 1.6 Applying Formatting to Cells
Skill 1.7 Changing Fonts
Skill 1.8 Applying Cell Styles
Skill 1.9 Applying Number Formats
Skill 1.10 Applying Date Formats
Skill 1.11 Entering Simple Formulas
Skill 1.12 Adding Borders
Skill 1.13 Adding Shading
Skill 1.14 Using Format Painter with Excel
Skill 1.15 Using Paste Options
Skill 1.16 Using Find and Replace in Excel
Skill 1.17 Clearing Cell Content
Skill 1.18 Changing the Zoom Level

skills

introduction

In this chapter, you will learn the skills to build an Excel 2010 worksheet by entering data, descriptions, and simple computations. Also you will learn how to enhance your worksheet's appearance with formatting.

1.1 Introduction to Excel 2010

Microsoft Excel 2010 is a spreadsheet program in which you enter, manipulate, calculate, and chart numerical and text data. An Excel file is referred to as a workbook. A **workbook** is a collection of worksheets. Each **worksheet** (also called a "sheet") is made up of rows and columns of data on which you can perform calculations. It's these calculations that make Excel such a powerful tool.

Some of the basic elements of a Microsoft Excel workbook include

- **Worksheet**—an electronic ledger where you enter data. The worksheet appears as a grid where you can enter and then manipulate data using functions, formulas, and formatting. Excel workbooks have three worksheets by default (named Sheet1, Sheet2, and Sheet3). You can rename, add, and delete worksheets as necessary. To navigate to a worksheet, click the appropriate tab at the bottom of the worksheet grid.
- **Row**—a horizontal group of cells. Rows are identified by numbers. For example, the third row is labeled with the number ***3.*** To select a row, click the row selector (the box with the row number at the left side of the worksheet grid).
- **Column**—a vertical group of cells. Columns are identified by letters. For example, the fourth column is labeled with the letter ***D.*** To select a column, click the column selector (the box with the column letter at the top of the worksheet grid).
- **Cell**—the intersection of a column and a row. A cell is identified by its address—its column and row position. For example, the cell at the intersection of column B and row 4 has a cell address of B4. To navigate from cell to cell, use the mouse to click the cell you want to go to. You can also use the arrow keys on the keyboard to navigate around the worksheet.
- **Formula Bar**—data entry area directly below the Ribbon and above the worksheet grid. Although you can type any data in the formula bar, the *Insert Function* fx button at the left side of the formula bar was designed to make it easier to create complex formulas.
- **Name Box**—appears at the left side of the formula bar and displays the address of the selected cell. If a group of cells is selected, the *Name* box displays the address of the first cell in the group. You can use the *Name* box to navigate to a specific cell in the worksheet by typing the cell address in the *Name* box and then pressing ←Enter.
- **Status Bar**—appears at the bottom of the worksheet grid and displays information about the selected data, including the number of cells selected that contain data (count) and the average and sum (total) of the selected values (when appropriate).

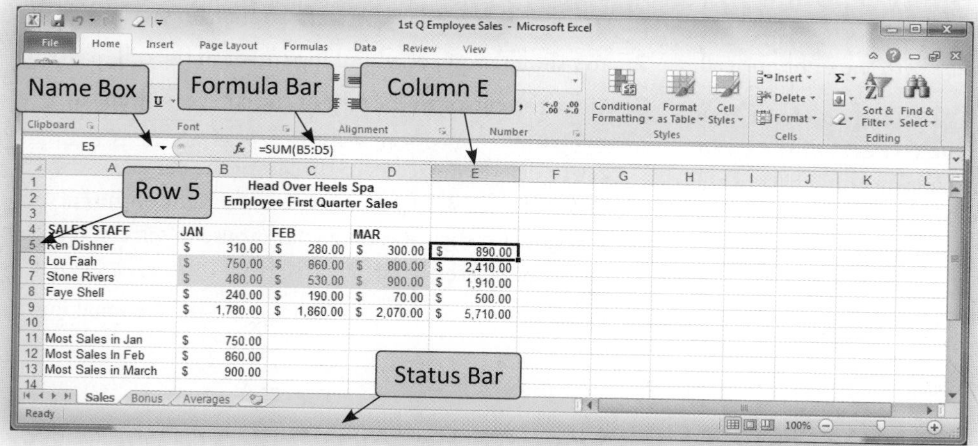

FIGURE EX 1.1

You can use Excel for a wide variety of purposes, from calculating payments for a personal loan, to creating a personal budget, to tracking employee sales and calculating bonuses for your business.

1.2 Entering and Editing Text and Numbers in Cells

The most basic task in Excel is entering data in your workbook. Entering numerical data is as easy as typing a number in a cell. Numbers can be displayed as dates, currency values, percentages, or other formats. (Later topics discuss number formatting and using functions and formulas to automate numerical calculations.)

Excel is not just about numbers, though. Without text headers, descriptions, and instructions, your workbook would consist of numbers and formulas without any structure. Adding text headers to your rows and columns creates the structure for you to enter data into your workbook.

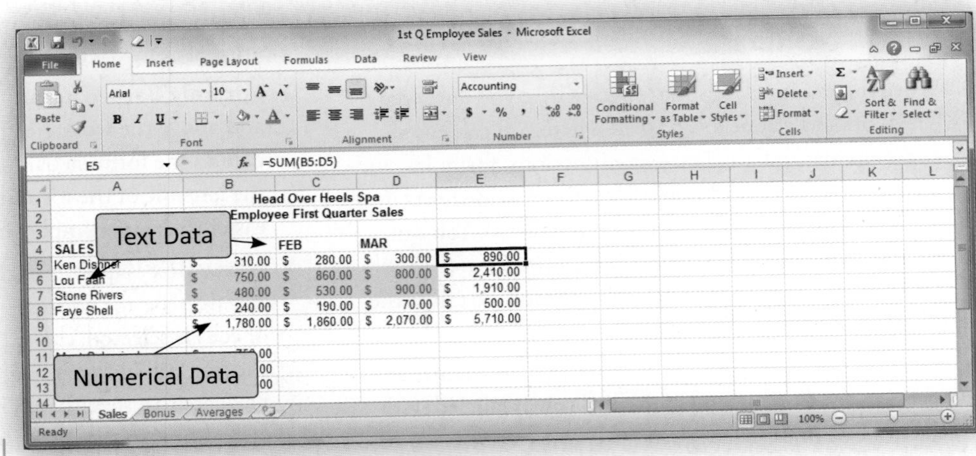

FIGURE EX 1.2

To enter data in a cell:

1. Click the cell where you want the data to appear.
2. Type the number or text.
3. Press the [←Enter] key or the [Tab] key on your keyboard.

   Pressing [←Enter] on the keyboard after entering text will move the cursor down one cell.

   Pressing [Tab] will move the cursor to the right one cell.

Excel gives you different ways to edit the data in your worksheet. If you want to change the contents of the entire cell, use **Ready mode**. If you want to change only part of the cell data, use **Edit mode**. The status bar, located at the lower-left corner of the Excel window, displays which mode you are in—Ready or Edit.

To use Ready mode to change text:

1. Click the cell you want to change.
2. Type the new contents for the cell.
3. Press [←Enter] or [Tab] when you are finished.
4. The old contents are completely removed and replaced with what you've typed.

To use Edit mode to change text:

1. Double-click the cell you want to change.
2. You should now see a blinking cursor in the cell.
3. Move the cursor to the part of the entry you want to change and make your changes. Use the [←Backspace] key to delete characters to the left of the cursor; use the [Delete] key to delete characters to the right of the cursor. You can also click and drag your mouse to select a section of text to delete.
4. Press [←Enter] or [Tab] when you are finished making your changes.

tips & tricks

To add a line break within the cell, press [Alt] while pressing [←Enter].

try this

As you type in a cell, the entry is displayed in the formula bar as well as in the active cell. Clicking the **Enter** icon ✓ next to the formula bar accepts your entry. Clicking the **Cancel** icon ✕ next to the formula bar removes your entry.

from the perspective of . . .

OFFICE MANAGER IN DOCTOR'S OFFICE

Spreadsheet software is perfect for creating documents to organize my office. I create schedules for projects, to-do lists, phone lists, and checklists. Using a variety of formatting including fonts and borders creates polished documents. It is also handy for keeping track of patient information.

1.3 Wrapping Text in Cells

When you type text in a cell, the text will appear to continue to the right as far as it can until there is another cell that contains data. At that point, the text will appear to be cut off. You could increase the width of the cell to show all the text, but do you really want the entire column to be that wide? If your worksheet includes cells with more text than will comfortably fit in the cell, you should use the **wrap text** feature. When wrap text is enabled for a cell, the text in the cell will automatically wrap to multiple lines, just as a paragraph would.

To wrap text in a cell:

On the *Home* tab, in the *Alignment* group, click the **Wrap Text** button. Notice the button appears selected when text wrapping is active for the cell.

To turn off text wrapping in a cell, click the **Wrap Text** button again to deselect it.

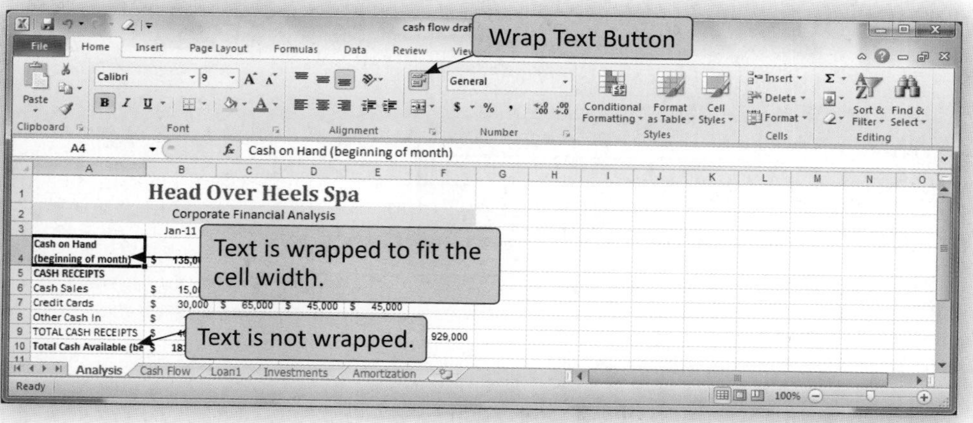

FIGURE EX 1.3

tips & tricks

The text wrapping feature only works for cells that contain text. If a column is too narrow to display its numerical data, Excel will not wrap it. Instead, the cell will show a series of # symbols, indicating that the cell contains numerical data, but the column is too narrow to display it.

tell me more

You can also turn on the text wrapping feature from the *Format Cells* dialog box.

1. Open the *Format Cells* dialog box.
2. Click the **Alignment** tab if necessary.
3. Click the **Wrap Text** check box.
4. Click **OK**.

1.4 Inserting Data Using AutoFill

Use the **AutoFill** feature to fill a group of cells with the same data or to extend a data series. With AutoFill, you can copy the same value or formula to a group of cells at once. This is much more efficient than using copy and paste over and over again. If you have a group of cells with similar data in a series, AutoFill can extend the series automatically. A **data series** is any sequence of cells with a recognizable pattern:

Numeric patterns:

1	2	3	4
1	3	5	7
Student 1	Student 2	Student 3	Student 4

Date patterns:

January	February	March	April
1/1/2010	2/1/2010	3/1/2010	4/1/2010
07/05/10	07/12/10	07/19/10	07/26/10

The easiest way to use AutoFill is to use the **Fill Handle tool** to fill data up or down in a column or to the left or right in a row.

To use the *Fill Handle* tool:

1. Enter the data you want in the first cell.
2. If you want to fill a series of cells with that same value, skip to step 5.
3. Enter the second value of the series in an adjacent cell.
4. Select the cell(s) you want to base the series on. (Click the first cell. Then holding ⇧Shift click the last cell you want to select.)
5. Click and drag the **Fill Handle** in the direction you want to fill the series. As you drag the *Fill Handle,* a tool tip appears displaying the value of the highlighted cell.
6. Release the mouse button when you have highlighted the last cell you want to fill.

Excel attempts to detect automatically if the data appear to be a series. Sometimes, however, the series doesn't fill with the data you expect or want. To change the type of data AutoFill inserts, click the **AutoFill Options** button and select a different option. From the *AutoFill Options* button, you can choose to copy the cells or fill the series. You can also choose to copy the cell formatting only or to fill or copy the data series without formatting.

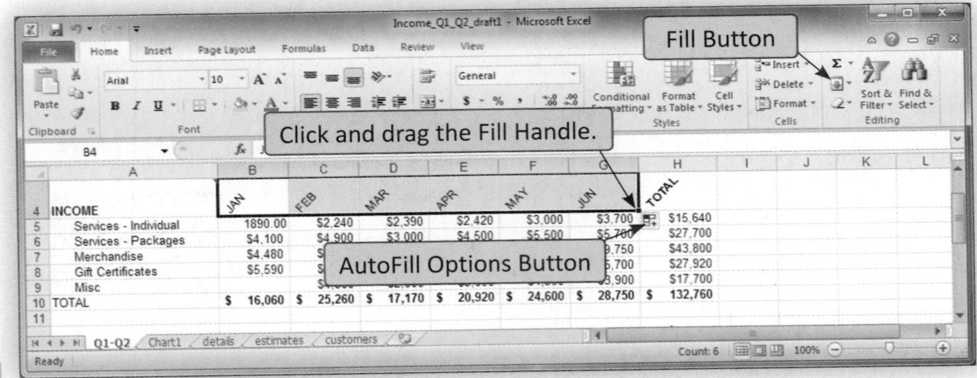

FIGURE EX 1.4

tips & tricks

Use AutoFill to enter repetitive data in your worksheet to avoid errors from entering data manually.

tell me more

The *Fill Handle* tool can be used to fill a series of dates by month as well as year. For example, if you start the series with Jan-2011 and Feb-2011, the *Fill Handle* will fill in the next cells with Mar-2011, Apr-2011, May-2011, etc. When the series reaches Dec-2011, the next cell will be filled in with Jan-2012.

If you are filling a series of dates, the *AutoFill Options* button will give you the options to fill by day, weekday, month, or year.

try this

You can also use the *Fill* command from the Ribbon. First, select the cells you want to fill. On the *Home* tab, in the *Editing* group, click the **Fill** button and select the type of fill you want: *Down, Right, Up, Left, Across Worksheets . . ., Series . . .,* or *Justify.*

Pressing Ctrl + D on the keyboard will fill the selected cell(s) with the value from the cell above it.

Pressing Ctrl + R on the keyboard will fill the selected cell(s) with the value from the cell to the left of it.

1.5 Inserting and Deleting Cells

You may find you want to add some extra space or more information into the middle of your worksheet. To do this, you must insert a new cell or group of cells. When you insert a new cell, you have the option to shift the existing cells to the right or down, allowing you to place the new cell exactly where you want it.

To insert a cell:

1. On the *Home* tab, in the *Cells* group, click the **Insert** button arrow.
2. Click **Insert Cells. . .**
3. Click the **Shift cells right** or **Shift cells down** radio button.
4. Click **OK.**

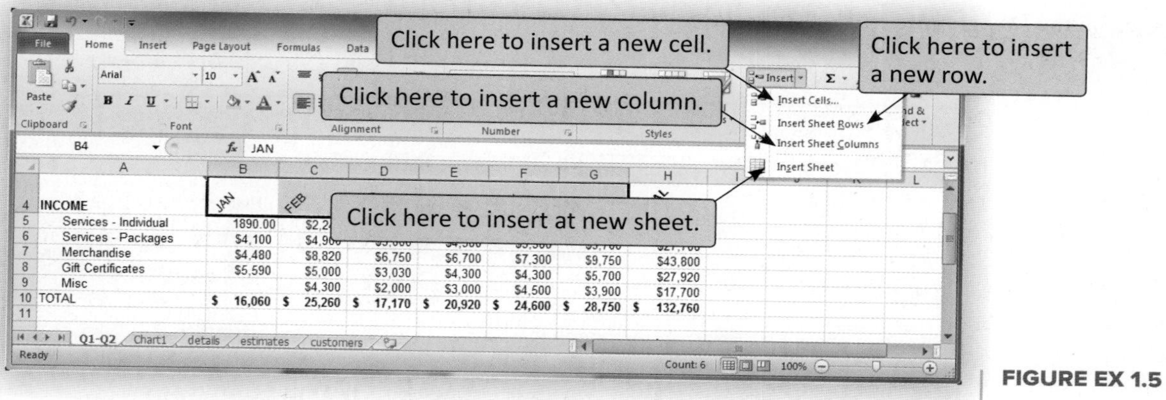

FIGURE EX 1.5

Of course, you can also delete cells. Deleting cells not only deletes the information and formatting in the cell, but also shifts the layout of the worksheet. Even if you delete an empty cell, you shift all the surrounding cells into new positions.

To delete a cell:

1. On the *Home* tab, in the *Cells* group, click the **Delete** button arrow.
2. Click **Delete Cells. . .**
3. Click the **Shift cells left** or **Shift cells up** radio button.
4. Click **OK.**

tips & tricks

Inserting and deleting cells may have unexpected consequences. Be careful not to delete cells that are referenced in formulas. Even though a new value may shift into the original cell's position, the formula will still be looking for the original cell (now deleted), causing an *invalid cell reference error.* When you insert a cell, any formulas referencing the cell address will update to reflect the new position of the original cell. Even if the formula uses absolute cell references, it will still update to reflect the updated cell reference.

tell me more

Pressing the Delete key on the keyboard will delete the contents of the cell but not the cell itself.

try this

Both **Insert . . .** and **Delete . . .** commands are available from the right-click menu.

1.6 Applying Formatting to Cells

You can apply common formatting to cells, such as **bold**, *italic*, and underline. Use bold, italic, and underline formatting to emphasize cells in your workbook.

To apply bold formatting:

› On the *Home* tab, in the *Font* group, click the **Bold** button.

To apply italic formatting:

› On the *Home* tab, in the *Font* group, click the **Italic** button.

To apply underline formatting:

› On the *Home* tab, in the *Font* group, click the **Underline** button.

› You can also click the **arrow** next to the **Underline** button to expand the underline options and apply the double-underline style.

Well-formatted spreadsheets have consistent formatting. When you select a row or column, you can apply formatting to the entire row or column at once.

1. Select the row or column by clicking the row heading or column heading (the number that represents the row or the letter than represents the column).
2. Select the formatting option(s) you want to apply.

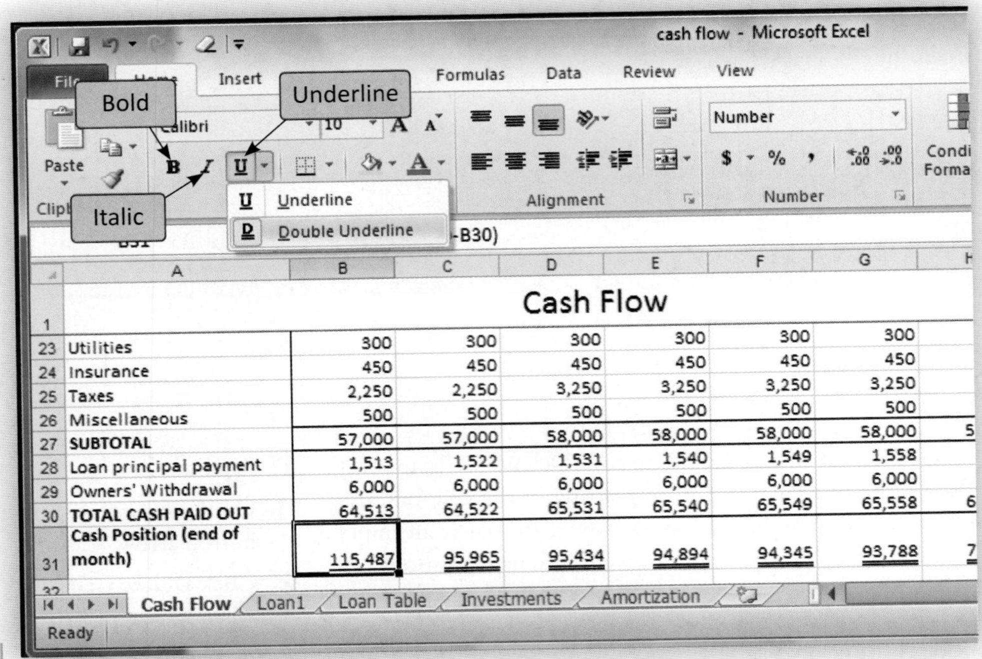

FIGURE EX 1.6

tips & tricks

Underline styles used in accounting spreadsheets are slightly different from "regular" underline styles. If you need to apply the accounting style of underline or double underline, do not use the *Underline* button on the Ribbon. Instead, use one of the accounting underline options from the *Format Cells* dialog:

1. Open the *Format Cells* dialog.
2. Click the arrow to expand the *Underline:* list and select **Single Accounting** or **Double Accounting.**
3. Click **OK** to apply the formatting.

tell me **more**

From the *Font* tab in the *Format Cells* dialog, you can apply additional character effects formatting such as strikethrough, superscript, and subscript.

try **this**

When you right-click a cell, the **Bold** and **Italic** buttons are available on the Mini toolbar.

You can also use the keyboard shortcuts:

› **Bold:** Ctrl + B

› **Italic:** Ctrl + I

› **Underline:** Ctrl + U

1.7 Changing Fonts

Use the commands from the *Home* tab, *Font* group to change font attributes such as font family, font size, and font color.

- To change the font, click the arrow next to the *Font* box to expand the list of available fonts, and then select the font you want.
- To change the font size, click the arrow next to the *Font Size* box and select the size you want.
- To change the font color, click the arrow next to the *Font Color* button to expand the color palette, and then select the color you want.

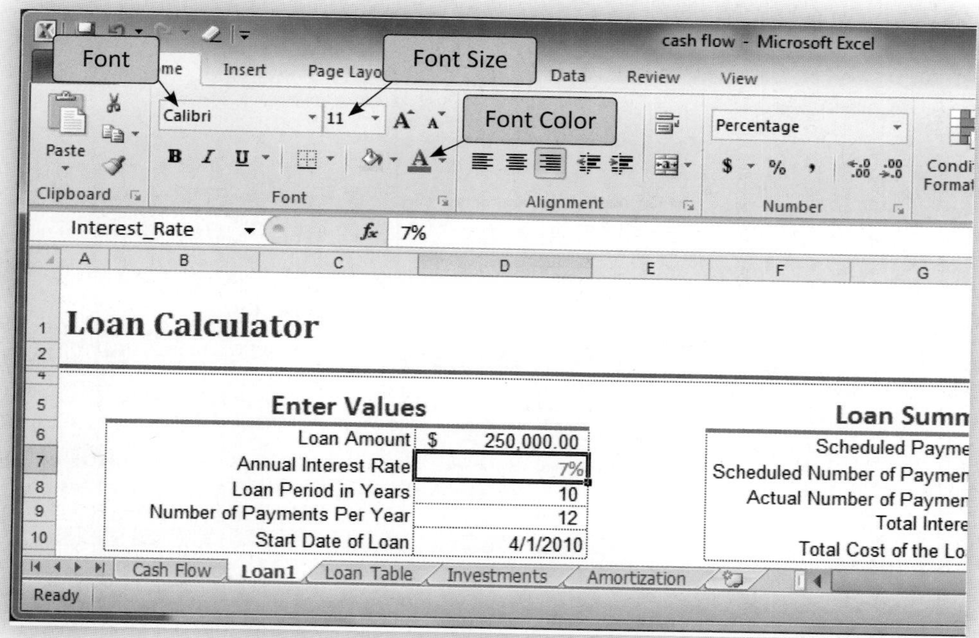

FIGURE EX 1.7

tips & tricks

The font color palette is divided into three parts:

- The top part shows the *Automatic* color choice (black or white, depending on the color of the background).
- The middle part shows the colors included in the theme that is applied well to the workbook. These colors are designed to work together.
- The bottom part of the palette shows the standard colors (dark red, red, orange, etc.) These colors are always available, no matter what theme is in use.

tell me more

You can pick a custom color by clicking **More Colors . . .** from the bottom of the font color palette.

try this

You can also change the font, font size, or font color by

- Opening the *Format Cells* dialog, clicking the **Font** tab, making the font selections you want, and then clicking **OK.**
- Right-clicking and making the font, font size, and font color selections you want from the Mini toolbar.

1.8 Applying Cell Styles

A **style** is a combination of effects that can be applied at one time. Styles can include formatting such as character effects, background color, typefaces, and number formatting.

Excel 2010 includes an extensive gallery of prebuilt cell styles. You can use these styles to help visualize your data by consistently applying them to your worksheet. For example, use the *Good* and *Bad* styles to highlight positive and negative data. Use text styles such as *Title* for the title of your worksheet and *Warning Text* to highlight crucial information about the data or worksheet.

To apply a cell style:

1. Select the cell or cells you want to apply the style to.
2. On the *Home* tab, in the *Styles* group, click the **Cell Styles** button.
3. Click the style you want to apply to your cells.

You can apply cell styles to an entire column or row at one time by first clicking the row or column selector, and then selecting the style you want from the *Cell Styles* gallery.

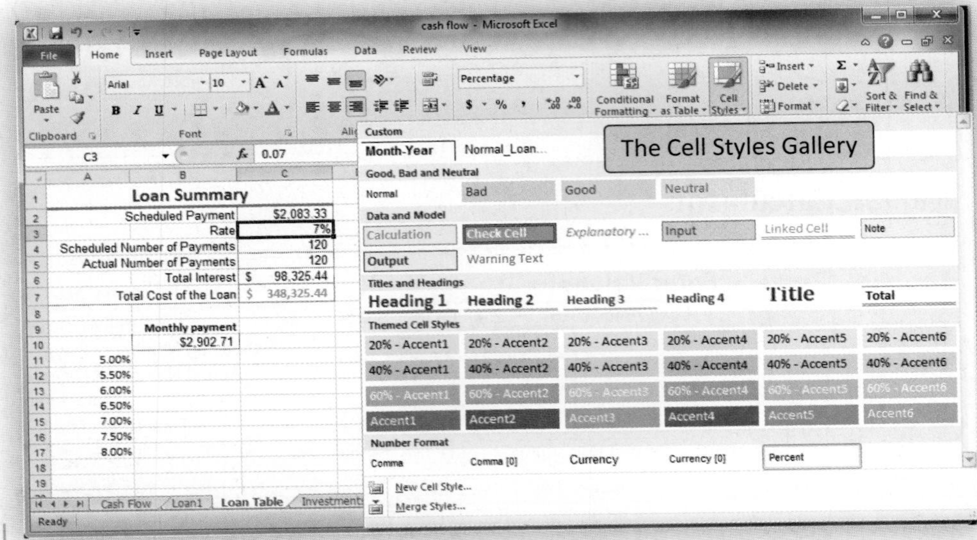

FIGURE EX 1.8

tips & tricks

If you have Live Preview enabled in Excel 2010, you can move your mouse over each style in the *Cell Styles* gallery to see a preview of how that style would look applied to your worksheet.

tell me more

You can create your own custom cell styles:

1. On the *Home* tab, in the *Styles* group, click the **Cell Styles** button.
2. Click **New Cell Style . . .**
3. Type the name of your style in the *Style name:* box.
4. Click the **Format . . .** button to open the *Format Cells* dialog.
5. In the *Format Cells* dialog, set all the formatting you want for your new style, and then click **OK.**
6. In the *Style* dialog, click the check boxes for the formatting types you want to include in your style (number format, alignment, etc.).
7. Click **OK** to save the new cell style.

Your new custom cell style will appear at the top of the *Cell Styles* gallery.

1.9 Applying Number Formats

When you first type numbers in a worksheet, Excel applies the *General* number format automatically. The *General* format right-aligns numbers in the cells but does not maintain a consistent number of decimal places (43.00 will appear as 43, while 42.25 appears as 42.25) and does not display commas (so 1,123,456 appears as 1123456). For consistency, and to make your worksheet easier to read, you should apply the specific number format that is most appropriate for your data. Excel provides several number formats for you to choose from.

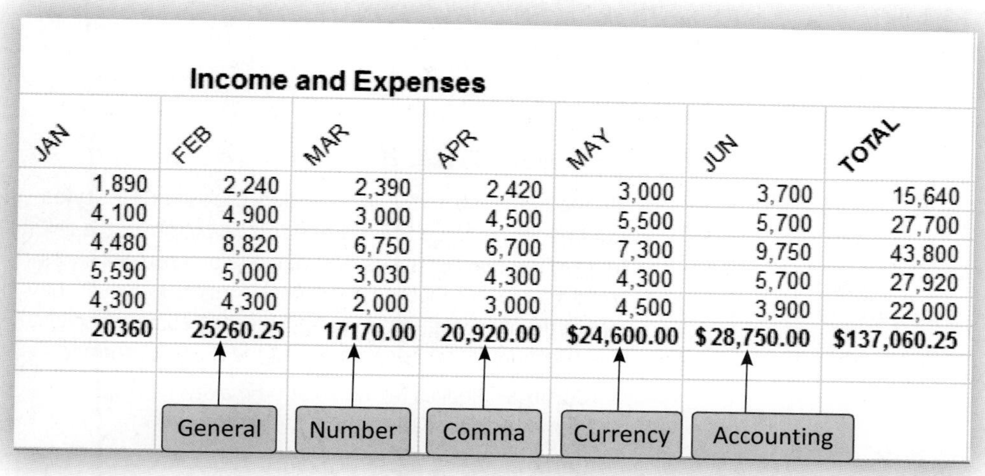

Income and Expenses

JAN	FEB	MAR	APR	MAY	JUN	TOTAL
1,890	2,240	2,390	2,420	3,000	3,700	15,640
4,100	4,900	3,000	4,500	5,500	5,700	27,700
4,480	8,820	6,750	6,700	7,300	9,750	43,800
5,590	5,000	3,030	4,300	4,300	5,700	27,920
4,300	4,300	2,000	3,000	4,500	3,900	22,000
20360	**25260.25**	**17170.00**	**20,920.00**	**$24,600.00**	**$ 28,750.00**	**$137,060.25**
	General	Number	Comma	Currency	Accounting	

FIGURE EX 1.9

Formatting numbers changes the appearance of the data in your worksheet but doesn't change the numerical values. The formatted number is displayed in the cell, and the actual value is displayed in the formula bar. Use the *Increase Decimal* and *Decrease Decimal* buttons from the *Number* group to increase or decrease the number of digits that appear to the right of the decimal point. For example, if a cell contains the number 1.234 and you click the *Decrease Decimal* button twice, the cell will now display 1.2. The number that displays in the formula bar will still be 1.234 because that is the number stored in the worksheet.

To apply the most common number formats, go to the *Home* tab, *Number* group, and click one of the following buttons:

$	Click the **Accounting Number Format** button to apply formatting appropriate for monetary values. The **Accounting Number Format** aligns the $ at the left side of the cell, displays two places after the decimal, and aligns all numbers at the decimal point. Zeros are displayed as dashes (–).
%	Click the **Percent Style** button to have your numbers appear as %. For example, the number .02 will appear as 2%. By default, **Percent Style** displays zero places to the right of the decimal point.
,	Click the **Comma Style** button to apply the same format as the *Accounting Number Format* but without the currency symbol. **Comma Style** is a good number format to use if your worksheet includes many rows of numbers, summed in a total row (like a budget or cash flow projection), where too many $ symbols could be distracting. Use *Comma Style* formatting for all numbers except the total row. *Use Accounting Number Format* for the total row.

For other common number formats, click the **Number Format** arrow above the buttons in the *Number* group to display the *Number Format* menu.

Number—The default **Number** format shows two decimal places by default (so 43 displays as 43.00) but does not include commas.

Currency—With the **Currency** format, columns of numbers do not align at the $ and at the decimal as they do with *Accounting Number Format*. Instead, the *Currency* format places the $ immediately to the left of the number.

More Number Formats . . .—This option opens the *Format Cells* dialog to the *Number* tab, where you can select from even more number formats and customize any format, including adding color, specifying the number of decimal places to display, and setting whether or not negative numbers should be enclosed in parentheses.

tips & tricks

If you type $ before a number, Excel automatically applies the *Currency* number format.

tell me **more**

On the *Home* tab, in the *Styles* group, click the **Cell Styles** button to expand the *Styles* gallery. At the bottom of the gallery are five number styles. Applying one of these cell styles is the same as applying a number format. However, be aware that applying the *Currency* cell style actually applies the *Accounting Number Format*, not the *Currency* format.

Comma—applies the default *Comma Style* format with two digits to the right of the decimal.

Comma [0]—applies the *Comma Style* format but with no digits to the right of the decimal.

Currency—applies the default *Accounting Number Format*, with two digits to the right of the decimal.

Currency [0]—applies the *Accounting Number Format* but with no digits to the right of the decimal.

Percent—applies the default *Percent Style* format.

try **this**

When you right-click a cell, these formats are available from the Mini toolbar:

- Accounting Number Format
- Percent Style
- Comma Style

To apply the *Percent Style*, you can also use the keyboard shortcut Ctrl + ⇧Shift + 5.

1.10 Applying Date Formats

When you enter numbers in a date format such as 9/5/2011 or September 5, 2011, Excel detects that you are entering a date and automatically applies one of the date formats. Excel treats dates as a special type of number, so cells formatted as dates can be used in calculations. There are many types of date formats available, but the underlying number for the date will always be the same.

There are two number formats available from the *Number Format* menu. To apply one of these formats, from the *Home* tab, click the **Number Format** arrow above the buttons in the *Number* group, and then click the format you want:

Short Date—Applies a simple format displaying the one- or two-digit number representing the month, followed by the one- or two-digit number representing the day, followed by the four-digit year (9/5/2011).

Long Date—Applies a longer format displaying the day of the week, and then the name of the month, the two-digit date, and the four-digit year (Monday, September 05, 2011).

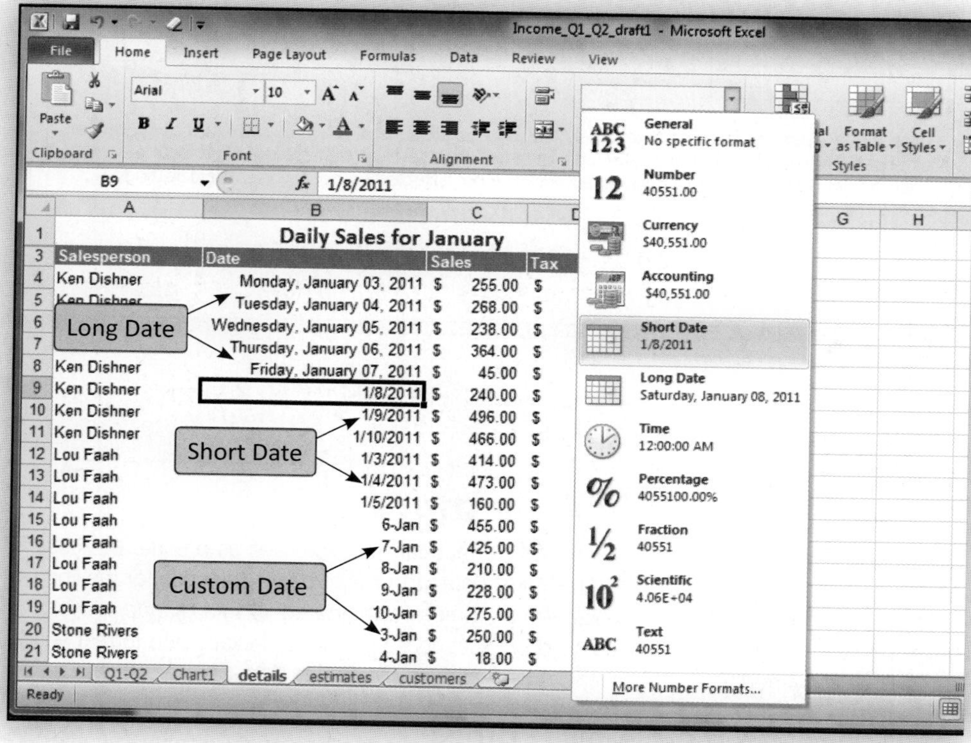

FIGURE EX 1.10

If you would like to use a different date format:

1. Select **More Number Formats. . .** from the *Number Format* list.
2. In the *Format Cells* dialog, from the *Number* tab, if necessary, click **Date** in the *Category:* list. Excel offers a variety of prebuilt date formats to choose from.
3. Notice that as you click each format in the *Type:* list, the *Sample* box shows how the active cell will display with the selected format.
4. Click the date format you would like, and click **OK.**

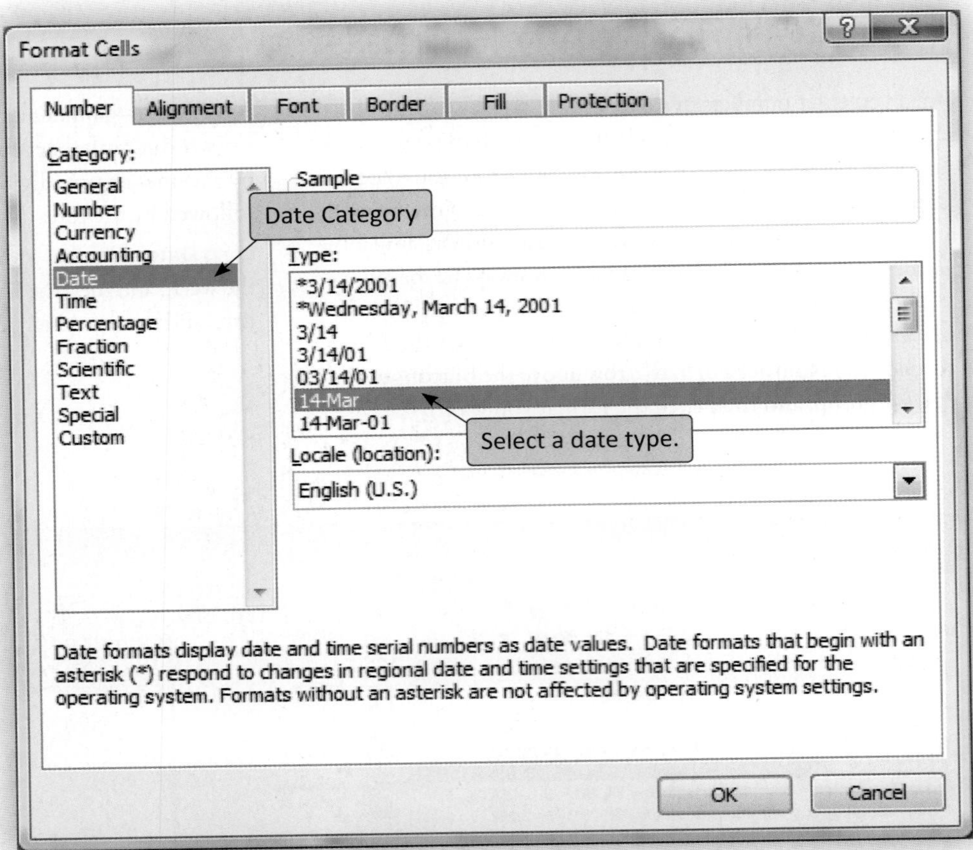

FIGURE EX 1.11

tips & tricks

Only dates from January 1, 1900, through December 31, 9999, are stored as numbers. Dates prior to January 1, 1900, are stored as text and cannot be used in calculations. To see the serial number for a date, change the cell format from *Date* to *General* or *Number*. The date will be converted to a "regular" number. For example, December 31, 2009, is the number 40178.

tell me **more**

Every date format can be expressed as a code. The code for the *Short Date* format is *m/d/yyy*. The code for the Long Date format is more complicated: *[$ –F800]dddd, mmmm dd, yyyy*. If Excel does not offer the exact date format you want to use, you can modify the date code using the *Custom* number option.

1. Select **More Number Formats . . .** from the *Number* list.
2. In the *Format Cells* dialog, from the *Number* tab, click **Custom** in the *Category:* list.
3. The *Custom* list includes the code for every number format offered. Click the code for the format closest to the format you want, and then make adjustments to the code in the *Type:* box. The *Sample* box shows how the number format will look in your worksheet.
4. Click **OK** to apply your new custom number format.

1.11 Entering Simple Formulas

A **formula** is an equation used to calculate a value. A formula can perform a mathematical calculation, such as displaying the sum of ***35 + 47,*** or a formula can calculate a value using cell references, such as displaying the sum of the values of cells ***A3 + B3*** or calculating the product of the value of cell ***A3 * 3.*** Formulas always begin with an equal sign (=).

Formulas may include functions. **Functions** are preprogrammed shortcuts for calculating complex equations (like the average of a group of numbers). Most functions require you to provide input called the **arguments** (numbers or cell references usually). Arguments are the parts of the formula that the function uses to calculate the value. Formulas that include functions always begin with an equal sign, followed by the function name, followed by the arguments enclosed in parentheses. If there are multiple arguments, separate them with a comma.

=AVERAGE(A2:A16)

The formula above uses the AVERAGE function to calculate the average value of cells A2 through A16.

When you select a cell that contains a formula, the cell will display the value and the formula bar will display the formula. You can edit the formula in the formula bar, or you can double-click the cell to edit the formula directly in the cell. Notice that when you edit the formula, any referenced cells are highlighted.

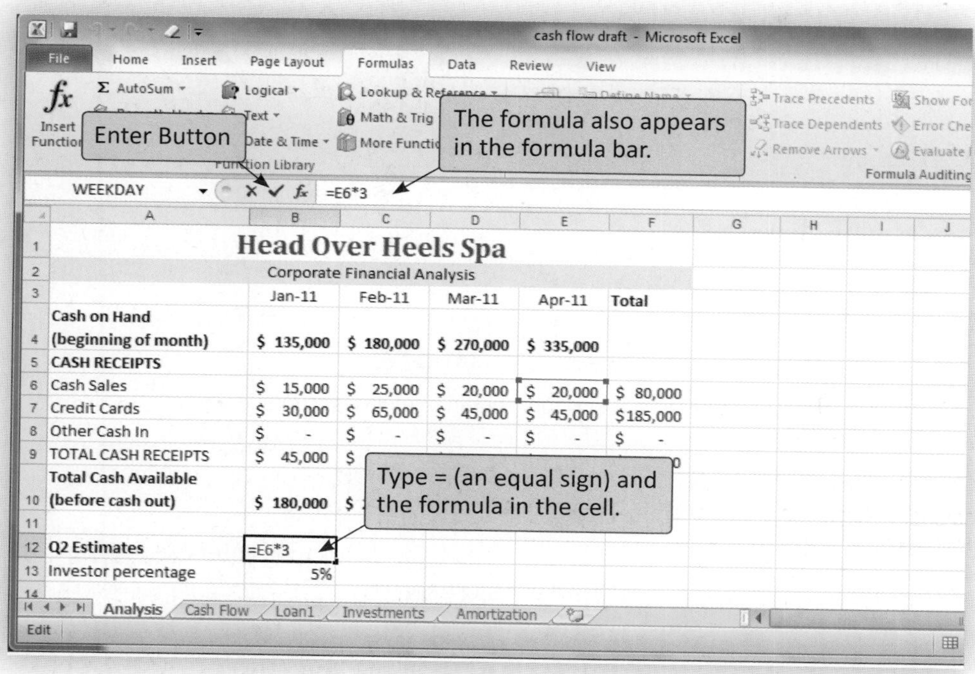

FIGURE EX 1.12

To enter a formula:

1. Click the cell in which you want to enter the formula.
2. Press the [=].
3. Type the formula.
4. To add a cell reference to a formula, you can type the cell address or click the cell. If you are in the middle of typing a formula and you click another cell in the worksheet, Excel knows to add that cell reference to the formula instead of moving to it.
5. Press [←Enter].

from the perspective of . . .

HIGH SCHOOL STUDENT

I use spreadsheets to do my math homework. I can use formulas to help me with my calculations.

tips & tricks

When you enter a formula with more than one mathematical operation, the formula is not necessarily calculated from left to right. Excel calculations follow the mathematical rules called the **order of operations** (also called **precedence**). The rules state that mathematical operations in a formula are calculated in this order:

1. Exponents and roots
2. Multiplication and division
3. Addition and subtraction

Adding parentheses around part of a formula will override the order of operations, forcing Excel to perform the calculation within the parentheses first.

4 + 5 * 2 = 14—Excel calculates 5 * 2 first (10) and then adds 4.

(4 + 5) * 2 = 18—Excel calculates 4 + 5 first (9), and then multiples by 2.

4 + 5^2 = 29—Excel calculates 5 to the 2nd power first (25), and then adds 4.

(4 + 5)^2 = 81—Excel calculates 4 + 5 first (9), and then raises that number to the 2nd power.

tell me **more**

Using functions in formulas is covered in depth in the lesson *Using Formulas and Functions.*

try **this**

To enter a formula, you can click the **Enter** button ✓ to the left of the formula bar.

1.12 Adding Borders

Add borders to your workbook to emphasize a cell or group of cells. You can use borders to make your workbook look more like a desktop publishing form, or to follow accounting conventions such as using a double-underline for cells displaying totals.

To add borders to your workbook:

1. Select the cell(s) you want to add a border to.
2. On the *Home* tab, in the *Font* group, click the **Borders** button arrow and select the border style you want.

To remove borders:

1. Select the cell(s) you want to remove the borders from.
2. On the *Home* tab, in the *Font* group, click the **Borders** button arrow and select **No Border** from the list of border styles.

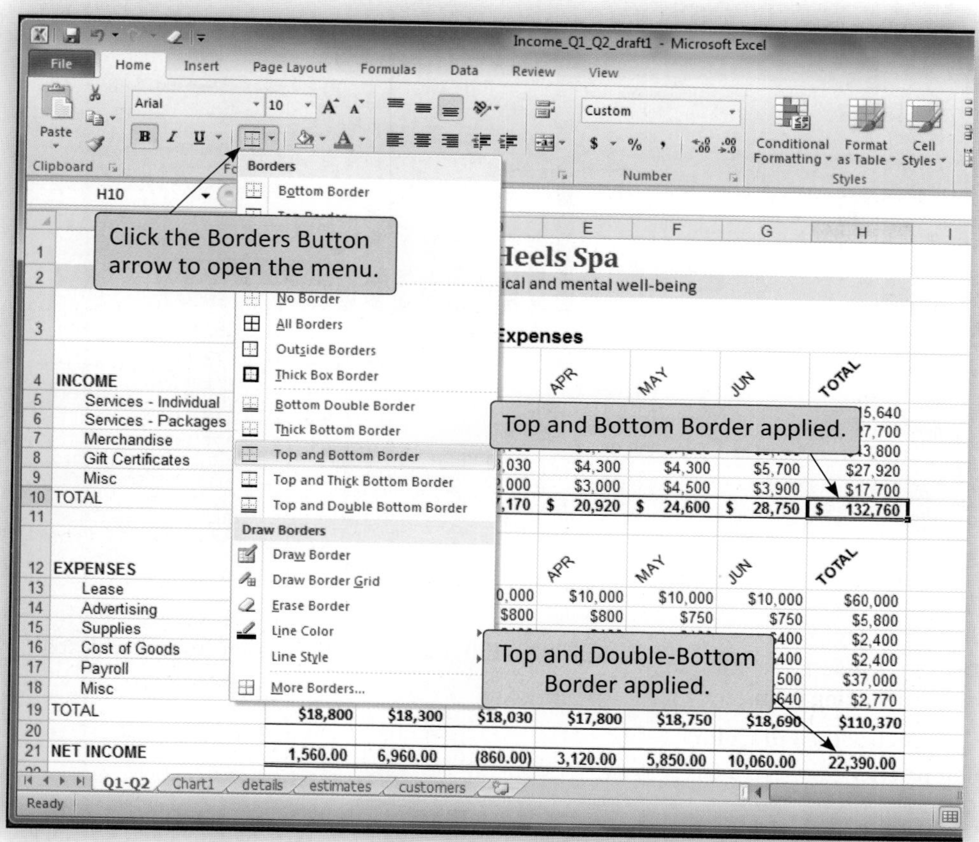

FIGURE EX 1.13

tips & tricks

The *Borders* button displays the most recently used border style. If you want to reuse this style, you can just click the button. You do not need to reselect the border style from the menu again.

tell me more

For more control over the look of cell borders, select **More Borders . . .** from the *Borders* menu to open the *Format Cells* dialog. From the *Border* tab, you can specify the line style and color for the border. You can also see a preview of how the border will look.

try this

The **Borders** button is also available from the Mini toolbar when you right-click a cell.

1.13 Adding Shading

Another way to emphasize cells in your workbook is to add shading. Shading is often used to differentiate alternating rows in a large table or to make the heading row stand out. If you use a dark color for shading, change the font color to white or another light color.

To add shading to your workbook:

1. Select the cell(s) you want to add shading to.
2. On the *Home* tab, in the *Font* group, click the **Fill Color** button arrow to display the color palette. The color palette includes colors from the workbook theme as well as a row of standard colors along the bottom. Notice that as you hold the mouse over each color in the palette, a tool tip appears displaying the color name.
3. Click the color you want.

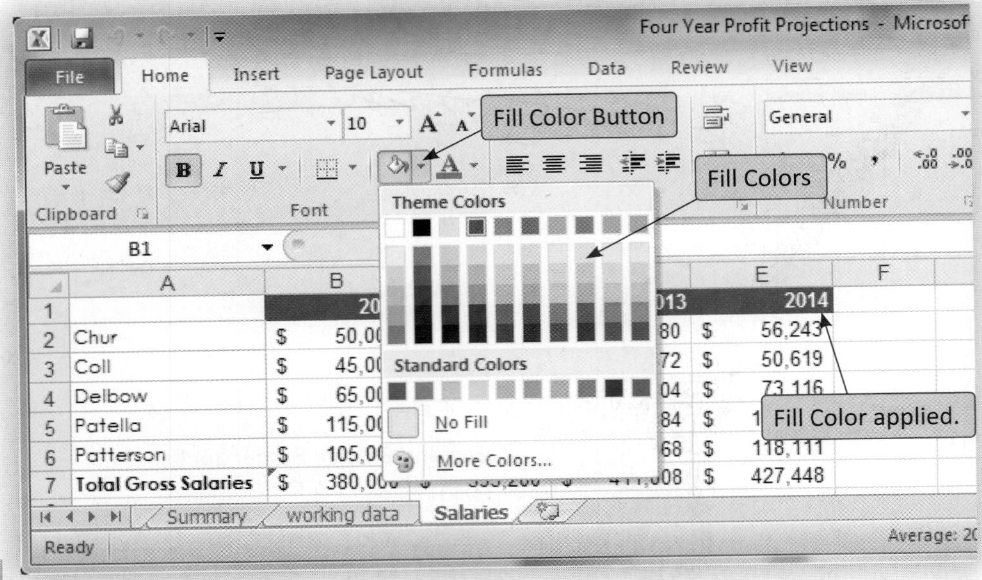

FIGURE EX 1.14

To remove shading:

1. Select the cell(s) you want to remove shading from.
2. On the *Home* tab, in the *Font* group, click the **Fill Color** button arrow to display the color palette.
3. Click **No Fill** to remove the fill color from the selected cells.

tips & tricks

Like the *Borders* button, the *Fill Color* button displays the most recently used shading color. If you want to reuse this color, just click the button. You do not need to reselect the color from the *Fill Color* palette.

Avoid overusing shading and using too many colors in your workbook. Shading should be used for emphasis and to make the workbook easier to read, not just to make the workbook more colorful.

tell me more

The *Fill* tab on the *Format Cells* dialog offers options for fill effects and pattern styles.

try this

The **Fill Color** button is also available from the Mini toolbar when you right-click a cell.

1.14 Using Format Painter with Excel

A professional, well-organized workbook uses consistent formatting. Use the **Format Painter** tool to copy formatting from one part of your worksheet to another, rather than trying to re-create the exact combination of font color and size, number formatting, borders, and shading to reuse.

To use *Format Painter:*

1. Select the cell that has the formatting you want to copy.
2. On the *Home* tab, in the *Clipboard* group, click the **Format Painter** button.
3. Click the cell that you want to apply the formatting to. To apply the formatting to a range of cells, click the first cell in the group, hold down the left mouse button, and drag across the cells. Notice that your mouse cursor changes to the *Format Painter* shape. When you reach the last cell in the group, release the mouse button.
4. The formatting is automatically applied to the selected cell(s).

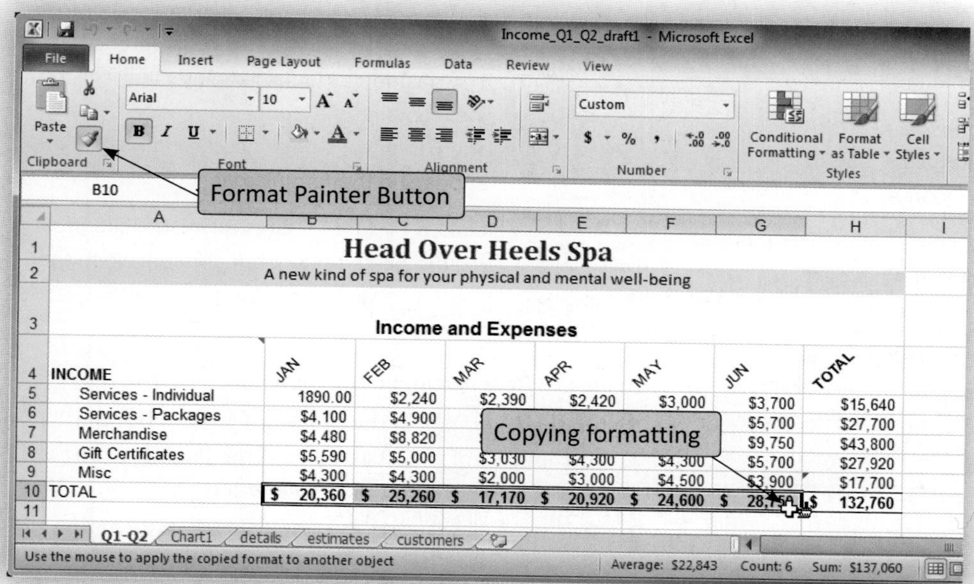

FIGURE EX 1.15

tell me **more**

If you want to apply the formatting to different parts of a worksheet or workbook, double-click the **Format Painter** button when you select it. It will stay on until you click the **Format Painter** button again or press Esc to deselect it.

try **this**

To activate *Format Painter,* you can also right-click the cell with formatting you want to copy and click the **Format Painter** button on the Mini toolbar.

1.15 Using Paste Options

When you paste data into Excel, you can use the default *Paste* option to insert the copied data (including formulas and formatting) into the selected cell, or you can select from the paste options to control more precisely what is pasted.

	Paste—The default paste command that pastes all of the source content and formatting.
	Formulas—Pastes the formulas but none of the formatting.
	Formula & Number Formatting—Pastes the formulas and number formatting but none of the cell formatting such as font size, borders, and shading.
	Keep Source Formatting—Pastes the content, including formulas, and all formatting from the source.
	No Borders—Pastes the content, including formulas, and all formatting *except* borders.
	Keep Source Column Widths—Pastes the copied cell, including formulas and all number and cell formatting. Also adjusts the column width to match the width of the source column.
	Transpose—Pastes the rows from the source into columns, and the columns from the source into rows.

When your source includes formulas, you also have the option to paste the calculated cell values without pasting the underlying formulas.

123	**Values**—Pastes only the values, not the underlying formula or cell formatting.
123%	**Values & Number Formatting**—Pastes only the values, not the underlying formulas. Includes number formatting but not other cell formatting such as borders and shading.
123	**Values & Source Formatting**—Pastes only the values, not the underlying formulas. Includes all formatting from the source.

The final group of paste options provides alternatives to pasting the actual contents of one cell into another.

%	**Formatting**—Pastes only the cell and number formatting, not the formula or cell value from the source.
	Link—Pastes a formula that references the source cell rather than pasting the contents of the source itself. When the source cell is updated, the linked cell displays the update automatically.
	Picture—Pastes an *image* of the source cell rather than the actual cell contents. The pasted cell looks like any other cell in the worksheet, except it cannot be edited, and when you select the cell, nothing appears in the formula bar.
	Linked Picture—Pastes an image, like the *Picture* paste option, but updates when the source cell is updated.

To use the *Paste* button on the Ribbon:

1. On the *Home* tab, in the *Clipboard* group, click the bottom part of the **Paste** button (the **Paste button arrow**) to expand the *Paste Options* menu.
2. Move your mouse over the icon for each paste option to see a preview of how the paste would look, and then click the icon for the paste option you want.

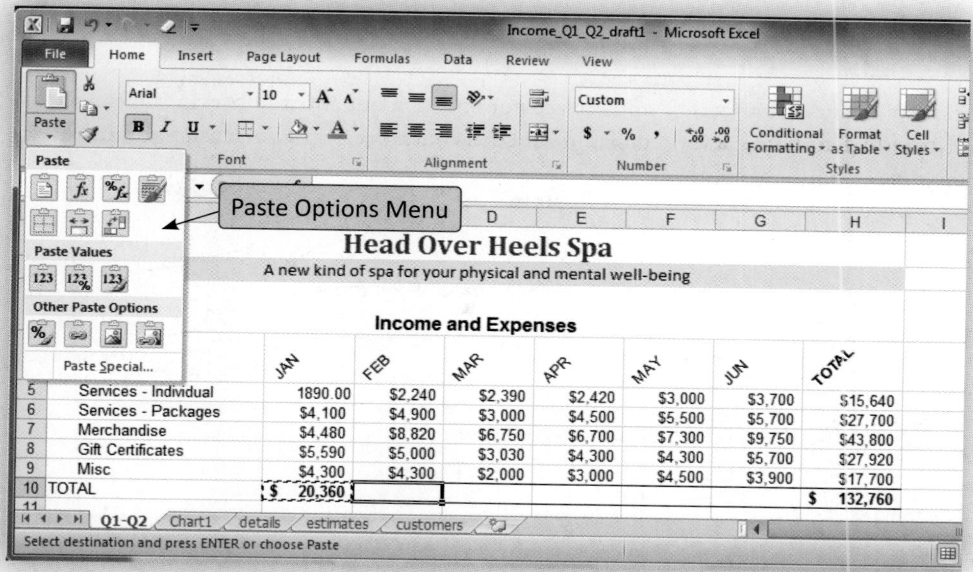

FIGURE EX 1.16

To use the keyboard shortcut:

1. Press Ctrl + V on the keyboard.
2. The source is pasted using the default *Paste* option, and the *Paste Options* button appears.
3. Click the **Paste Options** button (Ctrl) or press the Ctrl key to display the *Paste Options* menu. This is the same menu that is available from the *Paste* button on the Ribbon, but moving your mouse over the icons does not show a preview of how the paste would look.

tips & tricks

A useful paste option is *Keep Source Column Widths*. Often, when you paste data into a new worksheet, the default column width is too narrow to display the data. Use the *Keep Source Column Widths* paste option to maintain any column width adjustments you made in the source worksheet.

tell me more

If you do not want the *Paste Options* button to appear every time you paste with the keyboard shortcut, you can turn it off:

1. Click the **File** tab to open Backstage view.
2. Click **Options** to open the *Excel Options* dialog.
3. Click **Advanced.**
4. In the *Cut, copy, and paste* section near the bottom of the window, click the check box in front of **Show Paste Options button when content is pasted** to remove the check mark.
5. Click **OK.**

try this

You can also access the paste options from the right-click menu. Six of the paste options appear on the right-click menu (*Paste, Values, Formulas, Transpose, Formatting,* and *Paste Link*). To select an option from the full *Paste Options* menu, point to **Paste Special . . .,** and then click the paste option you want.

1.16 Using Find and Replace in Excel

All of the Microsoft Office applications include **Find** and **Replace** commands that allow you to search for and replace data in your file. In Excel, these commands can be used to find and replace not only text but also numbers in values and formulas in a single worksheet or across an entire workbook.

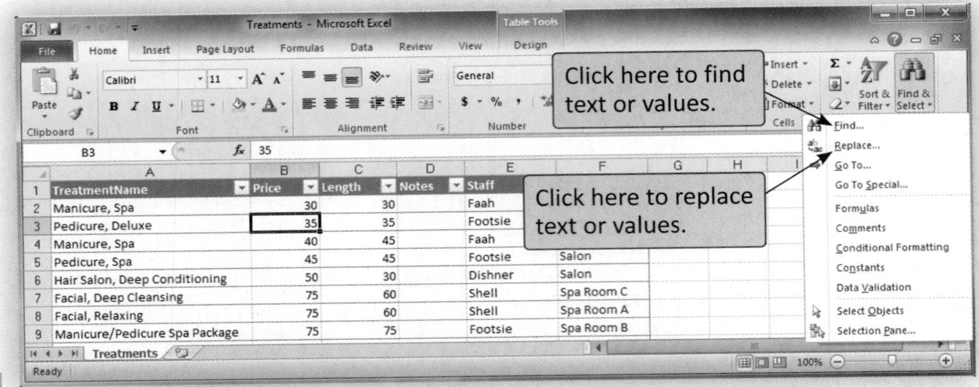

FIGURE EX 1.17

Before using the *Replace* command, you should use *Find* to make sure the data you are about to replace are what you expect:

1. On the *Home* tab, in the *Editing* group at the far right side of the Ribbon, click the **Find & Select** button.
2. From the *Find & Select* menu, click **Find. . .**
3. The *Find and Replace* dialog box opens, with the *Find* tab on top.
4. Type the word, phrase, or number you want to find in the *Find what:* box.
5. Click the **Find All** button. When you click *Find All,* Excel displays a list detailing every instance of the data—worksheet, cell address, the value of the cell, and the formula (if there is one).

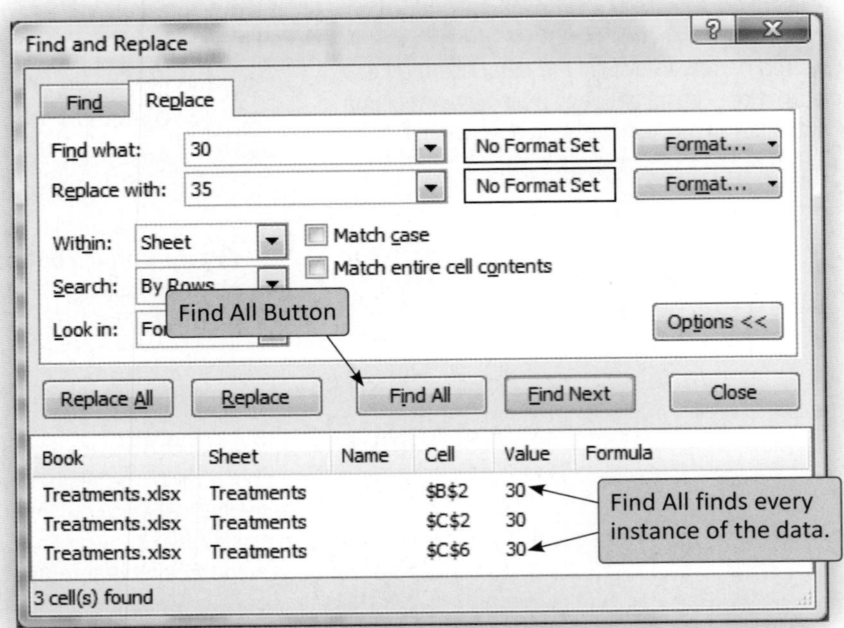

FIGURE EX 1.18

Once you have verified the data you want to replace, switch to the *Replace* tab in the *Find and Replace* dialog:

1. Click the **Replace** tab.
2. Excel keeps the data you typed in the *Find what:* box. Now type the replacement text or values in the *Replace with:* box.
3. Click the **Replace** button to replace one instance of the data at a time, or click **Replace All** to replace all instances at once.
4. Excel displays a message telling you how many replacements were made. Click **OK** to dismiss the message.
5. Click **Close** to close the *Find and Replace* dialog.

tips & tricks

By default, Excel searches for the data both in cell values and within formulas. If you want to limit the search to only cell values, first click the **Options**>> button in the *Find and Replace* dialog to display the find and replace optional settings. Next, expand the *Look in:* list by clicking the arrow, and select **Values.**

tell me more

Find and Replace allows you to find and replace formatting as well as data. This feature is especially helpful when replacing number formats throughout a workbook.

To find and replace formatting:

1. Open the *Find and Replace* dialog.
2. If necessary, click the **Options**>> button to display the find and replace optional settings. Notice that next to the *Find what:* and *Replace with:* boxes, the preview box displays "No Format Set."
3. Click the **Format . . .** button next to the *Find what:* box and use the *Find Format* dialog to define the formatting you want to find. The preview box now displays the word "Preview" using the formatting you defined. If you included number formatting, "Preview" will appear with an * after it (because the word "Preview" cannot display number formatting).
4. Click the **Format . . .** button next to the *Replace with:* box and repeat the same process to define the new format you want to use.
5. Click **Replace All.**
6. Click **OK** in the message that appears.
7. Click **Close** to close the *Find and Replace* dialog.

try this

Use the keyboard shortcut Ctrl + F to open the *Find and Replace* dialog with the *Find* tab on top.

Use the keyboard shortcut Ctrl + H to open the *Find and Replace* dialog with the *Replace* tab on top.

1.17 Clearing Cell Content

If you want to remove the contents of a cell without removing the cell from the structure of your workbook, you will need to **clear** the cell. In Excel, when you clear a cell, you remove its contents, formats, comments, and hyperlinks, but the blank cell remains in the worksheet. Clearing a cell does not affect the layout of your worksheet.

To clear a cell:

1. Select the cell you want to clear of formats or contents.
2. On the *Home* tab, in the *Editing* group, click the **Clear** button.
3. Click the command for the type of formatting or contents you want to remove from the cell.

Clear All—clears all cell contents and formatting and deletes any comments or hyperlinks attached to the cell.

Clear Formats—clears only the cell formatting and leaves the cell contents, comments, and hyperlinks.

Clear Contents—clears only the contents (including hyperlinks) and leaves the cell formatting and comments.

Clear Comments—deletes any comments attached to the cell while leaving the cell contents, formatting, and hyperlinks intact.

Clear Hyperlinks—removes the hyperlink action from the cell without removing the content or the hyperlink style of formatting.

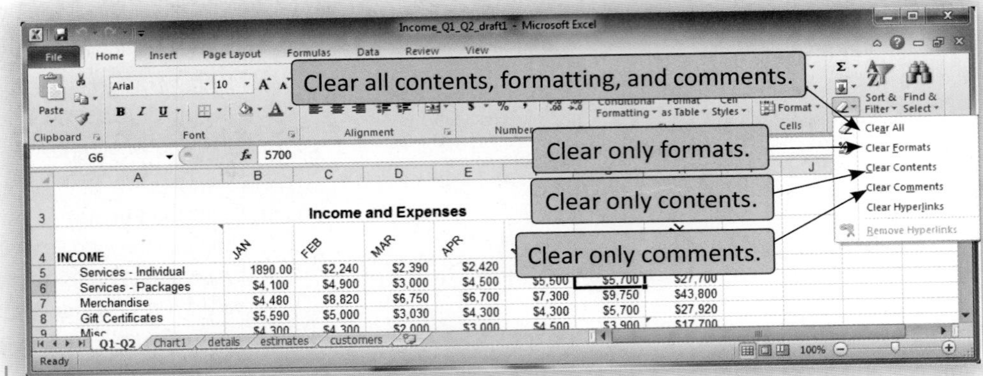

FIGURE EX 1.19

tell me **more**

A **hyperlink** is text or a graphic that when clicked jumps to another location in your workbook or opens another file or Web page. When a cell contains a hyperlink, the *Clear* menu option *Remove Hyperlinks* will appear active. Clicking **Remove Hyperlinks** deletes the link and the hyperlink formatting from the cell, leaving the cell content.

try **this**

To clear the contents of a cell, you can

- Right-click the cell and select **Clear Contents** from the menu. Using the right-click method, there are no options to clear formats or comments.
- Select the cell and then press the Delete key or the ←Backspace key to clear the cell contents but not the cell formatting.

1.18 Changing the Zoom Level

If you are working with a large spreadsheet, you may find that you need to see more of the spreadsheet at one time or that you would like a closer look at a cell or group of cells. You can use the **zoom slider** in the lower-right corner of the window to zoom in and out of a worksheet, changing the size of text and images on screen. As you move the slider, the zoom level displays the percentage the worksheet has been zoomed in or zoomed out. Zooming a worksheet only affects how the worksheet appears on screen. It does not affect how the worksheet will print.

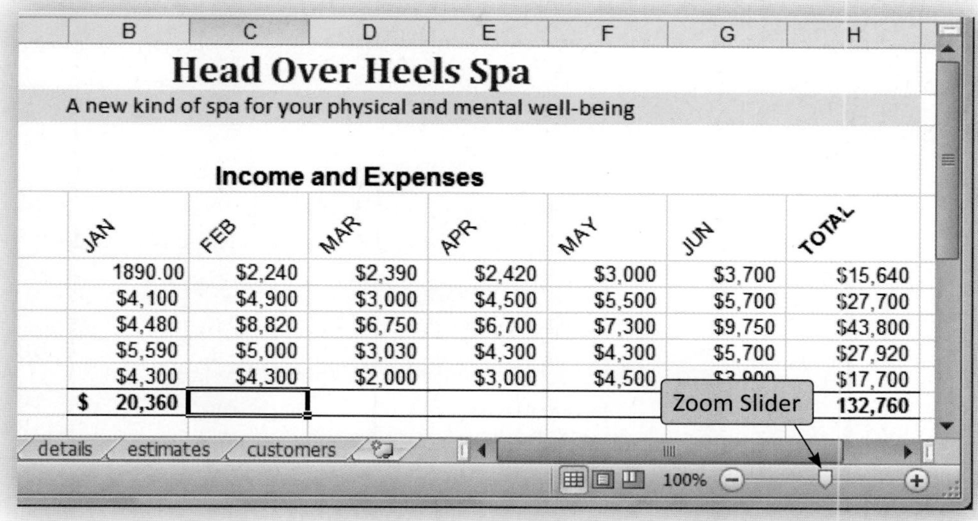

FIGURE EX 1.20

To zoom in on a worksheet, making the text and graphics appear larger:

- Click and drag the zoom slider to the right.
- Click the **Zoom In** button on the slider.

To zoom out of a worksheet, making the text and graphics appear smaller:

- Click and drag the zoom slider to the left.
- Click the **Zoom Out** button on the slider.

On the *View* tab, the *Zoom* group includes buttons for two of the most common zoom options:

- Click the **Zoom to Selection** button to zoom in as close as possible on the currently selected cell(s).
- Click the **100%** button to return the worksheet back to 100% of the normal size.

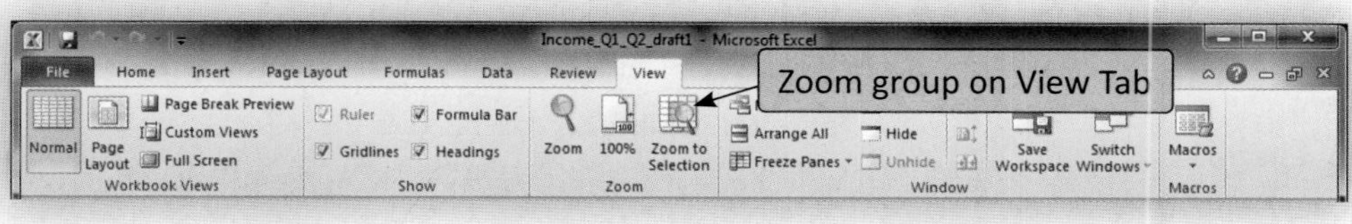

FIGURE EX 1.21

tips & tricks

When you create a new worksheet or open another worksheet, Excel will retain the zoom setting from the last active worksheet.

try this

You can also change the zoom level through the *Zoom* dialog box. To open the *Zoom* dialog:

- Click the zoom level number next to the zoom slider to open the *Zoom* dialog box.

or

- Click the **Zoom** button in the *Zoom* group on the *View* tab.

projects

Skill Review 1.1

Medication Schedule. In this review you will create a worksheet to keep track of a medication schedule.

1. Start a new Excel workbook and enter a title and labels as follows:

a. Click on the cell **A1.**

b. Type: `Medication Schedule`

c. Press **Enter** key on keyboard.

d. Save the file in an appropriate folder. Name the file: ***[your initials]*EX_SkillReview_1-1**

e. Enter the following word in cell **A2:** `Date`

f. In cell **A4** enter this text: `Patient Name`

g. In cell **A5** enter this text: `Medication`

h. In cell **A6** enter this text: `Dosage Amount`

i. Save the updates to the workbook. Click the **Save** button.

	A	B	C	D
1	Medication Schedule			
2	Date			
3				
4	Patient Name			
5	Medication			
6	Dosage Amount			
7				
8		1st dose	6:00 AM	
9				
10				
11				
12				
13				

FIGURE EX 1.22

2. Use AutoFill to enter data as follows:

a. In cell **B8,** enter this text: `1st dose`

b. In cell **C8,** enter the time for the first dose: `6:00 AM`

c. Drag the mouse to select both cells **B8** and **C8** to start the series.

d. Locate the little, black square called the **Fill Handle** (in lower right of selected cell). Click and drag it down to fill the series. Your mouse will look like a black plus sign.

e. Release the mouse button when you have highlighted the last cell to fill, cell **C13.**

f. Save the updates to the workbook by clicking the **Save** button.

3. Enter the date, patient, and medication information:

a. In cell **B2** enter this date: `Sept 24, 2011`

b. Select cell **B2.** On the *Home* tab, in the *Number* group, click the **Number Format** arrow. From the list, select the **Short Date** format.

c. In cell **C4** enter your first and last name as the patient name.

d. In cell **C5** enter the medication name: `dichlorephenezone`

e. In cell **C6** enter the medication dosage: `1 tablet every 4 hours`

f. Edit cell **A6** by deleting the word: *Amount*

g. Edit cell **C9** by changing the time of the second dose to: `10:00 AM`

	A	B	C	D
1	Medication Schedule			
2	Date	9/24/2011		
3				
4	Patient Name		Ima Student	
5	Medication		dichlorephenezone	
6	Dosage		1 tablet every 4 hours	
7				
8		1st dose	6:00 AM	
9		2nd dose	7:00 AM	
10		3rd dose	8:00 AM	
11		4th dose	9:00 AM	
12		5th dose	10:00 AM	
13		6th dose	11:00 AM	
14				
15				

FIGURE EX 1.23

h. Select both cells **C8** and **C9.** Drag the fill handle down to continue the pattern of 4-hour time intervals.

i. In cell **D8,** enter this number: `1`

j. In cell **E8,** enter this word: `tablet`

k. Select cells **D8** and **E8,** fill down.

l. Click the **AutoFill Options** button and select **Copy cells.**

4. Format the labels.

a. Drag your mouse to select (highlight) cells **A1** through **A6.** In Excel, we type this as *A1:A6.* The : colon character means "through."

b. Click the **Bold** button.

c. To change the font to Century Gothic, on the *Home* tab, in the *Font* group, click the arrow next to the **Font** box and select the **Century Gothic** font.

d. Save the updates to the workbook by clicking the **Save** button.

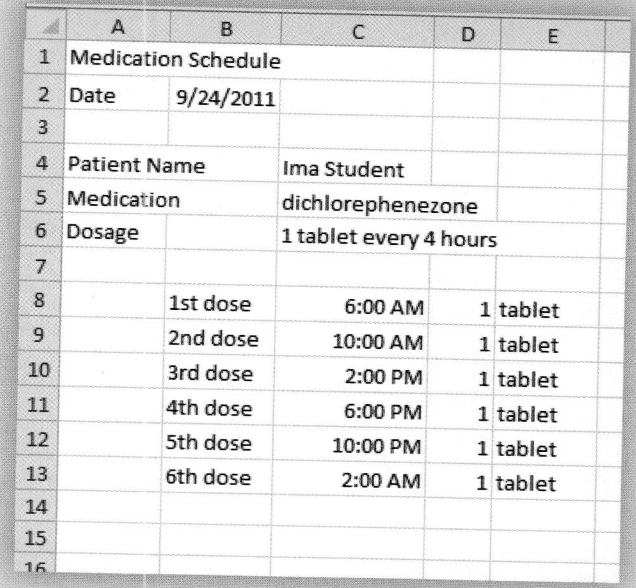

	A	B	C	D	E
1	Medication Schedule				
2	Date	9/24/2011			
3					
4	Patient Name		Ima Student		
5	Medication		dichlorephenezone		
6	Dosage		1 tablet every 4 hours		
7					
8		1st dose	6:00 AM	1	tablet
9		2nd dose	10:00 AM	1	tablet
10		3rd dose	2:00 PM	1	tablet
11		4th dose	6:00 PM	1	tablet
12		5th dose	10:00 PM	1	tablet
13		6th dose	2:00 AM	1	tablet
14					
15					
16					

FIGURE EX 1.24

5. Compute the total number of pills per day and the daily cost as follows:

a. Select cells **B8:E8.** Right-click on the selected area.

b. Choose **Insert . . .**; click **Shift cells down.** Repeat to insert 2 new blank rows.

c. In cell **A7** enter the text: `Cost per Tablet`

d. In cell **A8** enter the text: `Daily Cost`

e. In cell **C7,** enter this number: `.75`

f. Format cell C7 with dollar signs and 2 decimal places as follows:

(1) Select cell **C7.**

(2) Click the **Accounting Number Format** button, which looks like a dollar sign $.

g. In cell **D19** enter the following formula: `=D10 + D11 + D12 + D13 + D14 + D15 + D16.` Press **Enter.**

h. In cell **C8** enter the following formula: `= D19*C7.` Press **Enter.**

i. Save the updates to the workbook.

6. Format the worksheet as follows:

a. Format the worksheet title using cell styles as follows:

(1) Select the title cell **A1.**

(2) On the *Home* tab, in the *Styles* group, click the **Cell Styles** button to display the *Styles* gallery.

(3) Click the **Title** style to apply it to the cell.

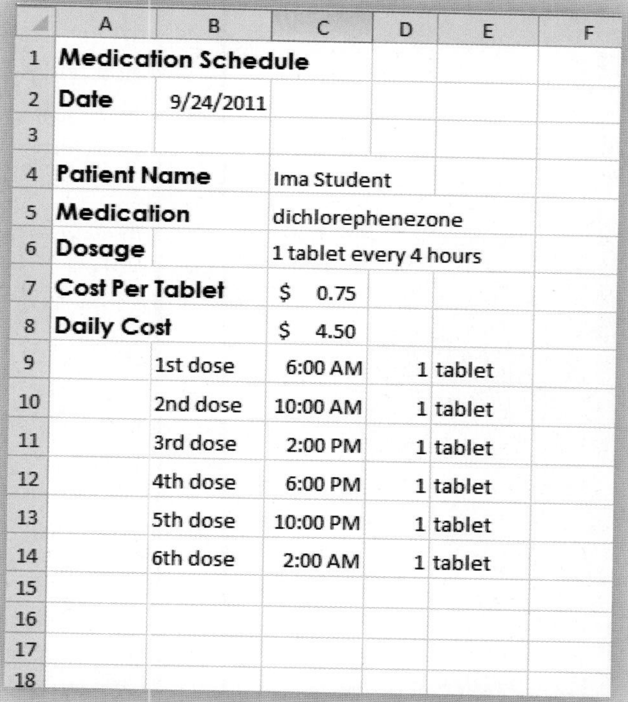

b. Use *Format Painter* as follows:

(1) Select the title in cell **A1.**

(2) Click the **Format Painter** button once.

(3) Drag the mouse over the dosage numbers in cells **B10:B15.**

(4) With the cells **B10:B15** selected, reduce the font size by clicking the arrow next to the **Font Size** box, and selecting **11** by clicking the **Decrease Font** button four times.

	A	B	C	D	E	F
1	**Medication Schedule**					
2	**Date**	9/24/2011				
3						
4	**Patient Name**		Ima Student			
5	**Medication**		dichlorephenezone			
6	**Dosage**		1 tablet every 4 hours			
7	**Cost Per Tablet**		$ 0.75			
8	**Daily Cost**		$ 4.50			
9		1st dose	6:00 AM	1	tablet	
10		2nd dose	10:00 AM	1	tablet	
11		3rd dose	2:00 PM	1	tablet	
12		4th dose	6:00 PM	1	tablet	
13		5th dose	10:00 PM	1	tablet	
14		6th dose	2:00 AM	1	tablet	
15						
16						
17						
18						

FIGURE EX 1.25

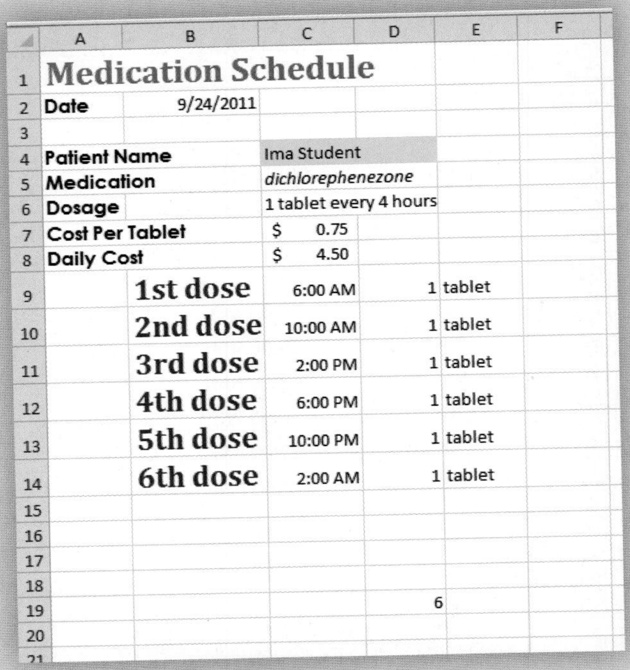

	A	B	C	D	E	F
1	**Medication Schedule**					
2	**Date**	9/24/2011				
3						
4	**Patient Name**		Ima Student			
5	**Medication**		*dichlorephenezone*			
6	**Dosage**		1 tablet every 4 hours			
7	**Cost Per Tablet**		$ 0.75			
8	**Daily Cost**		$ 4.50			
9		**1st dose**	6:00 AM	1	tablet	
10		**2nd dose**	10:00 AM	1	tablet	
11		**3rd dose**	2:00 PM	1	tablet	
12		**4th dose**	6:00 PM	1	tablet	
13		**5th dose**	10:00 PM	1	tablet	
14		**6th dose**	2:00 AM	1	tablet	
15						
16						
17						
18						
19				6		
20						
21						

FIGURE EX 1.26

c. Format the medication name with italic font.

(1) Click in cell **C5.**

(2) Click the **Italic** button. Press **Enter.**

d. Add shading to highlight the patient's name as follows:

(1) Select cells **C4:D4.**

(2) On the *Home* tab, in the *Font* group, click the **Fill Color** button arrow; choose yellow.

e. Save the updates to the workbook.

7. Edit the worksheet, making the following changes to it:

a. To make the title text larger, select cell **A1**, click the arrow next to the **Font Size** box, and select **20.**

b. To make the title text red, with cell **A1** still selected, click the arrow next to the **Font Color** button on the *Home* tab, in the *Font* group, and select red.

c. Add a border around the patient's name, medication, and dosage:

(1) Select cells **A4:E6.**

(2) On the *Home* tab, in the *Font* group, click the **Borders** button arrow and select **Thick Box Border.**

d. Use cell styles to accent the *Daily Cost.*

(1) Select cells **A8:C8.**

(2) On the *Home* tab, in the *Styles* group, click the **Cell Styles** button to display the *Styles* gallery and choose any of the **Accent** styles.

e. Save the updates to the workbook.

8. Use *Copy and Paste* to start another medication schedule for a different medication.

a. Select cells **A1:F21,** right-click on the selected cells, and select **Copy.**

b. Right-click in cell **H1,** point to **Paste Special,** move the mouse over various options to preview, and choose **Keep Source Column Widths.**

c. Zoom out, making the text and numbers appear smaller. To use the zoom slider in the lower-right corner of the window, click and drag the **zoom slider** to the left or click the **Minus** button until you can see all of your worksheet on your screen.

d. On the left half of your screen, delete the sixth dosage:

(1) Select the cells **B15:E15.**

(2) Right-click on the selected cells and choose **Clear Contents.**

e. On the right half of your screen, replace the old information with a new medication and dosage.

(1) Double-click the cell you want to change. You will see a blinking cursor in the cell.

(2) Make the appropriate change; press the **Enter** key.

(3) In cell **J5** enter the medication name: `hydrochlorathricida`

(4) In cell **J6** enter the medication dosage: `2 tablets every 6 hours`

(5) In cell **J7,** enter this number: `1.50`

(6) In cell **J11,** enter the second dose time: `12:00 PM`

(7) Select cells **J10** and **J11** and fill down the new times.

(8) Clear the contents of cells **I14:L15** to delete the 5th and 6th dosages.

f. Save the updates to the workbook.

FIGURE EX 1.27

9. Use *Find and Replace* as follows:

a. Select cells **H1:N21.**

b. On the *Home* tab, in the *Editing* group, click the **Find & Select** button arrow and select **Replace.**

c. In the **Find** box type: `tablet`

d. In the **Replace** box type: `capsule`

e. Click **Replace All.**

f. Verify accurate replacement throughout the right half of the worksheet and save the updates to the workbook.

g. Adjust column widths as needed.

h. Save the updates to the workbook by clicking the **Save** button.

10. Add *special instructions* information:

a. Select cells **A7:M7,** right-click on the selected area, choose **Insert. . .,** and click **Shift cells down.** Repeat to insert a new blank row.

b. In cell **A7** enter this label: `Special Instructions`

c. In cell **C7** enter: `Take with Food and plenty of Water`

d. Select cell **B7.** On the Home tab, in the *Alignment* group, click the **Wrap Text** button.

e. In cell **H7** enter this label: `Special Instructions`

f. In cell **J7** set to **wrap text** and enter: `Take on an Empty Stomach`

g. Adjust row heights as needed.

h. Save the updates to the workbook by clicking the **Save** button.

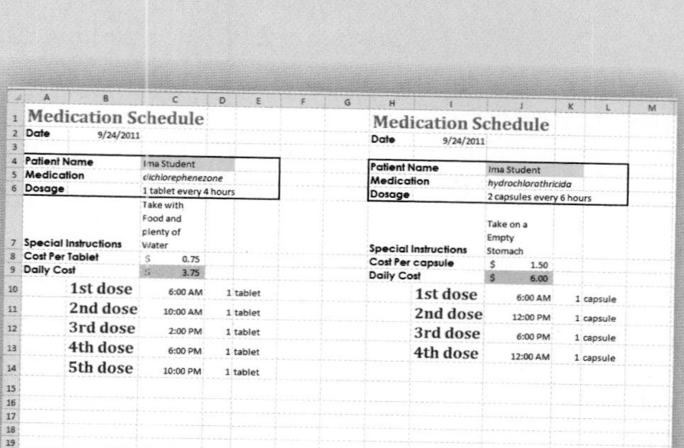

FIGURE EX 1.28

Skill Review 1.2

Textbook Purchases. In this review you will create a worksheet to track the cost of materials for your college classes.

1. Start a new Excel workbook and build the worksheet structure as follows:

a. Click on the cell **A1.**

b. Type: `College Book and Materials Purchases`

c. Press the **Enter** key on keyboard.

d. Enter the semester in cell **A3:** `Fall 2011` (or type in a recent semester/quarter or the current semester/quarter).

e. Enter the start date for the semester and the end date as follows:

(1) In cell **A4** type: `Aug 25`

(2) Press the **Enter** key on the keyboard.

(3) In cell **B4,** enter: `Dec 10.` Press **Enter.**

f. Save the file in an appropriate folder. Name the file:
***[your initials]*EX_SkillReview_1-2**

g. In row **6,** enter header labels to describe the column data:

	A	B	C	D	E	F
6	Item Number	Course	Books and Materials Purchased	Price Paid	Book Sell Back Amount	Net Cost

h. Some of the labels are too long to fully display; select the cells and click the **Wrap Text** button in the *Alignment* group on the *Home* tab.

2. Format the header labels:

a. Drag your mouse to select (highlight) just the cells A6, B6, C6, D6, E6, and F6. In Excel, we type this as `A6:F6`. The : colon character means "through."

b. Click the **Bold** button.

c. To change the font to Arial Narrow, click the arrow next to the **Font** box on the *Home* tab, in the *Font* group, and select the **Arial Narrow** font.

d. Save the updates to the workbook by clicking the **Save** button.

3. Enter the data to fill in the worksheet as follows:

a. In column **B** enter the course names; in column **C,** enter the books and materials; in column **D** enter the price; and in column **E** enter the book sell back amount.

COURSE	BOOKS AND MATERIALS PURCHASED	PRICE PAID	BOOK SELL BACK AMOUNT
History 17b	US History Reader, California History pamphlet	80.25	40
CIS30	Office Computer Applications book, course pack, USB drive	74.89	
English A	Composition Guide	52.50	25

b. Leave cell E8 blank.

c. Turn on cell wrapping as needed and adjust row and column widths appropriately.

d. Save the updates to the workbook by clicking the **Save** button.

4. Use AutoFill to enter all the item numbers:

a. Enter the following number in cell **A7:** `1`

b. Select cell **A7** to start the series.

c. Locate the little, black square called the **Fill Handle** (in lower right of the selected cell). Click and drag it down to fill the series. Your mouse will look like a black plus sign.

d. Release the mouse button when you have highlighted the last cell to fill, cell **A9.**

e. Excel just copied all ones. Instead number the items in sequence by clicking the **AutoFill Options** button [AutoFill Options icon] and then selecting **Fill the series.**

f. Save the updates to the workbook.

5. Compute the average sell back amount using two different formulas:

a. In cell **B11** enter the text: `Average Sell Back Amount`

b. In cell **E11** enter the Excel built-in function: `=AVERAGE(E7:E9)`

c. In cell **E12** enter the simple math formula: `= (E7+E9)/2`

d. Save the updates to the workbook.

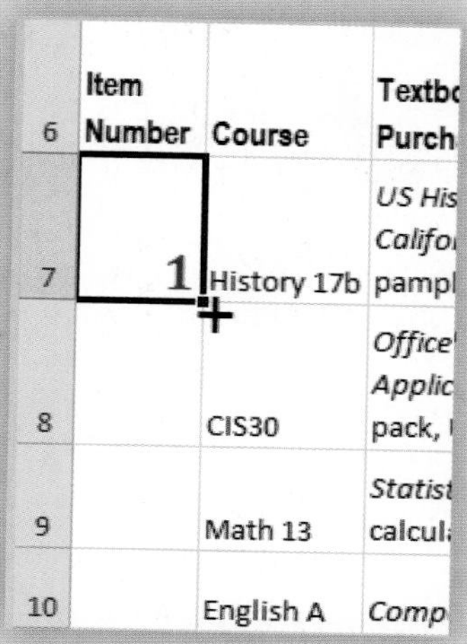

FIGURE EX 1.29

6. Compute the *Net Cost* per course using a simple math formula to subtract the *Sell Back Amount* from the original *Price Paid* as follows:

a. In cell **F7** enter the formula: `=D7-E7`

b. In cell **F8** enter the formula: `=D8-E8`

c. In cell **F9** enter the formula: `=D9-E9`

d. Save the updates to the workbook.

	A	B	C	D	E	F	G
1	College Textbook and Materials Purchases						
2							
3	Fall 2011						
4	25-Aug	10-Dec					
5							
6	Item Number	Course	Books and Materials Purchased	Price Paid	Book Sell Back Amount	Net Cost	
7	1	History 17b	US History Reader, California History pamphlet	80.25	40		
8	2	CIS30	Office Computer Applications book, course pack, USB drive	74.89			
9	3	English A	Composition Guide	52.50	25		
10							
11							

FIGURE EX 1.30

7. Format the worksheet as follows:

a. Format all the money numbers (*Price, Sell Back, Net Cost,* and *Average Sell Back Amount*) with dollar signs and 2 decimal places:

(1) Select the rectangular range of cells D7:F12 as follows: Drag from **D7** in the upper left through to **F12** in the lower right; then let go of the mouse button.

(2) On the *Home* tab, in the *Number* group, click the **Accounting Number Format** button, which looks like a dollar sign $.

(3) Adjust column widths as needed.

b. Format the worksheet title using cell styles:

(1) Select the title cell **A1**

(2) On the *Home* tab, in the *Styles* group, click the **Cell Styles** button to display the *Styles* gallery.

(3) Click the **Title** style to apply it to the cell.

c. Format the item numbers 1 through 3 to match the worksheet title using *Format Painter:*

(1) Select the title in cell **A1.**

(2) Click the **Format Painter** button once.

(3) Drag the mouse over the item numbers in cells **A7:A9.**

5						
6	Item Number	Course	Books and Materials Purchased	Price Paid	Book Sell Back Amount	Net Cost
7	1	History 17b	*US History Reader*, *California History* pamphlet	$ 80.25	$ 40.00	$ 40.25
8	2	CIS30	*Office Computer Applications* book, course pack, USB drive	$ 74.89		$ 74.89
9	3	English A	*Composition Guide*	$ 52.50	$ 25.00	$ 27.50
10						
11		Average Sell Back Amount			$ 32.50	
12					$ 32.50	
13						

FIGURE EX 1.31

d. Format the semester dates:

(1) Select the cells **A4** and **B4.**

(2) On the *Home* tab, in the *Number* group, click the **Number Format** arrow, and then select the **Short Date** format.

e. Book titles are typically typed with italic font.

(1) Click in cell **C7.**

(2) On the formula bar above the worksheet, drag to select just the words: *USHistory Reader*

(3) Click the **Italic** button. Press **Enter.**

(4) Continue to italicize all the book titles: *California History, Office Computer Applications,* and *Composition Guide.*

f. Add shading to highlight the semester and dates as follows:

(1) Select cells **A3:B4.**

(2) On the *Home* tab, in the *Font* group, click the **Fill Color** button arrow; choose yellow.

g. Save the updates to the workbook.

8. Edit the worksheet making the following changes to it:

a. Edit dates to include the correct year, as needed.

b. To make the title text larger, select cell **A1**. On the *Home* tab, in the *Font* group, click the arrow next to the **Font Size** box, and select **20.**

c. Make the title text purple: with cell **A1** still selected, on the *Home* tab, in the *Font* group, click the arrow next to the **Font Color** button and select purple.

d. Insert another course to the list after *CIS30* and before *English A* as follows:

(1) Select cells **B9:F9;** right-click on the selected area.

(2) Choose **Insert . . .** and click **Shift cells down.**

(3) Enter and format data for another course on row **9:** `Math 13, Statistics book, graphing calculator, $95.26 price, $45 sell back.`

(4) Clear the contents of cell **E13:** select it, then right-click **Clear Contents.**

(5) Enter the missing formula for net cost: *Price minus Sell Back Amount*

(6) Select cells **A7** and **A8** and drag the **Fill Handle** down to fill in item numbers for all the courses.

e. Add a border around this semester's data:

(1) Select cells **A3:F12.**

(2) On the *Home* tab, in the *Font* group, click the **Borders** button arrow and select **Thick Box Border.**

f. Use cell styles to accent the average sell back amount.

(1) Select cells **B12:E12.**

(2) On the *Home* tab, in the *Styles* group, click the **Cell Styles** button to display the *Styles* gallery and choose any of the **accent** styles.

g. Save the updates to the workbook.

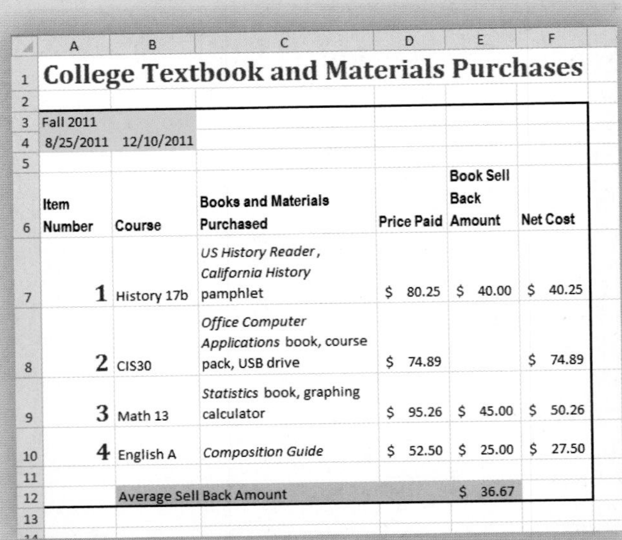

	A	B	C	D	E	F
1	College Textbook and Materials Purchases					
2						
3	Fall 2011					
4	8/25/2011	12/10/2011				
5						
6	Item Number	Course	Books and Materials Purchased	Price Paid	Book Sell Back Amount	Net Cost
7	1	History 17b	*US History Reader*, *California History* pamphlet	$ 80.25	$ 40.00	$ 40.25
8	2	CIS30	*Office Computer Applications* book, course pack, USB drive	$ 74.89		$ 74.89
9	3	Math 13	*Statistics* book, graphing calculator	$ 95.26	$ 45.00	$ 50.26
10	4	English A	*Composition Guide*	$ 52.50	$ 25.00	$ 27.50
11						
12		Average Sell Back Amount			$ 36.67	
13						

FIGURE EX 1.32

9. Use *Copy and Paste* to start another semester.

a. Select cells **A1:F13,** right-click anywhere in the selection, and press **Copy.**

b. Right-click in cell **H1** and point to Paste Special. Hover the mouse over the different options to see previews, then choose **Keep Source Column Widths.**

c. Zoom out, making the text and numbers appear smaller on screen. To use the zoom slider in the lower-right corner of the window, click and drag the **zoom slider** to the left or click the **Minus** button until you can see all of your worksheet on your screen.

d. On the right half of your screen, replace the old information with a new semester, new semester dates, new books, new prices, and new sell back amounts.

(1) Double-click the cell you want to change. You will see a blinking cursor in the cell.

(2) Make the appropriate change and press the **Enter** key.

e. Save the updates to the workbook.

10. Use *Find and Replace:*

a. Go to cell A1 by either clicking in it or using the keyboard shortcut **Ctrl+Home**.

b. On the *Home* tab, in the *Editing* group, click the **Find & Select** button and select **Replace.**

c. In the **Find** box type: `Book`

d. In the **Replace** box type: `Textbook`

e. If necessary, click the **Options** button. Check **Match Case** and click **Replace All.**

f. Verify accurate replacement throughout the worksheet and save the updates to the workbook.

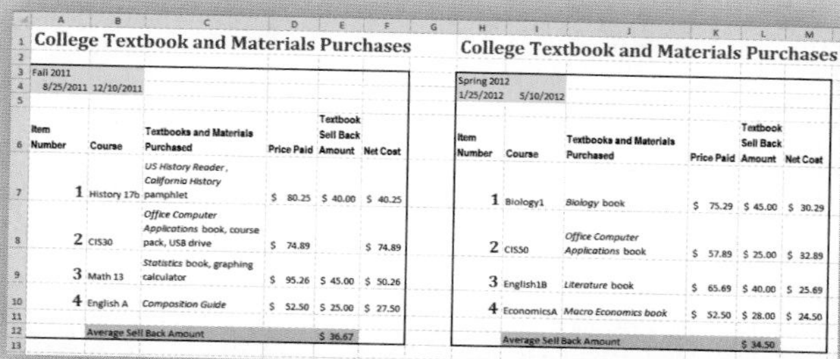

College Textbook and Materials Purchases

Fall 2011
8/25/2011 12/10/2011

Item Number	Course	Textbooks and Materials Purchased	Price Paid	Textbook Sell Back Amount	Net Cost
1	History 17b	*US History Reader, California History* pamphlet	$ 80.25	$ 40.00	$ 40.25
2	CIS30	*Office Computer Applications* book, course pack, USB drive	$ 74.89		$ 74.89
3	Math 13	*Statistics* book, graphing calculator	$ 95.26	$ 45.00	$ 50.26
4	English A	*Composition Guide*	$ 52.50	$ 25.00	$ 27.50
	Average Sell Back Amount			$ 36.67	

College Textbook and Materials Purchases

Spring 2012
1/25/2012 5/10/2012

Item Number	Course	Textbooks and Materials Purchased	Price Paid	Textbook Sell Back Amount	Net Cost
1	Biology1	*Biology* book	$ 75.29	$ 45.00	$ 30.29
2	CIS50	*Office Computer Applications* book	$ 57.89	$ 25.00	$ 32.89
3	English1B	*Literature* book	$ 65.69	$ 40.00	$ 25.69
4	EconomicsA	*Macro Economics book*	$ 52.50	$ 28.00	$ 24.50
	Average Sell Back Amount			$ 34.50	

FIGURE EX 1.33

challenge yourself **1**

Recipe Project. In this Challenge project you will apply your Excel skills to type up a recipe and compute the cost of ingredients.

1. Start a new Excel workbook and build a worksheet to match the model:

	A	B	C	D
1	# of servings		5	
2	Prep time	30	minutes	
3	Cook time	28	hours	
4	Ingredients			
5		Quantity	Unit of Measure	Food
6		0.5	gallon	non fat milk
7		4	ounce	plain active culture yogurt
8				
9				total ingredient cost
10				cost per serving
11				
12	Directions			
13	step 1	Heat H20 in the bottom of a double boiler over medium heat.		

a. Adjust column widths as needed.

b. Save your worksheet as `[your initials]EX_Challenge_1-3`

c. Change the format for the milk quantity to the **Fraction** number format.

d. In step 1 of the directions, apply **Subscript** font format to the **2** in H_2O.

e. Shift cells down several rows to add space for a title at the top of the worksheet.

(1) Title the page: `Greek Yogurt Recipe`

(2) Format the title with a distinctive font, large size and a different color.

f. Fill down the step numbers.

step 1	Heat H_2O in the bottom of a double boiler over medium heat.
step 2	Put non fat milk in top of double boiler.
step 3	Bring milk just to a boil.
step 4	Let non fat milk cool to about 100°.
step 5	Spoon yogurt into the pot.
step 6	Cover pot, wrap with a towel and place in a warm place.
step 7	After 24 hours, drain excess liquid.
step 8	Strain further in cheese cloth for 4-5 hours.
step 9	Refrigerate.

g. Enter the remaining direction step instructions.

2. In step 4 of the directions, apply the **Superscript** font format to a lowercase letter *o* to make the degree mark for *100°*.

3. Add a column to the right of the ingredients list called `Estimated Cost.` Set the column heading to **Wrap Text.**

4. Enter prices and format as currency.

FOOD	ESTIMATED COST
non fat milk	$2.50
plain active culture yogurt	$0.50

5. Enter a formula to compute the total ingredient cost by adding together the cells with the two costs.

6. Enter a formula to compute the cost per serving by dividing the total cost by the number of servings. Use the cell addresses in the formula.

7. Find and replace the text `non fat` with the text `whole` throughout the worksheet.

8. Use *Format Painter* to copy the formatting used for the title to the two cells with the text *Ingredients* and *Directions.*

9. Edit *step 2* to say: `Put whole milk in top of double boiler, bring it just to a boil.`

10. Step 3 is now redundant; it needs to be eliminated and the other steps shifted up. The *step 9* step number should be cleared.

11. Copy the entire recipe and paste it to the right using appropriate paste options. Make changes on the right to double the recipe. Enter formulas to multiply by 2 the cells with the numbers in the first recipe.

# of servings		10
Prep time	30	minutes
Cook time	28	hours
Ingredients		
	Quantity	Unit of Measure
	1	gallon
	8	ounce

12. Apply a box border around each recipe.
13. Use shading or cell styles to lightly background shade each recipe separately in different colors.
14. Below the first recipe leave a blank row or two and then enter the date in column A. Format with the **Short Date** format. In the next column, enter this text formatted in italic: `started this yogurt yesterday, ate it all up today, double recipe next time!` Adjust width of columns as necessary.
15. Save.
16. Copy the first recipe to another workbook using appropriate paste options.

Enter the ingredients and steps for a short recipe of your choice. Check the formulas and update as needed. Adjust formatting as needed for a neat appearance. Save the file using your initials and the recipe name as the file name.

challenge yourself 2

Weekly Schedule. In this Challenge project you will apply your Excel skills to create a weekly schedule for yourself, but the same skills could be applied to make an employees' work shift schedule.

1. Start a new Excel workbook and build a worksheet to match the model:
   a. Enter the first day of the week; then use AutoFill to make Excel fill in the rest of the days for you.
   b. Enter the very earliest time (on the hour or half hour) that you might ever get up and make sure it is formatted with an appropriate date format. Right below that, also enter and format a time half an hour later. Select both cells and AutoFill down to your latest bedtime.
   c. Save your worksheet as **`[your initials]EX_Challenge_1-4`**
   d. Format the day and time cells in a bold, dark, big font.
   e. Adjust column widths and row heights as desired.
   f. Apply **All Borders** to make boxes for each day and time.
   g. Save your worksheet.

	A	B	C	D	E	F	G	H
1		8/8/2011	8/9/2011	8/10/2011	8/11/2011	8/12/2011	8/13/2011	8/14/2011
2		Monday	Tuesday	Wednesday	Thursday	Friday	Saturday	Sunday
3	5:00 AM							
4	5:30 AM							
5	6:00 AM							
6	6:30 AM							
7	7:00 AM							
8	7:30 AM							
9	8:00 AM							
10	8:30 AM							
11	9:00 AM							
12	9:30 AM							
13	10:00 AM							
14	10:30 AM							
15	11:00 AM							
16	11:30 AM							
17	12:00 PM							
18	12:30 PM							
19	1:00 PM							
20	1:30 PM							
21	2:00 PM							
22	2:30 PM							

FIGURE EX 1.34

	8/8/2011	8/9/2011	8/10/2011	8/11/2011	8/12/2011	8/13/2011	8/14/2011
	Monday	Tuesday	Wednesday	Thursday	Friday	Saturday	Sunday
5:00 AM							
5:30 AM							
6:00 AM							
6:30 AM	get up	get up	get up	get up	get up		
7:00 AM	gym	gym		gym	gym		
7:30 AM	gym				gym		
8:00 AM							
8:30 AM		study		study			
9:00 AM		study		study			
9:30 AM		Spanish 1		Spanish 1		get up	get up
10:00 AM		Spanish 1	study	Spanish 1	study	gym	gym
10:30 AM		Spanish 1	study	Spanish 1	study	gym	gym
11:00 AM		study	CIS30	study	CIS30	gym	gym
11:30 AM		study	CIS30	study	CIS30	gym	gym
12:00 PM			CIS30		CIS30		
12:30 PM	work	work	CIS30	work	CIS30	work	
1:00 PM	work	work	CIS30	work	CIS30	work	
1:30 PM	work	work	CIS30	work	CIS30	work	
2:00 PM	work	work	study	work	study	work	
2:30 PM	work	work	study	work	study	work	
3:00 PM	work	work		work		work	
3:30 PM	work	work		work		work	
4:00 PM	work	work		work		work	
4:30 PM	work	work		work		work	
5:00 PM	work	work		work		work	
5:30 PM	work	work		work		work	
6:00 PM	work	work		work		work	
6:30 PM	work	work		work		work	
7:00 PM	work	work		work		work	
7:30 PM	work	work		work		work	

FIGURE EX 1.35

2. Shift cells down several rows to add space for a title and other information at the top of the worksheet. Use **Undo** as needed before proceeding.
   a. Title the page: `Weekly Schedule`
   b. Format the title font, size, and color.
3. Fill in the blank schedule to represent your regular weekly schedule. Color code your schedule, so that all your classes are one color, work hours are another, and personal time is another. Or make each class a different color.
   a. Select cells that represent times you have classes each week.
      (1) Use borders and shading or cell styles to color in each block of class time.
      (2) Enter the name of the class and other explanatory labels such as the start and end times, location, professor's name. Use wrapping as needed.
      (3) Use *Format Painter* and/or *Copy/Paste* and *Paste Options* to speed creation of this schedule.
   b. Select cells that represent times you have other commitments each week. Use shading or cell styles to color in each block of time.
   c. Select cells that represent times you plan to set aside to study each week. Use shading or cell styles to color in each block of study time.
   d. Also schedule other important regular events that you intend to implement to meet your own personal goals. Think about exercise, time to clean, time to get up and go to bed, time to pay attention to others, and so on.
   e. Save.

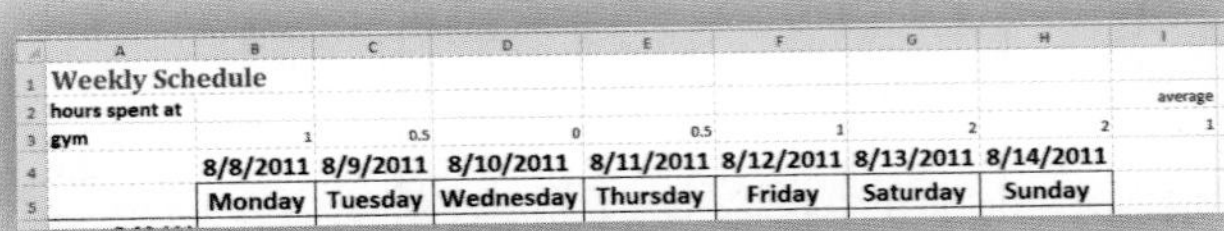

	A	B	C	D	E	F	G	H	I
1	Weekly Schedule								
2	hours spent at								average
3	gym	1	0.5	0	0.5	1	2	2	1
4		8/8/2011	8/9/2011	8/10/2011	8/11/2011	8/12/2011	8/13/2011	8/14/2011	
5		Monday	Tuesday	Wednesday	Thursday	Friday	Saturday	Sunday	

FIGURE EX 1.36

4. Copy your standard weekly schedule and paste it below, repeatedly, to create a schedule for each week this month. Adjust the zoom to view. Use paste options as needed. Then:
   a. For each week, enter actual dates above the days of the week. Speed this work by entering the first date and then filling across.
   b. Now, edit each week to include specific events, due dates, exams, appointments, and so on. Clear cells of regular events that do not occur during any particular week.
5. Use *Find and Replace* to replace `Weekly Schedule` with `Schedule for the Week` throughout the worksheet.
6. Save.

on your own

Auto Trip Cost. In this project, you will create a worksheet to record auto travel miles and compute costs. This worksheet could have a variety of uses from personal vacation planning to business expense reporting or shipping cost estimation.

1. Start with a new Excel workbook and save your file as `[your initials]EX_OnYourOwn_1-5`
   a. As always, save your worksheet periodically as you work.

2. Create the structure of the worksheet
   a. Leave several rows for a title and assumptions at the top.
   b. Enter column headers for: `Driving Date, Driving Starting Location, Driving Destination, Number of Miles`
   c. Wrap all column header text and narrow the columns.
   d. On the left, fill down the dates for the week, format with **Long Date Format,** and adjust column widths as needed.

DRIVING DATE	DRIVING STARTING LOCATION	DRIVING DESTINATION	NUMBER OF MILES
Monday, September 12, 2011			
Tuesday, September 13, 2011			
Wednesday, September 14, 2011			
Thursday, September 15, 2011			
Friday, September 16, 2011			
Saturday, September 17, 2011			
Sunday, September 18, 2011			

3. At the top of the sheet, enter your own assumption data. Shift cells down as needed to make enough room for assumptions. Format it appropriately and clearly label it so others will be able to understand your worksheet. Include:
   a. The `average cost per gallon` for fuel for the vehicle.
   b. The `make/model` of the vehicle or some other kind of vehicle identification such as fleet number.
   c. The `average miles per gallon` for the vehicle.
   d. The `average highway driving speed` in miles per hour.
   e. The `average city driving speed` in miles per hour.
   f. The `cents per mile allowed by the IRS`—If you don't know it, look it up later on the Web; for now just enter `.55`
4. Start entering travel data. Enter your own data for 5 to 10 start and end points. (Since you have not yet learned to copy formulas, you will be getting a lot of practice entering formulas, so do not enter too many trips in the worksheet.)
   a. Enter the name of the location from the travel beginning point to the destination. Adjust column widths or implement wrapping as needed to accommodate longer destination names.
   b. If you know the number of miles, enter that too. If not, use the Web to look up the mileage. Copy and paste numbers from the Web to Excel and don't forget your *Paste Options* button.
   c. If there are multiple stops on one day, insert cells to shift everything down so each trip from one place to another may be recorded on a separate row.

5. You decide to take a day without travel, so delete cells to remove the row for one date.
6. Insert cells to add columns for `Start Time` and `End Time`.
   a. Enter times for each trip and format with the appropriate time format.
7. Enter formulas in each row. Add wrapped column headers and format data with appropriate number formats.
   a. Add a column for `Number of Gallons Used`. For each trip, enter a simple math formula to compute the number of gallons used. Use the cell with your MPG assumption in the formulas.
   b. Add a column for `Fuel Cost`. Enter a simple math formula for each trip to compute the fuel cost. Use the cell with the cost per gallon assumption in the formulas.
   c. Add a column for `Estimated Driving Time in Hours`. Enter simple math formulas to compute the travel times. Use the cell with the appropriate average driving speed assumption in the formulas.
   d. Add a column for `Actual Driving Time`. Enter a simple math formula to compute each travel time. Subtract the start time from the end time in each row. Format the travel time number with the **13:30 Time** format or the **h:mm custom** format.
   e. Add a column for `IRS Allowance`. Enter simple math formulas to compute the IRS allowances for the miles traveled. Use the cell with the IRS allowance assumption in the formulas.
8. Format the worksheet:
   a. Add an appropriate title to the top of the worksheet.
   b. Carefully use cell styles, fonts, cell format, borders, and shading to make the worksheet attractive. Use *Format Painter* for consistency and neat appearance. Remember, "less is more"; professional worksheets are simple, not busy or garish.
   c. Adjust column widths and row heights as needed for neatness and balanced appearance.
9. Use *Find and Replace* to replace the word `Driving` with the word `Travel` throughout the worksheet.
10. Clear the contents of the cell with the IRS allowance assumption. Look up the allowance on the Web and enter it, or delete the cells with the IRS allowance column in the worksheet. Save.

fix it

Walking Running Log. In this project, you will fix up an imperfect worksheet that was intended for recording walking/running miles and times.

1. Open the provided file: *Jog Log.xlsx*
2. Save changes in a new file named ***[your initials]*EX_FixIt_1-6**
3. Increase the title size to 18 and bold.
4. Change the date format to *Long Date.* Change the year to 2011, filling the dates again.
5. Fix the font for the June 10th date to match the rest.
6. Add an additional run/walk on Wednesday—shift cells down to insert a row; select the Wednesday cells for date, minutes, miles, and MPH; then fill down; choose the **Copy Cells** fill option.

7. One of the *MPH* (miles per hour) formulas is wrong and needs to be fixed.
8. Change the heading *MPH* to `Miles per Hour` and set the cell format to **Wrap Text.** Adjust the column width and row height as needed.
9. Delete the Sunday run.
10. Find and replace all instances of the word `walk` with the word `jog`.
11. The font colors, borders, and shading are too busy. Clean up the worksheet to make it look nicer. Use no more than two colors in addition to black and white.
12. Save.

chapter 2

Using Formulas and Functions

In this chapter, you will learn the following skills:

- Use cell and range referencing options
- Use statistical functions
- Use date and time functions
- Use PMT function and VLOOKUP function
- Display, check, and print formulas

skills

introduction

It is time to go beyond simple formulas. In this chapter you will learn to use the functions built into Excel to compute statistics, work with date and time numbers, compute loan payments, and perform table lookups. Also you will create formulas that reference named ranges and other worksheets and formulas designed for fast replication.

2.1 Using Functions in Formulas

Functions are preprogrammed shortcuts for calculating complex equations (like the monthly payment amount for a loan). Most functions require you to provide input called the **arguments**. For example, when writing a formula using the PMT function to calculate a loan payment, the arguments include the interest rate, the number of payments, the amount of the loan at the beginning of the loan period, the amount of the loan left at the end of the loan period, and whether the loan payments will be made at the beginning or end of each payment period.

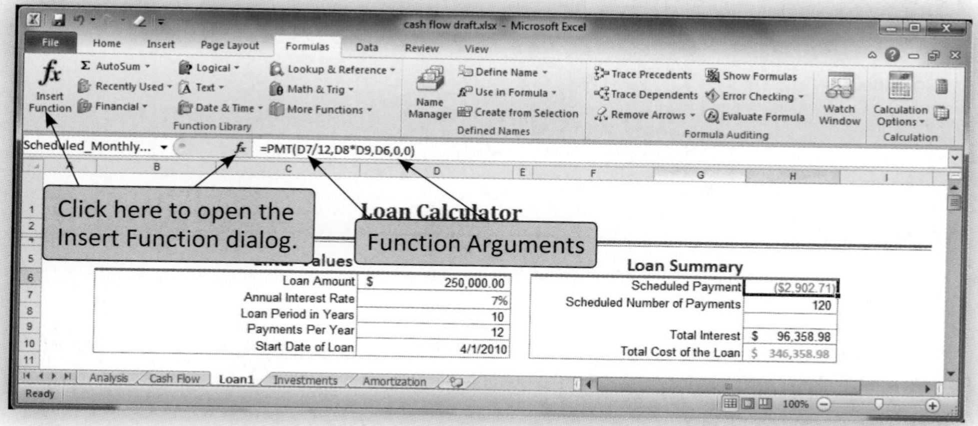

FIGURE EX 2.1

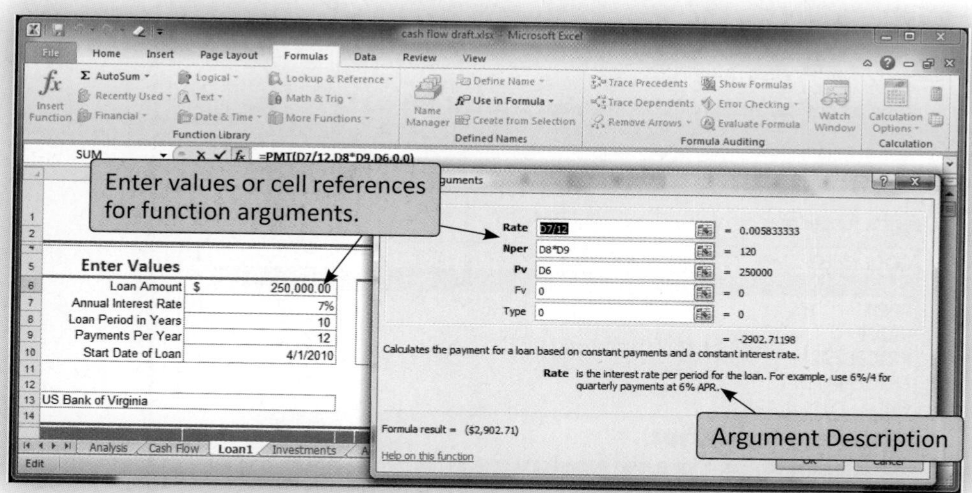

FIGURE EX 2.2

There are four basic ways to add a function to a formula:

1. Type the formula directly in the cell or the formula bar. Begin the formula by typing =, and then type the function name. After the function name, type (followed by the function arguments, separated by commas, and then). Press ←Enter to complete the formula.
2. Use **Formula AutoComplete**. When you type = and then a letter, Formula AutoComplete displays a list of potential matches (functions and other valid reference names). Type more letters to shorten the Formula AutoComplete list. Double-click a function name to enter it in your formula. Enter the expected arguments by typing values or selecting a cell or cell range. Press ←Enter to complete the formula.

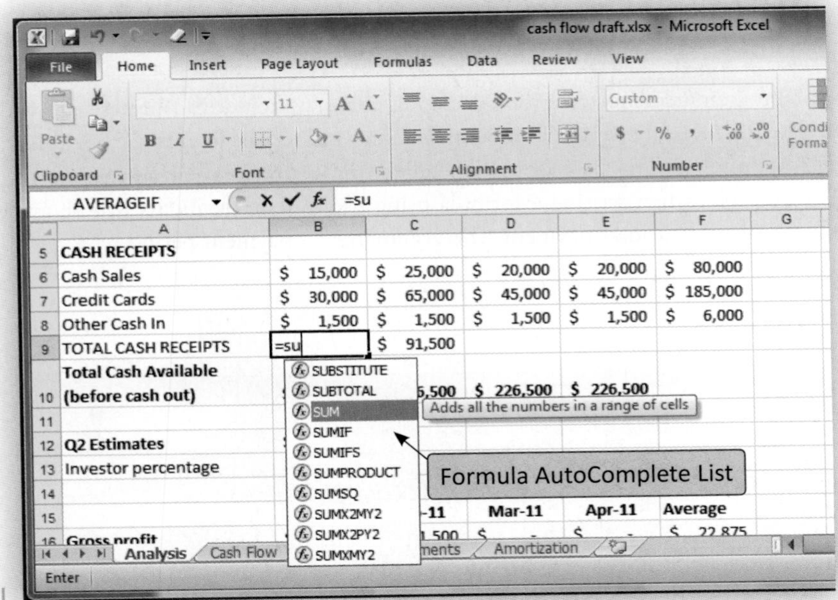

FIGURE EX 2.3

3. On the *Formulas* tab, select a function from the *Function Library* group, or click the **Insert Function** button to select a function from the *Insert Function* dialog. You can also click the **Insert Function** button f_x to the left of the formula bar.

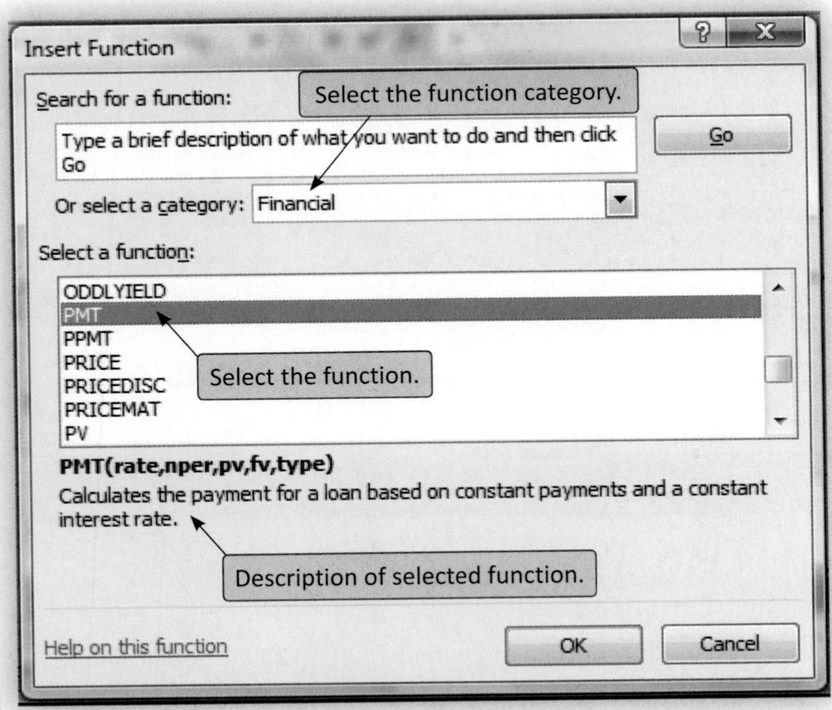

FIGURE EX 2.4

a. Functions are organized into categories such as *Financial* and *Statistical.* If necessary, expand the *Or select a category:* list and select the category you want. The category list will default to whatever category you used last, or it will show *Most Recently Used.*

b. Click a function in the *Select a function:* box to see a brief description of what it does and the arguments it takes.

c. Click **OK** to open the *Function Arguments* dialog. (This dialog is different for each function.)

d. Enter values in each of the argument boxes by typing or clicking outside the dialog and selecting the cell or cell range. As you click each argument box, a brief description of the argument appears near the bottom of the dialog.

e. When you are finished entering arguments, click **OK.**

4. Use **AutoSum**. The **AutoSum** button allows you to insert common functions (SUM, AVERAGE, COUNT, MIN, and MAX) with a single mouse click. It is available from both the *Home* tab and the *Formulas* tab. When you use the *AutoSum* button, Excel enters the function arguments for you, using the most likely range of cells based on the structure of your worksheet. Press ←Enter to complete the formula.

tips & tricks

When you use Formula AutoComplete, you can click the function name in the ScreenTip to open the Excel help topic for that function.

If you're not sure of the name of the function you want, open the *Insert Function* dialog and type keywords describing the function in the *Search for a function:* box, and then click the **Go** button. The *Or select a category:* box changes to *Recommended,* and the *Select a function:* box now displays a list of functions that match the keywords you typed.

try this

The *Name* box to the left of the formula bar normally displays the cell address or name. However, when you begin a formula by typing =, the *Name* box displays the name of the most recently used function. Click the arrow at the right side of the box to see a list of all the most recently used functions. Click any function name to open the *Function Arguments* dialog, or click **More Functions . . .** at the bottom of the list to open the *Insert Function* dialog.

2.2 Using AutoSum to Insert a SUM Function

The **SUM** mathematical function is used to add several cells together. Instead of writing a formula with several references separated by a plus sign, you can "sum" a range of cells. A formula using the SUM function looks like this:

=SUM(A3:A6)

The range **A3:A6** tells Excel to add the values in all of the cells between **A3** and **A6 (A3 + A4 + A5 + A6).**

Although you can create a SUM function using the *Function Arguments* dialog box or by using Formula AutoComplete, it is much easier to use the *AutoSum* button because Excel enters the function arguments for you.

To insert a SUM function using AutoSum:

1. Select the cell in which you want to enter the function.
2. On the *Formulas* tab, in the *Function Library* group, or on the *Home* tab, in the *Editing* group, click the **AutoSum** button.
3. Excel automatically inserts a formula with the SUM function, using the range of cells contiguous to (next to) the selected cell as the arguments for the function. You can increase or decrease the range of cells selected by clicking and dragging the corner of the highlighted cell range.
4. Press [←Enter] to accept the formula.

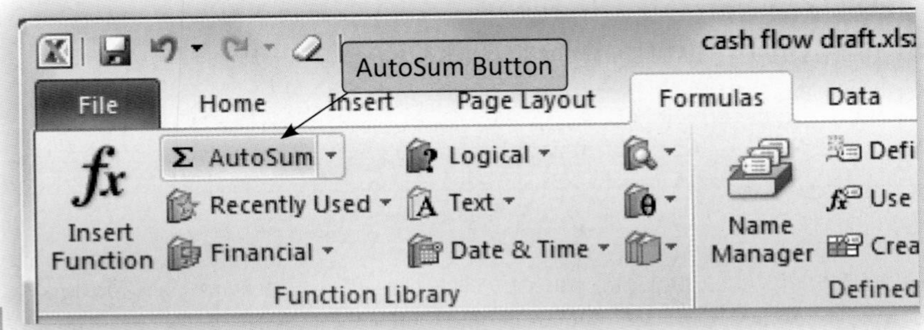

FIGURE EX 2.5

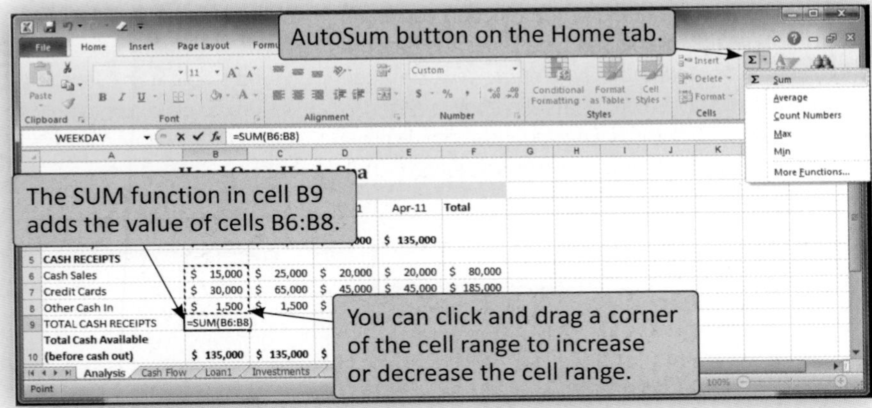

FIGURE EX 2.6

tips & tricks

When you use the *AutoSum* button, Excel enters the function arguments for you, using the most likely range of cells based on the structure of your worksheet. For example, if you use AutoSum at the bottom of a column of values, Excel will assume that you want to use the values in the column as the function arguments. If you use AutoSum at the end of a row of values, Excel will use the values in the row.

try this

You can also click the **AutoSum** button arrow and select **SUM** from the list.

Another way to use the AutoSum function is to select a range of cells, and then click the **AutoSum** button. Excel will insert the SUM function in the next available (empty) cell.

To use Formula AutoComplete to enter a SUM function, type =SU, and then double-click **SUM** in the list of available functions. Excel enters **=SUM(** in the cell for you. Click the first cell in the range of cells you want to add together, and then drag and release the mouse button when you reach the last cell in the range. Press [←Enter]. Excel enters the cell range as the function arguments, and adds **)** to the end of the formula.

2.3 Creating Formulas Using the AVERAGE Function

The **AVERAGE** statistical function is used to calculate the average value of a group of values. A formula using the AVERAGE function looks like this:

=AVERAGE(A3:A6)

The value of this formula is the average of the values of cells **A3 through A6: (A3 + A4 + A5 + A6)/4.** Average is calculated by adding the values, and then dividing the sum by the number of values.

If you want to calculate the average of the numbers in more than one range of values, use a comma to separate the arguments:

=AVERAGE(A3:A6,B3:B6)

The value of this formula is the average of the values of cells **A3 through A6** *and* **B3 through B6: (A3 + A4 + A5 + A6 + B3 + B4 + B5 + B6)/8.**

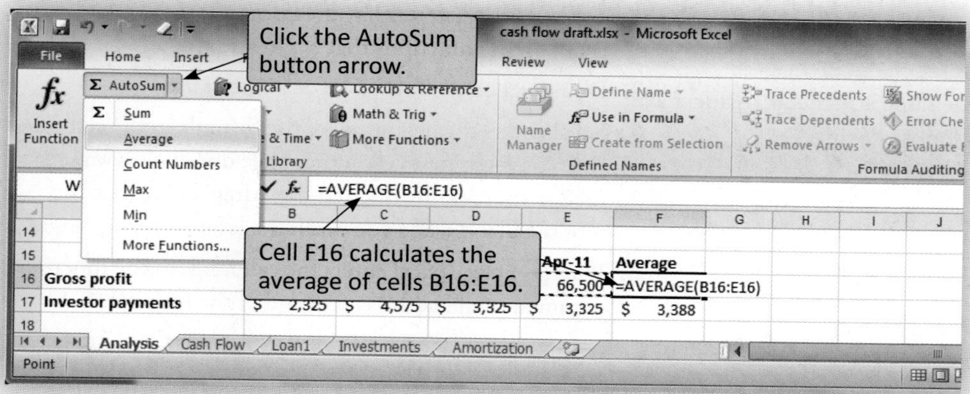

FIGURE EX 2.7

Although you can create an AVERAGE function using the *Function Arguments* dialog box or by using Formula AutoComplete, it is much easier to use the **AutoSum** button because Excel enters the function arguments for you.

To insert an AVERAGE function using AutoSum:

1. Select the cell in which you want to enter the function.
2. On the *Formulas* tab, in the *Function Library* group, click the **AutoSum** button arrow, or on the *Home* tab, in the *Editing* group, click the **AutoSum** button arrow, and then click **Average.**
3. Excel will automatically insert a formula using the AVERAGE function, using the range of cells contiguous to (next to) the selected cell as the arguments for the function. You can increase or decrease the range of cells selected by clicking and dragging the corner of the highlighted cell range. Press ←Enter to accept the formula.

tips & tricks

When calculating an average, Excel will ignore empty cells. If you want to include those cells in your average calculations, make sure they have a value of zero.

tell me more

What you might think of as the "average" is actually the statistical *mean. Average* is a general term in statistics that includes **mean** (the sum of a group of values divided by the number of values in the group), **median** (the middle value of a set of values) and **mode** (the value that appears most often in a group of values). In Excel, the AVERAGE function calculates the mean value. Most people say *average* when they really want to calculate the *mean* value.

try this

Another way to use AutoSum to calculate an average is to select a range of cells, and then click the **AutoSum** arrow and click **Average.** Excel will insert the AVERAGE function in the next available (empty) cell.

To use Formula AutoComplete to enter an AVERAGE function, type =AV, and then double-click **AVERAGE** in the list of available functions. Excel enters **=AVERAGE(** in the cell for you. Click the first cell in the range of cells you want to use for your arguments, and then drag and release the mouse button when you reach the last cell in the range. Press ←Enter. Excel enters the cell range as the function arguments, and adds **)** to the end of the formula.

2.4 Creating Formulas Using Counting Functions

There are three basic counting functions in Excel. These functions are useful when you need to know how many numbers or items are in a list, or how many rows are missing data for a particular column.

COUNT—Counts the number of cells that contain numbers within a specified range of cells.

COUNTA—Counts the number of cells that are not blank within a specified range of cells. Use COUNTA if your cell range includes both numbers and text data.

COUNTBLANK—Counts the number of blank cells within a specified range of cells.

All three of these functions take the same arguments. A formula using the COUNT function looks like this:

=COUNT(A2:A106)

The result of this formula is the number of cells in A2 through A106 that contain numerical values. If you want to include cells that contain text, use COUNTA instead.

=COUNTA(B2:B106)

The result of this formula is the number of cells in B2 through B106 that contain any data (numerical or text).

Use COUNTBLANK to find the number of rows missing values in a column.

=COUNTBLANK(D2:D106)

The result of this formula is the number of cells in D2 through D106 that are blank.

To use Formula AutoComplete to enter one of the counting functions:

1. Click in the cell where you want the formula.
2. Type =COUNT to display the Formula AutoComplete list of all the functions that begin with "count."
3. Double-click the function you want to use.
4. Excel enters the beginning of the formula in the cell for you. Click the first cell in the range of cells you want to use for your arguments, and then drag and release the mouse button when you reach the last cell in the range.
5. Press Enter. Excel enters the cell range as the function arguments, and adds) to the end of the formula.

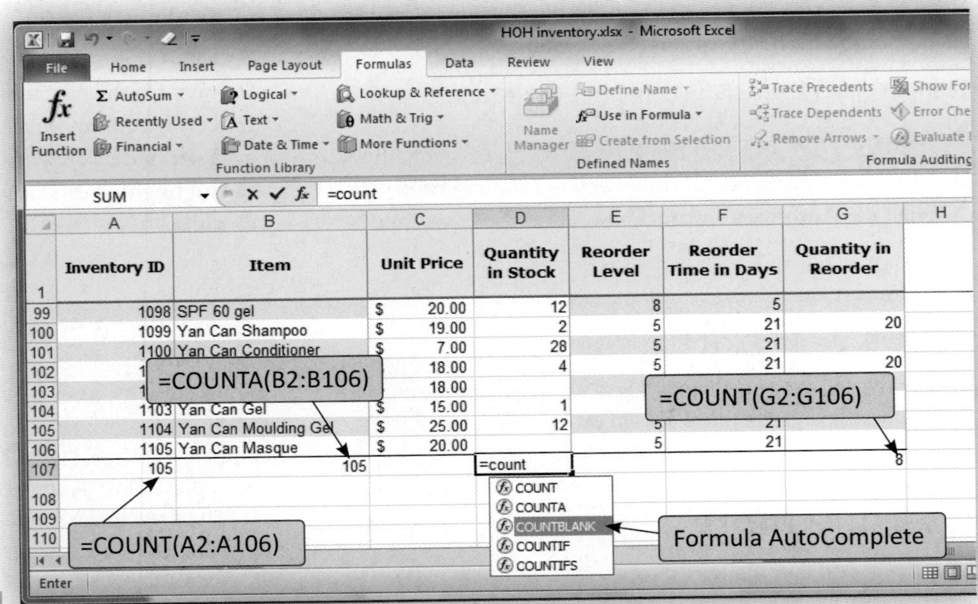

FIGURE EX 2.8

tips & tricks

Cells that contain a zero (0) are not considered blank.

2.5 Using Other Statistical Functions

In addition to AVERAGE and the counting functions, there are a few other statistical functions you may find useful in working with day-to-day spreadsheets.

The **MIN** (minimum) statistical function will give you the lowest value in a range of values. The **MAX** (maximum) statistical function will give you the highest value in a range of values. A formula using the MIN or MAX function looks like this:

=MIN(A3:A6)

=MAX(A3:A6)

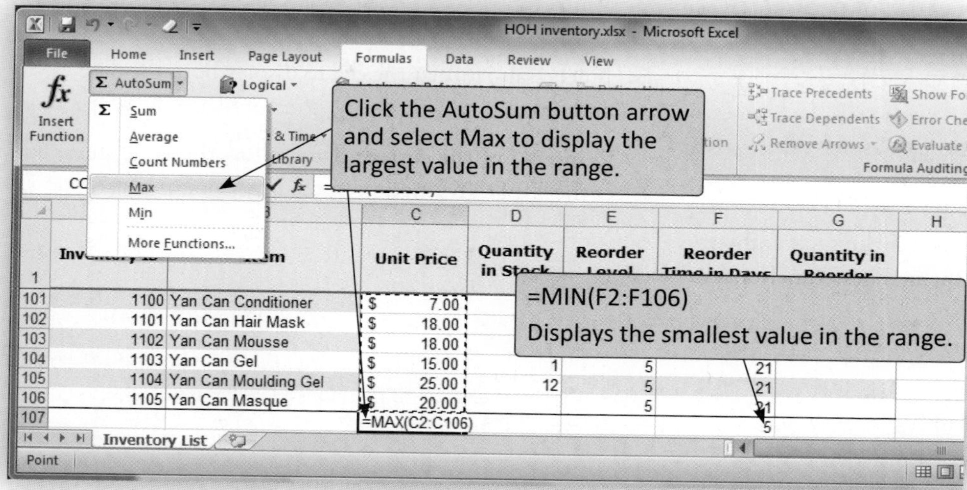

Click the AutoSum button arrow and select Max to display the largest value in the range.
=MIN(F2:F106)
Displays the smallest value in the range.

FIGURE EX 2.9

Although you can use the MIN and MAX functions from the *Function Arguments* dialog box or from the Formula AutoComplete list, it is sometimes easier to use the **AutoSum** button because Excel enters the function arguments for you.

1. Select the cell in which you want to enter the function.
2. On the *Formulas* tab, in the *Function Library* group, click the **AutoSum** button arrow, or on the *Home* tab, in the *Editing* group, click the **AutoSum** button arrow, and then click **Min** to display the smallest value or **Max** to display the highest value.
3. Excel automatically inserts a formula, using the range of cells contiguous to (next to) the selected cell as the arguments for the function. You can increase or decrease the range of cells selected by clicking and dragging the corner of the highlighted cell range.
4. Press ←Enter to accept the formula.

tell me **more**

To explore the wide variety of complex statistical functions available in Excel:

On the *Formulas* tab, in the *Function Library* group, click the **More Functions** button and point to **Statistical,** or open the *Insert Function* dialog box and select the *Statistical* category.

try **this**

Another way to use AutoSum to find the minimum or maximum value is to select a range of cells, and then click the **AutoSum** arrow and click **Min** or **Max.** Excel will insert the MIN or MAX function in the next available (empty) cell.

To use Formula AutoComplete to enter a MIN or MAX function, type `=m`, and then double-click the function you want. Excel enters the beginning of the formula in the cell for you. Click the first cell in the range of cells you want to use for your arguments, and then drag and release the mouse button when you reach the last cell in the range. Press ←Enter. Excel enters the cell range as the function arguments and adds **)** to the end of the formula.

2.6 Using Date and Time Functions

Excel includes two functions that insert the current date or date and time. The NOW function inserts the current date and time. The TODAY function inserts only the current date. Both of these functions are **volatile**—that is, they are not constant. They update with the current date or date and time each time the workbook is opened. This is useful if you want to keep track of the last time the workbook was edited or opened.

A formula using the NOW function looks like this:

=NOW()

A formula using the TODAY function looks like this:

=TODAY()

Notice that both of these functions include parentheses, but there are no arguments inside them. These functions do not require arguments.

To insert the current date and time:

1. Select the cell where you want the date and time to appear.
2. On the *Formulas* tab, in the *Function Library* group, click the **Date & Time** button.
3. Click **NOW.**
4. When the *Function Arguments* dialog box appears, click **OK.**
5. If necessary, format the cell to display both the date and time.

To insert just the current date, follow the same steps, but select the TODAY function instead.

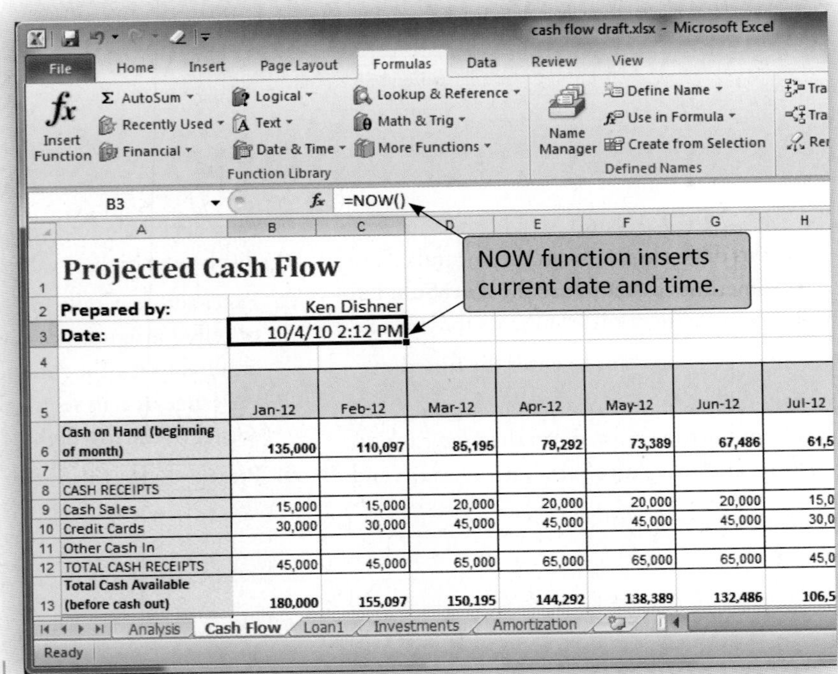

FIGURE EX 2.10

tips & tricks

Both NOW and TODAY use the date and time from your computer's clock. If your computer's clock is wrong, the date and time displayed in your workbook will be wrong as well.

tell me **more**

If the cell is formatted to use a date format that does not display the time, the result of the NOW and TODAY functions will appear the same. However, the underlying value will still be different. If you change the formatting of the cell to display the time, a cell using the TODAY function will always display a time of 12:00 AM, whereas a cell using the NOW function will display the correct time.

2.7 Using Absolute and Relative References

A cell's address, its position in the workbook, is referred to as a **cell reference** when it is used in a formula. In Excel, the $ character before a letter or number in the cell address means that part of the cell's address is *absolute* (nonchanging). Cell references can be relative, absolute, or mixed. A **relative reference** is a cell reference that adjusts to the new location in the worksheet when the formula is copied. An **absolute reference** is a cell reference whose location remains constant when the formula is copied. A **mixed reference** is a combination cell reference with a row position that stays constant with a changing column position (or vice versa).

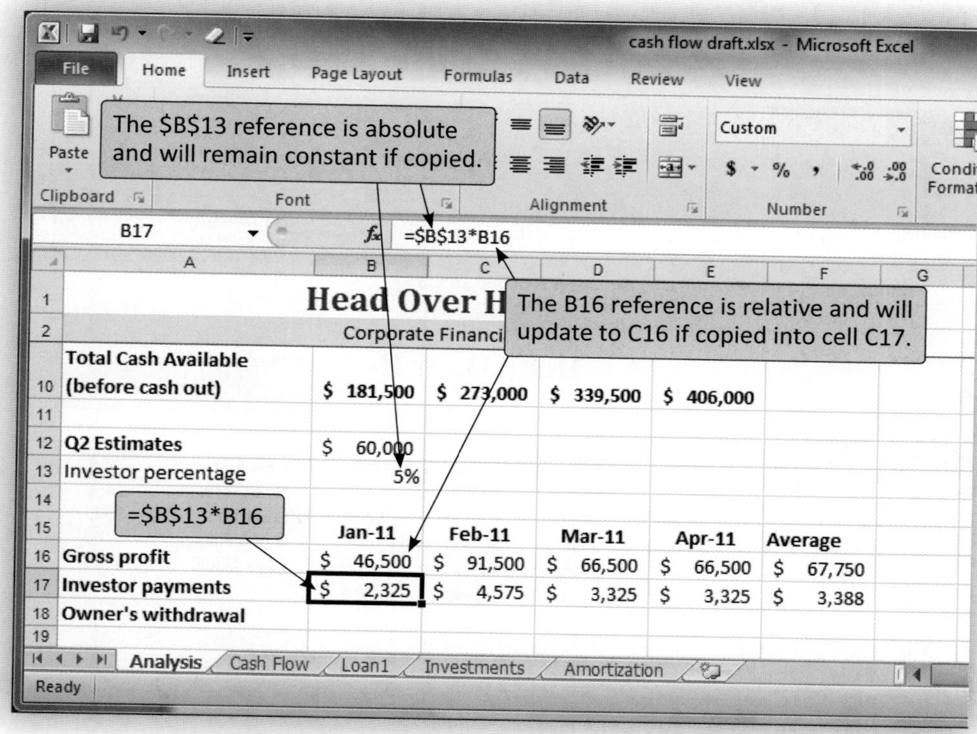

FIGURE EX 2.11

Relative reference—A1

Absolute reference—$A$1

Mixed reference—$A1

Here's how relative and absolute references work:

When you type a formula into a cell, it uses ***relative*** references by default. Excel calculates the position of the referenced cell ***relative*** to the active cell. For example, if cell B17 is the active cell and you type the formula **=B16,** Excel displays the value of the cell that is up one row from the active cell.

- If you add another row to your worksheet, shifting the position of cell B17 to cell B18, Excel automatically adjusts the reference in the formula to reflect the new cell address that is up one row from the current position.
- If you copy the formula **=B16** from cell B17 and paste it into cell C17, the pasted formula will update automatically to **=C16** to reflect the cell address that is up one row from the new position.
- If you *cut and paste* the formula, Excel assumes that you want the formula to maintain its previous value and treats the formula as if it had included absolute references, pasting the formula exactly as it was.

But what if you don't want the cell reference to adjust? For example, cell B13 contains a value that you want to use in calculations for multiple cells in a row. If you were to copy the formula **=B13*B16** from cell B17 to cell C17, the formula would update to **=C13*C16** (not what you intended) because both of the cell references are ***relative.*** Instead, you want the reference in cell B13 to be ***absolute,*** so it does not update when you copy it. If you use the formula **=$B$13*B16** instead and copy it from cell B17 to cell C17, the pasted formula will only update the relative reference ***(B16)***. The absolute reference ***($B$13)*** will remain constant. The formula in cell C17 will be **=$B$13*C16.**

2.8 Naming Ranges of Cells

Cell references like A4 and J34 do not provide much information about what data the cell contains—they just tell you where the cell is located in the worksheet. However, you can assign names to cells or ranges of cells to give your cell references names that are more user-friendly. These **names** (also called **range names** or **named ranges**) act as a list of shortcuts to the cell locations.

To create a named range:

1. Select the cell or range of cells to which you want to assign a name.
2. Type the name in the *Name* box to the left of the formula bar.
3. Press Enter to apply the name to the cell(s).

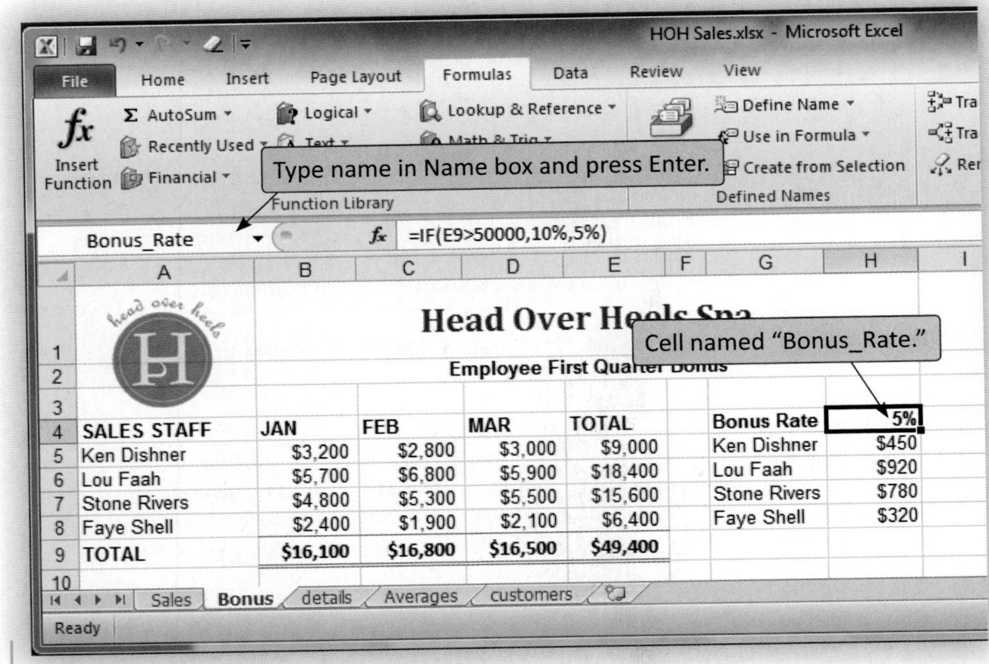

FIGURE EX 2.12

If your worksheet is organized in a table format, with column or row labels, you can automatically create named ranges using the labels as names:

1. Select the range of cells you want to name including the row or column label.
2. On the *Formulas* tab, in the *Defined Names* group, click the **Create from Selection** button Create from Selection.
3. In the *Create Names from Selection* dialog, click the check box(es) to indicate where the names are (top row, left column, bottom row, or right column).
4. Click **OK**.

Excel automatically creates named ranges for the groups of cells associated with each label.

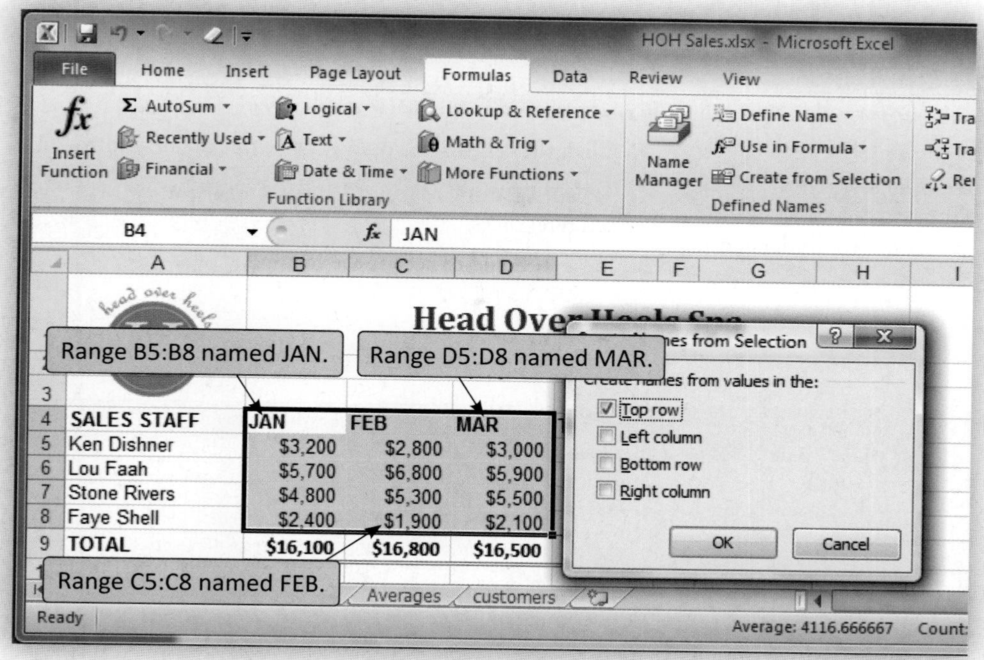

FIGURE EX 2.13

tips & tricks

Names may not include spaces. To make your names easier to read, try using an underscore character _ or a period . between words.

try this

You can also create new names through the *New Name* dialog.

1. On the *Formulas* tab, in the *Defined Names* group, click the **Define Name** button Define Name.
2. The selected cell(s) is entered in the *Refers to:* box.
3. Type the name you want in the *Name:* box. If the cell to the immediate left or immediately above the selected cell appears to include a label, Excel will pre-populate the *Name:* box with that text.
4. Click **OK.**

2.9 Working with Named Ranges

Rather than using a range of cells in your formulas, you can use a named range. The name will always refer to the cells, even if their position in the worksheet changes. Using named ranges in your formulas also makes it easier for others to use your workbook. Which formula is easier to understand: **SUM(B5:B8)** or **SUM(JAN)**?

To use a named range in a formula:

1. Click the cell where you want to enter the new formula.
2. Type the formula, substituting the range name for the cell references.
3. Press [←Enter] to accept the formula.

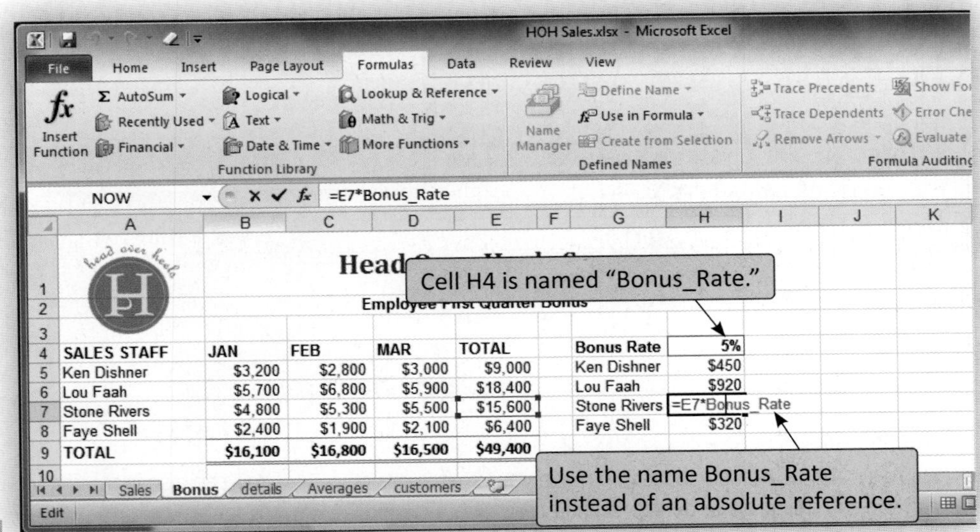

FIGURE EX 2.14

Formula AutoComplete lists named ranges as well as functions. Using the AutoComplete list is a good way to avoid typographical errors and ensure that you enter the name correctly.

To use Formula AutoComplete with names:

1. Type an = sign to begin the formula. As you type alphabetical characters, Excel will offer name suggestions.
2. When you find the name you want, double-click it.
3. Excel inserts the name into the formula.

FIGURE EX 2.15

tips & tricks

When you copy and paste a formula containing a named range, the name does not change with the new position in the workbook (similar to using an absolute reference).

If you move a named cell, the name updates with the new cell location automatically.

tell me more

You can also use named ranges to navigate your workbook:

1. Click the arrow next to the *Name* box to see the list of named ranges in your workbook.
2. To navigate to one of the named ranges, click the name in the list.

try this

- On the *Formulas* tab, in the *Defined Names* group, click the **Use in Formula** button to display a list of names in your workbook, and then click one of the names to insert it into your formula.
- You can also click **Paste Names . . .** from the bottom of the *Use in Formula* list. The *Paste Names* dialog opens and lists all of the names in your workbook. Click a name and then click **OK** to add it to your formula.

2.10 Using Logical Functions

The IF logical function returns one value if a condition is true and another value if the condition is false. The IF function can return a numerical value or display a text string. This formula uses the IF function to calculate a bonus rate (cell H4) based on the sales figure in cell E9 (named Total_Sales). If the value of cell E9 is greater than 50000, the formula will return 10%; if the value of cell E9 is not greater than 50000, the formula will return 5%:

=IF(TOTAL_SALES>50000,10%,5%)

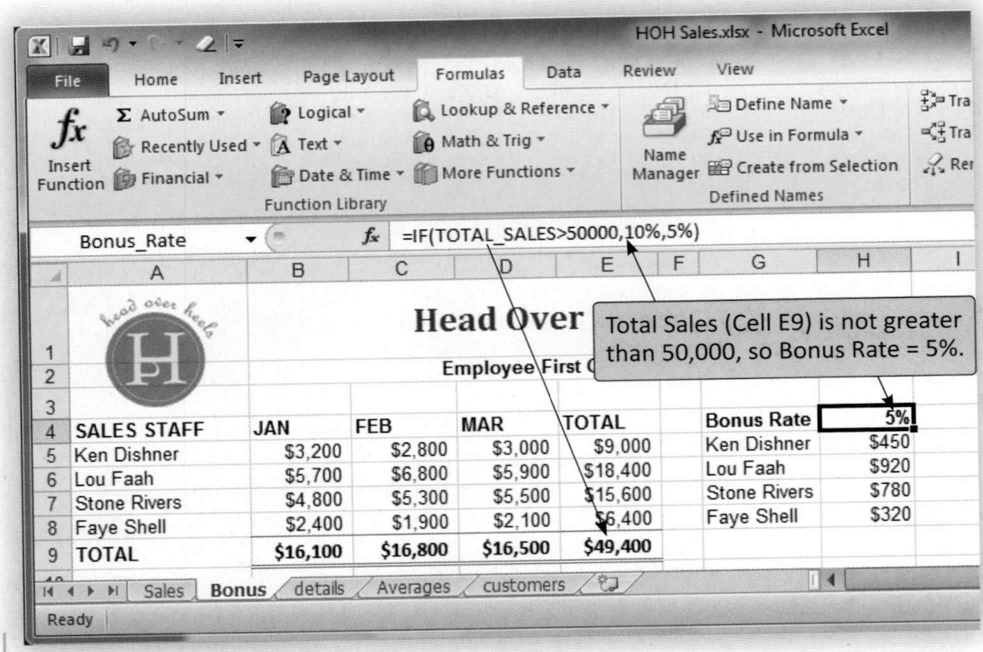

FIGURE EX 2.16

To use the IF function:

1. Select the cell where you want to enter the formula.
2. On the *Formulas* tab, in the *Function Library* group, click the **Logical** button.
3. Select **IF** from the list of functions. Excel displays the appropriate *Function Arguments* dialog where you can enter the function arguments.
4. Enter the *Logical_test* argument. This argument states the condition you want to test for. Use cell references and/or values with logical operators. For example, **TOTAL_SALES>50000** will return true if the value of the cell named TOTAL_SALES is greater than 50000 and false if the value is not greater than 50000.
5. Enter the *Value_if_true* argument. This is the text string or value that will be displayed if the *Logical_test* argument is true.
6. Enter the *Value_if_false* argument. This is the text string or value that will be displayed if the *Logical_test* argument is false.
7. Click **OK**.

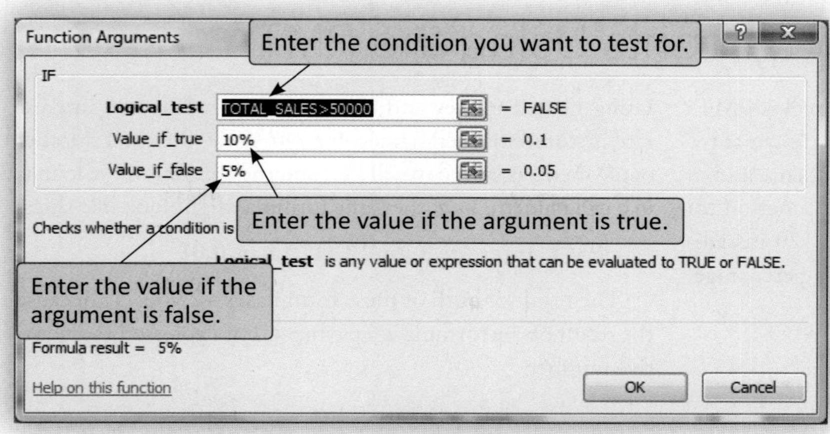

FIGURE EX 2.17

tips & tricks

When you click an argument box in the *Function Arguments* dialog, a description of the argument appears below the description of the function. As you enter arguments, the dialog box will display the results of your formula.

tell me more

In addition to the IF function, the logical functions group includes

- **AND**—Returns TRUE if the all of the arguments are true, and FALSE if at least one of the arguments is not true.
- **OR**—Returns TRUE if at least one of the arguments is true, and FALSE if all of the arguments are false.
- **NOT**—Returns TRUE if the argument is false, and FALSE if the argument is true.
- **IFERROR**—Returns an error message or specified value if the value of the referenced cell is an error; else it returns the value of the referenced cell.

try this

In the *Function Arguments* dialog, to enter arguments, you can type the cell reference in the argument box, or you can click the cell to add the cell reference to the dialog. If the position of the dialog box makes it difficult to click the cell you want, click the **Collapse Dialog** button. Click the cell to add the reference to the dialog, and then click the **Expand Dialog** button to return to the function dialog.

2.11 Calculating Loan Payments Using the PMT Function

One of the most useful financial functions in Excel is PMT (payment), which you can use to calculate loan payments. The PMT function is based upon constant payments and a constant interest rate. A formula using the PMT function to calculate payments for a $250,000 loan paid in 120 installments at 12 installments per year with an annual percentage interest rate of 7% looks like this:

=PMT(7%/12,120,250000)

Using named ranges and cell references, where the interest rate is stored in a cell named *Interest_Rate,* the total number of payments is stored in cell H7, and the amount of the loan is in a cell named *Loan,* the same formula might look like this:

=PMT(Interest_Rate/12,H7,Loan,0,0)

The result of both of these formulas is –2,902.71. Because the result of the formula is a payment, it is expressed as a negative number.

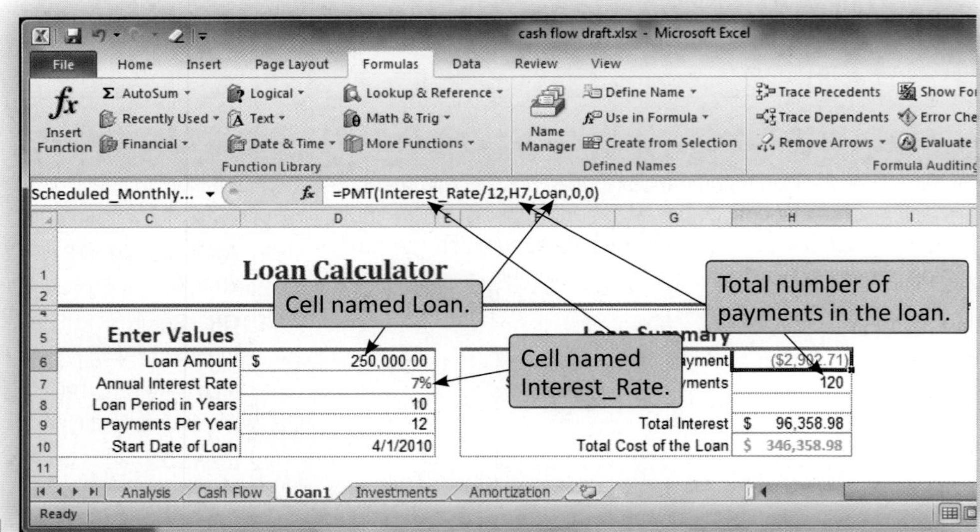

FIGURE EX 2.18

To use the PMT function:

1. Select the cell where you want to enter the formula.
2. On the *Formulas* tab, in the *Function Library* group, click the **Financial** button Financial.
3. Select **PMT** from the list. Excel displays the appropriate *Function Arguments* dialog.
4. In the *Rate* box, enter the interest rate divided by the number of payments per year. Usually, interest rate is expressed as an annual interest rate. If the loan requires a monthly payment, the annual interest rate should be divided by 12.
5. In the *Nper* box, enter the total number of payments over the life of the loan.
6. In the *Pv* box, enter the present value of the loan. This is how much you owe now (the loan principal).
7. (Optional) In the *Fv* box, enter the future value of the loan. Excel assumes a value of 0 unless you include the argument and specify a different value. If you will make payments on the loan until it is completely paid off, you can leave this argument blank or enter 0.
8. (Optional) In the *Type* box, enter `1` if the payment is at the beginning of the period. If you omit this argument, Excel assumes a value of 0 (meaning each payment is at the end of the period).
9. Notice that as you enter each argument, the value appears to the right of the argument box. The formula result (in this case, the loan payment amount) is displayed at the lower-left corner of the dialog box.
10. Click **OK** to enter the formula in your worksheet.

from the perspective of . . .

INSTRUCTOR

Spreadsheet software enables me to keep a grid of attendance information by student and by day. Using formulas and functions for grading gives me the flexibility to add scores, calculate averages, and provide feedback to my students.

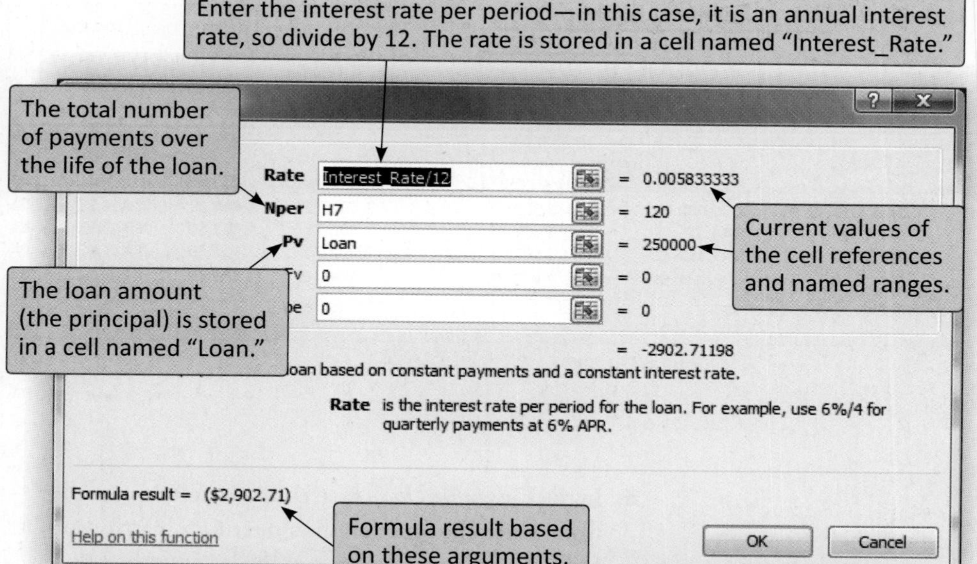

Enter the interest rate per period—in this case, it is an annual interest rate, so divide by 12. The rate is stored in a cell named "Interest_Rate."
The total number of payments over the life of the loan.
Rate
Interest_Rate/12
= 0.005833333
Nper
H7
= 120
Pv
Loan
= 250000
0
= 0
0
= 0
Current values of the cell references and named ranges.
The loan amount (the principal) is stored in a cell named "Loan."
= -2902.71198
oan based on constant payments and a constant interest rate.
Rate is the interest rate per period for the loan. For example, use 6%/4 for quarterly payments at 6% APR.
Formula result = ($2,902.71)
Help on this function
Formula result based on these arguments.
OK
Cancel

FIGURE EX 2.19

tips & tricks

When working with complex functions like PMT, use cell references as arguments rather than entering values directly. This way you can change values in your spreadsheet and see the results instantly without opening the *Function Arguments* dialog again. It can also be helpful to name the cells containing data for the function arguments. (It is easier to remember the cell name "Loan" than the cell reference D6.)

2.12 Finding Data Using the VLOOKUP Function

Excel includes a group of lookup and reference functions that return values based on a cell's position in a table or array. For example, this formula uses the VLOOKUP function to look up the part of a loan payment that is applied to the principal of the loan by returning the value of column 7 (the Principal column) within the range named Loan_Data (cells A20:I123), where the value in the first column of the data array (the PmtNo column) is the value in cell D13:

=VLOOKUP(D13,LoanRange,7)

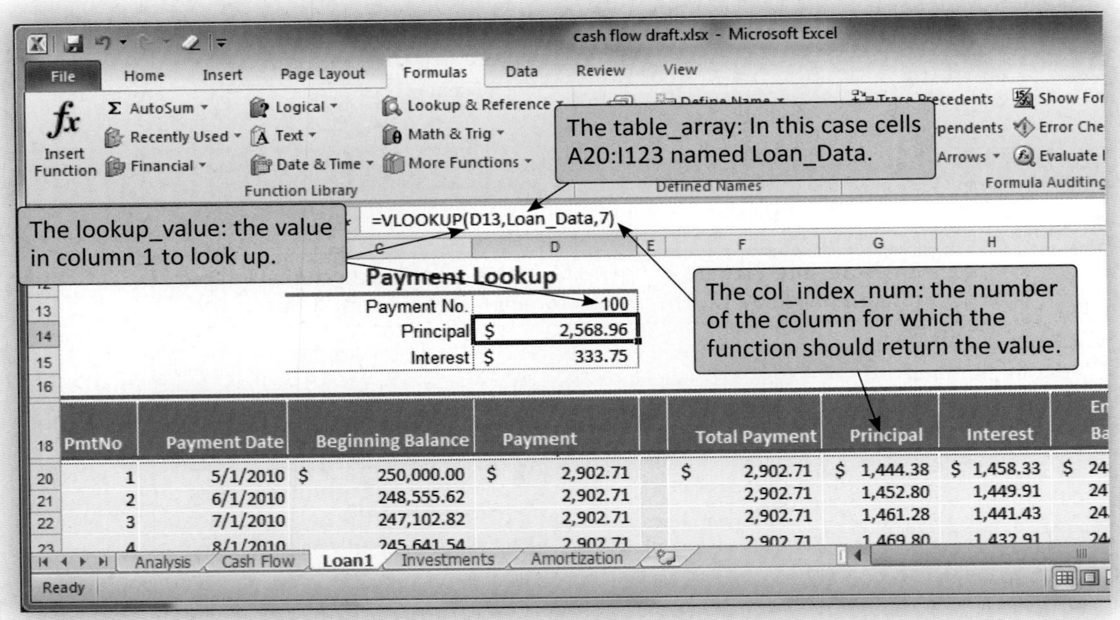

FIGURE EX 2.20

To use the VLOOKUP function:

1. Select the cell where you want to enter the formula.
2. On the *Formulas* tab, in the *Function Library* group, click the **Lookup & Reference** button.
3. Select **VLOOKUP** from the list. Excel displays the appropriate *Function Arguments* dialog.
4. In the *Lookup_value* box, enter the value in the first column that you want to return a corresponding value for. In other words, the value you want to look up.
5. In the *Table_array* box, enter the range of cells for the array (or the table or range name). If your worksheet includes a header row, do not include it in the range used for the *table_array* argument.
6. In the *Col_index_num* box, enter the column number from which the function should return a matching value. Enter the column number, not the letter or the column heading.
7. (optional) In the *Range_lookup* box, enter FALSE if you want to find only an exact match for the value entered in the *Lookup_value* box. If you omit this argument, Excel assumes a value of TRUE and will return the value for the closest match in the first column.
8. Click **OK.**

When using VLOOKUP, make sure the table or array is sorted A–Z by the first column (the lookup column). If your data are not sorted, you will see unexpected results.

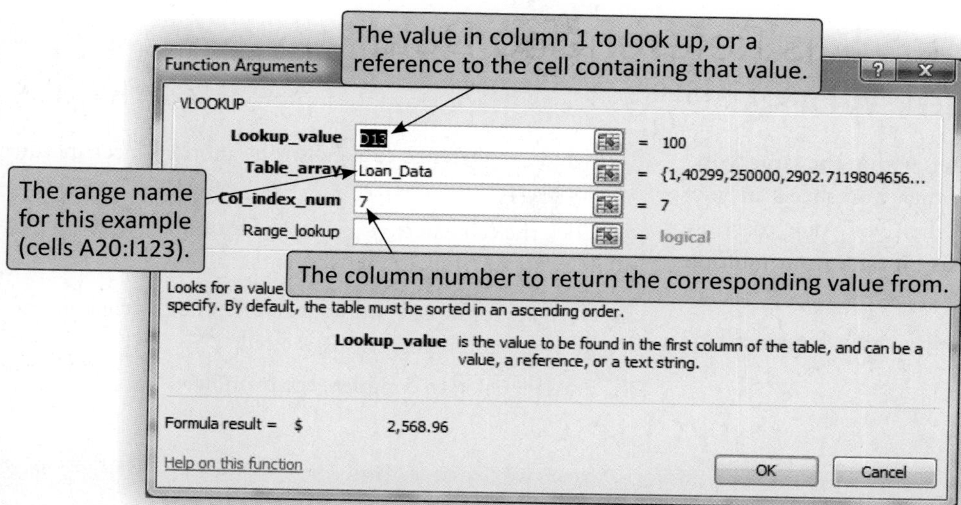

FIGURE EX 2.21

tips & tricks

Use a cell reference for the *Lookup_value* argument to give your formula more flexibility. This way you can change the value in the referenced cell instead of opening the *Function Arguments* dialog every time you want to look up a different value. Similarly, use table names and range names instead of cell references in the *Table_array* argument. When your workbook includes large amounts of data, it is much easier to use names in formulas rather than select a range of data that may be hundreds of rows long.

tell me **more**

The examples here all use the VLOOKUP function to find corresponding values in different *columns* within the same row (a *vertical* lookup). The HLOOKUP function works similarly, except you use it to find corresponding values in different rows within the same column (a *horizontal* lookup).

Use HLOOKUP when your worksheet uses a horizontal layout—few rows with many columns.

Use VLOOKUP when your worksheet uses a vertical layout—few columns with many rows.

2.13 Creating Formulas Referencing Data from Another Worksheet

Cell references are not limited to cells within the same worksheet. You can reference cells in other worksheets in your workbook. This feature is useful when you want to create summary sheets or perform analysis on data from multiple sheets at once.

For example, this formula will display the value of cell B3 from the Cash Flow worksheet:

='Cash Flow'!B3

To include a reference to a cell from another sheet in your workbook:

1. Click the cell where you want the formula.
2. Type an equal sign (=).
3. Navigate to the cell you want to reference by clicking the sheet tab and then clicking the cell.
4. Press ←Enter to complete the formula.

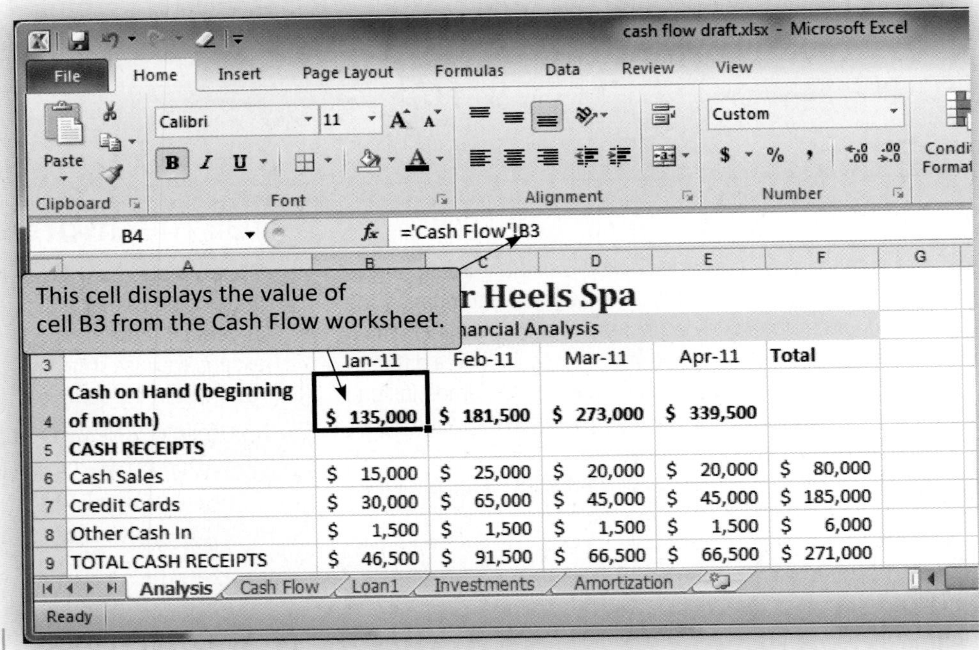

FIGURE EX 2.22

If you want to include the reference in a formula, enter the formula as normal. When you want to add a reference to a cell in another sheet, click the sheet tab, then click the cell(s) you want to add to the formula. Continue entering the formula in the formula bar or clicking cells throughout your workbook. When you are finished with the formula, press ←Enter.

tell me **more**

If your workbook includes multiple sheets with the same data structure, you can create a formula that references the same cell(s) on multiple sheets. This is called a **3-D reference**. For example, the formula **=SUM('2011 Projection:2013 Projection'!B24)** will calculate the sum of the value of cell **B24** on all sheets from **2011 Projection** to **2013 Projection.**

To add a 3-D reference to a formula, begin entering the formula as you would normally. Then, when you want to add the 3-D reference, select the sheet tabs for all the sheets you want included and click the specific cell(s) you want.

try **this**

You are not limited to referencing data within a single workbook. If you have multiple workbooks open, you can click a cell in another workbook to create an external reference. The reference will look like this:

=B17+'[Four Year Profit Projections.xlsx] Salaries'!$D$6

The file name of the referenced workbook is enclosed in brackets, followed by the sheet name, all enclosed in single quotes, followed by the specific cell reference. If the external file is not open, the reference will include the full path name to the file, not just the file name.

2.14 Displaying and Printing Formulas

How do you troubleshoot a worksheet that is displaying unexpected values? When you look at a worksheet, you see only the results of formulas—cells display the values, not the formulas themselves. When you click a cell, the formula is displayed in the formula bar. But what if you want to view all of the formulas in your worksheet at once?

› To display the formulas in the current worksheet instead of values, on the *Formulas* tab in the *Formula Auditing* group, click the **Show Formulas** button.

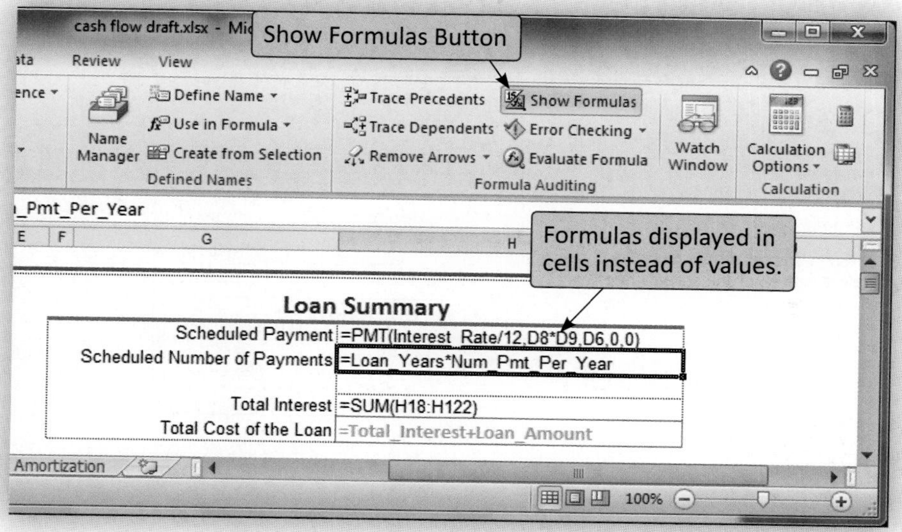

FIGURE EX 2.23

› To hide the formulas and display calculated values, click the **Show Formulas** button again.

To print a copy of the worksheet with formulas instead of values:

1. First display the formulas in the worksheet by clicking the **Show Formulas** button.
2. Next, print the worksheet:
   a. Click the **File** tab.
   b. Click **Print.**
   c. At the right side of the screen is a preview of how the printed file will look. Adjust the print settings if necessary.
   d. Click the **Print** button to send the file to your default printer.

tell me **more**

You can also set the worksheet option to display formulas instead of values, but this method is much less convenient than using the *Show Formulas* button on the Ribbon.

1. Click the **File** tab.
2. Click the **Options** button.
3. Click **Advanced,** and then scroll down to the *Display options for this worksheet:* section.
4. Click the check box for **Show formulas in cells instead of their calculated results.**
5. Select the worksheet for which you want to display only formulas.
6. Click **OK.**
7. Notice that the **Show Formulas** button on the Ribbon now appears highlighted.
8. To hide the formulas and display calculated values instead, click the **Show Formulas** button to turn the option off.

try **this**

The keyboard shortcut to display (or hide) formulas is Ctrl + ` (the ` key is directly to the left of 1 at the top of the keyboard).

2.15 Checking Formulas for Errors

Some worksheet errors are easily identifiable—such as divide by zero errors, which look like this in your worksheet: **#DIV/0!** (because Excel cannot calculate a value to display). Other potential errors, like formulas that leave out part of a cell range, are harder to find yourself. You can use Excel's Error Checking function to review your worksheet for errors. The *Error Checking* dialog displays each error it finds, allowing you to resolve or ignore each error in turn.

To use error checking to find errors in your worksheet:

1. On the *Formulas* tab in the *Formula Auditing* group, click the **Error Checking** button Error Checking.
2. The *Error Checking* dialog displays information about the first error. The buttons available in the dialog box will differ, depending on the type of error found.

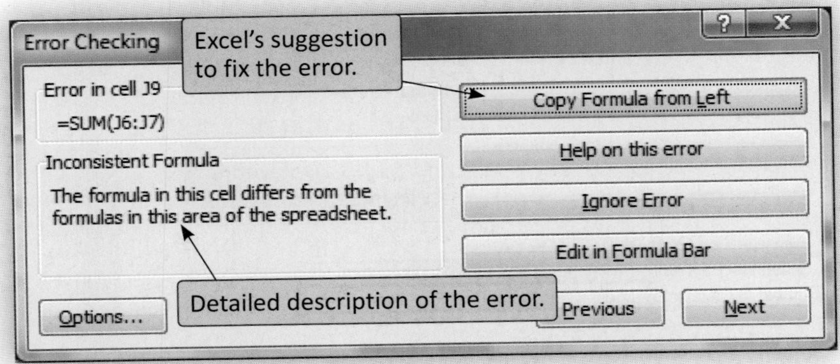

FIGURE EX 2.24

- If Excel is able to offer a solution to the error, the dialog will include a button to accept the suggested fix.
- Click the **Help on this error** button to open Microsoft Office Help.
- Click **Ignore Error** to dismiss the error. Excel will ignore this error until you manually reset ignored errors through Excel *Options*.
- Click **Edit in Formula Bar** to fix the error manually.

3. Click the **Next** button to see the next error in your worksheet.
4. When you have reviewed all errors, Excel displays a message that the error check is complete. Click **OK** to dismiss the message box.

Cells that include potential errors are marked with a green triangle in the upper-left corner of the cell. When you click the cell, Excel displays a **Smart Tag** to help you resolve the error.

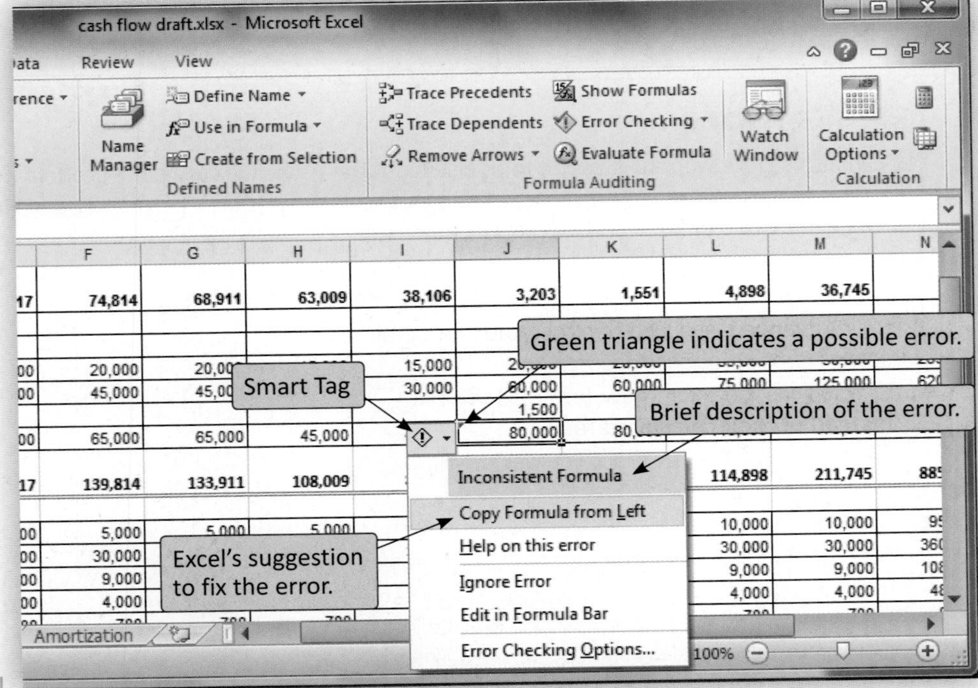

FIGURE EX 2.25

To use Smart Tags to resolve errors in formulas:

1. When a Smart Tag appears, move your mouse over the icon to display a tool tip describing the possible error ⚠ ▾.
2. Click the **Smart Tag** arrow to display the possible error resolutions.
3. If you want to keep the formula as it is, select **Ignore Error.**
4. If you want to resolve the error, select one of the options:
   - The first option is usually a suggestion of how to resolve the error. Click it to accept Excel's suggestion.
   - Select **Help on this error** to open Microsoft Office Help.
   - Select **Edit in Formula Bar** to manually edit the formula.
   - Select **Error Checking Options. . .** to open the *Options* dialog and modify the way that Excel checks for errors.
5. Once you have made a selection from the *Smart Tag* options, the Smart Tag is dismissed.

tips & tricks

You can make changes to your worksheet without closing the *Error Checking* dialog. When you click away from the dialog, one of the buttons changes to a *Resume* button and none of the other buttons in the dialog is available. When you are ready to return to error checking, click the **Resume** button.

tell me more

If the error is part of a complex formula, Excel may include a *Show Calculation Steps . . .* button in the *Error Checking* dialog. This button launches the *Evaluate Formula* dialog where you can walk through the formula step by step to try to find the cause of the error.

If the error is related to a reference to another cell, Excel will offer a *Trace Error* button to display precedent and dependent arrows showing dependencies between formulas in your worksheet.

try this

You can also start Error Checking by clicking the **Error Checking** arrow and selecting **Error Checking . . .**

projects

Skill Review 2.1

Client Bills and Staff Hours. In this project you will be completing a workbook for tracking staff hours on various clients' projects. The workbook generates client bills from the staff hours. This could be expanded and used for a legal office or consulting firm.

1. Open the provided file called *Clients.xlsx.*

   Use Save As to save an additional working copy of the file called `[your initials]EX_SkillReview_2-1.`

   Use this new copy of the file for the remainder of the project. If at any point, you would like to start over, you will be able to return to the original unaltered file.

2. Take a look at the various worksheets.

   a. There may be too many worksheets for all the sheet tabs to be visible at one time. Use the sheet tab scroll arrows in the bottom left of your screen as needed.

   b. Three staff members each have a worksheet for recording hours billed to different clients. Statistics are computed from the data. Two of the staff members' worksheets are completed; one you will be completing.

   c. There are four client bill worksheets as well. Three of them are complete and one you will complete.

   d. Finally there is a worksheet containing the staff members' billable rates.

3. Select the **Luz Hours** worksheet; enter formulas in each of the yellow cells.

   a. Count the number of clients. Click cell **H3.** Enter the formula: `=COUNTA(A10:A14)`

   b. Total the billable hours for each day. Select cells **B10:H15** and click the **AutoSum** button.

   c. Count the number of clients served on the first day. Click cell **B17.** Enter the function: `=COUNT(B10:B14)`

      Fill across to count the clients served each day.

   d. Average the number of billable hours per day during the first week, in cell **H19.** Click the **AutoSum** drop-down arrow, click **Average,** drag the mouse over cells **B15:H15,** then press the **Enter** key.

   e. Compute the total billable hours for the week in cell **H20.** Click the **AutoSum** button, drag the mouse over cells **B15:H15,** then press the **Enter** key.

   f. Find the lowest number of billable hours per day during the first week, in cell **H19.** Click the **AutoSum** drop-down arrow, click **Min,** drag the mouse over cells **B15:H15,** then press the **Enter** key.

   g. Find the highest number of billable hours per day during the first week, in cell **H19.** Click the **AutoSum** drop-down arrow, click **Max,** drag the mouse over cells **B15:H15,** then press the **Enter** key.

   h. Compute the Daily Bill amounts. Click cell **B24.** Enter the formula `=B15*$B$5.` Copy the formula to the right for each day of the week in cells C24:H24.

   i. In cell **B25,** enter the formula to total the bills for the week `=SUM(B24:H24).`

   j. Total the hours per week for each client. Click cell **K10.** Click the **AutoSum** button. Drag or use the keyboard to edit the selected argument cells to be **B10:H10,** then press the **Enter** key to complete the formula =SUM(B10:H10). Copy or fill the formula down for each of the clients in cells K11:K13.

k. Use an IF function to determine if the staff member is loaded with sufficient billable hours. In cell **K17,** enter: `=IF(H20>=$H$5,"yes","no")`

l. Repeat this process for all of the second week formulas.

m. In cell **H4,** use COUNTIF to find out how many days were billed at 8 hours or more. Enter: `=COUNTIF(B15:H15,">8")+COUNTIF(B36:H36,">8")`

n. Display your formulas temporarily to check for accuracy, comparing to the formulas on other staff hours sheets. On the *Formulas* tab, in the *Formula Auditing* group, click the **Show Formulas** button. Or use Ctrl + `. Return to the normal display when you are ready to go on. Use *Error Checking* as needed.

4. Assign a name to the range of cells containing the billing rates on the **Look Up** worksheet. Select cells **B4:C6.** On the *Formulas* tab, in the *Defined Names* group, click the **Define Name** drop-down arrow and click **Define Name.** Type the name: `Bill_Rates`

5. Select the **Proctor Bill** worksheet; enter formulas in each of the yellow cells.

a. Compute the bill due date 30 days from the day the bill is printed by entering the following formula: `=TODAY()+30`

b. Compute the number of hours Marshall billed to Proctor's project.

(1) Click in cell **B12,** type: =

(2) Click on the sheet tab for Marshall's hours and click the cell with Proctor's total for the first week, cell **K13.**

(3) Type: +

(4) Still on the sheet for Marshall's hours, click the cell with Proctor's total for the 2nd week, cell **K34.**

(5) Press the **Enter** key to complete the formula.

c. Repeat the process in column B to compute the number of hours Stevens billed to Proctor and the number of hours Luz billed to Proctor.

d. Use a lookup function to find the rates for each staff member.

(1) Start in cell **C12.** Click the **Insert Function** button *fx* to open the *Insert Function* dialog box; select the **Lookup & Reference** category and then select the **VLOOKUP** function. Click **OK.**

(2) Enter the function arguments in each box as pictured in Figure EX 2.28. Click **OK.**

(3) The resulting formula in **C12** should look like this: `=VLOOKUP(A12,Bill_Rates,2,FALSE)`

(4) Fill down column C to look up the rates for the other staff members as well.

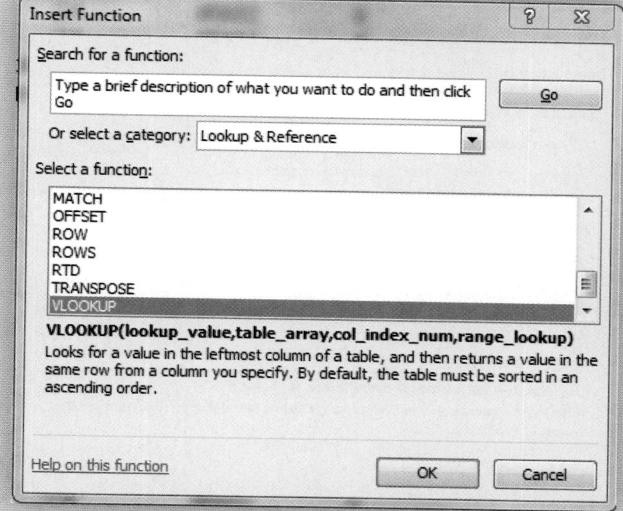

FIGURE EX 2.26

e. In column D, enter formulas multiplying the hours billed by the billing rate for each staff member.

f. Select cells **D12:D16,** then click the **AutoSum** button.

g. In cell **D25** compute the monthly payment.

(1) Either type in the function: `=PMT(D24/12,D23,-D16)`

(2) Or use the **Insert Function** button *fx* to open the *Insert Function* dialog box, select the **Financial** category, then select the **PMT** function. Enter the arguments in the boxes. Click **OK.**

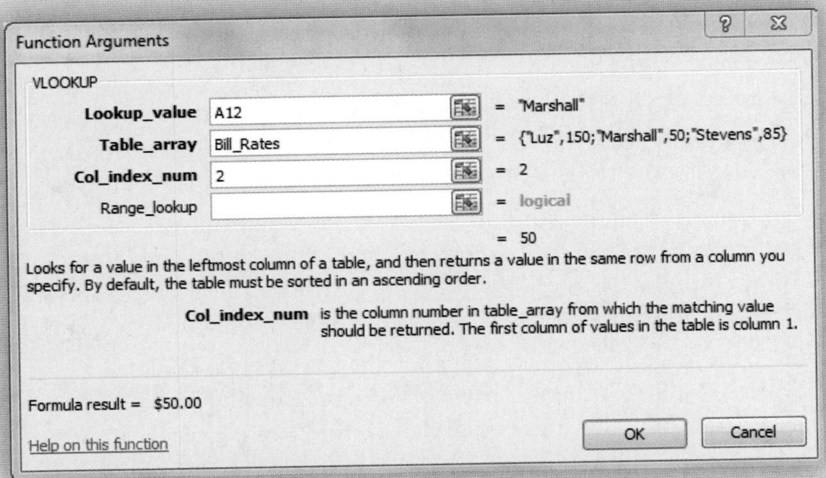

FIGURE EX 2.27

h. Display your formulas temporarily to check for accuracy, comparing to the formulas on other client bill sheets. On the *Formulas* tab, in the *Formula Auditing* group, click the **Show Formulas** button. Or use Ctrl + `. Return to the normal display when you are ready to go on. Use *Error Checking* as needed.

Skill Review 2.2

Teacher Grade Book. In this review you will edit a worksheet to compute student grades and grade statistics.

1. Open the provided file called *Grades.xlsx*.

a. Use Save As to save an additional working copy of the file called **[your initials]EX_SkillReview_2-2.** Use this new copy of the file for the remainder of the project. If at any point, you would like to start over, you will be able to return to the original unaltered file.

b. Take a look at the two sheets. The first sheet contains the students' names and their scores. The second sheet will be used to look up the letter grade for each student.

c. Save your work as you go along.

2. Enter a function to display the current date each time the worksheet is opened. Enter the `=NOW()` function in cell **T35** and format with a date and time format.

3. Count the number of students.

a. In cell **B5** type: `=cou`

b. Double-click **COUNTA.** Drag the mouse over the cells with the last names, **A14:A32,** to enter that range into the function. Press **Enter** to complete the formula.

c. Display your formulas temporarily to check for accuracy, comparing to the formula below:

`=COUNTA(A14:A32)`

Click cell **B5.** On the *Formulas* tab, in the *Formula Auditing* group, click the **Show Formulas** button. Or use Ctrl + `. Repeat to turn off the formula display and return to normal. Use *Error Checking* as needed.

FIGURE EX 2.28

4. Find out which students and how many students have a below C grade at the 7-week point.

a. Assign a name to the range of cells containing the possible points up through the midterm: Select cells **C11:R11.** On the *Formulas* tab, in the *Defined Names* group, click the **Define Name** drop-down arrow, then click **Define Name.** Type in the name: `Possible_Pts_MidTerm`. Click **OK.**

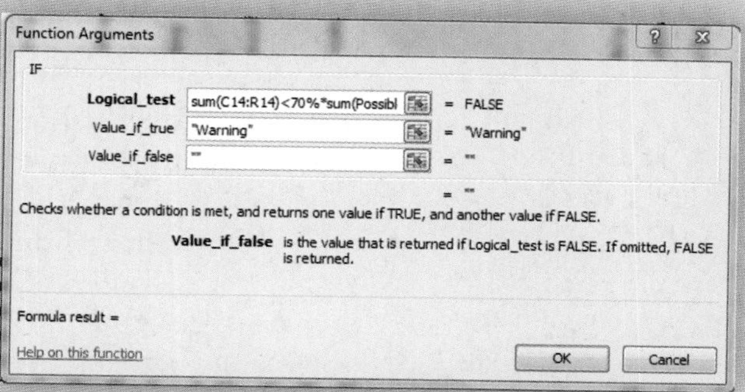

FIGURE EX 2.29

b. Enter an IF function in cell **T14** for the first student to see if his or her points are less than 70% of the total possible points through the midterm. If the student is below a C grade, display *Warning!* in the cell; otherwise leave the cell blank. Follow this format:

```
=IF(student points through midterm<70%*possible points through midterm, display Warning!, leave blank)
```

Either type in the function on the formula bar or use the **Insert Function** button *fx* to open the *Insert Function* dialog box, select the **Logical** category, then select the **IF** function.

c. Display your formulas temporarily to check for accuracy, comparing to the formula below.

```
=IF(SUM(C14:R14)<70%*SUM(Possible_Pts_
MidTerm),"Warning!","")
```

On the *Formulas* tab, in the *Formula Auditing* group, click the **Show Formulas** button. Or use Ctrl + `. Turn off the formula display. Use *Error Checking* as needed.

d. Fill the IF function in cell **T14** down for all students.

e. Assign a name to the range of cells that have the students' warning status. Select cells **T12:T32;** on the *Formulas* tab, in the *Defined Names* group, click **Create from Selection.** Select **Top Row,** then click **OK.**

f. Type a COUNTIF function in cell **U4** to count the number of students with a warning.

(1) Type: `=COUNTIF(Warn`

(2) Double-click **Warning_below_C_grade.**

(3) Type: `, "Warning!")` and press **Enter** to complete the function. The resulting function should be:

`=COUNTIF(Warning_below_C_grade, "Warning!")`

5. Compute statistics about the scores for each assignment.

a. Enter the statistical functions in column C:

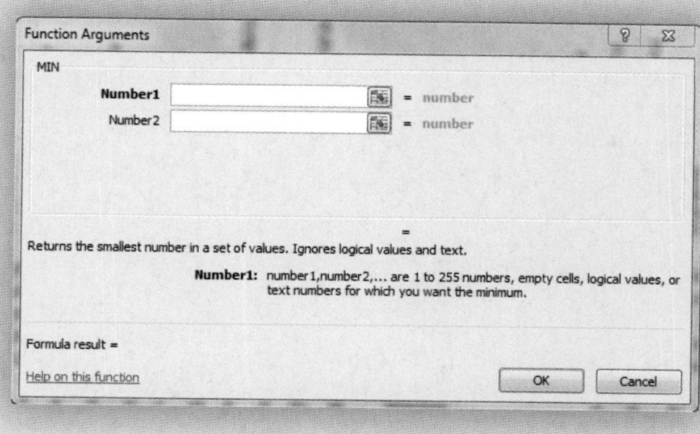

FIGURE EX 2.30

(1) In cell **C10,** enter the function to compute the average student score for the assignment in column C: `=AVERAGE(C14:C32)`

(2) In cell **C9,** type the function to compute the median student score for the assignment in column C: `=MEDIAN(C14:C32)`

(3) In cell **C8,** click the **Insert Function** button *fx* to build the function to compute the lowest student score for the assignment in column C. Choose the **Statistical** category, scroll down and select the **MIN** function, then click **OK.** In the *Number1* box, type: `C14:C32` and then click **OK.** The resulting function should look like this: `=MIN(C14:C32)`

(4) Click cell **C7.** On the *Home* tab, click the **AutoSum** button **drop-down arrow** and select **Max.** Drag the mouse over cells **C14:C32** to enter the range into the function. Press **Enter** to complete the formula.

(5) Display your formulas temporarily to check for accuracy, comparing to those in the table below. On the *Formulas* tab, in the *Formula Auditing* group, click the **Show Formulas** button. Or use Ctrl + `. Repeat to turn off the formula display. Use *Error Checking* as needed.

	B	C
7	Highest	=MAX(C14:C32)
8	Lowest	=MIN(C14:C32)
9	Median	=MEDIAN(C14:C32)
10	Average	=AVERAGE(C14:C32)

b. Use *AutoFill, Fill Options,* and *Copy/Paste* to fill the statistical functions across for the assignments, but leave columns S, T, and U blank.

6. Compute the students' total points and percentages.

a. Enter a SUM function in cell **AG14** to add all the points across for the first student. Select cells **C14:AG14,** the click the **AutoSum** button. The resulting formula in cell **AG14** should be: `=SUM(C14:AF14)`

b. Use *AutoFill* and *Fill Options* as needed to fill the SUM function down for all students. And copy the SUM function to cell **AG11** to total the points possible.

c. In cell **AH14,** enter a formula to compute the percentage for the first student. Divide the student's total points by the total possible points: `=AG14/AG11`

(1) Before entering the formula, prepare to copy this formula down for all the students. Set the total possible points to be an absolute reference. Click on the **AG11** part of the formula in the formula bar. Press the F4 key once to add the absolute reference $ symbols, changing it to $AG$11, then enter the formula. Now that part of the formula will stay the same and not adjust as the formula is filled down. The resulting formula should look like this: `=AG14/$AG$11`

d. Format cell **AH14** as a percent format with one decimal place. Then fill down for all students.

7. Look up the students' letter grades.

a. Enter the lookup function for the first student in cell **AI14** following this format:

=vlookup(cell with student percent, range of cells on second sheet that make up the grade table, second column has the letter grade)

(1) Type: `=VLOOKUP(`

(2) Click cell **AH14** to enter in the function the cell with the first student's percentage.

(3) Type: `,`

(4) Click on the *Grades* worksheet tab, drag the mouse over cells **B5:C9** to enter into the function the cells that make up the lookup table.

(5) Type the last piece of information needed, the column number within the lookup table that contains the letter grade: `,2)`

(6) Before entering the function, on the formula bar, select the part of the formula referencing the lookup table cells **B5:C9,** tap the F4 key to absolute reference the lookup table cells so they stay the same and are not adjusted as the formula is copied down for all the students.

b. Display your formulas temporarily to check for accuracy, comparing to the formula below.

```
=VLOOKUP(AH14,Grades!$B$5:$C$9,2)
```

Turn off the formula display. Use *Error Checking* as needed.

c. Fill down for all students.

challenge yourself 1

College GPA and Student Loan. In this project, you will record data about your completed and planned college courses. You will compute your GPA, college course costs, and various statistics. You will compute your expected college loan payment and count down the days to graduation and paying off the loan.

1. Open the provided file called *College.xlsx.* Save for yourself a copy of the file to use to complete this project. Call the copy ***[your initials]*EX_Challenge_2-3.**
2. There are three sheets. Start with the *GPA* sheet.
3. Assign a name to cell **A3.** Name it: `Student_Name`
4. Enter the formulas for the *GPA* worksheet as follows.
   a. Compute the **Cost** for the first course by multiplying the **Unit Cost** by the number of **Units** for the course. Use absolute referencing; then fill and copy to compute the cost for each course, both semesters.
   b. Use VLOOKUP to take the letter grade for the first course and look up the **Grade Points** in the second column of the lookup table. Use absolute referencing; then fill and copy to look up the grade points for each course, both semesters.
   c. Multiply the **Grade Points** by the **Units** to get the **Quality Points** for each course, for both semesters.
   d. Use AutoSum to get totals for **Cost, Units,** and **Quality Points** for each semester.
   e. Compute the **GPA** for each semester by dividing the total **Quality Points** by the total **Units.**
   f. At the top of the worksheet, total the **Cost** by using AutoSum to add all the numbers in the *Cost* column down to row **100** and divide that total by **2.** Do the same for the total **Units** and total **Quality Points.** (Note: This method of totaling will result in a worksheet ready to accept entry of additional semesters without the need to update the total formulas. Because the subtotals are also included in the columns, each amount is essentially counted twice, thus the need to divide by 2. Some Excel users may prefer to total the subtotal cells instead.)
   g. Use COUNTIF functions to count the number of General Ed and the number of non General Ed classes. (Again, in anticipation of adding more classes to the worksheet, select down through row **100.**)
   h. For the **Cumulative GPA,** divide the **Total Quality Points** by the **Total Units.** Format to **2** decimal places.
   i. Compare your results to Figure EX 2.31.

	A	B	C	D	E	F	G	H	I	J	K
1	**GPA Calculation**									Lookup Table	
2										**Letter Grade**	**Grade Points**
3	Ima Student						# of General Ed Classes	4		A	4
4							# of non General Ed Classes	3		B	3
5	Cumulative GPA		3.14							C	2
6	Total Units		21							D	1
7	Total Quality Points		66							F	0
8											
9	Total Cost		$504								
10											
11	**Community College**	**Unit Cost**	$24								
12											
13		**Cost**	**Term**	**Year**	**General Ed**	**Course**	**# Units**	**Grade**	**Grade Points**	**Quality Points**	**GPA**
14		$72	Fall	2010	yes	English A	3	B	3	9	
15		$72	Fall	2010	no	CIS 30	3	A	4	12	
16		$96	Fall	2010	yes	Bio 1	4	C	2	8	
17	Semester Total	$240					10			29	2.90
18											
19		$72	Spring	2011	yes	English 1A	3	A	4	12	
20		$96	Spring	2011	no	Math D	4	B	3	12	
21		$72	Spring	2011	yes	History 17	3	B	3	9	
22		$24	Spring	2011	no	PE 12	1	A	4	4	
23	Semester Total	$264					11			37	3.36
24											

FIGURE EX 2.31

j. As needed, switch to display formulas and compare to Figure EX 2.32.

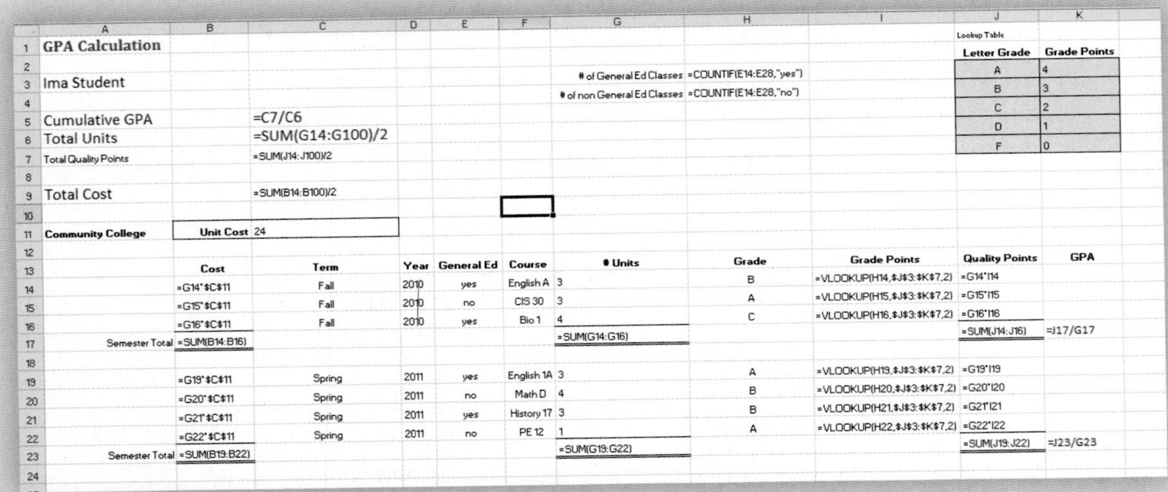

	A	B	C	D	E	F	G	H	I	J	K
1	**GPA Calculation**									Lookup Table	
2										**Letter Grade**	**Grade Points**
3	Ima Student						# of General Ed Classes	=COUNTIF(E14:E28,"yes")		A	4
4							# of non General Ed Classes	=COUNTIF(E14:E28,"no")		B	3
5	Cumulative GPA		=C7/C6							C	2
6	Total Units		=SUM(G14:G100)/2							D	1
7	Total Quality Points		=SUM(J14:J100)/2							F	0
8											
9	Total Cost		=SUM(B14:B100)/2								
10											
11	**Community College**	**Unit Cost**	24								
12											
13		**Cost**	**Term**	**Year**	**General Ed**	**Course**	**# Units**	**Grade**	**Grade Points**	**Quality Points**	**GPA**
14		=G14*$C$11	Fall	2010	yes	English A	3	B	=VLOOKUP(H14,$J$3:$K$7,2)	=G14*I14	
15		=G15*$C$11	Fall	2010	no	CIS 30	3	A	=VLOOKUP(H15,$J$3:$K$7,2)	=G15*I15	
16		=G16*$C$11	Fall	2010	yes	Bio 1	4	C	=VLOOKUP(H16,$J$3:$K$7,2)	=G16*I16	
17	Semester Total	=SUM(B14:B16)					=SUM(G14:G16)			=SUM(J14:J16)	=J17/G17
18											
19		=G19*$C$11	Spring	2011	yes	English 1A	3	A	=VLOOKUP(H19,$J$3:$K$7,2)	=G19*I19	
20		=G20*$C$11	Spring	2011	no	Math D	4	B	=VLOOKUP(H20,$J$3:$K$7,2)	=G20*I20	
21		=G21*$C$11	Spring	2011	yes	History 17	3	B	=VLOOKUP(H21,$J$3:$K$7,2)	=G21*I21	
22		=G22*$C$11	Spring	2011	no	PE 12	1	A	=VLOOKUP(H22,$J$3:$K$7,2)	=G22*I22	
23	Semester Total	=SUM(B19:B22)					=SUM(G19:G22)			=SUM(J19:J22)	=J23/G23
24											

FIGURE EX 2.32

k. Use *Error Checking* as needed. Make appropriate improvements to formatting.

5. Next go to the *Loan* worksheet.

a. In cell **H1,** set to right-align the student's name, then enter this formula: `=Student_Name`

b. Enter the formulas for the *Loan* sheet in column B.

(1) Use the lookup table to find the # of Years to Pay. Take the **Amount Owed,** then use the lookup table; you will find the number of **Years to Pay** in the second column.

(2) Use the payment function to determine the **Payment Amount.**

c. Enter your own loan information and calculations in column B.

(1) Enter a loan amount (at least $2,000), loan rate, and your graduation date.

(2) Enter a function to determine the current date each time the worksheet is opened.

(3) Compute the **# of Days Until Graduation** by subtracting today's date from your graduation date. Format the cell as a number with zero decimal places.

(4) To compute your first loan payment, add half a year, 182 days, to your graduation date.

(5) To estimate the date of the last loan payment, take the number of years to pay times 365.3 and add that to the date of the first loan payment.

(6) Subtract to estimate the # of days left until the loan is paid off.

d. Format cells appropriately.

6. Finally go to the *Summary* worksheet. Enter the formulas, most of which will reference the other two sheets. Format numbers appropriately.

a. Make a simple formula to reference the **Cumulative GPA** number from the *GPA* worksheet to display the **GPA** on the *Summary* sheet.

b. Do the Same for **Total Units.**

c. Create a formula to compute the **Total Cost** of all your college courses. This formula will reference the *GPA* sheet. Sum all the numbers in the *GPA* sheet **Cost** column and divide by **2.**

d. For **Total Debt,** reference the **Amount Owed** number from the *Loan* sheet.

e. Compute the **Average Cost Per Unit** by dividing the **Total Cost** by the **Total Units.** Compute **Average Debt Per Unit** in the same way.

f. Use COUNTIF to count the **Number of Classes** on the *GPA* worksheet in which you earned an A **Grade.** Do the same to count your Bs, Cs, Ds, and Fs as well.

g. Use a statistical function to find out the most paid for any semester.

h. Back at the top of the *Summary* sheet, enter IF functions to check to see if you met your GPA goal and your unit requirement. If your GPA is greater than or equal to the goal, display "Yes"; if not, display "No." If your total units are greater than or equal to the requirement, display "Yes"; if not, display "No."

i. Edit the goal and unit requirement to reflect your own GPA goal and unit requirement.

7. Edit the *GPA* worksheet to reflect your own college transcript information by entering at least all your college classes taken and those planned. Change *Ima A. Student* to your own name. Adjust, copy and fill in all the formulas to accurately complete the sheet and ensure that links to other sheets continue to work correctly. Assume that you will be attending university full time and for those semesters enter a flat fee for the **Semester Total Cost** number. You may need a new formula to compute university costs per course: `=Semester Cost/Semester Units*Course Units`

challenge yourself 2

Vehicle Purchase. Complete a vehicle shopping Excel workbook to compare the purchase of several vehicles of your choice.

1. Make a copy of the provided file called *Vehicle.xlsx* to use to complete this project. Call the copy ***[your initials]*EX_Challenge_2-4.**

2. In cell **E1** enter a time/date function to display an updated current date each time the worksheet is opened.

	A	B	C
1	**Vehicle Purchase**		Date of Vehi
2			
3			Vehicle 1
4	Description:		Ford Mustang 2010
5		Vehicle Type	Passenger
6			
7		Photo	
8			
9			
10		Seller	Car Max
11		Price	$33,140
12		MPG	22
13			
14	Yearly Costs		
15		Maintenance/Year	300
16		Registration Fee	100
17		Insurance/Year	1000
18			
19	Need Loan?		Yes
20		Amount to Borrow	$28,140
21		APR	4%
22		Years	4
23			
24	Monthly Costs		
25		Gas	
26		Loan Payment	$748.27
27		Maintenance/Month	$25.00
28		Insurance/Month	$83.33
29		Total Monthly	$856.60
30			
31		Can I Afford It?	No

FIGURE EX 2.33

3. On the *Purchase* worksheet, for the first vehicle, enter the formulas. Reference the assumption *cells,* which are found on the *Assumptions* sheet, in the formulas; do not enter the assumption *numbers* in the formulas. Be sure to use absolute references when needed so you will be able to fill across for additional vehicles.
   a. Enter a VLOOKUP function to look up the registration fee for the vehicle. Use the **Vehicle Type** in cell **C5** to look in the table on the *Assumptions* worksheet. Look in the second column for the fee.
   b. Use an IF function to determine if you need a loan, `Yes`, or if you have enough cash to buy the car right now, `No`.
   c. Subtract your car cash from the purchase price to compute how much you would need to borrow to purchase the car: `=C11-Assumptions!$A$3`
   d. Use the PMT function to compute the monthly loan payment.
   e. Compute the monthly cost of gas, maintenance, and insurance.
   f. Total all the monthly costs.
   g. Enter an IF function to determine `Yes` or `No` if you have enough money available each month to pay the loan and run the car.
   h. Compare your results to Figure EX 2.33.
   i. Where your results differ, use *Error Checking.* Also, display your formulas and compare with Figure EX 2.34.
4. On the *Assumptions* worksheet, replace the existing assumptions with your own assumptions for
   a. Total cash available for a vehicle purchase.
   b. Total monthly amount available to spend on a vehicle.
   c. Number of miles you expect to drive per month.
   d. Gas price per gallon.
5. Research vehicles online to enter in the *Purchase* worksheet.
   a. Replace the original data: Enter a brief description of the vehicle. Enter numbers for the price, MPG, expected yearly maintenance and insurance costs, loan rate, loan length, and so on.
   b. Repeat, entering data and filling formulas in the columns to the right with a few less and less expensive vehicles until you find a vehicle you can afford. You should have at least three or four vehicles and at least one that you can afford.
6. Enter COUNT functions to fill in the boxes in column G.
7. Change the number in cell **K7** to reflect a different MPG threshold.
8. Use **Create Names from Selection, Left column** to assign names to ranges for use in statistical analysis. Then use the **AutoSum drop-down arrow** to enter the functions for the averages and highest and lowest boxes in columns H, I, and J.

   Example: `=AVERAGE(Price)`

	A	B	C
1	**Vehicle Pu**		
2			
3			Vehicle 1
4	Description:		Ford Mustang 2010
5		Vehicle Type	Passenger
6			
7		Photo	
8			
9			
10		Seller	Car Max
11		Price	33140
12		MPG	22
13			
14	Yearly Costs		
15		Maintenance/Year	300
16		Registration Fee	=VLOOKUP(C5,Assumptions!$B$11:$C$18,2)
17		Insurance/Year	1000
18			
19	Need Loan?		=IF(C11>Assumptions!$A$3,"Yes", "No")
20		Amount to Borrow	=C11-Assumptions!$A$3
21		APR	0.04
22		Years	4
23			
24	Monthly Costs		
25		Gas	
26		Loan Payment	=-PMT(C21/12,C22*12,C11)
27		Maintenance/Month	=C15/12
28		Insurance/Month	=C17/12
29		Total Monthly	=SUM(C26:C28)
30			
31		Can I Afford It?	=IF(C29>Assumptions!$A$4,"No", "Yes")

FIGURE EX 2.34

9. After entering new data, if your formulas are entered correctly, you should see new results about affordability without any need to adjust your formulas. You should be able to enter new assumptions or data without any need to rework your formulas. For example, enter new numbers in your worksheet to reflect a bonus or large gift, a better deal on insurance, or a better auto loan rate. Use formula error checking tools as needed. Display your formulas and check for accuracy. Save after returning to display values in cells.

on your own

Dental Chart. Make yourself a copy of the provided file called *Teeth.xlsx* for this project in which you will be completing a dental chart workbook. Call the copy ***[your initials]*****EX_OnYourOwn_2-5**.

1. Start with the *Pocket Chart* worksheet. This dental chart is designed to be used to record measurements of the depth of gum pockets around the teeth. Each tooth is identified by number and name. The teeth of the upper and lower jaws are arranged across the worksheet from the patient's right side to the left. Pocket depth measurements have been entered.

a. Enter your name as the patient's name and enter the date of the examination.

b. Enter formulas in all of the empty boxes. Use statistical functions and VLOOKUP. Increase or reduce decimal places as needed.

c. Assign the name `Patient_Name` to the cell with the patient name and assign the name `Date_of_Examination` to the cell with the examination date.

2. On the *Treatment Plan* worksheet:

   a. Enter simple formulas referencing the patient name and the examination date named ranges. Format appropriately.

   b. Use COUNTIF to count the number of pockets that measure 1 mm (referencing the cell **B8**). To count the top and bottom jaws, add two COUNTIFs together. For example:

   ```
   =COUNTIF('Pocket Chart'!$B$14:$Q$14,B8)+COUNTIF
   ('Pocket Chart'!$B$20:$Q$20,B8)
   ```

   c. Do the same to count the number of pockets for each size though 7 mm.

   d. Use IF functions to recommend treatments:

   (1) In cell E9, if there are more than **five** 2 mm pockets, recommend "Sonic Toothbrush"; otherwise, make the recommendation "N/A."

   (2) If there are more than **seven** 3 mm pockets, recommend "Scaling and Planing"; otherwise, leave the recommendation "N/A."

   (3) If there are more than **three** 4 mm pockets, recommend "Laser Treatment"; otherwise, leave the recommendation "N/A."

   (4) If there are more than **three** 5 mm pockets, recommend "Surgery"; otherwise, leave the recommendation "N/A."

3. For each treatment, use VLOOKUP to find the **Cost.** The lookup table is on the *Look Up* sheet and it is already named **Treatment_Cost.** For example: `=VLOOKUP('Treatment Plan'!E9,Treatment_Cost,2,FALSE)`
4. For **Date of Consultation,** enter the TODAY function.
5. Use HLOOKUP to find the insurance coverage rate. Take the name of the insurance from cell **H3,** look in the horizontal lookup table on the *Look Up* sheet, and get the insurance rate from the second row in the lookup table.
6. Compute the amount the insurance will cover for each treatment. Use absolute referencing and fill.
7. Subtract what the insurance will pay from the **Cost** to get the **Billable Amount.**
8. Use AutoSum to total the billable amount.
9. Compute the **Payment Amount** for the payment option using the PMT function.
10. Display your formulas and check for errors. Use *Error Checking* as needed.

fix it

Party. In this project, you will correct function mistakes and other formula errors in a workbook designed for planning a large party or event.

1. Open and save yourself a copy of the provided file called *Party.xlsx* in which to periodically save your work. Call the copy ***[your initials]*EX_FixIt_2-6.**
2. On the *GuestList* sheet, check all the formulas. They all have box borders. Most of them need to be corrected. Use *Error Checking* as needed and/or display the formulas on-screen for easy viewing. When you have them right, it should look like Figure EX 2.35.

Guest List	
90	Total number of guests attending
65	Count of invitations sent
18	Count of invitations sent, but no one is coming
16	Count of invitations to guests outside of California
56	Count of invitations to guests outside of the 95677 zip code
23	Count of guests coming alone, not bringing a date or family member
$94.25	Total cost for purchasing and mailing invitations

FIGURE EX 2.35

3. On the *Shopping List* sheet, check all the formulas. They all have box borders. Most of them need to be corrected. Use *Error Checking* as needed and/or display the formulas on-screen for easy viewing. Be careful: Postage stamps are NOT taxed! When you have it right, it should look like Figure EX 2.36:

	A	B	C	D	E	F	G	H	I	J
1	**Shopping List**									
2			number of different items	24				$273	Average item cost	
3			# f items already purchsed	13				$1,500	Highest Item Cost	
4			# of items not yet puchased	11				$25	Lowest Item Cost	
5								$7,105.50	Total Cost with Tax	
6		as of	11/28/2010 21:42							
7									8.50%	
8	City	Source	Item Description	Quantity	Units	CostperUnit	Purchased	Cost	Tax	Total Cost
9	Roseville	Super Supermarket	Appetizers	25	pounds	$10.00	No	$250	$21.25	$271.25
10	Citrus Heights	CreativeBallons	Balloon Decorations	10	each	$45.00	No	$450	$38.25	$488.25
11	Sacramento	BevMO	Beers	3	case	$200.00	No	$600	$51.00	$651.00
12	Folsom	Sharons Bakery	Cake	1	Each	$350.00	No	$350	$29.75	$379.75
13	Roseville	Party Rentals	Coffee Pot	1	each	$25.00	Yes	$25	$2.13	$27.13
14	Citrus Heights	The Party Store	Dessert Forks, Cofee spoons	100	each	$0.50	Yes	$50	$4.25	$54.25
15	Citrus Heights	The Party Store	Dessert Plates	100	each	$1.00	Yes	$100	$8.50	$108.50
16	Citrus Heights	The Party Store	Dinner Plates	100	each	$1.25	Yes	$125	$10.63	$135.63
17	Citrus Heights	The Party Store	Dinner Silverware	100	sets	$1.00	Yes	$100	$8.50	$108.50
18	Folsom	Flower Power Florist	Flower Arangements	15	each	$40.00	No	$600	$51.00	$651.00
19	Roseville	Party Rentals	Glass Coffee Cups and Saucers	50	each	$2.00	Yes	$100	$8.50	$108.50
20	Citrus Heights	The Party Store	Glasses	100	each	$1.50	Yes	$150	$12.75	$162.75

FIGURE EX 2.36

4. On the *Summary* sheet, you will be entering all the formulas. They all have box borders.
5. You will need to name some cells on other sheets so that the formulas on this sheet will work. And you must reference cells on other sheets in the formulas on this sheet.
6. Use *Error Checking* as needed and/or display the formulas on-screen for easy viewing. When you have them right, it should look like Figure EX 2.37.

Party Financing	
As of	11/28/2010
# of Invitations	65
# of Guests	90
Cash Available for Event	$3,500.00
Do We Need to Borrow?	Yes
Amount to Borrow	$3,605.50
APR	4.5%
# Months to Pay	12
Monthly Payment Amount	$307.83

FIGURE EX 2.37

chapter 3

Formatting the Worksheet

In this chapter, you will learn the following skills:

- Apply themes
- Merge and split cells
- Modify rows and columns
- Work with worksheets in a workbook
- Set print options

Skill 3.1 Applying Themes
Skill 3.2 Merging Cells and Splitting Merged Cells
Skill 3.3 Modifying Row Heights and Column Widths
Skill 3.4 Inserting and Deleting Rows and Columns
Skill 3.5 Freezing and Unfreezing Rows and Columns
Skill 3.6 Hiding and Unhiding Rows and Columns
Skill 3.7 Naming Worksheets
Skill 3.8 Changing the Color of Tabs
Skill 3.9 Inserting and Deleting Worksheets
Skill 3.10 Moving and Copying Worksheets
Skill 3.11 Grouping Worksheets
Skill 3.12 Adding Headers and Footers
Skill 3.13 Splitting Workbooks
Skill 3.14 Showing and Hiding Worksheet Elements
Skill 3.15 Setting Up Margins for Printing
Skill 3.16 Scaling Worksheets for Printing
Skill 3.17 Changing Worksheet Orientation
Skill 3.18 Inserting Page Breaks
Skill 3.19 Printing Selections, Worksheets, and Workbooks
Skill 3.20 Printing Titles

Skills

introduction

As Excel projects get bigger and more complicated, more formatting skills are required. In this chapter learn about arranging data and formulas on separate worksheets, controlling how they appear on-screen and how they print on paper.

3.1 Applying Themes

A **theme** is a unified color, font, and effects scheme. When you apply a theme to the workbook, you ensure that all visual elements work well together, giving the workbook a polished, professional look.

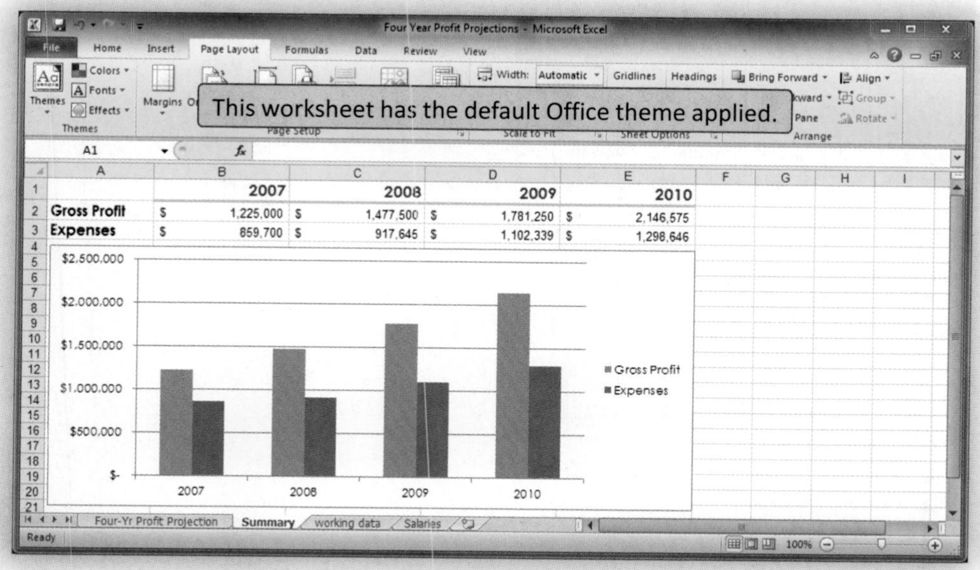

FIGURE EX 3.1

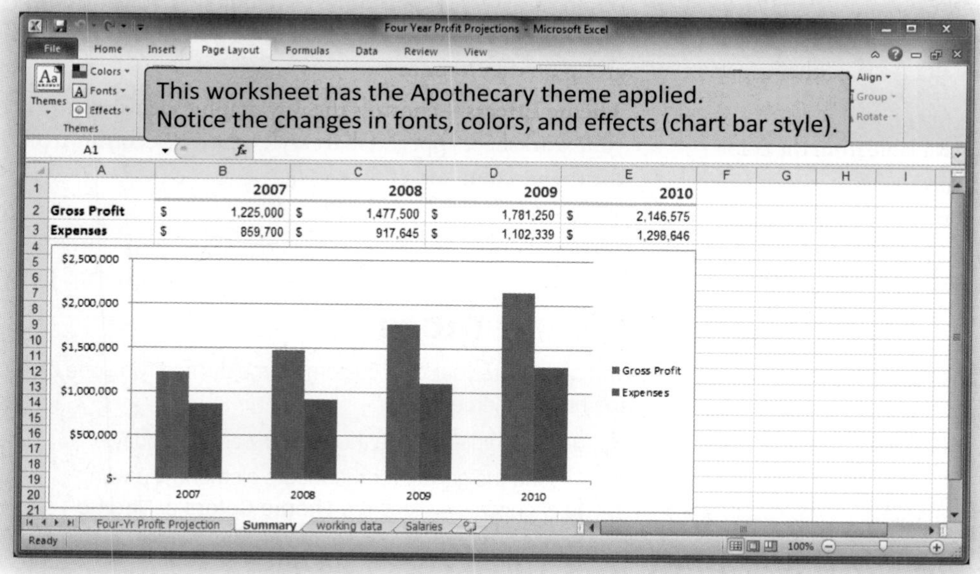

FIGURE EX 3.2

To apply a theme to a workbook:

1. Click the **Page Layout** tab.
2. In the *Themes* group, click the **Themes** button to expand the gallery.
3. Roll your mouse over each theme in the gallery to preview the formatting changes.
4. Click one of the themes to apply it to your workbook.

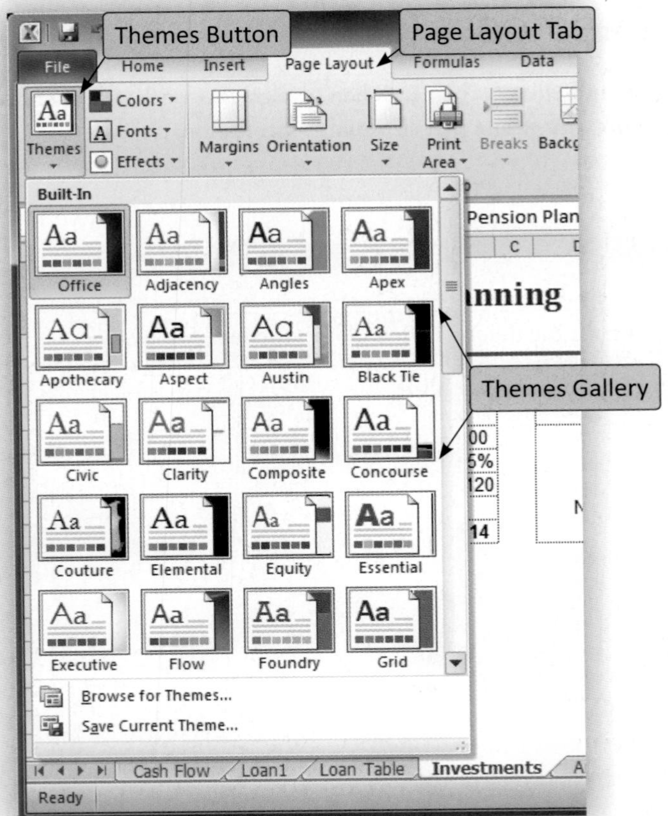

FIGURE EX 3.3

From the *Themes* group, you can apply specific aspects of a theme by making a selection from the *Theme Colors, Theme Fonts,* or *Theme Effects* gallery. Applying one aspect of a theme (for example, colors) will not change the other aspects (fonts and effects).

Theme Colors—limits the colors available from the color palette for fonts, borders, and cell shading. Notice that when you change themes, the colors in the color palette change.

Theme Fonts—affects the fonts used for cell styles (including titles and headings). Changing the theme fonts does not limit the fonts available to you from the *Font* group on the Ribbon.

Theme Effects—controls the way graphic elements in your worksheet appear. Chart styles change according to the theme color and effects.

tips & tricks

When you change the workbook theme, the look of the built-in cell styles changes. Be careful, as the change in style may increase the font size, causing some of your data to be too wide for the columns. If you change themes, you may need to adjust some of your column widths or row heights.

tell me **more**

You can create your own custom theme by modifying one of the built-in themes:

1. Begin by applying the theme you want to modify.
2. Expand the gallery for the theme element you want to change by clicking the **Theme Colors** or **Theme Fonts** button. (You cannot modify the theme effects.)
3. Click another built-in theme option to change that option for the current theme, or modify the existing theme options by clicking the **Create New Theme Colors . . .** or **Create New Theme Fonts . . .** link at the bottom of the gallery.
4. To save the modified theme so you can apply these exact settings to another workbook, click the **Save Current Theme . . .** link at the bottom of the *Themes* gallery.
5. Type a name for the theme, and then click **Save.**

3.2 Merging Cells and Splitting Merged Cells

Merging cells is one way to control the appearance of your worksheet. You can merge cells to create a header cell across multiple columns of data or center a title across your worksheet. The *Merge & Center* button automatically merges the selected cells and then centers the data from the first cell across the entire merged area. When you merge cells together, Excel will keep only the data in the uppermost left cell. All other data will be lost.

To merge cells and center their content:

1. Select the cells you want to merge, making sure the text you want to keep is in the uppermost left cell.
2. On the *Home* tab, in the *Alignment* group, click the **Merge & Center** button.

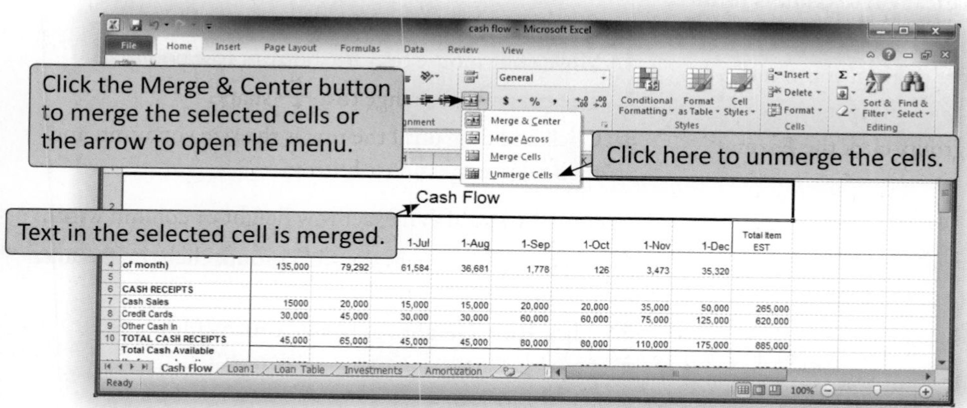

FIGURE EX 3.4

Click the arrow next to the **Merge & Center** button for additional merge commands:

Merge Across—lets you merge cells in multiple rows without merging the rows together. The cells in each row will be merged together, keeping the data in the leftmost cell in each row, but still keeping each row separate.

Merge Cells—lets you merge cells together without centering the data. Like the *Merge & Center* command, *Merge Cells* will combine all the selected cells into one cell, keeping only the data in the uppermost left cell.

Unmerge Cells—splits a merged cell back into its original cells. When the selected cell is a merged cell, clicking the *Merge & Center* button will also undo the merge.

tips & tricks

You cannot really split cells in Excel. You can unmerge a merged cell back into its original cells, but you cannot split a single cell into two new columns or two new rows (like you can with a table in Word or PowerPoint). However, if you have a column of data that you would like to split across multiple cells, you can use the *Text to Columns* command (from the *Data Tools* group on the *Data* tab).

try this

You can also merge and center cells from the *Format Cells* dialog box:

1. Click the **Alignment** tab in the *Format Cells* dialog box.
2. Under *Text alignment,* click the **Horizontal:** arrow, and select **Center Across Selection** from the drop-down list. (You can also select **Center.** When you merge the cells, it does not matter if the horizontal alignment is *Center Across Selection* or *Center.*)
3. Click the **Merge cells** check box.
4. Click **OK** to accept the changes.

To unmerge cells:

1. Click the **Alignment** tab in the *Format Cells* dialog box.
2. Under *Text alignment,* click the **Horizontal:** arrow, and select **General** from the drop-down list.
3. Click the **Merge cells** check box to uncheck it.
4. Click **OK** to accept the changes.

3.3 Modifying Row Heights and Column Widths

Some columns in your spreadsheet may be too narrow to display the data properly. If a cell contains text data, the text appears cut off. (If the cell to the right is empty, however, the text appears to extend into the empty cell.) If the cell contains numerical data, Excel displays a series of pound signs (#) when the cell is too narrow to display the entire number. You should adjust the column widths so the spreadsheet is easy to read.

Excel offers an easy way to automatically set columns to the optimum width for your data:

1. Click the column selector for the column you want to resize.
2. On the *Home* tab, in the *Cells* group, click the **Format** button.
3. Click **AutoFit Column Width.**

You can also modify column widths manually:

1. Move your mouse over the right column boundary.
2. The cursor will change to a ✛ shape.
3. Click and drag until the column is the size you want, and then release the mouse button.

Rows in Excel are automatically sized to fit the font size. However, there may be times you need to modify row heights. Use the same techniques you use for resizing columns:

1. Click the row selector for the row you want to resize.
2. On the *Home* tab, in the *Cells* group, click the **Format** button.
3. Click **AutoFit Row Height.**

To modify row heights manually:

1. Move your mouse over the bottom row boundary.
2. The cursor will change to a ✛ shape.
3. Click and drag until the row is the size you want, and then release the mouse button.

You can also specify an exact row height or column width:

1. On the *Home* tab, in the *Cells* group, click the **Format** button.
2. Click **Row Height . . .** or **Column Width . . .**
3. Enter the value you want.
4. Click **OK.**

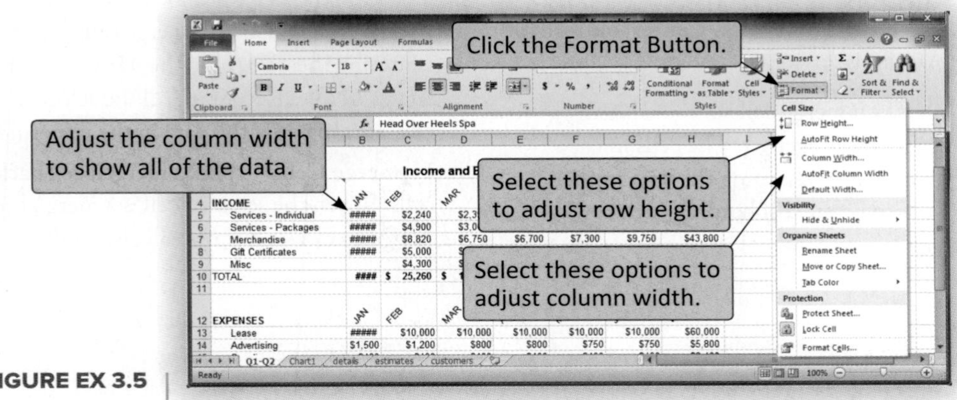

FIGURE EX 3.5

tips & tricks

Excel's default column width of 8.43 characters may not be wide enough to accommodate your data. If you know the cells in your spreadsheet need to be wider than 8.43, you can change the default width to any value between 0 and 255. (The number refers to the number of standard characters that can fit in a cell.) This command changes the width of all columns in the active worksheet that do not yet contain data. This does not change the default column width setting for Excel.

1. On the *Home* tab, in the *Cells* group, click the **Format** button.
2. Click **Default Width . . .**
3. Enter the value you want.
4. Click **OK.**

try this

- To make the column automatically fit the contents, double-click the right column boundary.
- To make the row automatically fit the contents, double-click the bottom row boundary.
- You can also select the column or row you want to resize. Then, from the right-click menu, select the **Column Width . . .** or **Row Height . . .** option to manually enter the size you want.

3.4 Inserting and Deleting Rows and Columns

You may find you need to add rows or columns of new information into or remove rows or columns from the middle of your workbook. Adding a new row will shift other rows down; adding a new column will shift other columns to the right. Deleting a row will shift other rows up; deleting a column will shift the remaining columns to the left.

To insert a row:

1. Place your cursor in a cell in the row below where you want the new row.
2. On the *Home* tab, in the *Cells* group, click the **Insert** button arrow and select **Insert Sheet Rows.**
3. The new row will appear above the selected cell.

To insert a column:

1. Place your cursor in a cell in the column to the right of where you want the new column.
2. On the *Home* tab, in the *Cells* group, click the **Insert** button arrow and select **Insert Sheet Columns.**
3. The new column will appear to the left of the selected cell.

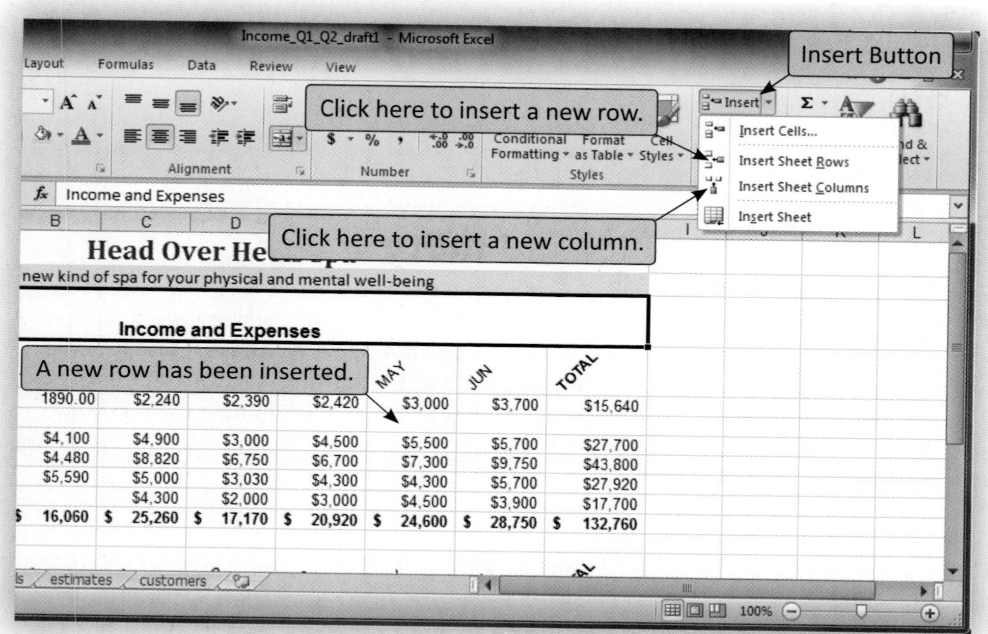

FIGURE EX 3.6

To delete a row:

1. Place your cursor in a cell in the row you want to delete.
2. On the *Home* tab, in the *Cells* group, click the **Delete** button arrow and select **Delete Sheet Rows.**
3. The row will be deleted and the rows below it will shift up.

To delete a column:

1. Place your cursor in a cell in the column you want to delete.
2. On the *Home* tab, in the *Cells* group, click the **Delete** button arrow and select **Delete Sheet Columns.**
3. The column will be deleted, and columns to the right of the deleted column will shift left.

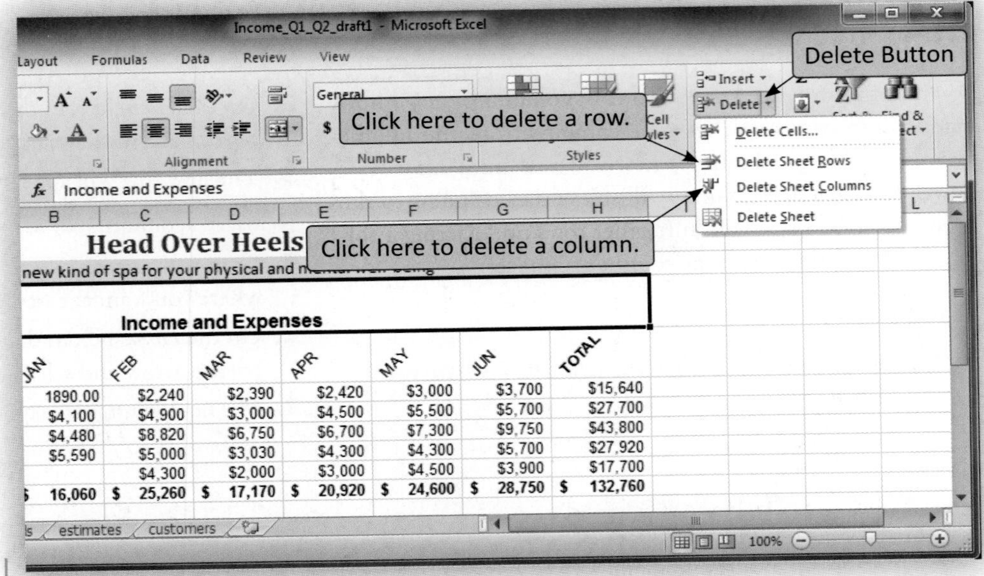

FIGURE EX 3.7

tips & tricks

Depending on whether you have a cell, a range of cells, a row, or a column selected, the behavior of the *Insert* and *Delete* commands will change. If you have a single cell selected and click the **Insert** button instead of the button arrow, Excel will insert a single cell, automatically moving cells down. However, if you select the entire column first, and then click the **Insert** button, Excel will automatically insert a column.

tell me more

When you insert a row or column, a Smart Tag will appear. Click the Smart Tag to choose formatting options for the new row or column—**Format Same as Above, Format Same as Below,** or **Clear Formatting** for rows and **Format Same as Left, Format Same as Right,** or **Clear Formatting** for columns.

try this

To insert or delete rows and columns, you can also:

1. Right-click in a cell, then select **Insert . . .** or **Delete . . .**
2. In the dialog box, select **Entire row** or **Entire column.**
3. Click **OK.**

You can also select an entire row or column by clicking the row or column selector, then right-click and select **Insert** or **Delete** from the menu. Because you have already selected an entire row or column, Excel will not ask you to specify what you want to insert or delete.

3.5 Freezing and Unfreezing Rows and Columns

If you have a large spreadsheet (very wide or very tall), you may want to **freeze** the top row or the left column. By doing this, you can keep column headings and row labels visible as you scroll through your data.

If you want the top row to always be visible:

1. Click the **View** tab.
2. In the *Window* group, click the **Freeze Panes** button.
3. Click **Freeze Top Row.**

If you want the first column to always be visible:

1. Click the **View** tab.
2. In the *Window* group, click the **Freeze Panes** button.
3. Click **Freeze First Column.**

To return your worksheet to normal, click the **Freeze Panes** button and select **Unfreeze Panes.**

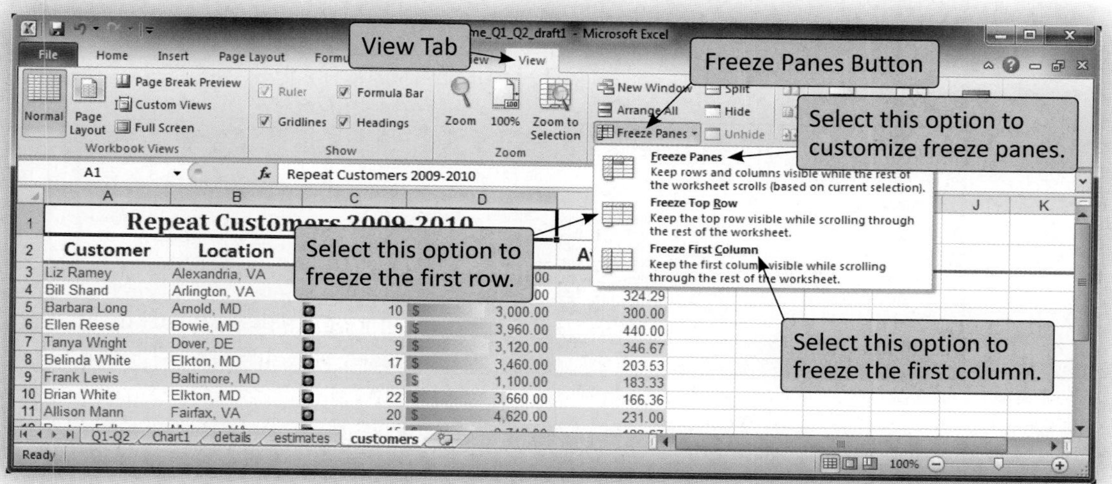

FIGURE EX 3.8

tips & tricks

If your worksheet has both a header row and a column of labels in the first column, freeze the worksheet from the cell immediately below the header row and immediately to the right of the label column (usually cell B2).

1. Click the **View** tab.
2. In the *Window* group, click the **Freeze Panes** button.
3. Select **Freeze Panes.**

Now when you scroll your worksheet, the first row and the first column will always be visible.

tell me more

Using the *Freeze Panes* option freezes the worksheet at the selected cell, so the rows above the cell and the columns to the left of the cell are always visible.

3.6 Hiding and Unhiding Rows and Columns

When you hide a row or column, the data still remain in your workbook, but they are no longer displayed on-screen and are not part of the printed workbook. Hiding rows can be helpful when you want to print a copy of your workbook for others but do not want to share all the information contained in your workbook. At any time, you can choose to "unhide" a row or column, which will redisplay the row or column.

To hide a row or column, you can select the entire row or column, or any cell or cells within that row or column.

1. Select any cell in the row or column you want to hide.
2. On the *Home* tab, in the *Cells* group, click the **Format** button.
3. Point to **Hide & Unhide,** and click **Hide Rows** or **Hide Columns.**

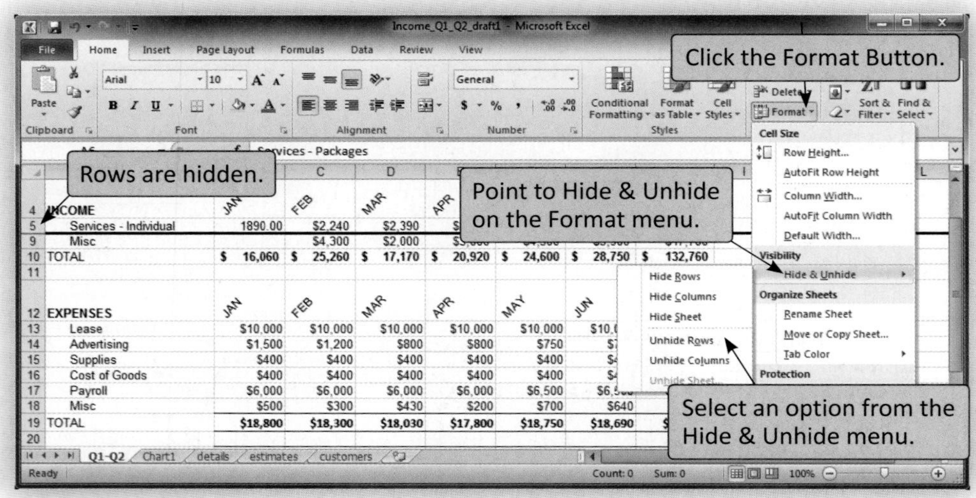

FIGURE EX 3.9

To unhide a row or column, you must select the entire row or column to either side of the hidden row or column.

1. Select the rows or columns on either side of the row or column you want to unhide.
2. On the *Home* tab, in the *Cells* group, click the **Format** button.
3. Point to **Hide & Unhide,** and click **Unhide Rows** or **Unhide Columns.**

tips & tricks

Hide rows and columns that may distract from the final data you are calculating. For example, if you are creating a budget estimate, and your boss wants to see only the final totals for each line, you can hide the columns containing estimated hours and hourly rates. If someone wants to see those details, you can unhide the columns later.

tell me more

You can hide an entire worksheet by selecting **Hide Worksheet** from the **Hide & Unhide** menu.

To unhide a hidden worksheet, select **Unhide Sheet . . .** from the **Hide & Unhide** menu. A dialog box will appear with a list of hidden worksheets. Click the sheet you want to unhide, and then click **OK.**

You can also hide and unhide worksheets by right-clicking the sheet tab and selecting **Hide** or **Unhide . . .**

try this

To hide a column, you can also:

- Press Ctrl + 0.
- Select the column, and then right-click and select **Hide.**

To hide a row, you can also:

- Press Ctrl + 9.
- Select the row, and then right-click and select **Hide.**

To unhide a column, you can also:

- Press Ctrl + ⇧Shift + 0.
- Select the columns on either side of the hidden one, and then right-click and select **Unhide.**

To unhide a row, you can also:

- Press Ctrl + ⇧Shift + 9.
- Select the rows on either side of the hidden one, and then right-click and select **Unhide.**

3.7 Naming Worksheets

When you create a new workbook, Excel automatically includes three worksheets named Sheet1, Sheet2, and Sheet3. It is a good idea to rename your worksheets to something more descriptive. Giving your worksheets descriptive names can help organize multiple worksheets, making it easier for you to find and use information.

To rename a worksheet:

1. On the *Home* tab, in the *Cells* group, click the **Format** button.
2. Click **Rename Sheet.**
3. Excel will highlight the sheet name. Just begin typing to overwrite the old name with the new one.
4. Press ←Enter to accept the name.

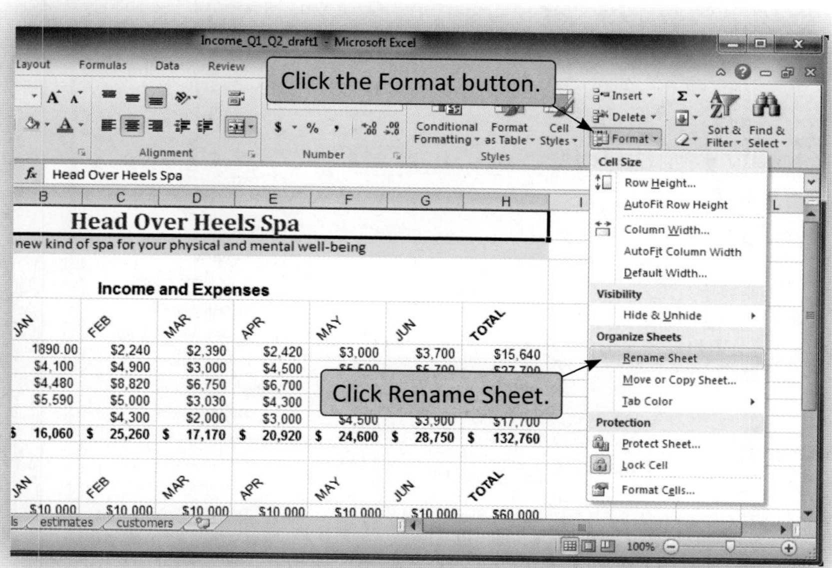

FIGURE EX 3.10

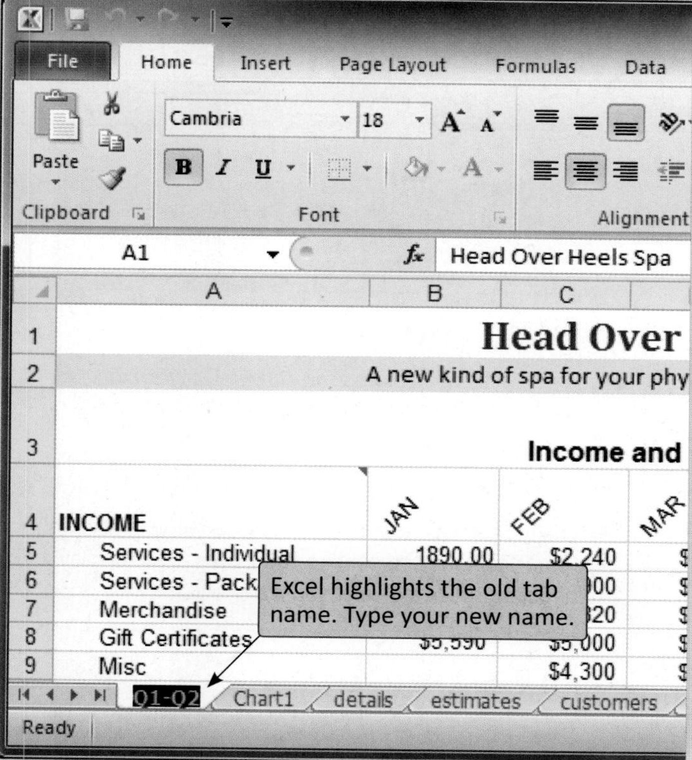

FIGURE EX 3.11

3.8 Changing the Color of Tabs

By default, all the worksheet tabs in Excel are white. If you have many sheets in your workbook, changing the tab colors can help you organize your data better. If you have sheets that contain related data, color them using different shades of the same color.

To change a worksheet tab color:

1. On the *Home* tab, in the *Cells* group, click the **Format** button.
2. Point to **Tab Color** to display the available color options.
3. Click the color you want.

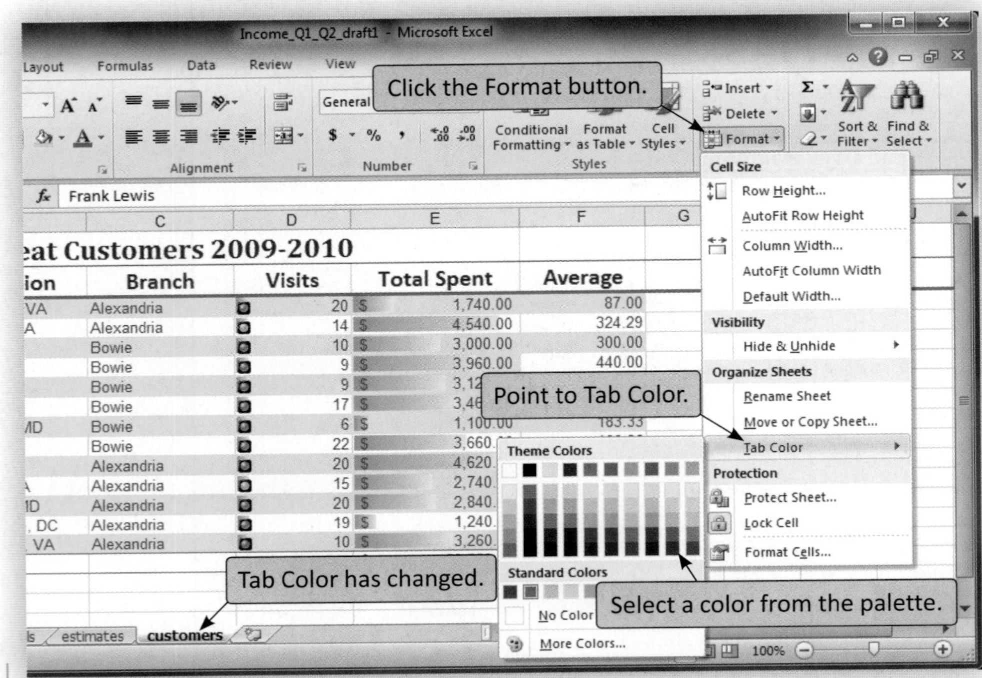

FIGURE EX 3.12

tips & tricks

In Excel 2010, you can select a theme color to ensure that your tab colors will coordinate with the rest of the styles in your workbook.

tell me more

When you select a colored tab, the tab will turn white with the text underlined with the assigned color.

try this

To change the tab color of a worksheet, you can also right-click the sheet tab and point to **Tab Color . . .** to display the color palette. Click the color you want.

3.9 Inserting and Deleting Worksheets

When you create a new workbook, it contains three worksheets (named Sheet1, Sheet2, and Sheet3). If you need more than three worksheets, you can add more. It is a good practice to keep all related information in the same workbook by adding more worksheets, rather than starting a new workbook.

To add a worksheet to the left of the current worksheet in your workbook:

1. On the *Home* tab, in the *Cells* group, click the **Insert** button arrow.
2. Click **Insert Sheet.** Blank worksheets are always added to the left of the current worksheet.
3. The new sheet is given the name Sheet# (where # is the next number available—for example, if your workbook contains the default Sheet1, Sheet2, and Sheet3, the next sheet inserted will be named Sheet4).

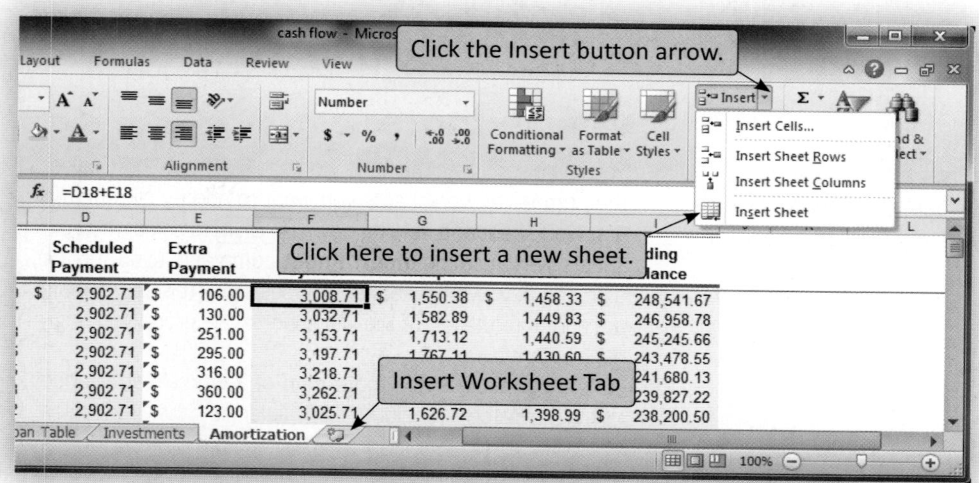

FIGURE EX 3.13

To add a new worksheet to the end of your workbook (to the right of the last worksheet tab), click the **Insert Worksheet** tab.

You can also delete unnecessary sheets from your workbook. To delete a sheet:

1. Select the sheet you want to delete.
2. On the *Home* tab, in the *Cells* group, click the **Delete** button arrow.
3. Click **Delete Sheet.**
4. If you try to delete a sheet that contains data, Excel will display a dialog box, warning that the sheet may contain data and asking if you are sure you want to permanently remove it from your workbook. Click the **Delete** button to continue and delete the worksheet. **Be careful—you cannot undo the *Delete Sheet* command.**

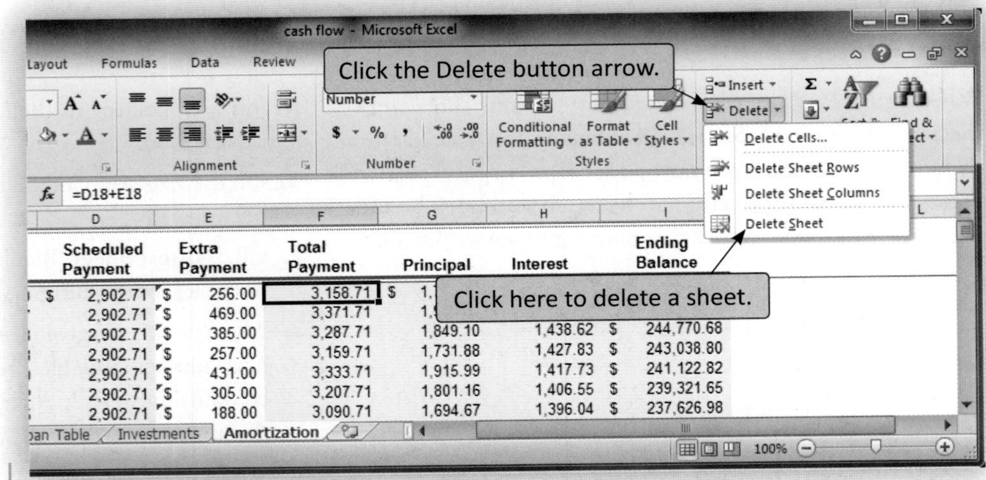

FIGURE EX 3.14

tips & tricks

Remove from your workbook any worksheets that you are not using. Limiting the sheets in your workbook to sheets that contain information can make your workbook appear organized and professional.

tell me more

You can insert more than one worksheet at once. First, select the number of worksheets you want to add by clicking the first worksheet and holding down Shift to select multiple sheets. Next, use the **Insert Sheet** command. Excel inserts as many new worksheets as you selected. The new sheets are added to the left of the last sheet in the group you originally selected.

You can also delete more than one worksheet at once using the same technique. First, select all the sheet tabs you want to remove, and then invoke the **Delete Sheet** command.

try this

To add a worksheet you can also:

1. Right-click on a sheet tab.
2. Select **Insert . . .** on the shortcut menu.
   - To insert a blank worksheet: Click the **Worksheet** icon in the dialog box.
   - To insert a formatted worksheet: Click the **Spreadsheet Solutions** tab, and click any of the template icons.
3. Click **OK.**

To delete a worksheet you can also right-click on a sheet tab and then select **Delete** from the shortcut menu.

3.10 Moving and Copying Worksheets

You can move worksheets around in a workbook, rearranging them into the most logical order. You can also copy worksheets within a workbook or to another workbook. But be careful—copying and moving worksheets can affect formulas and charts, and moving a worksheet may cause errors in your workbook.

To move or copy a worksheet:

1. On the *Home* tab, in the *Cells* group, click the **Format** button.
2. Click **Move or Copy Sheet . . .**
3. In the *Move or Copy* dialog box, click the name of the sheet you want to move the selected sheet before.
4. If you want to create a copy of the selected sheet, instead of moving the original, click the **Create a copy** check box.
5. If you want to move the sheet to the end of the workbook, select **(move to end)** in the *Before sheet:* box.
6. Click **OK.**

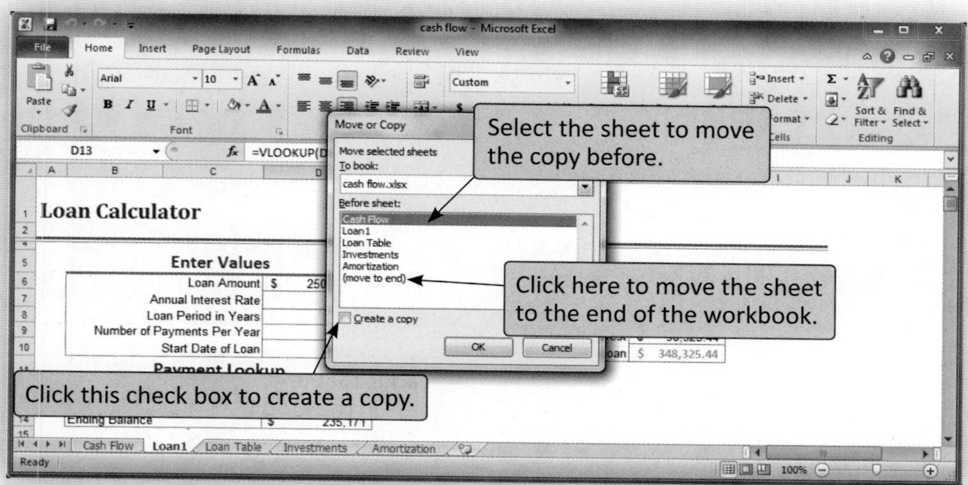

FIGURE EX 3.15

tips & tricks

You can move or copy a worksheet to another workbook. In the *Move or Copy* dialog box, click the **To book:** arrow. The *To book:* list shows all of the Excel workbooks you have open. Click the workbook you want. The list of sheets in the *Before sheet:* box will update to show the sheets available in the workbook you selected.

Moving a worksheet from one workbook to another deletes the worksheet from the original workbook. Consider ***copying*** the worksheet to the second workbook first, and then, once you are confident that formulas work as you intended, delete the worksheet from the original workbook.

tell me more

To move more than one worksheet, press Shift on the keyboard and click the worksheets you want to move. If the worksheets are not consecutive, then press Ctrl on the keyboard instead.

try this

To move a worksheet within a workbook:

1. Click the sheet tab of the worksheet you want to move.
2. When the cursor changes to a , drag the worksheet to the new position.

To copy a worksheet within a workbook:

1. Press Ctrl on the keyboard and click the sheet tab of the worksheet you want to copy.
2. When the cursor changes to a , drag the worksheet to the new position.

You can also right-click the sheet tab and select **Move or Copy . . .** from the shortcut menu to open the *Move or Copy* dialog box.

3.11 Grouping Worksheets

If you have multiple worksheets with the same structure, you can make changes to all of the worksheets at the same time by **grouping** them. This is convenient when you are setting up a series of worksheets with the same row or column headings. When sheets are grouped together, you can also change column widths and formatting, add formulas such as totals, or add headers and footers. Using grouping saves time and ensures that the sheets share a consistent style.

To group worksheets:

1. Click the first worksheet tab.
2. Hold down the ⇧Shift key and click the tab for the last worksheet you want included in the group. If you want to select noncontiguous worksheets (sheets that are not next to each other), click the Ctrl key instead, and then click each sheet tab.
3. Notice that the title bar now includes **[Group]** after the file name.
4. Make the change you want to the sheet. This same change will be made to the same cell in all sheets in the group.
5. To ungroup, click any sheet tab that is not part of the group.

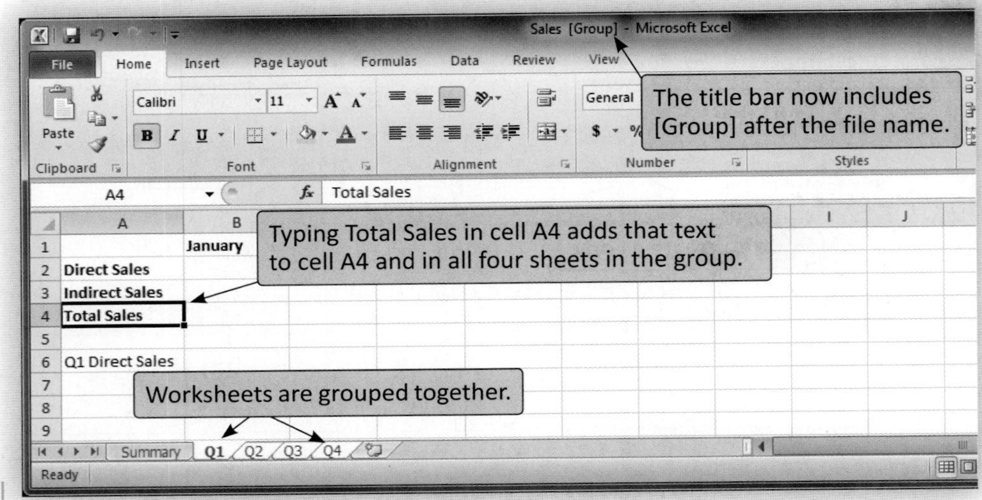

FIGURE EX 3.16

try **this**

To quickly group all the sheets in your workbook together, right-click any sheet tab and then click **Select All Sheets.**

To ungroup sheets, right-click one of the grouped sheet tabs and then click **Ungroup.** If all of the sheets in your workbook are grouped together, you will need to use this method to ungroup them.

3.12 Adding Headers and Footers

A **header** is text that appears at the *top* of every page, just below the top margin; a **footer** is text that appears at the *bottom* of every page, just above the bottom margin. Typically, headers and footers display such text as dates, page numbers, document titles, and authors' names. When you use Page Layout view to add headers and footers, you can see exactly how the header and footer will appear when you print the worksheet.

To add a header or footer to a worksheet from Page Layout view:

1. Switch to Page Layout view by clicking the **Page Layout** button on the status bar.
2. The header area has three sections: left, right, and center. Click the text **Click to add header** to activate the center section of the header box or click to either side of the text to activate the left or right header section. The contextual tab *Header & Footer Tools Design* appears.
3. In the *Header & Footer* group, click the **Header** button and select one of the predefined headers, or click a button in the *Header & Footer Elements* group to add a specific header element such as page number or the current date.
4. In the *Navigation* group, click the **Go to Footer** button to switch to the footer. Add footer elements the same way you added header elements.
5. When you are finished adding your header and footer elements, click anywhere in the worksheet and then switch back to Normal view. You cannot switch from Page Layout view to Normal view if you have one of the header or footer sections active. You must first select a cell in your worksheet, and then switch to Normal view.

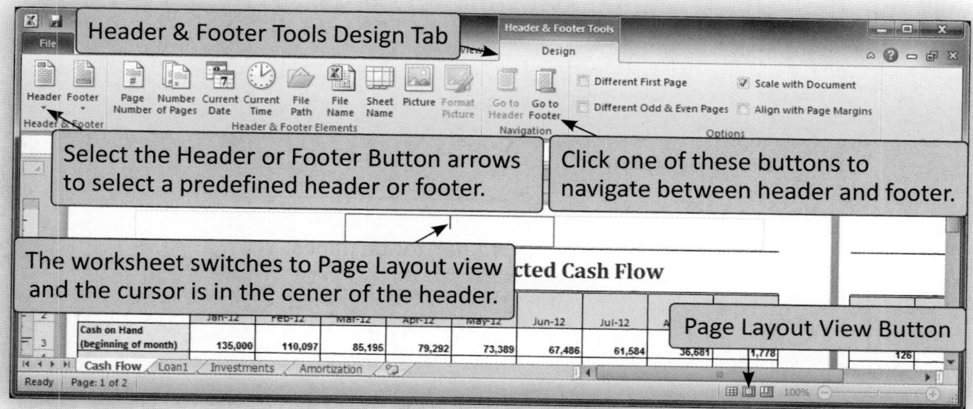

FIGURE EX 3.17

tips & tricks

To add the same header/footer to all of your worksheets at once, group the worksheets before adding the header/footer.

try this

Another way to add a header or footer to your worksheet is to click the **Insert** tab. In the *Text* group, click the **Header & Footer** button. (The worksheet will automatically switch to Page Layout view when you click the *Header & Footer* button.)

You can also switch to Page Layout view by clicking the **View** tab. In the *Workbook Views* section, click the **Page Layout** button.

tell me more

Another method for adding headers and footers uses the *Page Setup* dialog box. This method will be familiar to users who have worked with older versions of Excel.

To add a header or footer to a worksheet using the *Page Setup* dialog:

1. Click the **Page Layout** tab.
2. Open the *Page Setup* dialog by clicking the dialog launcher in the *Page Setup* group.
3. Click the **Header/Footer** tab.
4. Click the arrow beneath the *Header* or *Footer* area to expand the list of predefined header/footer options. Click the option you want to use.
5. You can also customize the header or footer by clicking the **Custom Header . . .** or **Custom Footer . . .** button and adding elements through the *Header* or *Footer* dialog.

3.13 Splitting Workbooks

In Excel, you can split the worksheet view into two or four panes. Each pane scrolls independently of the other(s), so you can see two (or four) different areas of the worksheet at the same time. This can be especially helpful if you want to change data in one part of the worksheet and immediately see the result in a formula in another part of the worksheet (for example, in a total row).

1. Click the cell in the worksheet where you would like to split the view.
   - If you want to split the worksheet into two horizontal panes, click a cell in column A.
   - If you want to split the worksheet into two vertical panes, click a cell in row 1.
   - If you want to split the worksheet into four panes, click any cell in the worksheet. The cell you selected will be the top left cell in the pane in the lower-right quadrant.
2. Click the **View** tab.
3. In the *Window* group, click the **Split** button.

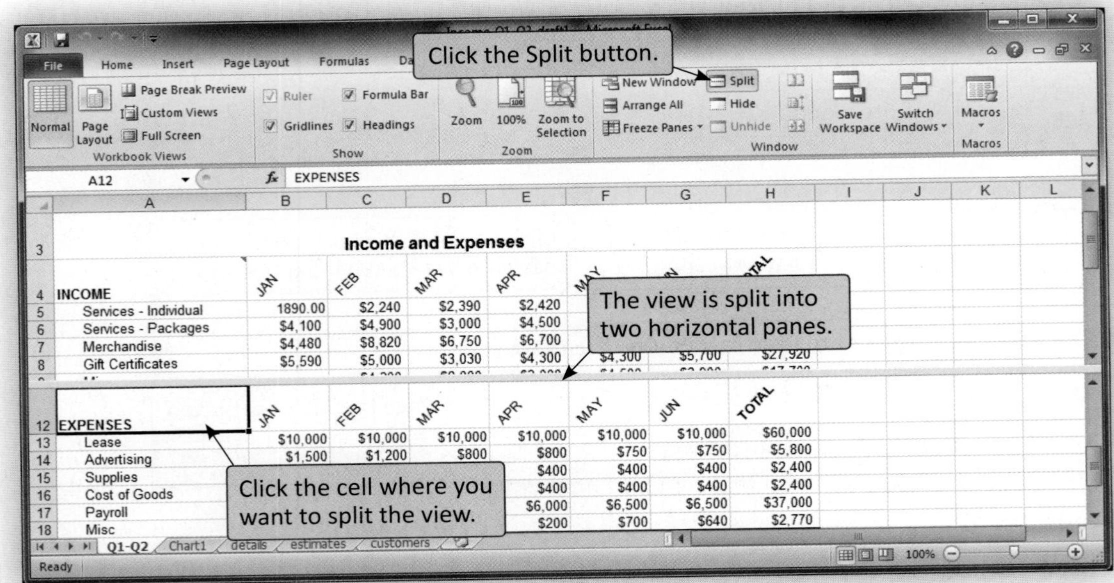

FIGURE EX 3.18

To undo the split and return the worksheet to a single view, click the **Split** button again.

tips & tricks

When you split a worksheet, the panes are just different views of the same data, not independent copies. If you make changes to a cell in one pane, the changes will be reflected in all the panes.

tell me more

To adjust the size of the panes, click and drag the pane border.

try this

You can select an entire row or column as the split point.

3.14 Showing and Hiding Worksheet Elements

Gridlines are the lines that appear on the worksheet defining the rows and columns. Gridlines make it easy to see the individual cells in your worksheet. There may be times, however, that you want to hide the gridlines to make your worksheet look less cluttered.

To hide gridlines:

1. Click the **View** tab.
2. In the *Show* group, click the **Gridlines** check box to remove the check mark and hide the gridlines.

To display the gridlines again, click to recheck the **Gridlines** check box.

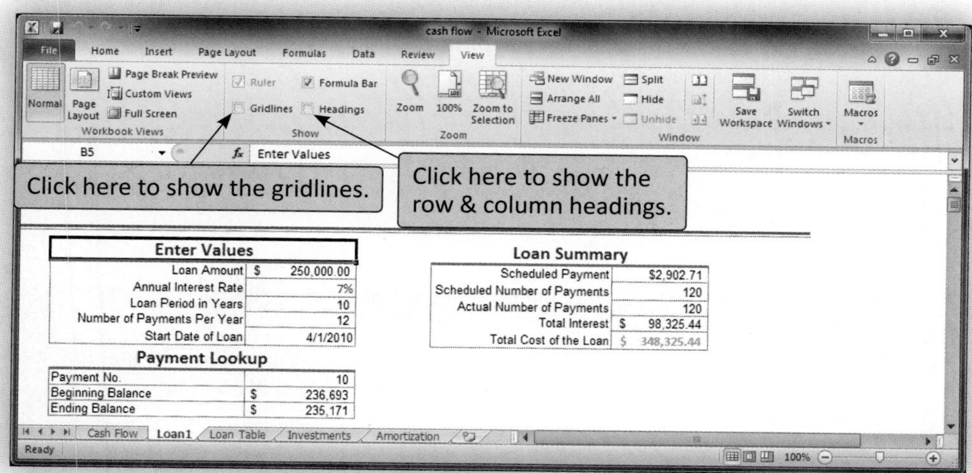

FIGURE EX 3.19

Headings are the numbers at the left of rows and the letters at the top of columns. By default, Excel displays the row and column headings to make it easy to identify cell references. Once your worksheet is finished, you may want to hide the headings.

To hide headings:

1. Click the **View** tab.
2. In the *Show* group, click the **Headings** check box to remove the check mark and hide the row and column headings.

To display the headings again, click to recheck the **Headings** check box.

Note: Depending on the size of your Excel window, the *Show* group may appear collapsed. If necessary, click the **Show** button to expand the group so you can click the check boxes.

tips & tricks

Hiding gridlines and headings can make your workbook look less like a spreadsheet and more like a form.

try this

To show or hide gridlines and headings on-screen, you can also:

1. Click the **Page Layout** tab.
2. In the *Sheet Options* group, click the **View** check box under *Gridlines* or *Headings.*

tell me more

By default, gridlines and row and column headings are visible on-screen when you are working in Excel, but they do not print. To print the gridlines and headings when you print the worksheet:

1. Click the **Page Layout** tab.
2. In the *Sheet Options* group, click the **Print** check box under *Gridlines* to print the gridlines.
3. In the *Sheet Options* group, click the **Print** check box under *Headings* to print the row and column headings.

3.15 Setting Up Margins for Printing

Margins are the blank spaces at the top, bottom, left, and right of a printed page. You may need to adjust the margins if you are printing on letterhead or if you want more or less blank space around your worksheet area. Because you will probably want to adjust margins once you are ready to print, Excel 2010 allows you to adjust the margins directly from the *Print* tab in Backstage view.

To set margins when printing:

1. Click the **File** tab to open Backstage view.
2. Click the **Print** tab.
3. In the *Settings* section, click the button displaying the current margins setting. There are three preset margins options. Click the setting you want to use.

Normal—uses Excel's default margins: 0.75 inch for the top and bottom and 0.7 inch for the left and right.

Wide—adds more space at the top, bottom, left, and right sides.

Narrow—reduces the amount of space at the top, bottom, left, and right sides, so more of your worksheet fits on each page

Notice that the Print Preview image adjusts to show how your worksheet will print with the new margins applied.

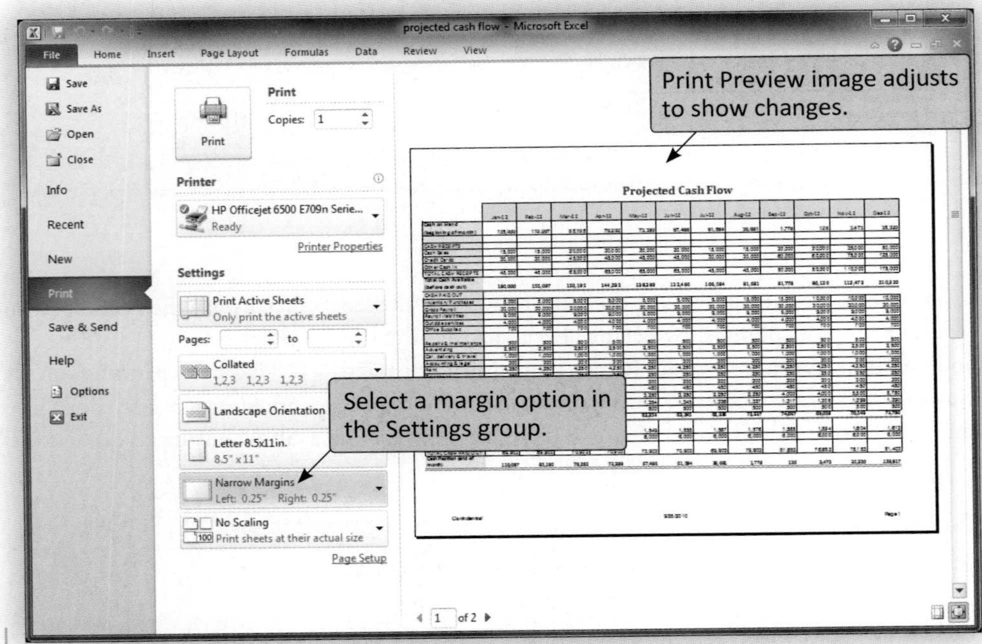

Print Preview image adjusts to show changes.
Select a margin option in the Settings group.

FIGURE EX 3.20

If none of the preset margins options is exactly what you want, click **Custom Margins . . .** at the end of the margins options list. This opens the *Page Setup* dialog where you can specify the exact margins you want.

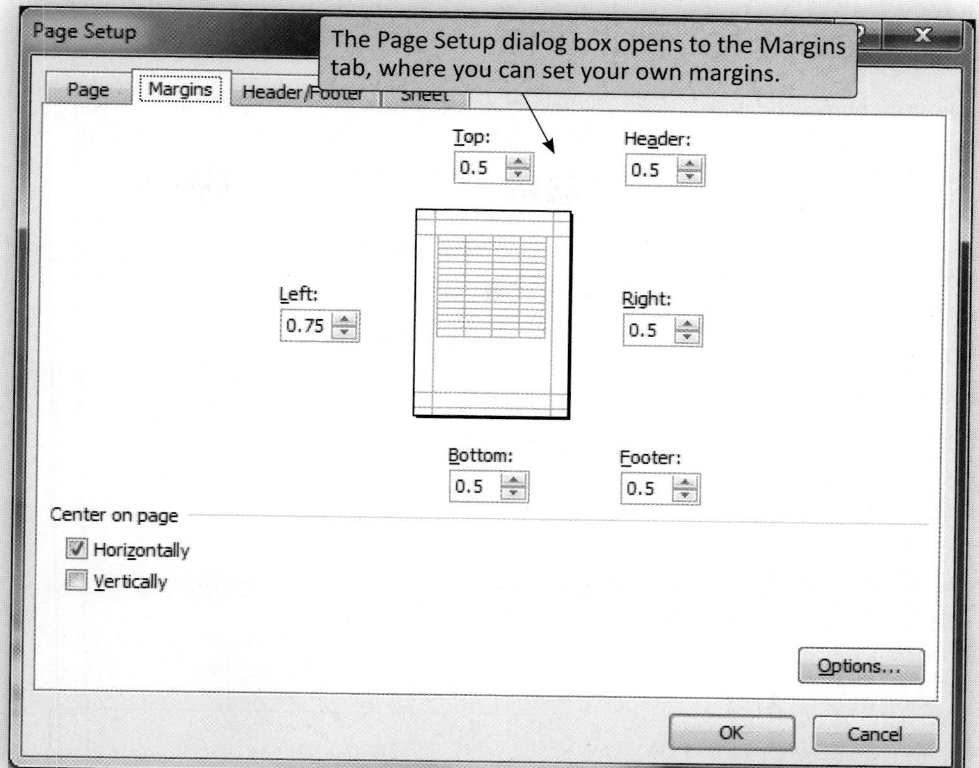

FIGURE EX 3.21

tips and tricks

If you would like to fit your worksheet on a certain number of printed pages, try using one of the scaling options instead of adjusting the margins. For more information about scaling options, refer to *Skill 3.16 Scaling Worksheets for Printing*.

try this

You can also set the scaling options from the *Page Layout* tab on the Ribbon:

1. Click the **Page Layout** tab.
2. In the *Page Setup* group, click the **Margins** button.
3. Click one of the preset margins options: **Normal, Wide,** or **Narrow** or click **Custom Margins . . .** to specify your own values.

3.16 Scaling Worksheets for Printing

When printing your worksheet, you can control the number of printed pages by specifying a maximum number of pages for the width or height. In previous versions of Excel, scaling options were available from the *Page Setup* dialog or the *Page Layout* tab on the Ribbon only. Because you really only need to adjust scaling once you are ready to print, Excel 2010 has included scaling options on the *Print* tab in Backstage view.

To set scaling options when printing:

1. Click the **File** tab to open Backstage view.
2. Click the **Print** tab.
3. In the *Settings* section, click the button displaying the current scaling setting. There are four preset scaling options. Click the setting you want to use.

   No Scaling

   Fit Sheet on One Page

   Fit All Columns on One Page

   Fit All Rows on One Page
4. Notice that the Print Preview image adjusts to show how your worksheet will print with the new scaling setting applied.

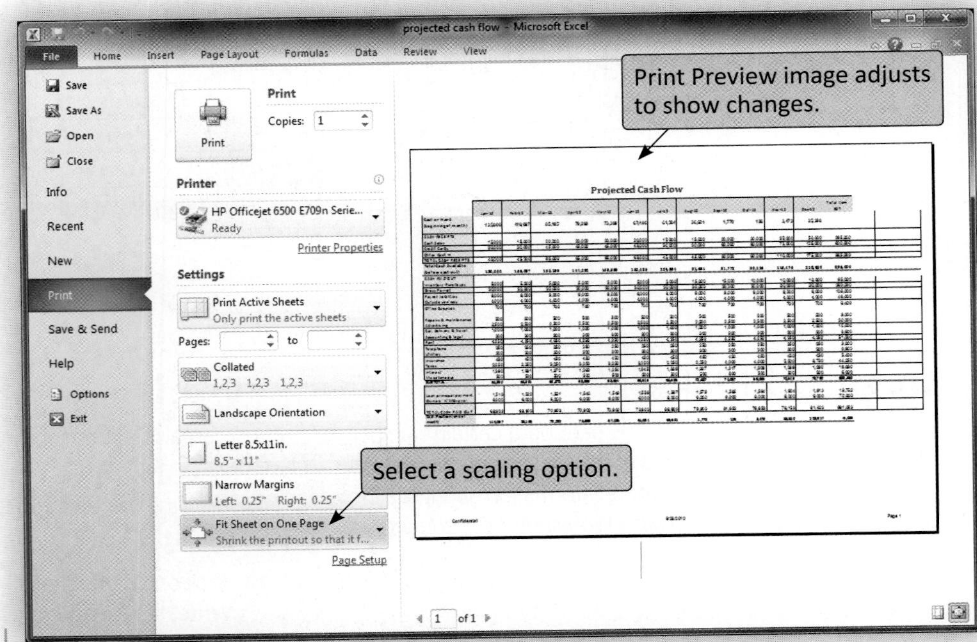

FIGURE EX 3.22

5. If none of the preset scaling options is exactly what you want, click **Custom Scaling Options . . .** at the end of the scaling options list. This opens the *Page Setup* dialog where you can specify the maximum number of pages for the width or height or a percentage by which the printed version of the worksheet will be smaller or larger than the original.

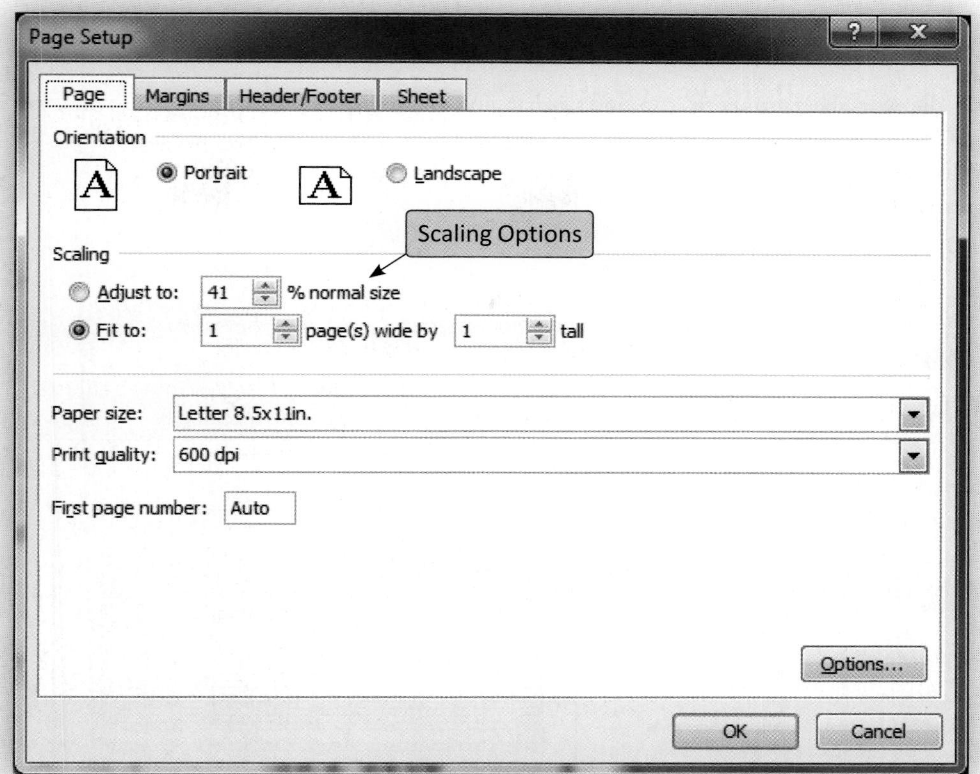

FIGURE EX 3.23

tips & tricks

When scaling your worksheet, be careful not to make the worksheet too small to read.

try this

You can also set the scaling options from the *Page Layout* tab on the Ribbon:

1. Click the **Page Layout** tab.
2. In the *Scale to Fit* group, select one of these options:

   Click the **Width:** arrow and select the maximum number of pages you want the worksheet to print across.

   Click the **Height:** arrow and select the maximum number of pages you want the worksheet to print vertically.

   Click the **Scale:** box and enter a percentage to grow or shrink the worksheet when printed.

3.17 Changing Worksheet Orientation

Orientation refers to the direction the worksheet prints. It doesn't affect the way the worksheet looks on your computer screen. The default print setting is for **portrait orientation**—when the height of the page is greater than the width (like a portrait hanging on a wall). If your workbook is wide, you may want to use **landscape orientation** instead, where the width of the page is greater than the height.

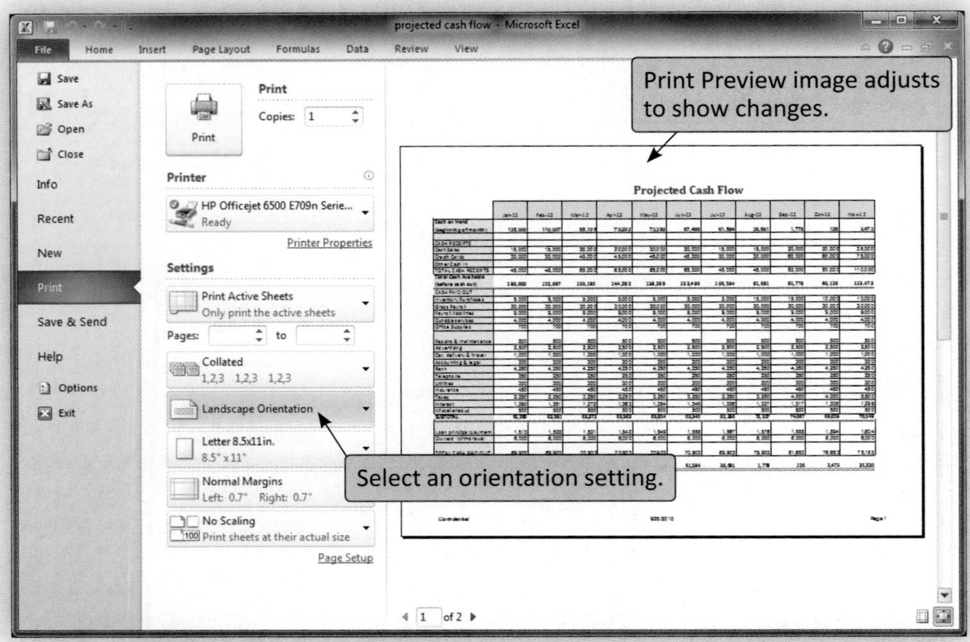

FIGURE EX 3.24

To change the orientation of a worksheet:

1. Click the **File** tab to open Backstage view.
2. Click the **Print** tab.
3. In the *Settings* section, click the button displaying the current orientation setting, and then click the orientation setting you want.
4. Notice that the Print Preview image adjusts to show how your worksheet will print with the new orientation setting applied.

try this

You can set the worksheet orientation from the *Page Layout* tab on the Ribbon:

1. Click the **Page Layout** tab.
2. In the *Page Setup* group, click the **Orientation** button.
3. Click the **Portrait** or **Landscape** option.

You can also use the *Page Setup* dialog box to change the orientation of your worksheet. On the *Page* tab, click the **Portrait** or **Landscape** radio button in the *Orientation* section.

3.18 Inserting Page Breaks

Excel automatically inserts page breaks so columns and rows are not split across pages when you print. However, you may want to control where page breaks happen so your worksheet prints in a more logical order.

To insert and remove page breaks, it is not necessary to switch to Page Break Preview view.

To manually insert a new page break:

1. If you want to add a horizontal page break, select the row below where you want the break. If you want to add a vertical page break, select the column to the right of where you want the break.
2. Click the **Page Layout** tab.
3. In the *Page Setup* group, click the **Breaks** button.
4. Click **Insert Page Break.**
5. A new page break is inserted to the left of the selected column or above the selected row.

To manually insert horizontal and vertical page breaks at the same time:

1. Begin by selecting the cell below and to the right of where you want the new page breaks.
2. Click the **Page Layout** tab.
3. In the *Page Setup* group, click the **Breaks** button.
4. Click **Insert Page Break.**
5. A new page break is inserted to the left of and above the selected cell.

To remove the page break, select any cell adjacent to (to the right of or below) the break, then:

1. Click the **Page Layout** tab.
2. In the *Page Setup* group, click the **Breaks** button.
3. Click **Remove Page Break.**

To remove all the manual page breaks at once:

1. Click the **Page Layout** tab.
2. In the *Page Setup* group, click the **Breaks** button.
3. Click **Reset All Page** Breaks.

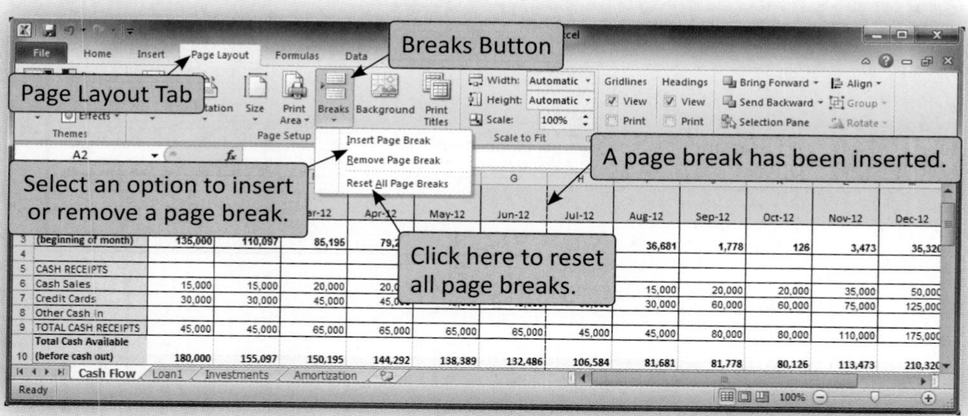

FIGURE EX 3.25

tips & tricks

If you insert a page break but nothing seems to happen, check to see if you have the scaling option set for printing. For example, if you have the worksheet set to print all columns on a single page, inserting a new page break between columns will not appear to have any effect on the worksheet. However, if you remove the scaling option, the new manual page break will appear.

tell me more

When the worksheet is in Page Break Preview view, automatic page breaks appear as blue dotted lines and manually inserted page breaks appear as solid blue lines. You can manually move a page break by clicking the page break line, and then dragging to the right or left or up or down. Release the mouse button when the line appears where you want the break. Notice that if you move an automatic page break, the line changes from dotted to solid.

3.19 Printing Selections, Worksheets, and Workbooks

Printing has changed significantly in Excel 2010. Previous versions of Excel relied on the *Print* dialog for setting printing options. In Excel 2010, the *Print* tab in Backstage view provides access to all of the printing options as well as a preview of what the printed worksheet will look like.

By default, Excel will print the current, active worksheet. You can change the printing options, however, to print only part of a worksheet or the entire workbook at once.

1. Click the **File** tab to open Backstage view.
2. Click the **Print** tab.
3. Verify that the correct printer name is displayed in the *Printer* section.
4. In the *Settings* section, the first button displays what part of the workbook will print. By default, *Print Active Sheets* is selected. To change the print selection, click the button, and then click one of the other options:

   Print Entire Workbook—prints all the sheets in the workbook.

   Print Selection—prints only the selected cells in the active worksheet, overriding any print area definitions in the active worksheet.

   Print Selected Table—prints the table only (only available if the current selection is within a defined table).

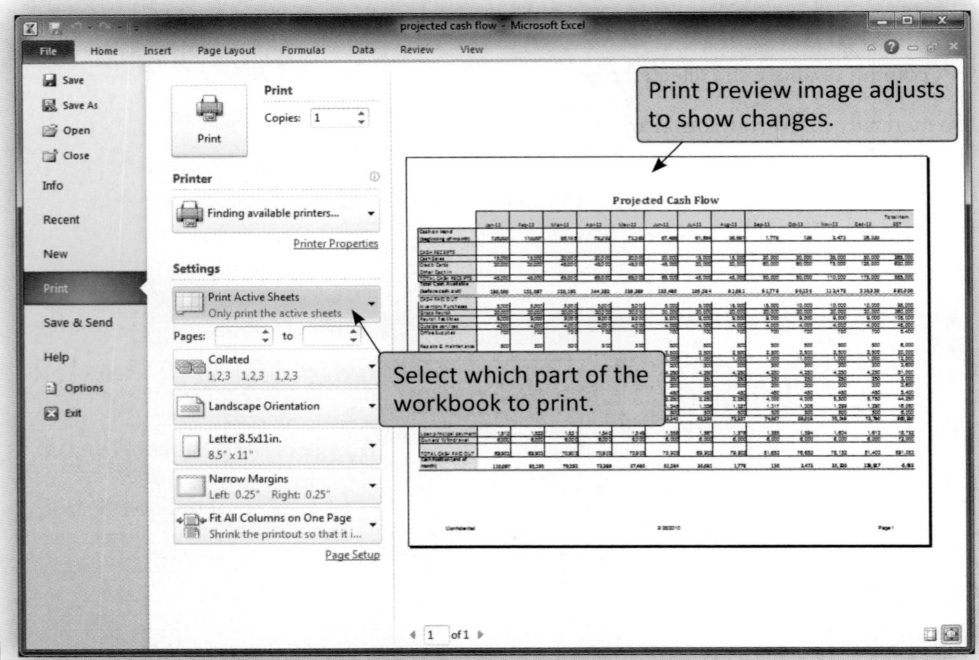

Print Preview image adjusts to show changes.
Select which part of the workbook to print.

FIGURE EX 3.26

5. If you want to ignore the defined print area, click **Ignore Print Area** at the bottom of the list.
6. Click the **Print** button to print.

tell me **more**

All of the options from the old *Print* dialog are available from the *Print* tab in Backstage view, including the settings for printing multiple copies of the worksheet or only selected pages.

try **this**

To open the *Print* tab in Backstage view, you can use the keyboard shortcut Ctrl + P.

3.20 Printing Titles

If your worksheet includes a large table of data that prints on more than one page, you should ensure that the column or row labels print on every page.

To repeat rows and columns on every printed page:

1. Click the **Page Layout** tab.
2. In the *Page Setup* group, click the **Print Titles** button.
3. In the *Page Setup* dialog box, in the *Rows to repeat at top:* box, type the row reference(s) using the format `$1:$1`. This example would repeat the first row only. `$1:$3` would repeat rows 1 through 3 on every printed page.
4. In the *Columns to repeat at left:* box, type the column reference(s) using the format `$A:$A`. This example would repeat the first column only. `$A:$C` would repeat columns A through C on every printed page.
5. Click **OK.**

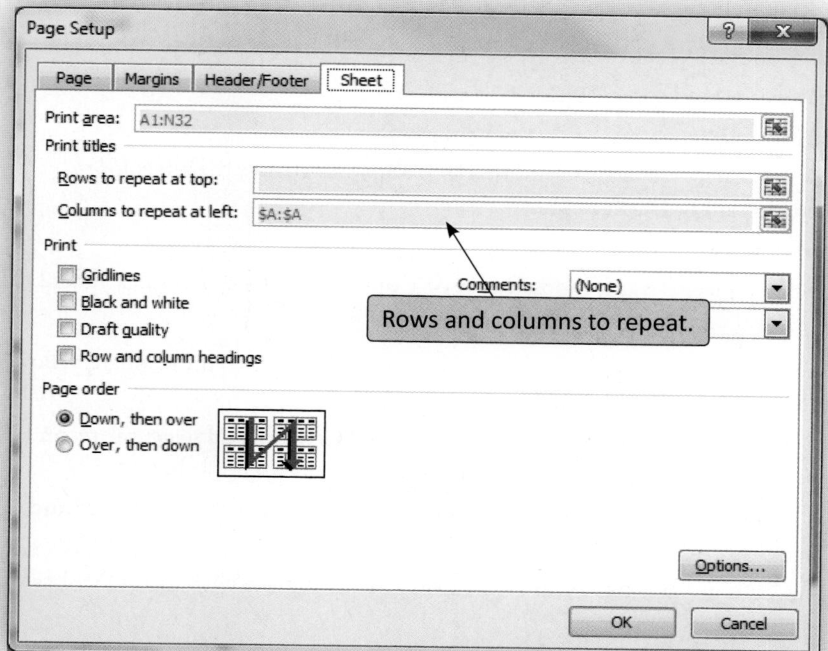

FIGURE EX 3.27

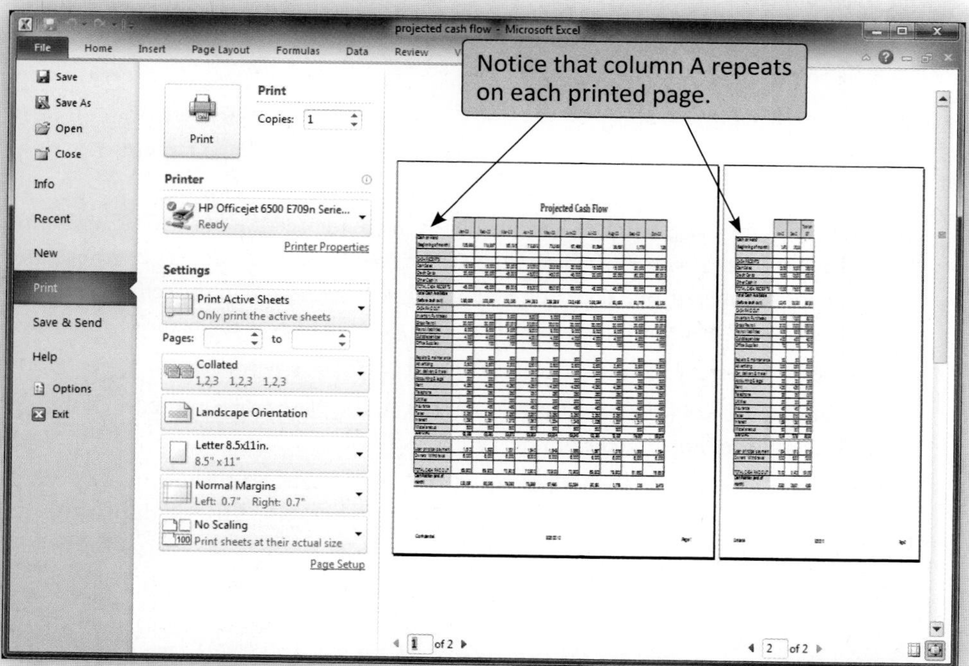

FIGURE EX 3.28

projects

Skill Review 3.1

Roll Project. In this Skill Review, you will be working with a workbook designed to be a class roll to keep track of students' attendance.

1. Make yourself a working copy of the provided file called *Roll.xlsx.* Call the copy `[your initials]EX_SkillReview_3-1.`
2. From time to time, save your file.
3. Rename Sheet1.
   a. Right-click on the **Sheet1** tab,
   b. Choose **Rename,** and enter `TTH1230`
   c. Press the **Enter** key.
   d. Right-click the sheet tab again, point to **Tab Color,** and change the tab color to **Dark Red, Accent 6, Darker 25%.**
4. Make a copy of the worksheet.
   a. Right-click the sheet tab and choose **Move or Copy;** for *Before sheet:* select **Sheet2.**
   b. Check **Create a copy** and click **OK.**
   c. Right-click the new **TTH1230 (2)** sheet tab, change the color to the standard yellow color, and change the name to `TTH340`
5. Select both sheets as a group—select the first one, hold **Ctrl** key, and select the second one. Now any changes made to one of the sheets will be made to both sheets.
   a. Select cells **D3** and **E3.** On the *Home* tab, in the *Alignment* group, click **Merge and Center.**
   b. Verify that both sheets are being formatted at the same time by clicking on the sheet tabs to view each sheet.
   c. Repeat the merge and center for each week.
   d. Select all the date columns by dragging over the letter column headings at the top of the screen. Drag the column boundary to make any one column narrower and all will adjust to match.
   e. From the *Page Layout* tab, apply the *Clarity* theme to both sheets.
   f. Using the buttons in the lower right of your screen, switch to **Page Layout** view to work on headers and footers.
      (1) Click where it says **Click to add header** in the center section of the header. From the *Header & Footer Tools Design* tab, in the *Header & Footer Elements* group, click the **File name** button. The code `&[File]` will be entered in the center section of the header. Once you click somewhere else, this will display the name of your file.
      (2) Click in the right section of the header and enter your own name.
      (3) From the *Header & Footer Tools Design* tab, in the *Navigation* group, click the **Go to Footer** button; click in the center section.
      (4) In the *Header & Footer Elements* group, click the **Sheet Name** button. The code `&[Tab]` will be entered. Once you click somewhere else, this will display the name on the sheet tab.
      (5) Click in the right section of the footer and click the **Current Date** button.
      (6) Click in any cell of the worksheet and click the **Normal view** button in the lower right of your screen.

6. Ungroup the sheets by clicking on any other sheet, such as **Sheet3.** Look at each sheet; they should both have been formatted. Make sure the sheets are now ungrouped.

7. Select the *TTH1230* sheet.

   a. It is hard to work with such a wide worksheet. Scroll to the right to see the end of the semester and you can no longer see the student names. Split the screen into two views of different parts of this worksheet.

      (1) Click cell **D1.** On the *View* tab, in the *Window* group, click the **Split** button. Now you can scroll each pane separately, but it is all still the same worksheet. You can drag the split bar to the right or left as needed.

      (2) Scroll to show the student names and the last few weeks of the semester on your screen.

      (3) Click the **Split** button again, to return to normal.

   b. You need to add and drop students.

      (1) Right-click on the row heading for row number 9. Choose **Insert.** The *Insert Options* button will appear; click it and choose **Format Same As Below.** Enter a new student named `Craig Alloy`. Use the same format as the other students. He attended the first day of class and you are adding him to the class. His student ID# is `1350699`.

      (2) **Justin Parry** has decided to drop the class; delete the entire row for Justin by right-clicking on the row heading number and choosing **Delete.**

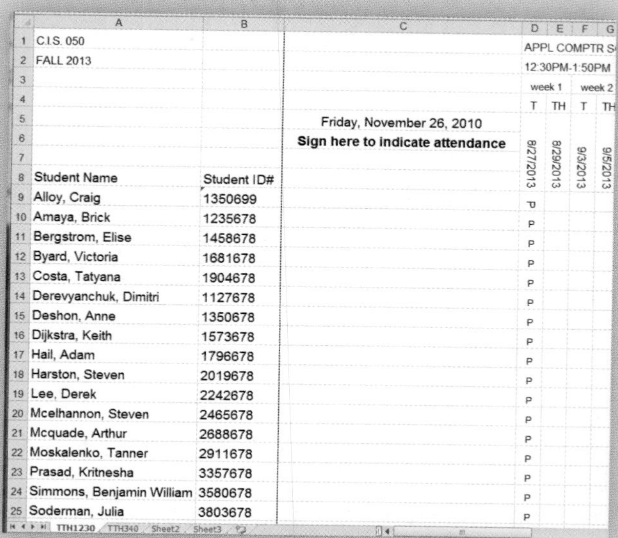

FIGURE EX 3.29

8. Select the *TTH340* sheet. Because this sheet was copied from the 12:30 pm class worksheet, the student names and ID#s are not those of the students in the 3:40 pm class.

   a. Copy the names and ID#s from *Sheet3* to the *TTH340* sheet.

   b. Delete **Sheet3** by right-clicking on the sheet name and choosing **Delete.**

9. On the *TTH340* sheet, click in cell **C9.** On the *View* tab, in the *Window* group, click **Freeze Panes,** then click **Freeze Panes** so that everything above and to the left of the cell will freeze on the screen no matter where you scroll. Try it; scroll to the right.

10. A portion of either of these worksheets may be printed to use as a class attendance sign in sheet.

   a. First we need to hide the student ID#s on the *TTH340* sheet. Right-click on the column B heading. Choose **Hide.**

   b. On the *Page Layout* tab, in the *Show* group, set the *Gridlines* to **Print.**

   c. On the *Page Layout* tab, in the *Page Setup* group, click the **Margins** button. Choose **Narrow.**

   d. On the *Page Layout* tab, in the *Scale to Fit* group, set the scaling to **1** page width by **1** page height.

   e. Scroll to the signature cell for the last student, drag the mouse to select from that cell up through **A1.**

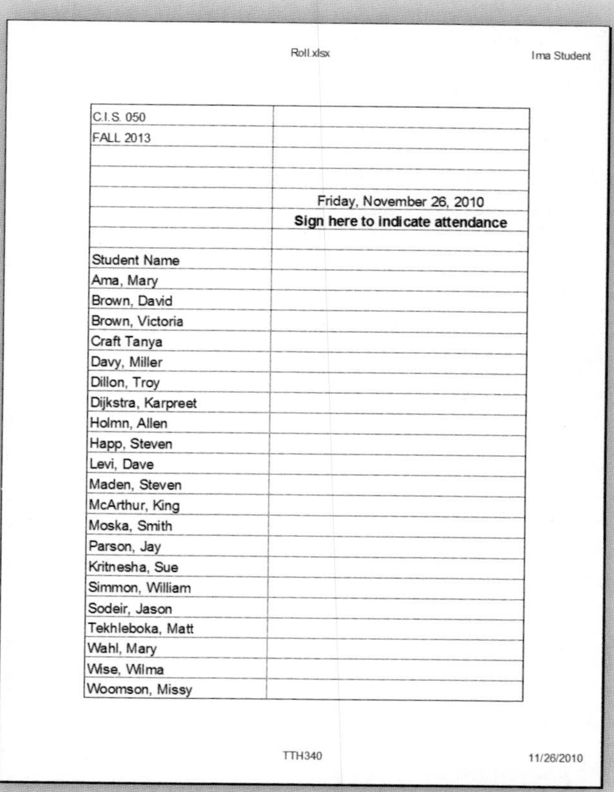

FIGURE EX 3.30

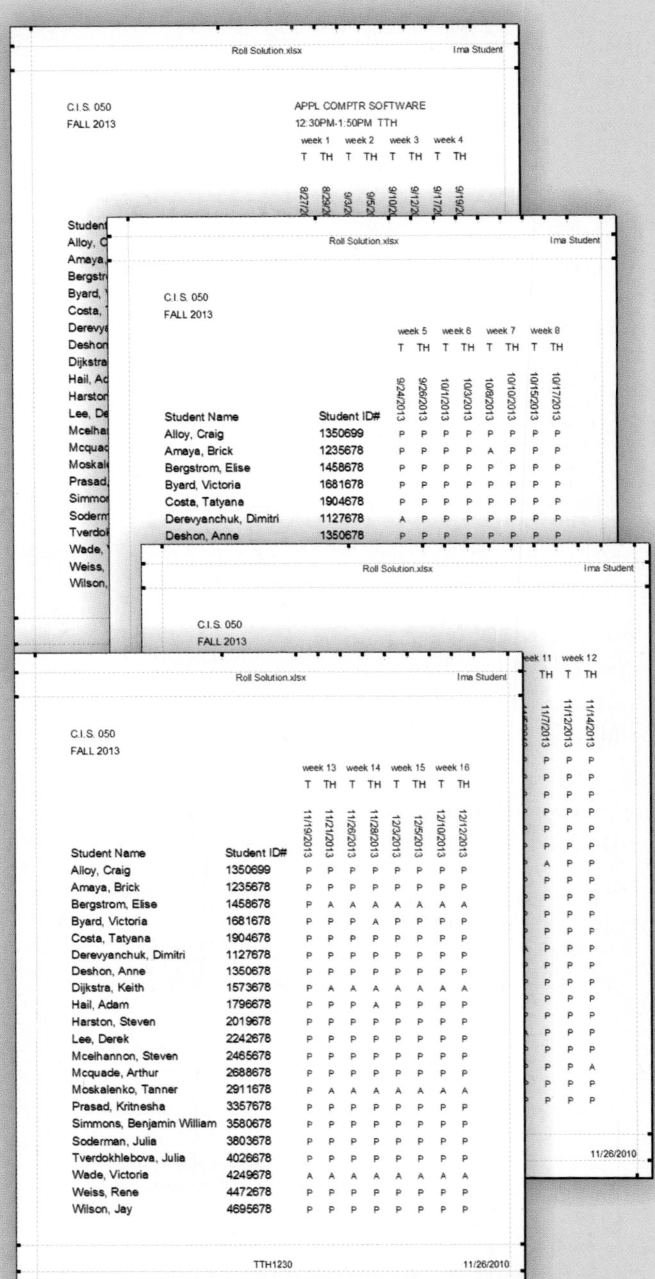

Roll Solution.xlsx   Ima Student

C.I.S. 050
FALL 2013

Student Name	Student ID#	week 13 T 11/19/2013	week 13 TH 11/21/2013	week 14 T 11/26/2013	week 14 TH 11/28/2013	week 15 T 12/3/2013	week 15 TH 12/5/2013	week 16 T 12/10/2013	week 16 TH 12/12/2013
Alloy, Craig	1350699	P	P	P	P	P	P	P	P
Amaya, Brick	1235678	P	P	P	P	P	P	P	P
Bergstrom, Elise	1458678	P	A	A	A	A	A	A	A
Byard, Victoria	1681678	P	P	P	A	P	P	P	P
Costa, Tatyana	1904678	P	P	P	P	P	P	P	P
Derevyanchuk, Dimitri	1127678	P	P	P	P	P	P	P	P
Deshon, Anne	1350678	P	P	P	P	P	P	P	P
Dijkstra, Keith	1573678	P	A	A	A	A	A	A	A
Hail, Adam	1796678	P	P	P	A	P	P	P	P
Harston, Steven	2019678	P	P	P	P	P	P	P	P
Lee, Derek	2242678	P	P	P	P	P	P	P	P
Mcelhannon, Steven	2465678	P	P	P	P	P	P	P	P
Mcquade, Arthur	2688678	P	P	P	P	P	P	P	P
Moskalenko, Tanner	2911678	P	A	A	A	A	A	A	A
Prasad, Kritnesha	3357678	P	P	P	P	P	P	P	P
Simmons, Benjamin William	3580678	P	P	P	P	P	P	P	P
Soderman, Julia	3803678	P	P	P	P	P	P	P	P
Tverdokhlebova, Julia	4026678	P	P	P	P	P	P	P	P
Wade, Victoria	4249678	A	A	A	A	A	A	A	A
Weiss, Rene	4472678	P	P	P	P	P	P	P	P
Wilson, Jay	4695678	P	P	P	P	P	P	P	P

TTH1230   11/26/2010

FIGURE EX 3.31

f. Click the **File** tab, and then click **Print.**

(1) Under *Settings,* click the drop-down arrow to change from *Print Active Sheets* to **Print Selection.**

(2) Click the **Page Setup** link to open the *Page Setup* dialog box.

(a) Click the **Margins** tab.

(b) Click the check boxes to *Center on page* **Horizontally** and **Vertically.** Click **OK.**

g. Finally click the **Print** button.

h. Drag to select columns A through C, right-click the selection, and choose **Unhide** so that the student ID# column will be unhidden.

11. At the end of the semester you will need to print all the attendance records to turn in to the administration office. Let's do this for the *TTH1230* class worksheet.

a. First, enter **P** for present or **A** for absent for each day and student.

b. Right-click on the column C heading and Hide the *Signature* column.

c. Set *Print Titles* so columns A and B and rows 1 through 8 will print on every page for all the worksheets.

(1) On the *Page Layout* tab, click the dialog launcher button to launch the *Page Setup* dialog box.

(2) Click the **Sheet** tab in the *Page Setup* dialog box.

(3) In the *Rows to repeat at top* box, enter: `$1:$8` OR click the button at the right end of the *Rows to repeat at top* box, drag the **1** row heading through the **8** row heading on the worksheet, then click the button again. You should see `$1:$8` in the box.

(4) In the *Columns to repeat at left* box, enter: `$A:$B` OR click the button at the right end of the *Columns to repeat at left* box, drag the **A** column heading and **B** column heading on the worksheet, then click the button again. You should see `$A:$B` in the box.

(5) Click **OK** in the *Page Setup* dialog box.

(6) On the *Page Layout* tab, in the *Scale to Fit* group, set the *Width* and *Height* to **Automatic.**

(7) On the *Page Layout* tab, in the *Show* group, uncheck so the **Gridlines** do NOT print.

(8) Click on cell **L1.** On the *Page Layout* tab, in the *Page Setup* group, click the **Breaks** button. This inserts a page break after week 4. Do the same after weeks 8 and 12. (If there are any additional page breaks clear them first.)

(9) Click the **File** tab, and then click **Print.** Under *Settings:*

(a) Click the drop-down arrow to change from *Print Selection* to **Print Active Sheets.**

(b) Click the *Orientation* drop-down arrow, choose **Portrait.**

(10) Click the **Show Margins** button in the lower right of the screen. Scroll down to see each of the pages.

(11) Click the **Print** button to print the 4 worksheet pages.

12. Four pages seems like too much paper. Fit the entire worksheet all on one piece of paper.

   a. On the *Page Layout* tab:

      (1) Change the *Orientation* to **Landscape.**

      (2) Change *Margins* to **Narrow.**

      (3) Click **Breaks** and choose **Reset All Page Breaks.**

      (4) In the *Scale to Fit* group, change the *Width* to **1 page.**

13. Click the **File** tab, and then click **Print.**

14. Click the **Print** button.

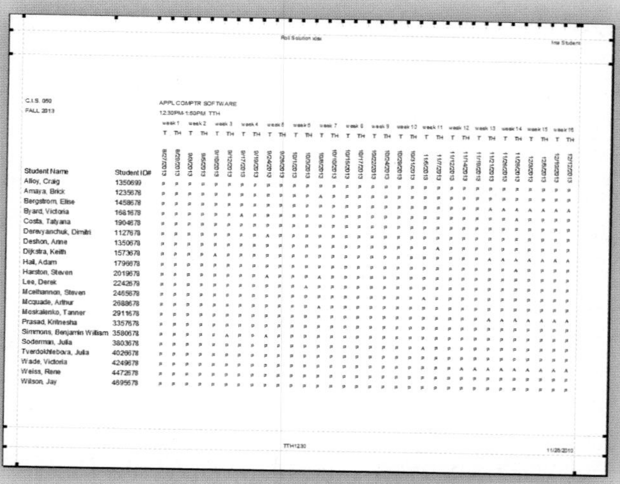

FIGURE EX 3.32

Skill Review 3.2

Work Schedule. In this Skill Review, you will be working with a workbook designed to plan employees' or volunteers' work schedules.

1. Open the provided file called *Schedule.xlsx*. Call the copy `[your initials]EX_SkillReview_3-2`.
2. As you complete some work and verify your accuracy, save your file now and then.
3. Look at the various worksheets. The monthly schedule worksheets need to be named and color coded.

   a. Double-click the tab for *Sheet1,* type: `January` and press the **Enter** key.

   b. Right-click the tab, point to **Tab Color,** and choose **Brown, Text 2, Lighter 40%.**

   c. Repeat for February and March for Sheet2 and Sheet3, naming the sheets and coloring February **Red, Accent 2, Lighter 40%** and March **Gray -50%, Accent 6, Lighter 40%.**

4. The monthly schedule sheets all need formatting. Group them and then format them all at once.

   a. Click the **January** sheet tab, hold down the **Shift** key, click the **March** sheet tab, then release the **Shift** key. Notice the three sheet tabs' appearance has changed to indicate that the three are selected. The *Regular Schedule* tab is not selected. Also notice that the title bar says [Group]. Any changes you make to the current sheet will be made to all three of the selected sheets, so be very careful.

   b. Click the *Page Layout* tab, then click the **Themes** button. Slide the mouse over different themes and notice the preview of the theme appearance on the worksheet. Choose the **Apothecary** theme.

   c. Adjust column widths and row heights to fit the contents and to make the worksheet more readable.

      (1) Look in column A. If you see ########### it means that the cell content is too wide for the column. Drag the column width double-headed arrow between the A and B at the top of the columns to enlarge the column so all the dates display.

      (2) Select all the time columns. Locate the column with the widest names. At the top of the column, double-click the right border between the letters to autosize the column. All the selected columns will size to match.

      (3) Select all the rows, drag any row height double-headed arrow a little (less than half of a row height) to make each row a little roomier.

5. Ungroup the sheets by clicking on any other sheet, such as the *Regular Schedule* sheet. Look at each sheet; they should all have been formatted. Make sure the sheets are now ungrouped.

6. Select just the *Regular Schedule* sheet.
   a. Insert a new row 2. Right-click on the header 2 for row two at the far left. Choose **Insert.**
   b. Drag the mouse over cells **B2:H2,** click the **Merge & Center** button in the *Alignment* group on the *Home* tab. Enter: `Morning Regular Schedule`
   c. Select cells **I2:M2,** merge, and enter: `Afternoon Regular Schedule`
   d. Select cells **N2:U2,** merge, and enter: `Night Regular Schedule`
   e. Click cell **A1** and press the **Delete** key to clear the cell's contents.
7. It is hard to work with such a wide worksheet. Scroll to the right to see the night shift and you can no longer see the dates. Split the screen into two views of different parts of this worksheet.
   a. Click cell **G1.** On the *View* tab, in the *Window* group, click the **Split** button. Now you can scroll each pane separately, but it is all still the same worksheet. You can drag the split bar to the right or left as needed.
   b. Scroll to show the morning and night shifts on your screen.
   c. Click the **Split** button again to return to normal.
8. Another way to deal with large worksheets is to freeze panes.
   a. Select any one of the month worksheets.
   b. Select cell **B5.** On the *View* tab, in the *Window* group, click **Freeze Panes,** and select **Freeze Panes.**
   c. Now you can scroll up or down and everything above and to the left of B6 remains visibly frozen on the screen.
   d. Freeze panes must be set on each of the month sheets separately. Grouping does not work for freeze panes. Repeat the freeze panes process for each of the month worksheets.
9. Make a sheet for April by copying the *March* sheet.
   a. Right-click on the **March** sheet tab. Choose **Move or Copy,** choose before sheet *Regular Schedule,* and check **Create a copy.** Click **OK.**
   b. Set up freeze panes on this sheet to make the sheet easier to work with. Name the sheet tab `April` and change the tab color to **Gold, Accent 5.**
   c. Make necessary changes to the sheet for April.
      (1) Edit the first date, changing it from March to April.
      (2) Add or delete days at the end of the month as appropriate by deleting rows or using fill.
      (3) Use copy and paste, drag and drop, and so forth to fill the appropriate days and times for each person as indicated on the *Regular Schedule.*
      (4) Mike has requested some special time off and Steve has agreed to work in his place on the second Saturday in April. Make this change on the April schedule and highlight the changed cells in yellow, so everyone notices the change.
10. Delete *Sheet4.* Right-click on the sheet tab and choose **Delete.**
11. Drag the sheet tab for *Regular Schedule* before the sheet tab for *January* so that *Regular Schedule* is the first worksheet in the workbook.
12. Look closely at the *Regular Schedule* sheet. There are several row numbers missing.
    a. Select the rows before and after the missing rows. Select the entire rows by dragging over the row heading numbers at the far left.

b. With both rows selected, right-click on the selection.

c. Choose **Unhide** to reveal the pay information that was hidden.

13. Click the *Page Layout* tab. In the *Sheet Options* group, click the **View Gridlines** check box to remove the check mark and see your worksheet without any gridlines. Click again to restore the gridlines on the screen.

14. Save your file.

15. Prepare to print your worksheets by adding headers and footers.

    a. Group all the worksheets to save time. This way the headers and footers may be added to all the sheets at once. Verify that all the sheets are selected.

    b. Click on the **Page Layout view** button in the lower right of your screen. If you see a message about *Freeze Panes* being incompatible with Page Layout view, continue.

    c. Click to add a header. (Adjust the zoom as needed in the lower-right corner of the screen.)

    d. From the *Header & Footer Tools Design* tab, in the *Header & Footer Elements* group, click the **File Name** button. The code `&[File]` will be entered in the center section of the header. Once you click somewhere else, this will display the name of your file.

    e. Click in the right section of the header and enter your own name.

    f. From the *Header & Footer Tools Design* tab, in the *Navigation* group, click the **Go to Footer** button; click in the center section.

    g. From the *Header & Footer Tools Design* tab, in the *Header & Footer Elements* group, click the **Sheet Name** button. The code `&[Tab]` will be entered. Once you click somewhere else, this will display the name on the sheet tab.

    h. Click in the right section of the footer and click the **Current Date** button.

    i. Click in any cell of the worksheet and click the **Normal view** button in the lower right of your screen.

16. Ungroup the sheets. Right-click on any sheet tab and choose **Ungroup Sheets.**

17. Select the *Regular Schedule* sheet. Click the **File** tab, and then click **Print.**

18. Scroll down to see all the pages for your worksheet. Scroll back up to the first page.

19. Click the drop-down arrow on the *Portrait Orientation* button and choose **Landscape.**

20. Click the drop-down arrow on the *Normal Margins* button and choose **Narrow.**

21. Click the drop-down arrow on the *No Scaling* button; click **Custom Scaling Options.** Choose **Fit Sheet on One page.**

22. This fits neatly on one page, but it is so small and hard to read.

23. Change the *Scale* from *Fit Sheet on One Page* to **No Scaling.**

24. It would be easier to read if the morning, afternoon, and night shifts each printed on a separate page in a reasonably large font size.

    a. Click the **Page Layout** tab. Click cell **I1.** In the *Page Setup* group, click the **Breaks** button. Choose **Insert Page Break.**

    b. Click in cell **N1.** On the *Page Layout* tab, in the *Page Setup* group, click the **Breaks** button. Choose **Insert Page Break.**

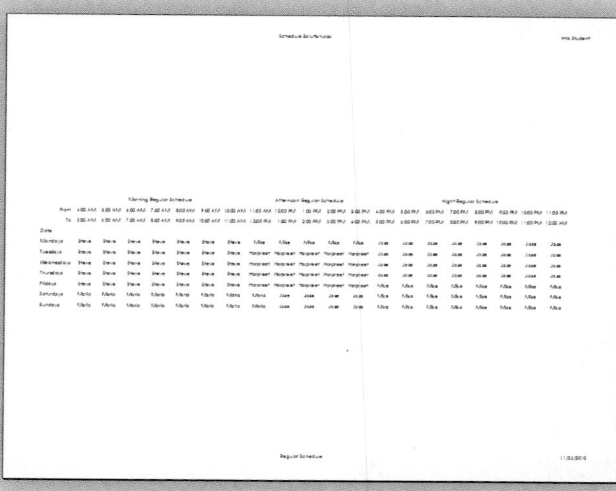

FIGURE EX 3.33

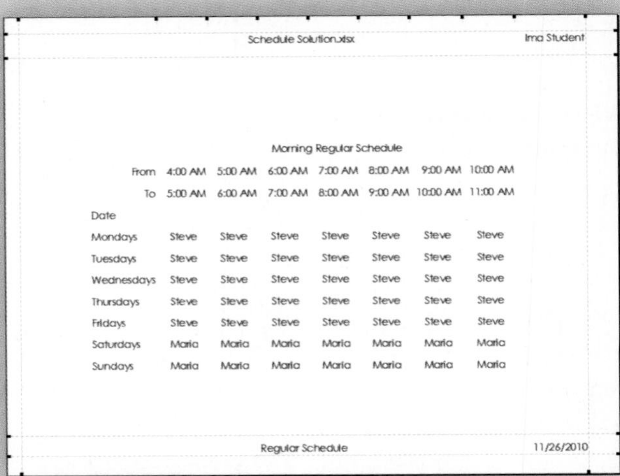
Schedule Solution.xlsx | Ima Student

Morning Regular Schedule

	From	4:00 AM	5:00 AM	6:00 AM	7:00 AM	8:00 AM	9:00 AM	10:00 AM
	To	5:00 AM	6:00 AM	7:00 AM	8:00 AM	9:00 AM	10:00 AM	11:00 AM
Date							
Mondays	Steve	Steve	Steve	Steve	Steve	Steve	Steve
Tuesdays	Steve	Steve	Steve	Steve	Steve	Steve	Steve
Wednesdays	Steve	Steve	Steve	Steve	Steve	Steve	Steve
Thursdays	Steve	Steve	Steve	Steve	Steve	Steve	Steve
Fridays	Steve	Steve	Steve	Steve	Steve	Steve	Steve
Saturdays	Maria	Maria	Maria	Maria	Maria	Maria	Maria
Sundays	Maria	Maria	Maria	Maria	Maria	Maria	Maria

Regular Schedule | 11/26/2010

FIGURE EX 3.34

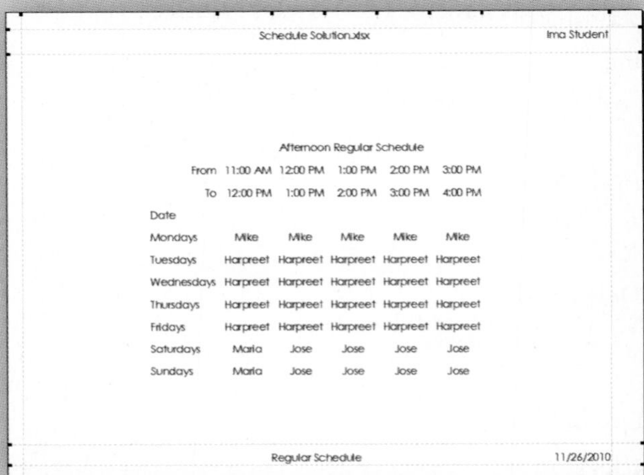
Schedule Solution.xlsx | Ima Student

Afternoon Regular Schedule

From	11:00 AM	12:00 PM	1:00 PM	2:00 PM	3:00 PM
To	12:00 PM	1:00 PM	2:00 PM	3:00 PM	4:00 PM
Date					
Mondays	Mike	Mike	Mike	Mike	Mike
Tuesdays	Harpreet	Harpreet	Harpreet	Harpreet	Harpreet
Wednesdays	Harpreet	Harpreet	Harpreet	Harpreet	Harpreet
Thursdays	Harpreet	Harpreet	Harpreet	Harpreet	Harpreet
Fridays	Harpreet	Harpreet	Harpreet	Harpreet	Harpreet
Saturdays	Maria	Jose	Jose	Jose	Jose
Sundays	Maria	Jose	Jose	Jose	Jose

Regular Schedule | 11/26/2010

FIGURE EX 3.35

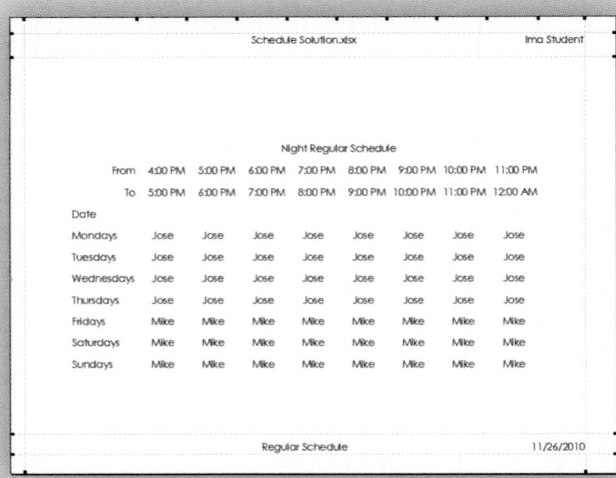
Schedule Solution.xlsx | Ima Student

Night Regular Schedule

From	4:00 PM	5:00 PM	6:00 PM	7:00 PM	8:00 PM	9:00 PM	10:00 PM	11:00 PM
To	5:00 PM	6:00 PM	7:00 PM	8:00 PM	9:00 PM	10:00 PM	11:00 PM	12:00 AM
Date								
Mondays	Jose	Jose	Jose	Jose	Jose	Jose	Jose	Jose
Tuesdays	Jose	Jose	Jose	Jose	Jose	Jose	Jose	Jose
Wednesdays	Jose	Jose	Jose	Jose	Jose	Jose	Jose	Jose
Thursdays	Jose	Jose	Jose	Jose	Jose	Jose	Jose	Jose
Fridays	Mike	Mike	Mike	Mike	Mike	Mike	Mike	Mike
Saturdays	Mike	Mike	Mike	Mike	Mike	Mike	Mike	Mike
Sundays	Mike	Mike	Mike	Mike	Mike	Mike	Mike	Mike

Regular Schedule | 11/26/2010

FIGURE EX 3.36

25. The days will only show on the first sheet, so the second and third sheets will make no sense. Set *Print Titles* so that column A will print on every page for all the worksheets.

a. On the *Page Setup* tab, in the *Page Setup* group, click the **Page Setup Dialog Launcher** button to launch the *Page Setup* dialog box.

b. Click the **Sheet** tab in the *Page Setup* dialog box.

c. In the *Columns to repeat at left* box enter: `$A:$A` OR click the button at the right end of the *Columns to repeat at left* box, click the **A** column heading on the worksheet, then click the button again. You should see `$A:$A` in the box.

d. Click **OK** in the *Page Setup* dialog box. Column A should now show on each page.

26. In the *Sheet Options* group, check the **Print Gridlines** check box to add gridlines to your printout.

27. Select rows **17** though **21,** then right-click and select **Hide.**

28. Click the **File** tab, and then click **Print** again. Click the **Page Setup** link.

a. Click the **Page** tab. In the *Scaling* section, click the *Adjust to: %* up arrow to choose **125.** This will make the text larger on the printed page.

b. Click the **Margins** tab. Check the boxes to *Center on page* **Horizontally** and **Vertically.** Click **OK.**

c. Click the **Show Margins** button in the lower right of your screen to display marks on the screen representing the margins and the column widths. Drag any of the lines a little to make adjustments on the printout.

d. Finally click the **Print** button.

29. Mike and Steve want printouts of the changed schedule for April.

a. On the *April* worksheet, set *Print Titles* so that column **A** and rows **1** through **4** will print on all pages.

(1) On the *Page Layout* tab, click the **Page Layout Dialog Launcher** button again to launch the *Page Setup* dialog box.

(2) Click the **Sheet** tab in the *Page Setup* dialog box.

(3) In the *Columns to repeat at left* box enter: `$A:$A` OR click the button at the right end of the *Columns to repeat at left* box, click the **A** column heading on the worksheet, then click the button again. You should see `$A:$A` in the box.

(4) In the *Rows to repeat at top* box enter: `$1:$4` OR click the button at the right end of the *Rows to repeat at top* box, drag the row headings for rows **1** through **4**

on the worksheet, then click the button again. You should see `$1:$4` in the box.

(5) Click **OK** in the *Page Setup* dialog box.

b. Select the highlighted cells.

c. Click the **File** tab, and then click **Print.**

(1) Click the drop-down arrow to change *Print Active Sheets* to **Print Selection.**

(2) Click the drop-down arrow to change *Portrait Orientation* to **Landscape** orientation.

(3) Click the **Print** button.

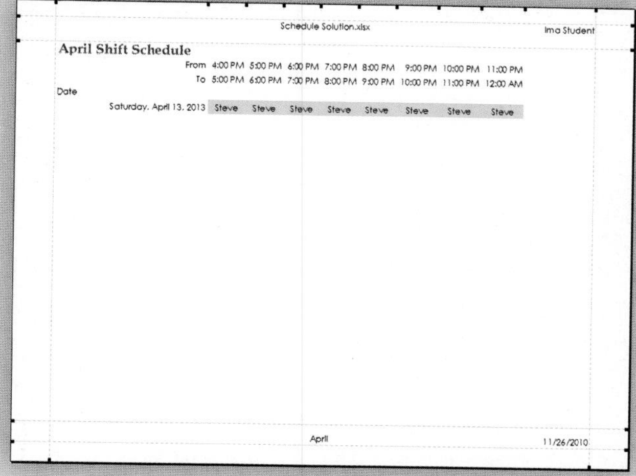

FIGURE EX 3.37

challenge yourself 1

Loan Schedule. In this Challenge project, you will be working with a workbook designed to keep track of loan repayment.

1. Save yourself a copy of the provided file called *Loan.xlsx.* Call the copy ***[your initials]*EX_Challenge_3-3.**
2. Change the name of *Sheet1* to: `Truck`
3. Change the *Truck* sheet tab color.
4. Make a copy the *Truck* sheet, placing it before *Sheet2.*
5. Change the name of the new sheet to: `House`
6. Change the *House* sheet tab color.
7. On the *House* sheet, change the title in cell **A1** to: `House Loan Amortization`
   a. Change the amount borrowed, years to pay, and the APR to reflect a reasonable home loan.
   b. Fill down the *Payment#*s to the end of the loan.
   c. In cell **C10,** enter the date of the first payment for the house. In cell **C11,** enter the date of the second payment. Select both dates and fill down.
   d. Edit the extra payment amounts to reflect an extra $500 paid twice a year.
   e. Fill down the *Payment Amount,* the *Interest,* the *Balance,* and the *Total Paid* to the end of the loan.
   f. Update the formula in cell **E5** as needed to total all the interest.
   g. Delete any extra rows at the bottom of the worksheet that would reflect overpayment of the loan. Edit the last *Payment Amount* to bring the balance to zero.
   h. Select cell **C9** and freeze panes. Scroll around the worksheet. Turn off freeze panes.
8. Group the *House* and *Truck* worksheets. Make the following changes to both sheets at once.
   a. Select a worksheet theme from the *Page Layout* tab.
   b. Merge and center the title in cell **A1** across cells **A1:I1.**
   c. Autosize all column widths.
   d. Hide the *Payment Amount* column.

e. In the center of the header, cause Excel to enter the *file name.*

f. To the right of the header, enter your name.

g. In the center of the footer, cause Excel to enter the *sheet name.*

h. In the right section of the footer, cause Excel to enter the *current date.*

i. Set the gridlines to print.

j. Ungroup the sheets.

9. Verify that the sheets are ungrouped. On the *Truck* sheet:

a. Split the screen so that you can look at the top of the worksheet and the bottom of the worksheet on the screen at the same time. (*Freeze Panes* must first be turned off.)

b. Delete extra rows at the bottom of the worksheet that would reflect overpayment of the loan. Edit the last *Payment Amount* to bring the balance to zero.

10. Delete the unused worksheets.

11. Print preview the *Truck* sheet. Notice that it does not fit on one page.

a. Set it to fit on **1** page **Height.**

b. Change orientation to **Portrait.**

c. Adjust margins and column widths as needed, and center on the page.

d. Print the *Truck* worksheet.

12. Print preview the *House* sheet. Notice that it does not fit on one page.

a. Set it to fit on **1** page **Width.**

b. Set the orientation to **Portrait.**

c. Set columns **A** and **B** as well as rows **1** through **8** as *print titles* so that they will print on every page.

d. Adjust page breaks as needed so that the last page contains at least one year of payments.

e. Adjust margins and column widths as needed, and center on the page.

f. Print just the last page of the *House* worksheet.

challenge yourself 2

Hobbies. In this Challenge project, you will be working with a workbook designed keep track of hobbies.

1. Make yourself a copy of the provided file called *Hobbies.xlsx.* Call the copy ***[your initials]*EX_Challenge_3-4.**

2. Change the names of the sheets as follows:

a. Change *Sheet1* to `Running`

b. Change *Sheet2* to `Football`

c. Change *Sheet3* to `Movies`

3. Change the color of each sheet tab.

4. Add a row at the top of each sheet and enter an appropriate title. Adjust column widths appropriately as needed.

5. On the *Football* sheet with the Super Bowl scores, use *Merge & Center* to center an appropriate title across the width of the columns used. Do the same with the *Movies* sheet about Academy Awards.

6. Group the worksheets and set a worksheet theme. Add headers and footers, then ungroup.
7. Freeze panes or split to make it easier to work with each worksheet. Add more Oscar and/or Super Bowl data. (Research to find this information on the Web.)
8. Insert a new worksheet after *Running* and enter data about your own hobby or interest.
9. Delete unused sheets. Rearrange the sheets in a different order.
10. Make an attractive readable printout of each worksheet. Each should fit neatly on one page or have logical page breaks and print titles when more than one page is required.
    a. Hide the least relevant columns as desired.
    b. Adjust column widths and row heights as needed.
    c. Set appropriate margins. Center on the page, where appropriate.
    d. Set the worksheets' orientation appropriately.
    e. Scale the worksheets appropriately.
    f. Print at least one of the sheets with gridlines and at least one without.
11. For one worksheet, make an additional printout consisting of a useful selection of just some cells, and fit all on one page.

on your own

Calendar Project. In this project, you will be working with calendar worksheets.

1. Make yourself a copy of the provided file called *Calendar.xlsx*. Call the copy **[your initials]EX_OnYourOwn_3-5.**
2. On *Sheet1* create a calendar for the current month or next month using Figure EX 3.38 as an example.
    a. Use column widths, row heights, cell merging, and cell alignment.
    b. Enter the date of the first day of the month in the title. Format the title using **Custom,** type: `mmm-yyyy`
    c. Enter the date of the first day of the month in the appropriate column. Format the date, choose **Custom,** enter `d` for the type.
    d. Use simple formulas, then fill and copy to compute the remaining dates. (Hint: Review the formulas used in the *2012-2013* sheet.)
3. Make a copy of the calendar sheet, placing it before *Sheet2.*
4. Edit *Sheet2,* to be the next month.
5. Change both sheet names to each reflect the month and year.
6. Change the color of the sheet tabs.
7. Group both month calendar worksheets:
    a. Set a worksheet theme.
    b. Set gridlines to print.
    c. Use margins settings and scaling and adjust column widths to fit neatly on two portrait pages as shown in Figure EX 3.39.

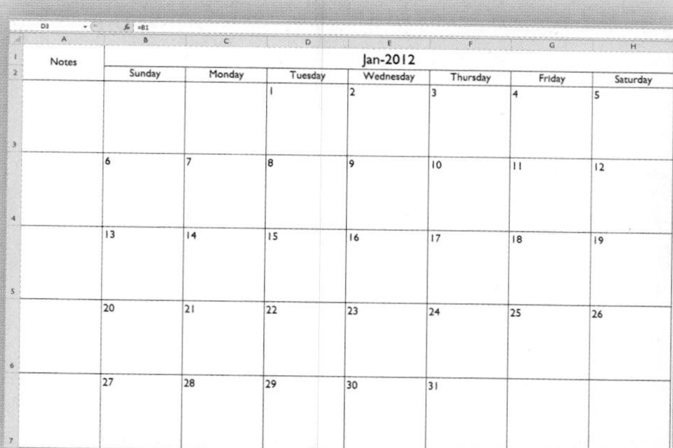

FIGURE EX 3.38

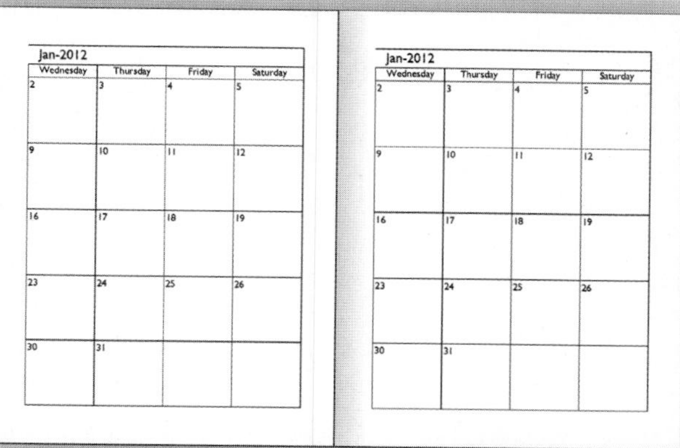

FIGURE EX 3.39

d. Add headers and footers—cause Excel to enter, using a small font, the file name in the center bottom and your name in the top center.

e. Print single sided. Ungroup the sheets.

8. Make the next two months' worksheets using worksheet copy.
9. Group the two new sheets and delete the *Notes* column. Move the *Sunday* column to the right. Ungroup the sheets.
10. Edit the new worksheet data, formulas, and sheet tabs to reflect the next two months.
11. This time, change the settings to neatly print each month on one landscape page.
12. Move the *2012-2013* worksheet to be the first worksheet in the workbook.
13. Using the academic calendar on the sheet called *2012-2013,* hide the *Saturday* and *Sunday* columns.
14. Split the screen to view August 2012 and August 2013 at the same time. Unsplit the screen.
15. Freeze panes so that the days of the week and the title are always visible, no matter where you scroll.
16. Insert a row above row 2 to match the formatting of the row above. Make up and enter the name of the school.
17. Set *Print Titles* so that the months, days of the week, and the title(s) will show on every printed page.
18. Insert page breaks and scale the worksheet to print neatly on 3 pages. Adjust margins, orientations, column widths, and so forth as needed. Print.
19. Delete the unused worksheets.

fix it

Green Car Data. In this project, you will be working with data about automobile emissions and fuel economy.

1. Make yourself a copy of the provided file called *Cars.xlsx*. Call the copy `[your initials]EX_FixIt_3-6.`

   These green car data were downloaded from the Web site http://www.data.gov/raw/2004 and are explained at this Web site: http://www.epa.gov/greenvehicles/Aboutratings.do. The scores range from 0 to 10, where 10 is best. The vehicles with the best scores on both air pollution and greenhouse gas receive the SmartWay designation. These raw data need formatting in order to be usable.
2. Color the worksheet tab and name the worksheet `Raw Data`
3. In the *Raw Data* worksheet begin entering page breaks after each manufacturer. You discover that there are really too many cars to try to do this with reasonable effort.
4. Copy the *Raw Data* worksheet placing the copy sheet before *Sheet4*. Color the worksheet tab and name the worksheet `Formatted All`
5. Freeze panes so that the titles show at the top of each row and at the start of each column no matter where you scroll. And set *Print Titles* for the same.
6. Copy all the rows for one car model or manufacturer (about a page worth of data) to *Sheet2,* and all the rows for another car model of manufacturer to *Sheet3.*
7. Move the *Raw Data* sheet after *Sheet3.*
8. Rename the sheets entering the model and/or manufacturer's name for the sheet name.

9. Group all the sheets except for the *Raw Data* sheet and begin to format them all at once.
   a. Apply a worksheet theme.
   b. Adjust row and column sizes as needed so that the data will display neatly and legibly.
   c. Hide the *Underhood ID* column.
   d. Set the worksheet *orientation* to **Portrait.**
   e. Set the worksheet *gridlines* to **Print.**
   f. Cause Excel to insert the *sheet name* into the center of the footer and *your name* in the upper-right section of the header.
   g. Set **Narrow** *margins* and set to *center* on the page.
   h. Scale the worksheet so that the *width* will fit on one paper.
   i. Reduce the font size in the header center section as needed.
   j. Insert a row at the top for entering sheet titles.
10. Ungroup the sheets, enter an appropriate title in cell **A1** of each of the worksheets, and then merge and center across all the used columns.
11. Split the *Raw Data* worksheet into four views and scroll around.
12. Delete the *Raw Data* worksheet.
13. Print each of the single model/manufacturer worksheets. Make sure each fits on one page.
14. Using the *Formatted All* worksheet, select all the data for a different manufacturer or model and print just the selected data. Make sure it fits on one page.

chapter 4

Adding Charts and Analyzing Data

In this chapter, you will learn the following skills:

- Create and edit charts
- Work with data tables
- Analyze data with Goal Seek
- Apply conditional formatting
- Use PivotTables and PivotCharts

skills

introduction

A picture is worth a thousand words; use Excel to create charts that make your data more easily understood. Also in this chapter, learn to use more advanced Excel tools for data analysis.

4.1 Inserting a Column Chart

A **chart** is a graphic that transforms numerical data into a more visual representation. Often, charts make it easier to see data trends and relationships. In Excel, you can create a wide variety of charts including column charts, pie charts, and line charts.

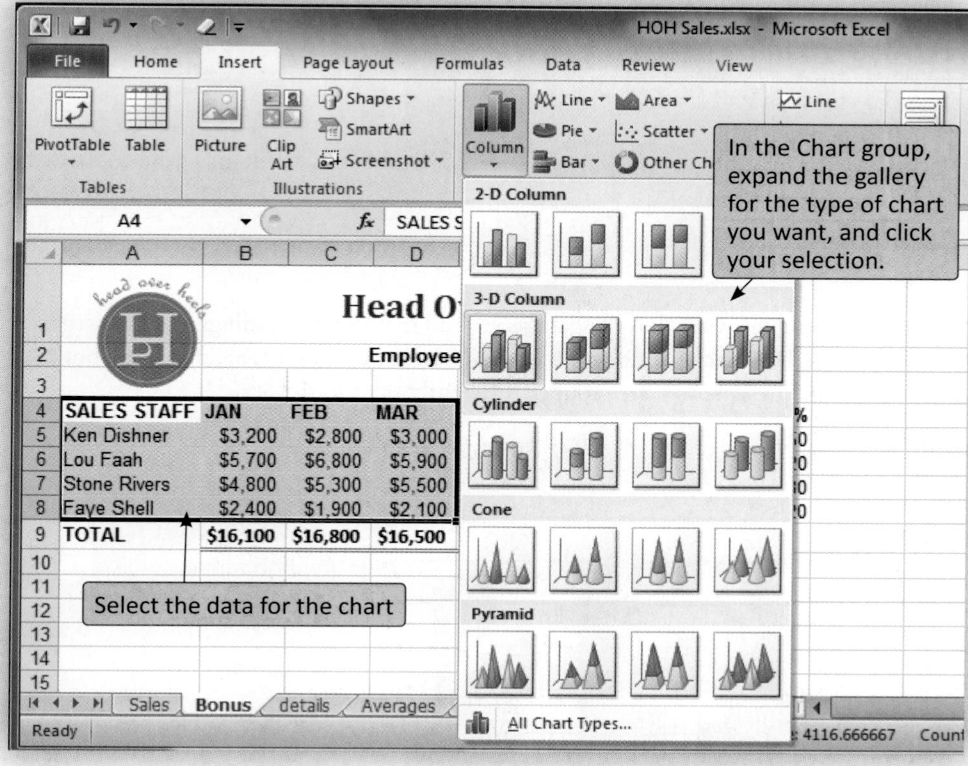

FIGURE EX 4.1

To add a chart to a workbook:

1. Select the data you want to visualize as a chart.
2. Click the **Insert** tab.
3. In the *Charts* group, click the button for the type of chart you want.
4. Click the specific chart type from the gallery.

Excel automatically inserts the chart into your active worksheet.

Column charts work best with data that are organized into rows and columns like a table. Excel automatically uses row headings as the categories on the horizontal (x) axis. For each category, columns represent the values of each cell in the row. Values in the cell range (**data points**) are grouped by column headings (the **data series**) and are plotted along the vertical (y) axis. The chart **legend** provides a key so you know which data series is represented by each color.

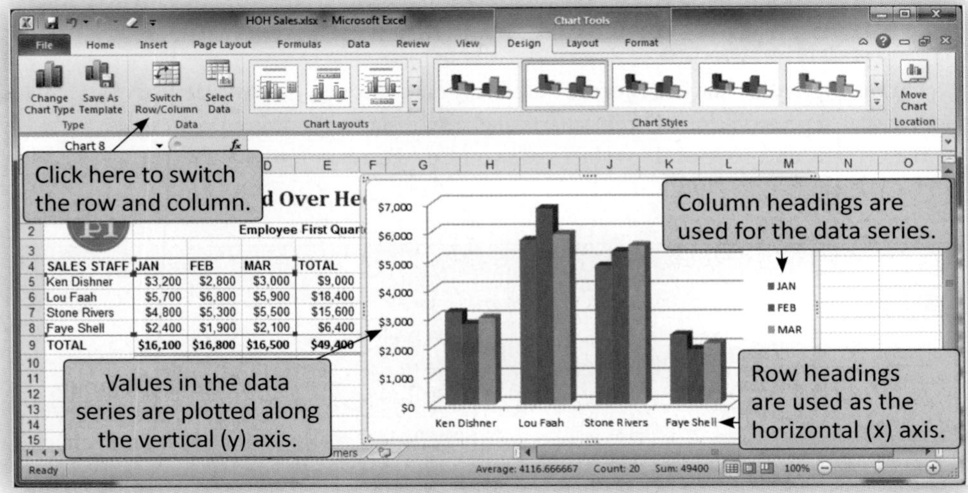
Click here to switch the row and column.
Column headings are used for the data series.
Values in the data series are plotted along the vertical (y) axis.
Row headings are used as the horizontal (x) axis.

FIGURE EX 4.2

You can change which way the data series is presented. On the *Chart Tools Design* tab, in the *Data* group, click the **Switch Row/Column** button. Now the row headings are presented as the data series, and the column headings are the categories along the *x* axis. The same data points are displayed, but they are grouped differently.

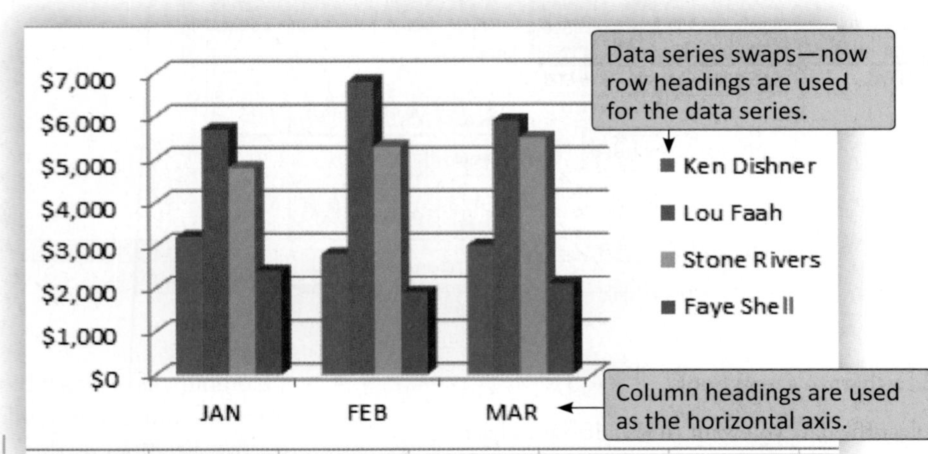
Data series swaps—now row headings are used for the data series.
Column headings are used as the horizontal axis.
$7,000
$6,000
$5,000
$4,000
$3,000
$2,000
$1,000
$0
JAN
FEB
MAR
Ken Dishner
Lou Faah
Stone Rivers
Faye Shell

FIGURE EX 4.3

tell me **more**

When the chart is selected, the *Chart Tools* contextual tabs are available. These tabs provide design, layout, and formatting options to customize the chart.

Design tab—Allows you to change the chart type, layout, and chart style. You can also modify the chart data from the *Design* tab.

Format tab—Allows you to change the individual formatting elements of the chart, such as fill, outline, and effects.

Layout tab—Allows you to change the individual elements of the chart layout, such as the appearance of the legend or chart title.

try **this**

You can also insert a chart from the *Insert Chart* dialog:

1. On the *Insert* tab, in the *Charts* group, click the **Chart** dialog launcher.
2. In the *Insert Chart* dialog box, click a chart type category to display that category in the right pane.
3. Click a chart type in the right pane to select it.
4. Click **OK** to add the chart to the worksheet.

4.2 Working with Pie Charts

Pie charts represent data as parts of a whole. They do not have *x* and *y* axes like column charts. Instead, each value is a visual "slice" of the pie. Pie charts work best when you want to evaluate values as they relate to a total value—for example, departmental budgets in relation to the entire budget, or each employee's bonus in relation to the entire bonus pool.

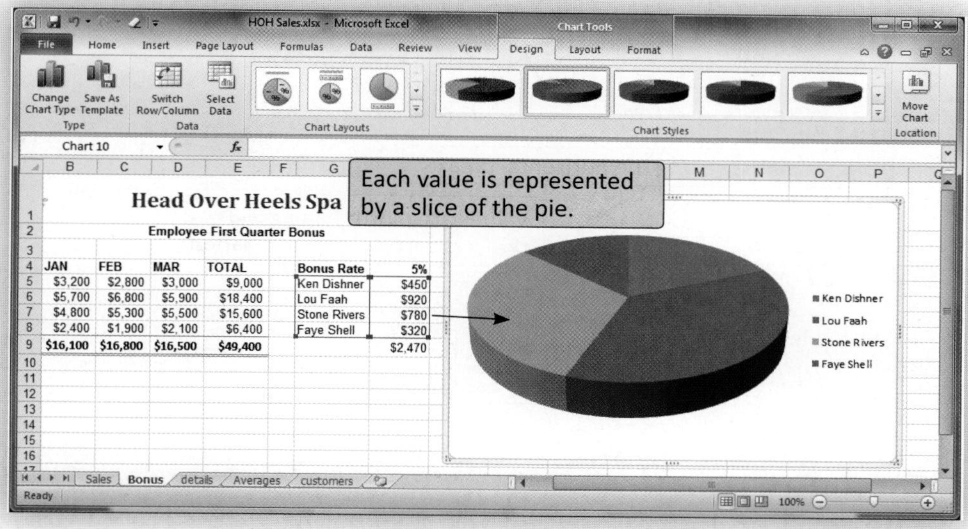

FIGURE EX 4.4

To add a pie chart:

1. Select the data you want to include in the pie chart.
2. Click the **Insert** tab.
3. In the *Charts* group, click the **Pie** button.
4. Click the specific pie chart type from the gallery.

Excel automatically inserts the chart into your active worksheet.

tell me **more**

In an "exploded" pie chart, each slice is slightly separated from the whole. You can "explode" a single slice by clicking it and dragging it away from the rest of the slices. Exploding a single slice of data gives it emphasis.

try **this**

You can also insert a pie chart from the *Insert Chart* dialog:

1. Click the **Chart dialog launcher** in the *Charts* group on the *Insert* tab.
2. In the *Insert Chart* dialog box, click **Pie** in the category list to display that category in the right pane.
3. Click a pie chart type in the right pane to select it.
4. Click **OK** to add the chart to the worksheet.

4.3 Working with Line Charts

Line charts feature a line connecting each data point—showing the movement of values over time. Line charts work best when data trends over time are important.

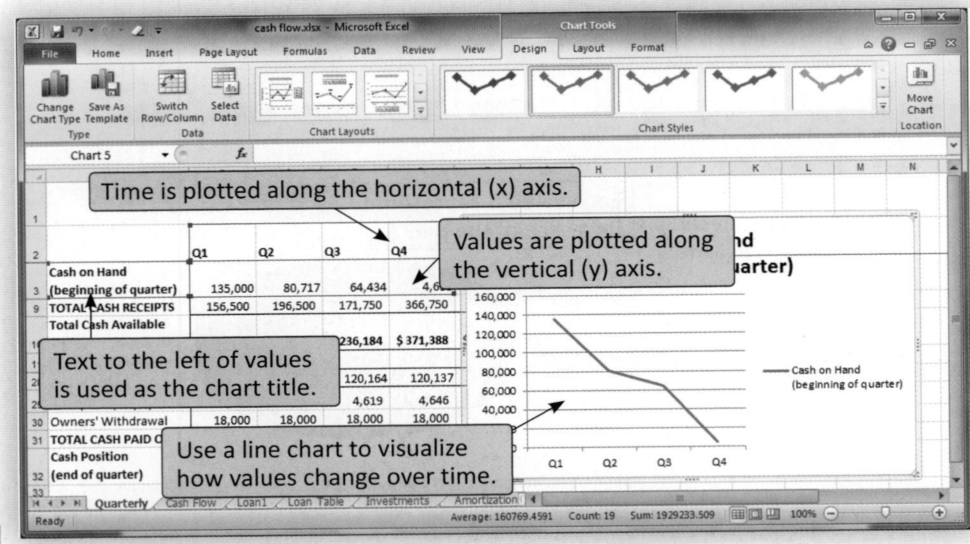

FIGURE EX 4.5

To add a line chart:

1. Select the data you want to include in the line chart. Be sure to include both values and the related cells that represent time segments (dates, calendar quarters, etc.).
2. Click the **Insert** tab.
3. In the *Charts* group, click the **Line** button.
4. Click the specific line chart type from the gallery.

Excel automatically inserts the chart into your active worksheet.

To add another data series to your line chart:

1. Select the chart by clicking anywhere in the **Chart Area** (any empty area of the chart).
2. In the *Chart Tools Design* tab, *Data* group, click the **Select Data** button 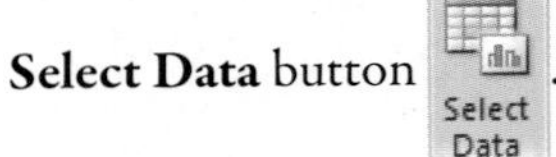.
3. The *Select Data Source* dialog opens showing the current data series.
4. Click the **Add** button.
5. The *Edit Series* dialog opens. Enter the appropriate cell reference in the *Series name:* box. Enter the appropriate cell range in the *Series values:* box. Click **OK.**
6. The *Select Data Source* dialog opens again with the new data series added. Click **OK** to add the data series to your line chart.

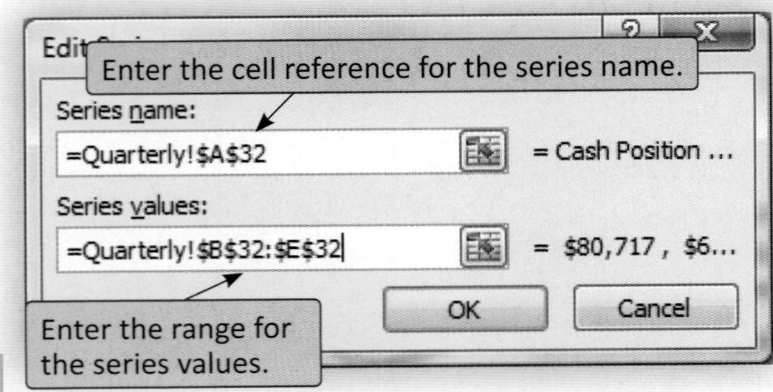

FIGURE EX 4.6

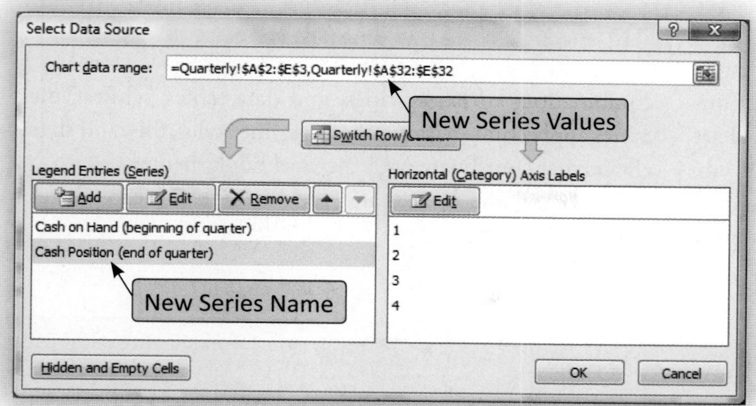

FIGURE EX 4.7

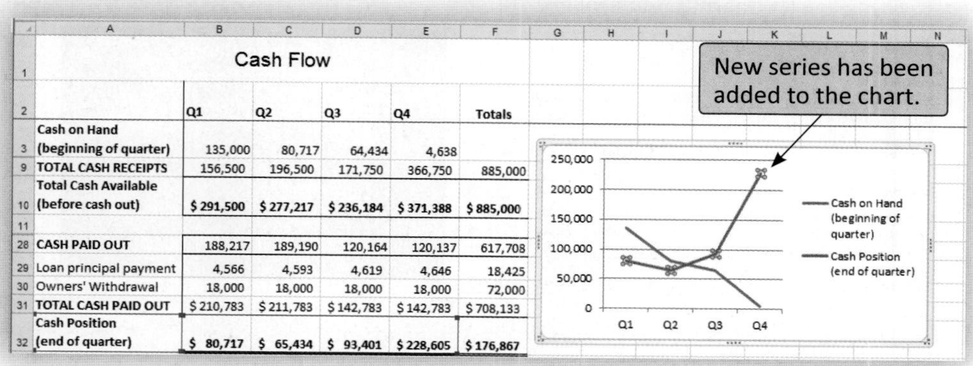

	A	B	C	D	E	F
1	Cash Flow					
2		Q1	Q2	Q3	Q4	Totals
3	Cash on Hand (beginning of quarter)	135,000	80,717	64,434	4,638	
9	TOTAL CASH RECEIPTS	156,500	196,500	171,750	366,750	885,000
10	Total Cash Available (before cash out)	$ 291,500	$ 277,217	$ 236,184	$ 371,388	$ 885,000
11						
28	CASH PAID OUT	188,217	189,190	120,164	120,137	617,708
29	Loan principal payment	4,566	4,593	4,619	4,646	18,425
30	Owners' Withdrawal	18,000	18,000	18,000	18,000	72,000
31	TOTAL CASH PAID OUT	$ 210,783	$ 211,783	$ 142,783	$ 142,783	$ 708,133
32	Cash Position (end of quarter)	$ 80,717	$ 65,434	$ 93,401	$ 228,605	$ 176,867

FIGURE EX 4.8

You can also insert a line chart from the *Insert Chart* dialog.	try **this**

4.4 Changing the Chart Design

When you insert a chart, Excel displays the *Chart Tools* contextual tabs. These tabs provide easy access to all the chart design, layout, and formatting tools. From the *Design* tab, you can change the chart layout or style using the predefined **Quick Layouts** and **Quick Styles**. Quick Layouts apply combinations of labels, titles, and data tables, while Quick Styles apply combinations of colors, line styles, fills, and shape effects that coordinate with the workbook theme.

Changing the layout and style of a chart can make a dramatic impact.

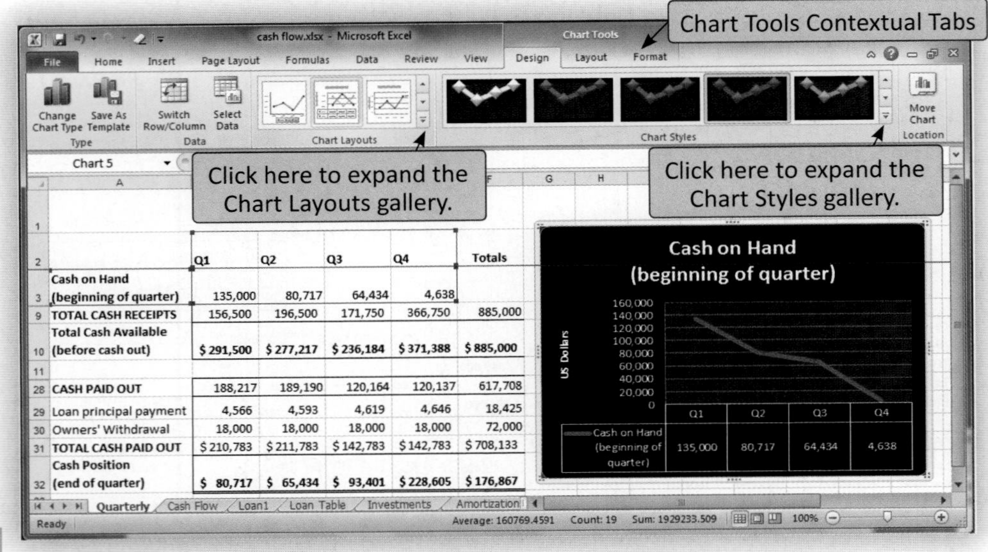

FIGURE EX 4.9

To change the chart layout using a Quick Layout:

1. Click the **Design** tab under *Chart Tools*.
2. In the *Chart Layouts* group, click one of the chart layouts, or click the **More** button to see all of the chart layouts available.

To change the chart style using a Quick Style:

1. Click the **Design** tab under *Chart Tools*.
2. In the *Chart Styles* group, click the style you want to use, or click the **More** button to see all of the chart styles available.

tell me more

The *Chart Tools Layout* tab allows you to change chart layout elements manually. The *Chart Tools Format* tab allows you to change chart style elements manually.

4.5 Changing the Chart Layout

Once you apply a Quick Layout to your chart, you may need to further modify layout elements such as the placement of titles, labels, and the chart legend. You can also specify whether or not the data table appears as part of the chart.

Chart Title—Hide or show and position the chart title.

Axis Titles—Hide or show the horizontal axis title and hide or show and control the appearance of the vertical axis title.

Legend—Control the appearance of the chart legend explaining how the various chart colors correspond to data elements.

Data Labels—Hide or show and position the values for chart elements.

Data Table—Hide or show the data table as part of the chart.

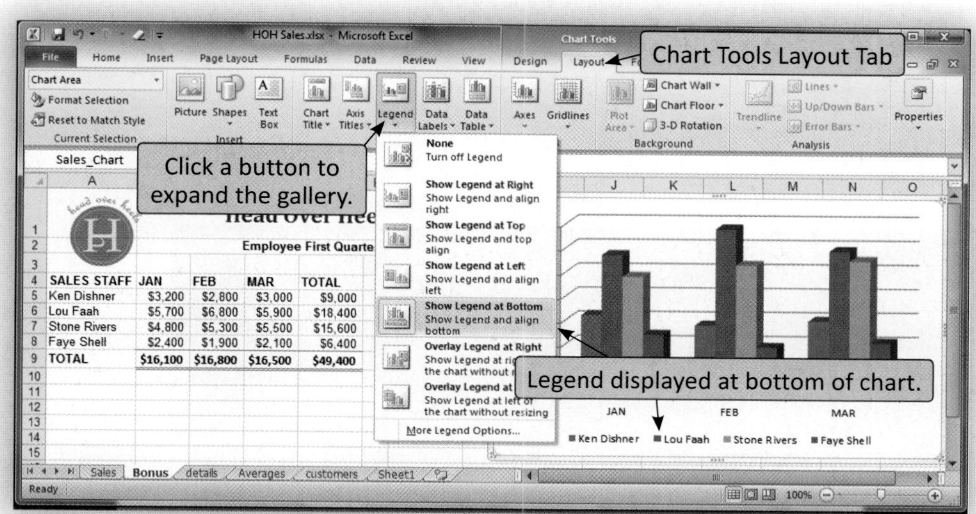

FIGURE EX 4.10

To change specific layout options:

1. Click the Chart Area to select the chart.
2. Click the **Chart Tools Layout** tab.
3. From the *Labels* group, click the button for the element you want to change, and then select the specific option you want.

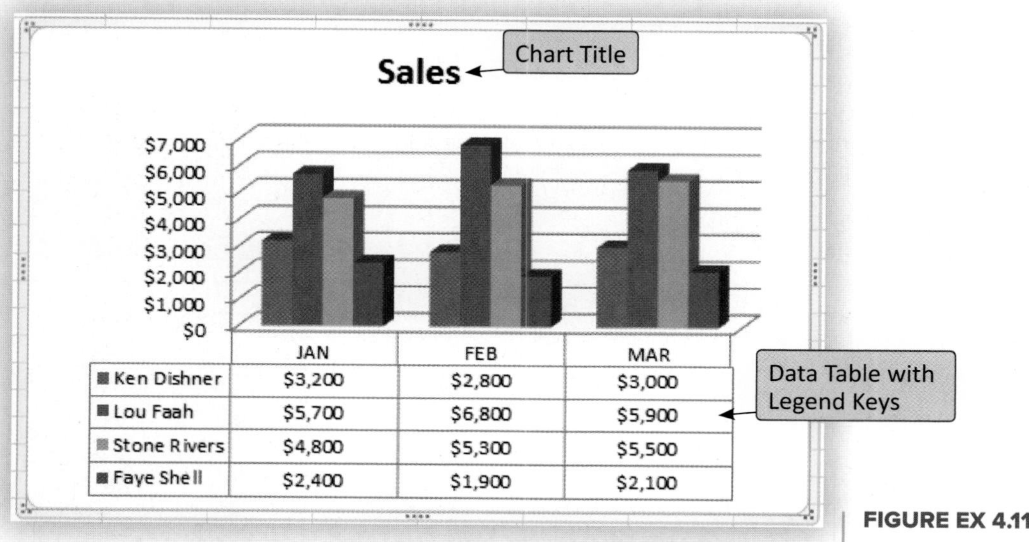

FIGURE EX 4.11

from the perspective of . . .

STUDENT ACCOUNTING CLERK

I use spreadsheet software to keep track of budgets, create accounts receivable schedules and financial reports. I can create charts to visually illustrate the costs for budget meetings.

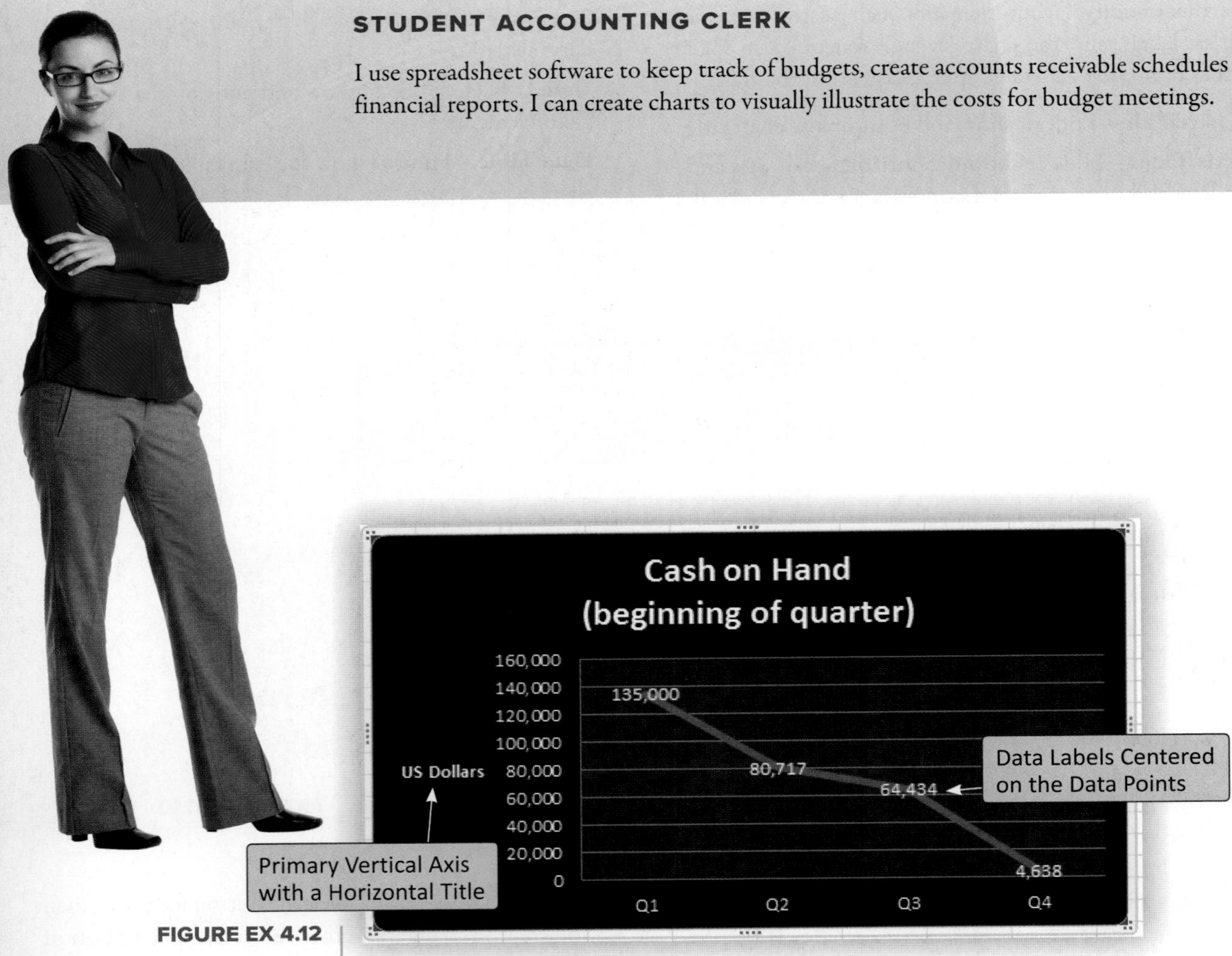

FIGURE EX 4.12

tell me **more**

The changes you make from the *Chart Tools Layout* tab apply only to the part of the chart you have selected. You can verify your selection (or change it) from the **Chart Elements** drop-down list at the top of the *Current Selection* group.

try **this**

You can add data labels to the chart by right-clicking the data and selecting **Add Data Labels** from the menu.

4.6 Changing the Chart Type

Often, when you insert a chart, your data do not appear exactly as you intended. After inserting a chart, you can quickly change the chart type from the *Chart Tools Design* tab.

To change the chart type:

1. Click the **Design** tab under *Chart Tools*.
2. In the *Type* group, click the **Change Chart Type** button.
3. In the *Change Chart Type* dialog box, click a chart type category to display that category in the right pane.
4. Click a chart type in the right pane to select it.
5. Click **OK** to change the chart type.

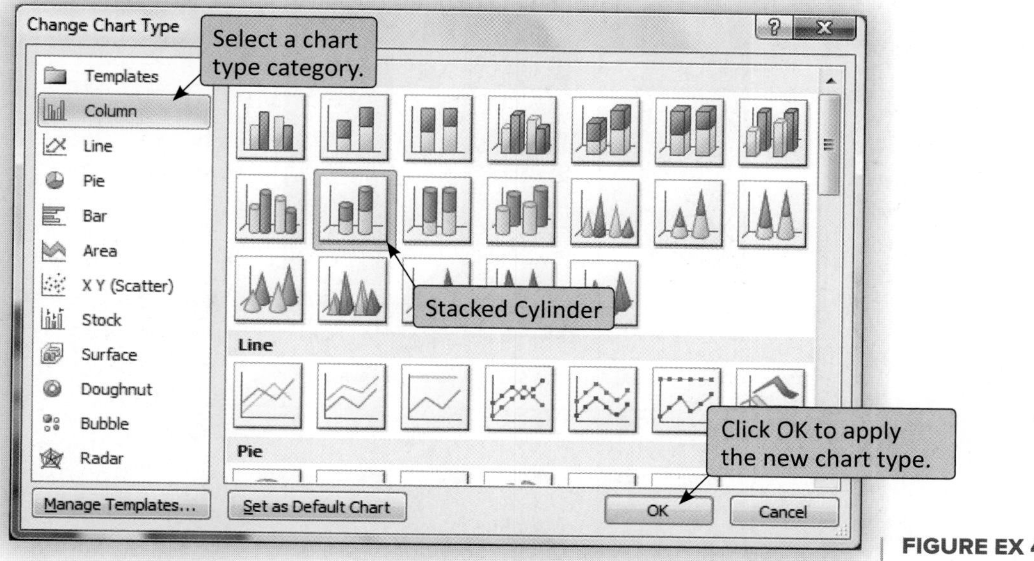

FIGURE EX 4.13

This clustered column chart shows a separate column for each salesperson's total sales per month, but it doesn't depict the total sales for everyone.

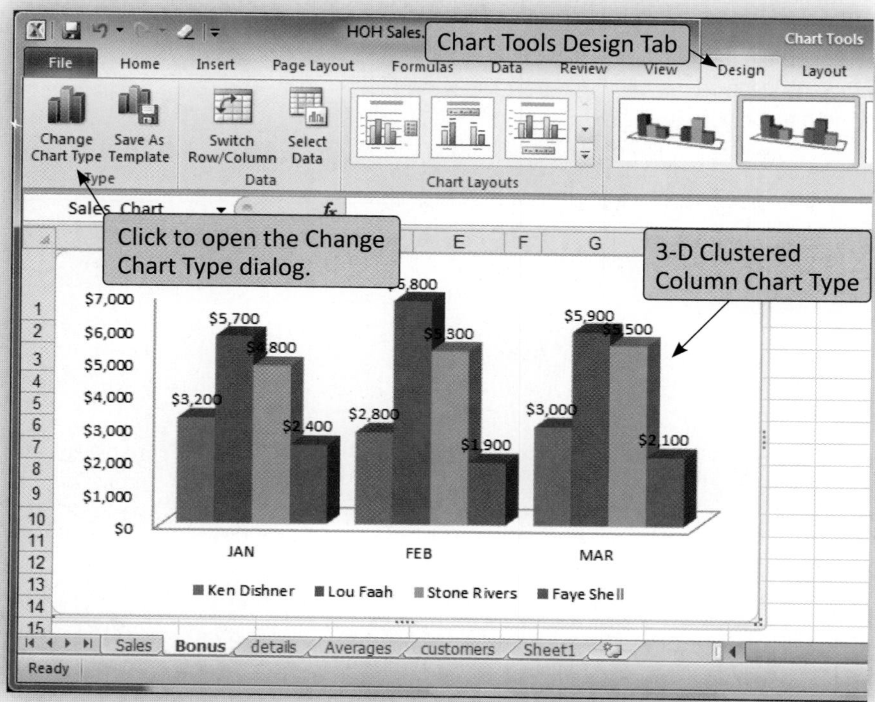

FIGURE EX 4.14

By changing the chart type to a stacked cylinder, you can compare each person's contribution to the total sales. Now, each column represents the total sales for the month, and individual sales for each person are represented by a piece of that column.

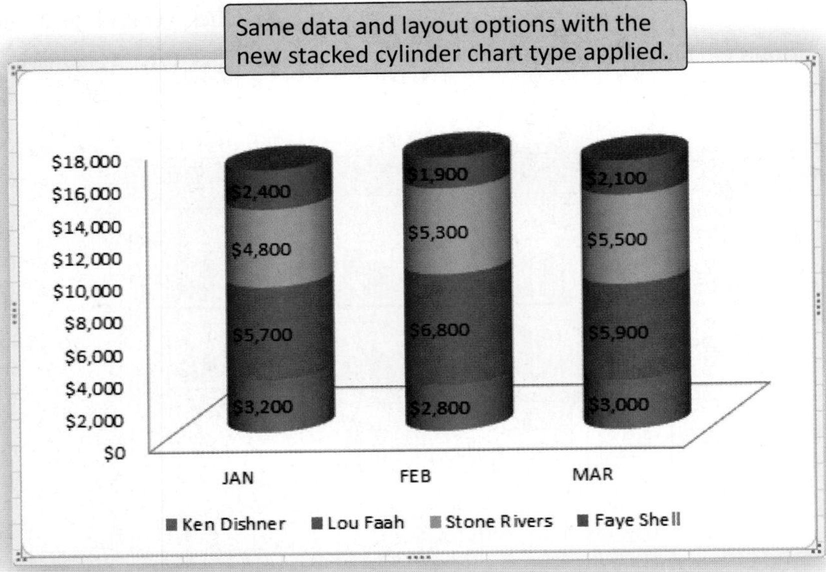

FIGURE EX 4.15

tips & tricks

If you typically use one type of chart, you can set that chart type as the default. In the *Change Chart Type* dialog box, select the chart type you want to set as the default. Next, click the **Set as Default Chart** button. Now when you create a new chart through the *Insert Chart* dialog, that chart type will automatically be selected and you won't need to search through the different chart types to find the one you want to use.

try this

To change the chart type, you can also right-click in the Chart Area of the chart and select **Change Chart Type . . .**

4.7 Moving a Chart

When you first create a chart, Excel places the chart in the middle of the worksheet. If your chart is large or complex, you may want the chart to appear on its own worksheet.

To move a chart to a new sheet:

1. If necessary, select the chart. If you just created the chart, it will still be selected.
2. From the *Chart Tools Design* contextual tab, click the **Move Chart** button from the *Location* group.
3. The *Move Chart* dialog opens.
4. In the *Move Chart* dialog box, click the **New sheet** radio button to move the chart to its own worksheet; or
5. Click the **Object in** radio button, and then select the name of the sheet you want to move the chart to from the drop-down list.
6. Click **OK.**

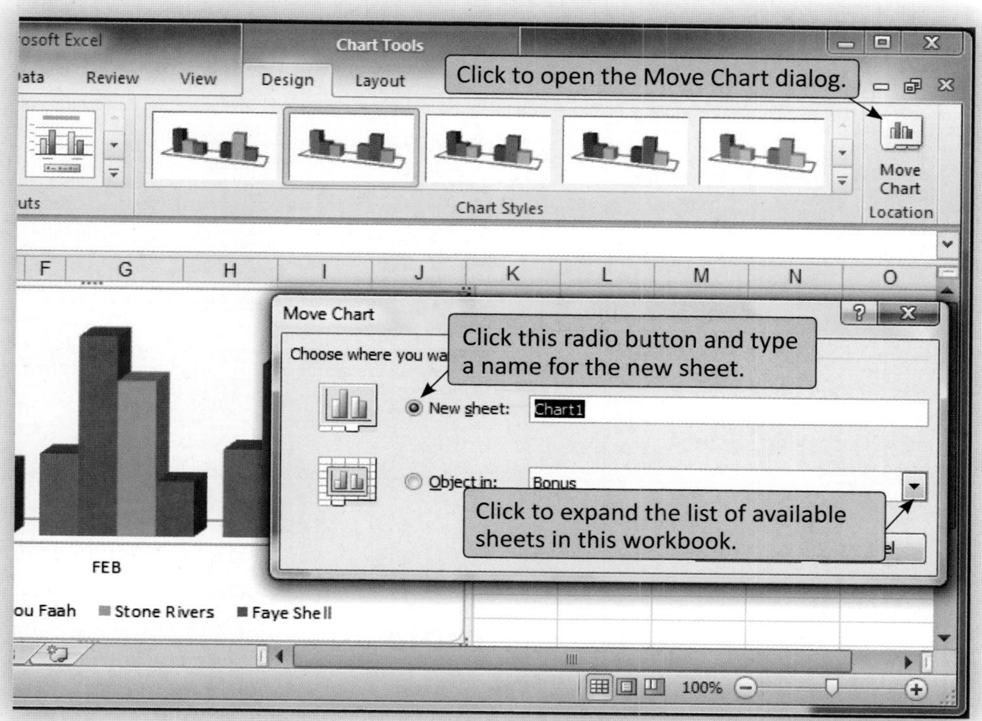

FIGURE EX 4.16

tips & tricks

If you move the chart to a new sheet, Excel automatically names the sheet **Chart1** (or Chart2, Chart3, etc., if you have multiple chart sheets in your workbook). If you want to use a different name for the new sheet, type the sheet name in the text box to the right of the *New sheet* radio button.

try this

Right-click in the Chart Area and select **Move Chart . . .** from the shortcut menu to open the *Move Chart* dialog.

tell me more

You can move a chart to a new position on the sheet by selecting it and then dragging it anywhere on the worksheet. To move a chart by dragging:

1. Click in the Chart Area of the chart you want to move. (Be careful not to click in the plot area, or you will move the chart plot area instead of the entire chart.) Your mouse cursor will change to the move cursor.
2. With your left mouse button depressed, drag the chart to the new location on the worksheet, and then release the mouse button to "drop" the chart at the new location.

4.8 Converting Data into Tables

In Excel, you can define a series of adjacent cells as a **table**. When you define data as a table, Excel provides a robust tool set for formatting and analyzing the data. In the table, the header row automatically includes filtering and sorting. When you add new data to the right of the table, Excel automatically includes the column in the table.

To define data as a table:

1. Select the data for your table.
2. On the *Home* tab, in the *Styles* group, click the **Format as Table** button to display the *Table Styles* gallery.
3. Click the style you want to use for your table.
4. Excel will automatically populate the *Format as Table* dialog with the selected data range.
5. Be sure to check the **My table has headers** check box if appropriate.
6. Click **OK** to create the table.

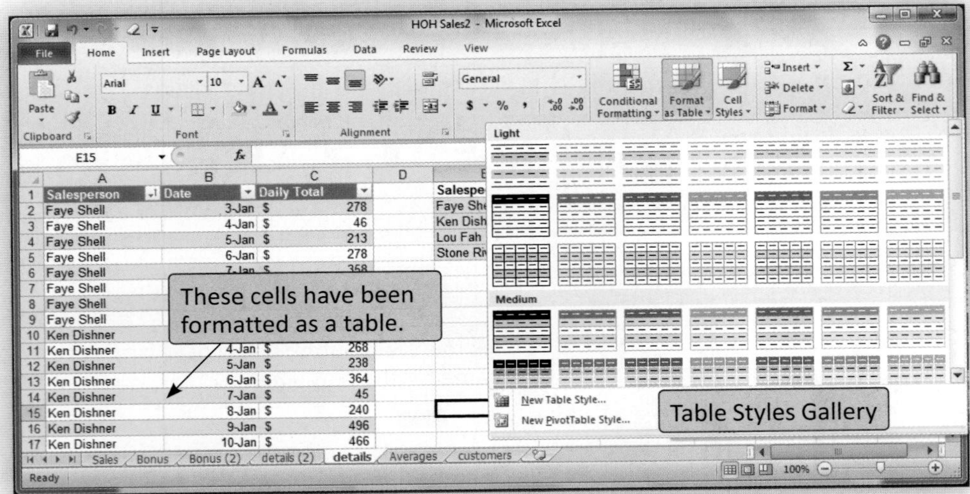

FIGURE EX 4.17

tips & tricks

You cannot create a table in a shared workbook. If your workbook contains a table, you will need to convert the table to a named range before sharing the workbook.

try this

To insert a table without specifying the table formatting:

1. Select the data for your table.
2. Click the **Insert** tab.
3. Click the **Table** button.
4. Excel will automatically populate the *Insert Table* dialog with the selected data range.
5. Be sure to check the **My table has headers** check box if appropriate.
6. Click **OK** to create the table. Excel will format the table with the most recent table style used.

tell me more

One of the most useful features of tables is the ability to reference table column names in formulas. When you enter a formula in a table, you can reference column names by enclosing the column header text in brackets: **[column name here]**. For example, to calculate the value of the **Total Spent** column divided by the **Visits** column, you would enter the formula =**[Total Spent]/[Visits]**.

To enter a formula referencing column names:

1. Click the first cell in the table column where you want to use a formula.
2. Begin typing the formula. When you are at the point in the formula where you want to reference a column name, type a [character. Excel automatically presents a list of available column names.
3. Double-click the column you want to add to the formula.
4. When you are finished entering the formula, press Enter. Excel automatically copies the formula to the remaining cells in the table column.

4.9 Adding Total Rows to Tables

If you have data formatted as a table, you can add a **Total row** to quickly calculate an aggregate function such as the sum or average of all the values in the column.

To add a Total row to a table:

1. On the *Table Tools Design* tab, in the *Table Style Options* group, click the **Total Row** check box.
2. In the Total row at the bottom of the table, click the column where you want to add a total.
3. Click the arrow, and select the function you want to use.

   Average—calculates the average value in the column.

   Count—counts the number of cells with data (text or number) in the column.

   Count Numbers—counts the number of cells containing numbers in the column.

   Max—returns the largest numerical value in the column.

   Min—returns the smallest numerical value in the column.

   Sum—calculates the total of all the values in the column.

   StdDev—calculates the statistical standard deviation.

   Var—calculates the statistical variance.

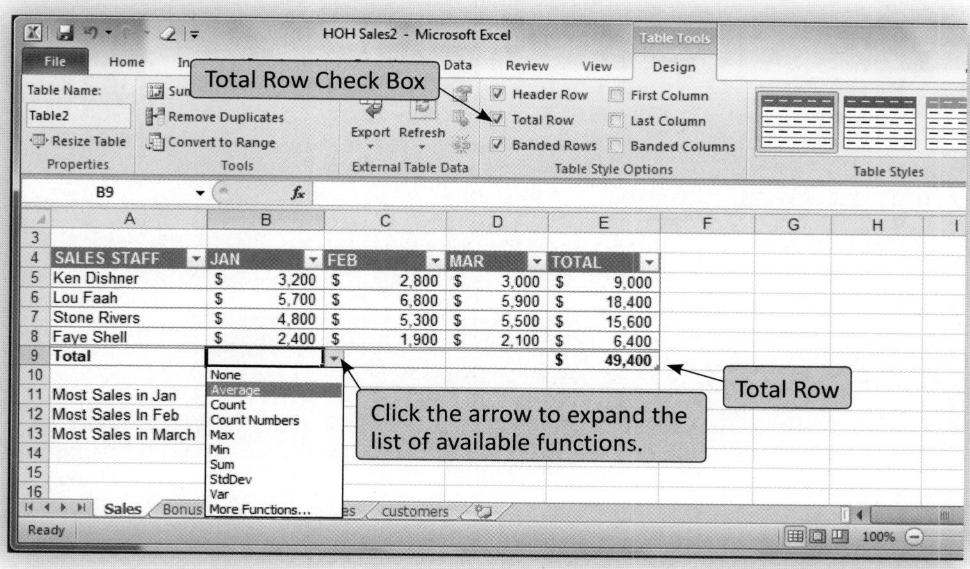

FIGURE EX 4.18

tips & tricks

The **Count** option can be useful when filtering records in a table. Count tells you how many records are included in the filtered table. The Count option from the Total row actually uses the COUNTA function.

tell me more

When you enable the Total row, the first cell in the Total row automatically displays the word "Total" and the last cell in the Total row automatically calculates the sum of the values in that column (if the column contains numbers).

try this

To add the Total row to the table, right-click any cell in the table, point to **Table,** and click **Total Row.**

4.10 Sorting Data

Sorting rearranges the rows in your worksheet by the data in a column or columns. You can sort alphabetically, by date, or by values.

To sort the data in your worksheet:

1. Click any cell in the column you want to sort.
2. On the *Home* tab, in the *Editing* group, click the **Sort & Filter** button.
3. Click the sorting option you want. The sorting options change depending on the type of data in the column you are sorting by.

› If the numbers in the column are formatted as dates, Excel detects this and offers sorting options **Sort Oldest to Newest** and **Sort Newest to Oldest.**

› If the column contains text, the sort options are **Sort A to Z** and **Sort Z to A.**

› If the column contains numbers, the sort options are **Sort Smallest to Largest** and **Sort Largest to Smallest.**

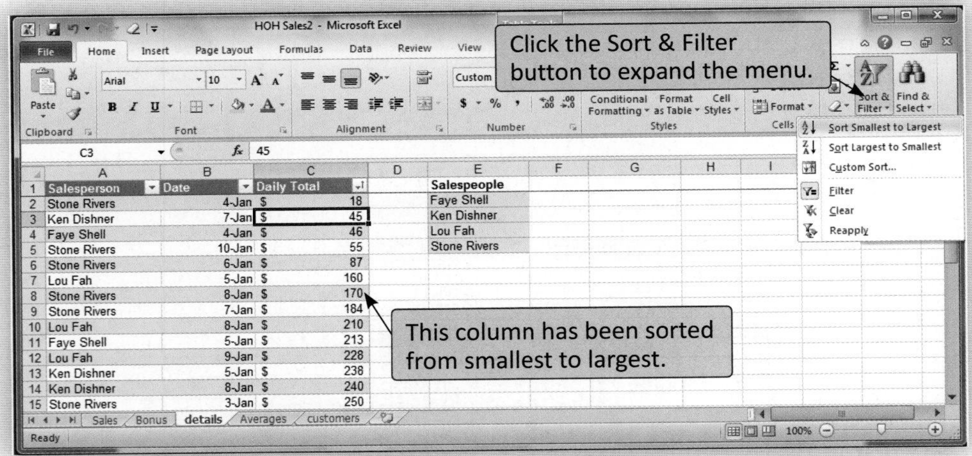

FIGURE EX 4.19

tell me **more**

With recent versions of Excel, the sorting and filtering options have been expanded to work with Excel's data visualization tools. If you have any of Excel's conditional formatting or cell styles applied to data in a table, you can sort and filter by color.

To sort data by color:

1. Click the arrow at the top of the column you want to sort.
2. Point to **Sort by Color** to expand the menu.
3. Click the color or icon you want to appear at the top of the column.

If you want to organize the column so that a certain cell color or cell icon appears at the top and another appears at the bottom, click the **Custom Sort . . .** option at the bottom of the *Sort by Color* menu. In the *Sort* dialog, you can add sorting levels. For Cell Color or Cell Icon, the *Order* options are **On Top** or **On Bottom.**

try **this**

If your columns are formatted as a table, you can click the arrow at the top of the column you want to sort by and then click the sort option you want.

You can also right-click any cell in the column you want to sort by. Point to **Sort,** and select the sorting option you want.

The sorting tools are also available from the *Sort & Filter* group on the *Data* tab.

› The [A→Z] button sorts alphabetically from A to Z, or by date from oldest to newest, or by value from smallest to largest.

› The [Z→A] button sorts alphabetically from Z to A, or by date from newest to oldest, or by value from largest to smallest.

4.11 Using AutoFilter

If your worksheet has many rows of data, you may want to filter the data to show only rows that meet criteria you specify. If your columns are not formatted as a table, you must first enable AutoFilter:

1. On the *Home* tab, in the *Editing* group, click the **Sort & Filter** button.
2. Click **Filter** to enable AutoFilter.

If your columns are formatted as a table, AutoFilter is enabled automatically. To filter data using AutoFilter:

1. Click the arrow at the top of the column that contains the data you want to filter for.
2. At first, all of the filter options are checked. Click the **(Select All)** check box to remove all of the check marks.
3. Click the check box or check boxes in front of the values you want to filter by.
4. Click **OK.** Excel displays only the rows that include the values you specified.

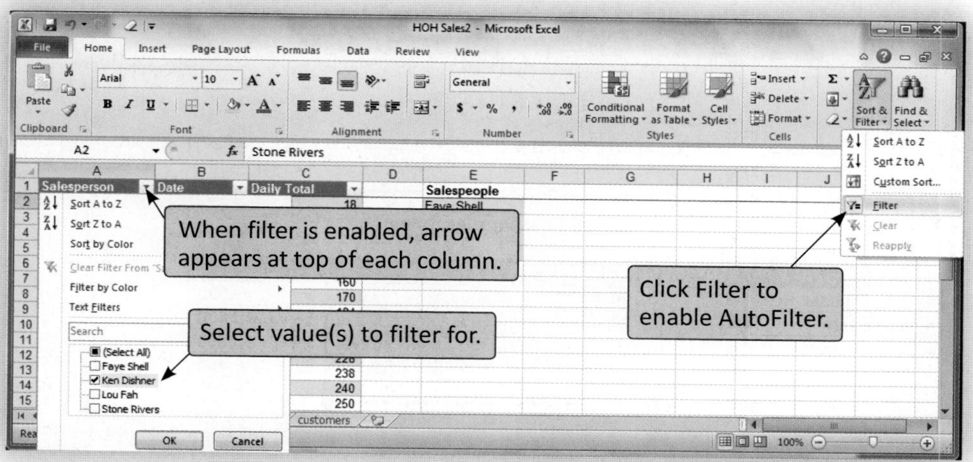
When filter is enabled, arrow appears at top of each column.
Select value(s) to filter for.
Click Filter to enable AutoFilter.

FIGURE EX 4.20

To clear the filter:

1. Click the arrow at the top of the column that you filtered by. In a table, when filtering is enabled, the column header includes a filter icon.
2. Click the **Clear Filter** option from the menu.

tips & tricks

Besides filtering by matching exact values, you can filter for values that meet broader criteria. Different columns with different data types will have different filtering criteria options available. For example, if the column contains dates, the AutoFilter menu includes a **Date Filters** submenu.

If you have applied conditional formatting to your data, you can also filter by cell color or cell icon.

try this

To enable filtering:

1. Click the *Data* tab.
2. In the *Sort & Filter* group, click the **Filter** button.

To clear the filter, you can:

- On the *Home* tab, in the *Sorting & Filtering* group, click the **Sort & Filter** button, and then click the **Clear Filter** button.
- Click the **Data** tab. In the *Sort & Filter* group, click the **Clear** button.

4.12 Working with Sparklines

Sparklines are a new type of chart available in Excel 2010. Sparklines represent each data series as an individual graphic within a single cell. As you update the underlying data series, the Sparklines update immediately.

To add Sparklines to your worksheet:

1. Select the data range with the data points for the Sparklines.
2. On the *Insert* tab, in the *Sparklines* group, click the button for the type of Sparkline you want to insert: **Line, Column,** or **Win/Loss.**

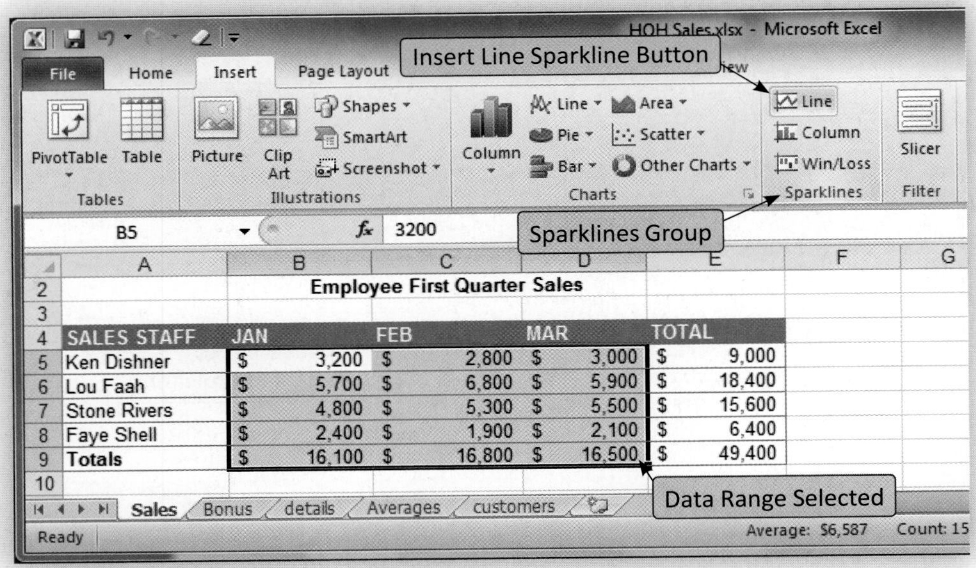

FIGURE EX 4.21

3. The *Create Sparklines* dialog opens with the selected range added to the *Data Range:* box.
4. In the *Location Range:* box, enter the cell range where you want the Sparklines to appear. If the location range is to the left or right of the data range, it should include the same number of rows as the data range. If the location range is above or below the data range, it should have the same number of columns as the data range.

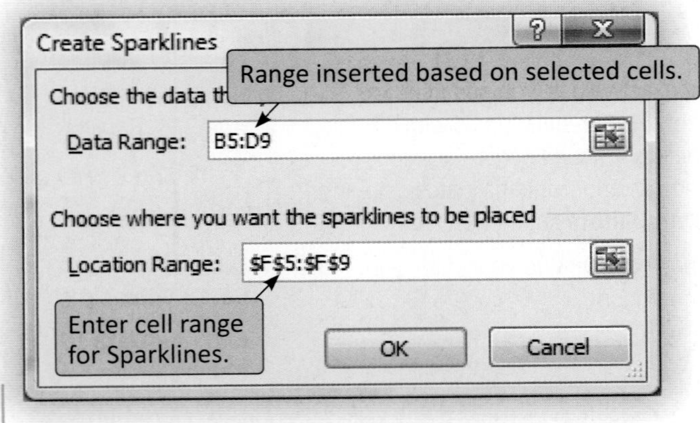

FIGURE EX 4.22

5. Click **OK** to insert the Sparklines.

In this example, the Sparklines show the trend for each person's sales over the selected three-month period.

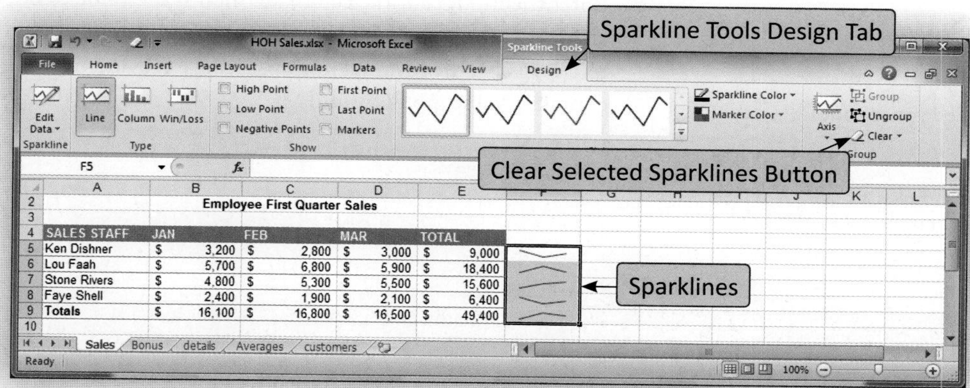

FIGURE EX 4.23

To remove Sparklines, you must select the cells containing the Sparklines, and then on the *Sparkline Tools Design* tab, in the *Group* group, click the **Clear** button.

tips & tricks

Sparklines are not actually chart objects—they are charts in the background of the cells. You can add text and other data to the cells that contain Sparklines. You can also extend the Sparklines over multiple cells using the **Merge & Center** commands.

tell me **more**

When cells containing Sparklines are selected, the *Sparkline Tools Design* contextual tab becomes active. From this tab you can customize the look of the Sparklines including emphasizing high or low points, changing the type of Sparkline used, and changing colors.

4.13 Analyzing Data with Goal Seek

Excel's **Goal Seek** function lets you enter a desired value (outcome) for a formula and specify an input cell that can be modified in order to reach that goal. Goal Seek changes the value of the input cell incrementally until the target outcome is reached.

To conduct a what-if analysis using Goal Seek:

1. Select the outcome cell. (This cell must contain a formula.)
2. On the *Data* tab, in the *Data Tools* group, click the **What-If Analysis** button, and then click **Goal Seek . . .**
3. Verify that the outcome cell is referenced in the *Set cell:* box.
4. Enter the outcome value you want in the *To value:* box.
5. Enter the input cell (the cell that contains the value to be changed) in the *By changing cell:* box. (This cell must be referenced in the formula in the outcome cell and must contain a value, not a formula.)
6. Click **OK.**

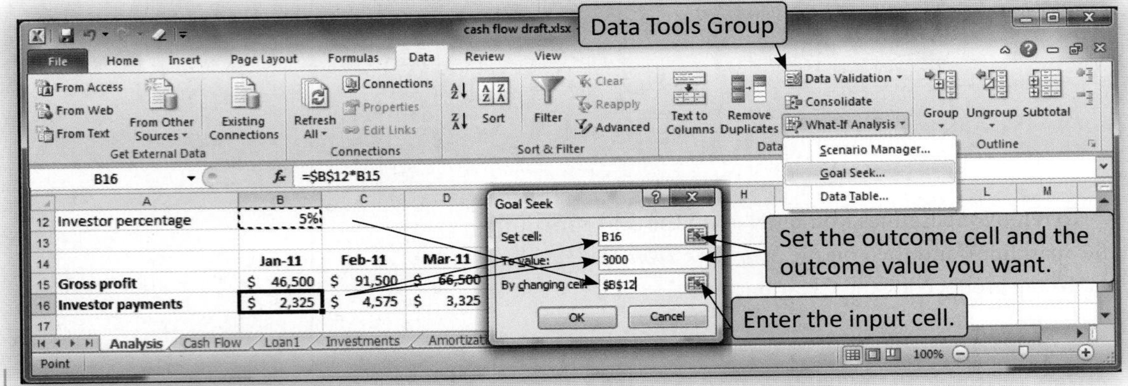

FIGURE EX 4.24

The *Goal Seek Status* box appears, letting you know if Goal Seek was able to find a solution. Click **OK** to accept the solution, or click **Cancel** to return the input cell to its original value.

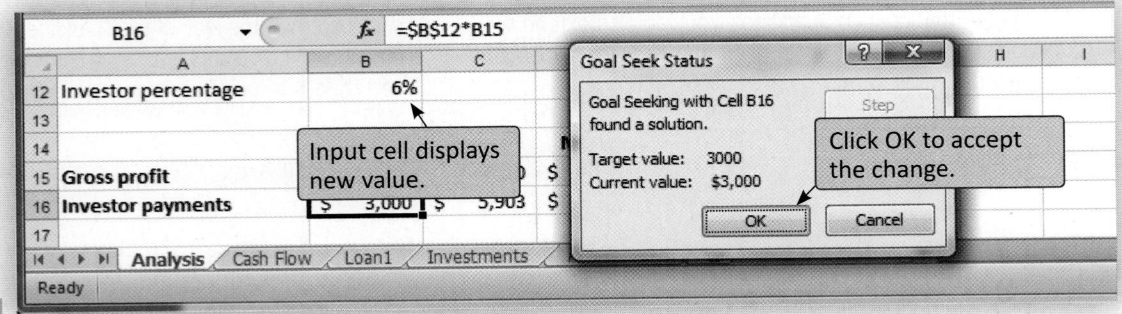

FIGURE EX 4.25

tips & tricks

Goal Seek works best in situations where there is only one variable, such as:

- Finding an optimal price point to reach a sales goal (when the number of units to sell is inflexible).
- Finding the required number of units to sell to reach a sales goal (when the price is inflexible).

If Goal Seek cannot find a solution, try using one of the other what-if scenario tools to analyze your data.

4.14 Analyzing Data with Data Tables

Data tables provide a quick what-if analysis of the effects of changing a single variable within a formula. The data table is organized with a series of values for the variable in either a column or a row. The formula referencing the original value is placed one cell above and to the right of the first value (for columns) or to the left and one row below (for rows).

To create a data table with a column input format:

1. In a column, type the series of values you want to substitute for the variable in your formula.
2. In the cell above and to the right of the first value, type the formula that references the cell you want to replace with the new values.
3. Select the data range, beginning with the empty cell above the first value you entered.
4. On the *Data* tab, in the *Data Tools* group, click the **What-If Analysis** button, and click **Data Table . . .**
5. In the *Data Table* dialog box, the input cell is the cell that contains the original value for which you want to substitute the values in the data table. If the data table values are listed in a column, enter the cell reference in the *Column input cell:* box. If the values are in a row, use the *Row input cell:* box.
6. Click **OK.**

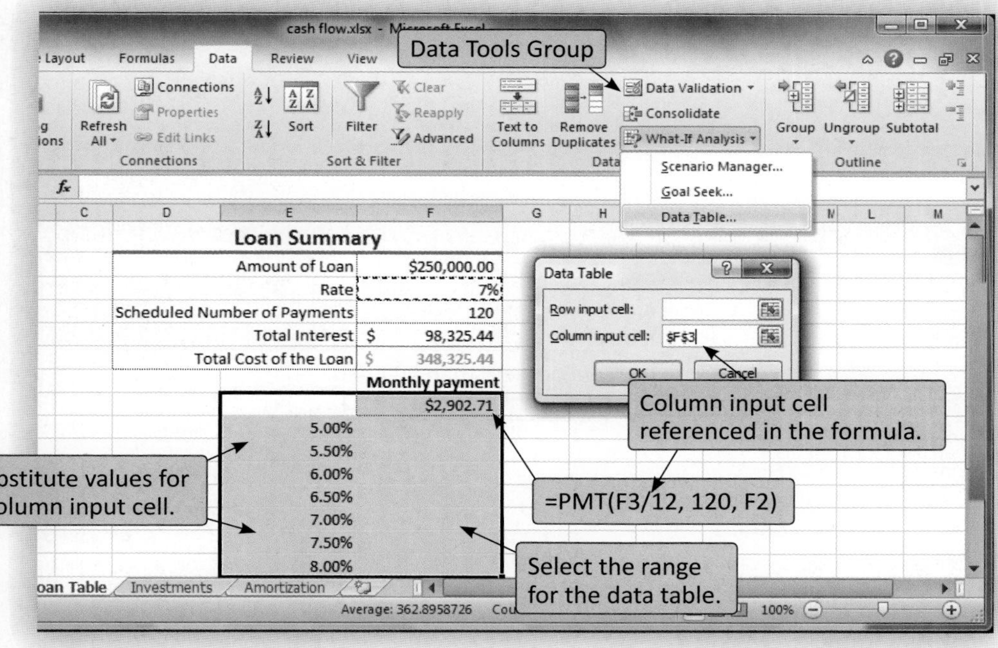

FIGURE EX 4.26

Excel completes the values in the table.

Loan Summary

Amount of Loan	$250,000.00
Rate	7%
Scheduled Number of Payments	120

Excel calculates the monthly payment by substituting the values in the data table.

	Monthly payment
	$2,902.71
5.00%	$ 2,651.64
5.50%	$ 2,713.16
6.00%	$ 2,775.51
6.50%	$ 2,838.70
7.00%	$ 2,902.71
7.50%	$ 2,967.54
8.00%	$ 3,033.19

FIGURE EX 4.27

4.15 Applying Conditional Formatting with Highlight Cells Rules

Conditional formatting with **Highlight Cells Rules** allows you to define formatting for cells that meet specific numerical or text criteria (e.g., greater than a specific value or containing a specific text string). Use this type of conditional formatting when you want to highlight cells based on criteria you define. Highlighting cells with duplicate values can be especially helpful when you are analyzing data.

To highlight cells with conditional formatting:

1. Select the data you want to apply conditional formatting to.
2. On the *Home* tab, in the *Styles* group, click the **Conditional Formatting** button.
3. From the menu, point to **Highlight Cells Rules** and click the option you want:

   Greater Than . . .

   Less Than . . .

   Between . . .

   Equal To . . .

   Text That Contains . . .

   A Date Occurring . . .

   Duplicate Values . . .

4. Each option opens a dialog where you can enter the condition to compare selected cells to and the formatting to apply when selected cells match the condition.
5. Click **OK** to apply the conditional formatting.

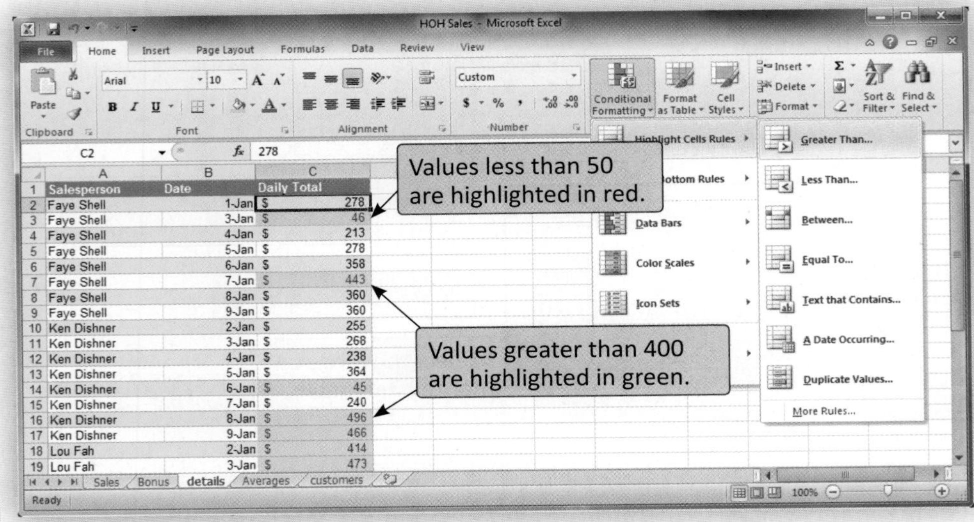

FIGURE EX 4.28

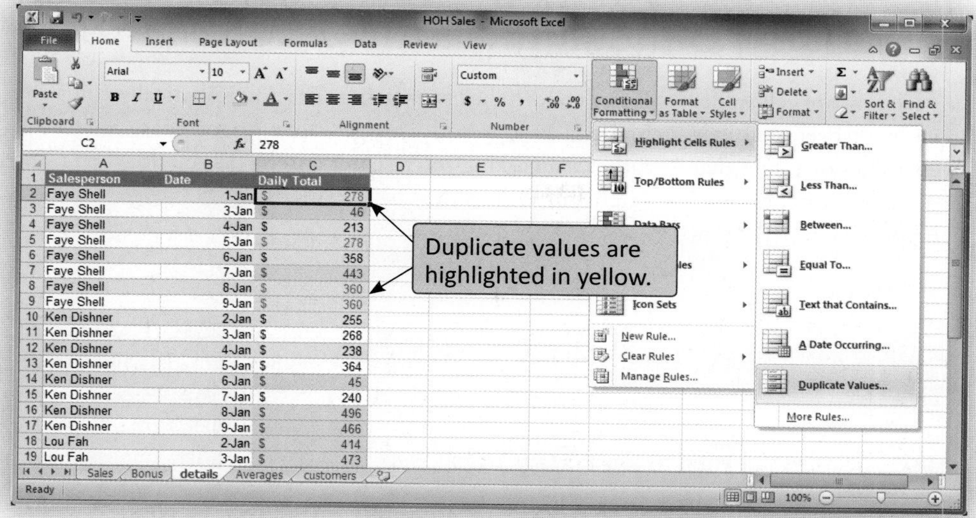

FIGURE EX 4.29

To remove conditional formatting:

1. Select the cells you want to remove the formatting from.
2. On the *Home* tab, in the *Styles* group, click the **Conditional Formatting** button.
3. Point to **Clear Rules,** and click the option you want from the menu:

   Clear Rules from Selected Cells

   Clear Rules from Entire Sheet

   Clear Rules from This Table (available if the selected cells are part of a table)

   Clear Rules from This PivotTable (available if the selected cells are part of a PivotTable)

tips & tricks

You should resist the temptation to overuse conditional formatting. Conditional formatting should be used to highlight important data or data trends, not colorize the entire worksheet.

4.16 Applying Conditional Formatting with Top/Bottom Rules

One way to analyze worksheet data is to compare cell values to other cell values. When analyzing a worksheet, you may want to highlight the highest or lowest values or values that are above or below the average. In these cases, use conditional formatting **Top/Bottom Rules**. When you use Top/Bottom Rules conditional formatting, Excel automatically finds the highest, lowest, and average values to compare values to, rather than asking you to enter criteria (as you do when using Highlight Cells Rules).

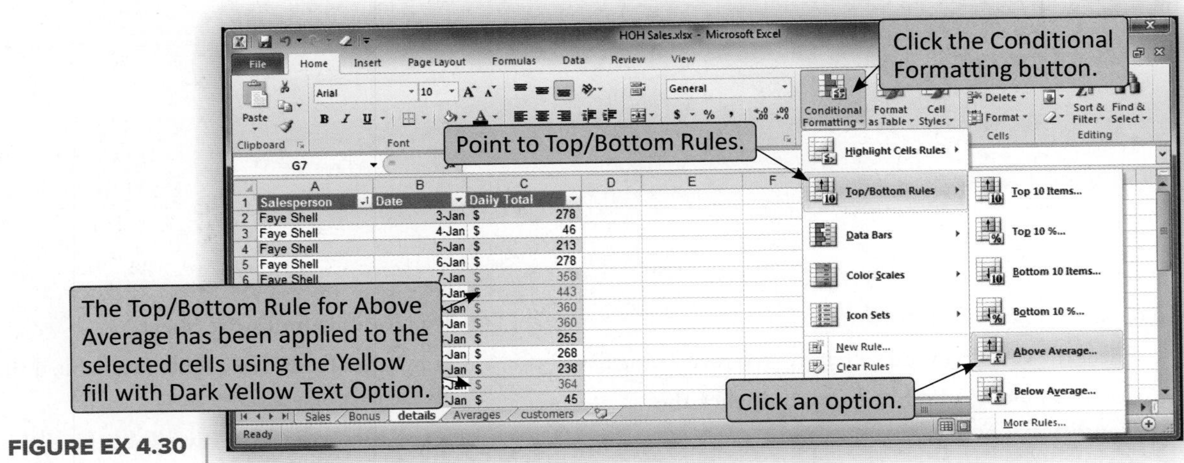

FIGURE EX 4.30

To highlight cells with conditional formatting Top/Bottom Rules:

1. Select the data you want to apply conditional formatting to.
2. On the *Home* tab, in the *Styles* group, click the **Conditional Formatting** button.
3. From the menu, point to **Top/Bottom Rules** and click the option you want:

   Top 10 Items . . .

   Top 10% . . .

   Bottom 10 Items . . .

   Bottom 10% . . .

   Above Average . . .

   Below Average . . .
4. Each option opens a dialog where you can modify the condition and select the formatting to apply when cells match the condition.
5. Click **OK** to apply the conditional formatting.

FIGURE EX 4.31

4.17 Applying Conditional Formatting with Data Bars, Color Scales, and Icon Sets

Conditional formatting can be used to visually represent relative values in your worksheet. Unlike Highlight Cells Rules and Top/Bottom Rules, there are no conditions to set. These types of conditional formatting apply formatting to all the selected cells.

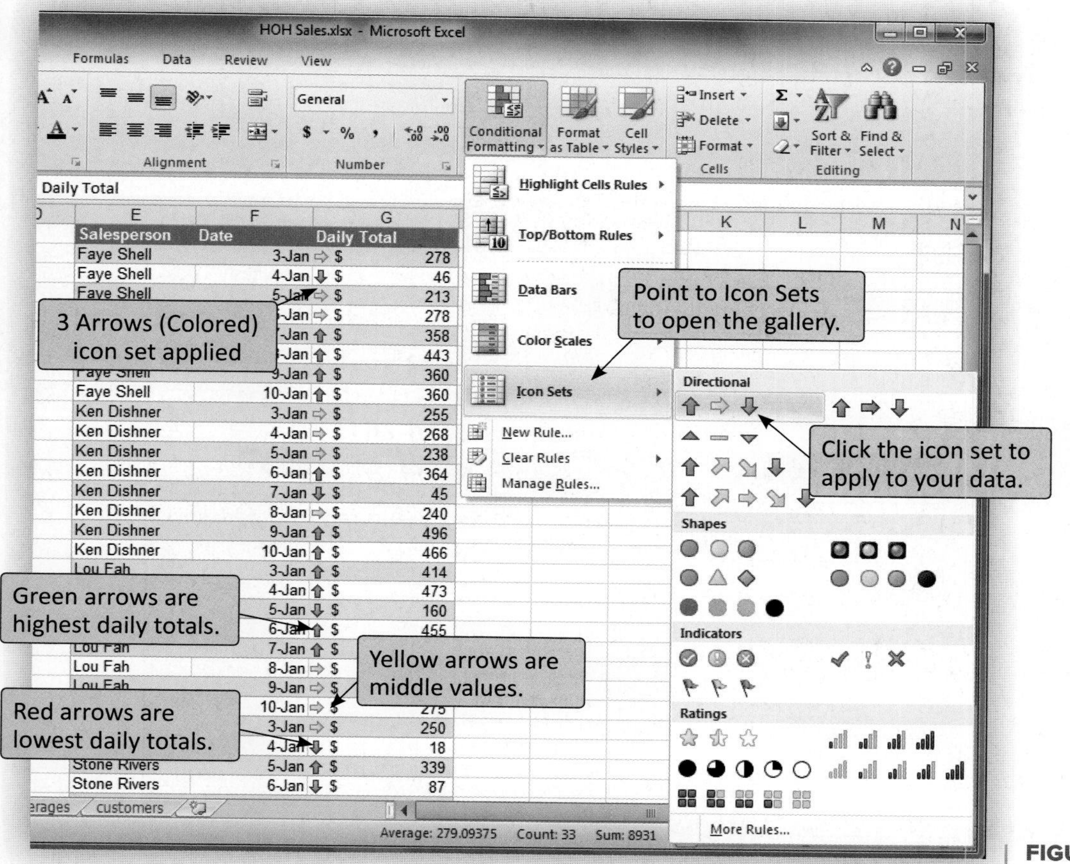

FIGURE EX 4.32

To highlight cells with conditional formatting:

1. Select the data you want to apply conditional formatting to.
2. On the *Home* tab, in the *Styles* group, click the **Conditional Formatting** button.
3. From the menu, point to one of the options, and then click the specific style of formatting you want.

Data Bars—Display a color bar (gradient or solid) representing the cell value in comparison to other values (cells with higher values have longer data bars).

Color Scales—Color the cells according to one of the color scales [e.g., red to green (bad/low to good/high) or blue to red (cold/low to hot/high)].

Icon Sets—Display a graphic in the cell representing the cell value in relation to other values.

tell me **more**

Through the **Conditional Formatting Rules Manager,** you can view all of your conditional formatting rules at one time and add, modify, or delete rules. Open the *Conditional Formatting Rules Manager* from the **Manage Rules . . .** option at the bottom of the *Conditional Formatting* menu.

4.18 Creating PivotTables

A **PivotTable** is a special report view that summarizes data and calculates the intersecting totals. PivotTables do not contain any data themselves—they summarize data from a range or a table in another part of your workbook. If the data underlying the PivotTable changes, you will need to manually refresh the PivotTable to display the updated data values.

To create a PivotTable:

1. Begin with any cell in a table selected or select the range you want to use in your PivotTable.
2. Click the **Insert** tab.
3. Click the **PivotTable** button in the *Tables* group.
4. The *Create PivotTable* dialog opens. Click **OK** to create a PivotTable in a new worksheet. (Notice the table or range you selected is entered in the *Select a table or range* box for you.)

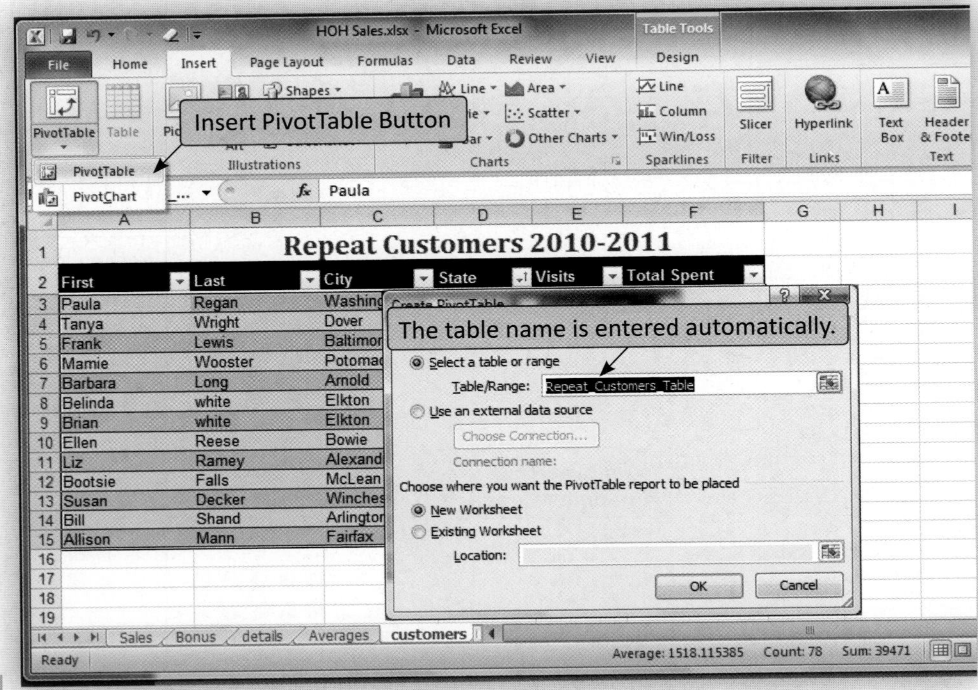

FIGURE EX 4.33

5. The empty PivotTable layout appears. The *PivotTable Field List* lists the column headings from your table or range.
6. Click the check box for each field you want included in the PivotTable. Excel will place fields with numeric data in the **Values** area and text fields in the **Row Labels** area. A sum of values for each row is calculated automatically.
7. If you add more than one row label, Excel will create subtotals, based on the order of the fields. For example, if you add a row label for State, and then a row label for Last name, the PivotTable will display subtotal rows for each customer's last name beneath each state.

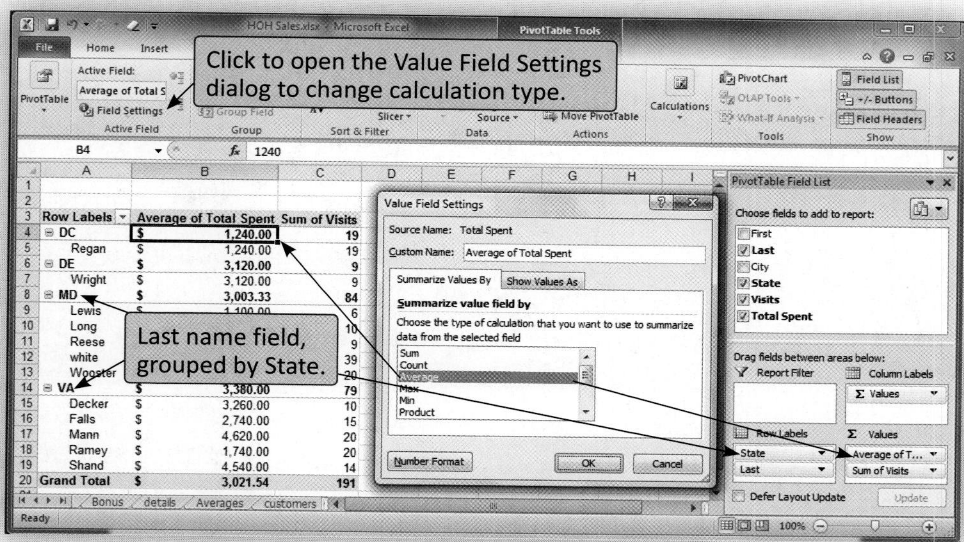

FIGURE EX 4.34

By default, PivotTables calculate totals using the SUM function. To change the calculation type:

1. Click anywhere in the field you want to change.
2. On the *PivotTable Tools Options* tab, in the *Active Field* group, click the **Field Settings** button.
3. The *Value Field Settings* dialog opens.
4. From the *Summarize Values By* tab, select the type of calculation you want.
5. When you select a new calculation type, the name in the *Custom Name:* box updates to reflect the new function. (For example, **Sum of Total Spent** changes to **Average of Total Spent** when you select the Average function.)
6. Click **OK.**

tips & tricks

You can click and drag fields in the *Row Labels* and *Values* boxes to reorder them.

try this

You can also create a PivotTable from a table by clicking the *Table Tools Design* tab. In the *Tools* group, click the **Summarize with PivotTable** button.

To open the *Value Field Settings* dialog, you can also click the arrow next to the field name in the *Values* box, and then select **Value Field Settings . . .**

4.19 Creating PivotCharts

A **PivotChart** is a graphic representation of a PivotTable. In a column chart, the Category fields are represented along the x (horizontal) axis while the data values are represented along the y (vertical) axis.

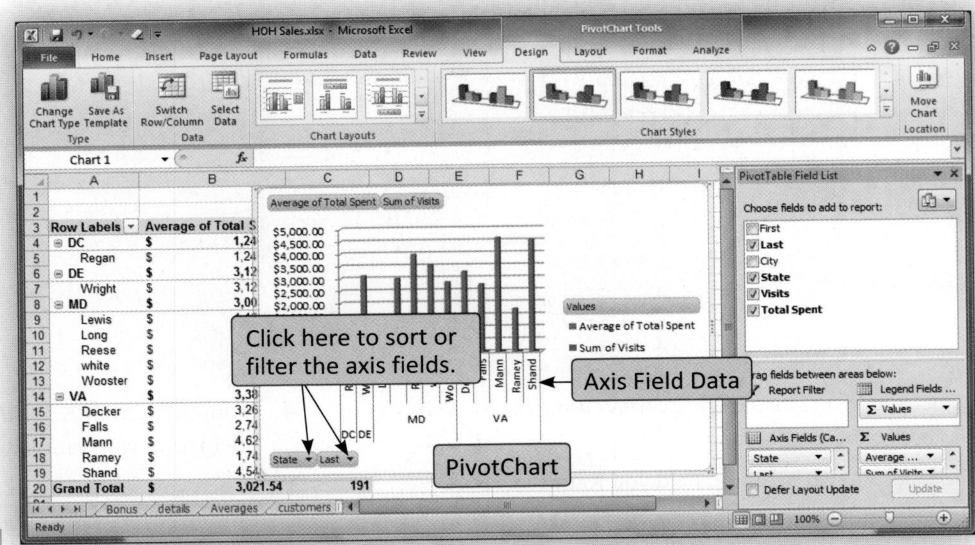

FIGURE EX 4.35

To create a PivotChart:

1. Select any cell in the PivotTable.
2. On the *PivotTable Tools Options* tab, in the *Tools* group, click the **PivotChart** button PivotChart.
3. Select a chart type from the *Insert Chart* dialog.
4. Click **OK.**
5. A new PivotChart is added to the worksheet.

PivotCharts include all the formatting options that regular charts do. You can apply built-in chart styles and layouts and modify chart elements such as the legend, data labels, and chart title.

To sort or filter the category data, click the button in the lower-left corner of the PivotChart with the name of the field you want to sort or filter. If your PivotTable used multiple row labels, you will see a button for each.

try **this**

You can also create a PivotChart without creating the PivotTable first.

1. Begin with any cell in a table selected or select the range you want to use in your PivotChart.
2. Click the **Insert** tab.
3. In the *Tables* group, click the **PivotTable** button arrow, and click **PivotChart.**
4. The *Create PivotTable with PivotChart* dialog opens. Click **OK** to create both the PivotTable and accompanying PivotChart in a new worksheet.
5. The empty PivotTable layout appears with an empty PivotChart next to it.
6. As you add fields to the PivotTable, the PivotChart builds automatically.

projects

Skill Review 4.1

Event Planning. In this project, you will be working with event planning data.

1. Open the provided file called: *Event.xlsx,* and save it as **`[your initials]EX_SkillReview_4-1`.**
2. Make the data on the *Table* worksheet into a table:
   a. Select all the data including the headings, being careful not to select any blank rows or columns.
   b. On the *Home* tab, in the *Styles* group, click the **Format as Table** button to display the *Table Styles* gallery.
   c. Pick the style you want to use for your table.
   d. Verify that the correct cells will be used. Check the **My table has headers** check box. Click **OK.**
   e. Add a *Total row* to the table:
      (1) On the *Table Tools Design* tab, in the *Table Style Options* group, click the **Total Row** check box.
      (2) In the Total row at the bottom of the table, notice the total count of guests attending.
      (3) In the Total row at the bottom of the table, click in the **Street** column, click the arrow, and select the **Count** function to count the invitations sent.
   f. Sort the data in last name alphabetical order:
      (1) Click anywhere in the **Last Name** column.
      (2) On the *Data* tab, in the *Sort & Filter* group, click the **A-Z** button.
   g. Change the sort order to sort the data alphabetically by city:
      (1) Click the drop down arrow at the top of the **City** column.
      (2) Click **Sort A-Z.**
   h. Use AutoFilter to filter data:
      (1) Click the little arrow in the **City** column header.
      (2) Click the **(Select All)** check box to remove all of the check marks.
      (3) Click the check box in front of **Rocklin** to filter for only guests from Rocklin.
      (4) Click **OK.** Excel displays only the rows for invitations sent to Rocklin.

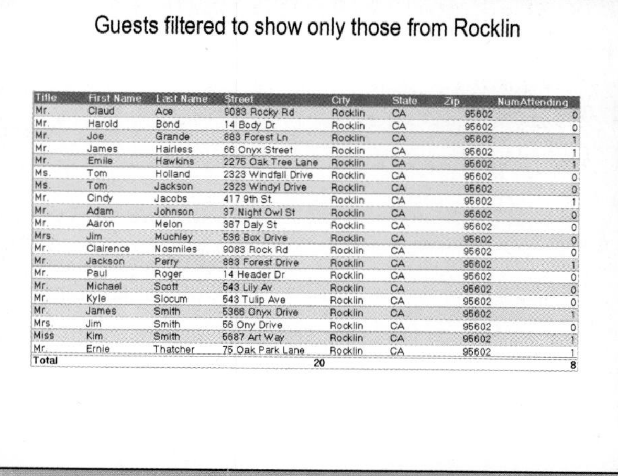

Guests filtered to show only those from Rocklin

Title	First Name	Last Name	Street	City	State	Zip	NumAttending
Mr.	Claud	Ace	9083 Rocky Rd	Rocklin	CA	95602	0
Mr.	Harold	Bond	14 Body Dr	Rocklin	CA	95602	0
Mr.	Joe	Grande	883 Forest Ln	Rocklin	CA	95602	1
Mr.	James	Hairless	66 Onyx Street	Rocklin	CA	95602	1
Mr.	Emile	Hawkins	2275 Oak Tree Lane	Rocklin	CA	95602	1
Ms.	Tom	Holland	2323 Windfall Drive	Rocklin	CA	95602	0
Ms.	Tom	Jackson	2323 Windyl Drive	Rocklin	CA	95602	0
Mr.	Cindy	Jacobs	417 9th St.	Rocklin	CA	95602	1
Mr.	Adam	Johnson	37 Night Owl St	Rocklin	CA	95602	0
Mr.	Aaron	Melon	387 Daly St	Rocklin	CA	95602	0
Mrs.	Jim	Muchley	536 Box Drive	Rocklin	CA	95602	0
Mr.	Clairence	Nosmiles	9083 Rock Rd	Rocklin	CA	95602	0
Mr.	Jackson	Perry	883 Forest Drive	Rocklin	CA	95602	1
Mr.	Paul	Roger	14 Header Dr	Rocklin	CA	95602	0
Mr.	Michael	Scott	543 Lily Av	Rocklin	CA	95602	0
Mr.	Kyle	Slocum	543 Tulip Ave	Rocklin	CA	95602	0
Mr.	James	Smith	5366 Onyx Drive	Rocklin	CA	95602	1
Mrs.	Jim	Smith	56 Ony Drive	Rocklin	CA	95602	0
Miss	Kim	Smith	5687 Art Way	Rocklin	CA	95602	1
Mr.	Ernie	Thatcher	75 Oak Park Lane	Rocklin	CA	95602	1
Total			20				8

FIGURE EX 4.36

   i. Print the Rocklin guests data, fitting neatly on one piece of paper.
   j. Clear the filter to restore all the hidden data:
      (1) Click the arrow at the top of the **City** column; when filtering is enabled, the column header includes a filter icon.
      (2) Click the **Clear Filter** option from the menu.
3. Format data with *Conditional Formatting:*
   a. Highlight all the invitations sent to females:
      (1) Select all the cells with the *Title* data. On the *Home* tab, in the Styles *group*, click the **Conditional Formatting** button. Do not select the header or total row of empty cells.
      (2) From the menu, point to **Highlight Cells Rules,** and click **More Rules . . .**

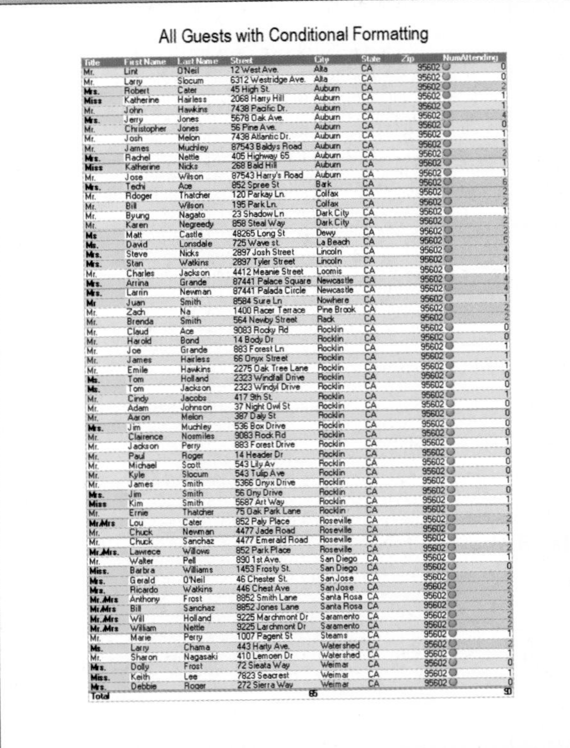

All Guests with Conditional Formatting

Title	First Name	Last Name	Street	City	State	Zip	NumAttending
Mr.	Link	O'Neil	12 West Ave.	Alta	CA	95602	0
Mr.	Larry	Slocum	6312 Westridge Ave.	Alta	CA	95602	0
Mrs.	Robert	Cater	45 High St.	Auburn	CA	95602	2
Miss	Katherine	Hairless	2068 Harry Hill	Auburn	CA	95602	1
Mr.	John	Hawkins	7438 Pacific Dr.	Auburn	CA	95602	1
Mrs.	Jerry	Jones	5678 Oak Ave.	Auburn	CA	95602	4
Mr.	Christopher	Jones	56 Pine Ave.	Auburn	CA	95602	0
Mr.	Josh	Melon	7438 Atlantic Dr.	Auburn	CA	95602	1
Mr.	James	Muchley	87543 Baldys Road	Auburn	CA	95602	1
Mrs.	Rachel	Nettle	405 Highway 65	Auburn	CA	95602	2
Miss	Katherine	Nicks	268 Bald Hill	Auburn	CA	95602	1
Mr.	Jose	Wilson	87543 Harry's Road	Auburn	CA	95602	1
Mrs.	Techi	Ace	852 Spree St	Bark	CA	95602	6
Mr.	Rdoger	Thatcher	120 Parkay Ln.	Colfax	CA	95602	2
Mr.	Bill	Wilson	195 Park Ln.	Colfax	CA	95602	2
Mr.	Byung	Nagato	23 Shadow Ln	Dark City	CA	95602	1
Mr.	Karen	Negreedy	858 Steal Way	Dark City	CA	95602	2
Ms	Matt	Castle	48265 Long St	Dewy	CA	95602	2
Ms.	David	Lonsdale	725 Wave st.	La Beach	CA	95602	5
Mrs.	Steve	Nicks	2897 Josh Street	Lincoln	CA	95602	4
Mrs.	Stan	Watkins	2897 Tyler Street	Lincoln	CA	95602	4
Mr.	Charles	Jackson	4412 Meanie Street	Loomis	CA	95602	1
Mrs.	Arrina	Grande	87441 Palace Square	Newcastle	CA	95602	4
Mrs.	Larrin	Newman	87441 Palada Circle	Newcastle	CA	95602	4
Mr	Juan	Smith	8584 Sure Ln	Nowhere	CA	95602	1
Mr.	Zach	Na	1400 Racer Terrace	Pine Brook	CA	95602	2
Mr.	Brenda	Smith	564 Newby Street	Rack	CA	95602	2
Mr.	Claud	Ace	9083 Rocky Rd	Rocklin	CA	95602	0
Mr.	Harold	Bond	14 Body Dr	Rocklin	CA	95602	0
Mr.	Joe	Grande	883 Forest Ln	Rocklin	CA	95602	1
Mr.	James	Hairless	66 Onyx Street	Rocklin	CA	95602	1
Mr.	Emile	Hawkins	2275 Oak Tree Lane	Rocklin	CA	95602	1
Ms.	Tom	Holland	2323 Windfall Drive	Rocklin	CA	95602	0
Ms.	Tom	Jackson	2323 Windyl Drive	Rocklin	CA	95602	0
Mr.	Cindy	Jacobs	417 9th St.	Rocklin	CA	95602	1
Mr.	Adam	Johnson	37 Night Owl St	Rocklin	CA	95602	0
Mr.	Aaron	Melon	387 Daly St	Rocklin	CA	95602	0
Mrs.	Jim	Muchley	536 Box Drive	Rocklin	CA	95602	0
Mr.	Clairence	Nosmiles	9083 Rock Rd	Rocklin	CA	95602	0
Mr.	Jackson	Perry	883 Forest Drive	Rocklin	CA	95602	1
Mr.	Paul	Roger	14 Header Dr	Rocklin	CA	95602	0
Mr.	Michael	Scott	543 Lily Av	Rocklin	CA	95602	0
Mr.	Kyle	Slocum	543 Tulip Ave	Rocklin	CA	95602	0
Mr.	James	Smith	5366 Onyx Drive	Rocklin	CA	95602	1
Mrs.	Jim	Smith	56 Ony Drive	Rocklin	CA	95602	0
Miss	Kim	Smith	5687 Art Way	Rocklin	CA	95602	1
Mr.	Ernie	Thatcher	75 Oak Park Lane	Rocklin	CA	95602	1
Mr/Mrs	Lou	Cater	852 Paly Place	Roseville	CA	95602	2
Mr.	Chuck	Newman	4477 Jade Road	Roseville	CA	95602	1
Mr.	Chuck	Sanchaz	4477 Emerald Road	Roseville	CA	95602	1
Mr./Mrs.	Lawrece	Willows	852 Park Place	Roseville	CA	95602	2
Mr.	Walter	Pell	890 1st Ave.	San Diego	CA	95602	1
Miss.	Barbra	Williams	1453 Frosty St.	San Diego	CA	95602	0
Mrs.	Gerald	O'Neil	46 Chester St.	San Jose	CA	95602	2
Mrs.	Ricardo	Watkins	446 Chest Ave	San Jose	CA	95602	2
Mr./Mrs	Anthony	Frost	8852 Smith Lane	Santa Rosa	CA	95602	3
Mr/Mrs	Bill	Sanchaz	8852 Jones Lane	Santa Rosa	CA	95602	3
Mr./Mrs	Will	Holland	9225 Marchmont Dr	Saramento	CA	95602	2
Mr./Mrs	William	Nettle	9225 Larchmont Dr	Saramento	CA	95602	2
Mr.	Marie	Perry	1007 Pagent St	Steams	CA	95602	1
Ms.	Larry	Chama	443 Harty Ave.	Watershed	CA	95602	2
Mr.	Sharon	Nagasaki	410 Lemoen Dr	Watershed	CA	95602	1
Mrs.	Dolly	Frost	72 Sieata Way	Weimar	CA	95602	0
Miss.	Keith	Lee	7823 Seacrest	Weimar	CA	95602	1
Mrs.	Debbie	Roger	272 Sierra Way	Weimar	CA	95602	0
Total				65			90

FIGURE EX 4.37

(3) Select the **Format only cells that contain** option.

(4) Click the little drop-down arrow to change **greater than** to **not equal to.**

(5) In the third text box, enter: `Mr`.

(6) Click the **Format** button.

(7) On the *Font* tab, choose **Bold;** on the *Fill* tab, choose **yellow.** Click **OK,** and then click **OK.**

b. Highlight the RSVPs for the largest groups of guests using the *Top/Bottom Rules:*

(1) Select the cells with the *Number Attending* data.

(2) On the *Home* tab, in the *Styles* group, click the **Conditional Formatting** button.

(3) From the menu, point to **Top/Bottom Rules** and click **Top 10 Items . . .**

(4) In the dialog box, click **OK.**

c. Identify those not attending versus those attending using *Icon Sets:*

(1) With all the *Number Attending* cells still selected, click the **Conditional Formatting** button, point to **Icon Sets,** and click **More Rules . . .**

(2) In the dialog box, make sure **Format all cells based on their values** is selected.

(3) In the dialog box, make sure the *Format Style* is set to **Icon Sets** and the *Icons Style* is set to **3 Traffic Lights.**

(4) Set the green light to show when the invited guests are attending:

(a) In the first *TYPE* box choose **Number.**

(b) In the first *Value* box enter: 1

(c) In the second *TYPE* box choose **Number.**

(d) In the second *Value* box enter: 1

d. Print the conditionally formatted data, fitting neatly on one page.

4. Switch to work with the *Data Table* worksheet. Examine the worksheet, notice the formulas that have been entered.

a. Select cells **B19:C26** to use the party cost formula in C19 and the various number of guest values in B20:B26.

b. On the *Data* tab, in the *Data Tools* group, click the **What-If Analysis** button.

c. Choose **Data Table.**

d. In the *Column input cell:* box, enter `C1`. Click **OK.**

e. Notice the party costs have now been computed for the various numbers of guests.

5. Add charts.

a. Make a column chart to compare the cost of various size parties:

(1) Select cells **B19:C26.**

(2) Click the **Insert** tab; in the *Charts* group, click the **Scatter** type drop down arrow.

(3) Choose the second specific scatter chart option from the gallery: **Scatter with smooth lines and markers.**

(4) Drag to move the chart object so that the worksheet data are not covered. (Be careful not to click in the plot area or you will move the chart plot area instead of the entire chart.)

b. Change the *Chart Type* to *Column:*

(1) Click to select the chart. On the *Chart Tools Design* tab, in the *Type* group, click the **Change Chart Type** button.

(2) In the *Change Chart Type* dialog box, scroll up to choose the first **Column** chart type. Click **OK.**

c. Change the *Chart Design* using *Quick Layout:*

(1) On the *Chart Tools Design* tab, in the *Chart Layout* group, choose **layout 9.**

(2) Click the bottom axis title on the chart. Enter: `Number of Guests`

d. Color and shade the chart using *Quick Style:*

(1) Click the **Chart Tools Design** tab.

(2) In the *Chart Styles* group, click a style.

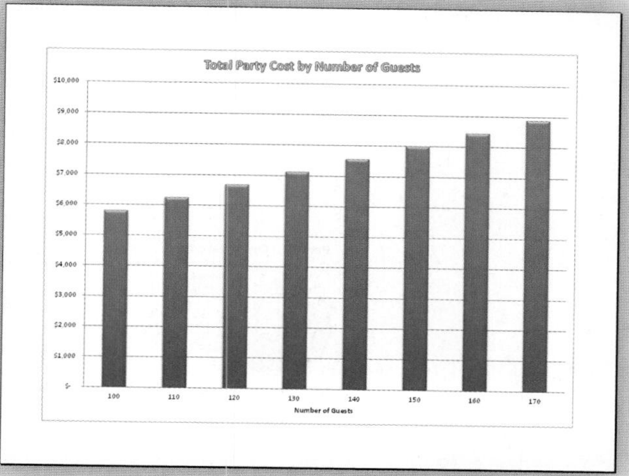

FIGURE EX 4.38

e. Use the *Chart Tools Layout* tab to change the chart layout.

(1) Select the chart; then click the **Chart Tools Layout** tab.

(2) In the *Labels* group, click the button for the **Legend** and choose **None.**

(3) Click the **Axis Title** button; choose **Primary Vertical Axis Title, None.**

f. Title text and the chart change the chart *Title* style:

(1) Click the chart title, click the first **WordArt Style** button on the *Chart Tools Format* tab.

(2) Click the chart title, click the first **WordArt Style** button on the *Chart Tools Format* tab.

g. Move the chart to its own sheet in the workbook.

(1) Select the chart. From the *Chart Tools Design* tab, in the *Location* group, click the **Move Chart** button.

(2) In the *Move Chart* dialog box, click the **New sheet** button and type in the new sheet name: `Chartsheet`. Click **OK.**

6. Use *Goal Seek* to determine the most you can afford for dinner per person, on a $6,000 budget for 100 guests:

a. On the *Data Table* sheet, select the outcome formula cell, **H19.**

b. On the *Data* tab, in the *Data Tools* group, click the **What-If Analysis** button and click **Goal Seek . . .**

c. Verify that the outcome cell **H19** is referenced in the *Set cell:* box.

d. Enter the outcome value of `6000` in the *To value:* box.

e. Enter the input cell `F4` in the *By changing cell:* box. Click **OK,** and then click **OK.**

f. Notice the per guest dinner price changed to $21.83. Highlight that cell **F4** with yellow.

g. Notice the total party costs changed to $6,000. Highlight cells **G18:H19** with yellow.

h. Change the worksheet tab to read: `Data Table & Goal Seek`

7. Make a *Pie Chart* breakdown of the per guest costs:

a. Select cells **G3:H11.**

b. On the *Insert* tab, in the *Charts* group, select **Pie;** then choose the first pie chart option.

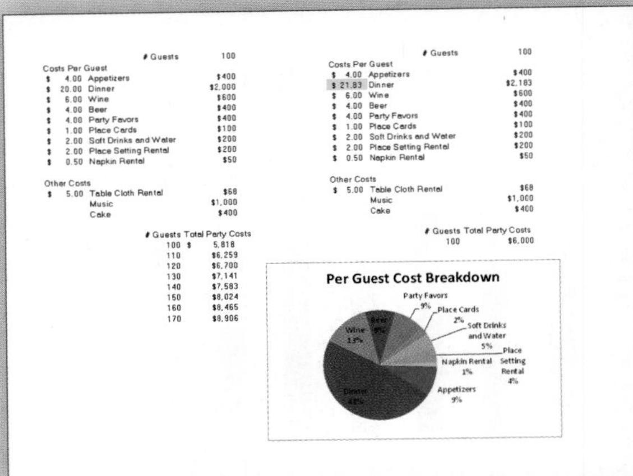

FIGURE EX 4.39

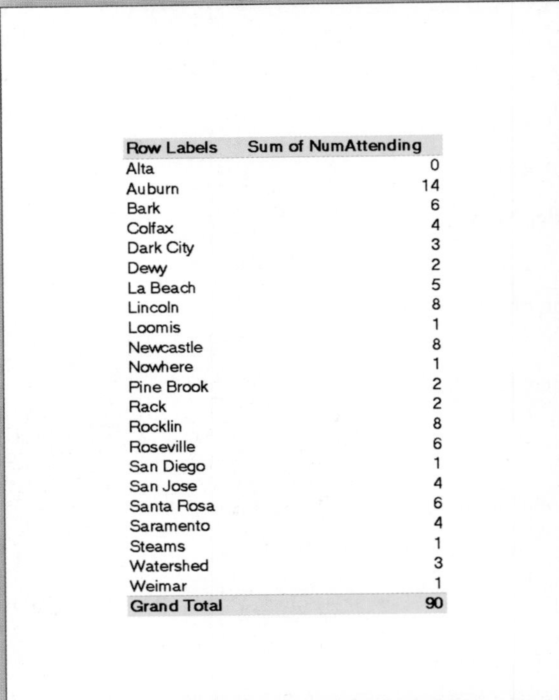

Row Labels	Sum of NumAttending
Alta	0
Auburn	14
Bark	6
Colfax	4
Dark City	3
Dewy	2
La Beach	5
Lincoln	8
Loomis	1
Newcastle	8
Nowhere	1
Pine Brook	2
Rack	2
Rocklin	8
Roseville	6
San Diego	1
San Jose	4
Santa Rosa	6
Saramento	4
Steams	1
Watershed	3
Weimar	1
Grand Total	90

FIGURE EX 4.40

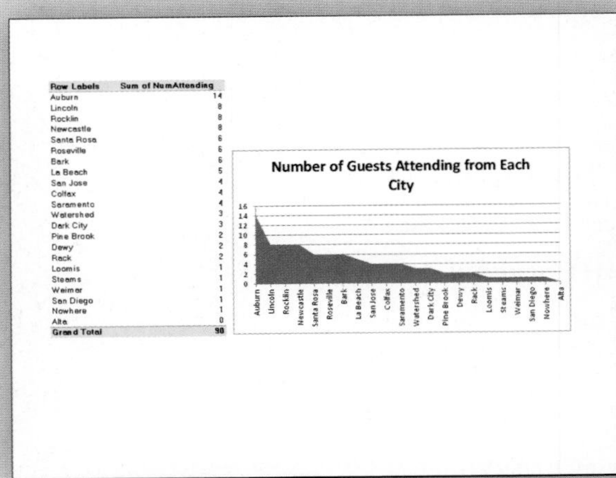

Row Labels	Sum of NumAttending
Auburn	14
Lincoln	8
Rocklin	8
Newcastle	8
Santa Rosa	6
Roseville	6
Bark	6
La Beach	5
San Jose	4
Colfax	4
Saramento	4
Watershed	3
Dark City	3
Pine Brook	2
Dewy	2
Rack	2
Loomis	1
Steams	1
Weimar	1
San Diego	1
Nowhere	1
Alta	0
Grand Total	90

FIGURE EX 4.41

c. Drag the object down so that no worksheet data are covered up.

d. On the *Chart Tools Design* tab, in the *Layout* group, choose **Chart Layout 1.**

e. Change the chart title to: `Per Guest Cost Breakdown`

8. Create a *PivotTable* listing the number attending from each city.

a. Return to the *Table* worksheet; click anywhere in the table of data.

b. Click the **Insert** tab, and then in the *Tables* group, click the **PivotTable** button.

c. The *Create PivotTable* dialog opens. (Notice the table or range you selected is entered in the *Select a table or range* box for you.)

d. Click **OK** to create a PivotTable in a new worksheet. The empty PivotTable layout appears on the right. The *PivotTable Field List* lists the column headings from your table or range.

e. Click the check box for the fields **City** and **NumAttending.**

f. Excel will place fields with numeric data in the *Values* area and text fields in the *Row Labels* area. A sum of values is calculated automatically.

g. Rename the sheet tab as: `Pivot Table`

9. Create a *PivotChart:*

a. Select any cell in the PivotTable.

b. From the *PivotTable Tools Options* tab, in the *Tools* group, click the **PivotChart** button.

c. Select the first column chart type from the *Insert Chart* dialog.

d. Click **OK.**

e. Click the title and change it to read: `Number of Guests Attending from Each City`

f. On the *PivotChart Tools Layout* tab, in the *Labels* group, click the **Legend** button; then click **None.**

g. Drag the PivotChart to position it neatly below or to the right of the PivotTable.

h. Change the sheet tab to read: `Pivot Table & Pivot Chart`

10. Sort the pivot data from high to low numbers attending:

a. In the PivotTable, click in the **Sum of NumAttending** column.

b. Right-click, then choose **Sort,** and then **Sort Largest to Smallest.**

11. Change the chart type:

a. Click the chart.

b. On the *PivotChart Tools Design* tab, in the *Type* group, click **Change Chart Type**, and then the first **Line** type. Click **OK.** This is a line chart, but line charts are generally used to show trends over time.

c. On the *PivotChart Tools Design* tab, in the *Type* group, click **Change Chart Type**, and then the first **Area** type. Click **OK.** Now we are showing the volume of guests by city.

12. Work with *Sparklines* on the *Sparklines* worksheet:

a. Select cells **E4:E6,** where we wish to display Sparklines.

b. On the *Insert* tab, in the *Sparklines* group, select the **Column** type of Sparkline.

c. In the *Create Sparklines* dialog box, enter `B4:D6` as the *Data Range* to use to create the Sparklines. Click **OK.**

d. Select one or more of the Sparklines to reveal the *Sparkline Tools Design* tab.

e. Change the *Type* to **Line.**

f. In the *Show* group, check the boxes to display value points like high and low points, negative points, and first and last points by selecting the corresponding options. Mark all value points by selecting **Markers.**

Event Cost Data

	Year			
Clients	2010	2011	2012	
Johnson's	$ 6,259	$ 7,583	$ 7,935	
Electronica Inc.	$ 6,700	$ 8,024	$ 8,376	
MakeAWish	$ 7,141	$ 8,381	$ 8,733	

FIGURE EX 4.42

Skill Review 4.2

Real Estate. In this project, you will be working with real estate data.

1. Open the provided file called *Houses.xlsx,* and save it as `[your initials]EX_SkillReview_4-2`.

2. Make the data on the *Table* worksheet into a table:

a. Select all the data including the headings, being careful not to select any blank rows or columns.

b. From the *Styles* group on the *Home* tab, click the **Format as Table** button to display the *Table Styles* gallery.

c. Pick the style you want to use for your table.

d. Check the **My table has headers** check box. Click **OK.**

e. Add a *Total row* to the table:

(1) Click the **Total Row** check box in the *Table Style Options* group on the *Table Tools Design* tab.

(2) In the Total row at the bottom of the table, click in the **Buyers** column, click the arrow, and select the **Count** function.

(3) In the Total row at the bottom of the table, click in the **Bedrooms** column, click the arrow, and select the **Average** function.

(4) In the Total row at the bottom of the table, click each of the remaining columns that contain numbers, click the arrow, and select the **Average** function.

(5) Format the cells with the averages for **Bedrooms, Bathrooms** and **Mortgage Years** to 1 decimal place.

f. Sort the data in *Agent* alphabetical order:

(1) Click anywhere in the **Agent** column.

(2) In the *Sort & Filter* group on the *Data* tab, click the **A-Z** button.

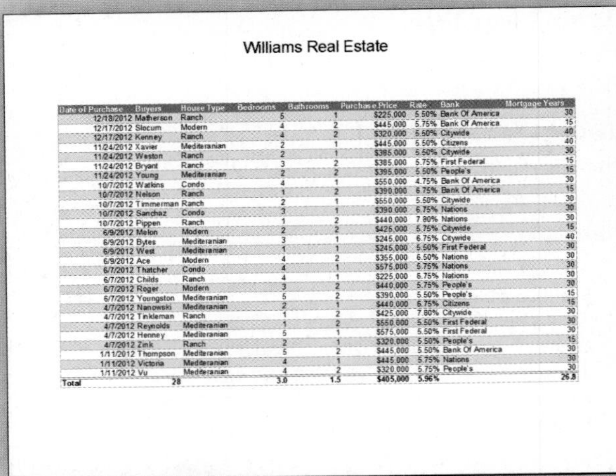

Williams Real Estate

Date of Purchase	Buyers	House Type	Bedrooms	Bathrooms	Purchase Price	Rate	Bank	Mortgage Years
12/18/2012	Matherson	Ranch	5	1	$225,000	5.50%	Bank Of America	30
12/17/2012	Slocum	Modern	4	2	$445,000	5.75%	Bank Of America	15
12/17/2012	Kenney	Ranch	4	2	$320,000	5.50%	Citywide	40
11/24/2012	Xavier	Mediteranian	2	1	$445,000	5.50%	Citizens	40
11/24/2012	Weston	Ranch	2	1	$385,000	5.50%	Citywide	30
11/24/2012	Bryant	Ranch	3	2	$385,000	5.75%	First Federal	15
11/24/2012	Young	Mediteranian	2	2	$395,000	5.50%	People's	15
10/7/2012	Watkins	Condo	4	1	$550,000	4.75%	Bank Of America	30
10/7/2012	Nelson	Ranch	1	2	$390,000	6.75%	Bank Of America	15
10/7/2012	Timmerman	Ranch	2	1	$550,000	5.50%	Citywide	30
10/7/2012	Sanchaz	Condo	3	1	$390,000	6.75%	Nations	30
10/7/2012	Pippen	Ranch	1	2	$440,000	7.80%	Nations	30
6/9/2012	Melon	Modern	2	2	$425,000	5.75%	Citywide	15
6/9/2012	Bytes	Mediteranian	3	1	$245,000	6.75%	Citywide	40
6/9/2012	West	Mediteranian	1	1	$245,000	5.50%	First Federal	30
6/9/2012	Ace	Modern	4	2	$355,000	6.50%	Nations	30
6/7/2012	Thatcher	Condo	4	1	$575,000	5.75%	Nations	30
6/7/2012	Childs	Ranch	4	1	$225,000	6.75%	Nations	30
6/7/2012	Roger	Modern	3	2	$440,000	5.75%	People's	30
6/7/2012	Youngston	Mediteranian	5	2	$390,000	5.50%	People's	15
4/7/2012	Nanowski	Mediteranian	2	1	$440,000	6.75%	Citizens	15
4/7/2012	Tinkleman	Ranch	1	2	$425,000	7.80%	Citywide	30
4/7/2012	Reynolds	Mediteranian	1	2	$550,000	5.50%	First Federal	30
4/7/2012	Henney	Mediteranian	5	1	$575,000	5.50%	First Federal	30
4/7/2012	Zink	Ranch	2	1	$320,000	5.50%	People's	15
1/11/2012	Thompson	Mediteranian	5	2	$445,000	5.50%	Bank Of America	30
1/11/2012	Victoria	Medderanian	4	1	$445,000	5.75%	Nations	30
1/11/2012	Vu	Medderanian	4	2	$320,000	5.75%	People's	30
Total	28		3.0	1.5	$405,000	5.96%		26.8

FIGURE EX 4.43

g. Change the sort order to sort the data alphabetically by *Bank:*

(1) Click the arrow at the top of the **Bank** column.

(2) Click **Sort A-Z.**

h. Change the sort to *Date* order:

(1) Right-click any cell in the **Date of Purchase** column.

(2) Point to **Sort,** and select **Newest to Oldest.**

i. Use AutoFilter to filter data:

(1) Click the arrow in the **Agent** column.

(2) Click the **(Select All)** check box to remove all of the check marks.

(3) Click the check box or check boxes in front of **William's** to filter for only houses sold by **William's.**

(4) Click **OK.** Excel displays only the rows for houses sold by **William's.**

j. Hide the **Agent** column, the **Fireplace** column, and the **Near School** column.

k. In the center of the header enter: `William's Real Estate.`

l. Print the *William's* data, fitting neatly on one piece of paper. Adjust column widths as needed.

m. Restore all the hidden data:

(1) Unhide the hidden columns.

(2) Click the arrow at the top of the **Agent** column; since filtering is enabled, the column header includes a filter icon. Click the **Clear Filter** option from the menu.

3. Format data with *Conditional Formatting:*

a. Highlight all the *"Condo"* cells in the **House Type** column with *Conditional Formatting.*

(1) Select all the cells with the **House Type** data. Do not select the heading, total row table statistics or any empty cells. In the *Styles* group on the *Home* tab, click the **Conditional Formatting** button.

(2) From the menu, point to **Highlight Cells Rules,** and click **More Rules . . .**

(3) Make sure this option is selected: **Format only cells that contain.**

(4) Click the little drop-down arrow to change **greater than** to **equal to.**

(5) In the third text box, enter: `Condo`

(6) Click the **Format** button.

(7) On the *Font* tab, choose **Bold;** on the *Fill* tab, choose **yellow.** Click **OK,** and then click **OK.**

b. Highlight cells using the *Top/Bottom Rules:*

(1) Select the cells with the **Purchase Price** data. Do not select the heading, total row table statistics or any empty cells.

(2) In the *Styles* group on the *Home* tab, click the **Conditional Formatting** button.

(3) From the menu, point to **Top/Bottom Rules,** and click **Top 10 Items . . .**

(4) In the dialog box, click **OK.**

4. Filter so only houses with five bedrooms show:
   a. Click the arrow in the **Bedrooms** column.
   b. Click the **(Select All)** check box to remove all of the check marks.
   c. Click the check box in front of **5** to filter for only houses with five bedrooms. Click **OK.**
5. Change the *Date* sort order:
   a. Right-click any cell in the **Date of Purchase** column.
   b. Point to **Sort,** and select **Oldest to Newest.**
6. Hide the **Rate, Bank,** and **Mortgage Years** columns. Print the worksheet with an appropriate header, neatly on one page.
7. Make a chart of the *Purchase Prices* by date:
   a. Select the **Date of Purchase** data cells, hold the **Ctrl** key, select the **Purchase Price** data cells.
   b. Click the **Insert** tab; in the *Charts* group, click the **Line** type drop down arrow.
   c. Choose the first line chart option from the gallery.

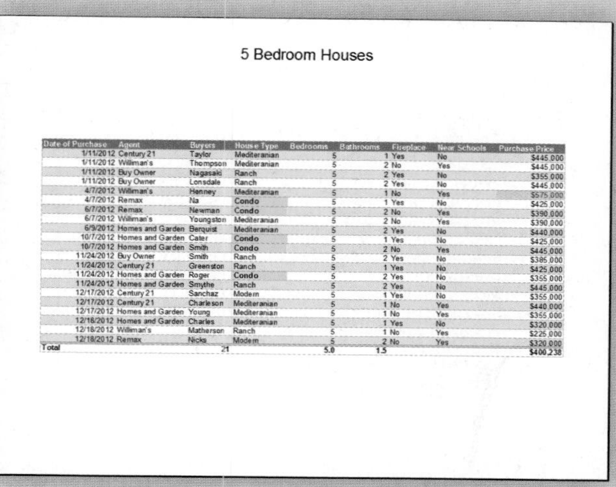

5 Bedroom Houses

Date of Purchase	Agent	Buyers	House Type	Bedrooms	Bathrooms	Fireplace	Near Schools	Purchase Price
1/11/2012	Century 21	Taylor	Mediteranian	5	1	Yes	No	$445,000
1/11/2012	Williman's	Thompson	Mediteranian	5	2	No	Yes	$445,000
1/11/2012	Buy Owner	Nagasaki	Ranch	5	2	Yes	No	$355,000
1/11/2012	Buy Owner	Lonsdale	Ranch	5	2	Yes	No	$445,000
4/7/2012	Williman's	Henney	Mediteranian	5	1	No	Yes	$575,000
4/7/2012	Remax	Na	Condo	5	1	Yes	No	$425,000
6/7/2012	Remax	Newman	Condo	5	2	No	Yes	$390,000
6/7/2012	Williman's	Youngston	Mediteranian	5	2	No	Yes	$390,000
6/9/2012	Homes and Garden	Berquist	Mediteranian	5	2	Yes	No	$440,000
10/7/2012	Homes and Garden	Cater	Condo	5	1	Yes	No	$425,000
10/7/2012	Homes and Garden	Smith	Condo	5	2	No	Yes	$445,000
11/24/2012	Buy Owner	Smith	Ranch	5	2	Yes	No	$385,000
11/24/2012	Century 21	Greenston	Ranch	5	1	Yes	No	$425,000
11/24/2012	Homes and Garden	Roger	Condo	5	2	Yes	No	$355,000
11/24/2012	Homes and Garden	Smythe	Ranch	5	2	Yes	No	$445,000
12/17/2012	Century 21	Sanchaz	Modern	5	1	Yes	No	$355,000
12/17/2012	Century 21	Charleson	Mediteranian	5	1	No	Yes	$440,000
12/17/2012	Homes and Garden	Young	Mediteranian	5	1	No	Yes	$355,000
12/18/2012	Homes and Garden	Charles	Mediteranian	5	1	Yes	No	$320,000
12/18/2012	Williman's	Matherson	Ranch	5	1	No	Yes	$225,000
12/18/2012	Remax	Nicks	Modern	5	2	No	Yes	$320,000
Total		21		5.0	1.5			$400,238

FIGURE EX 4.44

8. Move the chart to its own sheet in the workbook.
   a. Select the chart. From the *Chart Tools Design* tab, click the **Move Chart** button from the *Location* group.
   b. In the *Move Chart* dialog box, click the **New sheet** button and type in the new sheet name: `Chartsheet`. Click **OK.**
9. Use the *Chart Tools Layout* tab to change the chart layout.
   a. Select the chart; click the *Chart Tools Layout* tab.
   b. In the *Labels* group, click the button for the **Chart Title;** then choose **Above Chart.**
   c. On the chart, click the chart title, enter this title: `Purchase Price for five Bedroom Houses.`
   d. Click on some other part of the chart.
   e. In the *Labels* group, click the button for the **Legend,** then choose **None.**

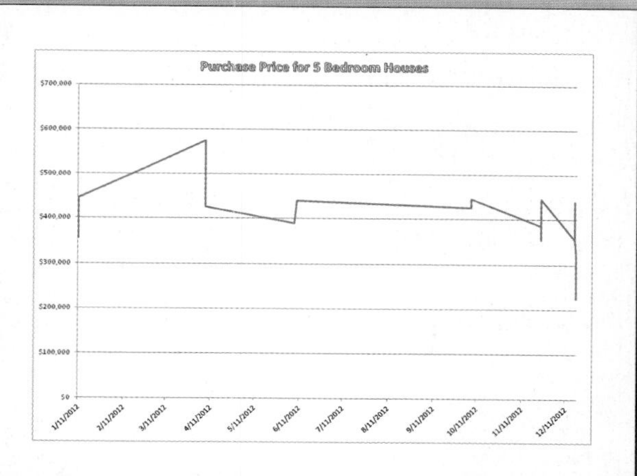

FIGURE EX 4.45

10. Click the **Design** tab under *Chart Tools.* In the *Chart Styles* group, click a style.
11. Use the *Chart Tools Format* tab to change chart *Title* style:
    a. Click the chart title, click the first *WordArt Style* button on the *Chart Tools Format* tab.
12. Print the *ChartSheet.*
13. Switch to work with the *Data Table* worksheet.
    a. Select cells **B5:E38** to use the payment formula in B5 and the various years and rates.
    b. On the *Data* tab, in the *Data Tools* group, click the **What-If Analysis** button.
    c. Choose **Data Table.**
    d. In the *Row input cell:* box, enter `C2`.
    e. In the *Column input cell:* box, enter `A2`. Click **OK.**
    f. Notice the payments have now been computed for the various years and rates.
    g. Format the payment amounts appropriately.

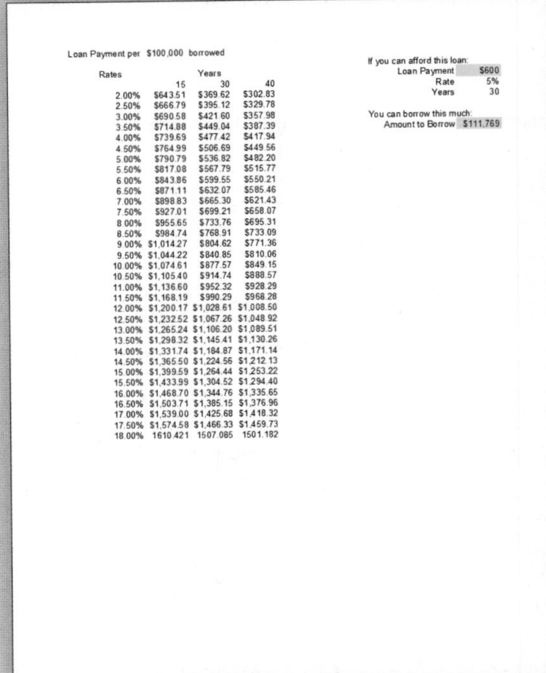

Loan Payment per $100,000 borrowed

Rates	15	30	40
	Years		
2.00%	$643.51	$369.62	$302.83
2.50%	$666.79	$395.12	$329.78
3.00%	$690.58	$421.60	$357.98
3.50%	$714.88	$449.04	$387.39
4.00%	$739.69	$477.42	$417.94
4.50%	$764.99	$506.69	$449.56
5.00%	$790.79	$536.82	$482.20
5.50%	$817.08	$567.79	$515.77
6.00%	$843.86	$599.55	$550.21
6.50%	$871.11	$632.07	$585.46
7.00%	$898.83	$665.30	$621.43
7.50%	$927.01	$699.21	$658.07
8.00%	$955.65	$733.76	$695.31
8.50%	$984.74	$768.91	$733.09
9.00%	$1,014.27	$804.62	$771.36
9.50%	$1,044.22	$840.85	$810.06
10.00%	$1,074.61	$877.57	$849.15
10.50%	$1,105.40	$914.74	$888.57
11.00%	$1,136.60	$952.32	$928.29
11.50%	$1,168.19	$990.29	$968.28
12.00%	$1,200.17	$1,028.61	$1,008.50
12.50%	$1,232.52	$1,067.26	$1,048.92
13.00%	$1,265.24	$1,106.20	$1,089.51
13.50%	$1,298.32	$1,145.41	$1,130.26
14.00%	$1,331.74	$1,184.87	$1,171.14
14.50%	$1,365.50	$1,224.56	$1,212.13
15.00%	$1,399.59	$1,264.44	$1,253.22
15.50%	$1,433.99	$1,304.52	$1,294.40
16.00%	$1,468.70	$1,344.76	$1,335.65
16.50%	$1,503.71	$1,385.15	$1,376.96
17.00%	$1,539.00	$1,425.68	$1,418.32
17.50%	$1,574.58	$1,466.33	$1,459.73
18.00%	1610.421	1507.085	1501.182

If you can afford this loan:

Loan Payment	$600
Rate	5%
Years	30

You can borrow this much:

Amount to Borrow	$111,769

FIGURE EX 4.46

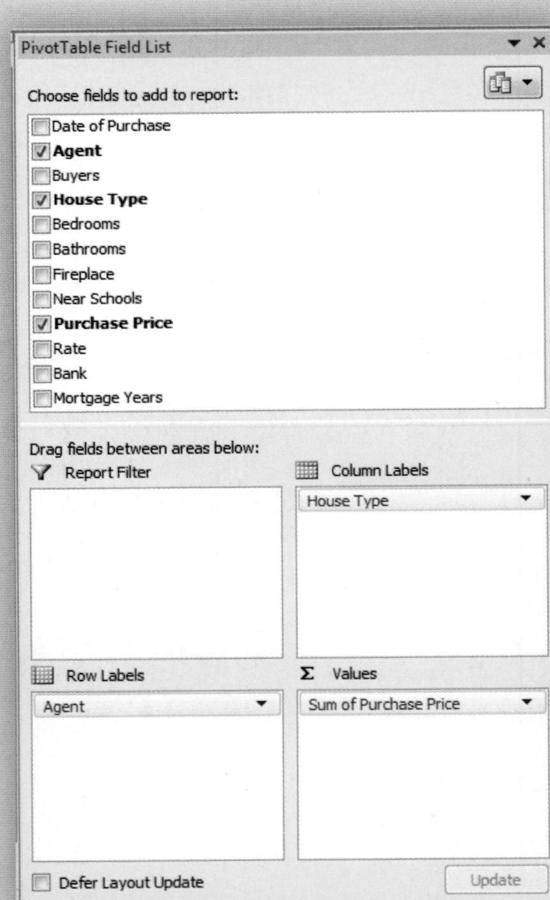

FIGURE EX 4.47

14. Use *Goal Seek* to determine the most you can afford to borrow, on a $600 per month repayment budget:

a. On the *Data Table* sheet, select the outcome formula cell, **J4.**

b. Click the **What-If Analysis** button in the *Data Tools* group on the *Data* tab, and click **Goal Seek . . .**

c. Verify that the outcome cell **J4** is referenced in the *Set cell:* box.

d. Enter the outcome value of `600` in the *To value:* box.

e. Enter the input cell `J9` in the *By changing cell:* box. Click **OK,** and then click **OK.**

f. Notice the loan payment changed to $600 and the amount to borrow was computed to be $111,769. Highlight cells **J9** and **J4** with yellow.

g. Change the worksheet tab to: `Data Table & Goal Seek`

h. Hide row 2.

i. Hide the contents of cell **B5** by setting a custom format of type: `;;;`

15. Print the worksheet with the data table and Goal Seek, fitting neatly on one page.

16. Create a *PivotTable* listing the average purchase price of different house types for each agent.

a. Return to the *Table* worksheet; click anywhere in the table of data.

b. Click the **Insert** tab; then click the **PivotTable** button in the *Tables* group. Click **PivotTable.**

c. The *Create PivotTable* dialog opens. Click **OK** to create a PivotTable in a new worksheet. The empty PivotTable layout appears.

d. The PivotTable Field List lists the column headings from your table or range. Click the check box for the fields: **Agent, House Type, Purchase Price.**

e. Drag **House Type** to the *Column Labels* box.

f. Click the little drop-down arrow for *Sum of Purchase Price* and choose **Value Field Settings, Average, Number format, Currency, 0** decimal places. Click **OK;** then click **OK.**

g. Rename the sheet tab as: `Pivot Table`

17. Make a *Pie* chart showing which agents sold which percent of condos.

a. Select cells **A5:B9.**

b. On the *Insert* tab, select **Pie** in the *Charts* group. Choose the first pie chart option.

c. Choose **Chart Layout 1** on the *Design* tab.

d. Click the chart title, type in a more descriptive title, and then press **Enter.**

e. Move the chart to its own sheet in the workbook.

(1) Select the chart. From the *Chart Tools Design* tab, click the **Move Chart** button from the *Location* group.

(2) In the *Move Chart* dialog box, click the **New sheet** button and type in the new sheet name: `PieChartsheet`. Click **OK.**

(3) Print the pie chart.

18. Create a *PivotChart:*

a. Select any cell in the PivotTable.

b. From the *PivotTable Tools Options* tab, click the **PivotChart** button in the *Tools* group.

c. Select the first column chart type from the *Insert Chart* dialog. Click **OK.**

d. Choose the chart **Layout 1.**

e. Click the title and change it to read: `Average Price by Type of House and Agent`

f. Drag the PivotChart to position it neatly below the PivotTable.

g. Change the sheet tab to read: `Pivot Table & Pivot Chart`

19. Work with *Sparklines:*

a. Select cells **G5:G9,** where we wish to display Sparklines.

b. On the *Insert* tab, select the **Line** type of Sparkline.

c. In the *Create Sparklines* dialog box, enter `B5:E9` as the *Data Range* to use to create the Sparklines. Click **OK.**

d. Select one of the Sparklines to reveal the *Design* tab.

e. Change the *Sparkline Type* to **Column.**

f. In the *Show* group, check the boxes to display value points for high and low points by selecting the corresponding options.

g. Select all the rows of the worksheet and make them all taller.

20. Print the PivotTable chart, PivotChart, and Sparklines, fitting neatly on one page.

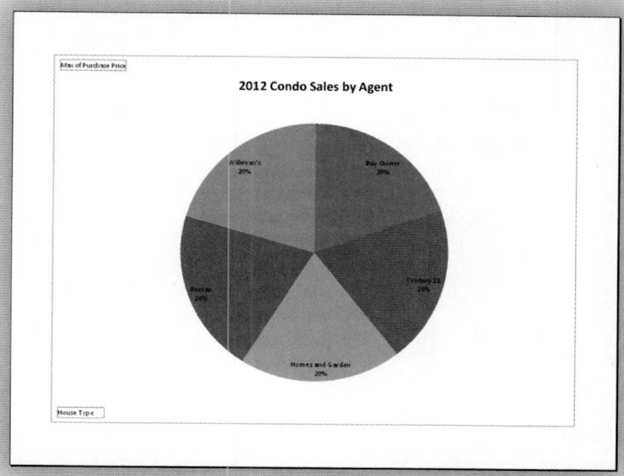

FIGURE EX 4.48

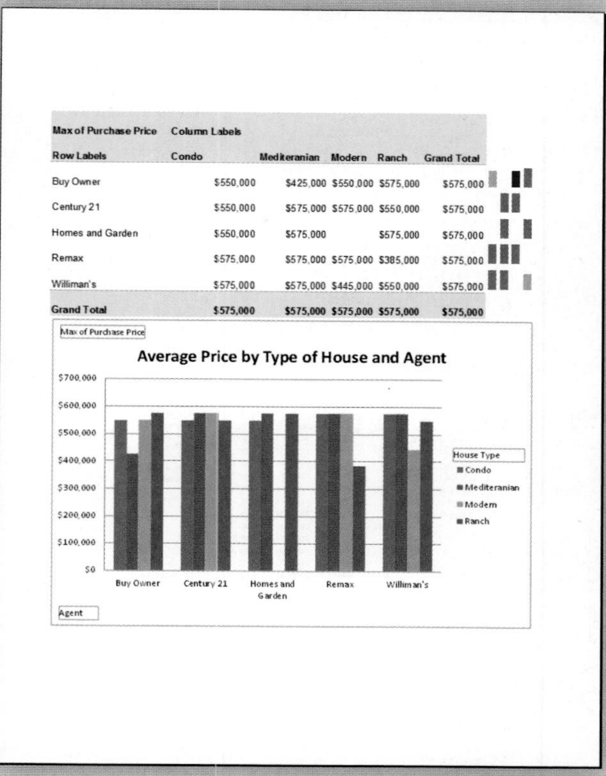

Max of Purchase Price	Column Labels				
Row Labels	Condo	Mediteranian	Modern	Ranch	Grand Total
Buy Owner	$550,000	$425,000	$550,000	$575,000	$575,000
Century 21	$550,000	$575,000	$575,000	$550,000	$575,000
Homes and Garden	$550,000	$575,000		$575,000	$575,000
Remax	$575,000	$575,000	$575,000	$385,000	$575,000
Williman's	$575,000	$575,000	$445,000	$550,000	$575,000
Grand Total	$575,000	$575,000	$575,000	$575,000	$575,000

FIGURE EX 4.49

challenge yourself 1

Shoe Sales. In this project, you will be pretending to have already graduated and to have started your first job selling shoes to retailers.

1. Open the provided file called *Shoe Sales.xlsx,* and save it as `[your initials]EX_Challenge_4-3`.

2. Make the shoe sales data into a table.

a. Sort by **Shoe.**

b. Sort by **Date, Newest to Oldest.**

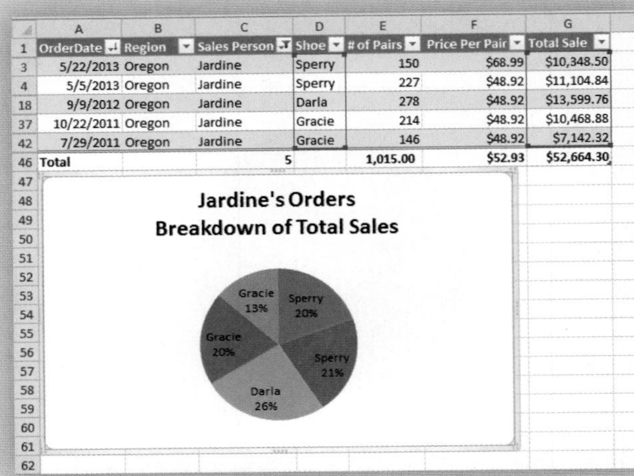

FIGURE EX 4.50

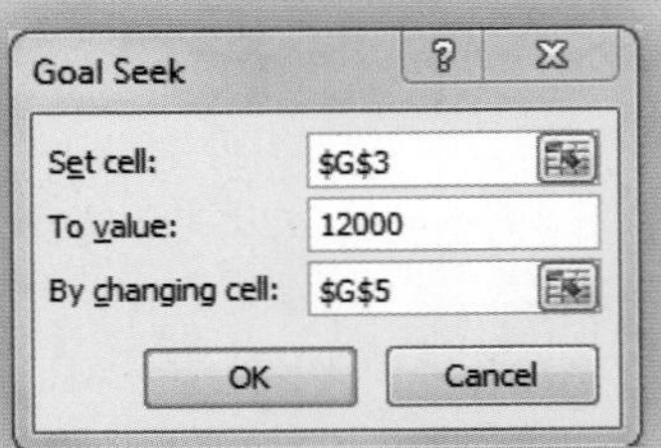

FIGURE EX 4.51

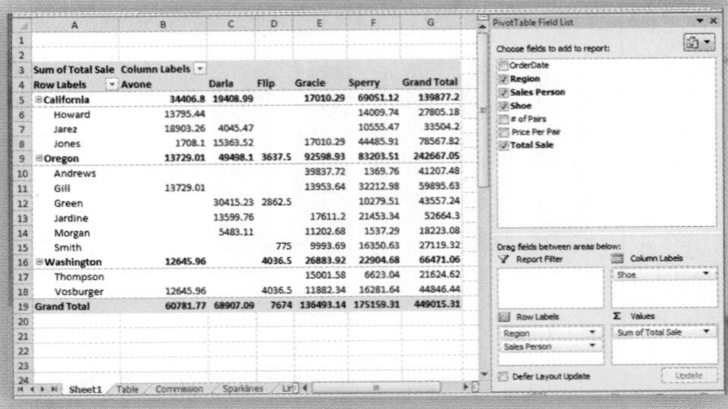

FIGURE EX 4.52

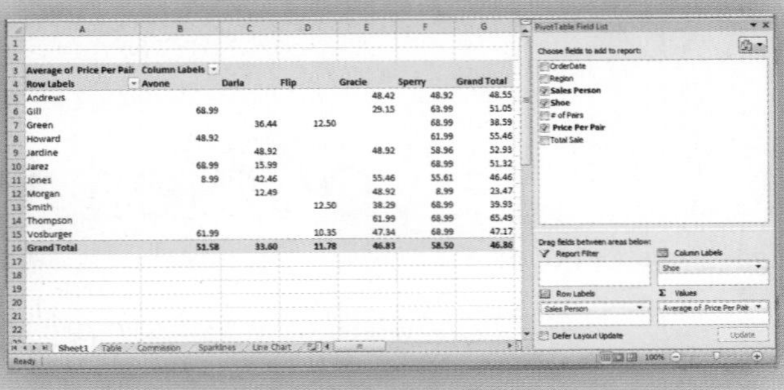

FIGURE EX 4.53

c. Add your first sale to the bottom of the table. Use one of the existing regions and shoes, make up the price, and compute the total sale.

d. Add a Total row to count the orders. Average the price per pair. Total the number of shoes sold and the total sales. Format the numbers appropriately.

3. Filter to show just the sales for Jardine. Make a *Pie* chart showing a slice for each order in terms of *Total Sale.*

a. Title and format appropriately.

b. Move the chart to its own chart sheet.

4. Use conditional formatting to highlight the top 10 orders in terms of # of pairs.

5. Use icon sets to show orders of $10,000 or more.

6. You have been told that you will receive a commission between 5 and 10 percent. On the *Commission* sheet, make a data table using cells **A:B14** to determine how much that commission may be.

a. The column input cell is **A4.**

b. Change the *Sales* amount in cell B1 match the amount of your first sale.

7. You owe $12,000 in student loans and would like to pay it all off with your commissions. Use *Goal Seek* to determine the amount you must sell to earn at least a commission of $12,000 and fully pay off your student loans.

8. On the *Sparklines* worksheet, add Sparklines in column **H.**

9. Create a PivotTable from the table of shoe sales data. Experiment with various options; then choose one that makes the most sense to you.

10. Make a *PivotChart.* Title and format it appropriately. Size and position it neatly on the same worksheet as the PivotTable.

11. On the *Line Chart* worksheet, make a line chart to show the sales of the number of pairs of the "Avone" shoe over time. Title and format appropriately. Change to a *Column* chart.

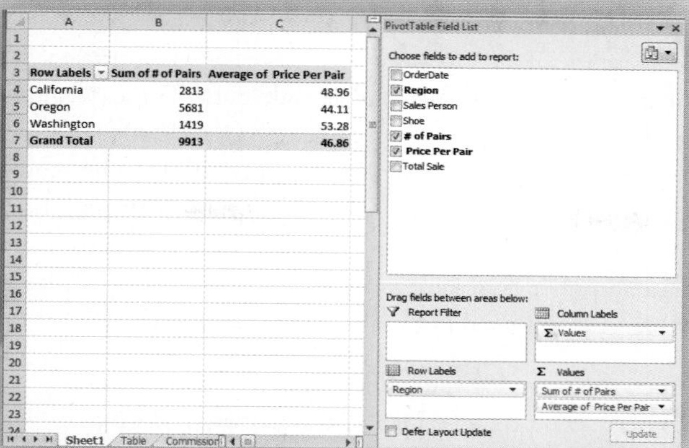

Row Labels	Sum of # of Pairs	Average of Price Per Pair
California	2813	48.96
Oregon	5681	44.11
Washington	1419	53.28
Grand Total	9913	46.86

FIGURE EX 4.54

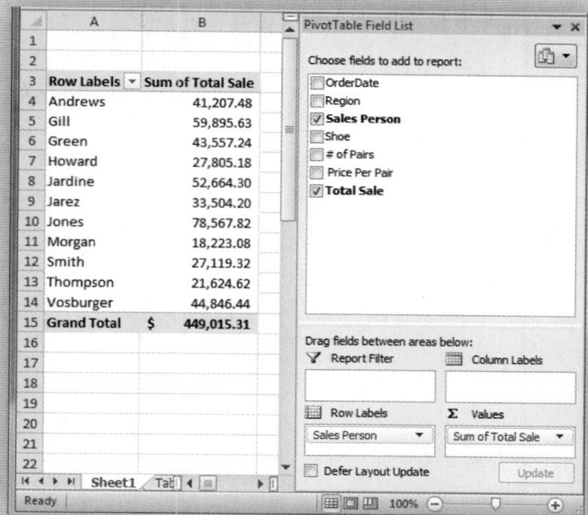

Row Labels	Sum of Total Sale
Andrews	41,207.48
Gill	59,895.63
Green	43,557.24
Howard	27,805.18
Jardine	52,664.30
Jarez	33,504.20
Jones	78,567.82
Morgan	18,223.08
Smith	27,119.32
Thompson	21,624.62
Vosburger	44,846.44
Grand Total	$ 449,015.31

FIGURE EX 4.55

challenge yourself 2

Video Project. In this project, you will be pretending to have amassed a significant collection of DVDs. You are a bit of a packrat and thought of possibly running a video rental business at one time. You enjoy sorting through them, but you are also considering cashing them in to launch a new hobby.

1. Open the provided file called *Videos.xlsx,* and save it as **`[your initials]EX_Challenge_4-4`.**
2. Make the *Video* data into a table with a Total row. Count the videos and average the purchase prices.
3. Highlight the G-rated movies.
4. Sort by *Category,* then change to sort by *Rating.*
5. Filter to show only the R movies. Remove the filter and then show only the comedies.
6. Create a PivotTable showing how many of each rating you have for each category, similar to Figure EX 4.56. Print it.
7. Change the category to just show Disney.
8. Create a pie chart showing the Disney moves by rating, similar to Figure EX 4.57. Print it.
9. Select all categories again on the PivotTable. Change the PivotTable so that the categories are rows and the ratings are columns.
10. Add column Sparklines on the right.
11. Make a stacked column PivotChart with categories listed on the horizontal axis and the number of each rating stacked in the columns.
12. Move the chart to its own chart sheet. Title, label, and format appropriately.
13. On the *Data Table* worksheet, make a data table to determine the amount of cash that would be raised if 100 videos were all sold at various prices.
14. Change the number sold to 175.
15. Assume that $3 is the most you can expect per video, when selling a portion of the collection. How many videos must be sold to raise $1,000 to launch a new hobby? Use *Goal Seek* to determine this.

Row Labels	Sum of # of Copies
Action	**471**
G	5
PG	56
PG 13	5
R	405
Comedy	**130**
PG	24
R	106
Disney	**64**
G	5
PG	19
PG 13	40
Drama	**113**
PG	17
PG 13	12
PG 14	5
R	79
Horror	**202**
PG	8
R	194
Romance	**33**
PG	2
R	31
Sci Fi	**17**
PG	5
R	12
Grand Total	**1030**

FIGURE EX 4.56

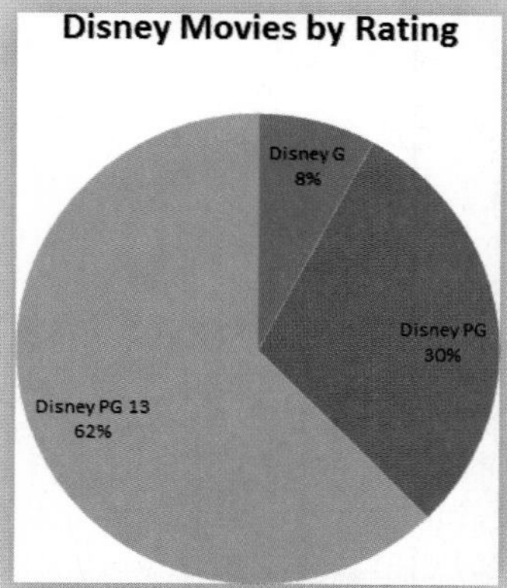

FIGURE EX 4.57

on your own

Autos Project. In this project, you will be working with automobile data. These automobile data were downloaded from the Web site http://www.data.gov/raw/2004 and are explained at the Web site http://www.epa.gov/greenvehicles/Aboutratings.do. The scores range from 0 to 10, where 10 is best. The vehicles with the best scores on both air pollution and greenhouse gas receive the SmartWay designation. These raw data were edited to make them usable. Rows with inappropriate number data such as an MPG of 13/17 or N/A were deleted. In order to make a PivotTable, you will need just a single number in each cell.

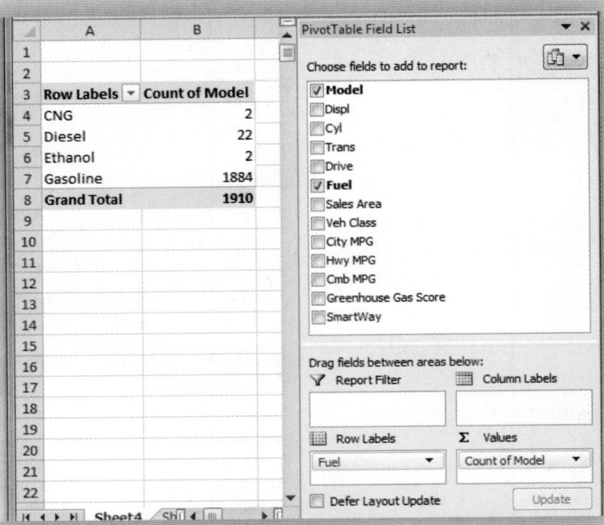

FIGURE EX 4.58

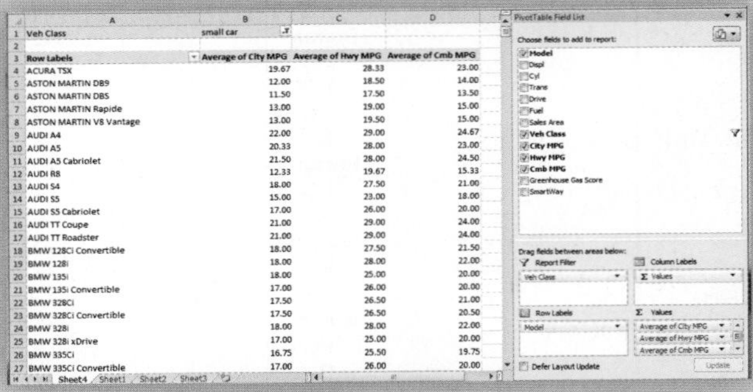

FIGURE EX 4.59

Miles	10,000			Total Gas Cost					
MPG				Price Per Gallon					
	$2.50	$2.75	$3.00	$3.25	$3.50	$3.75	$4.00	$4.25	$4.50
12									
12.5									
13									
13.5									
14									
14.5									
15									
15.5									
16									
16.5									
17									
17.5									
18									
18.5									
19									
19.5									
20									

FIGURE EX 4.60

1. Open the provided file called *Autos.xlsx,* and save it as `[your initials]EX_OnYourOwn_4-5.`
2. Make the auto data into a table.
3. Add a Total row to the table, with appropriate summary statistics including average, max, and count.
4. Add data bars to all the MPG cells.
5. Highlight the CA sales area cars with yellow.
6. Filter to show just one vehicle class. Print the worksheet.
7. Create a PivotTable to count the number of models using each fuel.
8. Copy the fuel data to another worksheet and create a pie chart from the data. Title, label, and position the chart appropriately on the worksheet. Print the worksheet.
9. Modify the PivotTable to show the average MPG data for all models in the small car class.
10. Set the PivotTable filter to show just the van vehicle class. Sort from lowest to highest on combined MPG. Make a PivotChart comparing the average MPG data for the two vans.
11. Format, title, label, and position the chart appropriately. Print the worksheet.
12. Change the filter on the PivotTable to show pickup trucks.
13. Move the chart to its own sheet and modify titles as needed. Change it to a line chart. Print the chart sheet
14. Add appropriate Sparklines to the right of the MPG data in the PivotTable. Print the worksheet.
15. On another worksheet, make a two-variable data table to determine total gas cost for driving any number of miles at various MPG and cost per gallon figures. For an example of the layout, see Figure EX 4.60. Print the worksheet.
16. On another worksheet, compute the cost of fuel for driving. Set up a place to enter the number of miles driven, the MPG, and the price per gallon of gas. Enter estimates for your own driving reality or fantasy. Use Goal Seek to determine how many miles you could drive if you received a gas card of $2,500. Print the worksheet.

Academy. In this project, you will be pretending to be on the staff of a private college preparation school. You are on the faculty, you are academic adviser to several students, and you are on a facilities planning committee.

1. Open the provided file called *Academy.xlsx,* and save it as **[your initials]EX_FixIt_4-6.**
2. On the *Faculty Pivot* worksheet, change the chart to a pie. Title, label, and format it appropriately. Move the chart to its own chart sheet.
3. Make the *Student Test Data* into a table.
   a. Try different sorts. Sort by student, then sort by subject, and then change the sort to score order.
   b. Filter to show only one student; change the filter to show only one subject; then remove the filter.
   c. Add a Total row to count the tests and average the scores.
   d. Highlight the top 10 scores and the bottom 10 scores.
4. On the *Student Test Data* worksheet, you want to see each student's scores for each month on each subject, similar to Figure EX 4.61.
   a. Fix the PivotTable.
   b. Make a PivotChart from it.
   c. Add Sparklines to plot the scores for each subject to the right.
   d. Make a PivotChart from the PivotTable. Title, label, and format it appropriately.
5. The committee has determined that a $14,000 facilities upgrade will be needed in 10 years. An alumnus has donated $10,000. If invested, will it grow to be enough? That depends on the rate of return.
   a. On the *Data Table* worksheet, an attempt has been made to use Excel's data table feature to determine the value of the investment after five years at different rates of return. Look over the worksheets, delete the zeros, and try the data table again.
   b. If you had a guaranteed rate of return of 3 percent, how many years would it take to grow the investment to $14,000? Use Goal Seek to find the number of years.

Row Labels	January	February	March	Quarter Average
⊟James	**77.83**	**82.33**	**85.33**	**81.83**
Art	92.00	86.00	95.00	91.00
English	90.00	85.00	86.00	87.00
French	65.00	75.00	79.00	73.00
History	84.00	87.00	94.00	88.33
Math	68.00	75.00	74.00	72.33
Science	68.00	86.00	84.00	79.33

FIGURE EX 4.61

access 2010

Getting Started with Access 2010

Working with Tables

Working with Forms and Reports

Using Queries and Organizing Information

chapter 1

Getting Started with Access 2010

In this chapter, you will learn the following skills:

- Learn about Access 2010
- Use the Navigation Pane to open, organize, and view database objects
- Use Quick Start Application Parts
- Learn views and how to navigate within Access 2010
- Enter and edit data in forms and tables
- Perform a backup and use the Compact & Repair tool

Skill 1.1 Introduction to Access 2010
Skill 1.2 Using Quick Start Application Parts
Skill 1.3 Using Views in Access 2010
Skill 1.4 Navigating Records in a Form or Table
Skill 1.5 Entering Data in a Table
Skill 1.6 Entering Data in a Form
Skill 1.7 Using Compact & Repair
Skill 1.8 Backing Up a Database

skills

introduction

This chapter is an introduction to databases and their role in the business world. Readers will learn how to navigate the Access 2010 interface and use the Navigation Pane to organize database objects. Database tables are used to manage records using various views in Access 2010. This chapter will also explain how to navigate, create, edit, and delete records in table and form objects. Readers also will learn the importance of database maintenance duties such as compact and repair and creating a backup.

1.1 Introduction to Access 2010

Microsoft Access is a powerful database program that allows you to enter and organize large amounts of data. Because Access allows you to relate tables and databases to one another, it is often referred to as a **relational database**.

A relational database is a group of tables related to one another by common fields. A table (or datasheet) looks similar to a spreadsheet. Each row in the table contains all the data for a single **record**. Each column in the table represents a specific data value called a **field**. All records in a table have the same fields.

For example, a table of employee data might include fields for *Employee ID, Last Name, First Name, E-mail Address, Staff Number,* and *Department.* Another table for tracking timesheets might have fields for *Timesheet Number, Employee ID, Week, Hours Worked,* and *Total Pay.* The two tables are related by the *Employee ID* field, so the database can generate reports combining information from the two tables.

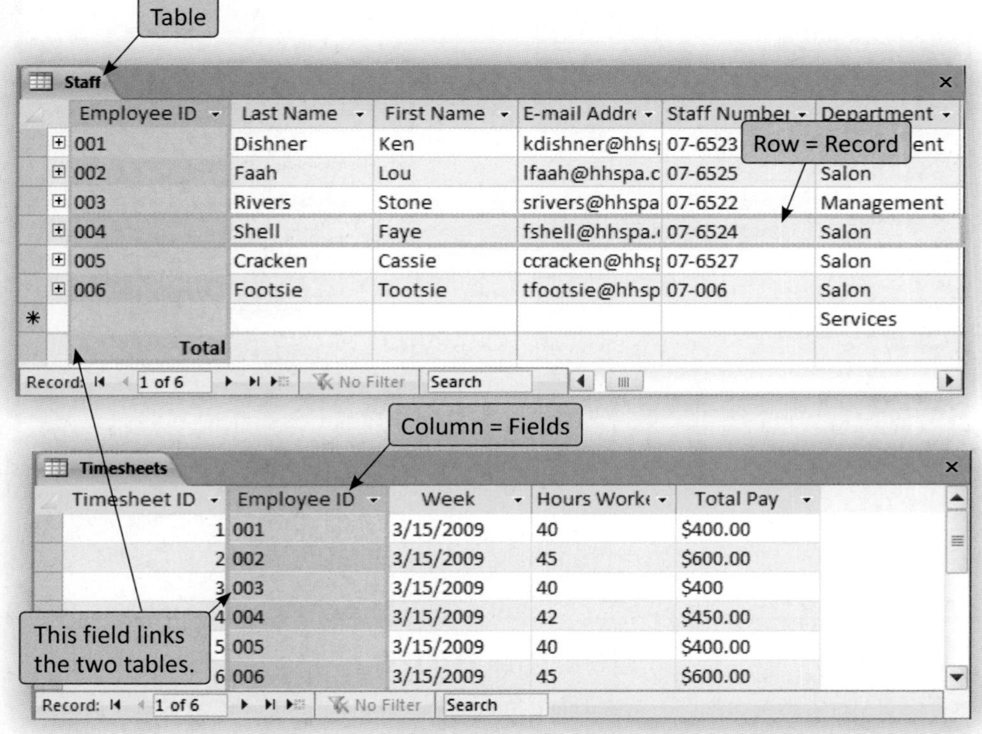

Employee ID	Last Name	First Name	E-mail Addr	Staff Number	Department
001	Dishner	Ken	kdishner@hhs	07-6523	ent
002	Faah	Lou	lfaah@hhspa.c	07-6525	Salon
003	Rivers	Stone	srivers@hhspa	07-6522	Management
004	Shell	Faye	fshell@hhspa.	07-6524	Salon
005	Cracken	Cassie	ccracken@hhs	07-6527	Salon
006	Footsie	Tootsie	tfootsie@hhsp	07-006	Salon
					Services
Total					

Timesheet ID	Employee ID	Week	Hours Work	Total Pay
1	001	3/15/2009	40	$400.00
2	002	3/15/2009	45	$600.00
3	003	3/15/2009	40	$400
4	004	3/15/2009	42	$450.00
5	005	3/15/2009	40	$400.00
6	006	3/15/2009	45	$600.00

FIGURE AC 1.1

Access is different from other Microsoft Office applications you may have used. Although you create and work with a single Access database file, inside the file, there are multiple **objects**. Within each Access database, you create, edit, and save (and delete) objects. The types of objects in an Access database are

Tables—store all the database data. Tables are the basic building blocks of the database.

Forms—allow users to input data through a friendly interface. Entering data through a form is easier than entering it directly into a table.

Queries—extract data from a table or related tables. Queries can include calculations.

Reports—display database information for printing or viewing on-screen.

Macros—are collections of programming code usually used within forms and reports.

The Access 2010 interface is significantly different from older versions of Access. All of the database objects are organized in the **Navigation Pane**, which is docked at the left side of the screen. The Navigation Pane is usually expanded when you open an Access database. If you need more room to work, you can collapse the Navigation Pane by clicking the **Shutter Bar Open/Close** button. To expand the Navigation Pane again, click the **Shutter Bar Open/Close** button.

You can change the way your database objects are grouped in the Navigation Pane. Click the arrow to expand the Navigation Pane menu, and click an option in the *Navigate to Category* list:

- **Object Type**—groups database objects by type (tables, forms, queries, reports).
- **Tables and Related Views**—displays tables grouped with the other database objects dependent upon them.
- **Created Date**—sorts database objects by the date they were created.
- **Modified Date**—sorts database objects by the date they were last changed.

To open a database object, double-click the object name in the Navigation Pane. The object will appear as a new tab within the Access work area unless it is specifically designed to open in a window format.

FIGURE AC 1.2

tips & tricks

If you are familiar with previous versions of Microsoft Access, keep in mind that the Navigation Pane can replace Switchboards. Use the Navigation Pane options to control which objects or groups of objects are available to your users.

tell me more

You can create your own custom categories and control what objects are visible to users through the *Navigation Options* dialog. Right-click the top of the Navigation Pane and click **Navigation Options . . .** Make the changes you want in the *Navigation Options* dialog, and then click **OK.**

try this

Press the F11 function key on your keyboard to open or close the Navigation Pane.

1.2 Using Quick Start Application Parts

Beginning a new blank database can be intimidating. **Quick Start Application Parts** provide predesigned tables, forms, and reports that you can use to start building a database. Some application parts, like Comments, are simple—containing only a single table. Others, like Contacts, are more complex and include tables, queries, forms, and reports designed to work together.

To use a Quick Start Application Part:

1. Click the **Create** tab.
2. In the *Templates* group, click the **Application Parts** button to expand the gallery.
3. In the *Quick Start* section, click the option you want to add.
4. If you have any objects open, Access will ask to close them. Click **Yes.**
5. Access will ask if you want to establish a relationship between the new table added by the application part and another table in your database. To add the new table without adding any table relationships, click the **There is no relationship.** radio button.
6. Click **Create.**
7. Access automatically adds the objects in the application part you selected to your database.

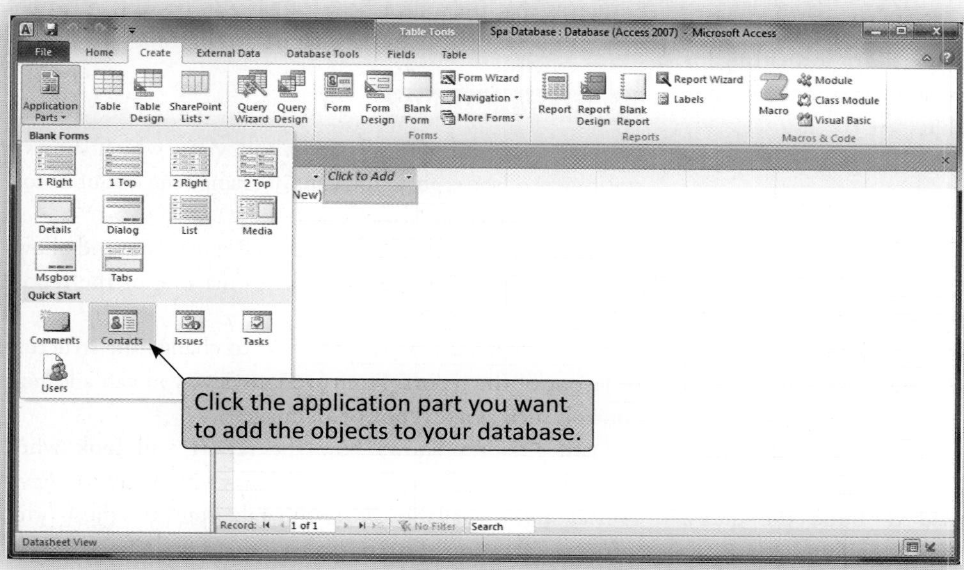

Click the application part you want to add the objects to your database.

FIGURE AC 1.3

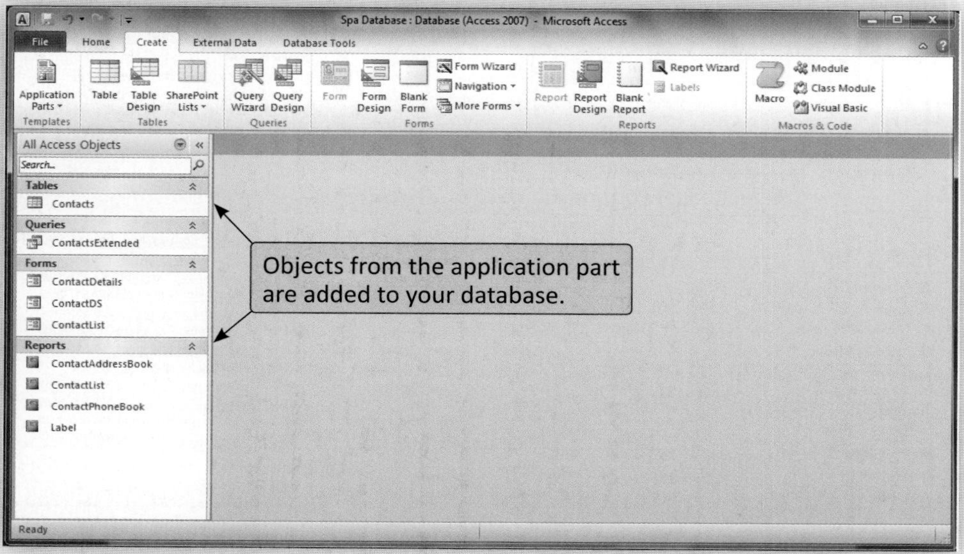

Objects from the application part are added to your database.

FIGURE AC 1.4

1.3 Using Views in Access 2010

You can open database objects in different views, depending on what you want to do. Each view has its own Ribbon tab(s) with commands available in that specific view.

To switch to another view:

› On the *Home* tab, in the *Views* group, click the **View** button arrow, and select the view you want.

TABLE VIEWS

By default, tables open in **Datasheet view.** Use Datasheet view when entering data in a table or to sort and filter data. From the *Datasheet* tab, you can add new fields or modify field properties without having to switch to Design view.

From **Design view,** you establish the table primary key and table properties as well as specific properties or formatting for individual fields. Use Design view when you want to change the structure or properties of the table.

PivotTable view and **PivotChart view** give you special tools for analyzing the table data.

QUERY VIEWS

By default, queries open in **Datasheet view,** showing the record set that matches the query criteria. Datasheet view for a query does not include the *Datasheet* tab that is available in a table.

Design view is where you build the query, adding fields and specifying criteria.

SQL view shows the code used to build the query. Advanced users may build queries directly in SQL view.

PivotTable view and **PivotChart view** provide the same data analysis tools that are available for tables.

FORM VIEWS

Most forms open automatically in **Form view.** Form view provides a user-friendly interface for entering data. From Form view, you cannot change the form layout or formatting.

Layout view looks very similar to Form view, except this view allows you to manipulate the layout and formatting of the form while viewing "live" data.

Use **Design view** when you want to change the structure or properties of the form. From Design view, you can add new controls such as a text box or a subform.

Forms that use a datasheet format also have a **Datasheet view** available. Not all forms include this option.

REPORT VIEWS

Reports open automatically in **Report view,** which shows a static view of the report. You cannot change the layout or formatting of the report from Report view.

Layout view looks very similar to Report view and allows you to manipulate the layout and formatting of the report while viewing "live" data.

Use **Design view** when you want to change the structure or layout of the report. From Design view, you can add new controls such as a text box or an image.

Print Preview shows how the report will look when printed. When you are in Print Preview view, only the *Print Preview* tab is available. From this tab, you can adjust print settings and export the report to another file format.

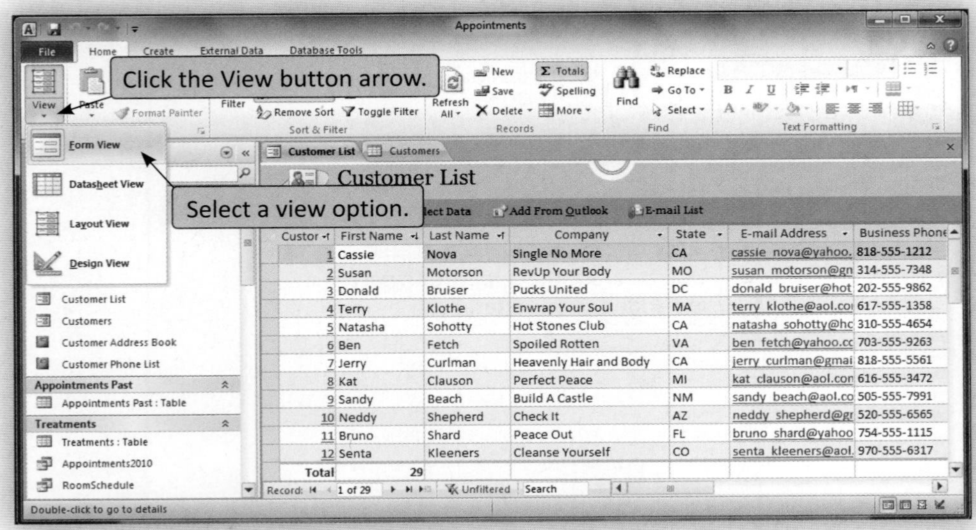

FIGURE AC 1.5

from the perspective of . . .

STUDENT

I use database software to store all my music. I can load the MP3 songs directly into a table. Later I can use the query feature to find my favorite song by title or singer.

tips & tricks

In previous versions of Access, modifying layouts in Design view required the user to switch back and forth between Design view and Form view or Report view to see how changes looked with real data. Now, with the Layout view you can modify the layout of a form or report while viewing data "live."

tell me **more**

If you try to make a change in Layout view that requires Design view instead, Access will prompt you to switch views.

try **this**

If the view you want to switch to is the default view available, you can switch views by going to the *Home* tab, in the *Views* group, and clicking the **View** button. It is not necessary to expand the list of views if the one you want is already visible.

To switch views you can also:

- Right-click the object tab and select the view you want.
- Click the appropriate view button in the status bar.

1.4 Navigating Records in a Form or Table

Tables often contain many records and can be difficult to navigate. At the bottom of the table window, you'll find navigation buttons to help you move quickly to the beginning or end of a table. You can jump to a specific record number or advance through the table one record at a time.

To navigate among records in a large table:

- Move to the next record by clicking the **Next Record** button ▶.
- Move to the last record by clicking the **Last Record** button ▶|.
- Move to the previous record by clicking the **Previous Record** button ◀.
- Return to the first record in the table by clicking the **First Record** button |◀.
- Move to a specific record number by typing the number in the *Current Record* box, then pressing [← Enter] or [Tab] on the keyboard.

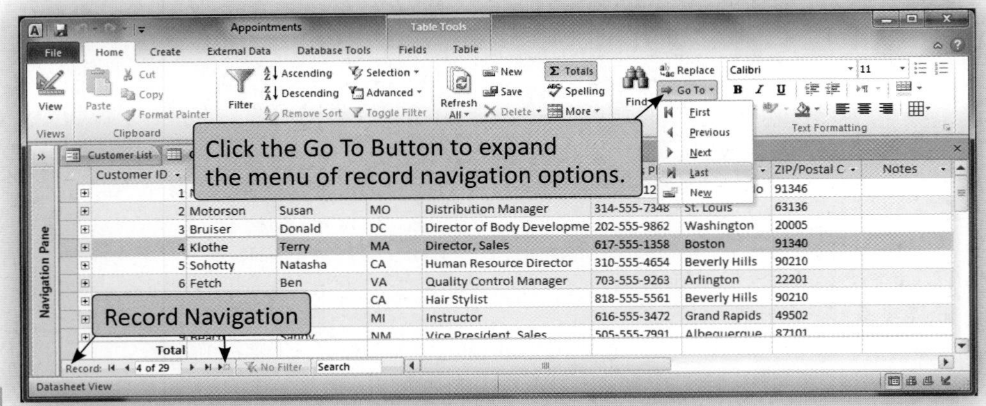

FIGURE AC 1.6

When you use a form to enter data, pressing [Tab] on the keyboard moves you from field to field. Pressing [Tab] from the last field in the record will move you to the next record or create a new blank record. You can also use the navigation buttons to move between records. The navigation buttons found at the bottom of the form window are the same as those in the table window.

tips & tricks

Navigating through a query is the same as navigating through a table. When you run a query, the results window includes record navigation buttons at the bottom of the window—just like a table.

tell me **more**

When entering data in a form, after you enter data in the last field, press [Tab] on the keyboard to open a new blank record.

try **this**

The record navigation commands are also available from the *Home* tab, in the *Find* group. Click the **Go To** button, and then click one of the navigation options from the menu.

You can use the arrow keys on your keyboard to navigate through fields in a record or between records.

- Press [Ctrl] + [↑] to go to the first record in the table.
- Press [Ctrl] + [↓] to go to the last record in the table.

1.5 Entering Data in a Table

Data are entered in records—through tables or forms. When entering records in a table, you must use ***Datasheet view.*** When you enter data in a table, Access commits the data (saves them) each time you move to a new field or begin a new record.

To enter records in a table:

1. Open the table in Datasheet view by double-clicking the table in the Navigation Pane.
2. If the last row of the table is visible, you can enter data by typing in the first field in the *(New)* row. Notice that once you enter data in a field, Access automatically adds a new *(New)* row.
3. If the last row of the table is not visible, insert a new record by clicking the **New (blank) record** button at the bottom of the table.
4. Type or select the data in the first field of the record. Press Tab or Enter on the keyboard to move to the next field. If the first field uses the AutoNumber format, you will not be able to type in that cell of the datasheet. Instead, move to the second cell to begin entering data.
5. When you've entered all the data for the new record, press Tab or Enter to start another new record.

FIGURE AC 1.7

tips & tricks

Not all fields allow you to enter data by typing. Some fields (called lookup fields) have lists from which you choose values; other fields allow you to insert a picture or other object.

If the field has rules to govern the type or format of data, Access will warn you if you enter invalid data.

try this

Other ways to add a new blank record to the table:

- On the *Home* tab, in the *Records* group, click the **New** button. If the *Records* group is collapsed, you will need to click the **Records** button first.
- On the *Home* tab, in the *Find* group, click the **Go To** button, and select **New** from the menu.
- Right-click any of the row selector buttons and select **New Record** from the menu.
- Use the keyboard shortcut Ctrl + +.

tell me more

You can delete records from tables. However, if your database has a complex structure, deleting records may not be as simple as the procedures listed below (as records in one table may be linked to records in another table). Access will prevent you from deleting records if the deletion would violate the integrity rules of the database.

There are multiple ways to delete a record. To delete a record, click the record selector for the record you want to delete, and do the following:

- On the *Home* tab, in the *Records* group, click the **Delete** button Delete. (If the *Records* group is collapsed, click the **Records** button to expand it.)
- Right-click the record selector and select **Delete Record** from the menu.
- Press the Delete key on your keyboard.
- Use the keyboard shortcut Ctrl + -.
- If the entire record is not selected, click the Delete button arrow and select **Delete Record.**

1.6 Entering Data in a Form

When you use a form to enter data, you are actually adding data to the underlying table. The form is a more convenient and user-friendly format for entering records. When you enter data in a form, Access commits the data (saves them) each time you move to a new field or begin a new record.

Access offers database designers a wide variety of tools for creating forms, so no two forms may look exactly alike. However, the process for entering data in a form is the same regardless of the format and layout of the form. Like the table Datasheet view, Form view includes a series of navigation buttons along the bottom of the form window.

To enter data in a form:

1. Open the form in Form view by double-clicking the form in the Navigation Pane.
2. Some forms are designed to automatically open to a new record where you can immediately begin entering data. If necessary, you can start a new blank record by clicking the **New (blank) record** button at the bottom of the form window.
3. Type or select the data in the first field of the record. Press Tab or ←Enter on the keyboard to move to the next field. The form design determines the tab order—that is, the order in which the Tab key moves from field to field in the form.
4. When you've entered all the data for the new record, press Tab or ←Enter to start another new record.

FIGURE AC 1.8

tips & tricks

If one of the fields is a memo field, you won't be able to use the ←Enter key to move to the next field. Pressing ←Enter will just keep adding blank lines to the memo. Use the Tab key or the mouse to move to the next field.

try this

Other ways to enter a new blank record in a form:

- Click the **New** button in the *Records* group on the *Home* tab. If the *Records* group is collapsed, you will need to click the **Records** button first.
- On the *Home* tab, in the *Find* group, click the **Go To** button, and select **New Record** from the menu.
- Right-click any of the row selector buttons and select **New Record** from the menu.
- Use the keyboard shortcut Ctrl + +.

tell me more

You can delete records from forms. However, if your database has a complex structure, deleting records may not be as simple as the procedures listed below (as records in one form/table may be linked to records in another form/table). Access will prevent you from deleting records if the deletion would violate the integrity rules of the database.

There are multiple ways to delete a record through a form. To delete a record, click the record selector so the record you want to delete is displayed on the form, and do one of the following:

- On the *Home* tab, in the *Records* group, click the **Delete** button. (If the *Records* group is collapsed, click the **Records** button to expand it.) If the entire record is not selected, click the **Delete** button arrow and select **Delete Record** instead.
- Right-click the record selector and select **Delete Record** from the menu. (If the form appears as a popup, right-click any blank area of the form.)
- Press the Delete key on your keyboard.
- Use the keyboard shortcut Ctrl + −.

1.7 Using Compact & Repair

To help your database run as efficiently as possible, it is a good practice to run the **Compact & Repair** tool on a regular basis.

When you delete records from an Access database, the database maintains space for the deleted data until you compact the database by removing unnecessary file space. Access also creates hidden, temporary database objects that take up database space unnecessarily. The longer your database is in use, the more of these unnecessary temporary objects there are. The Compact & Repair tool eliminates these unnecessary database objects for optimum efficiency.

To use the Compact & Repair tool:

1. Click the **File** tab.
2. Backstage view opens to the *Info* tab automatically.
3. Click the **Compact & Repair Database** button.

Access automatically returns to the database window when it has finished compacting the database.

If you need to interrupt the compact and repair process for any reason, press and hold the Esc key on your keyboard.

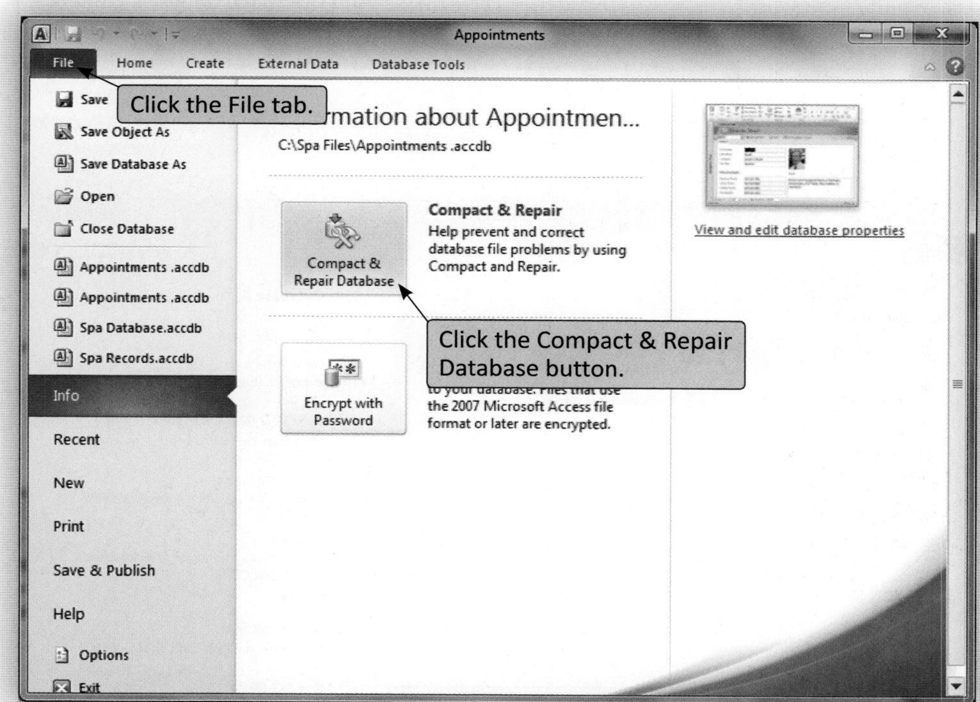

FIGURE AC 1.9

tell me more

You can set your database to automatically compact when you close it by changing the database options:

1. Click the **File** tab.
2. Click the **Options** button.
3. Click **Current Database** at the left side of the *Access Options* box.
4. Click the check box in front of **Compact on Close.**
5. Click **OK.**

1.8 Backing Up a Database

New records, tables, queries, and forms can be added to a database at any time. If you are about to add items or make changes that you may not want to keep, you should back up your database first. By backing up your database, you create a copy of the database and preserve the data at a certain point. At any time you can open the backup and restore your data from an earlier stage.

To create a backup of your database:

1. Close and save any open objects.
2. Click the **File** tab.
3. Click **Save and Publish.**
4. *Save Database As* is selected automatically in the *File Types* box.
5. Click **Backup Database** in the *Save Database As* list at the right side of the screen.
6. Click the **Save As** button.
7. The database will close, and the *Save As* dialog box opens.
8. If necessary, navigate to the location where you want to save the backup file. Access automatically creates a new file name for the backup using the original file name with the current date.
9. Click **Save** to create the backup file. When the backup is finished, Access opens your original database again.

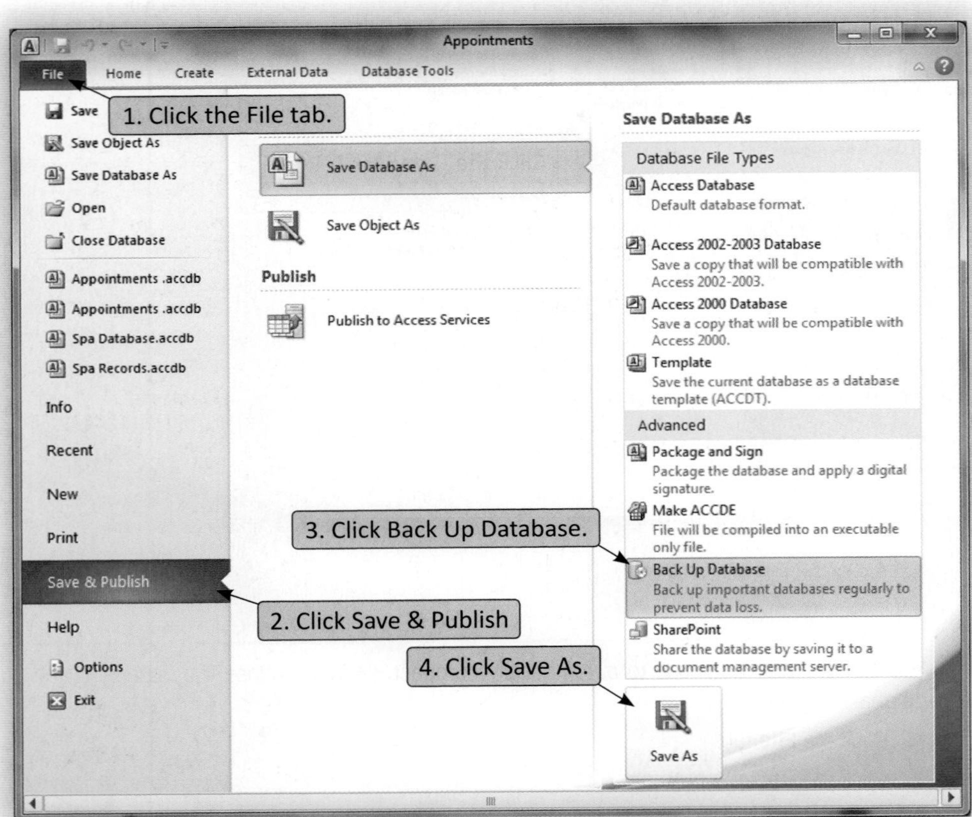

FIGURE AC 1.10

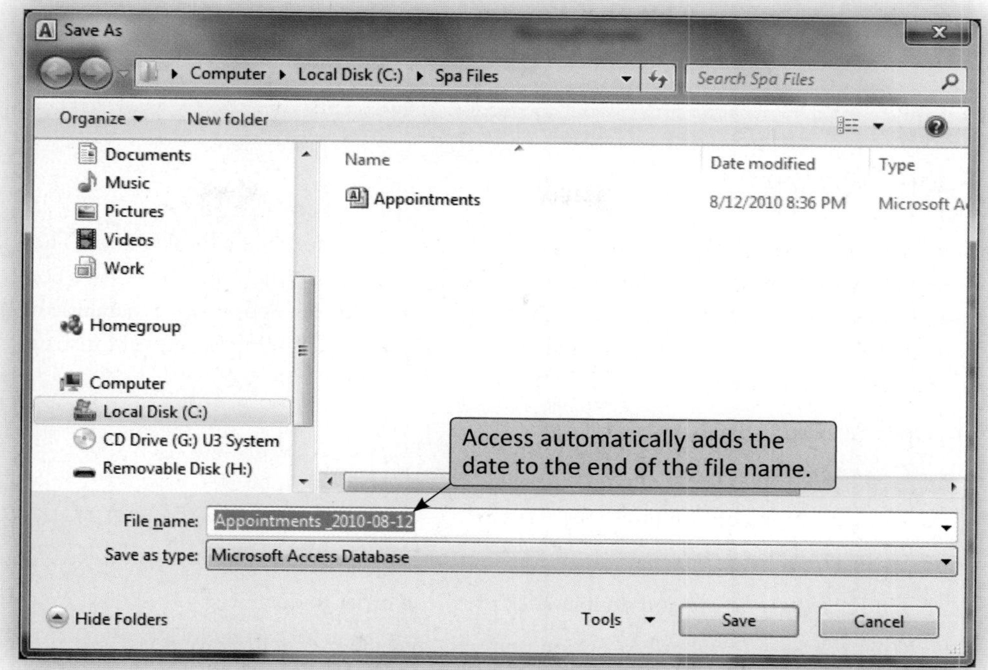

FIGURE AC 1.11

tips & tricks

Be sure to create a backup of your database before making any major changes to the database structure.

tell me more

If you find that you need to restore a database object (such as a table, query, form, or report) from a backup copy, click the **External Data** tab. In the *Import & Link* group, click the **Import Access Database** button to find and restore the database object you want.

If you want to completely replace a database with a backup copy, delete the database file you no longer want and then rename the backup so it has the original file name.

projects

Skill Review 1.1

You are a part-time employee in the Computer Science department of a local college. They would like your assistance in using Access 2010 to keep track of which employees have borrowed items from the department. Become comfortable with the department's database by completing the steps below. *Please note:* For any step that contains a question, your instructor may require a written response.

1. Open an existing database.

a. Open Microsoft Access 2010.

b. Click the **Open** option under the *File* tab.

c. In the *Open* dialog box, navigate to the location of your Access 2010 student files.

d. Find *collegedept.accdb* and double-click the file in order to open it.

e. Click the **Save Database As** option under the *File* tab in order to save this database as ***[your initials]*** **AC_SkillReview_1-1**.

2. Use the Navigation Pane.

a. Click the top of the Navigation Pane and observe the differences between the *Navigate To Category* and *Filter By Group* options.

b. Select **Object Type** and **All Access Objects** (if either of these options already contains a check mark to the left, then do not click it again).

c. Write down the names of all the objects now present in the Navigation Pane, as well as the category they are located under.

d. Click the top of the Navigation Pane again and select the **Tables and Related Views** option. Make sure **All Tables** is the checked option in the *Filter By Group* area.

e. Take a look at the objects in the Navigation Pane. What changed? Please write down the names of the objects inside the *Items* category.

f. Double-click the object named **Items : Table** in order to open it.

3. Switch views in an Access table.

a. You are now viewing the *Items* table in Datasheet view. *Home* should be the selected tab in the Ribbon.

b. Click the **View** arrow button located at the left side of the Ribbon. A menu with four options will appear below.

c. Select the **Design View** option from that menu.

d. What are the differences between this Design view and the previous Datasheet view? Write down your observations.

e. Go back to Datasheet view by using the **View** button of the Ribbon again.

4. Navigate records in a table.

a. Observe the record navigation buttons at the bottom of the table. Move your mouse over the different arrow buttons and observe the ScreenTips.

b. Observe which record in the table becomes highlighted as you click the following record navigation buttons: **Last record, First record, Next record, Previous record.**

c. Observe the *Current Record* box, which indicates the current record and the total number of records. Click to select the number in the *Current Record* box. Type the number 5 in this box and press the **Enter** key. Observe the record in your table that became highlighted.

d. Use the following shortcut keys on your keyboard and observe which field/record becomes highlighted: **Tab, Up Arrow, Down Arrow, Left Arrow, Right Arrow.** In addition, try holding the **Ctrl** key while pressing the **Up Arrow** or **Down Arrow** key.

5. Enter, edit, and delete records in a table.

a. Click the **New (blank) record** button at the bottom of the table.

b. Enter the following record into your table, using the **Tab** or **Right Arrow** key to move from one field to the next. When you reach the *Category* field, observe that it is a lookup field. Use the drop-down arrow on the right side to view and select from the available values.

ITEMID	ITEMNAME	DESCRIPTION	CATEGORY	COST
ACC1	Accounting 2.0	Accounting software for small businesses	Software	$149.00

c. Find the record with an *ItemID* of GRA1. Using your mouse, click to right of the word *Studio* in the *ItemName* field. Press the **Spacebar** and type: 10.1. The *ItemName* will now read *Graphics Studio 10.1.*

d. Find the record with an *ItemID* of SPH1. Click the **Record Selector** box on the left side of that row to highlight the entire record. Press the **Delete** key on your keyboard and then click the **Yes** button to permanently delete this record.

e. Close the *Items* table by clicking the small, black **x** at the top right of the table.

6. Enter, edit, and delete records in a form.

a. Double click **ItemsForm** in the Navigation Pane in order to open it.

b. Observe the record navigation buttons at the bottom of the form and note that they are the same as those in the table.

c. Click the **New (blank) record** button at the bottom of the form.

d. Enter the following record into your form, using the **Tab** key to move from one field to the next.

ITEMID	ITEMNAME	DESCRIPTION	CATEGORY	COST
CAM1	Digital Camera	10 megapixel SLR digital camera	Equipment	$499.00

e. Find the record with an *ItemID* of LAP1. Click inside the *Cost* field and change the amount from *$550* to $450.

f. Navigate to the record with an *ItemID* of PB03. Find the **Delete** button, which is in the *Record* group of the *Home* tab of the Ribbon. Click the drop-down arrow next to the **Delete** button and choose the **Delete Record** option. Click the **Yes** button in the dialog box that appears next in order to permanently delete this record.

g. Close *ItemsForm* by clicking the small, black **x** at the top right of the form.

7. Use *Compact & Repair.*
   a. Minimize the Access 2010 window and navigate to the folder where you saved this database. Observe the file size.
   b. Return to Access and click the **File** tab.
   c. Click the **Compact & Repair Database** button.
   d. Minimize Access 2010 and look at your database file again. How much did the file size decrease?
8. Backup a database.
   a. If necessary, maximize Access 2010 and click the **File** tab.
   b. Click the **Save & Publish** option.
   c. In the *Save Database As* area, under *Advanced,* double-click **Back Up Database.**
   d. Click the **Save** button in the *Save As* dialog box.

Skill Review 1.2

You have just been hired by a small health insurance company in the south Florida area. One of your duties is using Access 2010 to manage the company's list of in-network doctors and covered procedures. Become comfortable with the company's database by completing the steps below. *Please note:* For any step that contains a question, your instructor may require a written response.

1. Open an existing database.
   a. Open Microsoft Access 2010.
   b. Click the **Open** option under the *File* tab.
   c. In the *Open* dialog box, navigate to the location of your Access 2010 student files.
   d. Find *sfinsurance.accdb* and double-click the file in order to open it.
   e. Click the **Save Database As** option under the *File* tab in order to save this database as `[your initials]AC_SkillReview_1-2`.
2. Use the Navigation Pane.
   a. Click the top of the Navigation Pane and observe differences between the *Navigate To Category* and *Filter By Group* options.
   b. Select **Object Type** and **All Access Objects** (if either of these options already contains a check mark to the left, then do not click it again).
   c. Write down the names of all the objects now present in the Navigation Pane, as well as the category they are located under.
   d. Click the top of the Navigation Pane again and select the **Tables and Related Views** option. Make sure **All Tables** is the checked option in the *Filter By Group* area.
   e. Take a look at the objects in the Navigation Pane. What changed? Please write down the names of the objects inside the *Physicians* category.
   f. Double-click the object named **Physicians : Table** in order to open it.
3. Switch views in an Access table.
   a. You are now viewing the *Physicians* table in Datasheet view. *Home* should be the selected tab in the Ribbon.
   b. Click the **View** arrow button located at the left side of the Ribbon. A menu with four options will appear below.
   c. Select the **Design View** option from that menu.

d. What are the differences between this Design view and the previous Datasheet view? Write down your observations.

e. Go back to Datasheet view by using the **View** button of the Ribbon again.

4. Navigate records in a table.

a. Observe the record navigation buttons at the bottom of the table. Move your mouse over the different arrow buttons and observe the ScreenTips.

b. Observe which record in the table becomes highlighted as you click the following record navigation buttons: **Last record, First record, Next record, Previous record.**

c. Observe the *Current Record* box, which indicates the current record and the total number of records. Click to select the number in the *Current Record* box. Type the number `11` in this box and press the **Enter** key. Observe the record in your table that became highlighted.

d. Use the following shortcut keys on your keyboard and observe which field/record becomes highlighted: **Tab, Up Arrow, Down Arrow, Left Arrow, Right Arrow.** In addition, try holding the **Ctrl** key while pressing the **Up Arrow** or **Down Arrow** key.

5. Enter, edit, and delete records in a table.

a. Click the **New (blank) record** button at the bottom of the table.

b. Enter the following record into your table, using the **Tab** or **Right Arrow** key to move from one field to the next. When you reach the *City* field, observe that it is a lookup field. Use the drop-down arrow on the right side to view and select from the available values.

PHYSICIANID	FIRSTNAME	LASTNAME	STREETADDRESS	CITY	ZIPCODE	PHONE	MEMBERCOUNT
JB02	› James	› Bryant	› 3091 Main Street	› Miami	› 33143	› (305) 555-2122	› 16

c. Find the record with a *PhysicianID* of `HH01`. Using your mouse, click to right of the word *Avenue* in the *StreetAddress* field. Press **Backspace** a few times to erase it. Now type the word `Lane`. The *StreetAddress* will now read *2204 Plainfield Lane.*

d. Find the record with a *PhysicianID* of `JW01`. Click the **Record Selector** box on the left side of that row to highlight the entire record. Press the **Delete** key on your keyboard and then click the **Yes** button to permanently delete this record.

e. Close the *Physicians* table by clicking the small, black **x** at the top right of the table.

6. Enter, edit, and delete records in a form

a. Double-click **PhysiciansForm** in the Navigation Pane in order to open it.

b. Observe the record navigation buttons at the bottom of the form and note that they are the same as those in the table.

c. Click the **New (blank) record** button at the bottom of the form.

d. Enter the following record into your form, using the **Tab** key to move from one field to the next.

PHYSICIANID	FIRSTNAME	LASTNAME	STREETADDRESS	CITY	ZIPCODE	PHONE	MEMBERCOUNT
KS01	› Karen	› Singer	› 850 Tyler Street	› Miami	› 33155	› (305) 555-2490	› 21

e. Find the record with a *PhysicianID* of `SD01`. Click inside the *ZipCode* field and change the number from *33304* to `33309`.

f. Navigate to the record with a *PhysicianID* of AW01. Find the **Delete** button, which is in the *Record* group of the *Home* tab of the Ribbon. Click the drop-down arrow next to the **Delete** button and choose the **Delete Record** option. Click the **Yes** button in the dialog box that appears next in order to permanently delete this record.

g. Close *PhysiciansForm* by clicking the small, black **x** at the top right of the form.

7. Use *Compact & Repair.*

a. Minimize the Access 2010 window and navigate to the folder where you saved this database. Observe the file size.

b. Return to Access and click the **File** tab.

c. Click the **Compact & Repair Database** button.

d. Minimize Access 2010 and look at your database file again. How much did the file size decrease?

8. Backup a database.

a. Click the **File** tab.

b. Click the **Save & Publish** option.

c. In the *Save Database As* area, under *Advanced,* double-click **Back Up Database.**

d. Click the **Save** button in the *Save As* dialog box.

challenge yourself 1

You are a botany professor who was recently placed in charge of maintaining the department's greenhouse. You have inherited an Access 2010 database from the previous greenhouse supervisor. This database contains records of the plants in the greenhouse and the employees that assist you with maintenance duties. Become comfortable with the department's database by completing the exercises below. *Please note:* For any step that contains a question, your instructor may require a written response.

1. Open the *greenhouse.accdb* student file and save it as **[your initials]AC_Challenge_1-3.**

2. Write down the names of all the objects present in this database. Which three objects appear grouped together after selecting the **Tables and Related Views** option?

3. Open the **Employees** table and switch to Design view. Which of the five fields contains text in the *Description* area?

4. Switch to Datasheet view and browse the records using the record navigation buttons and keyboard shortcuts.

5. Enter the following record into your table and note that the *Position* field is a lookup field.

EMPLOYEEID	FIRSTNAME	LASTNAME	POSITION	WEEKLYHOURS
59267311	› Tracy	› Seidel	› Greenhouse Tech 2	› 15

6. Find the record with a *LastName* of Rojas and change the *WeeklyHours* from *35* to 30.

7. Delete the record with an *EmployeeID* of 23605379.

8. Close the *Employees* table and open **EmployeesForm.**

9. Enter the following record into your form:

EMPLOYEEID	FIRSTNAME	LASTNAME	POSITION	WEEKLYHOURS
77913350	George	Phillips	Greenhouse Tech 2	20

10. Find the employee named Gary and edit his last name so that it reads Mills.
11. Delete the record of the employee named Dale Barnes.
12. Close the *EmployeeForm.*
13. Observe the file size of your database. Use the *Compact & Repair Database* feature and check the file again. How much did the file size decrease?
14. Create a backup of this database using the default name chosen by Access.

challenge yourself 2

You work for a volunteer organization that ships and administers vaccines to various relief centers all over the world. It would like you to use Access 2010 to maintain a list of all approved vaccines and keep track of all shipments made to the relief centers. Become comfortable with the organization's database by completing the exercises below. *Please note:* For any step that contains a question, your instructor may require a written response.

1. Open the *vaccines.accdb* student file and save it as **[your initials]AC_Challenge_1-4.**
2. Write down the names of all the objects present in this database. Which two objects appear grouped together after selecting the **Tables and Related Views** option?
3. Open the **Vaccines** table and switch to Design view. What *data type* was selected for all three fields in that table?
4. Switch to Datasheet view and browse the records using the record navigation buttons and keyboard shortcuts.
5. Enter the following record into your table and note that the *TargetAudience* field is a lookup field.

VACCINEID	VACCINENAME	TARGETAUDIENCE
MAL	Malaria	At-risk individuals

6. Find the record with a *VaccineID* of TD and change the *TargetAudience* from *Adults* to *Teenagers.*
7. Delete the record with a *VaccineID* of LYD.
8. Close the *Vaccines* table and open **VaccinesForm.**
9. Enter the following record into your form:

VACCINEID	VACCINENAME	TARGETAUDIENCE
DF	Dengue Fever	At-risk individuals

10. Find the record with a *VaccineID* of FLU and add (Yearly Flu) after the word *Influenza.*

11. Delete the record with a *VaccineID* of JE.
12. Close *VaccinesForm.*
13. Observe the file size of your database. Use the *Compact & Repair Database* feature and check the file again. How much did the file size decrease?
14. Create a backup of this database using the default name chosen by Access.

on your own

You have an extensive movie collection at home. You have realized that Access 2010 is a great tool to help you keep a list of all the movies you own and keep track of which friends/relatives have borrowed your movies. Demonstrate your basic understanding of Access by completing the following exercises:

1. Open the *movie_collection.accdb* student file and save it as **[your initials]AC_OnYourOwn_1-5.**
2. Earlier this week, you acquired four new movies. Add these four movies to your database. You may use real or fake movies, but you must fill in all the fields and ensure your new data are consistent with the ones that are already there.
3. Find the movie with the word Lincoln in the title. Change the format to *Blu-Ray.*
4. You seem to have lost your solar system movie. Find and remove that movie from your database and make a note of which one you deleted for the instructor.
5. Make your database file size smaller and create a backup.

fix it

A local pet store has hired you to fix its database, which keeps track of inventory, customers, and store sales. Open the file named *petstore.accdb* and investigate the issues below. Fix the errors and save the file as **[your initials]AC_FixIt_1-6.** If your instructor requires that you justify your changes, please type them into a Word document and submit it along with your corrected database.

1. The employees can no longer see their forms and reports in the Navigation Pane. Why?
2. The owner tells you that a former employee would often make data entry errors, and he wants your help in finding and correcting these errors. Open the **Pets** table, find the three errors, and correct them. Hints: The first error is a misspelled animal type, the second error is a missing color, and the third error requires a swap between a particular record's breed and color.
3. The owner wonders why the database file size is so large. Help him reduce the file size.

chapter 2

Working with Tables

In this chapter, you will learn the following skills:

- **Skill 2.1** Designing a Table
- **Skill 2.2** Adding Fields to Tables in Datasheet View
- **Skill 2.3** Adding a Lookup Field from Another Table in Datasheet View
- **Skill 2.4** Adjusting Column Widths in Datasheet View
- **Skill 2.5** Changing Data Type in Datasheet View
- **Skill 2.6** Adding a Total Row
- **Skill 2.7** Using Attachment Fields
- **Skill 2.8** Modifying Field Properties in Datasheet View
- **Skill 2.9** Creating a Table in Design View
- **Skill 2.10** Setting the Primary Key
- **Skill 2.11** Adding and Deleting Fields in Design View
- **Skill 2.12** Modifying Field Properties in Design View
- **Skill 2.13** Adding a Lookup Field from a List in Design View
- **Skill 2.14** Modifying Lookup Field Properties
- **Skill 2.15** Modifying Table Properties
- **Skill 2.16** Renaming and Deleting Tables

skills

- **Design a table by adding fields, adjusting columns, and adding Lookup fields from other tables**
- **Work in Datasheet and Design views to create tables, modify field properties, and add lookup fields**
- **Learn to use attachment fields, set the primary key, and add a Total row to a table**
- **Modify table properties**
- **Rename and delete tables**

introduction

This chapter focuses on the Table object in Access 2010. New tables and their fields are created in both Datasheet and Design views. Various data types are introduced in order to determine the type of information stored in each field. Several field properties are changed to ensure that the data have the proper appearance and a primary key is set for one of the fields. The chapter also contains several exercises that focus on the formatting of the table in Datasheet view and the addition of Total rows.

2.1 Designing a Table

Remember that Access is a relational database—objects in your database are related to one another through relationships defined by common fields between tables. When you design a new table, consider how that table will relate to other tables in your database.

Design your database so that information is stored in one table only. For example, if your company has departments at different addresses, it makes more sense to create a Departments table to store the address for each department, and then create a Department field in your Employees table instead of storing the full department address in each employee record. That way, if the address of the department changes, you only need to update the Departments table instead of trying to update the record for each employee.

Field

Record

Table: Employees

ID	LastName	FirstName	Dept
001	Alberto	John	Sales
002	Smith	Mary	Sales
003	Mann	Terrance	Marketing
004	Jones	Margaret	Main

Table: Departments

Dept	Street	City	State
Sales	123 Main	Newton	CT
Marketing	55 Oak	Quincy	CT
Main	2 51st Street, NE	Wellington	CT

FIGURE AC 2.1

Even if you begin with one of the well-designed database templates included with Access, you may find that you need to add tables. One way to work with a new table is to add a blank table and add fields directly in Datasheet view.

1. Click the **Create** tab.
2. In the *Tables* group, click the **Table** button to insert a new table.

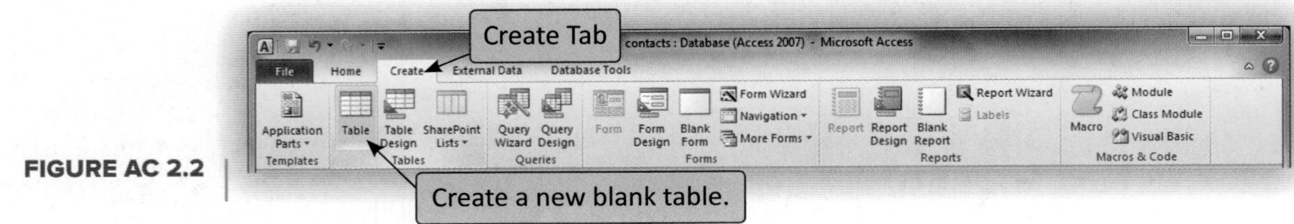

FIGURE AC 2.2

3. The new table opens in Datasheet view. The first field is automatically added as an AutoNumber field named *ID*.
4. To add a new field, begin typing. Access names the first field *Field1*.
5. Access will apply a data type based on what you type. For example, if you type a date, Access will automatically apply the Date/Time data type to the field.
6. Press Tab or Enter to add another field.
7. When you are finished, save the table by clicking the **Save** button on the Quick Access Toolbar. Type a meaningful name in the *Table Name:* box, and then click **OK**.

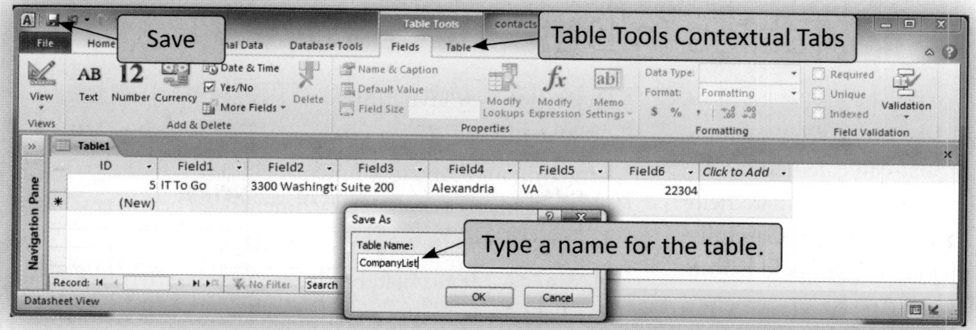

FIGURE AC 2.3

By default, the new fields are named Field1, Field2, etc. To rename a field:

1. Click anywhere in the field to select it.
2. On the *Table Tools Fields* tab, in the *Properties* group, click the **Name & Caption** button.
3. In the *Name* box, type the new field name. This is the name as it will be referenced by other objects in your database.
4. In the *Caption* box, type the field name as it should appear in labels and column headings. If you do not include a caption, Access will use the field name instead.
5. In the *Description* box, type additional information about the field (if necessary).
6. Click **OK.**

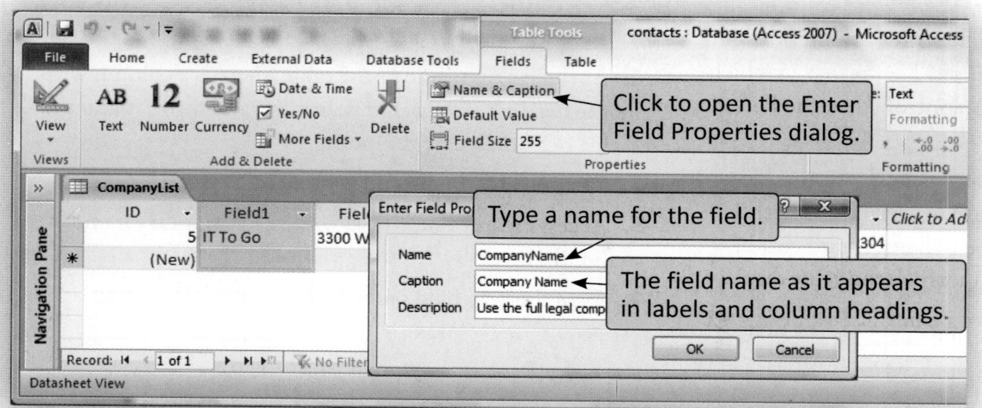

FIGURE AC 2.4

tips & tricks

A good practice is to avoid the use of spaces, hyphens, ampersands (&), and other unusual characters in field names. While Access can generally work with these characters, if you export data to another type of database, these characters might cause unexpected behavior. Use a mix of upper- and lowercase letters to make names easier to read—for example, use "CompanyName" instead of "Company Name."

tell me more

When you enter data in a table, the table is saved every time you move to a new field or record in the database. When you make changes to the database structure (such as adding a new field or changing a field name), you must actively save the table to commit the change. Access will prompt you to save your database changes whenever necessary. However, it is good practice to save manually as you make changes.

try this

To rename a field, right-click the field name at the top of the column in Datasheet view and select **Rename Field.** The field name appears highlighted. Type the new name, and then press Enter.

2.2 Adding Fields to Tables in Datasheet View

Each field in a table is assigned a specific data type. Specifying the appropriate data type for a field is crucial to designing a useful database. For example, you can't run calculations on a field with the text field type, and you can't sort a date field efficiently unless you use the date/time field type. Carefully consider the type of data you will include in each field before you decide on the data type.

AutoNumber—An AutoNumber field is automatically assigned its value by Access. Database users cannot edit or enter data in an AutoNumber field. AutoNumber fields are often used as a primary key if no other unique field exists in the table.

Text—A Text field can hold up to 255 characters. Text fields are used for short text data or numbers that should be treated as text.

Number—A Number field holds a numerical value. The default number is described as a *long integer,* a number between –2,147,483,648 and 2,147,483,647.

Date/Time—A Date/Time field stores a numerical value that is displayed as a date and time. The format in which the date and/or time displays is controlled by the Format property.

Currency—A Currency field stores a numerical value with a high degree of accuracy (up to four decimal places to the right of the decimal). Access will not round currency fields, regardless of the format in which the value displays.

Yes/No—A Yes/No field stores a true/false value as a –1 for yes and 0 for no.

Hyperlink—A Hyperlink field stores a Web address or e-mail address.

Attachment—An Attachment field stores files as attachments to records. Attachments can be images, Word documents, or almost any other type of data file.

Memo—A Memo field holds text and numbers like a text field, except you can enter up to 65,535 characters in a Memo field. Text in Memo fields can be formatted using Rich Text Formatting. When the Text Format field property is set to Rich Text, the text is stored as HTML code.

Calculated Field—A Calculated field uses an expression (a formula) to calculate a value. For example, a field named WeeklyWage might include the expression: [HoursPerWeek]*[HourlyRate]. In this case, [HoursPerWeek] and [HourlyRate] refer to two other fields in the same table. The value of WeeklyWage is the product of HoursPerWeek multiplied by HourlyRate.

To add a new field to a table:

1. At the far right side of the table, there is a column with the header *Click to Add.* Click the arrow to expand the list of available field types.
2. Click the field type you want to add.
3. Access creates a new field with the temporary name highlighted.
4. Type the new field name and then press [Enter].

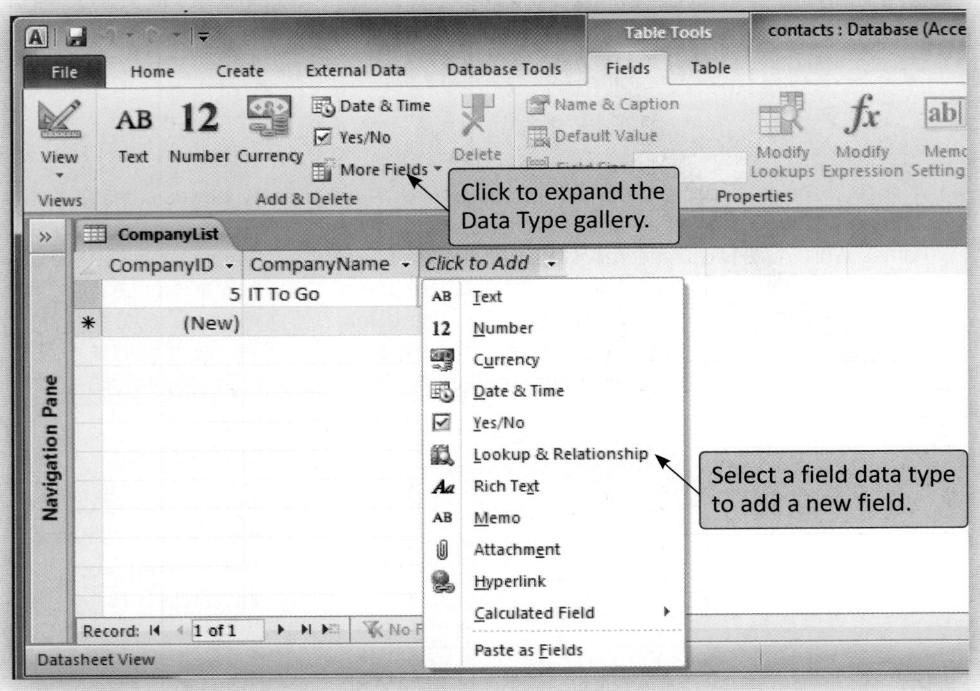

FIGURE AC 2.5

You can also add a new field by clicking the field type you want from the *Table Tools Fields* tab, *Add & Delete* group. If there isn't a button for the data type you want, click the **More Fields** button to expand the *Data Type* gallery.

The *Data Type* gallery organizes new fields by data type, such as Basic Types, Number, Date and Time, and Yes/No. The options in the last section in the gallery, *Quick Start,* insert a related group of fields. For example, select the **Address** option in the *Quick Start* section, and fields for Address, City, State Providence, Zip Postal, and Country Region are added to your table with one command.

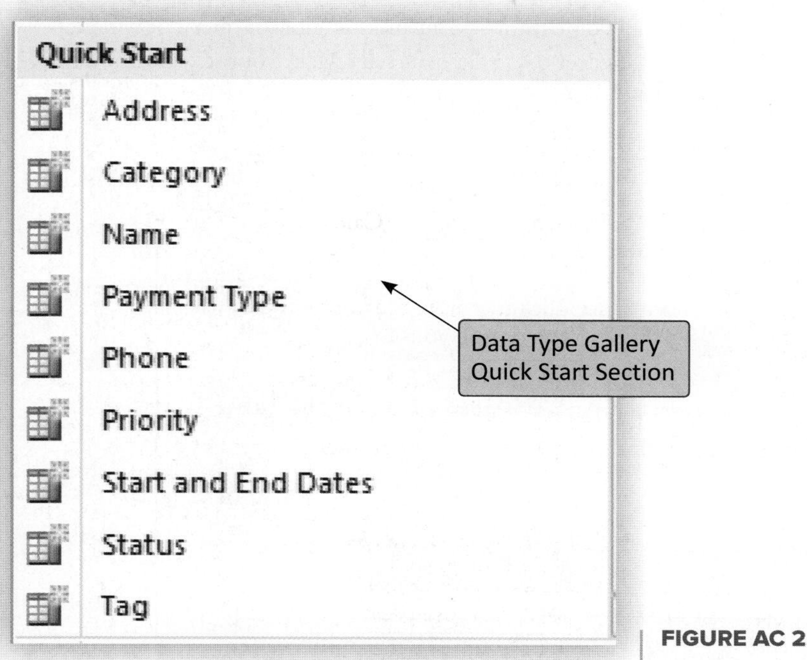

FIGURE AC 2.6

tips & tricks

The *Data Type* gallery replaces the *Add Field* task pane from Access 2007.

tell me more

In previous versions of Access, calculated fields could only be added to queries, but in Access 2010, you have the ability to add a calculated field directly to a table. Calculated fields cannot include references to fields in other tables or queries.

try this

You can also insert a new field by right-clicking any field name and selecting **Insert Field.** A new blank text field is inserted to the left of the field you selected.

2.3 Adding a Lookup Field from Another Table in Datasheet View

A **lookup field** allows the user to select data from a list of items. The list presented can be values from a field in another table or a query, or it can be values that you enter specifically in the lookup list. This skill shows how to create a lookup field that displays values from another table or a query.

To add a new lookup field in Datasheet view:

1. With the table open in Datasheet view, click the **Table Tools Fields** tab.
2. In the *Add & Delete* group, click the **More Fields** button.
3. From the *Basic Types* section, click **Lookup & Relationship.**
4. The *Lookup Wizard* opens. The first step of the wizard asks you to determine where your lookup list data will come from—from another table or query, or will you enter the values yourself? Make your selection and click **Next** to go to the next step.

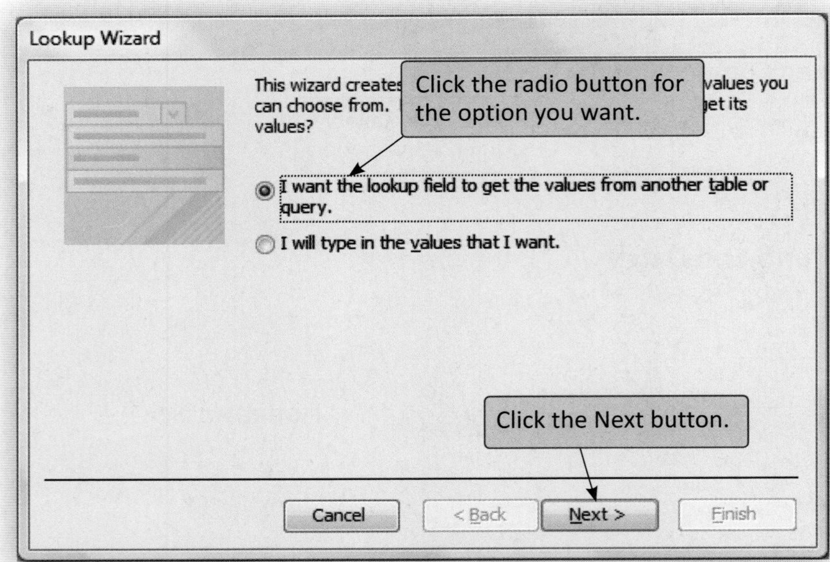

FIGURE AC 2.7

5. If the lookup values will come from a table or query, click the name of the table or query you want to use. Click **Next.**

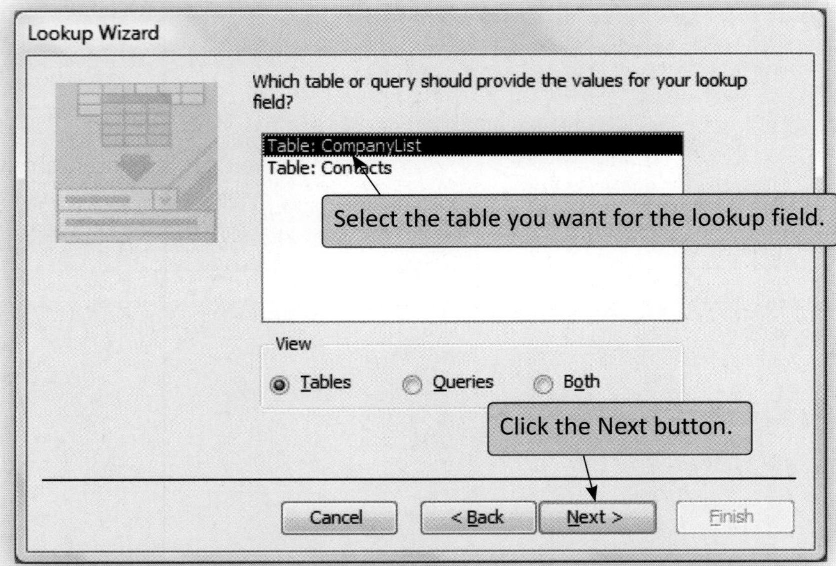

FIGURE AC 2.8

6. Double-click each field name you want to include in the lookup. When you have selected all the fields you want, click **Next.**

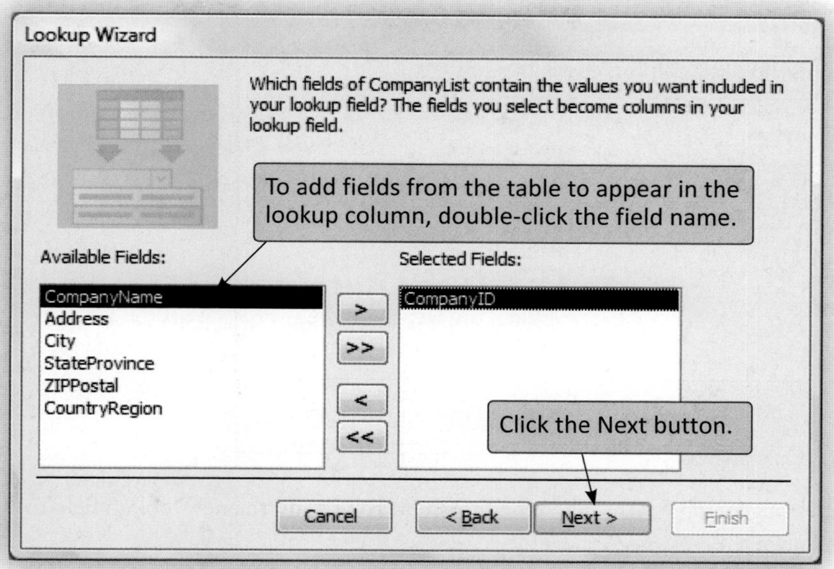

FIGURE AC 2.9

7. If you want items in the lookup list sorted in a particular order, select the field to sort by. The sort order is ascending by default. Click the **Ascending** button if you want to switch the sort order to descending. Click **Next.**

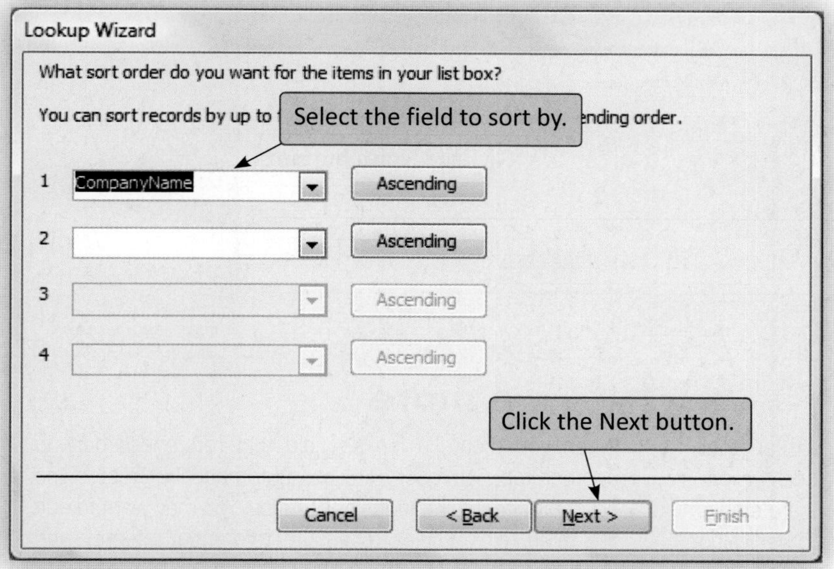

FIGURE AC 2.10

8. If you include a primary key field as one of the fields in the lookup field, Access will give you the option to hide that field during data entry. Click **Next.**

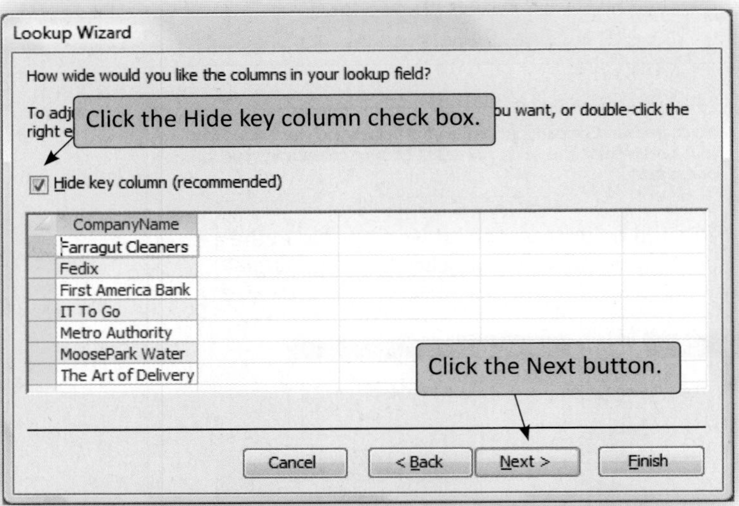

FIGURE AC 2.11

9. By default, Access will give the new lookup field a generic name (like Field1). You should change the name of the new field to something more meaningful.

10. Click the **Finish** button to add the new lookup field to the table.

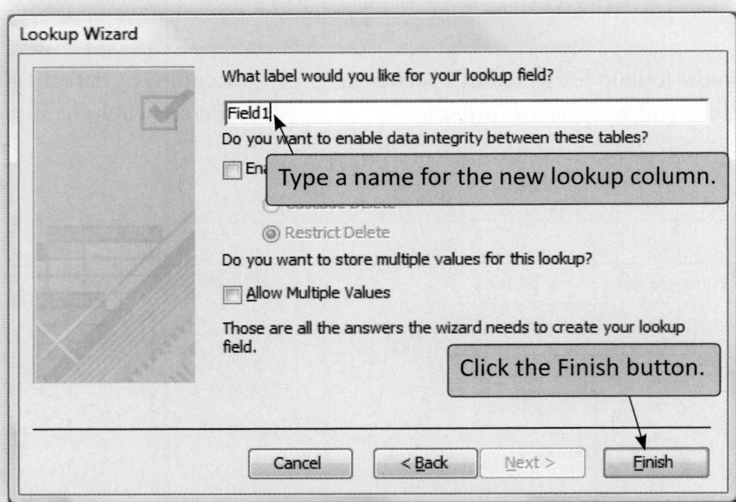

FIGURE AC 2.12

tips & tricks

When creating lookup fields that reference data in another table or query, you almost always want to include the primary key field to ensure that table relationships are stable. However, the primary key is often a number or other value that may not be helpful to someone entering data. In that case, you will also want to include at least one descriptive field in the lookup field to help database users select the correct item from the list.

tell me more

When you create a lookup field that references data in another table or query, Access automatically creates the appropriate table relationships for you. You may want to edit the table relationships to ensure referential integrity and enable cascade update and delete options.

try this

For more information on lookup fields that reference values from a list, refer to Skill 2.13, *Adding a Lookup Field from a List in Design View.*

2.4 Adjusting Column Widths in Datasheet View

When you insert a new field, it is created with the standard width, which may not be wide enough to display all of your data. Adjusting column widths in Datasheet view is similar to working with column widths in Excel.

To use the mouse to change the column size:

1. Move the mouse to the right border of the field header. The cursor changes to a ✛ shape.
2. Click and drag to resize the column width, or double-click the right column border to automatically resize the column to best fit the data.

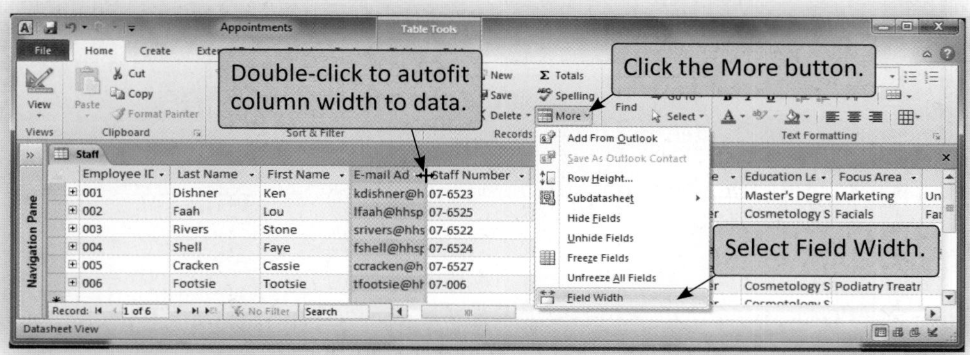

FIGURE AC 2.13

To use the *Column Width* dialog to change the column size:

1. On the *Home* tab, in the *Records* group, click the **More** button, and select **Field Width** to open the *Column Width* dialog box.
2. Type the width you want in the *Column Width:* box, or click the **Best Fit** button.
3. Click **OK.**

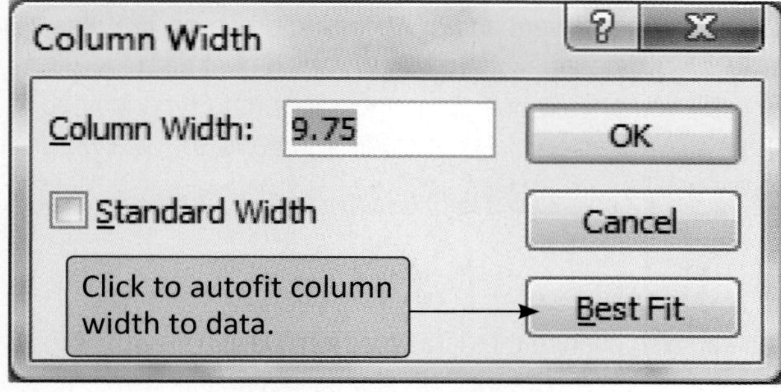

FIGURE AC 2.14

tips & tricks

Do not confuse field *size* with field *width.* Field *size* refers to the number of characters the field can hold in the database. Field *width* or column *width* refers to the number of characters that are visible on screen. This can be a little confusing because Access uses the terms *field width* and *column width* interchangeably.

try this

You can also open the *Column Width* dialog box by right-clicking the field column header and selecting **Field Width.**

2.5 Changing Data Type in Datasheet View

As discussed earlier, it is important to assign the correct data type to each field. For most fields, if necessary, you can change the data type after data have been entered. For example, if the E-mail Address field was originally created as a *text* field, and you want to add the ability to send e-mail messages directly from the database, you can change the data type to *hyperlink*.

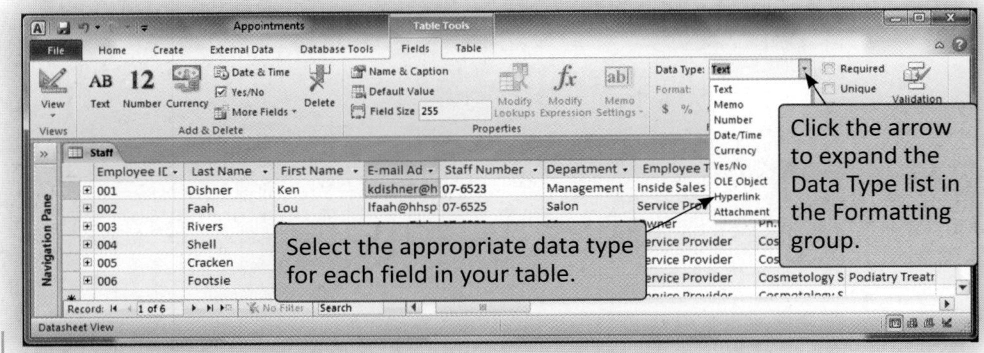

FIGURE AC 2.15

To change the data type for a field from Datasheet view:

1. Click anywhere in the field you want to change.
2. Click the **Table Tools Fields** tab.
3. In the *Formatting* group, expand the **Data Type:** list, and select the data type you want.
4. You must save the table to commit the change.

tips & tricks

- If you need a high degree of accuracy in your numerical calculations, use the Currency data type instead of the Number data type. A currency field is accurate to 15 digits to the left of the decimal point and 4 digits to the right. The number field is limited by the field size and format you choose.
- Attachment fields cannot be changed to another data type.

tell me more

An OLE Object field stores a graphic or file as part of the database. Recent versions of Access improve on the older OLE Object data type with the new Attachment data type. In general, you should use the Attachment data type instead of the OLE Object (which is included primarily for backward compatibility).

try this

You can also change the data type from Design view:

1. Click in the **Data Type** column for the field that you want to change.
2. Click the drop-down arrow to see the list of available data types.
3. Select the appropriate data type for your data.

2.6 Adding a Total Row

New to recent versions of Access is the ability to add a Total row to a datasheet. From the Total row, you can quickly calculate an aggregate function such as the sum or average of all the values in the column.

Sum—Calculates the total of all the values in the column. Sum works with the following field types: number, decimal, and currency.

Average—Calculates the average value, ignoring null values in the column. Average works with the following field types: number, decimal, date/time, and currency.

Count—Counts the number of items in the column. Count works for any data type.

Maximum—Returns the largest numerical value for number, decimal, date/time, and currency field types.

Minimum—Returns the smallest numerical value for number, decimal, date/time, and currency field types.

Standard Deviation—Calculates the statistical standard deviation for numeric field types only (number, decimal, and currency).

Variance—Calculates the statistical variance for numeric field types only (number, decimal, and currency).

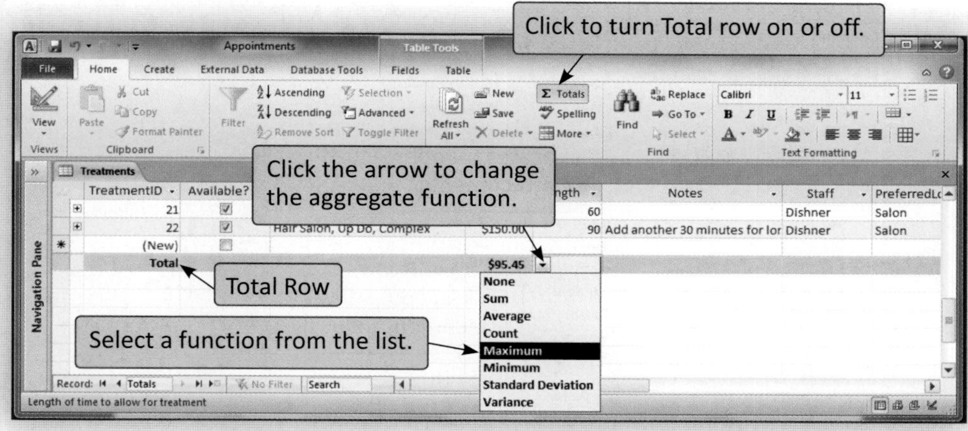

FIGURE AC 2.16

To add a Total row to a datasheet:

1. Click the **Totals** button in the *Records* group on the *Home* tab.
2. In the Total row at the bottom of the datasheet, click the column where you want to add a total.
3. Click the arrow, and select the function you want to use.

tips & tricks

Clicking the **Totals** button toggles the Total row on and off.

tell me **more**

The Total row is available for any database object in Datasheet view (table, form, or query).

2.7 Using Attachment Fields

One of the most useful enhancements to recent versions of Access is the ability to create Attachment fields to store files as attachments to records. Attachments can be pictures, Word documents, or almost any other type of data file. For security reasons, Access will not allow program files (for example, .exe or .bat files) or any files greater than 256 MB as attachments.

To add an Attachment field from Datasheet view:

1. At the far right side of the table, there is a column with the header *Click to Add.* Click the arrow to expand the list of available field types.
2. Click **Attachment.**
3. Notice that you cannot rename the attachment field. It is designated by a paperclip icon.

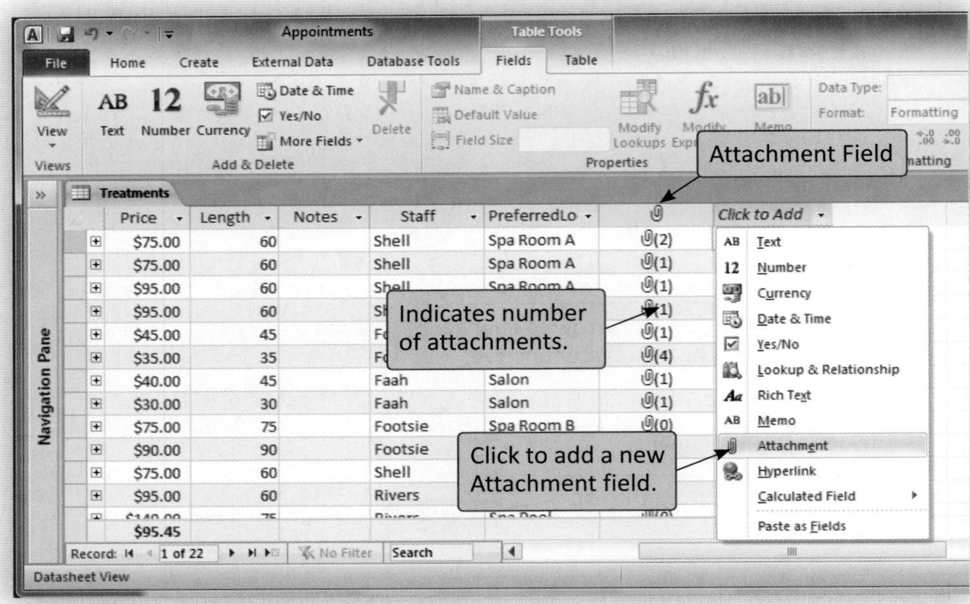

FIGURE AC 2.17

To add an attachment:

1. Double-click the Attachment field for the record you want to add the attachment to.
2. The *Attachments* dialog box opens.
3. Click the **Add . . .** button browse for the file you want to add.
4. Double-click the file to add it, or click the file once, and then click the **Open** button.
5. Click **OK** to save the attachment and close the *Attachments* dialog box.
6. The number next to the attachment icon in each record tells you how many attachments there are.

from the perspective of . . .

SMALL BUSINESS OWNER

I use database tables to keep track of business contacts, inventory, and sales. Customizing each table with virtually any type of data allows me flexibility to keep track of everything I need to run my business.

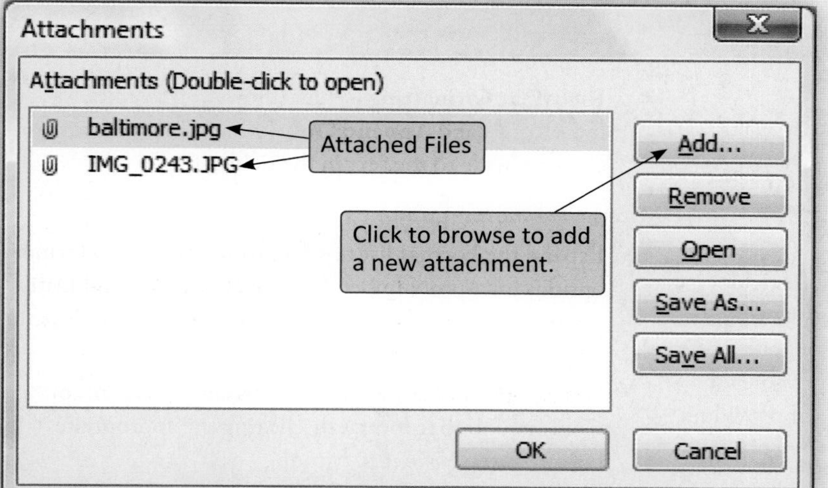

FIGURE AC 2.18

tips & tricks

You cannot see a preview of attachments in Datasheet view. However, most forms and reports will display the attachment (if it is an image) or an icon representing the type of file. For example, a Word document attachment will display a Word icon.

tell me more

From the *Attachments* dialog, you can remove attachments or view them in their native application or viewer program. For example, if the attachment is a Word document, double-click the attachment in the *Attachments* dialog to open it in Microsoft Word. You can then use the **Save As** command to save a copy of the document to another location external to Access.

try this

You can also add Attachment fields from Design view.

2.8 Modifying Field Properties in Datasheet View

When designing a table, you specify what type of data can be entered in each field by selecting the data type. You can also define specific field properties to control the appearance of data in the field or the way in which users enter data.

Most field properties can be changed in Datasheet view. Click anywhere in the field you want to change, and then on the *Table Tools Fields* tab make the selections you want. Not all properties are available for all field data types.

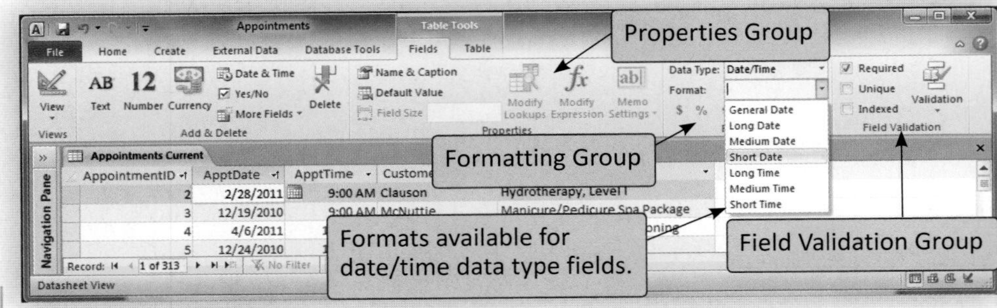

FIGURE AC 2.19

In the *Properties* group:

- Click **Name & Caption** to modify the field name and caption. The Caption property controls how the field is labeled in forms and reports. If you do not specify a caption, Access uses the field name.
- Click **Default Value** to add a preset value to the field. Entering a value in the Default Value property can save time during data entry. For example, if most of your employees live in Ohio, use OH as the default value for the State field. Default values are also useful for providing instructions in Text or Memo fields, such as "Enter customer preferences here."
- Enter a **Field Size** to limit the number of characters that can be entered in a text field. The default size for a text field is 255 (the maximum size for a text field). Limiting the field size can ensure that data are entered properly. For example, if you want entries in the State field to always use the two-letter state abbreviation, limit the field size to 2. You cannot limit the size of Memo fields.
- If the selected field is a lookup field, the **Modify Lookups** button opens the Lookup Wizard so you can adjust the lookup field settings. The ability to modify lookup fields from Datasheet view is new for Access 2010.
- If the selected field is a calculated field, the **Modify Expression** button opens the Expression Builder so you can adjust the formula.
- If the selected field is a memo field, the **Memo Settings** button controls two properties exclusive to memo fields: **Rich Text Formatting** (which allows you to add text formatting) and **Append Only** (which saves a history of changes made to the text in the field).

In the *Formatting* group:

- Expand the **Format** list to select from predefined format options for AutoNumber, Number, Currency, and Date/Time data types. Use these options to ensure that data are entered in a consistent format.
- You can also quickly apply the **Currency, Percent,** or **Comma Number** format by clicking the appropriate button in the *Formatting* group.
- Click the **Increase Decimals** or **Decrease Decimals** button to increase or decrease the number of digits that appear to the right of the decimal in your AutoNumber, Number, and Currency fields.

In the *Field Validation* group:

- Click the **Required** check box to require a value in the field for all records.
- Click the **Unique** check box to require that the value for the field be unique across all records in the table.
- Click the **Indexed** check box to add an index to the field. Indexing fields in a database generally increases efficiency. When the field is indexed, you specify whether or not duplicates are allowed. Primary key fields are always indexed and duplicates are not allowed.
- Click the **Validation** button to set validation rules and messages for both the selected field and record.

try **this**

Field properties can also be modified from the Field Properties pane in Design view (see Skill 2.12, *Modifying Field Properties in Design View*).

2.9 Creating a Table in Design View

When designing a table from Design view, you initially give each field a name, define the data type, and enter a description of the field. You then use the Field Properties pane to define formatting and other specifications for each field.

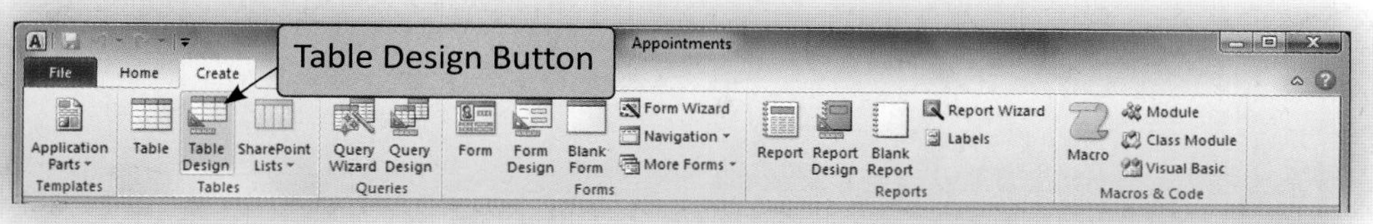

FIGURE AC 2.20

To create a table in Design view:

1. Click the **Create** tab.
2. In the *Tables* group, click the **Table Design** button.
3. Type the name of the first field.
4. Press Tab.
5. Expand the list of data types, and select the data type you want. Press Tab again.
6. Type a useful description of the field.
7. Press Tab to go to the next field.
8. Continue adding fields. When you are finished, save the table.

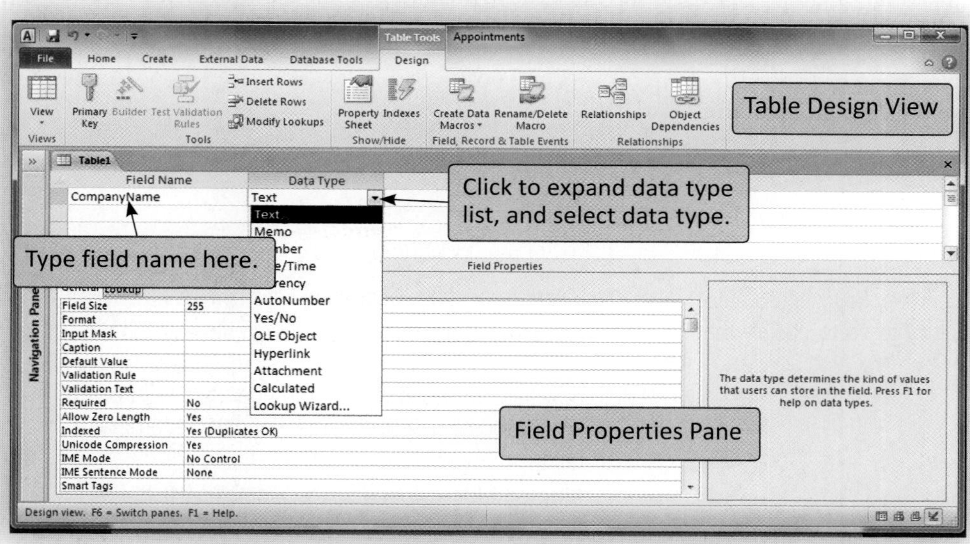

FIGURE AC 2.21

tips & tricks

Press the F6 key to switch back and forth between panes, including the Navigation Pane and the Ribbon.

2.10 Setting the Primary Key

Every Access table should have a primary key defined. The **primary key** is the field that contains data unique to that record. Primary keys are often IDs—product IDs, employee IDs, or record IDs. Remember that Access is a relational database—the primary key is the basis for relationships between different tables.

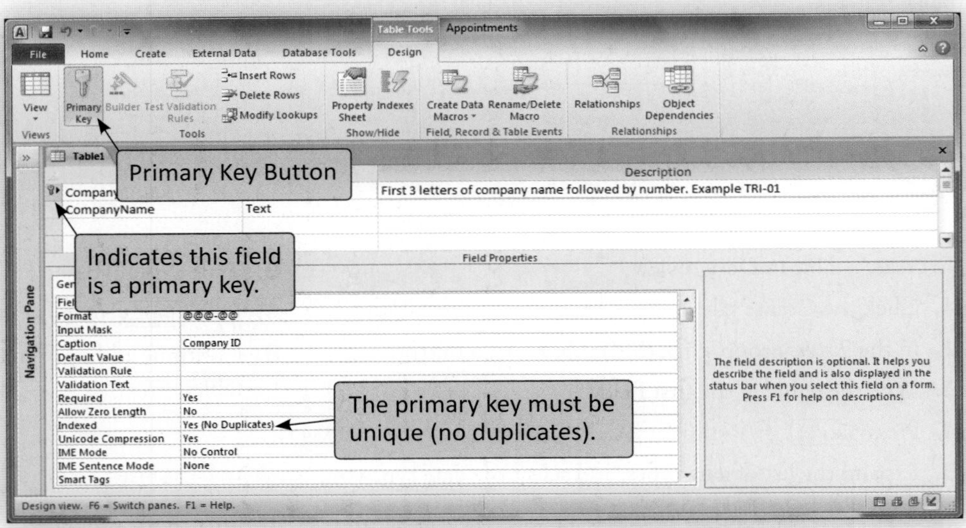

FIGURE AC 2.22

To set the primary key in a table:

1. In Design view, click the field that is going to be the primary key.
2. Click the **Primary Key** button in the *Tools* group of the *Table Tools Design* tab.
3. Click the **Primary Key** toolbar button again to remove the primary key designation.

tips & tricks

Once you establish a field as the primary key, Access automatically sets the *Duplicates* property to *no* to ensure that each record has a unique primary key.

tell me more

There are three types of primary keys:

AutoNumber—If your data do not already contain a field that is unique for each record, you can add a new field that uses the AutoNumber data type. Using an AutoNumber field ensures that each record has a unique numerical ID.

Single field—If your database contains a field that you know is unique for each record (such as a previously established product ID, employee ID, or part number), you can set this field as the primary key.

Multiple field—Some tables have records that do not have a single unique field. In this case, you need to create a multiple-field primary key. Select multiple fields by clicking the row selectors while holding down the Ctrl key on the keyboard; then click the **Primary Key** toolbar button.

try this

In Design view, right-click the row selector and select **Primary Key.**

2.11 Adding and Deleting Fields in Design View

Access makes it easy to add new fields to a table through Datasheet view. However, there may be times when you need more control when adding a field (such as setting field properties that are not available in Datasheet view). In those cases, it may be easier to add new fields from Design view.

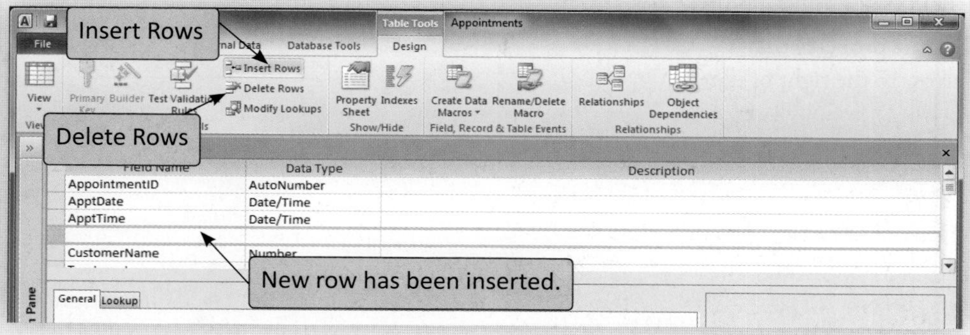

FIGURE AC 2.23

To add a new field in Design view:

1. If the table is already open in Datasheet view, switch to Design view. On the *Home* tab, in the *Views* group, click the **View** button. (You can also expand the *View* button and select **Design View.**)
2. To add a field at the end of the table, type the field name in the first blank row.
3. To add a field elsewhere in the table, click the field below where you want to insert the new field. On the *Table Tools Design* tab, in the *Tools* group, click the **Insert Rows** button.
4. Press Tab on the keyboard, and select the data type you want.
5. Press Tab again, and type a description of the field.
6. Review the field properties in the Field Properties pane and make any changes you want.
7. When you are finished, save the table.

To delete a field in Design view:

1. Select the field you want to delete by clicking the **Row Selector** box to the left of the field name. The entire field row will appear selected.
2. On the *Table Tools Design* tab, in the *Tools* group, click the **Delete Rows** button.

tips & tricks

If you make a structure change to the table in Design view, Access will prompt you to save the table before you switch to another view or close the table.

try this

You can also delete fields from Datasheet view:

- Right-click the field name at the top of the column and select **Delete Field.**
- Click in the field for any record, and then on the *Table Tools Fields* tab, in the *Add & Delete* group, click the **Delete** button.

2.12 Modifying Field Properties in Design View

Although you can modify most field properties from Datasheet view, the **Field Properties pane** in Design view offers some options that Datasheet view does not.

To modify field properties in Design view:

1. In table Design view, select the field you want to modify.
2. In the Field Properties pane, click the property that you want to change. Click the arrow to the right of the property box to expand the list of available options. The options available vary depending on the specific property you select. For some properties, you can type the format or value you want directly in the property box.
3. Don't forget to save the changes to the table design before switching to Datasheet view.

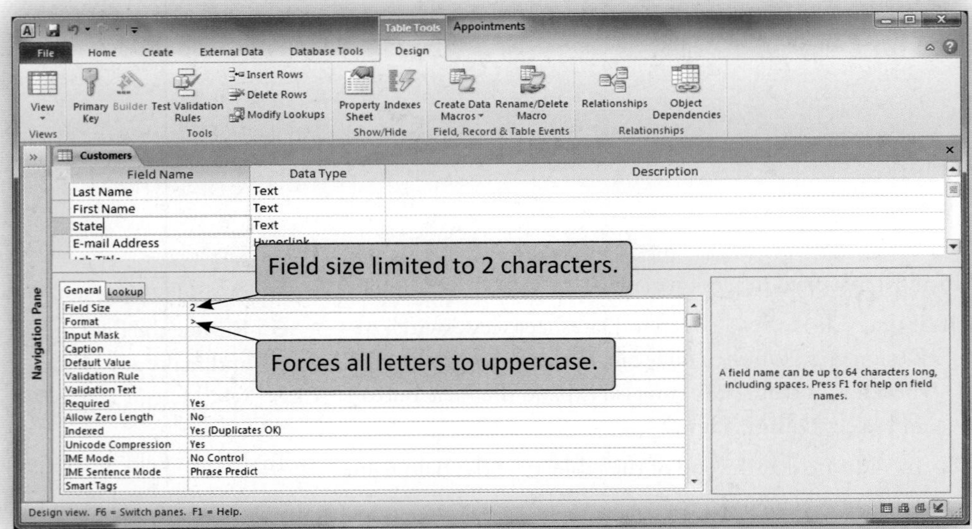

FIGURE AC 2.24

FORMAT

In addition to the preset format options for each data type, you can define your own formats through the Field Properties pane. For example, for fields with a text data type, you can enter < in the Format properties box to force text to appear in lowercase, or enter > to force text to appear in uppercase.

INPUT MASK

The **Input Mask** property ensures that users enter data in a particular format. For example, a field for social security numbers can use an input mask to force users to enter numbers in the format ###-##-#### (the standard format for Social Security numbers).

To use the Input Mask Wizard:

1. With the table open in Design view, click the field you want to apply the Input Mask property to.
2. Click in the **Input Mask** box in the Field Properties pane.
3. Click the **Input Mask Wizard** build button [...].
4. The Input Mask Wizard offers samples of the most common input masks. As you move through each step of the wizard, use the *Try It* box to see how the input mask will affect data entry. Through the wizard, you can modify the input mask or change the placeholder character.

ALLOW ZERO LENGTH

When Allow Zero Length is set to **Yes,** you can include a zero length string as field data. This indicates that the field is left empty on purpose. (A zero length string is entered as ""—two quotation marks with nothing between them.)

2.13 Adding a Lookup Field from a List in Design View

Lookup fields are useful for fields that reference a specific list of items. A lookup field does not need to reference data in another table or query. You can enter your own values to create a custom list.

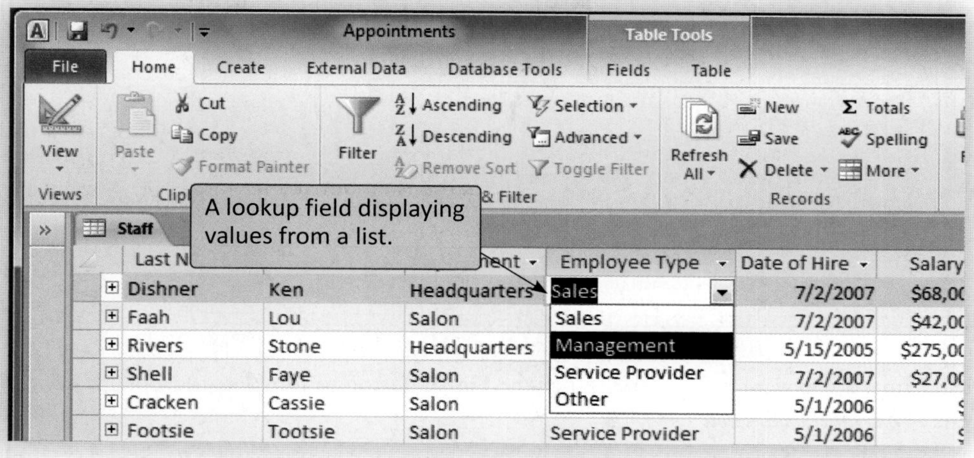

FIGURE AC 2.25

To modify an existing field to use a lookup field with values you specify:

1. Open the table in Design view.
2. Click the field that you want to modify to use a lookup list.
3. Click the **Data Type** drop-down arrow and select **Lookup Wizard . . .**
4. Click the radio button for the option to type in values for the list yourself. Click **Next** to go to the next step.

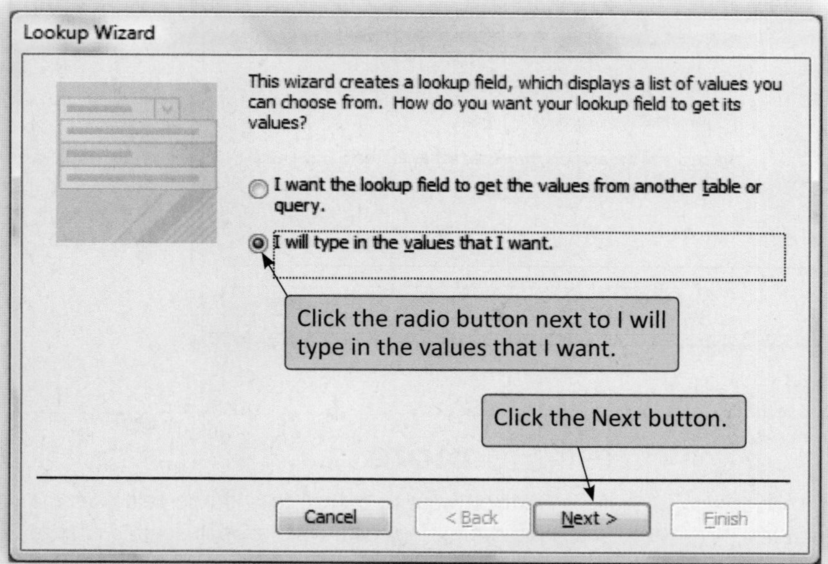

FIGURE AC 2.26

5. First, enter the number of columns you want in your lookup list.
6. Press Tab to go to the first cell in the first blank column.
7. Type the values in the table exactly as you want them to appear in the lookup field. When you are finished, click **Next** to go to the next step.

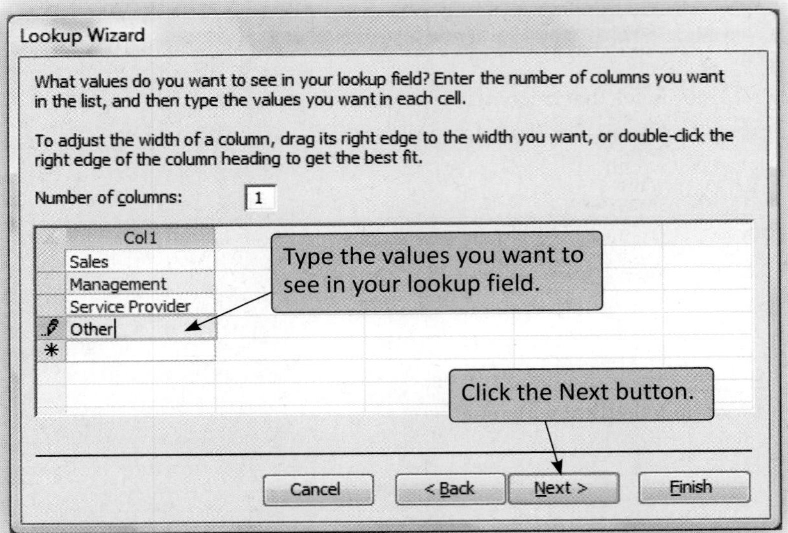

FIGURE AC 2.27

8. Access will keep the original field name. If you want to change it, type a new name in the *What label would you like for your lookup field?* box.
9. If you want to restrict data entry to only items in the list, click the **Limit To List** check box.
10. Click the **Finish** button to complete the lookup list.

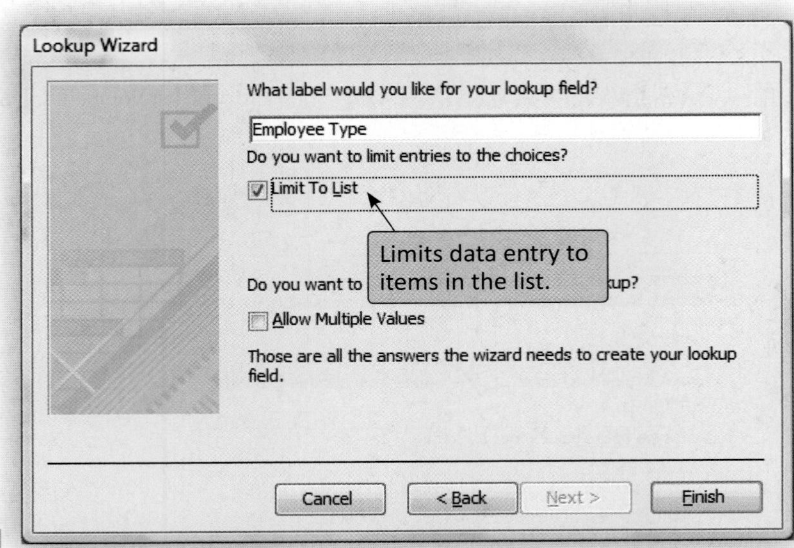

FIGURE AC 2.28

tips & tricks

When you enter values in the Lookup Wizard, you can adjust the width of the columns to make it easier to enter text.

tell me more

If the field you want to change to a lookup field uses the Date/Time or Currency data type, you will need to change the data type to Number before you can modify it to be a lookup field.

try this

For more information on lookup fields that reference values from a field in another table or query, refer to Skill 2.3, *Adding a Lookup field from Another Table in Datasheet View.*

2.14 Modifying Lookup Field Properties

Once you establish a lookup field, you can continue to refine it—adding and removing list items, adjusting the number of columns that display, and controlling how users interact with the list. In previous versions of Access, you could only modify lookup field properties in Design view. With Access 2010, you can make some adjustments from Datasheet view.

To modify a lookup field from Datasheet view:

› On the *Table Tools Fields* tab, in the *Properties* group, click the **Modify Lookups** button to open the Lookup Wizard. Complete the steps in the wizard, making the changes you want.

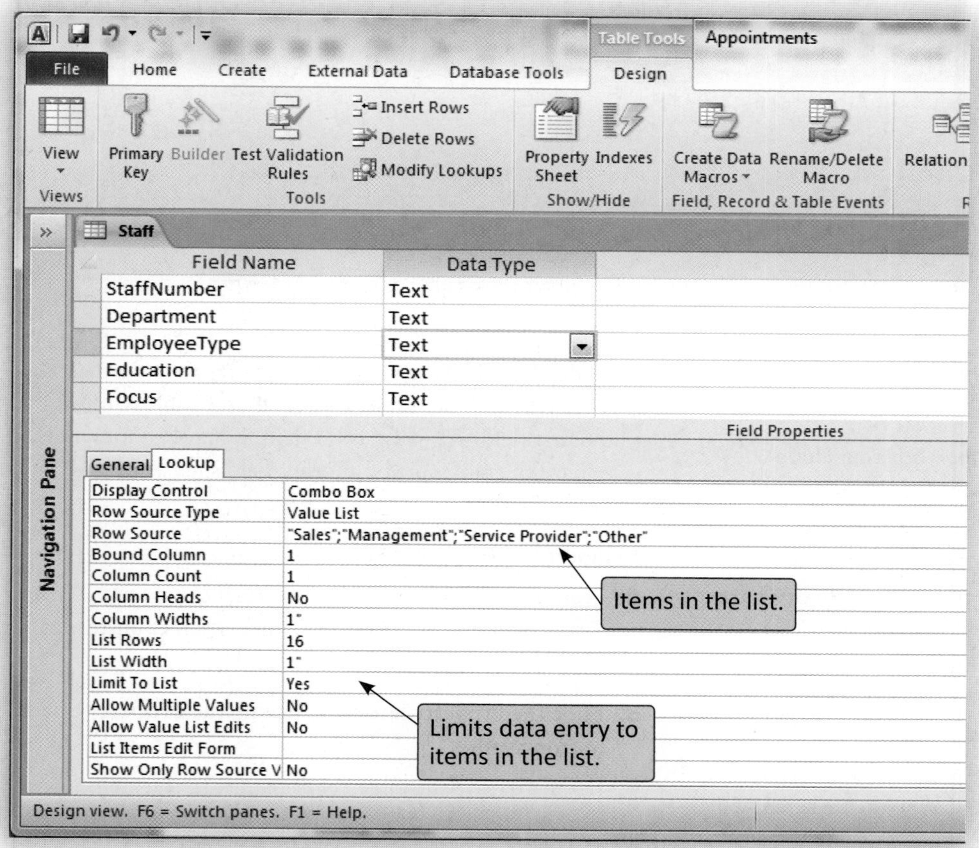

FIGURE AC 2.29

From Design view, you have more control over how the lookup field looks and behaves.

To modify the properties for a lookup field in Design view:

1. Select the field you want to modify.
2. In the Field Properties pane at the bottom of the screen, click the **Lookup** tab. The *Lookup* tab shows all the properties specific to the lookup field.
3. To add or remove items from the list without opening the Lookup Wizard again, edit the text in the *Row Source* box. Enclose each text item in quotation marks, and separate each list item with a semicolon. For example: `"Sales";"Management";"Service Provider";"Other"`
4. Adjust the width of the lookup list by entering a value in the *Column Widths* box.
5. To store multiple values for the field, click the **Allow Multiple Values** box, expand the list, and click **Yes.**
6. To restrict data entry to list items only, click the **Limit To List** box, expand the list, and click **Yes.**
7. Save the table to save your changes.

2.15 Modifying Table Properties

Through the table properties Property Sheet, you can modify some aspects of a table's behavior such as specifying a field for records to sort by or a filter to show only records that meet certain criteria.

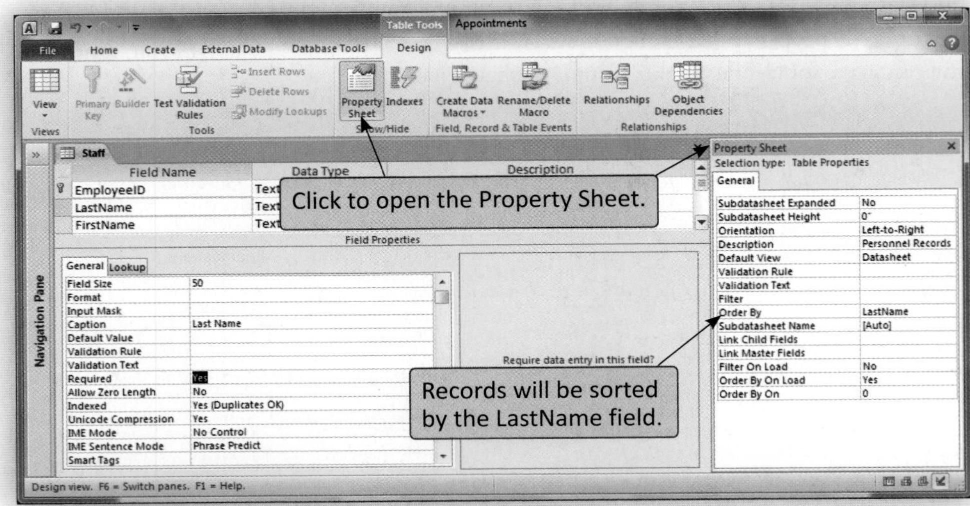
Click to open the Property Sheet.
Records will be sorted by the LastName field.

FIGURE AC 2.30

Some of the properties you can set through the table's Property Sheet are

Description—Use the *Description* box to include instructions about the table or more general information.

Default View—Tables are set to open in Datasheet view by default. To change this setting, expand the list in the *Default View* box and select **PivotTable** or **PivotChart.** (You cannot set a table to open in Design view.)

Validation Rule and Validation Text—Use the *Validation Rule* box to define rules for how fields in the table relate to one another (for example, if the value of one field must always be larger than the value in another field). In the *Validation Text* box, type the text that will appear if the user attempts to enter an invalid record.

Filter—The Filter property allows you to set a permanent filter on the table (to show only records that meet criteria that you define in this box).

Order By—Use the Order By property to define a default sort order for your table. By default, the table will sort by the first field—usually an ID field. It may be more useful to have the table sort by another field such as Last Name or Product Name.

To modify table properties:

1. From Design view, on the *Table Tools Design* tab, in the *Show/Hide* group, click the **Property Sheet** button.
2. Make the changes you want in the Property Sheet.
3. Hide the Property Sheet by clicking the **Property Sheet** button again.
4. Be sure to save the table. The changes to the table properties are saved when you save the table.

try **this**

Some table properties are available from Datasheet view. On the *Table Tools Table* tab, in the *Properties* group, click the **Table Properties** button to open the *Enter Table Properties* dialog box. From this dialog, you can enter Order By and Filter By properties and change the table orientation from left-to-right to right-to-left.

You can also add a table description by right-clicking the table name in the Navigation Pane, and then clicking **Table Properties.** The *Locations Properties* dialog opens. Type the description you want in the *Description:* box, and then click **OK.** This same description appears in the table Property Sheet.

2.16 Renaming and Deleting Tables

When you are in the process of designing your database, you may find that you have tables that you no longer need or that you want to use different names for objects. Access allows you to delete and rename tables and other database objects.

To delete a table (or other database object):

1. Right-click the table name in the Navigation Pane and select **Delete.**
2. Access displays a confirmation message, asking if you want to delete the object. Click **Yes** to delete the table or **No** to cancel the delete command.

Be careful! Once you delete a database object, you cannot undo the deletion.

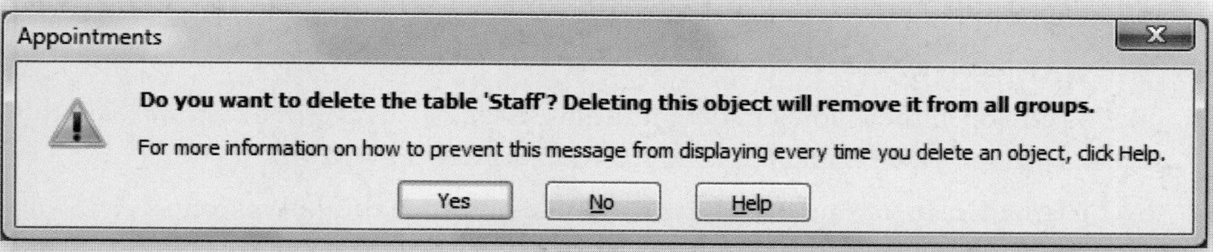

FIGURE AC 2.31

To rename a table (or other database object):

1. Right-click the table name in the Navigation Pane and select **Rename.**
2. Type the new table name, and press Enter.

When you rename a table (or other database object), the name change does not affect relationships.

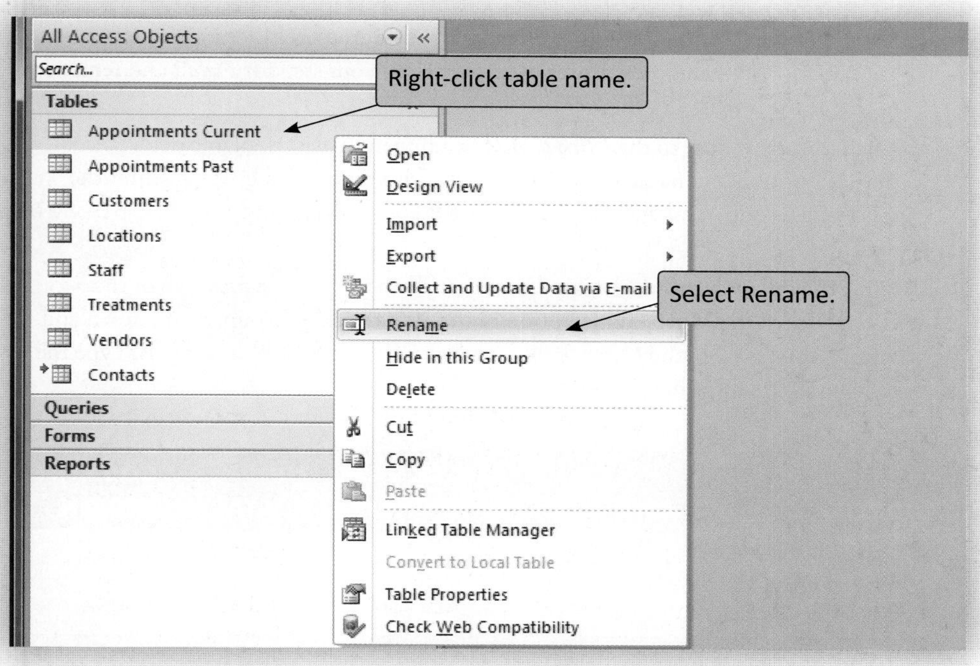

FIGURE AC 2.32

tell me **more**

Access will warn you if you try to delete a table that would invalidate relationships. If you are sure you want to delete the table, Access will automatically delete the relationships, and then delete the table. If you do not allow Access to delete the relationships, Access will not delete the table.

try **this**

You can delete a table or other database object by selecting it in the Navigation Pane, and then on the *Home* tab, in the *Records* group, click the **Delete** button Delete.

projects

Skill Review 2.1

You are a part-time employee in the Computer Science department of a local college. It uses Access 2010 to manage employees and various items that are often loaned out. It would like you to create two new tables in this database: one for the companies that the department frequently purchases from and another with a list of classrooms. Complete the steps below to create and modify these two tables.

1. Create a table in Datasheet view:

a. Find and open the following student file in Access 2010: *collegedept2.accdb.* Save this database as *[your initials]*AC_SkillReview_2-1.

b. Click the **Create** tab and then click the **Table** button in the *Tables* group.

c. You are now in the Datasheet view of a new table. Type `Greg's College Supplies` in the cell directly underneath the *Click to Add* heading. Do not modify the ID field. Press **Tab** to go to the next cell. Type: `http://www.gregscollegesupplies.com`. Press **Tab** again and notice that Access converts your text into a blue, underlined hyperlink. Go to the next row in the table and enter the following two items: `Cindy's Business Supplies` and `http://www.cindysbusinesssupplies.com`. Again, do not modify the ID field.

d. Right-click the *Field1* heading and choose the **Rename Field** option. Type `CompanyName` and press **Enter.** Repeat the previous step for *Field2* and rename it so that it reads `WebSite`.

e. Click the arrow next to the *Click to Add* heading in the last available field. Select the **Text** option and name this field `Phone`. Under this field heading, enter the following phone numbers: `(623) 555-6810` for Greg's and `(623) 555-8200` for Cindy's.

f. Click the cell underneath the last *Click to Add* heading. In the *Field* tab of the Ribbon, click the **More Fields** option in the *Add & Delete* group. Scroll down and select **Address** from the *Quick Start* category. Observe the five new fields. Type the following data into these new fields:

ADDRESS	CITY	STATE PROVINCE	ZIP POSTAL	COUNTRY REGION
› 370 Pine St	› Phoenix	› Arizona	› 85018	› USA
› 900 Finch Way	› Phoenix	› Arizona	› 85013	› USA

g. Close the table by clicking the **x** at the right edge of the table. Click **Yes** if it asks you to save the changes to the table. When Access prompts you to name the table, type `Vendors` and click **OK.**

2. Edit a table in Datasheet view:

a. Open the **Items** table.

b. Click the arrow next to the *Click to Add* heading in the last available field. Select the **Lookup & Relationship** option. In the *Lookup Wizard* dialog box, click **Next** immediately. In the following screen, select **Table: Vendors** from the list and click **Next.** Now, from the *Available Fields:* list, select the **CompanyName** field and click the single > button to add it to the right. Click **Next.** In the following screen, choose **CompanyName** as the sort field and click **Next.** Verify that the two companies you entered earlier appear on the next screen and click **Next.** In the last screen, type `CompanyName` as the label for this new field and click **Finish.** Test this new lookup field on the first three records by choosing **Greg's** for the first two and **Cindy's** for the third.

c. Notice that many of the columns are too narrow and the data are not fully visible. Resize the *ItemName, Description,* and *CompanyName* columns by double-clicking the right edge of their field headings.

d. Notice that the *Cost* field contains unformatted prices. Change this by clicking the **Cost** field heading, clicking the **Fields** tab in the Ribbon, and then changing the data type to **Currency** in the *Formatting* group.

e. Click the **ItemID** field heading. Click the **Fields** tab of the Ribbon and find the *Field Size* property. Change the value to `4`. Click **Yes** to continue.

f. Add a Total row to the datasheet by clicking the **Home** tab of the Ribbon and then clicking the **Totals** button in the *Records* group. In this new row, select the cell inside the *Cost* column and choose **Sum** from the drop-down menu.

g. Click the arrow next to the *Click to Add* heading in the last available field. Select the **Attachment** option. Find the record with an *ID* of `LAS1`. Double-click the paperclip icon for this record, which is located in the new *Attachment* column you just created. Click **Add** in the *Attachments* dialog box and then find the file named *laser_pointer.jpg* in your student folder. Double-click the file and then click **OK.**

3. Create a table in Design view:

a. Close all open tables. Go to the *Create* tab of the Ribbon and click the **Table Design** button in the *Tables* group.

b. Type `RoomNo` for the first *Field Name* and select a data type of **Text.** With the cursor still in this row, go to the *Design* tab of the Ribbon and click the **Primary Key** button.

c. Click the next row and type `Capacity` under *Field Name.* Choose the **Number** data type and then enter the following phrase in the *Description* column: `Maximum number of students`

d. In the next row, type `UpgradeDate` in the *Field Name,* choose the **Date/Time** data type, and enter the following phrase in the *Description* column: `Date in which the instructor's computer was last upgraded`

e. Save this table with the name `Classrooms` and close it.

4. Edit a table in Design view

a. Open the **Items** table in Design view.

b. Click the row that contains the *Location* field and click the **Delete Rows** button in the *Design* tab of the Ribbon. Click **Yes** to confirm the deletion.

c. Save and close the *Items* table.

d. Reopen the **Classrooms** table in Design view.

e. Click the row that contains the *UpgradeDate* field. In the *Field Properties* area at the bottom, change the *Format* property to **Medium Date** by using the drop-down arrow to the right. Now click the row that contains the *Capacity* field. In the *Field Properties* area at the bottom, change the *Default Value* property by typing `40` in the box provided.

f. Add a new field to the *Classroom* table named `Type`. In the *Data Type* menu, choose **Lookup Wizard.** In the dialog box, choose the second option (to enter your own value) and click **Next.** Use only 1 column and enter the following three values: `Auditorium`, `Computer Lab`, `Lecture Room`. Click **Finish.**

g. Edit this lookup field by clicking the **Lookup** tab in the *Field Properties* area of Design view. Click the **Limit To List** box, click the arrow to access the drop-down menu, and click **Yes.**

h. Remain in Design view and click the **Property Sheet** button in the *Design* tab of the Ribbon. In the *Description* box, enter the text: `Classrooms used by the CS Department`. In the *Order By* box, enter `Type`. Save and close the table.

5. Rename and delete tables:

a. Right-click the **Vendors** table in the Navigation Pane and select **Rename.** Type `Suppliers` and press **Enter.**

b. Right-click the **Officers** table in the Navigation Pane and select **Delete.** Confirm by clicking **Yes.**

Skill Review 2.2

You have just been hired by a small health insurance company in the south Florida area. One of your duties is using Access 2010 to manage the company's list of in-network doctors and covered procedures. It would like you to create two new tables in this database: one that contains a list of all the policyholders and another for the in-network hospitals that are affiliated with this insurance company. Complete the steps below to create and modify these two tables.

1. Create a table in Datasheet view:

a. Find and open the following student file in Access 2010: *sfinsurance2.accdb.* Save this database as ***[your initials]*****AC_SkillReview_2-2.**

b. Click the **Create** tab and then click the **Table** button in the *Tables* group.

c. You are now in the Datasheet view of a new table. Type `Miami City Hospital` in the cell directly underneath the *Click to Add* heading. Do not modify the ID field. Press **Tab** to go to the next cell. Type `87`. Go to the next row in the table and enter the following two items: `Central Lauderdale Hospital` and `59`. Finally, on the third row, enter these two values: `West Palm Hospital` and `61`.

d. Right-click the **Field1** heading and choose the **Rename Field** option. Type `HospitalName` and press **Enter.** Repeat the previous step for **Field2** and rename it so that it reads `MemberVisits`.

e. Click the arrow next to the *Click to Add* heading in the last available field. Select the **Text** option and name this field `Phone`. Under this field heading, enter the following phone numbers: `(305) 555-1100` for Miami; `(954) 555-2000` for Lauderdale; `(561) 555-6500` for West Palm.

f. Click the cell underneath the last *Click to Add* heading. In the *Field* tab of the Ribbon, click the **More Fields** option in the *Add & Delete* group. Scroll down and select **Address** from the *Quick Start* category. Observe the five new fields. Type the following data into these new fields:

ADDRESS	CITY	STATE PROVINCE	ZIP POSTAL	COUNTRY REGION
› 4500 Miami Blvd	› Miami	› FL	› 33126	› USA
› 320 Palmer Rd.	› Ft. Lauderdale	› FL	› 33301	› USA
› 800 Jefferson St.	› West Palm Beach	› FL	› 33403	› USA

g. Close the table by clicking the **x** at the right edge of the table. Click **Yes** if it asks you to save the changes to the table. When Access prompts you to name the table, type `Hospitals` and click **OK.**

2. Edit a table in Datasheet view:

a. Open the **Physicians** table.

b. Click the arrow next to the *Click to Add* heading in the last available field. Select the **Lookup & Relationship** option. In the *Lookup Wizard* dialog box, click **Next** immediately. In the following screen, select **Table: Hospitals** from the list and click **Next.** Now, from the *Available Fields:* list, select the **HospitalName** field and click the single > button to add it to the right. Click **Next.** In the following screen, choose **HospitalName** as the sort field and click **Next.** Verify that the three hospitals you entered earlier appear on the next screen and click **Next.** In the last screen, type `HospitalName` as the label for this new field and click **Finish.** Test this new lookup field on the first three records by choosing **West Palm Hospital** for the first two and **Central Lauderdale Hospital** for the third.

c. Notice that many of the columns are too narrow and the data are not fully visible. Resize the *LastName, StreetAddress,* and *City* columns by double-clicking the right edge of their field headings. Do the same for the new *HospitalName* field if necessary.

d. Notice that the *MemberCount* field incorrectly contains dollar amounts instead of quantities. Change this by clicking the **MemberCount** field heading, clicking the **Fields** tab in the Ribbon, and then changing the data type to **Number** in the *Formatting* group.

e. Close the *Physicians* table (click **Yes** if prompted to save changes) and open the **Hospitals** table.

f. Click the **State Province** field heading. Click the **Fields** tab of the Ribbon and find the *Field Size* property. Change the value to `2`. Click **Yes** to continue.

g. Add a Total row to the datasheet by clicking the *Home* tab of the Ribbon and then clicking the **Totals** button in the *Records* group. In this new row, select the cell inside the *MemberVisits* column and choose **Sum** from the drop-down menu.

h. Click the arrow next to the *Click to Add* heading in the last available field. Select the **Attachment** option. Go to the *Miami* record and double-click the paperclip icon, which is located in the new *Attachment* column you just created. Click **Add** in the *Attachments* dialog box and find the file named *miami_hospital.jpg* in your student folder. Double-click the file and then click **OK.**

3. Create a table in Design view:

a. Close all open tables. Go to the *Create* tab of the Ribbon and click the **Table Design** button in the *Tables* group.

b. Type `MemberID` for the first field name and select a data type of **Text.** With the cursor still in this row, go to the *Design* tab of the Ribbon and click the **Primary Key** button. Next, enter the following phrase in the *Description* column for this field: `First letter of last name followed by a randomly generated seven-digit number`

c. Finish creating this table by adding the following fields and setting their data types (indicated in parentheses): `FirstName` **(Text),** `LastName` **(Text),** `Address` **(Text),** `City` **(Text),** `State` **(Text),** `Zip` **(Number),** `DOB` **(Date/Time).**

d. Save this table with the name `Patients` and close it.

4. Edit a table in Design view:

a. Open the **Physicians** table in Design view.

b. Click the row that contains the *YearsInPractice* field and click the **Delete Rows** button in the *Design* tab of the Ribbon. Click **Yes** to confirm the deletion.

c. Save and close the *Physicians* table. Reopen the **Patients** table in Design view.

d. Click the row that contains the *DOB* field. In the *Field Properties* area at the bottom, change the *Format* property to **Medium Date** by using the drop-down arrow to the right. Now click the row that contains the *State* field. In the *Field Properties* area at the bottom, change the *Default Value* property by typing `FL` in the box provided.

e. Add a new field to the *Patients* table named `Sex`. In the *Data Type* menu, choose **Lookup Wizard.** In the dialog box, choose the second option (to enter your own value) and click **Next.** Use only 1 column and enter the following two values: `Female; Male`. Click **Finish.**

f. Edit this lookup field by clicking the **Lookup** tab in the *Field Properties* area of Design view. Click the **Limit To List** box, click the arrow to access the drop-down menu, and click **Yes.**

g. Remain in Design view and click the **Property Sheet** button in the *Design* tab of the Ribbon. In the *Description* box, enter the text: `Current Membership List`. In the *Order By* box, enter `LastName`. Save and close the table.

5. Rename and delete Tables:

a. Right-click the **Patients** table in the Navigation Pane and select **Rename.** Type `Policyholders` and press **Enter.**

b. Right-click the **Employees** table in the Navigation Pane and select **Delete.** Confirm by clicking **Yes.**

challenge yourself 1

You are a botany professor who was recently placed in charge of maintaining the department's greenhouse. This database contains records of the plants in the greenhouse and the employees that assist you with maintenance duties. You would now like to keep track of the fertilizers used in the greenhouse and the plants that use them. Complete the following exercises in order to create this table and make a few modifications to the greenhouse database.

1. Create a new table:

a. Open the *greenhouse2.accdb* student file and save it as **`[your initials]AC_Challenge_2-3`.**

b. Create a new table in Datasheet view, which you will be naming `Fertilizers`. Enter the following data and rename the fields as shown:

ID	FERTILIZERNAME	NUTRIENTRATIO	PRICE
1	› Monoammonium phosphate	› 11-52-0	› $25
2	› Polymer Coated Urea	› 44-0-0	› $35
3	› Nitrogen Solution	› 28-0-0	› $12

c. Go to Design view. Add a new lookup field named `Form`. Enter the following four values: `Granule, Liquid, Slow-Release, Organic`. Configure this lookup field to allow multiple values.

d. Delete the *ID* field in Design view. Insert a new field at the top named `FertID`. Set the *Data Type* to **Text.** Go back to Datasheet view and enter the following three values (in the appropriate record) under the *FertID* field: `MAP1, PCU1, NSO1`. Switch to Design view and make the *FertID* field the **Primary Key.**

e. In Datasheet view, add an *Attachment* field in the rightmost column. Attach the photo named *fertilizer_liquid.jpg* to the *Nitrogen Solution* record.

f. Add a Total row in Datasheet view that sums up all the fertilizer prices. Close the *Fertilizers* table.

2. Edit existing tables:

a. Open the **Plants** table. In Datasheet view, add a new lookup field that references the *FertilizerName* field in the *Fertilizers* table. Test this field by choosing any fertilizer for the first three plants.

b. Resize the *CommonName* and *ScientificName* columns.

c. Change the *Data Type* of the *MaxHeightFeet* field from *Text* to **Number.** If Access warns about potential data loss, just click **Yes** to proceed.

d. Go to Design view and change the *Format* of the *DatePlanted* field to **Medium Date.** Next, set the *Default Value* for the *FlowerColor* field to **white** and add a *Description* for this field that reads: `Main color only. Do not enter multiple colors.`

e. Change the *Table Properties* as follows:

(1) *Description:* `Plants only. No trees or shrubs.`

(2) *Order by:* `ScientificName`

f. Rename the *Plant* table to `ActivePlants`

g. Delete the *Equipment* table.

challenge yourself 2

You work for a volunteer organization that ships and administers vaccines to various relief centers all over the world. It currently uses Access 2010 to maintain the list of all approved vaccines and keep track of all shipments made to the relief centers. Now, it would like you to make a list of all the employees that work at its various relief centers.

1. Create a new table:

a. Open the *vaccines2.accdb* student file and save it as *`[your initials]`*`AC_Challenge_2-4.`

b. Create a new table in Datasheet view, which you will be naming `Volunteers.` Enter the following data and rename the fields as shown below. Be sure to use the **Name** *Quick Start* option to add the *First* and *Last Name* fields.

ID	LAST NAME	FIRST NAME	DOB
1	› Richardson	› Tyra	› 5/9/80
2	› Graham	› Susan	› 3/28/72
3	› Hernandez	› Mario	› 5/11/67

c. Go to Design view. Add a new lookup field named `Position`. Enter the following three values: `Clerical`, `Manager`, `Nurse`. Configure this lookup field to limit the values to this list.

d. Change the *Format* of the *DOB* field to **Medium Date.**

e. Set the *Default Value* for the *Position* field to **Nurse.**

f. Delete the *ID* field in Design view. Insert a new field at the top named `EmployeeID`. Set the *Data Type* to **Text.** Enter a *Description* for this field that reads: `First letter of last name followed by a random five-digit number`

g. Go back to Datasheet view and enter the following three values (in the appropriate record) under the *EmployeeID* field: `R87239`, `G31215`, `H55091`. Switch back to Design view and make the Employee*ID* the **Primary Key.**

h. In Datasheet view, add an *Attachment* field in the rightmost column. Attach the photo named *sgraham.jpg* to the *Susan Graham* record.

2. Edit existing tables:

a. Open the **Locations** table. In Datasheet view, add a new lookup field that references the *EmployeeID* field in the *Volunteers* table. Test this field by choosing employee **R87239** for the first location and employee **H55091** for the second. Close the table.

b. Open the **Shipments** table in Datasheet view. Resize the *DateShipped* and *Cost* columns.

c. Add a Total row that sums up all the amounts in the *Cost* field.

d. Change the *Data Type* of the *Quantity* field from *Text* to **Number.** If Access warns about potential data loss, just click **Yes** to proceed.

e. Change the *Table Properties* as follows:

(1) *Description:* `Vaccine shipments only. No other relief materials.`

(2) *Order by:* `LocationID`

f. Rename the *Volunteers* table to `Employees`

g. Delete the *Medication* table.

on your own

You have an extensive movie collection at home, and you have been using Access 2010 to manage this collection. You now want to add your home/vacation movies to this database. These are the movies you recorded with your camcorder, such as your son's first birthday and your vacation in Hawaii. You will create a table for these movies by following these guidelines:

1. Open the *movie_collection2.accdb* student file and save it as **`[your initials]AC_OnYourOwn_2-5.`**

2. Create a `HomeMovies` table and add at least six fields that you believe are appropriate for this type of collection. At a minimum, you must have

a. An ID for each movie. This field will serve as the primary key.

b. A name for each movie.

c. The running time for each movie in minutes.

d. The other three (or more) fields are your choice.

3. Demonstrate your knowledge of lookup fields by creating a value list in one of your fields.

4. Enter at least 10 home/vacation movies in Datasheet view. They can be real or fictional. Resize columns in Datasheet view if necessary.

5. Calculate the total number of minutes in your home movie collection using a Total row.

6. Modify at least two *Field Properties* for one or more fields in your table.

7. In the *Table Properties* pane, add a description for your table and define a default sort order of your choice.

8. Delete the *Stores* table and rename the existing *Movies* table to `PurchasedMovies`.

fix it

A local pet store has hired you to fix its database, which keeps track of inventory, customers, and store sales. Open the file named *petstore2.accdb* , save it as `[your initials]AC_FixIt_2-6`, and investigate the issues below. Fix the errors and save your work.

1. Fix the *Pets* table as follows:

a. In this store, there are only two types of pets sold: cats and dogs. Edit the *AnimalType* field so that these are the only two choices for this field. Do not allow any other type of animal to be entered.

b. The *Price* field should display the numbers using $ and two decimal places.

c. The store realizes it rarely types in the cage # for each animal it receives. Therefore, remove the *CageNum* field from the table.

d. The store needs to keep vaccination and photographic information. Add a new field named `Vaccines` that only accepts a yes or no value. Add another new field that can store photographs and insert the *poodle.jpg* image for the record with the *Poodle* breed.

e. The store needs to know the total price of its pet inventory. Calculate it for the store.

f. This table is incorrectly ordered by the age of the pet. Change this table's properties to sort by price instead.

2. Fix the *Sales* table as follows:

a. The *Salez* table is misspelled. Change the name to the correct spelling.

b. The dates in the *Sales* table should look like this: *30-Jun-10*

c. Add a new field in Datasheet view using the **Payment Type** *Quick Start* option.

3. Fix the *Customers* table as follows:

a. The default value for the *Newsletter* field in the *Customers* table should be `1` so that it appears checked every time you create a new record.

b. The *CustomerID* field should never have a value with more than 4 characters and it should be this table's primary key.

4. Fix the database as follows:

a. Open each table in Datasheet view and look at the columns closely. Two columns need to be larger. Find them and resize them.

b. This pet store only has a few individuals working for them. Therefore, it will not be using the *Employees* table. Remove the table.

chapter 3

Working with Forms and Reports

In this chapter, you will learn the following skills:

- Create forms based on tables and queries
- Create a Multiple Items form and a Split form
- Use the Form Wizard to create forms
- Add controls to forms and reports
- Learn to design forms and reports by adding design elements and editing themes
- Group records and discover how to use the total function to summarize data
- Print a report

Skill **3.1** Creating a Form Based on a Table or Query
Skill **3.2** Creating a Multiple Items Form
Skill **3.3** Creating a Split Form
Skill **3.4** Creating a Form Using the Form Wizard
Skill **3.5** Creating a Blank Form from an Application Part
Skill **3.6** Adding Controls to Forms
Skill **3.7** Creating a Simple Report
Skill **3.8** Using the Report Wizard
Skill **3.9** Adding Controls to a Report
Skill **3.10** Changing the Look of a Form or a Report by Applying a Theme
Skill **3.11** Adding Design Elements to Forms and Reports
Skill **3.12** Formatting Controls in Forms and Reports
Skill **3.13** Resizing and Arranging Controls
Skill **3.14** Grouping Records in a Report
Skill **3.15** Adding Totals to a Report in Layout View
Skill **3.16** Previewing and Printing a Report
Skill **3.17** Controlling the Page Setup of a Report for Printing

skills

introduction

This chapter focuses on the Form and Report objects in Access 2010. Various types of forms are created in order to work with the data stored in the linked table. Controls are added to the form and formatted. Several reports are created from the data in queries and tables. These reports are then formatted in order to create attractive printouts that both group and summarize the data.

3.1 Creating a Form Based on a Table or Query

While you can enter data directly in a table's Datasheet view, a **form** can provide a more user-friendly data entry format. A form displays data from an underlying table and allows database users to enter, edit, and delete data. A form does not contain records or data itself. It is only an interface to an underlying table or query.

To create a simple form based on a table or query:

1. In the Navigation Pane, select the table or query that provides the underlying records for your form.
2. Click the **Create** tab.
3. In the *Forms* group, click the **Form** button.

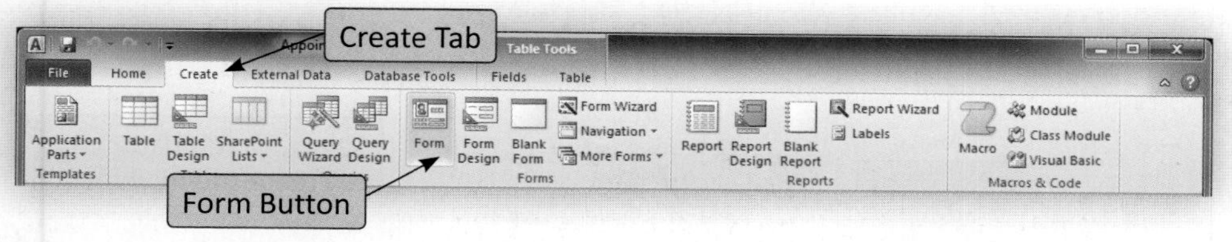

FIGURE AC 3.1

4. The new form opens in Layout view.
5. Save the form by clicking the **Save** button in the Quick Access Toolbar.
6. Notice that the default name in the *Form Name:* box is the same as the name of the table or query that you based the form on. Type a new name if you want to use something else.
7. Click **OK** to save the form and close the *Save As* dialog.

This form displays records one at a time (a *single record* form). Other form designs can display multiple records on a single page or use a tabbed interface to separate a single record into multiple parts.

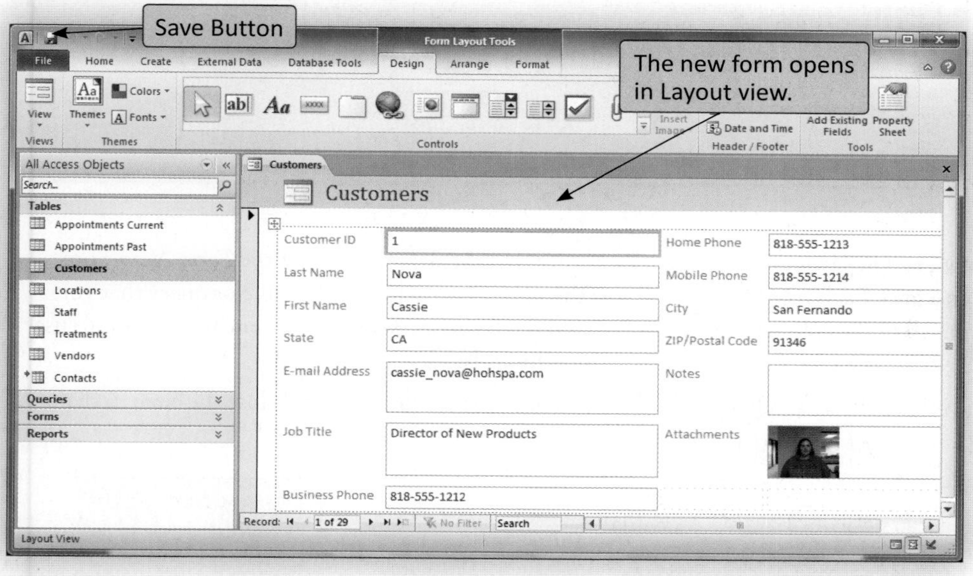

FIGURE AC 3.2

tips & tricks

If Access finds a one-to-many relationship between the table you are basing the form on and another table, Access automatically inserts a datasheet at the bottom of the form. The datasheet displays the records from the related table. (Access will only do this if there is only one one-to-many relationship available.)

tell me more

If you want to create a form that combines fields from more than one table or query, use the Form Wizard instead of the *Form* button.

try this

To create a new form directly in Design view, click the **Create** tab. In the *Forms* group, click the **Form Design** button.

To create a new form directly in Layout view, click the **Create** tab. In the *Forms* group, click the **Blank Form** button.

3.2 Creating a Multiple Items Form

Datasheet form reproduces the exact look and layout of the table datasheet as a form. A **Multiple Items form** has a similar layout displaying multiple records at once. However, a Multiple Items form is more flexible than a Datasheet form. You can easily modify the layout and design of a Multiple Items form.

To create a Multiple Items form:

1. In the Navigation Pane, select the table or query that provides the base for your form.
2. Click the **Create** tab.
3. In the *Forms* group, click the **More Forms** button.
4. Select **Multiple Items** from the menu.

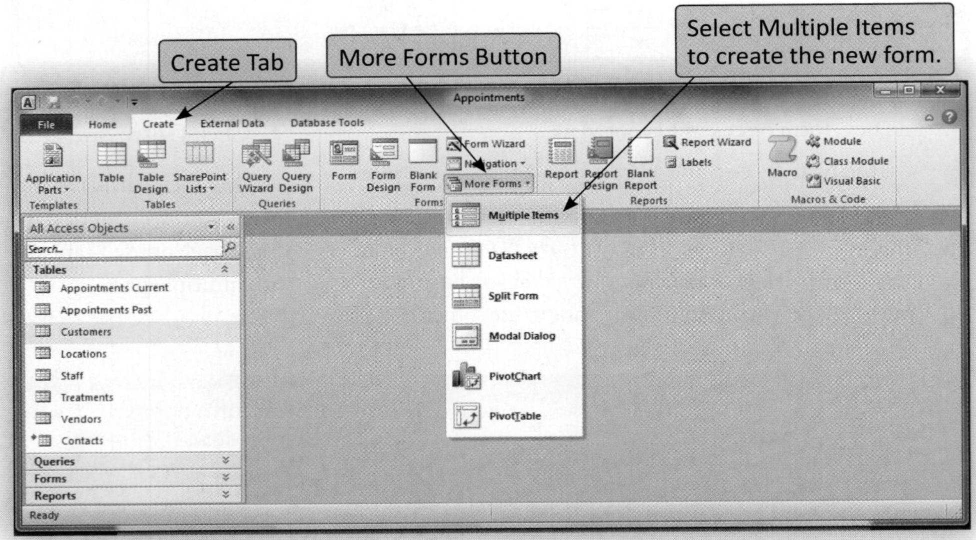

Create Tab
More Forms Button
Select Multiple Items to create the new form.

FIGURE AC 3.3

5. The new form opens in Layout view. The layout of the Multiple Items form is similar to a grid. Each record is a row, and each field is a column. All of the columns are the same width, and all of the rows are the same height.
6. Save the form by clicking the **Save** button in the Quick Access Toolbar.
7. Notice that the default name in the *Form Name:* box is the same as the name of the table or query that you based the form on. Type a new name if you want to use something else.
8. Click **OK** to save the form and close the *Save As* dialog.

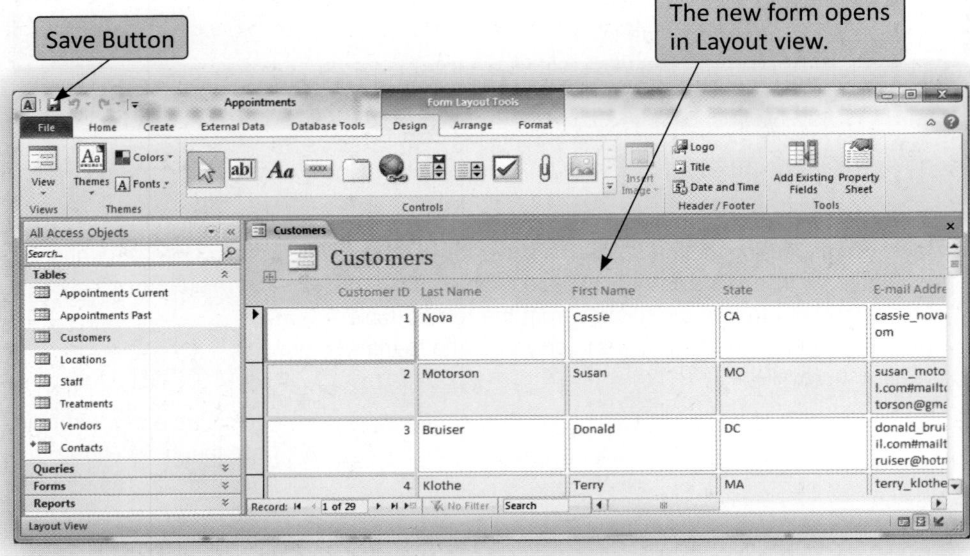

Save Button
The new form opens in Layout view.

FIGURE AC 3.4

3.3 Creating a Split Form

A **Split form** combines the convenience of a continuous Datasheet form with the usability of a single form displaying one record at a time. In a Split form, both formats are displayed and work together, so when you navigate records in one section, the other section automatically synchronizes. Use a Split form when you need to see a large group of records at one time while having quick access to an individual record's details.

To create a Split form:

1. In the Navigation Pane, select the table or query that provides the base for your form.
2. Click the **Create** tab.
3. In the *Forms* group, click the **More Forms** button.
4. Select **Split Form** from the menu.

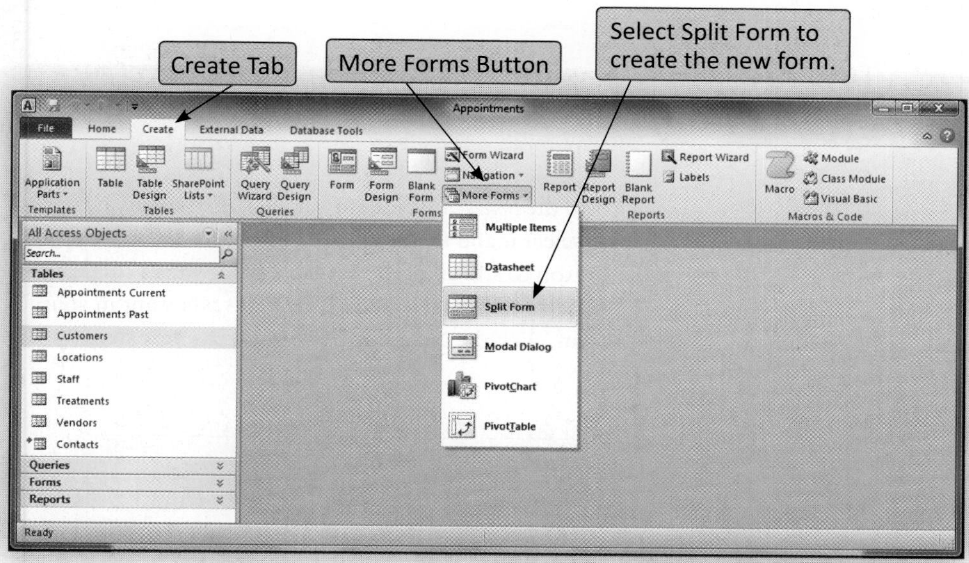

FIGURE AC 3.5

5. The new form opens in Layout view.
6. Save the form by clicking the **Save** button in the Quick Access Toolbar.
7. Notice that the default name in the *Form Name:* box is the same as the name of the table or query that you based the form on. Type a new name if you want to use something else.
8. Click **OK** to save the form and close the *Save As* dialog.

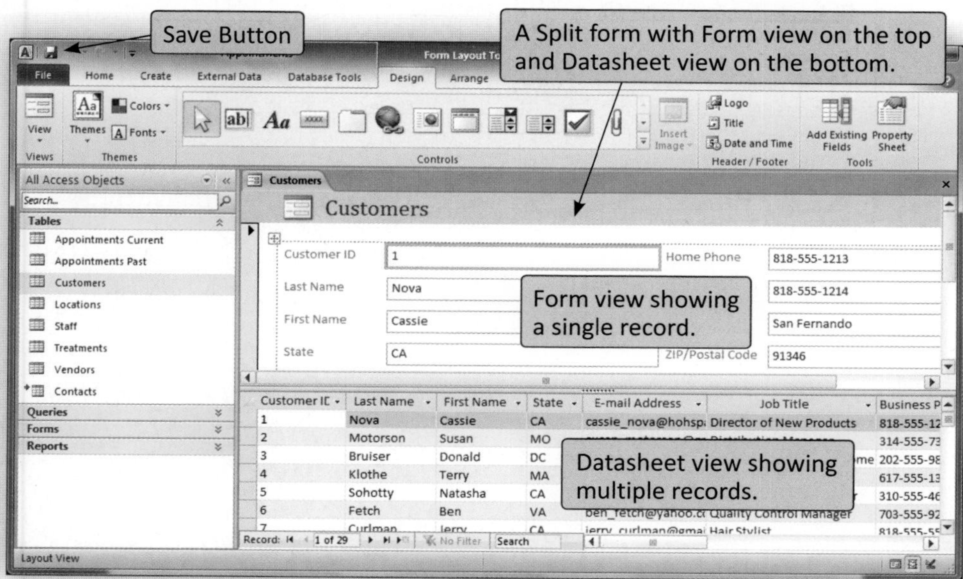

FIGURE AC 3.6

3.4 Creating a Form Using the Form Wizard

Another easy way to begin a new form is to use the Form Wizard. Instead of automatically creating a form that includes every field in the underlying table, the Form Wizard walks you through the steps of creating the form including selecting fields and a layout.

To create a new form using the Form Wizard:

1. Click the **Create** tab.
2. In the *Forms* group, click the **Form Wizard** button.

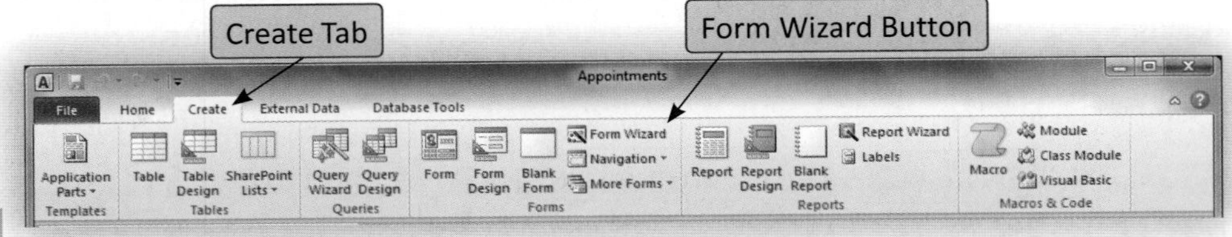

FIGURE AC 3.7

3. The Form Wizard opens. The first step is to expand the *Tables/Queries* list and select the underlying table or query for your form.
4. The *Available Fields:* box displays all the fields from the table or query you selected. Double-click a field to move it to the *Selected Fields:* box or click the field name once to select it and then click the > button. Click the >> button to add all of the available fields with a single click. When you have selected all the fields you want in your form, click the **Next** button to go to the next step.

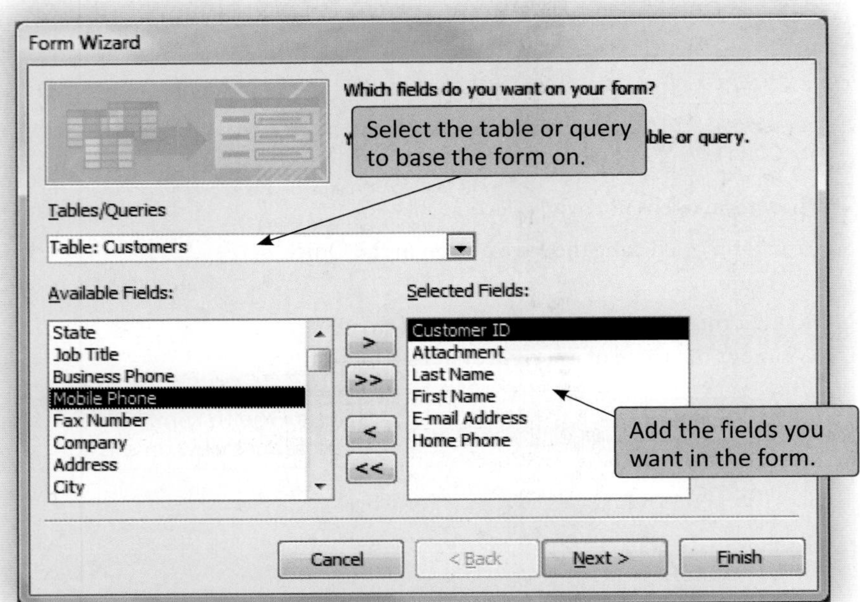

FIGURE AC 3.8

5. Select a layout for the form, and then click **Next.**

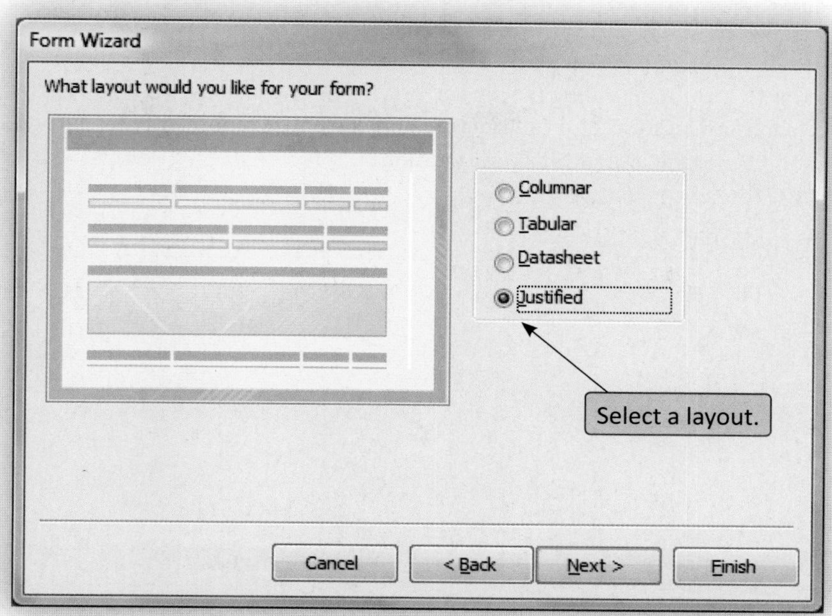

FIGURE AC 3.9

6. Enter a title for the form, and select whether you want to open the form to view and enter information (Form view) or modify the form's design (Layout view). Click **Finish** to save the form.

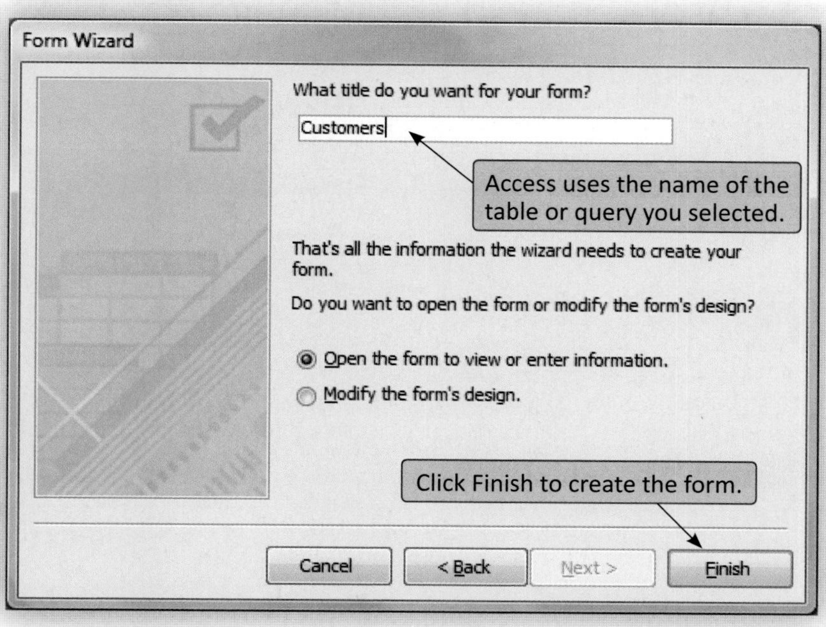

FIGURE AC 3.10

from the perspective of . . .

LAWYER

To keep track of time and billing for my law practice, I use database software. Forms make it easy to enter information into the database and customize reports for any purpose. I can organize my clients and billing, all in one location.

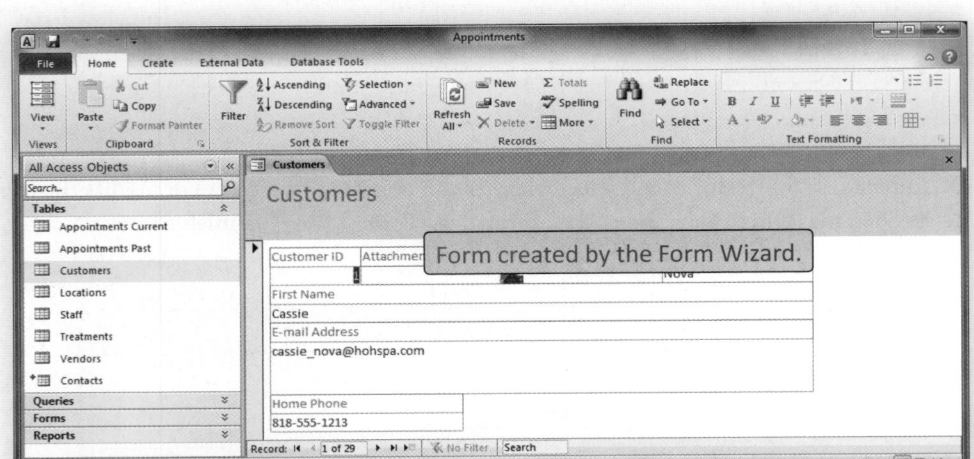

FIGURE AC 3.11

tell me **more**

Through the Form Wizard you can create more complex forms. When your form includes fields from multiple tables, the wizard includes additional steps asking you how the fields in the tables should relate to one another.

3.5 Creating a Blank Form from an Application Part

One way to start a new form is to begin with a blank form Application Part. These Application Parts are essentially form templates. They provide a blank form with a preset layout and placeholders for labels and other controls.

To create a new form based on an Application Part:

1. On the *Create* tab, in the *Templates* group, click the **Application Parts** button.
2. In the *Blank Forms* section, click the form template you want.
3. Access creates a new blank form for you.
4. Double-click the form name in the Navigation Pane to open it in Form view.

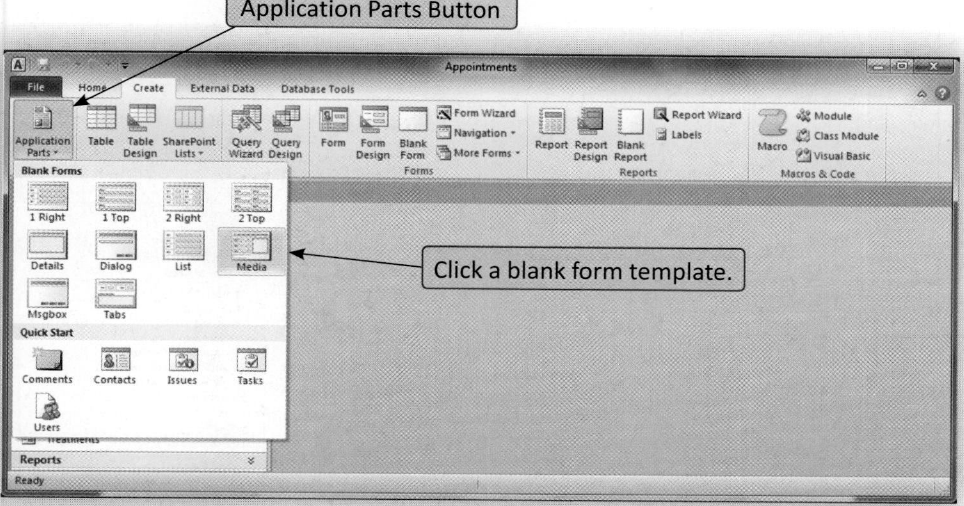

FIGURE AC 3.12

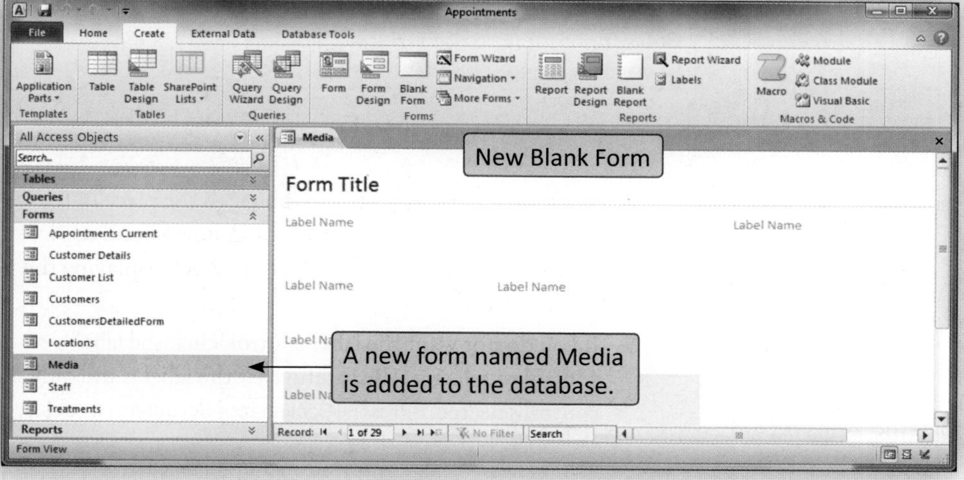

FIGURE AC 3.13

Notice that there are no records in the new form. The new blank form does not have a record source defined (an underlying table) and none of the controls in the form are bound to fields, so there are no records to display. The form is an empty layout until you modify it in Layout view and add bound controls.

tips & tricks

The Application Part layouts include label placeholders. When you add a control to display content from a table or a query, you will need to delete the label that is inserted automatically and update the text in the label placeholder instead.

3.6 Adding Controls to Forms

Once you have created a form, you may need to add more controls. A control can display data from a table or query field, or it can display static text or a graphic. Controls can also be used to display the current date and time or calculate a value.

When you create a new form based on a table or query, Access automatically creates two controls for each field in the table:

- A **label** control that displays the field name. A label control displays text that you can edit by clicking the control once to select it, and then clicking again to place the cursor in the control. A label is one example of a type of an **unbound control**—a control that is not linked to a field.
- A **bound control** that displays the field data. A control that displays data from a table or query is called a bound control because it is bound to the field.

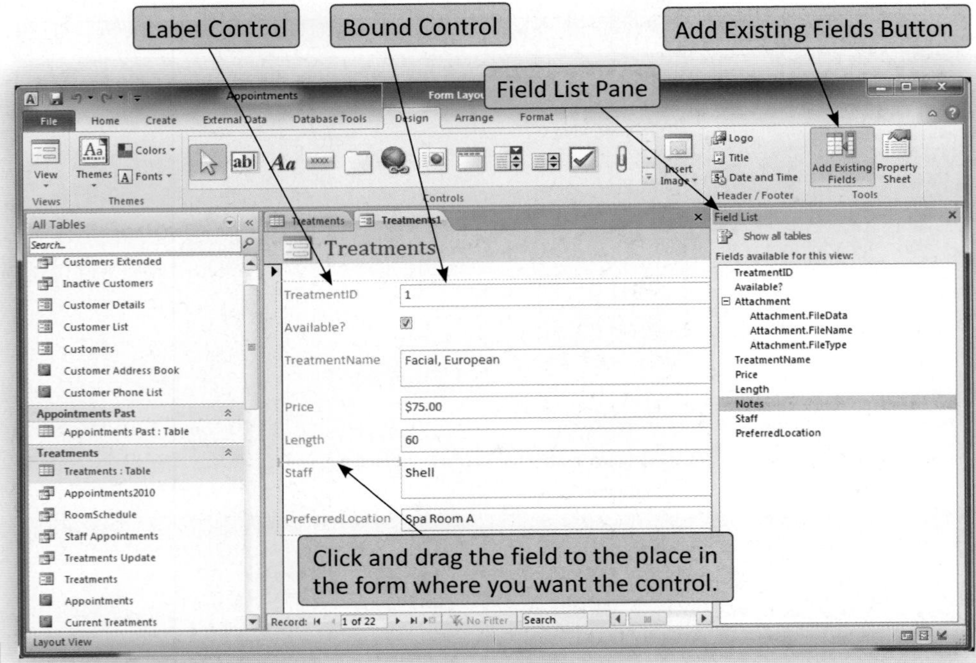

FIGURE AC 3.14

To add a new bound control to a form:

1. If necessary, switch to Layout view.
2. On the *Form Layout Tools Format* tab, in the *Controls* group, click the **Add Existing Fields** button to display the Field List pane.
3. The first box in the Field List pane lists the fields available from the associated table (the form's **record source**).
4. Click the field you want and drag it to the place in the form where you want the control. A new bound control is automatically created, including a label displaying the name of the field.
5. If you do not want the label control, click the label control to select it. (Be careful that the label is the only control selected.) Press ←Backspace or Delete to delete the label control.
6. Remember to save the form to save your changes.

tips & tricks

You can add controls from the Field List in Layout view or Design view, but it is generally easier to work in Layout view. If you need to add a more complex control, you will need to switch to Design view.

try this

Press Ctrl + F8 to display or hide the Field List pane.

You can also double-click a field name in the Field List pane to add it to your form. Double-clicking a field name automatically adds the new bound control to the right of whatever control is selected in the form. If nothing is selected, Access adds the new control to the end of the form.

3.7 Creating a Simple Report

A report displays data from a table or query in a format suitable for printing. Unlike forms, you cannot enter new data into a report. Access 2010 provides an easy process for creating a basic report that includes all the fields in a table or query.

To create a basic report based on a table or query:

1. In the Navigation Pane, select the table or query on which you want to base the report.
2. Click the **Create** tab.
3. In the *Reports* group, click the **Report** button.

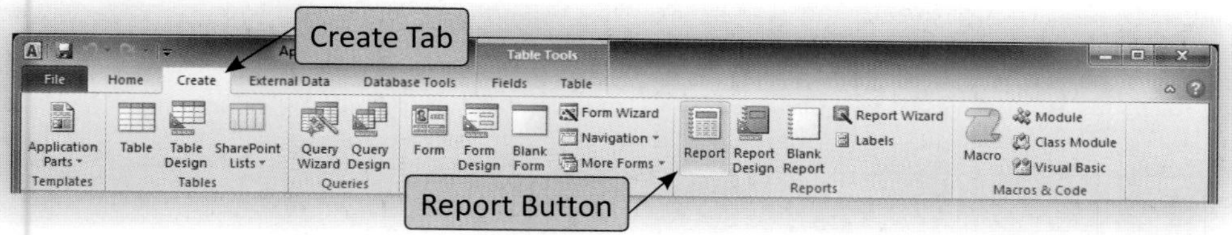

FIGURE AC 3.15

4. The new report opens in Layout view.
5. Click the **Save** button in the Quick Access Toolbar to save the report. Type a meaningful name in the *Report Name:* box. Click **OK.**

The report includes the date and time in the upper-right corner of the report header, and the page number centered in the page footer. If Access finds a field that contains values, it will add a total control for that field in the report footer.

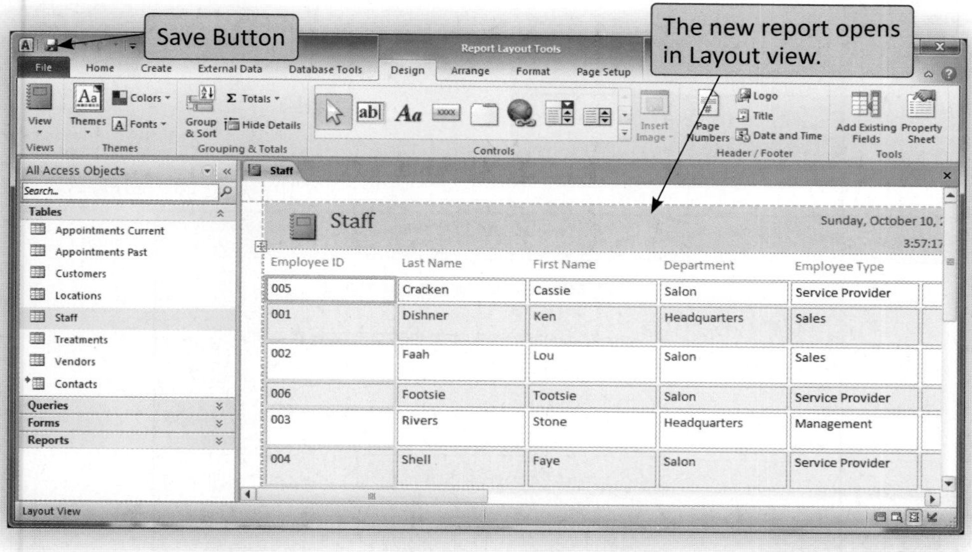

FIGURE AC 3.16

tips & tricks

The report layout is a simple grid similar to the Multiple Items form with each record displayed as a new row. If your report has many columns, this format may not fit on a single page.

tell me more

If you want to create a report that combines fields from more than one table or query, use the Report Wizard instead.

try this

To create a new report directly in Design view, click the **Create** tab. In the *Reports* group, click the **Report Design** button.

To create a new report directly in Layout view, click the **Create** tab. In the *Reports* group, click the **Blank Report** button.

3.8 Using the Report Wizard

The Report Wizard walks you step by step through the process of creating a report. The Report Wizard allows you to combine fields from more than one table or query and gives you more layout and design options than using the basic *Report* command from the **Create** button.

To create a report using the Report Wizard:

1. On the *Create* tab, in the *Reports* group, click the **Report Wizard** button.

FIGURE AC 3.17

2. Click the **Tables/Queries** drop-down arrow. Select the table or query to base your report on.
3. Double-click a field name to include it in the report, or click the name once and then click the [>] button.

Click the [>>] button to add all of the available fields with a single click.

FIGURE AC 3.18

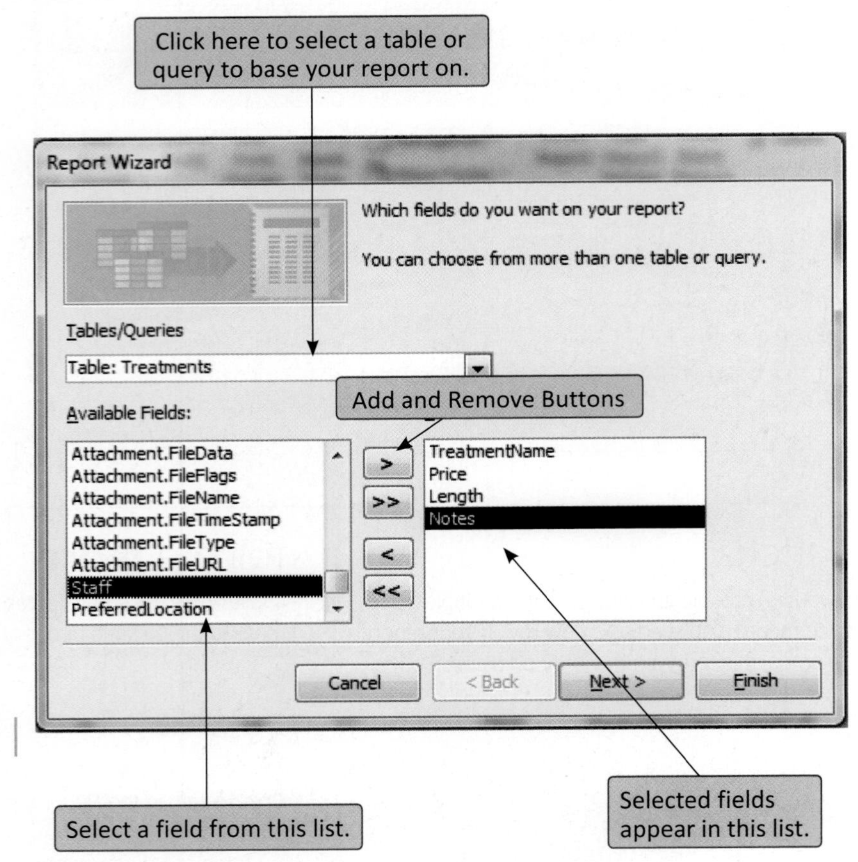

4. You can select another table or query from the *Tables/Queries* drop-down list and add other fields. When you have selected all the fields you want in your report, click the **Next** button to go to the next step.

5. Use grouping levels to organize the data into subgroups by the value of a specific field. You can add multiple grouping levels and reorder them if necessary. Click **Next.**

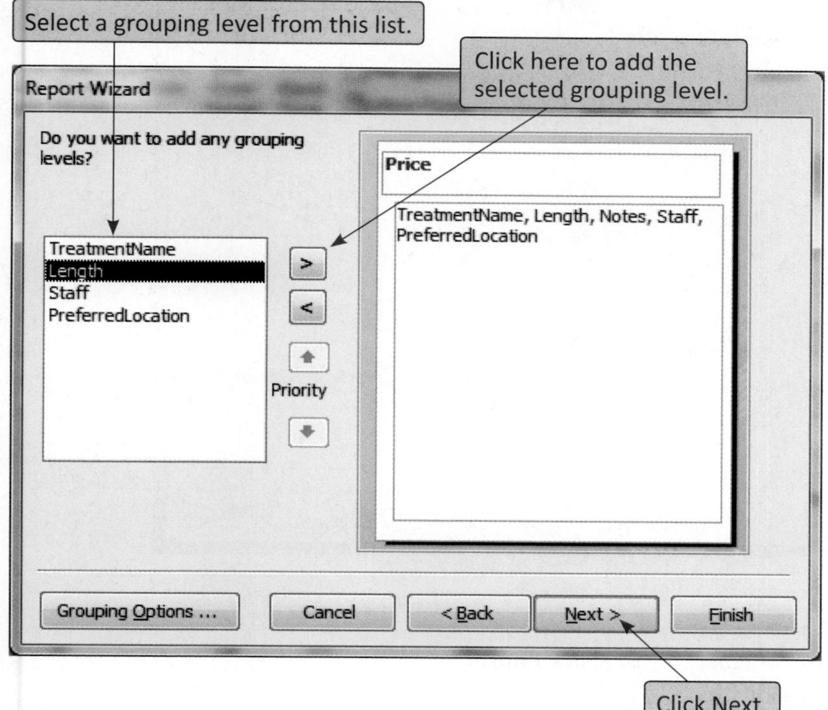

FIGURE AC 3.19

6. Next, specify how you want the data sorted. Click **Next.**

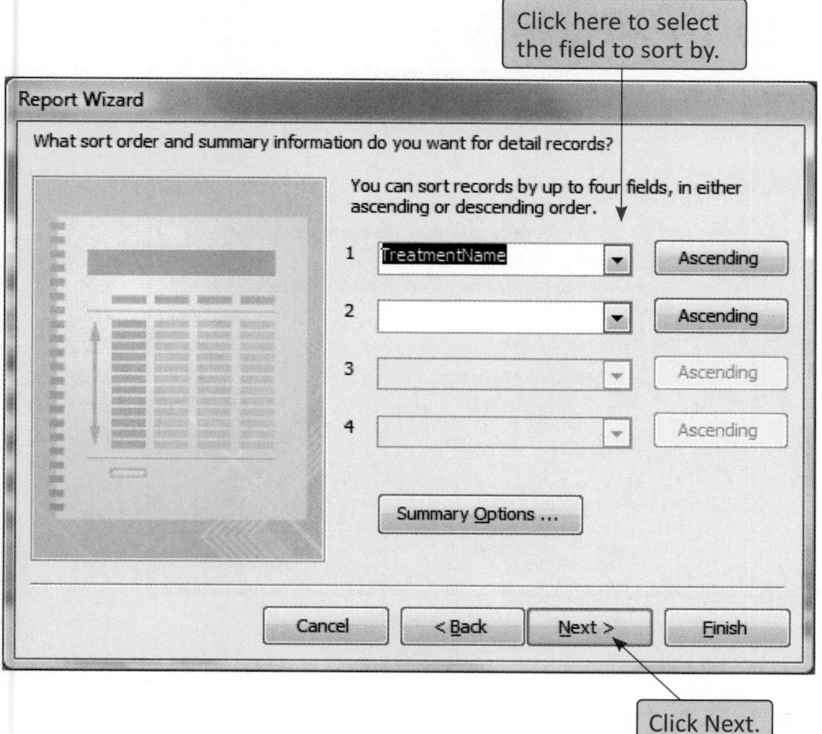

FIGURE AC 3.20

7. Select the report layout, and select whether you want to print in Portrait or Landscape orientation. Click **Next.**

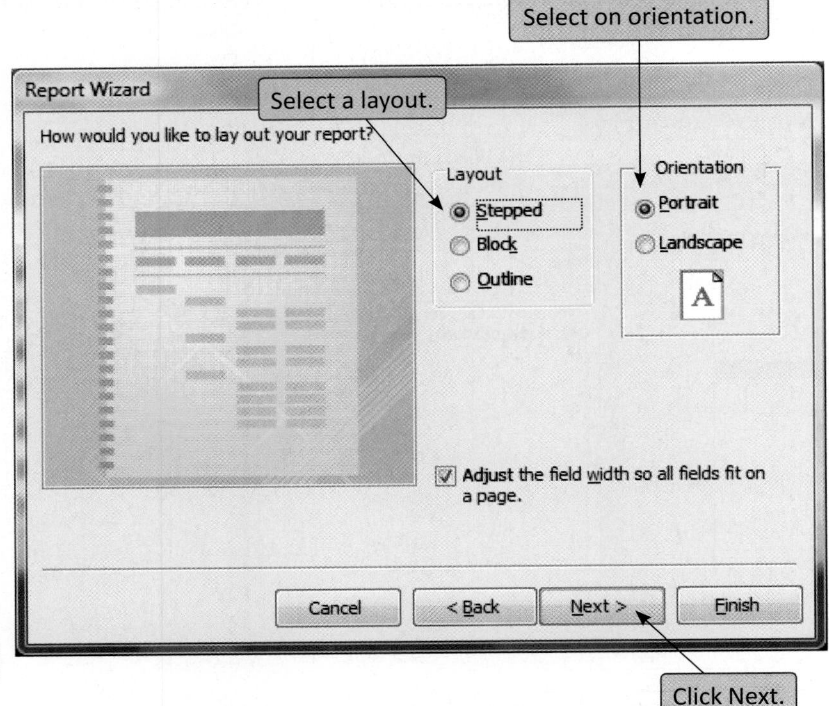

FIGURE AC 3.21

8. Give your report a meaningful title, and choose whether to view the report in Print Preview view or to modify its design.

9. Click **Finish.**

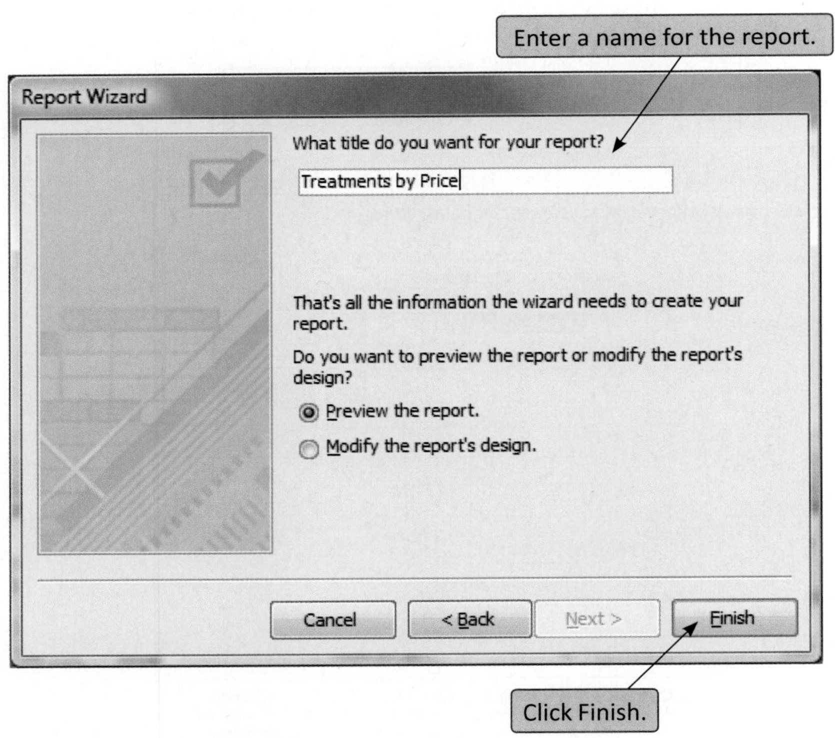

FIGURE AC 3.22

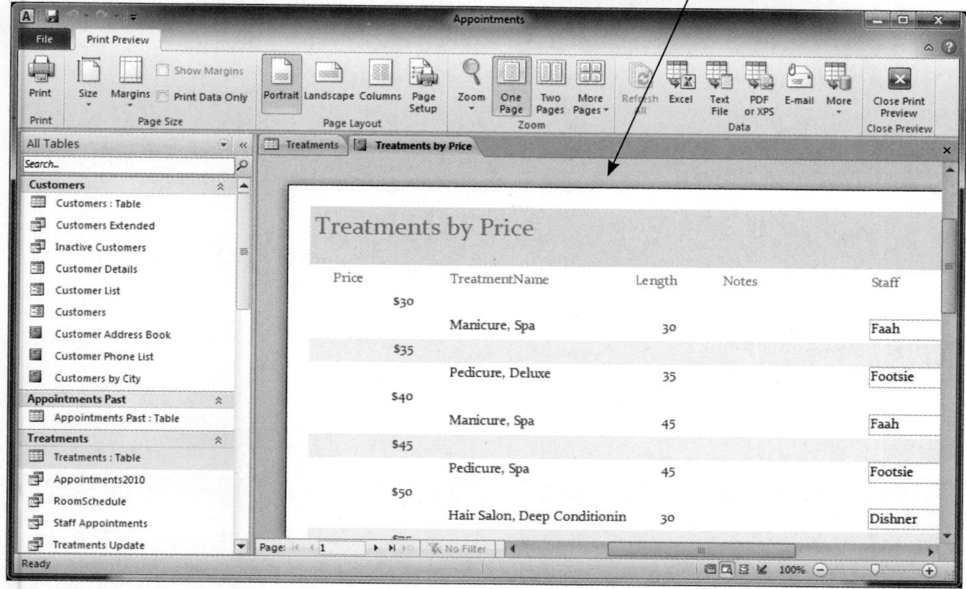

FIGURE AC 3.23

tips & tricks

You can modify your grouping or sorting choices later. To display the *Sort, Group, and Total* pane, click the **Sort & Group** button in the *Grouping & Totals* group on the *Report Layout Tools Design* tab.

3.9 Adding Controls to a Report

Once you have created a report, you may need to add more controls. A control can display data from a table or query field, or it can display static text or a graphic. Controls can also be used to display the current date and time or page numbers.

A control that displays data from a table or query is called a bound control because it is *bound* to the field.

To add a new bound control to a report:

1. If necessary, switch to Layout view.
2. On the *Report Layout Tools Design* tab, in the *Tools* group, click the **Add Existing Fields** button to display the Field List.
3. The Field List shows the tables available in your database. You may need to click the + in front of a table name to see the list of fields.
4. Click the field you want and drag it to the place in the report where you want the control. A new bound control is automatically created, including a label displaying the name of the field.
5. Remember to save the report to save your changes.

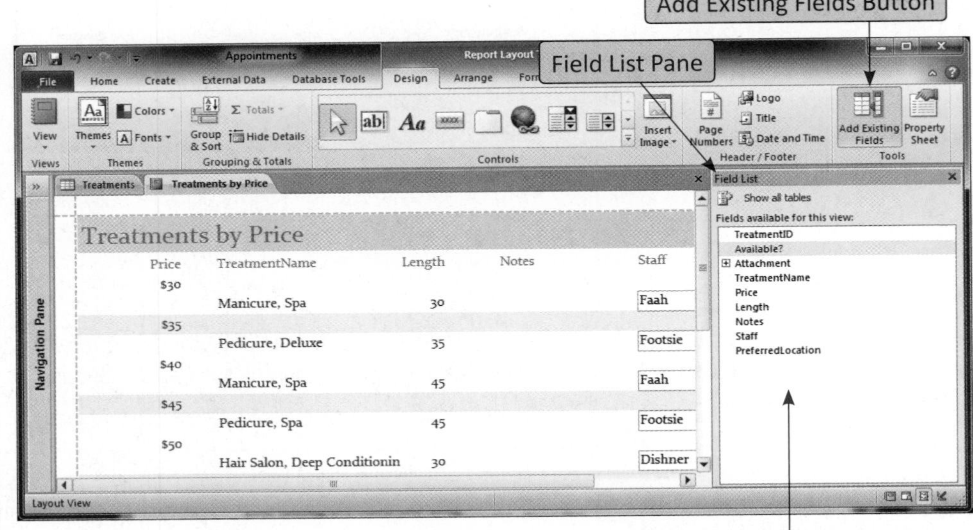

FIGURE AC 3.24

tips & tricks

If the Field List does not show all the tables in your database, click the **Show all tables** link right above the *Fields available for this view:* box.

try this

You can also double-click a field name in the Field List pane to add it to your report. Double-clicking a field name automatically adds the new bound control to the right of whatever control is selected in the report. If nothing is selected, Access adds the new control to the end of the report.

3.10 Changing the Look of a Form or a Report by Applying a Theme

A **theme** is a unified color, font, and effects scheme. When you apply a theme to a form, you ensure that all visual elements work well together, giving the form a polished, professional look.

To apply a theme to a form:

1. If you have the form open in Layout view, click the **Design** tab under *Form Layout Tools*. If you have the form open in Design view, click the **Design** tab under *Form Design Tools*.
2. In the *Themes* group, click the **Themes** button to expand the gallery.
3. Roll your mouse over each theme in the gallery to preview the formatting changes.
4. Click one of the themes to apply it to your form.

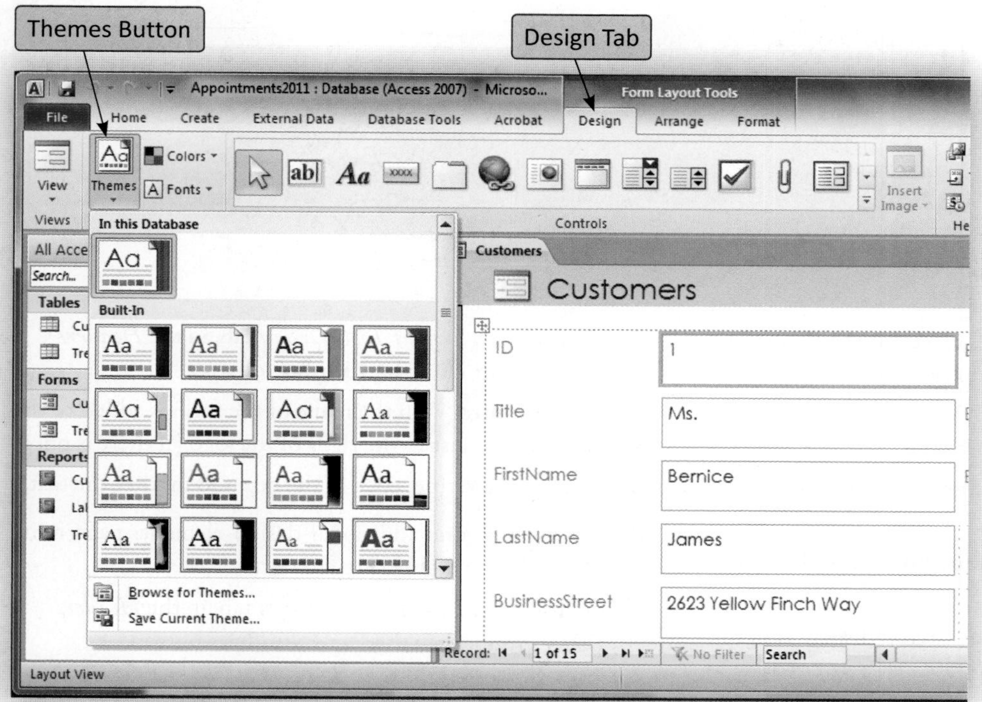

FIGURE AC 3.25

From the *Themes* group, you can apply specific aspects of a theme by making a selection from the *Theme Colors* or *Theme Fonts* gallery. Applying one aspect of a theme (for example, colors) will not change the other aspect (fonts).

Theme Colors—limits the colors available from the color palette for fonts, borders, and shading. Notice that when you change themes, the color palette changes for background colors, fills, outlines, and fonts.

Theme Fonts—affects the fonts used for titles, label controls, bound controls, and other text in the form. Changing the theme fonts does not limit the fonts available to you from the *Font* group on the *Format* tab under *Form Layout Tools*.

3.11 Adding Design Elements to Forms and Reports

Access 2010 has simplified the process of adding certain design elements to forms and reports. From Form Layout view and Report Layout view, you can add the date and time, a graphic logo, and a title without adding complicated controls yourself.

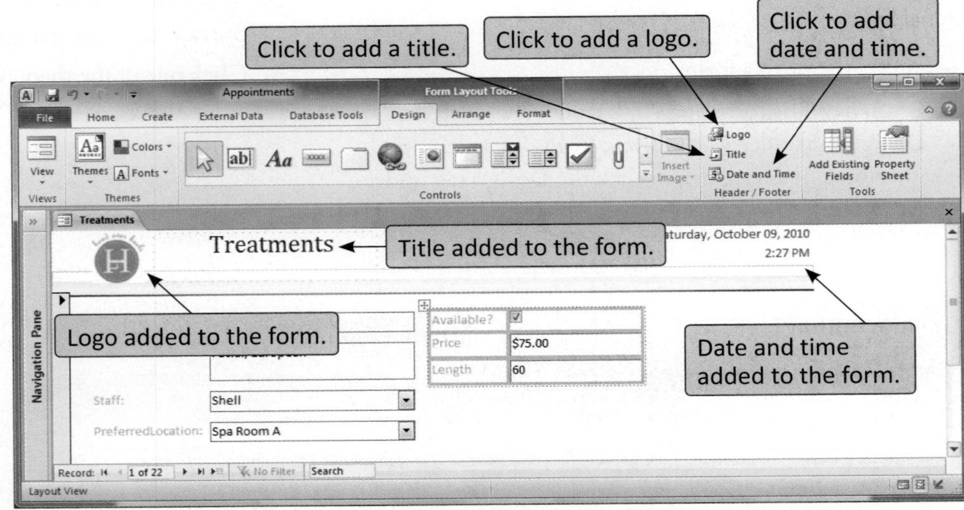

FIGURE AC 3.26

To add the date and/or time:

1. On the *Form Layout Tools Design* tab or the *Report Layout Tools Design* tab, in the *Header/Footer* group, click the **Date and Time** button.
2. The *Date and Time* dialog opens.
3. To include the date, click the **Include Date** check box, and then select a date format.
4. To include the time, click the **Include Time** check box, and then select a time format.
5. A sample of the formats you selected is displayed in the lower-left corner of the dialog.
6. Click **OK** to add the date and time options you selected to the upper-right corner of the form header.

To add a logo:

1. On the *Form Layout Tools Design* tab, in the *Header/Footer* group, click the **Logo** button.
2. The *Insert Picture* dialog opens.
3. Browse to find the graphic you want to use as the logo, select the file, and then click the **Open** button.
4. The graphic is added to the upper-left corner of the form header.

To add a title:

1. On the *Form Layout Tools Design* tab, in the *Header/Footer* group, click the **Title** button.
2. A label control with the name of the form is added to the form header, just to the right of the logo (if there is one).
3. To change the title, click in the box and modify the text.

Reports include one additional design element: page numbers. To add page numbers to a report:

1. On the *Form Layout Tools Design* tab, in the *Header/Footer* group, click the **Page Numbers** button.
2. The *Page Numbers* dialog opens.
3. Select the page number format, position, alignment, and whether or not to show the page number on the first page of the report, and then click **OK.**

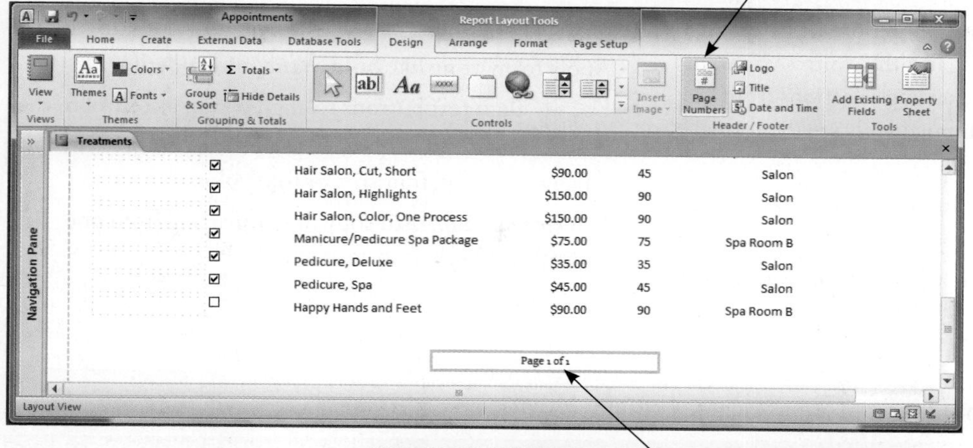

Page number centered at the bottom of the page.

FIGURE AC 3.27

try this

From Design view, to add a control that displays the current date, create an unbound text control and type `=Date()`.

From Design view, to add a control that displays the current time, create an unbound text control and type `=Time()`.

From Design view, to add a control that displays page numbers, create an unbound text control in the report page footer and type `= [Page]`. This will display a simple page number on every page in the report.

3.12 Formatting Controls in Forms and Reports

Once you have created your form or report, it is easy to change formatting in Layout view. Click the control you want to change, and then make your formatting selections from the Ribbon. In Layout view, you can immediately see the formatting change.

- For forms, these commands are found on the *Form Layout Tools Format* tab.
- For reports, these commands are found on the *Report Layout Tools Format* tab.

From the *Font* group, you can

- Apply formatting like **bold,** *italic,* and <u>underline</u>.
- Use the align text buttons to align text in a control to the left, center, or right side of the control box.
- Change the font, font size, or font color.
- Use *Format Painter* to copy the formatting from one control and apply it to another.

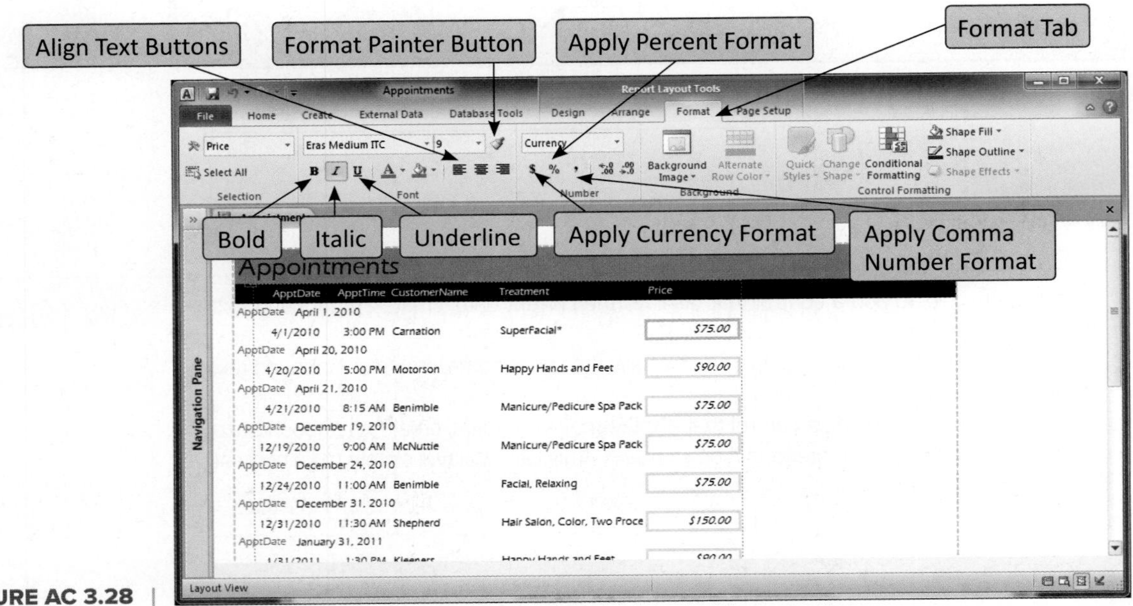

FIGURE AC 3.28

From the *Number* group, you can apply specific field type formatting by clicking one of these buttons:

- **Apply Currency Format**
- **Apply Percent Format**
- **Apply Comma Number Format**

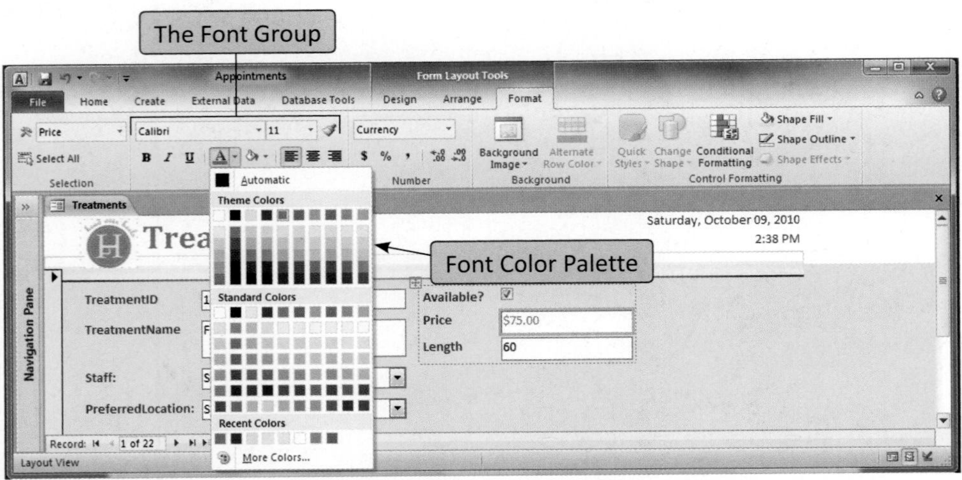

FIGURE AC 3.29

3.13 Resizing and Arranging Controls

A **control layout** combines multiple controls in your form or report into a single layout object in one of two formats:

- A **tabular** layout places labels across the top, with columns of data (similar to a datasheet or a spreadsheet).
- A **stacked** layout places the labels at the left side with data to the right (similar to many paper forms or reports).

Having controls grouped into control layouts makes it easy to add rows and columns to the layout and resize entire layout sections at once.

- To add a new row or column to the control layout, click one of the buttons from the *Arrange* tab, *Rows & Columns* group: **Insert Above, Insert Below, Insert Left,** or **Insert Right.**
- Use the **Select Column** and **Select Row** buttons to select parts of the layout to make changes to, or click the **Select Layout** button to select the entire layout.
- To change the width of part of the layout, move the cursor to the right or left edge of the column, and when the cursor changes to ⟷ click and drag to the right to make the control wider or to the left to make the control smaller. Release the mouse button when the control is the size you want. Use the same technique to make rows taller or shorter.
- To remove a column from the layout, select the column, and then press Delete.

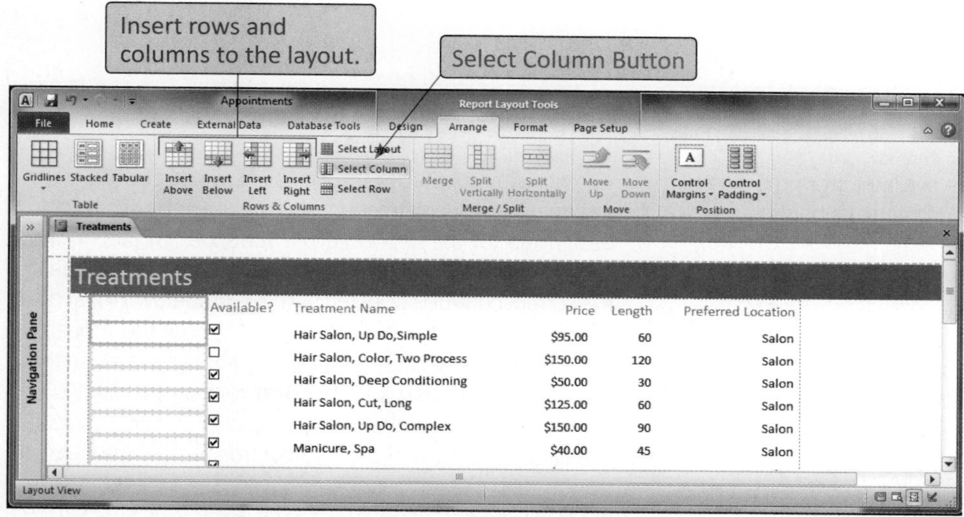

FIGURE AC 3.30

You can change the type of control layout applied to your form or report:

1. Click the **Layout Selector** to select all the controls in your layout at once.
2. Click the **Form Design Tools Arrange** tab or the **Form Layout Tools Arrange** tab or the **Report Design Tools Arrange** tab or the **Report Layout Tools Arrange** tab.
3. From the *Table* group, click the button for the control layout you want (**Stacked** or **Tabular**).

There may be times you want to move a single control separately from the rest of the control layout. You must remove the control from the layout before you can manipulate it individually.

1. From Design view, click the control you want to remove from the control layout. (You can select multiple controls at once by holding down the ⇧Shift key as you click each control.)
2. Click the **Form Design Tools Arrange** tab or the **Report Design Tools Arrange** tab.
3. Click the **Remove Layout** button to remove the control from the layout so it can be moved independent of the others.
4. Click the control you want to move and move the mouse to the center of the control. When the cursor changes to ✥, click and drag the control to the new location.

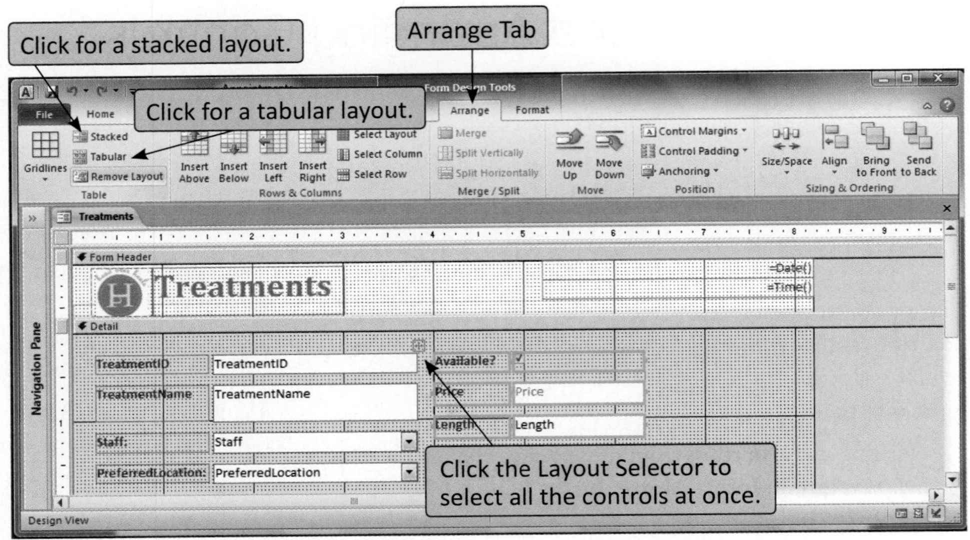

FIGURE AC 3.31

tips & tricks

The *Remove Layout* command is available from the right-click menu in Layout view, but not from the Ribbon.

tell me **more**

Another way to specify the height or width of controls is through the Property Sheet pane. On the *Form Layout Tools Design* tab (or the *Report Layout Tools Design* tab), in the *Tools* group, click the **Property Sheet** button. Ensure that the correct control is selected from the drop-down list at the top of the Property Sheet. If necessary, click the Property Sheet **Format** tab. Type the value you want (in inches) in the *Width* and *Height* boxes. Press **Enter** to apply the change.

Notice that when the control is part of a control layout, changing the height of a single control affects all the controls in the row, and changing the width of a single control affects all the controls in the column.

try **this**

You can also right-click a control, point to **Layout,** and click the control layout option you want.

3.14 Grouping Records in a Report

Adding grouping to your report defines the way records are displayed. When you add grouping to a report, you can also add a group header or footer. Group headers and footers differentiate the groups into distinct sections in the report.

To group records in a report:

1. Switch to Layout view if necessary
2. On the *Report Layout Tools Design* tab, in the *Grouping & Totals* group, click the **Group & Sort** button.
3. Click the **Add a group** button in the *Group, Sort, and Total* pane. Click the field you want to group by.

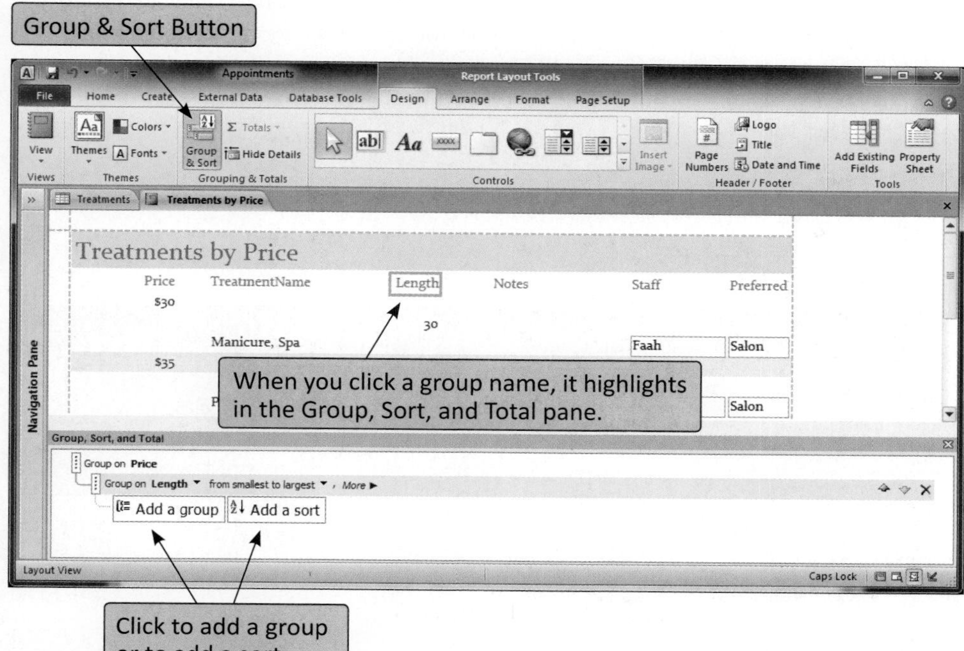

Group & Sort Button
When you click a group name, it highlights in the Group, Sort, and Total pane.
Click to add a group or to add a sort.

FIGURE AC 3.32

Groups are automatically sorted alphabetically with A first (or numerically with the smallest number first). To change the sort order for groups:

1. If necessary, click the group name in the *Group, Sort, and Total* pane. The line for the group will highlight.
2. Click the arrow next to the sort description to expand the list of sort options.
3. Select a new sorting option.

You can also control the sort order of records within each group. To specify a field to sort by within each group:

1. If necessary, click the group name in the *Group, Sort, and Total* pane. The line for the group will highlight.
2. Click the **Add a sort** button in the group you want to sort.
3. Click the field you want to sort by.

tell me **more**

Through the *Group, Sort, and Total* pane, you can control options for how groups are displayed, including formatting group headers and calculating aggregate functions for each group. To see the options available:

1. If necessary, click the group name in the *Group, Sort, and Total* pane. The line for the group will highlight.
2. Click the **More** button.
3. To close the *More Options* panel, click the **Less** button.

try **this**

You can also add groupings from the *Grouping & Totals* group in the *Report Design Tools Design* tab.

3.15 Adding Totals to a Report in Layout View

A **calculated control** is an unbound text control that contains an expression (formula). Calculated controls are often used to compute an aggregate value such as a total (sum), average, minimum, or maximum. You can add these types of controls to your reports from Layout view.

To add a calculated control from Layout view:

1. Open the report in Layout view.
2. Click the field you want to calculate an aggregate value for.
3. On the *Report Layout Tools Design* tab, in the *Grouping & Totals* group, click the **Totals** button.
4. Select the aggregate function you want: **Sum, Average, Count Records, Count Values, Max, Min, Standard Deviation,** and **Variance.** The functions available will vary, depending on the data type of the field you selected. For example, *Average* is only available for number and currency data types. *Count Records* is available for all data types.
5. Access automatically inserts the new calculated control into the report footer and the footer section for any group. The control in the report footer calculates a grand total, and the control in the group footer calculates the total for records in that group.

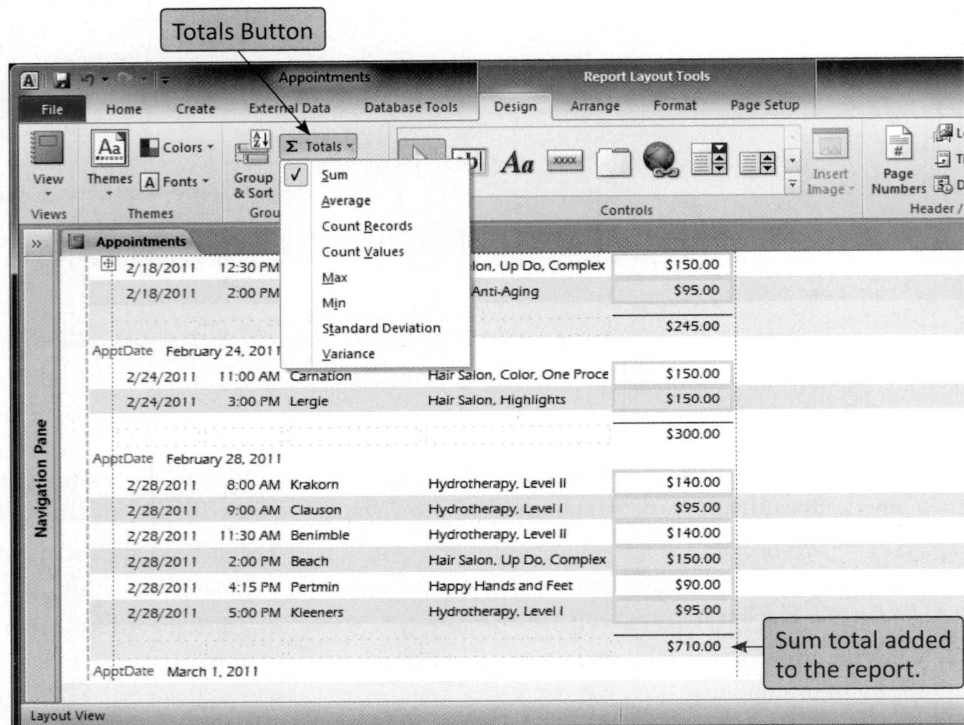

FIGURE AC 3.33

tips & tricks

Only the functions appropriate to the data type of the selected field are available in the *Totals* menu for reports. *Average, Min,* and *Max* are not available for date/time fields in reports (even though those functions are available when adding a Total row in Datasheet view for date/time fields).

3.16 Previewing and Printing a Report

Print Preview view shows you exactly how the report will look when it is printed. It is always a good idea to preview the report before printing.

To see how the report will print, switch to Print Preview view.

- Right-click the report tab, and select **Print Preview.**
- Click the **Print Preview** view button on the status bar.
- On the *Home* tab, in the *Views* group, click the **View** button, and select **Print Preview.**

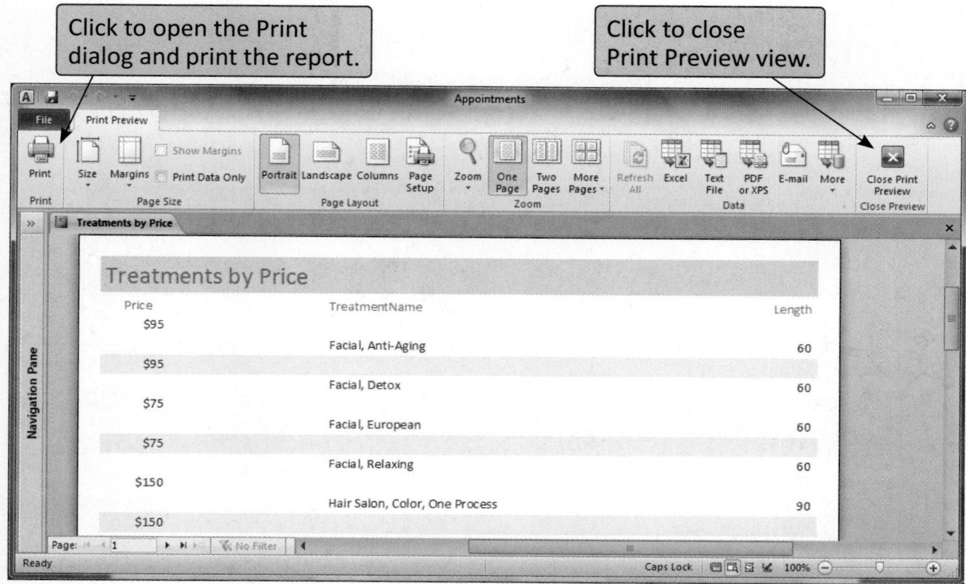

FIGURE AC 3.34

From Print Preview view, click the **Print** button at the far left side of the Ribbon to open the *Print* dialog. In the *Print* dialog you can specify which pages to print and how many copies to print. Click **OK** to send the report to the printer.

To close Print Preview view, click the **Close Print Preview** button at the far right side of the Ribbon.

You can print a report without opening Print Preview view first:

1. With the report open in any view, click the **File** tab to open Backstage view.
2. Click **Print.**
3. Select the print option you want.

Quick Print sends the report to the printer without opening the *Print* dialog first.

Print opens the *Print* dialog so you can make changes to the print settings before printing.

Print Preview opens the report in Print Preview view.

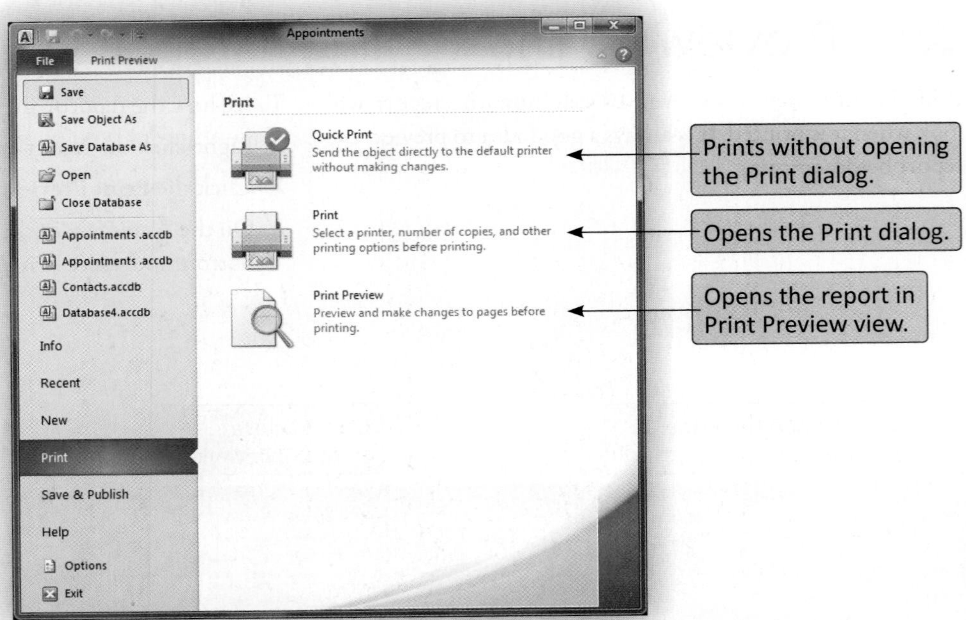

FIGURE AC 3.35

tell me **more**

You can print any type of database object. Open the table, form, or query you want to print, and then click the **File** tab, and click **Print.**

3.17 Controlling the Page Setup of a Report for Printing

When printing a report, the default page orientation for a report is **portrait.** This means the height of the page is greater than the width. You may want to change the page orientation to **landscape** to print sideways on the page if your report contains multiple columns of data.

Margins are the blank spaces at the top, bottom, left, and right of the printed page. By adjusting the margins, you can control the number of records printed on each page.

Use the *Page Setup* tab to adjust margins and page orientation for your reports:

1. From Layout view, click the **Page Setup** tab.
2. To change the page orientation, click the **Portrait** or **Landscape** button.
3. To use a preset margin option, click the **Margins** button, and select an option: **Normal, Wide,** or **Narrow.** If you need to set margins more precisely, click the **Page Setup** button and enter the margin measurements in the *Print Options* tab of the *Page Setup* dialog.

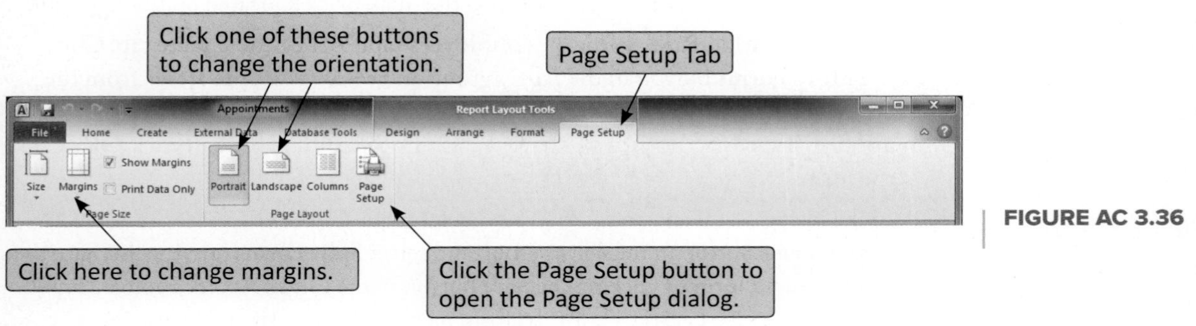

FIGURE AC 3.36

tips & tricks

When you print a report, Access prints the data along with all graphic elements associated with the report design. To print only the data and not the graphic elements of a report, select the **Print Data Only** check box on the *Page Setup* tab.

try this

The *Page Setup* tab is also available from Design view and from Print Preview view.

projects

Skill Review 3.1

You are a part-time employee in the Computer Science department of a local college. It uses Access 2010 to manage employees and various items that are often loaned out. It would like you to create forms in order to enter data into the table. It would also like to summarize and print its data using a few reports. Complete the steps below to create and modify these objects.

1. Creating forms:

a. Find and open the following student file in Access 2010: *collegedept3.accdb.* Save this database as ***[your initials]*****AC_SkillReview_3-1.**

b. In the Navigation Pane, select the **Employees** table. Click the **Create** tab. Click the **Form** button in the *Forms* group. Save the newly created form by clicking the **Save** button in the Quick Access Toolbar. Type `EmployeesForm` for the form name and click **OK.** Close the form by clicking the small black **x** located on the right side.

c. In the Navigation Pane, select the **Employees** table. Click the **Create** tab. Click the **More Forms** button in the *Forms* group and select **Multiple Items** from the list. Save the newly created form by clicking the **Save** button in the Quick Access Toolbar. Type `EmployeesFormMulti` for the form name and click **OK.** Close the form.

d. In the Navigation Pane, select the **Employees** table. Click the **Create** tab. Click the **More Forms** button in the *Forms* group and select **Split Form** from the list. Save the newly created form by clicking the **Save** button in the Quick Access Toolbar. Type `EmployeesFormSplit` for the form name and click **OK.** Close the form.

e. Click the **Create** tab. Click the **Application Parts** button in the *Templates* group and select **Tabs** from the list of blank forms. Notice the new form in the Navigation Pane. Double-click this new form, observe it, and close it. Leave the default name.

f. Click the **Create** tab. Click the **Form Wizard** button in the *Forms* group. In this new dialog box, select **Table: Items** from the *Tables/Queries* list box. Below that, click the >> button in order to add all the fields to your form. On the right side, click the **Description** field and click the < button in order to send it to the left. Click the **Next** button at the bottom.

g. You are now in the second step of the wizard. Select the **Columnar** radio button and click the **Next** button at the bottom to go to the third step. Type `ItemsForm` at the top and make sure that the **Open the form to view or enter information** option is selected. Click the **Finish** button at the bottom to exit the wizard. Do not close this form.

2. Edit a form:

a. On the Home tab, click the arrow below the **View** button in the *Views* group. Select **Layout View.** Click the **Design** tab if it is not already selected.

b. Click the arrow below the **Themes** button in the *Themes* group. Select the **Angles** theme, which is the third one in the first row of the Built-in category.

c. Click the **Add Existing Fields** button from the *Tools* group. In the *Field List* that now appears on the right side, double-click the **Description** field in order to add it to the form. Don't worry about the exact placement as you will modify it in the next few steps.

d. Drag the new *Description* control to an appropriate location to the right of the *ItemID* control. Align the top of the *Description* control with the top of the *ItemID* control.

e. Select the **Description** control and notice that it is divided into two parts: the left side is the label control while the right side is the bound control. Use the double-arrow pointer between these two controls to resize the label control so that it better matches the width of the other label controls. Use the same technique on the right side of the bound control to make it wide enough that its contents fit comfortably.

f. Right-click the **Description** control and select **Properties.** Change the value of *Height* so that it is **1.6".**

g. Click the **ItemID Label** control. Hold the **Shift** key and click the bound control to its right so that both are now selected. Go to the **Format** tab and click the **Bold** button in the *Font* group. Change the *Font* to **Arial** and the *Font Size* to **12.**

h. Save this form and close it.

i. Open the **EmployeesForm** that you created earlier. Click the arrow below the **View** button in the *Views* group. Select **Layout View.** Click the **Arrange** tab if it is not already selected.

j. Click the **LengthOfService Label** control. Hold the **Shift** key and click the bound control to its right so that both are now selected. Click the **Move Down** button in the *Move* group. Repeat until this control is the last one in the form's layout. Save this form and close it.

3. Creating reports:

a. In the Navigation Pane, select the **Items** table. Click the **Create** tab. In the *Reports* group, click the **Report** button. Click the **Save** button in the Quick Access Toolbar to save this newly created report. Type `ItemsReport` in the area provided. Click **OK.** Close the report by clicking the small black **x** located on the right side.

b. Click the **Create** tab. Click the **Report Wizard** button in the *Reports* group. In this new dialog box, select **Table: Employees** from the *Tables/Queries* drop-down box. Below that, click the >> button in order to add all the fields to your report. On the right side, click the **Email** field and click the < button in order to send it to the left. Do the same for the *LengthOfService* field. Click the **Next** button at the bottom.

c. In the second step of the Report Wizard, select the **Position** field and add it to the right by clicking the > button. This will group the records in your report by the various employee positions. Click the **Next** button at the bottom.

d. Next to the number *1* in this next step, click the list arrow and choose **LastName** from the list of choices. Click the **Next** button at the bottom.

e. You are now in the *Layout* step of the Report Wizard. Leave all options as they are except for the *Orientation.* Select the **Landscape** option. Click the **Next** button at the bottom.

f. In the final step, type `EmployeesReport` as the name and click the **Finish** button at the bottom. After the report displays, close it by clicking the small black **x** located on the right side.

g. In the Navigation Pane, select the **Loans** table. Click the **Create** tab. In the *Reports* group, click the **Blank Report** button.

h. Click the arrow below the **View** button in the *Views* group. Select **Layout View** if it isn't already selected. Also make sure the *Design* tab is the active one in the Ribbon.

i. Click the **Add Existing Fields** button from the *Tools* group to display the Field List pane. In the Field List pane, click the **Show all tables** link and then click the

[+] button to expand the *Loans* table. Double-click the following fields from the *Loans* table in order to add them to the report: **LoanID, ItemID, EmployeeID, LoanDate, Purpose.**

j. You decide that adding the *LoanID* field is not important. Right-click the bound control under the *LoanID* label and select **Delete Column** from the menu. The entire *LoanID* column should have disappeared, and all the other columns have now moved left.

k. Click the **Save** button in the Quick Access Toolbar to save this report. Type `LoansReport` in the area provided. Click **OK.** Close the report by clicking the small black **x** located on the right side.

4. Edit a report:

a. Double-click the **ItemsReport** to open it. Click the arrow below the **View** button in the *Views* group. Select **Layout View** if it isn't already selected.

b. Click the bound control below **ItemID** to select it.

c. Use the double-arrow pointer on the right edge of this control to make this column narrower since it only has four characters in any given cell.

d. Right-click the bound control below **Description** and select **Properties.** Change the value of *Width* so that it is **4.2".**

e. Right-click the bound control below **ItemID** and choose **Select Entire Column.** Move your mouse pointer over any part of this column and drag it so that it ends up to the right of the *ItemName* column.

f. Click the **Group & Sort** button from the *Grouping & Totals* group in the *Design* tab. Click the **Add a group** button in the *Group, Sort, and Total* pane. Choose the **Category** field. Now click the **Add a sort** button in the *Group, Sort, and Total* pane and choose the **ItemName** field. Close the *Group, Sort, and Total* pane.

g. Click the bound control under **Cost.** Click the **Totals** button from the *Grouping & Totals* group in the *Design* tab. Select **Sum** from the list. Observe the large total at the bottom of the report and the totals located at the end of each group. Resize these controls if necessary to make sure the number is fully displayed.

h. Select any of the **Category** bound controls. In the *Format* tab, click the **Bold** button in the *Font* group.

i. Right-click any of the **Category** bound controls and select **Properties.** Change the value of *Width* so that it is **1.0".**

j. Click the *Home* tab. Click the arrow below the **View** button in the *Views* group. Select **Design View.**

k. Select the control inside the *Page Footer* area. Click inside of it and delete all the text after the first occurrence of *[Page].* Press **Enter.**

l. Select the control that contains the word *Items* inside the *Report Header* area. Click inside of it and type the word `Report` next to it. Press **Enter.**

m. Go back to Layout view and move the **Page #** control to the left so that it appears centered at the bottom of the report.

n. Click the arrow below the **View** button in the *Views* group. Select **Print Preview View.** Click the **Landscape** button in the *Page Layout* group so that all of the columns in your report fit on the paper. If necessary, click **OK** to close the window containing a warning message. Feel free to return to Layout view and move/resize any controls that look strange in the print preview.

o. Return to *Print Preview* and click the **Print** button in the *Print* group. Click the **Close Print Preview** button, save your report, and close your database.

Skill Review 3.2

You have just been hired by a small health insurance company in the south Florida area. One of your duties is using Access 2010 to manage the company's list of in-network doctors and covered procedures. It would like you to create forms in order to enter new doctors and procedures. It would also like to summarize and print its data using a few reports. Complete the steps below to create and modify these objects.

1. Creating forms:

a. Find and open the following student file in Access 2010: *sfinsurance3.accdb.* Save this database as ***[your initials]*AC_SkillReview_3-2.**

b. In the Navigation Pane, select the **Physicians** table. Click the **Create** tab. Click the **Form** button in the *Forms* group. Save the newly created form by clicking the **Save** button in the Quick Access Toolbar. Type `PhysicianForm` for the form name and click **OK.** Close the form by clicking the small black **x** located on the right side.

c. In the Navigation Pane, select the **Physicians** table. Click the **Create** tab. Click the **More Forms** button in the *Forms* group and select **Multiple Items** from the list. Save the newly created form by clicking the **Save** button in the Quick Access Toolbar. Type `PhysiciansFormMulti` for the form name and click **OK.** Close the form.

d. In the Navigation Pane, select the **Physicians** table. Click the **Create** tab. Click the **More Forms** button in the *Forms* group and select **Split Form** from the list. Save the newly created form by clicking the **Save** button in the Quick Access Toolbar. Type `PhysiciansFormSplit` for the form name and click **OK.** Close the form.

e. Click the **Create** tab. Click the **Application Parts** button in the *Templates* group and select **Msgbox** (Message box form) from the list of blank forms. Notice the new form in the Navigation Pane. Double-click this new form, observe it, and close it. Leave the default name.

f. Click the **Create** tab. Click the **Form Wizard** button in the *Forms* group. In this new dialog box, select **Table: Orders** from the *Tables/Queries* list box. Below that, click the >> button in order to add all the fields to your form. On the right side, click the **OrderDate** field and click the < button in order to send it to the left. Click the **Next** button at the bottom.

g. You are now in the second step of the wizard. Select the **Columnar** radio button and click the **Next** button at the bottom to go to the third step. Type `OrdersForm` at the top and make sure that the **Open the form to view or enter information** option is selected. Click the **Finish** button at the bottom to exit the wizard. Do not close this form.

2. Edit a form:

a. Click the arrow below the **View** button in the *Views* group. Select **Layout View.** Click the **Design** tab if it is not already selected.

b. Click the arrow below the **Themes** button in the *Themes* group. Select the **Civic** theme, which is the third one in the first column of the Built-in category.

c. Click the **Add Existing Fields** button from the *Tools* group. In the *Field List* that now appears on the right side, double-click the **OrderDate** field in order to add it to the form. Don't worry about the exact placement as you will modify it in the next few steps.

d. Drag the new *OrderDate* control directly to the right of the *OrderID* control. Make sure the top and bottom are aligned with *OrderID.*

e. Select the **OrderDate** control and notice that it is divided into two parts: the left side is the label control while the right side is the bound control. Use the double-arrow pointer on the right edge of the bound control and drag it to the left to make it smaller. It should be wide enough to comfortably fit any date entered into it.

f. Use this same technique on the *PhysicianID* and *ProcedureID* bound controls. The right edge of these bound controls should be aligned with the right edge of the *OrderDate* bound control from the previous step.

g. Right-click the **OrderID** bound control and select **Properties.** Change the value of *Width* so that it is **0.5".**

h. Click the **OrderID** label control. Hold the **Shift** key and click the bound control to its right so that both are now selected. Go to the **Format** tab and click the **Bold** button in the *Font* group. Change the *Font Color* to a **dark blue** and the *Font Size* to **12.**

i. Save this form and close it.

j. Open the **PhysiciansForm** that you created earlier. Click the arrow below the **View** button in the *Views* group. Select **Layout View.** Click the **Arrange** tab if it is not already selected.

k. Click the **FirstName** label control. Hold the **Shift** key and click the bound control to its right so that both are now selected. Click the **Move Down** button in the *Move* group. The *FirstName* field is now located below the *LastName* field. Save this form and close it.

3. Creating reports:

a. In the Navigation Pane, select the **Physicians** table. Click the **Create** tab. In the *Reports* group, click the **Report** button. Click the **Save** button in the Quick Access Toolbar to save this newly created report. Type `PhysiciansReport` in the area provided. Click **OK.** Close the report by clicking the small black **x** located on the right side.

b. Click the **Create** tab. Click the **Report Wizard** button in the *Reports* group. In this new dialog box, select **Table: Procedures** from the *Tables/Queries* drop-down box. Below that, click the >> button in order to add all the fields to your report. On the right side, click the **ProcedureID** field and click the < button in order to send it to the left. Click the **Next** button at the bottom.

c. In the second step of the Report Wizard, select the **Covered** field and add it to the right by clicking the > button. This will group the records in your report into covered and noncovered procedures. Click the **Next** button at the bottom.

d. Next to the number *1* in this next step, click the list arrow and choose **ProcedureName** from the list of choices. Click the **Next** button at the bottom.

e. You are now in the *Layout* step of the Report Wizard. Leave all options as they are except for the *Orientation.* Select the **Landscape** option. Click the **Next** button at the bottom.

f. In the final step, type `ProceduresReport` as the name and click the **Finish** button at the bottom. After the report displays, close it by clicking the small black **x** located on the right side.

g. In the Navigation Pane, select the **Orders** table. Click the **Create** tab. In the *Reports* group, click the **Blank Report** button.

h. Click the arrow below the **View** button in the *Views* group. Select **Layout View** if it isn't already selected. Also make sure the *Design* tab is the active one in the Ribbon.

i. Click the **Add Existing Fields** button from the *Tools* group to display the Field List pane. In the Field List pane, click the **Show all tables** link and then click the [+] button to expand the *Orders* table. Double-click the following fields from the *Orders* table in order to add them to the report: **OrderID, PhysicianID, ProcedureID, OrderDate.**

j. Click the **Save** button in the Quick Access Toolbar to save this report. Type `OrdersReport` in the area provided. Click **OK.** Close the report by clicking the small black **x** located on the right side.

4. Edit a report:

a. Double-click the **PhysiciansReport** to open it. Click the arrow below the **View** button in the *Views* group. Select **Layout View** if it isn't already selected.

b. Right-click the bound control under the **PhysicianID** label and select **Delete Column** from the menu. The entire *PhysicianID* column should have disappeared, and all the other columns have now moved left.

c. Click the bound control below **ZipCode** to select it.

d. Use the double-arrow pointer on the left edge of this control to make this column narrower since it only has five characters in any given cell. Please be sure that it is still wide enough to fit the *ZipCode* label at the top of the column.

e. Right-click the bound control below **FirstName** and select **Properties.** Change the value of *Width* so that it is **1.2".** Repeat the same steps for the *LastName* and *Phone* columns. Alternatively, you could hold the **Ctrl** key to select all three columns at the same time and change the width in one step.

f. Right-click the bound control below **LastName** and choose **Select Entire Column.** Move your mouse pointer over any part of this column and drag it so that it ends up to the left of the *FirstName* column.

g. Click the **Group & Sort** button from the *Grouping & Totals* group in the *Design* tab. Click the **Add a group** button in the *Group, Sort, and Total* pane. Choose the **City** field. Now click the **Add a sort** button in the *Group, Sort, and Total* pane and choose the **LastName** field. Close the *Group, Sort, and Total* pane.

h. Click the bound control under **MemberCount.** Click the **Totals** button from the *Grouping & Totals* group in the *Design* tab. Select **Sum** from the list. Observe the overall total at the bottom of the report and the totals located at the end of each group. Resize these controls if necessary to make sure the number is fully displayed.

i. Select any of the **City** bound controls. In the *Format* tab, click the **Bold** button in the *Font* group.

j. Right-click any of the **City** bound controls and select **Properties.** Change the value of *Width* so that it is **1.3".**

k. Click the *Home* tab. Click the arrow below the **View** button in the *Views* group. Select **Design View.**

l. Select the control inside the *Page Footer* area. Click inside of it and delete all the text after the first occurrence of *[Page].* Press **Enter.**

m. Select the control that contains the word *Physicians* inside the *Report Header* area. Click inside of it and type the word `Report` next to it. Press **Enter.**

n. Go back to Layout view and move the *Page #* control to the left so that it appears centered at the bottom of the report.

o. Click the arrow below the **View** button in the *Views* group. Select **Print Preview View.** Click the **Landscape** button in the *Page Layout* group so that all of the columns in your report fit on the paper. If necessary, click **OK** to close the window containing a warning message. Feel free to return to Layout view and move/resize any controls that look strange in the print preview.

p. Return to *Print Preview* and click the **Print** button in the *Print* group. Click the **Close Print Preview** button, save your report, and close your database.

challenge yourself 1

You are a botany professor who was recently placed in charge of maintaining the department's greenhouse. This database contains records of the plants in the greenhouse and the employees that assist you with maintenance duties. You would like to create a few forms in order to easily enter new plants, employees, and maintenance information. You would also like to summarize and print the greenhouse records using a few reports. Complete the steps below to create and modify these objects.

1. Creating forms:
   a. Open the *greenhouse3.accdb* student file and save a copy as `[your initials]AC_Challenge_3-3`.
   b. Select the **Plants** table and create a form using the **Form** button in the *Forms* group. Save it using the name `PlantsForm` and close it.
   c. Create a **Multiple Items Form** for the *Plants* table. Save it with the name `PlantsFormMulti` and close it.
   d. Create a **Split Form** for the *MaintenanceLog* table. Save it with the name `MaintenanceFormSplit` and close it.
   e. Use the **Application Parts** button to create a **message box (Msgbox)** form. Leave the default name.
   f. Use the **Form Wizard** button to create a columnar form for the *Employees* table. Add all fields except *WeeklyHours.* Name this form `EmployeesForm` and leave it open for the upcoming exercises.
2. Editing forms:
   a. Apply the **Adjacency** theme, which is the second one in the first row of the Built-in group.
   b. Add the **WeeklyHours** field to the form. Position it next to the *EmployeeID* control. Align it properly.
   c. Resize all the controls so that they are appropriate for their content. Make sure that the right edge of *WeeklyHours, FirstName, LastName,* and *Position* are all aligned.
   d. The text in the *EmployeeID* control should be bold, size 12, and a dark green color.
   e. Save this form and close it.
   f. Open the **PlantsForm** that you created earlier. Move the **DatePlanted** field downward so that it is located directly above the *PurchasePrice* field. Save this form and close it.
3. Creating reports:
   a. Use the **Blank Report** button to generate a report based on the *MaintenanceLog* table. Add all fields except *MaintenanceID.* Save this report as `MaintenanceReport` and close it.
   b. Use the **Report Wizard** to create a report based on the *Employees* table. Add all fields except *EmployeeID.* Group by the *Position* field. Leave all other options with the default selections. Save the report as `EmployeesReport` and close it.
   c. Use the **Report** button to generate a report based on the *LightPlants* query. You will now modify this report.

4. Editing reports:

a. Delete the *PlantID* column. Rename the *MaxHeightFeet* label control to `MaxFt`.

b. Resize the *FlowerColor* column to an appropriate size. Resize the width of the *MaxFt* column to exactly **0.5"**.

c. Move the *DatePlanted* column all the way to left.

d. Group the report by *FlowerColor.* Sort it by *CommonName.* Resize the width of the *FlowerColor* column to exactly **1.0"**.

e. Add a total (sum) to each group and to the entire report. Increase the height of the total controls if necessary.

f. Make sure each of the *FlowerColor* controls is formatted in boldface. Format the *DatePlanted* label and bound controls so that they are aligned to the left.

g. In the *Page Footer* area, delete all the text after the first occurrence of *[Page]*. Format this control to be italicized. Move it to the left side of the report.

h. In the *Report Header* area, delete the *Date and Time* controls. Format the *LightPlants* control so that it is bold and a dark blue color.

i. Change the orientation to **Landscape.**

j. Review the layout and formatting of your report and make any necessary changes. Save the report as `LightPlantsReport` and print it if required by your instructor.

challenge yourself 2

You work for a volunteer organization that ships and administers vaccines to various relief centers all over the world. It currently uses Access 2010 to maintain the list of all approved vaccines and keep track of all shipments made to the relief centers. In order to make data entry easier, it would like you to create a few forms for the tables already present in the database. It would also like some printed reports of its data. Complete the steps below to create and modify these objects.

1. Creating forms:

a. Open the *vaccines3.accdb* student file and save a copy as **`[your initials]AC_Challenge_3-4`.**

b. Select the **Shipments** table and create a form using the **Form** button in the *Forms* group. Save it using the name `ShipmentsForm` and close it.

c. Create a **Multiple Items Form** for the *Locations* table. Save it with the name `LocationsFormMulti` and close it.

d. Create a **Split Form** for the *Locations* table. Save it with the name `LocationsFormSplit` and close it.

e. Use the **Application Parts** button to create a *Dialog* form. Leave the default name.

f. Use the **Form Wizard** button to create a columnar form for the *Vaccines* table. Add all fields except *Inventory.* Name this form `VaccinesForm` and leave it open for the upcoming exercises.

2. Editing forms:

a. Apply the **Black Tie** theme, which is the fourth one in the second row of the Built-in group.

b. Resize the *VaccineID* bound control (not the label) so that it is about 0.75" wide. Add the *Inventory* field to the form. Position it next to the *VaccineID* bound control. Move it so that the tops of these two controls are aligned.

c. Resize the *Inventory* bound control so that its right side is aligned with the two controls below it.

d. The *VaccineID* control should be bold, dark blue, and size 12.

e. Save this form and close it.

f. Open the **ShipmentsForm** that you created earlier. Move the *DateShipped* field upward so that it is located directly below the *ShipmentID* field. Save this form and close it.

3. Creating reports:

a. Use the **Blank Report** button to generate a report based on the *Shipments* table. Add all fields except *ShipmentID.* Move the *DateShipped* column all the way to the left side. Save this report as `ShipmentReport` and close it.

b. Use the **Report Wizard** to create a report based on the *LargerLocations* query. Add all fields except *LocationID.* Group by the *24-Hour* field. Sort by the *City* field. Leave all other options with the default selections. Save the report as `LargerLocationsReport` and close it.

c. Use the **Report** button to generate a report based on the *Vaccines* table. You will now modify this report.

4. Editing reports:

a. Delete the *VaccineID* column.

b. Resize the *Inventory* column to an appropriate size. Resize the *VaccineName* column width to exactly **3.5"**, as you anticipate some vaccines with longer names.

c. Group the report by *TargetAudience.* Sort it by *VaccineName.* Resize the *TargetAudience* column to exactly **2.0"**.

d. Add a total (sum) to each group and to the entire report. Increase the height of the total controls if necessary.

e. Make sure each of the *TargetAudience* controls is formatted in boldface and a black font color. Format the *TargetAudience* label only so that it is size **12.**

f. In the *Page Footer* area, delete all the text after the first occurrence of *[Page].* Move it to the center of the report.

g. In the *Report Header* area, format the *Date and Time* controls to be italicized. Format the *Vaccines* control so that it is bold and in a black font color. Add the word `Report` next to the word *Vaccines.*

h. Change the orientation to **Landscape.**

i. Review the layout and formatting of your report and make any necessary changes. Save the report as `VaccinesReport` and print it if required by your instructor.

j. Open the **LargerLocationsReport** you created earlier. Resize the *PatientAvg* label and bound controls so that they display properly. Save and close the report.

on your own

You have an extensive movie collection at home, and you have been using Access 2010 to manage this collection. You have just learned how to create forms, and you realize it is easier to enter new movies and loans using these Access objects. Additionally, you want to have a printout of these movies and loans when you are away from the computer. Create a few forms and reports as follows.

1. Open the *movie_collection3.accdb* student file and save a copy as `[your initials]AC_OnYourOwn_3-5`.
2. Create three forms: a standard form, a Multiple Items form, and a Split form.
3. Open your standard form and apply a new theme to it. Resize the controls, apply font formatting, and make a few changes to the layout.
4. Create two different reports for your *Movies* table. One should be grouped by *Genre* and the other by *Format.*
5. Resize the controls in both of your reports appropriately. Make sure the columns are arranged in an appropriate order.
6. In one report, use the Totals feature to calculate the total price (sum) of your collection. In the other report, calculate the average price of your movies.
7. Edit and format a few of your controls, as well as the report header and page footer.
8. Change the report orientation to **Landscape.**
9. Print the reports if required by your instructor.

A local pet store has hired you to fix the forms and reports in its database, which keeps track of inventory, customers, and store sales. Open the file named *petstore3.accdb* and investigate the issues below. Fix the errors and save your work as `[your initials]AC_FixIt_3-6`.

1. Fix the *CustomersForm* as follows:
   a. Add the `Newsletter` field to the form, right below the *Phone* control.
   b. Move the *LastName* controls so that they are just above *FirstName.*
   c. Apply the **Essential** theme, which is the fourth one in the fourth row of the Built-in group.
   d. Change the font of the entire form to **Verdana.**
   e. Resize the *StreetAddress* label control so that it is a bit wider. Resize all of the bound controls in the form (except for the *Newsletter* check box) so that they are exactly **4.0"** wide.
   f. Format the *CustomerID* label and bound controls so that they are bold.
   g. Format the *Newsletter* label control so that it has a red font and a size of **12.**
   h. Change the alignment of the *ZipCode* bound control to the left.
2. Fix *PetsReport* as follows:
   a. The *PetID* field is missing from this report. Add it to the report and move it all the way to the left so that it becomes the first column. Left-align the text inside all the controls in this new column. In addition, make them bold.
   b. It would like to see all the cats grouped together in the first part of the report, followed by all the dogs. Each group should be sorted by the breed and there should be a control that sums up the prices for each group.
   c. Resize the *AnimalType* and *MainColor* columns to a more appropriate size. Resize the total controls if the number is not fully displayed.
   d. Move the *PetID* column after the *Breed* column.

e. It doesn't need the pet's age for this report so delete the *AgeInMonths* column.

f. Change the alignment of all the column labels so that they are centered.

g. In the page footer, remove the *of 1* part of the page number control. Change the font color to black.

h. Fix the obvious spelling error "Pets Rport," located in the report header.

i. Change the orientation to **Landscape.**

3. Fix the database as follows:

a. The store would like a form for the *Sales* table that shows both a datasheet and a single record in one screen. Create this form.

b. The store would like a report for the *Customers* table. Create a simple report.

chapter **4**

Using Queries and Organizing Information

In this chapter, you will learn the following skills:

- **Skill 4.1** Using the Simple Query Wizard
- **Skill 4.2** Creating a Query in Design View
- **Skill 4.3** Adding Text Criteria to a Query
- **Skill 4.4** Adding Numeric Criteria to a Query
- **Skill 4.5** Using AND and OR in a Query
- **Skill 4.6** Specifying the Sort Order in a Query
- **Skill 4.7** Hiding and Showing Fields in a Query
- **Skill 4.8** Adding a Calculated Field to a Query
- **Skill 4.9** Finding Unmatched Data Using a Query
- **Skill 4.10** Finding Duplicate Data Using a Query
- **Skill 4.11** Using a Parameter Query
- **Skill 4.12** Importing Data from Excel
- **Skill 4.13** Creating Relationships
- **Skill 4.14** Viewing Dependencies
- **Skill 4.15** Filtering Data Using AutoFilter
- **Skill 4.16** Filtering Data Using Filter by Selection
- **Skill 4.17** Sorting Records in a Table
- **Skill 4.18** Using Find and Replace
- **Skill 4.19** Exporting Data

skills

- › Create a simple query
- › Add criteria to a query and organize data
- › Find data using a query and using find and replace
- › Import and export data from and to other sources
- › Filter and sort data and create relationships within Access

introduction

This chapter shows you how to find information quickly by using queries and filters in Access 2010. You can create various types of queries, each with its own specific role in your database. Queries can be customized in various ways, particularly with text and numeric criteria. This chapter also focuses on the use of related tables and the ability of Access to both import and export Excel files.

4.1 Using the Simple Query Wizard

Queries are powerful tools for presenting and manipulating the records in your database. You can use a query to bring together related fields from different tables, and then use the query as a basis for forms or reports. These queries are referred to as select queries (because you select fields from different tables).

Use the Simple Query Wizard to create a select query. A **select query** displays data from one or more tables or queries, based on the fields that you select. For example, if you want a list of appointments showing the location as well as the date and time of the appointment, use a simple query to show fields from both the Current Appointments and Locations tables.

To create a query using the Simple Query Wizard:

1. Click the **Create** tab.
2. In the *Queries* group, click the **Query Wizard** button.
3. In the *New Query* dialog, **Simple Query Wizard** is selected by default. Click **OK.**

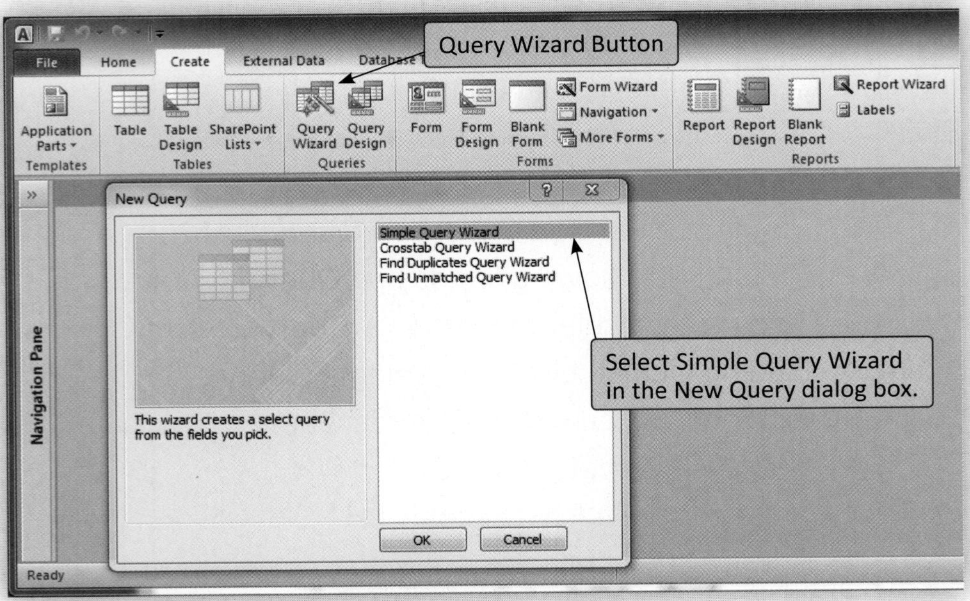

FIGURE AC 4.1

4. Click the **Tables/Queries** drop-down arrow. Click the first table or query that you want to select data from.
5. Add the field or fields in the order that you want them to display.

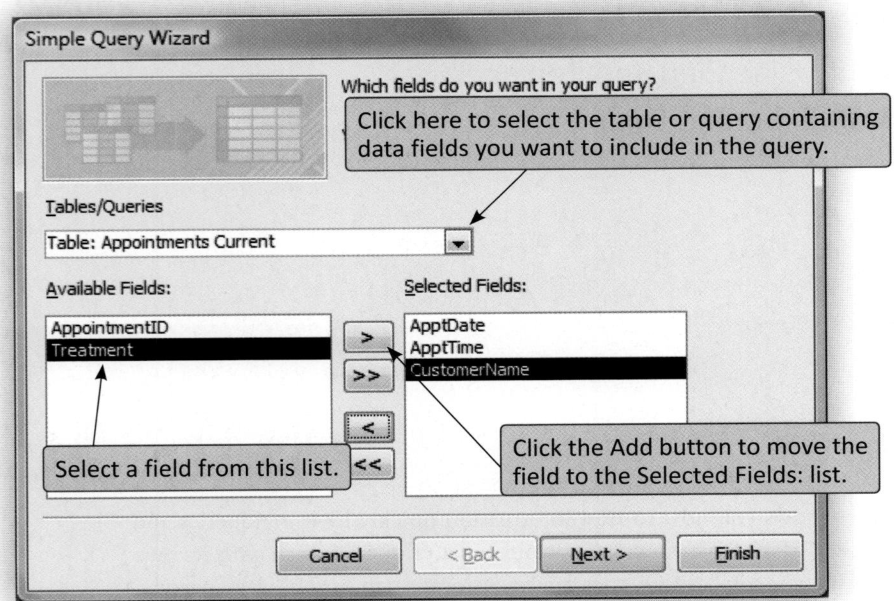

FIGURE AC 4.2

6. To add data fields from another table or query, click the **Tables/Queries** drop-down arrow again. Click the next table or query you want to select data from.

7. Add the field or fields you want to display.

8. When you have added all the fields you want, click **Next.**

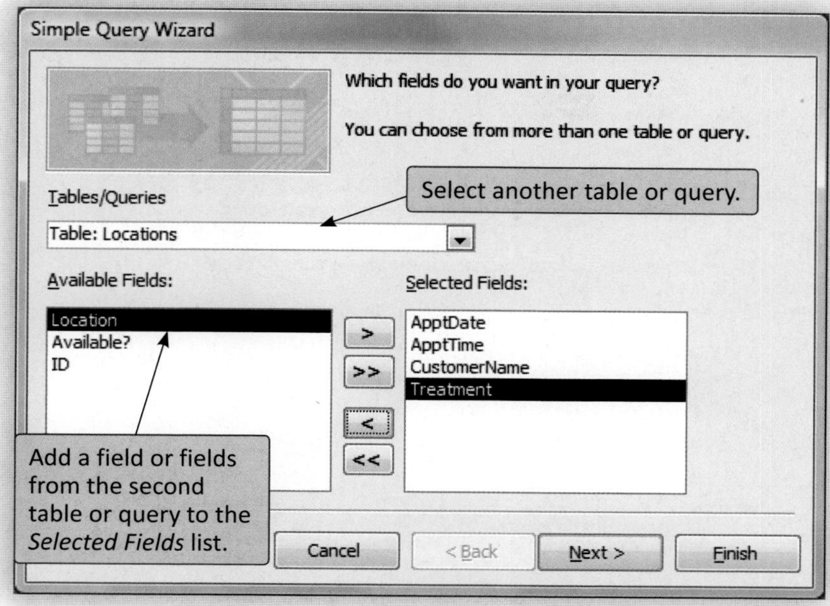

FIGURE AC 4.3

9. The radio button to create a detail query is selected by default. The detail query shows every field you selected for every record. Click **Next.**

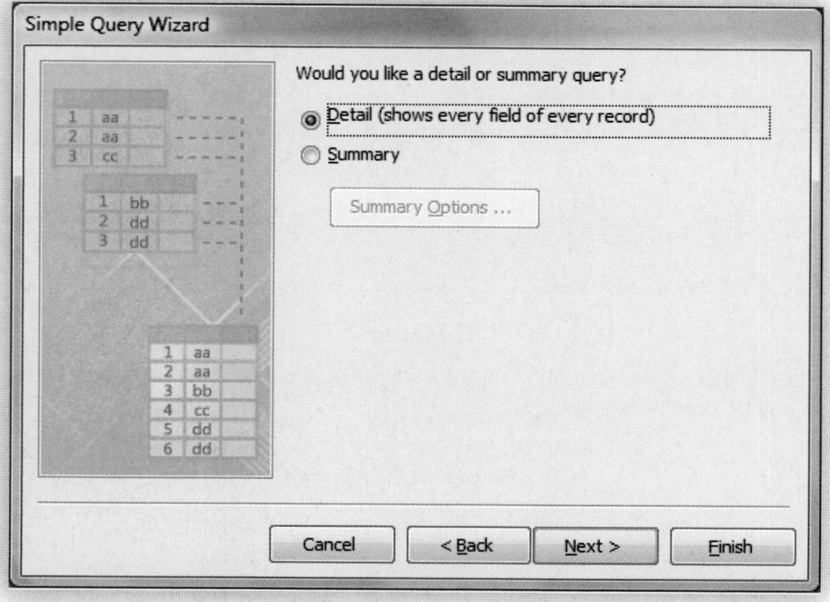

FIGURE AC 4.4

10. Give the query a meaningful title.

11. To see the results of the query immediately, select the radio button to **Open the query to view information.**

12. Click **Finish.**

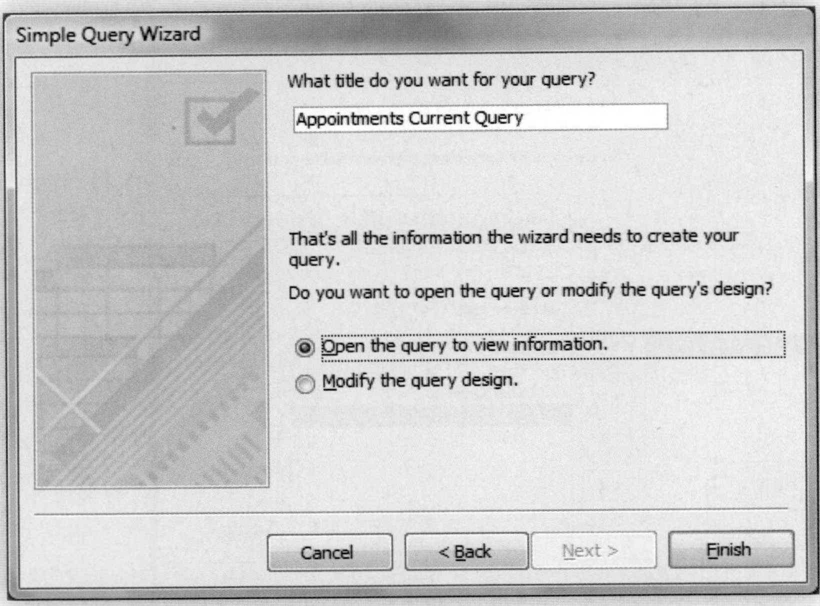

FIGURE AC 4.5

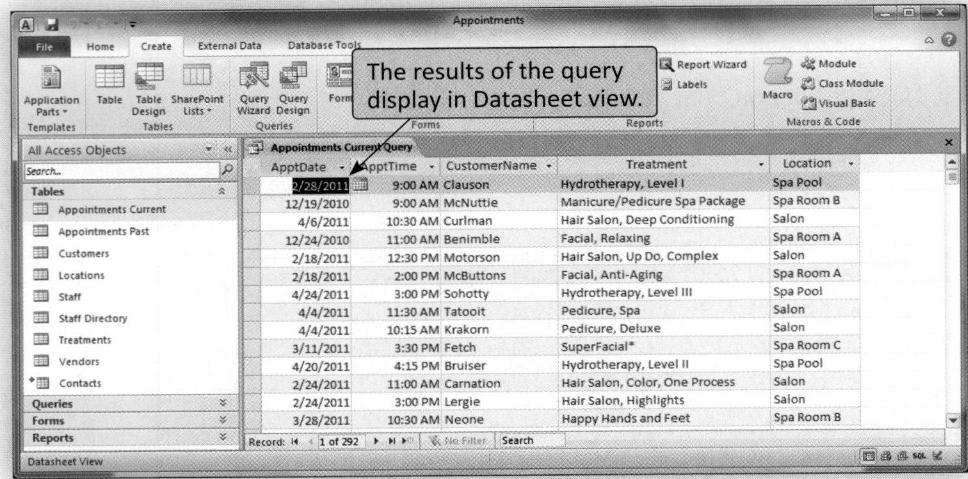

FIGURE AC 4.6

tips & tricks

By modifying the query in Design view, you can specify that the query display only records that meet certain criteria or that the query display records in a specific order.

tell me **more**

From the Query Wizard, you can create three other types of queries:

- **Crosstab Query**—presents data in a spreadsheet format, allowing you to specify fields to use for column headers and for row headers, and then automatically calculates totals for values in another field as related to the column and row headers.
- **Find Duplicates Query**—finds duplicate records in a table.
- **Find Unmatched Query**—finds records in one table that do not have matching records in another table.

4.2 Creating a Query in Design View

Query Design view has two parts. The upper pane shows the tables referenced in the query. The lower pane shows the **query grid** where you specify which fields to include in the query.

To create a select query in Design view:

1. Click the **Create** tab.
2. In the *Queries* group, click the **Query Design** button.
3. The *Show Table* dialog opens. Double-click the name of each table you want to include in the query (or click the table name once, and then click the **Add** button). Click the **Close** button when you have added the tables you want.

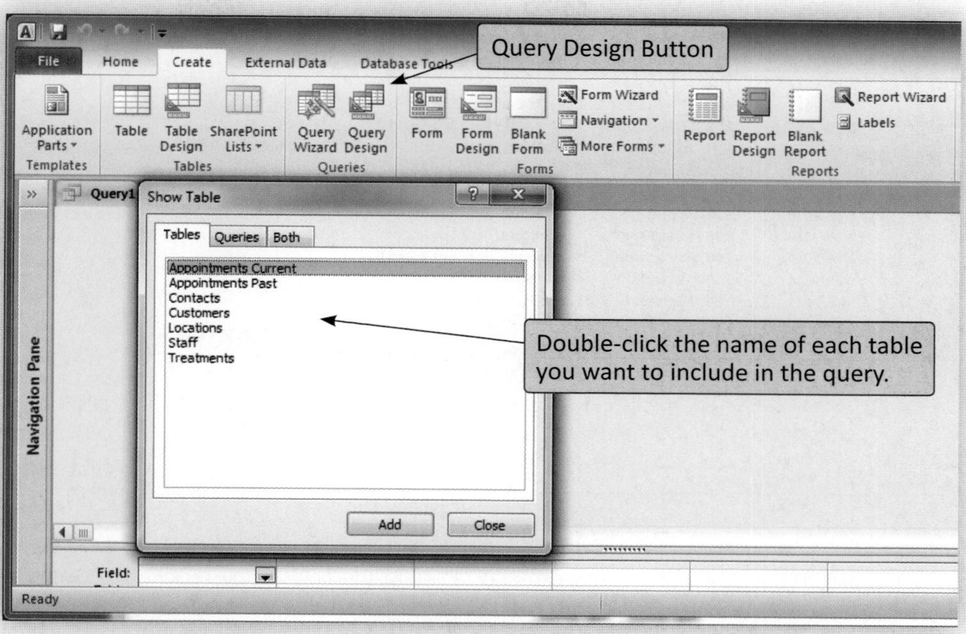

FIGURE AC 4.7

4. A complete field list for each table appears in the upper pane of the Query Design view. Add fields to the query using one of these methods:
   a. Double-click the field name in the field list.
   b. Click the field name and drag it to the design grid.
   c. Click in an empty cell in the *Field:* row of the design grid, expand the list of available fields by clicking the arrow, and click the field name you want.
5. When you have added all the fields you want, run the query by clicking the **Run** button near the left side of the Ribbon (on the *Query Tools Design* tab, in the *Results* group).

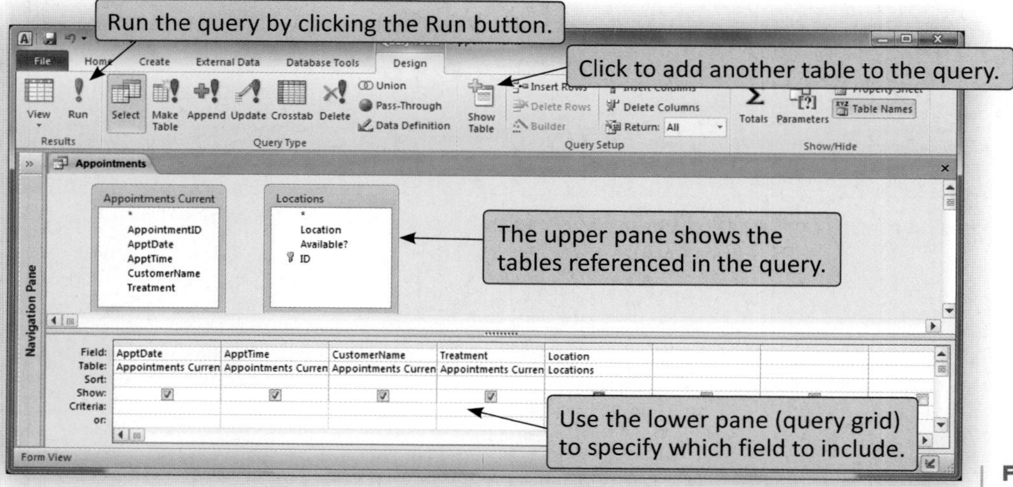

FIGURE AC 4.8

6. If you want to use the query again in the future, be sure to save the query, giving it a meaningful name.

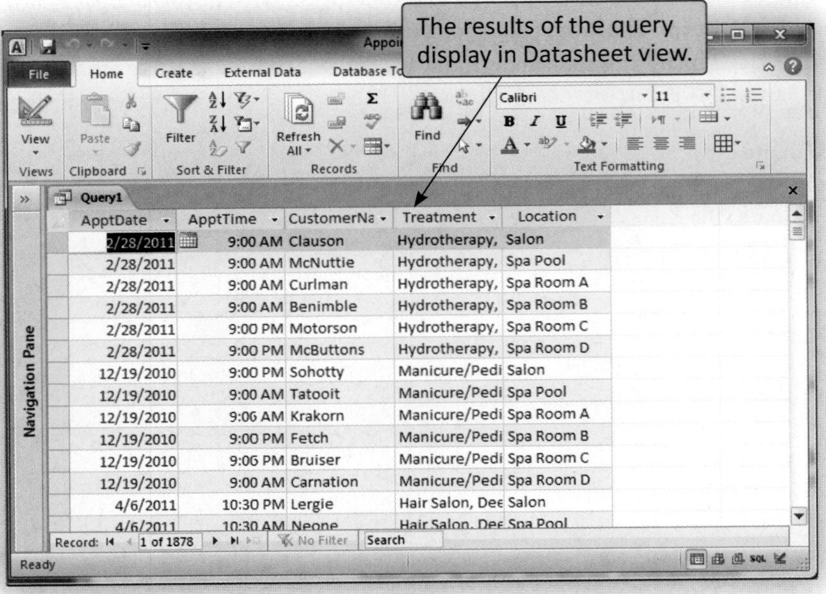

FIGURE AC 4.9

tips & tricks

If you want to include all the fields from a table in your query, click and drag the asterisk (*) to the field row. Notice that rather than listing each field from the table separately, there is only one field called table.* (where "table" is the name of the table). The * character represents a wildcard. Rather than look for specific field names, the query will look for all the fields in that table. So, if you later add or delete fields, you won't need to change the query design.

tell me **more**

You can add tables to the field list by clicking the **Show Table** button in the *Query Setup* group of the *Query Tools Design* tab, and then double-clicking the name of the table you want to add (or click the table name once, and then click the **Add** button). You must close the *Show Table* dialog before continuing to build the query.

try **this**

You can also view the results of a query by switching to Datasheet view.

- On the *Query Tools Design* tab, in the *Results* group, click the **View** button.
- Click the **View** button arrow, and select **Datasheet View.**
- Right-click the query tab, and select **Datasheet View.**
- Click **Datasheet View** in the status bar.

4.3 Adding Text Criteria to a Query

Although a select query displays only the fields you select, by default, it will show all of the records. By modifying the select query in Design view, you can refine the query so that it shows only records that meet specific criteria. **Criteria** are conditions that the records must meet in order to be included in the query results.

Each field data type takes a certain type of criterion. For example, text criteria are used for text, memo, and hyperlink fields.

To add text criteria to your query:

1. Open the query in Design view.
2. In the *Criteria:* row, enter the text you want to match in the column for the appropriate field. For example, to find all appointments that are scheduled for Spa Room A, enter the text criterion `"Spa Room A"` in the *Criteria:* row under the Location field. When you enter text in the *Criteria:* row, Access places the text in quotation marks for you.
3. Run the query to see the results.

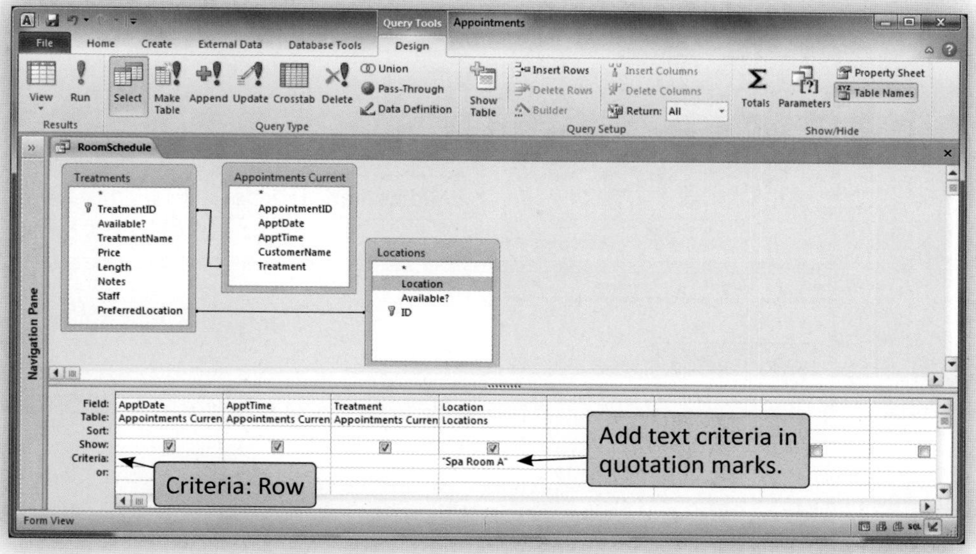

FIGURE AC 4.10

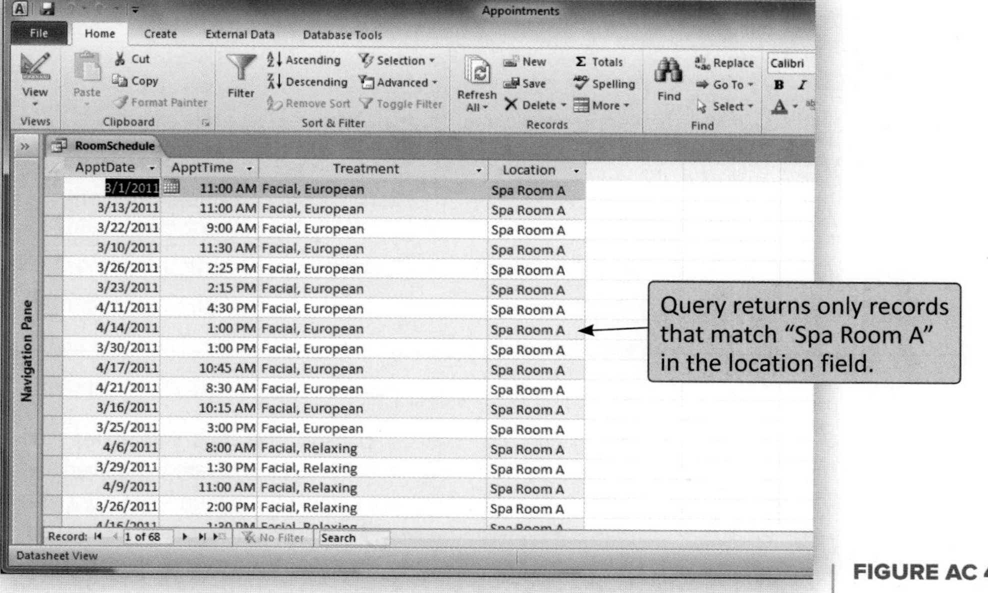

FIGURE AC 4.11

If you want the query to return all the records that have a value other than "Spa Room A" in the location field, type the criterion `Not "Spa Room A"` instead.

4.4 Adding Numeric Criteria to a Query

You can also add criteria to fields with number, currency, or date/time data types. When entering numeric criteria, you can enter values for exact matches, or you can enter an expression using comparison operators to broaden the criteria.

To add numeric criteria to your query:

1. Open the query in Design view.
2. In the *Criteria:* row, enter the value or the expression in the column for the appropriate field. For example, to find all appointments that are longer than 75 minutes, enter >75 in the criteria cell for the Length field.
3. Run the query to see the results.

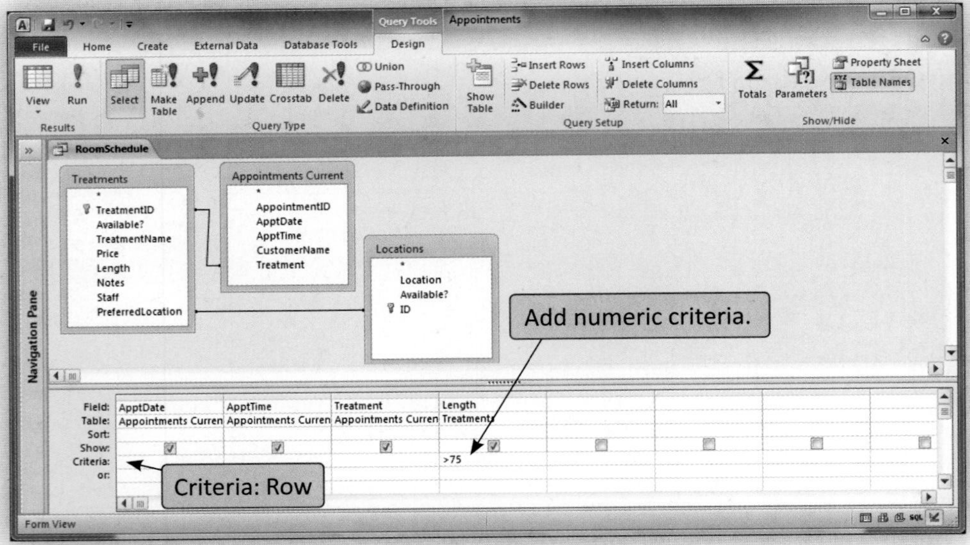

FIGURE AC 4.12

FIGURE AC 4.13

tips & tricks

Common comparison operators are

>	greater than
<	less than
=	equal to
< >	not equal to
>=	greater than or equal to
<=	less than or equal to

tell me more

You can also use comparison operators with dates. For example, to find all appointments that are scheduled for January 1, 2011 or later, enter the criterion >=1/1/2011 in the *Criteria:* row under the appointment date field. When you enter dates in the *Criteria:* row, Access places # symbols around the date.

4.5 Using AND and OR in a Query

To further refine a query, you can use multiple criteria.

To limit query results to only records that meet all the criteria, enter criteria for multiple fields on the *Criteria:* row, or enter multiple criteria for the same field separated by the word ***And.*** For example, enter `>12/1/2010` in the appointment date field and `>90` in the Length field to find all appointments with a date after December 1, 2010, AND a length greater than 90 minutes.

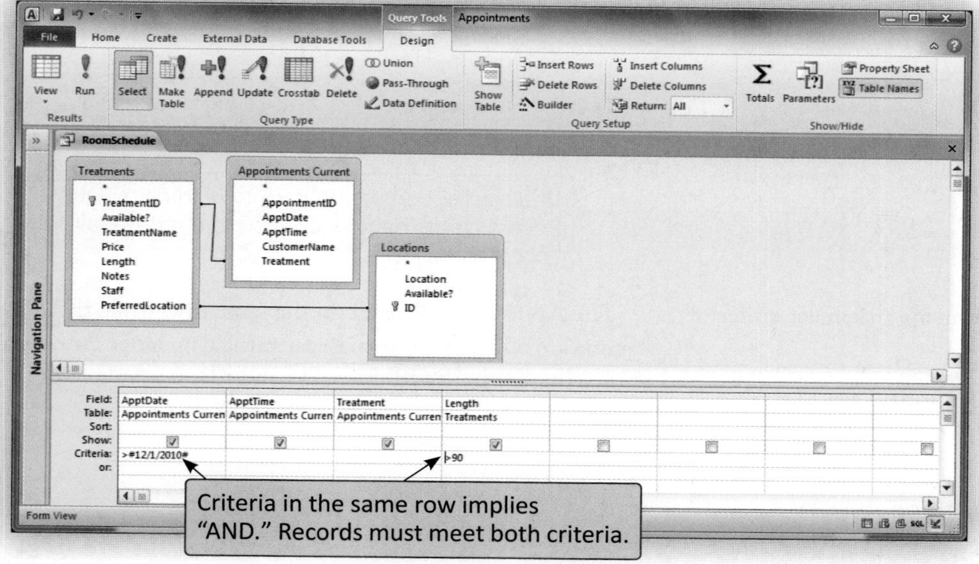

Criteria in the same row implies "AND." Records must meet both criteria.

FIGURE AC 4.14

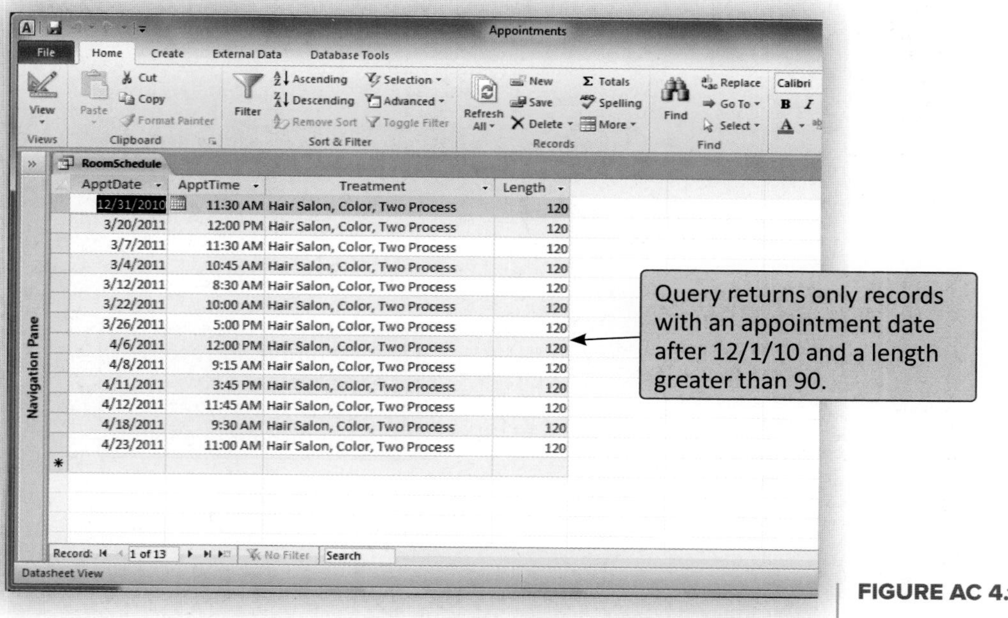

Query returns only records with an appointment date after 12/1/10 and a length greater than 90.

FIGURE AC 4.15

To expand query results to records that meet any of the criteria, enter criteria in both the *Criteria:* row and the *or:* row. You can enter multiple criteria for the same field or for different fields. When using an OR construction with multiple fields, make sure that each criterion is on its own row.

Let's look at a complex example: Staff members Ken Dishner and Faye Shell are both on vacation from April 2–14, 2011. You will need to reschedule all of their appointments for that time. The query might look like this:

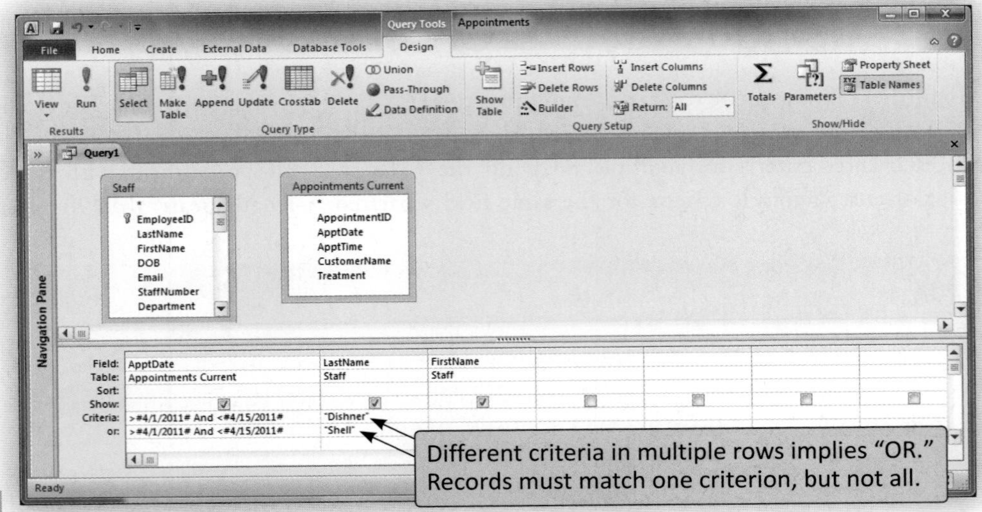

Different criteria in multiple rows implies "OR."
Records must match one criterion, but not all.

FIGURE AC 4.16

The query will return all appointments that meet either of these criteria:

After 4/1/2011 AND before 4/15/2011 AND assigned to Dishner

OR

After 4/1/2011 AND before 4/15/2011 AND assigned to Shell

The AND criteria are all on the same row, while the OR criteria are on separate rows. Because the date range criterion is the same for both OR criteria, it must be repeated in both rows.

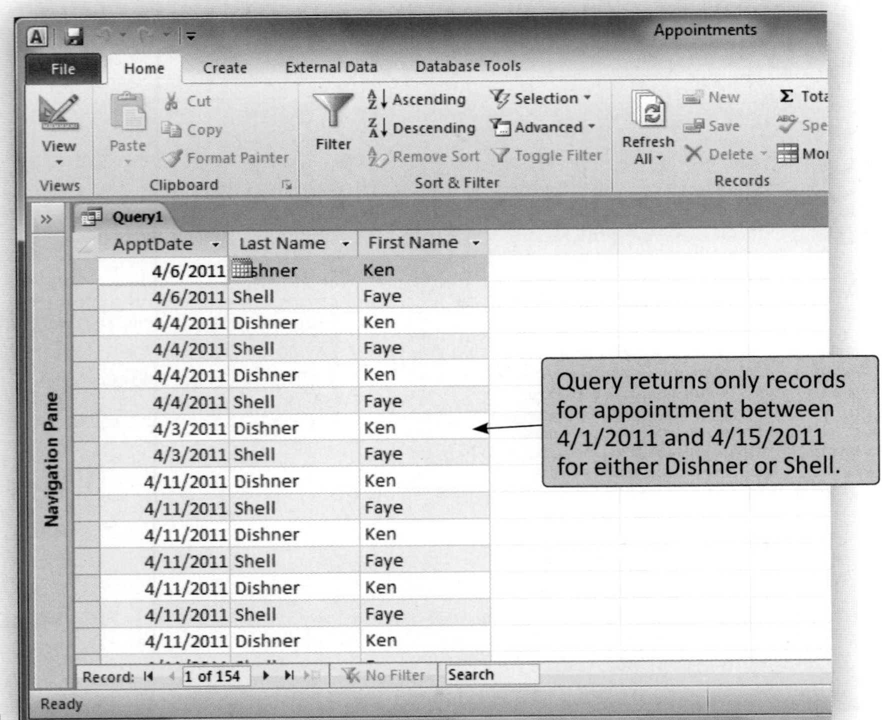

Query returns only records for appointment between 4/1/2011 and 4/15/2011 for either Dishner or Shell.

FIGURE AC 4.17

tips & tricks

You can add more OR criteria by continuing to add criteria to the rows under the *or:* row.

4.6 Specifying the Sort Order in a Query

Query results may display records in an unexpected order. If you want to control how records are displayed, set the sort order as part of the query design.

To add a sort order in query Design view:

1. Click in the *Sort:* row for the field you want to sort by.
2. Select **Ascending** or **Descending.**
3. Run the query.

If you want to sort by multiple fields, you can set the sort order for more than one field. Access will sort all the records first by the field farthest to the left (the ***outer*** sort). Records that have the same value in the first sort field will be sorted again by the next field with a sort order applied (the ***inner*** sort).

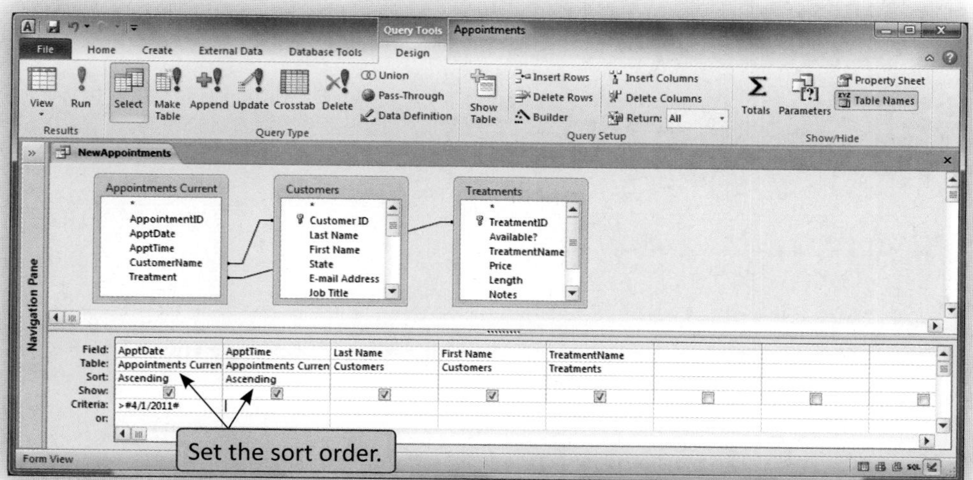
Set the sort order.

FIGURE AC 4.18

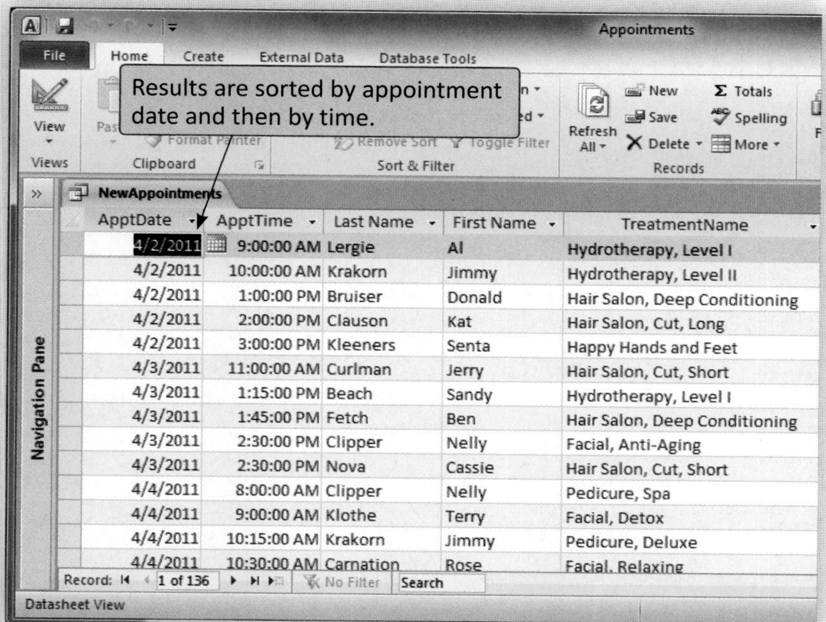
Results are sorted by appointment date and then by time.

FIGURE AC 4.19

Setting the sort order is especially helpful if you are going to use the query as the base for forms or reports. When the query is sorted, the records in forms and reports will appear in the same order.

tips & tricks

4.7 Hiding and Showing Fields in a Query

If you want to include a field in your query, but do not want that field to show in Datasheet view, click the **Show:** box to remove the check mark for the field you want to hide. This way you can use the field to define criteria for the query without making the field visible in the final query results.

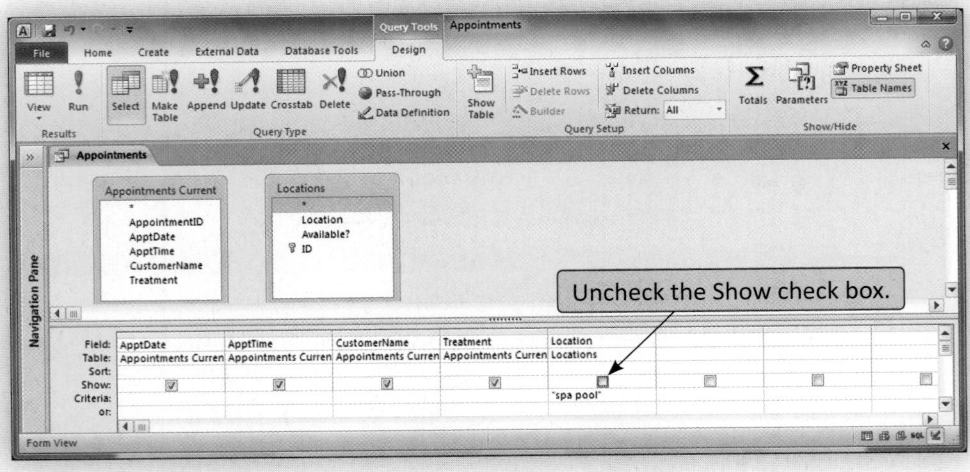

Uncheck the Show check box.

FIGURE AC 4.20

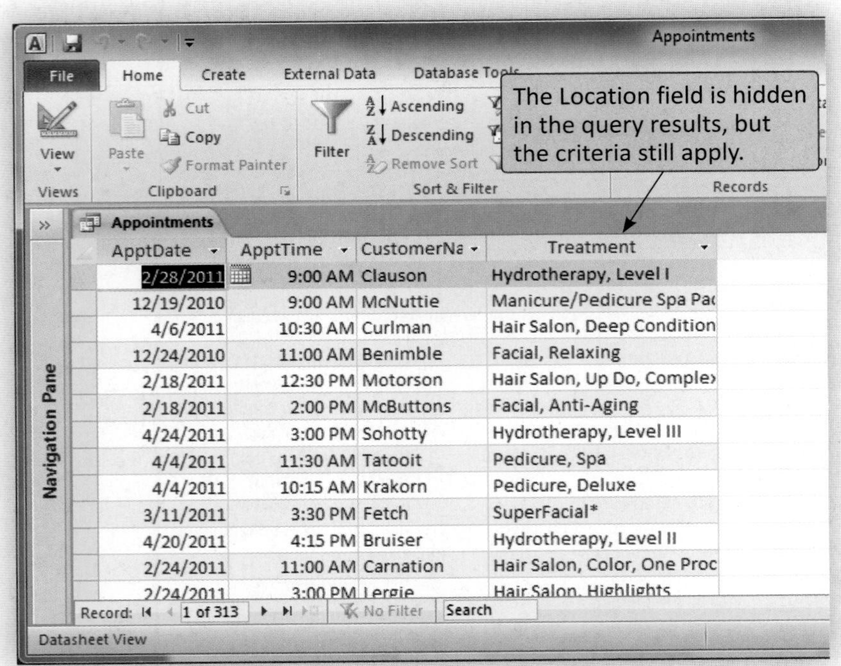

The Location field is hidden in the query results, but the criteria still apply.

FIGURE AC 4.21

4.8 Adding a Calculated Field to a Query

Database fields generally display the data that are entered into them. However, a **calculated field** displays a value returned by an **expression** (a formula). Expressions can reference fields, mathematical operators, and functions.

To create a calculated field in a query

1. Open the query in Design view.
2. Click the first empty cell in the *Field:* row.
3. On the *Query Tools Design* tab, in the *Query Setup* group, click the **Builder** button to open the Expression Builder.
4. In the *Expression Categories* box, double-click the name of the field you want to use in the expression. The field name is added to the expression box at the top of the dialog. When referencing a field name in an expression, the field name is always enclosed in brackets.
5. Finish entering the expression. For example, to calculate a 10 percent discount, type * .9 after the field name (to calculate a value that is 90 percent of the value of the field name—a 10 percent discount).
6. Click **OK** to add the expression to the query.
7. Notice that the new calculated field begins with *Expr1:*—this is the temporary name for the field. Click in the field and change the *Expr1* text to something more meaningful. Be careful not to delete the colon.
8. Run the query to see the results of the calculated field.

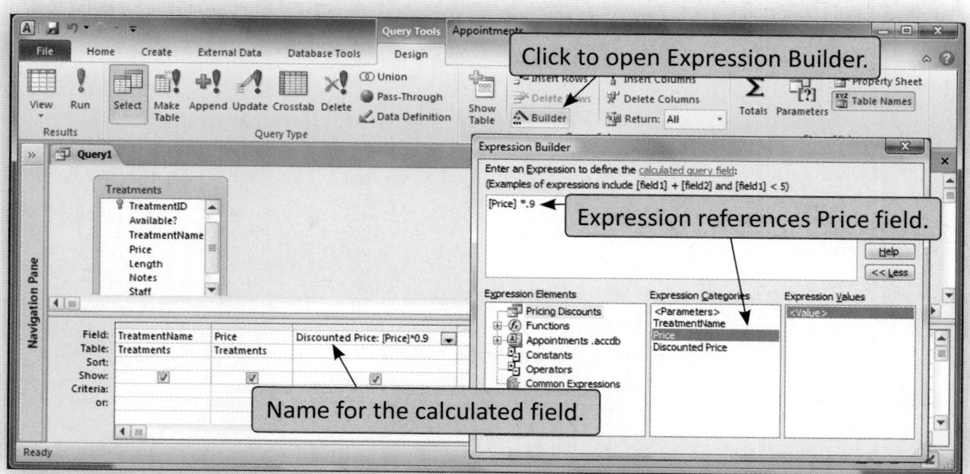

FIGURE AC 4.22

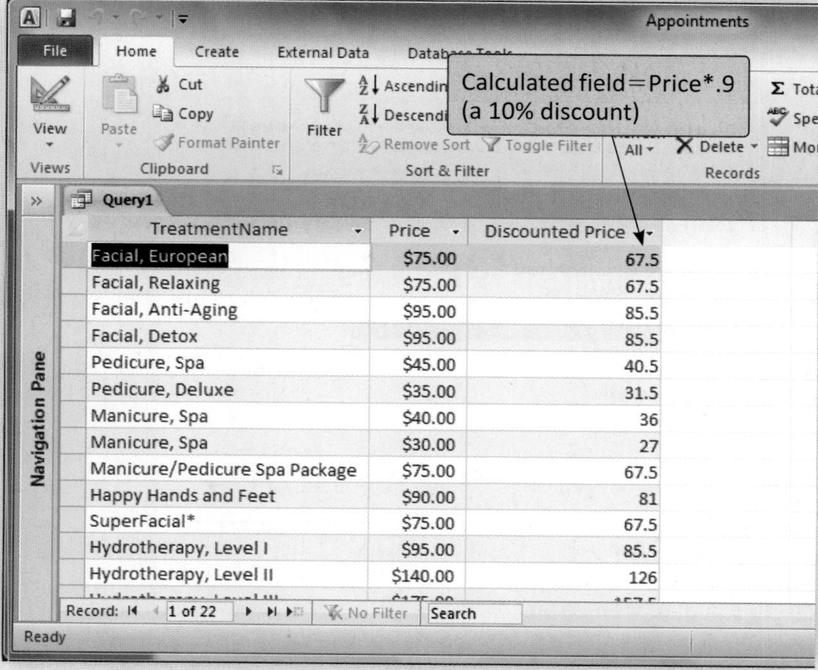

FIGURE AC 4.23

4.9 Finding Unmatched Data Using a Query

Use the Find Unmatched Query Wizard to create a query that shows records from one table that have no corresponding records in another table. This type of query is useful for scenarios such as finding employees who have no sales records or vendors who have no purchase orders.

To run the Find Unmatched Query Wizard:

1. Click the **Create** tab.
2. In the *Queries* group, click the **Query Wizard** button.
3. In the *New Query* dialog, click **Find Unmatched Query Wizard,** and click **OK.**

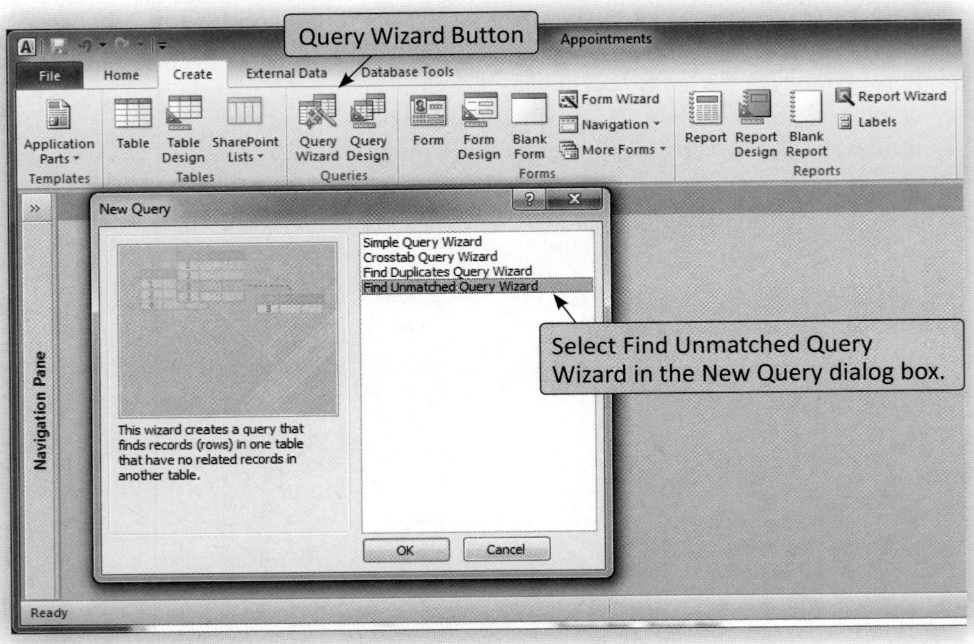

FIGURE AC 4.24

4. First, select the table or query that includes the records you want to match. Click **Next.**

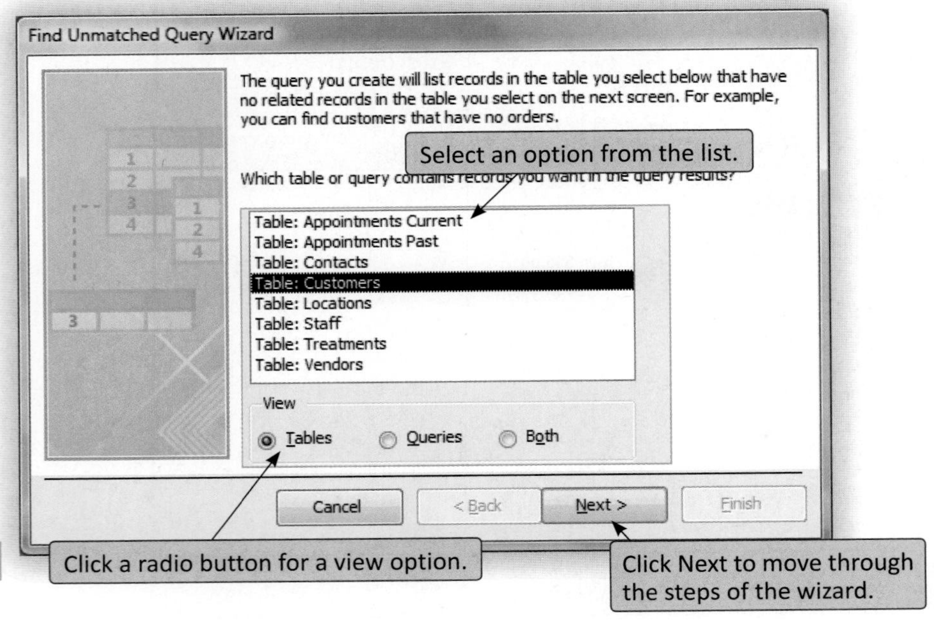

FIGURE AC 4.25

5. Select the table or query that contains the related records. The query will return results from the first table that do NOT have corresponding records in this table. Click **Next.**

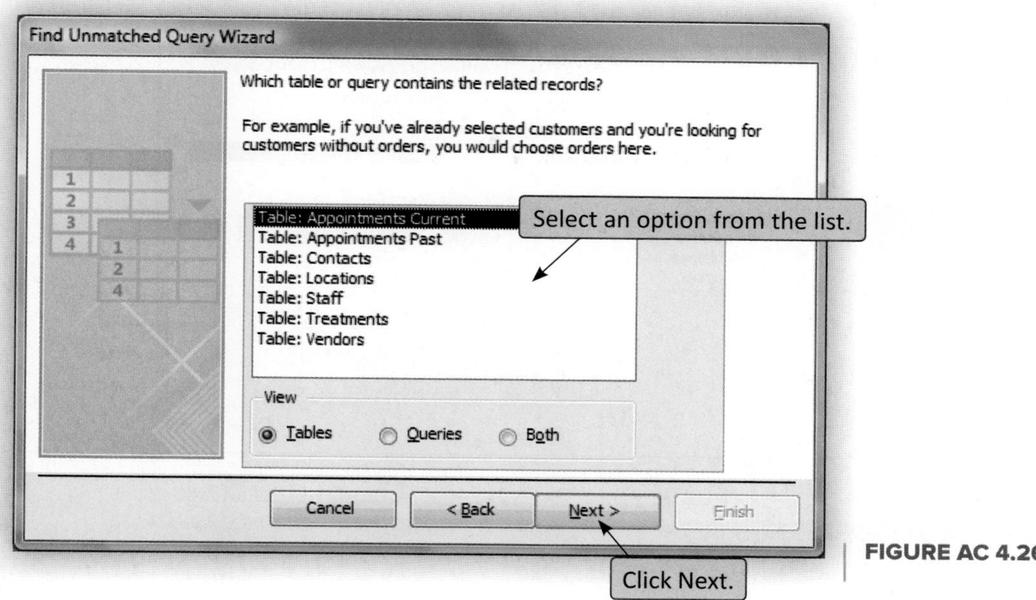

FIGURE AC 4.26

6. Now, find the fields in the two tables that might contain matches. If there is an obvious field (fields with the same name in both tables or fields with an established relationship), Access will automatically suggest it. Click **Next.**

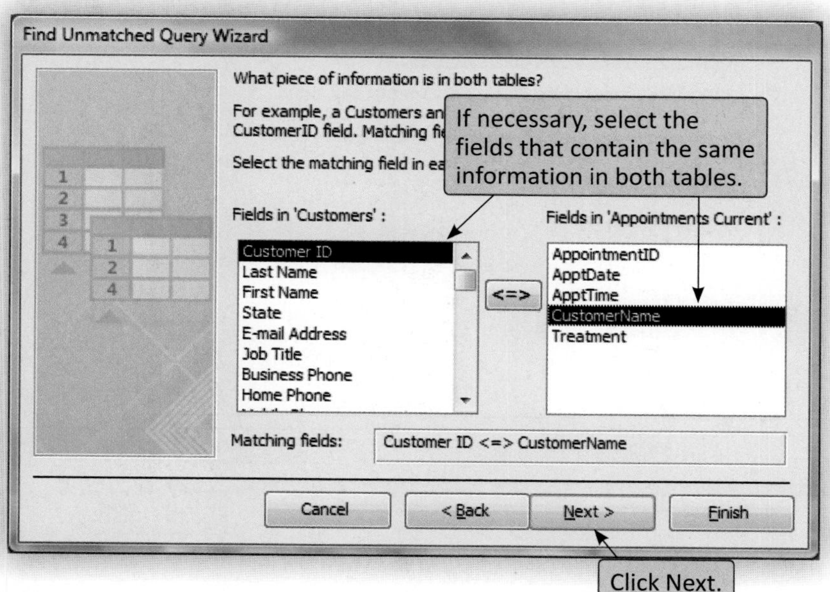

FIGURE AC 4.27

7. Add additional fields that you want to include in the query results. Add the fields that will help identify how the field values are related. Click **Next.**

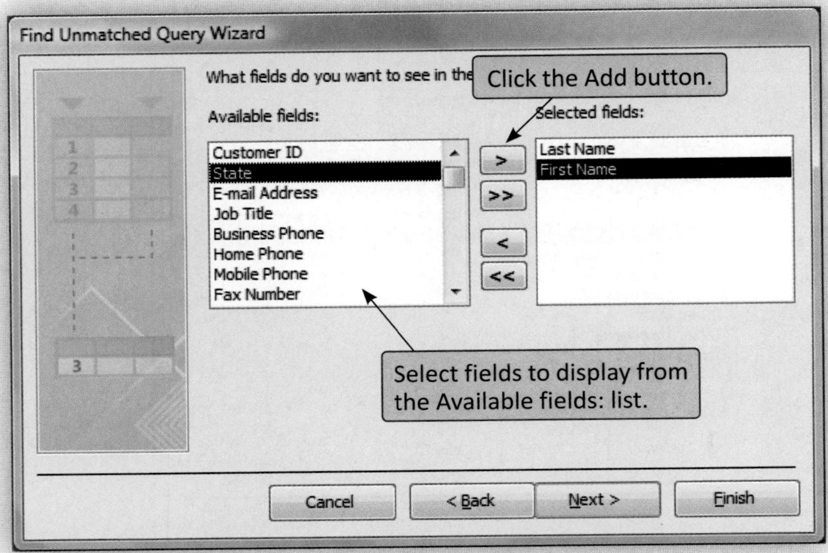

FIGURE AC 4.28

8. Give the query a title, and click **Finish** to view the results.

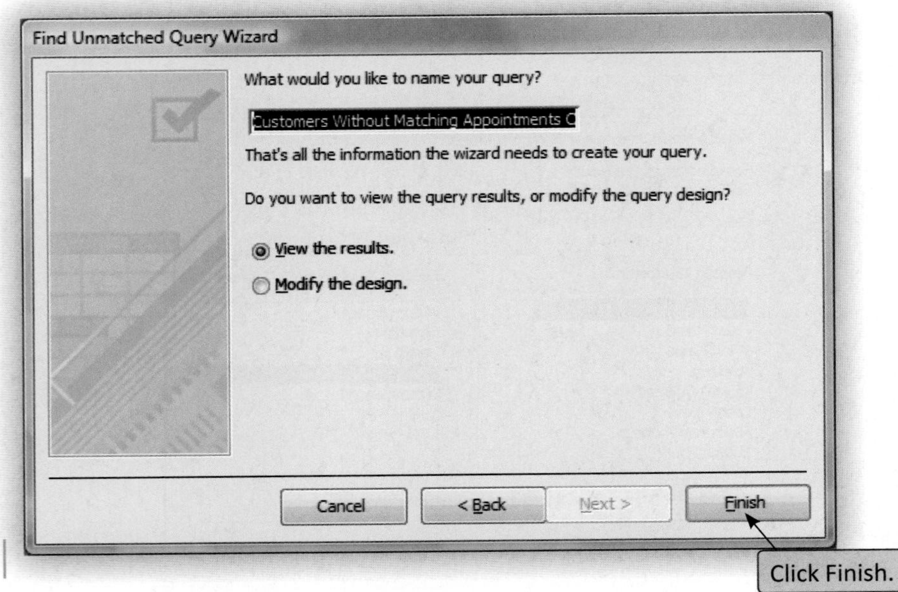

FIGURE AC 4.29

from the perspective of . . .

CONSTRUCTION WORKER

Working in construction involves keeping track of projects. Database software keeps track of hours, materials, and scheduling for our projects. The query feature enables us to determine if we are staying within the projected hours and budget, and still have materials needed to complete the job.

The results of the Unmatched Query Wizard display the specified fields from the first table for records that do not have corresponding records in the second table—in this case, the Last Name and First Name fields from the Customers table where the customer does not have any matching records in the Appointments Current table.

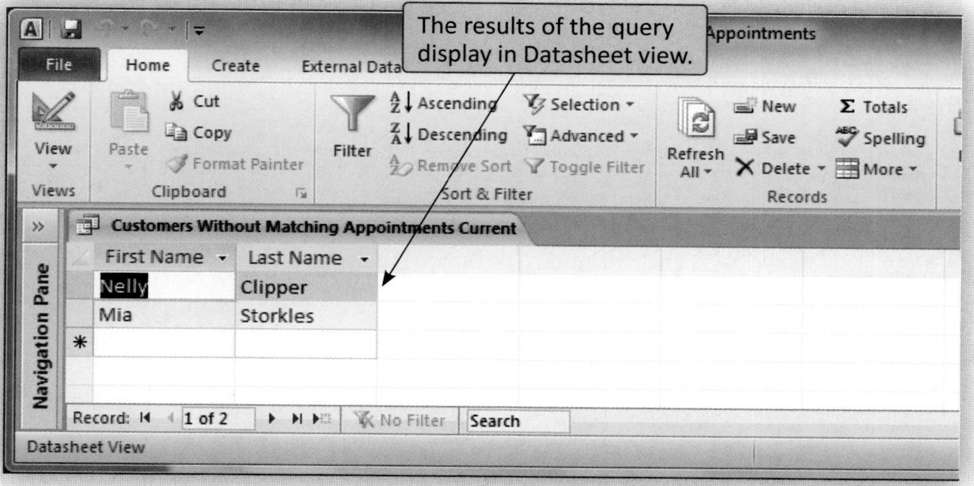

FIGURE AC 4.30

tips & tricks

When selecting the field(s) to search for unmatched values, remember that the fields might be named differently in the two tables. For example, the **CustomerID** field in the **Customers** table might contain the same values as the **CustomerName** field in the **Appointments** table.

tell me more

You can create a select query yourself to find records that are missing data in a particular field. Type `Is Null` in the *Criteria:* cell for the field you want to find. When you run the query, the results will show all records that are missing data in that field. To return only records that *have* data in the field, type `Is Not Null` in the *Criteria:* cell instead.

4.10 Finding Duplicate Data Using a Query

Mistakes can happen during data entry, and you may find that some records have been entered more than once. You can run a query to find all the records that have duplicate values in one or more fields. A Find Duplicates Query is also useful for scenarios such as finding all employees who live in the same city (duplicates in the city field) or locating appointments that are scheduled at the same time (duplicates in date and time fields).

To run the Find Duplicates Query Wizard:

1. Click the **Create** tab.
2. In the *Queries* group, click the **Query Wizard** button.
3. In the *New Query* dialog, click **Find Duplicates Query Wizard.** Click **OK.**

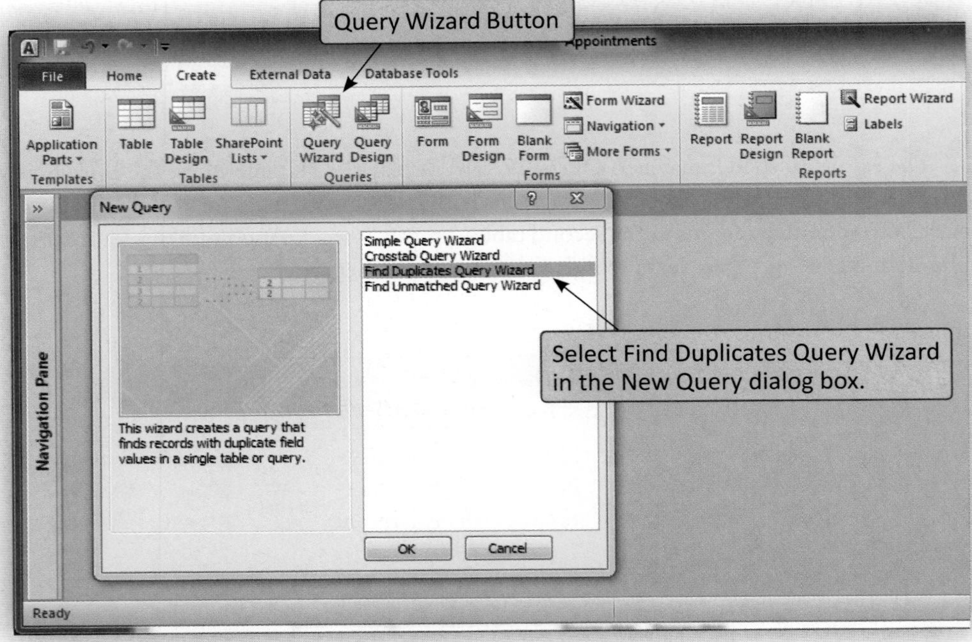

FIGURE AC 4.31

4. Select the table or query that you want to search for duplicate values. Click **Next.**

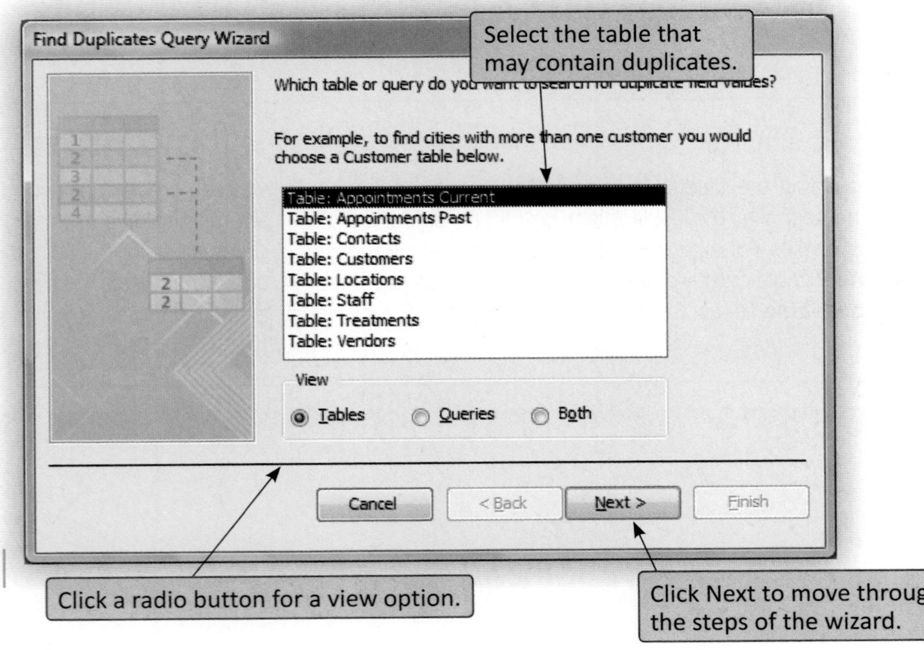

FIGURE AC 4.32

5. Add the field or fields that might contain duplicate values. Click **Next.**

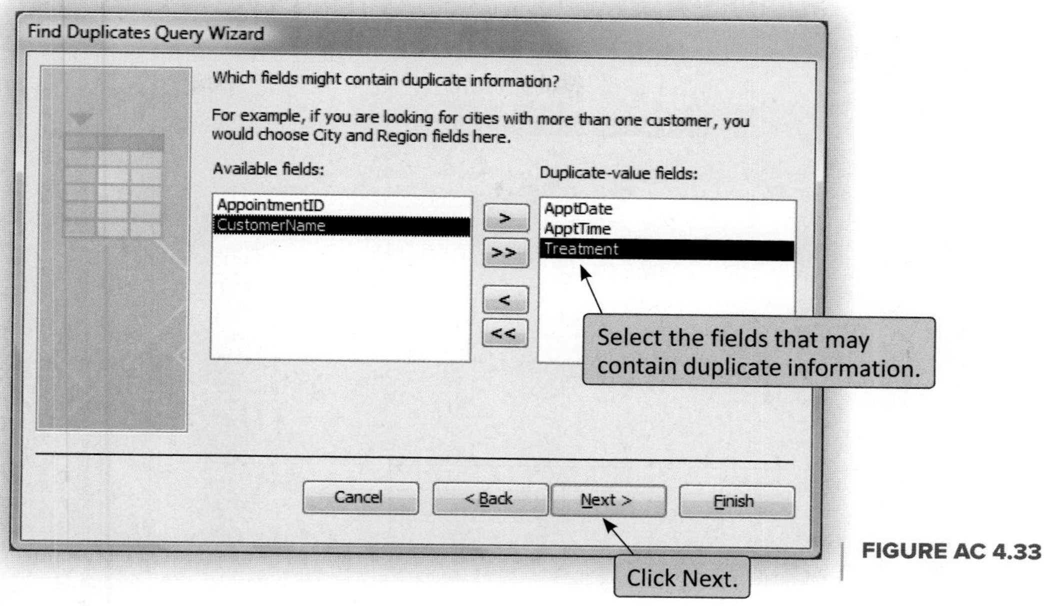

FIGURE AC 4.33

6. Add additional fields that you want to include in the query results. Add the fields that will help identify how the duplicate values are related. Click **Next.**

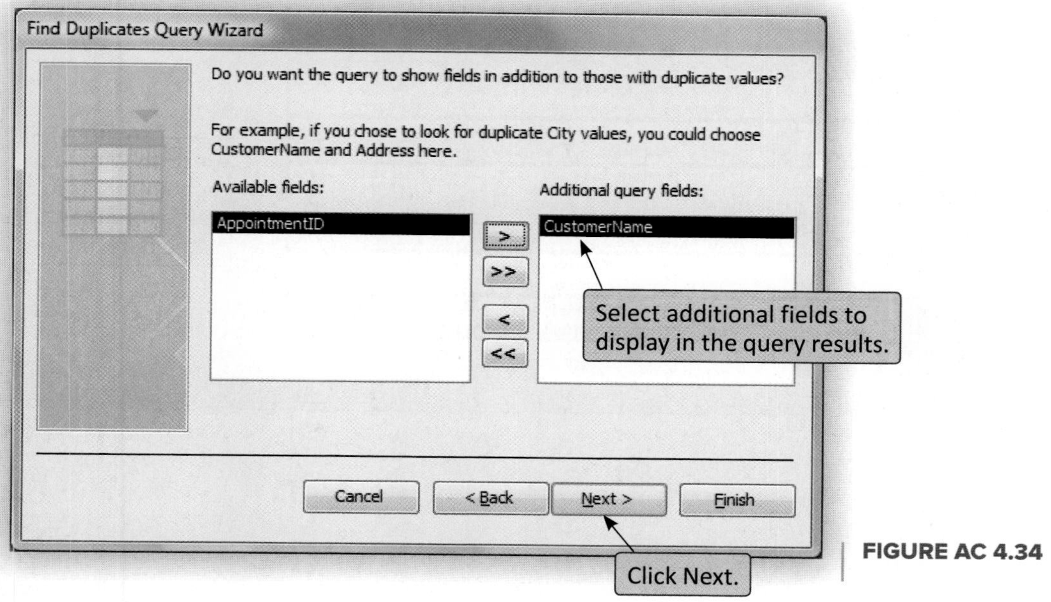

FIGURE AC 4.34

7. Give the query a title, and click **Finish** to view the results.

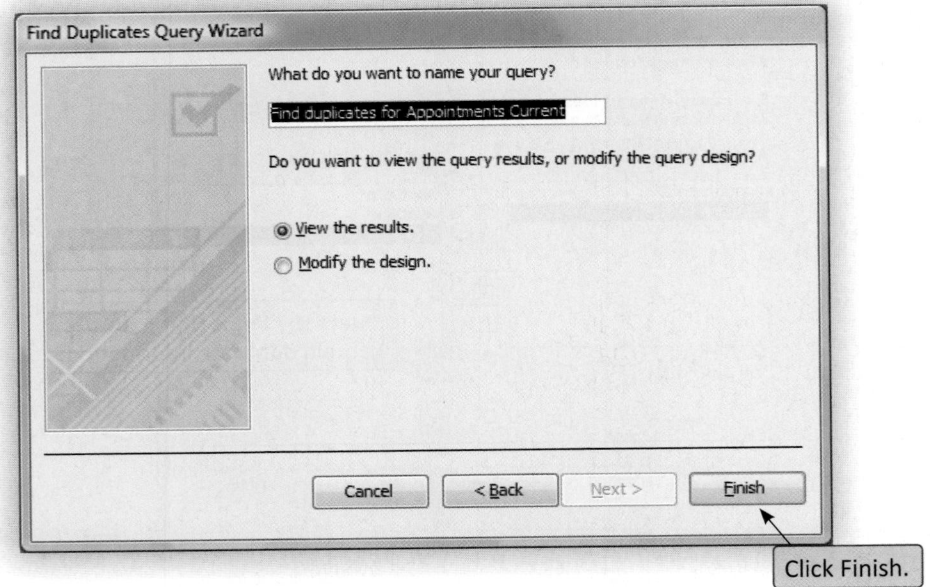

FIGURE AC 4.35

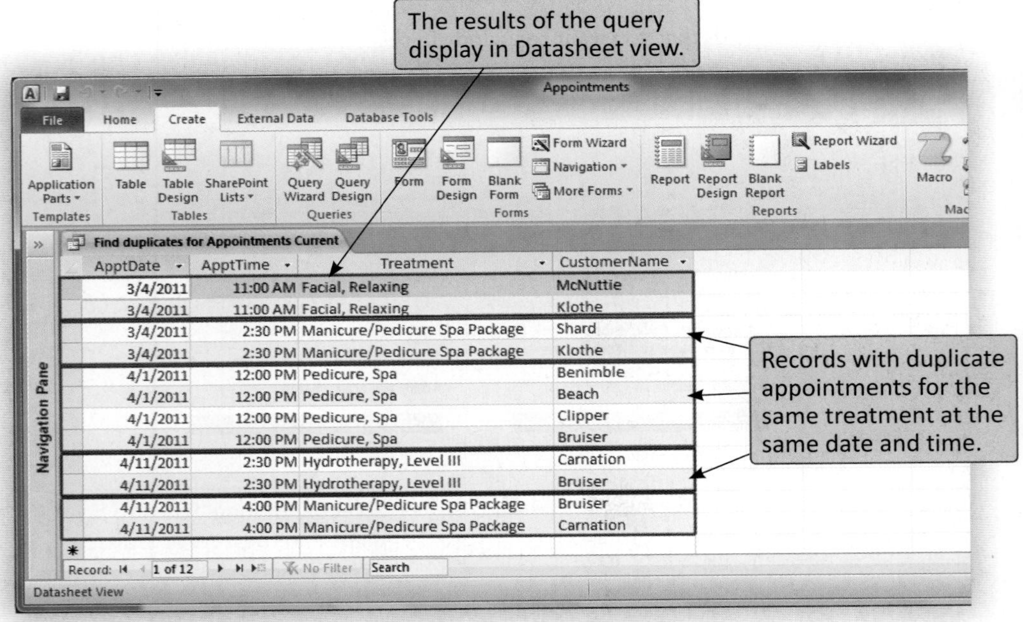

FIGURE AC 4.36

4.11 Using a Parameter Query

When you create a query, you specify the values that the query will display based on the criteria you enter. If you want to give your database users more flexibility, use a **parameter query**. When you create a parameter query, you specify the field or fields that the query will use, but you don't specify the exact criteria. Instead, you enter a prompt that the user will see when the query is run. Then the user can enter the exact value or values that he wants to search for.

To create a parameter query:

1. In Design view, create a select query.
2. In the *Criteria:* cell for the field you want to use for the parameter query, type the prompt the user will see, enclosed in brackets. Ideally, the prompt will give the user direction as to what data to enter. For example, `[Enter a customer last name]` or `[Enter a start date]`.
3. Run the query to test it. Notice that before results display, the *Enter Parameter Value* dialog appears with the prompt you created. Enter a value in the box, and then click **OK.**
4. The results of the query display only records that match the value (the input) you typed in the *Enter Parameter Value* dialog.

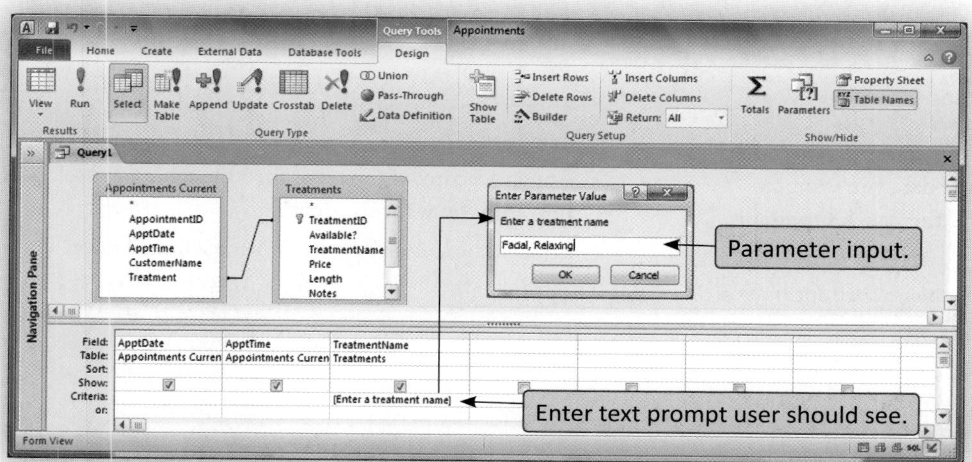

FIGURE AC 4.37

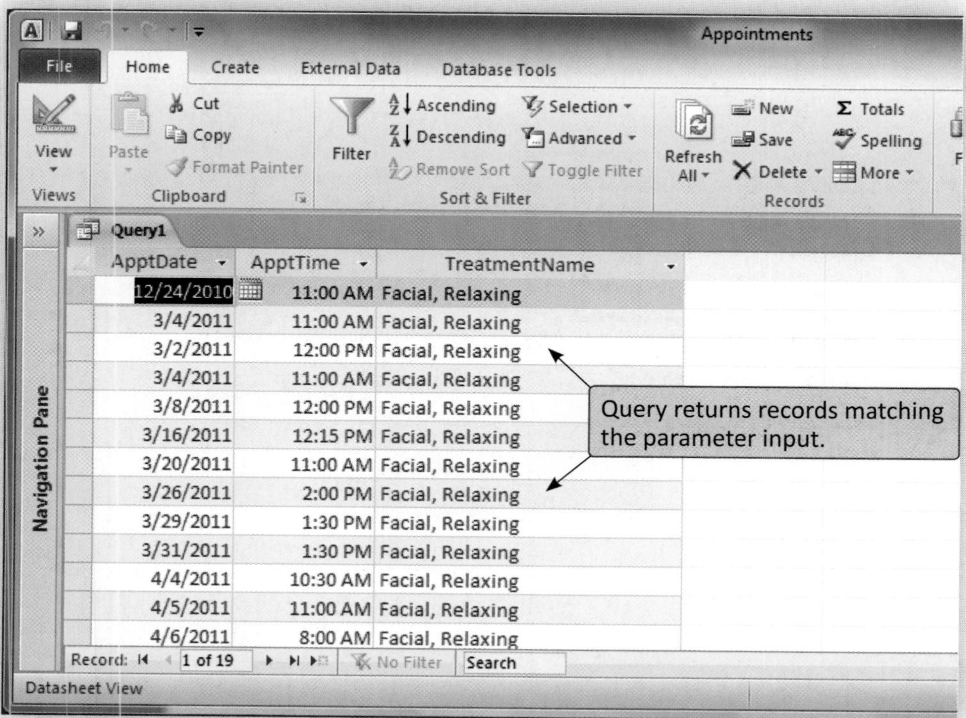

FIGURE AC 4.38

4.12 Importing Data from Excel

You can import data into Access from other Microsoft Office applications. When you select an Excel spreadsheet to import, Access will open the Import Spreadsheet Wizard to help you import the data.

To import data from Excel:

1. Click the **External Data** tab.
2. From the *Import & Link* group, click the **Excel** button.

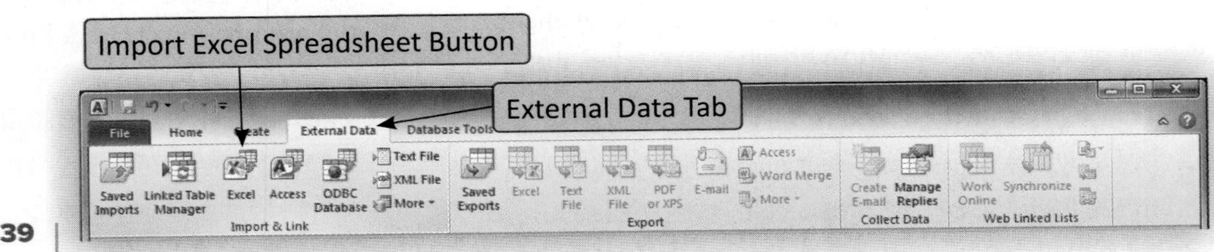

FIGURE AC 4.39

3. The *Get External Data–Excel Spreadsheet* dialog opens.
4. First, click the **Browse . . .** button and navigate to find the spreadsheet that contains the data you want to import. Click the file name, and then click **Open,** or double-click the file name.
5. Next, click the radio button for the import option you want:
   - Import the source data into a new table in the current database.
   - Append a copy of the records to the table (and select the table you want to append to).
   - Link to the source data by creating a linked table.
6. Click **OK.**

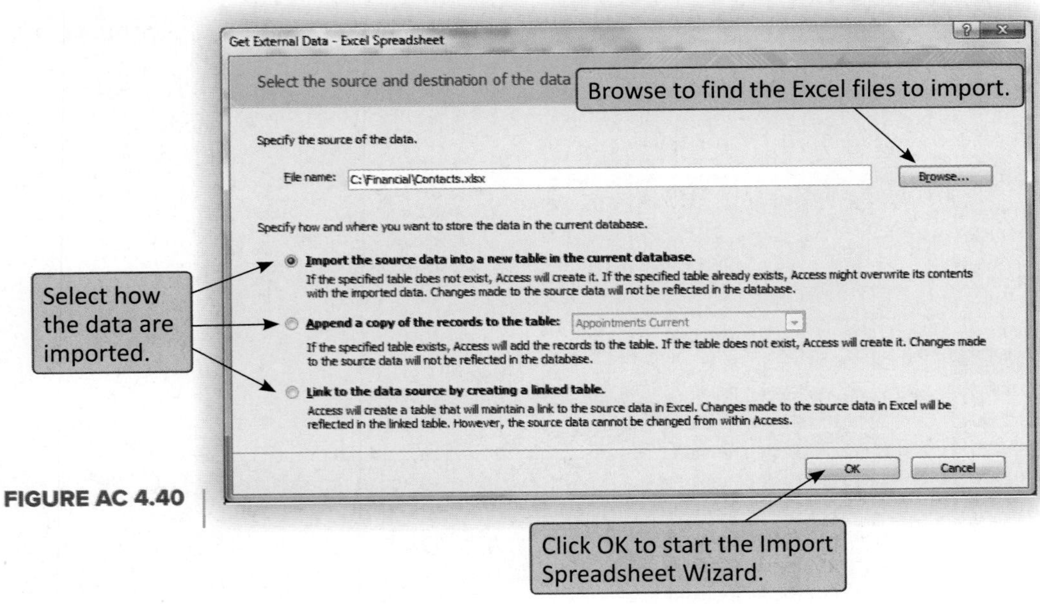

FIGURE AC 4.40

7. If your spreadsheet contains more than one worksheet or named range, select the worksheet or range you want to import. Click **Next.**

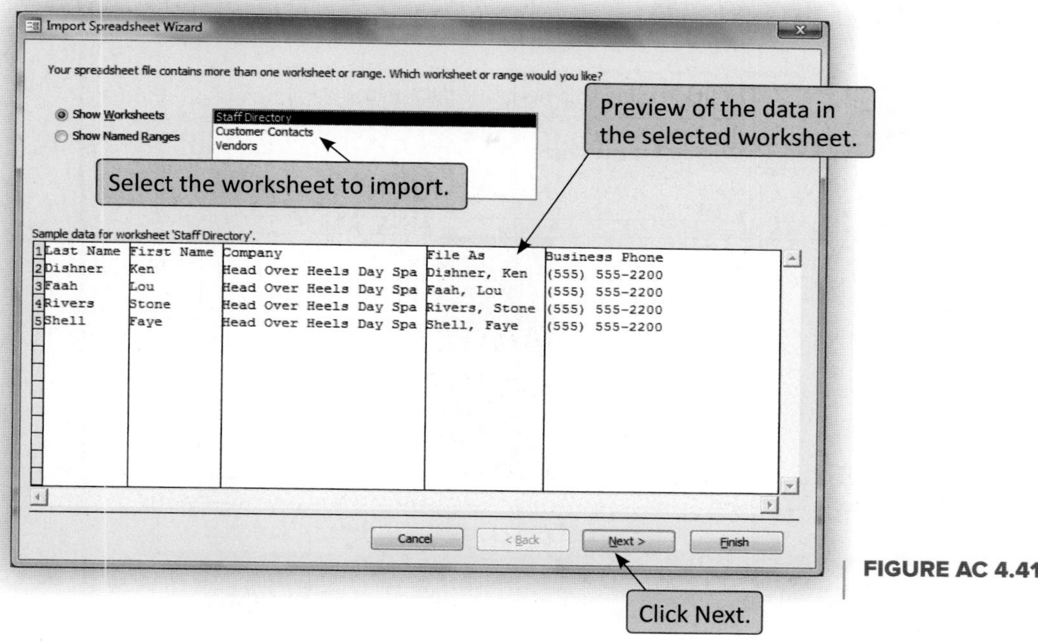

FIGURE AC 4.41

8. If the first row of your spreadsheet corresponds to field names, click the **First Row Contains Column Headings** check box. Access will automatically use the column headings as field names. Click **Next.**

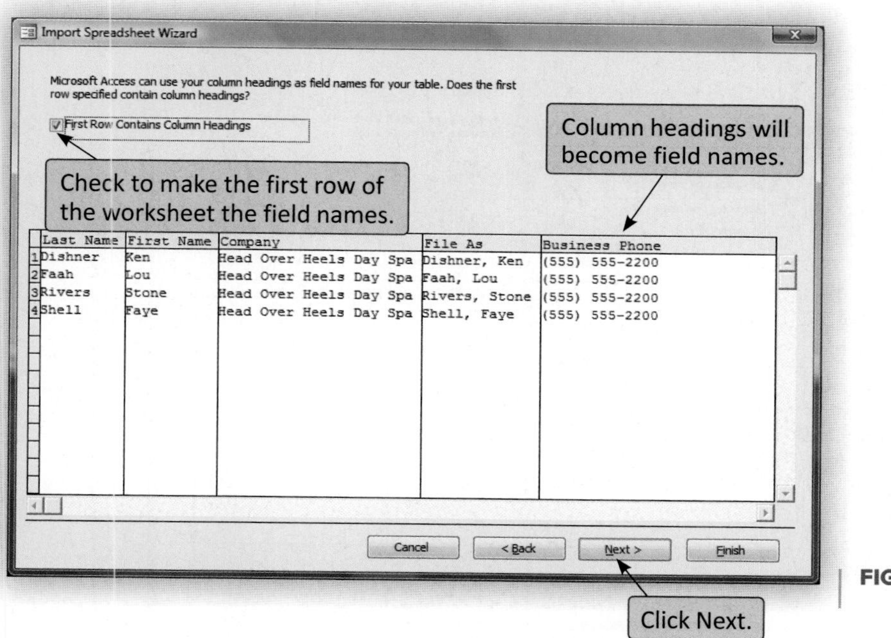

FIGURE AC 4.42

9. If you are creating a new table, the next page allows you to specify properties for each of the fields, such as data type. You can also select a field and click the **Skip Import** check box to exclude the column from the import. Make your choices and click **Next.**

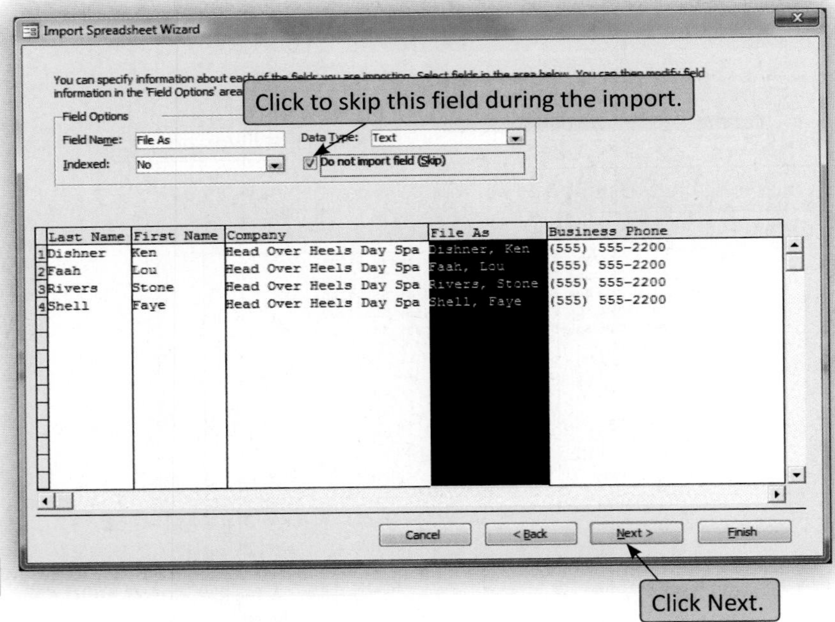

FIGURE AC 4.43

10. You can allow Access to choose the primary key, or you can select the primary key yourself. Set the primary key option and click **Next** to finish the import.

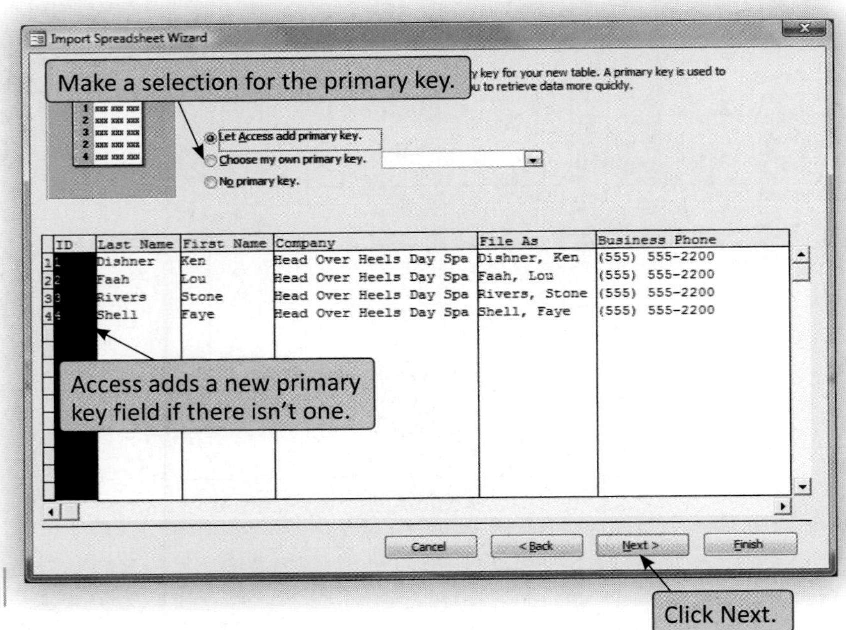

FIGURE AC 4.44

11. Give the table a name, and click **Finish.**

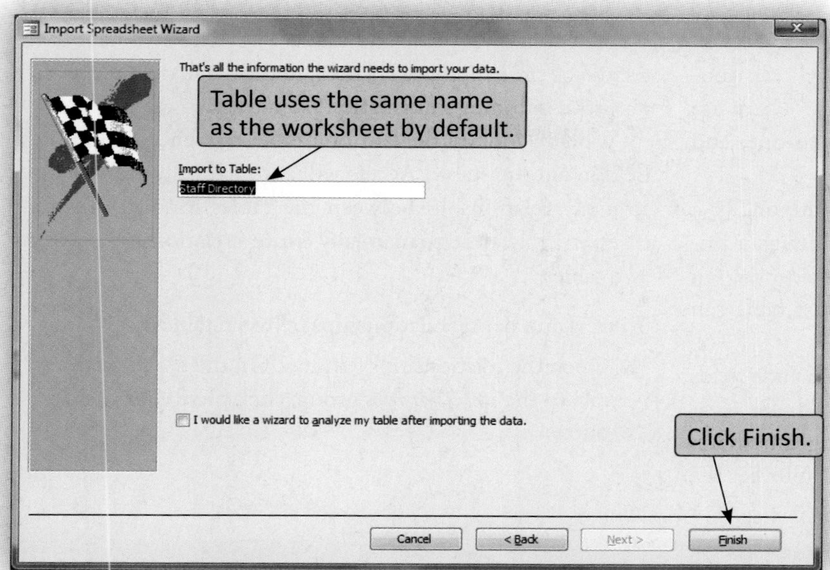

FIGURE AC 4.45

12. If you want to save these import steps to repeat again later, be sure to check the **Save import steps** check box.

13. Click the **Close** button to close the wizard.

14. The new data are imported to a new table, or appended to the table you specified. If there are errors, and Access is unable to import some of the data, you will see a warning message.

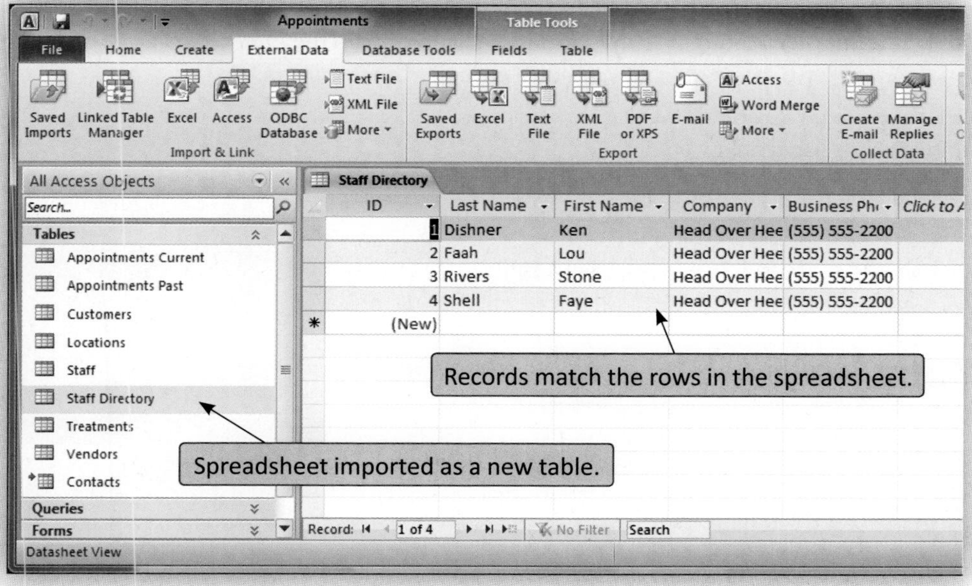

FIGURE AC 4.46

tips & tricks

If you import the source data into a new table, the Access table will be independent from the original Excel file.

If you plan to update the Excel file regularly, create a *linked* table instead. You can then use the **Linked Table Manager** from the *External Data* tab to update the Access table whenever you update the Excel file. The Navigation Pane shows a special icon next to linked tables to indicate the type of file that is linked.

tell me more

If you save your import (or export) specifications, you can run the import (or export) again later by clicking the **Saved Imports** or **Saved Exports** button from the *External Data* tab.

4.13 Creating Relationships

Remember that Access is a relational database. Objects in your database are related to one another through relationships defined by common fields between tables. There are three types of relationships: one-to-many, one-to-one, and many-to-many.

One-to-many relationships are the most common. In a one-to-many relationship, the primary table contains a primary key field that is included as a field (the **foreign key**) in the secondary table. Thus, one record in the first table can relate to many records in the second table.

For example, a table of employee data might include fields for Employee ID, Last Name, First Name, Address, City, State, and Zip Code. Another table for tracking timesheets might have fields for Timesheet Number, Employee ID, Week, Hours Worked, and Total Pay. The two tables are related by the Employee ID field, so the database can generate reports combining information from the two tables.

When a lookup field in one table references values in a field in another table, Access will automatically create a one-to-many relationship between the tables for you. In other cases, you may need to manually create a relationship between two tables.

To view and define relationships between tables:

1. Open the relationships window. On the *Database Tools* tab, in the *Relationships* group, click the **Relationships** button.

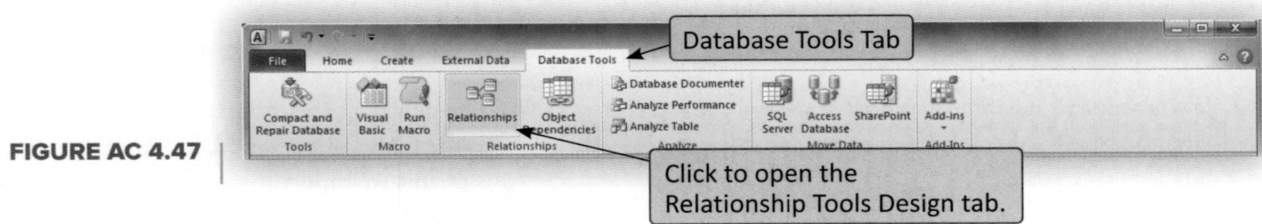

Database Tools Tab
Click to open the Relationship Tools Design tab.

FIGURE AC 4.47

2. You can see existing relationships by the lines connecting field names.
3. To create a new relationship, click the **primary key field name** in the primary table and drag to the related field name in the secondary table.
4. Review the relationship in the *Edit Relationships* dialog, and then click the **Create** button.

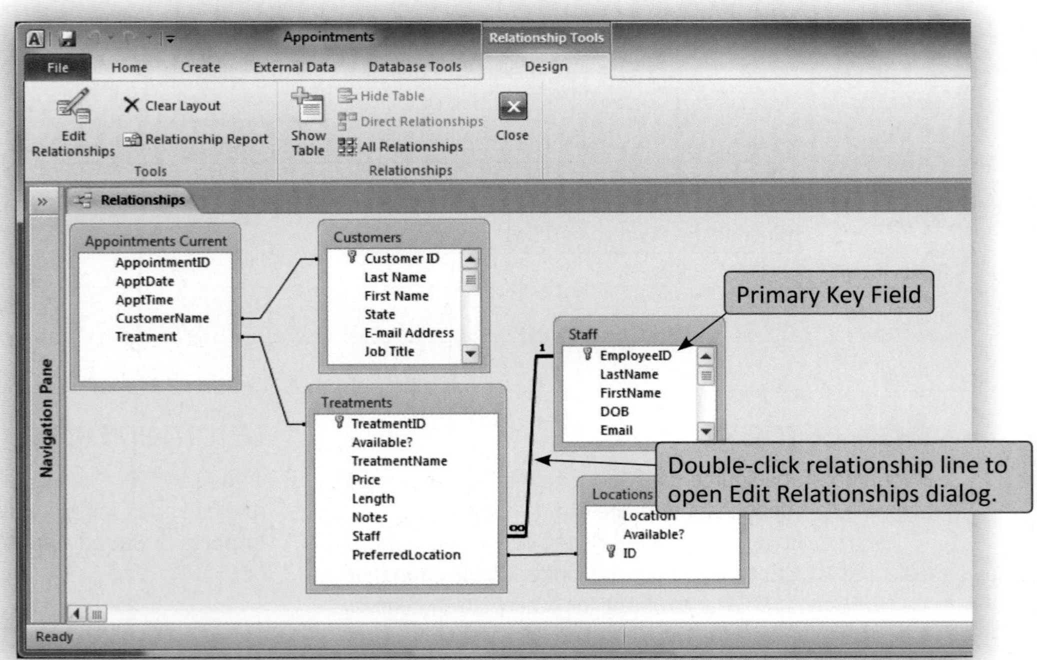

Primary Key Field
Double-click relationship line to open Edit Relationships dialog.

FIGURE AC 4.48

Enforcing **referential integrity** ensures that related database records remain accurate. If a relationship has **Enforce Referential Integrity** checked, then the tables will conform to the following rules:

1. You cannot add a record to the secondary table without an associated record in the primary table.
2. You cannot make changes to the primary table that would cause records in the secondary table to become unmatched.
3. You cannot delete records from the primary table if there are related records in the secondary table.

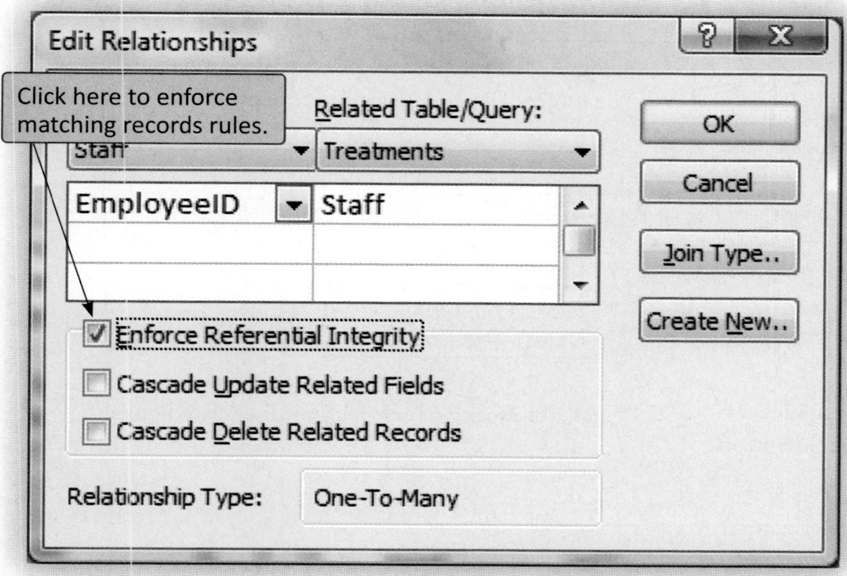

FIGURE AC 4.49

To enforce referential integrity in a relationship:

1. Double-click the **relationship line.**
2. Click the **Enforce Referential Integrity** check box in the *Edit Relationships* dialog.
3. Click **OK.**

Notice the change to the relationship line. The 1 indicates the "one" table in the one-to-many relationship. The infinity symbol indicates the "many" table. When these symbols appear, you know that the relationship has referential integrity enforced.

tell me **more**

To display a table or query that isn't already showing in the relationships window:

- On the *Relationship Tools Design* tab, in the *Relationships* group, click the **Show Table** button.
- Right-click anywhere in the relationships window and select **Show Table . . .** from the shortcut menu.

try **this**

To open the *Edit Relationships* dialog, you can also

- Double-click any field name showing in the Relationships window.
- Double-click any empty area of the Relationships window.

When you open the *Edit Relationships* dialog with either of these methods, you will need to select the primary table from the *Table/Query* list at the left side of the dialog. When you make a selection, Access will populate the dialog with the existing relationships.

4.14 Viewing Dependencies

When one database object depends on another, the relationship between the two objects causes an **object dependency**. For example, a form is dependent on the table it is based on. If you delete the table, the form will be invalid. In a complex database, dependencies are often nested—one object depends on another, which in turn depends on another database object.

Deleting objects with dependent objects can cause errors in your database. So, before deleting an object, it is a good idea to check to see if any objects are dependent on it. You can view object dependencies through the Object Dependencies pane.

To view the object dependencies in your database:

1. In the Navigation Pane, select the object you want to view dependencies for.
2. Click the **Database Tools** tab.
3. In the *Relationships* group, click the **Object Dependencies** button. It may be necessary for you to allow Access to update dependency information before the Object Dependencies pane opens.

FIGURE AC 4.50

4. To view the objects that depend on the selected object, make sure the **Objects that depend on me** radio button is selected.
5. Click the expand icon (+) to see the related objects.

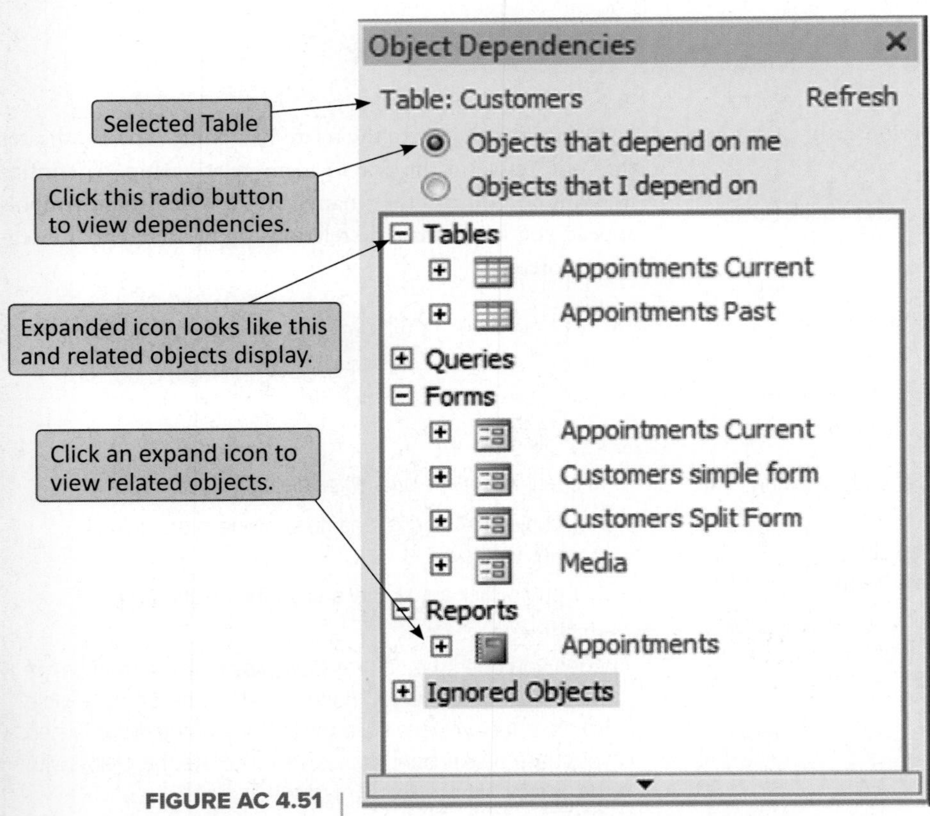

FIGURE AC 4.51

6. To view the objects used by the selected object, click the **Objects that I depend on** radio button.
7. Click the expand icon (+) to see the objects used by the selected object.
8. To hide the Object Dependencies pane, click the **Object Dependencies** button again, or click the Close **X** in the upper-right corner of the pane.

4.15 Filtering Data Using AutoFilter

By applying a **filter** to a database object, you display a subset of records that meet the filter criteria. You can apply a filter to a table, query, form, or report in Datasheet view, Form view, Report view, or Layout view. If you have used Microsoft Excel, some of these filtering tools will be familiar to you as they provide a list of values that you can check or uncheck to create a filter (similar to AutoFilter in Excel).

To filter a datasheet using AutoFilter:

1. Click the arrow in the column that contains the data you want to filter for.
2. At first, all of the filter options are checked. Click the **(Select All)** check box to remove all of the check marks.
3. Click the check box or check boxes in front of the values you want to filter by.
4. Click **OK.** Access displays only the records that include the values you specified.

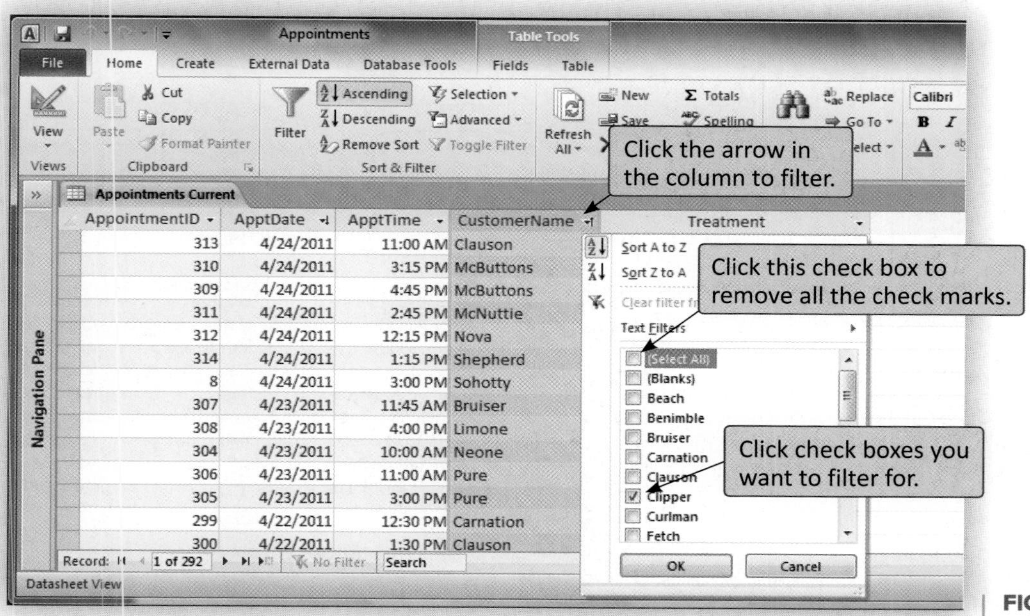

FIGURE AC 4.52

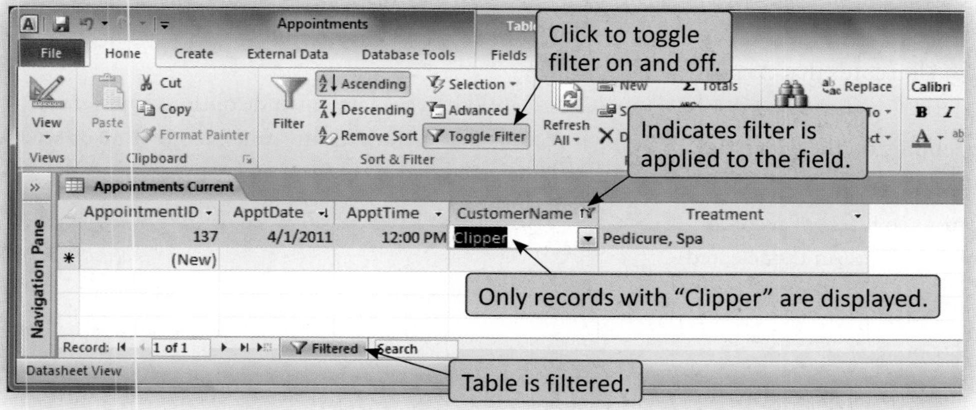

FIGURE AC 4.53

4.16 Filtering Data Using Filter by Selection

If a record that contains the data you want to filter for is visible, you can click the field and use the by selection filter options. Besides filtering by matching exact values, you can filter for values that meet broader criteria.

To filter by selection:

1. Select the data you want to use as the filter criteria. On the *Home* tab, in the *Sort & Filter* group, click the **Selection** button to view the filtering options available for the data you selected.

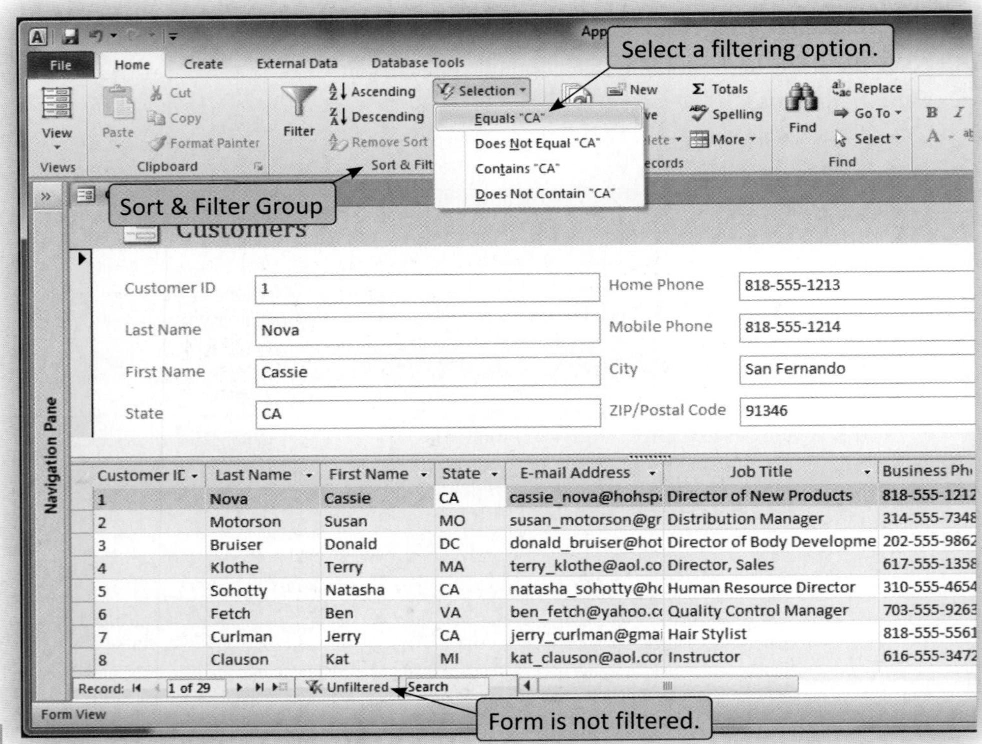

FIGURE AC 4.54

2. The first option is to filter for only records that match the selected field exactly.
3. The second option is to filter for all records that do not match the selected field.
4. The other options will vary depending on the data type of the selected field. For example:
   a. A text field will include options to filter for records that contain or do not contain the text in the selected field.
   b. A numeric field will include options to filter for records that are less than or greater than the selected field.
   c. A Date/Time field will include options to filter for records that include a date/time on or before or after the selected date.
5. Click a filtering option to apply it to the open database object.

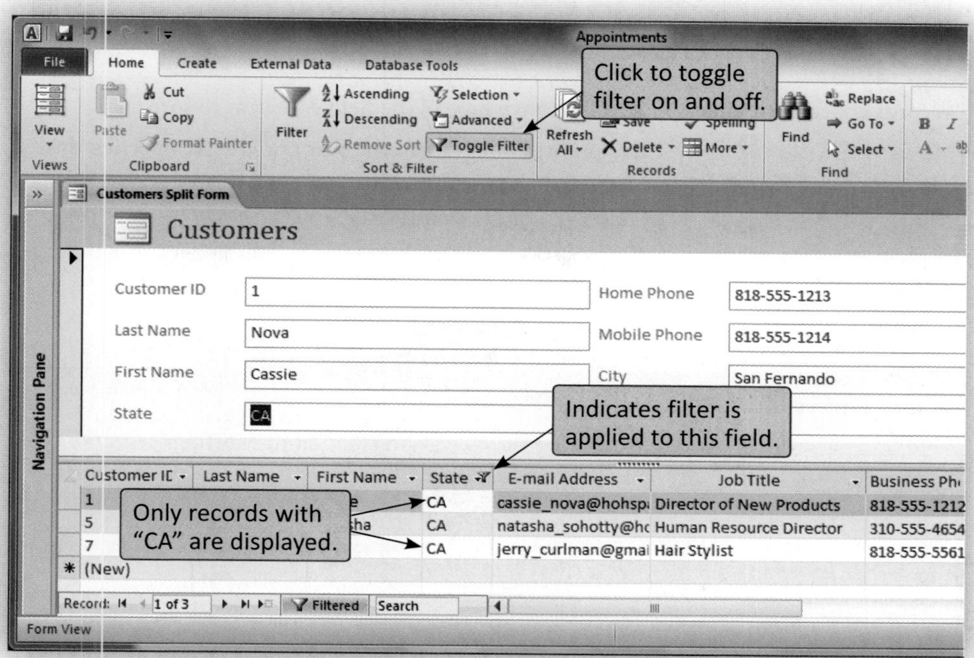

FIGURE AC 4.55

tell me **more**

To remove all filters from a database object, click the **Advanced Filter Options** button arrow and select **Clear All Filters.**

try **this**

Right-click the field that contains the data you want to filter for and select the filter option you want.

4.17 Sorting Records in a Table

You can control the order in which records appear in a table, query, or form by using the **Sort** feature. (See the **Tell Me More** box for more information on sorting records in a report.) Sorting records in Access is similar to sorting data in Excel.

To sort records in a table, query, or form:

1. Open the object you want to sort in Datasheet view, Form view, or Layout view.
2. Click anywhere in the field you want to sort.
3. On the *Home* tab, in the *Sort & Filter* group, click the button for the sort order you want to apply: **Ascending** (A–Z) or **Descending** (Z–A).

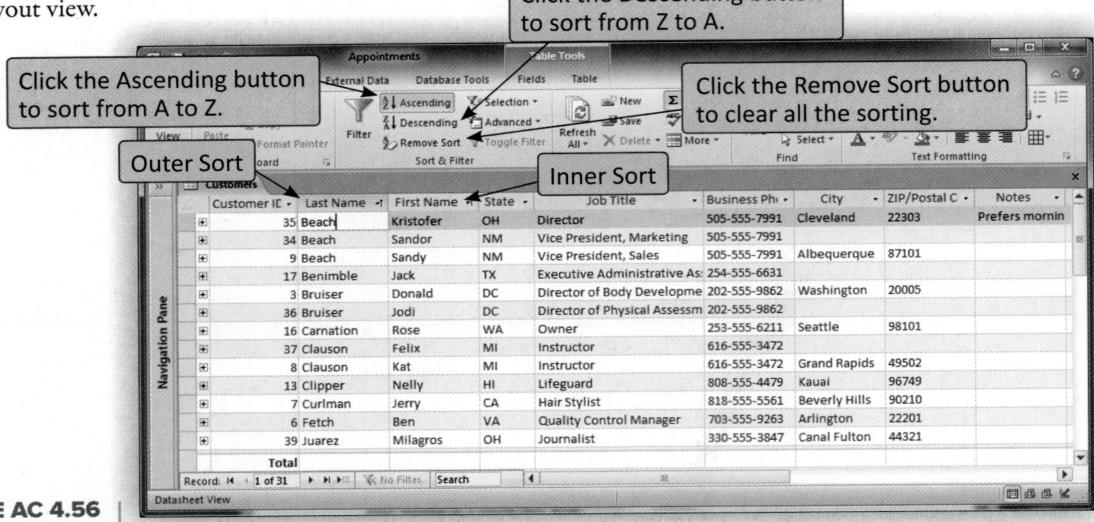

FIGURE AC 4.56

You can create multiple levels of sorting by applying the sort command to the fields in the order in which you want them sorted, from the inside out. For example, if you want records sorted by Last Name, and then by First Name, you would sort by the First Name field first. In this case, the First Name is used for the *inner* sort. The Last Name field is used for the *outer* sort. You can have as many sort levels as you want, but remember to begin with the innermost sort and work your way out.

To clear all sorting from the database object, click the **Remove Sort** button.

tips & tricks

The sort options will differ, depending on the data type of the field you are sorting:

- Text, Memo, and Hyperlink fields sort alphabetically from **A–Z** or **Z–A**.
- Number, Currency, and AutoNumber fields sort on their numeric values from **Smallest to Largest** or **Largest to Smallest**.
- Date/Time fields sort by time from **Oldest to Newest** or **Newest to Oldest.** If you want to show the most recent records first, use the **Z–A** button (Newest to Oldest).
- Yes/No fields are often displayed as check boxes and sort from **Selected to Cleared** or **Cleared to Selected.** A check mark or "yes" value is the "selected" state.

tell me more

To sort records within a report or within a group in a report:

1. Open the report in Layout view or Design view.
2. If necessary, click the group name in the *Group, Sort, and Total* pane. The line for the group will highlight.
3. Click the **Add a sort** button in the group you want to sort.
4. Click the field you want to sort by.

From Layout view, you can also right-click the field you want to sort by and select the sort order you want.

try this

If the database object is in datasheet format, you can click the arrow at the top of the column you want to sort and select a sort option.

You can also right-click a field and select a sort option.

4.18 Using Find and Replace

Access provides a number of ways to search for information in your database. You can *filter* a table, form, or report to display records that meet your search criteria, or for more complex searches, you can write a *query*. For a simple search in a table, form, or query, you can use the *Search* box next to the navigation buttons. Sometimes, the easiest way to search for records is to use the Find command. If you have used other Microsoft Office applications, the *Find and Replace* dialog will be familiar to you.

To search for specific records using the **Find** command:

1. Open the database object you want to search. The Find command is available for any object in Datasheet view, Form view, Report view, or Layout view.
2. On the *Home* tab, in the *Find* group, click the **Find** button to open the *Find and Replace* dialog.
3. Type the data you want to search for in the *Find What:* box. You can use wildcards if you are not sure of the exact data you want to find.
   a. Use an asterisk * when you know the beginning of the search word or phrase, but not the end. For example, **B*** will find records for **B**en, **B**ob, and **B**etty.
   b. Use question marks ? in place of specific letters or numbers. For example, **B??** will find records for **Ben** and **Bob** but not Betty.
4. To narrow your search parameters, you can also
   a. Use the **Look In:** list to specify whether to search only in the currently selected field or throughout the entire table.
   b. Use the **Match:** list to specify a match for the entire field, any part of the field, or only the beginning of the field.
   c. Use the **Search:** list to search only up or down from the current record or to specify to search all the records.
   d. Use the **Match Case** check box to find only records that match the case of your find text. (This check box is available even if you are searching for numerical data.)
5. Click **Find Next** to go to the first record that matches the search criteria. Continue clicking **Find Next** until Access displays a message that there are no more records that meet your search criteria.

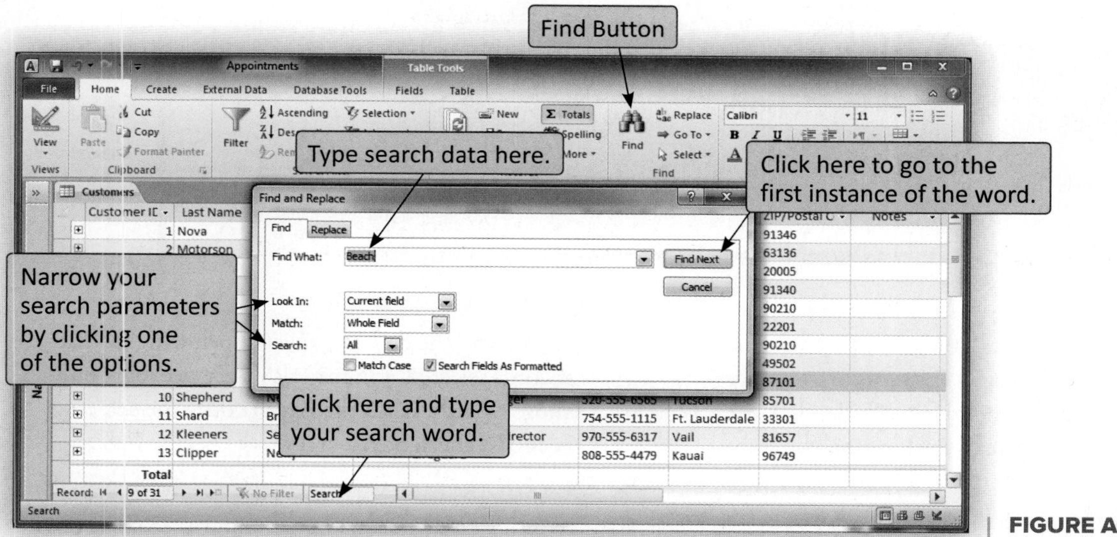

FIGURE AC 4.57

4.19 Exporting Data

You can export data from Access to a new Access database or to another type of file. In some cases, it may be useful to export an Access table, query, or form to an Excel spreadsheet. You can then forward the Excel file to someone who may not have Access or may not need to see the entire database.

To export an Access table, query, or form to a new Excel workbook:

1. In the Navigation Pane, click the object you want to export.
2. Click the **External Data** tab.
3. In the *Export* group, click the **Excel** button.

FIGURE AC 4.58

4. The Export Wizard opens.

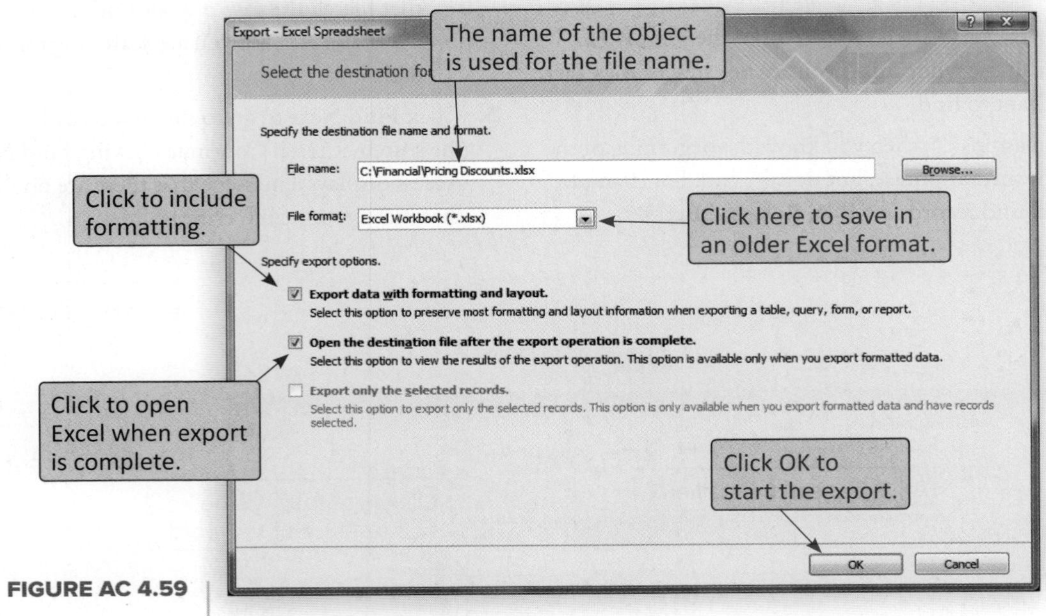

FIGURE AC 4.59

5. Access automatically suggests a file name based on the name of the object you selected. If you want to change the file name or the location of the saved file, click the **Browse . . .** button. Navigate to the location you want. Type a new name in the *File name:* box and click **Save.**
6. Access automatically selects the **Excel Workbook (*.xlsx)** format for the file. If you want to use an older Excel format, expand the *File format:* list and select the format you want.
7. If you want to export the data with formatting, click the **Export data with formatting and layout.** check box.
    a. When you select this option, you may also click the check box to **Open the destination file after the export operation is complete.**
    b. If you have the database object open with specific records selected, you may also elect to export only those records. Click the **Export only the selected records.** check box.
8. Click **OK.**
9. If you want to save these export steps to repeat again later, be sure to check the **Save export steps** check box.
10. Click the **Close** button to close the wizard.

Open the Excel file to see the Access data exported to the Excel format:

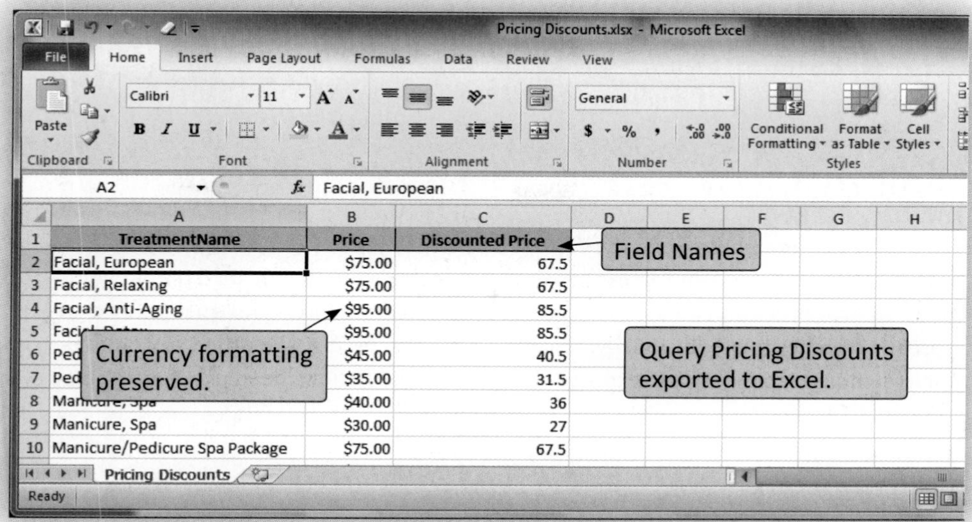

TreatmentName	Price	Discounted Price
Facial, European	$75.00	67.5
Facial, Relaxing	$75.00	67.5
Facial, Anti-Aging	$95.00	85.5
Faci[illegible]	$95.00	85.5
Ped[illegible]	$45.00	40.5
Ped[illegible]	$35.00	31.5
Man[illegible]	$40.00	36
Manicure, Spa	$30.00	27
Manicure/Pedicure Spa Package	$75.00	67.5

FIGURE AC 4.60

tips & tricks

If you save your export (or import) specifications, you can run the export (or import) again later by clicking the **Saved Exports** or **Saved Imports** button from the *External Data* tab.

try this

In the Navigation Pane, right-click the database object you want to export, point to **Export,** and select the export format you want to use.

projects

Skill Review 4.1

You are a part-time employee in the Computer Science department of a local college. It uses Access 2010 to manage employees and various items that are often loaned out. It would like you to improve the functionality of its database by creating filters and queries for data that it usually searches for. Additionally, since Excel is often used at the office, it would like for you to demonstrate the import-export features of Access. Follow the steps below to complete these tasks for the department.

1. Use the Query Wizard:

a. Find and open the following student file in Access 2010: *collegedept4.accdb.* Save this database as ***[your initials]*AC_SkillReview_4-1.**

b. Click the **Create** tab. Click the **Query Wizard** button in the *Queries* group. In the *New Query* dialog box, make sure that **Simple Query Wizard** is selected. Click **OK.**

c. Click the **Tables/Queries** drop-down arrow. Select **Table: Employees.** Click the >> button to add all the fields to the right. Use the < button to remove the *EmployeeID* field from the right side. Click **Next.**

d. In this step, make sure that **Detail** is selected and click **Next.** In the last step, type `InstructorsByTenure` for the title. Select the radio button to **Modify the query design** and click **Finish.**

e. Type `Adjunct` in the *Criteria:* area under the *Position* field. Below that, in the *or:* area, type `Faculty`.

f. Click the drop-down arrow in the **Sort:** area under the *LengthOfService* field. Select **Ascending.**

g. Click the **Run** button in the *Results* group. Click the **Save** button in the Quick Access Toolbar and then close the query by clicking the **x** in the right side of the window.

2. Create a query in Design view:

a. Click the **Create** tab. Click the **Query Design** button in the *Queries* group. In the *Show Table* dialog box, double-click the **Items** table. Click the **Close** button.

b. Notice the *Items* table in the upper pane of the Query Design view. Double-click each field name in the field list (except for *ItemID* and *SupplierID*) in order to add them to your query.

c. Type `Software` in the *Criteria:* area under the *Category* field. Type `>=199` in the *Criteria:* area under the *Price* field.

d. Uncheck the **Show** box under the *Category* field.

e. Next to the *Price* field, create a new calculated field by typing the following in the *Field:* area: `OurCost: [Price]*0.75`

f. Click the **Run** button in the *Results* group to check your work. Return to Design view by clicking the **View** button on the left side of the Ribbon.

g. Click the **Show Table** button in the *Query Setup* group. Double-click the **Loans** table and then click the **Close** button.

h. Click the **Run** button in the *Results* group and observe the new query results. Click the **Save** button in the Quick Access Toolbar and type `ExpensiveSoftwareOnLoan` for the query name. Close the query by clicking the **x** in the right side of the window.

3. Find unmatched and duplicate data:

a. Click the **Create** tab. Click the **Query Wizard** button in the *Queries* group. In the *New Query* dialog, click **Find Unmatched Query Wizard** and click **OK.**

b. Select **Table: Items.** Click **Next.** Select **Table: Loans.** Click **Next.** Confirm that Access has selected **ItemID** in both tables and then click **Next.**

c. Add the following fields to the right side by clicking the > button for each: **ItemName, Description, Category.** Click **Next.** Change the name to `ItemsNotOnLoan` and click **Finish.**

d. Observe the query results and then close the query by clicking the **x** in the right side of the window.

e. Click the **Create** tab. Click the **Query Wizard** button in the *Queries* group. In the *New Query* dialog, click **Find Duplicates Query Wizard** and click **OK.**

f. Select **Table: Loans.** Click **Next.** Select **EmployeeID** and add it to the right side by clicking the > button. Click **Next.** Add all fields by clicking the >> button. Click **Next.**

g. Change the name to `EmployeeMultipleLoans` and click **Finish.** Observe the query results and then close the query by clicking the **x** in the right side of the window.

4. Create a parameter query:

a. Click the **Create** tab. Click the **Query Design** button in the *Queries* group. In the *Show Table* dialog box, double-click the **Loans** table. Click the **Close** button.

b. Notice the *Loans* table in the upper pane of the Query Design view. Double-click each field name in the field list (except for *LoanID*) in order to add them to your query.

c. Click the **Criteria:** area under the *LoanDate* field and type the following: `Between [First Date] And [Last Date]`

d. Click the **Run** button in the *Results* group. In the first dialog box, type `4/1/10`. Click **OK.** In the next dialog box, type `4/30/10`. Click **OK.** Observe the query results.

e. Click the **Save** button in the Quick Access Toolbar and type `LoanDateSearch` for the query name. Close the query by clicking the **x** in the right side of the window.

5. Import from Excel:

a. Click the **External Data** tab. From the *Import & Link* group, click the **Excel** button. Click the **Browse** button and navigate to find the *suppliers4.xlsx* student file. Double-click the file name once you find it. Make sure that the following option is selected: **Import the source data into a new table in the current database.** Click **OK.**

b. Click the **First Row Contains Column Headings** check box. Click **Next.**

c. No changes are necessary in this step. Click **Next.**

d. Click the **Choose my own primary key** option and use the drop-down arrow to select the **SupplierID** field. Click **Next.**

e. Type `Suppliers` below *Import to Table* and click **Finish.** Click the **Close** button to close the wizard.

6. Work with relationships:

a. Click the **Database Tools** tab. Click the **Relationships** button in the *Relationships* group. Observe the existing relationships between the three tables.

b. Add the newly imported table by clicking the **Show Table** button in the *Relationships* group. Double-click the **Suppliers** table and then click **Close.**

c. Create a new one-to-many relationship by dragging the **SupplierID** field from the *Suppliers* table to the *SupplierID* field in the *Items* table.

d. In the *Edit Relationships* dialog box, select the **Enforce Referential Integrity** box. Click **Create.**

e. Click the **Close** button in the *Relationships* group and then click **Yes** to save your changes.

f. Return to the *Database Tools* tab and click the **Object Dependencies** button in the *Relationships* group. Observe the new pane on the right side. If required by your instructor, write down your observations about how various objects depend on each other.

7. Use filters, sort, and Find:

a. Double-click the **Employees** table in the Navigation Pane to open it in Datasheet view.

b. Click the arrow on the right side of the **Position** field. Use the check boxes to make sure that only the **Technicians** option is checked. Click **OK** and observe the results. Write down the number of records that show with this filter applied. Click the **Save** button in the Quick Access Toolbar and close the table by clicking the **x** in the right side of the window.

c. Double-click the **frmItems** form in the Navigation Pane to open it in Form view. Click the **Next Record** arrow at the bottom repeatedly in order to navigate to the fourth record (*ItemID* **DB02**).

d. Click inside the text box that reads **Textbook,** which is next to the *Category* field. On the *Home* tab, in the *Sort & Filter* group, click the **Selection** button in the *Sort & Filter* group. Select the **Equals "Textbook"** option and observe the results. Write down the number of records that display on the Record Navigator bar at the bottom of the form with this filter applied. Click the **Save** button in the Quick Access Toolbar and close the form by clicking the **x** in the right side of the window.

e. Double-click the **Items** table in the Navigation Pane to open it in Datasheet view.

f. Click anywhere inside the *Price* field. Click the **Ascending** button in the *Sort & Filter* group. Click anywhere inside the **Category** field. Click the **Ascending** button again in the *Sort & Filter* group.

g. Click anywhere inside the **ItemName** field. Click the **Replace** button in the *Find* group. Type `Laptop` next to *Find What:*. Type `Notebook` next to *Replace With:*. Select **Any Part of Field** from the drop-down menu next to *Match:*. Click **Replace All** and then click **Yes** to continue. Click the **Cancel** button to close the *Find and Replace* dialog box.

h. Click the **Save** button in the Quick Access Toolbar and close the table by clicking the **x** in the right side of the window.

8. Export a table to Excel:

a. Select the **Items** table in the Navigation Pane.

b. Click the **External Data** tab. Click the **Excel** button in the *Export* group.

c. If necessary, click the **Browse** button to select the location specified by your instructor. Make sure that the file name chosen by Access is **Items.xlsx.**

d. Confirm that the **Excel Workbook (*.xlsx)** option is shown for the file format.

e. Click the **Export data with formatting and layout** check box.

f. Click **OK;** then click the **Close** button to close the wizard.

Skill Review **4.2**

You have just been hired by a small health insurance company in the south Florida area. One of your duties is using Access 2010 to manage the company's list of in-network doctors and covered procedures. It would like you to improve the functionality of their database by creating filters and queries for data that it usually searches for. Additionally, since Excel is often used at the office, it would like for you to demonstrate the import-export features of Access. Follow the steps below to complete these tasks for the office.

1. Use the Query Wizard:

a. Find and open the following student file in Access 2010: *sfinsurance4.accdb.* Save this database as ***[your initials]*AC_SkillReview_4-2.**

b. Click the **Create** tab. Click the **Query Wizard** button in the *Queries* group. In the *New Query* dialog box, make sure that **Simple Query Wizard** is selected. Click **OK.**

c. Click the **Tables/Queries** drop-down arrow. Select **Table: Physicians.** Click the >> button to add all the fields to the right. Use the < button to remove the *PhysicianID* and *HospitalAffl* fields from the right side. Click **Next.**

d. In this step, make sure that **Detail** is selected and click **Next.** In the last step, type `PhysiciansByZipCode` for the title. Select the radio button to **Modify the query design** and click **Finish.**

e. Type `33176` in the *Criteria:* area under the *ZipCode* field. Below that, in the *or:* area, type `33186`.

f. Click the drop-down arrow in the **Sort:** area under the *LastName* field. Select **Ascending.**

g. Click the **Run** button in the *Results* group. Click the **Save** button in the Quick Access Toolbar and then close the query by clicking the **x** in the right side of the window.

2. Create a query in Design view:

a. Click the **Create** tab. Click the **Query Design** button in the *Queries* group. In the *Show Table* dialog box, double-click the **Procedures** table. Click the **Close** button.

b. Notice the *Procedures* table in the upper pane of the Query Design view. Double-click each field name in the field list (except for *ProcedureID*) in order to add them to your query.

c. Type `Yes` in the *Criteria:* area under the *Covered* field. Type `< = 30` in the *Criteria:* area under the *ReimbursementAmt* field.

d. Uncheck the **Show** box under the *Covered* field.

e. Next to the *ReimbursementAmt* field, create a new calculated field by typing the following in the *Field* area: `5% Increase: [ReimbursementAmt]*1.05`

f. Click the **Run** button in the *Results* group to check your work. Return to Design view by clicking the **View** button on the left side of the ribbon.

g. Click the **Show Table** button in the *Query Setup* group. Double-click the **Orders** table and then click the **Close** button. Double-click the **OrderDate** field in the *Orders* table in order to add it to the query.

h. Click the **Run** button in the *Results* group and observe the new query results. Click the **Save** button in the Quick Access Toolbar and type `CheapCoveredProcedures` for the query name. Close the query by clicking the **x** in the right side of the window.

3. Find unmatched and duplicate data:

a. Click the **Create** tab. Click the **Query Wizard** button in the *Queries* group. In the *New Query* dialog, click **Find Unmatched Query Wizard** and click **OK.**

b. Select **Table: Procedures.** Click **Next.** Select **Table: Orders.** Click **Next.** Confirm that Access has selected **ProcedureID** in both tables and then click **Next.**

c. Add all of the fields to the right side by clicking the >> button. Click **Next.** Change the name to `ProceduresNotOrdered` and click **Finish.**

d. Observe the query results and then close the query by clicking the **x** in the right side of the window.

e. Click the **Create** tab. Click the **Query Wizard** button in the *Queries* group. In the *New Query* dialog, click **Find Duplicates Query Wizard** and click **OK.**

f. Select **Table: Orders.** Click **Next.** Select **PhysicianID** and add it to the right side by clicking the > button. Do the same for **OrderDate.** Click **Next.** Add all fields by clicking the >> button. Click **Next.**

g. Change the name to `SameDateOrders` and click **Finish.** Observe the query results and then close the query by clicking the **x** in the right side of the window.

4. Create a parameter query:

a. Click the **Create** tab. Click the **Query Design** button in the *Queries* group. In the *Show Table* dialog box, double-click the **Physicians** table. Click the **Close** button.

b. Notice the *Physicians* table in the upper pane of the Query Design view. Double-click the following field names in order to add them to your query: **FirstName, LastName, City, Phone.**

c. Click the **Criteria:** area under the *City* field and type the following: `[Enter the city name]`

d. Click the **Run** button in the *Results* group. In the *Enter Parameter Value* dialog box, type `Miami.` Click **OK.** Observe the query results.

e. Click the **Save** button in the Quick Access Toolbar and type `PhysiciansByCity` for the query name. Close the query by clicking the **x** in the right side of the window.

5. Import from Excel:

a. Click the **External Data** tab. From the *Import & Link* group, click the **Excel** button. Click the **Browse** button and navigate to find the *hospitals4.xlsx* student file. Double-click the file name once you find it. Make sure that the following option is selected: **Import the source data into a new table in the current database.** Click **OK.**

b. Click the **First Row Contains Column Headings** check box. Click **Next.**

c. No changes are necessary in this step. Click **Next.**

d. Click the **Choose my own primary key** option and use the drop-down arrow to select the **HospitalID** field. Click **Next.**

e. Type `Hospitals` below *Import to Table* and click **Finish.** Click the **Close** button to close the wizard.

6. Work with relationships:

a. Click the **Database Tools** tab. Click the **Relationships** button in the *Relationships* group. Observe the existing relationships between the three tables.

b. Add the newly imported table by clicking the **Show Table** button in the *Relationships* group. Double-click the **Hospitals** table and then click **Close.**

c. Create a new one-to-many relationship by dragging the **HospitalID** field from the *Hospitals* table to the *HospitalAffl* field in the *Physicians* table. Note: You may need to scroll or resize the *Physicians* table in order to see the *HospitalAffl* field.

d. In the *Edit Relationships* dialog box, select the **Enforce Referential Integrity** box. Click **Create.**

e. Click the **Close** button in the *Relationships* group and then click **Yes** to save your changes.

f. Click any object in the Navigation Pane. Return to the *Database Tools* tab and click the **Object Dependencies** button in the *Relationships* group. Observe the new pane on the right side. If required by your instructor, write down your observations about how various objects depend on each other.

7. Use filters, sort, and Find:

   a. Double-click the **Orders** table in the Navigation Pane to open it in Datasheet view.

   b. Click the arrow on the right side of the **ProcedureID** field. Use the check boxes to make sure that only the **2325** and **3094** options are checked. Click **OK** and observe the results. Write down the number of records that show with this filter applied. Click the **Save** button in the Quick Access Toolbar and close the table by clicking the **x** in the right side of the window.

   c. Double-click the **frmPhysicians** form in the Navigation Pane to open it in Form view. You should be viewing the record that has a *PhysicianID* of **AG01.**

   d. Click inside the text box that reads **West Palm Beach,** which is next to the *City* field. Click the **Selection** button in the *Sort & Filter* group. Select the **Equals "West Palm Beach"** option and observe the results. Write down the number of records that display at the bottom with this filter applied. Click the **Save** button in the Quick Access Toolbar and close the form by clicking the **x** in the right side of the window.

   e. Double-click the **Physicians** table in the Navigation Pane to open it in Datasheet view.

   f. Click anywhere inside the **MemberCount** field. Click the **Ascending** button in the *Sort & Filter* group. Click anywhere inside the **City** field. Click the **Ascending** button again in the *Sort & Filter* group.

   g. Click anywhere inside the **Phone** field. Click the **Replace** button in the *Find* group. Type `(305)` next to *Find What:*. Type `(786)` next to *Replace With:*. Select **Any Part of Field** from the drop-down menu next to *Match.* Click **Replace All** and then click **Yes** to continue. Click the **Cancel** button to close the *Find and Replace* dialog box.

   h. Click the **Save** button in the Quick Access Toolbar and close the table by clicking the **x** in the right side of the window.

8. Export a table to Excel:

   a. Select the **Physicians** table in the Navigation Pane.

   b. Click the **External Data** tab. Click the **Excel** button in the *Export* group.

   c. If necessary, click the **Browse** button to select the location specified by your instructor. Make sure that the file name chosen by Access is **Physicians.xlsx.**

   d. Confirm that the **Excel Workbook (*.xlsx)** option is shown for the file format.

   e. Click the **Export data with formatting and layout** check box.

   f. Click **OK;** then click the **Close** button to close the wizard.

challenge yourself 1

You are a botany professor who was recently placed in charge of maintaining the department's greenhouse. This database contains records of the plants in the greenhouse and the employees that assist you with maintenance duties. You would like to improve the functionality of this database by creating filters and queries for information that is commonly searched for. Additionally, since Excel is often used in the department, you would like to practice importing data from Excel, as well as the exporting of Access objects. Complete the following exercises to enhance the department's database.

1. Creating queries:

   a. Find and open the following student file in Access 2010: *greenhouse4.accdb.* Save this database as `[your initials]AC_Challenge_4-3.`

b. Use the **Simple Query Wizard** to create a new query called GreenhouseTechsFT. Add all the fields from the *Employees* table. The query should list all employees whose *Position* contains the word greenhouse and whose *WeeklyHours* is greater than or equal to **30.** Sort the query by *LastName.* Add the *MaintenanceLog* table to this query and include the *Date_Time* field after the *WeeklyHours* field. Run it and save your work.

c. Use the **Query Design** button to create a new query called MediumSizePlants. Add all the fields from the *Plants* table except *ScientificName* and *PrefNutrient.* The query should list all white or yellow colored plants whose *MaxHeightFeet* is between **3** and **5.** Sort by the query by *MaxHeightFeet.* Run it and save your work.

d. Use the **Query Design** button to create a new query called RedPlantSale. Add the following fields from the *Plants* table to the query: **CommonName, FlowerColor, PurchasePrice.** Select only those plants with a red color, but don't show this field in the query results. Add a calculated field that displays a sale price that is 80 percent of the purchase price. Run the query and save your work.

e. Use the **Find Unmatched Query Wizard** to create a new query that identifies the plants that have no entry in the *MaintenanceLog.* Include all fields from the *Plants* table except the *PlantID* and *PrefNutrient.* Name this query PlantsMissingMaintenance.

f. Use the **Find Duplicates Query Wizard** to find out which plants have multiple maintenance entries. Show all fields from the *MaintenanceLog* table. Name this query RepeatedPlantMaintenance.

g. Create a new query that displays the first five fields from the *Plants* table. Configure the *DatePlanted* field so that it requests both start date and end date parameters from the user. Test the query and save it as DatePlantedSearch.

2. Excel importing/exporting:

a. Import the *nutrients4.xlsx* student file as a new table named Nutrients in this database. Note that the first row of the Excel file contains column headers. The primary key should be set to **NutrientID.**

b. Export the *Plants* table as an Excel file named Plants.xlsx. Make sure you export with formatting.

3. Working with relationships:

a. There should be a one-to-many relationship between the *NutrientID* field in the *Nutrients* table (one) and the *PrefNutrient* field in the *Plants* table (many). Be sure to **Enforce Referential Integrity** and save your changes.

b. Observe the *Object Dependencies* in your database. If required by your instructor, write down your observations about how various objects depend on each other.

4. Using filters, sorting, and Find:

a. Open the **MaintenanceLog** table. Apply a filter that shows only those plants that have been watered and pruned. Write down the number of records that show with this filter applied and save these changes.

b. Open the **frmPlants** form. You should be viewing the **AGPU5** record. Select the **purple** color and apply a filter based on your selection. Write down the number of records that show with this filter applied and save these changes.

c. Open the **Plants** table. Use sorting (in ascending order) so that the *DatePlanted* is the inner sort and the *FlowerColor* is the outer sort. After this, find any occurrence of the word Rhexia and replace it with Rexia.

challenge yourself 2

You work for a volunteer organization that ships and administers vaccines to various relief centers all over the world. It currently uses Access 2010 to maintain the list of all approved vaccines and keep track of all shipments made to the relief centers. It would like you to improve the functionality of this database by creating filters and queries for information that is commonly searched for. Additionally, since Excel is often used throughout the organization, it would like you to learn how to use the import and export features in Access. Complete the following exercises in order to enhance the organization's database.

1. Creating queries:

a. Find and open the following student file in Access 2010: *vaccines4.accdb.* Save this database as **[your initials]AC_Challenge_4-4.**

b. Use the **Simple Query Wizard** to create a new query called `MissingPatientAvg`. Add all the fields from the *Locations* table. The query should list all locations whose *PatientAvg* does not contain a value.

c. Use the **Query Design** button to create a new query called `LargeSeptShipments`. Add all the fields from the *Shipments* table except *Cost* and *ShipperID.* Configure the query so that it displays only those orders from **9/1/10** to **9/30/10** that have a quantity greater than **250.** Run it and save your work.

d. Use the **Query Design** button to create a new query called `YouthShipments`. Add all the fields from the *Vaccines* table. The query should list the vaccines whose target audience is either children or teenagers. Add the *Shipment* table to this query and include the *DateShipped* field after the *TargetAudience* field. Run it and save your work.

e. Use the **Query Design** button to create a new query called `PatientIncrease`. Add all the fields from the *Locations* table. Add a calculated field called PatientIncrease to calculate a patient increase that is 20 percent higher than the current *PatientAvg.* Sort the query (descending) by this new calculated field. Hide the *PatientAvg* field from the query results. Run the query and save your work.

f. Use the **Find Unmatched Query Wizard** to create a new query that identifies the vaccines that have no entry in the *Shipments* table. Include all fields from the *Vaccines* table except the *TargetAudience.* Name this query `VaccinesNotShipped`.

g. Use the **Find Duplicates Query Wizard** to find out which Location IDs have received multiple shipments. Show all fields from the *Shipments* table. Name this query `CountriesMultipleShipments`.

h. Create a new query that displays all the fields from the *Locations* table. Configure the *Country* field so that it requests the name of the country from the user when the query is run. Test the query and save it as `CountrySearch`.

2. Excel importing/exporting:

a. Import the *shipping4.xlsx* student file as a new table named `Shippers` in this database. Note that the first row of the Excel file contains column headers. The primary key should be set to **ShipperID.**

b. Export the *Vaccines* table as an Excel file named `Vaccines.xlsx`. Make sure you export with formatting.

3. Working with relationships:

a. There should be a one-to-many relationship between the *ShipperID* field in the *Shippers* table (one) and the *ShipperID* field in the *Shipments* table (many). Be sure to **Enforce Referential Integrity** and save your changes.

b. Observe the *Object Dependencies* in your database. If required by your instructor, write down your observations about how various objects depend on each other.

4. Using filters, sorting, and Find:

a. Open the **Shipments** table. Apply a filter that shows only those shipments that have a *VaccineID* of **YF.** Write down the number of records that show with this filter applied and save these changes.

b. Open the **frmVaccines** form. You should be viewing the **ATX** record. Select the **At-risk individuals** text next to *TargetAudience* and apply a filter based on your selection. Write down the number of records that show with this filter applied and save these changes.

c. Open the **Vaccines** table. Use sorting (in ascending order) so that the *VaccineName* field is the inner sort and the *TargetAudience* field is the outer sort. After this, find any occurrence of the letters `coccal` and replace it with `coccus`.

on your own

You have an extensive movie collection at home, and you have been using Access 2010 to manage this collection. Now that you have entered all of your movies, you want to search for particular data using queries and filters. Additionally, you want to learn how to connect new tables using relationships and link Access to Excel using import-export features. Open the *movie_collection4.accdb* student file, save it as **`[your initials]AC_OnYourOwn_4-5`**, and make changes to your database based on the following minimum requirements:

1. Import the *directors4.xlsx* file as a new table.

2. Create a one-to-many relationship between the imported table and the *Movies* table.

3. Export any of your tables as an **.xlsx** file.

4. Create at least six queries. Of those six, you must have at least one parameter, one unmatched, and one duplicate query. For the other three select queries, you must demonstrate the use of the following features in a way that creates meaningful/useful queries:

a. AND and OR criteria.

b. Text and numerical criteria.

c. Use of comparison operators, wildcards, and IS NULL.

d. Creation of one calculated field.

e. Show/hide and sorting.

f. Multiple tables.

5. Demonstrate the use of filters for one table and one form.

6. Sort at least two fields in any of your tables.

fix it

A local pet store has hired you to fix its database, which keeps track of inventory, customers, and store sales. It is currently having trouble with some queries and a table it imported from Excel. Open the file named *petstore4.accdb* and investigate the issues below. Fix the errors and save your work as **`[your initials]AC_FixIt_4-6`**.

1. Fix the queries as follows:

a. The **CustomersByPhone** query is not working properly. Fix it so that when this query is run, it prompts the user to enter a phone number in order to find a particular customer.

b. Fix the **PriceIncrease** query to correctly display a calculated field that increases the pet prices by 10 percent and hides the original pet price.

c. The **OlderDogSales** query has several problems. Fix it so that it correctly displays only dogs that are at least four months of age. Then, add the *Sales* table so that only those dogs that have been sold appear.

d. Fix the **AgeUnknown** query so that it only displays pets that have no data in the *AgeInMonths* field. Sort the results by the *PetID* field.

e. Fix the **Customers-W&B** query so that only customers whose last names begin with a **W** or a **B** appear in the query results.

2. Fix the forms and tables as follows:

a. When the *frmPets* form is opened, it displays the *No Filter* message at the bottom. Change this so that the form can be filtered by the *Cat* animal type.

b. The *Customers* table is currently configured to quickly filter the *Miami* customers. Change this so that only the *West Palm Beach* customers are filtered.

c. The *Pets* table is currently being sorted by *Price.* Remove this sort and change it so that the data are sorted primarily by animal type, followed by the breeds within each animal type (both ascending).

d. The **$20.00** prices in the *Pets* table are all errors. Change them all to **$25.00** using the replace feature.

3. Fix the relationships and Excel export as follows:

a. The store imported a table called *PetFoods* but forgot to relate it to another table. Fix this by creating a one-to-many relationship between the *FoodID* field and the *PreferredFood* field in the *Pets* table. Enforce referential integrity.

b. Open the *Customers.xlsx* file. Notice how the current format of the worksheet makes it difficult to understand the information. Fix this problem by deleting this file and doing the export correctly so that the Excel file is properly formatted.

powerpoint 2010

chapter 1

Getting Started with PowerPoint 2010

In this chapter, you will learn the following skills:

- Use the different view options
- Add slides and sections
- Change slide layouts and add transitions
- Work with the slide master and insert headers and footers
- Add notes for the speaker to use

skills

introduction

In this chapter you learn the skills necessary to navigate through and edit a basic PowerPoint 2010 presentation.

1.1 Introduction to PowerPoint 2010

Whether used for a sales pitch or as a teaching tool, a multimedia presentation incorporating graphics, animation, sound, and video is much more compelling than paper handouts or a "talking head" lecture. Microsoft Office PowerPoint 2010 enables you to create robust multimedia presentations. A **presentation** is made up of a series of **slides**. Each slide contains content, including text, graphics, audio, and video. You can then manipulate that content by adding transitions, animations, and graphic effects. Before diving in and creating a presentation, you should familiarize yourself with some of PowerPoint's basic features.

When you first start PowerPoint, you will notice the presentation window is divided into three areas:

Slides and Outline Tabs—Display all the slides in the presentation. The *Outline* tab displays only the text content of slides. The *Slides* tab displays thumbnail images of slides.

Slide Pane—Area where you can modify slides, including adding and formatting text, images, SmartArt, tables, charts, and media.

Notes Pane—Area where you can type notes about the current slide displayed in the *Slide* pane. The text you type in the *Notes* pane will not appear when you play your presentation. These notes can be printed as handouts for your audience or can be used by you during your presentation.

Each slide contains **placeholders** for you to add content to, including

Title—Use to display the title of the presentation or the title for the slide.

Subtitle—Use to display the subtitle of the presentation.

Text—Use to add text to a slide. Be sure to keep your points brief, and use bulleted lists to emphasize text.

SmartArt—Use to add a SmartArt diagram to a slide. SmartArt displays lists in a more graphic format, including, processes, cycles, hierarchical diagrams, and matrices.

Graphic—Add clip art, photographs, or other images to slides.

Charts and Tables—Organize information in a chart or table to give your audience a clear picture of your data.

Media Clips—Add sound and video to your presentation.

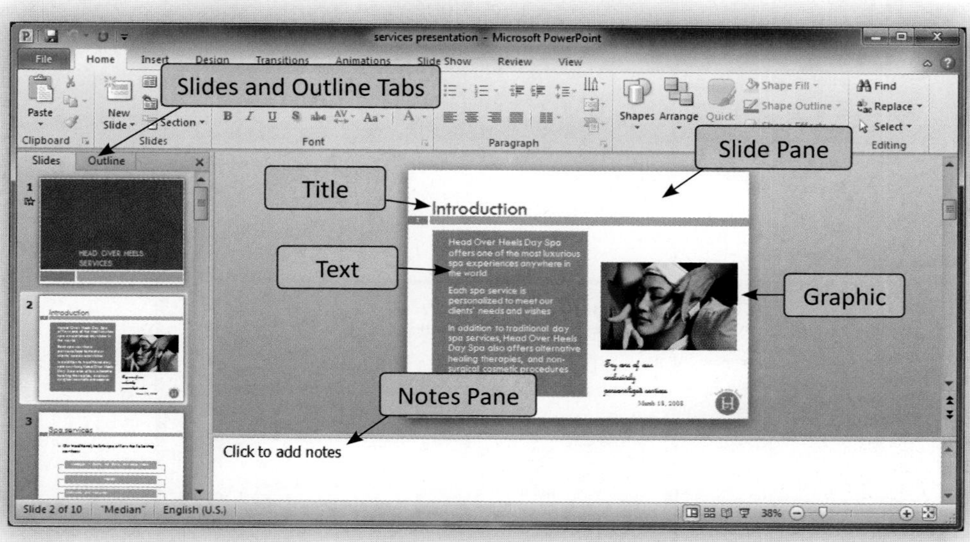

FIGURE PP 1.1

Presentations can be simple or complex, but they all follow some basic steps.

1. **Plan your presentation**—Decide what you want to include and in what order you want to present the information.
2. **Create your slides**—You can create slides from sophisticated templates, or start with blank slides and add formatting and effects to give your presentation a unique look.
3. **Review and rehearse**—Always check your slides for errors. You can also use special effects to add sizzle to your presentation.
4. **Practice**—Practicing your presentation will give you confidence when it comes time to give your presentation in front of an audience.

1.2 Understanding Views

PowerPoint has four main ways to view your presentation: Normal view, Slide Sorter view, Reading view, and Slide Show view. **Normal view** is the view where you will typically create and edit your content. **Slide Sorter view** displays thumbnail pictures of the slides in your presentation and is useful in rearranging the order of slides in a presentation. **Reading view** allows you to run your presentation within the PowerPoint application window. **Slide Show view** displays your slides full screen and allows you to see your presentation the way your audience will.

The easiest way to switch between views is to click one of the view buttons located at the right side of the status bar, near the zoom slider.

Click the **Normal view** button to add or edit content.

Click the **Slide Sorter view** button to view thumbnails of your presentation.

Click the **Reading view** button to view your presentation within the current PowerPoint window.

Click the **Slide Show view** button to view your presentation at full screen as your audience will. To exit Slide Show view, press the Esc key on the keyboard.

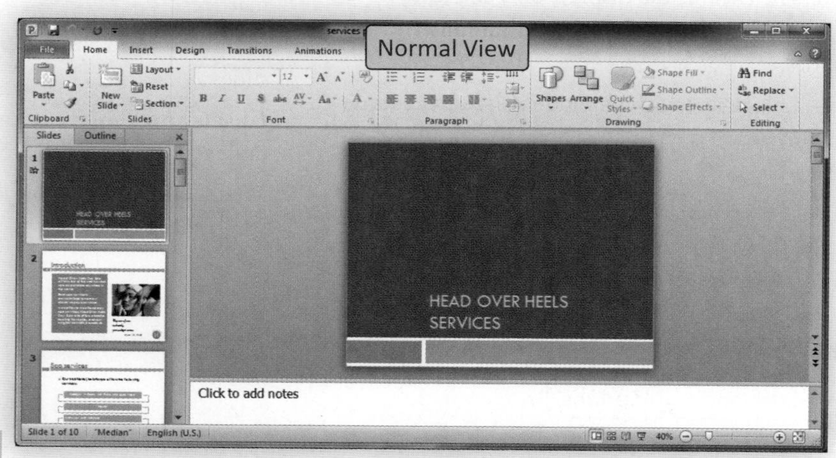

FIGURE PP 1.2

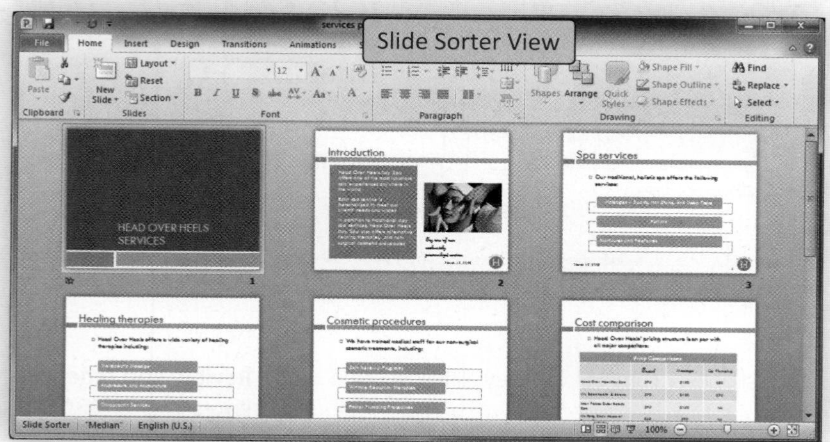

FIGURE PP 1.3

FIGURE PP 1.4

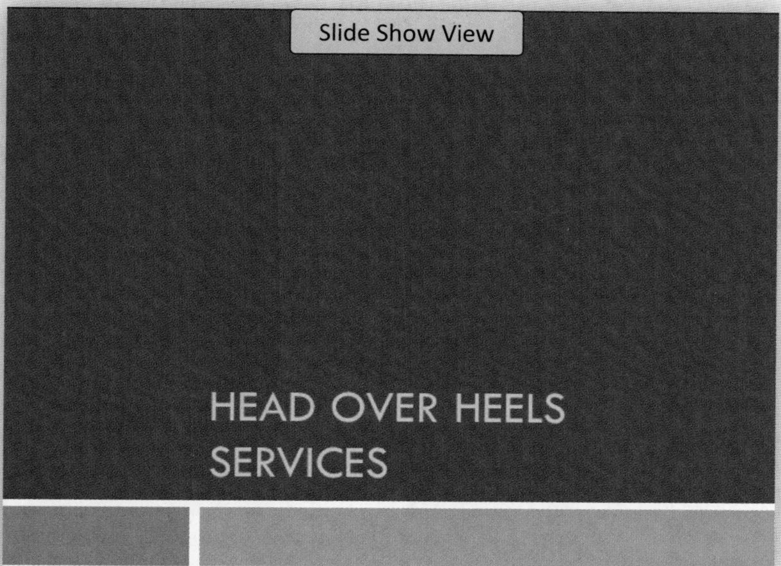

FIGURE PP 1.5

tips & tricks

When you first open a presentation, PowerPoint will display your slides so they fit in the Slide pane. When working in Normal view and Slide Sorter view, you may find you want to change the number of slides displayed onscreen. The **Zoom Bar** (located at the bottom of the PowerPoint window) allows you to change how your slides are displayed in the *Slide* pane. Use the Zoom Bar to magnify your slides to check alignment of text and graphics or to see how your slides will appear when you play your presentation.

try this

- To switch views, you can also click the **View** tab and click a view button in the *Presentation Views* group.
- To switch to Slide Show view, you can also click the **Slide Show** tab and click a button in the *Start Slide Show* group.

tell me more

In addition to the four main views, PowerPoint also includes the following:

Notes Page view—Allows you to add notes for each slide in your presentation. Each slide appears on its own screen with a large text area for your notes about the slide. The text you type in Notes Page view will not appear when you are playing your presentation. However, you can choose to print your notes along with your slides to hand out to your audience.

Master views—Includes Slide Master view, Handout Master view, and Notes Master view. The master views contain universal settings for the presentation. If you want to make changes that will affect the entire presentation, you should use the master view.

1.3 Using the Slides Tab

The Normal view in PowerPoint includes the *Outline* tab and the *Slides* tab to help you navigate between and work with slides. The **Slides tab** displays thumbnails of all your slides. Use the *Slides* tab to quickly navigate between slides, rearrange the slide order, and review and edit content. In order to make changes to a specific slide, it must first be displayed in the *Slide* pane.

To navigate to a slide using the *Slides* tab:

1. Verify that the ***Slides*** tab is displayed.
2. Click the thumbnail of the slide you want to display.
3. The slide appears in the *Slide* pane ready for editing.

To edit text on a slide:

1. Click the placeholder with the text you want to change.
2. Click and drag across the text to select it.
3. Type the new text for the placeholder.
4. Click outside the placeholder to deselect it.

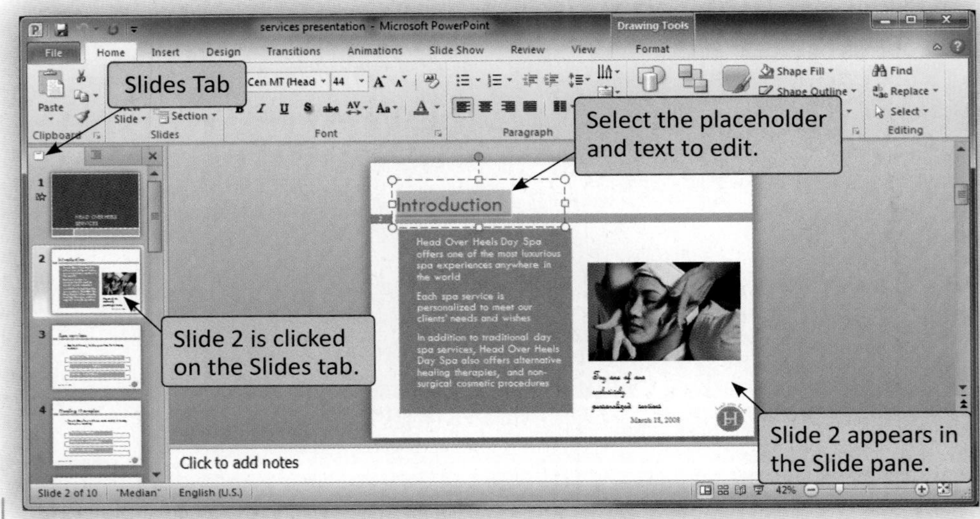

FIGURE PP 1.6

tips & tricks

Clicking in the middle of a text placeholder will select it and prepare it for editing. The placeholder will appear with a dotted line around it and a blinking cursor in the text. If you only want to resize or move the placeholder and not edit the text within it, click the edge of the placeholder. Instead of a dotted line around it, you will see a solid line surrounding the placeholder.

tell me more

The slide that is currently displayed in the *Slide* pane appears highlighted on the *Slides* tab, giving you a quick overview of the location of the slide in the presentation.

try this

To navigate between slides one slide at a time, you can also:

- Click the **Next Slide** and **Previous Slide** buttons on the vertical scroll bar in the *Slide* pane.
- Press the up and down arrow keys on the keyboard.

1.4 Using the Outline Tab

When working on a presentation it's easy to focus on the graphic elements of your slides. Adding graphics, transitions, and animations may seem important, but the foundation of an effective presentation is a focused message. When working with text on slides, it is a good idea to keep the amount of text on each slide balanced and to concentrate on one clear message per slide. The **Outline tab** displays the text from your slides in outline view, allowing you to concentrate on the text aspect of your slides without being distracted by the graphic elements. Use the *Outline* tab to enter and edit your text directly in the outline.

To use the *Outline* tab:

1. Click the tab labeled **Outline.**
2. Click in the text you want to change.
3. Type the new text for the slide.
4. Click the tab labeled **Slides.**
5. View the text you added in the slide's design.

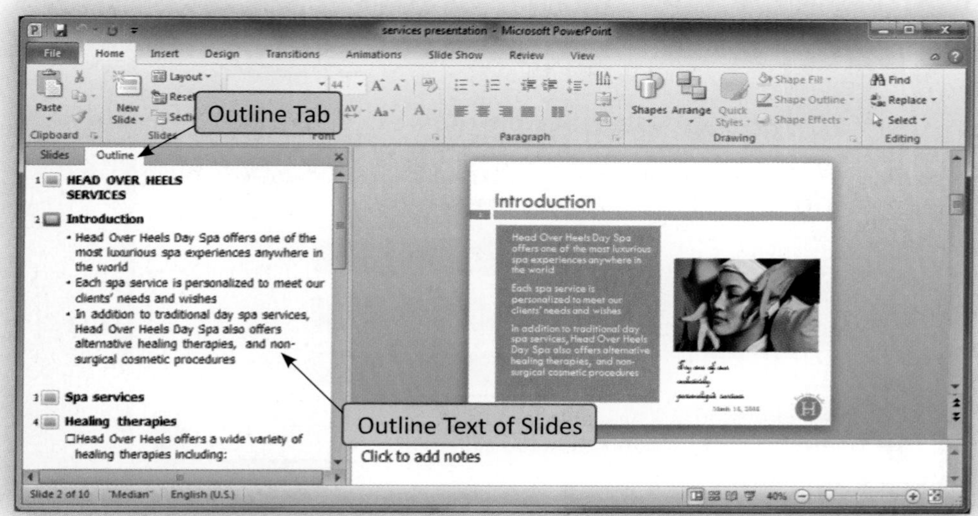

FIGURE PP 1.7

tips & tricks

If your slides include a large amount of text, you can make the *Outline* tab wider to make it easier to write and edit your content. To change the width of the *Outline* tab, place your cursor over the right edge of the pane. When the cursor changes to the resize cursor, click and drag the mouse to the right to make the pane wider or to the left to make the pane narrower.

tell me more

When the *Slides* or *Outline* tab is displayed, the *Slide* pane is sized to display the current slide in its entirety. If you resize either tab, the slide will be resized to fit in the newly sized *Slide* pane. By default, the *Outline* tab is wider than the *Slides* tab to accommodate the slides' text.

1.5 Adding Slides to Presentations

A presentation consists of several slides filled with text and graphics. If you start with a template, your presentation will already include several slides ready to add content. But what if you need to add more information to your presentation? How do you add more slides? PowerPoint makes it easy.

To add a slide to a presentation:

1. On the *Home* tab, in the *Slides* group, click the **New Slide** button arrow.
2. Select a slide layout from the *New Slide* gallery.
3. Add your content to the slide.
4. Continue adding and modifying slides until your presentation is complete.

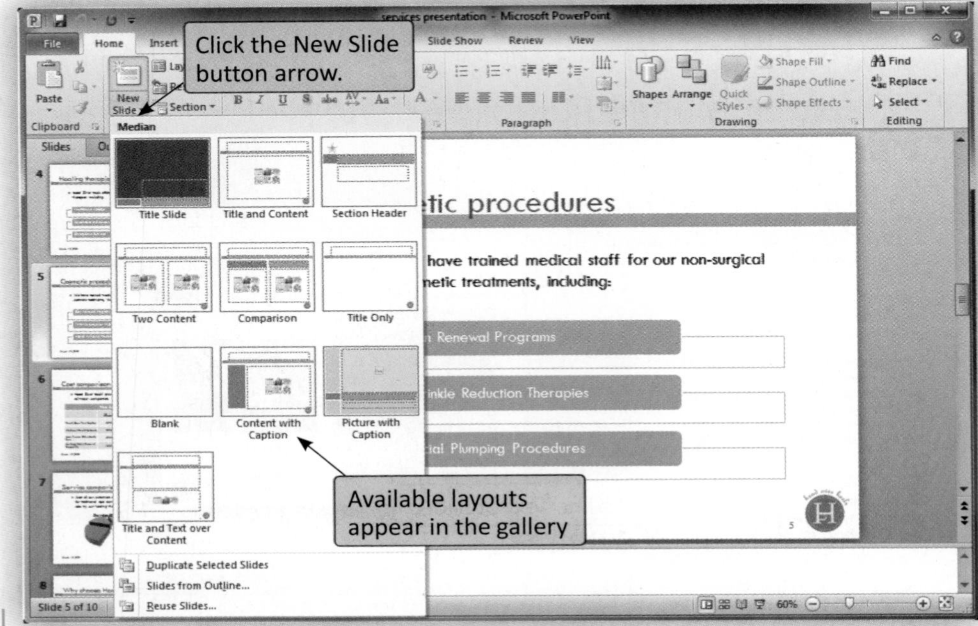

FIGURE PP 1.8

tips & tricks

When you add slides through the *New Slide* gallery, each slide layout includes design elements from the presentation's theme. This helps in creating a consistent look and feel for the entire presentation. If you switch themes, the look of the new slide layouts will change to match that theme.

tell me more

There are a number of slide layouts for you to choose from including title only slides, blank slides, title and content slides, side by side content slides, picture with caption slides, and content with caption slides.

try this

To add a slide to a presentation, you can also:

- Click the top half of the **New Slide** button.
- Press Ctrl + M on the keyboard.

Note: When you use either of these methods, the new slide added to the presentation will use the same layout as the last slide you added.

1.6 Adding Sections to Presentations

As you work on a presentation and add more slides, you may find it difficult to find a specific slide using the *Slides* tab. Scrolling through 20, 30, or even 40 thumbnails to find the content you are looking for is not a very efficient way to work. PowerPoint 2010 includes the ability to add **sections** to your presentation. You can use sections to create smaller groups of slides within your presentation to help you better organize your work. After you have added sections to your presentation, you can then hide and show the slides' thumbnails by expanding and collapsing the sections.

To add a section to a presentation:

1. On the *Slides* tab, click the thumbnail of the first slide for the section you want to create.
2. On the *Home* tab, in the *Slides* group, click the **Sections** button and select **Add Section.**
3. PowerPoint creates a new section.
4. To collapse the section and hide its slides, click the triangle next to the section name. To expand the section and show the slides, click the triangle again.

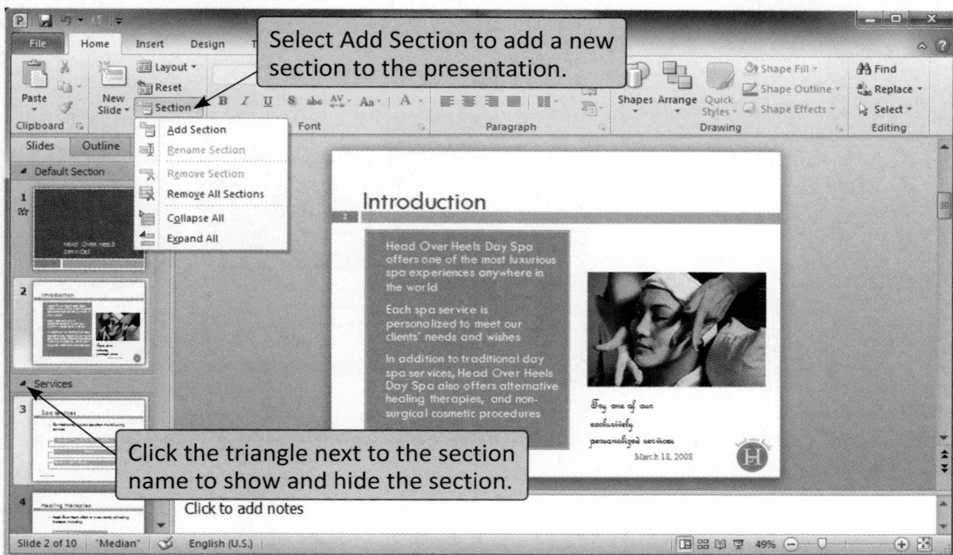

FIGURE PP 1.9

tips & tricks

If you have accidentally added a section, you can remove it by clicking the **Sections** button and select **Remove Section.** To quickly remove all the sections from your presentation, click **Remove All Sections** on the menu.

The **Expand All** command shows all the sections and slides in the presentation. The **Collapse All** command hides all the sections and slides in the presentation.

tell me more

When you first add a section to a presentation, it is given the name *Untitled Section.* To rename a section, first select the section to rename. Click the **Section** button and select **Rename Section.** In the *Rename Section* dialog box, type the name for the section and click **Rename.**

try this

- To add a section, you can also right-click a thumbnail on the *Slides* tab and select **Add Section.**
- You can also expand and collapse sections by double-clicking the section name.

1.7 Changing Slide Layouts

After you have created your presentation, you can modify the information displayed on an individual slide. If you add or delete elements, you may want to change the layout of the slide to accommodate the new content. PowerPoint comes with a number of slide layouts for you to use. Choose the one that best suits the content for each slide.

To change the slide layout:

1. Select the slide you want to change.
2. On the *Home* tab, in the *Slides* group, click the **Slide Layout** button.
3. Select a slide layout from the *Slide Layout* gallery.

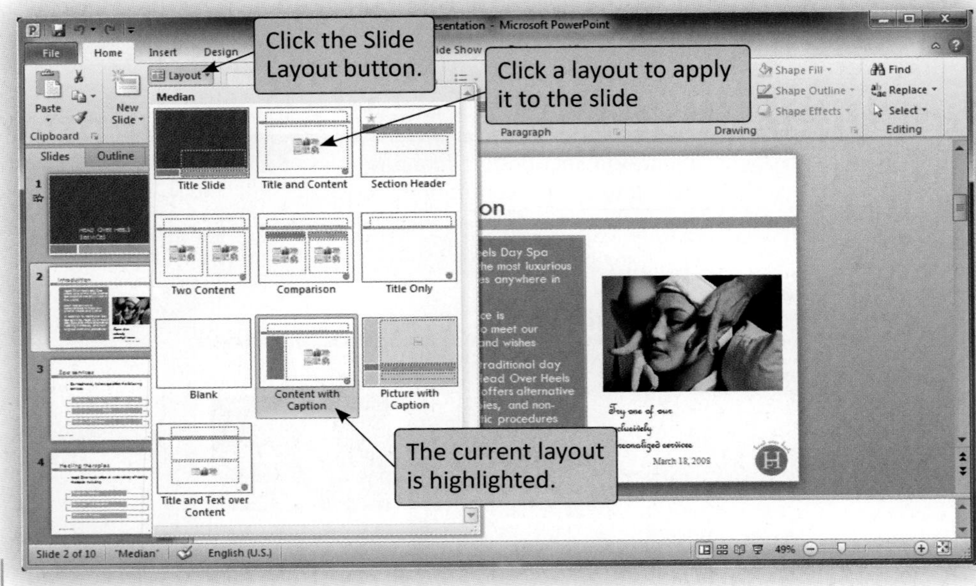

FIGURE PP 1.10

tips & tricks

Once you have selected a new slide layout, you can move and resize placeholders to fit your content. If you have made a number of changes and decide that you want to undo your changes, you can revert the slide to its original design. Click the **Reset** button on the *Home* tab in the *Slides* group to return the slide layout to its default layout.

tell me more

One way to share slide layouts with others is through a **Slide Library**. A Slide Library contains slides that have been uploaded to a server for others to view and use in their presentations. When you use a slide from a Slide Library in your presentation, the slide maintains a link to the original slide in the library. If the original slide is modified in any way, you will be notified of the change when you open the presentation. You can choose to update the slide, add the changed slide to your presentation, or keep the slide as it currently appears in the presentation. Using Slide Libraries for creating presentations can help ensure that presentation designs are consistent and up-to-date across large organizations.

try this

To change the layout of a slide, you can also right-click any area of the *Slide* pane without a placeholder, point to **Layout,** and select a slide layout.

1.8 Applying Slide Transitions

A **transition** is an effect that occurs when one slide leaves the screen and another one appears. Transitions add movement to your presentation and can keep audiences interested, but remember that overusing transitions can be distracting. Add transitions only where they will improve your presentation.

To apply transitions to a slide:

1. Select the slide to which you want to add the transition.
2. Click the **Transitions** tab.
3. In the *Transition to This Slide* group, click the **More** button and select a transition to apply to the slide.
4. PowerPoint automatically previews the transition for you.
5. Click the **Preview** button to play the transition again.
6. To add a sound effect to a slide, click the arrow next to the *Sound:* box.
7. To add the same transition to all the slides of a presentation, select the slide with the transition you want to apply, and click the **Apply to All** button.

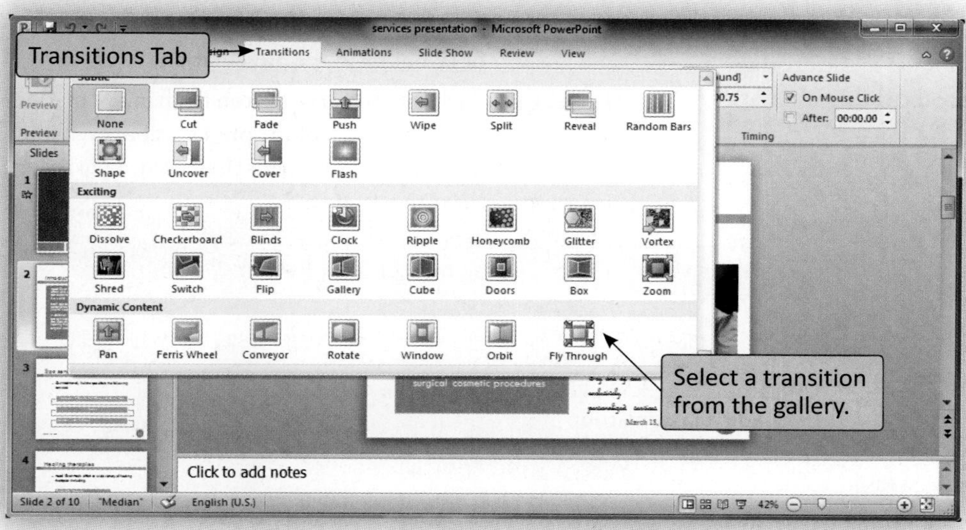

FIGURE PP 1.11

tips & tricks

When you select a transition, PowerPoint applies the default settings for that transition to the slide. You can customize the settings for a transition to create the exact effect you want:

- Click the **Effect Options** button to view the different options for the transition. When you select an option, PowerPoint will automatically play a preview of the new transition.
- Enter a time in seconds in the *Duration:* box or click the up or down arrows to adjust how quickly or slowly the transition happens. Click the **Preview** button to view the new transition speed.

tell me more

PowerPoint offers a number of transitions for you to choose from. There are simple fades and dissolves, any number of directional wipes (including shapes and rotations), pushes and covers, stripes and bars, and random transitions. When choosing transitions for your presentation, it is important to keep in mind who your audience will be. If you are presenting in a formal business environment, you will probably want to use more subtle transitions, such as fades and dissolves. If your audience expects more "sizzle" in the presentation, then you may want to choose a complex wipe, such as the Newsflash transition.

try this

To apply a transition, you can also click a transition in the *Transition to This Slide* group without opening the *Transitions* gallery.

1.9 Working with the Slide Master

Think of a **slide master** as a slide template that is used throughout your presentation to create a consistent look and feel. Slide masters make it easy to create a standard look throughout an entire presentation by controlling layouts and design elements, such as backgrounds and themes, at the presentation level rather than at the slide level. When you use a slide master to create slides in your presentation, you only need to modify the slide master in Slide Master view to make changes to all the slides in the presentation.

To switch to Slide Master view:

1. Click the **View** tab.
2. In the *Master Views* group, click the **Slide Master** button.
3. PowerPoint switches to Slide Master view. Here you can add more slide masters or new layouts to the existing slide master. You can also modify the slide master or individual layouts within the slide master.
4. Click the **Close Master View** button to return to Normal view.

When you are in Slide Master view, you will notice the second tab on the Ribbon is no longer the *Home* tab, but rather the *Slide Master* tab. The *Slide Master* tab contains the commands for working with the slide master. Specifically, the *Edit Master* group gives you access to the following commands:

Insert Slide Master—Presentations can have more than one slide master. To add another slide master, switch to Slide Master view. On the *Slide Master* tab, click the **Insert Slide Master** button.

Insert Layout—Each slide master contains several layouts that appear in the *New Slide* gallery in Normal view. Click the **Insert Layout** button to add a layout to the master.

Delete Slide—Click the **Delete Slide** button to remove a slide master or layout from the presentation.

Preserve—Click the **Preserve** button to change a master so that it will always be part of the presentation, even if it is not being used. When a master is preserved, a pushpin icon appears next to the slide.

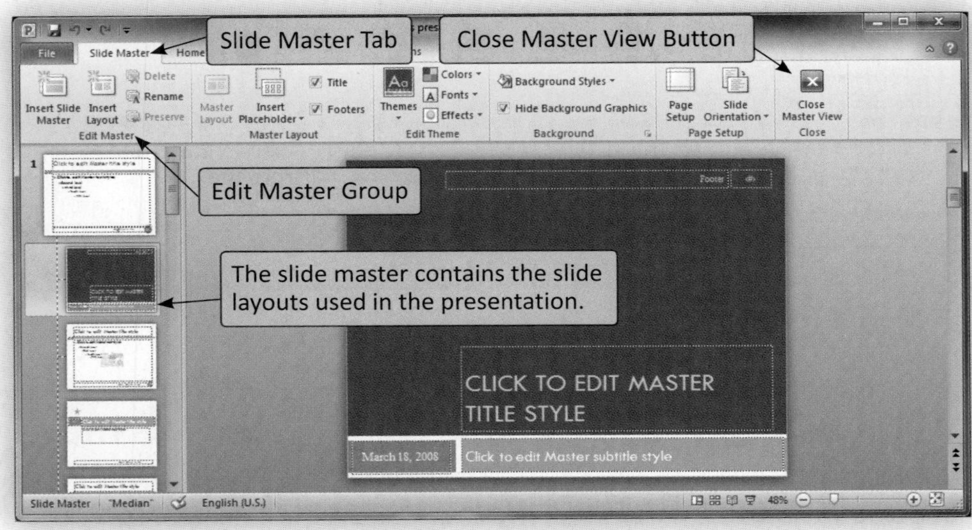

FIGURE PP 1.12

tips & tricks

If you want to use the design of your slide master in several presentations, save the slide master as a template (.potx file). Presentations you create using the template will be based on the slide master you saved.

try this

To close Slide Master view and return to Normal view, you can also:

- Click the **View** tab. In the *Presentations Views* group, click the **Normal View** button.
- Click the **Normal View** button on the status bar.

tell me more

In addition to slide masters, you can create handout masters and notes masters for your presentation. **Handout masters** control how the slides of your presentation look when printed. **Notes masters** control the look of your notes when printed along with the slides. From the Handout Master view and the Notes Master view you can choose to display the header, footer, date, and page number on your printed handouts. You can also change the background of the printed page or add images to the printouts that do not appear in the presentation.

1.10 Inserting Headers and Footers

Headers and **footers** are text that appear on every slide or handout. Typically, headers appear at the top of a handout and footers appear at the bottom. Slides only display footers. Use footers when you want to display the same text on every slide, such as the name of your company. When you add footers to the slide master, they are automatically added to every slide in the presentation.

To add text to the footer of all the slides in a presentation:

1. Verify that the slide master is selected.
2. Click the **Insert** tab.
3. In the *Text* group, click the **Header & Footer** button.
4. On the *Slide* tab of the *Header and Footer* dialog box, select the **Footer** check box.
5. Type the text for the footer in the *Footer* text box.
6. Click the **Apply** button to add the footer to the slide master.

Note: In order to change the footer for the slides associated with a slide master, you must use the *Header and Footer* dialog box. Adding text to the footer box directly on the slide master will not change the footer for the layouts associated with that slide master.

If you want a certain layout to use a different footer, first select the layout you want to change before opening the *Header and Footer* dialog box. When you change the footer, be sure to click the **Apply** button, not the **Apply to All** button.

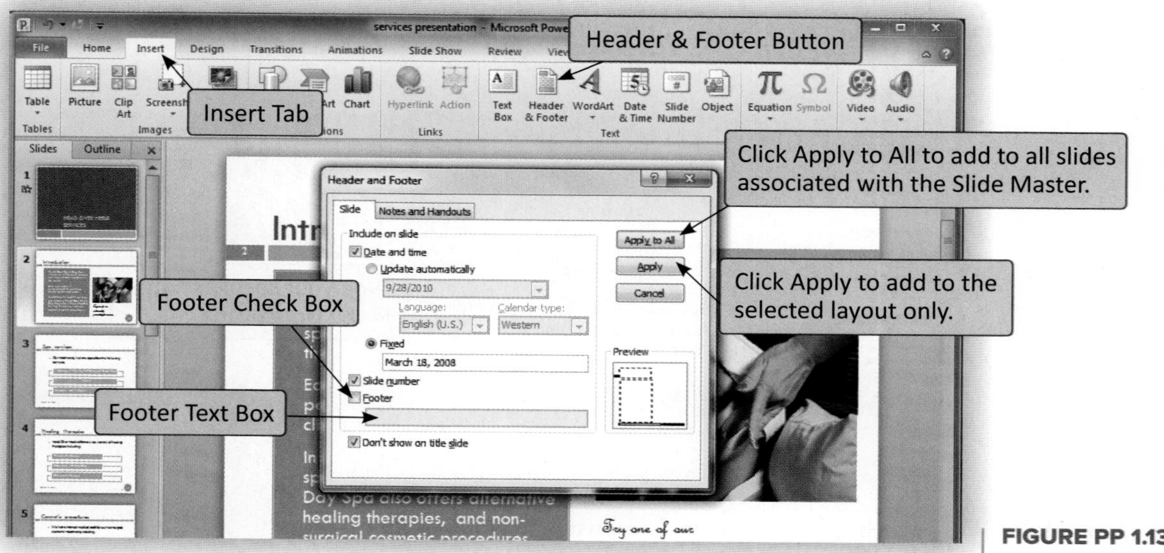

FIGURE PP 1.13

tips & tricks

- To display the date and time on slides, select the **Date and time** check box from the *Slide* tab in the *Header and Footer* dialog box. Click the **Update automatically** radio button to have the date update every time you give the presentation. Click the **Fixed** radio button to have the same date appear every time you present.
- To display the slide number on slides, select the **Slide number** check box.
- If you do not want your footer to display on the title slide of the presentation, select the **Don't show on title slide** check box.

tell me more

Notes pages and handouts use different footers than slides. To create a header or footer for your printouts, click the **Notes and Handouts** tab in the *Header and Footer* dialog box. From this tab you can add a header for the printed page, in addition to changing the date and time and footer. You can control whether or not the header, footer, date, or page numbers appear on the printed page from the Handout Master view.

try this

To change the header for all slides and layouts, you can also click the **Apply to All** button in the *Header and Footer* dialog box.

1.11 Adding and Printing Notes

Speaker notes are hidden notes you can add to slides. They do not appear as part of the presentation. Speaker notes can be used to help remind you to go to a certain slide in the presentation or to mention a specific detail that may not be included on the slide.

To add speaker notes to slides:

1. Verify you are in Normal view.
2. Click in the *Notes* pane. This is pane at the bottom of the screen with the text *Click to add notes.*
3. Type your note for the slide.

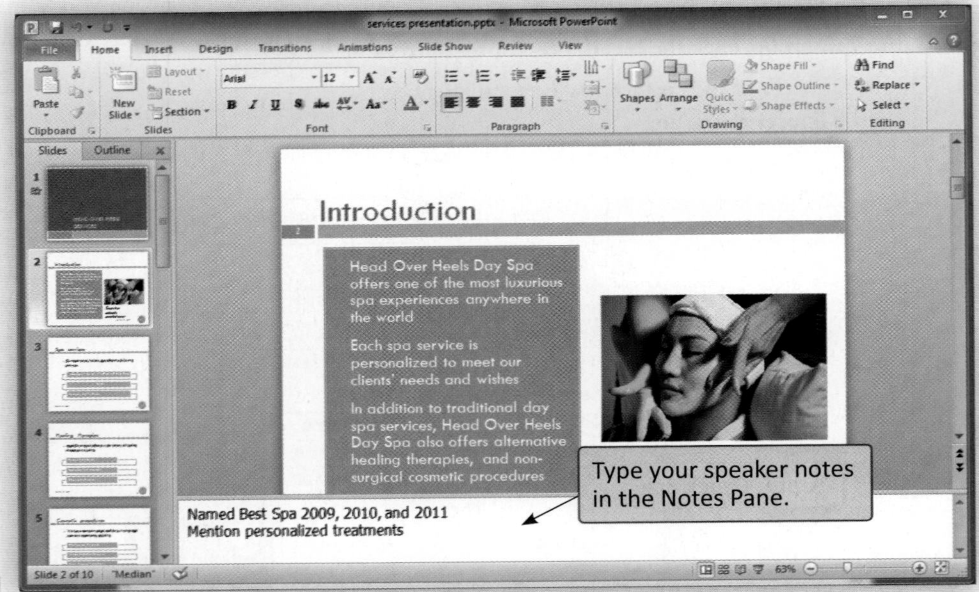

FIGURE PP 1.14

Speaker notes can also be used to create handouts for your audience. You can then print your speaker notes and distribute them to your audience. The Notes view allows you to view how your speaker notes will look when printed. In Notes view, the image of the slide appears at the top of the screen and the speaker notes appear directly below the slide. You can add and format text in Notes view, but you cannot edit the content of the slides.

To switch to Notes view:

1. Click the **View** tab.
2. In the *Presentation Views* group, click the **Notes Page** button.
3. PowerPoint displays your presentation in Notes view.
4. Select the speaker notes text and format the text as you want it to appear when printed.

from the perspective of . . .

TEACHER

Presentations enable me to provide handouts for my students, quickly cover lecture material, and give a professional, visual experience to keep their attention. I can even use presentation software to keep track of my notes by slide as I teach my class.

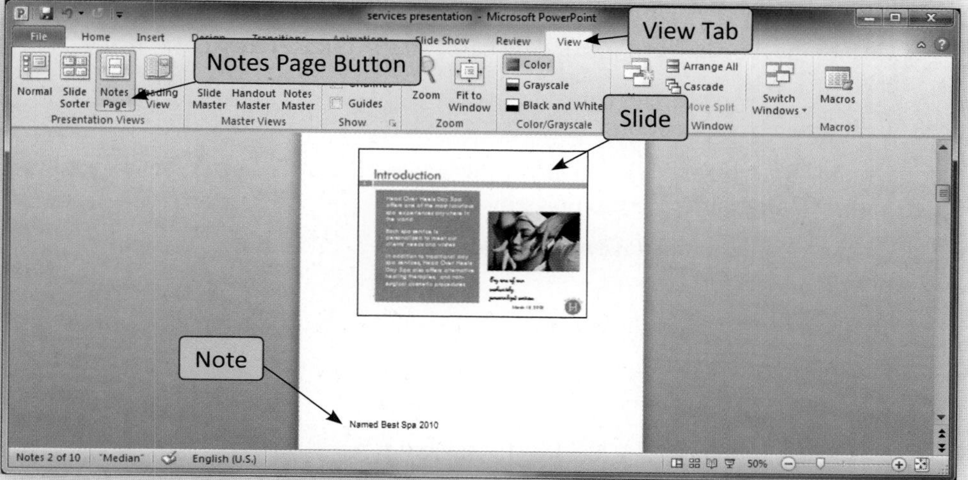

FIGURE PP 1.15

To print your speaker notes:

1. Click the **File** tab.
2. Click the **Print** tab in the Backstage view.
3. Click the first option under *Slides:*.
4. Under *Print Layout,* click **Notes Pages.**
5. Click the **Print** button.

tips & tricks

In PowerPoint 2010 you can use two monitors to display your presentation. When you use two monitors, your audience will see your presentation in Slide Show view, while you will see the presentation in Presenter view. Presenter view allows you to see your notes while you are giving your presentation, making it easier to refer to any notes you have added to slides.

tell me more

The **Notes master view** allows you to control how your printed notes pages will look. The Notes master includes placeholders for the header, date, footer, and page number, in addition to a slide image placeholder and a body placeholder. In the body placeholder, you can format the text (changing the font, font size, and other options) of the notes you have entered in the *Notes* pane of the presentation

try this

To display the *Print* tab in the Backstage view, you can also press Ctrl + P on the keyboard.

projects

Skill Review 1.1

In this review, you will use the skills learned in Chapter 1 to edit an existing presentation.

1. Open an existing presentation:

a. Open Microsoft PowerPoint 2010.

b. On the *File* tab, click **Open.**

c. In the *Open* dialog box, navigate to the location of your PowerPoint 2010 student files.

d. Find *Ch1_Review1_Design_Basics.pptx* and double-click the file to open it.

e. On the *File* tab, click the **Save As** option.

f. Change the file name to ***[your initials]*PP_SkillReview_1-1,** then click **OK.**

2. Use the different view options:

a. On the *View* tab, in the *Presentation Views* group, click **Slide Sorter** for an overall understanding of the presentation structure.

b. On the *View* tab, in the *Presentation Views* group, click **Reading** to view the presentation before edits.

c. On the status bar, click the **Normal view** button to add or edit content.

3. Add slides and sections:

a. Add a slide:

(1) On the *Slides* tab, click the thumbnail of **Slide 3.**

(2) On the *Home* tab, in the *Slides* group, click the **New Slide** button arrow.

(3) Select the **Title and Content** slide layout from the *New Slide* gallery.

(4) Click the **Title** placeholder and type: `Define your audience (Who?)`

(5) Click the **Text** placeholder and type: `What is the reason for the presentation?`

(6) Press the **Enter** key, then the **Tab** key on your keyboard, then type: `Goal`

(7) Press the **Enter** key, then the **Tab** key on your keyboard, then type: `Objectives`

b. Add sections to a presentation:

(1) On the *Slides* tab, click the thumbnail of **Slide 2.**

(2) On the *Home* tab, in the *Slides* group, click the **Sections** button and select **Add Section.**

(3) On the *Home* tab, in the *Slides* group, click the **Sections** button and select **Rename Section.**

(4) Type: `Plan`

(5) On the *Slides* tab, click the thumbnail of **Slide 6,** right-click, and select **Add Section.**

(6) On the *Untitled Section* label, right-click, and select **Rename Section.**

(7) Type: `Create and Present`

4. Change slide layouts and add transitions:

a. Change the slide layout:

(1) On the *Slides* tab, click the thumbnail of **Slide 5.**

(2) On the *Home* tab, in the *Slides* group, click the **Slide Layout** button.

(3) Select **Two Content** from the *Slide Layout* gallery.

(4) Select all of the items in the left text box.

(5) On the *Home* tab, in the *Paragraph* group, click the **Bullets** button.

(6) Select the last four items in the left text box (beginning with *Make it easy to follow*), right-click, and select **Cut.**

(7) Click in the right text box, right-click, and select **Paste.**

b. Apply transitions to a slide:

(1) On the *View* tab, in the *Presentation Views* group, click **Slide Sorter.**

(2) Click the thumbnail of **Slide 1.**

(3) Click the **Transitions** tab.

(4) In the *Transition to This Slide* group, click the **Fade** button.

(5) Click the **Plan** section bar.

(6) On the *Transitions* tab, in the *Transition to This Slide* group, click the **More** drop-down arrow, then click the **Shape** button.

(7) Click the **Create and Present** section bar.

(8) On the *Transitions* tab, in the *Transition to This Slide* group, click the **More** drop-down arrow, then click the **Clock** button.

5. Work with the slide master and insert footers:

a. Work with the slide master:

(1) Click the **View** tab.

(2) In the *Master Views* group, click the **Slide Master** button.

(3) Click the **Title and Content** slide master.

(4) Click the **Content** text box.

(5) On the *Home* tab in the *Font* group, click the **Increase Font Size** button twice.

(6) On the *Slide Master* tab, in the *Close* group, click the **Close Master View** button to return to Normal view.

b. Add text to the footer of all the slides in a presentation:

(1) Click the **View** tab.

(2) In the *Master Views* group, click the **Slide Master** button.

(3) Click the **Title and Content** slide master.

(4) Click the **Insert** tab.

(5) In the *Text* group, click the **Header & Footer** button.

(6) On the *Slide* tab of the *Header and Footer* dialog box, select the **Footer** check box.

(7) In the *Footer* text box, type: `PowerPoint Design Basics`

(8) Click the **Apply to All** button to add the footer to the slide master.

(9) On the *Slide Master* tab, in the *Close* group, click the **Close Master View** button to return to Normal view.

6. Add notes for the speaker to use:
   a. Add speaker notes to slides:
      (1) Verify you are in Normal view.
      (2) In the *Slide* pane, click on **Slide 4** (*Define your audience*).
      (3) Click in the *Notes* pane below the slide.
      (4) Type: `Explain that this matters when making a decision on the information included and the design and/or theme`
   b. Switch to Notes view:
      (1) Click the **View** tab.
      (2) In the *Presentation Views* group, click the **Notes Page** button.
      (3) PowerPoint displays your presentation in Notes view.
7. Save the file and close the presentation.
   a. On the *File* tab, click **Save.**
   b. On the *File* tab, click **Close.**

Skill Review 1.2

In this review, you will use the skills learned in Chapter 1 to edit an existing presentation.

1. Open an existing presentation:
   a. Open Microsoft PowerPoint 2010.
   b. On the *File* tab, click **Open.**
   c. In the *Open* dialog box, navigate to the location of your PowerPoint 2010 student files.
   d. Find *Ch1_Review2_Learning_Styles.pptx* and double-click the file to open it.
   e. On the *File* tab, click the **Save As** option.
   f. Change the file name to ***[your initials]*****PP_SkillReview_1-2,** then click **OK.**
2. Use the different view options:
   a. On the *View* tab, in the *Presentation Views* group, click **Slide Sorter** for an overall understanding of the presentation structure.
   b. On the *View* tab, in the *Presentation Views* group, click **Reading** to view the presentation before edits.
   c. On the status bar, click the **Normal view** button to add or edit content.
3. Add slides and sections:
   a. Add a slide:
      (1) On the *Slides* tab, click the thumbnail of **Slide 6.**
      (2) On the *Home* tab, in the *Slides* group, click the **New Slide** button arrow.
      (3) Select the **Title and Content** slide layout from the *New Slide* gallery.
      (4) Click the **Title** placeholder and type: `What Is Your Learning Style?`
      (5) Click the **Text** placeholder and type: `My Learning Style Is:`
      (6) Press the **Enter** key, then the **Tab** key on your keyboard, and then type one of the following based on your learning style: `Visual`, `Auditory`, or `Tactile/Kinesthetic`

b. Add sections to a presentation:

(1) On the *Slides* tab, click the thumbnail of **Slide 3.**

(2) On the *Home* tab, in the *Slides* group, click the **Sections** button and select **Add Section.**

(3) On the *Home* tab, in the *Slides* group, click the **Sections** button and select **Rename Section.**

(4) Type: `Style Types`

(5) On the *Slides* tab, click the thumbnail of **Slide 6,** right-click, and select **Add Section.**

(6) On the *Untitled Section* label, right-click, and select **Rename Section.**

(7) Type: `Why It Matters`

4. Change slide layouts and add transitions:

a. Change the slide layout:

(1) On the *Slides* tab, click the thumbnail of **Slide 4.**

(2) On the *Home* tab, in the *Slides* group, click the **Slide Layout** button.

(3) Select **Two Content** from the *Slide Layout* gallery.

(4) Select the second bullet and sub-bullets (beginning with *Increase Learning by*) in the left text box, right-click, and select **Cut.**

(5) Click in the right text box, right-click, and select **Paste.**

(6) On the *Slides* tab, click the thumbnail of **Slide 5.**

(7) On the *Home* tab, in the *Slides* group, click the **Slide Layout** button.

(8) Select **Two Content** from the *Slide Layout* gallery.

(9) Select the second bullet and sub-bullets (beginning with *Increase Learning by*) in the left text box, right-click, and select **Cut.**

(10) Click in the right text box, right-click, and select **Paste.**

b. Apply transitions to a slide:

(1) On the *View* tab, in the *Presentation Views* group, click **Slide Sorter.**

(2) Click the thumbnail of **Slide 2.**

(3) Click the **Transitions** tab.

(4) In the *Transition to This Slide* group, click the **Fade** button.

(5) Click the **Style Types** section bar.

(6) On the *Transitions* tab, in the *Transition to This Slide* group, click the **More** drop-down arrow, then click the **Gallery** button.

(7) Click the **Why It Matters** section bar.

(8) On the *Transitions* tab, in the *Transition to This Slide* group, click the **More** drop-down arrow, then click the **Doors** button.

5. Work with the slide master and insert footers:

a. Work with the slide master

(1) Click the **View** tab.

(2) In the *Master Views* group, click the **Slide Master** button.

(3) Click the **Title and Content** slide master.

(4) Click the *Content* text box.

(5) On the *Home* tab in the *Font* group, click the **Increase Font Size** button twice.

(6) Click the **Two Content** slide master.

(7) Click the left *Content* text box.

(8) On the *Home* tab in the *Font* group, click the **Increase Font Size** button twice.

(9) Click the right *Content* text box.

(10) On the *Home* tab in the *Font* group, click the **Increase Font Size** button twice.

(11) On the *Slide Master* tab, in the *Close* group, click the **Close Master View** button to return to Normal view.

b. Add text to the footer of all the slides in a presentation:

(1) Click the **View** tab.

(2) In the *Master Views* group, click the **Slide Master** button.

(3) Click the **Title and Content** slide master.

(4) Click the **Insert** tab.

(5) In the *Text* group, click the **Header & Footer** button.

(6) On the *Slide* tab of the *Header and Footer* dialog box, select the **Footer** check box.

(7) In the *Footer* text box, type: `My Learning Styles`

(8) Check the **Don't show on title slide** check box if it is not already checked.

(9) Click the **Apply to All** button to add the footer to the slide masters.

(10) On the *Slide Master* tab, in the *Close* group, click the **Close Master View** button to return to Normal view.

6. Add notes for the speaker to use

a. Add speaker notes to slides:

(1) Verify you are in Normal view.

(2) In the *Slide* pane, click on **Slide** 7 (*What is your learning style?*).

(3) Click in the *Notes* pane below the slide.

(4) Type: `Explain how you determined your learning style and what changes you will make in your study habits, if any.`

b. Switch to Notes view:

(1) Click the **View** tab.

(2) In the *Presentation Views* group, click the **Notes Page** button.

(3) PowerPoint displays your presentation in Notes view.

7. Save the file and close the presentation.

a. On the *File* tab, click **Save.**

b. On the *File* tab, click **Close.**

challenge yourself 1

In this challenge, you will use the skills learned in Chapter 1 to create a Fitness Plan presentation.

1. Create a new presentation:

a. Open Microsoft PowerPoint 2010.

b. Create a new presentation using the *Austin* theme.

c. Save the file as ***[your initials]*** `PP_Challenge_1-3`**.**

d. Use the **Normal view** button to add or edit content.

2. Add slides and sections:

a. Create slides using **Title** for the first slide and **Title and Content** layouts for the others to include the following:

SLIDE	TITLE TEXT	CONTENT TEXT
Title Slide	My Fitness Plan	Subtitle: Your Name
Slide 2	Diet	Food log More fruits/vegetables Fewer carbs Portion awareness
Slide 3	Exercise	Walk each day Park farther away Take the stairs Include aerobic activity
Slide 4	Rest	Regular bedtime Early start Take a nap when possible ☺
Slide 5	Relaxation	Find a new hobby Go hiking Vacation Read a book Time for "me" "Catch up" with a friend
Slide 6	Family/Personal Time	Schedule "date night" Manicure/pedicure/massage Quiet time
Slide 7	My Goal	*(Type in your fitness goal)*

b. Add sections to a presentation including:

(1) **Diet & Exercise** (Slides 2 and 3)

(2) **Rest/Relaxation/Family** (Slides 4 through 6)

(3) **My Goal** (Slide 7)

3. Change slide layouts and add transitions:

a. Change Slide 5 to *Two Content* layout with three bullets each.

b. Apply four transition types to the presentation: one for Slide 1 and one for each of the three sections.

4. Work with the slide master and insert footers:

a. Using the slide master, increase the font size for all but the title slide.

b. Add a footer with the presentation name. Ensure the footer displays on all but the title slide.

5. Add notes for the speaker to use

a. Add speaker notes to the last slide to explain why you selected this fitness goal.

6. Save the file and close the presentation.

a. Save and close your file.

challenge yourself 2

You are a member of a small group of friends involved in a wine tasting. In this challenge, you will use the skills learned in Chapter 1 to create a Wine Tasting presentation for your Wine Club.

1. Create a new presentation:
   a. Open Microsoft PowerPoint 2010.
   b. Create a new presentation using a theme of your choice.
   c. Save the file as *[your initials]*`PP_Challenge_1-4`.
   d. Use the **Normal view** button to add or edit content.
2. Add slides and sections:
   a. Create slides using **Title** for the first slide and **Title and Content** layouts for the others to include the following:

SLIDE	TITLE TEXT	CONTENT TEXT
Title Slide	**Wine Tasting Basics**	Subtitle: Your Name
Slide 2	**Varietals: A Sampling of Whites**	**Sauvignon Blanc (SO-vin-yon BLAHNK)** Light, crisp acidity and will often contain several fruit components. (Try New Zealand wines for a light citrus) **Chardonnay (shar-dun-NAY)** Full, golden and velvety with hints of fruit, nuts, butter, oak, spice or vanilla and have medium to high acidity. (Try both Oak and Steel Drum) **Riesling (REES-ling)** A bit sweeter and light
Slide 3	**Varietals: A Sampling of Reds**	**Cabernet Sauvignon (cab-er-NAY SO-vin-yon)** Dark purple or ruby in color, medium to full bodied with intense aromas and flavors Merlot (mur-LO) Low acidity and mellow softness with rich flavors of blackberry, plum and cherry **Pinot Noir (PEE-no NWA)** Light to moderate body with deliciously varied aromas and flavors
Slide 4	**The Process**	Look at color and clarity Swirl, then smell Taste Attack (alcohol content, tannin levels, acidity, and residual sugar) Evolution (flavor on your tongue/palate) The Finish (lingering taste) Select your favorites
Slide 5	**Enjoy**	Bring a buddy or a group Relax and enjoy the experience
Slide 6	**Be Safe**	Know your limits Identify a Designated Driver (or take a cab/tour bus)

b. Add sections to a presentation including:
   (1) **Varietals** (Slides 2 and 3)
   (2) **The Process** (Slides 4 through 6)

3. Change slide layouts and add transitions:
   a. Change slide 4 to *Two Content* layout.
   b. Apply three transition types to the presentation: one for Slide 1 and one for each of the two sections.

4. Work with the slide master and insert footers:
   a. Using the slide master, increase the font size for all but the title slide.
   b. Add a footer with the presentation name. Ensure the footer displays on all but the title slide.

5. Add notes for the speaker to use
   a. Add speaker notes to slide 5 to explain it is why your favorite wine and why you like it.

6. Save the file and close the presentation.
   a. Save and close your file.

on your own

You have just graduated from college and are ready to begin your new career. You would like to provide prospective employers with a PowerPoint résumé to "move beyond" the standard word-processed résumé.

1. Create a PowerPoint résumé that includes the following information:
   a. Contact Info (For this assignment you can include only your name and e-mail address.)
   b. Career Objective
   c. Key Skills
   d. Education
   e. Experience (Don't forget volunteer work.)

2. Add sections for each category.

3. Use multiple slide layouts and transitions.

4. Include your name in a footer for all slides except the title slide.

5. Add notes for the speaker to use.

6. Save your file as `[your initials]PP_OnYourOwn_1-5.`

You have been assigned the task of fixing an existing presentation based on the skills learned in Chapter 1.

1. Using Microsoft Office, open *Ch1_Fixit_Saving_Money.pptx*.

2. Save the file as `[your initials]PP_FixIt_1-6.`

3. Change the theme to **BlackTie.**

4. Add three sections: **Getting Started, Decrease Spending,** and **Increase Income**

5. Change the slide layout for the *Decrease Spending* slide to **Two Content.**

6. Add transitions.

7. Use the slide master to add bullets to the content slides.

8. Add a footer with the file name to all slides except the title slide.

9. Add a note with more suggestions for decreased spending.

chapter 2

Adding Content to Slides

In this chapter, you will learn the following skills:

- Work with text within slides including adding text, formatting lists, and using outlines
- Organize text with WordArt, the content placeholder, and tables
- Add interest through charts, SmartArt, and shapes with text
- Add graphics including clip art images, screenshots, and pictures
- Add media to slides including sounds and movies

skills

introduction

In this chapter you learn the skills necessary to edit and add content to a PowerPoint 2010 presentation.

2.1 Adding Text to Slides

A good presentation consists of a balance of text and graphics. It is important to remember to keep text brief. Short, clear points convey your message to your audience better than rambling paragraphs of text. You can add text to slides by using text placeholders and text boxes. **Text placeholders** are predefined areas in slide layouts where you enter text. **Text boxes** are boxes that you add to the slide layout to enter text where you want it.

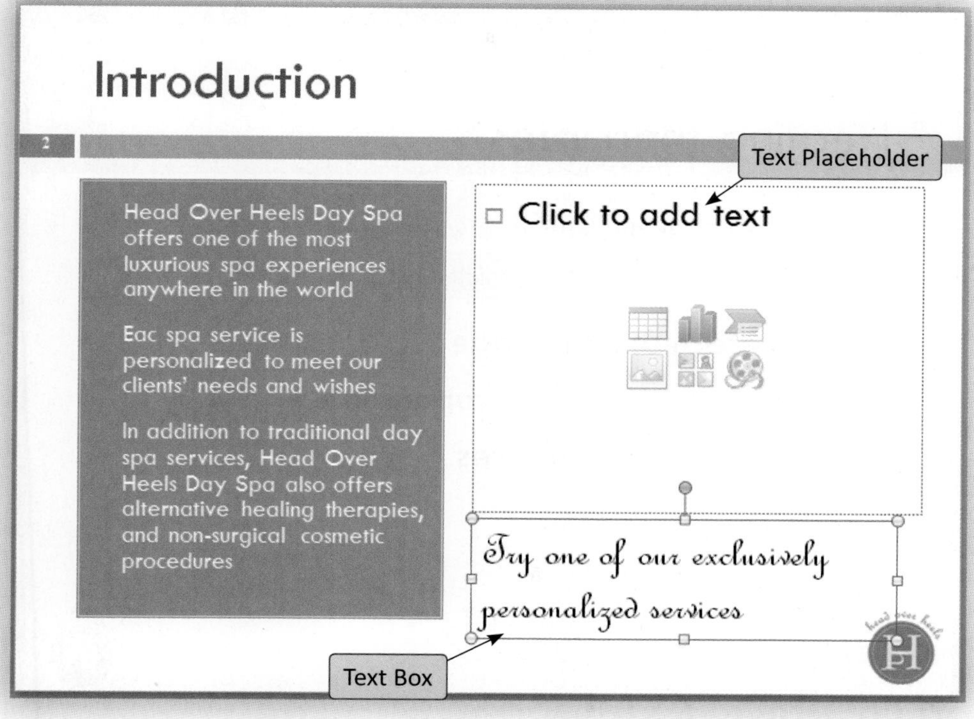

FIGURE PP 2.1

To add text to a text placeholder, click inside the text placeholder and type the text you want to add. Click outside the placeholder to deselect it.

To add a text box:

1. Click the **Insert** tab.
2. In the *Text* group, click the **Text Box** button.
3. Click on the slide where you want the text to appear.
4. Type your text.
5. Click outside the text box to deselect it.

FIGURE PP 2.2

tips & tricks

Text in a placeholder can be edited on the *Outline* tab or in the slide, but text you enter in a text box can only be edited on the slide.

try this

To enter text in a placeholder, you can also type the text on the *Outline* tab.

tell me more

Text placeholders are a part of the slide layout and cannot be added directly to a slide. You can only add text placeholders to slide layouts in Slide Master view. To add a text placeholder, first switch to Slide Master view. On the *Slide Master* tab, click the **Insert Placeholder** button and select **Text.** As you can see from the *Insert Placeholder* menu, you can add placeholders for pictures, charts, tables, SmartArt, media, and clip art, as well as text.

2.2 Adding Bulleted and Numbered Lists

Use bulleted and numbered lists to organize your information into brief points. **Bulleted lists** are used to organize information that does not have to be displayed in a particular order, such as features of a product. **Numbered lists** are used to organize information that must be presented in a certain order, such as step-by-step instructions.

Healing therapies

Head Over Heels offers a wide variety of healing therapies including:

Bulleted List

- Therapeutic Massage
- Acupressure and Acupuncture
- Chiropractic Services

4

Why choose Head Over Heels?

9

Numbered List

1. 5 star rating from Best Spas
2. Personalized services and maintenance plans
3. Dedicated, friendly staff to meet your every need
4. Wide range of services
5. Relaxing, luxurious surroundings

FIGURE PP 2.3

To add a bulleted list to a slide:

1. Select the text you want to display in a list.
2. On the *Home* tab, in the *Paragraph* group, click the arrow next to the **Bullets** button.
3. Select a bullet style from the gallery.

To add a numbered list to a slide:

1. Select the text you want to display in a list.
2. On the *Home* tab, in the *Paragraph* group, click the arrow next to the **Numbering** button.
3. Select a numbering style from the gallery.

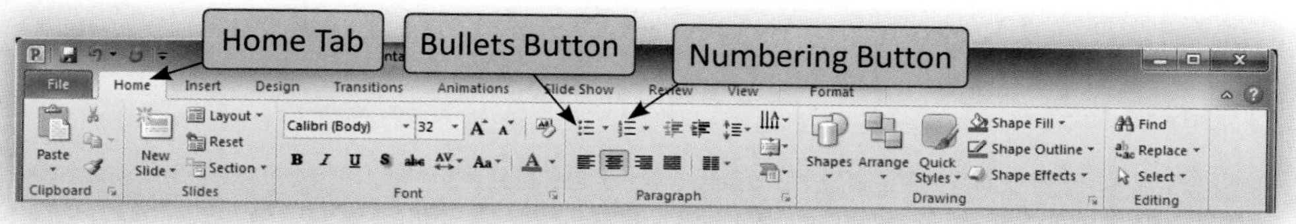

FIGURE PP 2.4

tips & tricks

Sometimes you will want to include subpoints in your bulleted and numbered lists. When a list includes point and subpoints, it is called a **multilevel list**. In PowerPoint, you can create a multilevel list by demoting and promoting points in lists. To move a point down a level in a list, click the **Increase Indent** button. To move a point up a level in a list, click the **Decrease Indent** button.

tell me more

The *Bullets and Numbering* dialog box allows you to modify the look of your lists. Click the **Bulleted** tab to change the style, size, and color of the bulleted list. Click the **Numbered** tab to change the type and color of the numbers or to change the starting point of the list. To open the *Bullets and Numbering* dialog box, click **Bullets and Numbering . . .** located below the *Bullets* gallery and the *Numbering* gallery.

try this

To add a bulleted list:

- Right-click the selected text, point to **Bullets,** and select a style from the submenu.
- Right-click the selected text. On the Mini toolbar, click the arrow next to the **Bullets** button and select a style.

To add a numbered list:

- Right-click the selected text, point to **Numbering,** and select a style from the submenu.

To apply the most recently used bullet or numbering style to a list, click the **Bullets** or **Numbering** button in the *Paragraph* group.

2.3 Opening a Word Outline as a Presentation

When organizing the content for a presentation, you may find it helpful to write your text in a Word document and then import it into PowerPoint. Use heading styles in the Word document to ensure that the content will convert to a presentation in a uniform manner. Each Heading 1 style becomes the title on the slide, and each Heading 2 style becomes the main text on the slide. After you have saved the Word document, you can then import the content, creating the base slides for your presentation.

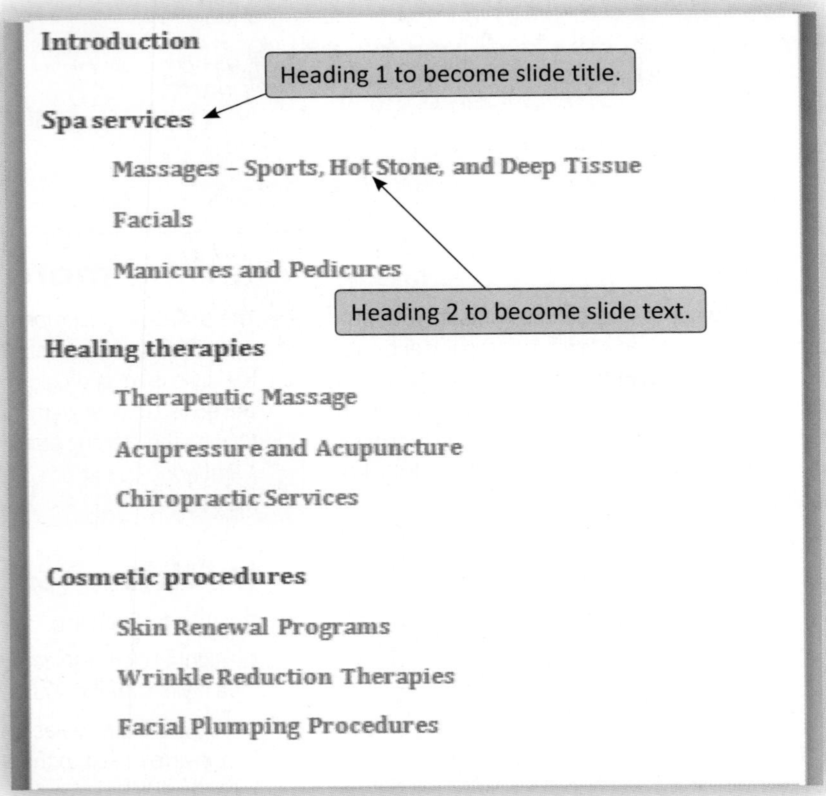

FIGURE PP 2.5

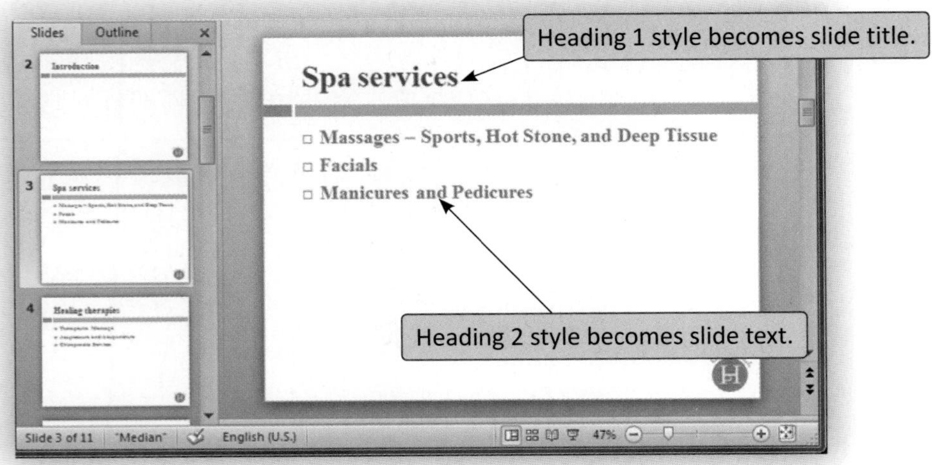

FIGURE PP 2.6

To insert slides from a Word outline:

1. Click in the presentation where you want to insert the slides.
2. On the *Home* tab, in the *Slides* group, click the arrow below the **New Slide** button and select **Slides from Outline . . .**
3. In the *Insert Outline* dialog box, select the file you want to insert.
4. Click the **Insert** button.
5. The slides are added to the presentation based on the heading styles in the Word document.

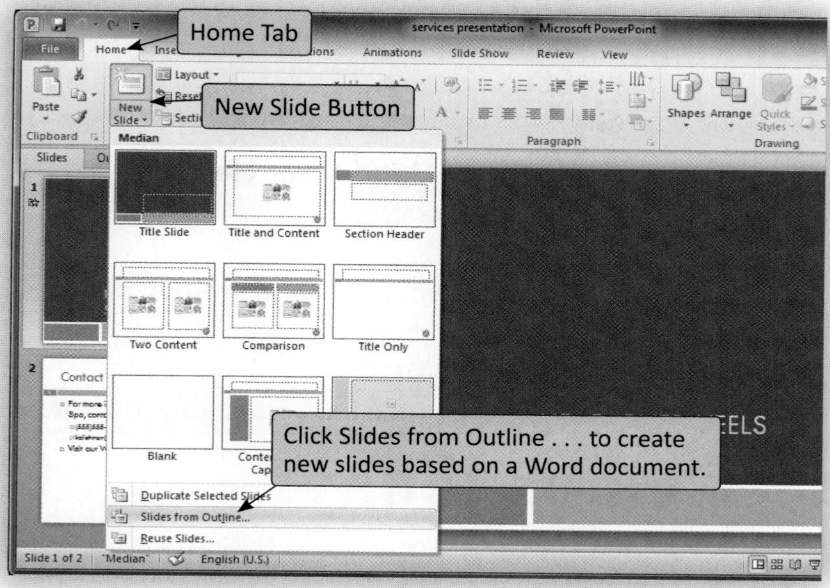

FIGURE PP 2.7

tips & tricks

When you insert an outline, all the slides will use the default slide design. Click the **Layout** button on the *Home* tab to change the layout of a slide. Click the **Design** tab to make any changes to a slide's design.

tell me **more**

You can import many file formats from Word, including Word documents (both .docx and .doc), plain text (.txt), rich text format (.rtf), and HTML (.htm).

2.4 Adding WordArt to Slides

Sometimes you'll want to call attention to text that you add to a slide. You can format the text by using character effects, or if you want the text to really stand out, you can use **WordArt.**

WordArt Quick Styles are predefined graphic styles you apply to text. These styles include a combination of color, fills, outlines, and effects.

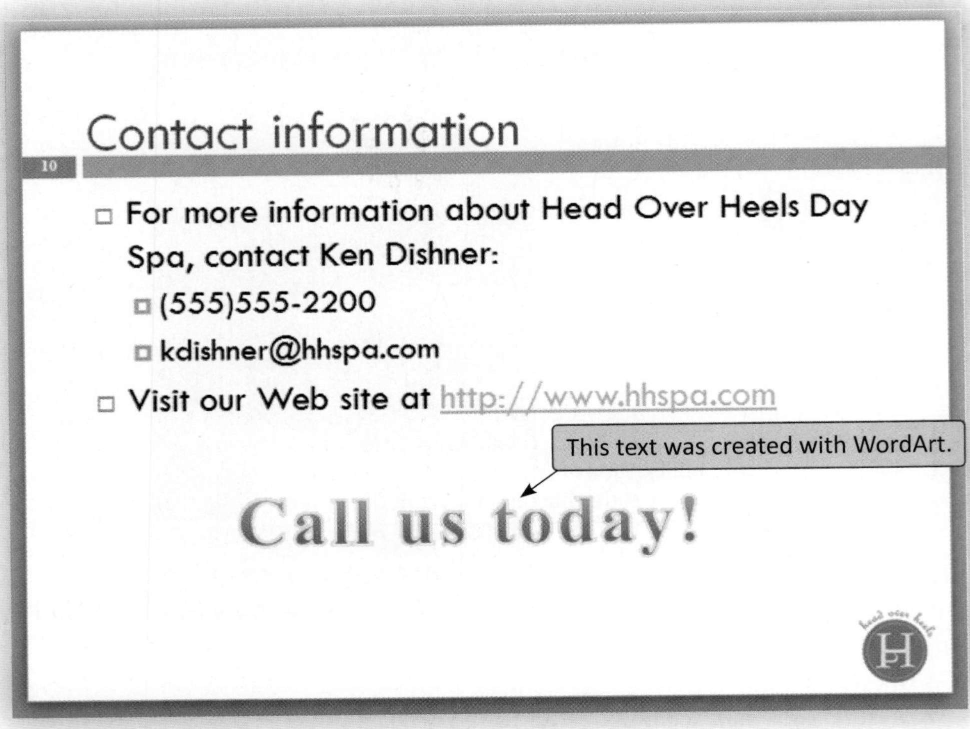

FIGURE PP 2.8

To add WordArt to slides:

1. Click the **Insert** tab.
2. In the *Text* group, click the **WordArt** button and select a Quick Style from the gallery.
3. Replace the text "Your Text Here" with the text for your slide.

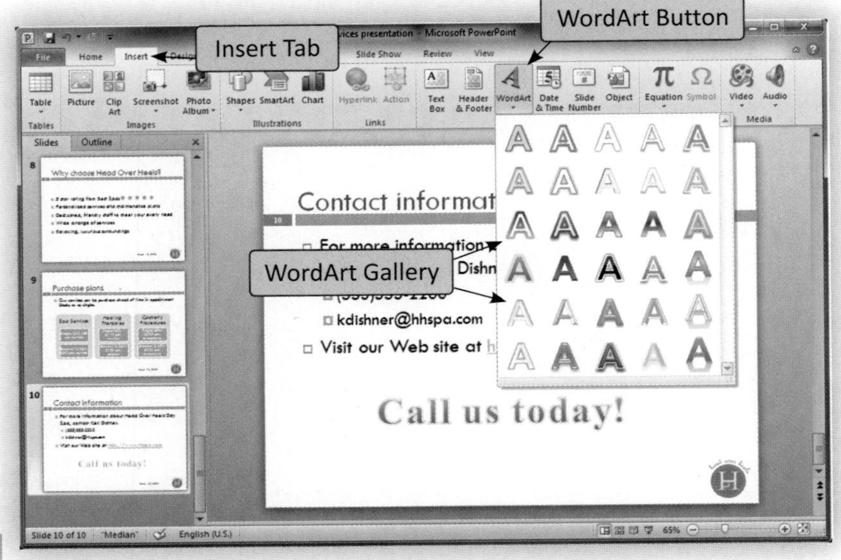

FIGURE PP 2.9

from the perspective of . . .

DENTAL HYGIENIST

In my profession as a dental hygienist, I created a fun presentation showing good oral hygiene habits. Using presentation software, I was able to add clip art, music, and cartoons. My young patients love it.

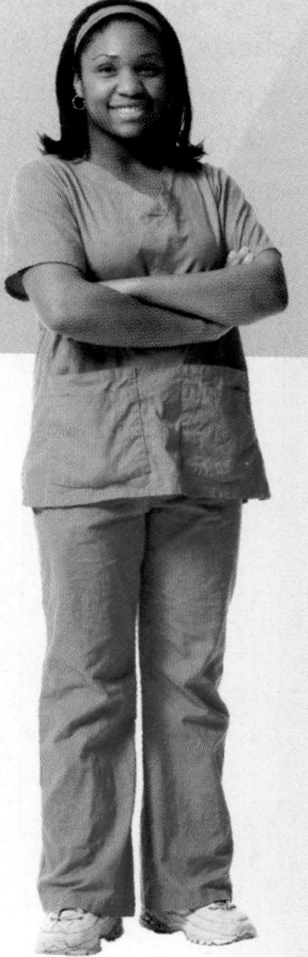

After you have added WordArt to your document, you can modify it just as you would any other text. Use the *Font* box and *Font Size* box on the *Home* tab to change the font or font size of WordArt.

In previous versions of Microsoft Office, WordArt came with a predefined set of graphic styles that could be formatted, but on a very limited basis. Beginning with PowerPoint 2007, WordArt was changed to allow a wide range of stylization. When you add WordArt to a slide, the *Drawing Tools Format* contextual tab appears. In the *WordArt Styles* group you can apply Quick Styles to your WordArt, or modify it further by changing the text fill, text outline, and text effects.

tips & tricks

Be sure to limit the use of WordArt to a small amount of text. Overuse of WordArt can be distracting to your audience.

tell me more

You can change the look of WordArt using the commands in the *Transform* gallery. You can choose to display the text along a path or to distort the letters, creating a warped effect. To transform WordArt, first click the **Format** tab under *Drawing Tools*. In the *WordArt Styles* group, click the **Text Effects** button. Point to **Transform** and select an option from the gallery.

2.5 Understanding the Content Placeholder

A good presentation contains a balance of text, graphics, charts, and other subject matter. The **content placeholder** is a special type of placeholder that gives you a quick way to add a variety of material to your presentations. In PowerPoint, you can add several types of content to your slides through the content placeholder:

	Insert Table
	Insert Chart
	Insert SmartArt Graphic
	Insert Picture from File
	Clip Art
	Insert Media from File

To add content to a slide through the content placeholder:

1. Click the icon of the type of content you want to add.
2. The associated dialog box or task pane appears.
3. Add the content in the same manner as if you accessed the command from the Ribbon.

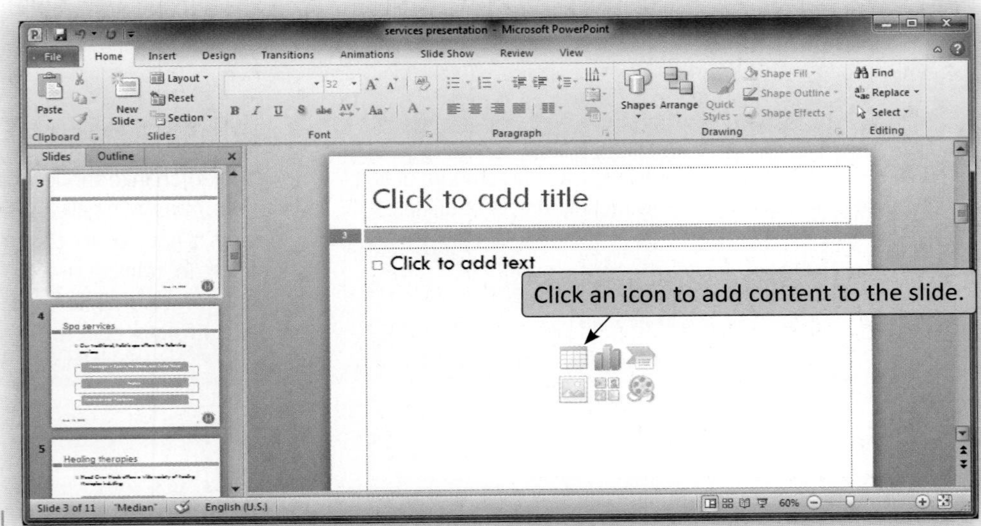

FIGURE PP 2.10

tips & tricks

When you add slides to a presentation, you can choose slides that are preformatted with content placeholders. Some slide layouts contain one content placeholder, but other layouts include multiple content placeholders, allowing you to add more than one content type to a slide.

2.6 Creating Tables in Presentations

When you have a large amount of data on one slide, you will want to organize the data so it is easier for your audience to understand. A **table** helps you organize information for effective display. Tables are organized by rows, which display horizontally, and columns, which display vertically. The intersection of a row and a column is referred to as a **cell**. Tables can be used to display everything from dates in a calendar to sales numbers to product inventory.

To add a table to a slide:

1. Click the **Insert** tab.
2. Click the **Table** button.
3. Select the number of cells you want by moving the cursor across and down the squares.
4. When the description at the top of the menu displays the number of rows and columns you want, click the mouse.
5. The table is inserted into your presentation.

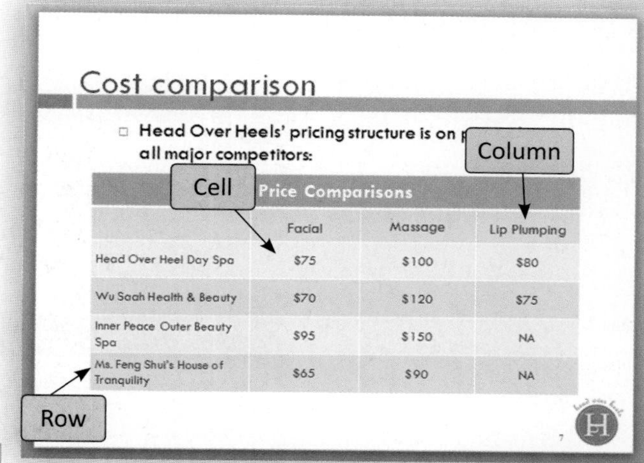

FIGURE PP 2.11

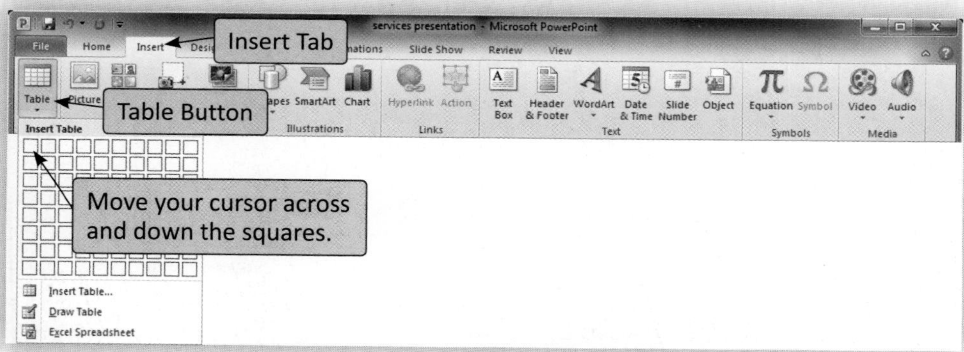

FIGURE PP 2.12

tell me **more**

When you add a table to a slide, the *Table Tools* contextual tabs display. These tabs contain commands for working with tables. From the *Design* tab, you can modify the rows and columns, apply table styles and effects, and change the table's borders. From the *Layout* tab, you can delete and add rows and columns, change the alignment of text in cells, change the size of cells, and change the size of the table.

try **this**

To add a table from the *Insert Table* dialog box:

› Click the **Table** button and select **Insert Table . . .**

› Click the **Insert Table** icon in the content placeholder.

In the *Insert Table* dialog box, enter the number of rows and columns for your table. Click **OK** to add the table to the slide.

2.7 Adding Charts to Slides

When creating a PowerPoint presentation, you will want to display your data in the most visual way possible. One way to display data graphically is by using charts. A **chart** takes the information you have entered in a spreadsheet and converts it to a visual representation. In PowerPoint, you can create a wide variety of charts including bar charts (both stack and 3-D), pie charts, column charts, scatter charts, and line charts.

To add a chart to a presentation:

1. Click the **Insert** tab.
2. In the *Illustrations* group, click the **Insert Chart** button.
3. In the *Insert Chart* dialog box, click a chart type category to display that category in the right pane.
4. Click a chart type in the right pane to select it.
5. Click **OK** to add the chart to the slide.

FIGURE PP 2.13

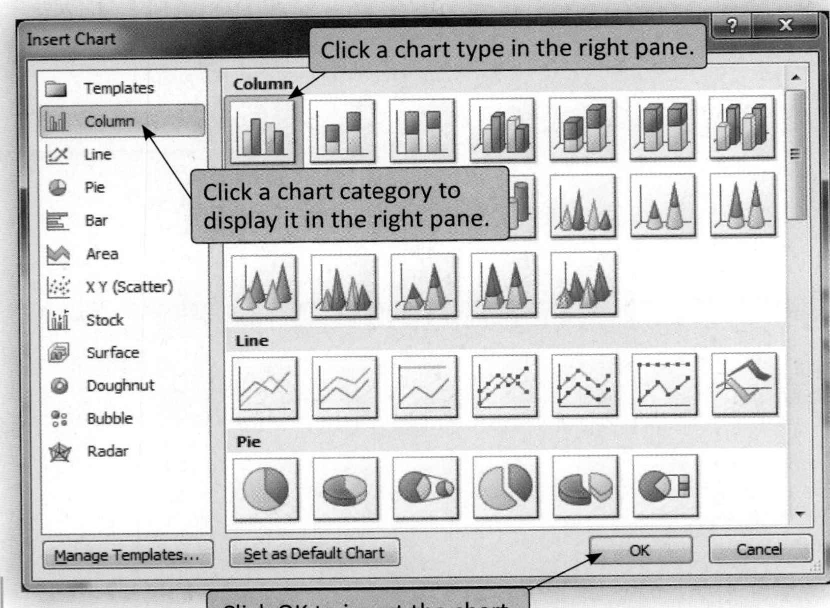

FIGURE PP 2.14

tips & tricks

If you typically use one type of chart for your presentations, you can set that chart type as the default chart type. In the *Insert Chart* dialog box, select the chart type you want to set as the default. Next, click the **Set as Default Chart** button. Now when you open the *Insert Chart* dialog box, that chart type will automatically be selected and you won't need to search through the different chart types to find the one you want to use.

tell me more

When you add a chart to a presentation, PowerPoint will automatically launch Microsoft Excel, with sample data for your chart entered for you. Just replace the sample data with your own data, close Excel, and return to PowerPoint to see your finished chart.

try this

To open the *Insert Chart* dialog box, you can also click the **Insert Chart** icon in the content placeholder on the slide.

2.8 Adding SmartArt to Slides

SmartArt is a way to take your ideas and make them visual. Where presentations used to have plain bulleted and ordered lists, now they can have SmartArt. SmartArt images are visual diagrams containing graphic elements with text boxes in which you enter information. Using SmartArt not only makes your presentation look better but helps convey the information in a more meaningful way.

There are eight categories of SmartArt for you to choose from:

List—Use to list items that ***do not*** need to be in a particular order.

Process—Use to list items that ***do*** need to be in a particular order.

Cycle—Use for a process that repeats over and over again.

Hierarchy—Use to show branching, in either a decision tree or an organization chart.

Relationship—Use to show relationships between items.

Matrix—Use to show how an item fits into the whole.

Pyramid—Use to illustrate how things relate to each other with the largest item being on the bottom and the smallest item being on the top.

Picture—Use to show a series of pictures along with text in the diagram.

To insert a SmartArt diagram:

1. Click the **Insert** tab.
2. In the *Illustrations* group, click the **Insert SmartArt Graphic** button.
3. In the *Choose a SmartArt Graphic* dialog box, click a SmartArt graphic type.
4. Click **OK.**
5. The SmartArt diagram is added to the slide.

FIGURE PP 2.15

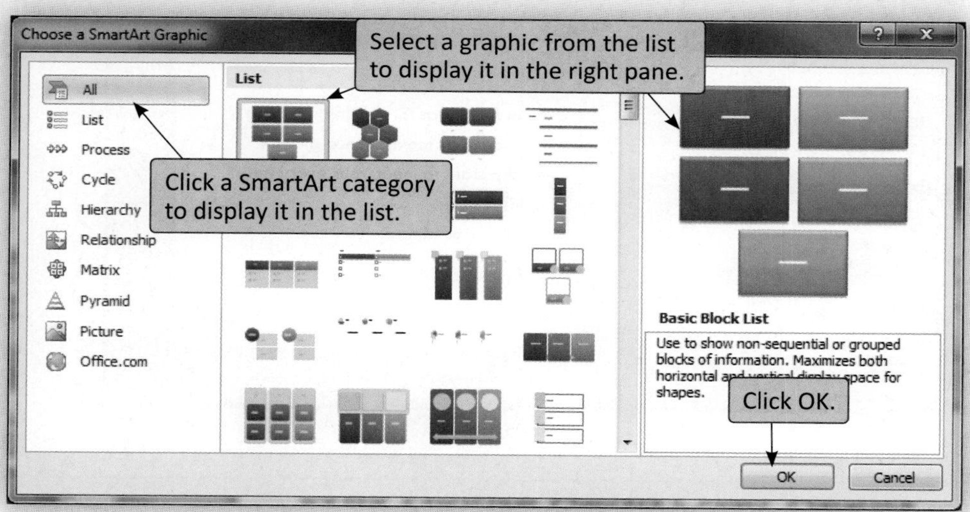

FIGURE PP 2.16

tips & tricks

When choosing a SmartArt diagram, it is important that the diagram type suits your content. In the *Choose a SmartArt Graphic* dialog box, click a SmartArt type to display a preview of the SmartArt. The preview displays not only what the diagram will look like, but also includes a description of the best uses for the diagram type.

tell me more

You can also convert existing text into SmartArt:

1. Select the text you want to convert.
2. On the *Home* tab, in the *Paragraph* group, click the **Convert to SmartArt Graphic** button and select a SmartArt style to apply to the text.

try this

To insert a SmartArt diagram, you can also click the **SmartArt** icon in a content placeholder.

2.9 Adding Shapes to Slides

A **shape** is a drawing object that you can quickly add to your presentation. The PowerPoint *Shapes* gallery gives you access to a number of prebuilt shapes to add to your presentation.

There are a number of types of shapes that you can add to slides, including

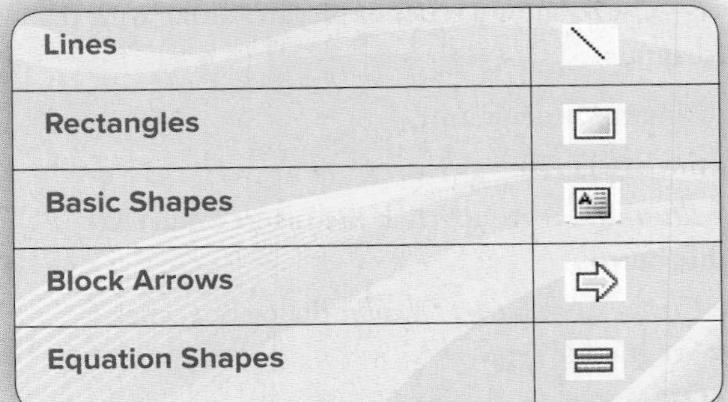

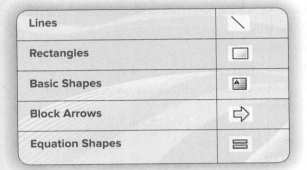

Lines	
Rectangles	
Basic Shapes	
Block Arrows	
Equation Shapes	

Flowcharts	
Stars and Banners	
Callouts	
Action Buttons	

To add a shape to a slide:

1. Click the **Insert** tab.
2. In the *Illustrations* group, click the **Shapes** button and select an option from the *Shapes* gallery.
3. The cursor changes to a crosshair.
4. Click anywhere on the document to add the shape.

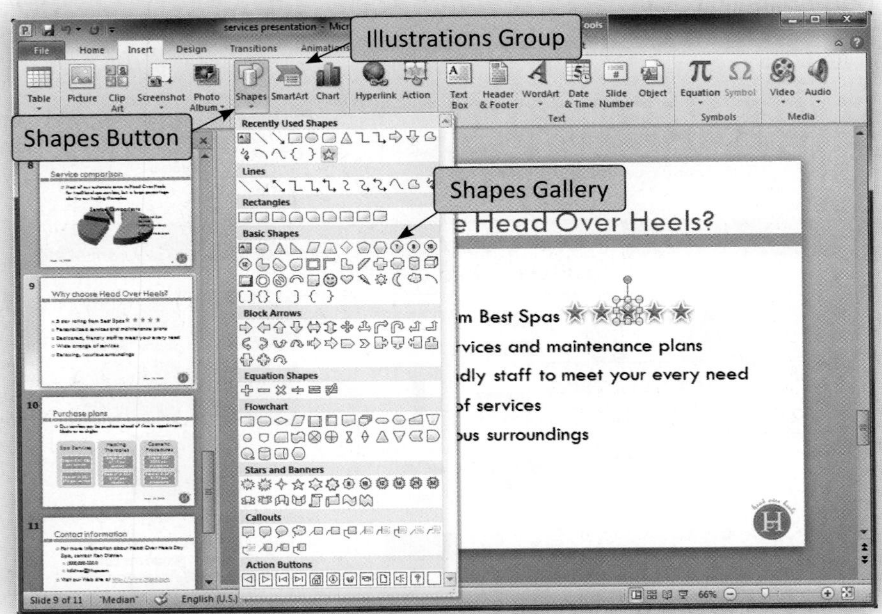

FIGURE PP 2.17

tips & tricks

Once you have added a shape to a document, there are a number of ways you can work with it:

› To resize a graphic: click a resize handle (or) and drag toward the center of the image to make it smaller or away from the center of the image to make it larger.

› To rotate a graphic: click the rotate handle and drag your mouse to the right to rotate the image clockwise or to the left to rotate the image counterclockwise.

› To move a graphic: point to the graphic and when the cursor changes to the move cursor, click and drag the image to the new location.

tell me more

When you insert a shape into a presentation, the *Format* tab under *Drawing Tools* displays. This tab is called a contextual tab because it only displays when a drawing object is the active element. The *Format* tab contains tools to change the look of the shape, such as shape styles, effects, and placement on the page.

try this

To add a shape, you can also click the **Shapes** button in the *Drawing* group on the *Home* tab.

2.10 Adding Text to Shapes

One way to bring attention to text on a slide is to include it as part of a shape. A shape will draw your audience's focus to whatever text you add to it. When you add a shape to a slide, the shape behaves as a text box. All you need to do to add text to the shape is begin typing. You can also go back and add text to shapes that you previously added to a slide.

To add text to an existing shape:

1. Select the shape you want to add text to.
2. Type the text you want to add to the shape.
3. Click outside the shape.

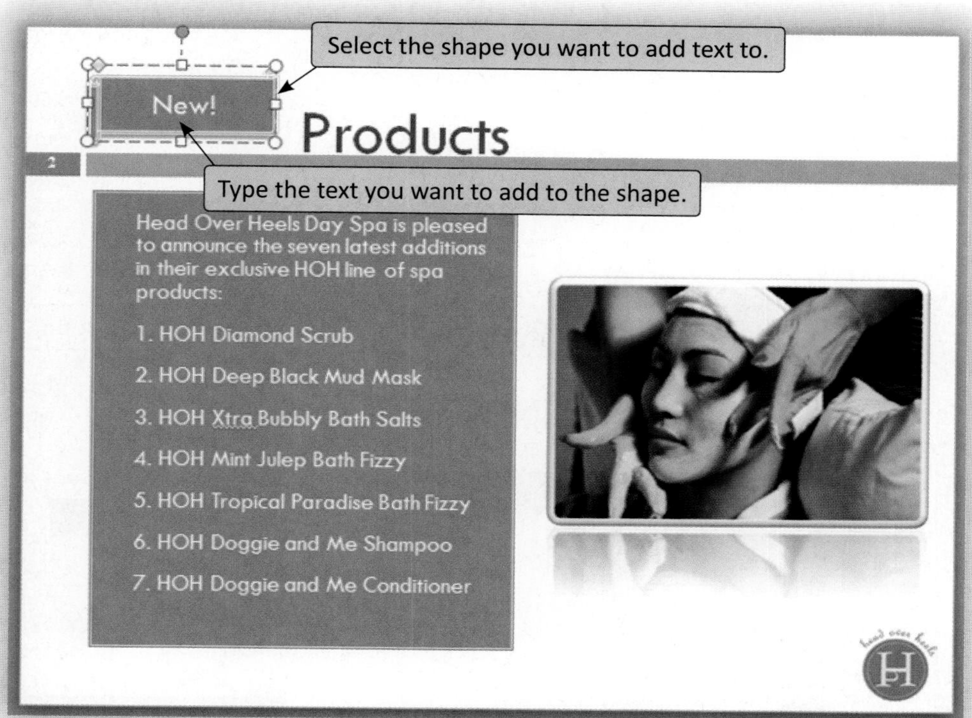

FIGURE PP 2.18

tips & tricks

When adding text to shapes, be sure not to use this design element too often. If every slide in your presentation has a shape with text, your presentation can seem too busy and the emphasis of the text is lost.

tell me more

Just as with any text box, you can add complex formatting to the text you add to a shape. You can apply bold, italic, and other character formatting to the shape's text. You can also change the font size and color. If you really want to make the text stand out, you can apply the WordArt formatting styles to add shadows, 3-D rotation, glows, and reflections to the text.

try this

To add text to a shape, right-click the shape and select **Edit Text.** The cursor appears in the shape ready for you to add your text.

2.11 Adding Clip Art Images to Slides

PowerPoint's **clip art** feature allows you to insert clips into your presentation. These clips include images, photographs, scanned material, animations, sound, and video. By default, PowerPoint inserts these clips as embedded objects, meaning they become part of the presentation (changing the source file will not change them in the new document). The *Clip Art* task pane allows you to search for different kinds of clips from many different sources.

To add clip art to a slide:

1. Click the **Insert** tab.
2. In the *Images* group, click the **Clip Art** button.
3. The *Clip Art* task pane appears.
4. Type a word or phrase describing the clip you want to add in the *Search for:* box.
5. Click the **Go** button.
6. Click the clip you want to add it to the slide.

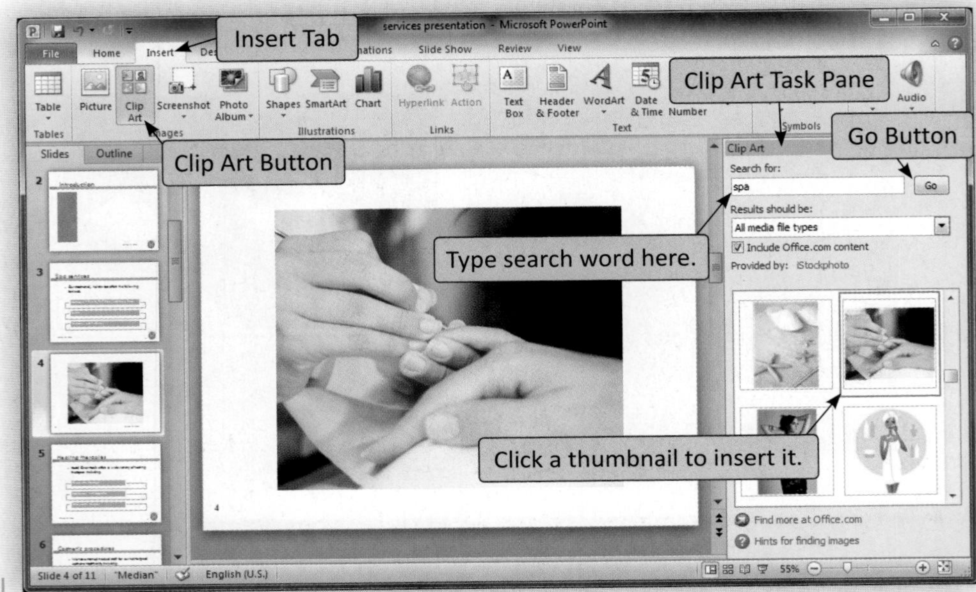

FIGURE PP 2.19

tips & tricks

You can narrow your search by media type, only searching for illustrations or photographs or videos or audio clips. Click the **Results should be:** arrow and click the check box in front of a media type to include or exclude those types of files from your search. Click the **All media types** check box to select and deselect all types at once.

tell me more

Microsoft's Web site for Office content, *Office.com,* contains more clips for you to use in your documents. If you are connected to the Internet, click the **Include Office.com content** check box to include content from the Web site in your search results.

try this

To display the *Clip Art* pane, you can also click the **Clip Art** icon in the content placeholder.

To insert an image from the *Clip Art* task pane, you can also point to the image and click the arrow that appears. A menu of options displays. Click **Insert** on the menu to add the clip to your document.

2.12 Adding Screenshots to Slides

A **screenshot** captures the image on the computer screen (such as an application's interface or a Web page) and creates an image that can then be used just as any other drawing or picture. With previous versions of PowerPoint, you had to use another application to create the screenshot and then insert the image through PowerPoint. In PowerPoint 2010, you can now use the *Insert Screenshot* command to capture and insert screenshots into presentations all from within the PowerPoint interface.

To add a screenshot to a presentation:

1. Click the **Insert** tab.
2. In the *Images* group, click the **Screenshot** button.
3. The *Available Windows* section displays a thumbnail image of each of the currently open windows.
4. Click a thumbnail to add the screenshot of that window to the presentation.

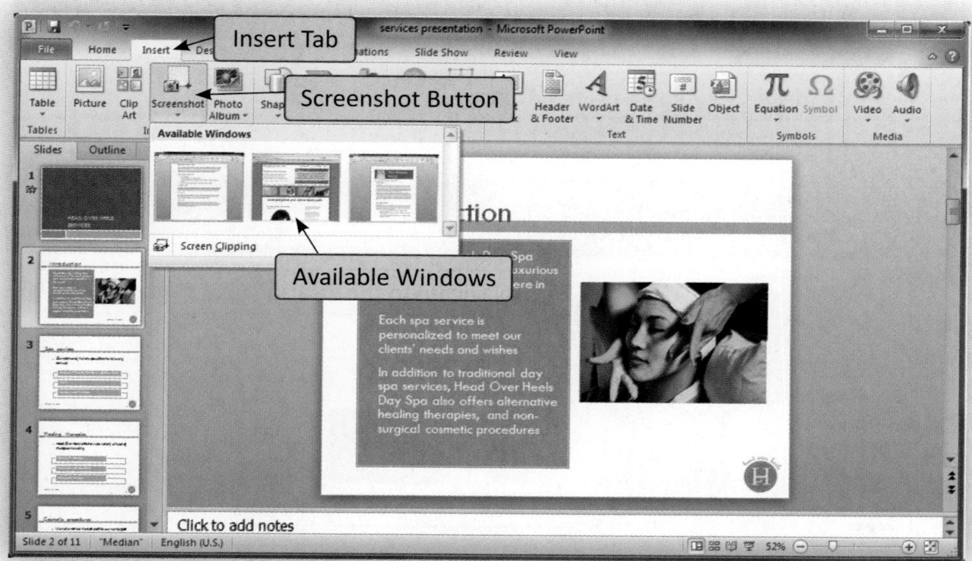

FIGURE PP 2.20

tips & tricks

The *Screenshot* gallery displays thumbnails of all the currently open windows. But what if you want to take a screenshot of only part of a window, or a screenshot of the entire desktop? You can use the *Screen Clipping* tool to take a screenshot of any part of the computer screen.

tell me more

After you have inserted a screenshot into a presentation, the *Format* tab under the *Picture Tools* contextual tab displays. This tab is called a contextual tab because it only displays when a drawing object is the active element. The *Format* tab contains tools to change the look of the image, such as color correction, artistic effects, and picture styles.

2.13 Adding Pictures to Slides

Sometimes adding a photograph or an illustration to a slide will convey a message better than text alone. Use the *Insert Picture* dialog box to insert pictures that you created in another program or downloaded from your smart phone or digital camera into your presentation.

To insert an image from a file:

1. Click the **Insert** tab.
2. In the *Images* group, click the **Insert Picture from File** button.
3. The *Insert Picture* dialog box opens.
4. Navigate to the file location, select the file, and click **Insert.**

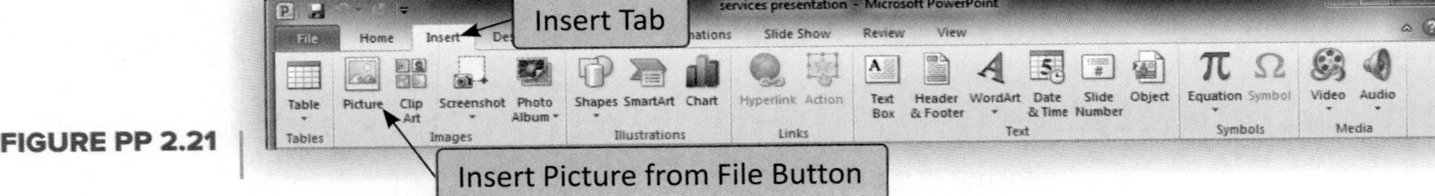

FIGURE PP 2.21

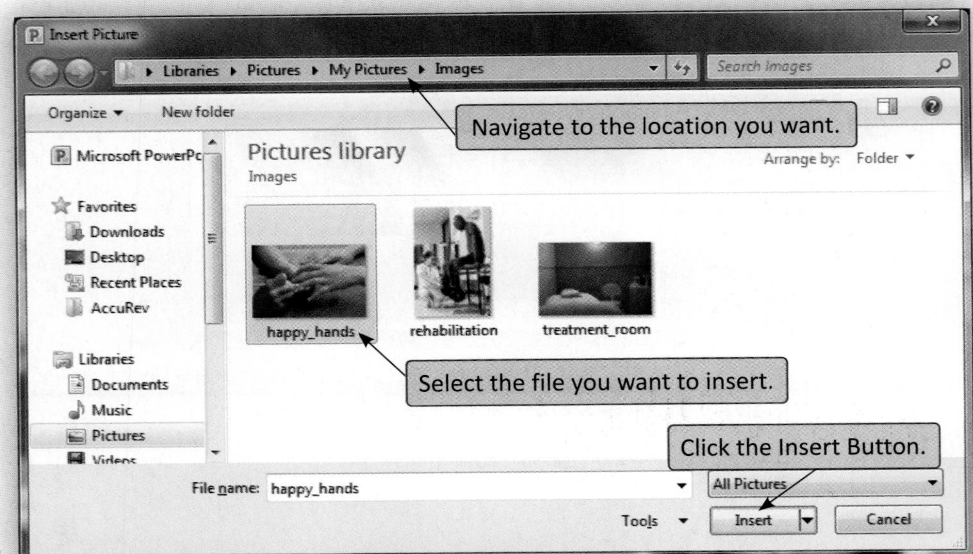

FIGURE PP 2.22

tips & tricks

By default, PowerPoint inserts pictures as embedded objects, meaning they become part of the new document. Changing the source file will not change or affect the newly inserted image.

tell me more

You can create photograph slide shows including captions using PowerPoint's **Photo Album** feature. On the *Insert* tab, in the *Images* group, click the **Photo Album** button. Use the *Photo Album* dialog box to add photos, create captions, and modify the layout. Click the **Create** button to create the photo album as a new presentation.

try this

To open the *Insert Picture* dialog box, you can also click the **Insert Picture from File** icon in the content placeholder.

2.14 Adding Sounds to Slides

Sound files, such as music or sound effects, can enhance your slides, making them more engaging to your audience. You can add sounds to your presentation from the Clip Organizer, from files you have downloaded from the Internet, or from files you've recorded yourself.

To insert a sound:

1. Click the **Insert** tab.
2. In the *Media* group, click the **Insert Audio** button.
3. In the *Insert Audio* dialog box, browse to find the file you want and click the sound file to select it.
4. Click **Insert** to add the sound file into your presentation.

FIGURE PP 2.23

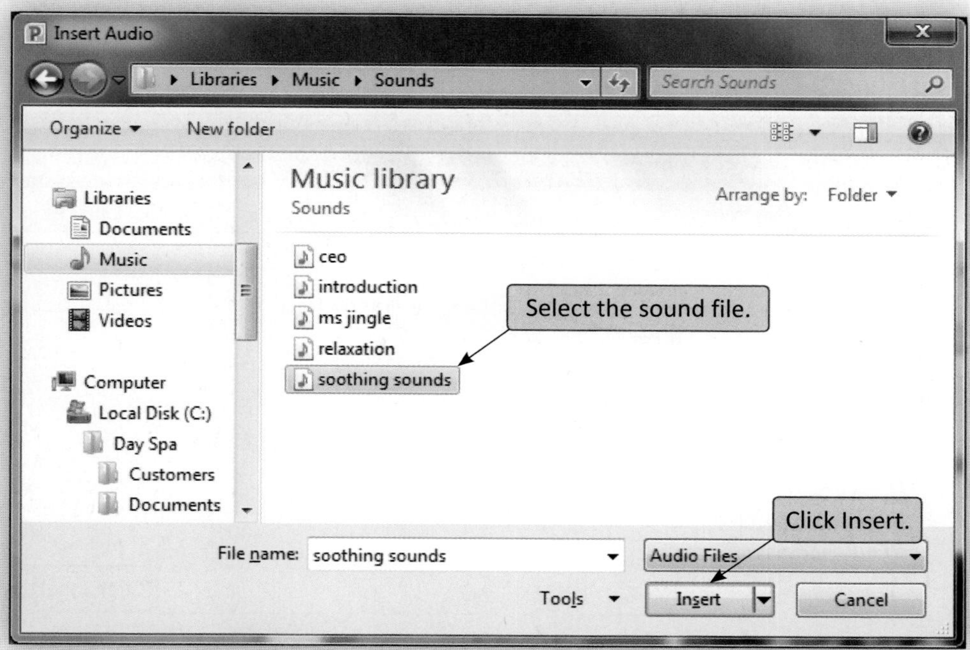

FIGURE PP 2.24

tips & tricks

When you add a sound to a slide, a sound icon is added to the slide. When you run your presentation, this icon will display as part of the slide, and a play bar will display when you rest your pointer over it. To hide the icon, click the **Playback** tab under *Audio Tools*. In the *Audio Options* group, click the **Hide During Show** check box.

try this

To open the *Insert Audio* dialog box, you can also click the arrow next to the **Insert Audio** button and select **Audio from File . . .**

tell me more

When you add a sound to a slide, the *Audio Tools* contextual tabs display. These tabs contain commands for working with sound objects in PowerPoint. The *Format* tab allows you to change the look of the sound icon in the presentation, including applying artistic effects and Quick Styles to the icon. The *Playback* tab provides tools for editing the audio file within PowerPoint. From the *Playback* tab, you can change the slide show volume, fade the audio in and out, loop the sound, and preview the sound.

2.15 Adding Movies to Slides

A **movie** is a multimedia clip that includes moving images and sounds. If you already have digital movies ready to go, you can add them directly into your presentation. If you don't have digital movies, PowerPoint comes with preset sound and animation files to add to your presentation.

To insert a movie:

1. Click the **Insert** tab.
2. In the *Media* group, click the **Insert Video** button.
3. In the *Insert Video* dialog box, browse to find the file you want and click the movie file to select it.
4. Click **Insert** to add the movie file into your presentation.

FIGURE PP 2.25

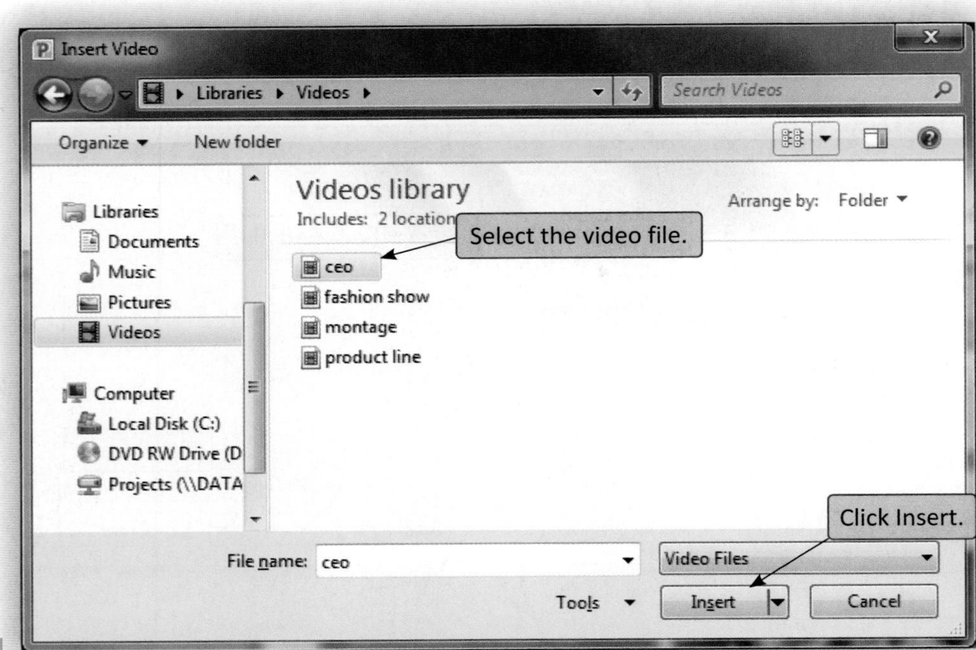

FIGURE 2.26

tell me **more**

Some of the movie formats that PowerPoint supports include

Windows video file format (.avi)
Windows media video format (.wmv)
MPEG format (.mpeg or .mpg)
MP4 video format (.mp4)
QuickTime movie format (.mov)

try **this**

To open the *Insert Movie* dialog box, you can also

- Click the **Insert Video** button arrow and select **Video from File . . .**
- Click the **Insert Media Clip** icon in the content placeholder.

Skill Review 2.1

In this review, you will use the skills learned in Chapter 2 to edit an existing presentation.

1. Open an existing presentation:
   a. Open Microsoft PowerPoint 2010.
   b. On the *File* tab, click **Open.**
   c. In the *Open* dialog box, navigate to the location of your PowerPoint 2010 student files.
   d. Find *Ch2_Review1_HealthFair.pptx* and double-click the file to open it.
   e. On the *File* tab, click the **Save As** option.
   f. Change the file name to ***[your initials]*PP_SkillReview_2-1,** then click **OK.**
2. Work with text within slides including adding text, formatting lists, and using outlines:
   a. Add a text box:
      (1) Click the **Insert** tab.
      (2) In the *Text* group, click the **Text Box** button.
      (3) Click on **Slide 1,** in the top center of the right panel.
      (4) Type: `January 24, 2011`
      (5) Click outside the text box to deselect it.
   b. Add a numbered list to a slide:
      (1) On **Slide 2,** click in the text box placeholder.
      (2) On the *Home* tab, click the arrow next to the **Numbering** button.
      (3) Select the **1., 2., 3.** style from the gallery.
      (4) Type: `Increase Health Awareness`, then press **Enter.**
      (5) Type: `Include Activities for All Ages`, then press **Enter.**
      (6) Type: `Motivate Participants to Make Positive Health Choices.`
   c. Add a bulleted list to a slide:
      (1) On **Slide 3,** click the edge of the **content text box** to select it.
      (2) On the *Home* tab, click the arrow next to the **Bullets** button.
      (3) Select the **Checkmark Bullets** style from the gallery.
   d. Insert slides from a Word outline:
      (1) In the *Slide* pane, click between **Slide 3** and **Slide 4.**
      (2) On the *Home* tab, in the *Slides* group, click the **New Slide** button arrow and select **Slides from Outline . . .**
      (3) In the *Insert Outline* dialog box, select the *Ch2_Review1_Target_Outline.docx* file.
      (4) Click the **Insert** button.
3. Organize text with WordArt, *Content* placeholder, and tables:
   a. Add WordArt to slides:

(1) Click on **Slide 5.**

(2) Click the **Insert** tab.

(3) In the *Text* group, click the **WordArt** button and select the **Fill–Olive Green, Accent 3, Outline–Text 2** Quick Style (last style in the first row) from the gallery.

(4) Replace the text **"Your Text Here"** with `Activities`.

(5) Select the **WordArt box** and drag it until it's centered across the top of the slide.

b. Use the *Content* placeholder to create a table and add a table to a slide:

(1) On **Slide 5,** click the **Insert Table** icon in the *Content* placeholder.

(2) In the *Insert Table* dialog box, use the arrow, to enter **3** columns and **4** rows. Click **OK.**

(3) The table is inserted into your presentation.

(4) On the *Table Tools Design* tab, in the *Table Styles* group, click the **More** button. In the gallery, select **Medium Style 2–Accent 3.**

(5) Add the following text:

ACTIVITY	TOPIC	TARGET AUDIENCE
Glo-Germ Demo	Hand Washing	ALL
You Booze, You Cruise, You Lose	Driver/Passenger	T, A
Bicycle Rodeo	Bicycle/Pedestrian Safety	C, T

4. Add interest through charts, SmartArt, and shapes with text:

a. Add a chart:

(1) Add a new slide.

(2) In the *Title* placeholder, type: `Attendance`

(3) Click in the *Content* placeholder.

(4) Click the **Insert** tab.

(5) In the *Illustrations* group, click the **Chart** button.

(6) In the *Insert Chart* dialog box, click the **Column** category to display that category in the right pane.

(7) Click the **Clustered Cylinder** type in the right pane to select it.

(8) Click **OK** to add the chart to the slide.

(9) Change the text in the *Chart in Microsoft PowerPoint Excel* pop-up from:

	Series 1	Series 2	Series 3
Category 1	4.3	2.4	2
Category 2	2.5	4.4	2
Category 3	3.5	1.8	3
Category 4	4.5	2.8	5

to:

	2010	2011	2012
Children	85	130	145
Teens	70	60	85
Adults	90	95	110

(10) Close the Excel window.

b. Use *SmartArt* objects:

(1) Add a new slide

(2) Delete the *Title* placeholder.

(3) In the *Content* placeholder, click the **Insert SmartArt Graphic** button.

(4) In the *Choose a SmartArt Graphic* dialog box, click the **Relationship** category.

(5) Click the **Funnel** icon in the right pane.

(6) Click **OK.**

(7) The SmartArt diagram has been added to the slide.

(8) In the *Type your text here* pane, type (one per line):

`Activities`

`Demos`

`Giveaways`

`Fun`

(9) Close the *Type your text here* pane.

c. Add shapes with text:

(1) Click above the Funnel SmartArt.

(2) Click the **Insert** tab.

(3) In the *Illustrations* group, click the **Shapes** button.

(4) In the *Stars and Banners* category, click the **Horizontal Scroll** shape in the gallery. Click above the Funnel SmartArt to add the shape to the slide.

(5) Type: `Join Us`.

5. Add graphics including clip art images and pictures:

a. Add *clip art* images:

(1) Click on **Slide 4.**

(2) Click the **Insert** tab.

(3) In the *Images* group, click the **Clip Art** button.

(4) In the *Clip Art* pane, type: `Target` in the *Search for:* box.

(5) Click the **Go** button.

(6) Click the clip of your choice to add it to the slide.

b. Add a picture from a file:

(1) Click on **Slide 6.**

(2) Click the **Insert** tab.

(3) In the *Images* group, click the **Picture** button.

(4) The *Insert Picture* dialog box opens.

(5) Navigate to the data files folder, select the *bikes.jpg* file, and click **Insert.**

(6) Click and drag the *bikes* picture to align below the *bicycle rodeo* text.

6. Add media to slides including sounds and movies:

a. Add sound:

(1) Click on **Slide 7.**

(2) Click the **Insert** tab.

(3) In the *Media* group, click the **Insert Audio** button.

(4) The *Insert Audio* dialog box opens.

(5) Navigate to the data files folder, select the *applause.mp3* sound file.

(6) Click **Insert** to insert the sound file into your presentation.

(7) Click the **Audio Tools Playback** tab.

(8) In the *Audio Options* group, click the **Start** drop-down list, select **Automatically,** and select the **Hide During Show** check box.

b. Insert a movie:

(1) Click on **Slide 6.**

(2) Click the **Insert** tab.

(3) In the *Media* group, click the **Insert Video** button.

(4) The *Insert Video* dialog box opens.

(5) Navigate to the data files folder, select the *activities.wmv* video file.

(6) Click **Insert** to insert the video file into your presentation.

(7) Select the movie clip and drag it below the table.

7. View the presentation:

(1) On the *View* tab, in the *Presentation Views* group, click **Slide Sorter** for an overall understanding of the presentation structure.

(2) On the status bar, click the **Normal** button to add or edit content.

(3) Save the file.

Skill Review 2.2

In this review, you will use the skills learned in Chapter 2 to edit an existing presentation.

1. Open an existing presentation:

a. Open Microsoft PowerPoint 2010.

b. On the *File* tab, click **Open.**

c. In the *Open* dialog box, navigate to the location of your PowerPoint 2010 student files.

d. Find *Ch2_Review2_IdentityTheft.pptx* and double-click the file to open it.

e. On the *File* tab, click the **Save As** option.

f. Change the file name to `[your initials]PP_SkillReview_2-2,` and then click **OK.**

2. Work with text within slides including adding text, formatting lists, and using outlines:

a. Add a text box:

(1) Click the **Insert** tab.

(2) In the *Text* group, click the **Text Box** button.

(3) Click on **Slide 1,** in the center, below the line.

(4) Type: `The Basics`

(5) Click outside the text box to deselect it.

b. Add a numbered list to a slide:

(1) On **Slide 2,** click in the text box placeholder.

(2) On the *Home* tab, click the arrow next to the **Numbering** button.

(3) Select the **1., 2., 3.** style from the gallery.

(4) Type: `Prevent`, then press **Enter.**

(5) Type: `Perceive`, then press **Enter.**

(6) Type: `Protect`, then press **Enter.**

c. Add a bulleted list to a slide:

(1) On **Slide 3,** click the edge of the **content text box** to select it.

(2) On the *Home* tab, click the arrow next to the **Bullets** button.

(3) Select the **Hollow Square** bullet style from the gallery.

d. Insert slides from a Word outline:

(1) In the *Slide* pane, click between **Slide 3** and **Slide 4.**

(2) On the *Home* tab, in the *Slides* group, click the **New Slide** button arrow and select **Slides from Outline . . .**

(3) In the *Insert Outline* dialog box, select the *Ch2_Review2_Target_Outline.docx* file.

(4) Click the **Insert** button.

(5) On the *Target Audience Key* slide (4), select *Title* placeholder and the *Content* placeholder.

(6) On the *Home* tab, in the *Font* group, click the **Font Color** drop-down arrow and select **White, Text 1.**

3. Organize text with WordArt, *Content* placeholder, and tables:

a. Add *WordArt* to slides:

(1) Click on **Slide 5.**

(2) Click the **Insert** tab.

(3) In the *Text* group, click the **WordArt** button and select the **Fill–White, Drop Shadow** (third style in the first row) from the gallery.

(4) Replace the text **"Your Text Here"** with `The Basics`

(5) Select the **WordArt box** and drag it until it's centered across the top of the slide.

b. Use the *Content* placeholder to create a table and add a table to a slide:

(1) On **Slide 5,** click the **Insert Table** icon in the *Content* placeholder.

(2) In the *Insert Table* dialog box, use the drop-down arrows to select **3** columns and **4** rows. Click **OK.**

(3) The table is inserted into your presentation.

(4) On the *Table Tools Design* tab, in the *Table Styles* group, click the **More** button. In the gallery, select **Medium Style 2.**

(5) Add the following text:

PREVENT	PERCEIVE	PULL THROUGH
Protect your Social Security number	Learn the signs of identity theft	Take the steps to recover
Be careful when using the Internet	Monitor your information	Freeze credit and set Fraud Alert
Treat your mail and trash carefully	Obtain and review free credit report	Prove you are a victim

(6) Select the last three rows.

(7) On the *Home* tab, in the *Font* group, click the **Font Color** arrow, and select **Black, Background 1.**

4. Add interest through charts, SmartArt, and shapes with text:

a. Add a chart:

(1) Add a new slide after **Slide 5.**

(2) In the *Title* placeholder, type: `FTC Top 10 Consumer Fraud Complaint Categories`

(3) Click in the *Content* placeholder.

(4) Click the **Insert** tab.

(5) In the *Illustrations* group, click the **Chart** button.

(6) In the *Insert Chart* dialog box, click the **Pie** category to display that category in the right pane.

(7) Click the **Pie in 3-D** type in the right pane to select it.

(8) Click **OK** to add the chart to the slide.

(9) Change the text in the *Chart in Microsoft PowerPoint Excel* pop-up from:

	Sales
1st Qtr	8.2
2nd Qtr	3.2
3rd Qtr	1.4
4th Qtr	1.2

to:

	%
Identity Theft	37
Internet Auctions	12
Foreign Money Offers	8
Shop-at-Home/Catalog Sales	7
Prizes/Sweepstakes and Lotteries	7
Internet Services and Computer Complaints	5
Business Opportunities and Work-at-Home Plans	2
Advance-Fee Loans and Credit Protection	2
Telephone Services	2
Other	17

(10) When you are finished, close the Excel window.

(11) Click the *Legend* text box in the chart to select it.

(12) On the *Home* tab, in the *Font* group, change the font size to **10.5.**

(13) Select the *Chart Title* text box and press **Delete.**

(14) Right-click the chart to display the shortcut menu; then select **Add Data Labels.**

The McGraw-Hill Companies

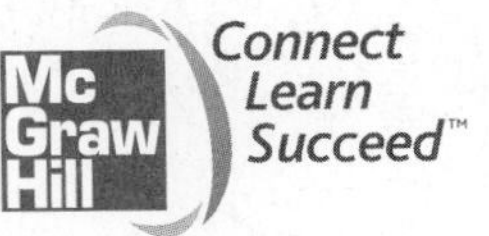

MICROSOFT® OFFICE 2010: A SKILLS APPROACH
Published by McGraw-Hill, a business unit of The McGraw-Hill Companies, Inc., 1221 Avenue of the Americas, New York, NY, 10020.

Some ancillaries, including electronic and print components, may not be available to customers outside the United States.

This book is printed on acid-free paper.

3 4 5 6 7 8 9 0 RMN/RMN 1 0 9 8 7 6 5 4 3 2

ISBN 978-0-07-351647-9
MHID 0-07-351647-3

Vice president/Editor in chief: *Elizabeth Haefele*
Vice president/Director of marketing: *Alice Harra*
Publisher: *Scott Davidson*
Sponsoring editor: *Paul Altier*
Outside development house: *Barrett Lyon*
Developmental editor: *Alan Palmer*
Editorial coordinator: *Allison McCabe*
Marketing manager: *Tiffany Wendt*
Lead digital product manager: *Damian Moshak*
Digital developmental editor: *Kevin White*
Director, Editing/Design/Production: *Jess Ann Kosic*
Project manager: *Marlena Pechan*
Buyer II: *Laura M. Fuller*
Senior designer: *Srdjan Savanovic*
Senior photo research coordinator: *Keri Johnson*
Digital production coordinator: *Brent dela Cruz*
Media project manager: *Cathy L. Tepper*
Cover design: *Maureen McCutcheon*
Interior design: *Maureen McCutcheon*
Typeface: *10.5/13 Garamond Premier Pro*
Compositor: *Laserwords Private Limited*
Printer: *R. R. Donnelley*
Cover credit: © *Plainview, iStockphoto; back cover:* © *Okea, iStockphoto*
Credits: The credits section for this book begins on page C-1 and is considered an extension of the copyright page.

Library of Congress Cataloging-in-Publication Data

Manning, Cheryl.
Microsoft Office 2010 : a skills approach / Cheri Manning, Catherine Manning Swinson.
p. cm.—(Connect, learn, succeed)
Includes index.
ISBN-13: 978-0-07-351647-9 (alk. paper)
ISBN-10: 0-07-351647-3 (alk. paper)
1. Microsoft Office. I. Swinson, Catherine Manning. II. Title.
HF5548.4.M525M349 2012
005.5—dc22
2010047628

The Internet addresses listed in the text were accurate at the time of publication. The inclusion of a Web site does not ›dicate an endorsement by the authors or McGraw-Hill, and McGraw-Hill does not guarantee the accuracy of the ›ormation presented at these sites.

com

soft® Office 2010

LS APPROACH

Cheri Manning

Catherine Manning Swinson

Triad Interactive, Inc.

b. Use *SmartArt* objects:

(1) Add a new slide.

(2) Delete the *Title* placeholder.

(3) In the *Content* placeholder, click the **Insert SmartArt Graphic** button.

(4) In the *Choose a SmartArt Graphic* dialog box, click the **Relationship** category.

(5) Click the **Basic Venn** icon in the right pane.

(6) Click **OK.**

(7) The SmartArt diagram has been added to the slide.

(8) In the *Type your text here* pane, type (one per line):

```
Prevent
Perceive
Pull Through
```

(9) Close the *Type your text here* pane.

c. Add shapes with text:

(1) Click the **Insert** tab.

(2) In the *Illustrations* group, click the **Shapes** button.

(3) In the *Stars and Banners* category, click the **Horizontal Scroll** shape in the gallery to add it to the slide.

(4) Type: `Remember`

5. Add graphics including clip art images and pictures:

a. Add *clip art* images:

(1) On **Slide 4,** click to the right of the bulleted list.

(2) Click the **Insert** tab.

(3) In the *Images* group, click the **Clip Art** button.

(4) In the *Clip Art* pane, type: `Target` in the *Search for:* box.

(5) Click the **Go** button.

(6) Click the clip of your choice to add it to the slide.

b. Add a *screenshot*:

(1) Open your Internet browser and go to http://www.ftc.gov/bcp/edu/microsites/idtheft/consumers/filing-a-report.html

(2) Maximize your *[your initials]PP_SkillReview_2-2.pptx* file.

(3) Select the **Filing a Complaint** slide.

(4) Click the **Insert** tab.

(5) In the *Images* group, click the **Screenshot** drop-down arrow and select the browser window with the FTC site.

(6) A screenshot of the Web page will display on your slide.

(7) If necessary, select the *screenshot* and resize and center it under the table.

c. Add a picture from a file:

(1) Click the **Objectives** slide.

(2) Click the **Insert** tab.

(3) In the *Images* group, click the **Picture** button.

(4) The *Insert Picture* dialog box opens.

(5) Navigate to the data files folder, select the *thief.png* file, and click **Insert.**

(6) Click and drag the *thief* picture to center it on the page.

6. View the presentation:
   a. On the *View* tab, in the *Presentation Views* group, click **Slide Sorter** for an overall understanding of the presentation structure.
   b. On the status bar, click the **Normal** button to add or edit content.
   c. Save the file.

challenge yourself **1**

In this challenge, you will use the skills learned in Chapter 2 to create a team orientation presentation.

1. Create a new presentation:
   a. Open Microsoft PowerPoint 2010.
   b. Create a new presentation using the *Perspective* theme.
   c. Save the file as ***[your initials]*****PP_Challenge_2-3.**
   d. Use the **Normal view** button to add or edit content.
2. Work with text within slides including adding text, formatting lists, and using outlines:
   a. Add text:
      (1) Type the title: `Team Orientation`
      (2) Add the subtitle: `The Basics`
   b. Add lists to slides:
      (1) Add a slide titled `Welcome & Introduction`
      (2) Create a *numbered* list including the following items:
         `1.Welcome`
         `2.Team objectives`
         `3.Member introduction`
      (3) Add a slide entitled `Topics`
      (4) Create a *bulleted* list using the **Checkmark Bullets** style from the gallery. Include the following items:
         - `Professional attitude`
         - `Quality work`
         - `Active participant`
         - `Provide constructive feedback`
   c. Insert slides from a Word outline:
      (1) Add a new *Slide from Outline*, using the *Ch2_Chall1_Outline.docx* file.
      (2) Change the *Title* text color to **Orange, Text 2** and the bullet text to **White, Text 1.**
3. Organize text with WordArt, *Content* placeholder, and tables:
   a. Add a new slide using the *Title and Content* layout.
   b. Replace the title with WordArt with the text: `SMART`. Use the style **Fill–White Drop Shadow** (third style in the first row) from the gallery.
   c. Select the **WordArt** box and drag it until it's centered across the top of the slide.
   d. Add a table using the *Content* placeholder with **2** columns and **6** rows with the **Medium Style, Accent 2.**

e. Add the following text:

GUIDELINE	TO BE EFFECTIVE
Specific	Is it clear?
Measurable	Can it be measured effectively?
Attainable	Can it be completed?
Relevant	Does it apply here?
Time Bound	When will it be completed?

4. Add interest through charts, SmartArt, and shapes with text:

a. Add a chart:

(1) Add a new slide titled `Time Commitment`

(2) Add a chart using the **Pie in 3-D** type.

(3) Include the following information:

`Preparation    30%`

`Communication 40%`

`Reporting      20%`

`Publishing     10%`

(4) Add data labels to the chart.

b. Use SmartArt objects:

(1) Add a new slide using the **Blank** layout.

(2) Insert a **SmartArt** graphic using the **Basic Cycle.**

(3) In the *Type your text here* pane, type (one per line), then resize the graphic if necessary.

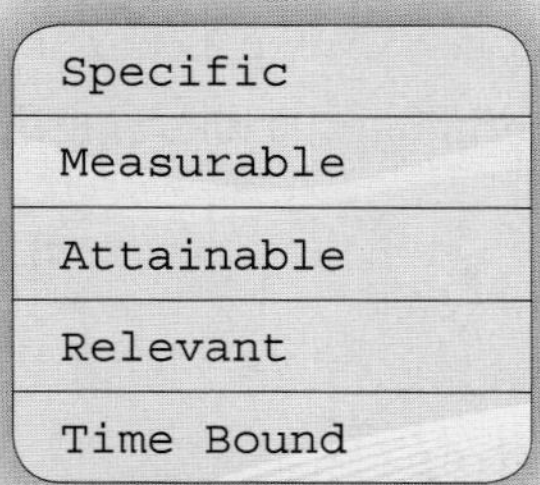

(4) Add a **Horizontal Scroll** shape above the SmartArt graphic with the text `SMART Review`

5. Add graphics including *clip art* images, screenshots, and pictures:

a. On **Slide 4,** add a **Target** clip art to the right of the bulleted list.

b. Add a new slide at the end of the presentation. Use the *Title and Content* layout.

c. Title the slide: `Teamwork Activities`

d. Open your Internet browser and go to: http://www.teampedia.net/

e. Use the **Screenshot** command to add a screenshot of the Teampedia site to the *Content* placeholder.

f. Click **Slide 5.**

g. Navigate to the data files folder and insert the *whistle.jpg* picture.

h. Click and drag the *whistle* picture to align it to the left of the *Title* text on the page, resizing if needed.

6. Add media to slides including sounds and movies:

a. Click the **Time Commitment** slide.

b. Navigate to the data files folder and insert the *time.mp3* audio file. Adjust options to hide it and run automatically.

c. Click the **Topics** slide.

d. Navigate to the data files folder and insert the *team.wmv* video file.

e. Select the video and drag it to center it after the bullets.

f. View the presentation, edit as needed, and then save the file.

challenge yourself **2**

You are a member of group that is tasked with planning a class reunion. In this challenge, you will use the skills learned in Chapter 2 to create a presentation for your group members.

1. Create a new presentation:

a. Open Microsoft PowerPoint 2010.

b. Create a new presentation using the *Oriel* theme.

c. Save the file as ***[your initials]*****PP_Challenge_2-4.**

d. Use the **Normal view** button to add or edit content.

2. Work with text within slides including adding text, formatting lists, and using outlines:

a. Add text:

(1) Type the title: `Class Reunion: 10th`

(2) Add the *name of your high school* as the subtitle.

b. Add lists to slides:

(1) Add a slide titled `Welcome & Introduction`

(2) Create a *numbered* list including the following items:

```
1.Welcome
2.Planning committee
3.Initial meeting objectives
4.Theme discussion
5.Task assignment
6.Action plan
```

(3) Add a slide titled `Planning Committee`

(4) Create a *bulleted* list using the **Hollow Square Bullets** style from the gallery. Include the following items:

- `Jane March`
- `Rob Walker`
- `John Patterson`
- `Michelle Johnson`
- `Mateo Ruiz`

c. Insert slides from a Word outline:

(1) Add a new *Slide from Outline*, using the *Ch2_Chall2_Obj_Outline.docx* file.

(2) Select the **Music, Food,** and **Decorations** bullets and indent them.

3. Organize text with WordArt, *Content* placeholder, and tables:

a. Add a new slide using the *Title and Content* layout.

b. Replace the title with a WordArt centered across the top of the slide with the text: `Initial Tasks`. Use the style **Fill–Orange, Transparent Accent 1, Outline–Accent1** from the gallery. It is the first style in the second row of the gallery.

c. Add a table using the *Content* placeholder with **3** columns and **10** rows with the **Medium Style, Accent 1.**

d. Add the following text:

TASK	ASSIGNED	DUE
Select date	All	Today
Select theme	All	Today
Location options	Jon & Sally	2nd Mtg
Menu options	Jon & Sally	2nd Mtg
Music options	Nikki & Preston	2nd Mtg
Decoration options	Stacy	2nd Mtg
Class list	Chance	2nd Mtg
Budget final	Alyssa	3rd Mtg
Invitations	Lalia	3rd Mtg

4. Add interest through charts, SmartArt, and shapes with text:

a. Add a chart:

(1) Add a new slide entitled `Budget`

(2) Add a *chart* using the **Pie in 3-D** type.

(3) Include the following information:

Venue	**30%**
Decorations	**20%**
Music	**10%**
Food	**30%**
Invitations	**10%**

(4) Add data labels to the chart.

b. Use *SmartArt* objects:

(1) Add a new slide using the **Blank** layout.

(2) Insert a **SmartArt** graphic using the **Radial Venn.** It is located in the *Relationship* category in the *Choose a SmartArt Graphic* dialog box.

(3) Type the following; then resize the graphic if necessary.

Theme (*center text line*)
Decorations
Music
Food
Invitations

(4) Add a **Horizontal Scroll** shape above the SmartArt graphic with the text `Theme Based`

5. Add graphics including clip art images, screenshots, and pictures:

a. On **Slide 4,** add a **Target** clip art to the right of the bulleted list.

b. Add a new slide at the end of the presentation. Use the *Title and Content* layout.

c. Title the slide: `Our School`

d. Open your Internet browser and go to your high school's Web page.

e. Use the **Screenshot** command to add a screenshot of the Web page to the *Content* placeholder.

f. Click the **Initial Tasks** slide.

g. Navigate to the data files folder and insert the *whistle.jpg* picture.

h. Click and drag the *whistle* picture to align it left of the *Title* text on the page, resizing if needed.

6. Add media to slides including sounds and movies.

a. Click the **Theme Based** slide.

b. Navigate to the data files folder and insert the *theme.mp3* audio file. Adjust options to hide it and run automatically.

c. Click the **Planning Committee** slide.

d. Navigate to the data files folder and insert the *reunion.wmv* video file.

e. Select the video and drag it to center it after the bullets.

7. View the presentation, edit as needed, and then save the file.

on your own

You have decided to begin an online business and need to create a preliminary business plan to share with prospective lenders

1. Create a PowerPoint business plan that includes the following information:

a. Prospective company name.

b. Contact info (for this assignment you can include only your name and e-mail address).

c. List of three objectives for your business (numbered list).

d. Key employee positions (bulleted list).

e. Use a Word outline to create a list of products (include the file with your PowerPoint file).

f. Include a table with at least three items or services and their prices.

g. Add a summary budget chart.

h. Use SmartArt to create a diagram to illustrate relationships among your services/ products.

i. Add a clip art image.

j. Include a screenshot of a Web page relating to your products/services.

k. Add a sound clip and a video clip to your presentation.

l. Save the file as ***[your initials]*PP_OnYourOwn_2-5.**

fix it

You have been assigned the task of fixing an existing presentation based on the skills learned in Chapter 2.

1. Using Microsoft Office, open *Ch2_Fixit_Careers.pptx*.
2. Save the file as ***[your initials]*PP_FixIt_2-6.**
3. Use a text box to add your name and the date to the *Title* slide.
4. Change the text to bullets on the *Desired Skills* slide.
5. Add a slide between slides 3 and 4. Include a table with two columns having the titles below and a list of at least three items under each:
   - **a. My Interests**
   - **b. Possible Careers**
6. Add a new slide with a chart with each of the careers you listed and the possibility percentage that you will select that career. (For example, teaching, 60%; computer repair, 10%; Web design, 30%). Add data labels and a slide title.
7. Add a SmartArt to illustrate the relationship(s) between your careers.
8. Add the *No Symbol* shape over the text *If it's not broken, don't fix it* on the last slide.
9. Add graphics including clip art images, screenshots, and pictures.
10. Add media to slides including sounds and movies.
11. Save the file.

chapter 3

Formatting Presentations

In this chapter, you will learn the following skills:

- Change themes and theme effects
- Apply Quick Styles to text boxes, tables, and shapes, and adjust the layout of SmartArt
- Show the ruler and gridlines, and change placeholder size
- Edit image alignment, grouping, rotating, and sizing
- Apply animation effects

Skill 3.1 Changing the Presentation Theme
Skill 3.2 Changing the Color Theme
Skill 3.3 Changing the Theme Effects
Skill 3.4 Changing the Slide Background
Skill 3.5 Changing Fonts
Skill 3.6 Changing the Look of Text Boxes
Skill 3.7 Applying Quick Styles to Text Boxes
Skill 3.8 Applying Quick Styles to Tables
Skill 3.9 Using the Shape Styles Gallery
Skill 3.10 Changing the Layout of SmartArt
Skill 3.11 Using the Picture Styles Gallery
Skill 3.12 Showing the Ruler and Gridlines
Skill 3.13 Changing the Size of Images
Skill 3.14 Changing the Size of a Placeholder
Skill 3.15 Aligning, Grouping, and Rotating Images
Skill 3.16 Applying Animation Effects
Skill 3.17 Modifying Animations

skills

introduction

In this chapter you learn the skills necessary to edit and format a PowerPoint 2010 presentation using themes, Quick Styles, text boxes, and animation effects. By incorporating pictures, animation, color, and backgrounds, you can create a very professional-looking presentation.

3.1 Changing the Presentation Theme

A **theme** is a group of formatting options that you apply to a presentation. Themes include font, color, and effect styles that are applied to specific elements of a presentation. In PowerPoint, themes also include background styles. When you apply a theme, all the slides in the presentation are affected.

To apply a theme to the presentation:

1. Click the **Design** tab.
2. In the *Themes* group, click the **More** button.
3. Select an option in the *Themes* gallery.
4. All the slides in your presentation now use the new theme.

FIGURE PP 3.1

tell me **more**

Although themes are designed to make it easy for you to create a cohesive look for presentations, you may find that the themes available in the Microsoft Office applications are close to what you want but not quite right for your presentation. To create your own version of a theme, all you need to do is change the theme's color, font, or effect styles. When you modify an existing theme, you can save it as your own custom theme. The file will be saved with the .thmx file extension. The theme will be saved in the *Document Themes* folder and will be available from Excel, Word, and Outlook as well as PowerPoint.

try **this**

To apply a theme, you can also click a theme on the Ribbon without opening the gallery.

You can also change the theme of a presentation from Slide Master view. On the *Slide Master* tab, in the *Edit Themes* group, click the **Themes** button, and select a theme.

3.2 Changing the Color Theme

When creating a presentation, it is important to choose colors that work well together. Poor color choices can detract from the message you are trying to convey in your presentation. If the colors you choose are too muted, your presentation may seem dull. If the colors you choose are too harsh and clash with each other, your presentation may seem busy and unfocused.

PowerPoint 2010 includes a number of color themes for you to choose from. A **color theme** is a set of colors that complement each other and are designed to work well in a presentation. A color theme will change the color of backgrounds, placeholders, text, tables, charts, SmartArt, and drawing objects in a presentation. When you apply a theme to a presentation, this includes a color theme, which includes default theme colors for presentation elements. You can change the color theme without affecting the other components of the theme.

To apply a color theme to a slide master:

1. Click the **Design** tab.
2. In the *Themes* group, click the **Theme Colors** button.
3. Select a color theme from the list that appears.

FIGURE PP 3.2

tips & tricks

You can create a new color theme, selecting your own colors for text and accents. To create a custom color theme, click the **Theme Colors** button and select **Create New Theme Colors . . .** Change the theme colors and give the theme a name.

tell me more

When you change the color theme for a presentation, the color options for presentation elements will change. The theme colors will appear in the *Font Color* menu, as well as in the *Table Styles* and *Shape Styles* galleries. Choose your colors from these preset theme colors to ensure your document has a consistent color design.

try this

You can also change the color theme of a presentation from Slide Master view. On the *Slide Master* tab, in the *Edit Themes* group, click the **Theme Colors** button, and select a color theme.

3.3 Changing the Theme Effects

In PowerPoint 2010, you can add graphic effects to drawing objects and text. These graphic effects give you the ability to create dynamic images without the help of a professional designer. You can create sophisticated fills for objects and control the shape outline for objects, including the color, weight, and line style.

Using these new effects can be overwhelming at first. How do you know which effects go well together? A part of a presentation's theme is the **theme effects**. The theme effects consist of line and fill effects that you apply to objects on your slides, giving you a starting point to create sophisticated images in your presentations.

To apply theme effects to the presentation:

1. Click the **Design** tab.
2. In the *Themes* group, click the **Theme Effects** button.
3. Select a theme effect from the gallery that appears.

FIGURE PP 3.3

tell me **more**

Theme effects are the same in the following Microsoft Office 2010 applications: Word, Excel, PowerPoint, and Outlook. These applications include 40 prebuilt theme effect combinations for you to choose from. Unlike theme fonts and theme colors, you cannot create your own theme effects in the Microsoft Office 2010 applications.

try **this**

You can also change the theme effects of a presentation from Slide Master view. On the *Slide Master* tab, in the *Edit Themes* group, click the **Theme Effects** button, and select an option.

3.4 Changing the Slide Background

A **background** is the graphic element that fills a slide. Backgrounds can be solid colors, textures, or even images. Each theme in PowerPoint provides a variety of background styles from which to choose. Background styles acquire their colors from the presentation's theme and range in color from light to dark. The background styles for themes also include different background textures, depending on the theme you choose. When you apply a theme to a presentation the default background styles will be applied to your slides. To change just the background of all the slides in a presentation (and not other theme elements such as fonts), you should change the background style for the presentation.

To change the background style:

1. Click the **Design** tab.
2. In the *Background* group, click the **Background Styles** button.
3. Select an option from the *Background Styles* gallery.

FIGURE PP 3.4

tips & tricks

You can create your own custom background style from the *Format Background* dialog box. To open the *Format Background* dialog box, select the **Format Background . . .** command at the bottom of the *Background Styles* gallery. Here you can change the fill to a solid fill, gradient fill, or picture fill. Use the tools in the dialog box to further customize the background, including colors and the amount of transparency.

tell me more

Since the background is tied to the presentation's theme, when you change the theme of a presentation, not only does the background of the slides change, but the *Background Styles* gallery also changes to reflect the new theme colors.

try this

You can also change the background for a presentation from Slide Master view. On the *Slide Master* tab, in the *Background* group, click the **Background Styles** button, and select a background.

3.5 Changing Fonts

A **font**, or typeface, refers to a set of characters of a certain design. The font is the shape of the character or number as it appears on-screen. You can change the look of text by changing the font, the font size, or the font color.

To change the font:

1. Select the text to be changed.
2. On the *Home* tab, in the *Font* group, click the arrow next to the **Font** box.
3. Scroll the list to find the new font.
4. Click the font name.

To change the size of the text:

1. Select the text to be changed.
2. On the *Home* tab, in the *Font* group, click the arrow next to the **Font Size** box.
3. Scroll the list to find the new font size.
4. Click the size you want.

To change the color of the text:

1. Select the text to be changed.
2. On the *Home* tab, in the *Font* group, click the arrow next to the **Font Color** button.
3. Click the color you want.

FIGURE PP 3.5

tips & tricks

Using different fonts, font sizes, and font colors can enhance your presentation, giving it a distinctive appearance. However, when you create a presentation it is best to limit the number of fonts, font sizes, and font colors you use. Using multiple fonts and effects in one presentation can give it a disorganized and unprofessional appearance.

tell me more

PowerPoint offers many fonts. Serif fonts, such as Cambria and Times New Roman, have an embellishment at the end of each stroke. They are used for notes pages, printed pages, and body text. Sans serif fonts, such as Calibri and Arial, do not have an embellishment at the end of each stroke. They are typically used for titles and subtitles in on-screen presentations since they have a clean look.

try this

To change the font, right-click the text, click the arrow next to the **Font** box on the Mini toolbar, and select an option.

To change the font size, right-click the text, click the arrow next to the **Font Size** box on the Mini toolbar, and select an option.

To change the font color, right-click the text, click the arrow next to the **Font Color** button on the Mini toolbar, and select an option.

3.6 Changing the Look of Text Boxes

Text boxes are content containers that allow you to place text anywhere on a slide. When you first add a text box to a slide, the text box uses the default font from the theme and has no background or border. If you want the text in a text box to stand out on a slide, you can customize the look of the text box by applying fill, outline, and shape effects.

To change the look of a text box:

1. Select the text box you want to change.
2. Click the **Format** tab under *Drawing Tools.*
3. To change the fill effects on a text box:
   a. In the *Shape Styles* group, click the **Shape Fill** button.
   b. Select an option from the color palette.
4. To change the shape outline of a text box:
   a. In the *Shape Styles* group, click the **Shape Outline** button.
   b. Select an option from the color palette.
   c. Point to **Weight** and select a thickness option for the outline.
   d. Point to **Dashes** and select a dash style for the outline.
5. To change the shape effects on a text box:
   a. In the *Shape Styles* group, click the **Shape Effects** button.
   b. Point to **Presets** and select a predetermined combination of shape effects.
   c. Point to any other options on the menu to choose from a variety of shadow, reflection, glow, soft edges, bevel, and 3-D rotation effects.

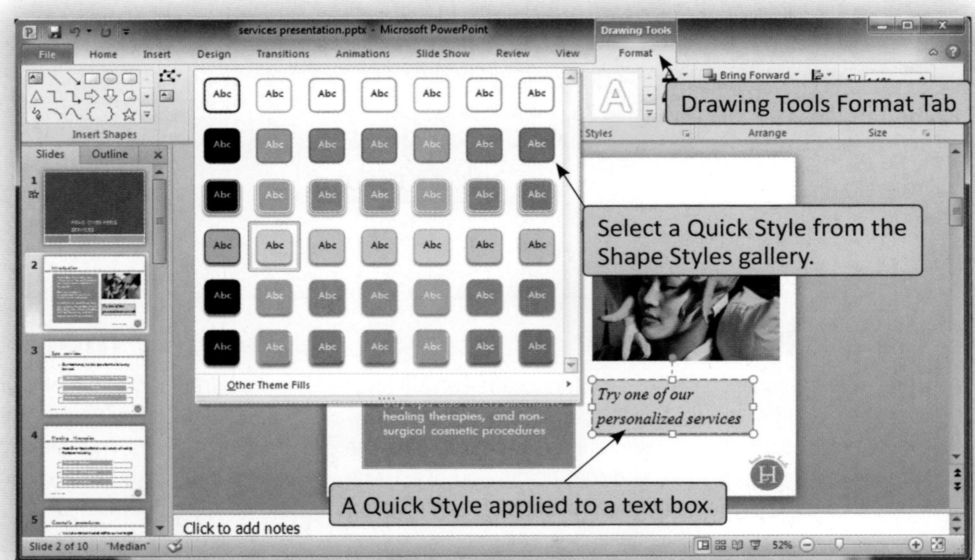

FIGURE PP 3.6

tips & tricks

You can resize text boxes just as you would resize any image in PowerPoint. First, point to one of the resize handles on the text box. When the mouse changes to the resize cursor, click and drag the mouse toward the center of the image to make it smaller, or drag the mouse away from the center of the image to make it larger. When the image is the size you want, release the mouse button.

tell me more

If you want to further adjust the visual effects of a text box, you can use the *Format Shape* dialog box. The *Format Shape* dialog box allows you to finely tune the graphic look of a shape by changing its fill, line color and style, shadow, and 3-D format. To open the *Format Shape* dialog box, click the dialog launcher in the *Shape Styles* group on the *Drawing Tools Format* tab. Click an effect category on the left to display the controls for the effect in the area on the right.

3.7 Applying Quick Styles to Text Boxes

Quick Styles are a combination of formatting that give elements of your presentation a more polished, graphical look without a lot of work. Quick Styles can be applied to text boxes and include a combination of borders, shadows, reflections, and picture shapes, such as rounded corners or skewed perspective. Instead of applying each of these formatting elements one at a time, you can apply a combination of elements at one time using a preset Quick Style.

To apply a Quick Style to a text box:

1. Select the text box you want to apply the Quick Style to.
2. Click the **Format** tab under *Drawing Tools.*
3. In the *Shape Styles* group, click the **More** button.
4. In the *Shape Styles* gallery, click a Quick Style to apply it to the text box.

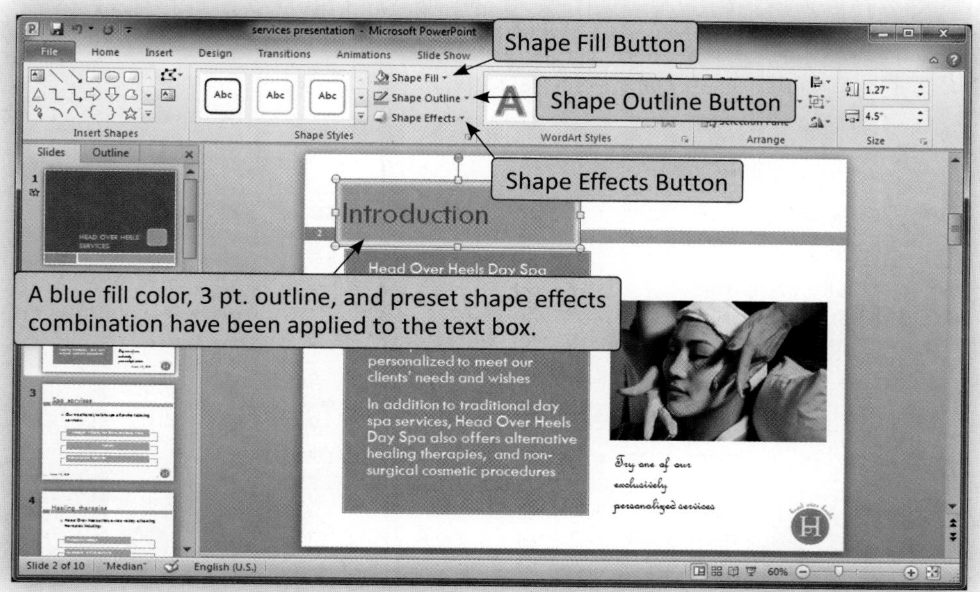

FIGURE PP 3.7

tips & tricks

You can further modify the look of text boxes by using the *Shading*, *Borders*, and *Effects* buttons in the *Shape Styles* group.

tell me more

When you insert a text box into a presentation, the *Format* tab under *Drawing Tools* displays. This tab is called a contextual tab because it only displays when a text box is the active element. The *Format* tab contains tools to change the look of the text box, such as shape styles, WordArt styles, sizing, and arrangement options.

try this

The *Shape Styles* group on the Ribbon displays the latest Quick Styles you have used. If you want to apply a recently used Quick Style, you can click the option directly from the Ribbon without opening the *Shape Styles* gallery.

3.8 Applying Quick Styles to Tables

Just as you can apply complex formatting to text boxes using Quick Styles for shapes, you can also apply complex formatting to tables using Quick Styles for tables. With Quick Styles for tables, you can apply the borders and shading for a table with one command, giving your table a professional, sophisticated look without a lot of work.

To apply a Quick Style to a table:

1. Click the **Design** tab under *Table Tools*.
2. In the *Table Styles* group, click the **More** button.
3. In the *Table Styles* gallery, click a Quick Style to apply it to the table.

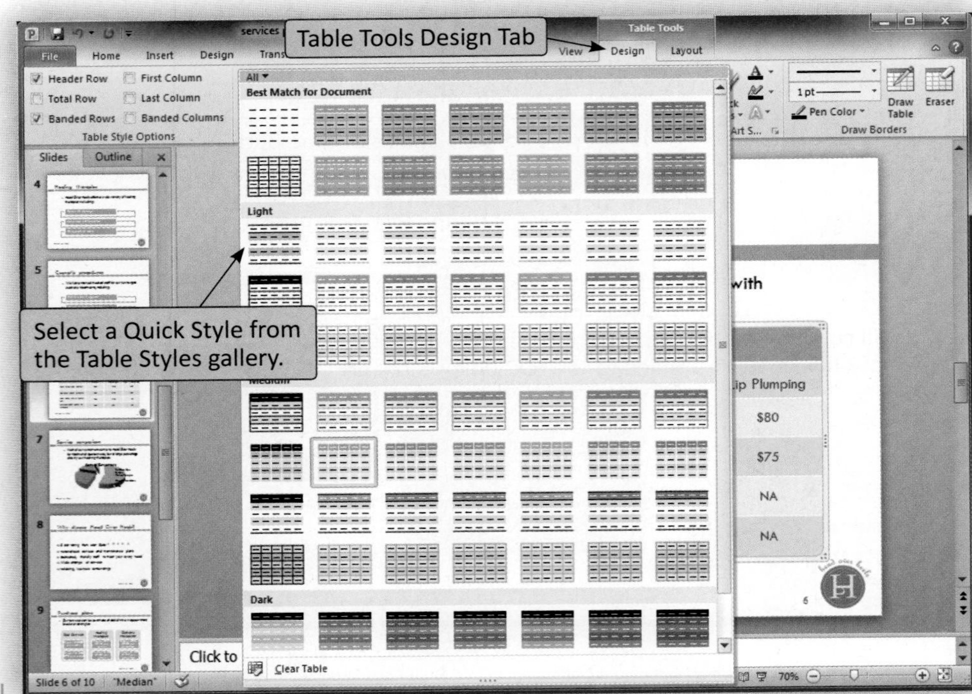

FIGURE PP 3.8

tips & tricks

To remove all formatting from the table, click the **Clear Table** button at the bottom of the *Table Quick Styles* gallery.

You can further modify the look of tables by using the *Shading*, *Borders*, and *Effects* buttons in the *Table Styles* group.

tell me more

When you insert a table into a presentation, the *Design* and *Layout* tabs under *Table Tools* display. These tabs are called contextual tabs because they only display when a table is the active element. The *Design* tab contains tools to change the look of the table, such as Quick Styles, Word Art, and borders. The *Layout* tab contains tools for changing the structure of a table, including adding and removing rows and columns, resizing the table, and changing the alignment of text.

try this

The *Table Styles* group on the Ribbon displays the latest Quick Styles set you chose. If you want to apply a recently used Quick Style, you can click the option directly from the Ribbon without opening the *Table Styles* gallery.

3.9 Using the Shape Styles Gallery

Once you have added a basic shape to a slide, you can apply complex formatting and styles to the shape. You can change the fill or outline color using one of the colors from your presentation's theme. You can also change the shape effects, applying shadows, reflections, glows, and 3-D effects to the shape. But the easiest way to format a shape is to apply a Quick Style. The *Shape Styles* gallery includes a number of Quick Styles, making it easy for you to apply complex formatting to shapes.

To apply a Quick Style to a shape:

1. Click the **Format** tab under *Drawing Tools*.
2. In the *Shape Styles* group, click the **More** button.
3. In the *Shape Styles* gallery, click a Quick Style to apply it to the shape.

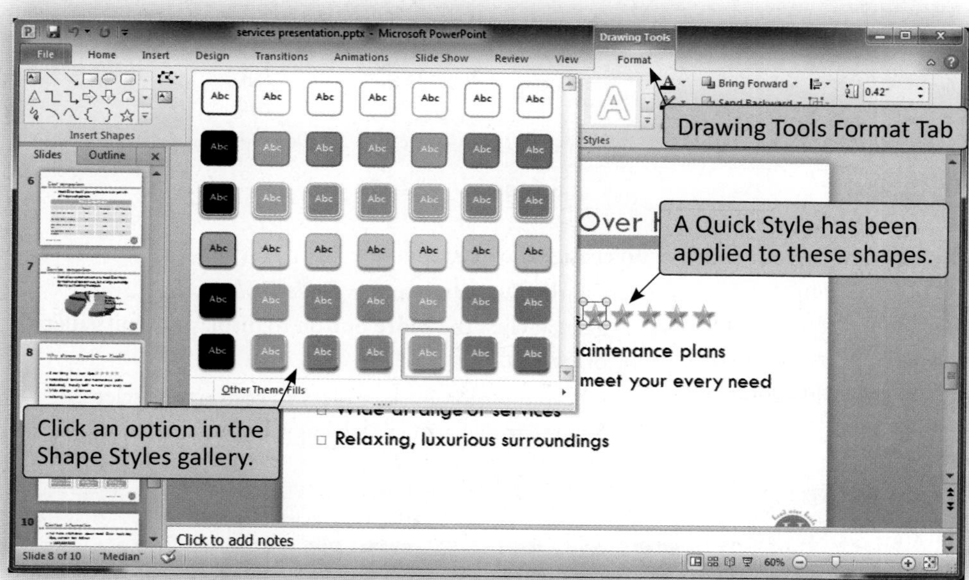

FIGURE PP 3.9

tips & tricks

To change a shape, click the **Edit Shape** button, point to **Change Shape,** and select an option.

You can further modify the look of shapes by using the *Shading*, *Borders*, and *Effects* buttons in the *Shape Styles* group.

tell me more

Once you have mastered applying the prebuilt shape styles to shapes, you can try further refining those styles using the *Format Shape* dialog box. The *Format Shape* dialog box allows you to finely tune the graphic look of a shape by changing its fill, line color and style, shadow, and 3-D format. To open the *Format Shape* dialog box, click the dialog launcher in the *Shape Styles* group on the *Format* tab under *Drawing Tools*.

try this

The *Shape Styles* group on the Ribbon displays the latest Quick Styles you have used. If you want to apply a recently used Quick Style, you can click the option directly from the Ribbon without opening the *Shape Styles* gallery.

3.10 Changing the Layout of SmartArt

SmartArt diagrams are designed to display specific types of data in a visual manner. Each SmartArt diagram includes a default layout for you to add data to. But what if your information does not fit the default layout? Or what if you want to add shapes under other shapes? You can use the *SmartArt Tools* contextual tab to add shapes and promote and demote shapes in SmartArt diagrams.

To change the layout of a SmartArt diagram:

1. On the *Design* tab under *Table Tools,* in the *Create Graphic* group, click the **Add Shape** button and select an option for adding a shape.
2. Click the **Demote Selection** button to move the new shape down one level in the diagram organization.
3. Click the **Promote Selection** button to move the new shape up one level in the diagram organization.

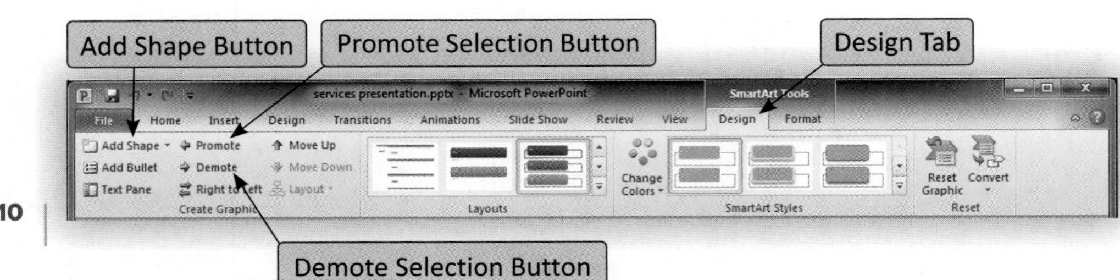

FIGURE PP 3.10

After you have added a SmartArt diagram to your slide, you may find a different layout would convey your information better. For example, you may have initially chosen a list diagram, but then later realized a cycle diagram is more appropriate for your information. You can change the diagram layout rather than re-creating the entire diagram over again.

To change the diagram type:

1. On the *Design* tab under *Table Tools,* in the *Layouts* gallery, click the **More** button to display the full gallery of layouts.
2. Click an option in the gallery to convert the selected SmartArt diagram into the new layout.

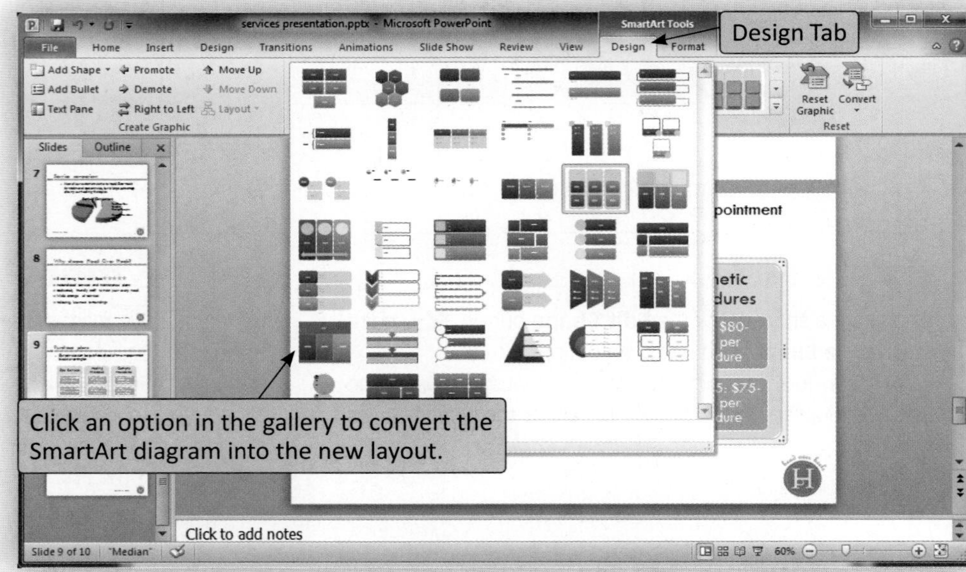

FIGURE PP 3.11

tips & tricks

By default SmartArt diagrams display information from left to right, as you would read text on a page. If you want to change the direction of information in the diagram, click the **Right to Left** button in the *Create Graphic* group. The diagram now flows from the right side of the slide to the left side.

try this

You can add more shapes to a SmartArt diagram by right-clicking the shape in the diagram, pointing to **Add Shape,** and selecting an option.

3.11 Using the Picture Styles Gallery

When creating a presentation, you want to grab the audience's attention. What makes one presentation stand out from another isn't necessarily the content of the slides, but the graphics used to convey that content. PowerPoint comes with a number of picture Quick Styles you can apply to images, instantly giving them a more sophisticated look. Picture Quick Styles include a combination of graphic effects, such as borders, shadows, 3-D rotation, and reflections.

To apply a picture Quick Style to an image:

1. Click the **Format** tab under *Picture Tools.*
2. In the *Picture Styles* group, click the **More** button.
3. In the *Picture Styles* gallery, click a Quick Style to apply it to the shape.

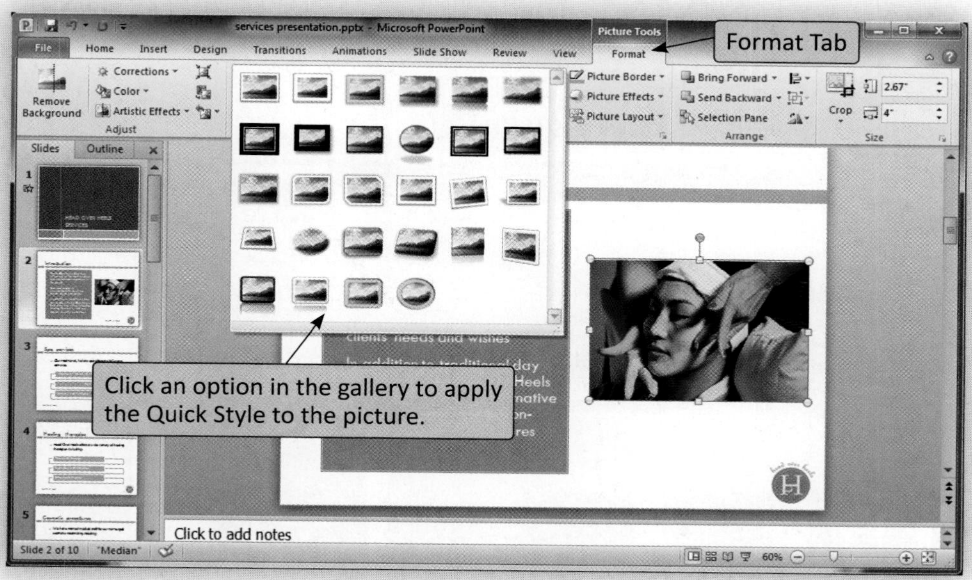

FIGURE PP 3.12

tips & tricks

You can further modify the look of pictures by using the *Picture Border* and *Picture Effects* buttons in the *Picture Styles* group.

tell me more

When you insert a picture into a presentation, the *Format* tab under *Picture Tools* displays. This tab is called a contextual tab because it only displays when a picture is the active element. The *Format* tab contains tools to change the look of a picture, such as applying artistic effects, changing the color, and cropping the image.

try this

The *Picture Styles* group on the Ribbon displays the latest Quick Styles you have used. If you want to apply a recently used Quick Style, you can click the option directly from the Ribbon without opening the *Picture Styles* gallery.

3.12 Showing the Ruler and Gridlines

When you are designing slides in your presentation, aligning placeholders and graphics can be the difference between a polished presentation and one that looks thrown together. Use PowerPoint's rulers and gridlines as visual tools to check the placement of text and graphics on your slides. The ruler allows you to control the placement of text in placeholders, including tabs and indents. **Gridlines** are a series of dotted vertical and horizontal lines that divide the slide into small boxes, giving you visual markers for aligning placeholders and graphics.

To display gridlines in PowerPoint:

1. Click the **View** tab.
2. In the *Show* group, click the **Gridlines** check box to select it.

To display the ruler in PowerPoint:

1. Click the **View** tab.
2. In the *Show* group, click the **Ruler** check box to select it.

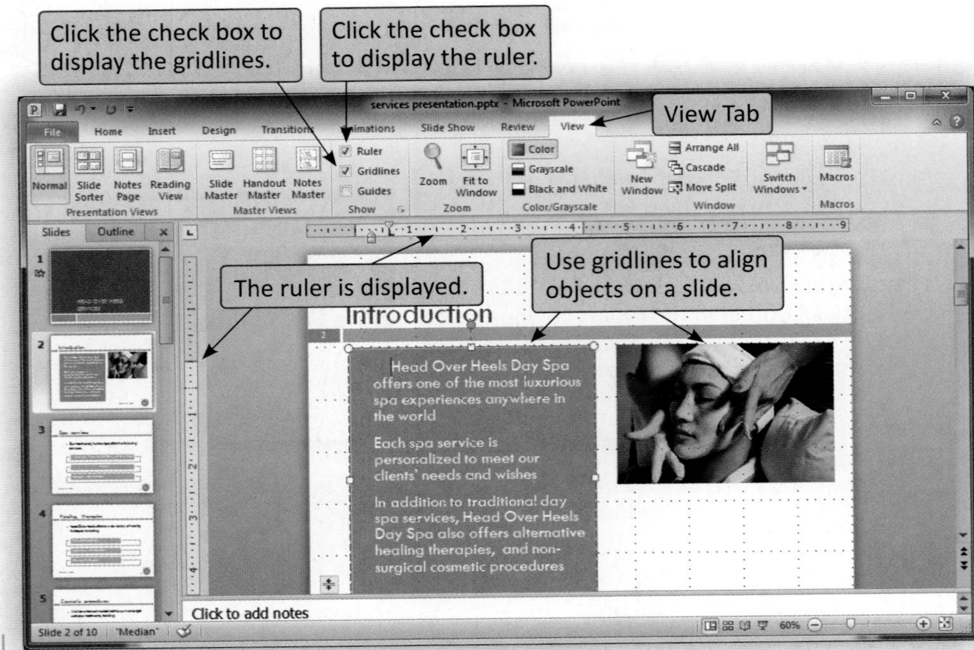

FIGURE PP 3.13

tips & tricks

You can modify the look and behavior of gridlines in the *Grid and Guides* dialog box. To open the *Grid and Guides* dialog box, click the dialog launcher in the *Show* group. Select the **Snap objects to grid** option to force objects to line up along an intersection in the grid when you insert or move them. For more precise layout, change the spacing in the grid to a smaller number.

tell me more

The grid and ruler are only visible when you are working on the presentation. They do not appear when you show the presentation in Slide Show view or when you print handouts.

try this

To display gridlines, you can also:

1. Click the **Format** tab under *Picture Tools*.
2. In the *Arrange* group, click the **Align** button and select **View Gridlines.**

3.13 Changing the Size of Images

When you first add an image to a slide, more than likely it is not the size you want. It will either be too small or too large. In PowerPoint, you can resize images using the resize handles that appear at the corners and sides of an image when it is selected.

To resize an image using the drag method:

1. Point to one of the resize handles on the image.
2. When the mouse changes to the resize cursor, click and drag the mouse:
   - Drag the mouse toward the center of the image to make it smaller.
   - Drag the mouse away from the center of the image to make it larger.
3. When the image is the size you want, release the mouse button.

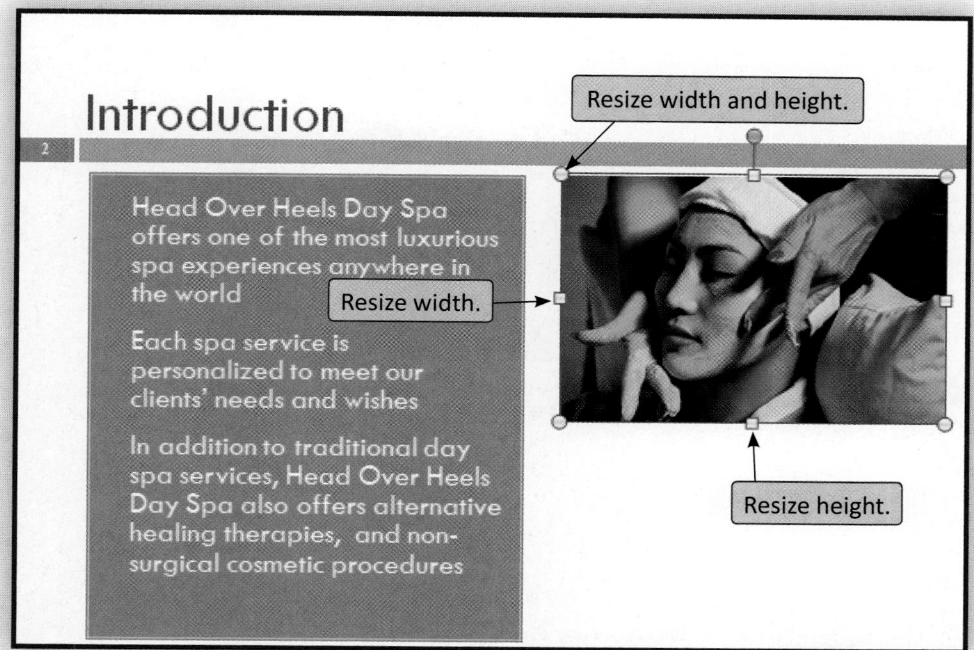

FIGURE PP 3.14

tips & tricks

When using one of the corner resize handles, press Shift on the keyboard as you drag the mouse to constrain the aspect ratio of the image. Constraining the aspect ratio resizes the width by the same percentage as the height. This prevents the image from becoming distorted.

tell me more

When an image is selected, you will see two types of resize handles:

Appears in the middle of one of the sides of the image. This allows you to resize the width or the height, but not both at the same time.

Appears at the four corners of the image. This allows you to change the width and height of the image at the same time.

try this

You can also resize an image by entering the width and height of the image in the **Width:** and **Height:** boxes in the *Size* group on the *Format* tab under *Picture Tools*.

3.14 Changing the Size of a Placeholder

A **placeholder** is a container on a slide that holds text or other content, such as a table, chart, or image. Placeholders are outlined with a dotted line that does not display in the presentation when it is running. You can use the same steps for changing the size of an image to change the size of a placeholder.

To change the size of a placeholder:

1. Point to one of the resize handles on the placeholder.
2. When the mouse changes to the resize cursor, click and drag the mouse:
   - Drag the mouse toward the center of the placeholder to make it smaller.
   - Drag the mouse away from the center of the placeholder to make it larger.
3. When the placeholder is the size you want, release the mouse button.

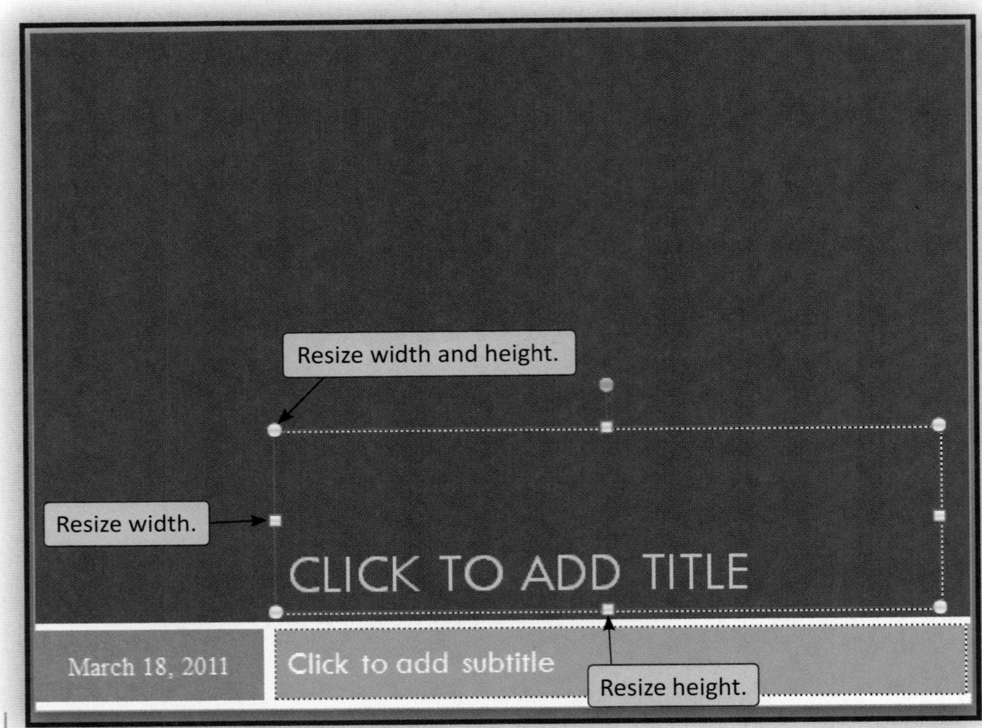

FIGURE PP 3.15

tips & tricks

When using one of the corner resize handles, press Shift on the keyboard as you drag the mouse to constrain the aspect ratio of the image and prevent the image from becoming distorted.

tell me more

You can only add placeholders from Slide Master view. To add a placeholder to a layout, click the **View** tab. In *Master Views* group, click the **Slide Master** button. PowerPoint switches to Slide Master view. In the *Master Layout* group, click the **Insert Placeholder** button and select an option.

try this

You can also resize a placeholder by entering the width and height of the placeholder in the **Width:** and **Height:** boxes in the *Size* group on the *Format* tab under *Picture Tools*.

3.15 Aligning, Grouping, and Rotating Images

When designing a presentation, it is important to place your graphics so that they will have the most impact on your audience. Any graphics that appear in a straight line should be aligned, to ensure that they are precisely placed. On the other hand, you may want to rotate one graphic to make it stand out on the slide. You can also select multiple images on a slide and group them together, thus turning multiple objects into a single object that you can easily move, rotate, or resize as one.

To align graphics on a slide:

1. Click the **Format** tab under *Picture Tools.*
2. In the *Arrange* group, click the **Align** button and select an option:
   - The **Align Left, Align Center,** and **Align Right** commands align graphics along an invisible vertical line.
   - The **Align Top, Align Middle,** and **Align Bottom** commands align graphics along an invisible horizontal line.
   - Click the **Align to Slide** option to align graphics along the edges and center of the slide, rather than relative to each other.
   - The **Distribute Horizontally** and **Distribute Vertically** options evenly space the graphics on the slide. In order to use these options, the **Align to Slide** option must be active.

To rotate graphics on a slide:

1. Click the **Format** tab under *Picture Tools.*
2. In the *Arrange* group, click the **Rotate** button and select an option:
   - **Rotate Left 90°**—rotates the graphic 90 degrees counterclockwise.
   - **Rotate Right 90°**—rotates the graphic 90 degrees clockwise.
   - **Flip Horizontal**—reflects the graphic along the vertical axis.
   - **Flip Vertical**—reflects the graphic along the horizontal axis.

To group graphics on a slide:

1. Select the graphics you want to group as one object.
2. Click the **Format** tab under *Picture Tools.*
3. In the *Arrange* group, click the **Group** button and select an option.

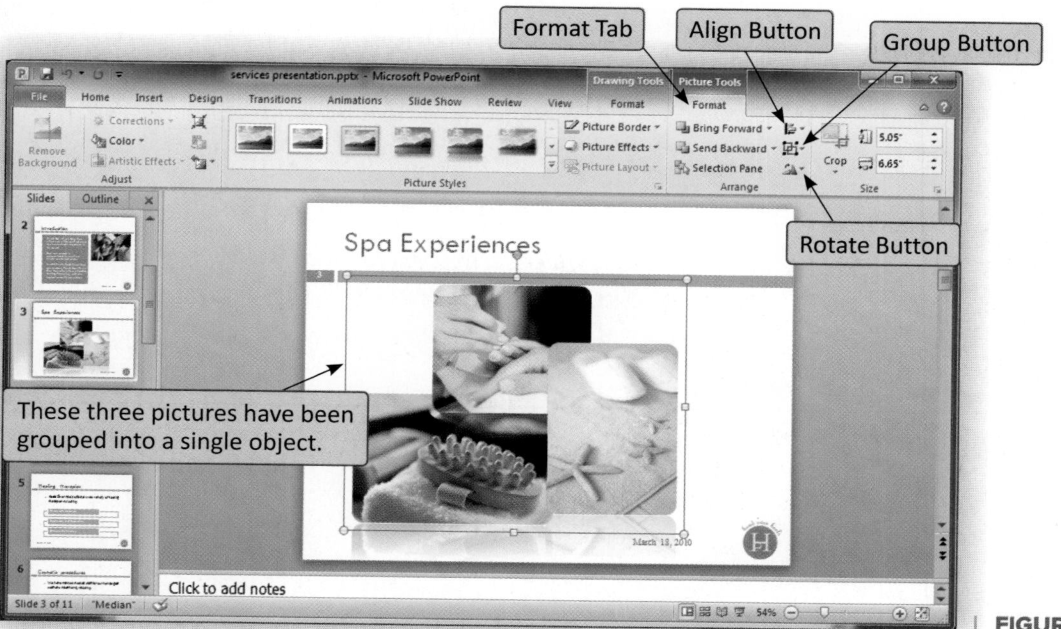

FIGURE PP 3.16

from the perspective of . . .

RETAIL MANAGER

Working in the marketing field, I need to advertise to clients and present at business meetings. With various formatting capabilities such as themes, animations, clip art, and SmartArt, presentation software enables me to quickly create and give professional presentations that incorporate multimedia.

tips & tricks

From the *View* tab you can display gridlines in the *Slide* pane, which is helpful when you have many graphics you want to align. To learn more about this feature, see the topic *Showing the Ruler and Gridlines* in this chapter.

tell me more

Placeholders cannot be grouped. Similarly, objects that have been added to a placeholder cannot be grouped with other objects. In order to group objects, you must add objects to the slide independent of a placeholder.

try this

To group graphics, you can also:

1. Select the graphics you want to group as one object.
2. Right-click the selected graphics, point to *Group*, and select **Group.**

3.16 Applying Animation Effects

Adding **animations** to slides can help emphasize important points and grab your audience's attention. In PowerPoint you can animate individual objects on a slide, including text, images, charts, tables, and SmartArt.

There are four basic types of animation schemes:

Entrance—animates the object coming on to the slide; starts with the object not visible and ends with the object visible. Examples of *Entrance* animations include *Fade In, Split, Fly In,* and *Appear.*

Emphasis—animates the object on the screen. Examples of *Emphasis* animations include *Pulse, Spin, Grow/Shrink,* and *Teeter.*

Exit—animates the object leaving the slide; starts with the object visible and ends with the object not visible. Examples of *Exit* animations include *Fade, Disappear, Float Out,* and *Wipe.*

Motion Paths—animates the object along an invisible line. Examples of *Motion Path* animations include *Lines, Arcs,* and *Loops.*

To add an animation to an object:

1. Select the object you want to animate.
2. Click the **Animations** tab.
3. In the *Animation* group, click the **More** button.
4. In the *Animation* gallery, click an option to apply it to the object.

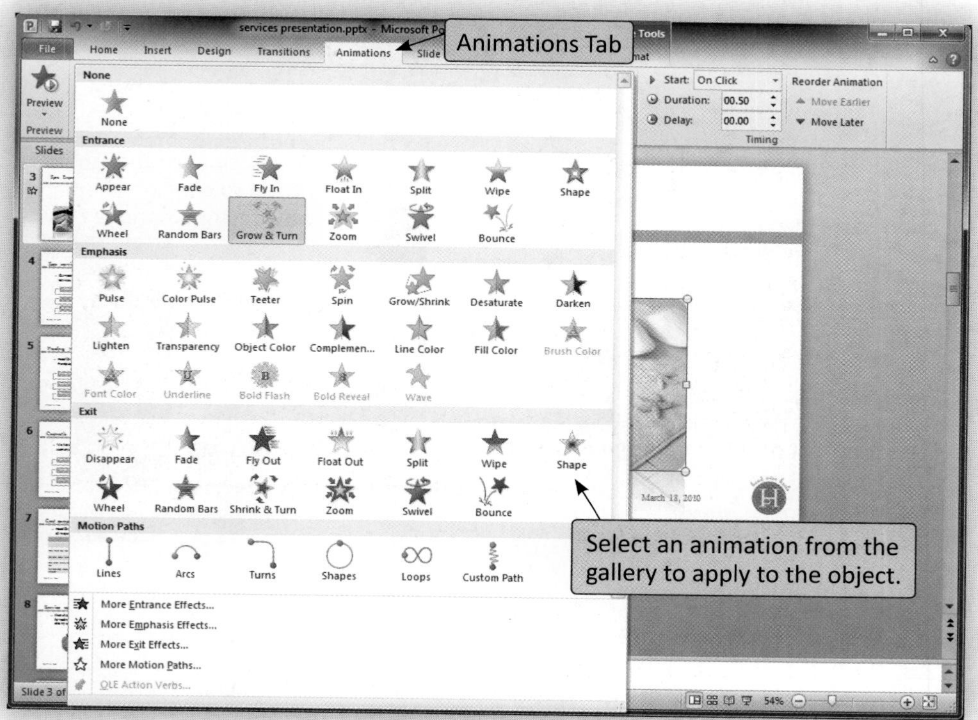

FIGURE PP 3.17

tips & tricks

To remove an animation, select **None** in the gallery.

try this

To add an animation, you can also select an animation option from the *Advanced Animation* gallery.

3.17 Modifying Animations

Although PowerPoint comes with a number of easy-to-use, prebuilt animations, you may find that you want to further customize those animations to better suit your needs. You can create complex animations by adding additional animations, changing the effect options, and modifying the timing of animations. All these properties can be changed from the *Animations* tab.

To customize an animation:

1. Select the object with the animation you want to modify.
2. Click the **Animations** tab on the Ribbon.
3. Click the **Effects Options** button to change the default behavior of the animation.
4. Click the **Add Animation** button to add more animations to an object, including entrance effects, emphasis effects, exit effects, and motion paths.
5. Click the arrow next to the *Start:* box and select when the animation will play—*On Click, With Previous,* or *After Previous*.
6. Enter a time in the *Duration:* box to control how fast or slow the animation plays. The higher the number, the slower the animation.
7. Enter a time in the *Delay:* box to add a break before the animation plays.

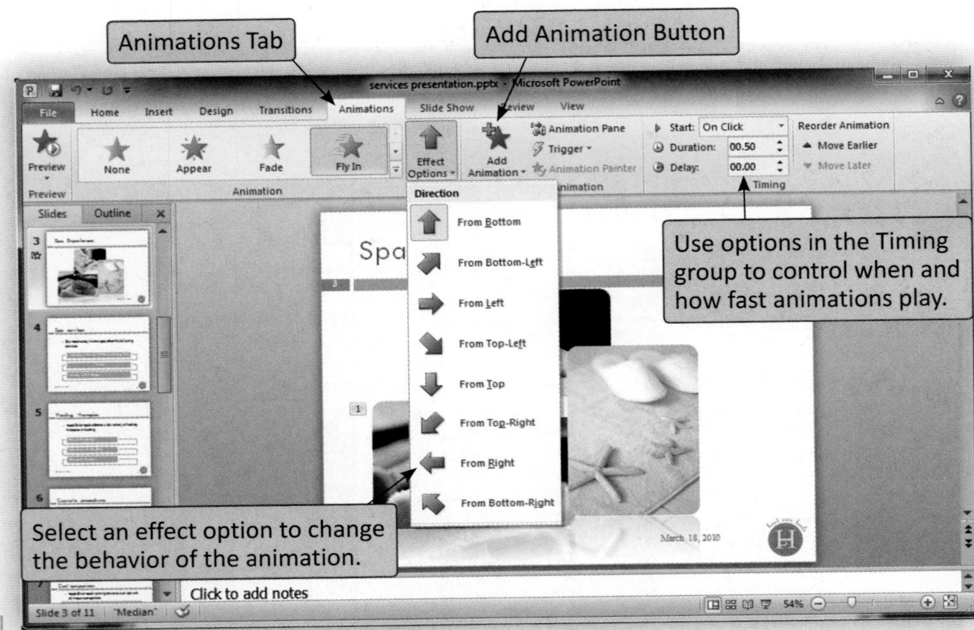

Animations Tab
Add Animation Button
Use options in the Timing group to control when and how fast animations play.
Select an effect option to change the behavior of the animation.

FIGURE PP 3.18

tips & tricks

When you add animations to objects, a number appears next to the object with the animation. This number indicates the order in which the animations will play. To reorder animations, click the **Move Earlier** or **Move Later** buttons in the *Timing* group.

tell me more

To see an overview of all the animation effects for a slide, click the **Animation Pane** button. The Animation pane lists each animation for the current slide and the order in which they will play. From the Animation pane, you can modify the behavior of each animation and then preview any changes you make.

projects

Skill Review 3.1

In this review, you will use the skills learned in Chapter 3 to edit an existing presentation.

1. Open an existing presentation:
   a. Open Microsoft PowerPoint 2010.
   b. On the *File* tab, click **Open.**
   c. In the *Open* dialog box, navigate to the location of your PowerPoint 2010 student files.
   d. Find *Ch3_Review1_NewPC.pptx* and double-click the file to open it.
   e. On the *File* tab, click the **Save As** option.
   f. Change the file name to ***[your initials]*****PP_SkillReview_3-1,** and then click **OK.**
2. Change themes and theme effects:
   a. Apply a theme to the slide master:
      (1) Verify that you are in Slide Master view and that the slide master is selected.
      (2) On the *Slide Master* tab, in the *Edit Theme* group, click the **Themes** button.
      (3) Click the **Metro** theme in the gallery.
      (4) All the slides in your presentation now use the new theme.
      (5) Close the Slide Master view.
   b. Apply a color theme in Normal view:
      (1) On the *Design* tab, in the *Themes* group, click the **Theme Colors** button.
      (2) Select the **Trek** color theme from the list that appears.
   c. Change the background style:
      (1) On the *Design* tab, in the *Background* group, click the **Background Styles** button.
      (2) Select **Style 8** from the *Background Styles* gallery.
   d. Change the font:
      (1) On **Slide 1,** select the **Title** placeholder.
      (2) On the *Home* tab, click the arrow next to the **Font** box.
      (3) Scroll the list to find **Corbel** and click the font name.
   e. Change the size of the text:
      (1) On the *Home* tab, click the arrow next to the **Font Size** box.
      (2) Scroll the list to find **60,** and then click it.
3. Apply *Quick Styles* to text boxes, tables, and shapes, and adjust the layout of SmartArt:
   a. Apply *Quick Styles* to a text box:
      (1) On **Slide 3,** select the **Title** text box.
      (2) On the *Home* tab, in the *Drawing* group, click the **Quick Styles** button and select **Moderate Effect–Brown, Accent 4** (fifth row, fifth effect).
   b. Change the look of a text box:
      (1) On the *Home* tab, in the *Drawing* group, click the **Shape Effects** button, point to **Bevel,** and select **Cool Slant** (first row, fourth effect).
      (2) On the *Home* tab, in the *Paragraph* group, click the **Center** button.

c. Apply *Quick Styles* to a table:

(1) On **Slide 3,** select all the cells in the table.

(2) On the *Table Tools Design* tab, in the *Table Styles* group, click the **More** button and select the **Themed Style 2–Accent 4** (second row, fifth effect) style.

(3) On the *Home* tab, in the *Font* group, click the **Bold** and **Shadow** buttons.

d. Use the *Shape Styles* gallery:

(1) On **Slide 3,** select the = shape. Press the **Ctrl** key and select the ≠ shape.

(2) Click the **Drawing Tools Format** tab.

(3) In the *Shape Styles* group, click the **More** button and select **Moderate Effect–Brown, Accent 4** (fifth row, fifth effect).

e. Change the layout of SmartArt:

(1) On **Slide 2,** select the **Process SmartArt** object.

(2) On the *SmartArt Tools Design* tab, in the *Layouts* group, click the **More** button and select the **Step-Up Process** layout.

(3) Place your mouse on one of the corners of the SmartArt object. When the mouse changes to the resize cursor, click and drag the mouse to decrease the size of the object.

(4) Move the SmartArt object to align to the right of the first bullet item.

4. Apply a picture style to an image:

a. On **Slide 1,** select the picture.

b. Click the **Format** tab under *Picture Tools.*

c. In the *Picture Styles* group, click the **More** button and select the **Soft Edge Oval** style.

5. Show the ruler and gridlines, and change placeholder size:

a. Show the ruler and gridlines:

(1) Display gridlines in PowerPoint:

(a) Click the **View** tab.

(b) In the *Show* group, click the **Gridlines** check box to select it.

(2) Display the ruler in PowerPoint:

(a) Click the **View** tab.

(b) In the *Show* group, click the **Ruler** check box to select it.

b. Change the size of a placeholder:

(1) On **Slide 2,** select the *Title* placeholder.

(2) Place your mouse on the middle right sizing tool.

(3) When the mouse changes to the resize cursor, click and drag the mouse to the left to decrease the size of the object until the right side aligns with **1″** on the horizontal ruler.

6. Edit image alignment, grouping, rotating, and sizing:

a. Align, group, and rotate images:

(1) Align graphics on a slide:

(a) On **Slide 4,** select the first image. Press the **Ctrl** key and select the second and third images.

(b) Click the **Format** tab under *Picture Tools.*

(c) In the *Arrange* group, click the **Align** button and select **Align Bottom.**

(2) Rotate graphics on a slide:

(a) On **Slide 4,** select the **shopping cart** image.

(b) In the *Arrange* group, click the **Rotate** button and select **Flip Horizontal.**

(3) Group graphics on a slide:

(a) On **Slide 4,** select the four graphics.

(b) In the *Arrange* group, click the **Group** button and select **Group.**

b. Change the size of images:

(1) On **Slide 4,** select the grouped graphic.

(2) Point to one of the resize handles on lower-right side of the image.

(3) When the mouse changes to the resize cursor, press the **Shift** key and drag the mouse until the image equals a height of **1.5** inches.

7. Apply animation effects to an object:

a. On **Slide 2,** select the **Content** placeholder.

b. Click the **Animations** tab.

c. In the *Animation* group, click the **More** button and select **Fly In.**

d. In the *Animation* group, click the **Effect Options** button and select **From Bottom-Left.**

e. View the presentation.

f. Save the presentation.

Skill Review **3.2**

In this review, you will use the skills learned in Chapter 3 to edit an existing presentation.

1. Open an existing presentation:

a. Open Microsoft PowerPoint 2010.

b. On the *File* tab, click **Open.**

c. In the *Open* dialog box, navigate to the location of your PowerPoint 2010 student files.

d. Find *Ch3_Review2_MedPlan.pptx* and double-click the file to open it.

e. On the *File* tab, click the **Save As** option.

f. Change the file name to ***[your initials]*** **`PP_SkillReview_3-2`,** and then click **OK.**

2. Change themes and theme effects:

a. Apply a theme to the slide master:

(1) Verify that you are in Slide Master view and that the slide master is selected.

(2) On the *Slide Master* tab, in the *Edit Theme* group, click the **Themes** button.

(3) Click the **Grid** theme in the gallery.

(4) All the slides in your presentation now use the new theme.

(5) Close the Slide Master view.

b. Apply a color theme in Normal view:

(1) On the *Design* tab, in the *Themes* group, click the **Theme Colors** button.

(2) Select the **Essential** color theme from the list that appears.

c. Change the background style:

(1) On the *Design* tab, in the *Background* group, click the **Background Styles** button.

(2) Select **Style 2** from the *Background Styles* gallery.

d. Change the font:

(1) Select **Slide 1.**

(2) Select the **Title** placeholder.

(3) On the *Home* tab, in the *Font* group, click the arrow next to the **Font** box.

(4) Scroll the list to find **Berlin Sans FB** and click the font name.

e. Change the size of the text:

(1) On the *Home* tab, in the *Font* group, click the arrow next to the **Font Size** box.

(2) Scroll the list to find **36,** and then click it.

3. Apply *Quick Styles* to text boxes, tables, and shapes, and adjust the layout of SmartArt:

a. Apply *Quick Styles* to a text box:

(1) On **Slide 3,** select the **Title** text box.

(2) On the *Home* tab, in the *Drawing* group, click the **Quick Styles** button and select **Subtle Effect–Orange, Accent 5** (fourth row, sixth effect).

b. Change the look of a text box:

(1) On the *Home* tab, in the *Drawing* group, click the **Shape Effect** button, point to **Soft Edges,** and select **5 Point.**

c. Apply *Quick Styles* to a table:

(1) On **Slide 3,** select all cells in the table.

(2) On the *Table Tools Design* tab, in the *Table Styles* group, click the **More** button and select **Themed Style 1–Accent 5** (the sixth option in the first row).

(3) Click the edge of the table and move it centered, below the title.

d. Use the *Shape Styles* gallery:

(1) On **Slide 3,** select the shape.

(2) Click the **Drawing Tools Format** tab.

(3) In the *Shape Styles* group, click the **More** button and select **Intense Effect–Orange, Accent 5** (the sixth option in the last row).

(4) In the *Shape Styles* group, click the **Shape Fill** button and select **Red, Text 2.**

e. Change the layout of SmartArt:

(1) On **Slide 2,** select the **SmartArt** object.

(2) On the *SmartArt Tools Design* tab, in the *Layouts* group, click the **More** button and select the **Vertical Curved List** layout (the third option in the sixth row).

(3) Place your mouse on one of the corners of the SmartArt object. When the mouse changes to the resize cursor, click and drag the mouse to increase the size of the object.

(4) On the *SmartArt Tools Design* tab, in the *SmartArt Styles* group, click the **Change Colors** button and select **Dark 2–Outline.**

(5) Move the SmartArt object to align to the right of the second bullet item.

4. Apply a picture style to an image:

a. On **Slide 1,** select the picture.

b. Click the **Format** tab under *Picture Tools.*

c. In the *Picture Styles* group, click the **More** button and select the **Rotated, White** style.

d. Select the picture and move it, centered near the top of the right panel.

5. Show the ruler and gridlines, and change placeholder size:

a. Show the ruler and gridlines:

(1) Display gridlines in PowerPoint:

(a) Click the **View** tab.

(b) In the *Show* group, click the **Gridlines** check box to select it.

(2) Display the ruler in PowerPoint:

(a) Click the **View** tab.

(b) In the *Show* group, click the **Ruler** check box to select it.

b. Change the size of a placeholder:

(1) On **Slide 3,** select the **Title** placeholder.

(2) Place your mouse on the middle right sizing tool.

(3) When the mouse changes to the resize cursor, click and drag the mouse to the left to decrease the size of the object until the right side aligns with the 3″ mark on the right side of the horizontal ruler.

(4) Repeat to decrease the size until the left side aligns with the 3″ mark on the left side of the horizontal ruler.

6. Edit image alignment, grouping, rotating, and sizing:

a. Align, group, and rotate images:

(1) Align graphics on a slide:

(a) On **Slide 4,** select the first image. Press the **Ctrl** key and select the second and third images.

(b) Click the **Format** tab under *Picture Tools.*

(c) In the *Arrange* group, click the **Align** button and **Align Middle.**

(2) Rotate graphics on a slide:

(a) On **Slide 4,** select the right image.

(b) On the *Picture Tools Format* tab, in the *Arrange* group, click the **Rotate** button and select **Flip Horizontal.**

(3) Group graphics on a slide:

(a) On **Slide 4,** select the three graphics.

(b) On the *Picture Tools Format* tab, in the *Arrange* group, click the **Group** button and select **Group.**

b. Change the size of images:

(1) Point to one of the resize handles on lower-right side of the image.

(2) When the mouse changes to the resize cursor, press the **Shift** key and drag the mouse until the image equals a height of **1.6** inches.

7. Apply animation effects to an object:

a. On **Slide 2,** select the **Content** placeholder.

b. Click the **Animations** tab.

c. In the *Animation* group, click the **More** button and select **Wheel** entrance effect.

d. In the *Animation* group, click the **Effect Options** button and select **4 Spokes.**

e. Save the presentation.

challenge yourself **1**

In this challenge, you will use the skills learned in Chapter 3 to format a presentation.

1. Open an existing presentation:

a. Open Microsoft PowerPoint 2010.

b. Navigate to the location of your PowerPoint 2010 student files.

c. Open *3_Chall1_Childproof.pptx.*

d. Save the file as `[your initials]PP_Challenge_3-3.`

2. Change themes and theme effects:

a. Apply a theme to the slide master:

(1) From Slide Master view, change the theme to the **Solstice** theme.

(2) Close the Slide Master view.

b. Apply a color theme in Normal view:

(1) From Normal view, change the theme colors for the presentation to use the **Waveform** color theme.

c. Change the background style:

(1) Change the background for the presentation to the **Style 2** background style.

d. Change the font and font size:

(1) Select the title on **Slide 1.**

(2) Change the font to **40 point Comic Sans MS.**

3. Apply *Quick Styles* to text boxes, tables, and shapes, and adjust the layout of SmartArt:

a. Apply *Quick Styles* to a text box and change the look of a text box:

(1) On **Slide 1,** change the *Title* text box to the **Moderate Effect–Blue, Accent 2** Quick Style.

(2) Change the shape effect to **Bevel** and select **Cool Slant.**

(3) Change the shape effect to **3-D Rotation** and select **Isometric Right Up.**

b. Apply *Quick Styles* to a table.

(1) On **Slide 3,** select the table.

(2) Change the table style to **Dark Style–Accent 1.**

(3) Center the table below the title.

c. Use the *Shape Styles* gallery:

(1) On **Slide 3,** change the shape's style to **Light 1 Outline, Colored Fill–Blue, Accent 2.**

(2) Change the shape's fill to **Blue–Accent 1.**

d. Changing the layout of SmartArt:

(1) On **Slide 2,** change the SmartArt object to the **Continuous Cycle** layout.

(2) Reduce the size of the SmartArt and align it to the right of the bullets.

(3) Change the color to **Colorful–Accent Colors.**

4. Apply a picture style to an image:

a. On **Slide 1,** change the picture style to **Bevel Cross.**

b. Enlarge the picture to a height of **4** inches.

5. Show the ruler and gridlines, and change placeholder size:

a. Show the ruler and gridlines:

(1) Display the **Gridlines.**

(2) Display the **Ruler.**

b. Change the size of a placeholder:

(1) On **Slide 1,** select the **Title** placeholder.

(2) Increase the size to encompass the text in one line.

6. Edit image alignment, grouping, rotating, and sizing:

a. Align, rotate, and group images:

(1) On **Slide 4,** select all of the images and **Align Middle.**

(2) Flip the left image horizontally.

(3) Group the three images.

b. Change the size of images:

(1) On **Slide 4,** select the grouped image.

(2) Enlarge the grouped image to a height of **3** inches.

7. Apply animation effects to an object:

a. On **Slide 2,** animate the bullets using the **Fly-In from Bottom Left** effect.

b. View and save the presentation.

challenge yourself **2**

In this challenge, you will use the skills learned in Chapter 3 to format a Web design presentation.

1. Open an existing presentation:

a. Open Microsoft PowerPoint 2010.

b. Navigate to the location of your PowerPoint 2010 student files.

c. Open *3_Chall2_WebDesign.pptx.*

d. Save the file as `[your initials]PP_Challenge_3-4`.

2. Change themes and theme effects:

a. Apply a theme to the slide master:

(1) Verify that you are in Slide Master view and that the slide master is selected.

(2) Change the theme to the **Concourse** theme.

(3) Close the Slide Master view.

b. Apply a color theme in Normal view:

(1) From the *Design* tab, change the theme colors for the presentation to use the **Technic** color theme.

c. Change the background style and font size:

(1) Change the background for the presentation to the **Style 8** background style.

(2) Select the title of **Slide 1.**

(3) Change the font to **54 point Century Gothic.**

3. Apply *Quick Styles* to text boxes, tables, and shapes, and adjust the layout of SmartArt:

a. Apply *Quick Styles* to a text box and change the look of a text box:

(1) On **Slide 1,** change the *Title* text box to the **Intense Effect–Aqua, Accent 1** Quick Style.

(2) Change the shape effect to **Bevel** and select **Aqua 18 pt glow–Accent color 1.**

(3) Change the shape effect to **3-D Rotation** and select **Off-Axis 1 Right.**

b. Apply *Quick Styles* to a table:

(1) On **Slide 3,** select the table.

(2) Change the table style to **Themed Style 2–Accent 1.**

(3) Center the table on the page.

c. Use the *Shape Styles* gallery:

(1) On **Slide 3,** change the shape's style to **Intense Effect–Aqua Accent 1.**

(2) Change the shape's fill to **Gray–80% Background 2.**

d. Change the layout of SmartArt:

(1) On **Slide 2,** change the SmartArt object to the **Step-Down Process** layout.

(2) Reduce the size of the SmartArt and center it below the bullets.

(3) Change the color to **Colorful Range–Accent Colors 3–4.**

4. Apply a picture style to an image:

a. On **Slide 1,** change the *Picture Style* to **Soft Edge oval.**

b. Adjust the picture's color to **Aqua–Accent 1 Light.**

5. Show the ruler and gridlines, and change placeholder size:

a. Show the ruler and gridlines:

(1) Display the **Gridlines.**

(2) Display the **Ruler.**

b. Change the size of a placeholder:

(1) On **Slide 1,** select the **Title** placeholder.

(2) Increase the size of the placeholder to fit well on the slide.

6. Edit image alignment, grouping, rotating, and sizing:

a. Align, rotate, and group images:

(1) On **Slide 4,** select both of the images and **Align Middle.**

(2) Flip the right image horizontally.

(3) Group the images.

b. Change the size of images:

(1) On **Slide 4,** select the grouped image.

(2) Enlarge the grouped image to a height of **2** inches.

7. Apply animation effects to an object:

a. On **Slide 2,** animate the bullets using the **Fly-In from Bottom Right** effect.

b. View and save the presentation.

on your own

Today is your first day teaching your class and you need to create an introductory presentation to share with your students.

1. Create a PowerPoint presentation entitled ***[your initials]*PP_OnYourOwn_3-5** that includes the following information and components:

2. Use the **Hardcover** theme.

3. Add slides.

SLIDE	TITLE	ADDITIONAL INFORMATION
Slide 1	Welcome & Introduction	Insert a Building Block graphic lower-right corner
Slide 2	The Plan	Bullets: › Welcome › Introductions › Course Schedule › Textbooks › Student Responsibilities
Slide 3	Introduction	Insert Table (1 column, 6 rows) First row—blank Rows 2–6 (one item per row): › Your Name › Birth place › Area of study › Favorite (or dream) vacation › Something interesting about you
Slide 4	Student Responsibilities	Bullets › To attend every class › Be in class on time and not leave early › Be prepared › Participate—it's your class—you are responsible for what you learn! › Contact instructor if problems occur › Courtesy and respect › Have fun!
Slide 5	Let's Get Started!	

4. On **Slide 1,** apply the **Beveled-Perspective** picture style.
5. On **Slide 2,** add a **SmartArt** for the bullet items using the **Basic Cycle** layout.
6. Apply the **Polished** SmartArt style.
7. On **Slide 3,** change the table to the **Medium Accent 2–Accent 5** table style.
8. On **Slide 4,** add a **5-point Star** shape in the lower-right corner.
9. Apply **Colored Fill–Dark Red Accent 5** shape style and a **Bevel Circle** shape effect.
10. On **Slide 5,** apply the **Title Slide** layout.
11. Insert two photographs from the *Clip Art* gallery that pertain to your class (i.e., globe and mouse).
12. **Align** the photographs in the middle.
13. **Group** the photographs.
14. Display the **Ruler** and **Gridlines.**
15. On **Slides 2 and 4,** animate the bullets using a **Fly-In from Bottom** animation.
16. View and save the presentation.

fix it

You have been assigned the task of fixing an existing presentation based on the skills learned in Chapter 3.

1. Using PowerPoint 2010, open *Ch3_Fixit_AutoSafety.pptx.*
2. Save the file as `[your initials]PP_FixIt_3-6.`
3. Change the *Master Slide Theme* to **Verve.**
4. Change the *Theme Color* to **Module.**
5. On **Slide 1,** apply the **Soft-Edged Oval** picture style.
6. On **Slide 2,** change the SmartArt layout to **Text Cycle.**
7. Apply the **Inset** SmartArt style.
8. On **Slide 3,** change the table to the **Light Style 1–Accent 2** table style.
9. Apply the **Colored Fill–Light Accent 1** shape style and the **Cool Slant** shape effect.
10. On **Slide 4, Align** the photographs in the middle.
11. **Group** the photographs.
12. Display the **Ruler** and **Gridlines.**
13. On **Slide 2,** animate the bullets using a **Fly-In from Bottom-Left** animation.
14. View and save the file.

chapter 4

Managing and Delivering Presentations

In this chapter, you will learn the following skills:

Skill 4.1 Deleting Slides from Presentations
Skill 4.2 Changing the Order of Slides
Skill 4.3 Copying and Pasting Slides
Skill 4.4 Using the Office Clipboard
Skill 4.5 Defining a Custom Show
Skill 4.6 Hiding Slides
Skill 4.7 Adding Hyperlinks to Slides
Skill 4.8 Adding Comments
Skill 4.9 Rehearsing Timings
Skill 4.10 Starting the Slide Show
Skill 4.11 Using Presentation Tools
Skill 4.12 Printing Presentations
Skill 4.13 Customizing Handout Masters
Skill 4.14 Previewing and Printing Handouts

skills

- **Delete, reorder, copy, and paste slides, and use the Office Clipboard**
- **Define a custom show and hide slides**
- **Add hyperlinks and comments**
- **Rehearse timings and use navigation tools**
- **Print presentations and handouts**

introduction

In this chapter, you will acquire the tools to give a professional presentation. Editing skills such as using the Office Clipboard, changing the order of slides, and copying and pasting slides will help you manage your presentation. Once the presentation is final, this chapter will guide you through the actual presentation process including rehearsing timing and creating handouts for your audience.

4.1 Deleting Slides from Presentations

After you have created all the content for your presentation, it is a good idea to carefully review the slides. As you make a final review, you may find that a slide you created is not really necessary, and you want to permanently remove it. You can remove an entire slide of content by deleting it from the *Slides* tab.

To delete a slide:

1. On the *Slides* tab, right-click the slide you want to delete.
2. Click **Delete Slide** on the menu that appears.

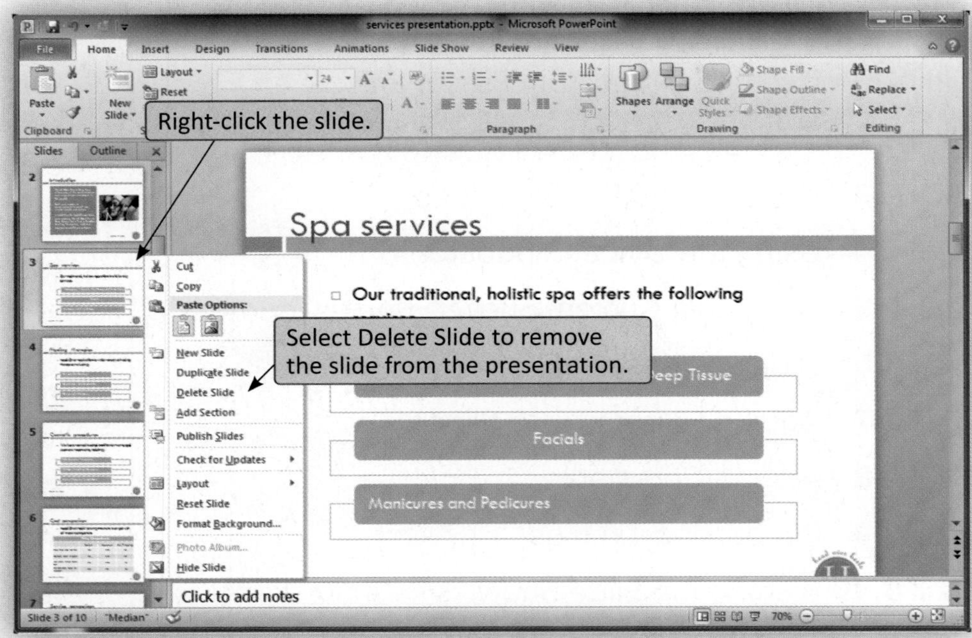

FIGURE PP 4.1

tips & tricks

You can delete multiple slides at once:

1. Click a slide you want to delete and press [⇧Shift] on the keyboard.
2. With the *Shift* key still pressed, click another slide. Notice, all the slides between the two slides you clicked have been selected.
3. Right-click any of the selected slides and select **Delete Slide.**

If you want to select slides that are not next to each other, press [Ctrl] on the keyboard instead of [⇧Shift] and click each slide you want to delete. Only the slides you clicked are selected.

try this

To delete a slide, you can also select the slide and press [Delete] on the keyboard.

4.2 Changing the Order of Slides

One of the most important aspects of a presentation is the flow of the information. It is important that your slides appear in a logical, grouped order for your audience to fully grasp the message you are trying to present. After you have reviewed your presentation, you may find that you want to switch the order of some of your slides. You can change the slide order from the *Slides* tab in Normal view or in Slide Sorter view.

To change the slide order from the *Slides* tab:

1. Select the thumbnail of the slide you want to move.
2. Click and drag until the gray line appears where you want the slide, and then release the mouse button.

The *Slides* tab in Normal view displays the thumbnails of your slides in a vertical pane. Slide Sorter view displays thumbnails of slides in a grid. Slide Sorter view is useful for seeing how your slides work together; you can then move slides around, experimenting with the order.

To change the slide order in Slide Sorter view:

1. Select the thumbnail of the slide you want to move.
2. Click and drag until the gray line appears where you want the slide, and then release the mouse button.

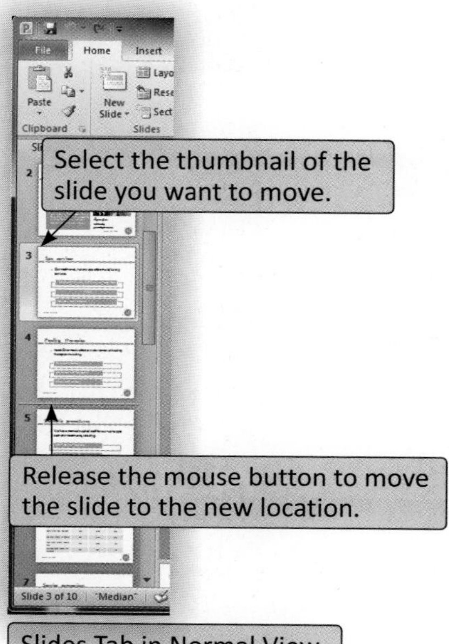
Select the thumbnail of the slide you want to move.
Release the mouse button to move the slide to the new location.
Slides Tab in Normal View.

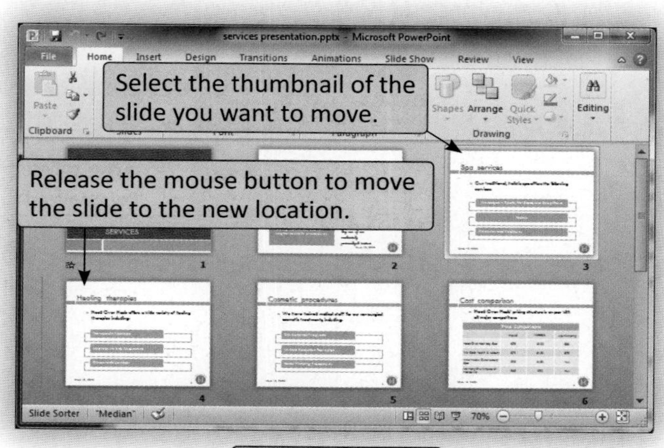
Select the thumbnail of the slide you want to move.
Release the mouse button to move the slide to the new location.
Slide Sorter View

FIGURE PP 4.2

tips & tricks

To select more than one slide to move, select the first slide, then press the ⇧Shift key, and then select the last slide in the set.

tell me more

Each slide thumbnail appears with a number next to it indicating its location in the presentation. When you change the order of slides, PowerPoint automatically renumbers the slides for you.

try this

To move or copy a slide by dragging, right-click the slide you want to move and drag it to the new location. When you release the mouse button, a menu of options will appear, allowing you to move the slide, copy the slide, or cancel the action.

4.3 Copying and Pasting Slides

You may find when you are creating your presentation that one slide's content and layout is similar to another slide's content and layout that you need to add. Instead of having to re-create all the content for the second slide, you can copy the first slide, paste it into the presentation where you want it to appear, and then change the content you need to change.

To copy and paste slides:

1. Select the slide you want to copy.
2. On the *Home* tab, in the *Clipboard* group, click the **Copy** button.
3. Click the slide that you want to appear before the new slide.
4. Click the **Paste** button.
5. The new slide has been added to the presentation.

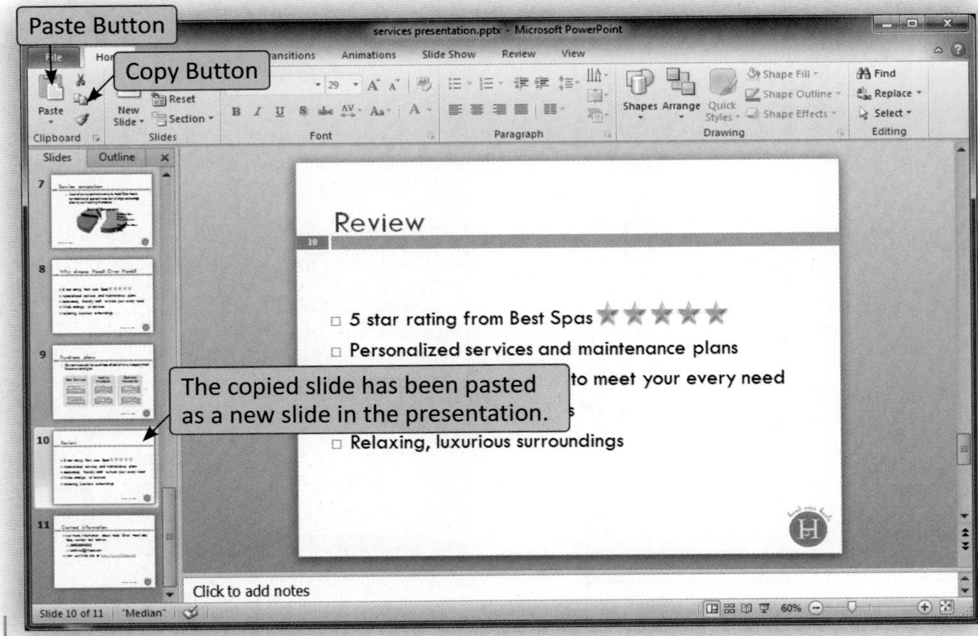

FIGURE PP 4.3

tips & tricks

If you want the copy of the slide to appear directly after the slide you are copying, click the arrow next to the *Copy* button and select **Duplicate.**

Click **Cut** in the *Clipboard* group to copy the slide to the Office Clipboard and remove it from its current location in the presentation.

tell me more

The *Paste* button now includes a menu of options for pasting slides. You can choose to use the current presentation's theme, keep the formatting for the copied slide, or paste the slide as a picture. If you paste the slide as a picture, it will be inserted as a single image and you will not be able to edit the content.

try this

To copy a slide:

- Click the arrow next to the *Copy* button and select **Copy.**
- Press Ctrl + C on the keyboard.
- Right-click the slide and select **Copy.**

To paste a slide:

- Click the arrow below the *Paste* button and select a paste option.
- Press Ctrl + V on the keyboard.
- Right-click the slide and select a paste option.

4.4 Using the Office Clipboard

When you cut or copy items, they are placed on the **Office Clipboard**. A short description or thumbnail of the item represents each item in the task pane, so you know which item you are pasting into your presentation. The Office Clipboard can store up to 24 items for use in the current presentation or any other Office application.

To paste an item from the Office Clipboard into a presentation:

1. Select the item you want to copy.
2. On the *Home* tab, in the *Clipboard* group, click the **Copy** button.
3. Place your cursor where you want to paste the item.
4. On the *Home* tab, in the *Clipboard* group, click the **Clipboard** dialog launcher.
5. The Clipboard task pane appears.
6. Click the item you want to paste.

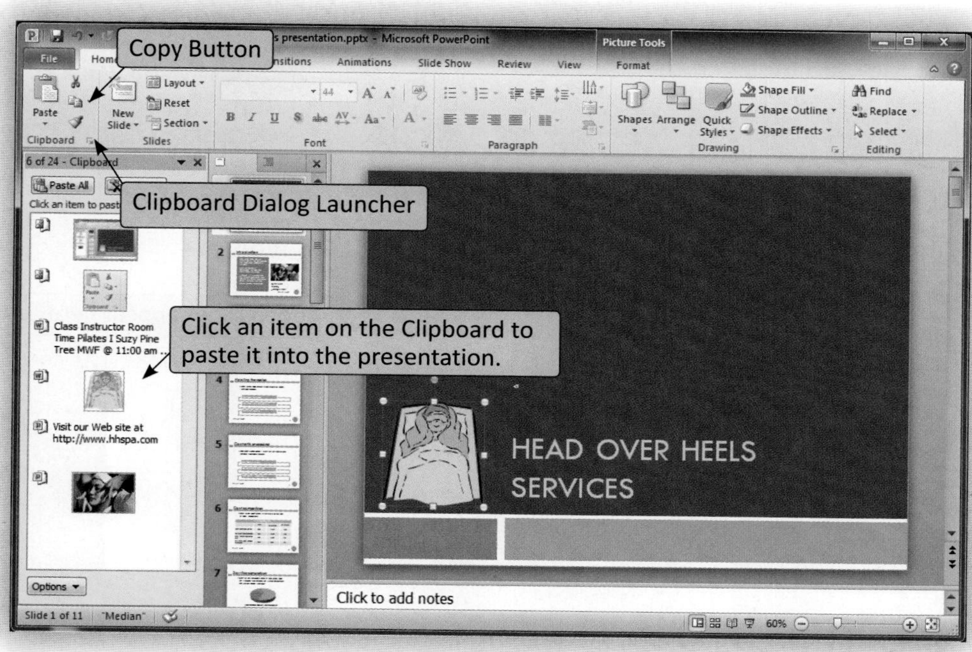

FIGURE PP 4.4

tips & tricks

- To remove an item from the Office Clipboard, point to the item, click the arrow that appears, and select **Delete.**
- To add all the items in the Office Clipboard at once, click the **Paste All** button at the top of the task pane.
- To remove all the items from the Office Clipboard at once, click the **Clear All** button at the top of the task pane.

tell me **more**

The Office Clipboard makes it easy to copy and paste items between presentations and between applications. The icons in the Office Clipboard identify the type of document from which each item originated (Word, Excel, Paint, etc.). When you copy an item in one application, such as Excel, the item will appear in the task pane when the Office Clipboard is opened in PowerPoint.

try **this**

To paste an item, you can also point to the item in the Clipboard task pane, click the arrow that appears, and select **Paste.**

4.5 Defining a Custom Show

A **custom slide show** is a slide show that runs inside another presentation. Custom shows give you the ability to customize your presentation for your audience. Instead of creating multiple presentations for different audiences, you can add custom shows to the original presentation and repurpose the presentation for different audiences.

To define a custom slide show:

1. Click the **Slide Show** tab.
2. In the *Start Slide Show* group, click the **Custom Slide Show** button and select **Custom Shows . . .**
3. In the *Custom Shows* dialog box, click the **New . . .** button.
4. In the *Define Custom Show* dialog box, select the slides you want in your custom show.
5. Click the **Add** button.
6. Click the up and down arrows to reorder your slides.
7. In the *Slide show name:* box, type the name of the custom show.
8. Click **OK** to add the custom show to your presentation.
9. To close the *Custom Shows* dialog box, click the **Close** button.

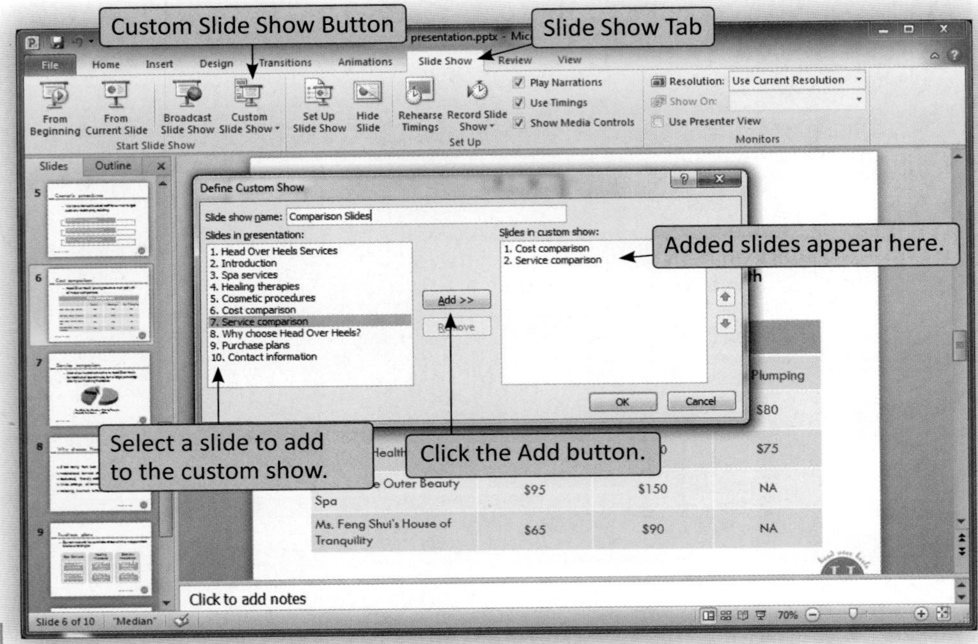

FIGURE PP 4.5

tips & tricks

- To play a custom show, click the **Custom Slide Show** button and select the name of the custom show you want to play. The custom show will open in Slide Show view, allowing you to run through the slides in the custom show.
- In the *Custom Shows* dialog box, click the **Show** button to preview the custom slide show.

tell me **more**

There are two main types of custom slide shows: basic and hyperlinked. Basic custom slide shows display a subset of slides of the main presentation. For example, if you only have 30 minutes to present, but your presentation is 45 minutes long, you could create two custom shows within the same presentation: one with 45 minutes of content and the other with 30 minutes of content. Hyperlinked custom slide shows display slides that are not part of the main presentation. Use hyperlinked custom slide shows for content that you may or may not want to access in the presentation.

4.6 Hiding Slides

When you practice your presentation, you may find that you want to omit certain slides, but that you do not want to delete them from your presentation, in case you need them later. Hiding slides allows you to prevent slides from being seen without permanently removing them.

To hide slides:

1. Select the slide you want to hide.
2. Click the **Slide Show** tab.
3. In the *Set Up* group, click the **Hide Slide** button.

When a slide is hidden, the hidden slide icon appears over the slide number in the *Slide* pane.

To unhide the slide, click the **Hide Slide** button again.

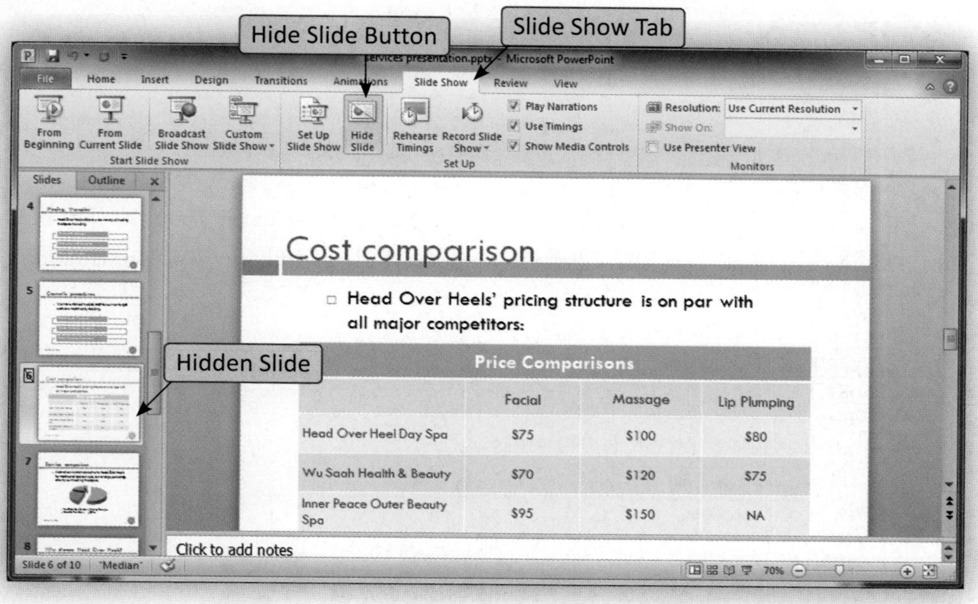

FIGURE PP 4.6

tips & tricks

To unhide a slide during a presentation, right-click any slide, point to **Go to Slide,** and select the slide you want to display. Hidden slides will appear in the list with parentheses around the number. For example, if the third slide in a presentation is hidden, the menu will display the number as (3).

try this

To hide a slide, you can also right-click the slide on the *Slides* tab and select **Hide Slide.** To unhide a slide, right-click the slide again and select **Unhide Slide.**

4.7 Adding Hyperlinks to Slides

A **hyperlink** is text or a graphic that when clicked takes you to a new location. You can use hyperlinks to navigate to Web pages, other PowerPoint presentations, custom shows, or any slide in the presentation. When you point to a hyperlink, your mouse cursor turns to a hand, indicating that it is something that can be clicked.

Some hyperlinks include ScreenTips. A **ScreenTip** is a bubble with text that appears when the mouse is placed over the link. Add a ScreenTip to include a more meaningful description of the hyperlink.

To add a hyperlink from one slide to another slide in the same presentation:

1. Select the text or object you want as the link.
2. Click the **Insert** tab.
3. In the *Links* group, click the **Insert Hyperlink** button.

FIGURE PP 4.7

4. The *Insert Hyperlink* dialog box opens.
5. Under *Link to:* select **Place in This Document.**
6. Select the slide to link to.
7. Type the text for the ScreenTip in the *Text to display:* box.
8. Click **OK** to insert the hyperlink into your presentation.

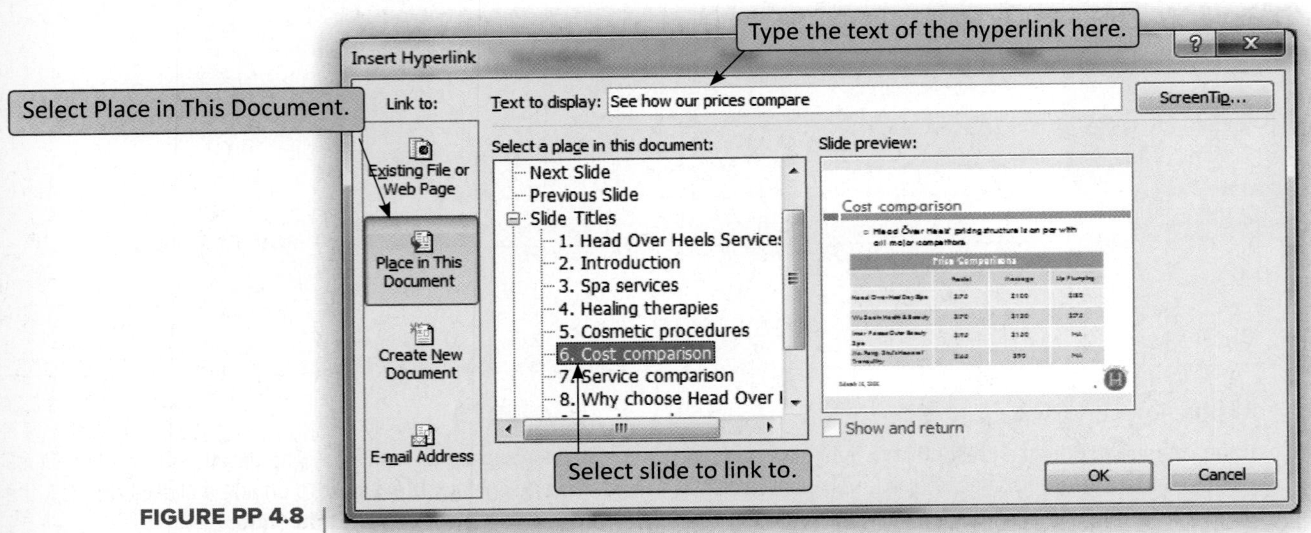

FIGURE PP 4.8

tips & tricks

To remove a hyperlink, first select the hyperlink you want to remove. In the *Links* group, click the **Hyperlink** button. In the *Edit Hyperlink* dialog box, click the **Remove Hyperlink** button.

tell me more

Text hyperlinks follow the color scheme of the presentation, and change color after they have been clicked.

try this

To open the *Insert Hyperlink* dialog box, you can also

- Right-click the object and select **Hyperlink . . .** from the menu.
- Press Ctrl + K on the keyboard.

4.8 Adding Comments

Comments are small messages you add to slides that are not meant to be a part of the presentation. Comments are useful when you are reviewing a presentation and want to add messages about changes or errors on a slide.

To insert a comment on a slide:

1. Click the **Review** tab.
2. In the *Comments* group, click the **New Comment** button.
3. A balloon appears on the screen with the cursor ready for you to enter your comment.
4. Type your comment.
5. Click outside the comment to minimize it.
6. To view the comment, click the comment's icon on the slide.

If you do not want your comments to display in the *Slide* pane, you can hide the comments in the presentation. On the *Review* tab, in the *Comments* group, click the **Show Markup** button to hide the comments in the presentation. Click the **Show Markup** button again to show the comments. The *Show Markup* button toggles between its normal and active state when clicked. When comments are displayed in a presentation, the *Show Markup* button appears in its active state. When comments are hidden, the *Show Markup* button returns to its normal state.

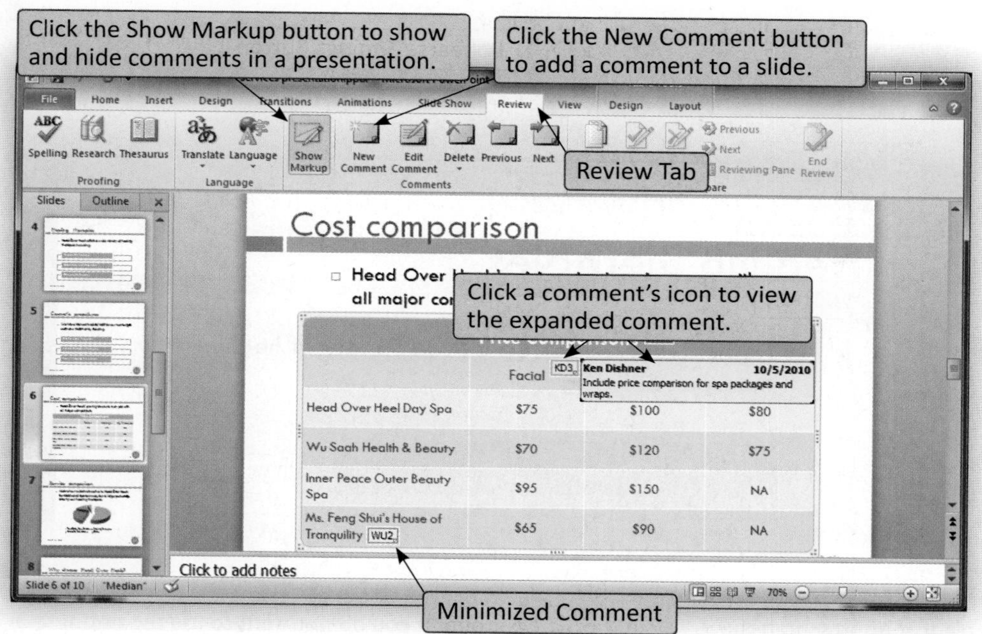

FIGURE PP 4.9

tips & tricks

Click the **Delete Comment** button on the Ribbon to delete a comment from the presentation.

tell me more

To edit a comment, first display the comment you want to edit. In the *Comments* group, click the **Edit Comment** button. Edit the comment in the balloon and click outside the comment to minimize it.

try this

To insert a comment, you can also right-click any comment and select **New Comment** from the menu.

4.9 Rehearsing Timings

Timing is an important part of your presentation. For example, you wouldn't want to be part way through explaining the content of a slide and have your presentation advance before you are ready. Before you give your presentation, it is a good idea to rehearse what you will say and set up the timing for the slide show. Use PowerPoint's **Rehearse Timings** feature to synchronize your verbal presentation with your slides.

To use PowerPoint's Rehearse Timing feature:

1. Click the **Slide Show** tab.
2. In the *Set Up* group, click the **Rehearse Timings** button.
3. When the first slide appears, begin rehearsing your presentation.
4. Click the **Pause** button if you want to stop the timer.
5. Click the **Next** button to advance to the next slide.
6. Continue rehearsing each slide, clicking the **Next** button to advance the slides, until you reach the end of the presentation.
7. At the end of the presentation, you will be asked if you want to keep the timing as part of your slide show. Click **Yes** to include the timings as part of the presentation.

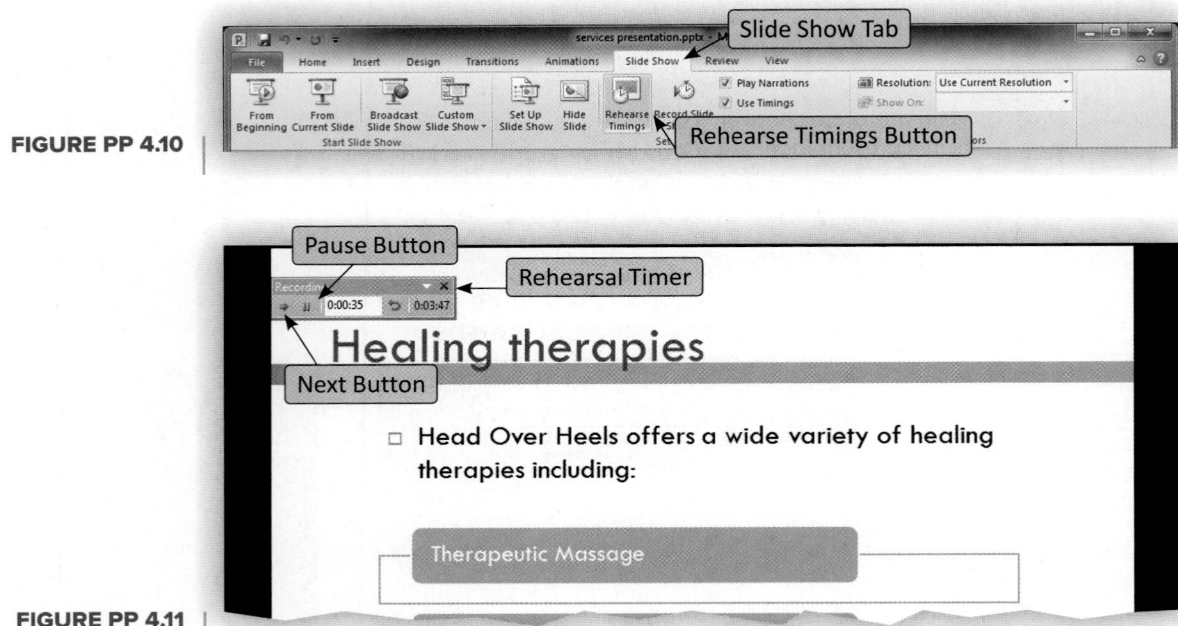

FIGURE PP 4.10

FIGURE PP 4.11

After you have rehearsed the timing of your presentation, you can choose to use the timings or not. If you want to use the timings, select the **Use Rehearsed Timings** check box in the *Set Up* group. If you do not want to use the timings, uncheck the box.

tips & tricks

When you are timing your presentation, be sure to speak slowly and carefully, and to pause slightly before you advance to the next slide.

tell me more

PowerPoint also includes the ability to record your own narration for a presentation and then include the narration as part of the presentation. Click the **Record Slide Show** button to record narration along with the timing for slides.

try this

You can enter the timing for a slide directly into the *Slide Time* box.

4.10 Starting the Slide Show

You can choose to start your presentation from the beginning, playing it all the way through. But what if you find you don't have as much time as you originally planned to present? You can also choose to start the presentation from any slide in the presentation.

To start a presentation from the beginning:

1. Click the **Slide Show** tab.
2. In the *Start Slide Show* group, click the **From Beginning** button.

To start a presentation from the current slide:

1. Click the **Slide Show** tab.
2. In the *Start Slide Show* group, click the **From Current Slide** button.

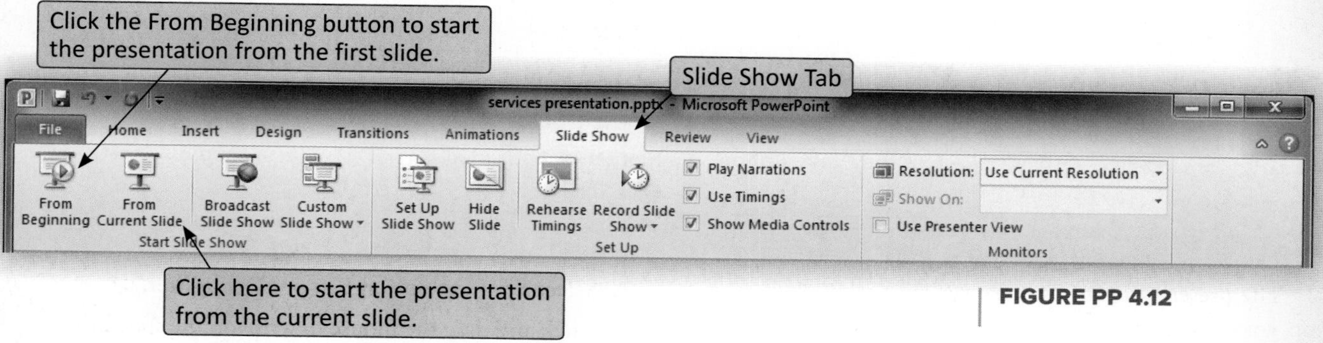

FIGURE PP 4.12

tips & tricks

Another way to start a presentation from the beginning is to select the first slide in the presentation and use any of the methods for playing the presentation from the current slide.

try this

To start a slide show from the current slide, you can also click the **Slide Show** view button on the status bar.

4.11 Using Presentation Tools

Once you have started the slide show, you will need a way to advance through the slides as you talk. You can use the Rehearse Timings feature to automatically advance the slide show for you. However, if you want the freedom to depart from your script, you will want to navigate the slide show yourself. This table lists commands for navigating a presentation in Slide Show view using the mouse and the keyboard:

Slide Show Navigation

COMMAND	MOUSE COMMAND	KEYBOARD COMMAND
Next Slide	Left-click on the slide. Right-click and select **Next.**	Press **Enter.** Press the **Spacebar.**
Previous Slide	Right-click and select **Previous.**	Press **Backspace.**
Specific Slide	Right-click, point to **Go to Slide,** and select the slide.	Press the number of the slide and press **Enter.**
Exit the Presentation	Right-click and select **End Show.**	Press **Escape.**

The presentation tools in PowerPoint allow you to write on your slides while you are giving your presentation. You can use the **Pen** tool to underline or circle important points as you discuss them. Use the **Highlighter** tool to add color behind text on slides and emphasize parts of your slides.

To make notations on slides using the presentation tools:

1. In Slide Show view, click the **Pointer Options** button.
2. Select a pointer option **Pen** or **Highlighter.**
3. Click and drag the mouse to write on the slide or highlight part of the slide.
4. Click the **Pointer Options** button and select **Arrow** to return to the arrow pointer.

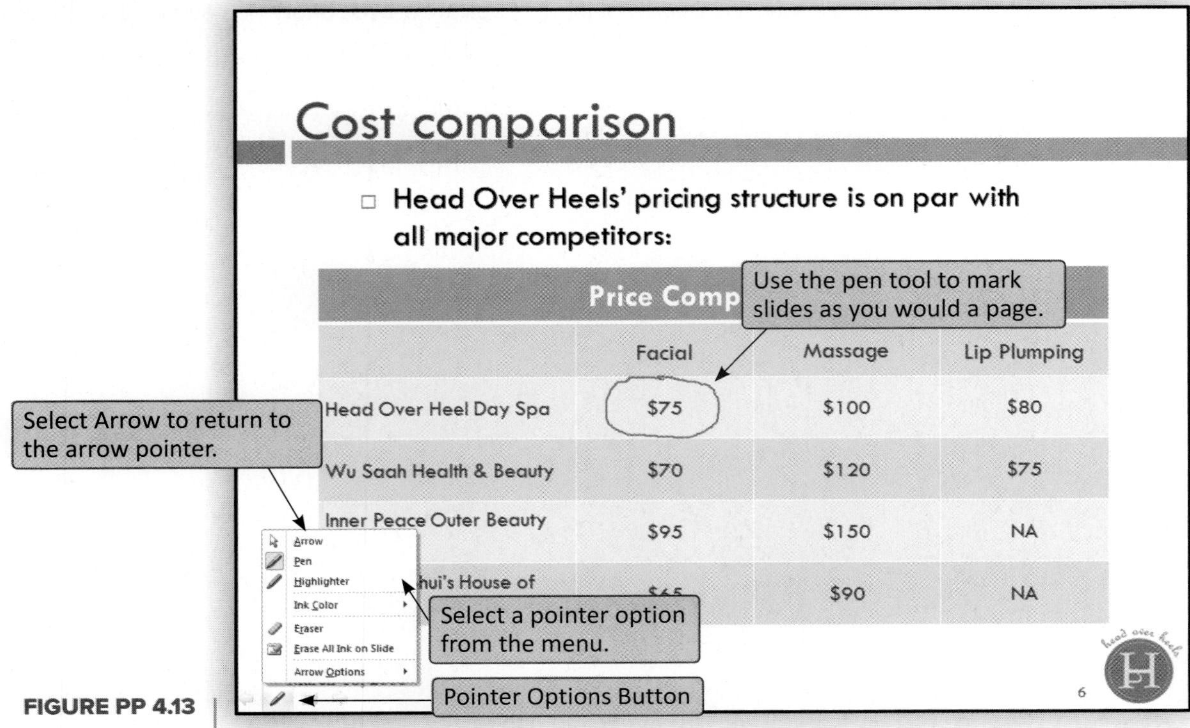

FIGURE PP 4.13

from the perspective of . . .

STUDENT

I was terrified at the idea of presenting in my oral communication class. Using presentation software I integrated tables, pictures, text, video, and sound, all in one presentation. The day I presented, I rocked!

tips & tricks

- If you want to see the last slide you viewed, but it is not part of the slide order, right-click the presentation and select **Last Viewed** on the menu.
- To view a custom show, right-click the presentation, point to **Custom Show,** and select a custom show.

try this

You can also use the *Slide Show* toolbar, located in the lower-left corner of the slide, to navigate through a presentation.

- Click the **Next** button to navigate to the next slide in the presentation.
- Click the **Previous** button to navigate to the previous slide in the presentation.
- Click the **Slide Show Menu** button for access to more powerful navigation commands, such as navigating to a specific slide.

4.12 Printing Presentations

Printing has changed significantly in PowerPoint 2010. Previous versions of PowerPoint relied on *Print Preview* for setting printing options. In PowerPoint 2010, the *Print* tab in Backstage view provides access to all of the printing options for presentations. From the *Print* tab in Backstage view, you can adjust your settings to print the slides in color, grayscale, or black and white. You can also adjust other elements of the slide, such as the header and footer.

To preview and print a presentation:

1. Click the **File** tab to open Backstage view.
2. Click the **Print** tab.
3. Verify that the correct printer name is displayed in the *Printer* section.
4. In the *Settings* section, the last button displays the color options for printing the presentation. By default, *Color* is selected. To change the print selection, click the button, and then click an option: **Color, Grayscale,** or **Pure Black and White.**
5. Click the **Print** button to print.

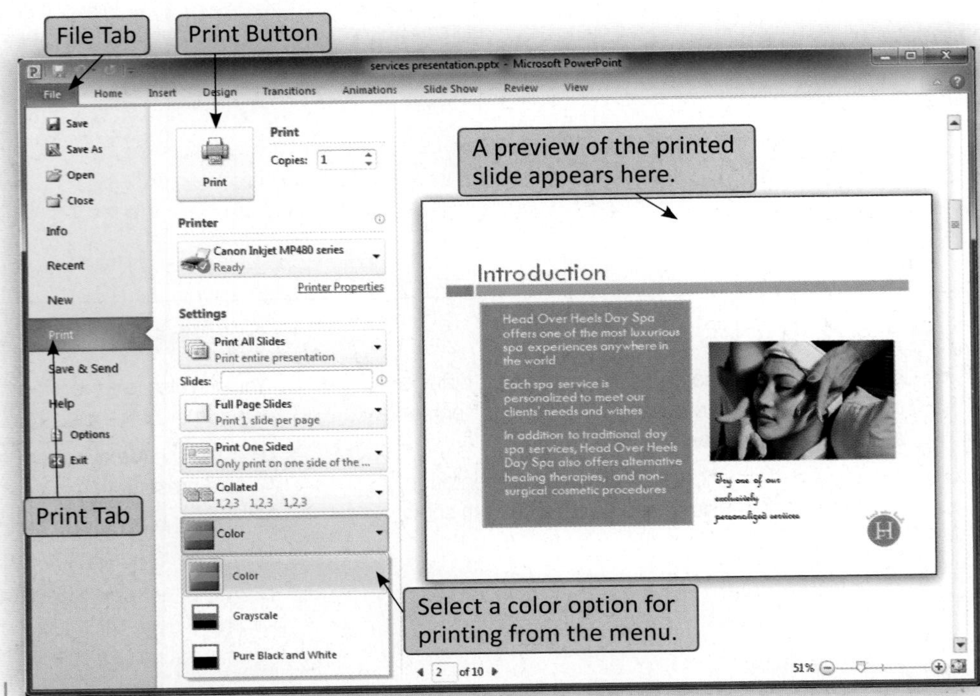

FIGURE PP 4.14

tips & tricks

Click the **Next Page** and **Previous Page** buttons at the bottom of the preview to navigate through your presentation to see how all the slides will appear when printed.

tell me more

All of the options from the old *Print Preview* window are available from the *Print* tab in Backstage view, including the settings for printing hidden slides, editing the header and footer, and printing handouts and notes.

try this

To open the *Print* tab in Backstage view, you can use the keyboard shortcut Ctrl + P.

4.13 Customizing Handout Masters

The **Handout Master** view allows you to modify how the printed version of your presentation will look. When you open the presentation in Handout Master view, you will see a preview of the printed page with dotted placeholders for the slides, header, footer, page number, and date.

To open Handout Master view:

1. Click the **View** tab.
2. In the *Master Views* group, click the **Handout Master** button.

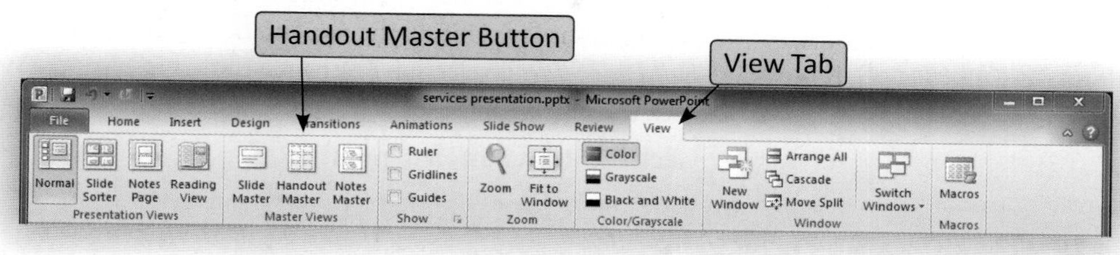

FIGURE PP 4.15

You can show and hide placeholders in Handout Master view. When you hide a placeholder, it no longer appears in the Handout Master view. To show and hide a placeholder, on the *Handout Master* tab, in the *Placeholders* group, click the placeholder's check box.

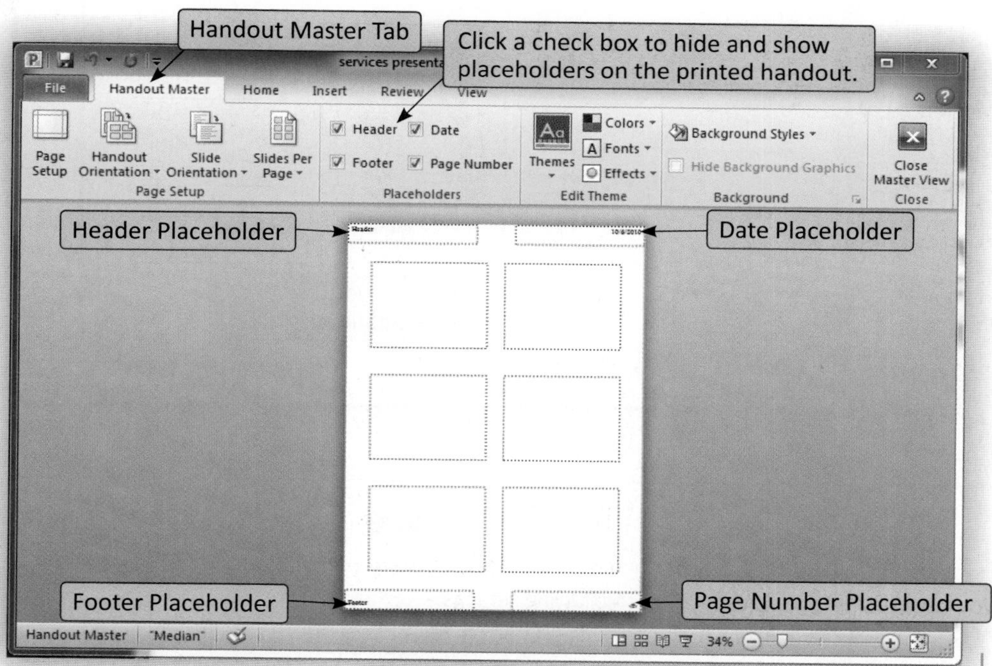

FIGURE PP 4.16

Placeholders you can hide and show include

Header—appears in the upper-left corner of the page and displays the text you entered for the header in the *Header and Footer* dialog box.

Date—appears in the upper-right corner of the page and displays the date.

Footer—appears in the lower-left corner of the page and displays the text you entered for the footer.

Page Number—appears in the lower-right corner of the page and displays the current number of the printed page (not the slide number).

4.14 Previewing and Printing Handouts

In addition to printing slides, PowerPoint also gives you the ability to print handouts, notes, and an outline of the presentation. A **handout** is a printout of your presentation with anywhere from one to nine slides per page and with areas for taking notes. The **Notes Pages** option will print a copy of the slide with its associated note, if there is one. Select **Outline View** when you want to print a text outline of your presentation. As with printing presentations, printing of handouts, notes pages, and outlines are all done from the *Print* tab in Backstage view.

To preview and print outlines, handouts, and notes:

1. Click the **File** tab to open Backstage view.
2. Click the **Print** tab.
3. Verify that the correct printer name is displayed in the *Printer* section.
4. In the *Settings* section, the second button displays the page options for printing the presentation. By default, *Full Page Slides* is selected. To change the print selection, click the button and then select an option.
5. Click the **Print** button to print.

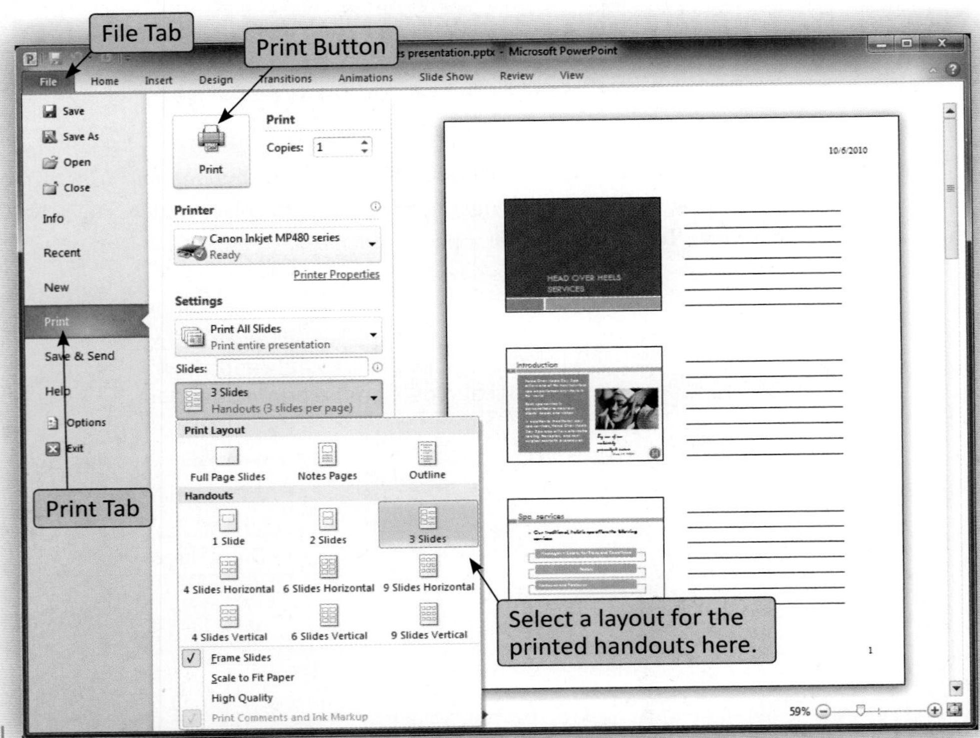

FIGURE PP 4.17

tips & tricks

The *Handouts (3 Slides)* layout includes lines next to the slide image. This layout is useful if you want to print your presentation for your audience and include an area where they can easily write notes to correspond with each slide.

try this

To open the *Print* tab in Backstage view, you can use the keyboard shortcut Ctrl + P.

tell me more

From the *Page Options* button, you can also adjust the following settings:

Scale to Fit Paper—resizes the slides to fit the paper size.

Frame Slides—draws a thin border around the slides for the printed version.

High Quality—prints slides in a higher resolution, allowing for more detailed images and effects.

Print Comments and Ink Markup—allows you to include comments and ink markup in your printed presentation.

projects

Skill Review 4.1

In this review, you will use the skills learned in Chapter 4 to manage and deliver an existing presentation.

1. Open an existing presentation:

a. Open Microsoft PowerPoint 2010.

b. On the *File* tab, click **Open.**

c. In the *Open* dialog box, navigate to the location of your PowerPoint 2010 student files.

d. Find *Ch4_Review1_Menu.pptx* and double-click the file to open it.

e. On the *File* tab, click the **Save As** option.

f. Change the file name to ***[your initials]*** **PP_SkillReview_4-1,** and then click **OK.**

2. Delete, reorder, copy, and paste slides, and use the Office Clipboard.

a. Delete and reorder slides:

(1) Right-click **Slide 6** on the *Slides* tab.

(2) Select **Delete Slide.**

(3) Click the **Undo** button to redisplay the slide.

b. Reorder slides from the *Slides* tab:

(1) Select the thumbnail of **Slide 7.**

(2) Click and drag until the gray line appears above **Slide 6,** and then release the mouse button.

c. Use the Office Clipboard to copy and paste slides:

(1) Select the thumbnail of **Slide 7.**

(2) On the *Home* tab, in the *Clipboard* group, click the **Copy** button.

(3) Click between the thumbnails of **Slide 1** and **Slide 2.**

(4) On the *Home* tab, in the *Clipboard* group, click the **Paste** button.

3. Define a custom show:

a. Click the **Slide Show** tab.

b. In the *Start Slide Show* group, click the **Custom Slide Show** button and select **Custom Shows . . .**

c. Click the **New . . .** button.

d. In the *Define Custom Show* dialog box, select **Slides 1, 3, 4, 5, 6, 7,** and **8.**

e. Click the **Add** button.

f. In the *Slide show name:* box, type Basic

g. Click **OK** to add the custom show to your presentation.

h. To close the *Custom Shows* dialog box, click the **Close** button.

4. Add hyperlinks and comments.

a. Add a hyperlink from one slide to another slide in the same presentation:

(1) On **Slide 3,** select the **Food Log** text.

(2) Click the **Insert** tab.

(3) In the *Links* group, click the **Insert Hyperlink** button.

(4) The *Insert Hyperlink* dialog box opens.

(5) Under *Link to:* select **Place in This Document**.

(6) Select **Slide 4** to link to.

(7) Click **OK** to insert the hyperlink into your worksheet.

b. Add comments:

(1) On **Slide 3,** select the **Fewer carbs** text; then click the **Review** tab.

(2) In the *Comments* group, click the **New Comment** button.

(3) A balloon appears on the screen with the cursor ready for you to enter your comment.

(4) Type: `Bad carbs - choose healthy carbs`

(5) Click outside the comment to hide it.

5. Rehearse timings and use navigation tools.

a. Use PowerPoint's Rehearse Timing feature:

(1) Click the **Slide Show** tab.

(2) In the *Set Up* group, click the **Rehearse Timings** button.

(3) When the first slide appears, begin rehearsing your presentation.

(4) Click the **Pause** button if you want to stop the timer.

(5) Click the **Next** button to advance to the next slide.

(6) Continue rehearsing each slide, clicking the **Next** button to advance the slides, until you reach the end of the presentation.

(7) At the end of the presentation, you will be asked if you want to keep the timing as part of your slide show. Click **No.**

b. Start a presentation from the beginning:

(1) Click the **Slide Show** tab.

(2) In the *Start Slide Show* group, click the **From Beginning** button.

(3) Exit the presentation by pressing the [Esc] key on the keyboard.

c. Start a presentation from the current slide:

(1) Click the **Slide Show** tab.

(2) In the *Start Slide Show* group, click the **From Current Slide** button.

d. Navigate through the presentation using the keyboard:

(1) To advance to the next slide: press [←Enter] or the **Spacebar.**

(2) To go to the previous slide: press [←Backspace].

(3) To jump to a specific slide: type the number of the slide and press [←Enter].

(4) To exit the presentation: press [Esc].

e. Navigate through your presentation using only the mouse:

(1) To advance to the next slide: click the mouse or right-click and select **Next.**

(2) To go to the previous slide: right-click and select **Previous.**

(3) To jump to a specific slide: right-click, point to **Go to Slide,** and select the name of the slide.

(4) To exit the presentation: right-click and select **End Show.**

6. Print presentations and handouts:

a. Print the presentation:

(1) Click the **File** tab to open Backstage view; then click the **Print** tab.

(2) In the *Settings* section, click the **Color** button and select **Grayscale** to change the color option for the presentation.

(3) Click the **Print** button to print your slides.

b. Customize *Handout Masters:*

(1) Click the **View** tab.

(2) In the *Master Views* group, click the **Handout Master** button.

(3) In the *Placeholders* group, click the **Date** check box to remove the date from the printed handout.

c. Preview and print outlines, handouts, and notes:

(1) Click the **File** tab to open Backstage view; then click the **Print** tab.

(2) In the *Settings* section, click the second button, and select **Outline.**

(3) Click the **Print** button and print your handouts.

(4) Save the presentation.

Skill Review **4.2**

In this review, you will use the skills learned in Chapter 4 to manage and deliver an existing presentation.

1. Open an existing presentation:

a. Open Microsoft PowerPoint 2010.

b. On the *File* tab, click **Open.**

c. In the *Open* dialog box, navigate to the location of your PowerPoint 2010 student files.

d. Find *Ch4_Review2_EmergingTech.pptx* and double-click the file to open it.

e. On the *File* tab, click the **Save As** option.

f. Change the file name to `[your initials]PP_SkillReview_4-2`, and then click **OK.**

2. Delete, reorder, copy, and paste slides, and use the Office Clipboard.

a. Delete a slide:

(1) Right-click **Slide 6** on the *Slides* tab.

(2) Select **Delete Slide.**

(3) Click the **Undo** button to redisplay the slide.

b. Reorder slides from the *Slides* tab:

(1) Select the thumbnail of **Slide 7.**

(2) Click and drag until the gray line appears above *Slide 6*, and then release the mouse button.

c. Use the Office Clipboard to copy and paste slides:

(1) Select the thumbnail of **Slide 7.**

(2) On the *Home* tab, in the *Clipboard* group, click the **Copy** button.

(3) Click between the thumbnails of **Slide 1** and **Slide 2.**

(4) On the *Home* tab, in the *Clipboard* group, click the **Paste** button.

3. Define a custom show and hide slides.

a. Define a custom show:

(1) Click the **Slide Show** tab.

(2) In the *Start Slide Show* group, click the **Custom Slide Show** button and select **Custom Shows . . .**

(3) Click the **New . . .** button.

(4) In the *Define Custom Show* dialog box, select **Slides 1, 3, 4, 5, 6, 7,** and **8.**

(5) Click the **Add** button.

(6) In the *Slide show name:* box, type `Basic`

(7) Click **OK** to add the custom show to your presentation.

(8) To close the *Custom Shows* dialog box, click the **Close** button.

b. Hide slides:

(1) Right-click **Slide 2** on the *Slides tab.*

(2) Select **Hide Slide.**

4. Add hyperlinks and comments.

a. Add a hyperlink from one slide to another slide in the same presentation:

(1) On **Slide 5,** select the **Communication** text.

(2) Click the **Insert** tab.

(3) In the *Links* group, click the **Insert Hyperlink** button.

(4) The *Insert Hyperlink* dialog box opens.

(5) Under *Link to:* select **Place in This Document.**

(6) Select **Slide 6** to link to.

(7) Click **OK** to insert the hyperlink into your worksheet.

b. Add comments:

(1) On **Slide 4,** select the **IPad** and **IPod** bullet points; then click the **Review** tab.

(2) In the *Comments* group, click the **New Comment** button.

(3) A balloon appears on the screen with the cursor ready for you to enter your comment.

(4) Type: `Change bullets to iPad and iPod`

(5) Click outside the comment to hide it.

5. Rehearse timings and use navigation tools.

a. Use PowerPoint's Rehearse Timing feature:

(1) Click the **Slide Show** tab.

(2) In the *Set Up* group, click the **Rehearse Timings** button.

(3) When the first slide appears, begin rehearsing your presentation.

(4) Click the **Pause** button if you want to stop the timer.

(5) Click the **Next** button to advance to the next slide.

(6) Continue rehearsing each slide, clicking the **Next** button to advance the slides, until you reach the end of the presentation.

(7) At the end of the presentation, you will be asked if you want to keep the timing as part of your slide show. Click **No.**

b. Start a presentation from the beginning:

(1) Click the **Slide Show** tab.

(2) In the *Start Slide Show* group, click the **From Beginning** button.

(3) Exit the presentation by pressing the Esc key on the keyboard.

c. Start a presentation from the current slide:

(1) Click the **Slide Show** tab.

(2) In the *Start Slide Show* group, click the **From Current Slide** button.

d. Navigate through the presentation using the keyboard:

(1) To advance to the next slide: press ←Enter or the **Spacebar.**

(2) To go to the previous slide: press ←Backspace.

(3) To jump to a specific slide: type the number of the slide and press ←Enter.

(4) To exit the presentation: press Esc.

e. Navigate through your presentation using only the mouse:

(1) To advance to the next slide: click the mouse or right-click and select **Next.**

(2) To go to the previous slide: right-click and select **Previous.**

(3) To jump to a specific slide: right-click, point to **Go to Slide,** and select the name of the slide.

(4) To exit the presentation: right-click and select **End Show.**

6. Print presentations and handouts.

a. Print the presentation:

(1) Click the **File** tab to open Backstage view; then click the **Print** tab.

(2) In the *Settings* section, click the **Color** button and select **Grayscale** to change the color option for the presentation.

(3) Click the **Print** button to print your slides.

b. Customize *Handout Masters:*

(1) Click the **View** tab.

(2) In the *Master Views* group, click the **Handout Master** button.

(3) In the *Placeholders* group, click the **Date** check box to remove the date from the printed handout.

c. Preview and print outlines, handouts, and notes:

(1) Click the **File** tab to open Backstage view; then click the **Print** tab.

(2) In the *Settings* section, click the second button, and select **Outline**.

(3) Click the **Print** button and print your handouts.

(4) Save the presentation.

challenge yourself 1

In this challenge, you will use the skills learned in Chapter 4 to manage and deliver an existing presentation.

1. Open an existing presentation:

a. Open Microsoft PowerPoint 2010.

b. Navigate to the location of your PowerPoint 2010 student files.

c. Open *Ch4_Chall1_FamilyReunion.pptx.*

d. Save the file as `[your initials]PP_Challenge_4-3.`

2. Delete, reorder, copy, and paste slides, and use the Office Clipboard.

a. Delete a slide:

(1) Delete **Slide 6.**

(2) Click the **Undo** button to redisplay the slide.

b. Reorder and copy slides:

(1) Move **Slide 7** before **Slide 6.**

(2) Copy **Slide 7** and paste it between **Slide 1** and **Slide 2**

3. Define a custom show and hide a slide:
   a. Define a new *Custom Slide Show* entitled `Basic` using **Slides 1, 3, 4, 5, 6, 7,** and **8.**
   b. View the custom show.
   c. Hide **Slide 2.**
4. Add hyperlinks and comments:
   a. On **Slide 5,** select the text **Select a theme** and hyperlink it to **Slide 6.**
   b. On **Slide 5,** select the **Photographer** text and add a **New Comment:** `Ask Uncle David`
5. Rehearse timings and use navigation tools:
   a. Rehearse the timings.
   b. Start a presentation from the beginning.
   c. Start a presentation from the current slide.
   d. Navigate through the presentation using the keyboard from slide to slide and directly to *Slide 5*.
   e. Navigate through your presentation using only the mouse.
6. Print presentations and handouts:
   a. Print the presentation in black and white.
   b. Print the *Handouts* **4 to a page.**
   c. Save the presentation.

challenge yourself **2**

In this challenge, you will use the skills learned in Chapter 4 to manage and deliver an existing presentation.

1. Open an existing presentation:
   a. Open Microsoft PowerPoint 2010.
   b. Navigate to the location of your PowerPoint 2010 student files.
   c. Open *Ch4_Chall2_Coffee.pptx.*
   d. Save the file as ***`[your initials]`*****`PP_Challenge_4-4`.**
2. Delete, reorder, copy, and paste slides, and use the Office Clipboard.
   a. Delete a slide:
      (1) Delete **Slide 5.**
      (2) Click the **Undo** button to redisplay the slide.
   b. Reorder and copy slides:
      (1) Move **Slide 6** before **Slide 5.**
      (2) Copy **Slide 6** and paste it between **Slide 1** and **Slide 2.**
3. Define a custom show and hide a slide:
   a. Define a new *Custom Slide Show* entitled `Basic` using **Slides 1, 3, 4, 5,** and **6.**
   b. View the custom show.
   c. Hide **Slide 2.**
4. Add hyperlinks and comments:
   a. On **Slide 5,** select the text **Service with a smile** and hyperlink it to **Slide 6.**
   b. On **Slide 5,** select the **Work with local farmers** text and add a **New Comment:** `Check with farmers association`

5. Rehearse timings and use navigation tools:
   a. Rehearse the timings.
   b. Start a presentation from the beginning.
   c. Start a presentation from the current slide.
   d. Navigate through the presentation using the keyboard from slide to slide and directly to *Slide 5*.
   e. Navigate through your presentation using only the mouse.
6. Print presentations and handouts:
   a. Print the presentation in black and white.
   b. Print the *Handouts* **4 to a page.**
   c. Save the presentation.

on your own

You are charged with holding the initial meeting for the local block watch committee and want to create an introductory presentation to share with your neighbors.

1. Navigate to the location of your PowerPoint 2010 student files.
2. Open *Ch4_OYO_Blockwatch.pptx.*
3. Save the file as `[your initials]PP_OnYourOwn_4-5.`
4. Delete **Slide 5.**
5. Click the **Undo** button to redisplay the slide.
6. Move **Slide 6** after *Slide 8.*
7. Copy **Slide 8** and paste it between **Slide 2** and **Slide 3.**
8. Define a new *Custom Slide Show* entitled `Basic` using all but **Slide 3.**
9. View the custom show.
10. Hide **Slide 2.**
11. On **Slide 6,** select the text **SMART** and hyperlink it to **Slide 8.**
12. On **Slide 4,** select the **Safety** text and add a **New Comment:** `Top Priority`
13. Rehearse the timings.
14. Start a presentation from the beginning.
15. Start a presentation from the current slide.
16. Navigate through the presentation using the keyboard from slide to slide and directly to *Slide 5.*
17. Navigate through your presentation using only the mouse.
18. Print the presentation in black and white.
19. Print the *Handouts* **4 to a page.**
20. Save the presentation.

fix it

You have been assigned the task of fixing an existing presentation based on the skills learned in Chapter 4.

1. Using PowerPoint 2010, open *Ch4_Fixit_Students.pptx.*
2. Save the file as `[your initials]PP_FixIt_4-6.`

3. Move **Slide 6** before **Slide 5.**
4. Copy **Slide 6** and paste it between **Slide 1** and **Slide 2.**
5. Define a new *Custom Slide Show* entitled `Basic` using all but **Slide 2.**
6. View the custom show.
7. Hide **Slide 2.**
8. On **Slide 3,** select the text **Preparation** and hyperlink it to **Slide 5.**
9. On **Slide 6,** select the **Responsibility** text and add a **New Comment:** `Learner success with learner responsibility`
10. Rehearse the timings.
11. Start a presentation from the beginning.
12. Start a presentation from the current slide.
13. Navigate through the presentation using the keyboard from slide to slide and directly to *Slide 5.*
14. Navigate through your presentation using only the mouse.
15. Print the presentation in black and white.
16. Print the *Handouts* **4 to a page.**
17. Save the presentation.

glossary of key terms

3-D reference: A formula that references the same cell(s) on multiple sheets.

a

Absolute reference: A cell reference whose location remains constant when the formula is copied. The $ character before a letter or number in the cell address means that part of the cell's address is *absolute* (nonchanging).

Accounting Number Format: Aligns the $ at the left side of the cell, displays two places after the decimal, and aligns all numbers at the decimal point. Zero amounts are displayed as dashes (–).

Animation: Movement of an object or text in a presentation. There are four basic types of animation schemes: Entrance, Emphasis, Exit, and Motion Paths.

Arguments: The parts of the formula (inputs) that the function uses to calculate a value.

Attachment field: Stores files as attachments to records. Attachments can be images, Word documents, or almost any other type of data file.

AutoCorrect: Feature that analyzes each word as it is entered in a document. Each word is compared to a list of common misspellings, symbols, and abbreviations. If a match is found, AutoCorrect automatically replaces the text in the document with the matching replacement entry.

AutoFill: Feature used to fill a group of cells with the same data or to extend a data series.

AutoFilter: Feature that allows you to show only rows that meet criteria you specify.

Automatic date stamp: Pulls the current date from the computer's system clock and displays the date in the document.

AutoNumber field: A field that is automatically assigned its value by Access. Database users cannot edit or enter data in an AutoNumber field. AutoNumber fields are often used as a primary key if no other unique field exists in the table.

AutoSum: Allows you to insert common functions (SUM, AVERAGE, COUNT, MIN, and MAX) with a single mouse click.

AVERAGE function: A statistical function that is used to calculate the average value of a group of values. A formula using the AVERAGE function looks like this: **=AVERAGE(A3:A6).**

b

Back Up: Creates a copy of the database and preserves the data at a certain point. At any time you can open the backup and restore your data from an earlier stage.

Background: The graphic element that fills a slide. Backgrounds can be solid colors, textures, or images.

Bibliography: A compiled list of sources referenced in a document.

Bound control: Control that displays data from a specific field.

Building block: A piece of content that is reusable in any document. Building blocks can be text, such as AutoText, or can include graphics, such as a cover page.

Building Blocks Organizer: Lists the building blocks in alphabetical order by the gallery in which they appear and includes Bibliographies, Cover Pages, Equations, Footers, Headers, Page Numbers, Table of Contents, Tables, Text Boxes, and Watermarks.

Bullet: A symbol that is displayed before each item in a list.

Bulleted list: List type used to organize information that does not have to be displayed in a particular order.

c

Calculated control: An unbound text control that contains an expression (formula).

Calculated field: A field in a table or query that displays a value returned by an *expression* (a formula).

Caption: A brief description of an illustration, chart, equation, or table.

Cell: The intersection of a row and column in a table or spreadsheet.

Cell reference: A cell's address when it is referred to in a formula.

Change Case command: Command in Word that manipulates the typed characters, changing how the letters are displayed.

Character effects: Special formatting applied to text to alter the text's appearance. Effects include **bold,** *italic,* and underline.

Chart: A graphic that transforms numerical data into a more visual representation.

Chart area: Any empty area of a chart.

Citation: A reference to source material in a document. Citations include information such as the author, title, publisher, and the publish date.

Clear: Command in Excel used to remove cell contents, formatting, comments, or hyperlink formatting.

Clear Formatting: Command that removes any formatting that has been applied to text, including character formatting, text effects, and styles, and leaves only plain text.

Clip art: Illustrations, photographs, audio clips, and video clips that are made available through Word, Excel, and PowerPoint to use in documents, spreadsheets, and presentations.

Clips: Images, photographs, scanned material, animations, sound, video, and other media files from an external source.

Color scales: A conditional formatting style in Excel that colors cells according to one of the color scales [e.g., red to green (bad/low to good/high) or blue to red (cold/low to hot/high].

Color theme: A set of colors that complement each other and are designed to work well together. See also *Theme Colors.*

Comma Style: Number format similar to the *Accounting Number Format,* but without the currency symbol.

Comment: A small text note similar to a Post-it note that can be added to a document, spreadsheet, or presentation.

Compact & Repair: Tool that eliminates hidden, temporary database objects that take up database space unnecessarily.

Compare Side by Side: Feature that allows two documents to be displayed and compared on-screen at the same time.

Content placeholder: A special type of placeholder that provides a quick way to add a variety of material to presentations, including tables, charts, SmartArt diagrams, pictures, clip art, and videos.

Contextual tabs: Contain commands specific to the type of object selected and are only visible when the commands might be useful.

Control layout: Combines multiple controls in your database form or report into a single layout object in one of two formats: tabular and stacked.

Copy: Command that places a duplicate of the selected text or object on the Clipboard without changing the file.

COUNT function: Counts the number of cells that contain numbers within a specified range of cells. A formula using the COUNT function looks like this: **=COUNT(A2:A106).**

COUNTA function: Counts the number of cells that are not blank within a specified range of cells. Use COUNTA if your cell range includes both numbers and text data. A formula using the COUNTA function looks like this: **=COUNTA(B2:B106).**

COUNTBLANK function: Counts the number of blank cells within a specified range of cells. A formula using the COUNTBLANK function looks like this: **=COUNTBLANK(D2:D106).**

Cover page: First page in a document that contains brief information about the document, including the title and the date.

Criteria: Conditions that the records must meet in order to be included in the query results. *Criteria* is a plural word that refers to more than one *criterion.*

Crosstab Query: Presents data in a spreadsheet format, allowing you to specify fields to use for column headers and for row headers, and then automatically calculating totals for values in another field as related to the column and row headers.

Currency field: Stores a numerical value with a high degree of accuracy (up to four decimal places to the right of the decimal). Access will not round Currency fields, regardless of the format in which the value displays.

Currency format: Number format that places the $ immediately to the left of the number, so columns of numbers do not align at the $ and at the decimal as they do with *Accounting Number Format.*

Custom slide show: A slide show that runs inside another slide show. Custom slide shows can be accessed through the *Custom Show* menu in Slide Show view or through a hyperlink.

Cut: Command that removes the selected text or object from the file and places it on the Office Clipboard for later use.

d

Data bars: A conditional formatting style in Excel that displays a color bar (gradient or solid) representing the cell value in comparison to other values (cells with higher values have longer data bars).

Data points: Values from a cell range plotted on a chart.

Data series: A sequence of cells with a recognizable pattern (used with the AutoFill feature).

Data series (chart): Groups of data points as plotted on a chart.

Datasheet form: An Access form that reproduces the exact look and layout of the table datasheet as a form.

Datasheet view, forms: Displays a Datasheet form in the same Datasheet view format used for tables. Available for Datasheet forms only.

Datasheet view, queries: View that shows the record set that matches the query criteria.

Datasheet view, tables: View to use when entering data in a table or to sort and filter data. By default, tables open in Datasheet view.

Date/Time field: Stores a numerical value that is displayed as a date and time. The format in which the date and/or time displays is controlled by the format property.

Design view, forms: Allows you to change the structure or layout of the form.

Design view, queries: View where you build the query, adding fields and specifying criteria.

Design view, reports: Allows you to change the structure or layout of the report.

Design view, tables: View where you establish the table primary key and table properties as well as specific properties or formatting for individual fields. Use Design view when you want to change the structure or properties of the table.

Draft view: Displays a simple version of the text in a document. Draft view does not display headers and footers, page edges, backgrounds, or drawing objects.

e

Edit mode: The data entry method used in Excel to change only part of the cell data by double-clicking the cell, and then moving the cursor within the cell to insert or delete data.

Endnote: A reference in a document that provides the reader with further information. Endnotes are comprised of two parts: a reference mark and the associated text. Endnotes appear at the end of the document.

Enhanced ScreenTip: A ScreenTip that displays not only the name of the command, but also the keyboard shortcut (if there is one) and a short description of what the button does and when it is used.

Expression: A formula used in a field in a table or query or a control in a form or report.

f

Field: Each column in a table in a database.

Field Properties pane: Allows you to set field properties in table Design view.

***File* tab:** Tab located at the far left side of the Ribbon. Opens the Microsoft Office Backstage view.

Fill Handle tool: Appears at the lower-right corner of a selected cell or group of cells and can be used to implement the AutoFill feature.

Filter: Limits the database records or spreadsheet rows displayed to only those that meet specific criteria.

Find: Command that locates specific text, data, or formatting in a document, spreadsheet, presentation, or database.

Find Duplicates Query: Finds duplicate records in a table.

Find Unmatched Query: Finds records in one table that do not have matching records in another table.

Font: Refers to a set of characters of a certain design. The font is the shape of the character or number as it appears on-screen.

Font theme: A set of fonts that complement each other and are designed to work well together. See also *Theme Fonts.*

Footer (PowerPoint): Text that appears on every slide or handout. Typically, a footer appears at the bottom of a slide or handout.

Footer (Word, Excel, Access): Text that appears at the bottom of every page, just above the bottom margin.

Footnote: A reference in a document that provides the reader with further information. Footnotes are comprised of two parts: a reference mark and the associated text. Footnotes appear at the bottom of a page.

Foreign key: In a one-to-many relationship, the field in the secondary table that relates to the primary key in the primary table.

Form view: Provides a user-friendly interface for entering data in a database. From Form view, you cannot change the form layout or formatting.

Format Painter: Tool that copies and pastes formatting styles.

Forms: Allow database users to input data through a friendly interface.

Formula: An equation used to calculate a value.

Formula AutoComplete: Displays a list of potential matches (functions and other valid reference names) after an = has been typed in a cell in Excel.

Freeze: Excel command that keeps column headings and row labels visible as you scroll through your data.

Full Screen Reading view: Displays the document in a simple easy-to-read format. In this view, the Ribbon is no longer visible.

Functions: Preprogrammed shortcuts for calculating complex equations (like the average of a group of numbers).

g

Goal Seek: Function that lets you enter a desired value (outcome) for a formula and specify an input cell that can be modified in order to reach that goal.

Graphics: Photographs, clip art, SmartArt, or line drawings that can be added to documents, spreadsheet, presentations, and database forms and reports.

Gridlines (Excel): The lines that appear on the worksheet defining the rows and columns.

Gridlines (PowerPoint): A series of dotted vertical and horizontal lines that divide the slide into small boxes. Used as visual markers for aligning placeholders and graphics.

Group: Subsection of a tab on the Ribbon; organizes commands with similar functions together.

Grouping (Excel): Combining multiple worksheets with the same structure into one object.

Grouping (Access): Feature that organizes records into distinct sections within an Access report.

h

Handout: A printout of a presentation with anywhere from one to nine slides per page and with areas for taking notes.

Handout master: Master that controls how the slides in a presentation look when printed.

Handout Master view: Master view where the printed version of a presentation is modified.

Hard page break: Command that forces the text to a new page no matter how much content is on the present page.

Header (PowerPoint): Text that appears on every slide or handout. Typically, a header appears at the top of a handout.

Header (Word, Excel, Access): Text that appears at the top of every page, just below the top margin.

Heading (Word): A word or brief phrase used to indicate the start of a new topic in a document. Word uses the built-in heading styles when generating a table of contents.

Headings (Excel): The numbers at the left of rows and the letters at the top of columns.

Highlight Cells Rules: A conditional formatting style in Excel that allows you to define formatting for cells that meet specific numerical or text criteria (e.g., greater than a specific value or containing a specific text string).

Highlighter tool: Slide show tool used to add color behind text on slides in Slide Show view and emphasize parts of a slide.

Highlighting: Tool in Word that changes the background color of the selected area to make it stand out on the page.

***Home* tab:** Contains the most commonly used commands for each Office application.

Hyperlink: Text or a graphic that, when clicked, opens another file or jumps to another place in the document, spreadsheet, or presentation.

Hyperlink field: Stores a Web address or e-mail address.

i

Icon sets: Conditional formatting style in Excel that displays a graphic in each cell representing the cell value in relation to other values.

IF function: Logical function that returns one value if a condition is true and another value if the condition is false. A formula using the IF function looks like this: **=IF(TOTAL_SALES > 50000,10%,5%).**

Index: A list of topics and associated page numbers that typically appears at the end of a document.

Input Mask property: Ensures that users enter data in a database field in a particular format.

k

Keyboard shortcuts: Keys or combinations of keys that when pressed execute a command.

l

Label: Control that displays the field name or other text.

Landscape: Page orientation where the width of the page is greater than the height.

Layout view, forms: Allows you to manipulate the layout and formatting of the form while viewing "live" data.

Layout view, reports: Allows you to manipulate the layout and formatting of the report while viewing "live" data.

Legend: A key for a chart defining which data series is represented by each color.

Line spacing: The white space between lines of text.

Live Preview: Displays formatting changes in a file before actually committing to the change.

Long Date: Excel date format that displays the day of the week, and then the name of the month, the two-digit date, and the four-digit year (Monday, September 05, 2011).

Lookup field: Allows the user to select data from a list of items.

m

Macros: Programming instructions that can be run from within a file. Macros are used to automate data entry and formatting processes and to execute commands from buttons in database forms and reports.

Mail merge: The process of creating several documents based on a main document, merge fields, and a recipients list.

Margins: The blank spaces at the top, bottom, left, and right of a page.

Master views: Contain universal settings for the presentation, and include the Slide Master view, the Handout Master view, and the Notes Master view.

MAX function: Statistical function that will give the highest value in a range of values. A formula using the MAX function looks like this: **=MAX(A3:A6).**

Mean: The sum of a group of values divided by the number of values in the group.

Median: The middle value of a set of values.

Memo field: Holds text and numbers like a text field, except you can enter up to 65,535 characters in a memo field. Text in memo fields can be formatted using rich text formatting.

Merge cells: Combines multiple cells in a table or spreadsheet into a single cell.

Merge fields: Placeholders that insert specific data from the recipients list you created in a mail merge.

Microsoft Office Backstage view: Tab that contains the commands for managing and protecting files including Save, Open, Close, New, and Print. Backstage replaces the Office Button menu from Office 2007 and the File menu from previous versions of Office.

MIN function: Statistical function that will give the lowest value in a range of values. A formula using the MIN function looks like this: **=MIN(A3:A6).**

Mini toolbar: Provides access to common tools for working with text. When text is selected and then the mouse is rested over the text, the Mini toolbar fades in.

Mixed reference: A combination cell reference with a row position that stays constant with a changing column position (or vice versa).

Mode: The value that appears most often in a group of values.

Movie: A multimedia clip that includes moving images and sounds.

Multilevel list: List type that divides the content into several levels of organization.

Multiple Items form: Displays multiple records at once. The layout and design of a Multiple Items form can be modified.

n

Named ranges: See *Names.*

Names: A word or group of words that is assigned to cells or ranges of cells to give your cell references names that are more user-friendly.

Navigation Pane: Pane that organizes all the objects for a database. The Navigation Pane is docked at the left side of the screen.

New command: Creates a new file in an Office application without exiting and reopening the program.

Normal view (PowerPoint): The view where content is created and edited. Normal view consists of the *Slide* and *Outline* tabs, *Slide* pane, and *Notes* pane.

Notes master: Master that controls the look of notes when printed along with the slides.

Notes Master view: View that controls how the printed notes pages will look.

Notes Page view: The view where notes are displayed along with slides in a presentation.

Notes pages: The printed copy of the slide with its associated note.

NOW function: Function that inserts the current date and time. A formula using the NOW function looks like this: **=NOW().**

Number field: Holds a numerical value. The default number is described as a *long integer,* a number between –2,147,483,648 and 2,147,483,647.

Number format: An Excel cell format that stores data as numbers and shows two decimal places by default (so 43 displays as 43.00) but does not include commas.

Numbered list: List type used to organize information that must be presented in a certain order.

o

Object dependency: The relationship between two database objects when one object is dependent upon the other. For example, a form is dependent on the table it is based on. If you delete the table, the form will be invalid.

Objects: The parts of an Access database. Objects include tables, forms, queries, reports, and macros.

Office Clipboard: Task pane that displays up to 24 copied or cut items for use in any Office application.

One-to-many relationship: A relationship between two database tables where the primary table contains a primary key field that is included as a field (the *foreign key*) in the secondary table. Thus, one record in the first table can relate to many records in the second table.

Order of operations: (Also called *precedence*). A mathematical rule stating that mathematical operations in a formula are calculated in this order: (1) exponents and roots, (2) multiplication and division, and (3) addition and subtraction.

***Outline* tab:** Displays only the text from the slides in a presentation in an outline format. Use the *Outline* tab to enter and edit text directly in the outline.

Outline view: Displays the document grouped by heading levels. Outline view is used to check the structure of a document.

p

Page border: The decorative graphic element along the top, right, bottom, and left edges of the page. Borders can be simple lines or include 3-D effects and shadows.

Paragraph: Any text separated by a hard return. A hard return refers to pressing the ←Enter key to create a new paragraph.

Paragraph alignment: How text is aligned with regard to the left and right margins of a document.

Parameter query: A query with user-controlled criteria input. When the query is run, the user is prompted to enter a value for a specific field (the parameter input) that will be used as the criterion when generating results.

Paste: Command that is used to insert text or an object from the Clipboard into a file.

Pen tool: Slide show tool used to underline or circle important points in Slide Show view as they are discussed.

Percent Style: Displays numbers as % with zero places to the right of the decimal point.

PivotChart: A graphic representation of a PivotTable.

PivotChart view: Access view that summarizes query or table data in a PivotChart.

PivotTable: A special report view that summarizes data and calculates the intersecting totals. In Excel, PivotTables do not contain any data themselves—they summarize data from a range or a table in another part of your workbook.

PivotTable view: Access view that summarizes query or table data in a PivotTable.

Placeholder: A container on a slide that holds text or other content, such as a table, chart, or image.

PMT (Payment) function: Function that can be used to calculate loan payments. The PMT function is based upon constant payments and a constant interest rate. A formula using the PMT function looks like this: **=PMT(7%/12,120,250000).**

Points: Measurement for the height of a font. Abbreviated "pt."

Portrait: Page orientation where the height of the page is greater than the width.

Precedence: (Also called *order of operations*). A mathematical rule stating that mathematical operations in a formula are calculated in this order: (1) exponents and roots, (2) multiplication and division, and (3) addition and subtraction.

Presentation: A multimedia slide show that combines text, images, charts, audio, video, animations, and transition effects to convey information.

Primary key: The field that contains data unique to each record in a table.

Print Layout view (Word): Displays how document elements will appear on a printed page.

Print Preview: In Access, Print Preview is a specific report view that shows how the database report will appear when printed. However, Print Preview is also a common command available from almost any application that allows you to see a preview of a file before you print it.

Property control: An element that is added to a document to save time entering the same information over and over again. Property controls can be used as shortcuts for entering long strings of text that are difficult to type, such as e-mail addresses, phone numbers, and street addresses.

q

Queries: Extract data from a table or multiple related tables.

Query grid: The lower pane in query Design view where the fields and criteria for the query are defined.

Quick Access Toolbar: Toolbar located at the top of the application window above the *File* tab. The Quick Access Toolbar gives quick one-click access to common commands.

Quick Layouts: Apply combinations of labels, titles, and data tables to charts.

Quick Parts: Snippets of text that can be saved and then added to any document.

Quick Start Application Parts: Predesigned tables, forms, and reports that you can use to start building a database.

Quick Style: A group of formatting, including character and paragraph formatting, that can easily apply to text, tables, drawings, or other objects.

r

Range names: See *Names.*

Reading view: The view that runs the presentation within the PowerPoint application window.

Ready mode: The data entry method used in Excel to change the contents of the entire cell by clicking the cell once and then typing the data.

Record: Each row in a table in a database.

Record source: The associated table or query for a database form or report.

Redo: Reverses the undo command and restores the file to its previous state.

Reference mark: The superscript character placed next to the text for a footnote or endnote.

Reference style: A set of rules used to display references in a bibliography. These rules include the order of information, when and how punctuation is used, and the use of character formatting.

Referential integrity: The policy that ensures that related database records remain accurate. If a relationship has referential integrity enforced, then no modification can be made to either table that would violate the relationship structure.

Rehearse Timings: Feature that runs the presentation while recording the time spent on each slide.

Relational database: A database that allows you to relate tables and databases to one another through common fields.

Relative reference: A cell reference that adjusts to the new location in the worksheet when the formula is copied.

Replace: Used with the *Find* command to replace specified data or formatting in a file with new data or formatting.

Report view: Shows a static view of the database report. You cannot change the layout or formatting of the report from Report view.

Reports: Display database information for printing or viewing on-screen.

Ribbon: Located across the top of the application window and organizes common features and commands into tabs.

S

Sans serif fonts: Fonts that do not have an embellishment at the end of each stroke. Includes Calibri and Arial.

Screenshot: An image of what is currently displayed on the computer screen (such as an application's interface or of a Web page).

ScreenTip (hyperlinks): A bubble with text that appears when the mouse hovers over a hyperlink. Typically, a ScreenTip provides a description of the hyperlink.

ScreenTip (Ribbon): A small information box that displays the name of the command when the mouse is rested over a button on the Ribbon.

Sections (PowerPoint): Smaller groups of slides within a presentation to help better organize the content.

Select query: Displays data from one or more tables or queries, based on the fields that you select.

Serif fonts: Fonts that have an embellishment at the end of each stroke. Includes Cambria and Times New Roman.

Shape: A drawing object that can be quickly added to a document, presentation, or worksheet.

Short Date: Excel number format that displays the one- or two-digit number representing the month, followed by the one- or two-digit number representing the day, followed by the four-digit year (9/5/2011).

Shortcut menus: Menus of commands that display when an area of the application window is right-clicked.

Slide: A unit within a presentation. Each slide contains content, including text, graphics, audio, and video.

Slide Library: Slides that have been uploaded to a server for others to view and use in their presentations.

Slide master: A slide template used throughout the presentation to create a consistent look and feel.

Slide Show view: The view that displays the slides full-screen and displays the presentation as the audience will see it.

Slide Sorter view: The view that displays a grid of thumbnail pictures of the slides in a presentation, and is useful in rearranging the order of slides in a presentation.

***Slides* tab:** Displays thumbnails of all the slides in a presentation. Use the *Slides* tab to quickly navigate between slides and rearrange the slide order of slides in a presentation.

Smart Tag (Excel): Icon that appears next to a formula with a potential error and displays a menu for resolving the issue.

SmartArt: Visual diagrams containing graphic elements with text boxes to enter information in.

Sort: Arranges the rows in a table, worksheet, or datasheet in either ascending (A–Z) or descending (Z–A) alphabetical or numeric order.

Sound files: Music or sound effects that can be added to slides.

Sparklines: A type of chart that represents each data series as an individual graphic within a single cell. Sparklines are a new type of chart available in Excel 2010.

Speaker notes: Hidden notes that do not appear as part of the presentation.

Split: Command that divides the worksheet view into two or four panes. Each pane scrolls independently of the other(s), so you can see two (or four) different areas of the worksheet at the same time.

Split cells: Divides a cell in a table in Word into multiple cells.

Split form: Combines the convenience of a continuous datasheet form with the usability of a single form displaying one record at a time.

SQL view: Shows the code used to build the query.

Stacked layout: Places the form or report labels at the left side with data to the right (similar to many paper forms or reports).

Styles: Complex formatting, including font, color, size, and spacing, that can be applied to Office files.

Synchronous scrolling: Feature that allows two documents to be scrolled at once. When the active document is scrolled, the other document will scroll at the same time.

t

Tab: Subsection of the Ribbon; organizes commands further into related groups.

Tab leader: Element that fills in the space between tab stops with solid, dotted, or dashed lines.

Tab stop: The location along the horizontal ruler that indicates how far to indent text when the Tab key is pressed.

Table (Excel): A range of cells may be explicitly defined as a table in Excel with additional functionality such as a Total row.

Table (Word, PowerPoint): Content element that helps to organize information by rows, which display horizontally, and columns, which display vertically.

Table of contents: Lists the topics in a document and the associated page numbers, so readers can easily locate information.

Tables (Access): Store all the database data. Tables are the basic building blocks of the database.

Tabular layout: Places the form or report labels across the top, with columns of data (similar to a datasheet or a spreadsheet).

Template: A file with predefined settings that can be used as a pattern to create a new file.

Text boxes (PowerPoint): Boxes that are added to the slide layout to enter text anywhere on the slide.

Text field: Database field that can hold up to 255 characters. Text fields are used for short text data or numbers that should be treated as text.

Text placeholders: Predefined areas in slide layouts where text is entered.

Theme: A group of formatting options that is applied to an entire Office file. Themes include font, color, and effect styles that are applied to specific elements in a file.

Theme colors: Aspect of the theme that limits the colors available from the color palette for fonts, borders, and shading.

Theme effects: Aspect of the theme that controls how graphic elements appear.

Theme fonts: Aspect of the theme that controls which fonts are used for built-in text styles. Changing the theme fonts does not limit the fonts available from the *Font* group on the Ribbon.

Thesaurus: Reference tool that provides a list of synonyms (words with the same meaning) and antonyms (words with the opposite meaning) for a selected word or phrase.

TODAY function: Function that inserts the current date. A formula using the TODAY function looks like this: **=TODAY().**

Top/Bottom Rules: Excel conditional formatting style that automatically finds and highlights the highest or lowest values or values that are above or below the average in the specified range of cells.

Total row: A row that calculates an aggregate function, such as the sum or average, of all the values in the column. Total rows can be added to defined tables in Excel and to tables and queries in Datasheet view in Access.

Transition: An effect that occurs when one slide leaves the screen and another one appears.

u

Unbound control: A control that is not linked to a field.

Undo: Reverses the last action performed.

v

VLOOKUP function: Function that returns values based on a cell's position in a table or array. A formula using the VLOOKUP function looks like this: **=VLOOKUP(D13,LoanRange,7).**

Volatile: Functions that do not return a constant value. For example, a function that displays the current date and time is volatile because the value of the function is constantly changing.

w

Watermark: A graphic or text that appears as part of the page background. Watermarks appear faded so that the text that appears on top of the watermark is legible when the document is viewed or printed.

Web Layout view: Displays all backgrounds, drawing objects, and graphics as they will appear on-screen if the document is saved as a Web page.

Word wrap (Word): Automatically places text on the next line when the right margin of the document has been reached.

WordArt: Predefined graphic styles that are applied to text. These styles include a combination of color, fills, outlines, and effects.

Workbook: An Excel file made up of a collection of worksheets.

Worksheet: An electronic ledger where you enter data in Excel (also called a *sheet*). The worksheet appears as a grid made up of rows and columns where you can enter and then manipulate data using functions, formulas, and formatting.

Wrap text (Excel): Automatically wraps text within a cell (similar to the Word Wrap feature in Word).

y

Yes/No field: Database field that stores a true/false value as a –1 for yes and 0 for no.

z

Zoom slider: Slider bar that controls how large or small the file appears in the application window.

Office Index

s

t

u

v

z

Word Index

g

h

i

j

l

m

U

V

W

X

Z

Excel Index

e

f

g

h

i

k

Access Index

g

h

i

l

m

n

t

u

v

w

y

z

PowerPoint Index

g

h

i

l

m

n

o

p

q

r

s

t

v

w

z

photo credits

Page OF-1, Maureen McCutcheon
Page OF-5, © Stockbyte/Getty Images

Page WD-1, Maureen McCutcheon
Page WD-12, © Ocean/Corbis
Page WD-26, © Juice Images/Alamy
Page WD-65, © Rubberball Productions
Page WD-94, © Jack Hollingsworth/Getty Images
Page WD-116, © Stockbyte/Getty Images
Page WD-117, © Ryan McVay/Getty Images

Page EX-1, Maureen McCutcheon
Page EX-5, © Design Pics Inc./Alamy
Page EX-16, © Blend Images/Getty Images
Page EX-57, © Ocean/Corbis
Page EX-122, © Burke/Triolo Productions/Brand X/Corbis

Page PP-1, Maureen McCutcheon
Page PP-15, © Comstock/Getty Images
Page PP-31, © Mike Kemp/Getty Images
Page PP-72, © Ocean/Corbis
Page PP-97, © Comstock/Getty Images

Page AC-1, Maureen McCutcheon
Page AC-7, © Rubberball/Mark Anderson/Getty Images
Page AC-33, © Rubberball Productions
Page AC-58, © Jose Luis Pelaez, Inc./Blend Images/Corbis
Page AC-105, © Rubberball Productions

Back cover credit: © Okea, iStockphoto.